Contemporary
Literary Criticism
Yearbook 1995

Guide to Gale Literary Criticism Series

For criticism on	Consult these Gale series
Authors now living or who died after December 31, 1959	*CONTEMPORARY LITERARY CRITICISM (CLC)*
Authors who died between 1900 and 1959	*TWENTIETH-CENTURY LITERARY CRITICISM (TCLC)*
Authors who died between 1800 and 1899	*NINETEENTH-CENTURY LITERATURE CRITICISM (NCLC)*
Authors who died between 1400 and 1799	*LITERATURE CRITICISM FROM 1400 TO 1800 (LC)* *SHAKESPEAREAN CRITICISM (SC)*
Authors who died before 1400	*CLASSICAL AND MEDIEVAL LITERATURE CRITICISM (CMLC)*
Black writers of the past two hundred years	*BLACK LITERATURE CRITICISM (BLC)*
Authors of books for children and young adults	*CHILDREN'S LITERATURE REVIEW (CLR)*
Dramatists	*DRAMA CRITICISM (DC)*
Hispanic writers of the late nineteenth and twentieth centuries	*HISPANIC LITERATURE CRITICISM (HLC)*
Native North American writers and orators of the eighteenth, nineteenth, and twentieth centuries	*NATIVE NORTH AMERICAN LITERATURE (NNAL)*
Poets	*POETRY CRITICISM (PC)*
Short story writers	*SHORT STORY CRITICISM (SSC)*
Major authors from the Renaissance to the present	*WORLD LITERATURE CRITICISM, 1500 TO THE PRESENT (WLC)*

ISSN 0091-3421

Volume 91

Contemporary Literary Criticism

Yearbook 1995

The Year in Fiction, Poetry, Drama, and
World Literature and the Year's
New Authors, Prizewinners, Obituaries,
and Outstanding Literary Events

Brigham Narins
Deborah A. Stanley
EDITORS

Jeff Chapman
Janet Witalec
ASSOCIATE EDITORS,
CLC YEARBOOK

Pamela S. Dear
John D. Jorgenson
Aarti D. Stephens
Polly A. Vedder
Thomas Wiloch
Kathleen Wilson
ASSOCIATE EDITORS

GALE

DETROIT · NEW YORK · TORONTO · LONDON

STAFF

_igham Narins and Deborah A. Stanley, *Editors*

_, Pamela S. Dear, John D. Jorgenson, Aarti D. Stephens,
_en Wilson, and Janet Witalec, *Contributing Editors*

George H. Blair, Polly A. Vedder, and Thomas Wiloch, *Associate Editors*

John P. Daniel, Daniel Jones, Annette Petrusso, Linda Quigley, and John Stanley, *Assistant Editors*

Marlene S. Hurst, *Permissions Manager*
Margaret A. Chamberlain, Maria Franklin, *Permissions Specialists*

Diane Cooper, Michele Lonoconus, Maureen Puhl, Susan Salas, Shalice Shah, Kimberly F. Smilay,
Barbara A. Wallace, *Permissions Associates*

Sarah Chesney, Edna Hedblad, Margaret McAvoy-Amato, Tyra Y. Phillips, Lori Schoenenberger,
Rita Velazquez, *Permissions Assistants*

Victoria B. Cariappa, *Research Manager*

Tamara C. Nott, Michele P. Pica, Tracie A. Richardson, Norma Sawaya, *Research Associates*

Alicia Noel Biggers, Julia C. Daniel, *Research Associates*

Mary Beth Trimper, *Production Director*
Deborah L. Milliken, *Production Assistant*

Sherrell Hobbs, *Macintosh Artist*
Randy Bassett, *Image Database Supervisor*
Robert Duncan, *Scanner Operator*
Pamela Hayes, *Photography Coordinator*

Library of Congress Catalog Card Number 76-46132
ISBN 0-8103-9269-0
ISSN 0276-8178

Printed in the United States of America
10 9 8 7 6 5 4 3 2 1

Contents

v

IN MEMORIAM

TOPICS IN LITERATURE: 1995

Preface

A Comprehensive Information Source
on Contemporary Literature

Scope of the *Yearbook*

*C*ontemporary Literary Criticism Yearbook is a part of the ongoing *Contemporary Literary Criticism (CLC)* series. *CLC* provides a comprehensive survey of modern literature by presenting excerpted criticism on the works of novelists, poets, playwrights, short story writers, scriptwriters, and other creative writers now living or who died after December 31, 1959. A strong emphasis is placed on including criticism of works by established authors who frequently appear on syllabuses of high school and college literature courses.

To complement this broad coverage, the *Yearbook* focuses more specifically on a given year's literary activities and features a larger number of currently noteworthy authors than is possible in standard *CLC* volumes. *CLC Yearbook* provides students, teachers, librarians, researchers, and general readers with information and commentary on the outstanding literary works and events of a given year.

Format of the Book

CLC, Volume 86: *Yearbook 1994*, which includes excerpted criticism on more than twenty authors and comprehensive coverage of three key issues in contemporary literature, is divided into five sections—"The Year in Review," "New Authors," "Prizewinners," "In Memoriam," and "Topics in Literature: 1994."

- **The Year in Review**—This section consists of specially commissioned essays by prominent writers who survey the year's works in their respective fields. Bruce Allen discusses "The Year in Fiction," Allen Hoey "The Year in Poetry," Julius Novick "The Year in Drama," and William Riggan "The Year in World Literature." For introductions to the essayists, please see the Notes on Contributors.

- **New Authors**—This section introduces eight writers who received significant critical recognition for their first major work of fiction in 1994 or whose work was translated into English or published in the United States for the first time. Authors were selected for inclusion if their work was reviewed in several prominent literary periodicals.

- **Prizewinners**—This section begins with a list of literary prizes and honors announced in 1994, citing the award, award criteria, the recipient, and the title of the prizewinning work. Following the listing of prizewinners is a presentation of eleven entries on individual award winners, representing a mixture of genres and nationalities as well as established prizes and those more recently introduced.

- **In Memoriam**—This section consists of reminiscences, tributes, retrospective articles, and obituary notices on six authors who died in 1994. In addition, an Obituary section provides information on other recently deceased literary figures.

- **Topics in Literature**—This section focuses on literary issues and events of considerable public interest, including Electronic "Books," Graphic Narratives, and Sylvia Plath and the Nature of Biography.

Features

With the exception of the four essays in "The Year in Review" section, which were written specifically for this publication, the *Yearbook* consists of excerpted criticism drawn from literary reviews, general magazines, newspapers, books, and scholarly journals. *Yearbook* entries variously contain the following items:

- An **Author Heading** in the "New Authors" and "Prizewinners" sections cites the name under which the author publishes and the title of the work discussed in the entry; the "In Memoriam" section includes the author's name and birth and death dates. The author's full name, pseudonyms (if any) under which the author has published, nationality, and principal genres are listed on the first line of the author entry.

- The **Subject Heading** defines the theme of each entry in "The Year in Review" and "Topics in Literature" sections.

- A brief **Biographical and Critical Introduction** to the author and his or her work precedes excerpted criticism in the "New Authors," "Prizewinners," and "In Memoriam" sections; the subjects, authors, and works in the "Topics in Literature" section are introduced in a similar manner.

- A listing of **Principal Works** is included for all entries in the "Prizewinners" and "In Memoriam" sections.

- A **Portrait** of the author is included in the "New Authors," "Prizewinners," and "In Memoriam" sections, and an **Excerpt from the Author's Work,** if available or applicable, is also provided. Whenever possible, a recent, previously unpublished **Author Interview** also accompanies each entry.

- The **Excerpted Criticism,** included in all entries except those in the "Year in Review" section, represents essays selected by editors to reflect the spectrum of opinion about a specific work or about an author's writing in general. The excerpts are typically arranged chronologically, adding a useful perspective to the entry. In the "Year in Review," "New Authors," "Prizewinners," and "In Memoriam" sections, all titles by the author being discussed are printed in boldface type, enabling the reader to more easily identify the author's work.

- A complete **Bibliographical Citation,** designed to help the user find the original essay or book, precedes each excerpt.

- **Cross-references** have been included in the "New Authors," "Prizewinners," and "In Memoriam" sections to direct readers to other useful sources published by Gale Research. Previous volumes of *CLC* in which the author has been featured are also listed.

Other Features

The *Yearbook* also includes the following features:

- An **Acknowledgments** section lists the copyright holders who have granted permission to reprint material in this volume of *CLC*. It does not, however, list every book or periodical reprinted or consulted during the preparation of this volume.

- A **Cumulative Author Index** lists all the authors who have appeared in the Literary Criticism Series published by Gale Research, with cross-references to Gale's Biographical and Autobiographical Series. A full listing of series referenced in the index appears at the beginning of the index. Readers will welcome this cumulated author index as a useful tool for locating an author within the various series. The index, which lists birth and death dates when available, is particularly valuable for locating references to those authors whose careers span two periods. For example, Ernest Hemingway is found in *CLC*, yet a writer often associated with him, F. Scott Fitzgerald, is found in *Twentieth-Century Literary Criticism*.

- Beginning with *CLC*, Vol. 65, each *Yearbook* contains a **Cumulative Topic Index,** which lists all literary topics treated in *CLC* as well as the topic volumes of *Twentieth-Century Literary Criticism, Nineteenth-Century Literature Criticism,* and *Literature Criticism from 1400 to 1800*.

- A **Cumulative Nationality Index** alphabetically lists all authors featured in *CLC* by nationality, followed by numbers corresponding to the volumes in which the authors appear.

- A **Title Index** alphabetically lists all titles reviewed in the current volume of *CLC*. Listings are followed by the author's name and the corresponding page numbers where the titles are discussed. English translations of foreign titles and variations of titles are cross-referenced to the title under which a work was originally published. Titles of novels, novellas, dramas, films, record albums, and poetry, short story, and essay collections are printed in italics, while all individual poems, short stories, essays, and songs are printed in roman type within quotation marks. When published separately, the titles of long poems (e.g., T. S. Eliot's *The Waste Land*) are printed in italics.

Citing *Contemporary Literary Criticism*

When writing papers, students who quote directly from any volume in the Literary Criticism Series may use the following general forms to footnote reprinted criticism. The first example is for material drawn from periodicals, the second for material reprinted from books:

[1]Alfred Cismaru, "Making the Best of It," *The New Republic,* 207, No. 24, (December 7, 1992), 30, 32; excerpted and reprinted in *Contemporary Literary Criticism,* Vol. 85, ed. Christopher Giroux (Detroit: Gale Research, 1995), pp. 73-4.

[2]Yvor Winters, *The Post-Symbolist Methods* (Allan Swallow, 1967); excerpted and reprinted in *Contemporary Literary Criticism,* Vol. 85, ed. Christopher Giroux (Detroit: Gale Research, 1995), pp. 223-26.

Suggestions Are Welcome

The editor hopes that readers will find *CLC Yearbook* a useful reference tool and welcomes comments about the work. Send comments and suggestions to: Editor, *Contemporary Literary Criticism,* Gale Research, 835 Penobscot Building, Detroit, MI 48226-4094.

Acknowledgments

The editors wish to thank the copyright holders of the excerpted criticism included in this volume and the permissions managers of many book and magazine publishing companies for assisting us in securing reprint rights. We are also grateful to the staffs of the Detroit Public Library, the Library of Congress, the University of Detroit Mercy Library, Wayne State University Purdy/Kresge Library Complex, and the University of Michigan Libraries for making their resources available to us. Following is a list of the copyright holders who have granted us permission to reprint material in this volume of *CLC*. Every effort has been made to trace copyright, but if omissions have been made, please let us know.

COPYRIGHTED EXCERPTS IN *CLC*, VOLUME 91, WERE REPRINTED FROM THE FOLLOWING PERIODICALS:

The American Poetry Review, v. 15, November-December, 1986 for "A Sense-Making Perspective in Recent Poetry by Vietnam Veterans" by Lorrie Smith. Copyright © 1986 by World Poetry Inc. Reprinted by permission of the author.—*Belles Lettres: A Review of Books by Women*, v. 6, Winter, 1991; v. 9, Winter, 1993-94; v. 9, July, 1994; v. 10, Fall, 1994. All reprinted by permission of the publisher.—*The Bloomsbury Review,* v. 9, March-April, 1989 for a review of "The Temple" by David Perkins; v. 13, September-October, 1993 for a review of "Encore: A Journal of the Eightieth Year" by Nancy Schwartzkopff; v. 15, September-October, 1995 for a review of "Atomic Ghost: Poets Respond to the Nuclear Age" by Erika Lenz. Copyright © by Owaissa Communications Company, Inc., 1989, 1993, 1995. All reprinted by permission of the respective authors.—*Book World—The Washington Post*, September 12, 1993; March 27, 1994; May 8, 1994; June 25, 1995. © 1993, 1994, 1995, Washington Post Writers Group. All reprinted by permission.—*Books Today—Chicago Tribune*, June 14, 1994 for "A 'Prince' of a First Novel" by Sanford Pinsker. Reprinted by permission of the author.—*The Boston Globe,* April 30, 1994; February 3, 1995. ©1994, 1995 Globe Newspaper Co. Both reprinted courtesy of *The Boston Globe.*—*Boston Review,* v. 20, April, 1995 for a review of "Reef" by Neil Gordon; v. XX, December-January, 1995 for "Race, Genes, and IQ" by Ned Block, abridged from "How Heritability Misleads About Race" in Cognition 56 (1995) 99-128 with the kind permission of Elsevier Science, Inc. Copyright © 1995 by the Boston Critic, Inc. Both reprinted by permission of the respective authors.—*Brockport Writers Forum,* February 14, 1978 for a transcription of a videotape interview with Stephen Spender by Peter Marchant and Stan Savel Rubin, edited by Earl G. Ingersoll. Copyright © 1987 by SUNY. All rights reserved. Reprinted by permission of the publisher.—*The Canadian Forum,* v. LXXII, January-February, 1994 for "Small is Beautiful" by Merna Summers. Reprinted by permission of the author.—*Canadian Literature,* n. 134, Autumn, 1992 for "Life After Death" by William J. Scheick; n. 144, Spring, 1995 for "Auto/Biographical Fictions" by Margery Fee. Both reprinted by permission of the respective authors.—*Chicago Tribune,* January 12, 1995 for "Murder Unveils an Island's Secrets" by Nancy Pate. © copyrighted 1995, Chicago Tribune Company. All rights reserved. Reprinted by permission of *The Orlando Sentinel.* / February 23, 1995. © copyrighted 1995, Chicago Tribune Company. All rights reserved. Used with permission.—*Children's Literature Association Quarterly,* v. 16, Summer, 1991. © 1991 Children's Literature Association. Reprinted by permission of the publisher.—*The Christian Science Monitor,* v. 86, March, 1994, for a review of "The Stone Diaries" by Laura Van Tuyl Clayton; September 23, 1994 for "First Forays Into Novel Writing" by Merle Rubin; November 15, 1994 for "Uncommon Women Ages Poorly, McNall's Latest Has Its Strengths" by Frank Scheck; March 15, 1995 for "Anne Frank, More Comprehensively" by Merle Rubin. © 1994, 1995 The Christian Science Publishing Society. All rights reserved. All reprinted by permission from the respective authors.—*Christianity Today,* v. XXXVIII, December 12, 1994 for "For Whom the Bell Curves" by Lisa Graham McMinn and Mark R. McMinn. © 1994 by Christianity Today, Inc. Reprinted by permission of the authors.—*Commonweal,* v. 71, September 9, 1994; v. XCCIII, February 10, 1995. Copyright © 1994, 1995 Commonweal Foundation. Both reprinted by permission of Commonweal Foundation.—*Daily News, New York*, February 15, 1995. © 1995 Copyright Daily News L. P. Reprinted with permission.—*The Economist,* v. 319, June 22, 1991. © 1991 The Economist Newspaper Group, Inc. Reprinted with permission. Further reproduction prohibited.—*The Globe and Mail,* Toronto, October 2, 1993 for "Straining to Fulfill Ambitions" by Geraldine

COPYRIGHTED EXCERPTS IN *CLC,* VOLUME 91, WERE REPRINTED FROM THE FOLLOWING BOOKS:

the Estate of Stanley Elkin.—Ergas, Yasmine. From "Growing up Banished: A Reading of Anne Frank and Ette Hillesum" in **Behind the Lines: Gender and the Two World Wars**. Margaret Randolph Higonnet and others, eds. Copyright © 1987 by Yale University. All rights reserved. Reprinted by permission of the publisher.—Fenn, J. W. From **Levitating the Pentagon: Evolutions in the American Theatre of the Vietnam War Era**. University of Delaware Press, 1992. © 1992 by Associated University Presses, Inc. All rights reserved. Reprinted by permission of Associated University Presses, Inc.—Gunesekera, Romesh. From **Reef**. Granta Books, 1994. © 1994 by Romesh Gunesekera. Reproduced by permission of the publisher.—Hart, Henry. From **Seamus Heaney: Poet of Contrary Progressions**. Syracuse University Press, 1992. Reprinted by permission of the publisher.—Herrnstein, Richard J., and Charles Murray. From "The Aristocracy of Intelligence: Race Pathology and IQ" in **The Bell Curve: Intelligence and Class Structure in American Life**. Free Press, 1994. Copyright © 1994 by Richard J. Herrnstein and Charles Murray. Reprinted with the permission of The Free Press, a division of Simon & Schuster, Inc.—Holbling, Walter. From "Literary Sense-Making: American Vietnam Fiction" in **Vietnam Images: War and Representation**. Edited by Jeffrey Walsh and James Aulich. The Macmillan Press, Ltd., 1989. © Editorial Board, Lumiere (Co-operative) Press Ltd 1989. All rights reserved. Reprinted by permission of Macmillan, London and Basingstoke. In the U.S. and dependencies by permission of St. Martin's Press, Incorporated.—Hug, W. J. From "Images of the Western Selected Vietnam Films" in **Continuities in Popular Culture: The Present in the Past & the Past in the Present and Future**. Edited by Ray B. Browne and Ronald J. Ambrosetti. Bowling Green State University Popular Press, 1993. Copyright © 1993 by Bowling Green State University Popular Press. Reprinted by permission of the publisher.—Isler, Alan. From **The Prince of West End Avenue: A Novel**. Bridge Works Publishing Co., 1994. Copyright © 1994 by Alan Isler. All rights reserved. Reprinted by permission of the publisher.—Jason, Philip K. From an introduction in **Fourteen Landing Zones: Approaches to Vietnam War Literature**. Edited by Philip K. Jason. University of Iowa Press, 1991. Copyright © 1991 by the University of Iowa. All rights reserved. Reprinted by permission of the publisher.—Klinkowitz, Jerome. From "Writing Under Fire: Postmodern Fiction and the Vietnam War" in **Postmodern Fiction: A Bio-Bibliographical Guide**. Edited by Larry McCaffery. Greenwood Press, 1986. Copyright © 1986 by Larry McCaffery. All rights reserved. Reprinted by permission of Greenwood Publishing Group, Inc., Westport, CT.—Kutler, Laurence. From "Holocaust Diaries and Memoirs" in **Holocaust Literature: A Handbook of Critical, Historical, and Literary Writings**. Edited by Saul S. Friedman. Greenwood Press, 1993. Copyright © 1993 by Saul S. Friedman. All rights reserved. Reprinted by permission of Greenwood Publishing Group, Inc., Westport, CT.—Lifton, Robert Jay and Greg Mitchell. From **Hiroshima in America: Fifty Years of Denial**. G. P. Putnam's Sons, 1995. Copyright © 1995 by Robert Jay Lifton and Greg Mitchell. All rights reserved. Reprinted by permission of The Putnam Publishing Group.—Miner, Valerie. From "Spinning Friends: May Sarton's Literary Spinsters" in **Old Maids to Radical Spinsters: Unmarried Women in the Twentieth-Century Novel**. Edited by Laura L. Doan. University of Illinois Press, 1991. © 1991 by the Board of Trustees of the University of Illinois. Reprinted by permission of the publisher and the author.—Noon, Jeff. From **Vurt**. Crown Publishers, Inc., 1993. Copyright © 1993 by Jeff Noon. All rights reserved. Reprinted by permission of Crown Publishers, a Division of Random House, Inc.—Sarton, May. From **Encore: A Journal of the Eightieth Year**. Norton, 1993. Copyright © 1993 by May Sarton. All rights reserved. Reprinted by permission of W. W. Norton & Company, Inc.

PHOTOGRAPHS AND ILLUSTRATIONS APPEARING IN *CLC*, VOLUME 91, WERE RECEIVED FROM THE FOLLOWING SOURCES:

Bauer, Jerry. Portrait of Romesh Gunesekera (wearing jacket, striped shirt, open at neck, two doorways in the background, medium length). © Jerry Bauer. Reproduced by permission.—Isler, Alan. From a jacket of *The Prince of West End Avenue: A Novel*. Portrait of Alan Isler. Bridge Works Publishing Co. Copyright © 1994 by Alan Isler. Reproduced by permission of the publisher.—Bauer, Jerry. Portrait of Jeff Noon (wearing a plaid shirt, seated indoors, medium length). © Jerry Bauer. Reproduced by permission.—Milligan, Debi. Portrait of Susan Power (head and shoulders, hand on chin, against a tree). © 1994 Debi Milligan. Reproduced by permission.—Werner, Honi. From a jacket of *The Grass Dancer*. By Susan Power. Putnam, 1994. Jacket design and illustration © 1994 Honi Werner. Reproduced by permission.—Foote, Horton, (hands cupping face, head shot), photograph. AP/Wide World Photos. Reproduced by permission.—Sabella, Jill. Portrait of David Guterson. Photograph by Jill Sabella. Reproduced by permission.—Giard, Robert. Portrait of Marilyn Hacker. Photograph by Robert Giard. Reproduced by

The Year in Review

The Year in Fiction

by Bruce Allen

The best American novel of 1995 was, beyond question, Philip Roth's **Sabbath's Theater,** which was lavishly praised throughout the review media, won the National Book Award, and in an oversight so stunning it amounts to a snub, was not even nominated for the Fiction Award presented annually by the—er, well—prestigious National Book Critics Circle (of which I am a member: *peccavi*).

It is arguable that Roth has already garnered more than his share of awards. What seems to me indisputable is that he has never written better—even in the comparably salacious and high-spirited *Portnoy's Complaint*—than in this compellingly funny and fierce portrayal of incipient old age in thunderous eruption.

Its protagonist is sixty-four-year-old Morris "Mickey" Sabbath, a former puppeteer and an unregenerate sexual gamesman whose appetitive energy and refusal to age gracefully, or even slow down minimally, sustains his rapturous zest for life and romance, both remembered and currently enjoyed—most memorably, however, with his late Croatian mistress Drenka, a Madonna, so to speak, of the gospel of sex who rivals the saturnine Sabbath himself as the most gloriously lustful character Roth has yet created.

Another career performance was produced by Madison Smartt Bell, the Tennessee-born novelist whose previous nine books have analyzed mostly urban discontents with grim irony and often feverish intensity. Bell's eighth novel **All Souls' Rising,** offers a wide-angled view of the eighteenth-century rebellion of Haiti's slave population against its French masters. The intricacies of the island's racial hierarchies are explored with meticulous specificity, and the dramatic narrative pulses with horrific excitement (the carnage is vividly detailed). Bell's characterization of the redoubtable slave leader Toussaint-Louverture seems perfunctory and predictable, but he has created in the thoughtful Doctor Hébert a protagonist of believably flawed understanding and mixed sympathies; and in the Arnauds, a slaveowning couple of almost inhuman viciousness, Bell has given us a pair of monsters that the author of *Uncle Tom's Cabin* might not have disclaimed. This will not be an easy book to forget.

It's a pleasure to realize that our final encounter with the work of the late Stanley Elkin (who died in 1995) will have been the beguiling **Mrs. Ted Bliss.** This is the story of a Jewish widow's retirement, and resignation to the approaching end of her days, in a Miami condominium complex where her serenity is comically challenged by the affectionate *kvetching* of her distant children and the romantic importunings of several distinctly unconventional

Latin would-be lovers. A climactic hurricane arrives on schedule, but it's no more a match than are any of these earlier distractions for the imperturbable Dorothy Bliss: a wonderful incarnation of her invaluable creator's explosive verbal wit and wry warmth. We'll miss Stanley Elkin.

A surprising reappearance was made in 1995 by Dorothy West, a veteran participant in the Harlem Renaissance of the 1920s scarcely heard from since her previous best known work, her 1948 novel *The Living is Easy.* No matter: West's **The Wedding,** produced in her late eighties, relates with almost casual mastery the story of a middle-class black family on Martha's Vineyard in the 1950s muddling through as its beloved daughter plans to marry her white fiancé and a rival black entrepreneur schemes to change her mind. It's the other side of *Guess Who's Coming to Dinner?,* and something more: a lyrically (if a bit stiffly) written comedy of manners that introduces us to a seldom-explored social milieu. Last year also saw the publication of West's **The Richer, The Poorer,** a nondescript collection of "Stories, Sketches, and Reminiscences" including several decades worth of very uneven pieces, only a few of which—such as the brilliant 1930 story "Funeral"—show that, at her best, Dorothy West is a sharp-eyed observer of the nuances of black experience in America. Her work deserves to be remembered.

In **The Education of Oscar Fairfax,** veteran novelist Louis Auchincloss composes one of his most telling portraits of professional and social rectitude challenged, though not changed, by the pressures of time's passage and society's demands. In an episodic series of encounters with friends and family members who are confronted by various moral dilemmas, the eponymous Oscar—a well-to-do lawyer who perceives in his recessive literary sensibility a kinship with that other protean blue blood Henry Adams (whom Auchincloss's title evokes)—subtly nudges them toward right action, while—amazingly—never settling into self-satisfaction. This elegant novel will seem retrograde to many readers, but it's a beautifully constructed story, and an appealing character study of great dignity and depth.

The Collected Stories of Evan S. Connell is a large omnibus volume of fifty-six short stories, many previously uncollected, by the unpredictable author of such disparate works as the paired suburban novels *Mrs. Bridge* and *Mr. Bridge* and his popular nonfiction study of General George Armstrong Custer, *Son of the Morning Star.* It's a very mixed bag, flawed by the highly artificial satirical "Leon and Bébert" stories but redeemed by such incisive parable-like tales as "The Yellow Raft" and "The Anatomy Lesson," and especially by several involving Connell's introverted "man of the world" Muhlbach (see "The Mountains of Guatemala" and "Saint Augustine's Pigeon"). Also the protagonist of his superb novel *The Connoisseur,* Muhlbach is, along with the Bridges, the most intriguing personality in Connell's sometimes excessively impersonal *oeuvre.*

I was less impressed by William H. Gass's **The Tunnel,** an elaborately rhetorical fiction in which the private lusts, guilt feelings, and convoluted personal history of a respected academic historian are ironically counterpointed against his recently completed study of Nazi Germany and his (numbingly symbolic) compulsion to dig a tunnel out from the foundations of his house (and hence, we infer, from the imprisoning cacophony of his thoughts). Gass varies the mix with high-octane prose, dirty limericks (some quite funny), and attention-getting graphics and typography—but there's an immense weariness at the core of this ponderously declamatory book. Gass spent thirty years writing it, and it feels as if it isn't finished yet.

Independence Day resumes the heartfelt though clear-eyed scrutiny Richard Ford focuses on Frank Bascombe, *The Sportswriter* of his 1986 novel, now a New Jersey real estate salesman who gets comically and frustratingly involved in the lives of his colleagues and clients (and a probable alter ego whom his author understands the way John Updike understands "Rabbit" Angstrom). Ford is not a stylish writer, but **Independence Day** bumps along building powerful momentum, and there's something painfully universal in Frank Bascombe's erratic passage into middle age and the intimation of his own mortality that makes it uncomfortable to look back as this tough-minded novel stares you down. Another of the year's best books.

T. Coraghessan Boyle's **The Tortilla Curtain,** his sixth novel and tenth book in just over fifteen years, forsakes this versatile author's trademark brazen comedy for a relentlessly serious examination of America Today. It's an altogether politically correct melodrama contrasting the lifestyles, experiences, and probable futures of a wealthy Los Angeles yuppie pair and a luckless Mexican "illegal" couple who collide, in several ways, yet can never bridge the socioeconomic gap that separates them—and that betrays the talented T. C. Boyle into leaden contrivance and blunt statement, making the book (which its publishers hint is a *Grapes of Wrath* for the 1990s) little more than smoothly written social-problem movie-of-the-week.

Moo is Jane Smiley's comic retake on the sobering view of midwestern America offered in her Pulitzer Prize-winning *A Thousand Acres.* It's a lighthearted and generally effervescent romp set on the campus of an agriculturally oriented university nicknamed "Moo U.," where the race for research grants and government contracts and the mechanics of departmental power struggles cross-pollinate amusingly with a farcical flowering of sexual combinations and recombinations worthy of a downhome Shakespearean comedy. Smiley expertly juggles these warring motifs, along with a large and attractive cast of characters featuring, most notably, a prize hog named Earl Butz and a prickly little martinet of a Texas billionaire

whom no reader of any political persuasion will fail to recognize, or appreciate. **Moo** is a hoot.

The delightful Minnesota novelist Jon Hassler has (since *Staggerford* in 1977) produced at agreeably regular intervals solidly plotted chronicles of midwestern *stürm und drang* populated by stoical-comical everymen and -women who'd be right at home in Garrison Keillor's Lake Wobegon. **Rookery Blues,** which documents the unrest that ensues when antiwar protest and a threatened teachers' strike besiege a small state college in the late 1960s, is Hassler's best yet. It's a perfect blending of serious and comic matters, told in the smoothest prose imaginable, and in detailing the interrelations among members of a faculty musical group who call themselves "the Icejam Quintet," Hassler has invented people so warm and real and frantic and funny you hope he'll return to them in subsequent novels.

Eric Kraft has been following the fortunes of his Babbington, Long Island protagonist Peter Leroy since the first Leroy novellas were published separately in the 1970s (they've since been collected as *Little Follies*). His latest, **At Home with the Glynns,** continues the middleaged Peter's informally Proustian recall of a boyhood that Tom Sawyer would have envied: growing up naive in "the clam capital of America" in the bosom of a townful of invincibly eccentric family and friends. This time around, Peter surrenders to the lure of the title family's pragmatic restructurings of reality: its father Andy's enlistment of Peter to "improve" the skills of Andy's art students, mother Rosetta's compulsive contest- entering, and—most formative of all—its twin pubescent daughters' bland appropriation of Peter as (what he thinks is) a sex object. It's a bewitching mixture of dreamy reminiscence and, as Peter cheerfully admits, therapeutically enhanced lies. Readers who haven't previously encountered the Peter Leroy books will find that it's certainly possible to start with this one. It's just that they won't find it easy to stop there.

Several American writers of more recent vintage produced memorable books last year. Michael Cunningham's second novel **Flesh and Blood,** for example, surveys four generations of a Greek-American family whose conflicted members are both united and divided by their hunger for success and their vagrant sexuality. It's an emotionally charged and involving story, distinguished by superb precision of statement and evocation of intricate emotion; a book that tugs at you and haunts you.

Michael Chabon whose witty coming-of-age novel *The Mysteries of Pittsburgh* was one of the brightest debuts of the 1980s, followed that cheerful chronicle of extended adolescence with **Wonder Boys,** a devious and deeply funny tale of literary skullduggery that takes place at a collegiate "literary festival" and features the disastrous interactions of an avaricious writer-teacher, his nervous editor, and a scheming graduate student who might accurately be labelled Unlucky Jim. One of the year's most entertaining novels.

There's also high entertainment value in Richard Powers's **Galatea 2.2,** the fifth imposingly brainy novel published in the last decade by a writer whose intellectual range and stylistic facility have earned him serious comparison with De Lillo, Pynchon, and Bellow. Powers's newest tells the story of a novelist named Richard Powers who recovers from romantic disappointment and self-imposed exile by participating in an academic experiment "training" a computer to master the study of English literature. The interrelations of artificial and human intelligence and the distinctive limitations of each are explored with insouciant wit and inventive lyricism in this highly original book from one of our most resourceful writers.

The House on the Lagoon, an ambitious family chronicle written in English by the Puerto Rican novelist Rosario Ferré, encapsulates that territory's precarious position throughout the twentieth century—midway between U.S. statehood and full independence—in the deliciously melodramatic relationship of a mutually suspicious wealthy couple. The aggrandizement practiced by Quintin Mendizabal's grasping family and the outraged exposure of their avarice proclaimed in his wife Isabel Monfort's accusatory *roman à clef* vividly embody the extremes of their culture's experience. Readers should note, too, that Ferré's lavish romance employs the ever-popular "magic realist" methods of Gabriel Garcia Marquez to stunning effect.

Yolk is a brilliant collection of interconnected short stories, both seemingly autobiographical and surreally comic, by Croatian-American author Josip Novakovich. His affectionate recall (assuming it is that) of Central European village life is enchantingly varied and deepened by his wry portrayals of expatriate sexual, political, and religious experience. "The Eye of God," "Wool," and "Honey in the Carcase"—the prize pieces in this praiseworthy collection—are about as good as contemporary stories get.

Thom Jones's *Cold Snap* collects ten more highpowered short stories by the author of the highly praised *The Pugilist at Rest.* They're extravagantly raw and vivid slabs of experience featuring prize-fighters, drunks and addicts, miscellaneous adventurers: people who travel beyond safe boundaries and plunge almost matter-of-factly into menacing liaisons and the scariest depths of themselves. "Dynamite Hands" and "Ooh Baby Baby," perhaps the best, dance along the dangerous edge of the seamy side of contemporary life with an unblinking concentration that's reminiscent of Hemingway and Algren in their prime.

In *The Summer Before the Summer of Love,* Marly Swick (author of one previous collection) examines the varieties and consequences of domestic intimacy and misunderstanding in generously observed and fully plotted stories that bring the whole weight of her complicated characters' histories and memories to bear on their present experiences. Rich, emotionally gratifying stories like "The Prodigal Father," "Crete," and especially the wonderful "Sleeping Dogs" offer an American near-equivalent to the uniquely layered tales of Canada's celebrated Alice Munro.

Exceptional first books of American fiction included Paula K. Gover's *White Boys and River Girls,* nine lively and gritty stories about love gone wrong, racial conflict and sheer damncussedness, and disappointed family hopes in

deep Southern and midwestern locales whose feisty characters sing the blues with an authoritative and funny mixture of resigned sadness and combative personal pride.

A similar buoyancy distinguishes the magical and realistic world of Alberto Alvaro Rios's *Pig Cookies,* which contains thirteen linked stories set in a nondescript Mexican town in the early years of this century. Rios is concerned with the continuity, and appealing human comedy, of his several families' on-going interrelations. "Pig Cookies" and "Five" are particularly delightful component parts of a splendid concoction that probably ought to be savored a story at a time—though most readers will probably swallow them all in a single gulp.

The Point by Charles D'Ambrosio gathers seven replete, patiently developed stories of failed relationships and personal losses, in which estrangement, addiction, and death push their protagonists gradually toward an understanding of what they must do to cope and survive. "Open House" and the intriguing title story are standouts in a nicely unified collection whose overall somber tone is effectively varied by its author's deft plotwork and sensitive observation.

The best American first novel of 1995 was Benjamin Taylor's *Tales Out of School.* This is the story of an immigrant Jewish family living in Galveston, Texas, in 1907 and struggling to adapt to their new land while also preserving their own culture and religion. Taylor exquisitely details his young protagonist Felix Mehmel's precarious adolescence and uncertain commitment to his family's business (a brewery), traditions, and expectations for him in a flexible and seductive narrative voice that might almost be called biblical-vernacular.

Its style is also a prominent distinguishing feature of Philip Graham's first novel, *How to Read an Unwritten Language,* the lyrical and episodic story of its protagonist Michael Kirby's development of an unusual and healing sensitivity. When Michael's eccentric mother challenges her children's imaginations through storytelling and role-playing, it is he who begins, as a result, to intuit the complex significances latent in familiar objects and the private feelings and fears that shape the lives of those nearest him. It's a haunting concept, brought memorably to life in a most unusual and original novel.

Don Kurtz's *South of the Big Four* is the solidly constructed and gripping tale of two parallel struggles that take place in Indiana's endangered farm country: that of stubbornly optimistic Gerry Maars to make a success of the land he now farms, against cruel odds; and that of the story's protagonist Arthur Conason (whose family once owned Maars's farm) to return to his origins and remake himself, against even steeper odds. The two men's intertwined fates, and the ways in which they challenge and change each other, are explored with unsentimental candor and force in a moving novel that is both satisfyingly "traditional" and disturbingly contemporary.

Raising Holy Hell is first novelist Bruce Olds's exhilarating portrayal of abolitionist John Brown, from the traumatic experiences that shaped his childhood sensitivity to injustice, to the climactic raid at Virginia's Harper's Ferry and its bloody aftermath. Olds combines fictionalized scenes and monologues, eyewitness accounts and "impressions" of unknown and famous contemporaries alike, and supporting documentary statements to produce a fascinating kaleidoscopic image of his complex central figure and a many-levelled picture of Civil War America.

Eric Zencey's *Panama* is a two-pronged mystery set in late nineteenth-century Paris at the time of the building of the Panama Canal (and of a scandal involving the French backers of that project). The novel features the eminent American intellectual Henry Adams recovering from his wife's suicide and pursuing an enigmatic woman whose fate will link his own "investigations" to that of the supposed scandal. If the resolution of these various mysteries proves less than fully satisfying, Zencey has nevertheless imagined his story's remote milieu with convincing particularity and given us a Henry Adams who is both a credible detective and an agreeably distracted and fallible human being.

The historical past is also a vivid presence in the most noteworthy novel from Great Britain to have appeared here last year. *A Dead Man in Deptford,* the last novel completed by Anthony Burgess before his death in 1993, is much more than a convincing reconstruction of the vigorous life and violent death of Elizabethan poet and playwright Christopher Marlowe. Like Burgess's earlier fictionalization of Shakespeare's love life *Nothing Like the Sun,* this superb novel offers a feast of gorgeous language and impertinent wit, and is especially noteworthy for its creation of an intricate espionage plot and its presentation of Marlowe's genuine intellectual nature and poetic power. Burgess's last novel may indeed be the best he ever wrote.

Peter Ackroyd's *The Trial of Elizabeth Cree* contrives splendid, if grisly entertainment in a hallucinatory recreation of Victorian England besieged by a series of savage murders of prostitutes in London's East End. Ackroyd's employment of a variety of narrative devices and rhetorical forms, and of the historical figures of Karl Marx and novelist George Gissing among others, add color and rapid-fire momentum to a lush tale whose ingenious resolution of several subsidiary mysteries introduced in its opening pages is only one of the story's interwoven satisfactions. A treat.

The Ghost Road, which won Britain's most recent Booker Prize, memorably concludes Pat Barker's First World War trilogy whose earlier volumes are *Regeneration* and *The Eye in the Door.* This novel counterpoints, to overpowering emotional effect, the winding-down of the war itself, the fateful resolution of its antagonist Lieutenant Billy Prior's sexual and social dysfunctioning, and her protagonist Dr. W.H.R. Rivers's meditative assessment of the ordeal his generation has endured and the lessons, if they be such, that it has to teach us. The best novel sequence since the similar work of Doris Lessing and Olivia Manning, and one of the great works of contemporary British fiction.

Another of Britain's best writers, the Anglo-Irish William Trevor, produced in *Felicia's Journey* one of his most elo-

quent dramatizations of the unfortunate collision of lonely souls unable to escape their own imprisoning natures. When the innocent and hopeful (and pregnant) Felicia accepts the "protection" of the sinister middleaged Mr. Hilditch, the stage is set for a precisely observed dual character study that is expertly wedded to a suspenseful and increasingly nerve-wracking plot. This skillfully modulated narrative displays the concision and focus for which Trevor's marvelous short stories are so noted, and it's his best full-length novel in many years.

Suspense and surprise are also essential ingredients which flavor *The Cunning Man,* the final novel from popular Canadian author Robertson Davies, who died in 1995. It's a rich brew of satirical comedy, Dickensian caricature/characterization, and enjoyably nonsensical melodrama, narrated by a retired police surgeon whose lavish episodic recall of his watchful involvement in the lives of (among others) an emotional clergyman and a curious pair of women artists has the relaxed, sprawling fascination of a nineteenth-century novel. Robertson Davies may have been a throwback, but it remains an incomparably rare pleasure to be thrown back into the crowded and colorful world of his addictive fiction.

Anita Desai's delicate and poetic portrayals of her native India reach a new level of complexity in her eleventh novel, *Journey to Ithaca.* This intricately woven story tracks forward and backward in time to recount the history of a western couple's confused introduction to Indian spirituality: the wife's recoiling from what she feels is the exploitation of their naivete, her husband's obsessive devotion to a popular Guru known as "the Mother," and the latter's own secular past and wavering religiosity. It's a novel whose several ambitions are only imperfectly realized, and does tend toward discursiveness, but it triumphs as a display of Desai's lyrically descriptive style and in its ironical presentation of outsiders' attitudes toward "the mystery that is at the heart of India."

The Shadow Bride is Guyanese-born novelist Roy Heath's absorbing narrative of an Indian physician's passionate efforts to heal the abused natives who labor on a Guyanese sugar plantation, and of his resistance to his domineering, wealthy widowed mother, who escapes her own alien status in this strange land by devoting herself to the calculating blandishments of a Hindu "holy man." Although the novel is suffused with exotic particulars, it focuses on three rather flat main characters who are all too recognizable in their hunger for self-definition and a sense of belonging. The neglected Roy Heath is, nonetheless, one of the foremost writers to have emerged from the Third World.

Japan's Kazuo Ishiguro has become one of the most popular and critically successful of the younger British novelists. His newest book (since the prizewinning *The Remains of the Day*), *The Unconsoled,* is a fable redolent of Kafka or Beckett, concerning a famous concert pianist's gradual understanding that the clamorous lives of those who perversely insist on intimacy with him (which, initially, he resists) are in fact unacknowledged or repressed aspects of his own sheltered psyche. The novel is dauntingly mysterious, but its expert pacing and frequent infusions of wry comedy make it a highly original and surprisingly accessible portrait of the vagaries and limitations of the artistic temperament.

1995 also saw a significant number of foreign-language novels and story collections from both younger writers and writers new to us: for example, Mexican novelist Francisco Rebolledo, whose *Rasero* won the fifteenth annual International Pegasus Prize for Literature. This is an elaborately contrived historical fiction, set primarily in eighteenth-century France and populated by such vividly reimagined real figures as Voltaire, Diderot, and Robespierre—and, centrally, its Mexican protagonist Fausto Rasero. He's a young, impressionable mixture of intellectual and sexual hungers which amusingly connect him, not just with the best minds—and bodies—of the Enlightenment, but with the promises and terrors of the future he is fated to have beckon him.

Rice is young Chinese writer Su Tong's harrowing melodrama of an ambitious young drifter's collision with a prosperous merchant family in the pre-Communist years, and of the self-destruction that inexorably engulfs them all. The greedy antihero Five Dragons and the two embittered sisters whose paths intertwine disastrously with his are painted in broad slashing strokes, but they are invested with a Zolaesque intensity that give this sordid story an irresistible narrative and thematic momentum.

Goran Tünstrom's *The Christmas Oratorio,* our first acquaintance with its acclaimed Swedish author, is an appealing generational saga about a closely-knit farm family altered for generations afterward by the accidental death of its loving and nurturing mother. The characters of Aron Nordensson, his alienated son Sidner, and the latter's estranged son Victor have a plaintive and haunting hyperreality, and the way in which each life is directed by the search to be loved and to become part of something larger, transcendent, confer on this charming novel a satisfying and moving unity. This is Tünstrom's ninth novel, and one hopes that more of this remarkable writer's work will be soon forthcoming in English translation.

In *Battlefields and Playgrounds,* Hungarian novelist Janos Nyiri offers an ironical perspective on the fate of his country's Jewish population during the Second World War. His protagonist, Jozsef Sondor, is a truculent hellion who's equally unfazed by the homilies urged upon his rebellious spirit by teachers and clergy, the impassive derelictions of his absent father, and, up to a point, the threat of Hitler's approaching armies. Jozsef is the survival instinct incarnate, and the central feature and strength of a vivid novel that shows us the Holocaust in an entirely new way.

Peter Hoeg's *The History of Danish Dreams* is the first novel written by the author of the spectacular international success *Smilla's Sense of Snow* (his third novel). It's an amusing and imaginative portrayal of his native country's distorted images of itself, covering nearly four centuries and examining the tension between languorous passivity and reformist agitation through the beguilingly told stories of such memorable individuals as an arrogant nobleman who believes he can control the passage of time and a family of thieves who are disgraced by their offspring's

perverse commitment to social justice. Hoeg's sly and unconventional novels are among the most interesting that have appeared in the 1990s.

Several prominent novelists of long-established international reputation also produced new books last year. Umberto Eco's *The Island of the Day Before* continues the technique of learned historicism employed so successfully in *The Name of the Rose* and less successfully in *Foucault's Pendulum,* with results somewhere in between. It's a tale of shipwreck in the South Seas, of the quest to master "the mystery of longitude," and of its protagonist's, highborn Roberto della Griva's, inevitably compromised recapture of his past and grasp of the knowledge he lives to acquire. The novel bogs down in various arcana, but is enlivened by Eco's witty polymathic approach and by the presence of such prodigious inventions as an Aristotelian memory machine and Roberto's impressively eccentric fellow traveler and mentor Father Caspar Wanderdrossel.

Of Love and Other Demons, an exquisite novella from Nobel Prize-winning Colombian novelist Gabriel Garcia Marquez, possesses in miniature form many of the virtues of his classic magical-realist romance *One Hundred Years of Solitude.* Set in a nameless town near the Caribbean Sea, this is the story of a disgraced marquis' daughter condemned as the devil's handmaiden, the introverted and lonely cleric who casts his fate with hers, and the destiny in store for a proud family whose wealth and prestige are built on the inequities of a notorious slave trade. The mixing of bloodlines becomes an act of liberation in this fascinating tale, at once a sardonic criticism of South America's ingenuous ruling classes and a brilliant evocation of the undercurrent natural world that opposes, and outlasts, all efforts to control it.

Extinction was the final book written by the great Austrian novelist Thomas Bernhard, and a fitting capstone to a uniquely consistent career during which Bernhard cast a baleful satirist's eye over the full depressing spectrum of what he perceived to be his culture's stultifying vanity and complacency. His familiar technique of virtually nonstop monologue here expresses the venomous sensibilities of Franz-Josef Murau, a self-styled aesthete whose abomination of his smothering provincial family is raised to blackly comic heights when the death of his parents in an automobile accident brings Murau back to his home to reclaim his inheritance. Murau's splenetic, self-justifying tirade becomes the vehicle for an unforgettable characterization: that of a lonely, vitriolic misanthrope for whom no human connection is satisfactory and no happiness is possible.

There also appeared in 1995 a first English translation of an interesting, if somewhat overwrought late novel by the dark genius of twentieth-century French fiction—and, almost certainly, a major influence on the pessimistic rhetoric of Thomas Bernhard: Louis-Ferdinand Céline (1894-1961). *London Bridge,* a sequel to his 1954 novel *Guignol's Band,* continues the ribald adventures of Céline's alter ego Ferdinand, having (in 1944) fled France where he was under attack for his anti-Semitism (as Céline himself was and continues to be) and found "refuge" in a hallucinatory wartime London populated by the manic grotesques and sexual predators familiar from his earlier days (and writings). Though not on the level of Céline's masterpieces *Journey to the End of Night* and *Death on the Installment Plan,* this comparatively more subdued picaresque forms a significant pendant to them and a necessary addition to its author's outrageous, inimitable, and controversial *oeuvre.*

Notice should also be taken of the appearance of **A Book That Was Lost,** a generous collection of twenty-five stories representing the long literary career of the great Israeli writer (and another Nobel Prize winner) S.Y. Agnon. Included among these powerful and vibrant tales of Jewish village life and survival throughout centuries of hardship are such intricate masterpieces as "Hill of Sand," "The Tale of the Menorah," and—what may as well be called Agnon's intellectual autobiography—the unforgettable title story.

Last year also brought the first complete English translation (of almost eighteen hundred pages) of Robert Musil's vast epic of the Austro-Hungarian Empire in the years immediately preceding World War I, **The Man Without Qualities.** It's a diffuse and exasperating work, marred not only by its incompleteness (though Musil wrote and rewrote it over a twenty-year period) but by its digressiveness and didacticism. Still, in Musil's exhaustive inventory of his confused title hero's mental and moral education, and especially in the vigorous satirical passages depicting the capture of a notorious mass murderer and his relation to a stunned bourgeois culture that thinks itself free of such imperfections, there is much to savor in this massive and forbidding work. Few will finish it in a year or less, but many may want to keep dipping into it over a lifetime; that's the way Robert Musil wrote it, and it seems the only rational way to read it.

Finally, I must pay tribute to three of the year's happiest literary surprises. *Imperfect Paradise* collects twenty-four short stories and two free-form nonfiction pieces by Shen Congwen (1902-88), an acclaimed Chinese writer whose vividly realistic stories of life in his native Hunan province date from the 1920s and 1930s but retain an astonishing freshness and modernity. Shen's work is permeated by a sober (though not somber) apprehension of time passing and things changing, observable both in his unillusioned looks at military service ("Black Night," "The Company Commander") and revolutionary ardor ("Big Ruan and Little Ruan") and in his deeply moving stories of embattled village denizens (the best of which, "The Husband,"

examines from its title character's anguished viewpoint the ordeal undergone by his wife, who works as a prostitute to support their impoverished family). But there are many other successes as well in this wonderful display of work by a superb writer who will be new to almost all American readers.

The Stories of Vladimir Nabokov includes sixty-five almost aggressively brilliant fictions from the late multilingual master who wrote with equal ease in Russian and English (and, occasionally, French). The book collects all of Nabokov's previously published short stories plus thirteen early works that are translated (and briefly annotated) here for the first time by his son and frequent collaborator, Dmitri. The chronological arrangement gives us the "new" thirteen first. These come from the 1920s when he was writing for and about Russian emigrés displaced from their culture and recreating themselves in Germany as artists, civilized souls, and lovers ("Wingstroke" and "Sound" are exemplary). Later stories display Nabokov's refreshing variety, sometimes expressed in accents of Chekhovian simplicity (in such stories as "Perfection" and "Christmas"). And, most distinctively of all, there are the ironical and expertly fashioned portrayals of deracination and alienation in a variety of stylistic and thematic forms (see "The Circle," "The Potato Elf," and "Signs and Symbols," to name only the finest) that are Nabokov's distinctive contribution. He knew what it was to be exiled from one's language and traditions (and, as a result, dissociated from oneself), and he wrote of it with a mingled plangency and inventiveness that were new to fiction when his work first appeared, and may never be equalled.

But nothing amazed me more in 1995 than the publication of **The First Man,** the uncompleted novel that was found in the wreckage of the automobile in which Albert Camus died in an accident in 1960 at the age of only forty-seven. At last released by Camus's daughter (having been previously withheld from publication out of fear it would lessen his reputation), this is an obviously autobiographical portrayal of its author's childhood and youth, and incipient yearnings toward a literary vocation, in Algeria in the time between the two World Wars. Unfinished or not, this is a heartfelt evocation of a brilliant literary sensibility just developing: an invaluable key to an understanding of Camus's family relations and intellectual affiliations, and a generous and unanticipated gift to we grateful readers.

The Year in Poetry

by Allen Hoey

Notable in 1995 was the selection of Seamus Heaney as Nobel laureate, the first time in a long time that an English-speaking poet has been awarded this honor. Heaney has worked, and worked well, in both received forms and free verse throughout his career, a feat which should put the lie to the notion that poets work best on just one side of the metrical fence.

While Heaney issued no volume of poems this year, he did publish a collection of lectures delivered during his tenure as Professor of Poetry at Oxford from 1989 to 1994. The subjects of the lectures demonstrate considerable range—from Christopher Marlowe's *Hero and Leander* to the poems of Dylan Thomas, from John Clare's local usage poems to Elizabeth Bishop, from the little-known *The Midnight Court* by Brian Merriman to the Synthetic Scots of Hugh MacDiarmid—yet running through these essays are notions of what Heaney calls, and titles the volume, *The Redress of Poetry.* He defines "redress" variously, following leads from the OED; in summary, however, while

> considering poetry's possible service to programmes of cultural and political realignment, or in reaffirming poetry as an upright, resistant, and self-bracing entity within the general flux and flex of language, I don't want to give the impression that its force must always be exercised in earnest, morally premeditated ways. On the contrary, I want to profess the surprise of poetry as well as its reliability; I want to celebrate its given, unforeseeable thereness, the way it enters our field of vision and animates our physical and intelligent being in much the same way as those bird-shapes stenciled on the transparent surfaces of glass walls or windows must suddenly enter the vision and change the direction of the real birds' flight. ("The Redress of Poetry")

To reinforce playfulness, Heaney argues, poetry must retain "its fundamentally self-delighting inventiveness, its joy in being a process of language as well as a representation of things in the world." As such, it provides "a glimpsed alternative, a revelation of potential that is denied or constantly threatened by circumstances." Poetry, however, "does not intervene in the actual but by offering consciousness a chance to recognize its predicaments, foreknow its capacities and rehearse its comebacks in all kinds of venturesome ways, it does constitute a beneficent event...." In short, Heaney argues that poetry at its best essays an almost spiritual enterprise.

Heaney's procedure through these lectures seems guided by his recognition that "[w]riters have to start out as read-ers, and before they put pen to paper, even the most disaffected of them will have internalized the norms and forms of the tradition from which they wish to secede." Heaney's acuity is gleaned from a career as a working poet; he neither romanticizes nor abstracts the process. (For an interesting contrast to Heaney's pragmatism, see the "Introduction" to Helen Vendler's *The Breaking of Style,* also a collection of lectures, in which she argues, with all the élan of an academic, "The fears and regrets attending the act of permanent stylistic change can be understood by analogy with divorce, expatriation, and other such painful spiritual or imaginative departures," an almost Wagnerian description of an activity that many poets, including Heaney, one of the subjects of her book, would regard as closer to the Yeatsian analog, which Vendler dismisses, of changing one's clothes to suit the occasion.) If poets' practice is shaped by their reading, the world, too, as Heaney asserts, "is different after it has been read by a Shakespeare or an Emily Dickinson or a Samuel Beckett because it has been augmented by their reading of it." For this reason, he further argues in "Joy or Night: Last Things in the Poetry of W. B. Yeats and Philip Larkin," "[w]e go to poetry, we go to literature in general, to be forwarded within ourselves."

The redress of poetry is not accomplished once and for all time but is undertaken each time poets take pen to page and readers read those words responsively. If such redressing is not always or entirely earnest, it is nonetheless a moral as well as spiritual labor, with all parties obliged to bring their all to the task. Through more than a dozen volumes of poems and translations of poems, Stephen Berg has not stinted in this regard, and *Oblivion* may be his strongest, most versatile offering yet. The offerings include highly idiosyncratic versions of Sappho, Rimbaud, and three Zen masters, Bankei, Seng Ts'an, and Daito. As with his versions of Zen Master Ikkyu and Anna Akhmatova, Berg's method seems more empathic than scholarly; he injects himself not so much into the writers' texts as into the flesh and fiber of their lives as revealed through the intricacies of the text, rebuilding outward versions that speak in charged English. The Sappho we encounter in the first section of this collection remains fragmentary, small points of brilliance such as the ancients believed shone through holes in heaven's canopy. In fragmentary texts, as in all texts only more obviously, the lacunae—or as Berg puts it, "the dark texts the spaces"—speak at least as loudly as the words. An aspect of this poem, and an undercurrent through the book, is revealed in this section, the sense that the poet and an other, however mythic or invented, come to create a greater whole. Berg expresses this in a fragment midway through the section:

> Stars in an
>
> unknown order   could it be this voice trying
>   to return
>
> my heart and your heart touch
> I can feel how we
> will always shine back
> fair face upon fair face
>
> deeper than flesh and blood

What remains unclear is the extent to which the above passage, like the other versions in the volume, reflects the actual language and concerns of the original and how much is Berg's "reinvention." The sequence "Rimbaud" consists of prose poems in which Berg "responds" to English versions of *Une Saison en Enfer*; in this case, readers with access to one or more bi-lingual translations can learn more about Berg's method. To appreciate more fully Berg's relationship with his correspondent others, however, readers would be served by somewhat more extensive notes. Finally, if Berg's responses are guided as much by his own obsessions as by Rimbaud's text, he brings across the insolence of the original; to accomplish this, Berg rearranges, trims, and invents with license, and we are enriched by an expanded sense of the originals in English.

In the poems and prose poems that constitute the remainder of *Oblivion*, Berg iterates the same themes, concerned with language, with the act of writing, with the urge to an impossible immediacy between thought and language. Still, he persists in the impossible task, looking back at his own words and realizing, as in "Written on a Blank Page in Schwerner's *Seaweed*," his own failures:

> What was I trying to explain?
> Why is everything I write not what I wanted to
>   write?
> Is love the catastrophe whose roots can't be
>   known?

Later in the poem, after introducing the idea of "the pure white void" out of which the world began, he asserts in a line that snakes across the page and doubles over: "A zone lurks behind the void, where seer and seen fuse into the trance of space between, and I'm in it." The sense of being "in it" (the title of an earlier collection) pervades Berg's work; whether we recognize it or not, we're always in the thick of the world, and Berg seeks to convey through his ragged lines and propulsive syntax a sense of that experience.

One technique for eliminating the emphasis of verse is the prose poem, a form which Berg uses to good effect in the several pieces included in this volume as well as those in his manuscript in progress, *Shaving*, parts of which were published in his *New & Selected Poems*. Particularly notable in this collection is "Burning," which begins by evoking the ordinary things encountered on the daily walk to work:

> . . . passed the hot dog and pretzel man by the
> library, strolled around Logan Square's Calder
> fountain by the Museum of Natural History, the

> huge bronze breasts and thighs of the goddesses
> gleaming water, Four Seasons, limos, Cigna, up
> 18th to Rittenhouse, it was all there as before,
> and why not, sweat started on my palms and
> forehead when I realized This is all there is, it
> began and it will end, they say, This is all there
> is, it is burning, birth death like a palace of
> leaves, burning. . .

The poem maintains this breathless pace for a full page, unpunctuated except for commas, carrying us like Molly's thoughts in *Ulysses*, a poetry of the commonplace elevated by observation to the verge of enlightened vision.

Regrettably, in **A Scattering of Salts,** his final completed book before his death on February 6, 1995, James Merrill seems too often satisfied with going through the motions, which makes this collection all the more unfortunate a testament to his work. Merrill, despite a highly mandarin style, has been one of our most accomplished metricists; that talent glimmers through some of these lines, but the mandarin quality almost sinks them. The Ouija-Board mysticism of *The Changing Light at Sandover* pushes the margins of credibility, but the over-arching concerns of the epic effort lent buoyancy to the high camp. "Nine Lives," his final foray into that territory, founders, alas, under its self-referential burden. For the unwary reader at a loss for what to make of the "familiars" given voice through the board, Merrill offers this advice:

> I hate to say it, but the neophyte
> Must take the full amazement of this news
> (At least till he can purchase and peruse
> A heavy volume called *The Changing Light
> At Sandover*) on faith.—What? Oh. My
>   muse,
> Smiling indulgently upon the wretch,
> Authorizes a quick background sketch.

Merrill's muse puts in another appearance in "Home Fires," where the speaker appeals, " 'The day I cease to serve you, let me die!' " Readers must judge for themselves who may have abandoned whom and take as too accurate the lines a few stanzas later in the poem: "Besides, the cramped flue of each stanza draws / Feeling *away*."

Merrill has not, however, entirely lost the satirist's touch. Moments gleam sharply from poem to poem, a little light escaping through the chinks. "Family Week at Oracle Ranch" manages a few spry jabs at New Age inanity. Of the psycho-babble mastered by the "connoisseur of feeling," Merrill writes that he is

> Used to depicting personal anguish
>
> With a full palette—hues, oils, glazes, thinner—
> He stares into these withered wells and feels,
> well. . .SAD and ANGRY?   Future lavender!
> An infant Monet blinks beneath his skin.

Would these glistening piths had marked the whole volume.

Readers familiar with Louise Glück's early work will find no surprises in **The First Four Books of Poems** which gathers, unaltered and in their entirety, *Firstborn, The House on Marshland, Descending Figure,* and *The Triumph of Achilles.* Indeed, the primary pleasure in the volume is the excuse for rereading these earlier poems in light of her magnificent 1993 collection, *The Wild Iris*, and her thought-provoking and astute volume of essays from last year, *Proofs & Theories*. One will strain mightily, however, and with little reward, if one seeks direct connections. In fact, what will strike the reader most is Glück's uncanny ability to alter her style, with all apparent deliberateness and none of the breast- or brow-beating angst Vendler insists must accompany such change. For Glück, the process is much more practical; as she explains in *Proofs & Theories*, "for the writer, thinking and writing (like thinking and feeling) are synonyms. Style changes when one has got to the end, willingly or not, of a train of thought" ("The Idea of Courage"). The brief "Author's Note," the singular gem for veteran Glück readers, describes the rationale for the present collection, again in very pragmatic terms, and candidly interjects Glück's feeling about some of these poems; the poems in her earliest volume, she confesses, leave her feeling "embarrassed tenderness," yet, should she try to revise them, some of them "might, in being reconstructed, evaporate." From many poets, this might seem coy protest; from Glück, however, it seems to mark a realistic apprehension of her successes and failures. Since the publication of these volumes between the same covers marks the end of their availability as individual books, readers interested in assaying Glück's entire oeuvre will need to avail themselves of this handsome collection.

In her "Author's Note," Glück explains that she shies away from editing a selected poems because she "cannot rid [her]self of attaching to that enterprise a valedictory taint." To that, I say "bravo." While many practical reasons exist for publishing a selected volume—gathering all one's poems under a single imprint, for instance—the venture does suggest that the poet has achieved some level of canonic prestige. The time has probably come for someone to debunk the entire game of selected poems, but, lacking that particular soapbox, let me reiterate that a selected poems is merited when a poet has shown consistent performance over the long haul—say a good five or six volumes over the course of at least twenty-five years—and the poet him- or herself should be somewhat venerable, which is to say, politely, over sixty. Otherwise, the endeavor smacks of pretension, whether the publisher's, the poet's, or both. Said volume should be a reasonable selection, weighing in at no longer than 150 pages. John Crowe Ransom managed Thomas Hardy in fewer, and his importance was already established. Finally, since a selected volume exists, at least in part, so that readers might assess the development over time of the poet's work, please—*please*—include adequate apparatus to let us know from which volume particular poems originated and when they were first published in book form.

That out of the way, let me say that no one deserves the valedictory aspect of a selected poems more than Stanley Kunitz, who has labored consistently for nearly seven decades in the gardens of the art. Happily, the National Book Award has vindicated itself this year with the (altogether safe) choice of Kunitz' ***Passing Through: The Later Poems New and Selected.*** Kunitz' reputation will survive whatever quibbles I might have about his fairly narrow

range and subject matter. Given his craft and talent, he makes good use of his gifts. The present selection begins with poems from his 1971 volume, *The Testing Tree*, and culls well from that and his succeeding three volumes. Most impressive are the new poems gathered here, always a danger in a selected volume, since the new poems often suffer by comparison, if only because they have not survived the test of time. I cannot say that these are the best poems I've read this year or even, necessarily, the strongest poems garnered in this volume, but these lines from "Touch Me," the last poem in the book, would be a credit to poets in their thirties, much less one in his nineties:

> Outdoors all afternoon
> under a gunmetal sky
> staking my garden down,
> I kneeled to the crickets trilling
> underfoot as if about
> to burst from their crusty shells;
> and like a child again
> marveled to hear so clear
> and brave a music pour
> from such a small machine.
> What makes the engine go?
> Desire, desire, desire.
> The longing for the dance
> stirs in the buried life.
> One season only,
>   and it's done.
> So let the battered old willow
> thrash against the windowpanes
> and the house timbers creak.
> Darling, do you remember
> the man you married?   Touch me,
> remind me who I am.

Beyond the felicities of such offerings, Kunitz gathers these twenty-five years worth of poems into reasonable length, and the volume clearly indicates vital data.

In many ways Sam Hamill's ***Destination Zero: Poems 1970-1995*** falls short of my stipulated criteria. While the period covered is extensive, and the number of volumes represented is apparently more than adequate, Hamill himself is not quite venerable, nor does the selection pare the work down to a manageable size or provide any apparatus beyond an author's note that serves as a kind of apologia. The volume gathers from all his published books in "roughly chronological order," includes many revised versions, and lacks much else by way of explanation. All rules require exceptions, and Hamill may be exhibit A. His work has been largely published by small presses, and most of those volumes, erratically distributed as they may have been, are currently out of print with little hope of resurrection. As publisher of Copper Canyon, the single most impressive independent poetry publisher in the U.S., he has long performed yeoman service, and his work deserves to be read more widely. If this volume can serve that end, all the better.

Hamill is not the strongest or the most widely skilled or diverse poet working today. His poems owe much to the work of two more gifted masters, Gary Snyder and Kenneth Rexroth, both of whom write about the Pacific Coast with similar love and background in Buddhist practice. For all of them, the act of poetry is also an act of conscience, which can lead to the weakest offerings of each, especially when the politics seem less at the service of poetry than vice versa, a sure recipe for propaganda, regardless of how sympathetic the cause. One does not have to skim too far to find examples of such well-intentioned failures. Consider the opening stanza of the randomly chosen "A Leaf":

> It is spring, full moon in a cloudless sky
> after a long dark winter, a year after
> another stupid war. Maybe these unconsoling
>   stars
> know the secret names of all we cannot know.

New Critics would have termed this last step "pathetic fallacy," and examples abound. Beyond that, the horribly weak "It is" gets the poem off to a slow start, which is not aided in the least by the clichéd "long dark winter" and regrettably lazy "stupid war." Finally, one is tempted to respond that those "unconsoling stars" are nothing but large gaseous thermonuclear reactors unlikely to know the "secret names" of anything.

Yet this same poet manages the eloquence of this passage from "A Dragon in the Clouds," in which he remarks of a finch:

> She knows two things:
> the world is flat,
> and that she lives
>
> on this side
> of the only river
> she cannot fly across.

No pathetic fallacy; rather, a sympathetic understanding of a bird's world. Similarly, the opening of "Gnostology" contains careful observation:

> Each return is a blessing,
> a birthing. I come back again in the last light of
>   evening
> and the blue cups camas raises to catch the mist
>   are dripping,
> blackberries turning blue from green, and down
> the narrow Strait of Juan de Fuca, foghorns
> faintly sound.

The lines are nicely balanced, demonstrating a good ear for effective enjambment, as well as the good sense to know when an end-stopped line creates the better rhythmic effect. Hamill's failings arise from a surfeit of feeling, and many contemporary American poets seem to have a difficult time knowing how to manage emotion in verse. Still, as Jack Gilbert writes at the end of "A Stubborn Ode," in the face of all this suffering, perhaps the best we can offer is "nevertheless."

Exemplary of the less is more school, William Bronk's *Selected Poems,* which gathers poems from publications as early as 1949 until his last collection in 1993, weighs in at a compact 80 pages. Perhaps because Bronk himself refused to make the selection, believing, like Glück, that his work needs to be taken "all in all," the more detached eye of an editor achieved what few poets seem able to do on their own—compile a concise yet complete sampler of a poet's work, leaving the reader hungry for more rather than bloated from an overly rich repast. In this regard,

Henry Weinfield is to be commended for his editorial rigor and care; not only is the volume trim, but the selections are arranged chronologically with clear notation, both in the table of contents and the text, of title and date of publication of original volumes. The austerity of the presentation mirrors the poems themselves, which manage more in a few lines than most contemporary poems can in several pages.

Bronk's task is unapologetically philosophical, though philosophy for him does not preclude the passions, reaching back to the Presocratics for correspondence rather than dialectical dichotomy between reason and feeling. As early as his first full-length collection, *Light and Dark* (1956), Bronk announces his fear and awe in the face of "the wilderness / of raw consciousness" and "the passion that we feel for forms" which manifest the world. As well, in "A Vase of Various Flowers," he celebrates "the many kinds of pleasure. . .there are / in just these yellow roses, open pink / single asters. . . ." Both impulses show clearly in this first stanza of "The Mind's Landscape on an Early Winter Day":

> Seeds and survivals are scattered in all the flaws
> of this raw day, even though these are perceived
> by being unperceived, until the mind
> tugs at the senses to remind them. The mind says
>   see.
> What the senses feel is the sharp immediate air
> and all this scene half emptied, opened out
> to admit the light, the thin, slight light.
> What the senses feel is loss, and not less loss
> for being neither final nor complete.
> The senses and the mind agree it seldom is.

What emerges is a sensibility akin to Stevens' in its need to know the world; as he writes in "Truth as a Far Country; as a Piteous Ogre," "the important thing / is to be here, to take it as it is." Unlike Stevens' operatic themes, however, Bronk makes a quieter music, perhaps a piece by Vivaldi for small ensemble.

The religious undertones of Bronk's work emerge more distinctly in the poems toward the middle of the book, beginning with the selections from *That Tantalus* (1971). "Civitas Dei," for instance, begins:

> When it was plain that there was never to be
> the City of God; after the line was clear
> that there was no line and none ever to be made;
> when it was plain that nothing at all was plain,
> we looked from side to side, we turned back,
> and no way there either, and here we were.

That sense of sufficiency in the face of what cannot be known, what cannot be certain, is a hallmark of Bronk's maturity. In contrast to Hamill's personified stars, in "The Limits of Knowledge," from *Silence and Metaphor* (1975), Bronk proposes a very different apprehension:

> The unpurposive lights in the sky at night, far
> from telling us what purpose is as, say
> *there is no purpose* (as may, perhaps, be so)
> say only how we don't know what it is.
>
> But Venus, tonight, was beautiful in the west.
> If I wake toward morning, as many times I do,
> and look in the east, Vega will be there.

What certainties are these? We don't know.

How easily we might overlook the careful music syntax makes, the counter-pointing of the sentence across the line, which isolates "far" and "say" at the line ends in the beginning of the poem, then allowing the qualifiers to accumulate, the punctuation interrupting the flow of the repeated words and phrases, forcing an emphasis. The correlation of line and sentence at the beginning of the second stanza prepares for the terse, emphatic final sentence. Yet that very brevity suggests a kind of certainty of purpose in the face of vast uncertainty. For readers unfamiliar with Bronk's work, this packed volume provides a taste that will whet the appetite for more of his less.

In *Spring Garden: New and Selected Poems,* Fred Chappell organizes his poems thematically rather than chronologically. Taking his inspiration from a poem by Ronsard, Chappell gathers his poems like

> Herbs for a salad, careful to select
> The healthful ones that might sustain a man
> Who'd suffered quartan fevers, disastrous love,
> The whims of kings and the unhappy fate
> Of being called by music when he'd gone deaf
> To tune his sonnets to an antique lute.

Like his renaissance precursor, Chappell most often—and most successfully—writes "poems in rhyme and measure," though the rhymes are often very slant (the passage above includes some of the more dramatic examples: "fate" and "lute," more a pararhyme, and, even more extreme, "love" and "deaf "). He handles meter, however, quite eloquently, with the colloquial grace of Frost.

Each of the volume's seven sections begins with a prologue, and the volume as a whole contains both a "General Prologue" and an "Epilogue," all written in rhymed octaves. These newer pieces show Chappell at his best, mixing narrative with epigram, and threading the whole together with an often wry sense of humor. While he takes the task of selecting from his life's work to date seriously, clearly he also does not take himself too seriously. The process of "heap[ing]. . .up" a selected poems marks him "as a certified Old Fart," he acknowledges in "The General Prologue," and in the "Epilogue" he notes,

> All in all, it's been a fair day's work,
> Selecting each poetic salad green,
> Pruning surplusage, trimming the borders clean.

And, all in all, he's made a creditable job of it. Readers unfamiliar with Chappell's work will find the accomplishment of an advanced journeyman and an altogether rewarding read.

The same might be said of Donald Justice's *New and Selected Poems,* his first volume containing new poems since the 1987 publication of *The Sunset Maker.* Paucity of publication has been a hallmark of Justice's career and sets him apart from most contemporary poets. What emerges from this volume is the sense of a scrupulous craftsman of modest but solid range. The new poems seem of a piece with the rest of the volume, no marked slacking off or unprecedented leap, laterally or forward. Justice emerges as a poet of quiet, almost melancholic reflection, typified by

this first section of the new poem "Body and Soul," titled "Hotel":

> If there was something one of them held back,
> It was too inadvertent or too small
> To matter to the other, after all.
>
> Afterwards, they were quiet, and lay apart,
> And heard the beating of the city's heart,
> Meaning the sirens and the street cries, meaning
> At dawn, the whispery great street-sweeper
>   cleaning
> The things of night up, almost silently.
>
> And all was as it had been and would be.

From the almost monosyllabic iambs of the first line, Justice sweeps into the quicker second line with the polysyllabic "inadvertent," then relaxes into the last line of the first stanza, throughout establishing an even iambic rhythm which he continues in the first two lines of the second stanza. Notice how effectively he breaks the rhythm at the same time as he breaks the mood; "the city's heart" seems almost clichéd, so the impact of "the sirens and the street cries" strikes all the more powerfully. Examples of such careful composition abound.

Ordinarily, I dislike the practice of beginning a selected volume with new poems; it skews the accumulation of a career. In this case, however, I find it difficult to complain about an organization that ends the book with "The Sunset Maker," the most successful conjoining of Justice's interests in music and poetry. Of the way one "hears" a piece of music while scanning the score, he writes:

> (Some duo of the mind produces them,
> Without error, ghost-music materializing;
> Faintly, of course, like whispers overheard.)

—This is the best description of the experience I have encountered. Consider also the following passage:

> The three plucked final chords—someone might
>   still
> Recall, if not the chords, then the effect
> They made—as if the air were troubled some-
>   how.
>
> *As if.* . .but everything there is is that.
> Impressions shimmering; broken light. The
>   world
> Is French, if it is anything. Or was.

The effective turn of the piece from one mood to another on the repeated "as if " demonstrates a highly proficient capacity for concision. The phrasing in this poem in particular—appropriate for a poem about musical composition—is a study in effective caesurae; the very different weights of the pauses in the last two lines quoted are a case in point. The fluid "Impressions shimmering" followed by a brief pause, then the staccato "broken light"; more sustained pause, "The world," hesitate, "Is French," brief catch of the breath, "if it is anything." Sustained pause. "Or was." Period. With his use of both high and pop culture, Justice seems a natural predecessor of the New Formalists, yet few of them (none, perhaps, excepting the Dana Gioia of *Daily Horoscope*) have learned from Justice such fluid metrical care.

Although Helen Vendler would clearly disagree, having hoisted Jorie Graham into the company of Gerard Manley Hopkins and Seamus Heaney in *The Breaking of Style,* the publication of *The Dream of the Unified Field: Selected Poems 1974-1994* seems premature to the point of pretension. Graham has published five volumes to date (*Region of Unlikeness* and *Materialism* reviewed here favorably in 1991 and 1993, respectively) and is a scant five years past Yale's cut-off for a younger poet. Each of her books remains readily available, so the only possible excuse is the publisher's desire to consolidate her work between two covers. This is not to diminish Graham's achievement; she is clearly an ambitious and talented poet, but not yet "a certified Old Fart." And, at 197 pages, albeit many of her poems are long, the volume seems gluttonous compared to Chappell's 155 pages or Justice's 173 pages, much less Bronk's bantam 80 pages.

As for the poems themselves, Vendler provides interesting access. Concerned with the ways in which poets break from an early style, Vendler examines Graham's use of long lines. Her earliest poems evidence "the young poet's approach, increment by increment, to a mastery of the world." In contrast, the later long-lined poems indicate a shift to a "lateral search," "the formal equivalent of mortality, dissolution, and unmeaning." Vendler rightly observes that "cinematic freeze-frame, by which an action sequence in film is divided. . .into minutely brief 'shots' " serves as a model for Graham's later poems. Such devices defer not only closure but often any sense of accumulation toward a whole. If, as Vendler argues, Graham's "fundamental measure" in many of her poems is "the gaze, rather than the breath," so that "utterance becomes. . .the tracking of the gaze, quantum-percept by quantum-percept," this indicates as well a prime weakness in the volume. By elevating vision over breath, Graham reinforces her preference for the cerebral over the visceral. Too many of her poems substitute sweeping lists of physical detail for felt experience of the physical world. Take, for example, this passage from the second section of the title poem in which she describes a tree full of starlings:

> All up and down the empty oak
> they stilled. Every limb sprouting. Every leafy
> backlit
>   body
> filling its part of the empty crown. I tried to
> count—
> then tried to estimate—
> but the leaves of this wet black tree at the heart
> of
>   the storm—shiny—
> river through limbs, back onto limbs,
> scatter, blow away, scatter, recollect—
> undoing again and again the tree without it ever
> ceasing to be
>   full.
> Foliage of the tree of the world's waiting.
> Of having waited a long time and
>   still having
> to wait. Of trailing and screaming.
> Of engulfed readjustments. Of blackness re-
> disappearing
>   into

> downdrafts of snow. Of indifference. Of indiffer-
> ent
>   reappearings.

What, one might reasonably inquire, happened to the starlings? The danger of such poetry, as Vendler notes but seems to feel Graham avoids, is that "the grand is always in danger of [becoming] the grandiose." The lyric sweep too easily loses the known world.

In *The Philosopher's Window and Other Poems,* his eighth collection, Allen Grossman takes a different tack toward the philosophical poem. In a prefatory note, Grossman explains that these poems "tell one story," from the point of view "of an old man compelled by the insistent questioning of the children to *explain* himself. On the long journey of his life, as he remembers it, everything speaks (which is only just) and teaches him by speaking to him (which is sheer good luck)." Grossman's approach draws on folk sources, biblical rhetoric, and what Coleridge would have called fancy. The voyage of the tale carries from a beginning, "The Great Work Farm Elegy," which opens "[i]n Adam's house, in Paradise," and establishes theme and premise:

> ". . .What, then, does it mean to begin again,
>   *dilectissimi,*
> As if from the beginning? It means just this:
> To be penetrated by a dark myth—in order
> To leave it empty at your death, like a book
> Forgotten on the asphalt that becomes, thereby,
> The one dark book which makes good
>   sense. . . ."

The rhetoric often sounds as if Wallace Stevens were attempting to tell a children's story, with its repetitions and embellishments, its intoxication with the physicality of language. And Grossman's enterprise, as he states in this first section, is likewise cut from the same cloth: to write "the extreme / Poem of the wind and rain, long letter of mind / Addressed to the abyss—*and sent.*"

Most sections of the book are organized in regular stanzas in almost regular pentameter lines. This armature serves well in a long poem that is both non-linear and frequently discursive. The artifice of the speaker also serves well, providing a keel for the poem that allows Grossman both to speak his mind and to preserve his privacy. This is especially true in the eponymous middle section, in which the speaker asserts, "It is time to begin the work. / The gods are done with it; but everything / Is left to do." Threaded through the fanciful tale of the speaker who becomes, as a boy, a ship's parrot, is the story of the building and launching of the *Great Eastern,* the largest steamship of its time, designed and constructed by the English civil engineer Isambard Kingdom Brunel. This story operates as metaphor for the poet's work, in the absence of gods, to make sense of a world left incomplete.

Another recurrent motif in this longest section is the philosopher at his window, gazing at the world. Stanza 132, from part XX., "A Short Walk to the Human End," exemplifies how Grossman handles his form:

> The philosopher rises from his window.
> He was staring at the ocean on its bed

Of stones, its turning, its falling in the eye
All night—as one might watch a sleepless soul
Forever passing away, and hear its cry
At the moment of passing. The philosopher
Turns at dawn from his window into the room
And walks through it into another room
And then another one, as into deeper snow.

From observation of the outer world, the poem turns inward, ever deeper inward. But as important is the way Grossman presents this idea, the variable pentameter line, occasional end-rhymes, and repeated phrasings—in short, the music of the expression reinforcing its sense.

From a beginning and middle, the volume leads to three possible endings, each with a slightly different mood. "The Snowfall" continues the mythic and prophetic vein of the middle section, while "Whoever Builds" extends the line of poet as *scop*, or maker, and the brief "June, June" provides the most lyrical conclusion. The second, however, which takes its title from Psalm 127, allows perhaps the greatest insight into Grossman's poetic premises, beginning with a poetic creed:

Whoever builds puts himself in service to materials
And becomes subject to the laws of materials.
Therefore, whoever builds of earth becomes subject
To the laws of earth. And whoever builds
Of air becomes subject to the laws of air.

By extension, of course, as more contemporary poets should understand, whoever builds of words becomes subject to the laws of words. This Grossman seems clearly to understand:

For things are known because
Of the laws they utter night and day. Thereof
Whoever builds, the poet first of all,
Does make his song.

Making such a song is an ambitious undertaking, demanding any poet's all. In this, his most rewarding collection to date, Allen Grossman makes an engaging go of it.

Time & Money, like the most recent of William Matthews' previous nine collections, is loosely organized around themes announced by the title and contains the poems about jazz and basketball that his fans have come to expect. This volume continues the course toward increased formality of line and stanza first seen in *Blues If You Want* (1991) and displays even greater felicity in several of the poems. This marks definite growth for Matthews, whose dry, often acerbic wit is best served by the constraints of rhyme and meter; Matthews himself observes, in "Time," that "what those critics like nicely to call 'wit' " is, in fact, "the whole compressed force of [his] rage / and love." Compression is exactly what received form facilitates in capable hands. If he seems disdainful of having written what critics call his "mature work," he has nonetheless progressed far from the youth of seventeen who, as he records in "Mingus at The Showplace," forced his poems on the jazz master. These lines, written from his misery, were "miserable, for that was how I thought / poetry worked: you digested experience and shat // literature." Instead, he understands, "Verse is easy, and poetry

is hard" ("The Rookery at Hawthornden"), which is true enough, as far as it goes. One might suggest, alternately, that, once learned, verse—i.e., composition by the line—may come easily, but that first caveat is crucial. Matthews' poems provide reasonable reward for the effort of reading them; that reward might be exponentially increased if he took the time before the next volume—and shredded the exercises, let me hasten to add—to get his numbers on his pulse.

Like Matthews, David Lee approaches his subject matter through humor. *My Town,* his fourth collection, consists of stories about the inhabitants of a small Utah town as told to the author by his friend John during the course of their workdays. Lee's ear for the rhythm and nuance of dialect seems unerring; although he largely eschews punctuation, his mastery of the line, as with the poems of Gary Snyder and Lucille Clifton, provides a clear sense of how to follow the syntactical flow. Because the poems are longish narratives, excerpting passages is difficult, but this verse paragraph from "Ugly" gives a sense of Lee's flair. The subject of the poem, Raphael Martinez, wakes one morning in excruciating pain, which he does not understand results from a kidney stone, and tries to take his life, unfortunately botching the job. Finally, he hoists himself onto the back of his mule and heads for town:

got him there by afternoon
passed out
people who found him was scairt to death
seen that one side
didn't have no face left
blood all over that mule
like he'd been swatting flies on him
with a icepick
they took him to the hospital
couldn't figure out what was wrong
saw all them holes in him
burnt off spots
blood everywhere
when they went
to lay him out straight he'd scream
like hell and they couldn't understand
a word of it
the only English he's speaking
was Spanish
couldn't wake him up enough
to shift his gear
tried to patch him up
best they could
without it costing much
they known it wasn't no insurance
nobody wanted the mule

The blend of pathos and hilarity, combined with wry delivery, recalls the Vermont monologues of Hayden Carruth, the contemporary master of the form. This book brings Lee a notch or two closer to that pinnacle.

Hayden Carruth selected *Infanta,* Erin Belieu's first collection, for the National Poetry Series, which might create a set of false expectations regarding these poems with their largely urban sensibility. Not uncommonly for a first book, Belieu stakes out a varied territory, from the domestic to the historical, the pastoral to the sophisticated, but themes of loyalty and memory run throughout. Her forms range from free verse and prose poems to the stricter requirements of rhyme and meter, as in the opening "Georgic on Memory":

> Lacking
> imagination, you'll take the pledge
>
> to remember—not the sexy, new
> idea of history, each moment
> swamped in legend, liable to judgment
> and erosion; still, an appealing view,
>
> to draft our lives, a series of vignettes
> where endings could be substituted—
> your father, unconvoluted
> by desire, not grown bonsai in regret,
>
> the bedroom of blue flowers left intact.

Vignettes, remembered or mis-remembered, or witnessed from a distance or felt from closest friends, comprise most of these poems. The poem which gives the volume its title, "For Catherine: Juana, Infanta of Navarre," braids the story of King Ferdinand's systematic stealing of his daughter's children to drive her mad with the less dramatic but equally poignant account of a friend trapped in an abusive marriage who "take[s] Prozac for depression, Ativan / for the buzz." Both women nurse dreams and loves about which the poet can only guess, imagining "the lost details of a life / that barely survives history."

Yet the volume is not all misery and bitterness; Belieu is equally comfortable with the lighter touch, suggesting more than her lines overtly reveal. In "The Problem of Fidelity," for instance, we might as easily believe that Belieu suggests as much about the process of composition as flirtation:

> It's the gamble, of course—
> the way the shot slips down when sent
> by a stranger; the conversation
>
> which, in itself, says nothing
> but all that isn't said; watching
> how a man takes off his shirt,
>
> unbuttons either collar
> or cuffs first or pulls the whole
> affair over, not careful about
>
> anything.

Such carelessness never mars these poems. The publication of *Infanta* signals the arrival of a poet worth watching.

In Alan Williamson's third collection, ***Love and the Soul***, neither love nor the soul emerges in clean, clear definition. This comes as little surprise when in the title poem Williamson notes, "T. S. Eliot called requited love 'the greater torment,' " a proposition for which this volume offers extensive proof. The mood is meditative, even elegiac, as signaled by the two opening poems, "The Author Reconsiders" and "Epilogue," respectively. Beginning with the end of things, however, does not necessarily imply the twenty-twenty hindsight of the Monday-morning quarterback; instead, Williamson uses distance to obtain a measure of objectivity which allows him to judge no one, neither himself nor any of the other parties, too harshly. What recrimina-

tion he offers results from the ambition of his reach, as suggested by these lines from the opening poem:

> What I mind most, in these pages,
> is having said so little to explain
> why things darken so quickly, between men and
> women,
> and not just in marriage; how soon,
> after the sheer balloon-like luck of the party,
> they're so huge to each other, niggled-at, unap-
> peasable. . .

"Epilogue" details in its tercets the evolution and dissolution of both marriage and subsequent affair with incisive analysis of motivation. Of himself and his wife, he notes,

> we had married each other
> in revenge, to destroy some hope in each other,
> as only siblings
>
> or parents should know enough to destroy.

The accuracy of observation is chilling and, extended through the volume, provides a contemporary equivalent of George Meredith's *Modern Love*. For Williamson, such treachery seems endemic to passion, as he writes later in the same poem:

> So in all things that descend
> there is an in-
> extricability, a pair of toothed gears, surface
>
> causing surface causing. . .

And neither party can truly communicate with the other. He provides a marvelous figure for this heart-wrenching separateness at the beginning of "Requited Love": "Two people in two houses on a hill, / the same record playing, think about a mystery." That mystery lies explored but finally undefined, as true mysteries should, at the heart of this collection.

Yet all is not hostile in this world; one accepts what comes. The opening lines of "Domestic Architecture" recall William Bronk's "A Vase of Various Flowers":

> There is no reason to be unhappy. Purplish flow-
> ers
> star the twigs out your window; it has a stately
> frame,
> eight small panes in procession above the great
> one,
> brown mullions like musical bars. And if the
> neighborhood's
> not what you asked for, still. . . Such things
> have woken you
> at almost every age, what is there more?

Such happiness through acceptance, however, is far from saintly. The third section of "Tidepools," the closing poem, provides an image for the all-too-human struggle:

> Suzuki Roshi
> says if you could think with a frog's mind,
> through and through,
>
> you would be Buddha.
> But what unremitting steadiness
> of wind the cormorants know themselves by,
> plunging

to their guano island. . .

Rereadings of this volume provide the satisfaction of sharing the experience of love and its attendant suffering presented in its complexity, even if we come away feeling it has all the clarity of mud.

Williamson's line in "Epilogue" could well have provided the epigraph for David Dooley's second collection: "*love becomes, incalculably, revenge. . . .*" Though very different in its forms, stance, and tone, **The Revenge by Love** ventures into the same territories. I should immediately note that my familiarity with the poems in this collection extends beyond that of reviewer; I have seen these poems in manuscript and provided an introduction to the volume. That said, I will attempt to approach the poems from the reviewer's rather than the advocate's stance, difficult as the task may be. Although often lumped with the so-called expansive poets (encompassing both new formalism and the new narrative), Dooley's work bears only superficial resemblance to the poems of these writers. One will scan the volume in vain for iambic pentameter or rhyme schemes; instead, one will find predominantly long-lined free verse narratives and monologues, prose poems, and even brief haiku-like poems. His references, also, are not as exclusively popular as those employed by many of the expansive poets, nor are his subjects as urban, nor his stance as urbane, though he is as comfortable writing about the French composer Camille Saint-Saens as about a rural mother who has lost her son to AIDS. Regardless of subject, Dooley withholds judgment, presenting enough detail to allow us to reach our own judgments about his characters, who, like their flesh-and-blood counterparts are an infuriating mix of the admirable and the inane. In "Zoramel," for instance, Dooley narrates the predicament of a student writer who has slept with his mentor's student girlfriend. Through the lens of the student's projected but, notably, unwritten fantasy novel set on the planet Zoramel, Dooley explores the student's confused feelings of guilt, denial, projection, and rationalization. In the end, we can neither condemn the student too harshly nor extend unqualified sympathy to the morose mentor.

Humor occupies a prominent place in Dooley's poetic toolbox, from the wry suggestiveness of "Politics," in which a speaker reminiscent of Gore Vidal flirts with a young man under the guise of discussing his aborted politic career, to the broader humor of "Dirt," a dramatic monologue whose apparent subject is the speaker's old and very messy friend; as with "Politics," however, the true subject, emerging from subtext, is seduction. Similarly, "A Little Hunger" explores a woman's rationalizations surrounding her diet as she thinks about her boyfriend, conflating the pleasures in ways that reveal much about her character:

> She hadn't wanted
> to marry anyone
> before law school and in law school who had
> time
> to do anything but order in pizza and read cases?
> Mushrooms
> and pepperoni with extra cheese. Yum. At work
> she could exist on microwave popcorn (unsalted,

unbuttered, as much as she wanted) and diet
Pepsi.
Eric said he loved her figure, which was sweet,
but
did anyone really love cellulite thighs?

As elsewhere in the volume, the humor does not exist to elicit a chuckle but to illuminate character and situation and to leaven the underlying pain.

The sequence "O'Keeffe and Steiglitz," which probes the relationship of the painter and photographer through poetic vignettes, comprises the second section of the book and marks Dooley's greatest accomplishment to date. Here, humor, objectivity, and facility with various forms allows Dooley to create fragments from which we can infer a greater whole. One of the strongest of these pieces is the prose poem, "Lake George at Winter," which evokes the wind-swept cinematography of *Doctor Zhivago* as it presents O'Keeffe's romance with poet and novelist Jean Toomer:

> Deep snow drifted around the farmhouse. The world seemed exceedingly pure, dazzlingly bright. They drove the Model T onto the surface of the ice and walked on the wide, glowing expanse till the bitter wind forced them back. Bits of dark green, ranges of brown, and white, white. Cerulean sky. Their breath carried their words out onto the wind. When she grew cold, he took one hand in each of his and rubbed them against each other. The ice could bear so much weight, themselves and the car made no impression. The day was blown glass of finest Venetian work. She showed him her favorite birch.

The implicit distancing of the prose poem allows Dooley to render their passion without falling into mere sentimentality; the details accumulate with the force of metaphor.

The final poem of the sequence, "Ghost Ranch," a dramatic monologue set after O'Keeffe's move to New Mexico, employs a very painterly sensibility. Dooley captures the landscape as O'Keeffe might have seen it—in both its particulars and its sweeping patterns. Most moving, however, is the gritty, hard-won optimism of the inveterate realist he has O'Keeffe voice at the end in imagined conversation with Steiglitz:

> My dear, I have a curious triumphant feeling
> about life.
> Seeing it bleak. Knowing it so and walking into
> it fearless
> because one has no choice. Enjoying one's consciousness.
> You spoiled me for other men, you know.
> How sharply the bonelight winks tonight!
> Far out in the dark are hills which turn angry
> red
> when a cloud passes. Oh, but in other lights
> they are pink as flesh. What will tomorrow's first
> colors be?
> Coral? Peach? Pale yellow? Opalescent blue?
> And then the sun will rise.

This second collection establishes Dooley as a significant voice in contemporary poetry, though the singular noun is somewhat belying, for Dooley's talent is having the strength and skill to speak in the many voices that compose our consciousness.

The Year in Drama

by Julius Novick

Because a play is not completely fulfilled until it is produced, and because theatrical production is a complicated, expensive, time-consuming, and above all a *public* process, drama is of all forms of literature the most dependent upon political, economic, and social factors. In 1995 these were not favorable.

The theater is the house that the drama lives in, and—to change the metaphor—the theater is a handicraft industry in a technological age. With only a few exceptions—mainly huge musicals, most of them British—professional theater in America cannot pay for itself. And the times are not friendly to anything that cannot pay for itself—especially anything with claims to be "art" or "culture," and thus subject to attack from right and left (but mostly right, these days) for being "elitist." The National Endowment for the Arts is being phased out. State and local arts subsidies are being cut back. Private givers are not taking up the slack. Not-for-profit theaters—where most new American plays originate—are tightening their belts and still going into deficit. The avant-garde, so vital and confident a few decades ago, is quiescent. And no one will ever know what masterpieces we may have lost because playwrights must spend their time writing for films or television, or waiting on tables, in order to make a living.

There was no new American play of really impressive stature in 1995, and there were some significant disappointments. Most of such excitement as there was came from foreign plays. And yet there were American plays in 1995 that were well-crafted, that were witty, that were entertaining, that were charming, that had something to say about the way we live now. All is not yet lost.

The most eagerly awaited new American play of the year was *Master Class* by Terrence McNally, whose *Love! Valour! Compassion!* was a major success of the previous year. A "master class" is a peculiar ritual of the classical-music world in which a celebrated artist, often a singer well past her prime, coaches young performers as an audience looks on. In McNally's play, the stage represents the stage of a hall in some unnamed conservatory; the audience of the play becomes the audience at such a master class; and the master musician, sharing her wisdom and experience, her malice and paranoia, with three young singers and with us, is Cecilia Sophia Anna Maria Kalogeropoulou, better known to the world as Maria Callas.

Proudly McNally's Callas preaches courage, fierce self-discipline, dramatic authenticity. One after the other she challenges her three pupil-victims, lectures them, bullies them, humiliates them, plays with them like a cat with a mouse. (Two are sopranos, one a tenor; she flirts a little with the tenor.) Self-absorbed, endlessly thirsty for attention, for applause, for revenge against what she perceives as a hostile world, this Callas is an imperious swan desperately demanding reassurance that she is no longer an ugly duckling.

As each young soprano launches into her showpiece aria, the lighting changes, the young singer becomes invisible and inaudible, and we hear the aging diva's reverie. She re-experiences her triumphs—but also the key moments of her affair with Aristotle Onassis, whom she remembers as a vulgar pig who demeaned her artistry, made her abort his baby, and refused to marry her. (The play's popular appeal is doubtlessly based in part on its gossip value.) These parts of the play are not innocent of sentimentality or melodrama. ("My song of love was for you, Ari!" she declares with a straight face.) Here, as in *The Lisbon Traviata*, his other play with an operatic background, McNally has clearly taken the open, bold, extravagant emotionality of opera as his standard.

Master Class is not a work of any great profundity: it is a Romantic glorification of the Suffering Artist, and above all the Suffering Lover, a Romantic exaltation of sheer intensity of experience. There is nothing much new about all that. The appeal is in the specifics, in the *presence* of this elegant, driven, pained, merciless woman.

Ever since the play's first reading at a new-play program in Big Fork, Montana, through engagements in Philadelphia, Los Angeles, Washington, D. C. and on to Broadway, the magnificent Zoe Caldwell has been McNally's Callas. She plays her with cool chic, dangerous, dulcet charm, and touches of mischievous understatement, through all of which we can feel the raging hurt that bursts forth at the climaxes. "This isn't just an opera—it's your life!" says Callas to one of her pupils, and whether she is enacting an aria or reliving a crisis of her own life, Caldwell gives herself up almost voluptuously to the emotion of the moment. There is a certain amount of repetitiveness built into *Master Class,* but the actress, the playwright, and their director (Leonard Foglia) have created a fascinating monster.

The Young Man from Atlanta, dark-horse winner of the 1995 Pulitzer Prize for Drama, is as unassuming as *Master Class* is flamboyant. Horton Foote, its author, has been writing plays for more than fifty years—mostly straightforward, scrupulously naturalistic plays about ordinary people in East Texas, the part of the country where he was born in 1916. Foote owns a couple of Oscars, for the screenplays of *To Kill a Mockingbird* and *Tender Mercies*;

as a playwright, he is a respected figure who has never broken through to a large audience. For the 1994-95 season, he was playwright-in-residence at the Signature Theater Company, a tiny off-Broadway enterprise in lower Manhattan that devotes its entire season to one playwright, a different one every year. Of the four Foote productions mounted by Signature, one was the world premiere of *The Young Man from Atlanta.*

Sometimes I have come away from a play of Horton Foote's thinking, "That was believable, all right—the author obviously knows his milieu—but what happens just isn't very interesting. Scrupulous ordinariness can go too far." (I thought that about *Laura Dennis,* another Foote play given its world premiere this year by the Signature Theater Company.) But *The Young Man from Atlanta* is more substantial.

Its central character, Will Kidder, is an aging businessman in Houston. Like Willy Loman in *Death of a Salesman,* he has worked many years for the same firm, and like Willy Loman he is fired by the son of his old boss. This aspect of the play is, to say the least, derivative. But Will has another trouble: his only son, who had left Houston and moved to Atlanta, has committed suicide at the age of 37. Now Will is being pestered by a young man from Atlanta, his son's "roommate" (the year is 1950).

The young man never actually appears in the play. Will refuses to see him, "Because there are things I'd have to ask him and I don't want to know the answer." How the truth about their son threatens Will and his wife, and how they deal with that threat, makes for modest, effective, and legitimate pathos.

From Eugene O'Neill onwards, American drama has often set out to indict America, to expose the hollowness of the American Dream. But one play of 1995 actually has the power to make people feel good about America, by introducing us to two actual, exemplary Americans. *Having Our Say* was adapted from the best-selling book of the same name; like the book, it recounts the memories and opinions of the Delaney sisters, two Negro maiden ladies, as they would call themselves. They have plenty to remember: the play takes place in 1993, the year the book was published, when Sadie was 104 and Bessie was 102 years old. (Bessie died during the run of the play; Sadie, at this writing, lives on.)

In the age of gangsta rap and commercial culture's nervous fascination with its own urban, black, margins, the Delaney sisters, somewhat like General Colin Powell, offer a reassuring counter-image (or so it might seem to well-disposed and anxious whites) of the African-American experience. As Bessie says, "I'm the kind of Negro most white Americans don't know about." Sadie Delaney was the first of her race to teach domestic science in a New York City high school; Bessie Delaney was that rare phenomenon, a black woman dentist. They are glad to be Americans, and at the same time proud of their race. They are not unaware of prejudice and discrimination, nor do they minimize it. They have suffered from it, and resented it, and fought it, and triumphed over it. But they are never sanctimonious. They share a sly wit—this is a

funny play, if not a conventional comedy—and a zest for life.

Not that they are interchangeable. "If Sadie is molasses, I am vinegar," says Bessie. When Sadie says, "Sometimes it's better to put up with it and live to tell about it," Bessie replies, "I told you, honey. I would rather die than back down." In the production that came to Broadway from the McCarter Theater in Princeton, N. J. (where adapter/director Emily Mann is the artistic director), Gloria Foster is warmly gracious as Sadie, and Mary Alice plays Bessie with sparkling mischief. As they welcome us to their home, as they cook the dinner that was their father's favorite (there is no real dramatic action, and it is not much missed), they play off each other with a lovely intimacy, like two women who have enjoyed one another's company for a hundred years. "Bessie is a naughty old girl," says Sadie. "I try to be good, ha ha ha ha ha," replies Bessie, with an irrepressible, irresistible giggle. Emily Mann and her two wonderful actresses make sure that whatever the Delaney sisters exemplify and represent, they are first of all two very particular and utterly delightful people.

The unluckiest play of the year was *Night and Her Stars* by Richard Greenberg. Graceful, witty, and intelligent like most of Greenberg's plays (of which *Eastern Standard* remains the best-known), it deals, like *Master Class* and *Having Our Say,* with real people and real events: in particular, the scandal that erupted when it was learned that America's favorite quiz show was fixed, and that Charles Van Doren, that clean-cut intellectual hero, had been fed the questions in advance. Commissioned and first produced by the South Coast Repertory in Costa Mesa, California, *Night and Her Stars* was produced in New York by the Manhattan Theater Club soon after the run of *Quiz Show,* Robert Redford's film about the same events. Greenberg's play seemed superfluous, and passed almost unnoticed. But, especially at this point in our history, how can we have too many plays, movies, novels, poems, whatever, that anatomize dishonesty?

The most interesting thing about *Night and Her Stars* is its characterization of Dan Enright, the man behind the fix. A trashy manipulator in the film, he emerges in the play as a brilliant manipulator, reflective, sardonic, and—thanks to Peter Frechette's quiet, strong acting—scary: Mephistopheles to Van Doren's Faust. *Night and Her Stars* deserved a better fate.

The most promising new American playwright of the year was, of all people, the actor-comedian-screenwriter Steve Martin, the erstwhile "wild and crazy guy" himself. His comedy *Picasso at the Lapin Agile,* first staged in 1993 at the Steppenwolf Theater in Chicago under Randall Arney's direction, transferred to Los Angeles and then, somewhat recast along the way, to an off-Broadway house in New York in 1995. (Another production was mounted at the American Repertory Theater in Cambridge, Mass.)

As its title implies, *Picasso* is another play that deals with people who actually existed—but it is very far from being a docu-drama. Taking place in 1904, it shows Pablo Picasso, aged 23, and Albert Einstein, aged 25, meeting in an artists' bar in Paris, competing for the attention of a young woman, and recognizing each other as a fellow genius. The comedy is based mainly on the difference between the eager, self-confident young men we see, and the venerated elders we know they will become. Nothing much happens for most of the play, but there is a beguiling offhand goofiness about the whole affair.

Then toward the end it shifts into a higher gear. The drab landscape painting over the bar is magically transformed into Picasso's huge, strange "Les Demoiselles d'Avignon"; a splendid night sky appears, in tribute to Einstein; everyone toasts the twentieth century. The contrast between the radiant optimism of this moment, and what we at the edge of the millennium know about the blood-soaked twentieth century, makes for poignant irony.

Steve Martin's other, and lesser, contribution as a playwright was a bill of four one-acts, presented by the Joseph Papp Public Theater/New York Shakespeare Festival (which surely deserves an award as the most awkwardly-named theater in America). The first of the four is a tiny, exquisite vaudeville sketch entitled **"Guillotine"**; the last and longest, entitled **"Wasp,"** is a tired and tiresome satire on the ideal of the American family; the other two are in between in both length and quality.

Other bills of one-act comedies had more to offer. *London Suite* will go down in history as the first play by Neil Simon—Neil Simon, for so many years the very symbol of commercial theater—ever to be given its New York premiere off-Broadway. This was widely, and not inaccurately, taken as a sign of Broadway's current inhospitality to non-musical plays, but it also suggests that Simon no longer commands the loyalty of as large an audience as he once did.

Following the pattern set by Simon's *Plaza Suite* and *California Suite*, *London Suite* is a bill of one-act plays that take place in the same luxury hotel room. It is not his best by any means, but it is good work, in an old-pro sort of way, with plenty of wisecracks, some sentiment (a famous actress has a reunion with her gay ex-husband), and some old-fashioned farce (including that ever-popular standby, the man who throws his back out and lies on the floor groaning while everything collapses into merry chaos around him). Deftly directed by Daniel Sullivan (artistic director of the Seattle Repertory Theater, where *London Suite* was first produced), with a cast led by Carole Shelley and Paxton Whitehead, two of the finest comic actors that England ever sent us, it had a disappointing five-month run, but it made a highly entertaining evening.

Death Defying Acts, the most popular of this year's off-Broadway bills of one-act comedies, consists of three plays by three different authors, united by a tart, unsentimental, tough-mouthed, big-city sensibility. **"An Interview"** by David Mamet is a brief, inconsequential sketch in which a lawyer is admitted to hell. In **"Hotline"** by Elaine May, a grouchy, depressed hooker calls a suicide hotline manned by a very inexperienced volunteer. The evening's last, longest and best work is **"Central Park West"** by Woody Allen, a hilarious festival of bracingly nasty wise-

cracks and at the same time a scathing portrait of moral bankruptcy among the Manhattan well-to-do.

Allen presents us with Phyllis, a formidable, middle-aged psychiatrist whose husband, Sam, has just left her, causing her to take refuge in alcohol, irony, and a little physical destructiveness. Enter Phyllis's friend Carol—whom Phyllis soon forces to admit to being the Other Woman. But it turns out that Sam doesn't want to go away with Carol after all. In view of Woody Allen's well-known personal life, it is interesting that Sam, who wants to leave his Central Park West wife for a beautiful twenty-one-year-old, gets decidedly the worst of it. Phyllis has the last line of the play: "Grow up, Sam—she shot you in the ass—it's called rejection!"

Two gentler American comedies, one by a veteran playwright and one by a neophyte, transferred to commercial off-Broadway runs from the Manhattan Theater Club. Like **"Central Park West,"** A. R. Gurney's *Sylvia* concerns a restless husband in a middle-aged, upper-middle-class Manhattan marriage. Unlike Allen's Sam, Gurney's Greg is not a philanderer. Instead, one day he brings home a dog. The dog's name is Sylvia, and she is a wonderful creation: eager, affectionate, impulsive, mercurial, bawdy, self-centered, manipulative, and pushy. Lassie she's not. She talks—which everyone in the play seems to take as a matter of course—and she is played, without disguise, by a very attractive young woman.

"Give a dog a woman's name," says another dog-owner, "you begin to think of her as a woman." Greg refuses to see that this applies to him, but how can he resist when Silvia says, "I think you're God, if you want to know," or sings, "Darling, je vous aime beaucoup," or says, "But even when you behave like a complete asshole, I love you completely"? "They do everything together," complains Kate, Greg's wife. "Once I caught them sharing an ice cream cone." Repeatedly Greg ignores Kate in order to pay attention to Sylvia. "Well, Sylvia, thanks a lot," says the rejected wife. "You've managed to chew a huge hole in a twenty-two-year-old marriage!"

All this could easily become sick and kinky and grotesque, but Gurney is not that kind of writer; tactfully, he keeps things bright and funny, with light, latent sexual electricity in the air. The problem is that he doesn't know how to end the play. Having devoted most of it to showing that Greg prefers his dog to his wife, he very implausibly has Greg agree to give up Sylvia at Kate's insistence, and then, equally implausibly, has Kate at the last minute agree to keeping Sylvia, so that, even more implausibly, all three of them can live together fairly happily ever after. It may seem preposterous to complain about this in a play with a talking dog played by a woman, but Aristotle pointed out long ago that it is not literal impossibility that destroys a play, but implausibility within the play's own context. In any case, up until those last few minutes, *Sylvia* is a playful fantasia, not without its share of shrewd truth, on the theme of male menopausal madness.

After-Play by Anne Meara—a veteran actress and comedienne, but a first-time playwright—puts us once again in upscale Manhattan, but the two couples who are the main characters are somewhat older than Greg and Kate, or Phyllis and Sam. They are having dinner together at a nice quiet restaurant, which is really some kind of vaguely supernatural space; Raziel, the gentle, dignified, unflappable waiter/bartender, is, as someone says, "an angel." The two couples discuss the play they have just seen; they bicker and make up; they complain about their kids; they drink far into the night. A third couple passes through; they have lost their son to AIDS, and the wife (powerfully played by Rochelle Oliver) has gotten bitterly, furiously drunk. But they are out the door in just a few minutes.

Nothing much happens in *After-Play*—as is true of several of this year's American plays—but fortunately, the conversation is snappy enough to sustain the evening. When one of the men refers to the women as "girls," one of them replies, "There are no girls here, Phil. Girls don't have wrinkles and mastectomies and children who hate them." Aging is the real subject of *After-Play.*

Along with these variously satisfying American plays of 1995, there were others, by writers of proven talents, that for one reason or another failed to meet expectations. (We won't even talk about the year's meager and dispiriting musical-theater activity.) The most eminent of these writers was David Mamet, whose play *The Cryptogram* was staged by the American Repertory Theater in Cambridge, Massachusetts and brought from there to New York for an unexpectedly brief commercial off-Broadway run. *The Cryptogram* was greatly admired by some; it seemed to me, however, that this portentous drama of a young boy failed by the adults around him was tiresomely mannered and cryptic, a festival of uncompleted sentences.

Donald Margulies, the author of *The Model Apartment,* is a thoughtful writer who specializes in bitterly ironic explorations of the sorrows and confusions of Jewish-American life. (His best-known play is *Sight Unseen*, that searching exposure of the contradictions in the life of a successful Jewish painter from Brooklyn.) First produced at the Los Angeles Theater Center in 1988, *The Model Apartment* came to New York in a new production at Primary Stages, an off-Broadway theater specializing in new plays. Its protagonist is a Holocaust survivor whose daughter—vividly imagined by the playwright and vividly played by Roberta Wallach—is an intolerably motor-mouthed schizophrenic, changing moods instantaneously and fantasizing feverishly. The father's grief is finely dramatized as he dreams of his older daughter, his daughter in another world, who was murdered by the Nazis. But it is never very clear what the Holocaust, and schizophrenia, and a "model apartment" in a Florida condo complex, furnished with fake appliances, have to do with one another. And where did the schizoid daughter's African-American boyfriend come from?

Another disappointment at Primary Stages was *Don Juan in Chicago,* a leaden rhyming comedy by David Ives, whose six-pack of comic playlets entitled *All in the Timing* was one of the delights of 1994. Don Juan can live forever if he beds a new woman every night; Donna Elvira pursues him down the centuries; the elaborately jokey situations just do not come off.

Even at the invaluable Manhattan Theater Club, not every play measured up to the hopes vested in it. Richard Nelson is a playwright more successful in London than at home. His *Some Americans Abroad,* a quietly merciless exposure of various kinds of dishonesty among American academics in England, was first produced at the Royal Shakespeare Company, as was *New England,* about a group of British expatriates in America. Given an American production by the MTC in 1995, *New England* had its share of admirers, but seemed to me unfocussed and repetitious. Clearly all the sneering at and grousing about America was meant to show how snooty the Brits are, not how barbaric the Americans are; but there was an awful lot of it.

Most of the theatrical excitement of 1995 was generated by foreign plays—from Ireland, from South Africa, from France, but mainly from England. The leading purveyor of English plays to American audiences is New York's Lincoln Center Theater—to the point where it is sometimes referred to as the Royal National Theater West. Trevor Nunn, who directed the original production of Tom Stoppard's *Arcadia* at the Royal National Theater in London, restaged the play at Lincoln Center with an American cast. (When *Arcadia* opened at Lincoln Center's Vivian Beaumont Theater, Stoppard's earlier play *Hapgood*—reviewed last year—was still running at the Center's smaller downstairs stage, creating a much-appreciated informal Stoppard Festival.) *Arcadia* won the New York Drama Critics Circle Award as the Best Play of 1994-95.

Tom Stoppard, as is well known, is not only intelligent but learned, and not only learned but fiendishly clever. All of these qualities have seldom been so abundantly displayed together as they are in *Arcadia.* The play is full of lore: about history, literature, science, mathematics, even gardening. But Stoppard's cleverness, at the service of his inborn, somersaulting playfulness, keeps *Arcadia* safely free of academic dust.

The play has two plots, ingeniously interconnected. "The action . . .", as Stoppard says, "shuttles back and forth between the early nineteenth century and the present day, always in this same room" in a splendid English country house. In the earlier time, Lady Thomasina Coverly, a brilliant girl—a genius—in early adolescence, is making staggering mathematical discoveries and becoming curious about "carnal embrace," which her tutor, a young man named Septimus Hodge, defines as "the practice of throwing one's arms around a side of beef." Septimus, however, does a good deal of carnal embracing himself, which gets him embroiled in various imbroglios.

In the present, a pushy, ambitious academic named Bernard Nightingale (played with neatly channeled comic energy by Victor Garber) is trying to find out what happened in the earlier time, believing himself on the verge of a sensational discovery about Lord Byron, who, as Stoppard has it, was a friend of Septimus. With triumphant flourishes, Bernard makes interpretations of the evidence that seem reasonable, but that, as Stoppard delights in showing us, are entirely erroneous. The satire on contemporary academic careerism is deftly hilarious.

Stoppard, however, is after bigger things: *Arcadia* is meant to be about the universe, and fate, and the sadness of things. But *what* about them? Hard to say. So much is going on in this intricate, two-tiered play that you would almost have to be Stoppard to be able to figure it all out. But *Arcadia* is wonderful even so, for its two neatly dovetailed stories, for the delicate note of sadness that emerges as the stories coalesce at the end, and most of all for the delights of Stoppard's dialogue: "Lending one's bicycle is a form of safe sex, possibly the safest there is." "Is the universe expanding? Is it contracting? Is it standing on one leg and singing 'When Father Painted the Parlour?' " "It is a defect of God's humour that he directs our hearts everywhere but to those who have a right to them."

Arcadia was followed into the Beaumont by David Hare's *Racing Demon*: another play from the National, again with the original director (this time Richard Eyre, head of the National) and an American cast. Hare is a very different sort of playwright from Stoppard: a blunt, angry lefty with comparatively little aptitude for playing with words or ideas. If Hare ever set a play in a great Stately Home, he would probably burn it down before the final curtain.

Part of a trilogy of plays about British institutions, *Racing Demon* examines the Church of England, which, it is universally conceded, is not in very good shape these days. According to a program note (reprinted, like the notes to *Arcadia,* from the National Theater program), in an average parish in 1985, 1.4% of the people went to C. of E. services on an average Sunday. "In general," said *The New York Times* recently, "the Church seems increasingly irrelevant to Britain's national life." But Hare is surprisingly sympathetic to the beleaguered Established Church, or at least to some of the clergyman who wrestle with the question of what the Church can and should mean in a contemporary, diminished, multi-racial, largely impoverished, overwhelmingly secular England. For a writer like David Hare to take the Church of England seriously—as he certainly does—is perhaps the finest compliment it has received lately.

Hare's protagonist, the Rev. Lionel Espy, is a parish priest in inner-city London, aging, overworked, oppressed by a sense of God's absence. Uninterested in doctrine and ritual, somewhat set in his ways, he tries to do what he can for his poverty-stricken parishioners—those few he can reach. Opposed to him is the Rev. Tony Ferris, an eager, impatient young man on fire with idealism and faith. "I want a full church," says Tony. "Is that so disgraceful? I want to see the whole community worshipping under one roof. That's what I want. And that's what I believe the Lord wants as well." And "Christ didn't come to sit on a committee. He didn't come to do social work. He came to preach repentance." And "People must be converted. There is only one religion. . . . And the only way to God is through Jesus Christ." Lionel becomes for Tony a symbol of what is wrong with the Church: "People don't go near him. He reeks of personal failure." And so Tony, the young zealot, enters into an unholy, incongruous alliance with a wily political bishop, and together they destroy Lionel.

There are a few clumsy Brechtian touches, and the whole play is a bit schematic, as if the theme came first, and then the characters. But the arguments have a Shavian urgency, complexity, and lucidity (though not much Shavian wit), and the struggle is compelling to watch, with personal destinies riding on moral and doctrinal disputes, and emotion driving the rhetoric. Josef Sommer, that quietly superb American actor, makes Lionel gentle but not weak, a man of dignity, integrity and grace; Michael Cumpsty gives Tony plenty of boyish charm, without stinting his dangerous ruthlessness. The arcane and ancient ways of the Church, the purple robes of the bishops, are not neglected, but the play, full of anguished inquiry as to what can be *done* about modern misery, seems anything but remote. We could use more *American* plays like this, in which institutions are examined and ideas are argued.

A third production from the National, recast for America, came not to Lincoln Center but to a commercial Broadway house. (As the veteran producer Robert Whitehead observed, surveying the plays that come to America from heavily-subsidized British institutions, "It's amazing how much our theater is depending on the taxpayer in England.") *Les Parents Terrible*, retitled *Indiscretions* for the American market, is a not-very-well-known play written in 1938 by Jean Cocteau. At least one scholar of French theater refers to it as a "tragedy," but especially in Sean Mathias's entertainingly over-the-top staging, it seemed to me (and to many other people) too preposterous to take altogether seriously. It concerns a young man who meets a young woman, falls in love with her, and is appalled to discover that she is the mistress of none other than his own father. Moreover, the father is secretly loved by his wife's sister, and the young man has a madly quasi-incestuous relationship with his mother. In Stephen Brimson Lewis's spectacular sets and costumes (also from the National), Eileen Atkins plays the sister-in-law with tart elegance, and young Jude Law, the only holdover from the English cast, gives a memorable portrait of the young man as a narcissistic puppy-dog. The whole thing is somewhat of a hoot.

A *fourth* play that came to America from the National Theater was *Mrs. Klein* by Nicholas Wright. But this one at least arrived off-Broadway in an all-American production. *Mrs. Klein* has something in common with *Master Class*: both are about real twentieth-century women, gifted, powerful, unhappy women, and both these women are spectacularly played by illustrious senior actresses.

"Mrs. Klein" is Melanie Klein, a celebrated and controversial pioneer of child psychoanalysis. As might perhaps be guessed, the play revolves around her destructive effect on her own children. Her son Hans has just died, and she manages not to go to the funeral. Did he commit suicide in order to get back at her? So thinks her daughter Melitta, also a psychoanalyst, and, according to a program note, "an implacable opponent of her mother's work. They were never reconciled." Mrs. Klein is in the process of replacing her daughter with a daughter-surrogate, another young woman who is, once again, a psychoanalyst.

Economically, classically, the play unfolds in one room, Mrs. Klein's living-room-work-room, over the course of one night and the following morning, as its three characters, the older woman and the two younger ones, work out their relationships to one another. There is a slight sense of gimmickry, as damaging revelations explode at neatly timed intervals, one reversing the other. But there is suspense, too, about how and why Hans died. And the playwright provides a brilliant demonstration of how psychoanalytic "insights" can be used by the adept as defensive and offensive weapons.

Best of all, *Mrs. Klein* provides a highly suitable role for Uta Hagen, one of this country's leading teachers of acting, and herself an actress much admired but not easy to cast. Born in Germany, Hagen has no trouble with Mrs. Klein's Central-European-ness; more important, she does justice to her arrogance, her rigidity, her wide-ranging changes of mood and emotion—and her charm. "She who can't, teaches" could never be said of Uta Hagen.

Not all the foreign plays that reached America in 1995 were from the National Theater (though it sometimes seemed so). The Roundabout Theater Company opened a new space for new plays in its premises overlooking Broadway, and inaugurated it with the American premiere of *Moonlight,* Harold Pinter's first new full-length play since 1978. It featured an elderly grouch (played by a miscast Jason Robards) lying and perhaps dying downstage left, watched over by his impassive wife (Blythe Danner), rejected by his two sons, and inconclusively visited by a middle-aged couple with whom he and his wife may have been sexually involved. At intervals, a young girl, presumably the putatively dying man's deceased daughter, wafts through the proceedings, being lyrical.

There are nice touches here and there, but except for the lyrical daughter, it mostly seems like Pinter imitating Pinter, complete with the usual Pinteresque haziness about what went on in the past. ("The past? What past?" says grouchy, bed-ridden Andy. "I don't remember any past. What kind of past did you have in mind?") The dialogue is typically Pinteresque: elliptical, pause-ridden, alternating passages of edgy, brittle banter with long verbal arias, altogether illustrating the old adage that words were given to us to conceal our thoughts. *Moonlight* makes it seem as if words were given to Pinter to conceal his play.

The Roundabout made amends with a beautiful production of a beautiful play: *Molly Sweeney,* written and directed by Ireland's leading playwright, Brian Friel. *Molly Sweeney* tells a simple story: Molly is an Irishwoman, living in a small town, getting on toward middle age. She has been blind since she was ten months old, but she is comfortable in her world of touch and hearing. At her husband's urging, she is operated on by a brilliant eye surgeon whose career has been ruined by drink, and who sees in Molly a chance to rehabilitate himself. Molly's sight is indeed restored, but the ultimate results are not what anyone hoped for. (The playwright acknowledges a debt to Dr. Oliver Sacks, for Sacks's article on the actual case of a man whose sight was restored, with unhappy results.) I was reminded of the title of a poem by Dr. Samuel Johnson: "The Vanity of Human Wishes."

It has been argued that *Molly Sweeney* is not a play at all,

since the story is not enacted but told. The three characters—Molly, her husband Frank, and the surgeon Mr. Rice—take turns telling the audience what happened. Their accounts do not conflict in Pinteresque fashion, but amplify and complement one another. The scope thus given to all three to reflect on their experience, and the grave, graceful, unobtrusive beauty of Friel's prose, justify his unusual choice of dramatic (if it is dramatic) method. Here, for instance, is Molly, remembering the eve of her first operation, when the possibility of losing her comfortable blind world loomed before her: "And then I knew, suddenly I knew why I was so desolate. It was the dread of exile, of being sent away. It was the desolation of homesickness." And here is Mr. Rice, remembering his years of success: "Insatiable years. Work. Airports. Dinners. Laughter. Operating theaters. Conferences. Gossip. Publications. The professional jealousies and the necessary vigilance. The relentless, devouring excitement. But above all, above all the hunger to accomplish, the greed for achievement."

It might be thought then that *Molly Sweeney* is really just a radio play, with only an aural dimension, but its presence onstage is justified by Friel's three remarkable actors, whose visible presence makes a compelling contribution. The serenity and stillness of Catherine Byrne, for whom the role of Molly was written, contrasts vividly with the eager, itchy, nervous energy of Alfred Molina as Frank (an "enthusiast" with a short attention span), and this in turn contrasts with the dry, distanced, medical manner, the stooped, shambling body, the beetling brows and cavernous eye-sockets of Jason Robards, admirably cast as Mr. Rice.

From South Africa, via the McCarter Theater in Princeton, New Jersey, to the Manhattan Theater Club came *Valley Song,* written and directed by Athol Fugard, with two-thirds of the dramatis personae played (and played very well) by Athol Fugard. *Valley Song* is Fugard's first post-*apartheid* play, and unless I've missed something, it is the first genuinely cheerful play in the long, honorable, and somber career of a writer who often seemed to be trying to take all the sins of white South Africa onto his own shoulders.

The play is set on a farm where an old "Colored" man lives with his beloved seventeen-year-old granddaughter, Veronica, who represents the new South Africa. Veronica objects to "bowing and scraping." "You will never see me on my knees," she cries, "scrubbing a white man's floor." Instead, she wants to be a singer. "When I sing," she says, "I'm alive. And my singing is my life."

The crux of the plot is rather Victorian: Veronica wants to go off to the big city and pursue her destiny, but the old man is dead set against it, fearing that the girl will come to a bad end there, like her mother before her. Finally he is persuaded that singing is to Veronica what planting seeds is to him. "Will you give me your blessing?" she asks. "God bless you, my child," he replies. "I love you, *Oupa!*" she says.

Valley Song is a sentimental, platitudinous, rather hokey play, slow-moving, as Fugard's plays tend to be. Veronica's little songs, scattered through this brief evening, have pleasant music by DiDi Kriel, but Fugard will never make it as a lyricist. And it is a little disturbing that the happy ending is brought about by a smiling, benevolent, patronizing *deus ex machina* described in the program as "The Author, a White man."

But the play's visual and structural unpretentiousness (ninety-minute running time, quick transitions, minimal scenery, a cast of two), and the charm of the performers, help us over the soggy spots. Fugard himself, as the old man and The Author, is a striking figure, with his furrowed brow, eagle nose, trim white beard, veined hands, and air of gentle intensity. Lisa Gay Hamilton as Veronica is a little too fond of standing with her legs apart and her knees bent, being a gawky teenager, but she has a genuine, radiant sweetness about her. And it is heartening to see Athol Fugard, after all these years, in such a good mood.

So, all in all, there was drama to keep the mind alive in 1995. But nearly all of it came, in one way or another, from theaters dependent on those ever-diminishing government subsidies. High ticket prices alienate the middle class, and as subsidies shrink, prices must inevitably rise. Moreover, a number of observers have noted that theater in America is no longer a common subject of serious discussion—a very dangerous sign. It is possible to be thankful for what we have, but it is difficult to be optimistic.

The Year in World Literature

by William Riggan

Significant new works by three German classics, important new fiction in French by a half-dozen major writers from outside France proper, a plethora of new titles in English from leading authors of Eastern Europe, East Asia, and the Middle East, and blockbuster returns by such literary icons as Salman Rushdie, Umberto Eco, Yevgeny Yevtushenko, the late Italo Calvino, and Nobel laureates Wole Soyinka, Kenzaburō Ōe, and Naguib Mahfouz highlighted the literary year 1995.

Germany

Two of the three German publications in question were posthumous. From the late great Uwe Johnson (d. 1984) came *Insel-Geschichten* (Island Stories), a collection of brief, whimsical, insightful, previously unpublished tales about the author's life of self-exile on the English coast and written primarily in an effort to overcome a serious case of writer's block which had halted progress on his massive tetralogy, *Jahrestage* (Anniversaries). The twelve stories by the late Nobel Prize winner Heinrich Böll (d. 1985) collected and issued for the first time in *Der blasse Hund* (The Pale Dog) date mostly from the immediate postwar years but also include one prewar piece from 1938; though stylistically different from his longer later works, they all bear the unmistakable mark of the author's critically detached engagement with current events, particularly with the social and psychological aftereffects of the war. *Ein weites Feld* (A Broad Field), Günter Grass's 781-page attempt at writing the Great German Historical Novel, sparked prolonged and heated controversy with its dark, bitter-edged portrait of German life and culture following the unifications of both 1989 and 1871. Grass is one of the few remaining unreconstructed leftists in Germany, and one of the few public figures who continue to view the latest effort at unification as a dangerous and utter failure, as nothing more than a campaign of plunder in which Western industrialists have enriched themselves by looting and destroying the poorer, weaker East. Using a modern-day counterpart of the nineteenth-century novelist (and chronicler of Prussia's rise to glory and power after the first unification) Theodor Fontane as his protagonist and alter ego, Grass takes particular aim at the Treuhand agency, which Bonn established to oversee the sale of the thousands of farms, factories, and businesses in the East that were "the people's" property under communist rule. For such a provocative infusion of politically unpopular views into his novel, Grass has been brutally savaged by critics across the entire ideological spectrum, from Western critical potentates like Marcel Reich-Ranicki to long-suffering Eastern writers such as Walter Kempowski.

Despite all the furor, the book has ridden high on the bestseller list since its release in April.

Africa and the West Indies

Francophone writing dominated the year's literary production from Africa and the Caribbean. Tahar Ben Jelloun of Morocco, a former Goncourt Prize winner, gathered twenty-one of his short stories from the last two decades in *Le premier amour est toujours le dernier* (The First Love Is Always the Last). As the title indicates, the focus here is not on politics or colonial oppression, as might be expected, but on love and tormented male-female relationships. Curiously, perhaps, for such an acclaimed author and persistent opponent of the oppression of women in North African and South European societies, Ben Jelloun here proves guilty of an insidious sexism, failing utterly to distance himself from the pronounced gender stereotyping and patronizing chauvinism of his various male protagonists, many of whom are even writers, no less. In *L'homme du livre* (The Book Man) Driss Chraïbi, also of Morocco, treads on potentially dangerous ground by offering an imaginary and personal account of the life of the Prophet Mohammed at the time of his first revelation; the overlay of a twentieth-century sensibility—Mohammed is shy, tolerant, introspective, sensitive, respectful of his wife Khadija, playful with his four children, and generally possessed of the qualities and attitudes inherent to the ideal twentieth-century man—on an otherwise straightforward account seems clearly intended to convey the message that every epoch is responsible for making sense of its received wisdom and eternal religious verities. Algeria's Mohammed Dib, long resident in France and Scandinavia, returns to his native land in the stories and novellas of *La nuit sauvage* (The Savage Night), all of which deal directly or indirectly with the violence and enmity that have marked the last forty years in North Africa.

Martinique's Raphaël Confiant, also a former Goncourt Prize winner, brought out another in his lengthening line of Creole-flavored French novels, *Commandeur du sucre* (Sugar Boss), centered on the professional activities and private world of a foreman or driver on a sugarcane plantation during a single growing season in 1936. For *créolistes* such as Confiant, it was precisely in such a milieu that their island culture was formed, and in the mulatto driver Firmin Léander, who narrates his own story in alternating chapters, the work features a protagonist situated midway between the white planters and the black workers—precisely where the transformation of the island society founded on the plantation occurs. Maryse Condé, the out-

26

standing francophone novelist from Guadeloupe, brought out *Crossing the Mangrove,* the English edition of *Traversée de la mangrove,* a powerful and complex generational novel that echoes Faulkner's *As I Lay Dying* and Carlos Fuentes's *Death of Artemio Cruz* in its posthumous reconstruction of the life of one Francis Sancher through the fragmented reminiscences and reveries of his fellow villagers as they file past his open casket. Denigrated and reviled in life by many as a vagabond and a cur, Sancher is gradually revealed as a powerful and mysterious individual who has variously liberated, oppressed, frightened, and consoled those who now gather to bid him farewell. The young Haitian-born Edwidge Danticat followed her first novel (*Breath, Eyes, Memory,* 1994) with *Krik? Krak!,* a collection of stories set both in rural and urban Haiti and in the Haitian community of New York City. Her principal themes prove to be "oppression, hope, fear, cultural identity, and the complex ties among women," as one critic noted, and the best of her stories "humanize, particularize, give poignancy to the lives of people we may have come to think of as faceless emblems of misery, poverty, and brutality."

From anglophone Africa came two new works by Nigeria's 1986 Nobel recipient Wole Soyinka: *Ibadan: The Penkelemes Years,* a memoir covering the "peculiarly messy" school years 1946-55 and continuing the lightly fictionalized autobiographical project the author began in 1981 with *Aké: Years of Childhood*; and *The Beatification of Area Boy,* a powerful full-length new play which satirically and "kaleidoscopically" examines post-oil-boom Lagos, the Nigerian capital, here depicted as a city in total turmoil, where everything, including the legal system, is breaking down and the future holds little if any hope for improvement.

Eastern Europe

The acclaimed Czech émigré writer Milan Kundera brought out his first-ever novel in French, *La lenteur* (Slowness), whose contemporary characters' obsessive desire for forgetting and their total surrender to "the demon of speed" embody the twentieth-century narcissism that the author holds in such obvious contempt. In *Waiting for the Dark, Waiting for the Light* Kundera's compatriot Ivan Klíma took up the theme of compromise and adaptation, familiar from his previous works: specifically, how the demands of a repressive state impose not only on people's domestic arrangements but also on their artistic activities and their spiritual lives. That theme is supplemented here with an examination of the impact on such arrangements of the collapse of the old repressive order as a result of the Velvet Revolution of 1989. Somewhat similarly, in *The Black Envelope,* Romania's Norman Manea offers a panüoüramic portrayal of Romanian society before the fall of Ceauşescu as well as an evocation of the ghosts of Romanian history back to World War II. As depicted here, twentieth-century Romania was a world of constant and complex surveillance, a monstrous realm more Kafkaesque than genuinely communistic and one that generated in its citizens only mania and alienation of the most futile and frustrating kind. In *A Little Hungarian Pornography* Péter Esterházy writes with extreme indi-

rection and allusiveness about the authoritarian Kádár years in Hungary, using the idea and practice of pornography as a metaphor for cowardice, compromise, complicity, and the general mendacious quality of life there during the communist era.

Regarding the year's best works in Russian, the way was led by the acclaimed poet and novelist Yevgeny Yevtushenko, whose sprawling and rambunctious novel *Don't Die Before You're Dead* offered a vast, emotionally satisfying panorama of Russian lives rooted in fear, as the August 1991 drama involving Gorbachev's house arrest in the Crimea and Yeltsin's bold defiance of the attempted putsch at the Russian White House played itself out before the eyes of the nation and indeed the entire world. The account mixes fact and fiction in vivid fashion, the prose is bright and unself-conscious, and the treatment of such now-vilified personages as Gorbachev is strikingly evenhanded. Andrei Bitov, in the "pilgrimage novel" *The Monkey Link,* offered an extremely complex, densely poetic satire on both socialist realism and the more recent Russian penchant for pulp fiction. *The Soul of a Patriot* by Evgeny Popov made for far more accessible and entertaining reading with its witty and brisk yet gritty and realistic epistolary account of the narrator's picaresque movements during the three-month period surrounding the 1982 death of Leonid Brezhnev. In *A Ring in a Case* Yuz Aleshkovsky updated Dostoevsky's classic novel *The Possessed,* using elements of the fantastic and the diabolic to expose the chaos, corruption, and militant nationalism of postcommunist Russia. Vladimir Makanin's *Baize-Covered Table with Decanter,* which garnered the first Russian Booker Prize and almost universal admiration among Russian readers and critics upon its original publication in 1993, made its appearance in English in 1995 to considerably less acclaim; one poor soul's rambling ruminations on interrogations past and future, filled with numbing details about the hellish existence of both the protagonist and his faceless, stereotyped inquisitioners (the Wise Old Man, the One Who Asks the Questions, etc.), the work unfortunately proves more dreary and dated than shocking and revelatory as an ideological model of the nightmare that was Soviet life in the 1980s.

Romance Languages

From elsewhere in Europe and the Americas in 1995 came new works by several prominent Romance-language writers. Italy's Umberto Eco weighed in with yet another lengthy novel (513 pages) set at a considerable historical remove from our own day—in this case the middle of the seventeenth century, the era of Descartes, of Galileo, and of the Baüroque in art and letters and music. *The Island of the Day Before* evokes the *conte philosophique* of Swift, Johnson, and Voltaire, taking a likable young hero on a remarkable series of physical and intellectual voyages as well as travels in time and memory and dream—all in the service of a profoundly humanist agenda that seeks to make the youthful protagonist (and the reader) aware of the uninterrupted continuity of human thought as well as of the authoritarian nature of narrative itself. *Numbers in the Dark* completed the Englishing of the late Italo Calvino with its presentation of a grab bag of juvenilia and previously untranslated stories and prose pieces from as early as 1943, ranging from philosophical tale to war vignette to scientific fable. Readers will find here a different Calvino from the familiar, wryly speculative, canonic author of such brilliant inventions as *Cosmicomics, Invisible Cities,* and *If on a Winter's Night a Traveler*—a writer more identifiably the product of his Italian cultural and political origins but still a fantasist of extraordinary precision and beauty. Mexico's Carlos Fuentes unfortunately did not fare quite so well with **Diana: The Goddess Who Hunts Alone,** the overwritten and self-indulgent account of a brief affair between a famous Mexican writer and a slightly mad American actress (based loosely on Jean Seberg) that serves principally as a metaphor for the artist's obsession with his work—the old Muse-as-mistress theme in modern intellectual-jet-set dress.

Middle East

New novels by two of Israel's most prominent authors and translations of recent novels by two of the Arab world's leading writers highlighted the literary year in the Middle East. Egypt's 1988 Nobel laureate, Naguib Mahfouz, weighed in with **Arabian Days and Nights,** taking up the question of what happened to the despotic King Shahriyar and his beautiful storytelling wife Shahrzad (Scheherazade) in the months and years that followed the original 1,001 Arabian nights. Thirteen unconnected tales from the *Arabian Nights* are here woven into a continuous narrative that traces Shahriyar's gradual and utterly convincing development from bloodthirsty tyrant to just ruler to self-exiled seeker of wisdom and salvation. In **Beirut Blues** the Lebanese-born author Hanan Al-Shaykh composed a book of mourning—for a city, a country, and the way things once were; through ten "sanity-saving and identity-preserving letters" the female narrator conveys in vivid and often squalidly quotidian terms the tragic plight of a wrecked society, an entire city and country destroyed by "gang warfare fought over religion, politics, money."

Amos Oz, one of Israel's most widely translated and internationally renowned writers, came out with a new novel in both Hebrew and English, **Don't Call It Night.** The accidental death of a lonely, introverted boy spurs his father and one of the youth's teachers to take stock of their lives and atone for missed opportunities during his lifetime by attempting to establish a drug-rehabilitation center for young people; although the project ultimately founders, both find a kind of fleeting fulfillment and discover some meaning to their lives through developing the capacity to give of themselves to and for others. In yet another epistolary novel of sorts, Aharon Megged's **Longing for Olga,** a frustrated municipal clerk retires with the dream of becoming a writer, only to find himself hopelessly blocked and literarily uninspired—until, that is, he glimpses a striking young Russian woman on the promenade at the Tel Aviv seashore. Epiphanically energized, he proceeds to compose imaginary letters to himself from this "Olga," letting his wife discover them and almost ending his marriage thereby. The letters eventually become his longed-for novel, however, and ultimately reinvigorate rather than terminate his marriage.

Asia

China's Su Tong, still basking in the afterglow of his success with *Raise the Red Lantern* (both book and film), saw his latest novel, **Rice,** released in English to similar acclaim in 1995; employing rice, the symbol of Chinese civilization and heavenly bounty, to daring iconoclastic effect and spinning a plot featuring blackmail, adultery, incest, and scandal, the author creates a visceral, fast-paced drama of poisonous family and social life in precommunist China. Mo Yan, author of the much-praised *Red Sorghum,* was again brought to the attention of the West with the release of his fifth novel, **The Garlic Ballads;** against the backdrop of the 1987 glut on the garlic market and the resulting devastation of individual farmers and entire communities dependent on this aromatic seasonal crop, three intricately intertwined tales of love and its consequences unfold as communist officialdom faces a potentially apocalyptic upheaval.

Standing above the crowd in a very productive literary year in Japan were two works by writers who boast both enormous popular followings as well as widespread critical acclaim. The celebrated author and director Ryu Murakami presented readers both at home and in the West with **Coin Locker Babies,** an offbeat tale recounting the lives and fortunes of two newborns abandoned by their mothers in the public lockers of train stations; via different paths (one becomes a bisexual rock star, the other a world-class pole vaulter), both eventually make their way to Tokyo and in the end destroy the women who so cruelly rejected them at birth. In the six stories of **Lizard** the appealing (and wonderfully named) young author Banana Yoshimoto remained within her familiar pop-culture milieu but also managed to deal substantively with matters of spirituality, selfhood, and time, in a style that some have compared favorably with that of Kazuo Ishiguro in its elegance and simplicity. The pervading theme here is that the individual is in some way inherently damaged and that growth can only come with a reconciliation of the past and the future. The 1994 Nobel laureate Kenzaburō Ōe and the eminent Catholic writer Shūsaku Endō both released first-time English editions of very early novels in 1995. Ōe's **Nip the Buds, Shoot the Kids** (**Memushiri kouchi,** 1958), contrary to its lightly colloquial title, is a gruesome, wrenching tale of betrayal and cruelty involving a group of orphaned and abandoned reformatory youths in wartime Japan and their doomed efforts to refashion their brutal world with some semblance of tenderness and compassion. Endō's sentimental tale **The Girl I Left Behind** is a flawed and awkward work filled with unlikely coincidences and heavy Christian symbolism, notable solely for the occasional flashes of sparkling intelligence and clarity that foreshadow the excellence of such later works as *Wonderful Fool* and *Silence.*

Footsteps, the third installment of a projected tetralogy (the Buru Quartet) by banned Indonesian novelist Pramoedya Ananta Toer, tracks the career of an expelled medical student turned journalist as he becomes a grassroots political organizer and eventually a crusading publisher of the nation's first native-owned daily; based on the experiences of journalist Tirto Adi Suryo in the first two decades of the twentieth century, the novel masterfully conveys one man's dream of a unified, multiethnic Indonesia free of colonial occupation. *Novel Without a Name* again brought the dissident yet popular Vietnamese woman novelist Duong Thu Huong to the attention of Western readers; thoughtful and provocative, her latest work is not so much a historical novel as an expression of retrospective disillusionment with two decades of postwar communist rule. An even more powerful story of love and combat was *The Sorrow of War: A Novel of North Vietnam* by Bao Ninh, a grim and graphically detailed account based on the author's own experiences in 1969-75 as one of only ten survivors from a 500-man youth brigade subjected to an unrelenting series of bloody encounters in the mountains and valleys of the South; Vietnamese readers from both sides of the North/South border and in the exile community have been comparing the novel to Remarque's classic *All Quiet on the Western Front* for its devastating portrait of the Vietnam War's horrors and waste of human life.

And lastly, from the famous/infamous Salman Rushdie came *East, West,* a wildly uneven and mostly unsatisfying collection of stories all revolving around the themes of cultural and geographic displacement and divided or dual loyalties; though a few of the tales are technically interesting or mildly diverting, none even begins to approach the masterful level of the author's novels, particularly *Midnight's Children* and *The Satanic Verses.* Far more successful among both critics and general readers alike was Rushdie's first full-blown novel since 1989, *The Moor's Last Sigh,* a huge and rambunctiously picaresque family saga told in richly allusive, pun-filled fashion by the exiled scion of a Portuguese merchant family from India. The parallels between the narrator's situation and the author's own are readily evident but do not intrude unduly on the reader's pleasure in following the myriad twists and turns of this antic tragedy-*cum*-political satire-*cum*-anti-creedal parable-*cum*-bitter cautionary tale all rolled into one magnificently entertaining package. Altogether a consummately brave and dazzling performance.

Notes on Contributors

Bruce Allen is a frequent contributor of reviews to the *Chicago Tribune*, *The New York Times Book Review*, the *Philadelphia Inquirer*, and Monitor Radio. He is currently at work on a critical history of the American short story.

Allen Hoey is the author of *A Fire in the Cold House of Being*, a verse collection chosen by Galway Kinnell for the 1985 Camden Poetry Award. An Associate Professor in the Department of Language and Literature at Bucks County Community College outside of Philadelphia, Hoey has contributed poems and essays to such journals as the *Georgia Review*, the *Hudson Review*, the *Ohio Review*, *Poetry*, *Southern Humanities Review*, and the *Southern Review*. He holds an M.A. and a D.A. from the English Department of Syracuse University. *What Persists*, his most recent collection of poetry, was published in 1992.

Julius Novick is Professor of Literature and Drama Studies at Purchase College of the State University of New York. The author of *Beyond Broadway: The Quest for Permanent Theaters*, Novick is the theater critic for *The Threepenny Review* and a winner of the George Jean Nathan Award for Dramatic Criticism.

William Riggan is Associate Editor of *World Literature Today* and an expert on Third World, Slavic, Anglo-American, and smaller European literatures. The author of *Picaros, Madmen, Naïfs, and Clowns: The Unreliable First-Person Narrator*, Riggan has written extensively on the history of both the Nobel and the Neustadt International Prizes in Literature. He also regularly reviews new foreign poetry and fiction for several journals and newspapers.

New Authors

Romesh Gunesekera
Reef

Gunesekera is a Sri Lankan-born English novelist and short story writer.

INTRODUCTION

Gunesekera's first novel, *Reef,* explores the transition from British rule to troubled independence in Sri Lanka (formerly Ceylon) through the eyes of the narrator, a young houseboy named Triton. Cook and caretaker for the remote and cerebral Mr. Salgado, a marine biologist educated in England, Triton embodies, with his cooking and mastery of "the art of good housekeeping," the island's increasingly forsaken traditions. The serenity of Salgado's life and household is disrupted, first, when he invites his mistress, the cosmopolitan Miss Nili, to live with him, and subsequently by the country's quickly encroaching political violence. Salgado and Triton eventually flee to London but find their old lives impossible to replicate. After several years of trying to give the devoted Triton a sense of independence, Salgado returns to Sri Lanka to care for Miss Nili, who has been paralyzed in the war's violence. Triton remains in England, using his culinary skills to become a successful restaurateur. Critical praise for the novel focuses on Gunesekera's rapturous descriptions of daily life in Sri Lanka, such as Triton's preparations for his first Christmas dinner and his delight in Miss Nili's reactions to his baking. Many critics applaud the contrast between the domestic details that form Triton's world and the larger themes of political and social strife. *Reef* was considered for Britain's Booker Prize and explores in greater depth some of the ideas encompassed in *Monkfish Moon* (1992), Gunesekera's previously published volume of short stories.

CRITICISM

Aamer Hussein   (review date 24 June 1994)

SOURCE: "The Destroying Sea," in *The Times Literary Supplement,* No. 4760, June 24, 1994, p. 23.

[*In the following essay, Hussein favorably reviews* Reef.]

In one of the finest stories in *Monkfish Moon,* Romesh Gunesekera's evocative and tantalizingly brief first collection, the narrator tells us of his deep and inarticulate relationship with an artisan who becomes his servant, managing, with startling sparseness, to convey the troubled state of Sri Lanka through the words and the silences of his characters. *Reef,* Gunesekera's first novel, reverses the story's central relationship to recount, this time in the words of the servant, the story of a similar relationship, explored in some depth with the author's customary precision and economy.

The novel begins with a London fragment. Triton, the narrator, now the self-possessed owner of a restaurant, meets, at a petrol station, a fellow-refugee. In spite of what they may have in common, they are divided by their mother tongues. But Triton can see that his Tamil compatriot, too, will "start with nothing", and is "painting a dream" of a lucrative future. Both have come from the "sea of pearls. Once a diver's dream. Now a landmark for gunrunners in a battle zone of army camps and Tigers". This encounter takes him on a return trip to where his life's journey effectively began: when, in 1962, he was brought, as a boy of eleven, by his uncle to the house of Mr Salgado, the kindly, intellectual marine biologist, with whom his destiny would be inextricably linked.

The first substantial section of the novel is the tale of Triton's apprenticeship. Hauntingly bleak and atmospheric, this is also the novel's most compelling and sustained piece of writing; Triton's sense of displacement from his rural milieu, and his adolescent terror of the lascivious, predatory head servant, Joseph, are deftly contrasted with their lush, tropical surroundings, vividly described. The lonely voice of the child interweaves with the more knowing tones of the adult narrator; practical reality and subterfuge combine with magical thinking to displace the demonic figure of Joseph, leaving Triton as sole auxiliary (and virtual manager) of his master's life. The effect of the chapter is reminiscent of Gunesekera's best short fiction; the author, a natural short-story writer, has cunningly contrived to compose his novel of fragments structured like complete stories; but each story is deliberately deprived of an essential element, which is later revealed at the right moment.

The two long central segments contain much of the novel's emotional and thematic development. The tautness of Gunesekera's tone gives way to a more relaxed rhythm, with set-pieces of gentle irony and telling banalities, as Triton, now growing into a masterly, self-taught chef, watches the flowering of Salgado's attraction to the seductive and volatile Miss Nili, a modern Sri Lankan woman. Triton plays culinary Cupid to the romantic duo, finding his master's—and possibly his own—way to her heart with his delicious food. Nili moves in, but their idyll is short-lived: stirrings of dissent, in the form of a distorted and disconcerting polyphony, the dinner-party conversations of Salgado's cronies as overheard by the inexperienced Triton, explode into full-scale violence. Death and destruction abound; the image of the island's fast disappearing reef is projected and re-projected with increasing clarity, juxtaposed with conflicting reports of reality.

Salgado's assistant tells the politically naive Triton: "You know, brother, our country really needs to be cleansed, radically. There is no alternative. We have to destroy in order to create. Understand? Like the sea. Whatever it destroys, it uses to grow something better."

But Triton, well trained by his moderate master and influenced, perhaps, by his Buddhist culture, fails to comprehend the need for violence, though he senses the potential for renewal and growth implicit in destruction. Asked by Salgado—now abandoned by Nili—to remind him of the parable of Anguli-Maala, the harmless prince turned by the machinations of ill-wishers into a vicious collector of human fingers, Triton finds no comfort in the happy ending of the fable, in which the prince repents and returns to contemplation and the Buddha. Instead, a vision of those killed and maimed by the prince, of corpses thrown up by the sea, is shared by teller and listener, and superimposes on the body of the legend a shroud of contemporary historical reality. For in 1971 the Reign of Terror, the "suppurating ethnic war", begins; "bodies would roll again in the surf, they would be washed in by the tide and be beached by the dozen. The lives of brothers, sisters, men and women, lovers, fathers and mothers and children

would be blighted time and again, unremembered." Recalling this era of violence in his English exile with his beloved mentor, Triton remembers his one visit to the real reef that Salgado had so diligently studied: "startling in its hidden brilliance. Suspended in the most primal of sensations, I slowly began to see that everything was perpetually devouring its surroundings." There are no simple answers to dilemmas political or philosophical.

But even in their "uprooted, overshadowed lives", Salgado and Triton are beleaguered by the call of home. Salgado is eventually summoned back by the memory of Nili, leaving behind with Triton the key to an independent future, the legacy of a painfully acquired blend of knowledge, bitter wisdom and a dream of origins and of the sea to which we all return: "The sea in our loins. A tear-drop for an island. A spinning blue globule for a planet. Salt. A wound."

Julian Evans   (review date 17 July 1994)

SOURCE: "Light as a Love Cake," in *Manchester Guardian Weekly*, July 17, 1994, p. 29.

[*In the following positive review of* Reef, *Evans discusses the relationship between the two main characters—Triton, the narrator, and his employer, Mr. Salgado—and examines the comedic aspects of the novel.*]

Mister Salgado's house has two white columns, and he asks about the failed coup as if it is unseasonable rain. The new houseboy "had never heard language so gently spoken . . . Ever after, when Mister Salgado spoke, I would be captivated". Salgado is a dreaming bachelor of impossible refinement. With a bachelor's deep sublimated passion for science, he collects endless data on the disappearing coral reef and, licking his lips with excitement, theorises to his friend Dias, the government accountant, about instruments of the future sensitive enough to record the still-circulating sound waves of his great-grandparents' conversation on their wedding night.

It's odd how familiar the distant, eccentric world of Romesh Gunesekera's first novel [*Reef*] is. (Eccentric politically as well as psychologically: the setting is Sri Lanka, which in the sixties was already wobbling badly on its post-colonial axis.) But the reader steps into the world of the houseboy, Triton, through the universally familiar perception of the child that doesn't know anything about what goes on past the garden gate, and latches on to new discoveries with the puzzlement, terror and wonder that every adult forgets. Halfway through the story, Mister Salgado gets a girlfriend. Miss Nili moves in, and Triton handles women's clothes for the first time:

> With one hand I was able to lift a whole pile of thin shiny material . . . Underneath I discovered little black pieces and white garments: satin cups with pointed ends where the seams met, coupled up with straps and hooks and bits of elastic. I picked up another squidgy bundle but felt perhaps that this was all getting a little out of hand. The material was like nothing I had ever come across before; not like Mister Salgado's under-

wear with pockets and pouches and little gaps for his pipe to shoot.

Like R K Narayan's novels about Malgudi, *Reef* is a comedy that reminds us of a framework of social conventions that we recognise but no longer share. This is another reason for its familiarity: human weakness brought out into the glare by misplaced aspirations, the frustrations of class, social taboos. Gunesekera's comedy is more tragic than Narayan's. There's a more brutal intrusion of politics, but there's the same mischievous ironic grace which stops short of judging.

When the 11-year-old Triton goes to work for "my Mister Salgado" he also thinks he "might find something more, something that would really change the world and make our lives worthwhile". The eventual revelation, brought about by his roughly simultaneous experience of Salgado's jealousy, the disappearance of Nili and the onset of the long-feared political violence—that the garden gate won't keep the world out—is his first and saddest adult experience.

Reef is a delightful novel. With no resolution (an escape from Sri Lanka to Earls Court hardly counts as a fictional resolution), *Reef* is a long story more than a novel, a long episode of childhood that ends with the characters fading out into real life on the last page, a comedy with a vein of sadness.

Native English writers seem to have little access to this world any more. Our world is liberated from these conventions; our aspirations of money and success have been converted to be part of the humourless material stock of human rights, not to be mocked. We had a comedy of recognition and we continue to have satire—comedy with attitude—but our popular satirists' aspirations are no different from ours. Most of them are successful businessmen. It could be argued that there aren't any English comedians now because real comedy, as in this novel, is never altogether happy. It needs the revealing presence of sadness.

In such a simple book one doesn't expect subtlety, and Triton appears to tell us nothing subtle. Yet his reflections on Salgado's yearning for impossibly sensitive scientific instruments to record 100-year-old conversations—things more accurately recorded by imagination and memory, the writer's instruments—are part of a cache of concealed maturity.

Mister Salgado himself, mysterious, kind, dreaming, depressive, is a complex creature on a par with Narayan's Margayya in *The Financial Expert* and Yusef in Greene's *The Heart of the Matter*. And to frame this depth, there is the view of Triton from the kitchen, expressed in a light voice of simplicity, loyalty and faint boyish cunning.

The kitchen is his main observation point, the place where he indulges his pride. "Triton made it," says Mister Salgado when Nili on her first visit asks him where he got the love cake. The food of seduction for Salgado, it is literally the food of memory for Triton. "Triton made it. It was the one phrase he would say with my name again and again like a refrain through those months, giving me such happiness . . . 'He makes a lovely cake,' she said." With these words Nili not only endears herself to him, but earns her place in his memory for the rest of his life. The observation, like the cake, is as light as a feather.

Guy Mannes-Abbott   (review date 2 September 1994)

SOURCE: "Sea Changes," in *New Statesman & Society,* Vol. 7, No. 318, September 2, 1994, p. 38.

[*In the following review, Mannes-Abbott comments that although* Reef *is "impressive," it displays somewhat less of the "Chekhovian clarity and brevity" found in his short story collection* Monkfish Moon *(1992).*]

In *The Location of Culture,* Homi Bhabha wrote that it is "from those who have suffered the sentence of history—subjugation, domination, diaspora, displacement—that we learn our most enduring lessons for living and thinking". Towards the end of his first novel, Romesh Gunesekera echoes Bhabha's wide thesis, while his preoccupation, made messy and dilute by the processes of fiction, is with the lessons for living and "enlarging the world with each flick of a tongue".

Reef displays many of the qualities of Gunesekera's assured collection of stories, *Monkfish Moon* (1992). In them he negotiated the terrain between Sri Lanka and Britain with a ventriloquist agility in sober, quietly crafted prose whose solution contained an eruptive intelligence.

In **"Ullswater",** for example, among the sheep and hollyhocks of a pastoral England, a young Sri Lankan encountered intimate truths about his dead, Anglophile father. The device is repeated in *Reef,* which begins with a section called "The Breach", in which Triton encounters a Sri Lankan refugee and recalls the "voyage of discovery" that landed him in London.

Reef returns 30 years, to a day in 1962 when Triton, aged 11, becomes a houseboy for Mister Salgado, a self-educated marine biologist and proto-environmentalist. Suddenly, "trapped inside what I could see", Triton realises that he had "no idea how much I did not know about the city." While Triton's limits remain undefined, Salgado will concede "no boundaries to knowledge" in his quest both to transform nature and to conserve the past in his imagined world. Salgado's appetites gain him a government commission to protect the coral reef that separates the south of Sri Lanka from the deep-water abyss.

Over the next eight years, Triton learns "the art of good housekeeping" while the world and the political culture of Sri Lanka changes. Salgado is changed too, swept up by a hungry passion for Miss Nili, who introduces him to a cosmopolitan, "bubbly world of gaiety" that conflicts with the murmurs of revolution that reach Triton.

Salgado's affair is charted in Triton's inclusive cooking. Beginning with a moist "love-cake", it settles oddly over a tangerine-stuffed Christmas turkey, and is destroyed after it peaks decadently with a bright blue-striped parrot fish known as a "coral cruncher".

Gunesekera's language, poetic and metaphorical in conception though deliberately less so in execution, fitted the short story perfectly. His stories are marked by Chekhovi-

An excerpt from *Reef*

Nili and six others, including some foreigners, were coming to our once and only Christmas party: a real dinner party. It was to be my big challenge. Nili had only come for snacks before; this was going to be a Christmas meal that had to meet a standard she, as a Christian, knew but which I had no idea of. Most of the preparation I did the night before, cooped up in the kitchen with the shrouded turkey. It was not too complicated. Only five dishes for the main course: turkey, potatoes, two green vegetables and the ham, then a ready-made Christmas pudding. A doddle compared with some of the meals I had had to do just for Mister Salgado and Dias on their own, when suddenly they would want this and that delectation as every mouthful detonated a memory in each of them sitting there eating and drinking and burping to kingdom come. With a little preparation and planning any emergency could be handled. Anything was possible.

The day of the party our Mister Salgado was maddeningly anxious. He kept coming into the kitchen to ask how I was doing. I didn't say much; there was no time to fool about explaining. I would just nod or say, 'Right. Everything fine,' and get on with the next job. He would watch me from the door until he felt reassured and then go back into the house until the nerve juice rose to the surface again and brought him back. 'OK,' I kept saying. 'Everything fine.'

'Turkey getting brown? Is it?' He looked around the kitchen, confused even as to where the oven was.

'Not yet, not yet. It will brown. Don't worry, Sir, I will get it nice and brown in the last hour.'

'Potatoes? What about the potatoes? You haven't forgotten the potatoes, have you?' His voice quavered. He had spotted them in a basin of water.

'Sir, potatoes go later.'

He reached for one, not convinced.

'Sir, I will get the clothes ready.'

He threw up his hands. 'No, no. I can do that. You concentrate on this. This turkey business everyone says is very tricky. Mustn't be too dry otherwise it will be like stale bread.'

'I know, Sir, I know. Mustn't be uncooked or it will be too bloody. But don't worry, everything will be fine.'

'She says even her mother never got it right.'

So? My heart opened inside me and spread a warm glow through my blood. My turkey was going to be the best she had ever had.

Romesh Gunesekera, in Reef, *The New Press, 1994.*

an clarity and brevity, occupied with the human scale and details of explosive significance. *Reef* is an impressive leap into novel writing, but the assured tone has dispersed and left a series of bright episodes unsure of their relative weight.

Similarly, metaphors jostle for dominance and expand erratically. While this is partly the novel's purpose, among such understated prose, the conflict is more accidental than instrumental. However, the lasting, and aptly liminal, image is of a breached but self-renewing reef: a holed survivor.

Richard Eder   (review date 19 February 1995)

SOURCE: "Cooking Up a Storm," in *Los Angeles Times Book Review,* February 19, 1995, pp. 3, 11.

[*An American critic and educator, Eder has received the National Book Critics Circle Award and the Pulitzer Prize for criticism. In the following review of* Reef, *he praises Gunesekera for providing the reader with a deeper understanding of the novel's characters and events than its narrator/protagonist possesses.*]

It was 10 years or so into the bloody political and ethnic violence that, since the late 1950s, has afflicted the beautiful island that once was Ceylon and now is Sri Lanka:

> All over the globe revolutions erupted, dominoes tottered and guerrilla war came of age; the world's first woman prime minister—Mrs. Bandaranaike—lost her spectacular premiership on our small island, and I learned the art of good housekeeping.

Reef, a novel about a youth who comes precariously together in a disintegrating world—like learning to fly in a plane that has already begun its fatal corkscrew plunge—shares the fragrant sweetness of its setting and its agony of change. It works them into the first-person narrative of a poor farmer's son for whom a job is wangled in Colombo as apprentice houseboy to Mr. Salgado, an eccentric intellectual who is the island's leading marine biologist.

Romesh Gunesekera has taken the risk of telling a large story in the tiny, almost cloying constriction of meals, recipes, furniture polishing and a boy's besotted reverence for the figure for whom he performed these tasks. There are times in *The Reef*—the loving preparation of a festive tea, a nerve-racking experiment with a Christmas turkey—when we could almost be reading a wry food-page feature about the perils and pleasures of Third World cookery. We are reading something quite different.

When Triton, the narrator, comes to work for Salgado, it is not simply a job. It is passage from the primitive countryside to the complex tasks and ceremonies that mark the highly civilized world where people read books, govern countries, enjoy wealth and travel to England. (And, as he will learn, where all these things wax and wane and collapse in struggles as bloody and primitive as any endured in the countryside.) Triton's reverence for his work and his master is the page's reverence for the knight he serves and for the order of chivalry that mastered the universe until the coming of the crossbow.

When the departure of Salgado's cook and principal houseboy leaves Triton to do everything alone, it is not a burden handed to him but a sword. Through ordeal and peril to glory: He works and studies to become the perfect cook, butler, valet and housecleaner, and to please Salgado and Salgado's ravishing girlfriend, Miss Nili. Thus, after a tea at which Nili ate every one of Triton's meat patties and lavishly praised—and consumed—his cashew-studded love-cake:

> "Triton made it," Mr. Salgado said. *Triton made it.* Clear, pure and unstinting. His voice at those moments would be a channel cut from heaven to earth right through the petrified morass of all our lives, releasing a blessing like water springing from a river-head, from a god's head. It was bliss. My coming of age.

It would be only the first coming of age. Triton's account begins long afterward on a cold night in London where he has lived for many years and has managed to set up, after hard struggles, a successful restaurant. Cooking is no longer a joyful salvation but simply a way to survive. It is the particular achievement of Gunesekera that he has been able to weave into Triton's buoyantly and comically ecstatic account of life as a servant, more complex glimpses of Salgado, Nili, Sri Lanka and himself, and of the hard things that change was bringing to all of them.

Salgado is a wonderful mix of abstraction and urgency. He drifts about the house like a cogitating wraith until Nili smites him; whereupon he fusses continually. He works himself into a tizzy over the Christmas turkey—16 pounds; will it burn? will it rot?—while the now-adept Triton handles things with Jeeves-like panache. Nili, sexy and frail, turns Triton into a buzzing circuitry of desire. The fact that he reveres her and his master too much to do anything about it only makes the erotic charge more powerful.

The growing strife and displacements of Sri Lanka and the world infiltrate the feudal glory of Triton's kitchen. Political polarization and radical urgencies endanger and ultimately destroy his scientific mission: the ecological preservation and careful development of the Sri Lankan coastal waters, with a particular view to protecting the fragile coral reefs offshore.

Coral is Salgado's passion and the book's central metaphor. A coral reef is alive, but only at its skin. Its billions of tiny organisms multiply and build on the surface, leaving their calcified bodies as the reef's mass. The violence of politics and change, in this image, destroy the living integument while seeking to give it more vital forms. Civilization is at the surface, not deep down; destroy the surface and the life that preserves it will die.

Gunesekera's point, like his coral, is not calcified but alive. As Salgado leaves his post and takes a modest job in Britain—a number of his friends have been killed in the growing violence—his life changes but does not come to an end. Neither does Triton's; he accompanies his master and continues to serve him, though more modestly. He shops at supermarkets and defrosts vegetables for supper. Encouraged and helped by Salgado, he reads, studies and starts a snack bar that will eventually grow.

The rich but fragile culture that the two of them had known has perished in violence and change. They retain their humanity. Triton will stay, work and prosper. Well, badly—the author makes no effort to say; the verb is now, the adverb comes later. Without prospects, Salgado returns to Sri Lanka to take care of Nili, who is now an invalid. Humanity means using whatever is left, even when it is only the past. Before Triton drives him to the airport, his former master tells him: "You know, Triton, we are only what we remember, nothing more . . . all we have is the memory of what we have done or not done; whom we might have touched, even for a moment." Perhaps, after all, coral would talk that way.

Edward Hower   (review date 26 March 1995)

SOURCE: "No Island Stays an Island," in *The New York Times Book Review,* March 26, 1995, p. 29.

[*Hower is an American short story writer, novelist, critic, and educator. In the following review he compares* Reef *to Kazuo Ishiguro's* Remains of the Day *(1989) and Michael Ondaatje's* Running the Family *(1982), praising Gunesekera's ability to cast "a spell of nostalgia."*]

"It was small, and yet its voice could fill the whole garden," says the narrator of **Reef,** describing an oriole that alights near his house. "In blissful ignorance it is completely beautiful; unruffled until its last moment." Lost innocence in the final years before a war is the theme of this eloquent first novel by Romesh Gunesekera, whose **Monkfish Moon,** a collection of stories about his homeland of Sri Lanka, attracted critical attention here in 1993. **Reef** was a finalist for Britain's Booker Prize last year.

Now an adult in exile in London, the novel's narrator remembers his Edenic childhood in Sri Lanka in the post-independence era of the 1960's, when at the age of 11 he became an apprentice houseboy for a marine biologist, Mr. Salgado. The boy—appropriately named Triton for the son of Poseidon, the sea god—loved the kindly oceanographer's home. "Even the sun seemed to rise out of the garage and sleep behind the *del* tree at night," he remembers. His master's praise thrilled him as if it had come from "a channel cut from heaven to earth right through the petrified morass of all our lives, releasing a blessing like water springing from a riverhead, from a god's head."

The aristocratic young scientist, as Mr. Gunesekera presents him, is himself an innocent, preoccupied with his studies of the sea and oblivious of the forces of darkness gathering around him. He has no understanding of the potential brutality of people like Joseph, his head house servant. But Triton does. Joseph terrorizes the boy, who can combat the older man's menace only with prayerful fantasies inspired by Buddhist folklore. He imagines the gods in the sky "crowded on a bamboo raft on a blue lake surrounded by rolling hills, holding silver spears and peering through peepholes in the clouds, searching for Joseph, determined to destroy him."

The prayer seems to work. Joseph, returning home drunk, is fired, and Triton is put in charge of the house. The pride he takes in his position brings to mind that of the butler-narrator of Kazuo Ishiguro's novel *The Remains of the Day*, but without any of the distancing irony of that work.

All the home lacks, Triton feels, is a woman's presence. Enter graceful Nili, a desk clerk from the local hotel, who captivates not only Mr. Salgado but the now teen-age Triton as well. The buttery "love cake" that the boy cooks for her and his employer has a magical effect: Mr. Salgado gives up his bachelor ways and invites Nili to move in. Their happy conversations on the veranda enchant Triton. "In the dark," he says, "the voices had a life of their own; they moved around me as if I were deep underwater and they were fish swimming, leaving a trail that could be felt but not seen, small currents, waves."

The novel is rich in sensuous descriptions not only of the gardenlike loveliness of the countryside, but also of the pleasures of cooking, which Triton discovers as a creative outlet. His culinary artistry, like Mr. Gunesekera's literary skill, produces "a kind of energy that revitalizes every cell. . . . Suddenly everything becomes possible and the whole world, that before seemed slowly to be coming apart at the seams, pulls together."

Other recurring themes, threaded subtly throughout the narrative, gradually become visible. The reef surrounding the island nation has always protected it from the outside world, but now the coral is being torn up by developers and turned into cement for tourist hotels. Capitalism is ravaging the country as aggressively as the revolutionary ideas spreading among the exploited people who insist that "we have to destroy in order to create."

The benign, protective aspects of Triton's religion are also shattered, as sectarian violence erupts, pitting Buddhist against Hindu. Triton recalls a folk tale about a gentle young prince who is told by his corrupt teacher to make a necklace out of a thousand human fingers and as a result becomes a blood-crazed mass murderer. He learns how naïve he was to assume that the tale was merely an exaggerated fantasy.

Triton's efforts to retain the harmonious atmosphere in the household, like Mr. Salgado's crusade to protect the reef and Nili's attempts to save him from despair, cannot preserve the innocence of his world. Nili leaves; Mr. Salgado takes to drink. The oriole in the garden will sing no more—except in memory.

Romesh Gunesekera's powerful novel preserves that memory beautifully. Like *Running in the Family,* Michael Ondaatje's reminiscences of his Sri Lankan childhood, *Reef* is peopled with colorful, memorable characters. Mr. Gunesekera, a masterly storyteller, writes about them with great affection, casting a spell of nostalgia with his lyrical prose.

At the story's end, Mr. Salgado, who has fled to England, returns to his homeland intent on finding his lost love—going after "a glimmer of hope in a faraway house of sorrow." For its exiled author, who now lives in London, this novel itself must represent such a glimmer. For his fortunate readers, the book is incandescent.

Neil Gordon (review date April 1995)

SOURCE: A review of *Reef,* in *Boston Review,* Vol. 20, No. 2, April, 1995, pp. 31-2.

[*In the following review, Gordon discusses the Sri Lankan political history that informs* Reef *and argues that although he feels Gunesekera is "one of the two or three best writers I've encountered among my contemporaries," he has not convincingly integrated the political and the emotional realities of the story.*]

In contemporary London, a Sri Lankan man stops at a gas station, pumps his gas, goes to pay. In the face of the boy in the cashier's booth, he sees a great familiarity, "almost a reflection" of his own. It is night, they are alone, and although compatriots, their only common language is English, of which the boy speaks little: the man is Sinhala, the boy Tamil, the two sides of their country's long civil war.

As they exchange a few words inside the lighted booth, the Sinhala envisages the Tamil's home, Silavatturai, "[o]nce a diver's paradise. Now a landmark for gunrunners in a battle zone of army camps and Tigers." Then the Tamil boy closes shop, flicking off the lights, and as the stars appear beyond the window in a London winter, the Sinhala experiences a long fugue of memory that transports him 30 years and 6000 miles away to his boyhood on an island off the southwest coast of India called, until 1972, Ceylon.

Romesh Gunesekera's acclaimed first novel, **Reef**—shortlisted for the Booker Prize in Gunesekera's adopted country, England—is this Sinhala man's narration in flashback of his life, from boyhood to young adulthood. It is a servant's life that he tells us: as a boy, Triton is steered into the service of Mister Salgado, a bourgeois Sinhala intellectual from a landowning family. At first he is a houseboy on a staff of three, but before long, with his cool efficiency, he supplants the other two, becoming Mister Salgado's cook and caretaker.

Over perhaps ten years Triton becomes indispensable to Mister Salgado and when, some time in the 70s, mounting Tamil terrorism forces Mister Salgado into exile, there is no question but that Triton, by now attending to all of Mister Salgado's domestic needs, will go with him. It is after twenty years in London that Triton stops at a gas station in Mister Salgado's car and meets the young Tamil refugee. But those twenty years in England are only briefly described: Triton is concerned with narrating, in detail, the ten years or so he lived with Mister Salgado in Sri Lanka.

Mister Salgado, in 60s Sri Lanka, is a marine biologist, and his tracking of the island's protective coral reef's slow destruction by pollution and over-fishing provides the title and central metaphor for this story—set, as we will very soon understand it to be, in a world heading for self-destruction. He is a kind man, and while he accepts without question the social hierarchy of his household— Triton's first job is to serve Mister Salgado his morning tea in bed—still Triton is never so much subservient to a master as he is respectful of a teacher.

Triton is a deeply creative and intelligent boy—the descriptions of his cooking and quiet command over the household are some of the novel's most satisfying passages—with some education, and he's smart enough to learn everything Mister Salgado can teach: ". . . I watched him, I watched him unendingly, all the time, and learned to become what I am." He learns his habits, the intimate details of his tastes for clothes and food; watches his work, listens to his conversations with his friends. When Mister Salgado travels on his marine studies, Triton travels with him. When, ultimately, Mister Salgado will go into exile, Triton will go with him. And when Mister Salgado falls in love with Miss Nili and so undergoes the great—the only—sentimental education of his life, Triton, never transgressing his observer's distance, falls in love with her too.

So far, it sounds like we're dealing with an essentially domestic tale, and that's true. But only to a point: there is another perspective within the narration that breaks the unity of the very young houseboy's view; Gunesekera insists on injecting references to the evolving disaster of Sri Lankan politics in the late 60s and early 70s. Of course, since independence from Britain in 1948—and even more so since the 1956 de-anglicizing of the country by the Sri Lankan Freedom Party, which so fatally decided on Sinhala as the national language—these politics are always immediately present in the story. This is a place on the verge of massive political upheaval, with social inequities and ideological rifts deep enough to find expression in terrorism, and then in decades of civil war. And yet when Gunesekera refers to the historical or political, always within the narrative point of view of this young boy, the integrity of the book's voice seems broken. Describing Mister Salgado's cook, he writes

> She had served Mister Salgado's grandfather whisky and coffee during the riots of 1915. She had seen politicians with handlebar moustaches and tortoiseshell topknots, morning coats and gold threaded sarongs, barefoot and church-shod. She had seen monkey suits give way to Nehru shirts; Sheffield silver replaced by coconut spoons.

Instances of terrorist violence, too, rock the placidity of Mister Salgado's household, a violence that not only in its occurrence but in its very nature is a harbinger of change.

> There were no death squads then, no thugs so callous in their killing that they felt no pleasure until they saw someone twitch against a succession of bullets. In my childhood no one dreamed of leaving a body to rot where it had been butchered, as people have had to learn to do more recently.

This is no doubt perfectly true, and a sense of the tragedy, the brute waste of the violence that will soon tear this island paradise apart, does inform the text. And yet, Gunesekera never really manages to make it an organic part of Triton's story. "I was trapped inside what I could see, what I could hear, what I could walk to without straying from my undefined boundaries, and in what I could remember from . . . my mud-walled school." So centrally important to the narrative voice is this limitation that the political observations—of the cook's background, of the

growth of terrorism—no matter how beautifully written, feel tendentiously imposed on the text instead of implicit to it, as if the author, more than the characters, feels the importance of the march of history on his plot. And it feels labored, as if, doubting the inherent dramatic interest of Triton's domestic life, the author were stretching for a Naipaul-esque relevancy to his story.

And in fact there are strong commonalities with Naipaul. There is the long reach of the British Empire, and there is the brutal irony of independence leading to violence beyond that which the British imposed. Gunesekera captures, like Naipaul, the peculiarly apt blend of British formality and tropical fecundity, as if the cold cultural eye of the English made even more movingly colorful the parrots, gekkos, orioles—the "promise of cinnamon, pepper, clove" in this "jungle of demons"; the "perpetual embrace of the shore and the sea, bounded by a fretwork of undulating coconut trees, pure unadorned forms framing the seascape into a kaleidoscope of bluish jewels"—of the island paradises they corrupted or, Gunesekera will suggest, were corrupted by.

But the prose is too original to allow much comparison. The story relies less on Naipaul-like telling detail than on the nostalgia, the regret that the prose captures in structure as well as subject, a careful progression of exactly described venues, like photographs of the past, a succession of tableaux more than a sequence of dramatic scenes. It seems forged in the timelessness of the tropical noon, etched on the eye by the sun. And the sensation is carried down to the nicest decisions of syntax, when in its subtlest and most impressive moments the language conjures a temporal suspension in its rhythms, constantly throwing the reader off guard in his expectation of lyricism with an unexpected word. This is wholly original, very ambitious language, and it is often, like the descriptions, exquisite.

> Most of all I missed the closeness of the . . . reservoir. The lapping of the dark water, flapping lotus leaves, the warm air rippling over it and the cormorants rising, the silent glide of the hornbill. And then those very still moments when the world would stop and only colour move like the blue breath of dawn lightening the sky, or the darkness of night misting the globe; a colour, a ray of curved light and nothing else.

As the book progresses, it is the prose rather than the wider political framework that involves the reader, the power of the descriptions and the emotional complexity of Triton's world that carry the story, and the wider perspective begins to seem less relevant. And that's difficult, to dismiss the central, tragic injustice of the political turmoil that is engulfing Sri Lanka as less important than a servant's domestic tale.

But emotional realities are what this book, in its perceptive, quiet voice, is most convincingly about. Of course the "distant thunder" of political events is always present, and often foregrounded: when it becomes loud enough, Triton and Mister Salgado go into exile. But in the continuum of Triton's consciousness, as it is here narrated, Gunesekera fails to assign these exterior political events a believable place. Of course the historic tragedy of Sri Lanka is implicit to the story—so implicit, perhaps, that Gunesekera's explicit insistence weakens its importance. History may be a nightmare in which Gunesekera is struggling to entrap us, and yet no matter how often he refers to these political realities, they never become as relevant as the more immediate, more compelling emotional realities of the story.

Nowhere is this better shown than in *Reef*'s central scene, the Christmas dinner that Mister Salgado hosts, and which will usher in his love affair with Miss Nili.

The preparation, serving, and consuming of the meal at Salgado's house—eight to dine with Miss Nili—compose the most sustained dramatic sequence of the book. Sitting at the middle of the story, the action of the dinner scene proceeds with sure logic, rising tension, and entire believability. And within its pace Gunesekera is able to make us understand something about the place he comes from, beyond its meticulously described locales, and far beyond its distant politics. As Triton listens to Mister Salgado talking to his guests, he is "spellbound."

> I could see the whole of our world come to life when he spoke. . . . The past resurrected in a pageant of long-haired princes clutching ebony rods; red-tailed mermaids; elephants adorned with tasselled canopies and silver bells raising their sheathed, gilded, curved tusks and circling the bronze painted cities of ancient warlords. His words conjured up adventurers from India north and south, the Portuguese, the Dutch and the British, each with their flotillas of disturbed hope and manic wanderlust. They had come full of the promise of cinnamon, pepper, clove, and found a refuge in this jungle of demons and vast quiet waters.

The tensions between the characters at the table—all revolving around Miss Nili—come as dramatically clear as the perfectly-cooked turkey cleanly parting from the bone under Mister Salgado's knife.

> Perfume rose up from her, and when I moved in to spoon the potatoes on to her plate it seemed the scent was stronger. It rose up from below her throat down inside her flapping dress. She had her elbows on the table; her body was concave. She must have smeared the perfume with her fingers, rubbing it in like honey paste to enrich the skin. . . . My sarong, tight around my hips, brushed her arm. She didn't notice. She was looking across the table. Robert had caught her eye; he was smiling, his head shyly cocked to one side. A piece of turkey tumbled from her fork. She quickly retrieved it and said, 'Jesus.'

Everything is here: the American Robert's attraction to Nili that will later cause Salgado's fit of jealousy and Nili's flight; Triton's deep attraction to Nili; the insistence on the British trappings of mashed potatoes and turkey that, with all it represents, has thrown this island country into permanent political turmoil; the deeply-felt background of jungle myths and generations of colonialists. An entire narrative at this pace, with this sure subtlety of touch, might sacrifice some of Gunesekera's description, as well as analysis, but in exchange it would gain a terrific level of intensity, and the payoff in terms of emotions it could encompass would be huge.

A writer who would have made this dinner his whole story is Joyce, and the result would be, like that other story of an evening's entertainment, "The Dead," both a classic of English language but also cinematic enough for John Huston to make it a film. Gunesekera is the only contemporary writer I have encountered good enough to do the same. The perceptive, thrilling drama of his narration seems to burst the limits of his framing device, a tribute to the power of his story. I look forward to reading every word he writes, not only for the pleasure of following one of the two or three best writers I've encountered among my contemporaries, but also in the hopes of seeing his stories escape his rather tendentious narrative bias toward literary relevance and speak more simply and dramatically for themselves.

Pico Iyer   (review date 22 June 1995)

SOURCE: "The Empire Strikes Back," in *The New York Review of Books,* June 22, 1995, pp. 30-1.

[*Iyer is an English-born Indian journalist and critic. In the following review, he analyzes* Reef *as an example of postcolonial fiction, comparing it to Shakespeare's play* The Tempest *(1611), Kazuo Ishiguro's novel* The Remains of the Day *(1989), and the work of other contemporary writers from former British colonies.*]

The Tempest has become a model for postcolonial fiction. Who, after all, can resist a tale of spirits and savages being tamed and taught by a fugitive European aristocrat (later joined by a mixed-up band of drifters and dreamers and drunkards)? And who could fail to see in it a metaphor for the way in which Western powers have long tried to bring their native ways and speech to untutored paradise islands? Shakespeare's experiment in magic realism offers an ideal prototype for the encounter between the civilized and the wild—or, as it would more often be called today, between two different kinds of civilizations, one drawn from Nature and one from books. It not only acknowledges both the angelic and the bestial sides of the subconscious world but also allows a visiting scholar to perform a kind of *mission civilisatrice* before returning home.

Whether or not the inspiration for the play came from the islands that have given us Derek Walcott and V.S. Naipaul, it is easy to see why many ex-colonials have seized upon its images of Ariel crying out for freedom; why the West Indian George Lamming, in his *Pleasures of Exile,* dwelt on the mysteries of Sycorax; or why Walcott, in his poetry, not only gives us Othello from the Moor's point of view but also describes how "Calibans howled down the barred streets of an empire that began with Caedmon's raceless dew, and is ending in the alleys of Brixton, burning like Turner's ships."

When Romesh Gunesekera begins his first novel, *Reef,* with an epigraph from *The Tempest,* we know that we are likely being ushered into a new version of the age-old colonial story. And, moreover, that it will probably be an example of "The Empire Strikes Back," the current shorthand for that increasingly visible phenomenon whereby much of the strongest writing in English—and especially in England—is coming from writers from the former colonies who are using the words they've learned at their masters' feet to turn their masters' literature on its head. Among the names to be found on the short list for England's Booker-Prize for Fiction—the clearest register of British literary fashion—are Salman Rushdie, Kazuo Ishiguro, Ben Okri, and Timothy Mo and it is more and more common to hear that, just as Spanish literature has been all but taken over by writers from Spain's former possessions (Gabriel García Márquez, Octavio Paz, Isabel Allende, and Carlos Fuentes, say), so Toronto and Sydney and Bombay have become new centers of English literature.

Gunesekera, a connoisseur of displacement, fits the description well, having been brought up on three separate islands—Sri Lanka, the Philippines, and England. And when you read his unusual prose-poem, you see exactly how the young "foreign" writers are flooding the English mainstream with their alien spices and colors and sounds. In this novel, Colombo comes to seem as close to us as Connecticut or Colchester.

On its surface—and it is an exquisitely sensuous surface—*Reef* simply tells the tale of Triton, a wide-eyed, earnest village boy, trained only in a "mud-walled school," who comes to Colombo to work in the junk-filled mansion of Mister Salgado, a quiet, rather dreamy amateur marine biologist. To Triton, Mister Salgado seems the last word in worldliness, though to us, as he sits on the veranda sighing over *The Mikado* and staring wordlessly at his mistress Nili, Salgado seems dangerously unworldly. These representatives of science and superstition combine to make their home a model of the island around them; and in every one of his exact details, Gunesekera acknowledges the mixed influences of an island in transition. Outside the house's entrance is a garden of "scarlet *rathmal* and white jasmine"; inside is a mix of "cane blinds, Formica surfaces and nylon mats." The master consumes soft-boiled eggs and plantain for breakfast, coconut cake and cucumber sandwiches for tea. And in perhaps the most revealing anomaly of all, the eleven-year-old boy confesses that such English as he knows he learned from a "poor, tormented schoolmaster, still under the spell of a junglified Victoria."

From the beginning, then, *Reef* presents us with an archetype of a master and his "boy," in a kind of tropical *Remains of the Day;* and, as in the Ishiguro novel, the story that unfolds is largely about the flatteries and follies of imitation (both parrots and parrot fish flit through the novel). For while Triton registers some of the ironies of the mongrel culture of his home (it is only foreigners who are vegetarians here, and it is only Sri Lankans who speak of "Ivy League men" and Las Vegas), he is so unquestioningly devoted to his master that he will not even eat until Mister Salgado has done so. Like Ishiguro's butler, he knows so little of the world outside that he believes his master to be omnipotent; and like Ishiguro's butler, he is not displeased when he is himself mistaken for a rich man on one of his rare forays outside his master's company. "I watched him, I watched him unendingly, all the time, and

learned to become what I am," the boy says, in the voice of Ariel, with something of the straightforwardness of Caliban.

The book's own spell arises from that very voice, one that we have seldom heard before—open, unlettered, eager to please—and from a perspective unclouded by ambiguity or distance. For even on the outskirts of the Sri Lankan capital, the young boy is living in a world of spirits. He sleeps at night under a small round window, and conjures demons out of the darkness. He rubs his "elephant-hair bracelet" for good luck, and makes spells to hex his enemies. The whole island is alive for him—this junglified Pip—with "mischievous little godlings" and malevolent sorcerers like the elder servant Joseph (whose head is "shaped like a devil-mask"). This is very much Prospero's isle—"a jungle of demons," as Triton calls it—as seen by a local sprite.

And because most of the book concerns Triton's life as chef to the languorous Salgado, it allows him to immerse the reader in the bewitching smells and flowers and fragrances of his spice-filled, wind-softened home. The book is lush with references to the smells of rosewater, almond essence, and cardamom, to white flame trees and temple trees and lily pads, to "the perfume of cinnamon in pearly rice, or the hum of a hummingbird sucking nectar from a pink shoe-flower." And because the world of the artless boy extends no further than the house, the reader's view, too, is circumscribed, and he mainly sees a Sri Lanka not of ethnic strife or social turmoil, but, rather, an enchanted garden of "red-beaked parrots and yellow-eared *salaleenas,*" where a boy freshens cupboards with drops of Moorish rosewater, and scrubs his hands with coconut hair and pink whalebone. Everything here is seen in local images, the sea "like a Madras pancake. *Thosai* flat," and a woman's ears "curled in like the edges of a puppadum when it hits hot oil." The novel takes place in the 1960s and the political tensions between Sinhalese and Tamils on an island that became independent in 1948 are present mostly as storm clouds on the horizon.

The strength of *Reef,* in fact, lies in its unforced and convincing depiction of a self-contained universe ("I didn't know what happened much beyond our lane," the boy admits) in which the beauties of an Elysian home can be taken for granted. Triton's work in the kitchen allows him to surround us with exotic flavors and seasonings, with *seeni-sambol* and *pol-sambol* and *pol-kiri-badun* curry; with *cadjan* fronds and *del* trees and *nelum* flowers. The first thing that strikes one about *Reef,* especially when compared with Gunesekera's earlier collection of short stories, *Monkfish Moon,* is that the pages here are lit up with italics, and every one of them seems to convey wild and unknown booty into our mother tongue. But Gunesekera deliberately chooses not to explain most of his Sinhalese terms, in much the same way that Vikram Seth, in *A Suitable Boy,* filled his pages with Indianisms, and yet declined to include a glossary. Puppadum and sari and nirvana are English terms now, these writers are saying; or, as Rushdie puts it in his more polemical way, "To conquer English may be to complete the process of making ourselves free."

The remarkable thing about this novel, indeed, is that it achieves nearly all of its effects silently, as it were, through almost imperceptible shadings of language and texture. The story it tells, of an island's fall from paradise, coinciding with a boy's fall into self-consciousness, is conventional enough; but the way it tells it, by showing how language itself gradually falls prey to more and more of the outside world, is original and heart-rending. Thus the early pages of *Reef* are luminous with local terms, like the central reef of the omnipresent "pearly sea" aglow with phosphorescent fish; and reading Triton's account of the omnipresence of the "pounding sea" one feels, in his inspired image, as if one is living "inside a conch." When people speak, it is in the particular, pungent cadences one would hear in a Sri Lanka village ("Big commotion was going on there with that Pando-*nona*"). But as the book goes on (and the boy grows up), more and more foreign influences start entering the sequestered house. The first comes with Mr. Dias, a friend of Mister Salgado, who speaks in the Wodehousian manner of the intellectual Anglo-Asian: "The rifle, you see . . . was resting like a fancy brolly on the tip of his shoe. In all the excitement, what with the din and all, the fellow pulled the trigger. Blew his own bloody big toe off!"

In the central scene of the book—again a little like the dinner party that is the centerpiece of *The Remains of the Day*—Triton faces his biggest culinary challenge as he cooks his first Christmas turkey (to be eaten near a plastic Christmas tree). It is a traditional bird for Salgado's foreign guests, but it is stuffed not only with raisins and liver but also with "Taufik's *ganja* and our own *jamanaran* mandarins" (much like the book itself). And though there is no apple in the turkey, it marks the end of Eden. This is the first time foreigners have been invited to Salgado's table and they bring to it their alien perspectives ("This extraordinary, I reckon, deeply *erotic* country. . . . So uninhibited. Really wild"). And, even sadder, the first foreign attitudes enter the language of the Sri Lankans, as they start to see themselves through foreign eyes. (Mister Salgado tells Triton that the dinner is to begin "at nine o'clock. Punctually. None of this lotus-eating business.") Before we know it, Mister Salgado and his friends are using secondhand terms and Western platitudes, chattering about "haves and have nots," "conspicuous consumption," and the "Fifth Column." The reader hears the gates of Eden closing as Mister Salgado discusses "the thermodynamics of the ocean in the Age of Aquarius."

From then on, the trajectory of *Reef* is, inevitably, an elegiac one, and the book, like Sri Lanka itself, fills up with engineers "trained in London and New England," "*nouveau* chefs," and references to Zeffirelli's *Romeo and Juliet* and "free love" in California. The government starts to plan inland seas and the diversion of enormous rivers; the eponymous reef—the one delicate system keeping the ocean and the forces of chaos at bay—is seen as a marketable resource. Marxists start burning buildings to purge the island, while pleasure-mongers open "batik boutiques" and roar around on "fluorescent motorbikes." But the singular courage of *Reef* is to suggest that the corruption lies deeper than any ism or fashion, and that it is not death squads, or nationalists, or Marxists, or greedy developers, that are the downfall of Sri Lanka: all are symptoms of a deeper malaise, the result of a too quick widening of horizons and too many foreign ideas. The flight from paradise begins when people start talking, too easily, of "the classic flight of capital."

Reef ends with Triton and his bewildered boss moving to London, and settling in a flat in an old Victorian house near the Gloucester Road. And like Ishiguro's butler, in a way, Triton comes to see that he has given his faith to a man who is himself ineffectual and naive. But the loss of innocence is again most tellingly conveyed just through language. When Triton visits the British seashore, he finds a gray and cormorant-haunted place with none of the color and music he knows, and his prose hardens into a brittle and crabbed kind of Anglo-Saxon as he describes how

> the sea shimmering between the black humps of barnacled rocks, mullioned with gold bladderwrack like beached whales, thickened into a great beast reaching landward, snuffing and gurgling. . . . In pock-marked, marooned rock pools speckled hermit-crabs and rubbery, red sea anemones dug in; limpets and periwinkles and bubble weed held fast waiting for the tide.

Reef proceeds so gently and lyrically—whispering around us like a murmurous sea—that it is easy to overlook just how subversive the book is. For it allows, and even forces, us to see Sri Lanka from a local boy's perspective, as we have never seen it before in English. As long as those of us in the West have been reading about the island, it has mainly been through the eyes of foreigners—and, moreover, foreigners highly aware of its alienness. "All jungles are evil," wrote Leonard Woolf of the island where he lived as a young civil servant, and Edward Lear complained that "the brown people of this island seem to me odiously inquisitive and bothery-idiotic." And this was all before the champions of global alienation, Paul Bowles and D.H. Lawrence, hit the place (the latter with his talk of "papaw-stinking buddhists").

Even the country's most famous contemporary writer, Michael Ondaatje, is himself a bemused half-outsider, a product of Dutch and English forebears who has lived all his adult life far away, most recently in Canada, and who, in *Running in the Family,* returns to his birthplace saying, "I am the foreigner. I am the prodigal who hates the foreigner." And the ancestors that Ondaatje portrays in his memoirs, playing billiards, going to the races, and dancing "in large living rooms to the music of a Bijou-Moutrie piano" are themselves the kind of deracinated cosmopolitans who seem almost extraterrestrial to the likes of Triton. (His father, Ondaatje mentions in passing, was briefly engaged to a Russian countess in Cambridge.)

Reef, then, like more and more of its contemporaries, is radical precisely in what it can take for granted: its very matter-of-factness about Embilipitiya grass and frangipani is part of its sedition. And at every turn, it performs a kind of counter-Orientalism, giving us the island as it appears from the servants' quarters, and so replacing Western views of the East with Eastern views of the West. For Triton, after all, it is not mynah birds or wizards that are exotic; it is copies of *Life* and the *Reader's Digest,* rumors of the Profumo affair and the Beatles. It is England that seems the dark and frightening country where one cannot speak the language. And when he describes the world around him, everything becomes transposed: he writes of "silver trays as big as the moon," and one realizes that one is accustomed to hearing English writers likening the moon to silver trays; elsewhere, reading in Mister Salgado's study, he describes the "sound of onion-skin rustling from story to story like trees blowing in a summer orchard." The very terms of familiarity and strangeness are turned around here.

Derek Walcott wrote once of an empire-haunted West Indian artist literally reversing the terms in an old poem, so that it would read, "Holy be / the white head of a Negro, / sacred be / the black flax of a black child." In this book's central episode—the dinner party for foreign guests—the Sri Lankans in attendance not only assert that their island was the original Garden of Eden but take the Bible itself and the story of Noah's ark and turn it into a Sri Lankan folk tale, of a "helluva bad monsoon" and a "*baasun-naha*—our carpenter with his boat." By the end of the scene, we are seeing things we thought we knew through the other side of the telescope.

In some ways, magic realism itself is nothing more than the conveying of everyday life to a world so distant that it takes realism for surrealism; as García Márquez discovered, the simple transcription of life in a superstitious and god-filled village will seem as otherworldly to us as our TV images and knickknacks seem to a Colombian villager: that is the *quid pro quo* of the modern imaginative trade routes. Magic realism is about transubstantiation—the turning of one man's water into another man's wine—and it adds to Kipling's famous line "The wildest dreams of Kew are the facts of Kathmandu," the rider that "The wildest facts of Kew are the dreams of Kathmandu." The lone, rather seedy American in Gunesekera's novel is described by the boy as a "film-star."

Though **Reef** is not strictly an example of magic realism, it is a glittering example of how Caliban is turning his master's speech upon him. A generation or so ago, V.S. Naipaul mastered the imperial voice and attitudes, and trained them upon the third world he had taken such fastidious pains to flee; born fifteen years later, on the eve of Independence, Salman Rushdie simply celebrated the polyglot mishmash of our mixed-up cultures, in which Bombay is as full of *Star Trek* fans as London is full of samosas. Now, though, even younger writers like Gunesekera are repatriating the skills and tactics they mastered in England to give new dignity and authority to their homelands. Ben Okri fills English with molue buses and Nigerian herbalists, all described in classic English sentences ("Under our intense gaze, he bit Mum's shoulder and pulled out a long needle and three cowries from her flesh"). The Caribbean-born Caryl Phillips writes a novel in flawless nineteenth-century prose and calls it *Cambridge,* to evoke not the bucolic English university town but a hideously mistreated black slave. And, like Rohinton Mistry, an Indian writer long resident in Toronto, Gunesekera looks back on the world he has left, from a

Western perch, and in a new kind of English describes "some itty-bitty *koreawa* road" and characters dancing "the cha-cha-cha or the *kukul kakul* wiggle."

The ultimate point of **Reef,** about how the East was lost, and with it a certain rough magic, is nothing new. But one strength of the book is that it doesn't belabor that point, that it never lets its story dwindle into a treatise or a polemic. When Mister Salgado is asked, by a foreign journalist, how "the lifestyle in coastal villages is changing as a result of this sea-erosion," he loses his composure for one of the only times in the book, simply because he loves his island too much to hear it subjected to Op-Ed clichés (even though he resorts to a few of his own). In the same way, Gunesekera refuses tidy explanations or easy rhetoric, and simply shows us the eroding flavors of his sea-washed home. For me, this is the best novel from the subcontinent since Rohinton Mistry's *Such a Long Journey,* and for much the same reason. Calmly, it gives us a new and unexpected world; and gradually it makes it feel like home.

Guy Amirthanayagam   (review date 25 June 1995)

SOURCE: "No Man Is an Island," in *Book World—The Washington Post,* June 25, 1995, p. 5.

[*Amirthanayagam is a Sri Lankan poet and essayist and the former ambassador from his country to England. In the following favorable review, he discusses* Reef *as a bildungs-roman in which the main character's maturation is mirrored by the political changes in Sri Lanka.*]

One of the impressive adventures of the 20th century is the rapidly burgeoning interpenetration of cultures. A rich fruit of this is a type of modern literature in which the central experience is cross-cultural and characters' destinies are shaped in some fashion by the cross-cultural encounter.

Romesh Gunesekera's debut novel, **Reef,** which was short-listed for Britain's prestigious Booker Prize, is a successful example of cross-cultural convergence. Sri Lanka, the book's setting and the land of Gunesekera's birth, has its own ethnic mix. The island nation, which is insulated from the rest of the world by the reef which girds its southern shore, has, however, undergone considerable change because of external influences during some centuries of colonization and foreign rule. Now, even its coral reef is in danger as it is being dug for use in building projects and the sea is fast eroding the frail land mass; the sea, "which would be the end of us all," is only waiting for the motion of its final wave. The sea and the reef have a symbolic weight in this novel, but the fortunes of the central characters are at the center of the stage.

There have been other novels written by Sri Lankans with the island as their setting, but this is the first to win international acclaim. Leonard Woolf's neglected masterpiece, *The Village in the Jungle,* is located in Sri Lanka, but Woolf was an Englishman. Michael Ondaatje's *Running in the Family,* though it uses the techniques of fiction, is a family history peopled by some exotic, larger-than-life characters. Besides, Ondaatje, though born in Sri Lanka, has long been a Canadian.

But it is important to see Gunesekera also as a Britisher, one of the expatriates who have written novels of diaspora and who are now at the forefront of London literary life. He bids fair to join the likes of V.S. Naipaul, Salman Rushdie, Timothy Mo and Kazuo Ishiguro.

Reef is a *Bildungsroman,* the story of a boy's maturation into an expert cook, an autodidact and even a philosopher. The boy is the narrator, named Triton after the son of the mythological god of the sea, Poseidon. He goes into service as a house boy in the employ of Salgado, an affluent marine biologist dedicated to the mission of saving the protective reef from its human predators, an able and well-meaning scientist but with little sense of what is going on in the country around him. Salgado's hypothesis is that the delicate polyp is affected even by a minor change in the immediate environment. "Then the whole thing will go. And if the structure is destroyed, the sea will rush in. The sand will go. The beach will disappear."

It is nature, red in tooth and claw: The human cruelty only mirrors nature and what goes on in the jungle on land and under the sea. In Triton's words:

> The one time I did swim out to Mister Salgado's real reef, back home, I was frightened by its exuberance. The shallow water seethed with creatures. Flickering eyes, whirling tails, fish of a hundred colours darting and digging, sea snakes, sea-slugs, tentacles sprouting and grasping everywhere. Suspended in the most primal of sensations, I slowly began to see that everything was perpetually devouring its surroundings.

This predaciousness in nature has its human parallel in the rumblings of national discontent that soon erupt into a suppurating class and ethnic war in the 1960s. Neither Triton—who plies the culinary arts, learns to make excellent love cakes and other pastries, and knows how to marinate tiger prawns and steam parrot fish—nor his master Salgado, who is a dedicated scientist but also a naif, realizes what is going on until it is too late.

The novel is further complicated by the entry into the bachelor household of Salgado's mistress, Nili, who lifts the monkishness from their house but does little to open their eyes to the real conditions in the country, preferring to bask in Salgado's love and to savor Triton's culinary delicacies.

Gunesekera's style is sensuous and impassioned, almost incandescent. Nature also has its benign and blessed aspect:

> The sand garden, the clumps of crotons, the vines around the trellises by the kitchen, all seemed to breathe life. Even the furniture seemed stained by the shade, but when I looked up again I would glimpse the sea between the trees bathed in a mulled gold light. The colour of it, the roar of it, was overwhelming. It was like living inside a conch: the endless pounding. Numinous.

But whatever is idyllic has to disappear. Nili proves unfaithful; the insurgency and the racial war make it necessary for Salgado to emigrate. Triton is led to reflect: "But are we not all refugees from something? Whether we stay or go or return, we all need refuge from the world beyond our fingertips at some time."

When Salgado hears in England that his former love Nili is homeless after her house was gutted by a mob incensed because she had given refuge to Tamil families, he decides to return to find her. Triton remains in London, "without a past, without a name," hoping to become a restaurateur. But he cannot forget the sights and sounds of his home country:

> "Most of all I missed the closeness of . . . the reservoir, the lapping of the dark water, flapping lotus leaves, the warm air rippling over it and the cormorants rising, the silent glide of the hornbill . . . An elephant swaying to a music of its own."

Alan Isler
The Prince of West End Avenue

Isler is an English-born American novelist and educator.

INTRODUCTION

A production of *Hamlet* in a retirement home in New York City provides the setting in which Isler, in the voice of his narrator Otto Korner—a once-promising poet and survivor of the Auschwitz death camp—explores memory, old age, and twentieth-century history. Korner becomes the play's leading man and director upon the death of Adolphe Sinsheimer, another resident at the home. When a cherished letter, in which the poet Rainer Maria Rilke praised his writing, disappears, and when a new physical therapist arrives at the home who looks like his first love, Korner is stirred to recall his experiences before and during World War II and the Holocaust, and thereafter in America. Critics note that Isler treats this potentially somber material with gentle wit and insight. As Anita Brookner commented: "[*The Prince of West End Avenue*] is an excellent novel, not merely because every sentence is alive but because the reader might be persuaded that what is on offer is a mere comedy of manners. In fact Isler is several steps ahead of that reader on all counts, and it is his craft that one finally salutes."

CRITICISM

Publishers Weekly (review date 14 March 1994)

SOURCE: A review of *The Prince of West End Avenue,* in *Publishers Weekly,* Vol. 241, No. 11, March 14, 1994, p. 63.

[*In the following review, the critic favorably assesses* The Prince of West End Avenue.]

Set in a retirement home in Manhattan's Upper West Side in 1978, Isler's haunting first novel [***The Prince of West End Avenue***] features Otto Korner, an Auschwitz survivor, who is directing his fellow retirees in a retirement home production of *Hamlet.* Otto blames his smug refusal to heed his first wife's desperate pleas to flee Nazi Germany for the tragedy that befell his family in the Holocaust. To keep his sanity, he searches everywhere for signs of a "greater Purpose," which constantly eludes him, even when the retirement home's new physical therapist turns out to be a dead ringer for Magda Damrosch, an old flame who broke his heart in Zurich in 1916. The retirees' sexual escapades, feuds, and political debates alternate with Otto's flashbacks to Hitler's Germany, or, much more often, to Zurich, where as a young literary journalist and emigré German poet, he met Lenin and mingled with Tristan Tzara, Hans Arp and their Dadaist circle. Isler, who teaches English literature at Queens College, has created a deeply cultured, fiercely articulate protagonist whose ironic voice hooks the reader as he ruminates on death and old age, love and libido, Mozart and the madness of history.

Kirkus Reviews (review date 15 March 1994)

SOURCE: A review of *The Prince of West End Avenue,* in *Kirkus Reviews,* Vol. LXII, No. 6, March 15, 1994, p. 324.

[*In the following favorable review, the critic recounts the plot of* The Prince of West End Avenue.]

Memories of past sorrow and misspent passion come unbidden to an elderly Holocaust survivor in this elegant novel [*The Prince of West End Avenue*] when a woman bearing a resemblance to an old love joins the staff at a retirement home located on Manhattan's Upper West Side.

While most of the residents of the Emma Lazarus home are busy squabbling over the casting and the direction of *Hamlet,* Otto Korner, challenging ghosts of his own, feels appropriately cast as the Gravedigger. A published poet at 19, and unable to serve in the army, he is sent to Zurich by his family at the advent of World War I. There he meets a thoughtful, bookish Lenin, an "unmannered oaf" named James Joyce, and is an unhappy midwife at Tristan Tzara's birthing of the Dadaist movement. It is there, too, that he becomes obsessed with the high-spirited, scornful Magda Damrosch, whose likeness he sees 60 years later in the "dull, empty-headed" physical therapist from Cleveland. His placid, unreflective life at the retirement home, already shaken, is further disturbed when a prized letter from the poet Rilke, praising his "precocious talent," is stolen. Someone begins sending clues in verse—"charades," he calls them—and they tax both his literary and personal memory. Isler moves smoothly from war to war and to the present, with Korner moving among memories of his youth; of his two wives ("both . . . were cremated, only one of them by her own request"); of his emigration in 1947 to New York, where he found his sister hanged in her kitchen ("I stuffed Lola's memory high on the closet shelf with the rest of my past and closed the door tightly"); and of his quiet, uneventful years at the New York Public Library where, ironically, he was placed in charge of materials published in Germany between 1929 and 1945.

A delicious, evocative, gentle debut, written in prose to be savored and cherished.

S. Schoenbaum   (review date 8 May 1994)

SOURCE: "The Readiness Is All," in *Book World—The Washington Post,* May 8, 1994, p. 5.

[*In the following review, Schoenbaum notes some of the historical references in* The Prince of West End Avenue *and praises Isler as "a novelist to be watched."*]

Yesterday, the narrator of this novel [*The Prince of West End Avenue*] tells us, he celebrated his 83rd birthday. The year is 1978. Eventually, he wryly observes, we'll find him just south of Mineola, Long Island, where he'll be taking up his subterranean residence. Otto Korner is his name—dropping the umlaut over the "o" being his first concession to America. These days he resides at the Emma Lazarus Retirement House on West End Avenue in Manhattan.

Who was Emma Lazarus? Students of New York's history and probably few others will know of her as a spokeswoman and forgotten poet ("Songs of a Semite") remembered, if at all, for a sonnet about the Statue of Liberty, "The New Colossus," which is engraved on the pedestal of the statue in New York City harbor. "That is no country for old men," begins a celebrated early modern poem. Korner

is an old man, but he has not sailed to Byzantium but to the New World.

Constipation besets him, as it does other elders: A local wag calls their little home the Enema Lazarus, a witticism from the house specialist in coprological humor. In houselingo Korner appears in a daily list of solo ambulants rather than sedentary residents, so he can still walk about and have coffee and play dominoes at Goldstein's Dairy Restaurant on Broadway, a short distance from the Emma Lazarus. Certainly Korner is not burning and raving at close of day (as another poem would have it); but he is not going gentle into that good night, either.

He is haunted by memories. Twice widowed, he finds solace taking part in the Emma Lazarus Old Vic, which specializes in performing the classics. In their recent production of *Romeo and Juliet,* Juliet was 73 and Romeo was 78. When Romeo killed Tybalt, it was Romeo who fell, and had to be carried on a stretcher from the stage. He can now be found in Mineola. Currently a production of *Hamlet* is in the works. The star, to guard against a midnight hunger pang, secreted away a lump of sugar, which he choked on in his room. Thus he discovered how sweet it is to die. Korner is set to play a Ghost or a Gravedigger, in any event a spectral presence. The text of *Hamlet* is savored with a plethora of allusions and quotations. For Korner is a literary gent, employed before retirement by the New York Public Library.

Reared in a comfortable middle-class Jewish Berlin household, some years before Schindler compiled his list, young Korner seemed destined for the literary life. A precocious poem by him elicited an encouraging letter from the great Rilke. Korner held on to his tattered letter even in an extermination camp of the Third Reich. Unlike his first love, Magda Damrosch, whose short life was snuffed out in a gas chamber, Korner is a Holocaust survivor. Not until late in the novel is the number on his wrist commented upon. The Rilke letter, by now almost undecipherable, mysteriously disappears at the Emma Lazarus. So what? It is only an old handwritten letter from what's-his-name. Ultimately it resurfaces.

The other woman in Korner's life is Mandy Dattner, a youthful Ph. th. (physical therapist) from Shaker Heights Community College in Cleveland, who works with him at the Emma Lazarus. Her presence reminds him of Magda, in part because of the analogous disyllables of their names.

In Korner's memory, celebrated personages make their entrances and exits at a Zurich restaurant, where a cadaverous-looking man with thick eyeglasses sits with others singing songs and telling jokes in sundry languages. Magda lifts her glass to toast him. Korner thinks him an unmannered oaf. He looks like a down-at-heels dandy: "A lifetime later," Korner observes, "leafing through the photographs in Ellman's [sic] classic biography, I discovered to my surprise and embarrassment that this 'unmannered oaf' had been the great Irish writer James Joyce, even then, in 1916, at work on his incomparable *Ulysses.*"

Also in Zurich he chatted and had a drink with Lenin at the Cafe Odeon. Zurich, Lenin, and Joyce—shades of

Tom Stoppard, a very different presence and literary talent from Isler.

"If it be now, it is not to come; if it be not to come, it will be now, if it be not now, yet it will come. The readiness is all." So Hamlet to Horatio, who has well-justified misgivings before the culminating duel with Laertes in the final scene of the play. "The readiness is all"—it is the last sentence of the novel. In time Korner becomes the director of the Emma Lazarus Old Vic and plays Hamlet. The Prince of West End Avenue becomes the Prince of Denmark.

And who is Alan Isler? A Brit by origin, he hobnobs with ex-colonials in the Big Apple. A member of the English Department at Queens College of the City University of New York, he is currently renewing acquaintance with the old country. I expect that *The Prince of West End Avenue* will deservedly delight many readers. Isler is a novelist to be watched.

An excerpt from *The Prince of West End Avenue*

The last few weeks have not been easy for me. After an absence of sixty years, Magda Damrosch has reentered my life and my system is in turmoil. I cannot sleep and I am troubled by constipation. How ironic that the release of the psychological mechanism should be accompanied by stoppages in the physical! And, of course, there are the headaches, two points of pain that gather behind the temples and converge at the base of the skull. No cause for alarm, however. I shall not die at the Emma Lazarus for want of a laxative and an aspirin. Not for nothing does Benno Hamburger call our little home the "Enema Lazarus." This witticism is still making the rounds. No doubt of it, he is our specialist in coprological humor, a man of unbounded cloacal enthusiasms.

But what sort of a way is this to begin, for heaven's sake? Even to talk of such things! I am ashamed of myself. First I should tell you who I am. My name is Otto Korner. Dropping the umlaut over the "o" was my first concession to America. Yesterday, September 13, 1978, I celebrated my 83rd birthday at the aforementioned Emma Lazarus, a retirement home on West End Avenue in Manhattan. Eventually, you'll find me just south of Mineola, Long Island, where I will be taking up permanent subterranean residence.

Alan Isler, in The Prince of West End Avenue, *Bridge Works Publishing Co., 1994.*

Bette Pesetsky   (review date 29 May 1994)

SOURCE: "Shakespeare Meets Emma Lazarus," in *The New York Times Book Review*, May 29, 1994, p. 9.

[*Pesetsky is an American novelist, short story writer, critic, and educator. In the following generally positive review, she notes that although Isler's novel has considerable emotional power, only Otto Korner, the narrator and protagonist, is a fully drawn character.*]

Alan Isler uses to advantage the mythic power of the theater in his first novel *The Prince of West End Avenue*. But it turns out to be a distinctly unconventional sort of theater. As the story begins, a production of *Hamlet* is in rehearsal by a troupe whose actors are drawn from the residents of the Emma Lazarus retirement home on New York's Upper West Side. The fate of the play itself is uncertain, and chaos reigns. Death, you see, has already decimated the cast and threatens to do so again. In addition, all the contretemps involved in putting on a play are present—jealousies, casting problems, politics.

The Emma Lazarus is a world largely dominated by an émigré culture rich with allusions to the past, yet also with romances and rivalries, with the sense that life is definitely not over. There is a kind of nostalgia in Mr. Isler's depiction of his characters and the complex web of their memories. But curtains are drawn over parts of their lives, shielding nightmare events they cannot bear to examine too closely. The darkness of the past animates their present.

Otto Korner, an engaging and erudite retired librarian, is the novel's narrator; originally, he is cast as the ghost in *Hamlet*. The octogenarian Korner, once a published poet and writer of articles on literary subjects, now keeps a journal, whose aim is to clarify once and for all certain truths about "*anti*-art: in brief, Dada." A Holocaust survivor, he has lived, since his rescue, in search of a purpose.

Korner's memories are rattled by the appearance of young Mandy Dattner, a newly hired physical therapist. Can she be a reincarnation of the beautiful Magda Damrosch, who perished at Auschwitz? Recollections pull Korner back to the early decades of the century when, unable to serve in the Kaiser's army in World War I and thus a visible target for sentiments directed against his family in Germany, he was sent to Switzerland to continue his studies. It was on the way to Zurich that he first glimpsed the unattainable Magda and fell in love with her.

If Korner moved cautiously on the fringes of a changing world, Magda was in the thick of events, holding court at the Cabaret Voltaire with the artists Hans Arp and Max Oppenheimer and the poet Tristan Tzara. In Korner's memories of Magda, we witness the birth of the Dada movement.

> **There is a kind of nostalgia in Mr. Isler's depiction of his characters and the complex web of their memories. But curtains are drawn over parts of their lives, shielding nightmare events they cannot bear to examine too closely. The darkness of the past animates their present.**
>
> **—Bette Pesetsky**

The exiled Korner also met and had a drink with Lenin: "What did we talk about, Lenin and I? Not about political economy or the rights of the proletariat. You will scarcely believe me if I tell you that we spoke of love—or, rather, that I spoke of it." Korner even spent an evening listening to a noisy and unimpressive James Joyce. But what did such meetings mean? They were, Korner concludes, like much of life, to be considered merely coincidences.

Moving back and forth from the world of his memories to the present world of the *Hamlet* production, Korner finds only turbulence and change. With the death of Adolphe Sinsheimer, who was both the play's director and its Hamlet and the only Emma Lazarus resident with professional acting experience (as "a Ruritanian soldier in the movie *The Prisoner of Zenda*), the stage is set for new intrigues. Cabals form at Goldstein's Dairy Restaurant, with plots to take over the floundering *Hamlet*.

Mr. Isler displays a sharp and original wit, with touches of black humor. Some jokes are genuinely funny, as when the play's self-appointed replacement director, who fears offending Orthodox members of the audience, changes the line "Is she to be buried in Christian burial?" to "Is she to be buried in Mineola?" But at whom are we laughing?

Although the other émigrés are skillfully drawn, not one holds the fascination of Otto Korner. And the men, like Korner's friend Benno Hamburger, have a depth and complexity not shown by the residence's vocal and conniving women, who seem more like stock characters. Korner's second wife, the Contessa, whom be marries during his early retirement, is an exception as we spy on his recollections of their failed physical union, we wince as he cruelly describes her aging body.

Gradually, though, **The Prince of West End Avenue** emerges as a paradoxical tale of how to make peace with an unbearable past and the sin of pride. In a powerful scene toward the end of the novel, when Korner at last speaks at length of his first wife, Meta, and his son, the pettier concerns of the Emma Lazarus home abruptly diminish. It is then that we realize how much Otto Korner's story is able to haunt us.

Elaine Kendall   (review date 13 June 1994)

SOURCE: "A Rich Meditation on Old Age, First Love and Tragic Loss," in *Los Angeles Times Book Review*, June 13, 1994, p. E5.

[*In the following review, Kendall offers a positive assessment of* The Prince of West End Avenue, *noting that although "the subtext [of the novel] is profound, the tone is kept buoyant" by the interaction of the many colorful characters.*]

The year is 1978, and the residents of the Emma Lazarus retirement home are planning an ambitious in-house production of *Hamlet*.

They're a spirited crew despite advancing age and encroaching infirmity, and although their theatrical backgrounds run a short gamut from nonexistent to sketchy, the drama society performs only the classics. Last year's

Romeo and Juliet was a triumph, even after Romeo fell after killing Tybalt and had to be carried off-stage on a stretcher. But as our narrator Otto Korner tells us, you have to make allowances.

This year, however, making allowances may not be quite enough. The man who was to have played Hamlet has just died and a substitute must be found at once. Still, the people who live at Emma Lazarus are experienced at dealing with adversity.

Several of the cast members fled Europe just before the war, while others were not so fortunate and barely escaped with their lives. To them, a dead Hamlet is merely a challenge. They've overcome far worse. Their star has departed for another stage, but the show will go on.

While the situation seems designed for comedy, resident Otto Korner is not only an extremely articulate observer but a man with an acute sense of irony. The result is a rich and complex novel; a meditation on age, love, loss and the enduring guilt felt by those who survived the European catastrophe.

You may forget you're reading a serious novel after encountering the lusty and sardonic Benno Hamburger and the unregenerate Bolshevik nicknamed "the Red Dwarf." Otto Korner's thoughtful commentary, still cadenced with European formality, keeps the humor firmly under control.

—Elaine Kendall

Before the war, Korner was a promising poet and literary journalist, happily married and the father of a son. Like many others with powerful ties to their homeland, he was reluctant to leave, ignoring the pleadings of his wife until flight was no longer possible.

His tragic personal story is revealed only gradually, when long-suppressed memories are aroused by a new young physical therapist at the Emma Lazarus house, a woman who bears an uncanny resemblance to his first, lost love. Each encounter with Mandy Dattner opens another locked door into Korner's past, reminding him of the dazzling Magda Damrosch and then, inevitably, of the family who perished in the Holocaust.

The fragments accumulate and slip into place, putting Korner in the foreground of the European artistic ferment between the wars. Introduced by the free-spirited Damrosch to the vibrant cafe life of Zurich before the First World War, Korner meets the avant-garde writers, artists and political figures of the era, encounters that continue to shape his view of the world. He treasures only one relic of his past—a letter from the great German poet Rilke praising Korner's youthful efforts in verse.

The mysterious disappearance and subsequent recovery of that letter will thrust Korner still further into the present, making it possible for him to relinquish his chosen role of Ghost and take the part of Hamlet. As the reader discovers, the parallels between the cynical 83-year-old refugee and the young Prince of Denmark are inescapable.

Although the subtext of **The Prince of West End Avenue** is profound, the tone is kept buoyant by the interaction among the Emma Lazarus residents, whose intrigues, passions and arguments provide a counterpoint of levity.

You may forget you're reading a serious novel after encountering the lusty and sardonic Benno Hamburger and the unregenerate Bolshevik nicknamed "the Red Dwarf." After you've attended one of the impromptu philosophical seminars led by the relentlessly cerebral Hermione Perlmutter and watched as Tosca Dawidowicz transforms herself from a pudgy virago into a superb Ophelia, you'll think for a moment that the author has intended only to entertain you with a cast of gifted, if inadvertent, comedians. The coffee hours in Goldstein's Dairy Restaurant are hilarious; the rivalries and romances among the actors continuously diverting. Otto Korner's thoughtful commentary, still cadenced with European formality, keeps the humor firmly under control.

As Korner tells us at the beginning of this supremely original book, his subject "is not amateur theatricals, it is art—or, more accurately, anti-art: in brief, dada." An ideal metaphor for the insoluble riddles of the 20th Century.

Sanford Pinsker　(review date 14 June 1994)

SOURCE: "A 'Prince' of a First Novel," in *Books Today—Chicago Tribune*, June 14, 1994, p. 5.

[*Pinsker is an American scholar, poet, and author of several books on contemporary American literature, including the critical study* Between Two Worlds: The American Novel in the 1960s *(1978), and two books on the works of novelist Philip Roth. In the following highly positive review, Pinsker notes the lessons learned by the novel's protagonist/ narrator.*]

Alan Isler's impressive first novel, **The Prince of West End Avenue,** is a tale of a group of retirement-home thespians trying to mount a production of *Hamlet*—against the long odds of death, failing health and internal bickering—that ultimately becomes an extended metaphor of our nightmarish century and the human race's capacity to survive its worst brutalization.

The novel's protagonist-narrator is Otto Korner, a Holocaust survivor, one-time poet (his book of poems, published in Germany when he was 19, was praised by none other than the Austrian poet Rainer Maria Rilke) and currently an 83-year-old resident of the Emma Lazarus House on West End Avenue in New York City.

Although he had been given the role of gravedigger, events conspire to make him mount the stage as Hamlet, the man of existential doubt and over-exercised mind.

Korner's narration is at once a history of how the Emma Lazarus *Hamlet* got to opening night and a series of flashbacks that follow him through his European past as he meets and interacts with the likes of Tristan Tzara (founder of Dadaism), Lenin and James Joyce.

The result is a novel dripping with cultural richness and generous measures of wit. When he encounters a young physical therapist who resembles a woman he wooed unsuccessfully 60 years earlier, Korner uses the occasion to engage in a series of speculations that, by increments, unblock his heart and send a torrent of regrets to the surface.

Not surprisingly, his affinities with Hamlet play a role in this process:

> Perhaps my objection to Lipschitz' [the director that Korner eventually replaces] mutilations has to do with the fact that in the Prince of Denmark I see much of myself. It is not to Hamlet's nobility of mind that I refer, not to the "courtier's, soldier's, scholar's eye, tongue, sword" or to "the glass of fashion and the mould of form," but to his hesitations, his vacillations, above all his egregious eagerness to play the antic. In this mirror that he holds up to nature, I see my own reflection. . . . No one would want to argue that Hamlet was good for women, whether the young Ophelia or the matronly Gertrude: one way or another, their deaths were on his head. As for me, both my wives were cremated, only one of them, the Contessa, by her own request.

Indeed, Korner has much to grieve about—not only for loved ones who met their deaths in the Holocaust but also for the way his articles urging German Jews to "stand fast" ("As a matter of right—legal, moral and religious—we belong on German soil") helped seal their fate. As he puts it: "How many besides my own flesh and blood have I on my conscience? I should have screamed from the rooftops, 'Jews, run for your lives!' "

What Korner discovers only at the moment before the curtain rises on the retirement-home *Hamlet* is that the present is infinitely precious: "What can we do but grasp the fleeting moment? For me, in this now, that moment is our play. I want to be Hamlet. And I care not a whit for the comical figure I shall cut."

In **The Prince of West End Avenue,** the play's the thing—and a thing of dazzling verbal richness and human complexity it is. Old age and love, loss and redemption, have seldom been cobbled into such an enormously satisfying whole.

Mary Cummings　(essay date 10 July 1994)

SOURCE: "25-Year Journey to Find Otto's 'Voice'," in *The New York Times*, July 10, 1994, sec. 13, p. 14.

[*In the following article, Cummings discusses Isler's background and his writing of* The Prince of West End Avenue.]

In Alan Isler's first novel, **The Prince of West End Avenue,** it is the arrival of the luscious Mandy Dattner at the Emma Lazarus retirement home on the Upper West Side of Manhattan that throws Otto Korner into a state of emotional turmoil and prompts him to start keeping a journal.

A physical therapist from Cleveland, the "unbearably beautiful" Ms. Dattner, is a dead ringer for the passion of Otto's youth, Magda Damrosch, the toast of Zurich's Cafe Voltaire in 1916 and the darling of the Dadaists, who made it their headquarters.

Ms. Dattner's appearance at the home for the aged, where Otto is a resident some 60 years later, sets off for him a flood of long-repressed memories. Otto is an Auschwitz survivor, and his flashbacks provide a counterpoint to his account of the comic opera that is life at the Emma Lazarus.

Mr. Isler's inspiration for writing the novel ostensibly written by Otto in the form of a journal was a much slower process. The seed for the idea was planted 25 years ago, the writer said in a telephone interview.

A professor of English literature at Queens College who usually divides his time between New York and Sag Harbor, Mr. Isler is spending most of a leave in his native London.

Twenty-five years ago Mr. Isler read a newspaper article about a home for the aged in Brooklyn whose residents were preparing a production of *Macbeth*. "They had gotten the essence of the play," he said, "but had otherwise rewritten it."

Mr. Isler said he felt that "something had to be done with the idea," but he was writing for scholarly journals and the "voice" that ultimately dictated the book, Otto's voice, was not nearly as insistent as it became later.

Until there was a voice there was no story, Mr. Isler said. But once the voice grew distinct and persistent, he said, the story, which had been in gestation for more than 20 years, spilled out in "no more than 15 months."

For a time, Mr. Isler recalled, Otto Korner seemed to whisper in his ear every night. "It was almost as if I woke the next day and it was there in my head, just waiting to be transcribed," he said. "It was a marvelous experience, very exciting, the happiest time of my life."

In the novel it is *Hamlet* that the denizens of the Emma Lazarus are rehearsing, squabbling over and tampering with as Otto, who has been cast as the Ghost, begins his journal.

The bonds of old age and Judaism notwithstanding—the "open-door policy" at the home is interpreted to mean that "all Jews are welcome"—the residents are anything but homogeneous. They feud over sexual rivalries, jockey for position and power on stage and off, nurse oversize egos and cultivate petty resentments.

Tosca Davidowicz, orthodox and exquisitely sensitive to anything that might make her appear otherwise, is prepared to go to the mats over Shakespeare's reference to a Christian burial for Ophelia. Unless the offending line is eliminated and replaced with, "Is she to be buried in Mineola?" La Davidowicz, as Otto invariably refers to her, will not play the part.

An erstwhile poet and intellectual, Otto is horrified at the idea of altering Shakespeare. His closest friend, Benno Hamburger, is mutinous. The "Red Dwarf," resident anarchist and trouble maker, is gleeful. "That's it," he says. "Don't knuckle under to the fascists."

The crisis is another in an apparently endless series of contretemps that threatens to delay the production permanently. Death, the ultimate contretemps and an impatient presence at the Emma Lazarus, has already claimed *Hamlet's* original director, who is buried in Mineola and could strike again at any moment.

Mr. Isler said he chose Mineola as the permanent resting place for his characters, and the favored substitute for Shakespeare's offending reference, not for any logical reason but because he liked the sound of the name. "I have no idea if there is a cemetery there," he said. "But I do know that Long Island is replete with them."

His characters, by contrast, were created from more personal material. With roots in the emigre culture of New York and England, they are based, albeit rather broadly at times, on real people whom the writer has known.

"They are a composite of many, many people whom I met over the years," Mr. Isler said, "people who could claim backgrounds similar to Otto and Benno, particularly the German-Austrian émigrés."

This was the circle in which his parents and their friends moved in London in Mr. Isler's earliest childhood, he said, "people who managed to flee Austria in 1938."

Later, in the 50's, after Mr. Isler had left England to come here at the age of 18, he found an émigré community molded by the same forces on the Upper West Side. He remembers sitting as a young guest at dinner tables "awed by their cynical worldliness and cultural savoir-faire, their casual references to the genuine articles and the big names, many of whom they actually knew."

Drawn into the past by the shock of seeing Magda in the person of Mandy, Otto moves back and forth in his journal between past and present. Painful memories surface—of his failure as a poet, of cruelties born of bitterness and frustration and inflicted on people he loved, of a terrible arrogance and pride that had the most terrible consequences for his family.

He gives himself little quarter and can find no "grand purpose" in the seemingly random, often ugly events of his life. What has kept the blackness from engulfing him has been his ability to live in the moment. "For the last 30 years I have existed in the present," he writes, "disposing of my life a day at a time."

The shifting focus from tragic past to comic present also keeps blackness from engulfing Mr. Isler's readers. The examined life goes on, after all.

At the Emma Lazarus, despite the byzantine plotting and scheming, life is filled with the unexpected and fraught with ambiguities. It does not surprise him, Mr. Isler said, that the word "gentle" has appeared in early reviews of his book.

True, he has spared his characters few of old age's unbecoming infirmities, but he also said he believed that he had created in them "a much livelier group of people than you would actually find in such a place."

"This is the world in which we live," Mr. Isler said. "There are certain absolute truths."

Given those unavoidable truths, what he admires most, he said, is a certain combination of awareness with an appreciation for the uncertainties that finds expression in amusement and laughter.

Certainly Otto, with his unvarnished view of his own behavior and unsentimental attitude toward the foolishness of his friends, possesses it. Nor does it seem likely that Otto will ever rid himself of a certain deep-rooted ambivalence that colors his outlook, try as he might. And in that, Mr. Isler said, he resembles his creator.

"There is a lot of Korner in me," he said. "Like him, I love the old verities. On the other hand I also admire the youthful Dadaists and their impudent disturbing of the status quo."

Not surprisingly, the voice that waited so long before it was ready is now refusing to be silenced. The book, which found a publisher "serendipitously" though East End connections who recommended to Bridge Works in Bridgehampton, has been completed for a couple of years now, Mr. Isler said.

And yet, he added: "The voice is still very much alive in me. I have to fight against it, because I don't want it in my next work of fiction."

The new book, now in "the revisions stage," according to Mr. Isler, is something that he prefers not to talk about at the moment, except to say, "It grows more obviously out of my experience than the first one." . . .

Anita Brookner   (review date 4 February 1995)

SOURCE: "Hamlet, Though Not Meant to Be," in *The Spectator,* Vol. 274, No. 8691, February 4, 1995, pp. 28-9.

[*Brookner is an English novelist, nonfiction writer, and critic. In the following review, she praises Isler's craft as a novelist and agrees with those critics who have favorably compared* The Prince of West End Avenue *with the works of Isaac Bashevis Singer and Saul Bellow.*]

Since new talent invariably comes garlanded with pre-publication encomia the potential reader is advised to adopt an attitude of caution. Alan Isler's novel [*The Prince of West End Avenue*], first published in America, has been compared with the works of Isaac Bashevis Singer and Saul Bellow: Cynthia Ozick has added her commendation. Can it possibly live up to such praise? It can, it does. The comparisons are not odious but they are very slightly wide of the mark. Singer is a mystic, Bellow an intellectual ruminant. Isler is a sharp-witted novelist who knows how to beguile his readers, and also to lay traps for them. Since the action of his story takes place in a Jewish retirement home, stuffed with argumentative and essentially like-minded characters, the result might have been

intolerably self-regarding. Yet what emerges from this account of their affairs, and after considerable and masterly delay, is an awful dignity. These people, roughnecks some of them, are nevertheless and at the same time sophisticates. That is the fact of their survival, although the hero and narrator, Otto Korner, may not appreciate this particular irony. He is wise enough, however, to realise that he has no choice in the matter.

The Emma Lazarus Retirement Home in Manhattan, a comfortable establishment which we might well do to emulate over here (excellent cuisine, resident doctor, cultural activities) is inhabited by elderly parties whose wits and appetites have remained intact. In the intervals of breakfasts at Goldstein's Dairy Restaurant they are preoccupied with their forthcoming production of *Hamlet,* for which a particularly close reading of the text is undertaken by Otto Korner. Cast first as the Ghost, then demoted to Gravedigger, he longs to play Hamlet himself. Never mind that he is 83 years old: he has the experience. He is, or rather was, a man of letters; not only did he have a volume of poems published in his native Nuremberg, which brought him a treasured letter from Rilke, he was a student in Zurich at the epochal moment when Lenin was speaking in one part of town and Ball, Tzara, Arp and friends were performing in another. Indeed he may even have invented the term Dada for which the group became famous. Certainly he remembers a shambling figure with thick glasses who turned out to be James Joyce.

The letter from Rilke and the memory of his own literary efforts give Korner an added incentive to direct the production, a task which eventually becomes his by default, since the occupants of the Emma Lazarus home are occasionally overtaken by mortality. His ruminations on the play are surprisingly worthwhile, and mark him out as a genuine man of letters. At the same time he has to contend with the day-to-day life of the home and the vagaries of his companions. These are all dealt with sympathetically, and here the comparison with Bellow is valid: the overdressed and plaintive widows, the cracked former communists, and the priapic elders of both sexes all emerge vigorously from their different backgrounds and are devoid of the vulgarity with which they might be charged by those not of their number. Since an additional motif of the novel is the life force this is not surprising.

Korner's story differs from those of his fellows only in being more extreme. By the time he is waiting in his room for the call to play Hamlet we have learnt all there is to know about him. The brevity with which the information is disclosed is admirable. Like Hamlet he is no hero—but perhaps, he reflects, Hamlet was ashamed of and irritated by that cuckolded father and his belated call for revenge? There are embarrassments so severe that they can be life-threatening. Korner's passage from the incomparable culture of the pre-war German Jewish bourgeoisie to the Emma Lazarus home might be accounted a logical progression, given the manner in which the century has evolved. But not all victims are innocent. It was Korner's literary ambitions which were his undoing, and even in the Emma Lazarus home there is a witness to accuse him. But accuse him to his face: even here there is no subterfuge.

This is an excellent novel, not merely because every sentence is alive but because the reader might be persuaded that what is on offer is a mere comedy of manners. In fact Isler is several steps ahead of that reader on all counts, and it is his craft that one finally salutes. All that is known of the author is that he is English by birth, that he moved to America when he was 18 years old, that he has taught at Queens College in New York, that he is 60 years old, and that this is his first novel. The good news is that he is working on another. His remarkable debut is a cause for congratulation not only for the author but for the small American press which originally published him and for Jonathan Cape for buying the book and bringing it out in trade paperback. All in all, a distinguished and creditable enterprise, and a reminder that big money is not necessarily a guide to the production of excellent work.

Chang-rae Lee
Native Speaker

Born in 1965, Lee is a Korean-born American novelist.

INTRODUCTION

Although it employs a spy-novel plot, *Native Speaker* (1995) focuses mainly on themes of cultural assimilation and language use among Korean Americans. Henry Park, the protagonist, who was born in New York City but raised in a traditional Korean household, works as a spy for a private, commercial intelligence agency. He is assigned to infiltrate and report on the political organization of the charismatic Korean-American New York City councilman, John Kwang. Over the course of the story, Henry must come to terms with his ethnicity and with his desire to be accepted by both American and Korean-American communities. These inner conflicts affect his career, his marriage to an Anglo-American woman, the impact of his son's death, and the way he relates to his Korean family and culture. While some critics argue that *Native Speaker* fails as a spy novel, most agree that Lee's prose style, well-drawn characters, and insights into the Asian-American immigrant experience make it a highly successful autobiographical novel. Representative of the critical reaction, Rand Richards Cooper writes that "[h]idden inside *Native Speaker* is a memoir struggling to get out—a rapturous evocation of a past life. . . . I wish Chang-rae Lee had scrapped the spy stuff and written that book."

CRITICISM

Kirkus Reviews (review date 1 December 1994)

SOURCE: A review of *Native Speaker*, in *Kirkus Reviews*, Vol. LXII, No. 23, December 1, 1994, p. 1565.

[*In the following review of* Native Speaker, *the critic lauds Lee's prose style and development of characters.*]

In quiet, rich tones, Korean-American Henry Park, the narrator of this debut, speaks more clearly about his estranged wife than about his work.

This is only natural, for Henry is employed as a sort of industrial spy, and his most recent assignment is to infiltrate the people surrounding John Kwang, a Korean-American New York City councilman who may be headed for bigger things. Dealing with the slick Kwang causes him to reminisce about his own father, who owned fruit and vegetable

stores and encouraged him to marry a white woman. Inadvertently following his father's advice, he ended up married to Lelia, a speech therapist. Their son died at seven when he participated in a "dog pile" gone wrong. Subsequently, Lelia wanders off periodically and then finally leaves Henry for good. Lee creates the perfect tone for Henry—distanced, but never ironic or snappish. His observations and memories have the discomfiting feel of revealing truth. He tells how his father made him recite Shakespeare to show off his English for customers, and how one day he was commanded to allow a regular customer to exit a store without paying for an apple she had bitten and returned to a shelf. "Mostly, though," says Henry, "I threw all my frustration into building those perfect, truncated pyramids of fruit." He also describes how his father employed recently arrived immigrants because they were the hardest workers. His grappling with his son's death ("You pale little boys are crushing him, your adoring mob of hands and feet, your necks and heads, your nostrils and knees, your still-sweet sweat and teeth and grunts") and the slow rapprochement between him and Lelia are wonderfully drawn. The sections on his work are somewhat more challenging, particularly since his exact job is not very clear in the beginning, but Lee's careful prose conveys an immigrant's ability to observe without participating, and an outsider's longing for place and identity.

A serious, masterful, and wholly innovative twist on first-generation-American fiction.

Jeff Yang (review date 7 March 1995)

SOURCE: "Secret Asian Man," in *The Village Voice,* Vol. XL, No. 10, March 7, 1995, pp. 26-8.

[*In the following excerpt, Yang presents a highly positive review of* Native Speaker *and discusses Lee's examination of the difficulties posed by language for non-native speakers of English in the United States.*]

Let me take this moment to confess to sins of the first and worst order for a writer: sins of language, my original sins. I was born in America but English wasn't my first tongue, not even my second. I was raised to toddlerhood in a three-room Brooklyn flat across from the hospital where I was born and where my mother and father worked. I received their native Chinese from an aunt who spoke little else, then frightened my weary immigrant parents by mangling it with Spanish. To their horror, I was experiencing multicultural meltdown, becoming a linguistic bastard. While my nanny-aunt was busy elsewhere, I'd been left to sample the forbidden fruits of public broadcasting—*Villa Alegre, Carrascolendas*—and, *gracias al televisor,* was stumbling ever further from their model of that good second-generational child who should be, must be, reared as *a bi gok lang* (American) speaking *ying gi* (English).

They sent me to nursery school early, to root out the traces of my parents' speech and of the polyglot electric box. Now I'm told that over the phone I don't sound Asian, that I sound just like . . . embarrassed pause, because in this day of recognized diversity, *American sounds as American does.* So now I'm a speaker of English without portfolio: I can't even successfully mimic the ching-chong mockery of others speaking yellow. I'm stuck in basic broadcast.

Which leads to my second, conscious sin: becoming an accomplice to the murder of my ancestral tongue, a language that could not be resurrected despite years of after-school remedial classes and the best efforts of my repentant parents. My Spanish is still better than my Chinese.

So reading Change-Rae Lee's debut novel was like being handed a confession to sign. I play the literary authority while hiding the suspicion that this name, this face, this carefully disciplined tongue will someday betray me. And half hoping someone will remember that I can't even read a Chinatown newspaper. Sorry, man. *Se habla* Asian American. Brother Lee too.

Which means we work the contradictions, and this is what we write: spools of cultural history looped and extended with spurious detail. Or immigrant fantasies embedding

nuggets of remembered fact. Or ethnic Everyman metaphors that want to recount the story of our selves more surely than we would or could ourselves. All Asian American stories, ultimately, are biocryptography—not fiction, not nonfiction, but *un*-fiction, coded answers to the question: Who Am I?

Lee does have irony. He gives **Native Speaker** the disguise of a spy story, lending generic form to the spirit of cultural surveillance that inhabits most Asian American literature. Though the form is only cosmetic: Lee knows full well (as you will, early on) that he won't deliver a thriller's payoff in blood, lead, and adrenalin. What Lee does is to take the bones of a so-American genre and build them into a work of tremendous grace and discomforting resonance.

Lee's protagonist, Henry Park, is a Korean American man born to immigrant parents, raised in ivory suburban upstate New York, educated—overeducated—and then married and employed, both against the grain. His wife is a WASP speech therapist named Lelia, and their relationship has become broken and distant since the death of their son, Mitt, in a tragic accident.

Lelia's mourning over Mitt is raw and melodramatically American, open in a way that Henry finds he cannot match; this she correctly takes as a lack of feeling, or at least emotional truth, on his part. Their daily communication has shrunk into empty terminology. "We were hardly talking then," he says, "sitting down to our evening meal like boarders in a rooming house, reciting the usual, drawn-out exchanges of familiar news, bits of the day. When she asked after my latest assignment I answered that it was *sensitive* and *evolving* but going well, and after a pause Lelia said down to her cold plate, *Oh good it's the Henryspeak.*"

If Henryspeak sounds disconcertingly like Company lingo—spook talk—that's no coincidence. Henry works as an ethnic intelligence expert, an identity-mole-for-hire. Working for Dennis Hoagland, a canny opportunist, he and his coworkers are assigned to get close to and observe their own, to speak their language and listen to their responses, reporting their secrets to unknown and invisible clients:

> Each of us engaged our own kind, more or less. Foreign workers, immigrants, first-generationals, neo-Americans. I worked with Koreans, Pete with Japanese. We split up the rest, the Chinese, Laotians, Singaporans, Filipinos, the whole transplanted Pacific Rim. . . . Hoagland had established the firm in the mid seventies, when another influx of newcomers was arriving. He said he knew a growth industry when he saw one; and there were no other firms with any ethnic coverage to speak of.

Henry is a very good agent. The same things that impair him as a husband make him a perfect spy. A closeted identity is a necessary tool in this field, and Henry's lifelong fear of appearing alien has been useful:

> If I may say this, I have always only ventured where I was invited or otherwise welcomed. When I was a boy, I wouldn't join any school club or organization before a member first ap-

proached me. I wouldn't eat or sleep at a friend's house if it weren't prearranged . . . call me what you will. An assimilist, a lackey. A duteous foreign-faced boy. I have already been whatever you can say or imagine, every version of the newcomer who is always fearing and bitter and sad.

Henry, friendly assimilist, cultural chameleon, has always been able to get close to others without being touched himself. But his most recent assignment has been a disastrous failure: asked to investigate a Filipino American psychotherapist named Luzon, he instead finds himself offering up revelations, blending facts from his life with the faux data of his cover. His son, his wife, his assembled artifacts of assimilation, have been stripped away, and he is all too vulnerable.

For Lee, "to speak or not to speak" and "to be or not to be" have identical meanings. Language is pandemic, it infects and pervades and mediates everything: Speech is culture, speech is power, speech is sex.

—Jeff Yang

John Kwang—Korean American Queens councilman, potential mayoral candidate and messiah apparent of the gorgeous mosaic—is Henry's second and last chance. Hoagland plants Henry as a mole in the Kwang campaign. It seems like a plum gig. Henry's long-disused ties of blood and language make it easy for him to gain Kwang's trust. But Henry himself is slowly seduced by this patriarch, this Moses out of Flushing, in whom so many have invested immigrant hope. Kwang calls Henry by his Korean name, weaves around him a cocoon of familiarity. By story's end, Henry must make a painful choice: *Should he tell Kwang's secrets, or should he keep them?* If he speaks, he will be returned to his former state of cultural denial—the good agent-American, condemned to a voiceless life. Silence, by contrast, might set him free.

Here as elsewhere, for Lee, "to speak or not to speak" and "to be or not to be" have identical meanings. Language is pandemic, it infects and pervades and mediates everything: Speech is culture, speech is power, speech is sex. It's Lelia's crispness of tongue, her confidence in lingua Americana, that first attracts Henry. "Even before I took measure of her face and her manner," Henry muses, remembering their original encounter,

> I noticed how closely I was listening to her. What I found was this: she could really speak. . . . Every letter had a border. I watched her wide full mouth sweep through her sentences like a figure touring a dark house, flipping on spots and banks of perfectly drawn light.

In contrast with Lelia's lack of verbal inhibition, Henry is emotionally ingrown, mute. He attributes this to being brought up within his father's culture of silent endurance, where pain must be swallowed in public (before the whites) and can only be expressed in private in the secret speech of home, in the father tongue which Henry, at the hands of his American education, has lost. Henry notes that what remains is "all that too-ready devotion and honoring, and the chilly pitch of my blood, and then all that burning language that I once presumed useless, never uttered and never lived."

Having smothered that burning tongue beneath the English of his teachers and peers, he's left with a language stacked against him: "There isn't anything good to say to an average white boy to make him feel small. The talk somehow works in their favor, there's a shield in the language, there's no fair way for us to fight." So is it any wonder that when grown-up Henry speaks, it is with a dissociation that suggests that the syllables and images flowing from his mouth sluice around his being without touching it? They come from some external source, the pen of an unseen author, some primeval phrase book; they aren't native to his heart. Henry has become living proof that man can be an island, even an Alcatraz. What he *wishes he could say* lies trapped behind the seal of the Good, the Silent, the Model Minority.

The spy in the house of culture: Lee's device works on so many levels, none deeper than as an examination of the position of the immigrant, and particularly of the Asian immigrant. Since World War II, of course, Asians in America have faced suspicions of divided or imperfect loyalty. The internment of Japanese Americans and, more recently, allegations in the news of Chinese immigrants acting as sleeper spies: these are examples of how the foreignness of Asians is seen as running deep as blood. We are not only different from whites, but also blacks. Thus, too frequently, our survival in America's bicameral politics of race means adopting one or another alias, smiling and wearing camouflage.

I remember a late night with an Asian American friend who'd been brought up midwestern; we were discussing Los Angeles's Museum of Tolerance, the identity theme park that had recently opened to mostly white, mostly uncritical acclaim. To enter its exhibit halls, you must pass through a set of doorways that damn you to self-definition, marked in cold letters WHITE and COLORED. Of course, we thought, this device would shock and "educate" only those for whom the recognition of this divide was not a fact of daily life, and how often is any person of color given a choice between these doors? And then we considered our own childhoods, marked by spot-moments of acceptance and rejection, by inane and desultory wranglings with identity.

"Which door would you've gone through?" my friend joked.

I thought for a moment before answering.

"In one, out the other, I think."

While I was being half facetious then, on another day I might have meant it—a more bitter or honest day. As

Henry notes in *Speaker,* "It's still a black-and-white world."

"It seems so, Henry, doesn't it?" Kwang agrees. "Thirty years ago it certainly was. I remember walking these very streets as a young man, watching the crowds and demonstrations. I felt welcomed by the parades of young black men and women. . . . I tried to feel what they were feeling. How could I know? I had visited Louisiana and Texas and sat where I wished on buses, I drank from whatever fountain was nearest. No one ever said anything."

"Soon there will be more brown and yellow than black and white," Kwang says. "And yet the politics, especially minority politics, remain cast in terms that barely acknowledge us. . . . [I]f I don't receive the blessing of African-Americans, am I still a *minority* politician? Who is the heavy now? I'm afraid that the world isn't governed by fiends and saints but by ten thousand dim souls in between. I am one of them."

Dim souls—finless, featherless creatures of the gray world. In the binary of our race politics, Asians are regularly seen as double agents, outsiders and in-betweeners harboring an enigmatic personal agenda; more so now, when anti-immigrant hysteria has brought back the interrogator's hot lights and the loyalty oath. In post-Proposition 187 California, to be yellow or brown invites accusation. To be a nonnative speaker becomes a daily confession. "Traitor" and "spy" and "false speaker of language" have become identical; and now more than ever we are tongue-tied.

Like every politician, Kwang has skeletons hidden in his closets; unlike many, he won't be allowed to keep them. Since he resolutely refuses to enter a door—WHITE or colored—Kwang will be swept off the stoop. This, Henry grows to realize, is the nature of his assignment. And so: speak or be silent? The time comes when Henry is asked to call his loyalty, an identity to keep and be damned. It's to Lee's credit—or is it?—that Henry gets a third option, and a resolution of his Who Am I? is withheld. After all, there are no easy answers, and admission through whichever door comes at a price that Asian Americans—that no one—should have to pay.

Speaker's world, with its New York precisely drawn as a mosaic cracked, its boycotts and bombings, the machinery and manipulation of its politics, is familiar enough to leave the reader wondering if chapters after the last will be played out in headlines.

Richard Eder   (review date 19 March 1995)

SOURCE: "Stranger in a Strange Land," in *Los Angeles Times Book Review,* March 19, 1995, pp. 3, 13.

[*Eder, a nationally known journalist and critic, won the Pulitzer Prize for criticism in 1987. In the following mixed review of* Native Speaker, *he praises Lee's depiction of the Korean-American immigrant experience but criticizes his handling of the novel's genre elements.*]

When she temporarily walks out, Henry's wife, Lelia, hands him "a list" of who he is. She writes, among other things: "You are surreptitious . . . B plus student of life . . . illegal alien . . . emotional alien . . . genre bug . . . yellow peril: neo-American . . . stranger . . . follower . . . traitor. . . ."

Like the author, Chang-rae Lee, Henry is a Korean-American. Instead of a writer he is a spy; but it is clear that his spy condition is more important as a symbol than as a plot element. The plot of *Native Speaker* is garish and strained, in fact. The novel's strength lies in its portrait of a man whose national and cultural identities live a double life inside him.

Over the past 20 years the fictional mosaic of America has been filled in by writers of Chinese, Japanese, Mexican and Caribbean origin, among others. Each depicts the shocks, gains, losses and alterations from the interplay of an immigrant culture with an established one; otherwise, each is entirely different.

The Cuban-American family matrix contains a civilization largely unlike that of a Mexican-American family—a fact that no longer ought to surprise us. The Chinese-American families depicted by Gish Jen and Maxine Hong Kingston—different from each other, of course—represent a rich and elaborate communal tradition. Chang-rae Lee's Korean-Americans offer a stark contrast: a painfully laborious and grimly isolated striving.

An excerpt from Native Speaker

"Henry Park," her voice would quiver. "Please recite our favorite verse." I'd choke, stumble inside myself. And this was her therapy, struck in sublime meter on my palms and the backs of my calves:

> Till, like one in slumber bound,
> Borne to ocean, I float down, around,
> Into a sea profound, of ever-spreading
>   sound . . .

Peanut Butter Shelley, I'd murmur beneath my breath, unable to remember all the poet's womanly names. It was my first year of school, my first days away from the private realm of our house and tongue. I thought English would be simply a version of our Korean. Like another kind of coat you could wear. I didn't know what a difference in language meant then. Or how my tongue would tie in the initial attempts, stiffen so, struggle like an animal booby-trapped and dying inside my head. Native speakers may not fully know this, but English is a scabrous mouthful. In Korean, there are no separate sounds for L and R, the sound is singular and without a baroque Spanish trill or roll. There is no B and V for us, no P and F. I always thought someone must have invented certain words to torture us. *Frivolous. Barbarian.* I remember my father saying, Your eyes all *led,* staring at me after I'd smoked pot the first time, and I went to my room and laughed until I wept.

Chang-rae Lee, in his Native Speaker, *Riverhead Books, 1995.*

The emotional heart of **Native Speaker** and by far its most interesting aspect is the narrator's—Henry's—recollections of his immigrant father, and the anchoring these recollections provide to his hyperactive and far less convincing present-day story.

The father's money was painfully acquired in a fruit and vegetable business that started with nothing but hard work, and ended up with five well-placed stores in Manhattan. It has allowed Henry to grow up in the suburbs, go to a good college, and get a job whose antiseptic and well-paid abstraction is the antithesis of fruit handling. Antiseptic, but hardly clean: Henry works for a private intelligence agency. Its specialty is infiltrating immigrant communities on behalf of financial or political establishments anxious to know about any threat they may pose to their interests.

At the point the book begins, Lelia, a remedial English teacher, leaves for a love affair in Italy—she is fed up with her husband's masks and with what she calls "Henryspeak." Also Henry has botched an assignment. He was to keep an eye on a Philippine psychoanalyst suspected of organizing support in the United States for the deposed (now dead) Ferdinand Marcos. Henry had enrolled as a patient but made the mistake of letting himself slide into sympathetic transference. His bosses—a chilly, blithe Wasp and a warm, avuncular Greek—all but abduct him from the case, and not long afterward the doctor dies in an "accident."

With the greatest solicitousness—and an edge of threat—Henry is given a second chance. He is to infiltrate the entourage of John Kwang, a charismatic Korean-American councilman from the New York City borough of Queens. Young and appealing, Kwang has made a fortune from a small empire that started with dry-cleaning equipment and built up to manufacturing and real estate holdings up and down the East Coast. More to the point, he has begun to unite the various ethnic communities in Queens and to win the confidence of black leaders whose following has been in bitter and sometimes violent conflict with Korean shopkeepers. He may become a threat to the mayor.

The book's life comes mainly from Henry's recollections of his father and of the harsh silence with which he made his way.

—Richard Eder

What follows is an elaborate chronicle of scheming, duplicity and violence. Henry will become more and more closely drawn to Kwang, who takes him into his confidence. For a while it seems that he may resolve his own internal split. Perhaps it will not be necessary to choose between his Korean heritage and his American ambitions, and to use the latter to betray the former. Perhaps Kwang proves you can make it as both a Korean and an Ameri-

can. Nothing is as it seems, though; corruption and disguise are the universal price of success. Henry will end by resigning ambition and helping Lelia—now returned and reconciled—in her job of teaching immigrant children to speak English.

Lee's story of political skulduggery, a chilly corruption and a paranoid world maneuvered by hidden forces is written with a fair amount of awkwardness and a fair lack of skill. Kwang could be any ambitious political idealist turned bad. Henry's ruthless spymasters have the deceptive geniality of Le Carré characters but lack their fine and particular needles of ice. Lelia is inert: a remedial instrument to help Henry abandon his masks. Their lovemaking is so remote that we may feel we have passed by a hotel door incautiously left open.

The book's life comes mainly from Henry's recollection of his father and of the harsh silence with which he made his way. He swept floors, worked 14 hours a day, and kept vigilant, relentless track of each day's incremental gains. For a while, the family would picnic with other struggling Koreans, all of whom contributed to an investment fund—a "ggeh"—from which each, by turn, could withdraw the capital to set up a small business. Once they all began to prosper, the community broke up. Henry's father moved the family to a suburb among American neighbors he never came to know.

While the struggle was still going on, Henry's mother—who died partway along—would greet her husband's return each night with the same three sentences: "You must be hungry." "You come home so late." "I hope we made enough money today." When, in his teens, Henry sought to engage his silent father in conversation by asking about his day, his mother erupted in fury. Don't you realize, she demanded, that he hates his work, that he cannot stand selling vegetables, that he gave up his college engineering degree and his entire idea of himself in order to make a place in the United States for his family?

Lee has written a bleak portrayal of an immigrant society newer and rawer than that, say, of the Chinese and Japanese who have been coming here for generations. His book is raw as well, in its story and much of its writing. Still, the figure of Henry's father, whose love is expressed in sacrifice, whose sacrifice is expressed in harshness and whose harshness distills into an odd hint of poetry, is a memorable one.

Rand Richards Cooper   (review date 9 April 1995)

SOURCE: "Excess Identities," in *The New York Times Book Review,* April 9, 1995, p. 24.

[*In the following review of* Native Speaker, *Cooper criticizes Lee's poorly developed spy plot and uneven prose style, but praises his depiction of Korean immigrant family life.*]

Henry Park, the narrator of Chang-rae Lee's first novel, **Native Speaker,** is the son of Korean immigrants, a boy known as Marble Mouth in kindergarten, when his tongue felt "booby-trapped and dying" as it wrapped itself around the agonies of English. Grown up now, Henry has taken the classic path of American assimilation while using his adopted language to clear the way to college and a career.

A curious career—for Henry is a spy. He works for Glimmer & Company, a New York dirty-tricks firm that specializes in what he wryly calls "ethnic coverage," hiring first-generation Americans to keep watch on the immigrant communities they still have a foot in. For its shadowy patrons, Glimmer & Company keeps tabs on labor organizers, radical students and the like. Henry's job, on behalf of an unnamed client, is to infiltrate the organization of John Kwang, a city councilman from Queens whose progressive rainbow-coalition appeal is gaining prominence on the New York political landscape.

Native Speaker brims with intrigue and political high jinks, but Mr. Lee, who came to this country from South Korea when he was 3 years old, is no spy novelist. His interest lies in language, culture and identity; for him, the spy makes a convenient symbol for the American immigrant.

"Speak enough so they can hear your voice and come to trust it," Henry's spymaster boss lectures him, "and no one will think twice about who you are." We may consider a spy, with his Zelig-like ability to fade into the background, to be a born assimilator, but Mr. Lee slyly suggests the opposite: the immigrant's assimilated son is a born spy.

Inside *Native Speaker* is a memoir struggling to get out.

—*Rand Richards Cooper*

What is the cost of being a born spy? Henry Park's American wife, Lelia, finds him detached and cold. One of the novel's best passages concerns the Korean housekeeper who raised Henry after his mother's death. All his life, Henry has treated her as a mere employee, and his wife is first bewildered, then horrified, to learn that he doesn't even know the woman's name; he has always called her by the Korean equivalent of "ma'am." Who is this man she has married? Lelia wonders. It's a moment of deep mutual strangeness. Like a spy, the truly multicultural person seems to have several identities; that's the flip side of being no one at all. Mr. Lee's novel delves adroitly into our fascination with the plasticity of identity.

Equally moving are scenes recalling Henry Park's estrangement from his father, a successful grocer so imbued with the habits of work that at home he'd take one bite of an apple—reflexively sampling for freshness—and then put it down. Mr. Lee treads this familiar immigrant ground with skill and feeling, showing how father and son wield their respective languages to wound each other, and how Mr. Park's creed of hard work initially appears to Henry as mindless sacrifice and stoicism. Yet after his father's death that creed creates deep anguish and remorse in the son. "What belief did I ever hold in my father," Henry asks, "whose daily life I so often ridiculed and looked upon with such abject shame?"

Somewhat surprisingly, given all this hurt, *Native Speaker* offers a hopeful take on America's traditional role as beacon to the world. When Lelia remarks to Henry's father that a Korean street in Queens must look and sound just like one in Korea itself, the grocer demurs. "My father explained to her how if she looked carefully at the people she'd see the extra spring in their steps, the little boost everyone had, just by the idea of where they were, 'Look, look,' he implored her, crouched, slapping the pavement with both hands. 'This is an American street.'"

Native Speaker has some glaring flaws. Its plot is implausible and overblown; the tense shifts unnecessarily in midnovel, producing sentences like "Yesterday we're in Ozone Park"; and central characters like John Kwang exist less in their own right than as father figures trucked in as therapy for the narrator. Mr. Lee's prose is wildly uneven as well, its tone now breezy and ironic, now ponderously melodramatic: "A good spy is but the secret writer of all moments imminent"; "I celebrate every order of silence borne of the tongue and the heart and the mind." Whole hunks of *Native Speaker* exist at a level of quality far below the novel's best moments. You feel like taking up a paring knife.

That Mr. Lee can make these mistakes and still have something fine to offer shows just how talented he is. When you're done with the paring knife, what you have left is a tender meditation on love, loss and family. Here, for example, is Henry Park recalling the table rituals of his childhood:

> As we sat down, my mother cracked two eggs into my father's bowl, one into mine, and then took her seat between us at the table before her Spartan plate of last night's rice and kimchi and cold mackerel (she only ate leftovers at lunch), and then we shut our eyes and clasped our hands, my mother always holding mine extra tight, and I could taste on my face the rich steam of soup and the call of my hungry father offering up his most patient prayers to his God.

Hidden inside *Native Speaker* is a memoir struggling to get out—a rapturous evocation of a past life, viewed across a great gap of time and culture. I wish Chang-rae Lee had scrapped the spy stuff and written that book.

Jeff Noon
Vurt

Born in 1958, Noon is an English novelist.

INTRODUCTION

Set in Manchester, England, in the near future, *Vurt* (1993) concerns a character named Scribble and a group of friends consumed with the search for legal and black market strains of "vurt," a hallucinogenic drug that transports the user into a dream-like world. By placing a colored feather in one's mouth, an individual is able to enter a multilayered world of virtual reality, or, in the Manchester slang of the future, vurt. Ostensibly a love story and mystery, *Vurt* focuses on Scribble's search for his sister and lover, Desdemona, who remains lost in the vurt; the siblings became separated while on a drug trip inspired by a combination of the "Curious Yellow" and black "English Voodoo" feathers, and Scribble must find a way to retrieve his sister. The novel also features such fantastic creatures as dreamsnakes, robot cops, mutants, and the "Thing-from-Outer-Space," a living, organic manifestation and materialization of the drug vurt.

Winner of the 1994 Arthur C. Clarke Award for Fiction, *Vurt* was first published in England in 1993 and has been praised for its bleak yet intriguingly conceived portrait of the future and its original and, at times, lyrical language. Much of the critical attention surrounding *Vurt* has focused on its fragmented narrative and on attempts to classify the novel within a specific genre. Detractors have argued that *Vurt* fails as a piece of science fiction because Noon refuses to examine the relationship between his dystopic future and the moral and ethical dilemmas posed by contemporary society and technological advancement. Other commentators, however, have favorably compared Noon's "cyberpunk" portrait of the future with other notable works of fantastic literature, including William Gibson's *Neuromancer* (1984), Anthony Burgess's *A Clockwork Orange* (1962), and Lewis Carroll's *Alice's Adventures in Wonderland* (1865) and *Through the Looking-Glass, and What Alice Found There* (1872). Many reviewers have also seen in Scribble's quest for his sibling an update of the Orpheus and Eurydice myth.

PRINCIPAL WORKS

Woundings (drama) 1986
*Vurt (novel) 1993
†Pollen (novel) 1995

*This work published in the United States in 1995.

†This work is a sequel to *Vurt*.

CRITICISM

David V. Barrett (review date 21 January 1994)

SOURCE: "Madchester," in *New Statesman & Society*, Vol. 7, No. 286, January 21, 1994, p. 41.

[*In the excerpt below, Barrett relates the plot of* Vurt, *praising it as "an astonishing novel in story, style and emotion."*]

[In Jeff Noon's *Vurt*] Vurt is a type of virtual reality (but without computers), and a kind of drug. You put a coloured feather in your mouth and you're in a dream-world—or a nightmare. Scribble is searching for his kid sister (and lover) who went into a Vurt world with him and never came back. He roams the backstreets with a gang of friends, trying to find a dealer who will supply him with a Curious Yellow feather, so he can go back to the same world to find her.

The Vurt worlds are appealing and terrifying, mystical and murderous; the real world is gritty and realistic. Noon's Manchester has Bottletown, a housing estate with a couple of unemptied bottle banks. "When the banks were full, and overflowing, still they came, breaking bottles on the pavements and the stairs and the landings. This is how the world fills up. Shard by shard, jag by jag, until the whole place is some kind of glitter palace, sharp and painful to the touch." The last sentence is a perfect description of the novel, as is this: "Such is beauty, in the midst of the city of tears. In Bottletown even our tears flicker like jewels."

Vurt is an astonishing novel in story, style and emotion. In places it has the lyricism of Elizabeth Smart's *By Grand Central Station I Sat Down and Wept,* mixed with the weird and wild fun of Chester Anderson's cult hippy-SF novel *The Butterfly Kid* and the streetwise cynicism of Kurt Vonnegut at his best. It may be too harsh for hippies, too beautiful for bikers; but its spikiness should appeal to the punks, and its obsession with danger and death should grab the goths.

Russell Letson   (review date April 1994)

SOURCE: A review of *Vurt,* in *Locus,* Vol. 32, No. 4, April, 1994, p. 23.

[*In the following review, Letson offers a mixed assessment of* Vurt, *arguing that the novel's disparate generic elements do not cohere.*]

I know I'm in for trouble when I'm able to finish a book, recognize its virtues, and still not like it—especially when it's an ambitious book that I know is going to be loved by some readers. In the case of *Vurt,* a first novel by Jeff Noon, and a finalist for the Arthur C. Clarke Award, it was mixed feelings at first sight. Take the following ingredients: a gritty welfare-state urban landscape; a gang of young people with not much to do except knock around looking for thrills; drugs or drug-like somethings that supply said thrills; sex and rock & roll (just to keep the trinity together); virtual reality, nanotechnology, artificial intelligences, robots, and bioengineering. Science fiction, right? In fact, probably cyberpunk or one of its cousins.

Now add a multiverse of dreamworlds of varying degrees of reality; a lost love swallowed up in one of those dreamworlds and replaced by a changeling Thing; a mysterious and powerful guide/guardian who knows the secrets of these worlds and can walk up and down in them; a search for an object of power that will give the protagonist access to the world where his lost love waits. Have we fallen through a rabbit hole into another genre? Should that matter?

"Vurt" is future-Brit slang for virtual-reality experiences: not individual drug-dreams, but something more like role-playing games that can be shared with one or more com-

panions. Vurts are products with standard titles and recognized levels of sophistication and danger. The language that describes them combines terminology from film, sound recording, and computer gaming: they are acted, edited, remixed; some have menus. But there is no indication of how they actually work, nor of the economy of which they are part. What's really strange is that the delivery medium for a vurt is a feather, placed in the mouth as if it contained a drug.

So in a near-future Manchester, Scribble and his gang, the Stash Riders, get most of their fun from doing Vurt. In the gradually-revealed back-story is the matter of how Scribble's sister/lover Desdemona got left behind in the dangerous English Voodoo world, and how the gang got, by the law of exchange, the live-drug Thing, an amorphous alien creature whose renewable flesh offers Vurt experiences even better than those from feathers. The armature of the story is Scribble's search for Desdemona and its point seems to be what finding her costs him and his companions. Along the way we get glimpses of a Manchester peopled by dog-humans, robo-dogs, Vurt changelings, real and virtual cops, and practically every combination of the basics.

Every so often the Game Cat (which/who is both a magazine and a person) breaks in to deliver just enough background to keep the whole thing from collapsing into incomprehensibility. All the same I kept asking questions, and only occasionally could I come up with answers. Is the Vurt experience based on a telepathy-inducing drug? On short-lived nano-agents that go right for the brain? The book doesn't supply an answer, or seem to care to. Most of all, I kept asking, *why feathers?* The only answer I could come up with was that they operate metaphorically or symbolically. (Joseph Campbell's *The Flight of the Wild Gander,* anyone?) It certainly doesn't make sense any other way.

In fact, metaphor drives everything in this book. Given that much fantastic literature is literalized metaphor to begin with, this should not be a problem, except that in sf one expects the metaphors to be not only literalized but rationalized—sf is dedicated to the proposition that the world makes sense, even if sometimes that sense escapes us for a while. *Vurt* is terminologically but not intellectually sf. For all the robo-this and nano-that, the sf motifs don't articulate as sf; the book's operational rules combine those of expressionist fantasy with the wizards, monsters, and magic spells of Dungeons and Dragons and the elf-land-logic of fairy tale. When Scribble hears Desdemona calling for help in the middle of a Vurt dream, he might as well be seeing her in a magic mirror or scrying stone and a Vurt feather might as well be a magic wand or talisman.

I do realize that sf and heroic fantasy share more than a few archetypes, and that mixing genre elements and structures can lead to interesting and illuminating new entities—Michael Swanwick's *The Iron Dragon's Daughter* is an illustrious recent example. But the key to a successful mixture—one with real hybrid vigor—is a deep coherence (we used to call this "organic unity") that holds the dissimilar materials together, and I'm not sure that *Vurt* manages that. I suspect that instead it aims at being un-classifiable, a sort of postmodern recursive roleplaying metaphysical cyberpunk fairytale.

Vurt is, despite my grumbling, an intermittently success-ful mélange. It is generally vivid, evocative, and linguisti-cally inventive. Nor is its imaginative world without reso-nances. It's just not coherent enough for my taste. But in seeing the conjunction between high-tech and the magical, Noon is an apt candidate for an award named for the in-ventor of Clarke's Law.

Faren Miller   (review date September 1994)

SOURCE: A review of *Vurt*, in *Locus*, Vol. 33, No. 3, Sep-tember, 1994, p. 21.

[*In the review below, Miller lauds Noon's use of language in* Vurt.]

[In Jeff Noon's Clarke Award-winner *Vurt*, we're] amongst the Stash Riders, a bunch of druggy kids on the dole in near-future Manchester UK, scruffy, unromanti-cized, as aimlessly amoral as the worst of Kress's Livers and considerably less picturesque than [William] Gibson's usual cyberpunk lowlives. The virtual reality that gives the book its title is the world of a strange drug (taken in the form of a feather), rather than a realm accessed by com-puter. The cybernetic element here is the prevalence of ro-bots and cyborged humans with random bits of tech in them—human/machine combinations just as seedy as the ordinary humans, as sad, as hungry for the dreams that only Vurt can provide. Even Gibson's hackers would seem a more energetic variety of outlaw, not content to sit and drool, bleed, or rust away in an inner-city doorway.

Vurt provides dream-triumphs, sensual pleasure, even knowledge, for a weary European country decades ahead of America in its acknowledgement of defeat. An expert known as Game Cat describes the effects of the drug known as English Voodoo: "There is a dream out there, of a nation's second rise: When the dragon is slain and the good queen awakens from her coma-sleep, to a land capa-ble of giving breath to her."

Vurt gradually comes to fascinate with its sad beauty, and a wayward form of mystery not to be confused with standard genre action, but found in some of the more haunted Raymond Chandler novels.

—Faren Miller

As this passage indicates, there's beauty in the sad nation under the sway of Vurt—it just lies in the language, more than in Noon's apparently unpromising subject matter. Witness this observation from Scribble, the narrator: "The emptiness inside of me reflected in the glass fragments. So I was a thousand times sad, with each footstep. *Sometimes*

even broken glass, cracked cement, sad lives; well, they seem like the good dreams of bad things." That last bit, italicized in the book, could easily pass for Noon's own re-sponse to his material—and to his characters as well (though Scribble isn't such a bad sort really; he's just been deprived of what we'd call "a life").

So, rather like the feather-drug itself, **Vurt** gradually comes to fascinate with its sad beauty, and a wayward form of mystery not to be confused with standard genre action, but found in some of the more haunted Raymond Chandler novels. I should emphasize that the book's plea-sures are not *all* matters of language. There's eventually a plot, involving Scribble's loss of his incestuous sister-lover Desdemona, Eurydice to his Orpheus, and the pow-ers of loss, madness, and other factors can drive the char-acters to actions as gripping as anything in our own more apparently purposeful society.

In all, **Vurt** is deserving of its prestigious award, and well worth reading, so long as you're into literary quality, con-vincing atmosphere, and a future animated more by age-old passions than by whatever high-tech lies behind those strange drug-feathers that lead to another world. . . .

Richard Gehr   (review date February 1995)

SOURCE: "Feather Underground," in *VLS*, No. 132, February, 1995, p. 14.

[*In the following highly favorable review, Gehr offers a sty-listic and thematic discussion of* Vurt.]

Right away I found myself describing **Vurt** to interested parties as—ahem—"the *Neuromancer* of psychedelics," knowing full well I was probably doing both of these so-called science fiction novels a virtual disservice. There would be no **Vurt** without *Neuromancer*, of course—just as there would be no *Neuromancer* without *The Crying of Lot 49* or *Goldfinger*. Like William Gibson's genre-warping cyberpunk howdy, Jeff Noon's debut novel comes nearly out of nowhere. A millennial fairy tale as entertain-ing as Gibson's wild ride through popular science, **Vurt** offers an equally mutant vision of consciousness-expanding technology. With its mean Manchester streets and twisted ontology, call it *A Clockwork Orange* meets *Alice in Wonderland*.

You could also read **Vurt** as a literary remix of cyber-punk—a dub version as important for what's been taken out as for what remains. A profound story about absence and loss, **Vurt** is set in a future Manchester that technolog-ical progress appears to have bypassed entirely. Give or take the ubiquitous presence of something called Vurt, a wryly romantic scene in which a pair of "twinned crus-ties" named Tristan and Suze wash their entwined dreadlocks with "nanoshampoo," a few genetic muta-tions, and some fractal bullets, **Vurt** depicts essentially the same dark, distressed Manchester that former punk rock-er Jeff Noon calls home. Where most SF projects the pres-ent into the future, he retrojects a few elements from the future into the present.

It's a rare book that can take you as high into the conceptual cosmos as it can toss you down into the harsh karmic sump, but *Vurt* manages to do precisely that,

—*Richard Gehr*

Apart from the absence of technofetishism, the novel diverges most radically from the cyberpunk template in its abundance of heart. "This is a love story. You got that already?" nags Scribble, the 20ish narrator, halfway through. By this point we've learned how Scribble has lost his younger sister-lover Desdemona to the Vurt world, which has sent back in exchange a lump of raw Vurt matter known affectionately by Scribble's gang, the Stash Riders, as the "Thing-from-Outer-Space." Mythic, operatic, and throwaway at once, *Vurt* riffs between myth, kitsch, and chaos through language embodying a sometimes excruciatingly elegant pop poetics. "If they can remix Madonna after she's dead," Scribble inquires, "why can't they remix the night?"

While the Vurt signifier pervades the novel, no one—not even, I suspect, the author himself—knows precisely what Vurt really is. *Vurt* begins like a sexually egalitarian *Clockwork Orange,* with a squeal of tires and a narrow escape from an "all-night Vurt-U-Want," where the Stash Riders have scored their contraband. Vurt sounds a lot like a drug here, especially in light of the algebra of need exhibited by the Riders' leader, Beetle. "The Beetle had this obsession about doing Vurt alone," says Scribble. "That you'd need help in there, friends in there. What he really means was—you need me in there." Yet Vurt is more than a drug: as punning a title as it is a concept, Vurt is that place dreams, stories, movies, television, video games, cyberspace, "adverts," and (eventually) virtual reality all take us with varying—and, some would say, generally decreasing—degrees of profundity.

Ingested orally (or sometimes anally) through the elegant medium of colored feathers, Vurt offers a range of potencies. At the bottom are pink "Pornovurts" and blue televisual "Soapvurts" like "Co-op Street"; "You bought it every Monday, Wednesday and Friday. It took you to a small Northern terrace, gave you a house to live in, gave you a home and a husband or a wife, and you got to interact with all the famous characters as their epic stories unfolded."

Aficionados such as the Stash Riders, however, prefer hard Vurt, dire black bootleg feathers like. "English Voodoo" and "Skull Shit." Among the book's strange pleasures are intermittent newsletters written by the Vurt-inhabiting Game Cat, who offers cautionary and consumer advice for his "kittlings" about such Vurt selections as "Skull Shit" ("aka The Synapse Murders, Head Fuck, Temple Vomit, Id Slayer").

Like Philip K. Dick's *A Scanner Darkly* (still the best drug

novel ever written), *Vurt* plays with states within states, gaming with textual reality and illusion in increasingly subtle ways. The "Curious Yellow" feather that captured Desdemona was contained within the world opened up by the black feather "English Voodoo," and the entire Vurt-verse can come to a screeching halt when a "player" enters a state of "meta-vurt." Part of *Vurt*'s mystique lies in how it blurs the boundaries dividing video games, psychedelics, and psychoanalysis, posing knotty questions about the ontological distinctions characterizing these common alternatives to consensual reality. As always, some make more of these states than do others. As Tristan argues, "They think Vurt's more than it is, you know? Like it's some higher way, or something. It's not. Vurt is just collective dreamings. That's all. Christ! Isn't that enough for them?"

When things get too weird in there, "the Haunting" signals a powerful wake-up call from objective-materialist reality. "The Haunting was the feeling you got sometimes, in the Vurt; the real world calling you home. *There's more to life than this. This is just a game.*" Of course, it both is and isn't. Although Vurt at times operates like a video game (silver feathers allow the user to scroll down an editing function), entities exist inside the realm. Apart from the Game Cat, these include the Sniffing General and the mysterious Hobart, the unseen feminine presence whose dreams generate not only Vurt but, the Game Cat implies, a dangerous yet exciting new England.

> There is a dream out there, of a nation's second rise: When the dragon is slain and the good queen awakens from her comasleep, to a land capable of giving breath to her. The followers of ENGLISH VOODOO worship the new queen. The queen is the keeper of our dreams. Through her portals you can see a paradise of change, where trees are green, birds do sing, and the trains run on time. Also, lots of sex; that special kind, with a delicious English thump.

An alternative universe potentially containing all humanity's stories, Vurt contains multitudes. A kingdom of snakes described through a Hindu fable also contains the Manchester police department's database. Since *Vurt* is only the first volume of a planned quartet, Noon has given himself plenty of space to work out the details. Inverting *Vurt* a dozen years later, Noon's follow-up, *Pollen,* will concern the dream world's desire to capture a portion of reality for itself by aggressively manufacturing a malevolent paradise so fecund it produces death by hayfever. So stick around. (How hot is *Vurt*? In an interview, Noon has mentioned seeing a treatment for the film version, wherein the retiring Scribble's protagonist has been usurped by the more conventionally heroic Tristan. And, naturally, a computer game is also in the works.)

In his quest to find another Curious Yellow feather and exchange the Thing for Desdemona, Scribble becomes a virtual white Orpheus who must wrest the blob back from *Vurt*'s version of Cerberus. Das Uberdog, therefore, is a sexually charismatic halfbreed who inhabits a hellishly squalid squat aptly named "Turdsville." So as not to suggest too pointed a racial allegory, I should probably add that *Vurt* is also populated by pathetic "robo-crusties" and telepathic shadow creatures. Most futurologists predict increasing tribal conflicts as the Western world spins toward millennial hysteria (unless you happen to be, you know, Muslim, or some other differently calendared believer). In Noon's future Manchester, where most residents are dependent on a dole he renames "dripfeed," these tribes include synthetically mutated new phyla containing varying combinations of dog, robot, "shadow," and Vurt (Scribble becomes part Vurt after he's bit by one of the realm's "dreamsnakes," which appear when players jerk out of the realm prematurely). "Pure is poor," reads the local graffiti, implying that the balance of power is changing.

Vurt reads brown and gray, if you know what I mean—like Samuel Delany's classic *Dhalgren.* You can read all the SF you want about high-tech future worlds, but it's positively refreshing to read something hovering around the fringes of the genre that embraces poverty as major thematic material. *Vurt* includes a thick grease trail in the omnipresence of a substance called simply Vaz. An all-purpose ointment, Vaz implies everything from a raver's mentholated buzz to quotidian urban scuzz. "Sometimes it feels like the whole world is smeared with Vaz," complains Scribble. A progressively more disorienting narrative experience, *Vurt* freaks out while maintaining material presence. It's a rare book that can take you as high into the conceptual cosmos as it can toss you down into the harsh karmic sump, but *Vurt* manages to do precisely that.

Scott L. Powers (review date 3 February 1995)

SOURCE: "Inventive *Vurt*: Getting High and Lost in Cyberland," in *The Boston Globe,* February 3, 1995, p. 50.

[*In the following positive assessment of* Vurt, *Powers argues that the novel breaks new ground in the genre of "cyberpunk" fiction and praises Noon's pacing, "visual style," and focus on music.*]

In the future—as in the past—there will be drugs. Lots of them. In the future of Jeff Noon's first novel, *Vurt,* bands of youths moving to techno-trance and occasional punk beats will devote their lives and deaths to drugs, determined to slip through cracks in this world to a separate reality, searching for continually different and higher highs.

Scribble is one of them. His friends (gang is too strong a word, they're after highs, not money or *A Clockwork Orange* ultraviolence) call themselves the Stash Riders, and they have just scored some non-legal vurt. But a shadow-cop has spotted them with an inpho, beaming onto their license plate. So Scribble, Beetle, Mandy, Bridget and the Thing-from-Outer-Space are on the run . . . again.

In classic science-fiction style, *Vurt* creates its own world and language. Noon has added to all this an inventive hook that propels a basic missing-person mystery story into a journey into a believable, distant future where computer science and biology have created a drug/computer/video game/movie ingested by placing a color-coded feather in one's mouth. Once the credits are over, legal vurt takes one on an enjoyable, and usually safe, ad-

venture. But also available under-the-counter from the Vurt-U-Want retail outlets are bootleg remixes—illegal and highly potent feathers that take users to other places, from where they may not return, or if they do, it might be with a being from the alternative world.

Scribble's search for his sister, Desdemona, who has been trapped in an illegal vurt, is the loose plot that propels *Vurt,* but it's Noon's vision of this constant acid-trip-of-a-world that is the book's strength. Set in a future Manchester, England, Noon's environment conjures *Max Headroom* and *Blade Runner.* Like Carlos Castaneda's Don Juan, Scribble has his guide into the vurt, Game Cat, who knows the vurt programs yet possesses wisdom beyond alternative existence. Noon's future world also includes beings that have slipped through one reality and into another: shadowgirls who know your thoughts, illegal live drugs whose body parts offer quick trips into the vurt and dog-people who possess an Adam Ant-like pop appeal.

That Noon would string music through spots of *Vurt* isn't surprising, given his background playing in bands around the influential Manchester music scene. Noon, now in his mid-30s, is reported to have written *Vurt* while kicking around as a clerk at the Waterstone's bookstore in Manchester. A friend published it in England; then an American literary agent came across it in a bookstore in Switzerland, became entranced and sold the book rights to Crown. *Vurt* won last year's Arthur C. Clarke award for science fiction, and Noon is finishing the second of a planned four-part book series based on this idea. A movie is under discussion.

A movie version of *Vurt* has promise, given Noon's visual style:

> Doorman at the Slithy Tove was a fat white rabbit. He had a blood-flecked head protruding from the beer-stained neck fur and a large pocket watch in his big white mittens. The big hand was pointed to twelve, the little hand pointed to three. That's three o'clock in the morning of the night just begun.
>
> Two door whores were trying to blag their way in without a coding symbol. Rabbit was dealing them grief. I flashed my laminated access-all-areas after-gig party passcode, formed to the shape of a small and cute puggy dog half-cut with a human baby, dappled in fur; overleaf, a photo of Dingo Tush, naked but for his (authorised) autograph. Around the edge of the pass ran the slogan—Dingo Tush. Barking for Britain tour. Presented by Das Uberdog Enterprises.

Writing science fiction can be liberating, with its creation of new worlds with new realities. But integrating those realities without blocking the plot can derail them. Noon pushes readers into his book with its music-video-paced plot, taking only phrases here and there to explain. Easing the way is Scribble, who is no punk, but a well-intentioned slacker with a few dirty secrets and an overpowering obsession with vurt. This reluctant hero—and the other characters who possess some depth—warms Noon's world away from the steel and flashing lights of the cyberpunk genre where *Vurt* has been lumped. Noon has stripped away detailed explanations, and by making vurt less machine and more organic, has moved his book into a fresher, post-cyber world.

Novels with strong drug influences are nothing new. In its approach, *Vurt* seems more influenced by Castaneda's voyage into knowledge with the aid of a teacher and organic ally and by Lewis Carroll than by the current cyberpunk of William Gibson. Like Alice racing through Wonderland in a broken-down van with the radio blaring, Noon's journey into the future is trippy and captivating.

Tom De Haven   (review date 5 February 1995)

SOURCE: "The Fickle Feather of Fate," in *The New York Times Book Review,* February 5, 1995, p. 19.

[*An American editor, author of books for children, and educator, De Haven has written several fantasy novels and was instrumental in adapting William Gibson's 1984 novel* Neuromancer *into a graphic, "comic book," format. In the negative review below, he laments* Vurt's *lack of moral and social vision, which are typically considered characteristics of science fiction.*]

Whether it's set on Planet Earth or Planet X, next week or next millennium, most science fiction pays close, even persnickety attention to the ethical, political and technological facts of life. Social context counts; always has. Without the anchor of a coherent culture, a science fiction novel becomes as disjointed and surreal as a music video, and just as solipsistic. It becomes, I'm afraid, a book like *Vurt*.

This first novel by Jeff Noon was originally published in England, where it won the Arthur C. Clarke Award for fiction. Yet despite its bizarre trappings and intriguing basic conceit, it fails to convince. Though we glimpse night streets, dance clubs and grim housing projects, everything in *Vurt* is rendered so generically, or glanced over with such glib neologisms, that it's impossible to place much credence in Mr. Noon's invented world.

Nor does his cast of characters (consisting almost entirely of Manchester street gangsters) have much connection to the continuum of history, either global or local; its members exist outside of politics as well. That's a romantic notion, but a deceitful one. To be an outlaw, after all, presumes the existence of law, and law presumes the confluence of morals and economics: a system. One cop named Murdoch, who shows up whenever the plot needs goosing, carries an unfair burden: she, and she alone, embodies prevailing, and presumably repressive, Authority.

Vurt appears to be set sometime in the relatively near future. Sharing the turf with Mr. Noon's scruffy humans are several meta-human species, including cyborgs and a feral half-canine race, one of whom calls himself Das Uberdog. ("Our great-grandfather was an Alsatian," explains another toothy brute.) But how did this world, this culture, this *biology* come to be? The author never even hints, and the reader is left to concoct the reality shell. Or, more likely, not to bother.

In this England-to-come, a mysterious new entertainment medium called Vurt has proliferated. Slip a computer-coded feather into your mouth, tickle your throat, and you're gone. While legal feathers plunge you into interactive soap operas or sensual scenarios, contraband ones drag you down to more dangerous realms. The oddest property of Vurt is its so-called exchange mechanism. A feather-dreamer can disappear while curled up asleep, to be replaced by a variety of living objects, including poisonous snakes, from a number of dream worlds.

Scribble, who narrates the novel, is a young Vurt devotee who has lost his beloved Desdemona (a younger sister and occasional bedmate) to a bad exchange. After swallowing a feather called Curious Yellow ("It makes the past into a nightmare, and then strands you there, with no hope of release"), Desdemona was replaced by a tentacled blob.

With his outlaw colleagues (Bridget, Mandy, Twinkle, the Beetle and a pair of lovers named Tristan and Suze, who share "six feet of thick entwined hair"), Scribble rackets around the city, hoping to score another copy of the rare Curious Yellow feather. Naturally, he intends to go after the lost Desdemona and bring her back.

Nearly 20 years ago, I was a member of a writers' workshop moderated by the novelist Craig Nova, who one evening explained his objection to science fiction. The trouble, he said, is that most of its plots are swiped from the Bible or mythology, then dressed up in future-speak. (I remember squirming, since at the time I was writing a science fiction novel based on the story of Cain and Abel.) Mr. Nova was exaggerating to make a point, I'm sure, but his criticism has some validity. And it's certainly true in this case.

For all of its dystopian huggermugger, *Vurt* is, of course, a retelling of the Orpheus myth. (Instead of Hades, Scribble must descend into virtual reality.) Its theme, however, more closely echoes that of *The Wizard of Oz*. Take away the novel's inconsequential murders, incest and punk cynicism, and what remains is a surprisingly ingenuous conservatism. Though Dorothy from Kansas would doubtless run screaming from a character like Scribble (or sic Toto on him), they both espouse, at the ends of their adventures, almost identical sentiments. "There's no place like home," says Dorothy, while Scribble declares, "The real world is not beautiful, but it's where you belong."

If only Mr. Noon had taken the trouble to give dimension and detail to that "real world," his story might have had resonance and power. Instead, it meanders on, garish and kooky, like a fever dream, a hallucination that Mr. Noon, choosing to ignore the glazed look in our eyes, insists on recounting in all its droning detail.

Hal Espen   (review date 13 February 1995)

SOURCE: "Virtual Reading," in *The New Yorker,* Vol. LXX, No. 49, February 13, 1995, pp. 86-7.

[*In the review below, Espen offers a negative assessment of* Vurt.]

Virtual reality, true to its name, continues to recede into the brave new digital future. Except for a few tacky theme-park versions, the technology remains a vaporware phenomenon that has yet to escape from the labs and into the

An excerpt from *Vurt*

Last time I saw my sister, for real, she was sitting opposite me, across an apple jam-smeared table, with a feather in her mouth, expecting to fly. It was me, the brother, holding the feather there, turning it all around inside of her mouth. And then moving it to my own mouth, and Desdemona's eyes were glazed already by the Vurt, as I twisted the feather deep, to follow her down. Wherever she was going, I was going too. I really believed that.

We went down together, sister and brother, falling into Vurt, watching the credits roll; WELCOME TO ENGLISH VOODOO. EXPECT TO FEEL PLEASURE. KNOWLEDGE IS SEXY. EXPECT TO FEEL PAIN. KNOWLEDGE IS TORTURE.

Last time I saw my sister, close up, intimate, in the Vurt world, she was falling through a hole in a garden, clutched at by yellow weeds, cut by thorns, screaming my name out loud. A small yellow feather was fluttering at her lips.

I told her not to go through that door. It was a NO GO door. She went anyway.

I told her not to. She went anyway.

'I want to go there, Scribble. I want you to come with me. Will you come?' My sister's last real words to me, before the yellow feather kicked in, and she was falling, screaming my name.

Some of us die, not in the living world, but in the dream world. Amounts to the same thing. Death is always the same. There are some dreams you never wake up from.

Desdemona . . .

The room, in silence.

Later that day. Hours of smoke uncounted, but now the mist was drifting apart, revealing tiny fragments of the real world. These little glimpses stung the eyes like needles. I could no longer tell the tale; its telling was too much for me. I was shaking from the memories; Desdemona was aching in my heart.

Tristan broke the mood. 'You found another feather in there?' he asked. 'Is that what you're saying?'

I just nodded. . . .

'I've been there,' he added.

'What?'

'I've been inside English Voodoo.'

'Tell me.' I was desperate for knowledge.

Jeff Noon, in his Vurt, *Crown Publishers, Inc., 1993.*

real world. For more than a decade, however—certainly since the publication of William Gibson's *Neuromancer,* in 1984—V.R.'s imaginary analogues have proliferated in the subgenre that Gardner Dozois, the editor of *Asimov's Science Fiction,* christened "cyberpunk." More recently, virtual-reality story lines have become hot properties in Hollywood: Michael Douglas watches a virtual Demi Moore delete his career in *Disclosure;* Keanu Reeves (in the forthcoming *Johnny Mnemonic*) and Denzel Washington (in *Virtuosity*) will soon jack into the cyberspace frontier on film; and Robin Williams has bought the rights to Alexander Besher's virtual-reality novel *Rim,* which *Wired* magazine is now serializing on the Internet. (Harper-Collins West published a hard-copy version in November.)

The mainstreaming of cyberpunk continues with Jeff Noon's first novel, ***Vurt***. Noon, a thirty-seven-year-old former rock musician, won Britain's Arthur C. Clarke Award for ***Vurt*** last year; his American publisher, calling the book "really commercial and almost literature," has ordered a big first printing and is trying to reach beyond the sci-fi ghetto. One of the presumably commercial things about ***Vurt*** is the absence of daunting electronic paraphernalia and programming jargon: its artificial realities are not computer generated but induced by a variety of designer drugs. Noon has come up with the baroque notion of having these drugs packaged in the form of feathers: tickle the back of your friends' throats and you can join them in a shared and utterly convincing dream world—the Vurt. While this novel observes most of the conventions of cyberpunk fiction, its imagery is insistently organic, and owes more to the underground pharmacology of the rave scene than to the world of hardwired chips and user interfaces.

Vurt is set in Manchester, in the not-too-distant future. (Madonna is dead, but Interactive Madonna is one of the stars at Woodstock Seven.) The narrator and hero is Scribble, who runs with a posse of feather-head proles who call themselves the Stash Riders. They live on public assistance—"the dripfeed"—and spend their time trying to score bootleg feathers. Blue feathers are safe and legal, pink feathers offer "Pornovurts," but black bootlegs are dangerous "knowledge feathers." (Much of the incidental pleasure in this kind of writing comes from the way catchphrases and throwaway references to brand names use the mundane to suggest the fantastic. Characters in ***Vurt*** smoke Napalm cigarettes, eat J.F.K. flakes for breakfast, and wear Showbiz cologne. A girl has hair "as blonde as the day is doomed," and a couple of "crusties" wash their greasy dreadlocks with Nanosham, a shampoo made of microscopic machines that turn "dirt into data, processing hair clean.") Naturally, the Stash Riders have a quest: to rescue Scribble's sister Desdemona from the Vurt, where she was trapped when a trip on English Voodoo, a bootleg, took a nasty turn.

By and large, Noon is a woefully clumsy writer, and he brings a minimal level of competence to bear on the car chases, street fights, and noir confrontations that take up much of the real-world plot. After the brisk and relatively engrossing opening chapters, Noon meanders back and forth between Scribble's Vurtual excursions and his desultory search for Desdemona; the Stash Riders are hassled by the police (both "fleshcops" and robots); and there are several long, pointless episodes involving a subculture of mongrel dog-people.

The book's most serious flaw is the flimsiness of the relationship between Scribble and Desdemona. Noon has tried to be daring by making the two siblings lovers, but he has no idea how to handle their incestuous passion, and his flashbacks to their lovemaking are pure Pornovurt. ("She was my sister, fifteen years old, but I loved her a lot. Too much. More than is good. More than is legal. She was stretched out and hot, and my right hand was stroking her leg way up, and she was smiling. . . .") In the end, when Scribble finally gets his chance to free Desdemona, there are hints that an abusive and (possibly virtual) father drove the siblings into each other's arms, but that doesn't explain why the author treats her like an inflatable love doll.

But Noon does make at least one valuable contribution to the metaphysics of virtual reality. In *Vurt,* fantasy has a cost. The relationship between the world and the Vurt is governed by a set of exchange mechanisms, and Game Cat, a Vurt sorcerer whose periodic pronouncements about the laws of Vurt function as a Greek chorus, defines the risks:

> Friends and colleagues, fellow travellers in the Vurt, sometimes we lose them; even lovers we sometimes lose. And get bad things in exchange; aliens, objects, snakes, and sometimes even death. Things we don't want. This is part of the deal, part of the game deal; all things, in all worlds, must be kept in balance. . . . Any given worth of reality can only be swapped for the equivalent worth of Vurtuality, plus or minus 0.267125 of the original worth.

When Scribble loses Desdemona, he is thrown back into reality with an amorphous blob of an alien—a poor substitute for his beloved sister. And then there are dreamsnakes: "Any time something small and worthless was lost to the Vurt, one of these snakes crept through in exchange." A growing number of poisonous Vurt vipers—part of the unintended cost of unfettered fantasy—lurk in the shadows of reality.

It's a suggestive notion, and an ingenious way to dramatize the fear of being overwhelmed by the mechanics of wish fulfillment. The plot of *Rim,* Alexander Besher's novel, is based on a similar trope: a computer virus causes a glitch that leaves scores of children bottled up in cyberspace, and Tokyo is replaced by its virtual counterpart. Soon enough, we're going to have to learn how to inhabit the wilds of cyberspace, but we're already preparing for the psychic economy of our virtual destination.

Additional coverage of Noon's life and career is contained in the following source published by Gale Research: *Contemporary Authors,* Vol. **148.**

Susan Power
The Grass Dancer

Power is an American novelist.

INTRODUCTION

Winner of the 1995 PEN/Ernest Hemingway Award for first fiction, *The Grass Dancer* is set in North Dakota on a Sioux reservation. Presented as a montage of stories told through the voices of several different narrators, the novel centers on Harley Wind Soldier's search for a sense of self and on the automobile accident that killed Harley's father and brother four weeks before Harley was born. Critics note that the movement of the stories between different time periods—including the 1980s, 1960s, 1930s, and 1860s—evokes the theme of the simultaneity of past and present, while the interaction of spirits in dreams and memories reinforces the idea that ancestors are continually present and active in everyday life. Magic also plays a major role in the novel, particularly in the actions of Red Dress, who exploited her magical powers of sexual attraction to kill a number of soldiers at Fort Laramie in the 1860s; Red Dress's grand-niece, Anna Thunder, also uses magical powers to bewitch young men, but she does so to exact revenge against others in the community. Anna is feared by everyone and her machinations against Harley's father contributed significantly to the accident that killed him. Critical reaction to *The Grass Dancer* has generally been favorable, with most commentators arguing that the novel's central concern is Native-American heritage and white society's treatment of Native-American history. In addition, critics have noted Power's portrayal of chance and its consequences as well as her depiction of the legacies of love and jealousy. As Linda Niemann has argued, Power "chooses to represent indigenous history not as a record of defeat but rather as a continuing process whose outcome is still uncertain."

CRITICISM

Michael Dorris (review date 4 August 1994)

SOURCE: "A Dynamic First Effort That Proves to Be the Real Thing," in *Los Angeles Times,* August 4, 1994, p. E7.

[*Dorris is an American novelist, short story writer, poet, and critic. In the following review, he remarks favorably on* The Grass Dancer.]

The Grass Dancer is a look through an inverted telescope

into the rich tapestry of Dakota society. Moving a century backward from the early 1980s and reclosing the loop in the present, its series of related, beautifully told tales unravel the intricate stitch of related lives, the far-reaching consequences of chance acts, the lasting legacies of love and jealousy.

Susan Power, an enrolled member of the Standing Rock Sioux tribe, has written a first novel that hums with serious intention and reads like a sad and lovely lament. The high plains reservation setting is rendered with the kind of authentic realism—the little but crucial details—that only the most acute observer notices, and her prose is both strong and lyrical.

As with other books that deal with the social dynamics of small communities, *The Grass Dancer* is concerned with the power of thwarted or stunted kinship—mothers who lose their daughters, fathers who die before they are known by their sons—and with marital love gone wrong or betrayed.

The bitterness of one generation literally haunts the next, and the next. Frustrated spirits often meddle in human affairs, and indeed the boundary dividing the living and the dead is occasionally so blurred that a man can marry his fiancee's ghost.

Magic suffuses the world that Power poetically describes. Eyelashes baked in chocolate cupcakes instantly turn high school boys lusty, a tiny fragment from the sheet of one bed sewed onto that of another is a prescription for unwilling adultery—or at least that's how people explain seemingly irrational occurrences to themselves and each other.

People, especially the young and innocent, can be puppets in the hands of unscrupulous elders whose manipulations, in the long run, are balanced only by the goodness of ancestors even older, even wiser in the ways of power.

In what might be the book's most powerful story—an archetypal tale of a sibling love-hate rivalry—two sisters do battle using their unfortunate children as pawns.

> They looked like two opposites, like people with blood running from separate rivers. Chaske, whose baptism name was Emery Bauer Jr., after his German father, was sturdy and tall for his age, his powerful calf muscles bulging like little crab apples under the skin. His hair was creamy yellow, the color of beeswax, and his eyes were a silvery gray, so pale they were almost white. . . .
>
> Dina, on the other hand, was a blueprint of the women in our family, long-legged and graceful, thick braids grazing her narrow hips. Her little heart-shaped face was dark brown, the color of a full-blood, and her eyes were black and onyx studs.

In the end, both perish, each from the meanness of their respective aunts—whose true animosities are toward each other, but whose children are too-easy targets.

The world that Power describes pulses with vitality and passion. Characters roll forward like gusts of wind, smacking into each other, changing direction, temporarily blowing the same way, exhausting themselves with the force of their will.

Even though they may pretend otherwise, everyone wants something—a lot—although achieving a goal is no guarantee of contentment. When they get what they wanted, they immediately want something else just as badly. And once in awhile, just when they teeter on the edge of finding satisfaction, they misread the signals, make a mistake, lose their chance—and forever regret their blunder.

Power is a terrific writer—energetic, fresh, political, daring. She succeeds most impressively when she relaxes into the simple rhythm of her stories, trusting the reader to understand their mythic elements without underlining them too boldly.

The symbolism at the heart of this striking novel—the grass whose beauty and movement, whose very soul the best dancers strive to catch and imitate—is unadorned, timeless: "She became a flexible stem, twisting toward the sky, dipping to the ground, bending with the wind. She

was dry and brittle, shattered by drought, and then she was heavy with rain."

The Grass Dancer is a book wonderful both for what it is and for what it promises. Susan Power is the real thing.

Richard Tyrrell on *The Grass Dancer*:

[*The Grass Dancer*] flows like a smooth waltz, flourishing, keeping balance, doubling back. Its structure—the tales are told from several viewpoints—owes a lot to William Faulkner. If there is one weakness, it is in the chapters in which Anna Thunder takes up the narrative. Thunder has been developed as such a talismanic character that to suddenly meet with her in the first person deflates her mystique. I could not help thinking these chapters would have been more effective as third-person tales.

Richard Tyrrell, in "Richer Than All Her Tribe," in Manchester Guardian Weekly, *January 22, 1995.*

Lawrence Thornton   (review date 21 August 1994)

SOURCE: "The Grandmother in the Moon," in *The New York Times Book Review,* August 21, 1994, p. 7.

[*Thornton is an American novelist, educator, and critic. In the review below, he discusses Power's integration of past and present in* The Grass Dancer.]

Near the beginning of *The Grass Dancer,* Susan Power's captivating first novel, an old medicine man tells his grandson to remember that there are "two kinds of grass dancing. There's the grass dancer who prepares the field for a powwow the old-time way, turning the grass over with his feet to flatten it down. Then there's the spiritual dancer, who wants to learn grass secrets by imitating it, moving his body with the wind." The second kind of dancing, both a complex art form and a resonant metaphor for the relationship between humans and nature, functions as the armature of this moving exploration of lives infused with the power of the spirit world.

Ms. Power, a member of the Sioux tribe, writes with an inventiveness that sets her writing apart from much recent American fiction. She is more interested in montage than the *progression d'effet* of traditional plot. Set on a North Dakota reservation, *The Grass Dancer* tells the story of Harley Wind Soldier, a young Sioux trying to understand his place among people whose intertwined lives and shared heritage move backward in time in the narrative from the 1980's to the middle of the last century.

The effect of the structure is manifold. The reader responds to the narrative as if it were a series of photographs ranging from the crisp images of a Nikon to grainy daguerreotypes spotted with age. But Ms. Power's method has thematic as well as technical brio, for it also replicates the tribal sense of time and connectedness, reifying a world where ancestors are continually present in everyday life as spirits, memories and dreams. There is a fine example early in the book when Harley paints his face with traditional markings in preparation for a traditional dance and suddenly thinks he hears the voices of "the dead grandfathers . . . scratching the house with hoarse whispers, rasping like static from the radio. *We are rising, we are rising,* the voices hummed. And when Harley's painted mask was in place, an angry magpie divebombed the bathroom window, screeching, *We are here, we are here.*" This is not magic realism, which consciously alters the world in order to expand its circumference, but a factual representation of reality as it is perceived by the characters—a single plane where past and present exist simultaneously.

The novel opens with Harley's father and brother dying in an accident after a drunk mistakes the headlights of their car for ghost eyes and drives his pickup truck "into their strange light, blinding them forever." From this stunning scene that sets the elegiac tone of Harley's life, *The Grass Dancer* leaps forward to 1981, the year Harley meets a young woman named Pumpkin, an accomplished dancer who finds him attractive. The problem is that Charlene Thunder also has designs on him, and her mother, Mercury, is endowed with powerful medicine. When Pumpkin is killed in a car wreck we have an uneasy feeling that Mercury had something to do with it. The reader is thus informed early on that bad as well as good medicine affects the lives of everyone on the reservation. Both are ever present as the spirits who chide and guide the living.

Mercury's witchery is countered by the ministrations of Herod Small War, a "famous Yuwipi man, the one who finds things: misplaced objects, missing persons, the answers to questions." Herod and Margaret Many Wounds, Harley's grandmother, are Harley's principal tutors, and while he learns much from Herod, Margaret Many Wounds has the greatest effect on her grandson's life. As she lies dying, the old woman leads Harley to one of his earliest visions. It is 1969 and Harley, who is 5 years old, is watching television, following the movements of Neil Armstrong and Buzz Aldrin on the moon. A moment later, Harley "saw his grandmother's figure emerging on the screen, dancing toward him from the far horizon behind the astronauts." Though he does not know it at the time, Harley will spend the early years of his adult life seeking to replicate this vision, which holds answers to questions he has not yet learned to ask.

As *The Grass Dancer* edges into the past, women's voices fill out the history of the community, and their wisdom leads Harley to a remarkable moment of reintegration with his ancestors. Besides Mercury Thunder, whose powers are inherited from Red Dress, a warrior woman who figures prominently in the story, there is also Lydia Wind Soldier, Harley's mother. She, too, is drawn in her dreams to Red Dress, whose powerful voice speaks from 1864. The chapter devoted to her is the strongest in the novel. Red Dress recreates the Old West in startling images that reveal irresolvable conflicts between Indians and settlers. Her strength is immediately apparent, her devotion to the religion of her people unswerving. But when her powers to kill soldiers with words and dreams are fully manifested at Fort Laramie, the post chaplain, a deranged fundamentalist named Pyke, enacts a chilling revenge that resonates into the present.

The single fault with *The Grass Dancer* is that many of the women's voices are indistinguishable from one another. Had Ms. Power found individual inflections for them, the novel would have soared. But this is a small flaw in an otherwise substantial achievement. Written with grace and dignity, *The Grass Dancer* offers a healing vision that goes to the core of our humanity.

Stephen Henighan   (review date 2 December 1994)

SOURCE: "The Sioux Sense of Self," in *The Times Literary Supplement,* No. 4783, December 2, 1994, p. 22.

[*In the review below, Henighan argues that* The Grass Dancer *fuses traditional storytelling with contemporary fictional forms and demonstrates the continuing vitality of Sioux culture.*]

The act of reclaiming a lost or suppressed cultural identity is often carried out with defiance. Histories that have been denigrated or marginalized tend to be reborn in the contentious language of rebellion. Susan Power's first novel, *The Grass Dancer,* set on a North Dakota reservation, reassembles the history of the Sioux Indians—a term Power seems to prefer to the currently favoured "Native Americans"—with disarming equanimity.

Four weeks before Harley Wind Soldier's birth, his father and brother are killed by a drunken driver. The driver is white, and, though Power makes little of this detail, the accident epitomizes the offhand way in which, throughout this novel, white society wipes out the Indian past more through carelessness than malice. Harley's mother, traumatized by the accident, becomes mute; Harley grows up feeling that he has a "black, empty hole squeezed in his chest between heart and lungs". When the novel opens, in 1981, he is an introverted seventeen-year-old. At a summer pow-wow, he meets Pumpkin, a red-haired Menominee dancer of Irish ancestry. "You shouldn't ever be too arrogant or too loud about who you are", she tells Harley, in response to his anger at having been denied knowledge of his past. Before their relationship can release Harley from his stunned resentment, a second road accident claims Pumpkin's life. Her successful projection of her heritage into the hybrid reality of the present serves as a model for the stories that follow.

Later chapters of the novel hop back and forth between 1961 and the early 1980s; one tale reaches back as far as the 1930s, and there is a full-blown historical re-creation of a tragic encounter between Sioux and missionaries in 1864. Each of these narratives contributes, in a subtle way, to the reader's understanding of the opening accident. Nearly all of the narrators are women. Power is anything but a racial purist; her heroines have their children by wayward Swedes and errant Japanese doctors, yet their offspring's claims to Sioux history are never in doubt. The narrating voices are tough and matter-of-fact, even when their vision elides the barrier separating life from death; spirits abound in this novel, yet their activities are depicted as unremarkable. The mingling of living and dead, like that of Indians and whites, is crucial to Power's integrated account of her community. If her various narrators all speak in similar language, at once frank and lyrical, this appears to be a strategy rather than a stylistic lapse: the complementary insights and images evoked by their respective stories forge the shared history which, in the novel's final pages, succeeds in restoring Harley Wind Soldier's sense of self.

Comparisons of *The Grass Dancer* to the work of Louise Erdrich are unavoidable. Despite the shared North Dakota settings, Indian themes and layering of voices, however, Power has succeeded in creating a universe resonant with its own obsessions. Her fiction is more introspective and less plot-driven than that of Erdrich. This novel concludes with the white woman whose meddling is indirectly responsible for the initial accident marrying and having a child with a Sioux man. Yet one of the reservation's elders discourages her from bringing up her daughter solely in the Sioux tradition: "She needs to know both sides . . . tell her two stories." Acceptance, here, grows out of a deep-seated indifference. The lure of white society fails to impress Power's Sioux characters; their culture rolls on, adapting prevailing modes to express a Sioux vision. This scrupulously wrought novel, deftly fusing traditional story-telling with the forms of contemporary fiction, provides a sparkling demonstration of that culture's continued vitality.

Linda Niemann   (review date January 1995)

SOURCE: "Healing History," in *The Women's Review of Books,* Vol. XII, No. 4, January, 1995, p. 23.

[*In the following review, Niemann focuses on the magical and supernatural aspects of* The Grass Dancer.]

The Grass Dancer flows along the page with the grace of its title character, a Menominee woman named Pumpkin who dances what is traditionally the male role of the grass dancer in powwows. The book as a whole becomes a place—the reservation where the series of stories that make up the novel are heard. Each chapter is as long as one night's storytelling, reflecting different points of view on the same set of events and characters. Susan Power draws on both novelistic technique and oral tradition to create a newly emerging form.

Storytelling, like grass dancing, is a tribal art: Power is working within her tradition to unfold spiritual secrets through the narrative. Each chapter is a discrete story in its own right, taking the reader from the 1860s to the 1980s as the lives of younger generations come to intersect with the still-present spirits of their ancestors.

This structuring of the novel as a series of overlapping stories is similar to Sherman Alexie's *The Lone Ranger and Tonto Fistfight in Heaven.* The difference is in focus: Alexie's stories are deeply rooted in reservation life and are triumphs over despair, while Power is more concerned with myth-making in all its new-car excitement. People get up from their deathbeds and walk on the moon with Neil Armstrong. They come back from the dead in pretty good shape, with consoling messages for the living. They give advice. History is not drenched in gore, as in Leslie Marmon Silko's *Almanac of the Dead;* it's less of a tragedy than we thought it was.

Power tells stories of how the Dakotas used white magic to defeat their enemies, such as the story about the "Medicine Hole"—the magical opening up of the earth that hid and protected warriors surrounded in a battle with US soldiers in the 1860s. She chooses to represent indigenous history not as a record of defeat but rather as a continuing process whose outcome is still uncertain. The past and the spirit world lie within and around the present.

The germinal story tells of Red Dress, a woman warrior who left her people to go to the US soldiers' Fort Laramie in 1864. There she pretended to accept their culture, but secretly used her magical powers of sexual attraction to lure and kill a number of them. Accepting this role separated her from her lover, Ghost Horse, and she died at the fort before they could be married. Ghost Horse married her spirit anyway, but in his grief he was unable to release her. He sought death in battle, and his spirit went to the place of the ancestors, while hers remained attached to the places of the living.

> **Power chooses to represent indigenous history not as a record of defeat but rather as a continuing process whose outcome is still uncertain.**
>
> **—Linda Niemann**

The modern inheritor of Red Dress' power is Anna Thunder, her grand-niece. Anna, however, uses her sexual power for her own ends rather than for the good of the tribe—to bewitch lovers and take revenge. This is not to say that her character is unsympathetic; Power presents her as a formidable, intelligent, intensely alive woman:

> "Too many people don't believe in their souls, don't recognize them when they feel the spirit twist against their heart or snap across their brain. And some that do believe hand their spirits over to the care of others, just give them blithely away, though they may be tightfisted when it comes to their coins. I own my spirit. Can you say that? How many can say that?"

Anna is grooming her teenage granddaughter, Charlene, to succeed her as a *bruja,* but Charlene prefers the approval of the tribe over the personal power a black magic worker possesses. It mortifies her that everyone is afraid to eat any of her grandmother's casseroles or to buy any of her beadwork for fear of bewitchment:

> Charlene trained her headlights on the dog, but he didn't look up. His front paws were planted in the macaroni casserole Charlene had baked. Two neat squares—the servings Charlene had carved for her grandmother and herself—were missing, but the pan . . . was otherwise full. "They must have thrown it out," Charlene thought. "And it was good, too." Tears pooled in her eyes, but she squinted fiercely to keep them from spilling down her face.

The other series of intercut stories concerns the descendants of Ghost Horse, the Wind Soldier family. Harley Wind Soldier, the great-great-nephew of Ghost Horse, is struggling for spiritual healing after the tragic death of his father, Calvin, and in the face of his mother's continuing vow of silence. The family tragedy is complicated by the involvement of Anna Thunder, whose witchcraft made Calvin sleep with his wife's twin sister. Harley turns to traditional medicine with the help of the tribe's practitioner, Herod Small War. In a vision quest ceremony he meets Ghost Horse and is given knowledge of himself and the history of the tribe:

> Harley Wind Soldier stood in the same deep pit his father had occupied thirty years before. Harley was more cooperative than Calvin had been, and wore only his gym shorts and a blanket. He clutched Herod Small War's pipe against his chest and watched the flags staked at the perimeter of the pit rise in the wind. His mother and Alberta Small War had made the long string of tobacco ties that encircled him.
>
> "I don't know how to pray," Harley mumbled, but he dismissed the idea. "I will learn," he told himself.

The title character, the grass dancer Pumpkin, appears only briefly in the narrative. She is in a way a cipher for the author, being a mixed-blood on her way to an Ivy League education. Grass dancers imitate the way the prairie grass moves; their costume is fringed, and they wear grass bundles on their backs. Early in the book Pumpkin turns up at a powwow, where she wins the heart of Harley Wind Soldier, whose emptiness she promises to fill with her own soul. Leaving the powwow she is killed in a car wreck, another victim of Anna Thunder's witchcraft.

Pumpkin beat Charlene in the powwow competition, and Charlene is haunted by the responsibility for her death. But the way in which she is relieved of this burden illustrates the philosophy permeating this novel—that life works itself out in ways not understandable to humans, but with a beauty, even in tragic events, that is accessible and healing.

> Pumpkin opened her mouth to speak, and Charlene flinched, dreading the beautiful little birds, which she knew would leave the dancer's lips only to die. This dream was different. The birds emerged, the same as always, but this time darted away. They were a neat flock, so miniature and close together that they looked to Charlene like a school of fish. Her mouth creaked open in surprise. Quickly, easily, the birds flew past her teeth, entering the cave of her jaws. Charlene coughed, but the birds coasted down her throat, tickling her with their fluttering wings.

Peter Quinn
Banished Children of Eve: A Novel of Civil War New York

Born in 1947, Quinn is an American novelist and speech-writer.

INTRODUCTION

Set in New York during the Civil War, *Banished Children of Eve* (1994) is an account of the city's economic and racial tensions at the time, which culminated in the bloody Draft Riots of 1863. Started by a predominantly poor Irish mob angry over the imposition of the nation's first military draft, the Riots quickly escalated, lasting five days and resulting in at least 119 deaths. Many of the victims were working-class blacks, largely targeted by the Irish mobs as their primary competition for low-paying jobs. Using an episodic narrative structure and brief character sketches to tell his story, Quinn ultimately offers several suggestions as to why social protest often degrades into naked acts of violent hatred. Kevin Cullen has described *Banished Children of Eve* as a "compelling, textured account of how those at the bottom inevitably turn on one another rather than join forces to challenge whoever or whatever it is that has kept them down."

CRITICISM

Michael O. Garvey   (review date 20 March 1994)

SOURCE: "A Historical Novel Nearly Disorienting in Its Authenticity," in *The Philadelphia Inquirer,* March 20, 1994, p. L2.

[*In the following review, Garvey praises* Banished Children of Eve, *calling it both "vividly imagined" and "scrupulously researched."*]

It is an impressive illustration of the power of television advertising that most 18-year-old American boys now submit to the Selective Service system and to the blandishments of MTV with equal docility. The subservience urged and apparently secured by those annoying commercials would amaze and probably disgust their mid-19th-century counterparts.

During the summer of 1863, the nation's first federal conscription law was greeted with riots in towns and cities throughout the Union.

Even among the most enthusiastic supporters of the war effort, a passion for civil liberties overmatched the impera-

> **The narrative sweep of *Banished Children of Eve*:**
>
> [The novel] is as vividly realized for its period (the Civil War) as *Bonfire of the Vanities* was for the 1980s. It also has much the same narrative drive and broad range of characters, and is as grandly cynical about most human activities. . . . We see an Irish con man at his work; a young actor who is an early minstrel star (audiences laugh at minstrels and weep at *Uncle Tom's Cabin* even as their behavior to the black people among them is appalling); a beautiful young mulatto woman making her delicate, dangerous way through life; a child runaway who becomes a successful broker, only to face losing his fortune if he bets wrong on which side will be victorious in the war; and poor Stephen Foster, his songs on everyone's lips but reduced to plundering what little is left of his talent to pay for the oblivion of drink.
>
> *From a review of* Banished Children of Eve, *in* Publishers Weekly, *Vol. 240, No. 50, December 13, 1993, p. 60.*

tives of military expediency. New York Gov. Horatio Seymour, in a Fourth of July speech that would haunt him for the rest of his political career—some historians insist that it guaranteed the failure of his presidential bid five years later—warned the administration: "Remember this, that the bloody, and treasonable, and revolutionary, doctrine of public necessity can be proclaimed by a mob as well as by a government."

Nine days later, Manhattan exploded. It took more than a week for Union troops, many of them fresh from the carnage at Gettysburg, to restore order. While it's been established that at least 105 New Yorkers, many of them black victims of lynch mobs, were killed during that week, the riot was surely responsible for some of the dozens of unidentifiable corpses that washed up on both banks of the East River during the rest of July. New York, convulsed by 16 major riots between 1834 and 1874, was that kind of city.

Peter Quinn, chief speechwriter for Time Warner, has

chosen to unfold his first novel against this gritty historical surface. Vividly imagined, scrupulously researched, and almost disorienting in its authenticity, *Banished Children of Eve* performs the function of a historical classic, which historian M. A. Fitzsimons described as "to make us conscious of a past, of an otherness outside ourselves but with which we are kin."

Quinn's richly peopled New York is refracted through the perceptions of real and imagined characters whose plights and gripes seem strikingly contemporary.

Stephen Foster, drinking himself to death while his popular music saturates the squalid and violent 19th-century urban environment, much as gangsta rap does today, brings to mind a dozen drug enfeebled, self-destructive rock heroes of our own time.

Catholic Archbishop John Hughes—called "Dagger John" by the True American nativist bigots and Irish-fearing Yankee aristocracy—clambers about on the scaffolding of an unfinished St. Patrick's Cathedral and broods over past oppressions.

It is a familiarly ungovernable city of impoverished Irish newcomers, fatherless households, illegal immigrants, brutal cops, organized and sporadic crime, collapsing infrastructure, speculative greed and war profiteering. There are even street gangs to parallel our Bloods and Crips—the Dead Rabbits and the Plug Uglies.

The draft riots themselves absorb remarkably little of Quinn's narrative, which concerns itself far more with cowardice, greed, racism, desperation and lust for power. Much like Mackinlay Kantor's 1955 book *Andersonville,* this story recaptures a past, seizes something nearly devoured by history, and invites wonder and even a little grief about it.

Here the riots, like the nationwide bloodletting they approximate, are a central catastrophe, a calvary that a variety of New Yorkers ascend and descend by a variety of tragic and farcical routes. A hasty and restrained summary of just one of Quinn's invented lives suggests the breadth and intricacy of the novel: Jimmy Dunne, a distracted Irish American thief, bungles a burglary at the height of the violence and reluctantly saves the life of Audley Ward, a benighted racist aristocrat. Dunne also falls in love with Margaret O'Driscoll, an immigrant maid in the household of Ward's niece's husband, a Yankee stockbroker, self-made man, compulsive gambler, embezzler and murderer named Charles Bedford. Dunne eventually marries Margaret O'Driscoll, gives up, or at least adjusts, his criminal career to become a Tammany Hall operative and saloon keeper. One of his children is ordained a Jesuit priest and elected president of Fordham University.

It would be equally suggestive to track the lives of Ward, O'Driscoll, or Bedford. Or, for that matter, of Maria Rose Pryor (alias Eliza) a mulatta actress starring in *Uncle Tom's Cabin.* Or of her spineless paramour, Jack Mulcahey, the star of a black-face minstrel show. Making immediate the passions that animated them nearly a century and a half ago, *Banished Children of Eve* bends these and

its better documented lives to the purposes of high art. The result is nothing short of splendid.

Noel Perrin   (review date 27 March 1994)

SOURCE: "On the Sidewalks of New York," in *Book World-The Washington Post,* March 27, 1994, p. 4.

[*Perrin is an American essayist, nonfiction writer, critic, and educator. In the following review of* Banished Children of Eve, *he praises the novel's "fascinating details about life in New York in 1863," but faults its "lurid" melodrama teeming with "too many characters involved in too many plots."*]

Banished Children of Eve is a panoramic novel about New York as it was 140 years ago, during the Civil War. But people who know 19th-century New York from the novels of Henry James or Edith Wharton will not easily recognize the city. A different cast is here.

The book opens in Mike Manning's saloon, in lower Manhattan. A young Irish immigrant named Jimmy Dunne, who has just burgled the downtown branch of Brooks Brothers, is having an early-morning shot of whiskey. From there the scene shifts to the Astor House, where Stephen Foster is downing a morning beer. Now we jump to evening and to a minor theater where a young Irish immigrant named Jack Mulcahey is preparing to go on stage. He's a blackface minstrel.

Soon we're at the muddy site of St. Patrick's Cathedral, which is only half-built. Archbishop Hughes (an Irish immigrant, of course) and Father Corrigan are up on the scaffolding.

By no means all the characters are Irish. Numerous WASPs appear, just as in James and Wharton, but they are seen from a very different angle. Take Bedford, the stockbroker. He begins as a liar, goes on to be a thief, winds up a murderer. Gets away with it, too. When last seen, he has fled to California and has made a second fortune.

There's also Eleanor Van Schaik, scion of one of the oldest and grandest families in New York, and currently a whore. And Sarah Ward, of another fine old family, who copulates with Bedford in a closed coach, going up Fifth Avenue. In modern terms, it is their third date.

In short, there is not much Jamesian sensibility here. Not in the WASP characters, uniformly known to the Irish as rat-noses. Not in the Irish characters, uniformly known to the WASPs as Paddies. There *is* some in Eliza, the beautiful black actress who lives with Mulcahey. And perhaps in some of the minor black characters, too. They have gained it because they are even worse exploited by the rat-noses than the Paddies are.

Banished Children of Eve is genuinely panoramic. It's loaded with historical characters—not just Stephen Foster and Archbishop Hughes but also General Meagher, commander of the Irish Brigade of the Union Army; Jay Gould; and 80-year-old General Wool, who is still on active duty. It has all kinds of exciting stories to tell, culminating with the draft riots of 1863, far worse than any riots that have occurred in New York since. Many sections are a pleasure to read.

But it also has an astonishing number of faults. For one, there are too many characters involved in too many plots. I counted 100 speaking parts just in the first half. It's hard to remember them all, especially since there are also hundreds of non-speaking parts, such as those of nine generations of Eliza's ancestors.

For another, the author is a little free in assigning behavior to his historical characters. How can he know that Stephen Foster was impotent at the time of his marriage, let alone how his young wife responded? Is it fair to quote from an 1863 book by a philanthropic New Yorker named Charles Loring Brace in such a way as to make him seem an ugly racist, when Brace's aim in the book is to demonstrate that all humanity has a common ancestry, and not the multiple ancestry that many people at the time asserted in order to justify prejudice?

But the big fault is the melodrama. When Jimmy Dunne, who is an orphan, is taken out west along with many other Irish orphans, to be placed with settlers' families, the Protestant clergyman who leads the party proves to be a hypocritical bastard. Mrs. Ellingwood, the wife of the settler who takes Jimmy, seduces the 14-year-old boy at the first opportunity. He gets back to New York a few months later because a tornado sucks up both Ellingwoods. When Eliza, the beautiful black actress, does a stint in a whorehouse (this is before she goes on stage), she gets the Prince of Wales as a customer.

If you like lurid, this is your book. If you don't, but are willing to overlook it for the sake of thousands of fascinating details about life in New York in 1863, it might also be your book. If you want plausible characters, I'm afraid it isn't.

Peter Quinn with Patricia Harty   (interview date March-April 1994)

SOURCE: "An Irish American Unearths His Past," in *Irish America Magazine*, March-April, 1994, pp. 64, 66.

[*In the following interview, Quinn discusses* Banished Children of Eve *and his identity as an Irish American.*]

Irish history, New York history and Civil War history are the three topics that most interest Peter Quinn. Put all three together, add a dollop of fiction, set the stage with a wide range of characters, hold them all together with writing reminiscent of William Faulkner and you have *Banished Children of Eve,* a novel set in New York in 1863 before and during the draft riots, that is so powerful and colorful and full of history that it is sure to put Quinn, 47, on a course for the rest of his life.

Insiders will know Quinn as the editor of *The Recorder,* the journal of the American Irish Historical Society, and have been waiting for this novel for years. Other will know him as a speechwriter for Governors Carey and Cuomo and now Time Warner, and may be surprised at his latent talent for novel writing.

Quinn, who wanted to write a novel since he was 12, does not regret the 15 years as a speechwriter, in fact, perhaps there wouldn't be a novel if it wasn't for his day job. "The one thing that you learn being a speechwriter is that you don't wait for the muse to come. If the governor is down the hall you get to it," he says.

Each day as he took the subway in from Brooklyn, to arrive at his workplace two hours early to write, he would look out over South Street where in the years 1845-46 alone 85,000 Irish landed. He would picture his ancestors mingling with the crowd on the dock and wonder what life was really like for them—these banished children seeking to find the promised land.

He considered writing a social history, and whenever he could he would wander around the Lower East Side where his grandmother had lived and worked as a seamstress. As part of the research process he read Adrian Cook's *Armies of the Street* about the Draft Riots which contained the records of people killed, one of whom was a Peter Quinn: 55-year-old laborer, and "it happened," he says. "In some way the characters came alive and they told me who they were. I didn't start out with a graph and say this is what's going to happen. I started with a general idea that the riot would reveal people—the riot would tell you.

"Writing a novel you have to brood a lot. My daughter would say, 'Daddy are you sad?' And I would say, 'No honey I'm just brooding.' Because I wanted these people to tell me what happens.

"When I first started to do the research I would look at prints and lithographs. And they looked so clean—the dirt and grime wasn't there, and that was something I wanted to bring out in the book. These aren't quaint people. They are as real as we are. With our complexities and our contradictions."

[*Harty*]: *Which of these characters did [you] feel closest to?*

[Quinn]: Maybe Margaret.

Is she an ancestor?

Margaret is a combination of different people. I wanted her to be earthy, and the earthy side of my family is my mother's side. My father's side were all rural puritans. The women were much more capable of talking about sexuality than men.

There's a subtle but powerful moment in the book when Margaret is called Brigid by the man of the house, and she says, "It's Margaret, sir. Me name."

That's the ultimate contempt. It's not that the rich look down on them—it's that they are not there—the faceless poor.

Walt Whitman used the term invisible man about the blacks. And you see references in the 19th century to Irish maids as Brigids, that's the name they gave them, and there's terrible contempt in there.

So really the Irish and the blacks have a lot in common?

Yes. I think they have an incredible amount in common. In the 1830s the Irish were almost all rural people, peasants. Fifty years later when you are talking about urban machines in the United States you are talking about the Irish. There was this tremendous transfer from the land to the city in a kind of panic, and the same thing happened in the black migration.

Today when you talk about urban youth you are talking about blacks. Their entry into power is through politics rather than through business, which is the Irish experience. The Irish in Ireland had a folk culture and the church. That's what gave them their dignity and their sense of organization. And you have the same thing with blacks. A fundamental institution that reflects who they are and a folk culture. And also the role of women. The women are the strongest part of both cultures.

At the end of the book the Irish have been allowed in. They have their own university [Fordham]. But the blacks are gone. You had black people who had lived in New York for over 100 years being driven out of the city.

And in the end of **Banished Children,** the question is still a racial question. We have admitted these immigrants but these banished children [the blacks] haven't been allowed in. There is a really bloody, violent, disturbing history of what we have done to immigrants, but in the end we have admitted most of them—after the anti-Semitism and after the anti-Catholicism—but blacks are still in question.

Because we Irish always want to present the lace curtain was it hard to look at this other side of our history?

Yes. I found when I first read the accounts of the draft riots—the lynching of blacks and the sexual mutilations—it was hard for me to think about, to understand. But one thing you have to realize is that there's only one mob in history. It doesn't matter if it's Irish or it's the red guard. When people get together en masse and they lose their individuality, they are capable of doing anything. It's not just Irish. What is a tragedy is what's happening to the blacks in the cities, and what happened to the Irish in the cities in the 1860s is a tragedy. These people are 15 years removed from the Famine and it's a class struggle about which group is going to wind up at the bottom and that's what I try and say in the book. The tragedy is that the people at the bottom are fighting each other. If you want to understand American urban life in the 1990s you have to look at Los Angeles—here you have the city of the future and it blows up.

Look at New York in 1863—this ferocious explosion—the Draft Riots—and the poverty it came out of, and look at New York now and see the poverty and the squalor and the new immigrants, and it may seem hopeless, but I would want people to come away from my book with a sense of hope that along with people's pain and struggle there's this life, this vibrancy, and ambition that is the heart of New York and it's bigger and stronger than the poverty and the struggle. The genius and curse of New York is that nothing is going to stay the same.

Why this interest in the Irish?

Because I am third generation. My father didn't have to ask himself those questions, because he lived in an essentially Irish American community. There was the church,

and the party, and the unions. That all dissolved in my lifetime. And you wanted to know what it was all about, just as you are about to leave it all behind. My mother is surprised at my interest in all of this. She thinks of herself as Irish American but moving into America, shedding this identity.

All the Irish studies programs have started in my lifetime. When I was a kid the Irish study program was parochial and Catholic education—that was what it meant to be Irish. I would say it's only since the seventies you have this systematic examination of the Irish American experience—how does it relate to Ireland? Who are we? As Ireland's role in the world is more obvious Irish Americans are asking themselves who they are. In one way after 130 years of emigration there is still a lot of Irishness left.

Irish people are surprised by this, to them you're American.

I was brought up in the Bronx where no one was brought up to think of themselves as American. You were Irish, you were Jewish or Italian, and then I went to school, for three months, in Galway and they didn't think I was Irish at all. And when I was a teacher in Kansas and they thought of me as a New Yorker rather than an American. I was an Irish New Yorker and I was caught—between two worlds. Ireland and America—both parts of me. And that's what this book is about, both parts.

Where do you see the Irish now?

I don't think you could say they are in one place. They have achieved economic success but they haven't told their story yet. And I think artists are just emerging like William Kennedy who are finally beginning to produce a body of Irish American literature. The Irish are such a big presence in America but the literature reflecting that presence isn't there. There's James T. Farrell, and writers with Irish names who don't write about Irish things like F. Scott Fitzgerald and John O'Hara. But really, the first great Irish Catholic novelist in this century is James Joyce. There aren't a lot of great Irish Catholic voices before that.

It may sound pretentious but *Ulysses* is the only book I ever read three times. There are several things in there [*Banished Children*] that I steal right from Joyce. Like the citizen in the bar—the cyclops. And Bedford on the toilet is Bloom on the toilet, but I didn't want anyone to think I was stealing without paying homage, so it opens in June 1904, which is the month of *Ulysses*. I wanted people to know that this is a tribute to the master. It is such a tremendous book to read even to this day, because it says you can try anything, any voice. I wanted a black character—a black woman, but then I said this is a pretty presumptuous thing to try to do. But I said a prayer to James Joyce and just let go.

John Crowley   (review date 3 April 1994)

SOURCE: "The Bowery Sphinx and Other Irishmen: A First Novel about Immigrant Life in New York City during the Civil War," in *The New York Times Book Review,* April 3, 1994, p. 29.

[*In the following positive review, Crowley describes* Ban-

QUINN

ished Children of Eve *as "the mature fruit of protracted labor."*]

There are two readers for any historical novel: the one who knows well the history on which it is based and the one who doesn't. Some novels depend for their effect on the reader's knowledge; some are spoiled by it. Readers of **Banished Children of Eve,** Peter Quinn's panoptic novel of New York City during the Civil War, need not know which of his many characters and incidents derive from his sources and which are invented, and he has worked those sources so artfully that readers who don't know already won't be able to guess.

The Irish who left for America in the black years of the famine are Mr. Quinn's banished children of Eve; by the time the war began they were the greater part of New York's underclass, despised not only by the old Dutch and Anglo-Saxon ascendancy but also by the other immigrants they competed with for jobs and living space. They in turn despised and feared the small but growing class of free blacks, who (they believed) threatened their place on the next-to-bottom rung.

In July 1863, the tensions in the city eventually spilled over into a days-long riot against the imposition of the military draft, a confrontation in which many blacks were lynched or murdered and many other people died as well. The riot, looming in the future like a summer storm, is the destination of all the book's characters.

Mr. Quinn's narrative method is the usual one for novels described as sweeping or panoramic, one that derives ultimately, I suppose, from the Dickens of *Our Mutual Friend* and *Bleak House*: we ride along on the consciousness of one character after another, each for a few pages, returning frequently to some and less frequently to others, building little blocks of story from shifting points of view. This method has all the advantages of prefab housing: it comes in units that are easy to read (and write), and it gives the impression of crowded liveliness—but it can tend toward sprawl, sameness and tedium.

Mr. Quinn deploys this method with great energy. The individual sections of the plot are convincing and intriguing, yet at the same time the ceaseless forward flow of event and emotion that carries them is always felt. One wonderful touch is to have the various characters continually appear, often unnoticed or disregarded, in the lives of others, which makes Mr. Quinn's city not only a living web of coincidence but an engine of unguessable fate.

The big cast is largely Irish, inhabitants of the *favelas* of an old New York that was never built to hold such a population. There is James Dunne, who will end up being called the Bowery Sphinx for his reticence about his life and livelihood; in fact, he is a skilled thief who survived the awful crossing and the cruel charity of the Children's Aid Society, which shipped unwanted orphans and abandoned children to the West by the trainload, to be given as wards—often as slaves—to overworked pioneer families. There is Margaret, the maid in the house that is Dunne's next objective, there is Jack (no longer Sean) Mulcahey, the greatest blackface minstrel of the day; there

are brutal gang leaders, heavy drinkers and upwardly mobile graspers.

There are others too: Eliza, a light-skinned black woman whose name was not at first Eliza but who now plays the role in the endlessly running production of *Uncle Tom's Cabin* with a cast otherwise white; and Charles Bedford, a Long Island farm boy on his way up, then down again, betting against the Union in the ferocious money market of Civil War Wall Street. He too has had more than one name, more than one life. All of Mr. Quinn's main characters are survivors, able to discard unrewarding lives, families, backgrounds, and invent or grab new ones; their efforts don't always keep them afloat. Learning who will go under and who will not in the coming disaster is, of course, one thing that keeps us reading.

We ride along on the consciousness of one character after another, each for a few pages, returning frequently to some and less frequently to others, building little blocks of story from shifting points of view.

—John Crowley

By the time the riot breaks out, Mr. Quinn has so many oranges, Indian clubs, flaming torches and wine-glasses in the air that we barely notice when he drops a few. Hardly a page of the book is without some revelation. We observe the origins of professional baseball at the same time as we watch Mr. Quinn's ruined broker turn to violence to save himself. Stephen Foster sinks into hopeless alcoholism even as he tries and fails to invent a new art form, the musical comedy.

This very long and quite accomplished book is, surprisingly, a first novel; **Banished Children of Eve** certainly seems the mature fruit of protracted labor. It is to be hoped that Peter Quinn hasn't shot his bolt. Historical fiction as well made and whole as this is not common.

Kevin Cullen (review date 30 April 1994)

SOURCE: "A Vivid First Novel Chronicles the Irish Draft Riots of 1863," in *The Boston Globe,* April 30, 1994, p. 23.

[*In the following review, Cullen offers praise for* Banished Children of Eve, *calling it "a compelling, textured account."*]

When Irish-Americans sit down to write fiction about their forebears, they tend to produce romantic epics, chronicling how their ancestors overcame overwhelming odds, poverty and oppression to prosper in the New World. They are comfortable books, warm respites.

Peter Quinn's first novel, **Banished Children of Eve,** is like a January dip in the Liffey or, more appropriately, New York's East River, on whose banks dozens of bodies washed up during the summer of 1863, when in a fit of anger and resentment Irish immigrants led riots against the nation's first draft and, because they had no one else to take out their frustrations on, lynched blacks.

Quinn is the chief speechwriter for Time-Warner and former speechwriter for New York governors Mario Cuomo and Hugh Carey. His grandfather arrived in New York 10 years after the Draft Riots. Quinn spent six years researching and four years writing his book. It shows.

Like the best historical novels, the book plucks one's consciousness, stirring old social studies lessons while creating characters and events, so it is hard to say what is based on fact and what is the fruit of Quinn's fertile imagination.

The novel is a vividly drawn chronology of New York's inexorable march into madness, when a protest over conscription into the Union Army degenerated into a frenzy of looting and murder.

The Irish had a point. They literally had been starved out of their own country by famine and indifferent British colonizers. Hundreds of thousands of them had endured great hardship for a new start in a new land only to be awarded society's lowest rung, positioned above only blacks. To add insult to insult, the Irish were ordered to fight for a Union that openly regarded them as inferior. And afflicted with that inferiority complex, many Irish saw themselves being asked to liberate slaves who would inevitably take the few crumbs they had scavenged for themselves. Meanwhile, they watched "true Americans" exploit the working class and pay $300 to avoid the draft.

But whatever principle motivated the resistance gave way quickly to unbridled hatred, much of it racist. There is a depressing undercurrent to *Banished Children of Eve.* Evil often triumphs over virtue. Yet the book is so relevant because it resonates in contemporary New York. Many people, especially those who don't live there, consider New York lost and irredeemable, anarchy in the USA. Through Quinn's prism, New York seems to be struggling with many of the same fundamental problems it had some 130 years ago. It is the ultimate melting pot, and pots tend to boil. If New York is hopeless, it is no more hopeless today than it was in 1863.

For all the import of its subject matter, Quinn's book is driven more by characters than plot. Some of the characters, such as Stephen Foster, the composer whose songs were on millions of Americans' lips even as cheap booze was on his, are real. Others, like Jimmy Dunne, an Irish-American hustler, are imagined. All of them are survivors, because only the fittest survived the summer of 1863 in New York.

Dunne would steal a hot stove, but he is likable in a way that charismatic criminals often are. And in a sobering story line, he alone is ultimately redeemed, changed by Margaret O'Driscoll, an Irish domestic for Charles Bedford, a self-made Wall Street broker who is about to be ruined, not by inside trading or a hostile takeover, but by bad investments and a gambling addiction. Dunne is determined to hustle Bedford but instead falls for Margaret, the maid. It seems fitting and not entirely implausible that a good woman leads Jimmy Dunne to give up his thieving, or at least most of it, for Tammany Hall politics. His career segue seems appropriate.

There is a moral in Quinn's book, though his work is too sophisticated to resort to blatant exposition. The parallels between the Irish and blacks in this country are unavoidable. Yet their histories, even to this day, suggest a relationship based more on hostility than common ground.

Besides creating a half-dozen characters who linger on long after the last page is turned, *Banished Children of Eve* is a compelling, textured account of how those at the bottom inevitably turn on one another rather than join forces to challenge whoever or whatever it is that has kept them down. It is a lesson with no shortage of examples today.

Judy Bass   (review date 9 May 1994)

SOURCE: "Struggling to Survive in a World of Hate," in *Los Angeles Times,* May 9, 1994, p. E2.

[In the following review, Bass commends Quinn for his "pungent style, refusal to romanticize and affinity for historical details."]

When most of us try to conjure up images of Civil War-era New York, we think of ornate drawing rooms populated by ladies in voluminous gowns and urbane, frock-coated men puffing on cigars. *Banished Children of Eve,* Peter Quinn's exceptional debut novel, presents the far more earthy New York of yesteryear. According to him, it was a grotesquely primitive and savage place or, as the book itself puts it, "a vast nether world of poverty, resentment and ethnic hatred."

Spanning 10 days in the spring and summer of 1863, this historical tale, a bit reminiscent of E.L. Doctorow's *Ragtime,* loosely interweaves the destinies of many fictitious and actual people.

We meet Jimmy Dunne, a wily con man whose brittle exterior camouflages vestiges of decency; Charles Bedford, the stockbroker with a troublesome appetite for gambling; volatile Jack Mulcahey, a minstrel performer who slathers burnt cork on his face and struts onstage disguised as a black man; Mulcahey's lover, Eliza, an actress of mixed ancestry whose spunk almost exceeds her beauty, and Stephen Foster, the nearly penniless tunesmith who guzzles

> **Through Quinn's prism, New York seems to be struggling with many of the same fundamental problems it had some 130 years ago. It is the ultimate melting pot, and pots tend to boil.**
>
> *—Kevin Cullen*

liquor to forget that his ebbing imagination won't even yield a tidbit of quality music.

Quinn, chief speech writer at Time Warner, enlivens his narrative with cameo appearances by Harriet Beecher Stowe, the Prince of Wales and Secretary of War Edwin Stanton, among others. The novel's intensity, however, stems from Quinn's wrenching portrayal of the dolorous existence of the Irish immigrants in America, who had already faced seemingly endless calamities in their native land.

One typical newcomer is Bedford's maid, Margaret O'Driscoll. Like thousands of others, she journeyed here because, as Quinn explains, there was virtually nothing worthwhile to aspire to in Ireland, "a country haunted by the memory of hunger, humiliated by the improvidence of its children, the wrath of God visited upon them."

Unfortunately, when the boat carrying Margaret docks at these shores, the first American she sees utters a greeting sour enough to disenchant the hardiest adventurer: "Well, ladies and gents, welcome to hell."

For Margaret, along with most of the Irish depicted in **Banished Children of Eve,** New York does resemble a nightmare. Although she anticipated a metropolis alive with opportunities, this earnest young woman quickly realizes that, at least to the have-nots, it is merely a hotbed of squalor and vice where saloons, music halls and brothels cater to individuals who might euphemistically be defined as "riffraff."

Before joining the Bedford household, Margaret lived in a roach-infested tenement and took a job at a factory where employees received pathetic wages for exhausting physical labor. Her situation brightens greatly after she starts work at the Bedfords', but Margaret's idealism has been permanently curbed, thanks to the knowledge that downtrodden folks like her could ascend in American society via only three routes: outright lawlessness, cunning or luck.

The lowly need all the good fortune they can muster. Overt antagonism flourishes between Protestant Yankees and Catholic immigrants, the gentry and the paupers, and especially Irish and blacks, writes Quinn, who sketches these hostilities in flashbacks.

For example, when Mulcahey sojourned in Boston as a boy, three ruffians his age taunted him, then gave him a wholly unwarranted beating. A kind passerby stopped the assault and dispensed some wisdom to Mulcahey, too. The Yankees "will ship the lot of us back to Ireland if they have the chance," the man declared, "but not before they've made sure they've wrung us dry."

Quinn has chosen to emphasize such historical themes instead of using his literary craftsmanship to concoct elaborate plot twists or spotlight character development and interaction. Thus, **Banished Children of Eve** is atmospheric and cerebral, rather than tautly suspenseful. Nevertheless, an offbeat cat-and-mouse chase is particularly gripping.

Bedford, who rises to the venerated position of director at a stockbrokerage mainly by lying about his humble family background, undergoes a series of war-related business fiascoes so dire that his usual swagger vanishes. To pay off his debts, he resorts to gambling and embezzlement, avenues by which he can secretly amass thousands of dollars.

But a hood named Waldo Capshaw learns about Bedford's plight and enlists the wary Dunne in a scheme to rob this ignoble titan of commerce of his ill-gotten treasure. Meanwhile, New York's prolonged social turmoil culminates in violence as feverish mobs jam the streets to air their loathing of a new law mandating conscription. Whether Bedford, Dunne, Mulcahey and everyone else will survive the widespread rampage known as the Draft Riots is a question left tantalizingly unresolved until the book's final scenes.

Quinn masterfully communicates the irony of the fact that men and women endured tremendous risks when they fled Ireland to seek better prospects in urban America, where further degradation, exploitation and oppression awaited them.

An equally painful irony applied to northern blacks during the Civil War, Quinn points out. Although free from metal shackles, they were subjected to symbolic bondage. Obliged to grapple with the racial prejudices of whites, blacks had scant economic mobility, therefore, they found themselves pitted against the Irish for the most menial jobs.

The author's pungent style, refusal to romanticize and affinity for historical details all blend to make **Banished Children of Eve** an achingly vibrant panorama of ethnic feuds and struggles.

Peter Quinn with Ken Emerson   (interview date 12 July 1994)

SOURCE: "Remembering New York's Deadliest Riot," in *Newsday,* July 12, 1994, p. 35.

[*In the following interview, Quinn and Emerson discuss the New York Draft Riots of 1863.*]

[*Emerson*]: *A hundred and thirty years ago tomorrow, a mob of New Yorkers, mostly Irish, hung a black man from a lamppost and cheered for Jefferson Davis, the president of the Confederacy. After the cops cut the corpse down, it was dragged by the genitals through the streets of New York. How could this have happened?*

[Quinn]: Well, the first thing to notice is the date: July 13, the day after Orangeman's Day, when the Protestants in Ireland celebrated—and still do—William of Orange's victory at the Boyne. It has often been a time of sectarian violence in Ireland, and that tradition was carried undiluted to New York. The bloodiest single day in New York City history is July 12, 1871, when there was a riot between the Irish Protestants and Irish Catholics on Eighth Avenue. The militia opened up and killed 41.

That's part of the text of the Draft Riots of 1863: this agrarian, this Irish resentment, and this explosion from below.

How long did the Draft Riots last?

An excerpt from *Banished Children of Eve*

In a room beneath the stairs, two of the colored women were pinning shirts. The other two were moving up and down the stairs with buckets of coal and starch. They moved from floor to floor, keeping the stoves tended, the sinks full, putting the tubs, irons, and ironing boards in order, sweeping the floors, mopping where they were wet.

Mrs. O'Sullivan stopped where Margaret was sitting. The older woman's wet blouse clung to her breasts. "Better get a move on," she said. The muscles in Margaret's calves were taut and sore.

The dark-colored woman whom Margaret had admired earlier came down the stairs carrying two empty buckets. Mrs. O'Sullivan was blocking her way. The black woman stood waiting for Mrs. O'Sullivan to move. Mrs. O'Sullivan ignored her.

"You're in the way," Margaret said to Mrs. O'Sullivan.

"It's a white man's right to stand where he wants, and the last time I looked, I was still white."

The black woman stood with her eyes straight ahead. The perspiration dripped from her chin onto her dress.

Margaret stood up. "Very well," she said, "I'm ready." She made room so that the black woman could pass.

Mrs. O'Sullivan watched the dark-skinned woman go into the room with the other colored women. "You'll learn," she said to Margaret.

"To be rude?"

"No, about niggers."

"She was doing nothing but her job."

"She's here because she wants your job. Niggers will steal any job they can."

"She's got a job of her own."

"She's got a job because when they tried to bring niggers in to work with us, we refused to work, all of us, even the German girls . . . . Finally the owner agreed not to hire them except as pin girls and sweepers that get paid a daily rate, a child's wage, and more than a nigger deserves."

"They have to feed themselves, don't they?" Margaret said.

"Not on our bread." Mrs. O'Sullivan went up the stairs. "Don't waste your sympathy on them," she said.

Peter Quinn, in his Banished Children of Eve, *Penguin Books, 1994.*

They started on Monday the thirteenth, and by Friday the army had regained control.

How many people had been killed by then?

They can identify 119 people. There was an armory on Second Avenue that blew up and burned down. How many bodies were not recovered? I would say the northern figure [for riot fatalities] would be 150.

Were these the deadliest riots in American history?

Yes.

Why are they called the Draft Riots?

In the spring of 1863, a lot of the two-year enlistments were coming up and casualties were such that the government didn't think they could fill the ranks with volunteers anymore. There would have to be a military draft. They put in a provision that you could either hire a substitute (which had always been true; it was true in the Revolutionary War) or you could pay $300 to get out of that round of the draft. Those alternatives were not accessible to working people or the poor—and 99 percent of the Irish were in that class. It was a race riot because class and race in America have always been intertwined, but it was also class warfare.

Then how come so many of the mobs' targets were blacks, even lower on the economic ladder?

The rich neighborhoods were less accessible. The blacks lived intermingled with the Irish, so you could serendipitously grab a black man and take out your resentment on him. Also, in April, 1863, there was a longshoremen's strike on the East Side where they brought in black strikebreakers—which seemed to some people like a deliberate provocation.

But rich white men were assaulted. They were forced to kneel before Irish workmen. This humiliation would never leave the consciousness of the upper classes.

Do you think this reinforced prejudice against the Irish?

It confirmed every impression of the Irish as rowdy, unreliable, drunken, violent. Like all stereotypes, it contains a grain of truth, but it substitutes a fraction of the truth for the whole. And [it contributed] to our vocabulary of "paddy wagons," "hooligans" and "Irish confetti" (which used to be what came off the rooftops when the police came in to any neighborhood).

Were African-Americans a real economic threat to the Irish?

There were newspapers that said, "Emancipation is going to bring the blacks north and take your jobs." But in reality blacks had occupied most of the servant and waiter positions in New York, and when the Irish flooded in after the Potato Famine, they took those jobs away from the blacks.

Why weren't New Yorkers rallying around the flag and Abe Lincoln?

The war enjoyed a great deal of popularity in the beginning, but the casualty lists and the reality of modern warfare dragged on. The war started inflation, the most punishing thing the poor can suffer. And the draft seemed to add to this. However central the struggle to end slavery is to American history, to a working person on the Lower East Side in the 1860s it was pretty distant.

How did the rioting affect relations between New York's Irish and African Americans?

It's not just New York. The same struggle was going on in Boston in the 1970s with busing. The Irish were the working class left in Boston, and they were fighting blacks. Race has often had that effect on the United States: Working-class groups who should get together don't because the most important thing is race rather than class.

In fact, a lot of Anglo-Americans would not have counted the Irish as white. Charles Loring Brace, the founder of the Children's Aid Society, in 1863 wrote a book in which he says that the Irish brain is halfway between that of an Englishman and Ethiopian. Every tester of intelligence from that time on has always proved that the poor are stupid, that the poor are poor not out of any fault in the system, but because of the fault of the poor. It makes it a lot easier for the rich to believe that.

I've read that a lot of the things we think of as the great achievements of New York—Central Park, for instance, —were largely the creations of white Republicans—and before that, Whigs—who were terrified of the teeming Irish masses and trying to create some kind of safety valve.

There's a real strain in American history: Americans don't like cities, and they don't trust them. That comes from Thomas Jefferson, and it goes through Frederick Law Olmsted [co-creator of Central Park] to Robert Moses. We do not have the same attitude to our cities Europeans have to theirs. We regard them as repositories of things that are foreign and dangerous. We're a suburban country in mentality.

Two of the people who had the greatest influence on New York—Olmsted and Moses—loathed cities?

They regarded them as dangerous places in which the job of the upper classes and government was to order people's conduct. The idea of Central Park was that they'd let the lower classes mingle with the upper classes, see their betters, and they'd learn how to behave. Moses had that attitude, too: Best to get people out of the cities.

As a student of a riot that took place 130 years ago, what do you think when you consider L.A. or Crown Heights, and racial tensions today?

In a weird way it makes you kind of optimistic. If you look back at what New York was in the 1860s—the sanitation, the poverty, the highest death rate of any city in the Western world—you might throw up your hands. But, you know, the struggle goes on. And if you look at New York in the 1990s, in some ways it's more a 19th-Century city than it was 50 years ago—the public squalor and decay of institutions. But I think you have a right to be hopeful. This is a process. Once a people arrive in the United States, there's a struggle to [become included]. Maybe Los Angeles is a hopeful sign. People have woken up.

There are many parallels between the Irish and the blacks. Maybe that's why they've had such difficulty—in a lot of ways they're alike. In their almost total transfer from the land to the cities in a very short time. That has happened with blacks since the Second World War. Of course, the Irish enjoyed a great advantage: they're white. But if any group of white ethnics should have a sense of what it is to be an outsider and underdog, it should be the Irish. The closer they come in contact with their own history, the more they can serve as a kind of a bridge between groups.

Lorraine Kreahling   (essay date 24 July 1994)

SOURCE: "A Long Historical View of What Foments Mob Rioting," in *The New York Times,* July 24, 1994, p. 8.

[*In the following, Kreahling discusses the historical background of* Banished Children of Eve, *placing special emphasis on the role of poverty in the New York Draft Riots of 1863.*]

A mass of sweating angry men storm New York City's summer streets, breaking windows and stealing property, murdering people with different skin colors and beating others whose clothing suggests middle-class comfort.

That racial riot in Peter Quinn's **Banished Children of Eve** a new novel that provides a detailed context for the four days in July 1863 when New York City exploded into a bloody riot.

"I believe in history that there's only been one mob, and all mobs act the same way," Mr. Quinn said in an interview as he compared the New York draft riots of 1863 to the riots in Los Angeles in 1992. "The reptilian brain somewhere on the evolutionary scale takes over, and when people go berserk for whatever reasons they do the same thing."

The mob in Mr. Quinn's novel and in history's record of the draft riots was mostly made up of impoverished Irish people rebelling against conscription into the Union Army during the Civil War. As they poured into the streets from tenements and shanties along the Hudson River, they not only burned and looted stores and homes, but also murdered any black person they could lay hands on and a few military men as well.

Records verify 119 deaths. Some historians estimate that up to 1,000 people died and property losses ran $1 million to $2 million.

Banished Children of Eve, a 612-page first novel, portrays the tensions between working-class blacks, who had been freed by the New York antislavery law of 1799, and the Irish, who, along with 2.1 million of their countrymen, had recently fled death and famine in Ireland.

As the two groups competed for low-paying jobs, the Irish used their skin color to push blacks out of their way. The paradox, Mr. Quinn said, is that the two groups had more in common than they realized.

"Irish culture was a popular culture," he said. "It was a

folk culture that resided in music, dance and storytelling, which is what black culture was in the South."

Both groups, he said, transmitted the traditions through the church and music and both spent generations farming land that did not belong to them.

Writing in *The Boston Globe*, Kevin Cullen called Mr. Quinn's book "a compelling account of how those at the bottom inevitably turn on one another, rather than join forces to challenge whomever or whatever it is that has kept them down."

Mr. Quinn said many Irish-Americans did not realize that their ancestors were social outcasts. "Almost every person in the establishment of New York in the middle of the last century was horrified by Irish immigration, from Herman Melville to Charles Loring Grace to Frederick Law Olmstead," Mr. Quinn said. "The only one who wasn't was Walt Whitman."

That may explain Mr. Quinn's use of a quotation from "Leaves of Grass" at the end of the book. It reads: "Each belongs here or anywhere as much as the well off. . . just as much as you. Each has his or her place in the procession."

Mr. Quinn shares another affinity with Whitman. Both were regular visitors to Greenport. "Walt Whitman's sister lived in Greenport," Mr. Quinn said. "He used to take the train out, and it took three and a half hours. So some things don't change."

Mr. Quinn, who was born in Greenport 46 years ago and raised in the Bronx, lives in Brooklyn with his wife and two children. His family owns a house on Shelter Island and regularly makes their way there through Greenport.

His parents were vacationing on Shelter Island the summer when he was born. "The doctor took an X-ray, and when he saw two tiny spines he put my mother in what was then the Greenport Hospital," Mr. Quinn said, explaining that he has a twin brother.

The author's interest in Civil War New York began when he was working as a speechwriter for Gov. Mario M. Cuomo and received a copy of "Armies in the Streets," a history of the draft riots. "In the back of it was a list of people killed, and one of them was Peter Quinn," Mr. Quinn said.

He began collecting pictures of mid-19th century New York City. "They all looked like South Street Seaport," he said. "You know, quaint."

When Mr. Quinn came across a copy of the first housing report to the State Legislature, he realized, he said, the "incredible squalor and misery" suffered by some people in that era.

The report documented "back-lot tenements, basements filled with people, no plumbing, no air," Mr. Quinn said. He started trying to recreate the lives of people forgotten not only by history, but also by the period fiction and seen in books like Henry James's "Washington Square."

Mr. Quinn counts among the "banished children" all who have been deprived of fertile ground on which they might have thrived.

—*Lorraine Kreahling*

Mr. Quinn researched his project for six years. He organized the information in notebooks in sections for each character. When he started writing, making up stories to go with the material came naturally, he said, adding:

"As a kid growing up in my family it was important that you could speak at the dinner table and tell stories. Speeches that work tell stories. Speeches that don't work are dead rhetoric."

He is now chief speech writer at Time Warner Inc.

Banished Children of Eve details characters of different races and classes, most fictional but some nonfictional. Stephen Foster, past his creative prime, stumbles in and out of the novel in a drunken stupor, the notes of scores and visions of the future music industry circulating in and out of his consciousness.

"Stephen Foster is a lot like Elvis," Mr. Quinn said. "He brought black music to white people, because they wouldn't take it from black people." The Irish, he said, did the same thing when they put on black face to perform in the minstrels.

In *Banished Children,* Mr. Quinn uses the theater as a symbol of how the races can get along if they share a common vision. A cunning mulatto woman, Eliza, finds her way out of a high-class brothel and into work as an actress in a presentation of *Uncle Tom's Cabin.* Her lover, Irishman Mulcahey, who survived the crossing of the Atlantic during the Potato Famine, becomes a minstrel performer through sheer will, Mulcahey's other closest friend is his black assistant, Squirt.

Drive and ambition are what the characters in Mr. Quinn's book share, regardless of their class and race. Spunk and exceptional resourcefulness, intermingled with a necessary callousness, often spell the difference between not only the characters' success, but also their survival.

There are a farm boy from Southampton who erases his past and eventually heads a Wall Street brokerage, an Irish teen-ager who ignores adult advice and lies her way into a maid's position in a "good house," an Irish-born con artist and petty burglar who finally establishes himself in a "legitimate" saloon and an elderly female fishmonger who uses will and feigned madness to keep her fish stall, the only one owned by a black person on Fulton Street.

As the portraits emerge and the stories intertwine, water becomes a symbol for a social rank. The broker knows that he has truly made it when the house he buys for his bride has flush toilets. "People's access to water—that was the real divide between the comfortable and the uncomfortable," Mr. Quinn said. "You could hook up to the Croton system for $10 a month. That means you didn't have to go to the privy in the yard."

Another liquid that flows steadily through *Banished Children* is low-quality liquor, which, Mr. Quinn points out, parallels the drugs in inner cities today. "We don't think of it as substance abuse," Mr. Quinn said of the alcohol that his characters consume. "But it really was the poor anesthetizing themselves against their poverty."

Mr. Quinn said a chief interest in writing the book was to convey the complexity of history that is lost in its retellings by the ruling classes. That helps explain Audley Ward, a comical figure who, despite his financial decline and need to rely on his son-in-law's "new money," spends most of his time writing essays that ennoble his family's history and confirm their aristocratic superiority.

Ward is obsessed with the notion that the size of the English cranium is larger than that of both the Irish and the blacks.

Banished Children of Eve ends with fictional historic documents that Mr. Quinn said purposefully erased the impoverished, black and female characters that he took such pains to create. "In the epilogue women and blacks disappear," he said. "Their history is totally lost and never recorded."

Mr. Quinn counts among the "banished children" all who have been deprived of fertile ground on which they might have thrived. The words are taken from a Roman Catholic prayer imploring the Virgin Mary.

"To thee," it says, "we cry poor banished children of Eve, to thee we send up our sighs, mourning and weeping in this valley of tears."

Mr. Quinn said he wrote *Banished Children of Eve* in three and a half years, working weekday mornings from 7:15 to 9:15. Part of his inspiration came while crossing the East River on the subway from Brooklyn. He said he would look down on South Street, where his ancestors probably landed when they arrived here.

"Taking that train every morning was part of my writing," he said. "Writers hope for some kind of grace, and that to me was mine."

Mr. Quinn is now working on a novel that focuses on a murder in September 1938. "It's about the Bund, a Nazi camp in Yaphank," he said. "It's about eugenics, selective breeding and forced sterilization of the retarded, which I think is one of the most horrific movements of the 20th century. The Eugenics Record Office was in Cold Spring Harbor."

Elizabeth Bartelme   (review date 9 September 1994)

SOURCE: "A Splendid Stew," in *Commonweal*, Vol. 71, No. 15, September 9, 1994, pp. 26-7.

[*In the following review, Bartelme offers a favorable assessment of* Banished Children of Eve.]

Irish history, like the history of the Jewish people, embraces diaspora, exile, suffering, and a vision of the promised land. In his remarkable first novel, Peter Quinn, chief speechwriter for Time Warner, brings a new and formidable talent to the chronicling of Irish wanderings and their outcome. Although the emphasis of the book is on the Irish experience in nineteenth-century New York, Quinn goes beyond it to include on a broader canvas the entire sweep of a history steeped in the bitter fruits of subjugation. Nor does he neglect the Yankees and the free blacks who were so much a part of the New York Civil War tumult, and who were respectively the masters and the foes of the Irish.

As he draws together the strands of his narrative, Quinn moves between Ireland and New York, turning the latter teeming metropolis into a village that becomes his own American Nighttown. Here the immigrants, the "Paddys," go about their dubious business, survival uppermost in their minds, displaced only by the oblivion of a night's drinking. Here, too, they vie with the blacks for the menial jobs they are terrified of losing, and vent their anger and hatred of the Yankee "ratnoses," the Know Nothings or true Americans, who are indifferent to the miserable poverty around them, or prey on it.

These antagonisms and fears erupt in the draft riots of 1863, when the poor of New York battle armed federal troops, using bottles, paving stones, and arson. Out of control, the rioters maim and murder a poor dwarf, Squirt, believed to be the offspring of the lovely Eliza La Plante and her white lover, Jack Mulcahey. When the carnage is over, and the dead are buried, a new direction is indicated for each of the main characters.

And what richly realized characters they are, almost Dickensian in their variety and quirkiness: Jimmy Dunne, likable and resourceful, though hardly the conventional hero, who is rescued from Great Plains servitude by a tornado to become a New York hustler; Eliza, beautiful and a gifted actress, starring in *Uncle Tom's Cabin* and as well, the light of Jack Mulcahey's life. Mulcahey himself is the greatest of the blackface minstrels, performing his routines nightly to the music of Stephen Foster. And what of Margaret O'Driscoll, devout maidservant ready for the main chance, which could be Dunne?

There are others: Charles Bedford, Wall Street entrepreneur and hustler in a different mode, taking his chances at the faro table in Morrissey's gambling establishment and losing to the implacable owner. And how will this sit with the whining fence, Capshaw, who has Bedford between a rock and knife for improper securities dealings? We encounter, too, Colonel Robert Noonan, administrator of the draft, an honorable man hated by his compatriots who see him as a threat to their independence. Stephen Foster lurches from saloon to saloon, accompanied by his fictional great friend, One-eyed Jack Cassidy.

Over these and a host of minor characters is the brooding figure of Archbishop John Hughes, who truly sees his "banished children of Eve" as the exiles they are, a people wandering in the wilderness, in need of saving. He is determined that it will be he who leads them out of their degraded situations and into the promised land and to this end he is building his cathedral. The scene of Hughes on the scaffolding of the just-begun Saint Patrick's, attended by his sycophantic auxiliary, is one of the most dramatic and at the same time most comical scenes in the novel.

The research that informs the narrative is so smoothly and seamlessly integrated that it would hardly be noticeable were it not for the ebb and flow of the historical underpinnings. Quinn handles with great skill the events of the months leading to the draft riots, and at the same time acquaints the reader with the history of the famine-cursed Irish, the terrible blight that brought about the migration. With tenderness and compassion he describes the pain and sorrow of those famine years in Ireland, the wrenching farewells of parents to children whom they would never see again, the panic and despair of the greenhorns landing at Castle Garden in New York. And the survivors—what of them? Pickpockets, whores, servants: Was being in service to the Protestant Ascendancy any better than starving in Ireland?

Well, yes. Although **Banished Children** arrives at no conclusions of this kind, the epilogue opens up possibilities for the future. Here Quinn's controlled sense of irony has full play as he draws the reader beyond the riots into calmer waters. And comedy, too, is one of his gifts, for who could resist his more raffish characters as they reel in and out of bars and brothels, declaiming, singing, cadging drinks. His creations, then, are living, breathing, original habitués of the dens and warrens of nineteenth-century Manhattan. Beyond that they are, some of them, men and women with aspirations, longing for a better life, and with only the thinnest slice of hope to keep them going.

That they have been celebrated in this splendid stew of a book is a tribute to their resilience and to the overflowing life with which they have been filled by their creator. His empathy, knowledge, and masterly narrative have brought them into being. Flawed and broken though they are, these "banished children" are irresistible. Peter Quinn's achievement is to have brought them alive in a historic moment and to have given us a historical novel of stature and breadth.

Maurice N. Hennessy   (review date Fall 1994)

SOURCE: "The New World Irish, Warts and All," in *The Irish Literary Supplement,* Vol. 13, No. 2, Fall, 1994, p. 7.

[*In the following review, Hennessy commends* Banished Children of Eve, *claiming that the novel "marks a new voice in the annals of Irish literacy."*]

To those who hold history as an uncompromising and sacred art, Peter Quinn's novel, structured around local incidents in the history of New York City during the Civil War, adds a new and surprising dimension. While literary ability has frequently found its source of fiction in history, Quinn's book deserves special recognition as a historical pathfinder. In essence, he appears to have followed in the tradition of Dostoevski rather than Tolstoy. The latter tended to pontificate from a God's eye view; Peter Quinn, using a Dostoevskian tradition, has presented his historical narratives from the point of view of the participants and devoid of any claim to objectivity by the author.

This work has as it major theme the intense hatred which existed between Irish immigrants and African-Americans. The freed slaves who fled the South and came to New York inflamed the passions of the Irish who were particular victims of the notorious draft laws implemented by Colonel Noonan, also an Irishman. However, Quinn cannot be accused of being chauvinistic; he refers to "Paddy" in the words of a former Congressman from New York who said,

> God bless his democratic soul, he is as pugnacious and resentful a creature as God put on this earth. And don't let the veneer of musicality fool you into believing otherwise. In his heart of hearts, every Paddy believes the same thing: that the Know-Nothing-Abolitionist-Protestant-Ascendancy has decided that in the contest between him and the nigger as to which would occupy the lowest station in life, Paddy must win.

A characteristic literary pattern, established by a number of Irish writers, appears in this novel. Quinn introduces as a prologue to each section, either a verse of poetry or an apt quotation. This reviewer applauds this format as an effective means to channel the reader in anticipatory fashion to related incidents.

Among Quinn's historical findings, which are both original and noteworthy, is the way the development of minstrel shows created a rivalry for the musical soul of New York, another sore point between the Irish and blacks. The music of African-Americans was much more popular than that of the Irish, who were frequently accused of turning musical only in their more drunken moods. Today we laud, justifiably, the musical genius of our African-American citizens; during the Civil War the music of the blues and the minstrels were already laying the foundation for the extraordinary talents of today's African-Americans.

The Irish in the United States have always been considered a diocese of the Vatican; however, the narratives dealing with religion not only give the distinct impression that many of the Irish women immigrants became prostitutes, but that they rose to the position of madams in a number of important New York brothels. Pungent observations in a similar vein are to be found throughout the book. Describing one Irish character, Quinn says of him. "He had the best training in the romantic arts that the young Republic could provide," and observes in another passage that "the women were given to amorous acrobatics that their counterparts in the East were incapable of." Certainly this is a new approach to the romantic reputation of the Irish!

Not all of Quinn's portraits are so unsparing. As a tribute to his alma mater, Quinn gives us a short note on the first president of Fordham University, one admirable Father Dunn who hailed from the Bronx, and was of course a descendant of Ireland. And one great Catholic stands out here: Archbishop Hughes, who spent many hours watching the building of St. Patrick's Cathedral: "A fine sight,

Archbishop Hughes and his secretary wrestling in the mudhole surrounding the Cathedral while his coachman yells at him, 'Your grace, please stand back.' " This was the man who was wont to admonish those of his flock who insisted on participating in public mayhem, "Keep out of the crowd where mortal souls are launched into eternity . . . Ireland has been the mother of heroes and poets, but never the mother of cowards." He was referring to the hanging of African-Americans by the Irish during the Draft Riots.

Quinn has taken daring license in fictionalizing famous characters, from the Prince of Wales slumming in brothels during a visit to the City in 1860, to other real-life characters such as Stephen Foster, who apparently careened around the city creating disturbances; apart from his musical ability he was known as something of a nuisance. Even then New York was very tolerant of drunken musicians like Foster. Quinn quotes from a well-known theatrical figure: "The dancer, the singer, the balladeer, the minstrel, the thespian, whether comedian or tragedian, those of us who compose music and those of you who play it, we know no qualification but ability. We accept no distinction but talent!"

It has often been said that the only thing we learn from history is that we learn nothing from history. The author offers further proof. A comparison of the City today and of the Civil War era shows up many fascinating parallels. Gangs were as prevalent in those days as now and were just as flamboyant. They had names like The Plug Uglies, The Buckaroos, The Slaughterhouses, The Daybreak Boys, The Underswamp Angels, and so forth. Even Wall Street comes in for its fair share of attention: bureaucratic robbery, white-collar pilfering and similar varieties of middle-class roguery are described as the order of the day. In one instance a leading Wall Street pundit was guilty of a personal act of murder and managed to get away with it. In fact, it is in the area of comparison that this book tells so much. In painting so terrifying a picture of the City as it was then, one can only wonder whether the violence, murder and extraordinary absence of conventional morality as it exists now did not have their origin in what some people call "the good old days."

One particularly affecting incident is the execution of a young, innocent black woman while a great crowd of New Yorkers gathered around the City's gallows, which was located in what was then Potter's Field. The woman's name was Maria Rose Prior, born on 20 January 1840. The presence of this level of detail is indicative of the enormous research which the author has done.

In painting this often unflattering picture of the immigrant Irish, Peter Quinn does not suggest that they had any corner on the arts of greed. Many of his seamiest characters were themselves victim of oppression by other New Yorkers. This raises the question: against whom can we cast the first stone? Certainly the Dutch immigrants who landed in the City in the middle of the 17th century were as voracious as many of the later arrivals, including the Germans. The English, who were hated by the Irish, added their own brand of cupidity, even though they were but a small segment of the immigrant population.

As an Irishman reading this book, I felt not the slightest urge to take pride in my people; at the same time, I was delighted to find someone who was sufficiently honest, even in fictional narrative, to paint a portrait of the New World Irish with all their warts, all their dishonesty, and above all, their appalling enslavement to the bottle.

In short, this book is a formidable and yet fascinating read. The author sweeps the reader along on an ever-changing tide of people, places and incidents. He indeed proves that far from being a melting pot, New York City in the days of the Civil War was a seething mass of intolerant and warring tribes. What emerges triumphant, however, is a sense of the vibrant and vital contest between good and evil which has made this country what it is.

One thing must be added: the writing in this book marks a new voice in the annals of Irish literacy. It is dark and brilliant, fateful and forceful, unsparing in its evocations of brutality and tender in bearing witness to the travails of the innocent. In style it forges into the new space created by the belief in local knowledge and local meaning. There are no overarching explanations, no overarching narratives. The reader is left to create out of vivid rags and snatches the world of a vanished period and the cry of a banished race.

Maurice Walsh   (review date 25 November 1994)

SOURCE: "A New York History," in *The Times Literary Supplement*, No. 4782, November 25, 1994, p. 20.

[*In the following mixed review of* Banished Children of Eve, *Walsh argues that Quinn is not entirely successful handling the vastness of his narrative and the large number of characters.*]

The lonely farmer's wife, in Peter Quinn's novel [*Banished Children of Eve*], who seduces a young Irish orphan from New York sent to the cold western prairies for moral re-education, shares with him her tantalized imaginings of the distant city: "My husband says it's a wicked place, noisy, dirty, impious. Says that most of the people don't work, live off politics and that criminals abound and whores and drunkards are everywhere. It belongs to the foreigners he says, and let them have it. America's got no use for it."

This anarchic vista is the mood with which Peter Quinn has infused his long novel about the city during the time of the Civil War. He seems to make a bet on controlled length, rich learned detail, historical verisimilitude and a wide spread of characters jostling across the page for our attention, in the manner of the Irish mobs massing on the Bowery. His bet seems to be that this teeming edifice will bring to life his imaginative vision of the city's history. That the more elaborate the structure, and the greater the length, the more compelling and irresistible will be the recreation for the reader of the stuff of life in New York during the critical moments of the mid-nineteenth century. It is a bet because there are pages in this book which suggest another, perhaps discarded, line of attack; a technique that is more concentrated, more imaginative, less discursive and expository. These are the pages which work best, and their suggestiveness and force diminish what is thinly stretched in plot and characterization.

The story of New York from April to May 1863, when the Union seemed to have been losing the war with the Confederates, is told through the individual deeds and histories of a long list of characters, some of them historical figures. There is Jimmy Dunne, the Irish orphan who grows up to be a resourceful and reflective thief: Charles Bedford, a cunning young broker who enriches himself only to gamble away his fortune; Bedford's drearily loquacious uncle-in-law, Audley Ward, relentlessly peddling his theories; the Irish minstrel, Jack Mulcahey, and his lover Eliza, a freed slave. Civil War generals and the popular composer Stephen Foster appear in person. As he describes the rise and fail of the stock market, the race wars between the Irish and the blacks, and the eventual victory of patrician Republicans over the Confederates, Quinn contrives to make the lives of his characters intersect, often subtly.

It is clear that Quinn has a command of the period. His narrative is particularly vivid in conveying the extraordinary pace of change. He hints, through his characters, at the growing power of the railroads. And Charles Bedford, desperately dreaming of some opportunity to rescue himself from debt, muses, while sitting on the lavatory, about the wealth represented by piped water: "the great divide between the haves and the have nots . . . the spawning pond of the bourgeoisie". But the author's chosen motif of rushing History, carrying his characters to intertwined destinies, ultimately engulfs their individuality. And we are left with particular passages which suggest he could have mined the rest of his historical material less predictably.

Early on in the novel, there is an eerie description of the triumphalist visit by Archbishop Hughes to the city's unfinished Catholic cathedral. The cranky old man wades through puddles and mud and climbs the scaffolding desperately pursued by his aide, Father Corrigan. When the Archbishop reaches the edge of the wall, a strong gust of wind tears away his hairpiece. Corrigan sees him standing there, his skull "shiny and knobby, his cheeks sunken. He was smiling, he beckoned to Corrigan to come forward. Then he turned around again." And later, with the orphan boy, Jimmy Dunne, there is a scene where he is brought by the farmer in the West to a place by the railroad where passengers take potshots at the herds of buffalo crossing the tracks. "Across the prairie in front of him were thousands of animal carcasses, some little more than skeletons, others swelling masses of decaying, putrid flesh. . . . Jimmy worked all morning at collecting bones, a rag soaked in cottonseed oil tied across his face to keep out the terrible odor. Toward late afternoon a strong wind came up and the sky clouded over." More of this close focus across a smaller cast of characters would have been a better bet.

Prizewinners

Literary Prizes and Honors
Announced in 1995

American Academy and Institute of Arts and Letters Awards

Academy Members (new)

Jules Feiffer
Brendan Gill
Murray Kempton
James Laughlin
Richard Serra

Charles Simic
Garry Wills
August Wilson
Olly Wilson
Charles Wright

Academy Awards in Literature
Given annually to encourage creative achievement in literature.

John Haines, Josephine Humphreys, Miller Williams, Louis Begley
R. V. Cassill, Jane Cooper, Stephen Dunn, Horton Foote

Award of Merit Medal for the Short Story
Larry Woiwode

Michael Braude Award for Light Verse
Wendy Cope

Witter Bynner Foundation Prize for Poetry
Established in 1979 and awarded annually to recognize an outstanding younger poet.

Franz Wright

E. M. Forster Award in Literature
Colm Tóibín

Gold Medal for Fiction
William Maxwell

The William Dean Howells Medal
John Updike
Rabbit at Rest

Sue Kaufman Prize for First Fiction
Awarded annually to the author of the best first fiction published during the preceding year.

Jim Grimsley
Winter Birds

Rome Fellowship in Literature
Henri Cole

Richard and Hilda Rosenthal Foundation Award
Awards given annually for accomplishments in art and literature. The literature award recognizes a work of fiction published in the preceding year which, while not a "commercial success," is considered a literary achievement.

Laura Hendrie
Stygo

Morton Dauwen Zabel Award
Presented in alternating years to poets, fiction writers, and critics, to encourage progressive, original, and experimental tendencies in American literature.

Frank Bidart
(poetry)

Eve Kosofsky Sedgwick
(criticism)

James Tait Black Memorial Book Prize
Sponsored by the University of Edinburgh and awarded annually for the best works of fiction and biography published during the previous year.

Alan Hollinghurst
The Folding Star
(fiction)
(see entry below)

Doris Lessing
Under My Skin
(biography)

Bollingen Prize for Poetry
Kenneth Koch

Booker Prize for Fiction
Britain's major literary prize awarded annually in recognition of a full-length novel.

Pat Barker
The Ghost Road

Hugo Awards
Established in 1953 to recognize notable science fiction works in several categories.

Lois McMaster Bujold
Mirror Dance
(novel)

Mike Resnick
Seven Views of Olduvai Gorge
(novella)

Joe Haldeman
"None So Blind"
(short story)

Lannan Literary Awards
Honors writers of distinctive literary merit. The award carries a cash prize of $50,000.

Louis de Bernières, Mary Morrissy, Alice Munro
(fiction)

Thomas Berry, Richard K. Nelson, Scott Russell Sanders
(nonfiction)

Hayden Carruth, Carol Ann Duffy, Li-Young Lee, Arthur Sze
(poetry)

Ruth Lilly Poetry Prize
Awarded annually to an outstanding American poet.

A. R. Ammons

Los Angeles Times Book Awards

Honors technique and vision in various categories.

William Boyd
The Blue Afternoon
(fiction)

Robert Pinsky
The Inferno of Dante
(translation)

Doris Lessing
Under My Skin
(biography)

Mark Merlis
American Studies
(Art Seidenbaum Award for First Fiction)

Lenore Marshall/*Nation* Poetry Prize

Established in 1974 to honor the author of the year's outstanding collection of poems published in the United States.

Marilyn Hacker
Winter Numbers
(see entry below)

National Book Awards

Established in 1950 to honor and promote American books of literary distinction in various categories.

Philip Roth
Sabbath's Theater
(fiction)

Stanley Kunitz
Passing Through: The Later Poems New and Selected
(poetry)

Tina Rosenberg
The Haunted Land: Facing Europe's Ghosts after Communism
(nonfiction)

National Book Critics Circle Awards

Founded in 1974 to recognize superior literary quality in American literature in several categories.

Carol Shields
The Stone Diaries
(fiction)
(see entry below)

Lynn H. Nicholas
The Rape of Europa
(nonfiction)

Mikal Gilmore
Shot in the Heart
(biography)

Nebula Awards

Established in 1965 to honor significant works in several categories of science fiction published in the United States.

Greg Bear
Moving Mars
(novel)

Mike Resnick
Seven Views of Olduvai Gorge
(novella)

David Gerrold
The Martian Child
(novellette)

Martha Soukup
"A Defense of Social Contracts"
(short story)

New York Drama Critics Circle Award

Presented annually in several categories to encourage excellence in playwriting.

Terrence McNally
Love! Valour! Compassion!
(Best New American Play)
(see entry below)

Tom Stoppard
Arcadia
(Best New Play)
(see entry below)

Nobel Prize in Literature

Awarded annually to recognize the most distinguished body of literary work of an idealistic nature.

Seamus Heaney
(see entry below)

Obie Awards

Given annually to recognize excellence in off-Broadway and off-off-Broadway theater productions in various categories.

David Mamet
Cryptogram
(best play)
(see entry below)

Ming Cho Lee
(sustained achievement)

David Hancock
The Convention of Cartography
(playwriting)

Tony Kushner
Slavs
(playwriting)

Terrence McNally
Love! Valour! Compassion!
(playwriting)
(see entry below)

Susan Miller
My Left Breast
(playwriting)

PEN American Center Awards

Faulkner Award for Fiction

David Guterson
Snow Falling on Cedars
(see entry below)

Ernest Hemingway Foundation Award

Susan Power
The Grass Dancer
(Best first book of fiction by an American writer)
(see entry below)

———————

Edgar Allan Poe Awards
Presented annually for outstanding achievement in mystery writing.

Mary Willis Walker
The Red Scream
(best novel)

George Dawes Green
The Caveman's Valentine
(best first mystery novel by an American writer)

Lisa Scottoline
Final Appeal
(best original paperback)

Doug Allyn
"The Dancing Bear"
(best short story)

Martin Greenberg
(Ellery Queen Award)

Mickey Spillane
(Grand Master)

———————

Pulitzer Prizes
Awarded in recognition of outstanding accomplishments by American authors in various categories within the fields of journalism, literature, music, and drama. Literary awards usually recognize excellence in works that concern American life.

Carol Shields
The Stone Diaries
(fiction)
(see entry below)

Horton Foote
The Young Man form Atlanta
(drama)
(see entry below)

Doris Kearns Goodwin
No Ordinary Time
(history)

Joan D. Hedrick
Harriet Beecher Stowe: A Life
(biography)

Philip Levine
The Simple Truth
(poetry)

Tony Awards

Officially titled the American Theatre Wing's Antoinette Perry Awards, prizes are presented in recognition of outstanding achievement on Broadway.

Terrence McNally
Love! Valour! Compassion!
(best play)
(see entry below)

United States Poet Laureate

Created in 1986 by an act of Congress to honor the career achievement of an American poet.

Robert Hass

Horton Foote
The Young Man from Atlanta

Award: Pulitzer Prize for Drama

Born in 1916, Foote is an American playwright, scriptwriter, and novelist.

For further information on his life and works, see *CLC*, Volume 51.

INTRODUCTION

Part of Foote's dramatic cycle "The Orphan's Home," *The Young Man from Atlanta* (1995) is noted for its examination of grief, family dynamics, and self-delusion. Set in the 1950s in Houston, Texas, the play centers on Will and Lily Dale Kidder following the death of their only son, Bill, who likely committed suicide. Refusing to discuss Bill's alleged homosexuality and the events surrounding his death, Will finds himself consumed with work; during the course of the play, however, Will is fired and replaced by a young executive-in-training. Meanwhile, to alleviate her grief, Lily Dale turns to religion and is comforted with stories of Bill's strong faith told by Bill's roommate, Randy Carter. Thankful for Randy's condolences and sympathetic to tales of his and his family's financial difficulties, Lily Dale gives him large sums of money despite her husband's protests and despite rumors that Randy took financial advantage of Bill and was his lover.

The Young Man from Atlanta has received a mixed reception. Negative reviews have faulted Foote's depiction of American society and quotidian concerns as limited in scope and criticized his colloquial dialogue as uninspired and clichéd. Other commentators, noting Foote's revelation of the truth surrounding Bill's death and lifestyle, have praised the work for its thematic focus on the American dream, blind optimism, self-denial, and the grieving process. The drama has also been lauded as an exercise in character development, a naturalistic piece succinctly evoking what is often thought to have been a more innocent time in contemporary American history, and an examination of the nature of familial ties and their inevitable secrets. Clive Barnes observed that *The Young Man from Atlanta* "is a simple, immensely satisfying play, crafted with elegance, alive with feeling, holding a mirror up if not to nature at least to the next best thing, our concept of nature."

PRINCIPAL WORKS

The Wharton Dance   (play)   1939-40
Texas Town   (play)   1941
Out of My House   (play)   1941-42
Only the Heart   (play)   1942
Ludie Brooks   (television play)   1951
The Chase   (play)   1952
The Old Beginning   (television play)   1952
The Travelers   (television play)   1952
The Death of the Old Man   (television play)   1953
John Turner Davis   (television play)   1953
The Midnight Caller   (television play)   1953
The Oil Well   (television play)   1953
Tears of My Sister   (television play)   1953
The Trip to Bountiful   (play)   1953
The Trip to Bountiful   (television play)   1953
A Young Lady of Property   (television play)   1953
The Traveling Lady   (play)   1954
The Chase   (novel)   1956

*Harrison, Texas (television plays) 1956
Storm Fear (screenplay) 1956
Old Man [adaptor; from the novella by William Faulkner] (television play) 1958
Tomorrow [adaptor; from the short story by William Faulkner] (television play) 1960
†Night of the Storm (play) 1961
To Kill a Mockingbird [adaptor; from the novel by Harper Lee] (screenplay) 1962
Tomorrow [adaptor; from the short story by William Faulkner] (play) 1963
‡Baby, the Rain Must Fall (screenplay) 1964
Hurry Sundown [adaptor, with Thomas Ryan; from the novel by K. B. Gilden] (screenplay) 1967
The Stalking Moon (screenplay) 1969
Gone with the Wind [adaptor; from the novel by Margaret Mitchell] (musical) 1972
Tomorrow [adaptor; based on the short story by William Faulkner] (screenplay) 1972
The Displaced Person [adaptor; based on the short story by Flannery O'Connor] (screenplay) 1977
§Courtship (play) 1978
§1918 (play) 1979
Barn Burning [adaptor; from the short story by William Faulkner] (screenplay) 1980
§On Valentine's Day (play) 1980
The Man Who Climbed Pecan Trees (play) 1982
**The Roads to Home (play) 1982
Tender Mercies (screenplay) 1983
Blind Date (play) 1985
1918 (screenplay) 1985
The One-Armed Man (play) 1985
The Prisoner's Song (play) 1985
The Road to the Graveyard (play) 1985
The Trip to Bountiful (screenplay) 1985
On Valentine's Day (screenplay) 1986
§Lily Dale (play) 1986-87
§The Widow Claire (play) 1986-87
The Habitation of Dragons (play) 1988
The Land of the Astronauts (play) 1988
§Cousins (play) 1989
§The Death of Papa (play) 1989
§Convicts (screenplay) 1991
Of Mice and Men [adaptor; based on the novella by John Steinbeck] (screenplay) 1992
Night Seasons (play) 1993
Talking Pictures (play) 1994
God's Pictures (play) 1995
Laura Dennis (play) 1995
§The Young Man from Atlanta (play) 1995

*This volume collects eight scripts Foote wrote for television.

†This work was later renamed *Roots in a Parched Ground* and is considered part of "The Orphan's Home" cycle.

‡This work is an adaptation of Foote's play *The Traveling Lady*.

§These works are part of the dramatic cycle known as "The Orphan's Home."

**This trilogy is composed of the works *The Roads to Home, The Dearest of Friends,* and *Spring Dance.*

CRITICISM

Clive Barnes (review date 30 January 1995)

SOURCE: "Foote's Giant Step Forward," in *New York Post,* January 30, 1995.

[*An English-born critic, Barnes is the author and editor of several books about the performing arts. In the following favorable review, he discusses the theme of self-delusion in* The Young Man from Atlanta.]

Things change suddenly, and with those changes, a life can unfurl in odd shapes, odd shapes casting odder shadows; as we recognize what we took to be true as not quite what we first thought. This is the world of playwright Horton Foote, whose plays are domestic variations on a common theme of relationships, man with his world, people with people, family with family.

The things that happen in that world are always on a human scale of possibility and disappointment. The latest variations are in **The Young Man From Atlanta,** given its world premiere this weekend at the Kampo Cultural Center by the Signature Theater Company as part of its season-long Horton Foote retrospective.

The play opens up with a dense slice of exposition, worthy of Ibsen or Arthur Miller.

In short order we learn that 64 year-old Will Kidder, chief executive with a wholesale produce company, is besotted with "wanting the biggest and the best," has just bought a $200,000 house (the time, by the way, is 1950; the place, Houston, Texas), has recently been diagnosed with a heart condition, and is still mourning the recent death by drowning of his 39-year-old son, which he reluctantly suspects was a suicide.

"I'm a realist," he says.

No sooner have we absorbed all this information when: bang! Out of a clearish blue sky, the owner of the company comes in, and after a minimum of throat-clearing politeness, fires Will, with three months notice. Will says he will leave at once, and determines to start up his own company.

But nothing is quite as it seems. The devoted office protégé who has been sympathetically listening to Will's troubles is, in fact, the new executive selected to supplant him. The banks, with whom he presumed to have close connections, refuse to lend him money.

And there is, above all, the mysterious way his son lived and died, and that title character **The Young Man From Atlanta,** whom we never meet, but is destined to play a key role in Will's life.

You see, Will really doesn't know his wife, or even himself—they have wrapped themselves within a cocoon of tiny lies, and now with Will's disaster everything starts to unravel. Is Will really a realist, or is that to be his final illusion?

Most playwrights succeed in making melodrama out of

drama; it is Foote's particular skill, reversing the process, to make drama out of melodrama.

His situations are often highly colored—obvious hubris, far-flung falls, deceptions, heart attacks—the only subtle thing about them being the low-keyed and realistic fashion with which they are faced.

Tone is everything, because without the right tone Foote's inner truth—that credibility coming from real people reacting to real events—will be lost.

The director Peter Masterson has done a beautifully layered and textured job. The acting is fine, particularly from a wonderful Ralph Waite as the blustering, self-deluded Will, and Carlyn Glynn as his weak and wavering toy-doll of a 60-year-old wife.

Here is a simple, immensely satisfying play, crafted with elegance, alive with feeling, holding a mirror up if not to nature at least to the next best thing, our concept of nature. Not to be missed.

Vincent Canby   (review date 30 January 1995)

SOURCE: "Nameless Menace in Latest by Foote," in *The New York Times,* January 30, 1995, pp. 13, 16.

[*For many years the chief film critic of* The New York Times, *Canby is also a novelist, playwright, and theater critic. In the following, he offers a favorable review of* The Young Man from Atlanta, *noting Foote's focus on the American dream, homosexuality, grief, and family dynamics.*]

A menacing secret lazes around, sharklike, just beneath the comparatively placid surface of *The Young Man From Atlanta,* the sorrowful, satiric new play by Horton Foote that opened on Friday night at the Kampo Cultural Center. The secret is never mentioned by the characters whose lives it threatens to ruin. Having no name, it can't be spoken even on a dare. Instead, it's always referred to indirectly, and with a kind of puzzled Christian innocence that denies the secret's corrosive effects. Mr. Foote's characters say that everything's all right, but he knows better.

After *Talking Pictures* and *Night Seasons,* the Signature Theater Company continues its season devoted to the playwright with a first-rate production of a work that will haunt you long after the performance. *The Young Man From Atlanta* is both quintessential Horton Foote and, in terms of subtext, one of his least characteristic works.

The director is Peter Masterson, who was responsible for the film adaptation of Mr. Foote's *Trip to Bountiful.* The excellent cast is headed by Ralph Waite and, in a role very different from the big-hearted madam she played in *The Best Little Whorehouse in Texas,* Carlin Glynn, who is married to the director. The Signature people know how to make a playwright feel at home.

The Young Man From Atlanta, which is to run through Feb. 26, forsakes Mr. Foote's usual rural Texas setting for the big city of Houston. The time is the spring of 1950, a few months before the outbreak of the Korean War, when American business was still adjusting to the jittery post-World War II economy. The principal characters are Will (Mr. Waite) and Lily Dale Kidder (Ms. Glynn), though a major presence is their only child, the 32-year-old Bill, who had been living in Atlanta until his recent death.

It seems that while on a business trip in Florida, Bill stopped for a swim, walked into a lake and drowned. Just like that. The curious thing is that he didn't know how to swim. His father acknowledges that it was a suicide, though for reasons he doesn't want to think about. Lily Dale is convinced that it was some kind of terrible accident.

As imagined by Mr. Foote and played with desperate heartiness by Mr. Waite, Will recalls the kind of middle-American boosters Sinclair Lewis wrote about in the 1920's. He's a Republican. He's self-made and proud of it. When first seen, he's reaping the rewards of a successful 40-year career with a wholesale grocery company. He has just built a $200,000 house, "the biggest and the best" that money can buy, in what he fondly calls the best city in the South. He has a slight heart condition, but his optimism is ironclad, even when he's reminded of Bill.

Bill's death has changed Lily Dale. She still plays the doll-wife to Will, whom she calls "Daddy." She dresses in clothes that look expensive but are not especially suitable. She keeps up appearances. Yet instead of devoting herself to her music as she once did, playing the piano and composing for family and friends, she has turned to religion.

At the start of the play, two things happen to wreck the accommodations that Will and Lily Dale have made to keep their marriage in balance: Will is fired from his job, which leaves him almost broke, and the title character turns up in Houston.

The Young Man From Atlanta refers to Randy Carter, Bill's room-mate. He remains offstage, but is an even more vivid presence in the play than the lost Bill. Randy has come to Houston in hopes that Will will give him a job. He was there for the funeral, Will remembers, crying harder and more noisily than Lily Dale during the service.

Though forbidden by Will to have any dealings with the young man, Lily Dale has not only been talking to him several times a week on the telephone, but she has also been advancing him money. First she felt compelled to help out when, being so upset over Bill's death, he couldn't work. Then his mother needed an operation, and his sister's husband disappeared, leaving her with three children to support. Lily Dale has so far shelled out $35,000.

In the work of any other play-wright, a character like Lily Dale would seem naïve to the point of simple-mindedness. As conceived by Mr. Foote and played by Ms. Carlin, she's far from simple-minded. In her own gentle way, she's furious and steely. She's willing to pay for the comfort provided by the young man, who tells her what a religious fellow Bill was and how his praying used to cheer the boarding house where they lived.

This being 1950, nobody in the play mentions the word "gay," or refers even euphemistically to the truth of the relationship between Bill and Randy. From the few details that we get, it seems to have been a stormy affair, possibly a platonic one, involving the prematurely old, balding, severely repressed Bill consumed by a passion for a fast-talking hustler 10 years his junior.

In *The Young Man from Atlanta* Foote gives us a portrait of parents who, to any independent child, would seem to be monsters, and of a child whose feckless life is beyond the comprehension of his sternly. Protestant parents.

—Vincent Canby

In much the same manner that Will and Lily Dale come to terms with the loss of their son, Mr. Foote comes to terms with them and with Bill and Randy. That is, obliquely. *The Young Man From Atlanta* is not a gay play. Yet the playwright gives us a portrait of parents who, to any independent child, would seem to be monsters, and of a child whose feckless life is beyond the comprehension of his sternly Protestant parents.

The Young Man From Atlanta can also be blunt. The opening is as overstuffed with exposition as the first scene of one of Shakespeare's histories. The rest of the play is more graceful. Mr. Foote avoids big scenes here. He creates rich characters that allow for rich performances by Mr. Waite, Ms. Glynn and the members of the supporting cast, particularly James Pritchett, who plays Lily Dale's observant, non-committal stepfather, and Beatrice Winde, who's stunning in the tiny role of a former maid.

Also noteworthy is E. David Cosier's principal set: a clean, new, depressingly impersonal living room framed in a way to look like a shadow box. it's a perfect reflection of a genteel world where money and property, which are supposed to signify happiness, are seen to be merely pieces of overstuffed furniture

The Young Man From Atlanta doesn't soothe or lift any hearts. It's tough, one of Mr. Foote's most serious and scathing works. The Signature Theater's estimable season goes on.

Michael Feingold   (review date 7 February 1995)

SOURCE: "The Normal Foote," in *The Village Voice,* Vol. XL, No. 6, February 7, 1995, p. 81.

[*Feingold is an American critic and educator. In the excerpt below, he questions the validity of Foote's portrait of contemporary American society in* The Young Man from Atlanta.]

Horton Foote's plays invariably amaze me. Characters come and go, a situation of some kind is broached, and something happens, or is said to happen, which does or doesn't resolve said situation, more often the latter. That's all there is, a very sparse return for the ticket price, yet

---

***The Young Man From Atlanta* is part of a nine-play cycle called *The Orphan's Home.* Set in 1950 and filled with echoes of both Arthur Miller and [Tennessee] Williams, the play concerns the mysterious circumstances surrounding a son's death, and a visit to his parents in Houston paid by the son's duplicitous Atlanta roommate.**

—Jeremy Gerard, in his "Foote Nabs Pulitzer for 'Man From Atlanta,' " in Variety, *24 April 1995*.

Foote's plays keep getting produced, applauded, praised. His work seems to fulfill some idea Americans have, incomprehensible to me, of what a play is, or maybe of what their lives are: a representation of people in a room, engaging in stilted, pro forma talk, mostly to impart data the audience either doesn't need or already has.

Superficially, the ambience of Foote's plays is naturalistic, but there is little detail and less personalizing. Though the setting is usually Texas, the dialogue rarely ventures into the wild, colloquial excess that gives Texas talk its charm and color; the people might as easily be new arrivals from Connecticut. The long speeches, replete with *he saids* and *I told hims*, often replay, unaltered, conversations we've just heard. Constantly reiterating their life stories for each other, Foote's people never appear to have any shared past—or, in some respects, any past at all. What shapes their fates is less destiny than coincidence.

Will Kidder (Ralph Waite), the retirement-age hero of *The Young Man From Atlanta,* has worked for the same firm 30 years, in an executive position, but seems to have no pension or investments. When he's fired—it's 1950 and the new boss wants younger, more competitive men—he gets three months' severance, which won't keep up the costly new home he's just built to distract himself and his wife Lily Dale (Carlin Glynn) from the gloom brought on by their son Bill's death.

Bill, an unmarried 37-year-old, who shared a room in an Atlanta boarding house with a younger man while working at a drudge job, has inexplicably walked into a lake and drowned; he was a non-swimmer. What this implies is self-evident, but Foote, like his characters, isn't about to discuss the matter. Instead, we get a coy game of was-Bill-or-wasn't-Bill, with the long arm of coincidence providing a dubious onstage witness—Lily Dale's stepfather's great-nephew, if you please—to counter the version of his life given by the (unseen) roommate, who has sponged extensively off Bill and is now trying to repeat the process with Lily.

Of course, the great-nephew's story—Bill was a straight upstanding chap being rooked by his fourflusher roommate—is as suspect as its opposite: He himself is hitting up Lily's stepfather for money, on various pretexts; maybe it's an Atlantan custom. It's anyone's guess if the young man of Foote's title is the one we see, or the one we don't see, just as we never know if Will and Lily's son was a major queer who killed himself in 1950s despair, or a generous; pious young fellow who abruptly decided to have a swim and got out of his depth. Will, having survived a heart attack, and settled for a lesser job in his old firm, decides that he'd rather not know: He makes Lily Dale send the roommate away, effectively banishing all future discussion of Bill.

This desperate desire not to face reality is certainly very American, but does Foote want us to indict it or empathize with it? His flat style, with its eerily empty, echolaliac lines, occasionally suggests that he thinks he's writing satire—the American family reduced to an Absurdist organism. That would explain Will's repeated boast, just before his firing, that he lives in "the greatest city in the greatest country in the world." And it might explain the presence of no less than two supportive, serenely pious, black female domestics. (Watching Frances Foster and Beatrice Winde, the two sublime actresses who play these roles, snatch eagerly at every scrap of individuality in their few lines is a disquieting experience in itself.)

At the same time, it's hard to imagine writing so flat-footed and colorless as a vehicle for irony; it's like calling Grandma Moses a political cartoonist. Foote's bland, featureless Texas, with its well-meaning souls reciting cliches to each other while dodging every dangerous fact or emotion, is neither naturalistic nor satiric, but a kind of urbanized folk legend, its figures less like dramatic characters than like patchwork dolls or the faces carved in apples, creations of unenlightened, mechanical craft rather than art. And because he offers full-scale images of life, not tiny objects to decorate a shelf, Foote's plays carry a considerably eerier resonance than the apple-carver's gargoyles. He hears America singing, and its song says, "I'm stupid, I'm comfortably off, I pay lip service to God, and I'm happy that way. Don't bother me about anything serious."

Richard Christiansen   (review date 23 February 1995)

SOURCE: "Foote's 'Young Man' Wonderfully Detailed," in *Chicago Tribune*, February 23, 1995, p. 6.

[*Christiansen is an American journalist, editor, and critic who frequently writes about Chicago's artistic community. In the following review, he praises Foote's use of characterization and dialogue, and discusses his treatment of family in* The Young Man from Atlanta.]

Horton Foote, the master miniaturist of American drama, has created a small but potent domestic tragedy with his new play, *The Young Man From Atlanta*.

A writer for more than 50 of his 78 years, Foote is perhaps best known for his Academy Award-winning screenplays of *To Kill a Mockingbird* and *Tender Mercies*. But he has been a diligent and prolific playwright, as well, turning out over the years a series of low-key, hand-polished family dramas, many of them reflecting his own heritage in southeastern Texas.

In recognition of his work, the enterprising off-off-

Broadway Signature Theatre Company this year is devoting its entire season to four Foote dramas, including this world premiere.

Here, as in much of his work, Foote works within a tight family circle and he builds his story with layers of small increments.

The central event of the play already has occurred when the story begins in Houston in the spring of 1950. It is the death by drowning of the 37-year-old bachelor son of Will and Lily Dale Kidder, a death that has left both parents traumatized.

In her grief over the loss of her only child, the sprightly Lily Dale has turned to religion, while Will, convinced that his son was a suicide, is wrestling with indications that he was a homosexual, living in an Atlanta YMCA with a gold-digging deadbeat 10 years his junior.

We never see this young man from Atlanta, and, though evidence points to the belief that he was indeed a liar and a cheat who sponged off the Kidder son, we do not know for sure whether he was more victim or victimizer.

In the end, he remains a mystery, a comfort to Lily Dale, who needs to believe the best of him (and her dead son) and a source of dread to Will, who fears to find out the answers to the questions raised by his son's suicide.

Clinging to each other in mutual misery, the grieving parents are frightened, battered survivors of their past, facing the future with a desperate, last-stand hope that all will somehow turn out well.

The Young Man from Atlanta is very strong and solid, its power carried by the author's remarkable writing skills and by his delicate probing of deep family truths.

—*Richard Christiansen*

Lasting a few minutes under two hours, and performed without intermission, the play is a wonder of strong drama built through ordinary talk and everyday incident.

Once the action gets past the *Death of a Salesman*-like expository first scene set in Will's office it moves to the Kidder living room and really grabs hold in the quiet, complex characterizations of the Kidders and their family.

The touching intimacy of the drama, directed by Peter Masterson, is beautifully captured on the small stage of the Signature's 80-seat auditorium.

Ralph Waite, the steadfast, resourceful father of TV's *The Waltons,* superbly portrays another weak and frail, parent here. With calmly modulated sensitivity and sharply honed timing, he shows us a bluff and optimistic man at the end of his tether, tapped out in spirit and body. Simply to see him collapse in weariness on the living room sofa is to understand precisely how drained of the old vigor his life has become.

Carlin Glynn, costumed to perfection in her '50s dresses, is an ideal counterpoint to Waite's gray lion. Red-haired and still kittenish (she calls her husband "Daddy"), she is a simple, spoiled woman who suddenly sees her secure world shattered beyond repair.

Backing them up is a fine ensemble cast in which even the smallest roles—a layabout great-nephew and an aged former housekeeper—cast light on the Kidder family secrets.

The drama in *The Young Man from Atlanta* is never stormy, and its humor, including a running joke about Eleanor Roosevelt is never uproarious.

But the play is very strong and solid, its power carried by the author's remarkable writing skills and by his delicate probing of deep family truths.

We should see more of his work in Chicago.

John Simon   (review date 27 February 1995)

SOURCE: "With Blunt Tools," in *New York* Magazine, Vol. 28, No. 9, February 27, 1995, pp. 115-17.

[*An American essayist and critic, Simon has served as a drama critic for* Esquire *and the* New Leader. *In the excerpt below, he offers a highly negative account of* The Young Man from Atlanta.]

"Where is the Christopher Columbus to whom we'll owe the forgetting of a continent?" asked the great poet Guillaume Apollinaire. Upon seeing *The Young Man From Atlanta,* I would not go so far as to ask its author, Horton Foote, to forget an entire continent; I'd settle for his corner of Texas, which he keeps chewing and rechewing: There is a point where mastication becomes masturbation. Do not think the title means that the play is set in Atlanta, or that the eponymous young man actually appears in the

play. No, we are again stuck in Texas, the Houston of this play no different from the Harrison of most of the others. Look, I'm not asking for Atlanta; I'd be satisfied even with Albuquerque or Baton Rouge. Or with Foote's quitting altogether. How many times can he, as prolific as Miss Oates and nearly 80, keep writing the same sentimental, pathetic, old-fashioned, terminally boring play?

Here we have the reckless Lily Dale (encountered previously in the Foote *oeuvre*) and her kind, long-suffering husband, Will Kidder, whose only son has just drowned. A young man from Atlanta, where he was the son's roommate, shows up in Houston (though not onstage) to sweet-talk the bereaved mother out of money just as he always did her son. But Will Kidder has just been let go by the bank where he'd toiled all his life, and Lily Dale can't go on spending as usual. And then another young Atlantan shows up (onstage), revealing that the son was a homosexual and a suicide. Can the Kidders live with this revelation?

This, more or less, is the play, except for a few subsidiary characters, most of them sweet. Everything about the play has a wistful sheen to it, like the pants seat of an old serge suit. "Life goes by so fast, Lily Dale," Will sighs; but the play somehow refuses to emulate it. As routinely directed by Peter Masterson, this world premiere feels more like a world dernière, though I have no doubt that there are regional theaters retrograde enough to be eager to mount it.

The acting is generally acceptable, with Ralph Waite (Will) and especially James Pritchett (Lily Dale's father) better than that. Perhaps the best thing about *Young Man From Atlanta* is that there is no role in it for Foote's untalented daughter, Hallie. But what joy there is in that quickly subsides at the performance of the director's wife, Carlin Glynn, who even goes up on her lines, as Lily Dale.

Additional coverage of Foote's life and career is contained in the following sources published by Gale Research: *Contemporary Authors,* Vols. 73-76; *Contemporary Authors New Revision Series,* Vol. 34; *Contemporary Literary Criticism,* Vol. 51; and *Dictionary of Literary Biography,* Vol. 26.

David Guterson
Snow Falling on Cedars

Award: PEN/Faulkner Prize for Fiction

Born in 1956, Guterson is an American novelist and short story writer.

INTRODUCTION

Snow Falling on Cedars is set on the Puget Sound island of San Piedro in 1954 and centers on the murder trial of Kabuo Miyomoto, accused of killing fisherman Carl Heine. Miyomoto and his family were sent in 1942 to Manzanar, one of the relocation camps in which many Japanese Americans were interned during World War II because—though many had lived in America for generations—the American government determined they represented a threat to national security due to their race. Perhaps surprisingly, upon his release Miyomoto joined the United States Army and fought in Italy. After the war he returned to San Piedro to find that the strawberry farm his family had been buying from the Heine family had been sold during the Miyomoto's absence. Miyomoto's obsession with the farm provides the apparent motive for his alleged murder of Heine. Although the action of the novel focuses on the investigation and testimony presented at the trial, Guterson's omniscient viewpoint allows for numerous flashbacks among several of the characters, including a subplot involving an adolescent romance between Ishmael Chambers, a war veteran who operates the local newspaper, and Hatsue, Miyomoto's wife. Critics have praised Guterson's subtle treatment of racial prejudice and have characterized the novel as a study of community, hypocrisy, and the debilitating effects of guilt and obsession. Miyomoto's drive to reclaim the farm, and the guilt he feels for having killed Germans in Italy, is contrasted throughout with Chambers's vague desire to rekindle his romance with Hatsue. Although some commentators contend that the novel lacks an intriguing protagonist and suffers from an overabundance of detail, most have lauded Guterson's prose, arguing that he invigorates his story with a dramatic and suspenseful pace and evokes a clear sense of the island's physical environment and the mood and way of life of its inhabitants.

PRINCIPAL WORKS

The Country Ahead of Us, the Country Behind (short stories) 1989
Snow Falling on Cedars (novel) 1994

CRITICISM

Michael Harris (review date 19 September 1994)

SOURCE: "Sometimes, Even Good People Must Coexist With Evil," in *Los Angeles Times,* September 19, 1994, p. E4.

[*In the review below, Harris comments on character and theme in* Snow Falling on Cedars.]

David Guterson's haunting first novel [*Snow Falling on Cedars*] works on at least two levels. It gives us a puzzle to solve—a whodunit complete with courtroom maneuvering and surprising turns of evidence—and at the same time it offers us a mystery, something altogether richer and deeper.

In 1954, off the island of San Piedro in Puget Sound, salmon fisherman Carl Heine is found drowned and entangled in his boat's gill net. It seems to be an accident. Soon, however, darker suspicions bubble to the surface, and a fisherman of Japanese descent, Kabuo Miyomoto, is put on trial for murder.

Heine, the coroner discovers, has a fractured skull; before drowning, he hit his head on something, or was hit. Evidence confirms that Miyomoto boarded Heine's boat on the foggy night when he died—a rare occurrence among these solitary and self-reliant men. Yet Miyomoto's initial statements to investigators failed to mention such a visit.

Besides, Miyomoto had a motive for foul play. When San Piedro's Japanese population was interned in 1942, his parents had nearly paid off their mortgage on a seven-acre strawberry farm bought from Heine's parents. Heine's mother, Etta, promptly sold the land to another farmer. Stoic in the face of legalized injustice, Miyomoto and his wife, Hatsue, waited patiently to repurchase the farm when its owner grew old, but instead Heine bought it just before his death.

This is the puzzle: We are led to believe that Miyomoto, who fought with the legendary 442nd Regimental Combat Team in Europe, is an honorable man, although his stern bearing revives anti-Japanese prejudices that nine postwar years have only lightly buried. We are led to believe that distrust of whites—his family and Hatsue's were shipped to the Manzanar camp in California's Owens Valley—and guilt over the German soldiers he has killed make him accept his arrest as fate.

But if Miyomoto *is* innocent, why does a net of circumstantial evidence bind him as tightly as any struggling fish?

Ishmael Chambers covers the trial for San Piedro's newspaper, which he inherited from his father. A former Marine who lost an arm fighting the Japanese at Tarawa, Chambers was Hatsue's high school sweetheart; before her crowning as Strawberry Festival Princess in 1941, they secretly met and necked in a hollow cedar tree. From Manzanar, however, Hatsue wrote denying that she loved him, and in the Pacific he felt his love turn into hate.

By now, love and hate alike have faded. "You went numb, Ishmael," his mother tells him. "And you've stayed numb all these years."

Just as Miyomoto is obsessed with getting back the exact acreage that his family lost, so Chambers sleepwalks through life in the vague hope of reclaiming Hatsue. The contrast between these two obsessions—one conscious and potentially fruitful, the other unconscious and debilitating—is Guterson's main device for leading us into the mystery.

Which is: How can people in a small, tightly knit community be neighbors for generations, even love one another, yet be torn apart by racism?

During the three-day trial, an epochal snowstorm intensifies San Piedro's isolation. Island people, Chambers' father once told him, can't afford to make enemies.

"No one trod easily upon the emotions of another. . . .

This was excellent and poor at the same time—excellent because most people took care, poor because it meant an inbreeding of the spirit, too much held in, regret and silent brooding . . . fear of opening up." The ordeal of the storm, coupled with the shock of Heine's death, forces them to confront the past and cracks the ice of their reserve.

Guterson (whose previous work includes a story collection, *The Country Ahead of Us, the Country Behind*) convinces us that he knows or has researched everything essential here—details of fishing, farming and lawyering; of Coast Guard and coroner's procedures; of Japanese American culture.

With a stately pace and an old-fashioned omniscient voice, he describes the beauty of the Puget Sound islands, the bloody chaos of Tarawa, the desolation of Manzanar and the inner life of every major character.

What he finds there is usually nobility. The only semi-villains are Etta Heine, a couple of FBI men and the anonymous callers who curse Chambers' father for his editorials defending the island's Japanese residents after Pearl Harbor.

Everyone else—Hatsue, Heine's widow, the judge, the sheriff, the aged defense attorney, tough and silent Heine himself—is human and often admirable.

How can so many good people coexist with a major historical evil? The mystery remains even after the puzzle is satisfyingly solved.

Merle Rubin (review date 23 September 1994)

SOURCE: "First Forays Into Novel Writing," in *The Christian Science Monitor,* September 23, 1994, p. 12.

[*In the following excerpt, Rubin offers an unfavorable review of* Snow Falling on Cedars, *stating* "*unfortunately, almost nothing in this novel comes alive.*"]

David Guterson, a contributing editor at Harper's Magazine and author of a story collection and a book on home schooling, would seem to have assembled the right elements for his first novel, *Snow Falling on Cedars,* about the murder trial of a Japanese-American fisherman set on Washington's scenic San Piedro Island in the 1950s. There's the issue of anti-Japanese bigotry, the unique beauty of the setting, and the added drama of a love triangle involving the accused man's lovely Japanese-American wife and a local reporter covering the trial.

Unfortunately, almost nothing in this novel comes alive. The leaden narrative fails to generate the suspense or the human empathy to propel the reader through an accretion of colorless details that would put even the most conscientious juror soundly to sleep. This is a pity, because somewhere in Guterson's overlong novel might have been a poignant story about the enduring, peculiarly human need to seek justice in a chaotic world.

Susan Kenney   (review date 16 October 1994)

SOURCE: "Their Fellow Americans," in *The New York Times Book Review,* October 16, 1994, pp. 12-13.

[*In the review below, Kenney praises Guterson's handling of* Snow Falling on Cedars' *complex narrative.*]

In March 1942, just before the 800 Japanese residents of San Piedro Island in Puget Sound are herded off to a California internment camp, 18-year-old Hatsue Imada gives what seems a naïve response to her mother's description of the deep racial bias that has surfaced in their small, isolated community in the wake of Pearl Harbor: "They don't all hate us," Hatsue says. "You're exaggerating, mother—you know you are. They're not so different from us, you know. Some hate, others don't. It isn't all of them." Hatsue should know; for four years she has been carrying on a clandestine romance with a boy named Ishmael Chambers, son of the local newspaper editor, the two of them meeting at odd moments in a huge old hollow cedar in the forest between their houses. But neither the romance nor the friendship that they have shared since childhood will survive the bitter division brought about by the war.

Successive waves of "wayward souls and eccentrics"— Canadian Englishmen, Scots-Irish, Scandinavians, Germans and most recently Japanese, who came originally as migrant labor to pick berries on the extensive strawberry fields and stayed on, aspiring for their American-born children to own their own plots—have resulted in an ethnically if not economically diverse population on this "island of five thousand damp souls." Their isolation within the spectacularly beautiful but harsh environment has fostered the illusion of community, an illusion abruptly shattered by the advent of World War II.

It's now the first week in December 1954, and snow is falling outside the courtroom in the "rainy, wind-beaten sea village" of Amity Harbor, the island's only town, "downtrodden and mildewed," where Hatsue's husband, Kabuo Miyomoto, is on trial. He is charged with the first-degree murder of Carl Heine, a fellow fisherman, whose body was found early on the morning of Sept. 16, entangled in his own gill net. Now the sole proprietor of his late father's newspaper, Ishmael Chambers, maimed both physically and psychically fighting against the Japanese in the South Pacific, looks out at the storm, hoping it will "snow recklessly and bring to the island the impossible winter purity, so rare and precious, he remembered fondly from his youth."

But the war has taken a terrible toll on the human spirit, and memories of that desperate conflict have exacerbated the racial intolerance subtly present even before the war. This is most clearly evidenced in the testimony of Carl's mother. Etta Heine, whose act in denying the Miyomoto family ownership of their all-but-paid-for seven acres of strawberry fields is revealed as the first link in a decade-long chain of events that has now apparently culminated in Carl's death at the hands of Kabuo.

Though the courtroom setting defines the present in *Snow Falling on Cedars,* David Guterson's finely wrought and flawlessly written first novel (he is the author of a book of short stories and a guide to home schooling), this meticulously drawn legal drama forms only the topmost layer of complex time strata, which Mr. Guterson proceeds to mine assiduously through an intricate series of flashbacks. Thus testimony slides ineluctably from merely verbal recollection into remembered incident into fully realized historical narrative—past events told from the numerous characters' points of view with all the detail and intensity of lives being lived before our very eyes.

The most immediate of these serial flashbacks recounts not only Sheriff Art Moran's investigation of the events surrounding Carl's death during the months preceding the trial, but also the personal histories of the people Moran has seen fit to interview and who are now being called as witnesses. Even minor characters—Ole Jurgensen, present owner of the disputed seven acres; Horace Whaley, the coroner; Carl's wife, Susan Marie; Army Sgt. Victor Maples, who testifies to Kabuo's expertise in kendo, the ancient military art of the samurai warrior—are dramatized well beyond their roles as participants in the trial.

Unlike many recent purveyors of courtroom calisthenics, Mr. Guterson does not stop there. Taking us back nearly a dozen years in both historical and personal time, he depicts the Allied invasion of the South Pacific island of Betio through the eyes of the 19-year-old Ishmael, as, lying gravely wounded on the beach, he sees the rest of his company wiped out, so that like his namesake he alone survives to tell the tale. Almost simultaneously, we accompany Hatsue and her family on their harrowing journey southward to California, and we share their deprivation and humiliation in the notorious internment camp of Manzanar, as well as the irony of Kabuo's turnabout military service fighting Germans in the European theater. Tunneling back even further, we witness Ishamel and Hatsue's secret meetings inside the hollow cedar, the development of their forbidden romance and its subsequent demise, adding emotional depth to their estrangement in the present.

> ***Snow Falling on Cedars* is a densely packed, multifaceted work that sometimes hovers on the verge of digressiveness, but in Mr. Guterson's skilled hands never succumbs to the fragmentation that might well have marred such an ambitious undertaking.**
>
> **—Susan Kenney**

As the exhaustive list of acknowledgments demonstrates, Mr. Guterson has done his homework on everything from autopsies to Zen Buddhism, taking on the enormous risk of crossing boundaries not just of time, but of sex and culture as well. The result is a densely packed, multifaceted work that sometimes hovers on the verge of digressiveness, but in Mr. Guterson's skilled hands never succumbs to the fragmentation that might well have marred such an ambitious undertaking. In fact, so compelling is the narrative that we almost lose sight of the central issue, which is, as the defense attorney Nels Gudmundsson reminds us in his summation, whether Kabuo Miyomoto is on trial for murder—even worse, will be found guilty—simply because he is Japanese.

Simply is not the right word. In a parallel to the case against Kabuo, the reader must sift back through the weight of the whole novel to determine not only whether Kabuo's accusation and trial are in fact racially motivated, but where the responsibility lies if this is in fact the case. Along with the clear manifestations of racism, there is enough evidence of people struggling with their own consciences, speaking out against prejudice, among them Ishmael's parents and Carl Heine's father, to support Hatsue's perception that "it isn't all of them" that hate.

The answer, finally, is equivocal at best. Is Kabuo's refusal to reveal his whereabouts on the fateful night a response to the prejudice he feels will condemn him out of hand, or a self-fulfilling prophecy that is in itself a form of racism? The key, Mr. Guterson seems to say, lies in the possibility of individual action. As Nels Gudmundsson instructs the jury: "Your task as you deliberate together on these proceedings is to insure that you do nothing to yield to a universe in which things go awry by happenstance. Let fate, coincidence and accident conspire; human beings must act on *reason.*"

In a heart-stopping demonstration of this, fate, coincidence and accident do conspire to supply a crucial bit of last-minute evidence, requiring one of the actors in this drama to choose whether to act on reason and compassion, or, by giving in to hatred and anger, let accident rule every corner of the universe. Thus the mystery plays itself out, along with the storm, leaving the human heart to shake free, as the hardiest cedars shake free of snow, of the chill of hatred and war—if it only will.

Nicci Gerrard   (review date 1 January 1995)

SOURCE: "Love for a Cold Climate," in *The Observer,* January 1, 1995, p. 9.

[*In the review below, Gerrard remarks favorably on* Snow Falling on Cedars.]

Urban thrillers are out; the thrills of the far north are now capturing the imagination of readers. E Annie Proulx did it with the award-winning *The Shipping News* set among the lowering skies, blistering winds and foggy, stunning bleakness of Newfoundland. Peter Høeg did it, too, with his best-selling *Miss Smilla's Feeling for Snow,* so full of northern bitterness the wintry recesses of the human spirit. And this year, first-time novelist David Guterson is set to burst in from the cold.

Snow Falling on Cedars, to be published by Bloomsbury in May, is a glorious whodunnit blown through by the elements and full of a seductive sense of grief. It takes place on San Piedro Island (north of Seattle), in the Pacific northwest. It is a finely written courtroom drama set in the

early Fifties. Inside an overheated court, a Japanese-American fisherman stands trial while the snow falls against the windows in thick flakes; outside there are soft drenching rains, deep fogs, the perfume of the cedars. Fishermen work their nets, smoke their pipes. An old love affair works its way back into the present. The shadow of war stains the present. The contrast between the murder that was done so suddenly and the landscape which endures, between hectic ugliness and calm beauty, dominates *Snow Falling on Cedars.*

David Guterson is in his thirties, lives on Puget Sound and is a contributing editor to *Harper's* magazine; he has never written a novel before. He grew up in the landscape of his novel, and says that his love of the place is central to his book. 'The setting for this novel, San Piedro Island, presented itself to me initially in black and white—like old, grainy celluloid, or like a daguerreotype . . . Then one day I happened to look closely at the bark of a cedar tree in the grove just outside my home. Later I placed this bark and the tree in the landscape of the novel and worked outward from there until San Piedro took on sepia and then hand-tinted hues.'

Guterson's novel is Bloomsbury's thriller for the late Nineties: like Scott Turow's extraordinarily successful *Presumed Innocent,* it closes like a fist around the captivated reader. It is riveting about wrongdoing, but set in a mythologised, forever unspoilt landscape of the melancholy past.

Nancy Pate   (review date 12 January 1995)

SOURCE: "Murder Unveils an Island's Secrets," in *Chicago Tribune,* January 12, 1995, p. 4.

[*In the review below, Pate remarks favorably on* Snow Falling on Cedars.]

It is December of 1954, and in the crowded courthouse on the Puget Sound island of San Piedro, a man is on trial for murder. Outside, a winter storm is brewing, the wind from the sea driving the snowflakes inland. Soon, the snow quietly blankets the island—much like the silent prejudice that shrouds its "five thousand damp souls."

The man accused of murdering salmon fisherman Carl Heine is another fisherman, Kabuo Miyomoto. He and Carl went to school together, but then Kabuo, like the 843 people of Japanese descent who lived on San Piedro in March of 1942, was exiled to the Manzanar internment camp. There he married a fellow islander, Hatsue, before joining the U.S. Army and fighting in Europe. After the war, Kabuo and Hatsue returned to San Piedro with dreams of having their own strawberry farm, only to find that Carl's mother, Etta, had foreclosed on the seven acres that Kabuo's late father had been buying.

This loss of the land, and a more recently foiled attempt to buy it again, is supposedly the motive for Kabuo having boarded Carl's fishing boat in the fog, bashed him on the head and pitched him overboard.

Listening to the state present its case, local reporter Ishmael Chambers, who lost an arm in the war, remembers the past. He went to school with Carl and Kabuo. But it was Hatsue who was his childhood friend, his teenage love, the girl he planned to marry in the innocent days before Pearl Harbor.

David Guterson's carefully crafted first novel [*Snow Falling on Cedars*] provides more than just courtroom drama. As the trial proceeds, he essentially puts the island on trial, alternating chapters of testimony and cross-examination with flashbacks—to the idyllic days when Ishmael and Hatsue dug for clams and wandered in the woods, to the deprivations of desolate Manzanar, to the horrors of war, to the investigation into Carl Heine's death. Prejudice takes many forms: the outright venom of Etta Heine; white fishermen joking that they can't tell one Japanese-American from another; islanders passively watching as their neighbors are loaded on ferries in Amity Harbor.

Guterson's prose is controlled and graceful, almost detached. But the accretion of small details gives his story weight. He's particularly good at evoking a sense of place—the yellow dust cloaking the barbed wire and barracks of Manzanar, the strawberry-scented summer on San Piedro, the slippery, kerosene-lanterned deck of a fishing boat at night. Then there is the snow falling on cedars. As the snow buries the island, Guterson's narrative begins to reveal the community's secret heart, the injustice that may break it in two.

Stephen Henighan   (review date 26 May 1995)

SOURCE: "Red and Yellow Necks," in *The Times Literary Supplement,* No. 4808, May 26, 1995, p. 23.

[*In the following review, Henighan discusses characterization and the theme of racism in* Snow Falling on Cedars.]

Set in 1954, on an island near Seattle, *Snow Falling on Cedars* describes the trial of a Japanese-American fisherman accused of murdering a white colleague. When Carl Heine's body is hauled up out of his own net, a wound on his head, combined with circumstantial evidence and racial suspicion, leads to the arrest of his neighbour and boyhood friend Kabuo Miyamoto. The trial's investigation of the tangled relations of the Heines and the Miyamotos reveals the hypocrisies and injustices of an entire era.

During the 1930s, Kabuo's parents, forbidden by law from owing land, sign a contract to buy from the Heines the seven acres on which the Miyamotos cultivate strawberries. The purchase is to be made by instalments that will culminate when Kabuo—American-born and hence permitted to own land—reaches the age of majority. The Miyamotos are only two payments short of proprietorship when the US government responds to the Japanese attack on Pearl Harbor by deporting them, along with all other residents of Japanese ancestry, to internment camps. They return in 1945 to find their land sold to a Scandinavian farmer, their money lost and their claim to a place in the community damaged by the racial hatred of the war years. When Kabuo sees a chance to get the land back, he grabs it; bad judgment exposes him to the charge of murder.

Guterson's handling of the theme of racial bigotry is effec-

tively low-key. In the eyes of the residents of San Piedro Island, there are no hyphenated Americans. Many of the white islanders—nearly all of German or Scandinavian ancestry—are immigrants; some still speak accented English. Yet they are "Americans", while second- and third-generation Japanese-Americans remain "Japs". Guterson portrays most of the islanders as stolidly well-intentioned citizens blind to their own prejudices; only Carl's strident mother conforms to the redneck stereotype.

The trial scenes, narrated with camera-eye impartiality, are dramatic and suspenseful. Cinematic dissolves into past events, mainly during the Second World War, fill in the background. Guterson, a contributing editor to *Harper's Magazine,* displays excellent research skills in reassembling the past. Yet, while every detail in this first novel feels credible, few surprise or astonish. *Snow Falling on Cedars* suffers from a throttling of the imagination by particulars. There is a failure to distinguish between telling detail and information. Guterson's attempt to heighten verisimilitude by listing groups of islanders by name—fishermen whom the reader does not meet, witnesses whose testimony is not recounted, citizens (who never become characters) whose cars have broken down in a snowstorm—reduces the reader's interest in the narrative. The story lacks an intriguing protagonist. Both warrior-like Kabuo and muscular Carl remain brawny enigmas. Ishmael Chambers, the embittered war-amputee journalist who was Kabuo's wife's secret boyfriend in adolescence, is the most fully realized character. Guterson writes evocatively of Ishmael's loneliness and his efforts to come to terms with the destruction of both his body (he loses an arm in battle) and his youthful love for a woman of another race.

The novel's closing words invoke "the chambers of the human heart". But as with the lyricism promised by the title, the heart plays little role in Guterson's dispassionately executed design. None the less, *Snow Falling on Cedars* announces the emergence of a skilful writer.

FURTHER READING

Criticism

Gehrman, Jody Elizabeth. "Hatching a Movie Egg." *The San Francisco Review of Books* 21, No. 1 (January/February 1996): 30.
> Mixed review of *Snow Falling on Cedars.* Gehrman praises the novel's suspense and dramatic tension, but finds its emotional content trite and its characterizations of Japanese Americans uninspired.

Howard, Jennifer. Review of *Snow Falling on Cedars,* by David Guterson. *Book World—The Washington Post* (16 October 1994): 8.
> Favorably reviews Guterson's novel.

Iyer, Pico. "Snowbound." *Time* 144, No. 13 (26 September 1994): 79.
> Praises Guterson's vivid descriptions in *Snow Falling on*

Cedars and calls the novel a "tender examination of fairness and forgiveness."

Streitfeld, David. "Where Winning Isn't Everything." *Book World—The Washington Post* (15 May 1995): B1, B7.
    Comments on the awarding of the PEN/Faulkner Prize to *Snow Falling on Cedars.*

Additional coverage of Guterson's life and career is contained in the following sources published by Gale Research: *Contemporary Authors,* Vol. 132.

Marilyn Hacker
Winter Numbers

Award: Lenore Marshall/*Nation* Poetry Prize

Born in 1942, Hacker is an American poet.

For further information on her life and works, see *CLC*, Volumes 5, 9, 23, and 72.

INTRODUCTION

The often painful exigencies of life and the inevitability of death are the subjects of Hacker's award-winning poetry collection, *Winter Numbers* (1994). Using traditional poetic forms and leavened with a sense of humor, Hacker writes about her daughter, homosexuality, her lovers, bigotry, the Holocaust, the AIDS crisis, and her breast cancer; this final subject is examined in the sequence of poems known as the "Cancer Winter" sonnets. Most critics have applauded the poetic maturity and thematic insight of *Winter Numbers,* noting in particular its structural craftsmanship, word images, and complex, multi-layered themes. As Grace Schulman observed, in *Winter Numbers* Hacker "is, paradoxically, less articulate than before. There are silences . . . , pauses, sudden turnings, juxtapositions that are more internalized, less explicit. She has deepened."

PRINCIPAL WORKS

Presentation Piece (poetry) 1974
Separations (poetry) 1976
Taking Notice (poetry) 1980
Assumptions (poetry) 1985
Love, Death, and the Changing of the Seasons (verse novel) 1986
Going Back to the River (poetry) 1990
The Hang-Glider's Daughter: New and Selected Poems (poetry) 1990
Selected Poems: 1965-1990 (poetry) 1994
Winter Numbers (poetry) 1994

CRITICISM

Grace Schulman   (review date 7 November 1994)

SOURCE: "Chiliastic Sapphic," in *The Nation,* New York, Vol. 259, No. 15, November 7, 1994, pp. 548-52.

[*Schulman is an American educator, writer, poet, and critic. In the following excerpt, she favorably assesses the poetic style and themes of* Winter Numbers.]

Marilyn Hacker's seventh book, ***Winter Numbers,*** strikes me as her strongest to date. From the beginning, she has used ironic antitheses, often yoking disparate entities ("Richter plays Bach. My baby daughter plays / with a Gauloise pack"; **"Geographer"**). Here, to darker ends, she sees discordances in a torn culture.

In **"Chiliastic Sapphics,"** a new poem that links daily activity with world slaughter, the poet sits in her Paris apartment reading of tanks, aircraft carriers and suicide squadrons. Intermittently, she hears the honk of a wedding car, and, on a cassette, nuns singing the Kyrie. In **"Street Scenes II,"** she writes of contradictions in her own neighborhood near the Marais, the Jewish quarter on the right bank:

> The French Jews mostly disappeared
> in forty-two: the Vélodrome d'Hiver,
> Beane-la-Rolande, Drancy—then the trains.
>
> Their street is being frosted to a myth.
> The cowboy-boot boutique rubs doorsills with
> a new shop selling Yemenite cassettes
> and hand-painted Israeli seder plates.

Powerful are her outcries against injustice, in poems whose intensity often is offset by casual titles such as **"August Journal"** or **"Days of 1992,"** their tone often a sardonic veil for despair: *"So, carpe diem*: eat, drink, fuck and write / to glean grace from these chiliastic days?"* (**"Letter to Julie in a New Decade"**). My favorite of these poems is **"Elysian Fields,"** in which the speaker, sitting at a New York cafe whose awning reads **"Champs Elysées of Broadway,"** watches the homeless and remembers her own youthful poverty:

> Five-fifteen
> and I walked east, walked south, walked up my
>   four
> flights. Poor was a neighborhood, was next door,
> is still a door away. The door is mine.
> Outside, the poor work Broadway in the rain.
> The cappuccino drinkers watch them pass
> under the awning from behind the glass.

Central to the new book is "Cancer Winter," a risky, dynamic sequence of crown sonnets. Replete with Hacker's mix of bitterness, irony, humor and praise, it tells of the poet's battle and is, further, a meditation on life, death and survival at the century's end.

A fascinating theme emerges in that poem and in **Winter Numbers** at large—the poet as a Jew in exile. Turning up the darker side of her earlier refrain, "another Jewish Lesbian in France," she cries, "Cell-shocked, I brace to do / what I can, an unimportant exiled Jew" ("Cancer Winter"). Elsewhere, she observes the Jews of Paris, once hidden and deported to the death camps, now seeking roots. The sight of them prods her, a privileged American, to consider her own heritage: her grandparents' grave, whose location is uncertain; the uncut gauze on her mother's tombstone; pogroms suffered by her ancestors; the Holocaust.

That isolation is only a phase of a recurring theme. In her first book, **Presentation Piece,** the word "exile" comes up in a title and in many lines. Early on, she identifies with wanderers of history, myth and literature, using personae of troubadours and metaphors of navigators. Those poems recount voyages into new territory and the dangers of gaining insight in exile. Early and late, she writes of place. She is at home in Regent's Park, in the Luxembourg Gardens and on Canal Street. And yet, familiar as those scenes may be, she is an alien, carrying the weighty baggage—and blessing—of the artist, the intellectual and the Jew. In **Winter Numbers,** realization of her own Jewish roots, and thereby her exile, allows her identification with not only murdered Jews but with Bosnia's raped, El Salvador's gutted and Broadway's homeless.

A problem for writers gifted with acute observation is to avoid intruding on the scenes they have created—that is, to write from the hurricane's eye, rather than report it from outside. Just so, in the new work, Hacker finds herself at the center of a life-and-death struggle, and is, paradoxically, less articulate than before. There are silences in "Cancer Winter"—pauses, sudden turnings, juxtapositions that are more internalized, less explicit. She has deepened.

Like the confessional poets of the fifties and sixties—Lowell, Berryman, Plath, Sexton—Hacker speaks from a self that also embodies the joys and sorrows of others. At the same time, she goes beyond the confessional aesthetic in creating fictions of exile: the wanderers of her early work; later, the lesbian who is worldly but estranged in London, Paris and even in her native New York; and finally, the "unimportant exiled Jew," a contemplative woman who sees "syllables shaped around the darkening day's contours." Through the lens of the stranger, she perceives kindness and cruelty, love and destruction. Now her **Selected Poems** and **Winter Numbers** show her progress clearly in the light of that thematic development. What's more, the books are dazzling.

Matthew Rothschild   (review date January 1995)

SOURCE: A review of *Winter Numbers,* in *The Progressive,* Vol. 59, No. 1, January, 1995, pp. 43-4.

[*In the following excerpt, Rothschild favorably reviews* Winter Numbers.]

This is the seventh volume of poems by Marilyn Hacker, who for the last few years was the editor—and a brilliant one at that—of *The Kenyon Review.* (It was she who brought Campo to my attention). But last summer she was cashiered, she told *The Advocate,* suspecting that her lesbian orientation and radical politics were too much for that tightly buttoned magazine—another brave moment in publishing.

Death stalks this book. The opening long poem, **"Against Elegies,"** sets the tone from the very first lines:

> James has cancer. Catherine has cancer.
> Melvin has AIDS.
> Whom will I call, and get no answer?

Halfway through the poem, Hacker mentions "the day I meet / the lump in my breast," and her cancer will return throughout the book. Intensely personal, this opening poem and others in the collection also reflect on the crimes of this century,

> in which we made death humanly obscene
> Soweto El Salvador Kurdistan
> Armenia Shatila Baghdad Hanoi
> Auschwitz. Each one, unique as our lives are,
> taints what's left with complicity,
> makes everyone living a survivor
> who will, or won't bear witness for the dead.

In **"Elysian Fields,"** she points out the gap between rich and poor in America. Set in an upscale café in Manhattan, the poem describes how "cappuccino drinkers" watch the poor from the comfort of the coffee house.

Lush with rhymes and modified traditional forms, Hacker's poetry echoes and reverberates. And her sense of humor is refined, as in the sendoff she gives her students in **"Groves of Academe,"** who want to write poems for *Vanity Fair.* Or take this throwaway update of Yeats: "The Left lacks all conviction, and the Right—capitalism with a human face?"

Hacker writes tenderly of her lesbian lovers, and of her daughter, now grown. But it is the specter of death that lends this work its unforgettable power. As a Jew who lives part-time in Paris, her "chosen diaspora," Hacker writes hauntingly of the Holocaust. As a lesbian who lives part-time in America, Hacker writes with tremendous force about bigotry, AIDS, and breast cancer.

The last section of the book, "Cancer Winter," contains three poems, and they are among the most draining I've ever read. In **"Year's End,"** she mourns:

> Men and women, mortally wounded where we
> love and nourish, dying at thirty, forty,
> fifty, not on barricades, but in beds of
> unfulfilled promise.

And in the final poem, **"August Journal,"** she acknowledges that "My future, though, is coming toward me fast / from elsewhere, and I cannot know where from." She concludes, quietly, beautifully:

> All I can know is the expanding moment,
> present, infinitesimal, infinite,
> in which the late sun enters without comment
> eight different sets of windows opposite.

Lawrence Joseph   (review date February 1995)

SOURCE: "A Formal Life: Marilyn Hacker's Deep Structure," in *VLS,* No. 132, February, 1995, p. 25.

[*In the following excerpt, Joseph favorably reviews* Winter Numbers, *focusing on the "Cancer Winter" sonnets.*]

[In Hacker's new book, ***Winter Numbers***], the central motifs of her poetry—the inner and outer furies of the physical world, and the ways in which poetry embodies them—revolve around, simultaneously, the destruction of one's own body and that of the body politic. Hacker's voices are more mellifluously startling and alive than ever. Positing that "sound more than sense determines words I choose, / invention mutes intention," the book's dialogical contentions take you right in. Hacker has been doing this so well, and for so long, that you hardly realize what you're reading is major work. Especially powerful is the sonnet sequence, "Cancer Winter"—"Syllables shaped around the darkening day's / contours." The textured compression of physical detail, the sensual world loved down to its essential form in language—and note the rhyme:

> All I can know is the expanding moment,
> present, infinitesimal, infinite,
> in which the late sun enters without comment
> eight different sets of windows opposite.

"Words crystallize despite our lives," the poet writes. That's only partly true. In this expanding social moment, in the infinitely challenging human world of the poem, Hacker's poems crystallize our lives, too.

David Kirby   (review date 12 March 1995)

SOURCE: "Glad-Handing Her Way Through the World," in *The New York Times Book Review,* March 12, 1995, pp. 6-7.

[*In the following excerpt, Kirby favorably assesses* Winter Numbers, *noting Hacker's "fluid" poetic style and her ability to handle ideas about death and middle age.*]

The history of recent literature is the history of the phrase "Only connect." Writers and readers have taken these words from E. M. Forster's *Howards End* as an exhortation, with "only" meaning "merely" or perhaps "exclusively." But the phrase can also be read ironically, despairingly, even interrogatively, with a rising borscht belt intonation, so that "Only connect?" becomes "Are you kidding me?"

At a time when so many writers seem to be measuring life from a considerable remove, it is invigorating to watch Marilyn Hacker glad-handing her way through the world with a warm facility. And a formalism so colloquial as to undo any readerly stereotypes. Indeed, Ms. Hacker is the best friend of anyone trying to learn the writing of formal verse. There are no ticktock rhymes in her work; her use of enjambment, slant rhyme and metrical variation produces a line so lissome and fluid that, once engaged, the reader glides on as swiftly as a child in a water slide. . . .

As the title of Ms. Hacker's latest book suggests, ***Winter Numbers*** takes both writer and reader into middle age and the shadows that fall across every life. "Cancer Winter," for example, is the account of her own struggle with the disease. An aptly named poem, **"Against Elegies,"** chronicles deaths both personal and impersonal, though the dying are people whose imminent extinctions are more incidental to their lives than central. One, Lidia, for example, gave up all her vices only to find out she had got AIDS from her husband:

> And Lidia, where's she
> who got her act so clean
> of rum and Salem Filters and cocaine
> after her passing husband passed it on?
> As soon as she knew
> she phoned and told her mother she had AIDS
> but no, she wouldn't come back to San Juan.
> Sipping Café con leche with dessert,
> in a blue robe, thick hair in braids,
> she beamed: her life was on the right
> track, now. But the cysts hurt
> too much to sleep through the night.

Once again Ms. Hacker's supple formalism gives backbone to ideas and images that might overwhelm a lesser poet, and once again one sees how good this poet is, so good that anyone else trying to do what she does would only look foolish.

Additional coverage of Hacker's life and career is contained in the following sources published by Gale Research: *Contemporary Authors,* Vols. 77-80, rev. ed.; *Contemporary Literary Criticism,* Vols. 5, 9, 23, 72; and *Dictionary of Literary Biography,* Vol. 120.

Seamus Heaney
Nobel Prize in Literature

(Full name Seamus Justin Heaney) Born in 1939, Heaney is an Irish poet, critic, essayist, translator, and editor.

For further information on Heaney's life and career, see *CLC,* Volumes 5, 7, 14, 25, 37, and 74.

INTRODUCTION

Widely considered Ireland's most accomplished contemporary poet, Heaney was awarded the Nobel Prize for what the Swedish Academy proclaimed his "works of lyrical beauty and ethical depth, which exalt everyday miracles and the living past." In his works, Heaney often considers the role and responsibility a poet should play in society, exploring themes of self-discovery and spiritual growth and addressing political and cultural issues related to Irish history. His poetry is characterized by sensuous language, sexual metaphors, and nature imagery. Many critics agree with Robert Lowell's assessment of him as "the greatest Irish poet since Yeats."

Biographical Information

The eldest of nine children, Heaney was raised a Roman Catholic in Mossbawn, County Derry, a rural community in Northern Ireland. He once described himself as one of a group of Catholics in Northern Ireland who "emerged from a hidden, a buried life and entered the realm of education." At age eleven, Heaney left his family's farm to study at Saint Columb's College in Londonderry, Northern Ireland, where he had received a scholarship. In 1957 he attended Queen's University in Belfast, where he was introduced to Irish, American, and English literature and was particularly influenced by such poets as Ted Hughes, Patrick Kavanagh, and Robert Frost, whose poetry was significantly informed by their childhood experiences. While in college, Heaney contributed poems to university literary magazines under the pseudonym Incertus. After graduating from Queen's University with a first-class honors degree in English language and literature and a teaching certificate, he held positions as a secondary school teacher and later returned to Queen's University as a lecturer. During this time he also established himself as a prominent literary figure with the publication in 1966 of *Death of a Naturalist,* his first major volume of poetry. As a Catholic living in Belfast when fighting erupted between Protestants and Catholics in 1969, Heaney took a personal interest in Ireland's social and political unrest, and he began to address the causes and effects of violence in his poetry. In 1972 Heaney moved from Belfast to a cottage outside Dublin and began writing full time. He returned

to teaching in 1975 as head of the English department at Caryfort College in Dublin. Heaney has traveled frequently to the United States to give poetry readings and, from 1989 to 1994, he served as a professor of poetry at Oxford and was appointed Boylston Professor of Rhetoric and Oratory at Harvard University.

Major Works

Heaney's earliest works evince sensuous memories associated with nature and with his childhood on his family's farm. In such poems as "Digging," from *Death of a Naturalist,* Heaney evokes the Irish countryside and comments on the care and skill with which his father and ancestors farmed the land. Nature is also a prominent theme in his next volume, *Door into the Dark* (1969) in which several poems focus on the work of rural laborers. Critics have praised the poem "Undine," for example, in which

Heaney describes the process of agricultural irrigation in the context of myth and sexuality. Much of Heaney's poetry addresses the history of social unrest in Northern Ireland and considers the relevance of poetry in the face of violence and political upheaval. Included in his collections *Wintering Out* (1972) and *North* (1975), for example, are a series of "bog poems" that were inspired by the archaeological excavation of Irish peat bogs containing preserved human bodies that had been ritually slaughtered during the Iron Age. Heaney depicts the victims of such ancient pagan rites as symbolic of the bloodshed caused by contemporary violence in Ireland. In such poems as "Ocean's Love to Ireland" and "Act of Union," Heaney portrays the English colonization of Ireland as an act of violent sexual conquest. Some critics believe that Heaney's most effective poetry emphasizes personal themes of self-determination and poetic imagination. While many of the poems in *Field Work* (1979)—including such elegies as "The Strand at Lough Beg," "A Post-Card from North Antrim," and "Casualty"—continue to address the unrest in Northern Ireland, they incorporate a personal tone as Heaney depicts the loss of friends and relatives to the violence. Irish history and myth are frequently incorporated in Heaney's works, including his prose poem *Sweeney Astray* (1984), which is based on the medieval Irish tale of King Sweeney, who was transformed from a warrior-king into a bird as the result of a curse. Some critics have interpreted the figure of King Sweeney as a representation of the artist torn between imaginative freedom and the constraints of religious, political, and domestic obligations, reflecting Heaney's concern with the role of the poet in society. Irish history is also an important motif in a sequence of allegorical poems entitled "Station Island," included in his 1984 collection of the same name. Patterned after Dante's *Commedia* (c.1307-c.1321; *Divine Comedy*) the sequence portrays a three-day spiritual pilgrimage undertaken by Irish Catholics to Station Island. While on the island, the narrator encounters the souls of dead acquaintances and Irish literary figures, who inspire him to reflect on his life and art. Critics have also praised the privately emotional tone of *The Haw Lantern* (1987), a collection that includes parables of Irish life and a series of poems entitled "Clearances" in which Heaney explores memories of his relationship with his mother. In such poems as "From the Republic of Conscience" and "From the Canton of Expectation," he meditates on spirituality in the context of a menacing political climate. *Seeing Things* (1991) also diverges from Heaney's previous emphasis on politics and civic responsibility, returning to the autobiographical themes of childhood experience and Irish community ritual. Feelings of loss and yearning are prominent motifs in the collection, as many poems evoke celebratory images of Heaney's deceased father, who appears frequently throughout the volume. Critics have cited "Squarings," a sequence comprising four sections each containing twelve twelve-line poems, as exemplary of Heaney's stylistic and technical virtuosity. Although some commentators have faulted *Seeing Things* for its presentation of elusive images and themes that eschew critical interpretation, many have praised the volume for its imaginative qualities and its focus on visionary transcendence experienced through ordinary life events.

Critical Response

Critical response to Heaney's work has been predominately positive and enthusiastic. Comparisons between his work and that of other Irish writers—William Butler Yeats in particular—but also James Joyce and Samuel Beckett have proliferated. Harold Bloom called Heaney's poem "The Harvest Bow," which praises marriage, "a perfect lyric." And John Gross has stated that Heaney "has all the primary gifts of a poet, and they are gifts put at the service of a constant meditation on primary themes, on nature and history and moral choice."

PRINCIPAL WORKS

Eleven Poems (poetry) 1965

Death of a Naturalist (poetry) 1966

Room to Rhyme [with Dairo Hammond and Michael Longley] (poetry) 1968

Door into the Dark (poetry) 1969

A Lough Neagh Sequence (poetry) 1969

Boy Driving His Father to Confession (poetry) 1970

Night Drive (poetry) 1970

Land (poetry) 1971

Servant Boy (poetry) 1971

Wintering Out (poetry) 1972

Bog Poems (poetry) 1975

Fire i' the Flint: Reflections on the Poetry of Gerard Manley Hopkins (criticism) 1975

North (poetry) 1975

Stations (poetry) 1975

In Their Element: A Selection of Poems [with Derek Mahon] (poetry) 1977

After Summer (poetry) 1978

The Making of a Music: Reflections on the Poetry of Wordsworth and Yeats (criticism) 1978

Robert Lowell: A Memorial Address and Elegy (nonfiction) 1978

Field Work (poetry) 1979

Hedge School: Sonnets from Glanmore (poetry) 1979

Ugolino (poetry) 1979

Poems: 1965-1975 (poetry) 1980; also published as *Selected Poems 1965-1975*, 1980

Preoccupations: Selected Prose 1968-1978 (essays) 1980

Sweeney Praises the Trees (poetry) 1981

An Open Letter (poetry) 1983

Hailstones (poetry) 1984

Station Island (poetry) 1984

Sweeney Astray: A Version from the Irish [translator and adaptor] (poetry and prose) 1984

Verses for a Fordham Commencement (poetry) 1984

From the Republic of Conscience (poetry) 1985

The Haw Lantern (poetry) 1987

The Government of the Tongue: The 1986 T. S. Eliot Memorial Lectures, and Other Critical Writings (essays) 1988; also published as *The Government of the Tongue: Selected Prose, 1978-1987*, 1988

OVERVIEWS

Mary Kinzie   (essay date Fall 1988)

SOURCE: "Deeper than Declared: On Seamus Heaney," in *Salmagundi,* No. 80, Fall, 1988, pp. 22-57.

[*Kinzie is an American poet, critic, and educator. In the following excerpt, she analyzes the imagery and syntax of Heaney's poetry, focusing on the epic poem, "Station Island."*]

"Was there a 'misalliance,' " asks Seamus Heaney of Robert Lowell, "between the gift and the work it was harnessed to do?" [see ***Preoccupations: Selected Prose 1968-1978***]. To ask the question is to suggest an affirmative reply: The vivid occasion in Lowell was ever straining toward meditation, the verbal breakdowns toward a state of Horatian health (and, one could say, vice versa). Heaney's sensitivity to this "misalliance" is revealing, since he, too, the best known poet to come out of Ireland since Yeats, hankers after a species of court dress and bardic intonation, for which almost everything in his unconscious music automatically disqualifies him. So, too, do Heaney's authentic gifts as a chronicler of the rough, marshy landscapes and family farms of Ulster ill prepare him to write the large-scale politico-religious work. Yet the misalliance is not without its hard-won triumphs.

"Station Island" is a curious poetic sequence, poignant in parts, powerful in others, but disjointed and bottled up, as if the poet could not commit himself to its deeper drift. Nor is emotion liberated by the liberal confidentiality of some of the poems. Feeling is still largely numbed with remorse, and the poems float in loose, nominal relation to one another despite Heaney's almost anxious reverence for nets and skeins of meaning. Allusions to more thoroughgoing systems of belief than his own are constantly made. Dante is present, both in the nagging background of current politics and in the variable terza rima of four of the twelve poems (the triplets of the fine poem about the young priest are near enough the terza rima norm to serve as a distant fifth); and Dante's presence is also felt in the grotesquerie of the premise that the dead masters and friends and political victims—those violently dead still bearing the marks of their deaths on their bodies—can come forward to speak with Heaney. But he does not judge, or assign his dead to circles, or give them activities that measure their sins, their expiation, or their blessedness. The afterlife is a convenient fiction, and Dante's influence a matter of shards, since his minor premise is honored, that the living may speak with the dead, but not his

theism, let alone his theology. [In a Footnote, Kinzie continues: "*Field Work* is also haunted by Dante. The two longest poems are the Dante translation called **'Ugolino'** and **'The Strand at Lough Beg,'** which gives us a new 'reading' of Vergil's tender washing of Dante's face with his hands dipped in dew from the grass near the inexhaustible reeds, as Heaney pictures bathing his murdered cousin in the moss strikingly pictured as 'Fine as a drizzle out of a low cloud.' A third poem, **'An Afterwards,'** is parodically based on Dante (the poet's wife consigns all poets to hell). There are three further allusions in the volume; the one in **'Leavings'** lightly captures the whole Dantean feeling of fatedness—in the crime, the penance, and the instigating personality—as Heaney wonders how Thomas Cromwell will be punished for the crime of smashing the idols, replacing stained glass in all the chapels of England with clear panes: 'Which circle does he tread, / scalding on cobbles, / each one a broken statue's head?' "]

Similarly, Heaney is pursuing a series of expiatory "stations" traditionally aimed at placing the moral weaknesses of the "pilgrim" under avid, pious attack. But although this pilgrim regrets his failings, primarily those that stem from apolitical indifference or disengagement, he is not interested in examining the flawed instrument. He does not aim to school the ego, nor to pacify the will. His penitential guise is almost prideful, as if to prove Johnson's dictum that "All censure of a man's self is oblique praise. It is in order to show how much he can spare."

Finally, Heaney's **"Station Island"** poems obsessively fasten on the idea of mortality, without seriously questioning its meaning. Whenever ultimate meaning is required, Poetry automatically steps in. Indeed, it is hygienically described, in a passage where putrefaction and decay are celebrated, as the process of cleaning out life's wounds as by the action of maggots: "another life that cleans our element." But this purifying role of verse is asserted rather than argued. There is some disappointment, therefore, when we catch the notes of disembodied reverence with which the poet-pilgrim "faces into" his stations. For he does not address the redemptive function of this other ritual, either. The nearest he comes to acknowledging the purpose of the Station Island retreat occurs in the young missionary's elliptical suggestion that Heaney must be here on the Island not to humble himself to God but to bid God farewell. " 'What possessed you?' " the dead priest asks the poet, his grammar twisting as his thought worms through:

> '. . . all this you were clear of you walked into
> over again. And the god has, as they say, withdrawn.
>
> What are you doing, going through these motions?
> Unless . . . Unless . . . ' Again he was short of breath
> and his whole fevered body yellowed and shook.
>
> 'Unless you are here taking the last look.'
>
> **("Station Island," IV)**

Nowhere else in the sequence do we find God even nostalgically brought in. Not that the poems lack their Satanic figures. A little-known writer named William Carleton, Protestant convert, angry, bitter, blustering, is one, who undertakes the rough, stressed Anglo-Saxon attitudes familiar from Heaney's earlier volumes:

> hard-mouthed Ribbonmen and Orange bigots
> made me into the old fork-tongued turncoat
> who mucked the byre of their politics.

Another minor demon is the tinker Simon Sweeney, who first appears with a bow-saw in his arms "held / stiffly up like a lyre," a gesture which should betoken blessing. But he shows his truer form when he reminds the poet of the latter's childhood fear of him in a simile that fairly shudders with the aversion his person inspired. When

> woodsmoke sharpened air
> or ditches rustled
> you sensed my trail there
> as if it had been sprayed.

Yet in the last six stanzas of this poem, which opens the **"Station Island"** suite, Heaney succumbs to the vaporous apparitions of shawled women moving in wet fields through the rags of moisture that make up this poet's atmospheric element. The women's chaunt convokes his dead in a "loosed congregation." We lose sight of the "old Sabbath-breaker"; a last chaffing command to " 'Stay clear of all processions!' " is Simon Sweeney's only attempt to shed light on his encounter with the poet, whose mind he can read. This bending of the poems' design under the weight of tangent and digression is a particular mark of the **"Station Island"** poems, showing how delicate a task of convocation Heaney has set himself.

Demonic too are the shadowy assassins, both Protestant and Catholic, whose victims confront Heaney with their accusing wounds. In fact, one might conjecture that his real demons are these self-accusations emanating from the world where others act and die. Even his style grows demonic in its exorbitance:

> Strange polyp floated like a huge corrupt
> Magnolia bloom, surreal as a shed breast,
> My softly awash and blanching self-disgust.

Self-disgust has a political cast, cowardice a wilting reminder of public reticence. "Forgive," he asks, "my timid circumspect involvement"; "I hate how quick I was to know my place." The affairs of Ulster (the older name of Northern Ireland that encodes the indigenous heroic tradition) press upon Seamus Heaney as matters of conscience, but no more strongly than it appears they have been pressed upon him by his more engaged readers. And **"Station Island"** was to have been the poem where he would "be facing the North and getting shut of it" [see Frances X. Clines, interview with Seamus Heaney, *The New York Times Magazine* (13 March 1983), p. 99]. Yet he draws a veil of inconclusive poignancy over the IRA killer whose whole life was lived in the context of weapons and guerrilla war. In a sleeping vision framed in elegant, moody pentameter whose unobtrusive and slant rhymes trace an equally unobtrusive sonnet pattern, Heaney sees the dead man laid out, smells the very mildew

> From the byre loft where he watched and hid
> From fields his draped coffin would raft through.

Unquiet soul, they should have buried you
In the bog where you threw your first grenade,
Where only helicopters and curlews
Make their maimed music, and sphagnum moss
Could teach you its medicinal repose.

(**"Station Island,"** IX)

Would his soul thereafter begin to be healed of its rancors, absolved of its crimes? Or would the invading helicopters, their blades slapping the air, drown even the interred one in their looming modern racket? The questions can be answered only by recognizing, first, how tempered the diction is, smoothing the roughness of *helicopters* by matching its consonants with a semantically more muffled lexicon whose sounds are metallic, but not whose meanings (*unquiet, coffin, curlews*), just as *grenade* is softened down among the wet places of *bog* and *sphagnum*. Next one would note how the metaphor of ghostly palimpsest lays future over past with an air of visionary mourning; the temporal carrier is the rural landscape, where the underground soldier grew up, and held out: "the byre loft where he watched and hid / From fields his draped coffin would raft through." The uncommon verb *raft* suggests not only the watery gliding of the bier but also the kindred sluicing audible in more common past participles like *reft* (bereft) and *rift*, both of which owe something to *tearing*, especially as extended to the heart.

Finally, one should remark how the natural world ironically opens to accept even insoluble paradoxes, burning them down to harmonies, recasting itself out of the contraries. The helicopters' cacophony is literally subdued to the level of the curlews' cries, the bog swallows the sound of the grenade, silence falls into the vacuum torn out by combat: " 'an ambush / Stillness I felt safe in settled around me.' " At times, it appears the only constant in Heaney's world is the natural landscape, moist, overcast, luxuriant, which lends itself to the individual's terms without infringing on its own enormities. In the moving elegy on Barney Murphy that forms the major part of **"Station Island,"** V (Murphy was Heaney's schoolmaster, whose school was razed to reclaim the land for farming), the old master's asthmatic breath "rushed the air softly as scythes in his lost meadows." The classical and biblical seriousness of the diction gives authority to the kindly overlap of natural with human processes. In a harsher style, the poor insurgent in IX speaks of his spiritual decay in somatic terms equally magnetized by the rural milieu; his tropes go back to Heaney's bog folk whose mummification in the peat was quite literal:

> 'My brain dried like spread turf, my stomach
> Shrank to a cinder and tightened and cracked.
> Often I was dogs on my own track
> Of blood on wet grass that I could have licked.'

Here is an overlay of a different sort, as the thirsty, starving, bleeding outlaw changes places with his ravenous trackers—yet another example of nature's polymorphous sway. And in more daring elegiac fashion, the most tawdry items of contemporary technology (car, helicopter, gun, bomb, grenade) are subsumed by the seasonal-natural machine. The first part of **"Station Island,"** IX can stand with **"The Tollund Man," "Funeral Rights,"** and **"Kinship"**; with the two strong laments in *Field Work,* **"The Toome Road"** and **"The Strand at Lough Beg"**; and, from the more recent volume, with **"The First Flight"** and the superbly ironic **"Sandstone Keepsake,"** as one of Seamus Heaney's finest politically oriented works.

But the rest of the poem raises the spectre of ambivalence on a second front as well. The entire last half, from the third sonnet to the fifth, makes no reference to the young warrior, but instead breaks into a medley of dream-anguishes with three different tenors and three different styles. First the dream shows the muddy flood of self-disgust (the polyp-breast image, quoted earlier), which is followed by a hiatus during which his heart revives, only to be oppressed by the tangential memory, still within the dream, of an old brass trumpet Heaney found in a barn but was too self-effacing to take ("a mystery / I shied from then for I thought such trove beyond me"—his boyhood persona is almost too good to be true). Then the last sonnet/paragraph, strewn with self-castigations, closes with the abrupt attempt, by means of a shorthand epiphany, to haul the whole complex weight of the preceding 70 lines under a dome of shining sweetness:

> 'I hate how quick I was to know my place.
> I hate where I was born, hate everything
> That made me biddable and unforthcoming,'
> I mouthed at my half-composed face
> In the shaving mirror, like somebody
> Drunk in the bathroom during a party,
> Lulled and repelled by his own reflection.
> As if the cairnstone could defy the cairn.
> As if the eddy could reform the pool.
> As if a stone swirled under a cascade,
> Eroded and eroding in its bed,
> Could grind itself down to a different core.
> Then I thought of the tribe whose dances never
>   fail
> For they keep dancing till they sight the deer.

To dance until something miraculous happens in the world, or until one drops, is a brave extreme to undergo, but I do not know that Heaney proposes to do this (he merely "thought of " it). Nor do I see the immediate link between the deer-invocation and the need to reform a weak character. There is a little casuistry under the attractive imagery of cascade and woodland dance, just as there is a little evasion in the stylishly flat self-confrontation in the shaving mirror, when Heaney at once mocks and approves his own chagrin. The question of responsibility is deflected, to one side determinism ("As if a cairnstone could defy the cairn"), to the other guilt ("Lulled and repelled by his own reflection").

Although they do not readily imply or support one another, the two halves of this poem do have the dim, infernal relation of photograph to negative. And perhaps what makes the young guerrilla of the first two sonnets attractive to Heaney is his complete lack of self-pity: His self-regard is of a cosmic sort, like the Croppies' of 1798: "The hillside blushed, soaked in our broken wave" [**"Requiem for the Croppies,"** *Door into the Dark* (1969)]. The two Irishmen touch by virtue of their temperamental exclusions. The barn where Heaney found the brass trumpet eerily reminds us of the bog where the other boy threw his

first grenade, one an object of white magic and sentimentality, the other of black magic and damnation. The polyp of self-disgust that luxuriates in sexual folds in the second half is the metaphoric and stylistic and, indeed, spiritual 'positive' of that dried-out brain and stomach tight as a cinder with which the poem strongly begins. It is as if action (dark, desiccated) were being opposed to thought (glistening and spongy).

But such oppositions are perhaps too beguiling in their dialectical neatness; they tend to smother thought. Had Heaney *not* known his place, for example (and who knows what conditions would have conspired in such a character change?), had he been more forthcoming, less docile ("biddable"), would he have joined the IRA and eschewed poetry? What, then? He hints, I think unconvincingly, that he might have been readier to make something of his tribal knowledge, to act or sympathize, independent of violent cadres—to dance—until he saw justice done. Although this might not have insured that justice was done, it would, the parable implies, have given him an easier conscience. Collaterally, the ambivalences that prompt such cutting of corners in the realm of self-knowledge rather mar this cumbersome second group of sonnets.

The same confrontation between beauty of thought and efficacy of deed—perfection of the work or of the life—occurs in the second half of another **"Station Island"** poem devoted to Heaney's cousin Colum McCartney, arbitrarily killed by Protestants. A kind youth who shied away even from the spent cartridges left by hunters, he accuses the poet of manipulating "artistic tact" until it becomes "evasion." He claims that his cousin, in his splendid elegy in *Field Work,* **"The Strand at Lough Beg,"**

> '. . . whitewashed ugliness and drew
> the lovely blinds of the *Purgatorio*
> and saccharined my death with morning dew.'

The deprecatory judgment is half-hearted: It is undercut by Heaney's style. The beauty for which he has his dead cousin castigate him irrepressibly enters the rhetoric and the stately prosody of the condemnation itself. Reminiscent of Robert Lowell's dismissal of his high rhetorical mode in "The Dolphin" as mere "set-piece, set-piece," McCartney's speech in **"Station Island,"** VIII is an attempt on the poet's part to devalue all fine speech, for it is not true grief. Then, as if to prove that he is not putting himself above his own experience, Heaney as the pilgrim lets his guard down and invites into the poem a note of whining and a flawed prosaism. When McCartney claims that even strangers showed more agitation than his cousin did, the poet replies in dialogue made doubly brittle by the recuperated grand cadences of the second pair of lines:

> 'But they were getting crisis
> first-hand, Colum, they had happened in on
> live sectarian assassination.
> I was dumb, encountering what was destined.'

Heaney countenances this patent ineptitude of emotion, and of style, in an effort to absolve himself of the finished flourish of his earlier elegy and, by "standing up for life against art, implicitly defend [ ] the bulk and flux of the less finished work."

117

Like Lowell, whom he thus describes, Heaney also has phases in which he would commit himself to the fragmentary over the finished. For anything more than fragments will falsify the brokenness and insolubility of experience—and do so in a way that amounts to complicity with the forces of repression, inactivity, and decay. (The only poem acceptable to the Left may eventually be the completely ill-written and inchoate one. Memory, tradition, and especially the literary memory, are suspect: Over a dismantled lobster in **"Away from It All,"** another poem of postprandial funk like the **"Oysters"** of *Field Work,* "quotations start to rise / / like rehearsed alibis.") Heaney is clearly ambivalent toward the grand modes and the traditional genres like elegy that permit breadth and sweep of utterance, because there one speaks from a stable position that can risk general statements, uphold with moderate confidence social and moral standards, relish aesthetic design, and reside in a context of literary history, hence comfortably make allusions. Ironically, it is these modes, designed to permit the poet to say what is possible on the categorically impossible occasions (of war, death, love, awe), which now indict the writer of conservatism. "The political implications of lyric art are quite reactionary," Heaney says. "You are saying to people, 'Everything's all right'" [Clines interview, p. 104].

But even in the beginning of Seamus Heaney's own lyric art, everything was not, in this sense, all right. His poems are not straightforward heterocosms, attentive solely to their own purity of form and feeling. Even when most absorbed in the lyrical moment, he has often been impelled to thicken and adulterate the brew. To label this impulse with political motives is to ignore the longstanding urge to roughen, which early on had personal rather than chauvinist motives. Heaney has always been drawn two ways, toward high rhetoric and toward low, toward expansive meditation and toward crippled epigram, toward standard speech and dialect. His poetry grounds itself in dichotomy—which has a decidedly unbalancing effect on the verse, like that of an unpaved track on a fragile carriage—yet the unbalancing itself falls pleasingly on his ear. This is a sign of the authenticity of his divided attention, torn between the attitudes of adult reason and childlike genius, between the sounds of English and of Irish speech, the claims of tradition and the individual psychology, and, as the well-known pair of poems in *North* embodies the dichotomy, between the figures of Hercules and Antaeus.

In one of the most splendid examples of poetic criticism by any writer since Eliot, Heaney in his prose collection *Preoccupations* constructs elegant and persuasive tension-emblems to elucidate the work of his forbears and contemporaries. Yeats and Wordsworth beautifully offset one another as examples of the combative and the entranced poet. Hopkins is countered by Keats, Dylan Thomas, even Blake, as if, whatever the angle he is seen from, Hopkins cannot help sounding artificial—however seductive one finds the artifice, as Heaney admits that he does. He opposes allegory to symbol as waking to sleeping consciousness, fire and flint to oozing matrix, Christian man to natural man, Latin to Celtic thinking, and the polysyllable to the monosyllable. To this roster of paired antinomies from the pages of *Preoccupations,* we can add:

reason	versus	feeling
assertion		suggestion
discourse		pre-verbal intimation
acting out		listening in
concept		imagination
proposition		incantation
England		Ireland
adult		child
consonants		vowels
male		female
the arched back		the copious lap (of language)
disciplina		*pagus*
library		lair
literacy (intellect)		illiteracy (instinct)
Patrick		Oisin
empire		local piety
flint		ooze
poem as conductor		poem as crucible
honeycomb		swarm
craft (tradition)		technique (individual)

"Poetry of any power," he writes in his essay on Irish nature poetry, "is always deeper than its declared meaning." According to the pattern of contraries above, the "declared meaning" of any work would be opposed to something like its "whispered meaning"—something hummed under the breath that makes the passage of the breath itself more touchingly apparent. For it is the gift of the undeclared and undeclarative poetic instinct to hear *how* it will say as the precondition to *what.*

Note that it is the author who identifies himself primarily with a fluent, feminine, pre-conscious, oozing, yielding mentality who is responsible for this tight trellis of opposing categories. I don't think this is unusual. Like many who live in tempo with the deeps (symbol, instinct, ooze, crucible), Heaney also thinks according to a few old dualisms collapsed into each other like a honeycomb, with surprisingly little intellectual resistance. Although not all the left- and right-hand items match up—for example, Patrick was not English, incantation is not audition—nevertheless, Catholicism shares with Protestantism a rigor which Oisin the natural man opposes: The convinced pagan recoils at the dank chill of *disciplina.* And in the context of the strong, active, masculine traits of acting-out and proposition-making, the right-hand items incantation and listening-in share the quality of receptive patience. Nor is Irish a vowel-oriented language; Heaney remarks that the Ulster accent is especially consonantal and Hopkinsian. Yet that fluidity, which the vowel requires the consonant to shape and to bound, is like the naive and passive aspects of the national character, which the English were so ruthless in exploiting. There is no doubt that the left-hand column is construed pejoratively.

So the Englishman in Heaney, the well-read, discursive, persuasive if not imperious and form-loving poet—the one who approved the antinomies on the list, the one who makes elegies and sonnets, whose poems are sharp and edged and inter-nested with meaning—is constantly being ambushed (to his own applause) by the woodkern who is all sound irrespective of sense, whose words are runes, magical but serrated, who was just born, hence remembers the oceanic feeling that links him with the ages prior to, or ignorant of, writing.

So which self is it who writes, in **"Old Pewter"** (*Station Island*):

> Glimmerings are what the soul's composed of,
> Fogged-up challenges, far conscience-glitters
> and hang-dog, half-truth earnests of true love?

The theme of evanescent soul-stuff and the pile-up of nonce-phrases could almost suggest Robert Browning, although the third line would then not come on us so sharply; Browning was more rangy and circumspect about his soft climaxes. Heaney has a similar way of secreting qualities, layer upon deeply embroidered layer, in the line. Now that his lines are so much longer than they were in *North,* the layering of descriptive design may sound more Victorian than it once did. Or which kind of poem is it—the poem that commands and transmits, or the poem that swarms and bubbles—in which the poet fondly relishes the mixed series that abound in *Station Island:* "Granite is jaggy, salty, punitive / / and exacting"; a woman's low neckline is "inviolable and affronting"; Thomas Hardy has a "ghost life" that is "unperturbed, reliable"; morning has a "distancing, inviolate expanse"? Or consider the simply baffling reference to "sexprimed and unfurtherable mosstalk." Clearly, these packed polysyllabic clusters engage the poet, at some level, in the process of *ratio,* the root of the propositional and conceptual column. But it is as if he wished to borrow from that range of speech-acts *only* the rhythms and nuances of diction, not the words' denotative function (although obviously meaning is not altogether ignored). Perhaps Heaney is hoping to reform these polysyllables by tumbling them down the ragged cataract of his lists. Reform them, that is, from their bureaucratic flatness, undo the process by which they were first compounded—paganize them. Unfortunately, as long as meaning clings to these polysyllables, sense will count, and the fancily involuted sound of "inanition" will not warrant its use in the recondite mixed metaphor, "between / balance and inanition," applied to "the light at the rim of the sea" in **"Away from It All."** On the level of *ratio,* the phrase is pedantic and obscure; on that of *inspiratio* (to coin a counterfeit etymology), it is part of some indigenous rhythm that goes on forever, deeper than what is being declared, when this poet works, and which elsewhere falls into happier synchrony with his rhetoric.

Heaney's sound has ever been hard rather than musical or melodic, just as his discursive authority had tended to extrude into density rather than strike through it. He is a poet of feelings that are the emotional counterpart to a regional dialect in speech, for he is entrained to very particular kinds of place, texture, tone, color, mood, weather, soil, and light, and able to say how their nuances relate, almost as a geologist might. The bond to his favorite locales would seem much deeper—for it seeps out everywhere—than the sympathy upheld by Auden in his "In Praise of Limestone." Heaney also sounds in his work remarkably good-tempered, despite the toughness of many poems. They are tough in their elocution, not in their sentiment. (The reverse is true of Ted Hughes, from whom he takes fire in many of his first poems.) So it is easy to see why Heaney is fired by contraries, for they provide a drama that is not inherent in his character. To the poems that otherwise tend toward exclamation and the hyperbole of repetition (the early **"Churning Day,"** with its lavish play on the short *u* among plosive consonants, is a good example), they add the electricity of argument-with-the-self (as happens in **"Blackberry-Picking,"** where the hard facts and the muffled antithetical claims of the couplet pull him out of the thick tangle of vegetative life toward general precept).

Thus at the same time as these tensions are honestly come by, they do have their redolence of the lamp. Heaney's solutions to what he perceives as a basic division in his being may differ from book to book, yet the forces between which he must negotiate remain surprisingly constant, almost as if refueled and refurbished from time to time. The

---

Sidney Borris on Heaney's struggle with politics and poetry:

From his early days as a civil rights activist, Heaney has been acutely aware of the demanding relation, particularly in Northern Ireland, between the literary life and the political, or engaged life. Throughout his career he has pondered this difficult relationship, and it often provides him with his subject matter, particularly in the poems written after he left Belfast. Delivered as one of the T. S. Eliot Memorial Lectures at the University of Kent in 1986, Heaney's assessment of Sylvia Plath's development posed the question that has haunted him throughout his own career: "To what extent should the tongue's hedonism and frolic be in the control of the noble rider of socially responsible intellect, ethics or morals?" The allusion to Wallace Stevens's essay "The Noble Rider and the Sound of Words" clears the way for the tempered aestheticism of his own answer: "I do not in fact see how poetry can survive as a category of human consciousness if it does not put poetic considerations first—expressive considerations, that is, based upon its own genetic laws which spring into operation at the moment of lyric conception."

Sidney Borris in his The Poetry of Resistance: Seamus Heaney and the Pastoral Tradition, *Ohio University Press, 1990.*

"Station Island" sequence is riddled with ambivalences of theme and tone pursuant to the effort to challenge the private being in light of the public, to make the intuitive self the measure of the learned public man.

Henry Hart   (essay date 1992)

SOURCE: An introduction to *Seamus Heaney: Poet of Contrary Progressions,* Syracuse University Press, 1992, pp. 1-8.

[*Hart is an American critic and educator. In the following essay, his introduction to* Seamus Heaney, *he examines Heaney's development as a poet, focusing on his position in—and his reactions to—Ireland's literary and political history.*]

Few twentieth-century poets writing in English have been able to secure a wide audience among general readers and critics alike. After W. B. Yeats, only Robert Frost achieved such bipartisan acclaim, although for many years scholars denigrated Frost beside the intellectually more sophisticated modernists. In a culture where films, television shows, and compact discs have usurped the monopoly on communication that books once enjoyed, a popular poet is rare. Maintaining an "international reputation," as a writer in *The Observer* recently commented, "is a tricky business. . . . It takes a special gift to win hearts on both sides of the Atlantic and no one now possesses it quite like Seamus Heaney" [21 June 1987, p. 7]. With the publication of each new volume, the critical consensus grows that Heaney is not only the most gifted poet in Ireland and Britain, but also the most critically respected poet writing in English today.

The anonymous *Observer* writer, echoing claims made by Robert Lowell, Helen Vendler, and Harold Bloom, entitled his article "Poet Wearing the Mantle of Yeats" and mischievously drew attention to those among the Irish who "suspect he's already a *better* poet than Yeats." Mantles obfuscate as well as illuminate, and Yeats's mantle on Heaney is both burden and honor. As Heaney's readers and critics proliferate, so do his different mantles—his different masks and identities—and so do the conflicting appraisals of his work. Those who suspect that Heaney's popularity lies in the common demand for *one* Irish bard per generation argue that he is a minor Dylan Thomas whose talent as a poetic "ornamentalist" with "a fine way with language" lacks substance [see A. Alvarez, "A Fine Way with the Language," *New York Review of Books,* 6 March 1980, pp. 16-17]. For others he is a pastoralist whose homely portraits of rural Irish life attract both curiosity and sympathy but are ultimately sentimental. Others believe his appeal arises from his position as political spokesman for Northern Ireland's perpetual Troubles, while those in the opposite camp claim that his poetry amounts to a culpable escape from those Troubles. For some he writes a romantic poetry of transcendence, for others a classic one of principled social engagement. With regard to the Catholic religion in which he was reared, some say his poetry is still regressively steeped in sacrificial symbols and rituals; others declare that, like James Joyce, he has flown above the nets of religion for a more objective anthropological view. For those critics who de-

mand allegories from their writers Heaney obliges by making his poems speak for religious, political, linguistic, sexual, and literary matters all at once. For those who believe allegory is mechanical and simplistic, bastardizing rather than legitimately representing history, Heaney is just the latest mythmaker in a long line of Irish mystifiers.

His complexity, understandably, leads to debate about what he stands for, what kind of poet he really is, and whether the ethical and aesthetic standards exemplified in his verse are meritorious or meretricious. He is so elusive, in fact, that while his wife can attest to his "magical ring of confidence" and his sense of security which, to her, is "like an egg contained within a shell, without any quality of otherness, without the sense of loss that this otherness brings" [see Polly Devlin, *All of Us There,* 1983, pp. 16-17] other less intimate observers declare that the personality behind the poems is wracked with anxiety, uncertainty, fear, anger, and painful self-consciousness. Heaney may not like wearing Yeats's mantle. Nevertheless, his poetry vacillates between antinomies as persistently as his precursor's. Like the Irish history that saturates it from beginning to end, his poetry is a battleground of competing affiliations. In a passage Heaney likes to quote from Yeats, and one that applies to much of his own work, his countryman remarked: "We make out of the quarrel with others, rhetoric, but of the quarrel with ourselves, poetry. Unlike the rhetoricians, who get a confident voice from remembering the crowd they have won or may win, we sing amid our uncertainty" [*Mythologies,* 1959, p. 331]. Yet for Heaney poetry and rhetoric, art and politics, are entangled rather than distinct, merging and emerging as rhythmically as the uncertainty that underlies them.

At the root of his work is a multifaceted argument with himself, with others, with sectarian Northern Ireland, with his Anglo-Irish heritage, and with his Roman Catholic, nationalist upbringing on a farm in County Derry. As he follows Yeats in striving for "unity of being," mapping out the embattled factions in his nation and psyche, he is descriptive as well as prescriptive. He diagnoses Irish ills, suggests cures (like dismantling his country's archaic hierarchies so that different religious and political groups can engage creatively rather than murderously), then withdraws to let legislators and law enforcers put the plan into practice. He realizes his agenda may be utopian and that his personal renunciation of overt political action may be taken as a cop-out (at least by "the noisy set / Of bankers, school-masters, and clergymen / The martyrs call the world" in Yeats's "Adam's Curse" [in *The Poems,* 1983, p. 80]). Nevertheless, he stands by the artist's right to choose one devotion over another. With Stephen Dedalus he will "forge the uncreated conscience of his race" [*A Portrait of the Artist as a Young Man,* 1916] in art rather than in government, although the blueprint for better governance will be scored into his poems for anybody to examine.

Behind Heaney's noble principles, however, is the worry that, as W. H. Auden proclaimed, "poetry makes nothing happen," that "it survives / In the valley of its making where executives / Would never want to tamper" [*Selected Poetry of W. H. Auden,* 1971, p. 53], that art rather than reform only exacerbates the dominant authorities. So Heaney's poems, to borrow current critical terms, are assiduously self-reflexive, self-consuming, self-deconstructing. They search for images and answers for Irish problems and submit them to intense critical scrutiny. What they set up they tend to knock down. Deploying a different metaphor, Heaney likes to quote Robert Frost on this process of composition by decomposition: "like a piece of ice on a hot stove the poem must ride on its own melting." Similarly, "the poem . . . a linguistic exploration whose tracks melt as it maps its own progress" [*Preoccupations,* pp. 80-1]. The moral value of this poetry that vigilantly investigates cultural dilemmas but then dissolves its solutions and that deconstructs the ancient hierarchies and oedipal struggles between "patriarchal" British Protestants and "matriarchal" Irish Catholics bothers Heaney because it fails to articulate concrete political resolutions for Ireland. Of Yeats, Auden elegiacally commented in "In Memory of W. B. Yeats," "Mad Ireland hurt you into poetry" [*Selected Poetry,* p. 53]. Looking back on his career, which gained momentum during the Catholic civil rights movement in the sixties and the resurgence of I.R.A. attacks and Protestant counterattacks in the early seventies, Heaney intimates that if "Mad Ireland" had hurt him into politics he would feel less anxious. Politics, for better or for worse, makes things happen.

This kind of argument in which opposite views compel and repel Heaney with equal force begins with his first book, *Death of a Naturalist*. Here and in some of the uncollected poems printed when he was a student at Queen's University in Belfast he expresses a bittersweet nostalgia for his childhood on the farm in Derry. As in the pastoral tradition that stretches from Frost and Dylan Thomas (two of Heaney's early models) back to Virgil and Theocritus, Heaney depicts his rural, agrarian home ground as his golden age or Eden. As soon as pastoral enchantment wells up in him, however, he represses it with grim recognitions of farming in Ireland and the sectarian battles erupting or about to erupt just outside the farms' ditches and hedges. As he struggles to free himself from Mother Ireland's womblike pastures and reconcile himself with the historical facts of Father Britain's depredations, Heaney imagines himself as both an Adam falling from Eden into a knowledge of agonizing divisions and an oedipal child contending with both biological and cultural parents. His quest for fatherhood and poethood travels a dialectical path between pastoral and antipastoral traditions. Although he elegizes his early, innocent naturalism, which is traditional pastoralism thinly disguised, its death prepares the way for a more mature naturalism in tune with the struggles raging all around him.

Without the recognition of rural hardship, Heaney's poetry of agrarian ways would have floundered in the mists of another Celtic Twilight. Similarly, his meditational *via negativas* in *Door into the Dark* would have seemed solipsistic or narcissistic if they did not illuminate the psychological motives and consequences of meditation. While Heaney draws on the sort of Catholic meditation institutionalized by such divines as St. Ignatius Loyola and St. John of the Cross and updated for him by Evelyn Underhill and Thomas Merton, and while he sympathetically

records sacred moments in the mystic's "dark night" (the altarlike anvil wreathed with sparks in **"The Forge,"** the grass flaming in **"In Gallarus Oratory"**), his spiritual marriages are between imagination and unconscious rather than soul and Christ. His argumentative and iconoclastic way is to counter orthodox Catholic meditations by emphasizing their secular correlatives. As poetry replaces religion, Heaney demystifies the divine Word by transforming it into the poetic word. If Platonic and Judeo-Christian tradition has tended to denigrate writing as a cumbersome, improper medium for communicating sacred mysteries, Heaney, like his poststructuralist peers, contradicts that bias by deploying writing as a principal way to excavate the ground from which mysteries and prejudices have always burgeoned.

Realizing that pastoralism and mysticism have flourished primarily because of linguistic conventions and their power to evade or transcend the real world's troubles, Heaney in *Wintering Out* plunges even more methodically into language in order to expose its collusions with those troubles. In his poems on Northern Irish place names, etymology recapitulates history. An archaeologist of language, Heaney unearths signs of Scottish and English invasions lingering in the lexicon and pronunciation of his Irish compatriots. Focusing on British words transported to Ulster by colonizers and often fused with native Gaelic words, Heaney devises miniature allegories in which even the different syllables radiate political, religious, literary, and sexual significance. As he composed these poems, Heaney felt increasing pressure from the Catholic, nationalist community in his homeland to act as its propagandist. Yet his poems subvert partisan jingoism and strive to fashion in its place new emblems of sectarian cooperation.

As the bombs began to explode once again in the early seventies in Northern Ireland, Heaney responded with *North,* his most gruesome account of the tragic and mythical aspects of the sectarian hostilities. Some critics accused him of wallowing in rituals of sacrificial purgation and sexual renewal, as if he were emulating Yeats's more bellicose moods. Rather than clamber after the apocalyptic rapacity of Yeats's Zeus or Jehovah, Heaney typically identifies with and elegiacally mourns the victims of such myths. He repeatedly invokes ancient fertility cults and apocalyptic expectations to implicate them in the apocalyptic atrocities that have afflicted his country for centuries. Because Protestant and Catholic paramilitary groups shed blood in order to preserve their sacred ideals of Mother Ireland, she emerges more as a femme fatale or "terrible beauty" than as a benevolent fertility goddess. Heaney understands the devotion to the Mother among Catholics and the I.R.A., and sympathizes with their anger over her repeated desecration at the hands of Britain's Protestant Fathers. Still, he hopes for an oedipal resolution that is as political as it is psychological. To move toward civilized compromise, he suggests, both sides must realize that Ireland can be an old sow that eats her farrow, a tyrannical patriarch devouring sow and piglets alike, and also the androgynous, ecumenical humanist envisioned by Joyce in Leopold Bloom.

Heaney's year at Berkeley between 1970 and 1971 reinforced his liberal sentiments and loosened his early formalist constraints. In California he tried to incorporate the expansive American forms of Walt Whitman, Ezra Pound, William Carlos Williams, Robert Duncan, and Gary Snyder. If historically poetry has been an aristocratic art and prose a more democratic one, Heaney, following the experiments of the Americans, sought to yoke the two in a series of prose poems called *Stations,* which he published in pamphlet form in 1975. The title recalls the Stations of the Cross, but rather than focus on Christ's agonizing Passion and Crucifixion, Heaney dwells on personal and political crises. Again he secularizes the cross so that it refers to his own multifarious crossings—between Ireland and America, Ulster and the Republic, Protestantism and Catholicism, and even between prose and poetry. Although his sequence of prose poems can be read as a spiritual autobiography *in imitatione Christi,* it is more specifically a confessional narrative of a boy growing up in Northern Ireland after World War II and gradually recognizing that for centuries the Christian cross has inspired rancorous division rather than divine unity.

After the controversial move from Belfast to Glanmore in 1972, Heaney seemed prepared to shut his "door into the dark" and open "a door into the light" [see "An Interview with Seamus Heaney," by James Randall, in *Ploughshares,* Vol. 5, No. 3, 1979, pp. 7-22]. In essays and interviews he spoke of trusting a more lucid, conversational voice and of trusting his new, more enlightened audience in the South (which was predominantly Catholic, unlike the predominantly Protestant society in the North). Christopher Ricks in a penetrating review of *Field Work* ["The Mouth, the Meal and the Book," *London Review of Books,* November 8, 1979, pp. 4-5], the book that grew out of this transition, rang the changes on this theme of trust. In poetry, politics, and marriage Heaney elevates trust to the status of faith. Still, his faith in a recently acquired freedom, voice, and audience in the South is nevertheless undermined at nearly every point by doubt and distrust. In the North he sought to transcend political responsibilities imposed on him; in the South he equates transcendence with political escapism. Accepting Dante and Robert Lowell as his models, he places his trust in art's ability to confront conflicts between freedom and responsibility, private craft and public involvement, but continually chastises himself for evading commitments and failing to have more impact on the situation he left behind.

The medieval Gaelic poem, *Buile Suibhne,* which he translates as *Sweeney Astray* during this period, provides an ancient mask for his contemporary dilemma. Confronted by the horrors of the battle of Moira in Ulster (A.D. 637) and cursed because of his contempt for the invading Christian empire, Suibhne Geilt metamorphoses into a guilt-ridden bird and, like his Icarian heir, Stephen Dedalus, attempts to fly over nation, religion, and language and to survive by silence, exile, and cunning. He resembles the stock character of medieval iconography, the pagan wild man, although at the end he is converted by his friend, St. Moling, and comes to resemble that other stock figure of medieval Irish lore, the ascetic saint negotiating a penitential *peregrinatio* through the wilderness. For Heaney, Sweeney acts as a half-pagan, half-Christian persona that, especially in his "Sweeney Redivivus" poems, allows him to

dramatize his own guilty feelings aroused by his flight from Ulster to the woods of Wicklow. But if Suibhne takes a penitential journey to atone for his murderous sins against insurgent Christians, Heaney's sin is that he *takes* a journey—that he abandons his embattled homeland. Once again he seizes on a character and narrative, implicates his own experience in ancient paradigms, and then critically assails them.

The same ironic sense of sin and guilt predominate in that other long poem based on medieval precedents, **"Station Island."** In Dantesque tones and stanzas, Heaney records his early pilgrimages to the island in Lough Derg where St. Patrick supposedly initiated a three-day vigil of fasting, praying, and mortification. Imitating Dante's journey through the circles of hell and purgatory, Heaney traipses over circles of rocks on the island, communing with tutelary ghosts as he goes. In typical self-reflexive fashion, his pilgrimage engenders an argument about pilgrimages; he journeys to a holy island in order to purge the guilt and anxiety that such journeys create. As he fares forth, most of the prominent figures he summons from the dead (Simon Sweeney, Patrick Kavanagh, William Carleton, Joyce) accuse him of groveling through old rituals that are masochistic, life-denying, meaningless, or simply distracting. They form a formidable opposition but really speak for Heaney's artistic conscience, which is painfully at odds with those two other internal gorgons, his political conscience and his religious conscience. Divided against himself, he once again launches an ambitious investigation into his ambivalent motives, assaulting his ideals and then shoring their fragments into a brilliant poem.

For a postcolonial poet who feels that the religious, political, and linguistic hierarchies imposed on his country by a foreign empire still watermark his psyche, deconstruction is as much a gut response as a well-thoughtout strategy of exposure and demolition. In *The Haw Lantern,* Heaney mounts his most sustained attack on the binary oppositions that have stratified and oppressed his society in the past, tracing them, as Jacques Derrida and others have done, back to the Platonic and Judeo-Christian origins of Western civilization. Addressing such loaded terms as presence and absence, speech and writing, he deploys his deconstructive maneuvers along a *via negativa* that negates age-old prejudices in order to affirm the productive interplay of differences. In a country where one sectarian faction pretends to hold a monopoly on truth and justice and historically has chosen to kill those who oppose the "one true way," deconstruction is not simply an abstract hermeneutic strategy designed for clever critics. It has ethical relevance for the reorganization of all aspects of culture.

In *The Haw Lantern,* however, Heaney criticizes deconstruction, as others have done, for its reckless flirtation with nihilism and frivolous play. As he reinscribes absences with new presences and makes marginal cultures (like Northern Ireland's) central rather than peripheral, he also argues for reconstruction. The book, he proposes in terms borrowed from Mercea Eliade, charts the deconstruction of sacred by profane space. He uses an architectural metaphor of decentering to represent the cultural metamorphosis that he and his generation in Ireland witnessed: "I watched it happen in Irish homes when I first saw a house built where there was no chimney, and then you'd go into rooms without a grate—so no hearth, which in Latin means no focus. So the hearth going away means the house is unfocused. . . . it represents a reality: the unfocusing of space and the desacralizing of it" ["An Interview with Seamus Heaney," by Randy Brandes, in *Salmagundi,* Fall, 1988, pp. 4-21]. The generic deconstructionist applauds the unfocused, the decentered, and the indeterminate, concluding that all reading and writing is a ludic exercise of negative capability. Heaney responds by celebrating affirmative capability. He seeks "images of a definite space which is both empty and full of potential" and principled ways of tapping and governing that potential. His collection of essays, *The Government of the Tongue,* elaborates on these poetic preoccupations, speaking eloquently of the always difficult balance between linguistic constraint and freedom, orderly space and unleashed potential, political dictate and private rebuke.

Heaney's former status as a "noncitizen" in Protestant-dominated Northern Ireland derived at least in part from his decision to choose writing as his mode of expression rather than the more customary political organ, speech. Domestic and social authorities repressed his will to speak out; poetry became the oracle for his impassioned sense of justice and injustice. His poetry notebook records a passage from the late French philosopher, Gaston Bachelard: "What is the source of our first suffering? It lies in the fact that we hesitated to speak. It was born in the moment when we accumulated silent things within us" [quoted in "Poet of the Boys: Seamus Heaney, Ireland's Foremost Living Poet Commands a Growing Audience," by Francis X. Clines, in *The New York Times Magazine,* March 13, 1983, pp. 42-3, 98-9, 104]. He told Francis Clines from the *New York Times,* "If I could make poetry that could touch into that kind of thing, that is what I would like to do." Few other poets today articulate as self-consciously and judiciously the difficult issues of language and silence, and especially how they relate to poetic expression and political repression. In a century when major writers have espoused nazism, fascism, monarchism, and other antidemocratic creeds, Heaney's hesitancy to speak out politically seems noble rather than culpable. That his writing dramatizes bipartisan arguments in which historical differences continue to clash gives it an urgency that much contemporary poetry lacks and makes it even more worthy of attentive study.

AWARD ANNOUNCEMENTS

William Grimes **(essay date 6 October 1995)**

SOURCE: "Irish Poet Wins the Nobel Prize in Literature," in *The New York Times,* October 6, 1995, pp. B1, B18.

[In the following article, Grimes summarizes Heaney's life and career.]

The Irish poet Seamus Heaney has been awarded the Nobel Prize in Literature. In conferring the prize, the Swedish Academy praised Mr. Heaney "for works of lyrical beauty and ethical depth, which exalt everyday miracles and the living past."

It also praised Mr. Heaney, a Roman Catholic, for analyzing the violence in Northern Ireland without recourse to conventional terms.

The poet (whose name is pronounced SHAY-muss HEE-nee) will receive the award on Dec. 10 at a ceremony in Stockholm, along with the Nobel winners in physics, chemistry, economics and medicine, who will be announced next week. This year the prize is worth more than $1 million, the highest it has ever been.

The poet Derek Walcott, who won the Nobel Prize in 1992, issued a statement through Farrar, Straus & Giroux, Mr. Heaney's American publishers: "As the guardian spirit of Irish poetry, Seamus Heaney has, like his predecessor Yeats, received his just recognition."

Paul Muldoon, an Irish poet teaching at Princeton University, said, "This is a great day for Irish poetry and for poetry throughout the world."

Mr. Heaney's son, Michael, said in Dublin that his father was on vacation in rural Greece and that not even family members had been able to reach him.

Mr. Heaney, 56, was born on a farm west of Belfast in County Derry, Northern Ireland, the eldest of nine children. He received a bachelor's degree in English language and literature at Queen's University, Belfast, and after earning a teaching certificate from St. Joseph's College of Education, taught at a secondary school in Ballymurphy and at St. Joseph's.

He began publishing poems as a student, using the pseudonym Incertus. In Belfast he became associated with the Group, a circle of young writers that included Derek Mahon, Michael Longley and James Simmons.

His first poetry collections, *Death of a Naturalist* (1966) and *Door Into the Dark,* (1969), immediately marked Mr. Heaney as a gifted lyric poet. In pared-down, tactile language, his verse gave off the scent and savor of his rural surroundings. The comparisons to William Butler Yeats and Robert Frost came early and often.

In an almost literal sense, Mr. Heaney's poetry is rooted in the Irish soil. He has often written of the poet as a kind of farmer, digging and rooting, as though Ireland's wet peat were a storehouse of images and memories. At the same time, Mr. Heaney moves easily from the homely images of farm and village to larger issues of history, language and national identity, creating what he once called "the music of what happens."

In 1972, he moved from Belfast to the Irish Republic, eventually settling in Dublin, and his poetry from the 1970's, collected in *North* (1975) and *Field Work* (1979), bears witness to the political turmoil in Northern Ireland, although from after. "He took a lot of flak for moving," said Henry Hart, an associate professor of English at William and Mary College and the author of *Seamus Heaney: Poet of Contrary Progressions.* "The Catholics saw it as a betrayal, and he himself experienced a great deal of guilt over it."

Although all his works have been well received, he won lavish critical praise for **Station Island** (1984), the title poem of which, a narrative sequence, drew on Dante to dramatize the torment of Irish politics and history.

In a review of **Station Island** in The New York Times, John Gross enumerated Mr. Heaney's poetic arsenal: "powerful images; compelling rhythms; a distinctive palette; phrases packed tight with meaning." Mr. Heaney, he said, "has all the primary gifts of a poet, and they are gifts put at the service of a constant meditation on primary themes, on nature and history and moral choice."

Mr. Heaney's most recent poetry collections are **The Haw Lantern** (1987), **Selected Poems 1966-1987** (1990) and **Seeing Things** (1991). **The Spirit Level,** a new collection of poetry, is to be published in May 1996 by Farrar, Straus.

His essays have been collected in two volumes, **Preoccupations: Selected Prose 1968-1978** (1980) and **The Government of the Tongue** (1989). **The Redress of Poetry,** consisting of his poetry lectures at Oxford, is scheduled to be published in the United States next month by Farrar, Straus.

Mr. Heaney has also ventured into translation, beginning with **Sweeney Astray** (1984), a version of the medieval Irish narrative poem *Buile Suibhne,* about an ancient Irish king who, cursed by a Christian cleric, wanders the countryside as a mad outcast, half-man, half-bird.

He also rendered Sophocles' *Philoctetes* into blank verse under the title **The Cure at Troy** (1990).

Laments, a translation of elegiac poems by the 16th-century Polish poet Jan Kochanowski that Mr. Heaney undertook with Stanislaw Baranczak, is also to be published this fall.

Mr. Heaney is a member of the Irish Academy of Letters. His many awards include the E. M. Forster Award of the American Academy and Institute of Arts and Letters.

He was professor of poetry at Oxford University from 1989 to 1994.

He is currently on a leave of absence from Harvard University, where he has been Boylston Professor of Rhetoric and Oratory since 1985.

Mr. Heaney is the third Irishman to win the Nobel Prize. Yeats was awarded the prize in 1923 and Samuel Beckett in 1969.

James F. Clarity (essay date 9 October 1995)

SOURCE: "Laureate and Symbol, Heaney Returns Home," in *The New York Times,* October 9, 1995, p. B4.

[*In the following article, Clarity reports Heaney's reactions to winning the Nobel Prize.*]

Seamus Heaney, the winner of the Nobel Prize in Literature, arrived home last night and was welcomed not only as a great poet in a land that loves writers and writing, but also as a symbol of hope for lasting peace in Northern Ireland.

Mr. Heaney, who was born in Northern Ireland 56 years ago but now lives in Dublin, was on vacation in Greece when his award was announced on Thursday. For a full day, neither his children nor the scores of reporters seeking interviews could find him. He was invited to a dinner party on Friday at the residence of the American Ambassador, Jean Kennedy Smith, but did not appear.

But when he arrived at Dublin's airport on Saturday night, after cutting his trip short upon learning about the prize, Prime Minister John Bruton was there to praise him as a literary symbol of the Northern peace effort, and to have the poet autograph a book of his lectures.

Asked at the airport how he felt about joining the other Irish Nobel winners, William Butler Yeats, George Bernard Shaw and Samuel Beckett, he said: "It's like being a little foothill at the bottom of a mountain range. You hope you just live up to it. It's extraordinary." He did not mention Ireland's literary giant, James Joyce (a figure in his poetry), who never won the Nobel.

Mr. Heaney and his wife, Marie, were whisked from the airport to the residence of President Mary Robinson for champagne and more praise. He has been the main story on national television since Thursday, and he read three of his poems on the radio today at the start of the main afternoon news program.

"It was entirely bewildering," he said in an Irish television interview before he left the Greek port of Kalamata, "and still a bit incredible. It's an awesome dimension." Asked how he felt about being considered a peace symbol, he showed none of the annoyance of some of his friends, who thought he should have won solely as a poet. Mr. Heaney has dealt with Northern Ireland in his work and acknowledges that his point of view supports Roman Catholic charges of harsh discrimination by the Protestant majority. He left the British-ruled province in the early 1970's after he was threatened by Protestant paramilitary guerrillas.

"There has been a new mood in the country since last year," he said, clearly referring to the peace effort that accelerated when the Irish Republican Army declared a cease-fire more than 13 months ago. "It's a very precious mood because it promises new energy. I'm also gratified that I've been honored as part of that. I've a very strong sense of belonging to the North, and of course I insist on being Irish." Referring to the province of his birth and the 25 years of sectarian warfare between Catholics and Protestants there, he added, "One doesn't want one's identity coerced. But I've said the British Irish in the North shouldn't be coerced out of their identity, either."

When the award was first announced, Mr. Heaney's childhood friend, John Hume, the Roman Catholic political leader instrumental in starting the current peace effort, said he hoped the prize was for poetry, not politics. Mr. Hume has been nominated for this year's Nobel Peace

Prize, as has former Prime Minister Albert Reynolds, also for his work toward peace.

The Irish Times said in an editorial: "No doubt there will be mutterings from many quarters that the Nobel committee has once again made a political choice by awarding the prize to an Irishman at the end of a year which has been one of the most hopeful yet perilously balanced periods in the history of our two states. Such begrudgery, though typical of us as a nation, will only shame us in the eyes of an admiring world."

At the airport, Prime Minister Bruton said that in the peace effort, "I draw encouragement and inspiration from Seamus's writing."

Mr. Heaney, recognized in the streets of Dublin by his frizzy white hair, spoke about growing up in the North, where his friends, in addition to Mr. Hume, included the playwright Brian Friel and the poet Seamus Deane, who is now a lecturer at Notre Dame University in Indiana. "Teen-age lads rampant," he said. "There was a lot of energy, but there was no sense of a future of destiny or anything like that.

"I'm very moved to hear about the pleasure in the country at home. I feel myself part of something. Not only being part of a community, but part of an actual moment and a movement of Irish writing and art. That sense of being part of the whole thing is the deepest joy."

INTERVIEWS

Seamus Heaney with *The Economist* (interview date 22 June 1991)

SOURCE: A conversation in *The Economist,* Vol. 319, June 22, 1991, pp. 98-102.

[*In the following interview, Heaney discusses his philosophy of language and the influence his father and his home in Ireland have had on his poetry.*]

Seamus Heaney is one of the best known and most widely read of modern poets. His latest collection of poems, *Seeing Things,* has been both praised and damned: the *Spectator* has called it "a glass precipice without toehold". In conversation recently, he explained himself to *The Economist.*

[*The Economist*]: *You were raised a Catholic in County Derry, one of nine children, and your father was a cattle dealer. Were words revered in your household?*

[Heaney]: Not in any conscious way at all, no. There was no self-consciousness about the use of language. But there was an unself-conscious relish of excellence in it. I wouldn't say this was particular to the family. It was common to a kind of rural subculture—remarks made were reported. It wasn't the felicity of adjectives that was relished, more the aptness and succinctness and usually slightly elegant cruelty of the remarks.

Your father, who died five years ago, is evoked very vividly in this new collection—and yet you seem to be circling his memory somewhat warily. How would you describe your relationship with him?

For the first ten or 12 years of my life it was uncomplicated but distant. In my teens it was not hostile, but it was definitely complicated . . . It was just that he was completely wordless . . .

You mean he was taciturn . . .

Yes, he was, but he was not a sour person at all. He was simply in terror of misrepresenting things by speaking of them. In a sense I think he believed—he never expressed this, but all his activity bore witness to such a belief—that to speak a thing out, to confess it, to name it, in some way disabled it.

Time and again in your new collection you begin by describing the very simple, almost thoughtless, excitements of childhood and adolescence—fishing, playing football, sliding on ice—and then they are weighed in the mind and seem to take on a totally different kind of significance.

You describe very exactly the desire I would have for a reader—this suspension in an element that is hallucinatory; that is both weightless and weighty. The idea of free fall. The idea of that buoyancy in the spacecraft, of getting light and at the same time retaining a relationship with gravity . . . One of the earliest poems I wrote in the collection, **"Fosterling",** includes the words, "me waiting until I was nearly 50 to credit marvels", and that too is about things going up, lifting and lightening, in spite of sluggish surroundings. In my first book, ***Death of a Naturalist,*** the whole effort of the writing was to solidify the thing in language, block it out, make it embossed, until it became a kind of language braille of sorts . . . In this case, I think you could say I was trying to call it in . . . not to make it insubstantial, but to do something akin to beaming it up, like in "Startrek".

There is not much politics in this book, but there is a more generalised eschewal of violence, particularly at the end of **"The Pitchfork."**

That poem and one other, **"The Ashplant,"** were the earliest poems written and I worked on them in County Derry, in the house where my father was dying. It contains an image of space which I meant to be silent and eerie—but it could, as you say, be sinister and aggressive. The pitchfork becomes a sort of missile—as well as everything else. But I wanted to bring the pitchfork through even that, you know. The last stanza is quite explicit. It says: let's keep going to another set of experiences. The opening hand is meant to be an image of unclenching and generosity . . . as Czeslaw Milosz says, "Open the clenched fist of the past." Hard to do.

The other poem that has political possibilities, this time more explicit, is **"The Settle Bed."** A settle bed is a very heavy thing, a very Ulster, rural thing, a burdensomely heavy inheritance. But you don't have to be utterly burdened. There are ways of handling this, you know.

> **The kinds of truth that art gives us many, many times are small truths. They don't have the resonance of an encyclical from the Pope stating an eternal truth, but they partake of the quality of eternity. There is a sort of timeless delight in them.**
>
> *—Seamus Heaney*

The book contains a very affectionate sequence of poems about Glanmore, your home in the country—the second time you've written about the house.

The house came back to me—quite unexpectedly. When we lived in it first [after leaving Belfast in the early 1970s] we were only tenants, and it was a moment of our lives which was provisional and temporary anyway. There was that sense of being in transition, at the edge, feeling slightly menaced and slightly free, more than slightly free.

The relationship with Glanmore is completely different now. I got into a good situation in terms of breadwinning, in terms of parent-and-citizen life. I'd go four months to the States, able to earn my keep there, and come back home. But by being between an apartment in Harvard University and a family home in Dublin, and the family house getting constantly invaded by telephone calls, the balance of where I was—you know: was I in America? Was I in Dublin?—became upset. I found the needles wavering, you know. And when I was able to get to Glanmore, I found true north again. I felt completely in place. I felt secure. I felt I had a starting point and an ending point.

I'd like to ask you about the poem in which you're addressing questions to Yeats's ghost, the one that begins, "Where does spirit live?"

It began completely whimsically. All these 12-line poems were written swiftly. They were like plunges in. They were . . . experimental, always, almost always, and a number of them didn't survive their own experiments. The poem addressed to Yeats ends with the line: "What's the use of a held note or held line / That cannot be assailed for reassurance?" And I think that is one of the functions of a certain kind of art—form, the abstract, the platonic type, the thing, the original and last shape, all this is a necessity, and we want it to be there. We want it to withstand our scepticisms, you know. And some of the satisfactions that a Yeats poem gives include the feeling of being empowered and thrilled by all that. It's like getting on a bronze horse, almost of becoming a bronze horseman. Yeats's music is overbearing in that way and resonantly so. And you want to—another part of you, the flesh and blood part of you wants to—refuse that, but it will sustain, it will survive all refusals.

Does it worry you that some regard you as an ambassador for poetry, as a type of representative English-language poet? Can you cope with this?

It is indeed an anxiety. I mean I hadn't anticipated or envisaged the amount of representative status or eye-catching profile that, for example, the Oxford professorship would yield. I had a strong sense of previous Oxford professors *being* there—but not actually being noticed. You know, it was a nice skyline further away, but it wasn't a hill in the foreground. And I suddenly feel that it has been foregrounded, you know . . . but at the same time it's not an area where I want to wear my heart on my sleeve or have my heart bleed or indeed to plead about it.

What is your own apology for poetry? What is poetry good for?

To quote my friend Derek Mahon, they keep the colours new. They rinse things. . .

What sort of things?

Well, first of all rinse the words, yes. But also perhaps rinse—and hang out again on the line—values, values of freedom of spirit and play, but also values which are fundamental to the culture, the myth values of the culture . . . You see, I think poetry's also domestic. It lives within certain cultural borders. It can transcend them, it can broadcast beyond them, but its first life is within its language borders and then maybe within a certain domain of that language . . . The kind of poet who founds and reconstitutes values is somebody like Yeats or Whitman—these are public value-founders. Then you can put beside Whitman in 19th-century America Emily Dickinson, who is a reconstitutor of an inner metaphysic for human creatures . . . The poet is on the side of undeceiving the world. It means being vigilant in the public realm. But you can go further still and say that poetry tries to help you to be a truer, purer, wholer being, you know. This doesn't mean that each poem has to be something like Eliot's "Four Quartets" . . . It can mean a *haiku* such as "Twilight / Farmer pointing the way / With a radish". You suddenly see the world renewed.

The kinds of truth that art gives us many, many times are small truths. They don't have the resonance of an encyclical from the Pope stating an eternal truth, but they partake of the quality of eternity. There is a sort of timeless delight in them. And it's that timeless delighting, the timeless rightness of 2 little thing or the resonant rightness of a bigger thing—that's what it can do. Let a blind up for a moment.

You've talked about the public role of poetry, but you have also said that poetry can't afford—as it did in the 19th century—to indulge in exhortation any more.

Yes. That is true, I was talking about the suspicion that Irish poets in particular had had induced in them by the scoldings of Patrick Kavanagh against a national theme. And Kavanagh said: there's nothing as damned as the important thing. But then there was also the caution that came upon us in the late 1960s, early 1970s because of the collusion between high national rhetoric and possibly low, dangerous activities—the IRA and so on . . . The appetite for uttering a big truth shouldn't be altogether rebuked, you know. But how is it to be uttered? That is the question.

To go back to the present collection, you seem to use bigger words than you've ever dared use before—soul and spirit, for example. There is one line in particular where the soul is hung out like a white . . .

. . . handkerchief, which, in a sense, goes back to the very beginnings of religious instruction, to the school catechism, where the innocent soul was a white handkerchief—and then sin came along like a stain of soot or a piece of tar and the soul had to be cleansed at confession. It was pretty coarse stuff . . . I think that those primary images retain—as Wordsworth would have said—a vivifying force, but they can also be constricting—in a subliminal way—right throughout your life. And that poem was a discovery of a delight in realising that eternal life is credible, you know . . . One associated it, first of all, with a mystery, and it was, in the first world. The religious language was entirely radiant and mysterious—but it was unquestioned. Then you come to the detached, self-secularising period, and you say: eternal life? It's all language, you know. There's no afterlife. There's no paved floor of heaven. The seraphim aren't there.

And then, suddenly, you say: well, wait! Eternal life can mean utter reverence for life itself. And that's what there is. And our care in a green age, so to speak, in an age that's conscious of the ravages that have been done to the planet, the sacred value is actually eternal life. So that language is perfectly proper. It can be used again. It can be revived. It's not necessarily a mystifying language. It's a purifying language. And I suppose that's what I would like to do . . . This was not an ambition, but it is a kind of apologia for using words like soul and spirit. You want them to . . . yes, to be available, to purify possibilities again.

Jonathan Bing (essay date 4 December 1995)

SOURCE: "Seamus Heaney: Vindication of the Word 'Poet'," in *Publishers Weekly,* Vol. 242, No. 49, December 4, 1995, pp. 42-3.

[In the following essay, which is based on an interview with Heaney, Bing discusses the poet's early work and the ideas that led to his book, The Redress of Poetry.*]*

There is a Gaelic superstition still associated with Seamus Heaney's ancestral home in County Derry in Northern Ireland. According to Heaney, a St. Muredach O'Heney once presided over a monastic site affiliated with his family. It's said that if soil is dug from the ground of that site by a Heaney, it carries an aura of magic and beneficence.

Heaney, too, has an aura, if not a star power, shared by few contemporary poets, emanating as much from his leonine features and unpompous sense of civic responsibility as from the immediate accessibility of his lines. Since Robert Lowell dubbed Heaney "the most important Irish poet since Yeats," his poems have entered the core curricula of schools around the world. Listeners jam the rafters at his readings. He has published more than 10 volumes of poetry in 30 years, as well as three collections of essays, one play and a host of translations, chapbooks and other ephemera.

Commanding a great range of voices, idioms and metric conventions, Heaney's poetry nevertheless remains rooted in the soil of his native country-side, in the clash of ancient myth and modern politics, in domestic rituals and elegies for friends, family members and those lost to sectarian violence in Northern Ireland. Despite his oft-invoked pet name, "Famous Seamus," Heaney prefers the solace of his phoneless Wicklow cottage and the toilsome pleasures of teaching to the glare of the limelight. His new volume of critical prose, ***The Redress of Poetry,*** is a collection of lectures delivered at Oxford, where he is the Professor of Poetry.

Citing Heaney's "works of lyrical beauty and ethical depth, which exalt everyday miracles and the living past," the Nobel committee announced on Oct. 5 that Heaney is to receive this year's prize of $1.1 million. On that day, however, the 56-year-old poet was vacationing with his wife, Marie, in Greece, well beyond the reach of the international media. "We had just passed from Argus into Arcadia," he recalls, when—two days after the announcement—he happened to phone his children in Dublin (there are three, Michael, Christopher and Catherine, all in their 20s). "They were under siege."

When [*Publishers Weekly*] meets Heaney in Cambridge, Mass., a month later, the public's enchantment with him is unabated. The previous night, 2000 admirers waited in the rain in Harvard Yard to see Heaney read at the centenary celebration of the Harvard art museums.

There's clandestine air to our late-morning rendezvous. Slouched in a chair in a heavy tweed suit in his secluded room in the Harvard Inn, Heaney looks a bit haggard. Under his unruly plume of white hair, his face is tinged with apprehension. As a vacuum cleaner sounds in the hall, he confesses a "weariness" about the "pure publicity" associated with the prize, preferring instead to discuss the poetry itself and the landscape from which it emerged.

The eldest of nine siblings, Heaney was born at Mossbawn, a farm in Derry, 30 miles outside of Belfast. "It was a farming household," he recalls, "with enlightened values [and] a special sense of worth." He attended boarding school from the age of 12, and there he met Seamus Deane, now the Keough Professor of Irish Studies at the University of Notre Dame and the editor of *The Field Day Anthology of Irish Writing;* the two became fast friends, both entering Queen's University in Belfast in the same class. For 10 years, that intimacy shaped and sustained both writers' formative love of the written word ("Deane was the star in our literary firmament," Heaney recalls). In the early 1960s, Heaney taught literature at Queen's University and began placing poems in the *New Statesmen,* whose editor was Karl Miller ("one of the great editors of our time," notes Heaney), leading to a solicitation from Charles Monty, an editor at Faber & Faber in London. The publisher of Eliot, Auden, MacNeice and Lowell, Faber "was a much more translunar address in 1965," Heaney points out. "It was like getting a letter from God the Father."

Faber brought out ***Death of a Naturalist*** in 1966; it won several prizes, including the Somerset Maugham Award. Evincing the influence of Frost, Hopkins and Ted Hughes, these poems evoked his early years at Mossbawn, the tactile fluidity of the farmland, a fascination with buried things and the delights and terrors of childhood. He was to revisit that landscape often in subsequent books, but with *Door into the Dark* (1969), *Wintering Out* (1972) and, especially, *North* (1975), another Heaney emerged: an allegorist of national politics and mythology. In a series of "bog" poems, Heaney wrote of the mummified, iron-age corpses exhumed from the bogland, emblems of Ireland's first conquerors and martyrs. Other poems dealt with the politics of Ulster, its ethnic humiliations and poetry's role in confronting its terrible history.

In 1972, Heaney moved his family from Belfast to a cottage in Wicklow in the Irish Republic. As *North* took shape, he stopped teaching for three years. It was then, he recalls, resolutely raising his fist, that the full import of a life devoted to language and poetry grew clear. "I felt that I had vindicated poetry in myself and vindicated the word 'poet' for myself, and when I stood up, it was with the full force of my being," he says. The critic Helen Vendler, among the academy's staunchest Heaney fans, believes *North* is "one of the greatest of 20th century books of poetry, right up there with *Prufrock* or *Harmonium*."

Heaney marked the 1970s with teaching stints at Berkeley and Carysfort College in Dublin, and in 1981, he became a visiting professor at Harvard. Early on, he notes, "I made a choice, for better or worse, to work in the university in order to preserve a kind of nonchalance with regard to publication. I have an old-fashioned ethic of earning my keep. I also have a kind of poetic, protective notion that the poetry should not be a meal ticket."

Heaney also turned out prose—lambent memoirs of Mossbawn and critical essays on poetry—the first collection of which, *Preoccupations,* appeared in 1980. Asked about the difficulties involved in switching gears from poetry to prose, Heaney shrugs. "It's a different part of your being. That's what the muse means. To some extent [the essays] are my persona as teacher. They're my job. Poetry is completely different. It's a force that feeds off everything else," he says.

Tenured in the halls of academe, however, Heaney was not insulated from the unrest in Northern Ireland, which came to a head in the hunger strikes of the early 1980s. Prompted by the staging in Derry in 1980 of Brian Friel's play, *Translations,* which showed English surveyors traveling through 18th-century Ireland Anglicizing all the place names, Heaney cofounded the Field Day Theater Group with Friel, Deane, the actor Stephen Rea and others. "That play was a play of wondrous discovery and renewal," recalls Heaney. "It did what theater should do in a society. It was an intravenous shot for people." A pamphleteering campaign followed, as Heaney and Deane began publishing Field Day chapbooks on Irish politics and culture.

While cautiously optimistic about the ongoing peace process, Heaney credits Ulster's poets with a subtler grasp of the dualities of Irish history than the diplomats in Dublin and London. "I think the poetry is ahead of the peace. If you take writers like [Paul] Muldoon and [Ciaran] Carson

who live there, their language, their plays and their ploys as writers have to do with outstripping the binary condition that they were offered," he says. "Through changing the language, opening trap doors inside every statement and going into a postmodernist double-take, they have in a sense prefigured the kinds of society that's called for."

If the vitality of Northern Irish literature springs, in part, from political friction, does Heaney worry that the poetry will slacken, as ancient enmities are soothed? "Peace talks don't necessarily mean the disappearance of the causes of the collisions," he says. "It means the onset of civilized ways of handling it, you know, rather than barbaric ways of handling it." He pauses. "I think that every writer in Ireland, North and South, has gone through elegy and tragedy. Stylistically speaking, the challenge is to move it on forward into adept and skeptical playfulness. A post-Beckettian poetics is called for."

It is in the context of Heaney's vexed relationship to art and politics that *The Redress of Poetry* is best appreciated. When Heaney's tenure at Oxford began in 1989, he says, "I know I was expected to do a kind of postcolonial resentment of English literature, which seems to me predictable, and other people are doing it better than I can."

Heaney chose instead a less fashionable plan: to redeem a few canonical, British and Irish poets from the simplifications and neglect of academic ideologues. Heaney's thesis: that poetry of the highest order shouldn't be fettered to political crusades. Through its "fine excess," its power to outstrip the circumstances it observes and broaden the horizons of its readers, great poetry redresses the profounder spiritual imbalances of its age. This credo is delineated in *Redress* in chapters on Herbert, Wilde, Yeats, Dylan Thomas and others.

"I think literature is there to open the spaces, not to erect tariff barriers," Heaney explains. "The notion of balance, of one form of life redressing another, of the imagined redressing the endured, that is just a central trope. But it also seems observably true that the sense of proportion, the sense of joy, the sense of irony, depends upon a certain amphibiousness between what we can conceive of and what we have to put up with."

The idea that anything that amplifies the spirit can be tied down with a dainty, politically correct label—it's damning, it's deadly. Rapture is its own good.

—Seamus Heaney

His favorite chapter, on Christopher Marlowe, recovers *Tamberlaine* and "Hero and Leander" from critics whose sole interest has been to read these texts as complicitous in the bloody legacy of English imperialism. "It's just a corrective to a kind of constricting panic in people that they will give offense," Heaney says. "The language that people are offered in the academy is totally a language of suspicion. Of course, that was a very salubrious language from my generation. But if you teach suspicion to people who have nothing within their minds to suspect, I think it proceeds toward the nihilistic." He pauses, his eyes at-winkle. "The idea that anything that amplifies the spirit can be tied down with a dainty, politically correct label—it's damning, it's deadly. Rapture is its own good."

In the U.S., Oxford published Heaney's first five volumes before he was discovered by Farrar, Straus and Giroux, which now handles all of his work. His editor is Jonathan Galassi, who succeeded Michael di Capua and Pat Strachan. Faber serves as his American agent. No appearances are planned to mark publication of *The Redress,* but come January, Heaney, who teaches at Harvard one semester each year, will again be stationed in his office at Widener Library, and wending his usual way through Harvard Square. "I keep dropping in on the Grolier Poetry Bookshop, run by Louisa Solano," he says. "She valiantly keeps going in what I think is a perilous enough situation for po-etry-only [booksellers]."

Meanwhile, he hopes that the Nobel Prize money (which is untaxed in Ireland) will buy him some solitude. With five days a week at his Dublin home and two at the cottage in Wicklow, "I have a fairly constant domestic life," he says. But the creative spirit demands sufficient time for germination and slow revision. "I'm not a kind of spillage system of verse," he laughs. In May, FSG will issue *The Spirit Level,* Heaney's first volume of poetry in five years. The poet is only middle-aged, after all, and the level of *his* spirit remains very high, indeed.

REVIEW OF HEANEY'S MOST RECENT WORK

John Bayley   **(review date 20 October 1995)**

SOURCE: "Professing Poetry," in *The Times Literary Supplement,* No. 4829, October 20, 1995, pp. 9-10.

[*In the following review of* The Redress of Poetry, *Bayley maintains that though Heaney's criticism is sound and fair, it offers no new startling insights.*]

Seamus Heaney's slim book of offerings as Oxford Professor of Poetry gives the impression of being adjusted with courtly discretion to an audience who expect the familiar rather than the new. His most interesting essays are an introduction on the *The Redress of Poetry,* and its follow-up on *Hero and Leander* in an Irish context. Later pieces on MacDiarmid and Dylan Thomas, Brian Merriman and John Clare, are sound but conventional, as if Heaney as a poet can only be saying the proper things about other poets, as he does in passing about contemporaries like Holub, Brodsky and the Europeans. The poet as diplomat is an honourable and unusual role (and Heaney's success in it has been suitably and deservedly recognized, along with his achievement in poetry, by the Nobel Committee);

but the critic exercising the same kind of function runs the risk of giving pleasure without surprise or illumination.

And yet the essays are rich in good things, one of the best being Heaney's discussion of Marlowe's erotic verse, in which he points out that "the reader is enticed towards a tolerant attitude by having his or her sexual preferences toyed with, and having the opposite preference discreetly insinuated at the same time". Heaney's own enticements are equally admirable, as if political correctness, in sexual as in other matters, came as naturally to him as breathing. It seems even to come to him naturally on the matter of death. Though never censorious, he cannot stomach Larkin's great "Aubade", in which the hopelessness of the situation is redeemed only by the grim Anglo-drabness of work that has to be done and the hope of receiving letters—"postmen like doctors go from house to house". Heaney prefers the rhetorical consolations of Yeats ("O Rocky Voice / Shall we in that great night rejoice?") and, more surprisingly, of Samuel Beckett, both of whom he considers, in contrast to Larkin, to be "on the side of life".

Heaney's infallible courtliness goes none the less with an uninsistent but ultimate criterion, which can seem a bit like a poetic version of political correctness. What was lost in the later Dylan Thomas was a quality that might be called "tonal rectitude", "taking tone in the radically vindicating sense attributed to it by Eavan Boland". The origins of such rectitude "must always be in a suffered world rather than a conscious craft". An ambiguous claim, which might mean much or nothing, and yet Heaney endorses Boland's judgment in a prose as persuasive as his poetry. The power of a "poet's undermusic" should come from "a kind of veteran knowledge which has gathered to a phonetic and rhythmic head, and forced an utterance":

> It is, for example, the undermusic of just such knowledge that makes Emily Dickinson devastating as well as endearing, and makes the best of John Ashbery's poetry the common unrarefied expression of a disappointment that is beyond self-pity.

That is eloquently said, although the attribution of "rectitude", of any sort, to these or any other poets may seem superfluous and even dubious. Larkin's sardonic shade is yet once again in the background. Does he, one wonders, possess "tonal rectitude"—TR as it might be called, an excuse for PCness, which he certainly did not possess? Like all other such attempts at a general criterion—Matthew Arnold's "touchstones" for instance—this one dissolves into mere concept when confronted with the realities of poetry.

And yet apart from things which Larkin himself would not have bothered about (he always refused to give any kind of lecture on poetry), both as poets and human beings Heaney and Larkin have much in common. Heaney's rectitude (also a more diplomatic term than correctness) is never nationalistic; as he movingly tells us in his last brief lecture, **"Frontiers of Writing"**, which includes a poem in which he takes leave of his professorial duties, he and Larkin, the English poet who loved Ulster, and once worked over there, "are part / Of some new commonwealth of art" and can salute each other "with independent heart". In the same way, he says, Louis MacNeice was "an Irish protestant writer with Anglocentric tendencies, who managed to be faithful to his Ulster inheritance, his Irish affections, and his English predilections". Still more important is the homeliness and love of domestic detail which Heaney and Larkin share, as poets and as men, including a relish for those "small blameless pleasures" praised by Larkin as typical of the art of Barbara Pym. And it is a fine as well as a humane critic who has noticed, as Heaney has, the homely touches that humanize those elegantly Ovidian and androgynous antics in Marlowe's *Hero and Leander:*

> If not for love, yet, love, for pity sake
> Me in thy bed and maiden bosom take;
> At least vouchsafe those arms some little room,
> Who hoping to embrace thee, cheerly swum . . .
> Herewith affrighted Hero shrunk away,
> And in her lukewarm place Leander lay.

A flagrant case of sexual harassment, but never mind that—Heaney shows just what it is in the scene that is so touching. "The lukewarm place that Leander slips into under the bedclothes was probably never warmed again, in exactly the right way, until Molly Bloom jingled the bedstrings more than three hundred years later."

FURTHER READING

Burris, Sidney. *The Poetry of Resistance: Seamus Heaney and the Pastoral Tradition.* Athens, OH: Ohio University Press, 1990, 165 p.

Analyzes Heaney's work in relation to the tradition of pastoral poetry, a form outwardly concerned with nature but encompassing many other philosophical and social concerns. Burris calls Heaney "a deeply literary poet, one whose consolations often lie in the invigorating strains of the poetic tradition itself."

Guenther, Charles. "Strong, Singular Voice Thrives Amid Turmoil." *St. Louis Post-Dispatch* (5 April 1992): 5C

Positive review of Heaney's *Seeing Things.*

————. "Irish Poet Who Chronicled 2 Cultures Wins Nobel Prize." *St. Louis Post-Dispatch* (6 October 1995): 3A.

Report on Heaney's winning the Nobel Prize.

Tapscott, Stephen. "Poetry and Trouble: Seamus Heaney's *Irish Purgatorio.*" *Southwest Review* 71, No. 4 (Autumn 1986): 519-35.

Discusses the relation of Heaney's work to that of William Butler Yeats and James Joyce, focusing on their contrasting views of Ireland.

Additional coverage of Heaney's life and career is contained in the following sources published by Gale Research: *Concise Dictionary of Literary Biography, 1960 to the Present; Contemporary Authors,* **Vols. 85-88, rev. ed.;** *Contemporary Authors New Revision Series,* **Vols. 25, 48;** *Contemporary Literary Criticism,* **Vols. 5, 7, 14, 25, 37, 74;** *Dictionary of Literary Biography,* **Vol. 40;** *DISCovering Authors: British; DISCovering Authors Modules: Most-Studied Authors* **and** *Poets;* **and** *Major Twentieth-Century Writers.*

Alan Hollinghurst
The Folding Star

Award: James Tait Black Memorial Book Prize for Fiction

Born in 1954, Hollinghurst is an English novelist, editor, poet, and critic.

For further information on his life and works, see *CLC,* Volume 55.

INTRODUCTION

Described as a homosexual version of Vladimir Nabokov's novel, *Lolita* (1955), *The Folding Star* (1994) concerns Edward Manners, a gay British teacher who leaves his birthplace to begin a tutoring job in Belgium. Although he engages in various affairs with men of questionable intentions, Manners becomes so enamored and obsessed with one of his young paramours, Luc Altidore, that he follows him, spies on him, and steals articles of his clothing. After consummating their relationship—an event initiated by Luc—the teenager runs away and Manners, still preoccupied with his student, begins a search for him. Hollinghurst interweaves the story of Manners and Luc with that of a Symbolist painter of Flemish origins named Edgard Orst, who, like Manners, was infatuated with one of his young models.

Noted for its focus on physical attraction, sex and sexuality, fixation, and the feelings of anticipation and loss associated with desire, *The Folding Star* has received a mixed reception. Hollinghurst has occasionally been castigated for introducing the historical story line concerning Orst instead of focusing on gay characters in a contemporary setting and for refusing to examine the sanctity of the student-teacher relationship. The novel's main characters and its depiction of romantic love have also been faulted as unconvincing and undeveloped. Nevertheless, Hollinghurst has been praised for his examination of art and desire, and his use of a gay protagonist. Nominated for the Booker Prize as well as the James Tait Black Memorial Prize, *The Folding Star* has also been lauded for its elegiac depiction of English society and culture—particularly in those sections recounting Manners's childhood—and for its literary richness. The novel, for example, has been compared to *Lolita,* Thomas Mann's *Der Tod in Venedig* (1912; *Death in Venice*), and Marcel Proust's *A la recherche du temps perdu* (1954; *Remembrance of Things Past*); the story also takes its title from a poem by John Milton, which relates, in part, a shepherd's obligations to his flock. Gabriele Annan has noted, however, that these intertextual aspects of the book do "not make the novel a quilt of pastiches. . . . The texture of [*The Folding Star*] is as

densely sophisticated as a Flemish tapestry (though tapestry is the one form of Flemish art that doesn't figure in it). That is one reason why it is an immense pleasure to read; the others are funniness and poetry, both handled with amazing sensitivity and accuracy."

PRINCIPAL WORKS

Confidential Chats with Boys (poems) 1982
The Swimming-Pool Library (novel) 1988
The Folding Star (novel) 1994

CRITICISM

Peter Kemp   (review date 27 May 1994)

SOURCE: "Aesthetic Obsessions," in *The Times Literary Supplement,* No. 4756, May 27, 1994, p. 19.

[*In the following review, Kemp lauds stylistic and thematic aspects of* The Folding Star.]

Alan Hollinghurst's new novel is chock-a-block with visual artefacts: Symbolist paintings, still-lifes, pensive Virgins, country scenes, portraits, murals, etchings, engravings, waxen-looking historical tableaux, blackened Victorian allegories, charcoal drawings, townscapes, seascapes. The most significant of them, done by a turn-of-the-century Belgian painter, Edgard Orst, exhibit an imagination dwelling on the same patterns, but rendering them in different tones.

Not dissimilarly, *The Folding Star* reproduces—with one major new motif and pervasive alterations of shading and highlight—the distinctive configurations of Hollinghurst's first novel, *The Swimming-Pool Library* (1988). That novel silhouetted a gay man against a city that was graphically portrayed and vividly populated. So does this book. But, this time, the setting isn't the flamboyant London of the early 1980s but a Flemish backwater in the early 1990s. The spring and summer of the earlier novel are replaced by autumn and winter. Instead of a wealthy, glamorous young swaggerer round the metropolis, this book takes as its narrator a slightly pudgy, bespectacled older man, teaching English in a silted-up museum city, whose carillons, stepped gables, canals, swans and Memling paintings suggest Bruges. As yet unheard-of in the hectic homosexual milieux of *The Swimming-Pool Library,* AIDS and AZT now cast shadows.

This more twilight atmosphere is appropriate to *The Folding Star,* in that the novel counterpoints two *fin-de-siècle* fixations: the 1890s obsession of Edgard Orst, with a flame-haired actress who inspired the Sphinxes, Herodiases and other hieratic temptresses on his crepuscular canvases, and the 1990s obsession of an English tutor, Edward Manners, with his seventeen-year-old pupil, Luc Altidore.

Rather as William Beckwith, who narrated *The Swimming-Pool Library,* gradually uncovered secrets from the life of a figure of a much earlier generation, so here Manners becomes increasingly acquainted with Orst's past. The perversities, betrayals and culminating Nazi murderousness he learns of parallel the perversities, betrayals and culminating racist murderousness that came to light in the earlier book.

Orst is, though, primarily seen as an instance of an infatuated imagination, projecting his enthralment with his actress-lover—sometimes powerfully, sometimes absurdly, sometimes repellently—into his art. A later, homosexual counterpart to him, Manners does the same thing in his story. Captivated by blond, clever Luc, he alternates spasms of swoony besottedness ("We had never walked up a flight of stairs together before") with fantasy sessions in

which they enjoy fabulous sex. A rather creepy roguishness towards the teenager he is twice as old as ("a feeling of being linked with him in some wonderful delinquency") works itself up into heated contortions.

Salaciously salivating over his love-object's name ("Luc's cul a dream palindrome—the two round cheeks of it and the lick of the s between"), Manners can occasionally resemble a gay variant on Humbert Humbert ("Lo-lee-ta: the tip of the tongue taking a trip of three steps down the palate to tap, at three, on the teeth"). Not merely a teacher but uncommonly entranced with school and schoolboys—he's charmed to find the room he rents overlooks a boys' college; the novel's central section is a lengthy, vivid flashback to his boarding-school days—he's revealed as, behind the subtlety and sophistication he elsewhere displays, in some respects still puerile.

What makes his narrative engrossing, despite this, isn't its twists of plot or the closing revelations that here, as in *The Swimming-Pool Library,* retrospectively re-slant events. It's the honesty about himself and his life that Manners admirably maintains. Openness to and about a diverse range of experience intensely vivifies this book.

As its title indicates—compacting together connotations of "embrace . . . implosion . . . something ancient but evanescent"—*The Folding Star* highlights doomed rapture. But more mundane manifestations of sexuality are arranged about it, too. Though Manners's fervour for Luc keeps hazing into a blur of bedazzlement, there's sharp-eyed perceiving of different physical, emotional and psychological elements melded into sexual attraction in the sections of the novel concerned with his other affairs (again like Beckwith, he has two regular lovers along with numerous temporary pleasurings). Like Hollinghurst's earlier novel, this book excels at near-documentary portrayal—lusty, sardonic, beguiled, unillusioned—of the public and private rituals, routines, excitements and disappointments of gay life. Like that book too, it swings between rarefied aesthetic satisfactions and thrills of a more fundamental kind.

Even in its sexiest moments, it never loses its intellectual poise. Dry witticisms intersperse sweaty couplings. Along with strong responsiveness to male physique and appeal goes informed receptivity to art: Manners is as adept at appraising Old Masters as he is at sizing up young men. With his urbane, ironic—rather Jamesian—disposition, he's also an ideal figure to do justice to the book's scenes of slyly funny social comedy.

Ranging from romantic obsession to anonymous sex in the undergrowth, from amused observation of a dinner-party to submersion in the symbolic shadows of nineteenth-century Decadent painting, making detours down literary and musical by-ways of the twentieth century, inspecting Gothic architecture and gay bars, two-way mirrors and differences between the placings of the eyes in Flemish and Italian Renaissance pictures, *The Folding Star* is a novel of considerable breadth. What gives it its depth is the candour, wit, sensuous immediacy and melancholy intelligence applied to it.

Nicholson Baker   (review date 9 June 1994)

SOURCE: "Lost Youth," in *London Review of Books,* Vol. 16, No. 11, June 9, 1994, p. 6.

[*An American novelist, nonfiction writer, and short story writer, Baker is the author of* The Mezzanine *(1988),* Room Temperature *(1990),* U and I *(1991),* Vox *(1992), and* The Fermata *(1994). In the review below, he offers a favorable assessment of* The Folding Star.]

Alan Hollinghurst is better at bees than Oscar Wilde. On the opening page of *The Picture of Dorian Gray,* Wilde has them 'shouldering their way through the long unmown grass'. A bee must never be allowed to 'shoulder'. Later that afternoon, Dorian Gray, alarmed by Lord Henry Wotton's graphic talk of youth's inevitable degeneration, drops a lilac blossom that he has been 'feverishly' sniffing. Bee *numero due* appears, taking most of a paragraph to 'scramble all over the stellated globe of the tiny blossoms' and further interrogate the 'stained trumpet of a Tyrian convolvulus'. Here again, when you're talking about bee-legs and their prehensile dealings with plant tissue, 'scramble' doesn't quite do the trick.

In *The Folding Star,* on the other hand, Alan Hollinghurst's narrator (who has several traits in common with Wilde's disillusioned, youth-seducing Lord Henry) describes lying on a bench in the sun, 'breathing the seedy vanilla smell of a bush on which half a dozen late bees still dropped and toppled'. 'Dropped and toppled', with its slumping music, is brief and extremely good: avoiding the mention of blossoms altogether, it nicely captures the heavy, dangled, abdominal clumsiness of those end-of-shift pollen-packers.

There are things like this, and better than this, to be grateful for on almost every page of Hollinghurst's new book—in almost every paragraph, in fact. And yet it isn't glutting to read because its excellences are so varied and multiplanar. Hollinghurst, it seems, has an entirely sane and unmanic wish to supply seriatim all the pleasures that the novel is capable of supplying. The conversation, especially, is brilliant, but everything—depraved or refined or both—is tuned and compensated for, held forth and plucked away, allusively waved at when there's no time for a thorough work-over, and neatly parsed when there is. The narrator is a sad man, past-besotted, unachieving and 'drinky' if not drunken, with moments of misanthropic Larkinism ('Books are a load of crap,' he unconvincingly quotes near the beginning), but his lost-youth mood is the opposite of depressing because he describes whatever suits him with an intelligence that cheers itself up as it goes.

He—Edward Manners—has come to a mythical, silt-choked, fallen Flemish city (Ghentwerp? Brugeselles? some hybrid, anyway) to start fresh by tutoring two boys in English. One is the son of an art historian who has been plugging away at a *catalogue raisonné* of a minor (and fictional) Burne-Jonesite Symbolist and syphilitic with the wonderful name of Orst—Edgard Orst, that is, depicter of fabric-draped interiors, spare seascapes, and allegorical women with orange hair and racy chokers made of Roman medals. But this first boy has asthma and is plump, so for-

get him. The other 'lad', Luc Altidore, 17, he of the wide shoulders and wondrously puffy upper lip, is the descendant of an eccentric luminary named Anthonis Altidore, a 16th-century printer (Christophe Plantin?) who, so we learn, successfully traced his ancestry straight back to the Virgin Mary. ('One imagines some pretty murky areas around, say, the third century,' somebody comments.) Despite the presence of a bewildering array of men and their variously sized and angled organalia in Edward Manners's gay bar-coded sensibility, young Luc, though he may possibly be a heterosexual (mixed blessing!), and though the thought that he is related to Jesus Christ is 'slightly unnerving', utterly appropriates our likeable if occasionally glum hero's romantic imagination. Luc is no rocket scientist. 'I could have impressed him, even gently squashed him with my knowledge,' Manners thinks, but allowances must be made for the language problem, and anyway, as Lord Henry Wotton explains, 'Beauty is a form of Genius—is higher, indeed, than Genius as it needs no explanation.' Manners, in a fever of early-thirties infatuation, can't stop thinking about that cursed 'molten trumpeter's lip' which blows all the available competition away; like some 'creepy old hetero', he finds himself sniffing used lad-undies and crusty lad-hankies, tasting dry toothbrushes and stealing negatives in order to get closer to this unattainable Altidorian Gray, who though he is at his best in white jeans can 'ironise' even a pair of khakis, leggy piece of work that he is.

The Folding Star turns out to be one of the few satisfying books around that treats the relationship between art and life and the secrets they keep from each other.

—Nicholson Baker

Like Hollinghurst's great first book, *The Swimming-Pool Library, The Folding Star* has many characters but few women. The author takes pains to greet them and make them feel welcome in a chapter or two, and he clearly bears them no ill-will, but he can't focus on them for longer than half an hour. It's too bad that we don't have a little more time with the charming (and page-boyish) Edie, for example, who is willing to listen to any lurid sketch of gay fetishism with 'the open-minded expression of someone on holiday good-naturedly learning the rules of a foreign national game'. But Edward is fundamentally suspicious of, or at least uninterested in, the 'never fully plausible world of heterosexual feeling'. An awed or intrigued reference to the male 'genital ensemble' occurs every fifteen pages or so, as well it should. (For instance: 'sometimes modest and strong, sometimes lolloping and heavy-headed, its only constants an easy foreskin, a certain presence, and a heather-honey beauty'; or, he 'pissed fiercely in the bushes; then stood for a while slapping his dick in his palm as a doctor smacks a vein he wants to rise'.) An analogous visual insatiability within the straight world, however, Edward views with fastidious distaste. Presented with some antique dirty pictures of a laundry-woman, he says: 'I made my interest scientific, dimly thinking what a prig I was when it came to women and the indignities men demanded of them.'

All this seems both true and very funny—there is a deep chasm, no doubt essentially vulval, of reciprocal incomprehensibility that normally separates the gay cosmology from the prevailing straightgeist; we might as well recognise the obvious cleavage and wrest some entertainment out of (for example) our mutually baffling pornography. Manners, with refreshing intolerance, goes so far as to say that 'there was always something lacking in those men who had never had a queer phase as boys, it showed in a certain dryness of imagination, a bland tolerance uncoloured by any suppression of their own, a blindness to the spectrum's violet end.'

Blind and violet-deprived though we few remaining creepy heteros are (and sleep-deprived, as well—Hollinghurst includes a glimpse of a new father, who 'yawned like a dog, with a whine too'), we nonetheless do our best to learn as much as we can about our cross-pollinating betters, and we welcome, or ought to welcome, with foot-stamping and cheers and the earnest rattling of our model-airplane kits, the inspired historical verisimilitude that Hollinghurst brings to bear in both his books on the making of an alternative creation-myth of artistic evolution. The retroactive homosexualisation of poetic history, and especially of the tradition of pastoral elegy and rustic reflection as it works its way down through Milton, William Collins, Wordsworth and Shelley all the way to the fictional Georgian poet 'Sir Perry Dawlish', is accomplished with astonishing ease and plausibility in *The Folding Star.*

In one scene, the adolescent Edward waits outdoors for the evening star to come out and thinks over his phrase-hoard of nature poetry and 'becomes a connoisseur of the last lonely gradings of blue into black'; and in doing so somehow leads us to the conviction that all the grunting, groping and 'stubbly frenching' that apparently goes on at dusk between men and boys in decrepit parks and over-grown commons, in ruined abbeys and hermitages and other handy arcadias, has always gone on and is good and worthwhile—is, indeed, the secret triumphant under-theme of all pastoral verse. Edward looks over the trees at that trope of tropes, Hesperus, star of the muse and of poetic attainment, the 'folding-star' of Collins's 'Ode to Evening' or (as in Milton's 'Comus') the 'Star that bids the shepherd fold', and it seems to become for him the wink-ing lure and symbol of all things perseveringly evanescent, immortally short-lived, bravely tearful and impeccably campy. Edward never goes so far as to say that his private muse, his beloved vespertine twinkler, is actually *puck-ered,* forthrightly anal, but he is too visually on the ball not to want to allow us to infer that cinctured sense of 'folding star', as well—he refers to Luc (the name is a bro-ken spangle from 'Lucinda', perhaps) as a 'star' and as 'starlit' and we concede the point. And it's a star of mourning, too; the Aidsy sadness of so much recent loss, the disappearance of brilliant youths and the disappear-ance of one's own youth's brilliance, and the more general sadness of the unknowable generations of self-stifled and closeted poets that preceded our outspoken time, and then, too, the simple asexual unattainability of much of what we really want and the unretrievability of what we best remember, are some of the emotions toward which Hollinghurst shepherds us.

The Folding Star turns out to be one of the few satisfying books around that treats the relationship between art and life and the secrets they keep from each other. In the 13th century, the English exported wool to Bruges, where Flemish guild-members wove it into cloth and tapestry. Edward Manners here exports himself, his native language, his wool-gathered raw-material of educated reading, his sexual appetite, to a Brugesed and battered city that goes to work on him and knots him as we read into a figure in its ancient hieratic carpet. The allegory in the book is thick and ambiguous and un-Jamesian: like a well-hung (shall we say) Flemish tapestry—like the Flemish tapestry, perhaps, that hangs in the childhood room where Dorian Gray secretly stores his horrifying portrait, or like the tapestries Edgard Orst paints behind his mysterious orange-haired models—it's decorative and plush and fine, exuberantly pictorial but uninsistently in the background.

Given the man-boy theme, we may be forgiven for keeping half an eye out for gender-flipped Lolitanisms. There are at least two: a pointed passage about the pronunciation of 'Lucasta' ('the darting buss with which it began, the up-ward and downward flicker of the tongue against the teeth'); and the Frenchified 'dream palindrome' of 'Luc' and 'cul'. One could conceivably call these defects, but they aren't—as a matter of fact, the play on 'Luc' and 'cul' helps dissolve another minuscule potential reproof, which is that there are a few too many uses of the vogue word 'clueless'. For 'clueless' is only a dream anagram of 'Luc-less'—and the pain of Luc-lessness is what this clue-laden book, lucky for us, is all about.

Victoria Hollander   (review date 10 June 1994)

SOURCE: "Dawdling Gay," in *New Statesman & Society,* Vol. 7, No. 306, June 10, 1994, p. 37.

[*In the review below, Hollander provides a mixed assess-ment of* The Folding Star.]

It is odd that nothing more in the way of an aesthetic has emerged from our *fin de siècle* than those cod modes desig-nated by the drab prefixes post- or de-. The last end-of-century produced the movements of Symbolism and Dec-adence, from which emerged the modern sensibility. In *The Folding Star,* Alan Hollinghurst tips his hat to them, while enlisting their help to build an aesthetic and, indeed, an aestheticism for our time.

A large part of that aesthetic is homosexuality, of a partic-ular kind. Like the similar narrating "I" of Hollinghurst's debut novel, *The Swimming Pool Library,* Edward Man-ners—the hero of his second—seesaws between affectless cruising and an obsessional yearning for a non-negotiable love-object, again an adolescent.

Whereas the earlier hero was an aristocratic golden boy,

a swimmer in all elements, Edward is bespectacled, dark, 33, running to fat and possessed of a distancing erudition—a step on towards that portrait that lurks in the Hollinghurst attic. More monomaniacal, nay hysterical, in his pursuit of a fetishised beloved, he embodies the severance of emotion from carnality; a gay version of the Madonna vs whore sort of love much favoured by the Decadents.

We meet him on the evening of his arrival in an historic Belgian city (probably Bruges) where after a vain shot at a heterosexual labourer, he lands in the gay bar where much of the novel will revolve. By page ten, he is busy with speedy fast-food sex, an activity stilled by the revelation of the two-way mirror in his hotel room. This is a city of secrets, of betrayals, of grey moodiness, a sort of hyperbolic England where Edward is both spy and spied-upon. It is a correlative for his dandyism, which throws on the peacockery of lush but "finical" (a favourite word) prose as a means not only of display but also of concealment.

The hyper-intelligent Edward, a writer manqué, has come to this country to give English conversation lessons to two school-boys whose reported English, in one case, is perfect. One of the boys is Luc, a "blond Aztec" whose photograph has already determined his teacher's infatuation; the other an unattractive asthmatic called Marcel (Proust Ha Ha Ha: one of the many referential or anagrammatic sideshows).

Both boys can lay claim to Belgium's great Symbolist flowering. Luc's ancient family (descended directly, somehow, from the Virgin Mary) published Maeterlinck and Verhaeren; Marcel's father has more or less inherited the curatorship of the local museum consecrated to Edgard (equals Edward) Orst, a Symbolist painter and "aesthete par excellence" whose devotion to his dead (female) lover took on ever more elaborate and perverted forms.

While Edward makes merry with rough trade, his unrequited lust for Luc ascends to a screech of self-abasement. Ranging secretly about the boy's rooms, he tastes his inamorato's toothbrush, sniffs his bed and paws through the laundry basket, stealing some Calvins (which he wears). With a porn-merchant lover, he breaks into the house beside the one where Luc and the others of his trio of shimmering *jeunes gens en fleurs* are holidaying, training binoculars on the 17-year-old as he sunbathes, his excitement relieved by a bit of friendly masturbation from his pal.

One imagines that Edward is doomed never to fuck Luc, but in one graphic scene we at long last get a glimpse of tenderness and real eroticism, in which response outweighs the anatomical detail. But even here is a disjunction: the narrative abruptly devolves from the present to the past, and Edward's consummation is prefaced by grief for the "desolate undertow of success".

Fuir, là-bas fuir!, as Mallarmé wrote. Anywhere but here, any time but now, anyone but you: the great beautifying No. From the Symbolists and the Decadents through to Proust, the mode was escape, the destination the unattainable, but the result was an unexpected wisdom.

Although *The Folding Star* twins Edward with Orst in a carefully documented history that conjoins the gravitas of Nazism with the lurid reclusiveness of the painter (heavily modelled on Huysmans' Des Esseintes), the parallels persist more as a ratification of the novel than as a true deepening of it. Orst's work, Edward tells us, was "hideous, poignant or shocking . . . perhaps all these things at once". Paul, the curator, claims for it a poetry of mysterious contrasts, "like images in a dream".

Ricocheting from *nostalgie de la boue* to *nostalgie du snob,* from arcania to *Hot Hunks* demotic, from empurpled swoon to social comedy, Hollinghurst nevertheless fails to discover in the mannerisms of a previous age a satisfying manner for his own. The novel fizzles out after the love scene, when Luc dies, or disappears, or dissolves; while Edward remains in his frenzy of stasis. Even our own lousy *fin de siècle* deserves more vitality than this.

James Wood   (review date 28 August 1994)

SOURCE: "England Calling," in *Manchester Guardian Weekly,* August 28, 1994, p. 29.

[*Woods is chief literary critic for the* Guardian. *In the review below, he lauds Hollinghurst's focus on and elegiac evocation of England, English society, and childhood in* The Folding Star.]

A lot of people have noticed that Alan Hollinghurst's second novel [*The Folding Star*] is "beautifully written" of course—people now use this phrase very soothingly, as if it were the solution to a puzzle. Certainly, Hollinghurst's language, with its patrician roll, and its self-savouring languor, is worth keen attention; but the novel's real achievement is to have created a viable contemporary *English* prose, peachy with remembered glows, but not mopingly retrospective.

This is not a negligible or insular achievement. Post-war English fiction has, largely, been unable to tell convincing national epics; instead of English novels, we have novels of Englishness (most egregiously in Peter Ackroyd's work). Balzac called fiction "the secret history of nations", and Alan Hollinghurst seems to know this secret epic cannot be blustered into being. On the contrary, nationalism in art is like a medieval town: it radiates outwards from a neglected centre.

The Folding Star begins foggily. Edward Manners, an old and seedily fatigued 33, arrives in a Bruges-like Flemish city. He is teaching English to two teenage boys, one of whom, the pure and fair Luc Altidore, he has fallen in love with. Edward is quickly inducted into the city's gay life, but the milieu seems too easy for Hollinghurst—Edward's round of bars and clubs seems a way of avoiding a necessary fattening of detail and theme. Initially, the book seems heavy and opaque. But it deepens slowly, and it soon teaches you to move at its own rich, slippered pace. The reader realises at length that this is a book that must dawdle, for the novel's dreamy theme is the elusiveness of romance, the elsewhere of childhood, the ungraspability of memory.

Luc is fabulously unattainable, and his unattainability slowly comes to represent (though this is too forceful a word) the glowing blank of Edward's own childhood. The impossibility of declaring love inflates the agony: "I felt my throat streaming, pulsing like a dove's with unspoken 'I love you's." Luc is unattainable not just for numerous practical reasons, but because he is the spirit of innocence. At one moment, Edward recalls seeing Luc's bedroom for the first time—"how young it all still looked, and how unguarded, and hence reproachful". Reproachful, because innocence is always a reproach to corruption, and Edward is undeniably corrupt. His corruption is not just the murderous, obliterating lust he hoards for Luc; it is the corruption of no longer being innocent.

This is the elegiac corridor through which Hollinghurst's lovely words swim like dust in sunlight; and it is not hard to hear their Larkinian music. In Hollinghurst's "how young it all still looked, and how unguarded . . ." we are reminded of Larkin's poem "Maiden Name": "How beautiful you were, and near, and young". It is in the book's middle section, when Edward returns to his childhood town, Rough Common, just south of London, that the book finds its secret pivot and rockingly swells. Edward has returned for a funeral, and recalls his lost childhood—the summery boredom of youth.

Late in the novel, Edward, trying to keep himself awake, recites half-remembered poems to himself. Suddenly the book delivers itself of its Larkinian theme of memory and elegiac betrayal:

> I tried to remember the whole of poems I'd once learned by heart . . . but memory was tarnished, words were spotted over, image blurred into image . . . When they faltered I left them and went drowsily towards the mirage they had conjured up, of summer dusks, funny old anecdotes, old embarrassments that still made me burn, boys' cocks and kisses under elms that had died with boyhood's end.

Kisses under elms that had died with boyhood's end—the softened syntax and phrasing is almost shamelessly English (though one shouldn't miss the slyness with which Hollinghurst slips "boys' cocks" into this pastoral bed). The novel's great achievement is to nuzzle this theme without rubbing it too hard. Edward remembers, for example, a family ritual—how, every summer, they would open the windows, close the curtains, and watch Wimbledon on television. Occasionally, one could hear a plane— "the sonic wallow of a plane distancing in slow gusts above". The whole experience seemed "an English limbo of light and shade, near and far, subtly muddled and displaced."

In some intangible but exquisite way, the novel's prose actually enacts this English limbo—it basks drowsily, it has its own kind of sonic wallow. Hollinghurst partly does this by avoiding the fetish of detail and choosing instead the mellower and more abstract approximateness of adjectives. And stunning adjectives these are—a first kiss, the mouths "open and sour with need"; "the loose purr of a car over cobbles"; "the mackintosh-scented gloom" of a tent's interior; a ski-jacket's "whispering cocoon", and on and on. There is something dreamy about this adjectival conjuring, and at length the novel's Flemish town—at one point likened to "a city in a book of hours"—becomes a

kind of dream city. Indeed, the novel's language floats beautifully away into the passionate reticence of all romance. And this is also the passionate reticence, the forceful hesitation of true art—this novel proves so gladdeningly.

Felice Picano (review date September 1994)

SOURCE: "The Tutor's Tale," in *Lambda Book Report*, Vol. 4, September, 1994, pp. 18-20.

[*An American novelist, poet, editor, memoirist, playwright, nonfiction writer, and scriptwriter, Picano frequently writes on gay culture and issues. In the following, he assesses the strengths and weaknesses of* The Folding Star.]

Alan Hollinghurst's debut with **The Swimming Pool Library** was so sudden and complete a few years back that many Americans were surprised to discover that he didn't just pop out of nowhere, but in fact had been the editor of the prestigious *Times Literary Supplement* for some time. This fact may have explained the rapture with which the book was received in England, but it didn't explain what a wonderful first novel it was, and how, after an excruciatingly long wait, there was finally another gay British novel fit to place next to *A Single Man,* not to mention a dozen American gay novels in between.

The Folding Star is Hollinghurst's newest book and already garnering high praise across the Atlantic. For American fans, it may prove more problematic. I suspect it's an earlier book than **The Swimming Pool Library,** one he returned to after that book's success. Like the other novel, it opens with a casually related gay pickup and its narrator is a good-looking, youthful, over-educated fellow. Also like the earlier book, unsavory incidents from the past are pulled in to complete the book's story. In that lies **The Folding Star**'s considerable interest, charm, and ultimately for this reader, its failure.

Why I think it's an earlier book is its greater ambition, its open-weave texture and its willingness to be inclusive of so much: despite the tight point-of-view, it might almost be an old-fashioned "plum pudding" book in the style of Dickens or Thackeray.

Edward Manners has come to a small Flemish city to privately tutor two boys in English. One, Marcel, is a fat, asthmatic youth, son of the local museum curator. The other, Luc Altidore, is the lean, blond, sexy teenage scion of an old noble line with a possibly criminal past, recently thrown out of the local school, and part of a mysterious little Trinity that also includes the palely beautiful Sybille and the darkly hunky Patrick. Manners becomes instantly and totally obsessed with Luc, follows him and his little group around, at the same time he's sleeping with other men he meets at the town's gay bars. He eventually beds Luc, thus setting in motion the boy's flight. Manners chases after him—*in loco parentis*—via auto across the Belgian countryside, and a series of not completely comprehensible surprises about Luc, Marcel, Sybille and in fact virtually everyone Manners has met so far in the town ensues.

Simultaneous with the obsession with Luc, Manners is befriended by Marcel's father, Paul Echevin, a man of sixty, himself obsessed with retaining and elevating the memory and reputation of the late local Symbolist artist, Edgard Orst. Early on, Echevin draws Manners into sharing his enthusiasm by narrating to him—and showing him paintings and photographs in great detail—of Orst's own great obsession, a red-haired actress who became his model, and when she died young, his muse and inspiration. Slowly, during the course of the novel, Echevin's relationship to the infirm and nearly blind old artist when Paul was a youth during World War II is revealed to be far more ambiguous and crucial than Manners or the readers has any reason to suspect.

In the middle of all this, Manners returns to England for the funeral of a former schoolboy crush, killed with his current lover in a car crash, and their early relationship, its own ambiguities and delights, its various small and larger betrayals occurring simultaneously with the decline and death of Manners' father—a famous classical tenor—is explored at a leisurely novelette length.

The Folding Star is like a giant Victorian sofa you keep in a back room: awkwardly constructed, a bit ugly, somewhat ungainly, yet dear for all that, comfy and fun to wallow in on rainy afternoons, with deep pockets and cushions among which one can find all sorts of ingratiating discoveries.

—*Felice Picano*

What makes *The Folding Star* intriguing and constantly readable, besides all this complexity and the author's quiet insistence that everyone carries some secret like a viper in his bosom, is his willingness to take on big themes—and of course the writing's delicious intelligence. Hollinghurst's prose can be erotic, athletic, funny and very dishy. Describing someone's crotch he writes, "the pleated, bum-hugging slacks appeared to shelter, down front, something of remarkable, even tedious length." Referring to Luc's mother's craft—embroidery—he remarks on her "terrible industry." Janacek's music is "convulsively life-like." Of a color used by Orst he writes "there were splashes of the intense blue that Paul said was the costly blue of the Bellini Madonna, but given a further resonance, the Symbolist's *infinite azure*." And describing a photo of Luc, Manners observes, "He was looking through me, eyes narrowed but translucent in sunshine, sea-wet hair pushed oddly, darkly back, lips apart but firm, as if trying out his own name, naked to the bottom edge of the photograph, just below his navel, and his long hands stretched wide, some ordinary gesture caught half-way through so that he looked like Nijinsky resting in air."

Equally delightful are Hollinghurst's splendidly realized minor characters—Manners' over-amorous, possessive,

naive, Moroccan sometime boyfriend, Cherif; his less serious boyfriend, Matt, assiduously handsome and a born capitalist, who steals underwear from his tricks and sells it to middle-aged men who call his phone-sex service, telling them they belong to the schoolboy and pornography objects of the men's lust. Also well-rendered are the nervous, ill, secretly romantic Marcel; Luc's dizzy and solicitous mother; the Echevins' silent and mysterious housekeeper, Mme. Vivier; someone he meets in a bar who's reviving Medieval Flemish music on original instruments. Even the German soldier Paul Echevin has a boyhood affair with comes vividly to life.

Less successful is Hollinghurst's portrayal of the objects of Manners' and Echevin's obsessions. Despite his constant presence in the book, Luc comes off as bland and really quite ordinary. Perhaps that was the author's point: like Swann who's obsessed by the ordinary Odette (but is she, really?), we often obsess on those unworthy of our attention. But that doesn't at all excuse Hollinghurst from doing something more with the legendary Edgard Orst to make him memorable. While we have page after page of his art, and of his affair with first the actress and then her later more vulgar counterpart, we never really get to understand what sets Orst apart, or above, what makes him worthy of Echevin's obsession.

That and the fact that no matter how skillfully the two stories—present and past, Luc and Orst—have been woven, they don't ever really come together, explicate each other, or in fact resonate. It's all slightly off. Like the book's title itself, which alludes to the planet Venus, the Evening Star, but which Manners explains is taken from lines by Milton: "The Star that bids the shepherd fold. 'As when the folding star arising shows his palely circlet'," which I suspect is also supposed to have amatory significance. Yet, in those cultures in which it *was* of utmost importance—the Mayan, the Assyrian—Venus, the brightest light in the sky, was usually an omen of war and disaster.

I can point out all these near-misses and still not be disappointed with the novel, because Hollinghurst gives the reader so very much more in the book that will delight and entertain and make you think. *The Swimming Pool Library* was one of those ingenious Queen Anne card tables, small, perfect, emblazoned in enigmatic marquetry, with sudden little doors and drawers and shelves that opened out to reveal all sorts of things, yet perfectly smooth and of a glittering high polish. *The Folding Star* is more like a giant Victorian sofa you keep in a back room: awkwardly constructed, a bit ugly, somewhat ungainly, yet dear for all that, comfy and fun to wallow in on rainy afternoons, with deep pockets and cushions among which on can find all sorts of ingratiating discoveries.

Craig Seligman   (review date 24 October 1994)

SOURCE: "Sex and the Single Man," in *The New Yorker*, Vol. LXX, No. 34, October 24, 1994, pp. 95-100.

[*In the excerpt below, in which he compares* The Folding Star *to Hollinghurst's first novel*, The Swimming-Pool Library, *Seligman faults the author's development of charac-*

ter in The Folding-Star *and argues that his depiction of homosexual love is unconvincing.*]

Alan Hollinghurst's 1988 début, **The Swimming-Pool Library,** made a bigger splash than anyone might have expected of a book that could be labelled, uncharitably but not inaccurately, a gay sex novel. Nicholson Baker documented his enthusiasm in the fourth chapter of *U and I* and it was typical of the reaction: "Once you get used to the initially kind of disgusting level of homosexual sex, which quickly becomes really interesting as a kind of ethnography, you realize that this is really one of the best first novels to come along in years and years!" But even allowing for the element of self-parody in Baker's response (which the context makes clear) and tiptoeing around that "disgusting," I think his evaluation misses the point: without all the gay sex, there wouldn't *be* any novel. It's the book's reason for being, its one distinguishing note. From a formal standpoint, **The Swimming-Pool Library** might have made its appearance in a much earlier era. Hollinghurst produces an easy, artful, gabby prose that is cushioned with euphony, like one of those grandmotherly English sitting rooms littered with plumped-up pillows. The sedative quality of his language probably isn't incidental to his popularity: if there are readers who might be shocked by what he writes about, they would be reassured by the way he writes about it. But the sex, pervasive and explicit as it is, is so oddly hygienic, so serene, so *pleasant,* that it seems like a cheat. It lacks the undercurrents of anxiety and neurosis that give choice pornography its thrill. William Beckwith, the aristocratic young man-about-London who is Hollinghurst's narrator and protagonist, approaches every carnal encounter with a gourmand's passion for an enticing new snack. Despite all the evidence he offers of his sensual prowess, I never could believe that he was a very good lay.

Will is meant to be an unreliable and deeply flawed (vain, selfish, shallow) narrator but nevertheless an irresistibly seductive one—both to the succession of beautiful men who start unzipping in their heads the minute their eyes meet his and to his readers, many of whom are clearly taken with his good humor, his fondness for his friends, and the Emma Woodhouse-like improvability that he exhibits when his comeuppance comes. Maybe a decent heart does beat inside that smug cocksman, but I couldn't get past his unkindness. Both Will and his creator have a cold, sharp eye for human imperfections: everyone gets looked at in the unforgiving light of the grading process, and those who are too old or too fat or too poor or shy or sad to measure up—well, somebody has to be on the bottom.

The narrator of Hollinghurst's high-aspiring new novel, **The Folding Star**—nominated for the Booker Prize in England—looks very different from Will Beckwith, at first: he's not rich, he's got no social position to speak of, and at thirty-three he's suffering the first indignities of middle-age spread. But aging and spreading though Edward Manners may be, when he walks into a bar you can be certain that he'll walk out with the most gorgeous trick in the place. Only the truly, incurably heterosexual can resist his lust. Will Beckwith lives. Or at least Edward and Will, un-

like the frustrated souls who people the rest of the world, get what they desire. The writing strives for a tone of autumnal resignation—not so premature for a character whose friends are dying of AIDS—but it isn't warmed by much humility.

Partly to put the devastation of his circle in England behind him, Edward has fled to a small Flemish city (a version of Bruges) to tutor two students in English. Sixteen-year-old Marcel Echevin, pudgy and sad, is too asthmatic to go to school; Luc Altidore, troubled, luscious, and seventeen, has been thrown out. Edward at once becomes infatuated, and then obsessed, with Luc. (About the only feeling that he can work up for Marcel, apart from distaste, is pity.) The most serious lapse in **The Folding Star** is Hollinghurst's failure to develop Luc into an interesting character. Actually, you could argue that it's no lapse at all—that Luc isn't undeveloped, just dull. There are multidimensional characters in both of Hollinghurst's novels, but they're never the male nymphets that Will and Edward drool over. The two men share the J. R. Ackerley syndrome, that peculiarly English ardor for barely schooled lower-class youths, dumb but pretty tabulae rasae on which older men can inscribe their fantasies. Luc differs superficially from the other boys in being richer and more literate, but he's just as big a blank—which is, I suppose, why he's such a turn-on for Edward. (Cherif, a Parisian Moroccan with whom Edward carries on a lackadaisical affair for most of the novel, fits the usual mold.)

Neither Edward nor his creator sees anything too unseemly in a thirtyish teacher slavering after his teen-age charge, and the age split wouldn't be such a problem if Edward weren't so oblivious of ethical borders or so deliriously fetishistic: prying, spying, raiding the bathroom hamper for Luc's dirty underwear, nibbling on his excreta. "I groped for a handkerchief," he remembers, "and of course it was Luc's, not altogether clean, with a trouser-pocket staleness, gummed up with snot which clung in the creases in hard translucent grains, like rice: I placed one on my tongue, half-expecting it to liquefy as in some miracle with a saint's salved fluids." He wants us to regard the object of his fixation as Albertine, when it's obvious, to us and to him, that Lolita is more like it. Nabokov, naturally, doesn't go unacknowledged; there are some halfhearted stabs at Humbertesque farce, with Edward scurrying around out of sight and peeping through curtained windows, and there are flights of purulent poetry like that handkerchief passage. But a fog of wistfulness settles damply over every page. Where Nabokov stokes Humbert's perversity and then demands that we recognize his vileness, Hollinghurst hums mopey little ditties to unrequited love.

And yet there's no convincing portrait of romantic love in either of the novels. There's only hot sex or—when the object is unavailable—mooning, swooning adoration. Edward has fond memories of his parents' devotion to each other, but they belong, in a phrase he uses elsewhere, to "the never fully plausible world of heterosexual feeling." The one gay marriage he mentions involves an old flame with AIDs and his dreary antique-dealer lover, the unavoidable implication being that domestic commitment is

> **The most serious lapse in *The Folding
> Star* is Hollinghurst's failure to develop
> Luc into an interesting character.
> Actually, you could argue that it's no
> lapse at all—that Luc isn't undeveloped,
> just dull.**
>
> *—Craig Seligman*

a fallback position for those who have been cast out of the disco-bunny life style. Hollinghurst doesn't draw any distinction—I don't think he sees any—between satyriasis and passion, and so the emptiness of Edward's fixation never really strikes him, even though he gives no indication of what Edward wants Luc for except to screw him to death.

Still, no one regards Edward as anything but upstanding and, bizarrely, trustworthy. Even characters who barely know him feel impelled to tell him everything. Their loquacity might make sense if Hollinghurst were offering a wry comment on the social marginality of sexual minorities—playing with the gay-best-friend scenario that's become familiar in the movies—but he has too much ego invested in Edward to see him as anything but central. The reason everyone opens up to Edward isn't psychological but structural: *The Folding Star* is a Jamesian jigsaw puzzle in which pieces—confessions, in this case—slowly accrete until, by the end, the reader has the big picture. It's such an outmoded way to construct a book, and Hollinghurst lets the machinery show through so nakedly, that there were moments when I wondered if he wasn't being archly, intentionally postmodern. He does all manner of literary acrobatics: word games, mirror images, character parallels, repeated triads—you name it. But the effect of all this meticulous craftsmanship is mainly prissy. It's easy to see why he might feel a kinship with Robert Mapplethorpe, whom he once extolled in a catalogue essay as "both hot and cold, horny and classical, detached and passionate," adding that "the aesthetic and pornographic impulses in him are identified with each other to an extraordinary degree." But Hollinghurst, a highly refined editor of the *TLS* sunk up to his ears in culture, doesn't have the edge of scary nuttiness that explodes Mapplethorpe's formalism. His amiable jabber is anathema to the subject of obsession. This is not the voice of a man who could take a nosedive into the abyss—any abyss.

It's surprising that Hollinghurst never sets off an erotic spark between Edward and Paul Echevin, the cultivated father of Marcel and the most engaging character in the novel, even though Edward and Paul are drawn to each other intellectually and develop an affection far more substantial than any feeling between Edward and Luc. But intellectual passion isn't Hollinghurst's idea of passion, and older men don't inflame his sexual imagination. He has a different use in mind for Paul: gatekeeper to his subplot. Hollinghurst loves elaborate, important subplots. In *The Swimming-Pool Library,* the papers of the elderly Lord

Charles Nantwich, given to Will to read and organize, become a periscope into the gay world of England and the English before Will's birth. The plan of *The Folding Star* is considerably more ambitious. Paul serves as the curator of an art museum devoted to a fin-de-siècle Symbolist named Edgard Orst, and, as the Edward-Edgard correspondence suggests, the subplot parallels the main plot; Orst is supposed to have been erotically fixated on a youthful object, too. In time, Edward learns that Orst perished at the hands of the Nazis: as his story unfolds piece by piece, the Holocaust lies waiting at the end. The troubled history of Europe in this century makes an impressive foundation for the novel, which is structured as a journey toward twin revelations, one intimate (Luc), the other world-historical (Orst). But how can you trust revelations from a narrator who is unrevealed to himself?

David L. Kirp   (review date 23 January 1995)

SOURCE: "A Man's Own Story," in *The Nation,* New York, Vol. 260, No. 3, January 23, 1995, pp. 101-02.

[*An American critic and educator, Kirp frequently writes about educational matters and issues related to gay culture and politics. In the following negative review of* The Folding Star, *he compares the novel to other recent works by gay writers. Acknowledging that Hollinghurst occasionally offers telling moments and details in his portrait of gay culture, he describes the novel's protagonist as pathetic and the plotline as "crudely visible" and "patently artificial."*]

During the dozen years between the 1969 Stonewall riot and the advent of AIDS, a host of writers reinvented gay fiction. (Lesbian fiction was also being reconceived, but that's another story.) Banished were the accounts of wracked consciences and suicides in the making, tear-stained tales of tea and sympathy. Gone as well were the coded references and coy asides of writers who, afraid for their livelihoods in straight America, dared not even reveal their names.

"Come out! Come out!": The political anthem of that era echoed in fiction that unceremoniously tossed out the old conventions as if they were last year's Halloween drag. Storytellers of varied persuasions—among them Andrew Holleran in the almost mythical *Dancer from the Dance;* David Leavitt in the *New Yorker*-ish short-story collection *Family Dancing;* and Larry Kramer in the blunt, in-your-face *Faggots*—found a new subject to write about. They paid attention not to the swooning and the doomed but instead to gay men who had ripped the doors off their closets and were hellbent on discovering their own true selves.

Alan Hollinghurst's first novel, **The Swimming Pool Library,** caused waves of excitement when it appeared in 1988—deservedly so, for it is the best account of contemporary gay life by an English novelist, perhaps the best in the English language. The dish is as good as anything Armistead Maupin serves up in *Tales of the City,* the bedroom romps as frequent and explicit as (if lots more imaginative than) vintage gay porn. This is vintage gay shtick, but it is also so much more. The novel mainly takes place on the eve of the AIDS era, when neither death nor disclosure but wrinkles and paunches—the stigmata of sexual undesirability linked to the inevitable, brute fact of growing older—haunt life in the gay fast lane. Its story line, which swerves from high life among the London glitterati to encounters between colonials and natives in Africa half a century earlier, is as intricately constructed as a nested set of matryoshka dolls. In less capable hands, such an ambitious amalgam of sex and sensibility could easily have gotten out of hand, become self-parodic. Yet Hollinghurst succeeds, as each of his episodes—black-tie nights at the opera; fag-bashing punks in East London council housing; a scene at Heaven, the London gay nightclub of the moment where stars flame and gutter; and cruising, in both senses, on the Nile—is a finely etched Hogarth sketch for our times, these sketches building on one another to form a powerful, unexpectedly moving narrative.

Although the narrator, Will Beckwith, is a perpetually triumphant cocksman for whom love and lust are entirely synonymous, this is no mere toting up of the sexual numbers. James, a harried doctor and a friend since Oxford days who lives much of his social life vicariously through Will, hovers over the proceedings as a kind of conscience. Stealing a read of James's diaries, Will comes upon a description of himself as at once luminous and

> "insufferable. . . . What a jerk! no regard for my feelings." . . . It was like suddenly finding out that someone I knew quite well had been leading a double life: the delectable blond super-stud I loved so much was really a selfish little rich boy, vain, spoilt and even, on one stinging occasion, "grotesque."

When Will undertakes to write the biography of the aging Lord Charles Nantwich, he discovers a personal history splashed with poignancy, even tragedy: Will's grandfather, himself a Lord and the doyen of the opera box Will frequents, turns out to have ruined Nantwich's life through exposure and criminal prosecution. As James, the moral compass in the here-and-now, is threatened with prosecution for some modest debauchery (the historical revelations setting up the modern as echo), Will realizes that he is a privileged member of a gay world that, for all its claims to liberation, still depends overmuch on the winking tolerance of the powerful. That abrupt awakening prompts a tentative stirring of conscience—even as Will, sexually insatiable as ever, spots a promising new adolescent conquest.

Perhaps nothing could have topped this debut, though in **The Folding Star,** his new novel, Hollinghurst tries very hard. Some of the literary tricks are familiar: Down-and-dirty sex gets played off against high art; complex narratives are constructed to run in tandem; and a mysterious past is replayed with a new cast of present-day characters (similar in some respects to William Vollman's attempts to fuse past and present plot lines, as in *The Rifles* most recently).

As the story begins in 1988, the narrator, slightly paunchy 33-year-old Edward Manners, has fled from England, where so many of his contemporaries are dead or dying of AIDS, to an unnamed Flemish city. He has agreed to give English lessons to two adolescents: Marcel Echevin, a timid and pudgy specimen whose asthma keeps him from attending school; and Luc Altidore, well-read and high-spirited, ravishing in a fair-haired, high-cheekboned sort of way, expelled from the (unsubtly named) St. Narcissus School for sins that, though never specified, are plainly of the flesh.

These boys transform Edward's life, one indirectly and the other frontally. While Marcel himself doesn't interest Edward, it is through Marcel's father, Paul, the curator of a local art museum, that Edward grows fascinated with the paintings of a turn-of-the-century symbolist named Edgard Orst, eventually relating his own fate to Orst's life-long obsession with his mistress. Meanwhile, Luc becomes Edward's own obsession. Even as Edward takes up in a desultory sort of way with Cherif, a sexy Moroccan, and later with Matt, a shady but drop-dead gorgeous young man, the tutor endlessly imagines himself as Luc's lover, torturing himself like a lovesick flagellant.

The two stories, Orst's and Edward's, play out contrapuntally, each with its little astonishments and each ending in revelation. In the course of his biographical researches, Edward discovers that Orst was so undone when his young mistress drowned in the ocean at Ostend that he had to select an almost perfect physical replica—this time, though, a syphilitic whore—to replace her, both in his life and as the subject for his canvases. Meanwhile, in time present, Luc turns out not to be the blushing innocent of Edward's ruminations but rather the sexual plaything of Matt, his sometime trick. Luc disappears, with Edward in fervent if feckless pursuit. He is last seen, contrivedly in Ostend, "robbed of his beauty," a face on a missing persons photo.

Hollinghurst can be a brilliant miniaturist, and at its best **The Folding Star** pitilessly captures the minutiae of gay life. In a bar on the very first night of his self-imposed exile, Edward Manners tries to pick up a man with the letters R-O-S-E tattooed on four fingers—a man whose "dangerous quality . . . unspecified challenge, spittle at the corner of his mouth" he finds seductive. It's unsteady going, though, in this tango of approach and avoidance. The stranger stares into his drink, "wave[s] his marked hand dismissively," and Edward wonders why he is bothering with this unpromising specimen; but then the marked man smiles a bit and, following the tired convention, asks Edward what he does for a living. The news that Edward is a teacher "didn't thrill him, it only ever touched those who had liked being taught: I saw a kind of wariness in his eyes, as if he might have owed me an essay." The denouement of this unsuccessful seduction—this hustle that Edward has misread—is painful in its exactitude. "I stroked his forearm," Edward reports, "which I felt actually vibrate with the mastered desire to withdraw it."

There are a number of such shining moments, including a slapstick scene when Edward finds himself playing the role of a hunky American adolescent in a phone sex-line conversation, and a pathetic interlude when the frustrated tutor roots around in Luc's dirty laundry, risking ridicule in his search for a relic to carry off.

> There were some white Hom briefs, tiny, damp from a towel they were bundled in with. I picked

them out and covered my face with them. They seemed spotless, hardly worth changing for new ones, with only a ghost of a smell. . . . I buried them at the bottom of the basket, but then some awful compulsion made me plunge my arm in for them again.

But these are only moments, set pieces that don't resonate with each other, in the midst of a narrative that goes on and on without ever signifying. The plot line, with its many forced coincidences, is as crudely visible and as patently artificial as the outlines on a paint-by-numbers canvas. The saga of Edgard Orst is seen through too many literary conceits, and its critical events give off a whiff of melodrama. The flat sameness that pervades Edward Manners's Flemish days—a little tutoring, more sex, lots of pining—is merely pathetic. A trip back to England, for the funeral of his first lover, becomes an occasion for more jokey naming (Rough Common, the old cruising ground), a nod to Mum, an encounter with yet another artist, and clichéd schoolboy reminiscences.

Nor are the characters of *The Folding Star* especially memorable. While Paul Echevin, the curator, has a richly complex personal history and a multichambered mind, the mind doesn't matter overmuch to Edward, except as a channel into sex. Paul, as it turns out, has his own gay past, but the fact that he is a grown-up makes him undesirable in Edward's eyes, so he is dropped from the narrative as unceremoniously as a jilted lover. Cherif, the young Moroccan, serves as a vessel for Edward's passing lust, another in the lengthening procession of Hollinghurst's boy love-objects. Luc Altidore, the object of abiding veneration, is a set of puns (Luc-*Cul,* Altidore-*t'adore*) but otherwise a cipher, a teenager with oddly shaped lips memorable only because he drives Edward wild with longing. Perhaps this vacuousness is intended—after all, Lolita, Luc's literary forebear, was not so scintillating. Yet while Humbert Humbert is rendered by Nabokov as an irredeemably vile body, Hollinghurst has Edward Manners forever moping around, uttering treacle that, though meant to convey a sense of humanity, is merely tedious.

In the decade since AIDS, the transformation of gay literature, its emergence from the shtetl, continues apace. In *Martin and John,* for instance, Dale Peck has written as wittily complex a narrative as any of Philip Roth's counter-lives. Fenton Johnson in *Scissors, Paper, Rock* has taken a familiar form, the American generational saga, and bent it into a fine new shape by making its narrator a gay member of the family. There has also been a turning back to explore pre-Stonewall history. Martin Duberman's autobiography, *Cures,* portrays a survivor of the 1950s psychoquackery; historian George Chauncey unearths a flourishing gay life during the early years of this century in *Gay New York;* and novelist Mark Merlis, in *American Studies,* manages to turn the tea-and-sympathy story on its ear, giving a decidedly postmodern twist to the miserable last days of a 1950s closet case.

The hope, after *The Swimming Pool Library,* was that Alan Hollinghurst would be the very best of this fine new generation of gay writers, exploring themes that would add nuance and range to the corpus of their literature. Be-

cause expectations were so high, that *The Folding Star* burns out disappoints all the more.

Chris Goodrich   (review date 27 January 1995)

SOURCE: "A 'Lolita' Tale but without the Conscience," in *Los Angeles Times,* January 27, 1995, p. E4.

[*Goodrich is an American critic and nonfiction writer. In the review below, he discusses similarities between* The Folding Star *and Vladimir Nabokov's* Lolita *(1955), focusing on the ethical questions posed by Hollinghurst's novel.*]

Vladimir Nabokov knew very well that *Lolita* would provoke an enormous scandal upon its U.S. publication in 1958. A teacher so infatuated with a 12-year-old girl that he determines to marry the girl's mother—imagine!

But the novel works, and brilliantly, for Nabokov knew just how far to push his material, how to make it echo with understanding—of the Western romantic tradition, of the tragi-comedy inherent in obsession, of taboo and vice and self-delusion. Humbert Humbert's love for Lolita is pathetic and wrong but also powerfully real, and it's a thrill to watch Nabokov walk the tightrope between pornography and art, indulgence and illumination.

Alan Hollinghurst, author of the widely praised *The Swimming Pool Library,* attempts to walk a similar tightrope in *The Folding Star,* but in this novel, at least, he shows little of Nabokov's acrobatic skill.

Edward Manners, a gay, well-educated, 32-year-old Englishman, has moved to Belgium to tutor high-school boys Luc and Marcel, and even before leaving Britain had developed, from photographs, something of a crush on Luc. Luc, 17, appears even more beautiful to Edward in person: The teacher is smitten, and soon tells his readers—the novel, like *Lolita,* is narrated in the first person—about his exquisitely unrequited love.

The differences between the *The Folding Star* and *Lolita* soon become evident, however. They may be traced to any number of causes—the rudimentary traditions of the openly gay novel: Hollinghurst's rambling, somber prose; the gulf between straight and gay culture; the novel's emphasis of pain over philosophy, due to its taking place in the immediate rather than the distant past. In any case, *The Folding Star* becomes repetitive and confessional rather than engaging and clarifying, proving to be more about sex than love (a charge frequently leveled, wrongly, at *Lolita*).

At first, one thinks the modest, self-conscious Edward will be much easier to identify with than the vain, professorial Humbert Humbert. But in time, Hollinghurst's hero seems dull, somewhat dim, and surprisingly shallow. He thinks constantly about getting into Luc's pants and never about the act's propriety, despite the fact that Edward has been placed in a position of great professional trust; on a personal level, too, he doesn't mind deceiving friends about his true motives and desires.

That Edward eventually commits minor criminal acts in

pursuit of Luc is altogether appropriate (Humbert Humbert's love for Lolita, after all, turns him into a killer).

Entwined with the main plot of *The Folding Star* is the story of Paul Echevin, Marcel's father, who runs a museum dedicated to a Symbolist painter, Edgard Orst, whom he worked for as a youth. Paul befriends Edward for no apparent reason, and ends up telling him of Orst's obsession with an actress and the painter's death while hiding from the Germans who occupied Belgium during World War II.

The two stories are brought together, rather awkwardly, by Paul's confession at the end of the novel of his inadvertent betrayal of Orst.

One of the great themes of literature is how a longed-for goal, once achieved, turns to ashes. In *The Folding Star,* consequently, one expects Luc will either elude Edward altogether or prove a terrible disappointment.

Hollinghurst takes a more sentimental route. Three hundred pages into the book, Edward has his night of bliss with Luc—initiated by the student, no less—who then disappears. Luc shows up again on the novel's last page, but there's no happy reunion. Edward describes Luc as "robbed of his beauty," as "a victim, to be stared at and pitied" . . . yet doesn't show the slightest sense that he may be responsible in any way for Luc's plight.

If Edward has been playing shepherd to Luc's sheep—and that's the implication of the novel's title, which refers to a Milton lyric in which a star bids the shepherd gather his flock—he seems not only to be miscast, but to have misconceived the nature of the task.

FURTHER READING

Review of *The Folding Star,* by Alan Hollinghurst. *Kirkus Reviews* LXII, No. 13 (1 July 1994): 871.
    Brief plot summary and critique of *The Folding Star.*

Shone, Tom. "Manners Maketh Boy?" *The Spectator* 272, No. 8655 (28 May 1994): 38.
    Mixed assessment of *The Folding Star.* Shone praises Hollinghurst's portrait of his gay protagonist as well-defined, but laments the novel's focus on history: "How can someone who has single-handedly done so much to put a contemporary gay sensibility on the map, not find enough adventure in exploring it?"

Additional coverage of Hollinghurst's life and career is contained in the following sources published by Gale Research: *Contemporary Authors,* **Vol. 114; and** *Contemporary Literary Criticism,* **Vol. 55.**

David Mamet
The Cryptogram

Award: OBIE Award for Best Play

(Full name David Alan Mamet) Born in 1947, Mamet is an American playwright, screenwriter, novelist, essayist, memoirist, and author of children's books.

For further information on his life and works, see *CLC,* Volumes 9, 15, 34, and 46.

INTRODUCTION

The Cryptogram (1994) focuses on the theme of betrayal and continues Mamet's innovative use of dialogue as a means of creating and representing conflict. Set in the late 1950s, the play depicts a month in the lives of a precocious ten-year-old named John, his mother Donny, his father Robert, and a family friend named Del. The play opens with John unable to fall asleep, too excited about an impending camping trip with his father. It is soon revealed that Robert, who never appears onstage, has abandoned his wife and child, and that Del has assisted in his deceptions. Struggling with the emotional consequences of Robert's departure and the nature of their own friendship, Del and Donny are unable or unwilling to meet John's most basic needs. Fearing that the truth would be too overwhelming, they avoid John's questions, which only increases his anxiety and sense of isolation.

Emphasizing issues of betrayal, abandonment, emotional abuse, and childhood angst, *The Cryptogram* has received mixed reviews. Mamet's use of language—which is marked by repetitiveness, interruptions, and long pauses—has been variously assessed by critics. While some commentators have faulted the minimalism of the dialogue as evasive, stilted, and fragmentary, others, such as Jack Kroll, have noted that the cryptic nature of the play reveals the characters' muddled perceptions of their world and their subsequent search for meaning and emotional stability. Kroll observed that "as we listen to [John] try to bring his broken world to order we realize that Mamet's language is at bottom a child's lingo, the trial-and-error, stop-and-start, nonresponsive speech tactic of kids. It's the sound of tainted innocence." Reviewers have also acknowledged the importance of *The Cryptogram* in Mamet's body of work, noting its autobiographical influences and disturbing portrait of the effects of divorce on families; they have particularly cited the emotional shock generated in the play's final scenes. As John Lahr has asserted: "With remarkable concision and insight, Mamet has mapped out the dynamics of a soul murder."

PRINCIPAL WORKS

Lakeboat (drama) 1970
Duck Variations (drama) 1972
*Sexual Perversity in Chicago (drama) 1974
Squirrels (drama) 1974
American Buffalo (drama) 1975
Reunion (drama) 1976
Dark Pony (drama) 1977
A Life in the Theatre (drama) 1977
The Revenge of the Space Pandas, or Binky Rudich and the Two-Speed Clock (drama for children) 1977
The Water Engine: An American Fable (drama) 1977
The Woods (drama) 1977
Mr. Happiness (drama) 1978
Lone Canoe, or the Explorer (musical) 1979
The Sanctity of Marriage (drama) 1979
Shoeshine (drama) 1979
The Postman Always Rings Twice [adaptor; from the novel by James M. Cain] (screenplay) 1981

Edmond (drama) 1982

The Verdict [adaptor; from the novel by Barry Reed] (screenplay) 1982

Glengarry Glen Ross (drama) 1983

The Cherry Orchard [adaptor; from the play by Anton Chekhov] (drama) 1985

Prairie du chien (drama) 1985

The Shawl (drama) 1985

The Untouchables (screenplay) 1986

Writing in Restaurants (essays) 1986

†House of Games (film) 1987

Speed-the-Plow (drama) 1988

†Things Change [with Shel Silverstein] (film) 1988

Uncle Vanya [adpator; from the play by Anton Chekhov] (drama) 1988

Some Freaks (essays) 1989

We're No Angels (screenplay) 1989

Three Sisters [adaptor; from the play by Anton Chekhov] (drama) 1990

†Homicide (film) 1991

The Cabin: Reminiscence and Diversions (memoirs) 1992

Glengarry Glen Ross (screenplay) 1992

Hoffa (screenplay) 1992

Oleanna (drama) 1992

The Cryptogram (drama) 1994

†Oleanna (film) 1994

Vanya on 42nd Street (screenplay) 1994

The Village (novel) 1994

A Whore's Profession (notes and essays) 1994

Passover (novella) 1995

*This play was adapted by Tim Kazurinsky and Denise DeClue for the 1986 film *About Last Night*.

†Mamet both wrote and directed these films. Bracketed information refers to screenwriting credit.

CRITICISM

John Lahr   (review date 1 August 1994)

SOURCE: "Betrayals," in *The New Yorker*, Vol. LXX, No. 23, August 1, 1994, pp. 70-3.

[*Lahr is a prizewinning American critic, nonfiction writer, playwright, novelist, biographer, and editor. In the review below, he offers a highly favorable assessment of* The Cryptogram, *lauding the work's dramatic intensity and focus on betrayal, death, and emotional abuse.*]

David Mamet, like the characters he puts onstage, tells us only so much about himself, and no more. We know, for instance, that he likes tricksters and magic. We know that he enjoys guys' things, like hunting and poker and cigars. We also know that he's divorced, and that, like any divorced parent, he has had to live with the grief of imposing on his children the bewildering pain of separation which he felt when his own parents divorced. In "The Rake," the first chapter of a 1992 memoir entitled ***The Cabin: Remi-***

niscence and Diversions, Mamet has provided a rare and chilling snapshot of himself and his sister, Lynn, growing up with their new stepfather in a Chicago suburb. Mamet dredges up from the mystery of childhood a few images and scraps of half-understood conversation which have etched themselves on his imagination. He tells of his sister's hearing raised voices and following them down the corridor to the master bedroom, where she pushed open the door to see their mother coiled in a fetal position on the floor of the closet "moaning and crying and hugging herself," and their tyrannical stepfather gesturing toward the bed, on which the children's grandfather, their mother's father, was slumped. "Say the words," the stepfather was saying to the grandfather. "Say the words, Jack. Please. Just say you love her." Mamet writes, "And my grandfather said, 'I can't.' " Mamet's sister was hit in the face with a hairbrush for bearing witness to this humiliation. Such bleak and brutal terrain—full of cloaked threat and blighted feeling—is a large part of Mamet's emotional inheritance. He survived to dramatize its wary and perverse psychological climate—a ferocious, repressed atmosphere in which, out of fear and impotence and shame, people become willed strangers to themselves, and in which the cunning thrust and parry of language becomes a carapace that cuts them off from both the world and their own murky feelings.

The Cryptogram, Mamet's newest play, which recently had its world première at the Ambassadors Theatre, in London, is a difficult but important drama, in which Mamet works his way back to childhood—specifically, to that irrevocable, buried moment in a child's life when the safety net of the parental embrace collapses, and the world, once full of blessing, is suddenly full of danger. The play, which consists of three terse scenes, takes place in 1959 (Mamet was born in 1947), and Mamet's surrogate, John, is "about ten." Bob Crowley's beautifully painted set is dominated by a huge stairway, which winds its way up toward the flies, and a backcloth of behemoth zones of blue-green and charcoal gray separated by a band of pink. Like a Rothko painting (which the backcloth resembles), the play is about the resonance of contradictory and puzzling emotional intensities; and the staircase becomes an image of the almost unbridgeable space between the muffled grownup world downstairs and the child's insecure purdah upstairs.

Mamet foreshadows the play's moral debate in the opening beats. Here, in Gregory Mosher's vivid production, John's first words are "I couldn't find 'em." John (superbly played by the precocious Richard Claxton, who alternates in the role with the equally adroit Danny Worters) is apparently talking about a pair of slippers he has packed for a camping trip with his father, which is scheduled for the next day; but what John really can't find in the environment of subterfuge and coded speech which engulfs him is the reality of his parents and of his own emotional life. John can't sleep. This is a familiar enough childhood complaint, and the family friend Del (well played by the pudgy, weak-faced comedian Eddie Izzard) tries to jolly him out of it in a cozy late-night man-to-man. "Where were we?" Del asks. John answers with a formal phrase obviously borrowed from earlier arguments with the adults. "Issues of sleep," he says. The phrase turns panic into a debating point, but we soon learn that John's sleeplessness is chronic. "*Every* night. *Every* night. There's some excuse. Some *reason*," says Donny, John's mother, played by the subtle Lindsay Duncan, whose pale elegance here disguises a steely detachment. Despite Del's special pleading and the excitement of the upcoming trip, Donny wants John upstairs and in bed. "Why aren't you asleep?" is her entrance line. John has picked up some anxiety that the household refuses to acknowledge. "Why isn't Dad home?" he asks Del, who takes the conversation in another direction. Later in the scene, John tells his mother, "I want to wait til he comes home." His request is stonewalled by apparent reasonableness. "Well, yes, I'm sure you do," Donny says. "But you need your sleep. And if you don't get it, you're not . . ."

Sleeplessness, not John's fear, is what Del and Donny want to contain. No one deals with John's feelings or tries to alleviate them. The audience starts to feel a certain highly charged and unspoken frustration—a kind of emotional static. Mamet puts the audience where the child sits, taking the characters at face value, only to have its will to believe confounded by those characters' mixed messages. Psychological truth is never acknowledged. In fact, it is scrambled—like a cryptogram—so that everything means something else. The play's uncluttered living room, composed merely of two sofas covered with red blankets, becomes an impenetrable landscape of denial. Mamet announces the pattern brilliantly, with the offstage crash of Donny's teapot, which precedes her first entrance. "I'm alright!" Donny shouts from the wings. "I'm alright!" Clearly she's not all right, and Del uses the shattered teapot to draw an avuncular parallel between the anticipated camping trip and John's edginess:

> DEL: Well, there you go.
>
> JOHN: What?
>
> DEL: . . . a human *being* . . .
>
> JOHN: . . . yes?
>
> DEL: . . . cannot conceal himself.
>
> JOHN: that, that's, that's an example?
>
> DEL: Well, hell, look at it: anything, when it is *changed* . . . *any,* um um, "upheaval," do you see? All of a sudden . . .

A broken teapot an "upheaval"? Del seems to be trying to ascribe John's sleeplessness to the prospect of a change of scenery, but his stumbling and inappropriate choice of words is confusing. Something—everything—is being concealed. But what? Nothing is ever directly stated. Even John's straightforward question about his father— "Where is he?" —gets a confused and confusing answer from Donny. "I don't know. Yes, I do, yes. He's at the Office. And he'll be home soon." She seems to know, and yet not to know, that something is awry. John's situation is never resolved; his anxieties and his questions are never answered. When John is sent to tidy up the attic, and reappears with a blanket—a totemic family object in which he

was wrapped as a baby—the blanket turns out to be torn. John thinks he has torn it, but Donny knows he hasn't. Even this projection of John's unspoken fear of having caused a rip in the fabric of the family is muddied by Del. "Because we *think* a thing is one way does not mean that this is the way that this thing must be," Del says. The evasions are confusing, and are meant to be. John's caretakers interrupt him, and confound him with doubletalk. At the end of the scene, John's worst fears are confirmed. A note somehow materializes. "When did this get here?" Donny asks, and after she's read it she sends John to bed. "Alright. I understand. I'm going," he says, knowing, without quite knowing, that the worst has happened. His father will not be going on the camping trip, or coming home. The dialogue that ends the first scene has a flat, matter-of-fact tone, but in the subsequent scenes it turns out to be part of a whole narrative of fraudulence:

> DEL: What is it?
>
> DONNY: It's a letter. (*Pause.*) Robert's leaving me.
>
> DEL: He's leaving you. (*Pause.*) Why would he want to do that . . . ?

"I thought that maybe there was nothing there," John says to Donny at the beginning of Scene 2, explaining a kind of brainstorm about the nature of reality. And, of course, he's right: what Mamet is about to unravel is the charade of human connection. John is starting to fragment before our eyes, and his night sweats—in this case, voices and spectres that accompany his fear of abandonment and his sense of annihilation—are now coming out in his questions. "And how do we *know* the things we know?" he says. "And, and we don't know what's real. And all we do is *say* things." What Del says when he enters is that he has looked all over town for Robert and can't find him. He brings medicine for John. (The medicine that John really needs is love, but this is never offered.) John finally breaks down and buries his head in his mother's lap. "What's happening to me?" he says. Donny embraces him. "It's alright," she says "Hush. You go to bed. It's alright. John. Shh. You've only got a fever. Shhh." It's a fierce and ironic moment: an act of violence couched in the language of love. Donny acts as if the truth would kill her son, but what's killing him is untruth.

The Cryptogram **may be short, but it is not miniature. The oblique, brilliant dialogue is not underwritten, nor are the characters unexplored. With remarkable concision and insight, Mamet has mapped out the dynamics of a soul murder.**

—*John Lahr*

The truth—a network of betrayals—is hard to admit or discover. Once John is safely upstairs, Del opens a bottle of whiskey, and he and Donny toast their friendship—a kind of strangulated toast, in which Del, who is gay but later confesses love for Donny, angles clumsily for some acknowledgment of deeper feeling from her:

> DONNY: May We Always be as . . .
> DEL: Yes.
>
> DONNY: As . . .
>
> DEL: Unified . . .
>
> DONNY: Well, let's pick something more moving than that.
>
> DEL: Alright . . . be. be. be. be. be-*nighted?* No, that's not the word I want to use   . . . be-*trothed* . . . ? No.
>
> DONNY: Close . . .
>
> DEL: Yes.
>
> DONNY: Close to each other.
>
> DEL: As we happen to be right now.

Within a few minutes, though, Del is caught out in a lie about a knife he has used to open the whiskey. He claims that Robert gave it to him on a camping trip the previous week, but Donny has seen it more recently, in the attic. This leads to the revelation that Del lent Robert his apartment for a tryst and used the camping trip as a decoy—a collusion for which he was rewarded with the knife, Robert's cherished "war memento," which proves later to be as inauthentic as Del's shows of sincerity. Del, it turns out, is caught between an allegiance to the absent Robert and a yearning for Donny, who flirts with him but is finally uninterested. The audience hardly has time to tally up the extent of his fabrications. Del, who planted the "Dear Donny" letter, has known all along about Robert's adultery and abandonment of his family. Del's badinage with John, the story about looking for Robert, the toast to Donny and friendship—all are flimflam. "I'm sorry that it came out like this," he says to her. Then, having deliberately lied to Donny, he proceeds to lie to himself. "But we can't always choose the . . ." These revelations are interrupted by John's returning from upstairs to recount his own revelation: "I'm perfectly alone." And he is.

We see just how alone John is in the last, and best, scene, which takes place a month later, with Donny and John packing up to leave the house. Here, especially, Lindsay Duncan—one of England's finest actresses—brings Donny into bold, monstrous relief. John has suicide on his mind. "Do you ever wish that you could die?" he asks his mother, who replies ambivalently, "How can I help you, John?" She is, as Mamet shows, killing him slowly with kindness. "Things occur," she tells him. "And the meaning of them . . . the *meaning* of them . . . is not clear." But meaning, we see, is being consciously and unconsciously subverted. "If I could find one man," Donny bleats to Del, who has returned with the knife to "attune" for his sins. "In my life. Who would not betray me." Donny's rancor has a self-hypnotic power, but in fact Donny has betrayed John and Del, just as Del has betrayed Donny and John; and Robert, it turns out, has betrayed all three. When John appears on the stairway to interrupt her aria of victimization, Donny turns on her boy

with unbridled fury. "Do you have no *feelings?*" she says. "I don't CARE. Go away. Leave me. Do you hear? You *lied.* You *lied* to me. I love you, but I can't like you. I'm sorry." Of course, it's Donny (and the other adults) who has lied to John; but John stands there, bewildered, trying vainly to make himself heard above Donny's double binds. All he wants is the blanket—his security blanket—but it has been packed. In a gesture typical of the adults' psychological obtuseness, Del gives John the knife to open the package. John, who has already broadcast suicidal thoughts, is called to attention on the stairway by Donny; she doesn't want to disarm him but, instead, to accuse him furiously of doing to *her* what she in fact is doing to him. "What are you *standing* there for?" she says. "Can't you see that I need *comfort?* Are you *blind?* Are you *blind?* That you treat me like an *animal?* What must I do?" It is a searing moment of emotional abuse. At the finale, John is looking down over the bannister at Donny and Del. He flicks the knife. The blade jolts into view with a startling *thwack*—a chilling sound that holds out the promise, as the lights fade, of murderous fury directed at John fade, of murderous fury directed at John himself or at the world.

Mamet chose to attack the world, and *The Cryptogram* goes some way toward illuminating the source of the cruelty and faithlessness that his characters generally find in it. The shifting ground of the play makes it hard to engage with, but its aftershock is enormous. *The Cryptogram* may be short, but it is not miniature. The oblique, brilliant dialogue is not underwritten, nor are the characters unexplored. With remarkable concision and insight, Mamet has mapped out the dynamics of a soul murder. This daring, dark, complex play got respectful though mixed notices in London, but I suspect that in time it will take its place among Mamet's major works.

Robert L. King   (review date November-December 1994)

SOURCE: A review of *The Cryptogram,* in *The North American Review,* Vol. CCLXXIX, No. 6, November-December, 1994, p. 51.

[*In the following review, King provides a negative assessment of* The Cryptogram.]

In London's West End, David Mamet's *Cryptogram* had its world premiere. Set in Chicago in 1959, the piece centers around the anxieties of John, a ten-year-old boy. The clues in character, time and place all point to a personal allusion in the coded title—Mamet must be revealing something about himself. His director of twenty years standing, Gregory Mosher, claims not to have raised the question; after all, he says, "The pleasure of the play lies not, of course, in whether the young boy's journey was Mamet's, but in whether it is ours." *The Cryptogram* runs for under seventy minutes, a brief journey at best; two of the three characters deliver set speeches at a high emotional level, enough to measure acting but not enough to equal a play.

In each of the three scenes, the boy, John, can't sleep. At first, he is excited in anticipation of the next day's outing with his father; the curtain lines to the end of scene one, however, tip us off to expect a less pleasant revelation. His mother reads a note and says, "Robert's leaving me," and her friend Del replies, "Why would he want to do that?" At the opening of scene two, the young boy is speculating on the nature of reality and the meaning of meaning, Del having helped him earlier with "Words can mean what you want them to." With John upstairs, Del comes to realize that a knife given to him by Robert was bought on the street after the war and was a payoff to him, a self-styled "sad queen," for letting Robert use his room for an affair. Robert has deceived all of them. At the very end of the play, John stops half way up the long flight of stairs that rises right to left against the stage's back wall; he opens the knife by letting the blade drop. His last words reveal some dark anxiety about the voices he hears as he would sleep: "They're calling my name." Some darkly creative power must be waiting to shape his future; armed with a parachutist's escape knife, he will presumably confront his destiny.

"Each of us is alone," Donny tells her son in the third and last scene. *The Cryptogram* is too slight to raise such generalities above bumper-sticker level and too single-minded to question their validity in the language of the stage. The actors arc given little more than try-out monologues, preludes to a real part. Unless Mamet expands this piece into a play, be warned. With his reputation, the enthusiasm of some reviewers, the part for a young boy, only two other characters and a single set, *The Cryptogram* could pop up in regional theaters for several years.

The master Mametian idea in [*The Cryptogram*] is that the breakup of family can be expressed in a breakdown of language. Words here are as dysfunctional as people.

—Donald Lyons, in his "To Paris and Back in a '20s Dream," in The Wall Street Journal, *14 April 1995*.

Vincent Canby   (review date 10 February 1995)

SOURCE: "Mamet in a Bleak Living Room of Childhood," in *The New York Times,* February 10, 1995, p. C3.

[*Canby is a novelist, playwright, and film critic. Here, he offers a highly favorable assessment of* The Cryptogram.]

The Cryptogram, David Mamet's spooky, very good new play, is elliptical but far less minimal than it initially looks. It's stuffed with the emotional bric-a-brac that leaves permanent scars on children, splits husbands from wives and rests lifelong friendships.

Under Mr. Mamet's direction *The Cryptogram* had its American premiere here on Wednesday night at the C. Walsh Theater. Though the American Repertory The-

ater's home is the Loeb Drama Center in Cambridge, it's presenting the play at the smaller theater in Boston, just behind the State House, as part of its New Stages '95 series. *The Cryptogram,* which has three characters and runs a scant 75 minutes without intermission, should be something of a coup for the group, which presented the first production of Mr. Mamet's *Oleanna* in 1992.

The new work doesn't have the topical kick of *Oleanna,* the temper-testing box-office hit about sexual harassment. Instead, it's a characteristically condensed Mamet consideration of matters that seem both more timeless and, in view of the playwright's stories about his own hair-raising childhood, more personal.

The Cryptogram takes place in a living room, which, as designed by John Lee Beatty, is a bleak commentary on every television sitcom set you have every seen. This living room, with the obligatory stairway at the back, looks as if it were in a permanent state of dismantlement, awaiting the movers. It contains one rump-sprung sofa and one easy chair with an ottoman. Nothing else, No lamps, no pictures on the walls. There aren't even any visible windows or doors.

Yet two floors above, there's an attic that, from what we hear, is stuffed with things hidden, stored, forgotten or abandoned: clothes, faded photographs, tackle boxes, old blankets. As various objects are retrieved from the attic during the play, it becomes evident that it not only is the repository of shared possessions but also functions as the collective unconscious of the characters. They are 10-year-old John (Shelton Dane), his mother, Donny (Felicity Huffman), and the family's best friend, Del (Ed Begley Jr.). Next to the boy, the most important figure in the piece is his father, Robert, who, having just abandoned his family, remains unseen.

Donny is a well-meaning but chilly woman who is furious when she learns her husband has departed, though not, it seems, totally surprised. Del, a feckless and aging librarian, a homosexual without any apparent social life of his own, has been Donny and Robert's pal since high school. He lives in a hotel room but, for lack of any impulse to do otherwise, hangs around their house. As things turn out, we learn that Robert has been using Del as casually as he has used Donny and the boy.

Young John is the play's focal point. He's an astonishing character. Not in any contemporary stage literature that I know has childhood been as movingly evoked as it is in *The Cryptogram.* John is certainly not an average child, but he's not necessarily some budding genius of a playwright. He's a particular child whose loneliness and prescience about doom give his mind a special alertness.

John is the kind of boy who's fascinated by the concept of thought. What are thoughts? Why do thoughts keep him awake? Do thoughts make real something that is dreaded? It isn't long before John is wondering aloud whether he's the dreamer or the dream.

He's the principal victim when Robert walks out on Donny. His mother is not a wicked woman, but she's so devastated by her abandonment that she hasn't the patience or the interest to deal with a precocious child. "I love you," she tells the boy at one point, "but I can't like you." She comes to see Del as Robert's partner in disloyalty, which is to give the poor fellow more credit than he deserves.

The Cryptogram is full of wit, though it's not exactly a barrel of laughs. At the beginning of the performance I attended, the audience was inclined to laugh easily, as if to announce its recognition of the playwright's idiosyncratic locutions. Indeed, those locutions seem so pronounced at the beginning that they border on self-parody. As the performance continued, however, that sort of laughter vanished. The script didn't become better (it's all of a piece), but the intensity of the performances made its sorrowful intentions clear.

It's not easy even for adult actors to play Mamet. As his own director, the playwright has done a remarkable job integrating young Mr. Dane's performance with those of the boy's far more experienced colleagues. Ms. Huffman, Mr. Begley and Mr. Dane are a splendid ensemble.

When you laugh in the course of *The Cryptogram,* it's less often because the lines are comic than because of the pleasurable skill with which the actors handle them. The dialogue tracks like a ball in an especially eccentric pinball machine. Speeches bounce off one another in totally unexpected directions, seemingly at random, for effects that prompt shudders even as they satisfy.

The Cryptogram is first-rate.

Markland Taylor   (review date 13 February 1995)

SOURCE: A review of *The Cryptogram,* in *Variety,* February 13, 1995, pp. 59-60.

[*In the excerpt below, Taylor offers a mixed assessment of* The Cryptogram. *Taylor praises Mamet's directing and writing abilities, but argues that the play seems incomplete and borders on the banal.*]

Directed and acted with exactly the right Mametic rhythms, harmony and counterpoint, this American premiere of David Mamet's *The Cryptogram* reveals it as a prime example of style triumphing over content that teeters on the brink of banality. Unlike the play's world premiere in London in June, which was helmed by American director Gregory Mosher, this version is directed by the author and gives every evidence of being precisely what he wants. As such it's almost always verbally fascinating, but it also raises the strong possibility that other productions not directed and acted with such apt precision would have a high irritation factor.

Set in 1959, with references to World War II, the play is not the puzzling matter of codes or ciphers its title suggests. What unfolds is a familiar tale of a marriage breaking up, betrayal by a friend of the separating couple, and the impact of the breakup and betrayal on the wife, 10-year-old son and friend. Neither the three characters seen in the play nor their tale is of riveting interest per se. But that's not taking into account Mamet's highly quirky dialogue. Minimalist, halting, fractured, repetitive, syncopat-

ed, staccato, overlapping, it has a life of its own that, in the hands of the playwright/director and his cast, almost convinces that there's more here than meets the ear.

The first of the play's three scenes opens with Del (Ed Begley Jr.) seated, leafing through a magazine. John (Shelton Dane), the 10-year-old who lives in the house, comes downstairs in his pajamas and strikes up a conversation, at first about having packed his slippers for a trip into the woods with his father. The father, a former World War II pilot, never appears onstage, and as is so often the case with catalytic unseen characters, had the potential to be the play's most interesting character. The further the story proceeds, the more he's missed.

The mother (Felicity Huffman) eventually emerges from the kitchen, where she's broken the teapot while making tea, and the dialogue spirals more and more urgently, often swallowing and regurgitating itself. The scene ends with the boy, who can't sleep, handing his mother a letter. It's from her husband, announcing that he's leaving her.

In scene two the son doggedly continues his search for meaning in words and life, suggesting the possibility that to children, adults speak in codes or ciphers. Del admits he's a "geek" and then delivers a cruel blow to the woman by announcing that rather than having recently been on a fishing trip with her husband he was allowing the husband to use the hotel room in which Del lives for an assignation with another woman. The wife orders him out of the house.

In scene three, Del returns to apologize. The wife is showing clear emotional and physical deterioration, her relationship with her son prickly and overwrought. "Each of us is alone," she tells him while assuring Del that all the men in her life have betrayed her. The play ends abruptly. . . .

What unfolds on this set does not have the controversy quotient of Mamet's previous play, *Oleanna.* It almost suggests that it's the first three scenes of a longer play waiting to be completed by the arrival of the husband.

Jonathan Kalb   (review date 28 February 1995)

SOURCE: "Crypto-Mamet," in *The Village Voice,* Vol. XL, No. 9, February 28, 1995, p. 83.

[*An American educator and critic who frequently writes on drama, Kalb has served as managing editor of* Theater *and is the author of the 1989* Beckett in Performance. *In the following, he offers a negative review of* The Cryptogram, *arguing that in the play, particularly as staged by Mamet, Mamet focuses more on mood and atmosphere than on plot development and character motivation.*]

David Mamet has always had his detractors, but until this misbegotten premiere I have never known him to offer them succor himself. In directing this desiccated production of *The Cryptogram,* he seems at loggerheads with actors who either cannot or have been told not to animate his mannered language, invest it with their own creativity. And the result is that his style comes off forced, overdetermined, a sort of overwriting camouflaged as austerity—

just as the skeptical critics used to say in the 1970s, before performers such as Al Pacino and Joe Mantegna gave them reasons to look closer.

The Cryptogram is what its title implies—an encrypted dramatic puzzle in the tradition of Pinter, designed to entice us into an obsessive search for solutions. Set in a cheaply furnished, nondescript living room in 1959 (when Mamet was 10 years old), the play deals with the effect of a father's leaving on 10-year-old John, his mother Donny, and a gay family friend named Del. It is not my favorite Mamet play—the spareness and studious avoidance of social context feel a bit derivative (of Beckett, Pinter, and Mamet himself), the self-conscious chilliness a bit trite (by Mamet's own standards)—but it is as dense and tightly constructed as any of his other texts, which I learned only by reading it on the train home.

As usual, Mamet's focus is less on organizing events than on creating atmosphere, faithfully reproducing that world of missed signals, incomplete connections, and irredeemable coldness he seems perpetually to see in his mind's eye. The coldness has a different flavor this time because it envelops a child, as do his familiar cloaking devices—those odd modes of speech and behavior he uses to obscure surface action and redirect our attention beneath—since they keep our interest in the mystery fueled.

What mystery? Take your pick of a hundred questions about situation and motivation that have no definite answers yet beg to be asked. What went wrong between Donny and her husband Robert (who never appears), and when? Were Del and Robert lovers, and if so, what is Del's place in the house now? Why is he there all the time? And why are the adults oblivious to the obvious mental nosedive of the child? The key to deciphering the cryptic action—it would give away the finale to say more—is realizing that no questions of this sort are of the essence.

One must look behind and between the sparse and fragmentary facts. The three characters talk over and through one another, for instance, continuing what they were saying two lines or two pages before, regardless of what the other person just said, so that even the basic plot is hard to follow in performance. It's as if everyone, including callow John, were infected with a sort of contagious pigheadedness, insisting on finishing their thoughts as a shield against really being heard or achieving closeness—ordinary conversation as a potential door to chaos.

Mamet also leans heavily, as he has before, on the dramatic value of simple frustration, peppering each of the three scenes with exasperating repeated questions ("What?" "When is my father coming home?") and interruptions that recall the infuriating phone rings in *Oleanna.* Every time someone is on the verge of a personal revelation, or a spiritual connection, someone else enters, usually the boy—who cannot sleep and whom no one ever tucks in. In another production, John's numerous reappearances (his thoughts increasingly ominous) might bring a dark chuckle or two—here they are utterly humorless, barely evoking weak pathos.

Which brings me back to the subject of acting. For reasons that can only be guessed at, Mamet apparently instructed his performers to maintain neutrally expressionless faces and venerate his pauses like holy writ—with the result that the play is deprived not only of suspense but of every other hook that might have held the audience's interest in the mystery. Felicity Huffman and Ed Begley Jr. as Donny and Del are so preoccupied with inserting requisite silences after every half-line ("Oh. Oh . . ." "To, um . . . to, um, what is the word . . . ?" "Look what I found") that their characters don't even make sense as ciphers for emotional stinginess. Worse still, Shelton Dane as John starts out with an affectless monotone and works himself up to near catatonia, as if Mamet were so afraid of the child actor's cuteness that he decided not to let him act.

Heaven knows what conceit about highlighting the indeterminacy of his characters' emotional bonds caused Mamet to eliminate all emotional continuity this way. In any case, there is such a failure of energy among this cast—really a palpable sense of defeat and demoralization—that the whole affair cries out to be started over from scratch.

[In *The Cryptogram*] we realize that Mamet's language is at bottom a child's lingo, the trial-and-error, stop-and-start, nonresponsive speech tactic of kids. It's the sound of tainted innocence.

—*Jack Kroll, in his "Phantoms in the Dark," in* Newsweek, *20 February 1995.*

The New Yorker (essay date 10 April 1995)

SOURCE: "David Mamet's Child's Play," in *The New Yorker,* Vol. LXXI, No. 7, April 10, 1995, pp. 33-4.

[*In the essay below, the critic relates Mamet's thoughts on his childhood and family life, language, and unhappiness, particularly as revealed in* The Cryptogram.]

At the far end of the pine table in the basement kitchen of David Mamet's town house, in Cambridge, Massachusetts, his six-month-old daughter, Clara, bobs in her baby bouncer; at the near end, the playwright himself is also bobbing, but with his mouth open to snare the mushrooms being lobbed at him from the other side of the stove by his actress wife, Rebecca Pidgeon (Becs to him), who is whipping up a pasta primavera. In the mushroom-catching department, Mamet is all chin and playfulness, but in the playwriting department he is all heart and ferocity. At home, Mamet seems to have found his bliss, and in his latest play, *The Cryptogram,* he seems to have faced the source of his fury.

The play, which Mamet is directing, and which arrives Off Broadway, at the Westside Arts Theatre, on April 13th, dramatizes a child's emotional abuse in a way that no other American play has ever attempted: from the child's point of view. Mamet's gift for dramatic dialogue may be

God-given, but his scrutiny of language—that nervy vigilance in which the pauses, the coded words, and the sludge of speech are registered, picked over, and served up with gripping accuracy—is the wary habit of a lifetime of on-the-job training in his own abusive household. In "The Rake," the first [chapter] of his 1992 memoir, **The Cabin: Reminiscence and Diversions,** with its chilling boyhood anecdotes of betrayal and viciousness, Mamet offered a glimpse into the puzzle of his family misery. For the moment, however, in order not to diminish his considerable achievement in **The Cryptogram** by reducing its power to mere autobiography, Mamet is staying *stumm* about his past—being, as he says, "charming and, I trust, evasive."

Childhood is the cryptogram that John, the agitated ten-year-old hero of Mamet's play, who has problems sleeping, and whose father is or is not coming home to take him on a camping trip, is trying to fathom from the mixed messages, lies, and double binds of his caretakers. In Mamet's words: "What happened in childhood? What did it mean? How much is invented? How much of it is distorted? How much suppressed?" Mamet sees myth and drama and dream coming down to the same childhood issues—"the terrors and pleasures of existence before we learned to repress and to filter and to abstract that into conscious perception"—and he says, "What art does is to reverse the process: to re-abstract our conscious perception back into experience." John's quest taps into the audience's own search. Unlike Mamet's polemical **Oleanna,** which prompted argument, the new play bypasses reason and prompts deep, visceral feelings about the past which have a way of making the memory of the play implode in the imagination.

"People may or may not say what they mean," Mamet says. "But they *always* say something designed to get what they want." The gift for cunning gab, he will admit, "seems to gallop in my family." His Polish grandfather, Naphthali, was a daydreamer, who sold ten-cent insurance policies in America, and who could "charm the birds off the trees." Mamet's father, Bernie, a labor lawyer who graduated first in his class from Northwestern Law School, "had a gift for crisp conversation—very colorful and very precise. We all had a vast vocabulary." But in Mamet's plays it's not just how people speak but how they listen that betrays the influence of the emotional abuse about which he's loath to elaborate. "Tolstoy says that all happy families are alike, and every unhappy family is unhappy according to its own ways. I think the same is true of language," Mamet says. "The language of love is, finally, fairly limited. 'You're beautiful,' 'I need you,' 'I love you,' 'I want you.' Love expresses itself, so it doesn't need a lot of words. On the other hand, aggression has an unlimited vocabulary. The unhappy family has myriad ways in which to be unhappy, in which to torture its members. In a happy family, the denotations and connotations of words are fairly close to the surface. But in an unhappy family relationship/political situation/trial, you are dealing with an adversary, and you have to be on guard. You listen with a much more attenuated decimal point of meaning to gauge the other's intent."

Clive Barnes   (review date 14 April 1995)

SOURCE: "A Tale of the Cryptic," in *New York Post,* April 14, 1995.

[*An English-born editor and critic, Barnes is the author and editor of several books about the performing arts. In the following excerpt, he praises Mamet's emphasis on childhood and the pain associated with the dissolution of a family in* The Cryptogram.]

A Cryptogram—a message in code or cipher. Code, mystery, solution. What we are is what we were, and our present is largely a secret message from our past.

Things happen to a child. A father leaves. A family friend disappoints. A mother goes shrewish into the bad night. We need to understand, to grapple with the frozen moments of the past, the moments that stopped us in our tracks and made us what we are.

Psychobabble? Of course! If you go to David Mamet's new play **The Cryptogram** expecting anything more than conventional enlightenment you may well be disappointed.

Mamet is no original thinker, but he is an original playwright. Using time-stained materials, he has invented an original and vastly interesting play that opened at the Westside Theater/Upstairs last night (pushing out Charles Busch's *You Should Be So Lucky* and igniting a controversy in the process).

It has been suggested that this very brief play, set in 1959, is partly autobiographical, because some of its facts—primarily a father leaving home—apparently coincide with those of Mamet's own Chicago childhood.

True or false, it's irrelevant, an irrelevance perhaps pointed up by the author, who after the London production, removed program-mention of Chicago from the play, leaving it placelessly anonymous.

The important thing here is not memoir, but how powerfully Mamet has evoked the pain and process of childhood—the way we learn "the meaning of things that have occurred."

The language is intentionally portentous—the three actors talk around one another with oddly artificial locutions, as if they were conversing in a translation from the telegraphese. At times the dialogue sounds like an oddly unsubtle and unfunny parody of Pinter or even Albee.

But it's not—the influences are there sure enough, yet Mamet is providing a stilted validity to his own very personal concept of lost innocence and bruised experience. As the play puts it: "Everyone has a story . . . And finally you are going to have to learn how you will deal with it . . . At some point we have to face ourselves."

The Cryptogram is the story of 10-year-old John's story. The story he must live with. And die with. And absorb.

To the play text, Mamet has appended a verse from a camping song: "Late last night when you were all in bed / Mrs. O'Leary left a lantern in her shed." John is the transfixed victim of yet another "Chicago fire," a calamity of which he has no part and less understanding.

The outer story surrounding John's confrontational inner story, is simple—a man (we don't meet him) leaves a letter for his wife telling her he is never returning home.

At first, she finds some solace in the couple's homosexual friend, but feels betrayed when she learns that the friend instead of going off earlier on a hunting trip with the husband had actually during that time loaned his hotel room for the husband's assignation with his girlfriend.

The play's original production was staged by Gregory Mosher in London last year, where it had a critical rather than popular success. The text has since been slightly revised—for one thing I think the friend is now more overtly homosexual than before, and the boy has lost the model airplane he once had in his room.

This time round, the play has been directed by Mamet himself—possibly a mistake, because the play seemed somewhat stronger in London. The action moved at a less formal gait, and the playing was altogether more naturalistic, which added to the story's poignancy, and the sense of a child looking back mostly into his life and finding, if only vaguely, that defining point of character. . . .

So finally, what is the cryptogram of the title? It's surely the Sphinx's riddle we all, like Oedipus, have to answer. And it is the mystery of what really happened at our own personal crossroads.

[*The Cryptogram* is] easily Mamet's most haunting and emotionally wrenching play, and the playwright's few enigmatic comments about its origin give rise to speculation that *Cryptogram* parallels some events in his own childhood. If that is true, one should pity the Mamet household.

—*April Austin, in her "Mamet Fires Off a Scorching Play," in* The Christian Science Monitor, *24 February 1995.*

Vincent Canby   (review date 14 April 1995)

SOURCE: "David Mamet's Attempt to Decode Family Life," in *The New York Times*, April 14, 1995, p. C3.

[*In the review below, Canby offers a laudatory assessment of* The Cryptogram, *extolling Mamet's use of language and disturbing dramatization of family life and "emotional games."*]

The Cryptogram, David Mamet's radical, elliptical new work as both playwright and director, is not casually titled: it speaks in code.

The play is thick with spare Mamet language, which is delivered in such a relentless way that commonplace words take on an edge and a ferocity that have little to do with the meanings and emotions they usually evoke. The words sometimes punish. They also illuminate, creating a child's vision of the world with a poignancy seldom experienced in the contemporary theater.

At the end of the 75 intermission-free minutes, you may be moved and mesmerized, as I was. Or, like some others, you may be as ready to leap in front of a cruising taxi as to hail it. *The Cryptogram* is tough, but it rewards. The production, which opened last night at the Westside Theater Upstairs, is a virtual replica of the first-rate production staged by Mr. Mamet in February for the American Repertory Theater in Boston.

The Cryptogram is a family drama so pared down that it almost seems generic, though it's not. It's specific and idiosyncratic. There are three characters: John (Shelton Dane), a 10-year-old boy who is the son, Donny (Felicity Huffman), the mother and abandoned wife, and Del (Ed Begley Jr.), the unmarried family friend who represents Robert, the offstage father, husband and betrayer.

The year is said to be 1959, though the play appears to be taking place in the timelessness of a remembered childhood. Except for references to "the war," nothing attaches events to a particular period. Nor does anything in John Lee Beatty's scenic design suggest that these characters have much in the way of quotidian lives.

The single set looks stripped, devoid of details that might invite sentimental identification. It contains an inexpensive couch at center stage, a chair with an ottoman to the right, a rug on the floor and, at the back, a stairway to the second floor. There are no pictures, books or magazines, no windows or doors, no forgotten detritus of daily life.

Mr. Mamet is dealing in basics. It's as if we were seeing an American living room for the first time, possibly the barren truth behind the nothing décor of *Father Knows Best.* In the course of the play's three scenes, covering one month's time, this living room becomes an arena where John begins to grow up.

He's a bright child without being preternaturally precocious. He knows enough not to question the reasons for his father's departure, (Robert has fallen in love with another woman.) At the beginning of the play John and his father are planning to go on a camping trip the next day. After Robert vanishes, John seldom mentions him. The boy's on his own as his mother deals with her own abandonment.

Donny is not a cruel woman, but she's too involved with her own fury to pay much attention to John. Del, the feckless friend, is blamed for having been aware of Robert's affair, and for having provided the room where Robert and his new love would meet.

Such are the events of *The Cryptogram,* which is played out in a series of oblique encounters between the son and his mother, the mother and the best friend, and the best friend and the son. The dialogue is sometimes brutal in its banality. Del to Donny: "What are you going to do this weekend?" Donny: "This weekend?" Del: "Yes." Donny: "Well, I don't know." Del: "You don't know what you're doing this weekend." Donny: "I'm going to sit." Del: "To sit here." Donny: "Yes."

Much of this talk between the adults is simply sparring, not for time but to avoid facing truth. It also allows the voice of the boy to be heard with piercing, unexpected emotional impact. As he becomes increasingly aware of the collapse of the life he has known, he questions the truth of everything, the existence of things he has been told about but has never seen, including the cities on his globe. "Maybe," he says, "there's nothing on the thing that it is of," And, "We don't know what's real. All we do is say things."

These are not the sorts of philosophical questions that a distraught American mom wants to ponder. When John asks Donny if she ever wished that she could die, he briefly gets through to her. "Everyone has a story," she says. "This is yours. You're going to have to learn how to deal with it." Toward the end of the play, her patience, like Hitler's before he obliterated an entire country, is exhausted. She claims John has lied to her by not staying in bed. "I love you," she tells him, "but I can't like you."

The Cryptogram is a horror story that also appears to be one of Mr. Mamet's most personal plays. It's not about the sort of physical abuse we see in television docudramas, but about the high cost of the emotional games played in what are otherwise considered to be fairly well-adjusted families.

That's not easy to dramatize, Mr. Mamet's method is to create an insular world in which words are weapons that can maim. His direction is as cool and formal as his intricately designed dialogue. This is spoken by Ms. Huffman, Mr. Begley and Mr. Dane, the members of his extraordinary ensemble cast, with the sort of intense dispassion that allows us to understand the sense of things while being aware of every syllable. It's as if Mr. Mamet were deconstructing language to make us think more clearly.

I'm not sure that he entirely succeeds, but the effort is fascinating. *The Cryptogram* is a fine new American play.

Jeremy Gerard   (review date 17 April 1995)

SOURCE: A review of *The Cryptogram,* in *Variety,* April 17, 1995, p. 45.

[*In the following, Gerard positively reviews* The Cryptogram, *discussing, in particular, the horror generated by the play's final scene.*]

It's impossible to imagine anyone being prepared for the closing seconds of *The Cryptogram,* a quietly shattering finale that caps 80 of the most densely packed, emotionally searing minutes this season—or any recent season, for that matter—has offered. As one would expect from David Mamet, the scene is played with a spareness of affect that belies an ambiguity beneath the surface: It is only a young boy climbing a staircase to the attic of his home, as his mother and a family friend look on. But the boy is carrying a hunting knife, and what use he will make of it is almost unbearable to imagine.

As the play's title demands, we find ourselves searching for the meaning of the scenes in *The Cryptogram* leading to that moment. Yet the play is one of the least elliptical Mamet has written; indeed, it's skeleton key to the work of a playwright who has electrified the stage for more than 20 years, provoking fist fights as often as praise along the way.

Skeleton key, hell—it's the key, the door and the whole closet, an unflinching look at the depthless emotional fractures that occur with the dissolution of a family, and, by inference, at wounds that will inevitably pass down through succeeding generations, as in a Greek tragedy. Make no mistake: This is the play that sets the season on fire.

How that talk will translate at the box office is another matter, for *The Cryptogram* is soul-rattlingly bleak. But no play since Michael Weller's 1987 *Spoils of War* has so rivetingly captured the paralyzing pain of a child and a parent in the face of irreparable rupture, and certainly none in memory has done it with Mamet's acuity.

The stairway dominates John Lee Beatty's simple set, and it's where the boy, John (Shelton Dane), spends much of the play. In the first scene, he's waiting for his father, unable to sleep in anticipation of a camping trip they are about to take. He banters with Del (Ed Begley Jr.), a gay family friend. John's mother, Donny (Felicity Huffman), is impatient with his reluctance to go to sleep—"It's grown into this minuet every night," she says, telling Del that John "has to learn the world does not revolve around him."

But in the railing John finds an envelope addressed to his mother, and after he finally departs, she reads the note from her husband telling them he has gone for good. The next night, the story grows even darker as Del confesses that he has allowed the husband to use his shabby hotel room as a trysting place with another woman.

"This is the only bad thing that I've ever done to you," Del tells the sobbing Donny, her cheeks, already hollow with misery, now seeming drawn to the point of stretching.

The final scene takes place a month later, as Donny and John are preparing to move out. "Things occur in our lives, and the meaning of them is not clear," she says, though in truth there is nothing unclear about the desertion from which they will never recover.

John is still wracked with sleeplessness, and by voices he cannot identify, beckoning him to the attic, where he wishes to retrieve a blanket that has already been packed. His repetitious insistence on getting the blanket grows in effect into an incantatory wail, yet it cannot penetrate Donny's own hurt. Her inability to hear, let alone comfort, him horrifies us; it makes us want to take to the stage and save both of them before they are lost to a despair beyond salvation. And when Donny allows Del to give John his father's knife—ostensibly to open the box holding the blanket—she seems to be giving him implicit permission to do something quite different.

The absent father's story is necessarily insignificant. All that matters is his leaving, the ultimate abuse of child and spouse. We wonder, of course, if John will survive, only, like so many sons of divorced parents, to someday leave his own wife and children.

Indeed, what's overwhelming about that final scene is how Mamet's signature speech rhythms—the halting, staccato delivery, the half-finished sentences, the constipated emotional outbursts—seem completely natural, pouring forth from a confused, hurt boy, the fitful patterns of a child who cannot—who will never be able to—comprehend why he has been treated so cruelly. It's as if the playwright were telling us: This is the way it has been, all along. Suddenly the obsessiveness of Mamet's style is revealed in the thwarted, truncated attempts at communication by a baffled child.

It's a stunning revelation that Mamet himself drives home by eliciting perfectly modulated performances from a mesmerizing cast. That's especially true of young Dane, who speaks this language of abandonment as if born to it. Perhaps he's lucky enough not to have been. But for any child or parent who has survived what is in so many ways a commonplace in our society, *The Cryptogram* holds no secrets. The meaning is there for all to see, drawn in pure anguish.

As the title suggests, [Mamet's] play exists to be decoded, and those attuned to the writer's ever-darkening palette will find it a hypnotic task. Involving three characters over three short scenes. *The Cryptogram* cloaks its painful story of abandonment and betrayal in language acknowledging its obliqueness; at times, the play seems to be deconstructing itself.

—*Matt Wolf, in his "Mamet's Bleak New 'Cryptogram' a Mystery Waiting to Be Decoded," in* Chicago Tribune, *5 July 1994.*

John Simon　(review date 24 April 1995)

SOURCE: "Broadway Goes Off," in *New York* Magazine, Vol. 28, No. 17, April 24, 1995, pp. 76, 79.

[*An American essayist and critic, Simon has served as a drama critic for* New York *Magazine as well as a film critic for* Esquire *and the* New Leader. *In the excerpt below, he faults* The Cryptogram *for its lack of content and Mamet's use of language and dialogue.*]

"A playwright who imprisons his characters within crippling verbal debris" is how Jeanette Malkin of Jerusalem's Hebrew University describes David Mamet in a book. I agree with this completely—except that she intends it as praise. It's one thing to imprison Mamet's characters—in Sing Sing, an underground oubliette, or crippling verbal debris—but another to so incarcerate the audience. Mamet's characters, after all, are guilty of having become involved with one of our most pretentiously vacuous playwrights; the audience, however, save for having been suckered into a shell game, is relatively innocent.

The Cryptogram starts out with what appears to be a typical middle-class family on the eve of a stay in their cottage in the woods. The seeming paterfamilias, Del, is reading on a sofa in their living room in 1959. The date, given by the program, is meaningless except perhaps to Mamet, but let's not quibble about a minor meaninglessness here. Offstage upstairs, John, circa 10, should be asleep. Offstage downstairs, mother Donny is making tea. But John is kept awake by excitement about the trip and comes down the exposed stairs to start pestering. And Donny, as she announces four times offstage and at least once on, has broken the teapot.

Further, Del is not Donny's husband and John's dad despite being patriarchally ensconced on that 1959 sofa. The real daddy is Robert, who is working overtime at the office—at least that's what Donny keeps telling John; actually, he'll never return. Del is a family friend, vague father surrogate, and something else I can't tell you without giving away the *crypto* and leaving you with only a couple of grams of *gram*.

Mamet is up—or down—to his usual verbal games. It begins with why John isn't wearing his slippers: They're already packed. This piece of information is chewed and rechewed. So is the fact that John couldn't sleep: "What does it mean, you couldn't sleep? It means nothing other than the meaning you choose to assign to it." Later, the kid says, "I'm perfectly alone; that is what I was saying to myself—because I didn't have a pen to write it down." This is stated three times; it all sounds writ by a nitwit who read Wittgenstein. Or just heard about him.

The form is dramatic fetishism: Object after object is verbally idolized. The slippers, the teapot, the blanket John wraps himself in against the cold. This blanket has a hole in it: freshly made, as John claims, or an old tear, as Donny maintains? This problem is good for many lines, though not quite so many as which coat John should take, an agon meriting at least twelve speeches. But even the coat cannot hold a candle to the knife: the German army knife Robert may have captured in the war (or may not have); the knife he may have given Del when they went camping together (or may not have—as, indeed, they may not have gone camping); the knife that may be in two different locations and may in fact be two knives. And should this knife be entrusted to John, to cut the twine around the package that contains . . .

But who cares what it contains: Contents is not what Mamet is about. About language, then? Yes, if you like rambling monologues that, merely because they occasionally connect, pretend to be dialogue—and don't even connect so much as encroach on one another. Mamet is the man who mistook the hat he was talking through for his muse.

Felicity Huffman moved me: Here is a capable actress who clearly believes in what she is doing to the point of imagining a role where there is none. She does not even mind mouthing Mamet's solecisms: "The older I get, the less that I know" and "If you do not sleep, lay there." Ed Begley Jr. also grapples touchingly with such lines as "Who am I? Some poor queen who lives in a hotel." Granted, Mamet dialogue should be inflicted on a kid only as punishment; but Shelton Dane betrays no charm or talent whatever and suggests that John must be Childe Mamet.

Michael Feingold   (review date 25 April 1995)

SOURCE: "Codehearted," in *The Village Voice*, Vol. XL, No. 17, April 25, 1995, p. 97.

[*Feingold is an American critic and educator. In the following, he offers a favorable review of* The Cryptogram.]

"Auch kleine Dinge können teuer sein," runs Wolf 's best-loved song, "Even little things can be precious to us." David Mamet's **The Cryptogram** is made up of little things—memories, household objects, verbal slips—that are precious as clues to the explanation of a childhood trauma. Magnified by it, they become objects of both veneration and horror, things that are not so much cherished as burned into the awareness.

The central figure is a child, but the action is conducted in rigidly adult terms, a puzzle that a child can only decipher in retrospect. It feels like a deep-buried memory of the playwright's own, striking with a force at once more personal and more profound than his other works: Under the cold, terse phrases, the spare structure, the formalized tableaux, its vulnerability is tangible, almost unbearable.

The adult's secret code that the child will have to crack in the future is paralleled by a puzzle to be solved in the play's present: Why isn't Daddy home? Del, the only man on the scene, is neither father nor husband, one of those spinsterish, sexually wavering "friends of the family" who is supportive to the absent man's wife, affectionate to the son, but, as it turns out, not really a friend to either. His love has led him into duplicity; under cover of his evasions, the husband has escaped forever from the marriage, betraying his friend as both have betrayed the wife.

The son, barely grasping any of this, feels betrayed by all three. No wonder he can't sleep, and hears voices in his dark bedroom. He thinks the dead are calling to him—but, of course, he doesn't know what "dead" is: When his mother, Donny, throws deceitful Del out the door and breaks down crying, the boy asks her, "Are you dead?" In a sense, he's not wrong. The house is full of dead things: love, marriage, friendship, affection between mother and son.

Mamet echoes their absence, visually, by staging the play in a creepily grave, arid style—naturalism with pieces inexplicably missing: The living room has a sofa and chair, but no tables. The staircase on John Lee Beatty's Hopperish set seems to stretch up to a dark infinity; the son's last slow ascent of it—on his way to the attic, with his father's hunting knife—makes the audience gasp as intensely as Cherry Jones's final-curtain climb in *The Heiress*.

Like other objects in the play, the knife too turns out to be a deceit, its obvious meaning false, the ones it will carry in retrospect more complex and numerous: a parting gift, a death wish, a symbol of the father's phallic betrayal, a memento that's also a manufactured lie. This is man's inheritance: Every memory is bittersweet, every object from the past as false as it is precious. The present is a cryptogram which we only solve years later, when its message is no longer any use. "Ye must become as a little child again," said the fellow who allegedly rose last Sunday. But when you do so, you find, not salvation, but the hell your parents unintentionally wished on you, to be passed on as unintentionally to your children. "Myself am Hell," as somebody else once remarked.

Once or twice, Mamet's austere language stiffens up into the stilted; a few of the terser exchanges slip down into ordinary Mametese. Beyond that, both his script and staging seem dauntingly, chillingly perfect, even in such weird details as Del's ornate struggle to handle a bottle and two glasses with no surface to rest them on. Begley, making his stage debut, is convincing, if occasionally a shade tentative. The play's emotional weight rests on Huffman, whose fierce, precise assurance on every elliptical line makes you marvel even while she's wrenching your heart out. And Shelton Dane's eerie, grave concentration as the child is so attuned to the Mamet style, you might almost believe he understands the play, which I sincerely hope for his own peace of mind he doesn't. Some future director will probably have this taxing role played by an adult actor in child's clothes—looking, I expect, a great deal like David Mamet.

Additional coverage of Mamet's life and career is contained in the following sources published by Gale Research: *Authors and Artists for Young Adults,* Vol. 3; *Contemporary Authors,* Vols. 81-84; *Contemporary Authors Bibliographical Series,* Vol. 3; *Contemporary Authors New Revision Series,* Vols. 15, 41; *Contemporary Literary Criticism,* Vols. 9, 15, 34, 46; *Dictionary of Literary Biography,* Vol. 7; *Drama Criticism,* Vol. 4; and *Major 20th-Century Writers.*

Terrence McNally
Love! Valour! Compassion!

Awards: Tony Award for Best Play, New York Drama Critics Award for Best New American Play, OBIE Award for Playwriting, Drama Desk Award for Outstanding Play, and Outer Critics Circle Award for Best Play.

Born in 1939, McNally is an American playwright.

For further information on his life and works, see *CLC*, Volumes 4, 7, and 41.

INTRODUCTION

Love! Valour! Compassion! (1994) is about gay life in America and the search for true love and happiness. The play unfolds at Gregory's summerhouse in upstate New York over three holiday weekends: Memorial Day, the Fourth of July, and Labor Day. The eight male characters alternately narrate the events of the weekends, each from his own perspective. The characters relate experiences from their relationships as well as the ways in which they deal with the effects of the AIDS epidemic. Favorably assessed as a ground-breaking work about gay life, *Love! Valour! Compassion!* has been compared to Mart Crowley's play about a group of homosexual men, *The Boys in the Band* (1969), as well as to the works of Thornton Wilder, Eugene O'Neill, and Anton Chekhov. While a few critics have suggested that the drama's themes are not well developed and that it relies too heavily on frank sexual humor and nudity, most agree with David Kaufman who wrote that McNally's "play refutes many myths regarding a gay lifestyle: above all by demonstrating that there can be more love—and yes, courage and compassion—within an extended family than many nuclear ones possess."

PRINCIPAL WORKS

The Roller Coaster (drama) 1960
*There Is Something Out There (drama) 1962; revised as *And Things That Go Bump in the Night,* 1964
The Lady of the Camellias [adaptor; from Giles Cooper's dramatic adaptation of the novel and play *La Dame aux camélias* (1848 and 1852) by Alexandre Dumas *fils*] (drama) 1963
†Next (drama) 1967
Tour (drama) 1967
‡Apple Pie: Three One-Act Plays (dramas) 1968
†Botticelli (television play) 1968
†¡Cuba Si! (drama) 1968
Here's Where I Belong (drama) 1968

Noon (drama) 1968
†Sweet Eros (drama) 1968
†Witness (drama) 1968
*Bringing It All Back Home (drama) 1969
*Last Gasps (television play) 1969
*Bad Habits: Ravenswood and Dunelawn (drama) 1971
†Where Has Tommy Flowers Gone? (drama) 1971
Let It Bleed (drama) 1972
*Whiskey (drama) 1973
The Tubs (drama) 1974; revised as *The Ritz,* 1975
The Golden Age (drama) 1975
The Ritz (screenplay) 1977
Broadway, Broadway (drama) 1979
The 5:48 [adaptor; from the short story by John Cheever] (television play) 1979
The Lisbon Traviata (radio play) 1979; adapted for the stage in 1985
It's Only a Play: A Comedy (drama) 1982
The Rink: A New Musical (drama) 1984

Frankie and Johnny in the Clair de Lune   (drama)   1987
Andre's Mother   (television play)   1990
Frankie and Johnny   (screenplay)   1991
Kiss of the Spider Woman [adaptor; from the Manuel Puig novel]   (drama)   1992
Lips Together, Teeth Apart   (drama)   1992
A Perfect Ganesh   (drama)   1993
Terrence McNally: 15 Short Plays   (drama)   1994
Love! Valour! Compassion!   (drama)   1994

*These works were collectively published as *The Ritz, and Other Plays* (1969).

†These works were collectively published as *Sweet Eros, Next, and Other Plays* (1969).

‡This work includes *Tour, Next,* and *Botticelli.*

CRITICISM

John Simon   (review date 14 November 1994)

SOURCE: "Saucy! Schmaltzy! Slow Moving!," in *New York* Magazine, Vol. 27, No. 45, November 14, 1994, pp. 79-80.

[*In the following excerpt, Simon reviews* Love! Valour! Compassion!, *examining the play's reliance on sexual humor and contending that the themes are poorly developed*.]

When, over three centuries ago, John Dryden initiated heroic drama, he declared that "love and valour ought to be the subject of it." To this program, Terrence McNally has added compassion and three exclamation points. Thus we get ***Love! Valour! Compassion!**,* a long play about three long weekends (Memorial Day, Fourth of July, Labor Day). Encapsulating the lives of eight homosexuals, two of them played by the same actor, it means to be memorable, forthcoming, a labor of love.

The locale is an isolated Dutchess County lakeside summer house, where Gregory, a famous but fading choreographer, is struggling with a new ballet while also planning a drag version of *Swan Lake* for an AIDS benefit. His lover, the blind and boyish Bobby, is seduced by the naughty Hispanic dancer Ramon, who is the boyfriend of John Jeckyll, a nasty British rehearsal pianist, who hides a Hyde just under his skin. His twin, James, however, is the sweetest of dithering queens, liked by everybody, but dying of AIDS. The gang's cutup is HIV-positive Buzz, who designs costumes for Gregory. Fat, loverless, and yearning, Buzz is a wizard at musical-comedy trivia and a wellspring of campy jokes. Representing non-show business are Arthur and Perry, an accountant and a laywer, married to each other for fourteen years. Perry is the raisonneur of the group, though he is scarcely less campy than Buzz.

These are not wholly carefree holidays. Ramon's fling with Bobby stirs up trouble for himself with the vindictive John, and for Bobby with the heartbroken Gregory. Even the motherly Arthur evinces a yen for Ramon, especially when, both naked, they share a raft on the lake. Tempers flare and taunts are taunted. Defiance circulates among the group. John reads and reveals Gregory's private diary. Somebody gets spat at. Somebody's sister dies in India. The group goes skinny-dipping. Two guys hide in a closet to watch two others carry on. Buzz and James find each other. John plays classical piano music, giving McNally a chance to show off his knowledge of serious music, even as Buzz's show-biz jokes allow him to parade his musical-comedy erudition. It rains a lot, but there is also smooching in the moonlight. And a few comic dance turns.

There is no denying that McNally can write funny lines as well as anyone. Often they are catty, but sometimes actually human. Buzz complains about his room: "That little horror under the eaves—I call it the Patty Hearst Memorial Closet." He gripes, "I'm sick of straight people. There's too goddamn many of them. . . . They're taking over, I'm telling you!" Or "I'm so intense. I need someone like Dennis Hopper." Someone asks, "Is there no British equivalent to *machismo?*" "No. None at all," affirms James, adding the ruminative topper: "Maybe Glenda Jackson."

Sometimes, however, he overreaches. " 'Nocturnal emissions' is so much nicer than 'wet dreams.' It made me think of Chopin: Nocturnal Emission in B-flat." The joke falls (non-B) flat. Someone is called a kibitz. "What's a kibitz?" asks Ramon. "A kibbutz is a place where old gay Jewish couples live." Somehow the kibitz-kibbutz homophone gets in the hair of those "old gay Jewish couples," which is itself stretching things a bit. And all the jokes are, one way or another, sexual. Is there no other kind of humor?

A bigger problem is McNally's waxing poetic every so often. There is intrinsically nothing wrong with waxing poetic, except when the waxing is more like a waning. For example, Perry has a habit of saying when the situation gets hairy, "Anyway. . . ." It is an aposiopesis all pick up and play variations on. The device is harped on until it loses its poetic charm and becomes a sweaty factotum, having to provide even the curtain line. No way. Also, I find kissing a relative stranger's AIDS lesion more frivolous than Franciscan.

Perhaps he is just giving us a slice of life, or two, or three.

—John Simon

What is McNally trying to say with this play? True, ever since he burst on the Broadway scene with ***And Things That Go Bump in the Night,*** he has been gnawing away at the closet door, which, finally nibbled away, reveals even the various ways three parallel gay couples are entwined in their sleep. (No differently from straight ones.) But, surely, there must be more to it, otherwise why the grandiose title? Though, frankly, I don't see much compassion here, and still less valour, with or without a "u."

Erich Kästner once published his poems as an anthology, *Lyrische Hausapotheke* ("Lyrical Medicine Chest"). In the index, he listed all possible emotional disasters, along with the page numbers for the poems that might soothe those ills. McNally may be trying for something similar. If so, his situations are not quite inclusive enough, his solutions not sufficiently solacing. But perhaps he is just giving us a slice of life, or two, or three. Anyway. . . .

Nancy Franklin   (review date 14 November 1994)

SOURCE: "McNally Men, Wasserstein Women," in *The New Yorker,* Vol. LXX, No. 37, November 14, 1994, pp. 129-31.

[*In the following excerpt, Franklin favorably reviews* Love! Valour! Compassion!, *focusing on the play's structure, characters, and themes.*]

The eight characters in Terrence McNally's new play, ***Love! Valour! Compassion!*** (terrible! title!), which just opened at his longtime theatrical home, the Manhattan Theatre Club, all happen to be gay, but they connect in ways that almost any nuclear family would envy. Most of them have a long history with each other—they have slept together, roomed together, worked together—and their relationships are rich and resonant. This is no uncomplicated idyll, though: some real ugliness comes out in the course of the play, and there are a number of betrayals, large and small. Yet in this beautifully written work McNally and his actors, under the direction of Joe Mantello, present humbling evidence of what human love is and can be.

The play is set in and around a house in the country in upstate New York on the three holiday weekends that punctuate the summer, and the three acts are punctuated by the men singing, in a-cappella harmony, songs from bygone days—"Beautiful Dreamer," "In the Good Old Summertime," and "Shine On, Harvest Moon." Gregory (Stephen Bogardus), a dancer, whose house we are in, addresses the audience and speaks with pride of his home, which was built in the early years of this century—the "golden age of American housebuilding." At the end of the play, the men, swimming naked in a lake, call up the image of a famous American painting, Eakins' "The Swimming Hole." The feeling of timelessness that imbues this play cuts both ways: as we're absorbing the lulling thought that there were others here before us and there will be others here after us, we're struck sharply by its unavoidable corollary—that we won't be here forever.

Early on, we're told outright that one of the guests, Buzz, who does costumes for Gregory's dance company, won't be here forever: he's H.I.V.-positive. But Buzz himself doesn't talk about it; in fact, his policy is that anyone who mentions AIDS this summer has to put five dollars into a kitty. Buzz, in yet another wonderful performance by Nathan Lane, eats, sleeps, and dreams musical comedy. When we first meet him, he's just woken up in a panic: "I was having a musical-comedy nightmare. They were going

to revive *The King and I* for Tommy Tune and Elaine Stritch. We've got to stop them!" (Buzz could have designed the set of ***L! V! C!,*** which is peculiarly *Carousel*-esque: a green hillock on one side of an almost bare stage, and a backdrop of stars against a night sky.) But the character goes beyond camp stereotype. As the summer has progressed, Buzz has found a new boyfriend, who has AIDS, and suddenly his world of happy endings, a world he can "get my hands around," breaks permanently loose from his grasp. In a rage, he shouts:

> I want to see a *Sound of Music* where the entire von Trapp family dies in an authentic Alpine avalanche. A *Kiss Me, Kate* where she's got a big coldsore on her mouth. A *Funny Thing Happened on the Way to the Forum* where the only thing that happens is nothing and it's not funny and they all go down waiting, waiting for what? Waiting for nothing, waiting for death, like everyone I know and care about is, including me.

It's hilarious, and it's devastating, but it's by no means the only painful probing of the wounds that being alive causes. Over a dinner table, the men argue about whether people really can or do care about each other—an argument set off by a discussion of the news photograph of a starving Sudanese child being watched over by a waiting vulture—and an infidelity is confessed at a particularly unfortunate time.

All the actors bring something vivid to their roles. John Glover, playing identical twin brothers—a nasty Englishman and his sweet counterpart (who becomes Buzz's boyfriend in the second act)—goes easily and believably between extremes, and even seems to look different in the two parts. Bogardus, as the aging dancer, whose body has begun to protest, has a kind of embracing tenderness about him; for the duration of the play, you feel that you, too, are a welcome guest in his house. Justin Kirk and Randy Becker, as the youngest members of the group, offer mainly youth and beauty. (And plenty of it: those who complain about the lack of male nudity in the movies need look no further than this play.) Stephen Spinella and John Benjamin Hickey are touching as Perry and Arthur, a lawyer and an accountant, who have been together for fourteen years. "We're role models," Perry says. "It's very stressful." We know by the end of the play that they will stay together. Earlier, we see Perry trimming the hair in Arthur's ears, and Arthur says, only half-jokingly, "You know, if you really think about it, this is what it all comes down to." Perhaps McNally has put his finger on what it is that parents are talking about when they say that all they want is for their children to be happy.

Frank Scheck   (review date 15 November 1994)

SOURCE: "*Uncommon Women* Ages Poorly, McNally's Latest Has Its Strengths," in *The Christian Science Monitor,* November 15, 1994, p. 14.

[*In the following excerpt, Scheck favorably reviews the character development, staging techniques, and performances in* Love! Valour! Compassion!, *while faulting the play's lack of "real dramatic structure or plot."*]

There's love, valour, and compassion aplenty in Terrence McNally's play, which has opened Off Broadway to the strongest reviews so far this season. There's also plenty of darker emotions. No contemporary playwright is as effective in blending high comedy with pathos, in giving us characters that will make you laugh and break your heart.

McNally's impact on both the New York stage and in Hollywood films is considerable. He is adept at creating emotional balancing acts.

In his screenplay for the 1991 film *Frankie and Johnny,* which starred Al Pacino and Michelle Pfeiffer, he paired an unlikely short-order cook with an emotionally withdrawn waitress. In the book for the musical version of *Kiss of the Spider Woman,* McNally juxtaposed a political revolutionary's single-mindedness against the escapism of his homosexual cellmate. His most recent Off Broadway hit was *Lips Together, Teeth Apart,* which pitted two mismatched married couples against one another.

Love! Valour! Compassion! is a rondelet among seven homosexual men spending summer weekends together at a house in upstate New York. This is the playwright's most insularly gay-themed play, but in its emotional concerns it is also one of his most universal.

If there's a fault with the play, it's that McNally, even more than usual, seems unconcerned with finding any real dramatic structure or plot. The play, which hits the three-hour mark, is a succession of vignettes that have all the narrative drive of one of those lazy summer weekends. The play's up-front and at times crass attitude toward nudity and sexuality will put off many theatergoers, but the characters are delineated with compassion and humor.

Director Joe Mantello, (an actor who was excellent in last season's *Angels in America*) has directed with a fine comic flair and imagination.

McNally's writing here is extremely fluid—a character might suddenly slip into the role of narrator, but the audience never loses its bearings. There are nice stylistic touches as well: the men sweetly harmonizing on various songs to open or close the acts; the opening image, with the group standing over a small model house that represents the play's setting.

What truly makes the play work are the performances. No one is less than superb, from the better-known actors like Stephen Spinella (fresh from two Tonys for *Angels in America*) and John Glover (familiar to television audiences and a five-time Emmy nominee) to relative newcomers like Justin Kirk and Randy Becker.

Nathan Lane, who is quickly establishing himself as one of the foremost comic acting talents of our time (he will soon be co-starring with Robin Williams in the movie remake of *La Cage Aux Folles*) continues to score huge laughs just about every time he opens his mouth.

The other players include Stephen Bogardus and John Benjamin Hickey.

David Kaufman   (review date 19 December 1994)

SOURCE: A review of *Love! Valour! Compassion!,* in *The Nation,* New York, Vol. 259, No. 21, December 19, 1994, pp. 774-76.

[*In the following favorable review, Kaufman examines the themes, characters, and plot development in* Love! Valour! Compassion!]

"You show me a happy homosexual and I'll show you a gay corpse." Though it was supposed to be sardonic, this tragic line from *The Boys in the Band* has acquired a grim, unintended meaning long after it was uttered by a gay character in 1968, a year before the Stonewall uprising. Generally perceived as the first "homosexual play"—as opposed to merely being a play about homosexuals—Mart Crowley's drama was steeped in a self-loathing that stereotyped homosexuality and branded all homosexuals at the time. But we've come a long way since then, both on stage and off. In terms of the theater, however, never has our progress seemed more assured or more richly proclaimed than it does today, with the arrival of Terrence McNally's new play, *Love! Valour! Compassion!,* which in some respects resembles a *Boys in the Band* twenty-five years later, and may become as much of a landmark. Even as important and recent a play as Tony Kushner's *Angels in America* is still riddled with self-loathing issues for homosexuals, which begins to explain why it has been more of a success with straight audiences than with gay. And the more current *Blade to the Heat,* by Oliver Mayer, which opened at the Joseph Papp Public Theater within a week of *Love! Valour! Compassion!,* focuses on closeted homosexuality and gay-baiting as well, in the professional boxing world of 1959.

Beginning with the fact that both *Love! Valour! Compassion!* and *The Boys in the Band* have eight gay characters, there are enough similarities to suggest McNally is paying homage. But beyond any tribute we might detect, his new offering functions more like a public exorcism, a stunning assertion that the self-hatred which ostensibly accompanied homosexuality has been buried once and for all.

For three decades, McNally has been one of our most reliable playwrights. From *It's Only a Play* to *The Lisbon Traviata* and *Frankie and Johnny in the Clair de Lune,* he could be counted on time and again to supply another sturdy play, practically guaranteed to amuse and move us in equal parts. Consistency need not imply greatness—think of Neil Simon—but this new venture achieves it.

Artistically speaking, *Love! Valour! Compassion!* owes very little to McNally's last overtly gay play, *The Lisbon Traviata,* first produced in 1985. But it follows very naturally from his most recent plays, *Lips Together, Teeth Apart* and *A Perfect Ganesh.* Both of those dared, as McNally does now, to ask profound questions about the meaning of life, and they also employed unconventional theatrical techniques whenever, for instance, their characters interrupted the exposition to lapse into internal reveries or stream-of-consciousness musings. While *Ganesh* sent two elderly women on a spiritual mission to India and *Lips Together* situated two married couples in a beach house, each of those plays trafficked in gay issues, albeit in relatively discreet ways. (In the first, one of the characters is trying to forgive herself for not accepting her son's homosexuality before he was murdered in a gay-bashing incident. In the second, the posh beach house has been inherited by the sister of a gay man who died of AIDS, and it is surrounded by gay characters offstage on both sides.)

Given his long-term association with the Manhattan Theatre Club, it seemed that McNally was deliberately writing gay plays from a straight perspective in order to better reach and educate its subscription audience, composed predominantly of elderly middle-class couples. If that were the case, he apparently feels they've learned enough by now to immerse them, finally, in a thoroughly homosexual milieu. In bringing together an octet of gay characters in a country house over three successive holiday weekends (Memorial Day, Fourth of July and Labor Day), *Love! Valour! Compassion!* features a lot of camping it up, bitchy humor and extensive full frontal nudity.

Yet, like the best gay fiction in the post-Stonewall era, this play is more about characters who happen to be gay than it is about gay characters. Though they are all men, they're engrossed in familiar McNally themes that have less to do with gender than with the human condition: finding intimacy or sustaining loving relationships in the midst of fear and loss. This particular group is so vividly drawn it transcends anything that we might find to say about the characters individually, even as the play that contains them transcends anything McNally has produced before.

What's difficult to convey in any discussion of *Love! Valour! Compassion!* is the grace with which the characters become people as their stories unfold. It's not only that they're vividly rendered, but that they're revealed gradually, in a layered and richly textured fashion. Evoking at times Thornton Wilder, at others the interior monologues of Eugene O'Neill, McNally has derived a unique voice that allows each of his characters to shift in and out of commenting on the action they are simultaneously a part of. They take turns, in other words, being part-time narrators even as they're playing themselves. They also share their inner feelings at certain moments, and eventually tell us what's to become of them long after the play is over. Though this all might sound awkward, it's accomplished naturally, free of any devices that smack of contrivance.

Located near a lake in upstate New York, the isolated country house is owned by Gregory (Stephen Bogardus), a celebrated choreographer, and his considerably younger lover, Bobby (Justin Kirk), who is blind. Their regular guests include the desperately funny Buzz (Nathan Lane), a costume designer who is eager to be in a relationship ("I'm so intense," he says, "I need someone like Dennis Hopper"). Buzz had an affair some years ago with John (John Glover), an unsuccessful composer who is now a rehearsal pianist for Gregory's dance company and who brings along Ramon (Randy Becker), a hot young Latino dancer he's been having a fling with for a few weeks. As if to confirm that not everyone who is gay is a professional artist, there are also Perry (Stephen Spinella), a lawyer, and his lover, Arthur (John Benjamin Hickey), an accoun-

tant. They have been together fourteen years ("We're role models—it's very stressful," says Perry).

During the course of their trinity of holiday weekends (separated by two intermissions), these lovers and friends engage in lively discussions about social responsibility, reveal their innermost yearnings, swim and go for walks, betray and spy on one another, lash out and reaffirm their love. What emerges is a group portrait of an extended family that remains connected and concerned despite any fallings-out it endures.

Though Gregory is 43 and beginning to stiffen in the joints, he's struggling with a new dance piece to be premiered in the fall. He's also rehearsing his guests for an AIDS benefit in which they'll perform a selection from *Swan Lake* in drag—wonderfully realized in the last act.

Whenever epiphanies occur, McNally posits them in the midst of mundane circumstances, which reduces the poetic weight they otherwise bear. The wicked John periodically reads his host's private diary entries, thereby discovering how much he's disliked by the others. One of the evenings is interrupted by a phone call informing Bobby that his beloved sister has died in a freak accident in India. And life goes on.

The HIV-positive Buzz is so tired of thinking and hearing about AIDS that he's invented a game whereby anyone who mentions the word has to contribute five dollars to a fund. Buzz believes that "everybody's gay—or they should be," and he is, stereotypically, a musical comedy fanatic. He awakens startled the first night to report, "I was having a musical comedy nightmare. They were going to revive *The King and I* for Tommy Tune and Elaine Stritch. We've got to stop them!"

Buzz is deliciously acerbic and tends to lift everyone's spirits with his wild and wacky declarations, such as: "I'm sick of straight people. Tell the truth, aren't you? There's too goddamn many of them. I was in the bank yesterday. They were everywhere. Writing checks, making deposits. Two of them were applying for a mortgage. It was disgusting. They're taking over. No one wants to talk about it, but it's true."

This inverted homophobia becomes one of the ways McNally negates the differences between gays and straights, even as he dwells on homosexual behavior. It's over Memorial Day that Ramon seduces Bobby. By July 4 their tryst has developed into an affair that everyone but Gregory seems to know about. Also by July 4, John's twin brother, James, has arrived from London, where he sews costumes for a theater company. (The twins are portrayed by the same actor: When James makes his first appearance in the second of three acts, he winningly tells the audience, "It's not who you think—I'm the other one.") James is as sweet and goodnatured as John is selfish and nasty. In a *coup de théâtre* requiring directorial sleight of hand, the brothers confront each other on stage as John divulges how much he has always resented James.

Buzz and James, who has full-blown AIDS, proceed to fall in love. In one of the more touching scenes, Arthur and Perry are in a canoe passing Buzz and James in another boat on the lake. While the longtime couple are talking about their sense of survivor's guilt at having remained HIV-negative, Buzz has to deal with James, who just soiled himself and needs to be rushed back to the house.

Though Buzz has managed to fend off AIDS-related anxiety by retreating to the escapist world of musical comedies, his frustration only escalates now that he's finally in love with someone who is evidently close to death. In the play's most dramatic moment, Buzz pours his outrage into an explosive monologue that mocks his greatest passion. After tending to James, he screams, "I want to see a *Sound of Music* where the entire von Trapp family dies in an authentic Alpine avalanche. A *Kiss Me, Kate* where she's got a big cold sore on her mouth. A *Funny Thing Happened on the Way to the Forum* where the only thing that happens is nothing and it's not funny and they all go down waiting, waiting for what? Waiting for nothing, waiting for death, like everyone I know and care about is, including me."

McNally clearly has compassion for each of his characters, and effectively transfers it to the audience. Some of the credit must go to the team involved in putting together this premiere production at the Manhattan Theatre Club, where its extended run through January has led to plans for a move to Broadway. From the uniformly exquisite ensemble to Joe Mantello's fluid direction, it's difficult to imagine any improvements. Loy Arcenas's abstract set design is an additional asset, permitting the stage to serve as many different interior and exterior locations, including a lake the group literally splashes around in at the end.

Though it seems unfair to single out any of the players, Nathan Lane's Buzz is further testimony that he is perhaps our greatest comic actor. And as both the resentful John and the gentle James, John Glover simply has more of an opportunity to display his range. But then, Stephen Spinella finds a range as well, given some inherent contradictions in Perry.

For the ways in which it's told no less than for what it has to say, *Love! Valour! Compassion!* is a remarkably Chekhovian work—which is to say vital and capacious, extremely natural yet poetic and crafted at the same time. (To borrow from Cynthia Ozick's remarks on Chekhov, this makes McNally a master of the observed as well as the unobserved.) While the title *Love! Valour! Compassion!,* which McNally found in one of Cheever's journal entries, is about as unfortunate as *Lips Together, Teeth Apart,* it is a perfect summary of the play's themes. Whether it was one of McNally's intentions or not, his play refutes many myths regarding a gay lifestyle: above all by demonstrating that there can be more love—and yes, courage and compassion—within an extended family than many nuclear ones possess.

Stefan Karfér **(review date 13 February 1995)**

SOURCE: A review of *Love! Valour! Compassion!,* in *The New Leader,* Vol. LXVIII, No. 2, February 13, 1995, p. 23.

[*In the following mixed review of* Love! Valour! Compas-

What's difficult to convey in any discussion of *Love! Valour! Compassion!* is the grace with which the characters become people as their stories unfold.

—David Kaufman

---

sion!, *Karfér states that "McNally shows little originality or audacity."*]

The progress and regress of homosexual life is usually left to the political propagandists on either side. You can get a more accurate (and less shrill) summary by comparing two comedies, staged 25 years apart.

In 1969, Mart Crowley's *The Boys in the Band* featured a group of nine gay men in the crosscurrents of professional and social life. Some were tragic, some funny, some faithful, some promiscuous. Almost all stayed in the closet. "Show me a happy homosexual," said a character, articulating the play's most famous line, "and I'll show you a gay corpse."

In 1995, Terrence McNally's **Love! Valour! Compassion!** features a group of eight gay men in the crosscurrents of professional and social life. Some are tragic, some funny, some faithful, some promiscuous. None has hidden his sexual identity; no need for dissembling in our enlightened era. That's the good news. The bad news, of course, is the spread of AIDS. The plague throws its shadow across everyone present.

The action takes place at a summer house over three long weekends, Memorial Day, July Fourth and Labor Day. The place is owned by Gregory (Stephen Bogardus), a regal dancemeister suffering from choreographer's block. This creative crisis has not diminished his generous nature, however, and he regularly opens his door to a gaggle of friends. Chief among them is the hyperthyroid Buzz Hauser (Nathan Lane), connoisseur of musicals and monger of gossip: "You mean her Ladyship Derek Jacobi and Dame Ian McKellen?"

The other visitors are markedly quieter; then again, junkyard dogs produce fewer decibels than Buzz. Among the guests: vile-tempered pianist John; his kindly, lisping twin brother James (both played by John Glover); uptight lawyer Perry (Anthony Heald); his WASPish lover Arthur (John Benjamin Hickey); young, blind Bobby (Justin Kirk); and overheated Latino dancer Ramon (Randy Becker).

As the play unfolds, characters and crises begin to define themselves. Bobby professes his loyalty to Gregory, a man whose work he can never witness. But all Ramon has to do is touch him and the sightless youth succumbs. Perry and Arthur bicker constantly. Yet the couple would rather fight than switch; arguments and jealousies cement their relationship.

Throughout most of the action Buzz is loveless at the top

of his lungs. HIV positive, he prefers to keep the world at bay—until the AIDS-afflicted James abruptly catches his eye and heart. Gregory finds that he can no longer do the leaps and arabesques of last year. Is he also suffering from the fatal virus? No, he's just another victim of that universal disease, middle age.

Clearly, McNally is offering two proposals.

1. Homosexuals are different in their humor (most of the group wants to don women's costumes for a campy ballet, in order to raise money for a favorite charity). They vary as well from the straight world in their position as outsiders, and, in this era, their terror of early death. Special attention must be paid to their predicament.

2. Homosexuals are just like everyone else. They are faithful and they sleep around, they drink too much and regret it the next morning, they prize youth and they grow old. If you prick them, do they not bleed? If you tickle them, do they not laugh?

Amid all this moral confusion, Joe Mantello's direction is unfailingly lucid; Loy Arcenas' set uses the best of Monet and Van Gogh; John Kilgore's sound design truly evokes the natural aura of summer and fall; and the playwright offers some poignant moments and coruscating lines. He has also written some inexcusably tasteless ones ("This is like Adolf Hitler *shtooping* Anne Frank").

Even at his infrequent best, though, McNally shows little originality or audacity. For all its psychological candor and physical nudity, *Love! Valour! Compassion!* is actually nothing more than *The Big Chill* seen from the other side of the bed, complete with nostalgic angst and bitchy asides.

As the holy fool, Lane is a standup, situp, liedown comic par excellence; his most pedestrian speeches are given unexpected emphases and uncanny timing. Of the supporting crew, Bogardus is the most credible and Heald the least. Nevertheless, the character of Perry engaged my sympathy from start to finale. He is the only one—speaking of taste—who steadfastly refuses to wear a tutu for Act III's inevitable and cloying after dinner mince.

Howard Kissel (review date 15 February 1995)

SOURCE: A review of *Love! Valour! Compassion!*, in *National Theatre Critic's Review,* Vol. LVI, No. 3, 1995.

[*In the following review, Kissel favorably assesses* Love! Valour! Compassion!]

To a certain extent, the history of New York theater in the last decade has been the history of gay theater. Terrence McNally's *Love! Valour! Compassion!* which has made the journey from Manhattan Theater Club to the Walter Kerr with all its virtues intact, is a key moment in that history.

Unlike many recent gay plays, whose tone was accusatory and shrill, *Love* is not a political statement. It documents the moment when the word "gay," which used to mean merry and mirthful as well as "homosexual," has come to mean bittersweet, if not sorrowful.

The play, about eight men—lovers, former lovers, would-be lovers—spending three holiday weekends together over a summer in an old house in Duchess County, is full of scenes that, 20 years ago, might have seemed silly but are now tinged with sadness.

I was again deeply moved by the sight of six men in tutus doing the dance of the little swans from *Swan Lake,* which seems in this context, an elegy for an innocence, a giddiness now lost and irreplaceable. The play is mostly hilarious, but the laughter is never unalloyed.

If anything, *Love!* seem sharper than it did before. Perhaps this is because Nathan Lane, as a costume designer who has AIDS, gets even more mileage out of McNally's great zingers about the dying art of musical theater. Or perhaps it is because Anthony Heald, the one new cast member, is far more engaging than his predecessor as an irritable lawyer.

All of the other performances have retained their potency, especially John Glover as twins and Stephen Bogardus as the choreographer in midlife crisis.

Incidentally, I am amused by how much tongue-wagging the abundant nudity has caused. Is this New York or Peoria?

Besides, did Jayne Mansfield steal the show 40 years ago in *Will Success Spoil Rock Hunter?* because she could act?

Vincent Canby (review date 15 February 1995)

SOURCE: "*Love!* Hits Broadway Running Like a Broadway Hit," in *The New York Times,* February 15, 1995, pp. C9, C12.

[*Canby is a highly acclaimed theater critic for* The New York Times. *In the following favorable review, he applauds the structure, plot, and characters of* Love! Valour! Compassion!]

The Manhattan Theater Club's production of Terrence McNally's *Love! Valour! Compassion!* was enthusiastically received when it opened Off Broadway in November. At that time even its admirers, including me, could not have dreamed that this proudly gay play stood a chance of becoming a mainstream hit.

That seems a distinct possibility now that *Love! Valour! Compassion!* has transferred, virtually intact (one cast change), to the Walter Kerr Theater, where it opened last night.

By coincidence, this is the same theater that housed *Angels in America,* Tony Kushner's award-winning "gay fantasia on national themes." Though both deal with gay characters and concerns, they're otherwise very different. Mr. Kushner's play is a bold attempt to create a theatrical epic, a slangy American equivalent to *Paradise Lost* and *Paradise Regained.*

Love! Valour! Compassion! is something else. Its roots are in old-fashioned Broadway theater, specifically in the house-party comedy, brought up to date and to brand-new life. Set in a comfortable farmhouse in Dutchess County,

N. Y., it's about eight mostly upper-middle-class homosexual men, most of them in their early middle age, in the time of AIDS. Over three successive holiday weekends in one summer, they gather to relax, celebrate their friendship and consider their lives while making accommodations to survive.

This is not the sort of thing you might expect to draw Broadway's usual big spenders. Yet *Love! Valour! Compassion!* is written, directed and acted with such theatrical skill and emotional range that it's as broadly entertaining as it is moving.

I don't mean to denigrate the gifts of both Mr. McNally and Joe Mantello, the director, to suggest that this production was made for Broadway: it's utterly contemporary; its one-liners are sometimes hysterical and are slammed home with style, most often by the incomparable Nathan Lane; it has genuine pathos that's only slightly tinged with sentimentality, and, as a singular talking point, it offers more male nudity than has probably ever been seen in a legitimate Broadway theater.

Is the nudity essential? Does it turn men into sex objects? Is it cheap exploitation? Discuss amongst yourselves. If you do become obsessed by what is, in effect, a carefully calculated, decidedly intrusive staging decision, you will miss a most adventurous new comedy by a playwright who has paid his dues and learned his craft well.

Mr. McNally's credits are long and include *The Ritz* (1975), one of the few authentic American farces of our time, and the book for the current *Kiss of the Spider Woman*. With *Love! Valour! Compassion!* he has finally created what might be his chef d'oeuvre: a play as funny as anything he has done before, wrapped in melancholy and written with a freedom that equals Dennis Potter's high-handed treatment of time in *The Singing Detective*.

As the narrative unfolds, Mr. McNally's characters not only talk directly to the audience, but they also comment on what the other characters are saying to the audience. They feed us facts they couldn't possibly know at the time they reveal them. They see into the future to illuminate the past and to give the frequently rocky present added poignancy.

The result is a theatrical experience of unusual richness, about characters of unexpected dimension. Most important: Gregory Mitchell (Stephen Bogardus), a successful dancer and choreographer who is the host of these weekends and is haunted by age; John Jeckyll and his twin brother James (both played by John Glover), one a self-loathing bully, the other a genteel queen dying of AIDS; and Buzz Hauser (Mr. Lane), who is H.I.V. positive, desperately lonely and not about to go quietly into the night.

The self-described role models for the group are Arthur Pape (John Benjamin Hickey), an accountant, and Perry Sellars (Anthony Heald), a lawyer, the role played in the original production by Stephen Spinella. Arthur and Perry have been together 14 years. As a couple, they are idealized and, in these circumstances, boringly conventional. On his own, though, Perry seethes with the fear and anger that only John Jeckyll expresses, which may be the

reason the two men so thoroughly detest each other. Creating the sexual tension in this demi-paradise are two younger fellows: Gregory's lover Bobby Brahms (Justin Kirk), who is blind, and Ramon Fornos (Randy Becker), a Puerto Rican dancer and John's lover of the moment.

Love! Valour! Compassion! runs three hours with two intermissions, but don't worry. Under Mr. Mantello's direction, on Loy Arcenas's beautiful, spare, Magritte-like unit set, the play sweeps effortlessly along as the characters fall in and out of love, argue, swim, dine, sleep, flirt and talk, which they do especially well.

The performances seem even better than they did at the Manhattan Theater Club, if only because the actors have had an extended try-out period. Mr. Heald, the only newcomer, is an edgier, far more tense Perry than Mr. Spinella, which works fine.

The play sweeps effortlessly along as the characters fall in and out of love, argue, swim, dine, sleep, flirt, and talk, which they do especially well.

—*Vincent Canby*

The danger now is that the actors will continue to improve too much. At the Saturday afternoon preview I attended, Mr. Glover, who is splendid in his dual role, received what seemed to be a spontaneous response from one member of the audience during a monologue addressed to the house. Whether that's good or bad, I'm not sure. It's impressive when a patron becomes so heedlessly involved in what's happening on the stage, but it could lead to chaos for everybody else.

Mr. Lane remains the center of this production, at least in part because he has the best lines. His Buzz can't be torn from the television set during a showing of the remake of *Lost Horizon*. Or, as he says, "I never miss the chance to watch Liv Ullmann sing and dance." Yet Mr. Lane is such an accomplished actor that he carries off the quiet moments with as much brio as he does his comic turns.

Would *Love! Valour! Compassion!* have the same impact if it were about heterosexuals instead of homosexuals? Of course not. Mr. McNally hasn't written a play about gay people living straight lives. It's a comedy about some comparatively privileged gay people in a world whose problems are ultimately shared by everyone. Though particular, as all good plays are, it's not parochial.

Love! Valour! Compassion! is the kind of solid, serious, non-musical American comedy that Broadway hasn't seen in years.

Jeremy Gerard (review date 20 February 1995)

SOURCE: A review of *Love! Valour! Compassion!*, in *Variety*, February 20, 1995, p. 84.

[*In the following favorable review, Gerard discusses the humor and pathos in* Love! Valour! Compassion!]

Terrence McNally's play arrives on Broadway with one major cast change, but otherwise, *Love! Valour! Compassion!* makes a smooth transition from the Manhattan Theater Club's City Center Stage I, where it opened mostly to acclaim in November, to Broadway's Walter Kerr Theater. Produced under the reduced costs/reduced ticket prices Broadway Alliance plan, the play looks like an attractive box office player and a shoo-in for all the top awards nominations.

Love is that rarity these days, a three-act play, full of humor and pathos. It's set outside New York over three summer holiday weekends at the Dutchess County dacha of choreographer Gregory (Stephen Bogardus) and his blind lover, Bobby (Justin Kirk). They're joined by two other gay couples: Arthur (John Benjamin Hickey) and Perry (Anthony Heald), an accountant and a lawyer who have been together for 14 years; and John (John Glover, who, in the later acts doubles as John's twin, James), an unlikable expatriate Brit who once wrote a flop musical and now is Gregory's rehearsal pianist, and Ramon (Randy Becker), a predatory Puerto Rican-born dancer who's John's boy toy.

But the linchpin of the group, its resident wit, clown and gadfly, is Gregory's costumier, Buzz (Nathan Lane), an AIDS sufferer and activist, not to mention repository of musical theater arcana who mourns the death of Broadway and its stars nearly as deeply as he mourns the death of everyone around him.

Love! flows with heartfelt writing and becomes quite moving in the relationship that develops between Buzz and the "good" twin, James, who is sick, too. It's also very, very funny, thanks in no small measure to Lane, who plays venerable comic business with freshness and authority, his voice a post horn, his eyebrows a drawbridge forever stuck in the up position. And he is by no means alone in praiseworthiness: The ensemble is altogether winning, and if Heald—like Lane, an old McNally hand—lacks some of the fine-shading brought to the role originally by Stephen Spinella, that will hardly be noticeable to the play's newcomers. Moreover, Heald brings a greater measure of anger to an unruly part, which is altogether to the good.

As it was at the smaller City Center, the play has been directed with elegiac tenderness by Joe Mantello, who appeared on this same stage as Louis Ironson in *Angels in America*. Good as it is, however, *Love! Valour! Compassion!* is no *Angels in America*, and the differences are even more striking here: Where *Angels* embraced a whole world—indeed, several worlds, real and imagined, political, sexual, religious and social—*Love!* is self-referential and cramped, and flirts with being maudlin. Suffused with sadness and death along with the laughs, it's also occasionally tasteless, and the flaunted nudity may prove a major turnoff to a part of the audience, whether straight

or gay, that the play will need to attract if it is to have a long run.

Nevertheless, even if Broadway weren't such parched territory for new plays, *Love! Valour! Compassion!* would be an outstanding entry. The sense of loss it summons is heartbreaking.

Robert Brustein (review date 3 April 1995)

SOURCE: "Aspects of Love and Compassion," in *The New Republic*, Vol. 212, No. 14, April 3, 1995, pp. 30-2.

[*Brustein is an actor, director, theater critic, and author of several books about acting and the social responsibilities of the theater. In the following excerpt, he reviews* Love! Valour! Compassion!, *faulting its plot, characterizations, and themes as examples of "Yuppie Realism."*]

I'm still disappointed in the direction of McNally's career. . . . *Love! Valour! Compassion!* is simply another example of what, in reviewing his *Lips Together, Teeth Apart,* I called Yuppie Realism, a genre that focuses "on upwardly mobile middle-class professionals, usually on vacation, in the act of exchanging witticisms while examining faulty relationships and compromised principles." Instead of being an advance in gay playwrighting, *Love! Valour! Compassion!* looks more like a regression to *Boys in the Band*. McNally is now stroking the gay audience in much the same way that Neil Simon used to pander to Jewish matinee ladies. There's obviously a lot of complacent consensual recognition between the spectators and the stage. What is lost is the penetrating particularity of the independent artist. The only thing that kept me sentient during this long evening was wondering about the exclamation marks in the title and why *Valour* was spelled with the British "u."

Love! Valour! Compassion! is less a play than a treatment for a T.V. series. It has everything required of a sitcom except a laugh track, and even this is provided by the live audience, which offers its Pavlovian response before an actor completes his line. Revolving around seven gay men vacationing at a house in Dutchess County on three summer holiday weekends, the play has no real subject other than sexual relationships—who is sleeping with whom, and how the who and the whom can be rearranged. Almost everyone in the play breathes the helium of high camp; virtually every action is the occasion for a smart remark.

The most explosive jokes of the evening belong to Nathan Lane, an irrepressible actor who should be forcibly repressed, and virtually all of them are based on references to show business. In the tradition of most McNally characters, Lane gets the laugh track spinning either by imagining unlikely Broadway revivals (a production of *The King and I* starring Tommy Tune and Elaine Stritch) or "outing" such unlikely people as Dan Rather and John Foster Dulles ("Ethel Merman was gay you know—so was Irving Berlin"), or invoking the recognition value of such favorites as Judy Garland and Glenda Jackson. Lane increases the decibel count to a painful level when he performs a version of the cancan, shouting "Eat your heart out, Donna McKechnie." At least the volume on your television set is controllable.

Except that they bear no resemblance whatever to recognizable human behavior, I don't have any fundamental objection to Broadway sitcoms, if that's what it takes to get people out of the house. McNally has a sharp edgy wit and he certainly knows how to feed bananas to hungry spectators. I probably wouldn't have found this evening so unappetizing were it not for the author's compulsion to shovel serious issues into the comic casing, in the manner of a butcher stuffing feed down the neck of a goose in order to enlarge its liver. It is manipulative to introduce such a painful reality as AIDS into a laugh-riot devoted to such artificial characters and events. Nathan Lane's HIV-positive Buzz Hauser stops camping just loud enough to plant a kiss on the lesion he has discovered on the breast of John Glover's AIDS-infected John Jeckyll, in much the same way that Sally in *Lips Together, Teeth Apart* stopped trading barbs for a moment to drink the water out of an AIDS-infected pool.

The major innovation of this play is that virtually everybody in it—and not just the muscled Latino youth (Randy Becker) whom everybody lusts after—eventually gets to take his clothes off. I haven't seen so many pecs and peckers on stage since *Oh! Calcutta*. If that's your cup of tea, or piece of cheesecake, then you may find some value in *Love! Valour! Compassion!* One character, the dancer Gregory Mitchell who owns this week-end house, seems to have some human dimension and is nicely played by Stephen Bogardus. The others, cast with very good actors, will undoubtedly soon be joining the play in the electronic media. Not since *Hot L Baltimore* has the Broadway theater provided such a successful tryout venue for network T.V.

Additional coverage of McNally's life and career is contained in the following sources published by Gale Research: *Contemporary Authors,* Vols. 45-48, rev. ed.; *Contemporary Authors New Revision Series,* Vol. 2; *Contemporary Literary Criticism,* Vols. 4, 7, 41; and *Dictionary of Literary Biography,* Vol. 7.

Carol Shields
The Stone Diaries

Awards: Pulitzer Prize for Fiction, National Book Critics Circle Award, and 1993 Governor General's Award for Fiction

Born in 1935, Shields is an American-born Canadian novelist, poet, playwright, and critic.

INTRODUCTION

The Stone Diaries (1993) is the unique fictional autobiography of Daisy Goodwill Flett, whose story encompasses time both before her birth and after her death and covers the more than eight decades of her life in Canada and the United States. Narrated by Daisy but written in the third person (with periodic breaks into the first), the story begins with her birth in 1905 in rural Manitoba, Canada. Daisy's mother, extremely overweight and unaware that she is pregnant, dies moments after Daisy is born. Unable to care for his daughter, Cuyler Goodwill convinces his neighbor Clarentine Flett to raise the child. Soon afterward, Clarentine leaves her husband and, taking Daisy with her, travels to Winnipeg, where she moves in with her son, Barker. Clarentine dies several years later, and Cuyler takes Daisy to Bloomington, Indiana, where he becomes a highly successful stonecarver. There, Daisy matures and enters into a "socially correct" marriage with a wealthy young man who dies during their honeymoon. In 1936 she returns to Canada in search of a life change and marries Barker Flett, who has become renowned for his agricultural research. Daisy finds fulfillment in her role as wife and mother; but after Barker dies, she takes over the rather staid and technical gardening column he wrote for the *Ottawa Recorder,* and, writing as the lively Mrs. Greenthumb, develops a devoted readership and experiences the most meaningful and rewarding time of her life. Her joy is short-lived, however, as the editor allows himself to be convinced that a more senior staff writer should handle the column. Daisy suffers through a period of depression, eventually recovering and moving to Sarasota, Florida, where she settles into a comfortable, retired life.

Critical reaction to *The Stone Diaries* has been overwhelmingly favorable. Commentators have praised Shields for exploring such universal problems as loneliness and lost opportunities, and for demonstrating that all lives are vital and significant regardless of outward appearances. The novel has been seen as a brilliant examination of the relationship between one's inner and outer "selves." Critics also note Shields's subtle blurring of the distinctions between fiction, biography, and autobiography. Allyson F. McGill writes: "Shields and Daisy challenge us to review our lives, to try and see life honestly, even while

'their' act of authorship only reveals how impossible it is to see and speak objective truth."

PRINCIPAL WORKS

Others (poetry) 1972
Intersect (poetry) 1974
Susanna Moodie: Voice and Vision (criticism) 1976
Small Ceremonies (novel) 1976
The Box Garden (novel) 1977
Happenstance (novel) 1980
A Fairly Conventional Woman (novel) 1982
Various Miracles (short stories) 1985
Swann: A Mystery (novel) 1987
The Orange Fish (short stories) 1989
A Celibate Season [with Blanche Howard] (novel) 1991

CRITICISM

Anita Brookner   **(review date 4 September 1993)**

SOURCE: "A Family and Its Good Fortune," in *The Spectator,* Vol. 271, No. 8617, September 4, 1993, pp. 28-9.

[*Brookner is an English novelist, nonfiction writer, critic, and translator. In the following review, she remarks favorably on* The Stone Diaries, *noting Shield's characterization and optimism.*]

'I have said that Mrs Flett recovered from the nervous torment she suffered some years ago, and yet a kind of rancour underlies her existence still: the recognition that she belongs to no one.' This marvellous sentence is extracted at random from [*The Stone Diaries,*] Carol Shields's account of an unremarkable life, one which will fill her readers with amazed gratitude for a novel which fulfils its promise to the very end, and, more, one which will put them in mind of a more established social order, now apparently lost, in which there was an element of honour in upward mobility, and in which all ends happily, or at least as happily as final dissolution will allow.

'Feisty' say the nurses admiringly in the Canary Palms Convalescent Home, but Mrs Flett, born Daisy Goodwill, is ordinary in every particular except her birth, which occurred in the kitchen of her parents' home at Grange Road, Tyndall, Manitoba, one very hot summer afternoon. Her mother had not known she was pregnant, and died, presumably of shock, minutes after the birth. The father, Cuyler Goodwill, who worked at the local stone quarry and had a gift for carving which was later to make him a renowned figure in the larger America to which he emigrated, was unable to care for the child, and handed her over to a neighbour, Mrs Clarentine Flett ('Aunt Clarentine') to be brought up.

The child came to no harm: no Freudian nightmares attended her, apart from the unavoidable sensation of solitude which filtered through as the years advanced. Indeed, what is remarkable about this narrative is that all the characters do well for themselves. Aunt Clarentine leaves her husband, moves in with her son Barker in Winnipeg, and starts a cut flower enterprise which flourishes. The illiterate Jewish pedlar who happened to be passing when the child was about to be born, and who pressed a foreign coin on the minutes'-old infant's forehead, summons up the courage to request a loan from the bank and ends up a millionaire with a network of hardware shops. Cuyler Goodwill, on the strength of a strange drystone tower he has built as a memorial to his wife, is headhunted by an international limestone concern in Bloomington, Indiana. Barker Flett, whom Daisy Flett knew as a child, and

whom she subsequently marries, rises to a senior post in agricultural research. Somewhere along the way Daisy manages a contented life as a wife, mother, gardening correspondent for the local paper, and finally blue-rinsed bridgeplayer in Sarasota, Florida. There is of course that bleak insight which visited her unannounced some time in her later years and is still there—but it is almost a comfort now—as she lies dying.

The Stone Diaries is principally a novel with an appeal to women readers, but of an altogether superior kind. It is also a novel about the acquisition of language.

—Anita Brookner

I restrain myself from filling in the abundant details of this exemplary story (there is a formidable family tree served up, as if this were the *Forsythe Saga*) because the details are not allowed to encroach on the main thrust of the narrative, which is seamlessly developed. But there is one authorial addition which will be eagerly appropriated by many women writers compelled to make a fiction out of their autobiography, although as a genre this may well be out of date. I refer to the inclusion of a set of photographs, all suitably aged, and purporting to be of the characters in the novel. These look authentic, save for one instance, and one wonders whether the account might not be a true family history, until one reflects that Carol Shields, who can teach her younger sisters a thing or two, has probably acquired the photographs first—a job lot?—and constructed her novel around them. Whatever the genesis of the story, the photographs add potency to what is already a poignant mix of fact and fantasy.

Here is grim Hannah Goodwill, the graceless mother of Cuyler Goodwill, who put her savings in a jam jar, where the dollar bills grew soft and limp. Here is a flirtatious Aunt Clarentine, surely taken from one of the sentimental postcards that were amorous currency in 1916. Barker, with his loosely knotted tie, stares fixedly into space, while Mrs Flett's friend, Elfreda ('Fraidy') Hoyt, smiles invitingly through her kiss-curls. Various toddlers and adolescents, brought unerringly up to date, represent Mrs Flett's grandchildren, not all of whom figure in the story. This innocent device, unsignalled in the text, connects with everyone's recall of half-forgotten faces, perhaps unrecognised in old family albums, and resurrected only by the names inscribed beneath the photographs, perhaps by a hand consigned to memory, itself half forgotten.

This is principally a novel with an appeal to women readers, but of an altogether superior kind. It is also a novel about the acquisition of language. Cuyler Goodwill discovers language when making love to his wife, Daisy Flett through writing her gardening column, Magnus Flett (Aunt Clarentine's deserted husband) through reading *Jane Eyre*. Barker Flett, in his last letter to his wife, becomes eloquent only when dying. There is a dignity here which is unusual in these ruffianly times. There is also an optimism (all those millionaires). I found my response softening as I read on, although the *leitmotif*—the stone of the title, the limestone of the quarries—is a hard one. If durability is what finally counts in Mrs Flett's life it is also a quality which attaches to the novel itself. An impeccable performance.

[*The Stone Diaries*] is a box within a box within a box. . . . I've made the big box; Daisy is the box inside, and the box inside Daisy is empty.

Carol Shields, as quoted by Laurel Graeber, in "Inside Daisy Flett," in The New York Times Book Review, *March 27, 1994.*

Penelope Fitzgerald   (review date 9 September 1993)

SOURCE: "Sunny Side Up," in *London Review of Books,* Vol. 15, No. 17, September 9, 1993, p. 19.

[*Fitzgerald is an English novelist, biographer, and journalist. In the review below, she remarks favorably on* The Stone Diaries.]

The Stone Diaries (though there are in fact no diaries, they are said to have been lost) because everyone raised in the Orphans' Home in Stonewall Township, Manitoba is given the name of Stone, because Mercy Stone's husband, Cuyler Goodwill, works in the limestone quarries, because her neighbour, the dour Magnus Flett, comes from the stony Orkneys, because Mrs Flett is killed when she falls against the sharp stone corner of the Bank, because for all of us the living cells will be replaced in death by 'the insentience of mineral deposition'. A train of imagery, then, which recalls the mermaid metaphors, 'giving off the fishy perfume of ambiguity' in Shields's last novel, *The Republic of Love.* The present book is just as readable, but more disconcerting.

The section headings—Birth, 1905; Childhood, 1916; Marriage, 1927; Love, 1936; Motherhood, 1947; Work, 1955-64; Sorrow, 1965; Ease, 1977; Illness and Decline, 1985; Death—cover all the grand old topics of *McCall's, Good Housekeeping* and the *Canadian Home Companion* which for so many decades gave social and moral counsel and explained how to turn out a jellied veal loaf. The protagonist is Daisy Goodwill. Her mother, Mercy Stone, dies in childbirth. Clarentine Flett, the next-door neighbour's fed-up wife, takes the baby and flees to Winnipeg 'with a dollar bill taken the night before from her husband's collar-box'. Reclaimed by her father, Daisy goes to Bloomington, Indiana, where in the Twenties stonecarvers are still needed. She marries a rich young goldhatted lover who throws himself out of a window; in 1936 she becomes the wife of Barker Flett, 22 years older than her-

self, an expert on hybrid grains. When her three children are grown she launches for the first time on a career—'working outside the home', as people said in those days; she becomes Mrs Green Thumb, the gardening consultant on the *Ottawa Recorder.* But the editor—who has taken fright at the idea that he might be expected to marry Daisy—gives her column back to a staffer. She takes a while to get over the resultant depression, but emerges in old age as a 'wearer of turquoise pants suits' in a condo in Sarasota, Florida. During her terminal illness she is moved to the Canary Palms Care Facility. Her last words (unspoken) are 'I am not at peace.'

I have summarised this plot to show how faultlessly Carol Shields has devised Daisy's story. It would in fact have been readily accepted, with a trivial change of ending, by the dear old *Canadian Home Companion.* Daisy is precisely what her son Warren calls her, 'a middle-class woman, a woman of moderate intelligence and medium-sized ego and average good luck', and Shields herself has said: 'I am interested in reality, in the texture of ordinary life, and the way people appear and relate.' *The Stone Diaries* could only have been written by an expert in sensuous detail, from the blood-drenched kitchen sofa where poor Mercy dies to Daisy's longing, as she recovers her nerve, for 'the feel of a new toothbrush against her gums, for instance. Such a little thing.' Shields also likes, she says, to write about survivors. Daisy Goodwill Flett surely survives for eighty years thanks to the overwhelming force of her ordinariness.

This, however, brings us to the most interesting though perhaps not the most successful element in the book. Daisy, member of the Mother's Union, the Arrowroots, Ottawa Horticultural Society, Bay Ladies' Craft Group (she even has a diploma in Liberal Arts somewhere, but can't remember which drawer she put it in), is also a closet Post-Modernist. Aware that her life is drifting harmlessly past her, she is determined to acquire power over it by standing apart and reporting on it as an independent witness. She begins with her birth. 'Why am I unable to look at it calmly? Because I long to bring symmetry to the various discordant elements, though I know before I begin that my efforts will seem a form of pleading.' She is aware, too, that 'the recording of life is a cheat' and that she will never be able to recount the whole truth. 'She understood that if she was going to hold onto her life at all, she would have to rescue it by a primary act of imagination, supplementing, modifying, summoning up the necessary connections, conjuring the pastoral or heroic or whatever ... getting the details wrong occasionally, exaggerating or lying outright, inventing letters or conversations of impossible generality, or casting conjecture in a pretty light.' Very well, then, Daisy knows that she will have to do this, but now a narrator appears, in corrective mode, to tell us that she is often wider off the mark than she thinks. She has translated (for instance) her uncle's 'long brooding sexual state' into an attack of indigestion. Later, this same narrator tells us that Daisy's is the only account there is, 'written on air, written with imagination's invisible ink'. But we cannot trust her, since she insists on showing herself in a sunny light, 'hardly ever giving us a glimpse of those dark premonitions we all experience'. Indeed, after the loss of her gardening column Daisy's consciousness seems to disintegrate altogether, for a time leaving her friends and family to interpret the situation as best they can. (This is reminiscent of the method of Shields's brilliant literary mystery story, **Mary Swann.**)

The Stone Diaries, it seems, is a novel, among other things, about the limitations of autobiography. As far as Daisy is concerned, it never gets away from them, even when the narration changes from the first person in 1905 ('My mother's name was Mercy Stone Goodman. She was only 30 years old when she took sick') to the third person in 1916 ('the infant—a little girl of placid disposition—was clothed in a white tucked nainsook day slip'). All the change really does is to mark the last point when she can truly establish her identity, before her mother dies and she herself, new-hatched, begins to live. This failure to find a language—as she realises at the very end—frustrates heaven knows how many. Her eyes 'stare icy as marbles, wide open but seeing nothing, nothing, that is, but the deep, shared, common distress of men and women, and how little, finally, they are allowed to say'. Carol Shields, however, believes that women have been much harder done by, in this matter of silence, than men. It is of their limitations that she is thinking.

Daisy has something important in common with Mrs Morel in *Sons and Lovers.* 'Sometimes life takes hold of one, carries the body along, accomplishes one's history, and yet is not real, but leaves oneself as it were slurred over.' Mrs Morel sets herself to live through her sons, but Daisy does not even contemplate doing this. She makes her own sortie into the world of earning money and respect, is unkindly rejected, recovers, and maintains a certain dignity without asking help from anybody, 'and yet a kind of rancour underlies her existence still: the recognition that she belongs to no one.' Her children are moderately fond of her, her great-niece Victoria very fond. Victoria, in fact, bids fair to bring the whole book to a happy resolution. She is the daughter of a gone-astray niece whom Daisy has taken in, with her baby, out of pure good nature, and this baby has grown up to become a paleobotanist, classifying traces of fossil plants in the rock. In other words, Victoria combines Shields's stone and her plant imagery, just as Daisy Stone does when she becomes the well-liked gardening correspondent, Mrs Green Thumb. But here Daisy does not deceive herself. She is certain that none of her descendants will do more than look back on her with forbearance. This gives her a frightening feeling of inauthenticity.

In the process of growing up, of becoming a middle-aged woman and an old woman, Daisy has failed either to understand or to explain herself. If you were to ask her the story of her life, says the narrator, and one can hear the exasperated sigh, 'she would stutter out an edited hybrid version, handing it to you somewhat shyly, but without apology, without equivocation that is: this is what happened, she would say from the unreachable recesses of her 72 years, and this is what happened next.' She is accustomed to her own version, and so, sadly enough, are we, all of us, accustomed to ours.

An exception, of course, is the witty, cautious, sometimes lyrical narrator, who knows all the words, all the versions and all the weak places. For fear we might doubt the reality of her characters, convincing though they are, Shields supplies a section of attractive-looking, faded photographs of five generations. Daisy herself, as might be expected, doesn't appear, but by comparing the family snaps with the portrait on the back dust-jacket we can make out that Carol Shields must be the mother of Alice, the most difficult of Daisy's children. (Alice becomes an academic, whose first novel is everywhere unfavourably reviewed, But she is able to rise above this, because she knows she is making up her own life as she goes along.)

Talking recently at Edinburgh about her books and her motivation for writing them, Carol Shields spoke of her care to establish the narrator's credentials and said that Daisy's inability to express herself was the true subject of **The Stone Diaries.** This would make it the tragedy of someone incapable of being tragic. But the novel as it stands suggests something more complex. The publishers tell us that Daisy's signal achievement is to write herself out of her own story. 'Somewhere along the line she made the decision to live outside of events'—that is, to accept her own insignificance. But the reader is also asked to decide whether this is 'a triumphant act of resistance or a surrendering to circumstances'. In novelist's terms, did she do right or wrong? Daisy is described as summoning up her 'stone self' so that even her brain becomes transparent—'you can hold it up to the window and the light shines through. Empty, though, there's the catch.' She is shown as breathing her own death and contriving it, taking charge of it, in fact, as though in exasperation with what has so far been suppressed in her. If she is capable of this, there was no need, perhaps, for the narrator to pity her quite so much.

Carol Shields is asking us to play a game—a game for adults—but she is also playing it against herself. The epigraph, attributed to Alice's daughter, says that nothing Grandma Daisy did was quite what she meant to do.

> but still her life
> could be called a monument

and that, in the end, is what the novel makes her.

Geraldine Sherman   (review date 2 October 1993)

SOURCE: "Straining to Fulfill Ambitions," in *The Globe and Mail,* Toronto, October 2, 1993, p. C23.

[*Below, Sherman offers a mixed review of* The Stone Diaries.]

A single question sits at the heart of all Carol Shields' fiction: How can we ever truly understand another person's life? In **Swann,** a scholar tries to explain how a simple Kingston farm wife managed to write a slim volume of unaccountably fine poetry. In **Small Ceremonies,** a biographer with "an unhealthy lust for the lives of other people" rummages through the house she's rented to learn all she can about the absent owners.

In **The Stone Diaries,** Shields examines the evidence of a woman's life the way a geologist might study fossils. Each piece is excavated and meticulously scrutinized by relatives and friends in an attempt to construct a credible version of the past, telling a story that sweeps back and forth across a century and several generations.

Much of that narrative material will be familiar to admirers of the author's nine previous works of fiction, rich in domestic detail and intelligent compassion for her characters. Here, Shields seems to be striving for something grander. Along with her attempt to solve the mysteries of a single life is the intention to reflect the moral complexities of an age. But in the end, Daisy Goodwill's tiny secrets and personal disappointments cannot bear the strain of the novel's high ambitions and overbearing technique.

The material is simply arranged in a series of milestones, chapters from Birth, 1905 to Death, 1985. Six generations of Goodwills and Fletts are shown on a detailed family tree, and there are eight pages of family photographs—men and women, young and old, dressed in bustles and bathing suits. One bright-eyed teen-ager, identified as "Lissa Taylor," born 1974, looks remarkably like the author herself.

What are we to think? Is Daisy Goodwill the real mother, or grandmother, of Carol Shields? Is this the story of her own family? A work of biography, autobiography, or fiction? Or is it, perhaps, all three, real and imagined events shuffled together, storytelling for "the documentary age" which, according to Shields, "can never get enough facts"?

Daisy's birth is brutal and unexpected. Her father, Cuyler Goodwill, a limestone cutter in rural Manitoba, doesn't know that Mercy, his bulky, kind-hearted wife, is pregnant. Neither, it seems, does she. One summer in 1905, in the presence of a neighbour and a passing Jewish pedlar, she falls to the kitchen floor, gives birth to a baby girl, and dies. Daisy is handed over to the neighbour, Mrs. Clarentine Flett, who moves to Winnipeg to live with her son Barker, a professor of botany, the man destined to marry the little girl he helps to raise.

Alone with his grief, Cuyler Goodwill erects a giant tower above his wife's grave, carving each piece of limestone with a hieroglyph illustrating their love. This rough-hewn Taj Mahal attracts sightseers from the city and brings him a lucrative job offer from a limestone company in Indiana.

Carol Shields loves characters like Cuyler, people able to create something beautiful in otherwise humdrum lives. Mrs. Flett, too, has the gift. She transforms her Winnipeg garden into a showplace and makes money selling flowers until she is struck and killed by a careless delivery boy.

When Cuyler takes his six-year-old daughter to the United States, he becomes obsessed with telling her his life story. "He felt, rightly, that he owed her a complete accounting for his years of absence. Owed her the whole story, his life prised out of the fossil field and brought up to light." Daisy, unfortunately, never finds her own voice, or it seems, her own face; her picture is notably absent from the family album. She passes through life like a baffled spectator, "outside events," something of a puzzle to her friends, a child to her husband, a shadow-figure to her own children. To her son she's simply a middle-class woman of moderate intelligence, a housewife who inherited her husband's gardening column and became, briefly, Mrs. Green Thumb. One of her daughters, sitting beside her deathbed, wants to ask her mother (but knows she mustn't), "Have you been happy in your life?"

Two world wars, the Depression, Lindbergh's transatlantic flight, and the birth of the Dionne quintuplets all flicker in the background of this domestic story. But large events play little part in Daisy's life. Far more important are the accumulated lists her children discover after her death, traces of her life in a series of messages—things to be done, the garden club luncheon menu, addresses, illnesses. "The recounting of a life is a cheat, of course," Shields writes. "I admit the truth of this; even our own stories are obscenely distorted."

Real life, unlike fiction, is messy and haphazard, explanations often elusive. But Shields hates loose ends; as a novelist (or biographer) she's overly eager to tie all the bits together. She takes too seriously the advice attributed to Chekhov; a gun pulled out in the first act must be fired by the third. The delivery boy, for example, who accidentally killed Clarentine Flett, returns as a guilt-ridden millionaire meatpacker who erects a glass-domed horticultural conservatory bearing his victim's name. We even pick up the story of the pedlar who witnessed Daisy's birth.

To hold our interest in Daisy's life and to extend the story's range, Shields inflates her language. She pumps up the metaphors until, literally and figuratively, no stone is left unturned. Despite its ambition and the Booker Prize nomination, *The Stone Diaries* fails in its attempt to break new ground.

Claire Messud   (review date 3 October 1993)

SOURCE: "Redeemed by an Act of Imagination," in *Manchester Guardian Weekly,* October 3, 1993, p. 28.

[*In the following review, Messud remarks favorably on* The Stone Diaries.]

"Things begin, things end. Just when we seem to arrive at a quiet place we are swept up, suddenly, between the body's smooth, functioning predictability and the need for disruption." Thus comments the narrator of *The Stone Diaries,* Carol Shields's latest accomplished and moving offering. Such ebb and flow, the relentless abruptness of change—it is the rhythm of life itself that Shields is addressing, its variety, the ordinariness of its idiosyncracies and the reassuring way it can accommodate astonishing, divergent paths.

To address these large paradoxes, Shields has chosen to follow the life of a Canadian woman named Daisy Goodwill, born in rural Manitoba at the start of the century to a mother who dies in childbirth and a bewildered father who cannot initially cope with his child. Around Daisy's life accrue the stories and histories of other lives—of her father, of her unknown mother, of Barker Flett (whom she eventually marries), of her friends and her children—and she wills all these stories into existence in the telling of her own.

This record of her own story, though, as Shields makes clear, is a triumph of Daisy's imagination, that has created a tale out of a life the world might not think worth recording. Already when sick and bedridden as a child, Daisy is conscious of the magnitude of her undertaking: "That was what kept coming back to her as she lay in her hot, darkened room: the knowledge that here, this place, was where she would continue to live all her life—blinded, throttled, erased from the record of her own existence . . ."

In this world, Shields suggests, in an ordinary life, the imagination can offer redemption. Perhaps it is enough; it is, in the end, all we are left with: Daisy "is not always reliable when it comes to the details of her life. Still, hers is the only account there is, written on air, written with imagination's invisible ink." But Daisy can and does wish for more than that: in her seventies she seeks, in tracing her father-in-law's footsteps back to the Orkney islands, to find someone who has imagined her life, and in so doing, made it real, in the way that she has imagined her mother's life, or her father's. But even she knows ahead of time that her mission is destined for disappointment.

This said, Shields, if not quite like Daisy ("one of life's fortunates, a woman born with a voice that lacks a tragic register"), is nonetheless a writer who, while acknowledging the bathos of tragedy, will not allow it to triumph. Unbeknownst to Daisy, Shields has ensured that she does have witnesses: not only the pedlar who blesses her at birth and passes on the story of her arrival to his children; but also Shields herself, and Shields' readers.

The principal images which she weaves through the book of Daisy's life are of flowers and of stone. The former, like Daisy (a flower herself), are destined to pass from this earth but they are regenerative. And the latter, like the human will and the redemptive power of the imagination, are indestructible.

The Stone Diaries—one of this year's Booker nominees—is a work of great but unconventional ambition which succeeds in almost all that it attempts.

Merna Summers   (review date January-February 1994)

SOURCE: "Small Is Beautiful," in *The Canadian Forum*, Vol. 72, No. 826, January-February, 1994, pp. 44-5.

[*Summers is a Canadian journalist and short story writer. In the review below, she discusses the characters in* The Stone Diaries.]

When **The Stone Diaries** was short-listed for the Booker Award earlier this fall, those of us who have long admired Carol Shields' work felt joy, but also what I can only describe as a glad combativeness. Maybe *now* Shields' books would get the admiration they deserve in Canada, we told one another. Maybe *now* the jury that neglected even to shortlist Shields' splendid novel, **The Republic of Love,** for a Governor General's Award would blush with shame. [In November, after this review was received, Carol Shields was awarded the Governor General's Award for Fiction, for **The Stone Diaries.**]

As I suppose everyone must know by now, **The Stone Dia-**

ries is the fictional biography of a woman whom the author has described as being "erased from her own life", the kind of woman who usually gets a four-inch obituary when she dies. Shields has tried to understand this life by the traces it leaves, to present the life and times of her character, Daisy Goodwill Flett, "prised out of the fossil field and brought up to life". Not surprisingly, the Booker judges commended Shields for "giving us a new kind of heroine".

Human beings are defined as much by the things that don't happen to them as by the things that do, and part of what Shields is doing here is honouring the restricted life, declaring that attention must be paid to the lives of women like Daisy.

Daisy Goodwill lived in an era when women were expected to make the best of things, not to ask for too much for themselves. If each woman in her time plays many parts, Daisy's roles were chiefly those of "daughter of ", "wife of ", and "mother of ". Later, in a brilliantly rendered old age, Daisy is troubled by the "deep, shared common distress of men and women, and how little they are allowed, finally, to say".

The Stone Diaries is a great outpouring of a novel, full of acute insights, generous in spirit and managing to turn our attention in directions it had not thought of going before. There are enough surprising stories, sharply sketched characters and entertaining and eccentric details to fill a dozen novels.

Shields' characters paint their own portraits in thought and action. One thinks of love as "mostly the avoidance of hurt". Another never wants to be surprised by life. Still another reflects that: "A childhood is what anyone wants to remember of it. It leaves no fossils."

There are images of fossils and of stones everywhere in this novel, but there are also green things growing, flowers being brought to bloom. These things are metaphors, but elusive ones. Does stone encase the dead? Is it a symbol of permanence? Do men build things to last, in stone, while women cultivate beauty that is transitory? Partly, but it is never quite as tidy as that. The reader is given considerable freedom to play with the resonances.

In middle age, Daisy Flett takes over her dead husband's gardening column for the local paper—writing under the name of "Mrs. Green Thumb"—and discovers that this work is deeply meaningful to her. "It was as though she had veered, accidentally, into her own life," her daughter says.

The most painful part of Daisy's life—or so one assumes from the "traces" recorded here—is not the dislocation of her childhood, nor her marriage to a boorish and masochistic young man who "longs for correction, for love like a scalpel". It is the loss of her work. When the newspaper decides to let a staffer take over her gardening column, Daisy—for the only time in her life—puts up a fight. When she loses the battle, she sinks into depression, and then old age.

One suspects that it is Shields' elegance as a writer, as well as her *brio,* that has won her such a high level of recognition in England. There is not a page in this novel that does not delight, does not contain something quotable. There are opening sequences that are worthy of a Jane Austen:

> Barker Flett at thirty-three is stooped of shoulder and sad of expression, but women who set eyes on him think: now here is a man who might easily be made happy.

It is this author's habit of paying humorous and loving attention to her characters that her readers value most of all in her work. Carol Shields demonstrates there are no small lives, no lives out of which significance does not shine. She makes us aware that banality, ultimately, is in the eye of the beholder.

An excerpt from *The Stone Diaries*

Now, at the age of fifty-nine, sadness flows through every cell of her body, yet leaves her curiously untouched. She knows how memory gets smoothed down with time, everything flattened by the iron of acceptance and rejection—it comes to the same thing, she thinks. This sorrowing of hers has limits, just as there's a limit to how tangled she'll let her hair get or how much dust she'll allow to pile up on her dressing table. That's Daisy for you. Daisy's resignation belongs to the phylum of exhaustion, the problem of how to get through a thousand ordinary days. Or, to be more accurate, ten thousand such days. In a sense I see her as one of life's fortunates, a woman born with a voice that lacks a tragic register. Someone who's learned to dig a hole in her own life story.

But she's tired of being sad, and tired of not even minding being sad, of not even in a sense knowing. And in the thin bony box of her head she understands, and accepts, the fact that her immense unhappiness is doomed to irrelevance anyway. Already, right this minute, I feel a part of her wanting to go back to the things she used to like, the feel of a new toothbrush against her gums, for instance. Such a little thing. She'd like to tie a crisp clean apron around her waist once again, peel a pound of potatoes in three minutes flat and put them soaking in cold water. Polish a jelly jar and set it on the top shelf with its mates. Lick an envelope, stick a stamp in its corner, drop it in the mail box. She'd like to clean her body out with a hoot of laughter and give way to the pull of gravity. It's going to happen. All this suffering will be washed away. Any day now.

Carol Shields, in her The Stone Diaries, *Viking, 1994.*

Rhoda Koenig (review date 7 March 1994)

SOURCE: "Rock-Solid, Stone-Cold," in *New York* Magazine, Vol. 27, No. 10, March 7, 1994, p. 62.

[*In the following excerpt, Koenig discusses the plot and themes of* The Stone Diaries.]

Speaking at her college-graduation ceremony, Daisy Goodwill's father asks his audience to think of the knowledge they have acquired as if it were Salem limestone, the pride of Indiana. "You are the stone carver. The tools of intelligence are in your hand. You can make of your lives one thing or the other. . . . The choice, young citizens of the world, is yours." The following June, however, he tells Daisy's engagement party that the fossil stone itself exists because of "the lucky presence" 300 million years before of a warm, shallow sea. Whether our lives are formed by conscious acts or by the accretion of numerous tiny accidents is the theme of *The Stone Diaries.*

Daisy Stone Goodwill's life begins one day in 1905 when her father comes home from working a quarry in central Manitoba to find that his wife has died giving birth. It is not only a shock but a surprise, since he didn't know his immensely fat wife was pregnant—but, then, neither did she. Daisy remains in Canada for her childhood, travels with her father to the Midwest for an agreeable, if mostly uneventful youth, then returns to Canada for middle age, marriage, and an unexpected, successful career. She ends up in Florida playing bridge with the gals, having her hair permed until it's "springy as Easter basket grass." She loathes the word *feisty,* but personifies it: A young man asks her if he should tell his mother he is gay. When she urges him to button his lip, he protests, "But I can't go on living a lie." "Why not?" says Daisy. "Most people do."

Daisy's own lie is the popular one that love, or even intimacy, naturally arises from years of tender association. She regards her elderly husband with benign detachment; he never speaks to her of his feelings until after he is dead: "Do you remember," he says in a letter found at his hospital bed, "that day last October when I experienced my first terrible headache? I found you in the kitchen wearing one of those new and dreadful plastic aprons. You put your arms around me at once and reached up to smooth my temples. I loved you terribly at that moment. The crackling of your apron against my body seemed like an operatic response to the longings which even then I felt. It was like something whispering at us to hurry, to stop wasting time." Daisy's grown daughter, at her mother's deathbed, wants to ask her, " 'Have you had moments of genuine ecstasy? Has it been worth it?' . . . Instead they speak of apple juice, gravy, screams in the corridor." Her children state, in their death notice of this passionate gardener, "Flowers gratefully declined."

Carol Shields complicates her picture of this simple life with multiple angles, shifting perspectives. Daisy's relatives and colleagues, her flapper school friend who has had "fifty-three lovers, possibly fifty-four," weigh in with letters and testimony; the novel contains poems, family photographs, and grocery lists, and closes, as it begins, with a recipe. Yet, while giving the story density, this approach also adds a sense of contrivance, the Olympian at times jarring with the homely rather than enhancing it. Shields's in-your-face metaphor (Daisy's father builds monuments of stone; her grandniece studies fossil plants; on a trip to Scotland, Daisy visits cemeteries and rock formations) can also feel too heavily overlaid on its subjects, more of a comment on their condition than a fact of their nature.

For the most part, however, this is a novel of innumerable small but genuine pleasures. Shields finds the poetry in domestic life but maintains a tone of astringency as well as regret over the way it can build us a comfortable cage. "Now there's a woman," reads one of the many epitaphs of Daisy Goodwill, "who made a terrific meatloaf, who knew how to repot a drooping rubber plant, who bid a smart no-trump hand, who wore a hat well, who looked after her personal hygiene, who wrote her thank-you notes promptly . . . who missed the point."

Jay Parini   (review date 27 March 1994)

SOURCE: "Men and Women, Forever Misaligned," in *The New York Times Book Review,* March 27, 1994, pp. 3, 14.

[Parini is an American poet, novelist, critic, and educator. In the following review, he favorably assesses The Stone Diaries.*]*

Carol Shields, the American-born Canadian novelist and story writer, is often mentioned in the same breath with Margaret Atwood and Alice Munro, and her last novel, **The Republic of Love,** attracted a small but enthusiastic band of admirers, myself among them. Last year **The Stone Diaries** was nominated for Britain's Booker Prize and acclaimed by many reviewers there. Now it has been published here, and it deserves our fullest attention.

The novel provides, glancingly, a panorama of 20th-century life in North America. Written in diary format, it traces the life of one seemingly unremarkable woman: Daisy Goodwill Flett, who is born in 1905 and lives into the 1990's. **The Stone Diaries** includes an elaborate family tree of the sort usually found in biographies as well as eight pages of family photographs. Surveying the faces in these photos of Ms. Shields's sharply drawn characters, the reader naturally wonders: are these "real" people or the made-up kind?

The question soon becomes irrelevant: indeed, the novel willfully smudges the already blurred distinctions between fact and fiction. "When we say a thing or an event is real, never mind how suspect it sounds, we honor it," writes one of Ms. Shields's several diarists. "But when a thing is made up—regardless of how true and just it seems—we turn up our noses. That's the age we live in. The documentary age."

So the novelist inserts her tongue deeply into her cheek and documents everything. But unlike the historian, who must cling to the enameled outer layer of reality, Ms. Shields plunges into the interior life of her characters with all the ferocity of a major novelist. As her readers, we are allowed to peer into the hearts of Daisy Flett and her family with gaudy indiscretion, and this voyeurism is at times unsettling. Humankind, as T. S. Eliot noted, cannot bear very much reality.

Poor Daisy, our hapless flower, arrives in this world in the least hospitable of circumstances. Her mother the absurdly fat Mercy Stone, expires at the moment of Daisy's birth. Before she does, however, there is plenty of time for Ms. Shields to offer a startling portrait of the erotic life of Mercy and her uxorious husband, Cuyler Goodwill. He is a stone mason (all puns are probably intentional) whose

creative energies were focused on his profession until he was 26, when he stunned the small Manitoba community (and himself) by marrying an obese orphan. He revels in Mercy's vast regions of pink flesh: "He is not repelled by the trembling generosity of her arms and thighs and breasts, not at all; he wants to bury himself in her exalting abundance, as though, deprived all his life of flesh, he will now never get enough. He knows that without the comfort of Mercy Stone's lavish body he would never have learned to feel the reality of the world or understand the particularities of sense and reflection that others have taken as their right."

Here, as in her previous fiction, Ms. Shields writes with an almost painfully attuned ear for the nuances of language and the way they attach to feelings and probe the most delicate layers of human consciousness. Her words ring like stones in a brook, chilled and perfected; the syntax rushes like water, tumbling with the slight forward tilt that makes for narrative. The reader is caught in whirlpools and eddies, swirled, then launched farther downstream.

After her mother's death, Daisy is adopted by a neighbor, Clarentine Flett, who is about to leave her husband, Magnus, a dour immigrant from the Orkney Islands. Clarentine moves with the infant Daisy to live with her son Barker in Winnipeg, where a cozy family group is established. Barker becomes one of the major figures in Daisy's life: guardian, then—after a lapse of decades—husband. A botanist, he is obsessed with "the western lady's-slipper, genus Cypripedium," thus sublimating his most primitive urges. The intensity of his gaze on this particular organism summons other complex longings, and botanical metaphors abound as the author lets one narrative strand lengthen and twine with others.

Cuyler Goodwill eventually flees Canada and the memory of his poor dead Mercy to Bloomington, Ind., where his talents as a stone cutter are in demand. He becomes a pillar of the community and a moderately wealthy man. The course of his life is summarized by his daughter: "In his 20's he was a captive of Eros, in his 30's he belonged to God, and, still later, to Art. Now, in his 50's, he champions Commerce." He is eloquent if somewhat voluble, given to saying things like, "The miracle of stone is that a rigid, inert mass can be lifted out of the ground and given wings." We follow his life tangentially through his daughter's eyes, right up to the splendid scene of his death beside a lake in spring.

As he lies "on a patch of Indiana grass like a window screen about to be rinsed off by the garden hose," he comes to a lovely sense of his place in the scheme of creation. In a touching moment, he fights through the gauze of a failing memory to recall the name of his beloved Mercy, at last finding it. "Ah, Mercy," he says to himself. "Mercy, hold me in your soft arms, cover me with your body, keep me warm."

The diaries leap from decade to decade, tracing the stages of Daisy's life: her first, tragic marriage to a boy from Bloomington, her second marriage to her old guardian, Barker, and the birth of her children. The fact that her life fits the familiar contours is, somehow, refreshing: Daisy is Everywoman, and her crises are the normal ones. "The real troubles in this world tend to settle on the misalignment between men and women," the diarist tells us as she discovers something like love with Barker Flett. Daisy's own "misalignment," in particular, is evoked with inspired circumspection, not only from her own point of view but from others' as well.

Barker, who has been turned into a "voyeur in his own life" after "decades of parched solitude," meditates on his relationship to Daisy as they fall asleep:

> Is this what love is, he wonders, this substance that lies so pressingly between them, so neutral in color yet so palpable it need never be mentioned? Or is love something less, something slippery and odorless, a transparent gas riding through the world on the back of a breeze, or else—and this is what he more and more believes—just a word trying to remember another word.

The novel ends with the death of Daisy as images are torn from a long life and pinned to the spinning wheel of her mind. Fragments of overheard conversation cross the page—disembodied, eerily displaced; lost recipes, bits of official paper, shopping lists, book titles: the *disjecta membra* of a life float by. Slipping in and out of a coma toward the end, she begins to imagine her own extinction: "You might say that she breathed it into existence, then fell in love with it."

There is little in the way of conventional plot here, but its absence does nothing to diminish the narrative compulsion of this novel. Carol Shields has explored the mysteries of life with abandon, taking unusual risks along the way. *The Stone Diaries* reminds us again why literature matters.

Laura Van Tuyl Clayton   (review date 30 March 1994)

SOURCE: A review of *The Stone Diaries,* in *The Christian Science Monitor,* March 30, 1994, p. 19.

[*In the following review, Van Tuyl Clayton asserts that* The Stone Diaries *concerns "the universal problem of how ordinary men and women connect with one another and whether they are living authentic lives in an age of frightening change and equally frightening superficiality."*]

Bestseller lists these days are flush with stories involving characters of monolithic courage or titanic ambition caught up in strange adventure or romantic exploit.

For those of us fatigued by all this fictional heroism, author Carol Shields has torpedoed the notion that only nervous excitement and derring-do can generate a gripping story. Instead, she meticulously depicts the life of a lone woman, Daisy Goodwill Flett, a character so remarkably ordinary she could be anyone's mother or grandmother.

Despite all this ordinariness, a quality both chilling and fascinating emerges from **The Stone Diaries,** a novel in which every day of this woman's life is a self-enclosed drama of its own, but performed before no appreciative audience.

From her birth in 1905 in rural Manitoba to her widowhood and death 85 years later, Daisy (named for the most common of flowers) moves across the flickering backdrop of the 20th century, a woman resigned to her "sphere" of domestic toil, wifely duty, and civic responsibility.

As the years roll by, Daisy's outward life appears to be increasingly at odds with an inner life of secrets and hidden yearnings. Like the flower garden and house plants she expertly nurtures, Daisy has fundamental needs, but sadly, they go unnoticed by those around her (and even by herself at times).

The Stone Diaries, nominated for Britain's Booker Prize, unfolds exquisitely through a mixture of first and third person narratives, letters, newspaper clippings—even recipes and short poems. A family tree and several pages of reproduced family photos lend an amusing air of authenticity.

Flashbacks, intentional digressions, and gaps in the plot never confuse the reader, but intensify the novel's central theme: What is the story of a life and who is qualified to tell it? Even Daisy herself admits to the reader that she is unreliable with details and subject to exaggeration.

At one point, after Daisy's husband dies, she becomes a successful gardening columnist for the city paper. Household chores become less important, and one senses she is at last beginning to live for herself, to write her own story. Touching letters from her faithful readers show she's making real and authentic connections to others.

When the editor abruptly hands over the column to a male employee of senior status (but vastly inferior talent), Daisy enters a period of depression and physical decline. No one is able to help her. Or, perhaps, she isn't allowing anyone to help. The last thing she wants to hear is "everything's going to be OK." She wants to write her own story.

One is never sure, however, whether Daisy truly has the courage to live for herself.

We follow her past this crisis and into her retirement days in Sarasota, Fla., where she plays out "the story" of widowhood as the world tells it—ease, bridge games, shuffleboard, and health problems.

The lush gardens and botanical richness that decorated and sustained Daisy's life metaphorically give way in her last moments as she imagines herself turning inch by inch into cold stone. Not even Christian beliefs of salvation hold any solace. Her death is as haunting as her birth, which was similarly tragic and physically agonizing.

Shields smoothly weaves into the story interesting snippets of the advancing century—world wars, the marriage of Princess Elizabeth and Prince Philip, the publication of Betty Friedan's *The Feminine Mystique.*

Daisy one time stops in Callander, Ontario, to gawk with other tourists at the Dionne quintuplets at play in their yard. In a telling moment, she becomes filled with indignation at the absurdity of the scene and how society so quickly glances at a person's life and sums it all up.

Shields, an American, has spent most of her life in Canada and invests this tale with an appreciation of its people and history.

Having raised five children before becoming a professional writer, she is penetrating in her gaze when it comes to traditional "women's work"—cooking, cleaning, child rearing—never belittling, but always searching for the woman behind it.

Still, *The Stone Diaries* is more than a woman's tale. Though there are moments of happiness and humor along the way, it is ultimately a story of lost opportunities and loneliness.

It looks beyond the accumulation of events, dates, and sterile facts a diary so faithfully records, to the universal problem of how ordinary men and women connect with one another and whether they are living authentic lives in an age of frightening change and equally frightening superficiality.

The author's outlook may be less than comforting, but it forces to the surface emotions that stir and rarefy, rather than merely titillate.

Allyson F. McGill   (review date Fall 1994)

SOURCE: "A Tangle of Underground Streams," in *Belles Lettres: A Review of Books by Women,* Vol. 10, No. 1, Fall, 1994, pp. 32, 34.

[*In the following review, McGill discusses the main themes in* The Stone Diaries.]

Daisy Stone Goodwill, heroine and chronicler of Carol Shields's *The Stone Diaries,* never knew her mother, but this does not stop her from envisioning her mother's death on the day of her own birth. In a mesmerizing examination of the nature of fiction and autobiography, Shields puts the pen into Daisy's hand, thus posing many puzzles, some forthright, others more oblique. So caught up are we in Daisy's story that only gradually do we realize what she is doing—nothing less than creating the totality of her life, reaching far beyond what she can truly know, and taking liberties with what she does.

The Stone Diaries, nominated for the 1993 Booker Prize, begins with Daisy's birth and extends to beyond her death some 90 years later. Ignore what you have read elsewhere about this being the story of an ordinary woman. No one in a Shields novel is ordinary. Her people, touched by some outside awareness, transcend the everyday. Somehow Shields always elevates her characters from the prosaic, commingling the darkness and the light in their lives. Daisy's darkness begins when her mother, Mercy—an orphan of elephantine size beloved by her young stonecutter husband, Cuyler—gives birth in her kitchen on a blazingly hot day, not knowing until the baby comes that she is pregnant, and dying even as her daughter draws a first breath.

Daisy's life is extraordinary as it follows the familiar tra-

jectory of birth, adolescence, marriage, motherhood, old age, and death. She is raised by a neighbor woman, Clarentine, who, having reached the midpoint of her own life, recognizes the emptiness of her marriage and decamps with the baby to Winnipeg. There they move in on the solitary life of her son, Barker, a botany professor. So do lives suddenly change, with resounding repercussions.

From the quarry's dust to her surrogate mother's lush gardens, Daisy's life returns to stone when her father reclaims her in adolescence, and they move to Bloomington, Indiana, from whose limestone will rise the Empire State Building and the gleaming buildings of Washington, D.C. In Bloomington Daisy grows to young womanhood and marries the pick of the town's youths, only to discover that he is an alcoholic and watch him plunge to his death on their honeymoon. Hers is a life where routine events are touched by the grotesque. It is Daisy's awareness of this and her growing realization of her motherless and thus anchorless state that propel her back to Winnipeg and Barker when her loneliness becomes unbearable. It is also what inspires her to write her life story.

But what *is* our life story? "Biography, even autobiography, is full of systematic error, of holes that connect like a tangle of underground streams," Daisy warns us, forcing us to question her story's validity. She imagines her birth and, decades apart, her parents' deaths. She concocts the life of Clarentine's husband after his abandonment in images that are both absurd and heartbreaking. But these are her fantasies, not eyewitness accounts, and in reading Daisy's "autobiography" we begin to question our own assumptions about the lives of people all around us. What is it we glimpse, what is always kept hidden from us, and what really motivates the human heart?

Ignore what you have read elsewhere about *The Stone Diaries* being the story of an ordinary woman. No one in a Shields novel is ordinary. Her people, touched by some outside awareness, transcend the everyday.

—Allyson F. McGill

Daisy's questioning is as much self-directed. By writing her life in the third person she becomes her own observer, knowing that the outer person and the inner self often diverge. And Daisy, born in 1905, is a product of her generation, that peculiar hybrid person who, brought up Victorian, must undergo bewildering transformations as society changes its rules with seemingly lightning speed. In the space of one lifetime a tightly corsetted girl with plaited hair and long skirts can metamorphosize into the polyester bridge-player who instead of cash carries credit cards in her purse.

Such appearances signify the duality of Daisy's life: the spirit within unable to find true expression in the conventions allowed to her. There is a note of pathos running throughout Daisy's narrative, the sense that both she and her culture are boxing her in. She recognizes this, perhaps through the very act of writing her own story: "The larger loneliness of our lives evolves from our unwillingness to spend ourselves, stir ourselves. We are always damping down our inner weather, permitting ourselves the comforts of postponements, of rehearsals." Is it that life is ultimately disappointing? Or that life's inevitable disappointments are mitigated by moments of pleasure, even joy? The seemingly mundane in Shields's world is continually irradiated by love: Cuyler's for Mercy; Clarentine's, and later Barker's, for Daisy. Out of a marriage of love dulled by familiarity come moments of rare poetry and the added poignancy of love's depth revealed after death. It is all mixed up together: lives that are too brief side by side with the love of people long together; grief at sudden loss and the lingering regret of words unsaid when a long life ends; the equal portions of sadness and grace when we recognize what we have. We take so much for granted. Shields and Daisy challenge us to review our lives, to try and see life honestly, even while "their" act of authorship only reveals how impossible it is to see and speak objective truth. We create our lives as much as they are created for us, and then we recreate it all in our retelling.

Carol Shields with Idella Sturino (interview date 9 December 1994)

SOURCE: An interview in *Scrivener,* Spring, 1995, pp. 76-85.

[*In the following interview, which was conducted in December 1994, Shields discusses* The Stone Diaries *and her writing process.*]

[*Sturino*]: **The Stone Diaries** *was a huge success for you. How did that feel? It was on the best-seller list for over a year, I think.*

[Shields]: It still is, in fact. I'm just amazed. I had no expectations for anything like this.

Have you been doing a lot of readings related to that (i.e. readings from **The Stone Diaries***)?*

I have done quite a few, now we're sort of at the end of that for a while until it comes out in the States, in paperback in the spring, and I'll do just a little bit of it then.

Do you enjoy that type of thing?

Well, I don't enjoy traveling that much anymore; I've sort of fainted as far as traveling goes.

I read in an interview you did with Eleanor Watchel in 1989 for A Room of One's Own, *and in that you described the period during which you wrote your first novel,* **Small Ceremonies** *as a very happy sort of time, and obviously* **Diaries** *was written many years later. That must have come from a very different place in your life; I'm wondering how the experiences of writing them compared? If it required a different sort of energy to write* **Diaries***?*

Well, probably it did, because my life is very different now because my children have grown up, but I loved writing

that book (**The Stone Diaries**); I was conscious of that . . . I don't always, I often find it terribly hard work and I put off getting down to it, but for some reason I loved writing that one. And I think because, once I found the structure, my chapters and so on, I felt it was going well, and I always felt it was about something important. I was never quite sure what the thing was, but it seemed to me it was about something important. So it was different of course, because I have a lot more time now to write. But I still produce at about the same rate. It took me two years to write the book. That seems . . .

Quick.

Does that seem quick to you?

Yes, I think so.

It seemed to go steadily, I never got stuck.

You mentioned, about the first novel I think, that you would sit down and write two pages a day, that it took you nine months. Did you find yourself on that same sort of schedule?

Yes, except . . . now it seems to take two years instead of nine months, even though I have more time, and partly it's because I'm teaching and have other obligations and have more interruptions, and maybe I'm not as disciplined as I was then.

You said that the structure (of **Diaries***) was something you were really happy about, and I loved the structure of the book, it was so different. I'm wondering where you thought of that idea?*

Well, you know, I love those old nineteenth century biographies and that's how they structure them. They have a chapter on birth, childhood, marriage, just really more or less the chapter headings that I used. And I wanted mine to be just slightly off, you know, a little bit slant, but to use those old ones to kind of gesture back to that nineteenth century biography.

It worked, it really did.

Good.

Are you working on anything right now?

Well, I'm just at the beginning of a novel. And I've done the film script for **The Republic of Love.** So that was what I worked on this year.

Wow, that's great. When will that be coming out?

Well, it isn't even in production yet, but apparently everything is ready to roll soon, so who knows. It's quite a different business that writing a book and sending it to your publisher.

Is there a genre that you are more comfortable writing in? Do you feel more comfortable writing poetry than fiction?

Oh, certainly, writing fiction, writing novels.

Novels as opposed to short fiction?

I think so.

How do you write? When you're set in that mode, do you

listen to music or do you only write at certain times of the day? Do you find yourself writing only under certain conditions?

No, well, these days . . . I used to write at home . . .

You don't now?

No, well, not as much. I mostly go to the university where I have an office, and just shut the door and try to spend half my day, the first half, writing. The second half is always consumed with mail and other tasks taken on. But I do try to get back to it late in the afternoon, to go over it again, what I've done for that day. And you know I'm still a very modest producer, maybe two, sometimes on a very good day I can do three pages. But I try not to go racing ahead, I go fairly slowly, and I tend to—it hasn't always worked so neatly—but I tend to start at the beginning and write through this way. Sometimes I find I have to go back and write a different beginning, but I try to feel my way as I go. And when I'm not writing, of course, I'm thinking about it, or talking about it. I talked about *The Stone Diaries* a lot to other people while I was writing it, and tried to find out what old age felt like, for example. Or I would try to talk to my colleagues at lunch about—I'm very interested in phrases from different decades—so it was fun to talk and chat with them about what they remembered. So I just loved all that.

When you were young you read a lot, and in the same interview that I mentioned earlier, you said that almost all of the books you read came from the library. I imagine by this point you have a little library of your own. I'm wondering, if you had to pick a favourite title of a book, or a favourite author off your shelf, what that would be?

As a child?

No, now.

Well, I love the poet Philip Larkin, so I sometimes take that down from the shelf. And of course I like anything by Alice Munro, so I have all her books, I can see them from here.

You've been compared to her.

Well, we're very different writers. I think when we're compared it's because we're both Canadians (she laughs), and we're both women, about the same age.

I guess that narrows the choices for comparison down.

Yes.

Do you see your work as influenced by certain writers?

Oh, I've probably been influenced by every writer I've ever read, I would think.

But not particularly one?

No, I wouldn't say particularly one, but I certainly think that other writers can show you what's possible, you know, what's allowed. And what's wonderful, when that happens.

Is there a piece of advice you can offer to young writers?

Oh, I love to give advice.

Good. It's such a cliche question, but . . .

Well, I certainly think reading is the way, and reading attentively, and reading to find out how the novels that you like are put together. And then I think that the novel you should try to write, or the book you should write, is the book that you can't find. The book you'd love to have, you know, so that if you imagine you're in bed with the flu, what would be the book that you'd want to read. And then write that book. I think there's a certain amount of sense to that.

Diaries is set up as an autobiographical narrative, but the first-person narrative slips into the third and also the book contains pictures which convey that biographical idea. This is a theme that's constantly talked about in the reviews of the book, this sort of tension between the subjective and objective. Why was this important for you? I've noticed in some of your short stories a similar theme.

Yes. In fact, in my early novels, the first novel I wrote, for example, is about a woman writing a biography (*Small Ceremonies*). I guess I'm just interested in how people tell their life stories, or if it's even possible to tell your life story. It wasn't something I set out to write about, it was something I found myself writing about.

The Stone Diaries **started with this love I have of stone, especially limestone. I'm interested in limestone because it's an inorganic material that's made of organic material. So there's something about the metaphor, of the organic and the inorganic, the expressed and the unexpressed, that I liked.**

—Carol Shields

Do you think that in telling life stories we re-invent ourselves? There's a phrase in the book about that.

I think people do re-invent themselves, so that's part of the life story. I'm told by some of my friends that in fact I'm wrong about this, that the personality is set at age, whatever, four or five. But I don't believe it. I simply don't believe it. I think that people make efforts to change themselves, and also events occur that change one, and responsibilities. You know, anyone who has children tells you that having children changes you enormously.

I had a teacher once who said that our perceptions of ourselves are very much defined by how others perceive us. This seems very applicable to Daisy. She seems very much defined for us, and for herself, by how other people perceive her. How does this sort of idea play itself out for you in your writing?

Well, I think I see it all around me. When I read the obituaries I always see women as defined as the wife of, the loving grandmother of, and so on. So I think traditionally women have been defined by other people rather than making their own definitions. I certainly see this as something that has inhibited women and their willingness to engage with the world.

I see it as time appropriate too . . .

Yes.

The recurring images in this book are of stone, flower and light. How are these important?

I hadn't realized light was a recurring image.

Not as much, I think . . .

The book started with this love I have of stone, especially limestone. I'm interested in limestone because it's an inorganic material that's made of organic material, it's made of sea creatures, actually, that have been crushed and cemented together. So there's something about the metaphor, of the organic and the inorganic, the expressed and the unexpressed, that I liked. Why flowers? It's hard to say. I don't know quite how, but I did see it slipping in as a kind of second spine, as it were. But I was very anxious that flowers not represent women, and stone men. I wanted to scramble that representation.

Well, it certainly was scrambled, we saw that with Daisy's husband.

Yes.

Daisy is very shaped by her orphanhood, and it seems she is always searching for that sense of home. What made you decide to use that theme?

To make her an orphan?

Yes, because it's such an important part of who she is.

Yes, of course she's very specifically an orphan, but I suppose you could say there's a sense in which we are all alone in the world, and always conscious of the absence of what we were once directly attached to. I also love the idea of someone having a child who didn't know she was pregnant. I've always followed those accounts in the newspaper, there's usually one or two a year. I'm just interested in that whole phenomenon, why it happens, so I just wanted to write about that.

Do you often get ideas like that, from newspapers?

Yes, often.

One of the other things about Daisy is that it seems that the story you're telling about her is one that isn't usually told. She's very recognizable and common in a lot of ways: I read a review that called her a sort of "everywoman" for her context, her time and class, and so on . . . I know you're interested in writing about the lives of women. How much were you trying to sort of unearth untold lives of women like Daisy, women like my grandmother . . . ?

I've seen this reference to an "everywoman" too, and I don't know quite what it means, or whether I should accept that or not. I was certainly never conscious of that. But I guess I am interested in the notion of fiction as redemption, and it seems to me that that's a part of our society that hasn't been redeemed—women who don't have a

public life, who belong to bridge clubs, who don't even have a working life, who are just women in our society. I wrote a play that was produced years ago called *Thirteen Hands* and I guess it's just something I'm thinking about as I'm getting older, or thinking about my mother's life, or all those millions of lives that somehow were never realized. And then, of course, the question begs itself of, well, maybe they were in ways. I don't know. So I was just interested in all that part of life.

In **Thirteen Hands,** *one thing that struck me—and I think this comes out in some of your other writing as well—was in the bonds of friendship, how for the women you write about they are such an important support system, in a way a life-support system.*

Yes, I'm fascinated by that. Women friendship has been very important in my life, it has always been important. You know, I'm still in touch with my old childhood friends, and friends from high school, always women, because women of my generation didn't have men friends. So, yes, it is something that I wanted to write about, and I think it is what sustains Daisy in her life, one of the things that sustains her.

Do you think that for characters you might draw from a present-day context, that friendship with women would be something which would still be as important to them? Or do you see it, as you mentioned, as a result of the fact that women in Daisy's time just didn't have male friends?

I don't know. I look at my daughters, who are young women now, and I think their friendships with women are very important too. I see it not as something that is over, or lost.

One of the things you mentioned in an interview I read was that you specifically want to write about women you can recognize, and this was one of the most pleasurable things for me about reading **Diaries,** *was that I could recognize my grandmother and my mother throughout. How much of it was drawn from memories of your own maternal figures?*

Surprisingly, not very much, directly. I suppose I drew indirectly on memories, not particularly of my mother, or my mother-in-law, but about the kind of world they inhabited. Naturally, I've had access to that world through them and through their friends, and of course I'm still part of this. A lot of women my age are doing exactly what Daisy did in her life, which was not very much, as we measure those accomplishments.

You've probably done so many interviews, more than you can count, and I'm wondering if there's one question as a writer that you would really like to be asked that you aren't, usually, or that interviewers just never seem to come up with?

(laughs) Actually, I was signing books in a shopping mall a couple of weeks ago in Toronto, and a woman asked me a question that no one else had asked me. And it comes up in the last chapter . . . it's a little paragraph about Daisy missing the point of it all, missing the point of her own life. And this woman came up to me; she was a woman of, I'd say, about thirty or thirty-five, and she was a little bit distraught and she opened the book and she said, "I want you to explain something to me." So, she pointed this out, and she said, "I think I've missed the point. What is the point?" (laughs) So it stopped me, because no one had asked me that question. I guess the big existential question, "Why are we in life and what are our lives to mean?" Of course, that's a question I can't answer. I have a friend . . . who's a writer, and we often talk on these things, and she has promised me that the minute she finds out what the point of it all is, that she'll send me a fax . . . so I'm waiting!

Margery Fee   (review date Spring 1995)

SOURCE: "Auto/Biographical Fictions," in *Canadian Literature*, No. 144, Spring, 1995, pp. 173-74.

[*In the review below, Fee examines narration and the theme of domesticity in* The Stone Diaries.]

The Stone Diaries begins: "My mother's name was Mercy Stone Goodwill." Daisy Goodwill Flett appears to be telling the story of her life, beginning with the day of her birth, a birth which almost immediately leads to her mother's death. That this is a novel about the limitations of biography and autobiography is a point made in almost every review and publisher's summary of this novel, reinforced by the book's use of photographs, the family tree on the endpapers, the title, format and many direct comments on the subject. However, *The Stone Diaries* is, one must point out, a work of fiction, neither autobiography or biography (or it could not have been nominated for a Booker Prize or have won the Governor General's Award for Fiction!) Significantly, the book contains no photograph of Daisy herself, only of her relatives, husbands and friends. And in a sense, the narrative figures Daisy as a hole in a complex social network. Lying delirious with pneumonia at the age of 11, Daisy realizes that the world is going on without her and concludes "that if she was going to hold on to her life at all, she would have to rescue it by a primary act of imagination, supplementing, modifying, summoning up the necessary connections, conjuring the pastoral or heroic or whatever . . . getting the details wrong occasionally, exaggerating or lying outright. . . ."

Thus, the narration itself is highlighted. The reader quickly realizes that Daisy, the ostensible narrator, could only have been present in the first scene in the novel in the most vestigial way, as a bloodied bundle squeezed out by a woman who may never have realized she was pregnant. "Blood and ignorance, what can be shaped from blood and ignorance" asks the narrator. What can we know even of ourselves, let alone the impenetrable mysteries posed by lovers, spouses, parents and children, despite the closest of biological and emotional ties? There is no "thyself" to know, even in retrospect. Thus it is ironic that Daisy's description of the time just preceding her own birth, an account of her young, overweight mother making Malvern Pudding on a sticky summer day, is one of the most sensual and striking in the novel, filled with images of heat, fruit, cream, flesh and sex. This memorable, convincing and detailed part of the narrative, given the narrator's position, is thus highlighted as doubly fictional, an emphasis

both autobiography and biography avoid. The novel veers between adopting autobiographical conventions and violating them; for example, the first-person narrator is sometimes clearly Daisy the autobiographer and yet also shifts to the third-person omniscience typical of the novel or biography. Yet despite this omniscience, which allows access to the inner thoughts of others (for example, the reader shares Daisy's father's thoughts as he dies), Daisy herself is oddly lacking in introspection and the third person narrator rarely recounts her thoughts. She apparently retains the reticence typical of the autobiographer about personal matters, voicing few negative opinions of family or friends and mentioning sex only briefly. Further, the novel is filled with passages that read like interviews conducted after her death with her friends and family.

The reader is challenged to discover a position Daisy could have taken to narrate such an account and ultimately it appears that the account is, in fact, a kind of fantasy she has during her long decline into death after a heart attack at 80: "she shuts her eyes . . . regarding something infinitely complex printed on the thin skin of her eyelids, a secret, a dream." Daisy has certainly had the time to fill in most of the "dark voids and unbridgable gaps" that are supposedly intrinsic to autobiography. In fact, she clearly has not produced an autobiography at all, but a fiction that mimics some of the conventions of autobiography and violates others. Daisy's stonemason father builds an intricately carved tower as a memorial to her mother; Daisy dreams a memorial for herself: "Stone is how she finally sees herself, her living cells replaced by the insentience of mineral deposition. . . . She lies, in her last dreams, flat on her back on a thick slab, as hugely imposing as the bishops and saints she'd seen years earlier in the great pink cathedral of Kirkwall. . . .

Although *The Stone Diaries* does highlight the limitations of life writing—currently a fairly fashionable project—it far more interestingly problematizes the split between the central character's life and her narrative voice. Unlike Margaret Laurence's *The Stone Angel,* where Hagar's account of her life from the perspective of old age conveys the effect of complete authenticity, Daisy and her narrative voice seem to be jarringly disparate. The Daisy we read about appears far too unselfconscious, far too unanalytic, to produce the fascinating narrative that we are reading, even in the context of a kind of deathbed conversion from dullness to brilliance. Her son Warren's speculations on her life underscore the problem. Apropos of a university essay Daisy wrote in 1926 on the struggle for Italian independence he asks:

> Where did it go, my mother's intellectual ease and energy? . . . When I think about my mother's essay on Camillo Cavour, I can't help feeling cheated, as if there's some wily subversion going on, a glittering joke locked in a box and buried underground. And then I think: if I feel cheated, how much more cheated she must feel. She must be in mourning for the squandering of herself. Something, someone, cut off her head, yanked out her tongue.

The narrative technique makes up, in a way, for the squandering of Daisy's intellectual, imaginative and spiritual self in middle-class domesticity; Daisy gets her intellectual ease back, but only as a glittering joke in the failing body of an old woman who has no real audience for her reclaimed life. The degree of her oppression is the difference between what her narrative proves she can think and what others saw of her. The reader, like her children, never sees anything but the domestic Daisy; only the reader hears the voice of the liberated Daisy. From a feminist perspective, Daisy's life can be figured as a triumph, but such a perspective cannot disguise its terrible limitations.

Nonetheless, feminism scarcely affected Daisy; what this text does is allow her to reveal the beauties and contributions of a life spent in nurturing men, children and plants. Domesticity is the heart of this novel; surprising a husband with a new recipe, counting pillow cases, producing a marvellous garden, these are the important feats, the memorable feats. Not to mention giving birth to the children and creating for them a peaceful home. Daisy's one venture into paid employment, the gardening column she writes for nine years, pales into insignificance by comparison. Domesticity is never rejected, but the text makes it clear what Daisy's generation missed. It is the next generation, exemplified by Daisy's elder daughter Alice, divorcée, mother of three, grandmother of three, failed novelist and noted Chekhov scholar, who will begin to overcome the patriarchal prohibition against women who combine a domestic life with an intellectual and spiritual one. Alice has been able to see her life as something "she's making . . . up as she goes along" rather than a fixed pattern laid out by convention, *Good Housekeeping, McCall's* and *The Canadian Home Companion.*

FURTHER READING

Benedict, Elizabeth. "Below the Surface." *The Los Angeles Times Book Review* (17 April 1994): 3, 7.
> Favorably reviews *Happenstance* and *The Stone Diaries,* noting that the latter work "has the scope of a Dickens novel, the wit of Muriel Spark and the stylistic inventiveness of Graham Swift's *Waterland.*"

Casey, Constance. "The Times of Her Life." *Book World— The Washington Post* 24, No. 20 (15 May 1994): 5, 10.
> Remarks on the themes of *The Stone Diaries.*

Clapp, Susannah. "Flowers and Fruit." *The Times Literary Supplement,* No. 4717 (27 August 1993): 22.
> Discusses theme and imagery in *The Stone Diaries.*

Denoon, Anne. "A Singular Life." *Books in Canada* XXII, No. 7 (October 1993): 32-3.
> Comments on narration in *The Stone Diaries.*

Hughes, Kathryn. "Life Studies." *New Statesman & Society* 6, No. 266 (20 August 1993): 40.
> Positive review. Hughes notes that throughout *The Stone Diaries,* "Shields holds fast to the conceit that this is no novel, but rather a documentary life of the type that became so central to recuperative feminist history in the 1970s."

Pool, Gail. "Imagination's Invisible Ink." *The Women's Review of Books* XI, No. 8 (May 1994): 20.
> Favorable review of *Happenstance* and *The Stone Diaries,* which Pool describes as "an intricate novel and complex commentary on living and telling lives."

Turbide, Diane. "A Prairie Pulitzer." *Macleans* 108, No. 18 (1 May 1995): 76-7.
> Comments on the awarding of the Pulitzer Prize to Shields for *The Stone Diaries* and her success as a novelist.

Tom Stoppard
Arcadia

Award: New York Drama Critics Circle Award for Best New Play

Born in 1937, Stoppard is an English playwright, screenwriter, and novelist.

For further information on his life and works, see *CLC,* Volumes 1, 3, 4, 5, 8, 15, 29, 34, and 63.

INTRODUCTION

Arcadia (1993) is set in the schoolroom of Sidley Park, a country house in Derbyshire, England, and covers three distinct points in time—three days in 1809, one day in the present, and one in 1812. For the first six of the play's seven scenes, the action alternates between the nineteenth and twentieth centuries, leading up to the final scene in which characters from the two centuries appear on stage simultaneously. The nineteenth-century story centers on Thomasina Coverly and her tutor, Septimus Hodge. A classmate and friend of Lord Byron, Hodge has an affair with Lady Chater, the wife of the untalented poet Ezra Chater, and, to avoid a duel, promises to review favorably Chater's "The Couch of Eros," which the poet subsequently inscribes. Thomasina, whose love for her tutor remains unrequited, discovers the proof for Pierre Fermat's last mathematical theorem, thereby calling the assumptions of Newtonian physics into question and paving the way for the Second Law of Thermodynamics, fractal mathematics, and chaos theory. On reviewing her proof, which she presents to him on the day before her seventeenth birthday, Hodge recognizes humankind's ultimate doom, as the theorem postulates the perpetual cooling of the universe. Thomasina dies in a fire later that night and Septimus sequesters himself in the Coverly's hermitage for the remainder of his life. The twentieth-century story centers on Hannah Jarvis, who is researching the mysterious recluse that lived in the Coverly hermitage, and Bernard Nightingale, who believes he can prove Byron killed Chater in a duel at Sidley Park. Nightingale's erroneous theory is based on Hodge's inscribed copy of Chater's poem—which also contains Chater's challenge—that Nightingale has traced to Byron's library.

Critical reaction to *Arcadia* has generally been favorable. Although a few reviewers have faulted the play as overly cerebral and lacking emotional impact, most commentators have praised it as a thought-provoking and engaging depiction of the dialogue between past and present and humankind's endless search for order. Remarking on the play's structure, John Lahr has stated that "Stoppard utilizes the ironies of history—the symmetries and accidents

that lead, nonetheless, to a kind of order—as a way of demonstrating the outcome of chaos theory." Other critics have praised Stoppard's extensive wordplay. Tom Appelo, commenting on Thomasina's calculations, has suggested that "her theme is the point of the play: that determinism is false, that fate and free will are like waltzing mice, that life is messy, so eat it over the sink."

PRINCIPAL WORKS

A Walk on the Water (radio play) 1963
A Walk on the Water (television play) 1963; also produced as *The Preservation of George Riley* [revised version], 1964
The Dissolution of Dominic Boot (radio play) 1964
"M" Is for Moon among Other Things (radio play) 1964

A Walk on the Water (drama) 1964; also produced as *Enter a Free Man* [revised version], 1968
The Gamblers (drama) 1965
If You're Glad I'll Be Frank (radio play) 1966
Lord Malquist and Mr. Moon (novel) 1966
Rosencrantz and Guildenstern Are Dead (drama) 1966
A Separate Peace (television play) 1966
Tango [adaptor; from the play by Slawomir Mrozek] (drama) 1966
Albert's Bridge (radio play) 1967
Another Moon Called Earth (television play) 1967
Teeth (television play) 1967
Neutral Ground (television play) 1968
The Real Inspector Hound (drama) 1968
Albert's Bridge (drama) 1969
If You're Glad I'll Be Frank (drama) 1969
After Magritte (drama) 1970
*The Engagement (television play) 1970
Where Are They Now? (radio play) 1970
Dogg's Our Pet (drama) 1971
Artist Descending a Staircase (radio play) 1972
Jumpers (drama) 1972
One Pair of Eyes (television play) 1972
The House of Bernarda Alba [adaptor; from a play by Federico García Lorca] (drama) 1973
Travesties (drama) 1974
The Boundary [with Clive Exton] (television play) 1975
Eleventh House [with Clive Exton] (television play) 1975
The Romantic Englishwoman [with Thomas Wiseman] (screenplay) 1975
Three Men in a Boat [adaptor; from the novel by Jerome K. Jerome] (television play) 1975
Dirty Linen and New-Found-Land (drama) 1976
Every Good Boy Deserves Favour (drama) 1977
Professional Foul (television play) 1977
Night and Day (drama) 1978
Despair [adaptor; with Rainer Werner Fassbinder; from the novel by Vladimir Nabokov] (screenplay) 1978
‡Dogg's Hamlet, Cahoot's Macbeth (dramas) 1979
Undiscovered Country [adaptor; from Arthur Schnitzler's play *Das Weite Land*] (drama) 1979
The Human Factor [adaptor; with Otto Preminger; from the novel by Graham Greene] (screenplay) 1980
On the Razzle [adaptor; from Johann Nestroy's *Einin Jux will er sich machen*] (drama) 1981
The Dog It Was That Died (radio play) 1982
The Real Thing (drama) 1982
Brazil [with Terry Gilliam and Charles McKeown] (screenplay) 1985
Rough Crossing [adaptor; from a play by Ferenc Molnár] (drama) 1984; revised version, 1990
Squaring the Circle (television play) 1984
Dalliance [adaptor; from a play by Arthur Schnitzler] (drama) 1986
Largo Desolato [adaptor; from the play by Vaclav Havel] (drama) 1986
Empire of the Sun [adaptor; from the novel by J. G. Ballard] (screenplay) 1987
Artist Descending a Staircase (drama) 1988

Hapgood (drama) 1988
The Russia House [adaptor; from the novel by John le Carré] (screenplay) 1989
Billy Bathgate [adaptor; from the novel by E. L. Doctorow] (screenplay) 1991
In the Native State (radio play) 1991
Rosencrantz and Guildenstern Are Dead (screenplay) 1991
Arcadia (drama) 1993
†Indian Ink (drama) 1995

*This work is an adaptation of Stoppard's 1964 radio play *The Dissolution of Dominic Boot.*

†This work is an adaptation of Stoppard's 1991 radio play *In the Native State.*

‡*Dogg's Hamlet*—a conflation of *Dogg's Our Pet* and *The 15 Minute Dogg's Troupe Hamlet*—and *Cahoot's Macbeth* are interconnected one-act plays.

CRITICISM

Vincent Canby (review date 31 March 1995)

SOURCE: "Stoppard Comedy Bridges Centuries and States of Mind," in *The New York Times,* March 31, 1995, pp. B1, B10.

[*For many years the chief film critic of* The New York Times, *Canby is also a novelist, playwright, and theater critic. In the following excerpt, he favorably reviews* Arcadia.]

There's no doubt about it. **Arcadia** is Tom Stoppard's richest, most ravishing comedy to date, a play of wit, intellect, language, brio and, new for him, emotion. It's like a dream of levitation: you're instantaneously aloft, soaring, banking, doing loop-the-loops and then, when you think you're about to plummet to earth, swooping to a gentle touchdown of not easily described sweetness and sorrow.

That's the play.

Trevor Nunn's Lincoln Center Theater production, which opened last night in the Beaumont, is a reasonable American facsimile of those he staged in London, first at the Royal National in 1993, then at the Haymarket in the West End transfer last year. The Beaumont production looks gorgeous and is true to the letter and spirit of the Stoppard words, but it should be better.

Arcadia demands something more than a reasonable facsimile if American audiences are to be consistently beguiled by this most ambitious of English comedies. It's a complicated piece, played in two time frames (1809 and the present) by two sets of characters. They share the same great country house, Sidley Park, and occasionally the same stage props, including a tortoise that's named Plautus in 1809 and Lightning today.

Mr. Stoppard's theatrical conceits are exhilarating; his interests are diverse but interlocking, always riveting and sometimes brazenly deep-dish, which is part of the fun. Among his concerns here: first love, Newtonian physics, hustling pedants, landscape gardening, sexual infidelity, class, the mathematics of deterministic chaos, manners and the absolute end of the universe when, one character observes, "We're all going to wind up at room temperature."

Mr. Stoppard pushes the audience to the edge of delicious bewilderment, then he suddenly pulls back to make all as clear as need be. The playwright is a daredevil pilot who's steady at the controls.

At the center of *Arcadia* is a mystery that is the consuming passion of a contemporary literary don, Bernard Nightingale (Victor Garber): did Lord Byron, while visiting Lord and Lady Croom at Sidley Park in 1809, fight a duel in which he killed a grossly untalented poet, Ezra Chater, over the honor of Chater's wife? And was that the reason for Byron's hasty, heretofore unexplained departure from England for the Continent?

Bernard is hungry for acceptance in academe, and even hungrier for the celebrity that comes with publication and the inevitable talk-show appearances. He's a loose cannon, a dangerously quick-minded, noisily self-centered man who doesn't care whom he insults or makes passes at. Chief among his victims: Hannah Jarvis (Blair Brown), a best-selling author and landscape historian; Valentine Coverly (Robert Sean Leonard), an Oxford student of scientific mind, and his sister Chloë (Haviland Morris), two children of the present Lord and Lady Croom.

In the course of his research, Bernard becomes convinced he has made "the most sensational literary discovery of this century." He has, of course, got it all wrong. *Arcadia* crosscuts between the present-day shenanigans at Sidley Park and the events that took place there nearly 200 years earlier. These involve poor Ezra Chater (Paul Giamatti), though only in a helplessly funny subsidiary role. Byron himself remains off-stage.

The more important players in the 1809 mystery are Septimus Hodge (Billy Crudup), a randy young man and part-time literary critic who is the tutor of 13-year-old Thomasina Coverly (Jennifer Dundas); Lady Croom (Lisa Banes), Thomasina's mother, who has never put off a man who had the good taste to presume on her virtue, and a celebrated landscape architect, Richard Noakes (Peter Maloney). Noakes is transforming Sidley Park's grounds from their comparatively natural look to a picturesque style that Hannah Jarvis in 1995 calls "the Gothic novel as landscape."

Hannah, too, becomes intent on solving a mystery: the identity of the hermit whom the earlier Crooms installed in their picturesque hermitage, built by Noakes as he was making mountains on land that had always been flat, and constructing ruins where no castle had ever existed.

The principal Stoppard characters are often driven, not always self-aware, very intelligent and furiously articulate, which is not to say they mean everything that comes out of their mouths. Bernard's vitriol is both hilarious and mean. Of scientists, he says to Valentine: "I'd push the

whole lot of you over a cliff myself. Except the one in the wheelchair; I think I'd lose the sympathy vote."

The play's most affecting characters are Thomasina and Septimus, who affectionately regards his pupil as the child she is.

Thomasina, who doesn't yet know what "carnal embrace" means, doodles away in her notebook, apparently to stumble onto today's new, nonlinear mathematics. She has the gift, sometimes possessed by the young, to conceive abstract concepts beyond the comprehension of those whose minds have been made soggy with received wisdom. She is also in love with Septimus, which has melancholy consequences.

As Bernard continues his investigations, it's clear to the audience, if not to him, that both Thomasina and Septimus are part of the mystery whose solution he so thoroughly muddles.

At the beginning of *Arcadia,* the two time frames are presented in separate, usually alternating scenes. As the play progresses, the times begin to merge, at first when the present-day characters are seen in 1809 costumes for a fancy dress ball. Further along, the characters from each section occupy the stage at the same time.

As Thomasina, Septimus and Lady Croom, and Bernard, Hannah and Valentine play around and through one another, they create the contrapuntal effect of a piece of music. It's tricky but hugely effective. The two stories come together in a way to give dramatic dimension to some of the more esoteric notions that have been bandied about earlier.

[In *Arcadia,* Stoppard] intriguingly demonstrates the ineluctable nature of history to repeat itself while simultaneously arguing the impossibility of events in the past yielding to valid interpretation in the present. Despite efforts to interpret, Stoppard maintains, the past exists as an alien world, essentially unknowable.

—*Craig Clinton, in a review of* Arcadia, *in* Theatre Journal, *May, 1994.*

John Simon   (review date 10 April 1995)

SOURCE: "Wits' End," in *New York* Magazine, Vol. 28, No. 15, April 10, 1995, pp. 74-5.

[*In the following excerpt, Simon argues that although* Arcadia *is clever, the play suffers from too much erudition.*]

"Its ingenuity is stupendous," wrote Harold Hobson in the London *Sunday Times* about Tom Stoppard's first hit, and so is that of his latest, *Arcadia:* stupendous and sometimes, I'm afraid, stupefying. To say that Stoppard is the cleverest playwright active in English is probably a platitude. But cleverness engenders its own problems: It is almost as hard for a clever playwright to create an unclever character as it is for a plodding playwright to create a clever one.

But some characters, even in a Stoppard play, cannot be clever. The only way the author can manage this is to make them into fools or near-mutes. There is nothing in between, where most of the real world situates itself. This, to be sure, is also true of Oscar Wilde, Stoppard's inspiration; there are passages in *Arcadia* that are distant but distinct echoes of *The Importance of Being Earnest.* Wilde, however, did not cheat: He would not have an Englishman in 1809 use the Yiddishism *tush,* or have two characters—including the 13-year-old Thomasina—interpret Poussin's famous *Et in Arcadia Ego* ("I too have lived in Arcadia") as being spoken by Death, i.e., the skull in the picture, a theory first proposed by Erwin Panofsky a century and a half later.

Arcadia takes place—first alternatingly, then simultaneously—in 1809 and today. The constant is a garden room at Sidley Park, the Derbyshire manor of Lord and Lady Croom. Their daughter, Thomasina Coverly, is being tutored by a young scientist, Septimus Hodge, a classmate of Lord Byron, who is visiting at Sidley Park. Lady Croom, whose other child is the tongue-tied Augustus, is witty and imperious, and has a yen for the handsome Hodge. Also present are Richard Noakes, the landscape architect (who is striving to convert the classically natural gardens into picturesque Gothic), and Ezra Chater, the resident poetaster (who is married to a beautiful flirt with whom Hodge, like Captain Brice, Royal Navy, her ladyship's brother, has an affair). The catch is that we are shown some of the less interesting characters (the foolish Chater, the brainless Brice) but not some of the more promising ones (Mrs. Chater, Lord Byron).

In the modern scenes, we get the three young Coverlys of today: Valentine, a mathematician in love with Hannah Jarvis, the author of a book about Lady Caroline Lamb, Byron's mistress; his younger brother, the autistic Gus, also taken with Hannah; and their sister, Chloë, a flighty young woman with a crush on Bernard Nightingale, a literary don doing research on Byron at Sidley Park. And we get Hannah herself, doing research for her next book on the life of the mysterious hermit of Sidley Park, and thus on the entire Coverly clan.

There are all kinds of parallels and divergences between the "old" story and the "new"; also some curious misreadings of the past by the present-day researchers, which contrast with the true story as we see it unfurl. The concinnity with which the two stories correspond or don't (with interesting insights into the triumphs and fiascoes of scholarship), and the way past and present—even if only figuratively—finally intermingle, are almost fiendishly crafty. But in the end, Stoppard—who never went to university and has an autodidact's infatuation with his homemade erudition—overdoes it: There are goodly chunks of the play that seem to have been written for the delectation of graduate students in literature and science, and you often wish Stoppard would rein in his parade.

Take this, for example: "English landscape was invented by gardeners imitating foreign painters who were evoking classical authors. The whole thing was brought home in the luggage from the grand tour. Here, look—Capability Brown doing Claude, who was doing Virgil. Arcadia! And here, superimposed by Richard Noakes, untamed nature in the style of Salvator Rosa. It's the gothic novel expressed in landscape." And then all those references to Francis Jeffrey and *The Edinburgh Review,* Southey's verse epics, Fermat's last theorem, iterated algorithms, etc., etc. —some of which was cut from the New York production, but much of which remains *pour épater les bourgeois.* Stoppard may end up like the man, cited by the physicist, philosopher, and wit Georg Christoph Lichtenberg, who "had so much intellect [*Verstand*] that he could be put to almost no earthly use."

In the London production, the much finer English cast (having, moreover, no problems with accents) just about managed the almost impossible task of making these distilled, volatile words become flesh; under the same canny director, Trevor Nunn, the American cast finds it a lot harder to cope.

John Lahr   (review date 17 April 1995)

SOURCE: "Blowing Hot and Cold," in *The New Yorker,* Vol. LXXI, No. 8, April 17, 1995, pp. 111-13.

[*Lahr is an award-winning American critic, nonfiction writer, playwright, novelist, biographer, and editor. In the review below, he discusses the interplay between chaos and order as well as the past and present in* Arcadia.]

In Tom Stoppard's 1966 novel, *Lord Malquist and Mr. Moon,* Malquist remarks, "Since we cannot hope for order, let us withdraw with style from the chaos." This notion has made Stoppard a very rich man. He says that his favorite line in modern English drama is from Christopher Hampton's *The Philanthropist*: "I'm a man of no convictions—at least, I *think* I am." Over the years, in twenty-one plays, Stoppard has turned his spectacular neutrality into a high-wire act of doubt. "I write plays because dialogue is the most respectable way of contradicting myself," he once explained. The three-ring circus of Stoppard's mind pulls them in at the box office, where news of the intellect, as opposed to the emotions, is a rarity. Marvel at his marriage of Beckett and Shakespeare in the death-defying clown act of *Rosencrantz and Guildenstern Are Dead* (1967). Watch him play with logical positivism and the meaning of God in *Jumpers* (1972). See him juggle Oscar Wilde, James Joyce, and Lenin in *Travesties* (1974). Stoppard's mental acrobatics flatter an audience's intelligence and camouflage the avowed limits of his plotting and his heart.

In *Arcadia,* at the Vivian Beaumont—to my mind, his best play so far—Stoppard is serving up another intellectual stew (the recipe includes "a seasoning of chaos and a pinch of thermodynamics following a dash of quantum mechanics," he says), but with a difference. Stoppard, whose stock-in-trade is parody, which is skepticism in cap and bells, has found a metaphor that takes him beyond parody to vision. Here, despite some casting glitches, Trevor

Nunn's elegant production pits the heart against the head in a subtle theatrical equation, which factors out into a moving ambiguity.

The play begins and ends with an image of Eden before the Fall. In this lush, tranquil landscape, painted onto a curtain, lit from behind, that wraps around the thrust stage like a kind of illuminated lampshade, no animals and no fear intrude on perfect pastoral harmony as Eve holds out to Adam the Apple of Knowledge. Only scudding gray clouds in the background suggest the confusion about to beset mankind once Adam takes a bite. The consequence of curiosity, once the curtain goes up, is a vaudeville of consciousness in a fallen world. "Septimus, what is carnal embrace?" the thirteen-year-old math brain truster Thomasina Coverly (the pert Jennifer Dundas) asks her handsome tutor, Septimus Hodge, in the play's first line. The question mirrors the image of Paradise about to be lost, and Stoppard's play goes on to answer her question. To embrace the flesh is also to embrace all the sins that the flesh is heir to—the sins to which Stoppard's labyrinthine plot, whose ingenious twists and turns involve greed, rapacity, vainglory, skulduggery, cruelty, delusion, confusion, and genius, bears ample witness.

The brilliance of **Arcadia** is not so much in the wordplay as it is in the construction. Stoppard has built his story along two time lines: life at Sidley Park, the Coverlys' country house in Derbyshire, in 1809, and life at present in the same house, where a couple of academics are picking over the bric-a-brac of Coverly family history. The action is set in a high-ceilinged room of grand Georgian design, which is dominated by a large oblong table cluttered with books, implements of learning, and a dozy pet turtle. A fissure in the cupola of Mark Thompson's shrewdly designed interior is the only physical hint of the skewing of world views that takes place around the table as the play shuttles back and forth in a nanosecond between centuries. (Actors in one time frame exit as actors from the other enter.) By crosscutting the Coverly family story and the story of the contemporaries trying to reconstruct it, Stoppard utilizes the ironies of history—the symmetries and accidents that lead, nonetheless, to a kind of order—as a way of demonstrating the outcome of chaos theory; that is, as the program note explains to us scientific simpletons, how reality "can be both deterministic and unpredictable." This is an enormous theatrical feat—a kind of intellectual mystery story—in which Stoppard provides the audience with the exhilarating illusion of omniscience. We become cosmic detectives, outside time, solving the riddle of history from the clues and connections that we see but the characters, who are caught in time, do not. For instance, the equation that Thomasina works out to explain the asymmetry of a leaf, her "New Geometry of Irregular Forms," later turns out, with the help of computers, to undo the assumptions of Newtonian physics. She is to classical mathematics what Picasso is to art history. The spirited youngster, who shouts "Phooey to Death!" in the first scene, works out a formula that, by the last scene, prophesies the ultimate doom of the universe, which is collapsing like a chocolate soufflé from the slow loss of heat. Even Thomasina's offhand doodle on the landscape architect's plans for a Gothic vista at Sidley

Park—she sketches a hermit to inhabit the planned Romantic hermitage—turns out to have been a prophecy of Septimus Hodge's destiny. The caprices of history, like the accidents that become inevitabilities in a plot, are the charms of chance that Stoppard and the audience stand in awe of.

Life's terrifying randomness is a mystery that compels mankind to impose order. Chaos is psychologically intolerable; man's need for coherence is greater than his need for truth. Landscape, like ritual, is consoling because it holds the magical promise of permanence. "English landscape was invented by gardeners imitating foreign painters who were evoking classical authors," says Hannah Jarvis (Blair Brown), a modern who is writing a book about the Sidley Park hermitage and the garden. The imaginative ideal is made into a reality; and Stoppard contrives to dramatize a moment in the life of the estate when the old illusion of reality is being adapted to fit a new one. At Sidley Park, Nature was originally tamed according to a neoclassical symmetry. The projected Romantic version, for which Stoppard supplies fascinating visual aids, is a triumph of the picturesque over the well proportioned. The planned irregularity and "naturalness" of the reimagined landscape capture the nineteenth-century drift toward Romantic individualism: from formality to spontaneity, from aristocratic public space to middle-class privacy, from the balance that reflects the Enlightenment's God of Reason to the brooding Romantic freedom that makes a god of the self. "The decline from thinking to feeling, you see," Hannah says. No wonder Septimus (Billy Crudup, making a persuasive Broadway début) refers to the landscape architect who engineers the loss of this particular version of Paradise as the Devil. "In the scheme of the garden he is as the serpent," Septimus says. The wildness of the picturesque style is an attempt to contain chaos by building the unpredictable into the landscape, just as Thomasina, in her algebraic equation, is unwittingly introducing chaos into the physical laws of life.

Meanwhile, the lives and loves of these citizens take their apparently ordinary lustful course. The philandering Septimus cunningly evades a duel with the cuckolded poet Ezra Chater (Paul Giamatti), who enters in fury and exits in flattery, inscribing Hodge's copy of his poem "The Couch of Eros," after the tutor, lying, promises to review it favorably. "Did Mrs. Chater know of this before she—before you—" Chater sputters, seeing his wife's infidelity not as a leg over for her but as a leg up the literary ladder for him. Septimus encourages this delusion, and Chater is triumphant. "There is nothing that woman would not do for me," he crows, thereby illustrating Stoppard's larger theme—that people will rationalize anything to avoid chaos.

The compulsion for coherence has its comic apotheosis in the biographical sleuthing of Bernard Nightingale, a don from Sussex University who is a whirlwind of spurious intellectual connections. Nightingale (played with swaggering and hilarious arrogance by Victor Garber) has stumbled on the copy of Chater's "The Couch of Eros" that contains both the poet's inscription and an unnamed challenge to a duel, and he has traced the volume to Byron's

> **The brilliance of *Arcadia* is not so much in the wordplay as it is in the construction. Stoppard has built his story along two time lines: life at Sidley Park in 1809, and life at present in the same house.**
>
> —*John Lahr*

library. A literary climber of the first order, Nightingale sniffs a mother lode of lit-crit kudos in making the connection between Byron and Chater. No one is better at this kind of academic flimflammery than Stoppard, and he has a good time teasing the literary second-guessing that too often passes for biography. Within minutes of insinuating himself into Sidley Park, and Hannah's orbit, Nightingale is spinning his academic wheels and turning what we know to be Septimus's face-saving deceit into a sensational case of adultery, literary infighting, and the death of Chater in a duel with Byron after the latter poet's devastating review of Chater's work appears in *Piccadilly Recreation.* "Without question, Ezra Chater issued a challenge to *somebody,*" Nightingale says, reading from his completed paper in the tour-de-force opening of Act II. "Without question, Lord Byron, in the very season of his emergence as a literary figure, quit the country in a cloud of panic and mystery, and stayed abroad for two years at a time when Continental travel was unusual and dangerous. If we seek his reason—*do we need to look far?*" Hellbent on literary glory, Nightingale rushes past the truth—"Is it likely that the man Chater calls his friend Septimus Hodge is the same man who screwed his wife and kicked the shit out of his last book?" The paper is proof positive of the cynic's adage that "history is something that never happened written by someone who was never there."

Arcadia uses intellectual argument as a kind of riptide to pull the audience under the playful surface of romance with which the characters in both time frames fill their days and nights. In *Arcadia*'s comic conceit, seismic intellectual shifts are treated as superficial, while superficial changes of the heart are treated as monumental. For the evening to work, the audience must feel the pull of sexuality as well as the play of knowledge. In London, with Felicity Kendal, Emma Fielding, and Harriet Walter in the major female roles, the erotic amperage was high; here, though, the American actresses can articulate the words but not the sexy twinkle beneath them. As Hannah, Blair Brown shows a sharp intelligence, but she can't give Stoppard's lines that nervy bluestocking spin which flirts with learning and turns the alarming into the charming. "Oh, shut up," she tells Nightingale, when he is upbraiding her after discovering she has written a letter to the London *Times* giving the facts of Chater's death. (He was killed by a monkey bite in Martinique after discovering the dwarf dahlia.) "It'll be very short, very dry, absolutely gloat-free," she says of her letter. "Would you rather it were one of your friends?" The strut of Stoppard's epi-

grams is also missed by Lisa Banes as Lady Croom, who delivers some of the most delightful *mots* without the louche aristocratic aura of entitlement that makes them properly pay off. "Do not dabble in paradox," she says to Captain Brice (David Manis). "It puts you in danger of fortuitous wit." Even the pint-size Jennifer Dundas, who has the smarts to make Thomasina a credible, if cloying, prodigy, hasn't the stature to make her a compelling object of desire. The cumulative effect is not to undermine the production but to dim it.

Still, the brilliance of Stoppard's metaphor shines through. In the final scene, Thomasina is horsing around with her brother when Septimus enters with her latest diagrams under his arm. "Order, order!" Septimus shouts to his rambunctious pupil, now nearly seventeen years old, who would rather waltz than work. By the end of the scene, when Septimus comprehends her latest equation, he sees that order—the Enlightenment notion of it—has entirely collapsed. Now the time frames merge, with the characters in the present overlapping with and commenting on the issues raised by characters in the past. "It's a diagram of heat exchange," says Valentine Coverly, a graduate student of mathematics (played expertly by Robert Sean Leonard), looking at the same diagrams that Septimus is studying. Septimus looks up. "So, we are all doomed," he says. "Yes," Thomasina answers cheerfully, not knowing that she is soon to become another integer in her equation of chaos. (She will perish the same night in a fire; and Septimus will become the hermit of Sidley Park, speaking to no one except his pet turtle.) But for the moment, with the geometry of the universe's doom in his hand, Septimus says, "When we have found all the mysteries and lost all the meaning, we will be alone, on an empty shore."

At the prospect of such an awesome, godless void, Thomasina suggests that they dance, and finally gets Septimus to his feet. The audience knows the outcome but the dancers don't: they live in the comedy of the moment, not in the tragedy of history. Hannah waltzes with Gus Coverly (John Griffin), a smitten teen-ager who has given her the final piece of the puzzle of Septimus's story. Together, the couples whirl around the old table covered with the inventory of centuries of learning. The ravishing image moves the play, in its last beats, from story to statement. The dance becomes the dance of time: one awkward, one graceful; one in celebration, one in resignation. The waltz, an act of grace in the face of gloom, is a perfect embodiment of Stoppard's spiritual standoff. Playwriting, like the dancing, is a way of giving off heat in a cooling universe: an assertion and an abdication at the same time. It's the dance of a stoic, and, from where I sit, it is brave and very beautiful.

Tim Appelo   (review date 1 May 1995)

SOURCE: A review of *Arcadia,* in *The Nation,* New York, Vol. 260, No. 17, May 1, 1995, pp. 612-13.

> [*Arcadia's*] vaulting erudition, the sorites of Chinese boxes cunningly ensconced within one another, become too much: Allusions and metaphors zoom across the stage like comets and meteors, and constellations of characters regroup in dizzying configurations. What gets totally lost in Stoppard's dramaturgy is people.
>
> —*John Simon, in "A Little Suff'ring," in* New York, *July 26, 1993.*

[*In the review below, Appelo remarks favorably on* Arcadia.]

In *Ulysses,* there is an Oxford don who goes around pushing a lawnmower that chuffs "Clevercleverclever." Though he quit school at 17 and ran off to the circus of newspaper journalism, Tom Stoppard has always been very like Joyce's professor, forever cramming his head with arcane books and emitting their more entertaining notions in clipped, endlessly articulate, witty disputations. The question has always been whether Stoppard is anything more than clevercleverclever—is he simply a prestidigitator of prose and a joke mechanic, a whiz kid staging fantastically elaborate intellectual collisions as if they were toy-train wrecks? Or is he in it for deeper satisfactions than the transitory sparks a nice crackup tosses off?

Stoppard himself has admitted that his early play *The Real Inspector Hound* (1968) was "a mechanical toy," but his work has been getting more human ever since. There's more of *him* in his later work, too; he is a recovering drama critic who began as a playwright by occupying other people's plays like a hermit crab. Pre-fame, he aped Robert Bolt and Arthur Miller; in *Rosencrantz and Guildenstern Are Dead* it was Beckett and Shakespeare; in *Hound,* Agatha Christie; in *Travesties,* Oscar Wilde. Starting with *Night and Day* (1978), he's tended to cling less to coattails and be more his own man, owning up to real emotions. He retains a perverse sense of humor akin to Beckett's; he's debate-besotted like Shaw, but he can see both sides of most questions; he's unearthly fluent and funny like Wilde, though he's grown more earnest. Yet his dramatic ideal remains what it was back in 1960, when he raved Richard Attenborough's *The Angry Silence* because it fused "entertainment and education as completely as a row of chorus girls explaining Einstein's theory of light." His plays are, I think, a highly refined, mutant strain of journalism.

If all we had to go on was *Hapgood,* the 1988 faux-spy thriller that recently closed at Lincoln Center after a smash production, we might think the old rap on Stoppard still had some currency. The gratuitous beauty of the staging and the performances by David Straithairn as a droll physicist-philosopher and Stockard Channing as the eponymous spymaster heroine (whose name, according to Stoppard scholar Katherine E. Kelly, refers to turn-of-the-century Russian literature translator and *Nation* contributor Isabel Florence Hapgood) might blind us to the fact that *Hapgood* is lively without being good. Stoppard seems not to give a rip about his incomprehensibly intricate le Carré-pastiche plot, let alone his characters. ("I'm no good at character," he once confessed, amazingly. "It doesn't interest me very much.") What has interested him lately is post-Newtonian physics, and *Hapgood* is a physics essay masquerading as a play. As Updike said of Bellow's *The Dean's December,* a novel that began as an essay, "This book has swallowed the earlier one but has transparent sides, so that we can see the non-fiction book inside the novel and can observe how incomplete the digestion process has been."

Incomplete intellectual digestion is a besetting sin of authors who read too much. Stoppard has been the chief of sinners in this regard, conducting his education at public expense; but he now redeems himself with *Arcadia,* at the Vivian Beaumont at Lincoln Center, his most important work since *The Real Thing* (1983). Unlike the spy-jive macguffins he juggles in *Hapgood,* the mystery addressed in *Arcadia* is one to which Stoppard is fully emotionally committed. If all those cigarettes kill him shortly, *Arcadia* is almost good enough to serve as the capstone to his career.

The setting, nicely realized by Mark Thompson, is the English country house of the Coverlys (I assume Stoppard alludes to Addison's squire Roger). There are two dueling story lines, exhilaratingly orchestrated by director Trevor Nunn, concerning the Coverlys of 1809 and of today. In the earlier frame, we are introduced to chaos theory by teenager Thomasina Coverly, who is based on its modern prophet, Benoit Mandelbrot, whose "Mandelbrot set," infinitely iterated images of the order lurking within nature's seeming disorder, you have seen depicted in a million articles about chaos. Like Mandelbrot, Thomasina (fetching but conventionally so, as played by Jennifer Dundas) is no math prodigy, but she can actually see the subtle geometry of chaos in her head. Her tutor is the Newtonian college math major Septimus Hodge. (Hodge was the name of Samuel Johnson's spoiled, oyster-eating cat, and this cat, smartly portrayed by Billy Crudup, is the spoiled, horny house guest of the Coverlys.) Hodge is baffled by Thomasina's dazzling musings about how post-Newtonian physics demolishes determinism. Forget Euclid and his lovely inviolable rules, Thomasina pouts, and let's look at the real world: "Mountains are not pyramids and trees are not cones."

Hodge is more preoccupied with brassiere cones, and the calculations necessary to remove them while dallying with another's wife in the gazebo by night. His machinations after being discovered *in flagrante* with fellow house guest Charity Chater by her sputtering husband, Ezra, propel the Feydeau-style Restoration comedy that leavens the mathematical debate. But the sex farce isn't purely frivolous—in Stoppard's mind, romance is the welcome snake that saves Eden from the overdetermination of natural law. As one character puts it, illicit sex is "the attraction that Newton left out. All the way back to the apple in the garden."

Arcadia's twentieth-century scenes are devoted to two interrelated detective stories about the 1809 characters. In the first, Thomasina's modern relative and fellow mathematician Valentine (the vulnerably lovely Robert Sean Leonard of *Dead Poets Society* fame) incredulously discovers Thomasina's eerily prescient equations (just as Mandelbrot rediscovered Gaston Julia's World War I-era documents in 1979), and, like Mandelbrot, uses a computer to extend and validate the earlier work.

Thomasina's vindication is a foregone conclusion, because her "New Geometry of Irregular Forms" is simply modern physics, and because her theme is the point of the play: that determinism is false, that fate and free will are like waltzing mice, that life is messy, so eat it over the sink. A similar lesson is learned by the second set of modern-day detectives: two literary historians, Hannah Jarvis (brassy Blair Brown) and Bernard Nightingale (vainglorious Victor Garber), who have descended on the Coverlys' Arcadia to mine the place for career advancement. Nightingale's ingeniously erroneous theory about what really happened in the house in 1809—he believes Lord Byron shot Ezra Chater dead in a duel—is the entertainment engine of *Arcadia,* a tour de force of scholarly folly that sets up Garber as the star of the show. We may have to struggle to keep the rest of the plot straight, but since we've seen what really happened in 1809, we can have great fun watching Nightingale pump up his ego until it explodes. "Is the universe expanding?" he demands. "Is it contracting? Is it standing on one leg and singing 'When Father Painted the Parlour'? Leave me out. I can expand my universe without you."

In making a laughingstock of Nightingale, a Euclidean type without a trace of humility in the face of nature, Stoppard is really recanting his old line about maintaining "the courage of my lack of convictions" through a scrupulous aestheticism. Now he seems more on the level, less distanced from his material, as the art-for-art's-sake, inflexibly arrogant argument loses big.

Nowhere is this clearer than in *Arcadia*'s deeply moving final scene, where the worlds of 1809 and the present do not so much collide as coincide. It is the night before Thomasina's 17th birthday, and if she knows something about the future of physics that nobody else does, the modern Valentine and Hannah (and we in the audience) know a terrible secret about her future that she does not. I can't indicate on the page just how he does this, but Stoppard blends the dialogue and actions of modern and long-vanished characters in a way quite different from his usual comic convergences. He's long been the master of people talking past each other, but here their conversations embrace across the centuries. Valentine finally figures out Thomasina's immortal discovery—that she, and we, are demonstrably, mathematically, doomed—but instead of going for the sixties-style cosmic laugh, Stoppard makes the revelation a moment of rueful acceptance. The dia-

logue pointedly echoes Eliot's *Four Quartets,* and the vibe is that of the late Shakespearean fables, spectral but deeply charged with feeling.

David Merrick, the producer of Stoppard's first hit, *Rosencrantz and Guildenstern Are Dead,* complained that if you took the main characters and put them on a graph, "they would all come out as one line." *Arcadia*'s plots may leave the play with more characters than it can comfortably handle, but the main ones describe an elegant arabesque worthy of Mandelbrot himself.

Anne Barton   (review date 8 June 1995)

SOURCE: "Twice Around the Grounds," in *The New York Review of Books,* Vol. XLII, No. 10, June 8, 1995, pp. 28-30, 32.

[*An American-born English educator and critic, Barton has written extensively on English drama. In the review below, she discusses language and theme in* Arcadia, *particularly the interaction between the past and present.*]

> "Allow me," said Mr. Gall. "I distinguish the picturesque and the beautiful, and I add to them, in the laying out of grounds, a third and distinct character, which I call *unexpectedness.*"
>
> "Pray, sir," said Mr. Milestone, "by what name do you distinguish this character, when a person walks round the grounds for the second time?"
>
> Mr. Gall bit his lips, and inwardly vowed to revenge himself on Milestone, by cutting up his next publication.
>
> —Thomas Love Peacock, *Headlong Hall* (1815)

In *Headlong Hall,* the earliest of Peacock's satirical novels, a motley collection of guests assembles at Squire Headlong's country estate for the Christmas season. Among them are Mr. Gall, the vitriolic reviewer, Philomela Poppyseed, the best-selling novelist, the poet Nightshade, Marmaduke Milestone, the landscape architect and "improver" of gentlemen's grounds, Mr. Cranium, exponent of the new "science" of phrenology, and his lovely daughter Cephalis, Mr. Escot, the embattled vegetarian and believer in the steady deterioration of the world, and his opponent Mr. Foster, who maintains that mankind is progressing steadily toward perfection.

Real people can be glimpsed behind many of these characters as they argue, and pair off in marriage. Gall, for instance, is Francis Jeffrey of the contemporary *Edinburgh Review;* Miss Poppyseed is based on the novelist Amelia Opie; Escot and Foster embody different aspects of Peacock's friend Shelley, while in Milestone he has amalgamated Humphry Repton (1752-1818) with his famous predecessor Lancelot "Capability" Brown (1716-1783). Repton liked to present clients with a book bound in red leather in which watercolor sketches of their estate could be folded back to reveal cutout projections of how it might look after his improvements. Brown, some of whose work still survives at Stowe and Blenheim Palace, acquired his nickname from a habit of assuring prospective patrons of the great "capabilities" of their grounds. The most celebrated of those eighteenth- and early nineteenth-century landscape gardeners who attempted to smooth out and compose nature until it resembled an idealized painting of Arcadia or the Elysian Fields by Poussin or Claude Lorrain, he once encountered a gentleman who expressed an earnest desire to predecease Brown, "because I want to see Heaven before you have 'improved' it."

Tom Stoppard claims that for some years now he has seldom picked up a novel. But *Headlong Hall,* whenever he read it, clearly left a powerful impression. Squire Headlong's country estate relates to Sidley Park, the equally fictitious setting for *Arcadia,* rather like one of the paired "before" and "after" views in Repton's Red Books. Stoppard, indeed, wittily half-acknowledges his indebtedness in Act I, by way of an account of Sidley Park around 1830, written (we are told) "by the author of *Headlong Hall.*" When Bernard Nightingale, Stoppard's pushy academic, requires an alias in a hurry, "Peacock," not accidentally, turns out to be the chosen name. Like *Headlong Hall,* Stoppard's play assembles disputatious visitors—among them a landscape architect, two poets, a female author, and a savage book reviewer—in a great country house. There they proceed to argue with the family and each other, not only about matters of taste in the formal landscaping of a park but about writers and literary critics, new scientific discoveries, and the future of the human race. They also find time to make love.

Arcadia is, at last, the full-length work Stoppard said in 1974—after the success of *Jumpers* (1972) and *Travesties* (1974)—he really wanted to write: "Something that takes place in a whitewashed room with no music and no jumping about . . . so that the energy can go into the literary side of what I do. I'd like to write a quiet play" [interview with Ronald Hayman (June 1974), in *Tom Stoppard,* by Ronald Hayman, 1982]. The schoolroom at Sidley Park, where all of *Arcadia* takes place, is not exactly a "whitewashed room"—it has scale and a certain architectural grandeur—but in Mark Thompson's set at Lincoln Center, as in London, it "looks bare," just as Stoppard specifies it should. Certainly, its furnishings are minimal. In Trevor Nunn's New York restaging with American actors of his original (1993) English production, the landscape framed by the room's French windows (some trailing foliage, and beyond it an expanse of grass obscured by mist that, between scenes, becomes low, fast-moving clouds) suggests extensive, hidden vistas.

The backdrop itself, however, remains timelessly noncommittal. Stoppard's play alternates for six of its seven scenes between 1809 and now. Then, in a long final movement, the present is hauntingly made to coexist on stage with the year 1812. Only the theater audience is privileged to participate in both: seeing and overhearing all these characters, the living and the dead, whose voices Stoppard brilliantly interweaves across the gap of 183 years, in a room that all of them have known. Like the backdrop, the room scarcely alters. The few scattered objects visible in 1809 and 1812 are still present at the end of the twentieth century, including Plautus the pet tortoise, even if someone has changed his name. As for music, although Stoppard has certainly not abandoned it, Jeremy Sams's score is for the most part unobtrusive and subdued: a clarinet, a saxo-

phone, an early piano sometimes played badly, sometimes well, but always offstage.

In theatrical terms, too, *Arcadia* is muted by comparison with most of Stoppard's previous work. No yellow-suited gymnasts dangerously construct and implode human pyramids (*Jumpers*); nor does an entire troupe of traveling actors stow away—and improbably contrive a musical performance—inside three barrels (*Rosencrantz and Guildenstern Are Dead,* 1967); no drama critic gets surprised and killed by the play he is reviewing (*The Real Inspector Hound,* 1968), nor is there any equivalent to the public librarian in *Travesties,* who seems to strip on top of her desk while delivering a heartfelt panegyric on Lenin.

Visually, nothing in *Arcadia* even approaches the dizzying play with briefcases and Russian twins in *Hapgood* (1988), let alone the surrealist tableau which confronts audiences at the start of *After Magritte* (1970)—Mother stretched out on the ironing board, while a man standing on a wooden chair, and wearing green rubber fishing waders over evening-dress trousers, apparently tries to blow out the electric light. In *Arcadia,* not only do two of the most important guests at Sidley Park, Lord Byron and the lascivious Mrs. Chater, remain tantalizingly offstage; all the really arresting events are invisible. It is typical of this play that the most startling (and also the most heart-wrenching) thing to happen in it should be the almost casual disclosure, close to the end, that nearly two hundred years earlier an exceptionally talented young girl met an accidental and senseless death.

Arcadia is wonderfully inventive and funny, full of the epigrams, puns, and verbal pyrotechnics characteristic of this dramatist. From the interchange between thirteen-year-old Thomasina Coverly and her tutor with which the play begins—"Septimus, what is carnal embrace?" "Carnal embrace is the practice of throwing one's arms around a side of beef"—to the end, Stoppard's highly individual love affair with the English language never slackens. For the very existence of that relationship, one is obliged to thank a combination of global warfare and pure chance. He was born Tomas Straussler, in the Czechoslovakia of 1937, and his family's removal to Singapore, evacuation to India, then residence in England itself from 1946, after Stoppard's widowed mother remarried, have determined the language in which he writes. Stoppard's fascination with twentieth-century linguistic philosophy—Wittgenstein, G.E. Moore, A.J. Ayer—and with the perplexed relationship of words to the "reality" they purport to describe, is manifest in a number of his plays. It has always been partnered, however, by a freewheeling delight in words that seems distinctively Elizabethan.

Stoppard's puns, far from being drearily Derridean, are something Shakespeare would have understood. He loves to demonstrate how exciting it can be when two meanings (as Tony Tanner puts it in *Adultery and the Novel*) lie down together irregularly in the same bed: as they do when Thomasina's "carnal," meaning "sensual," cohabits disconcertingly with its other connotation of "meat." *Arcadia* carries on and extends Stoppard's long-term association of wordplay with sexual transgression. What is new here is that elegiac, almost Virgilian quality signaled in the title of the comedy itself. This "quiet play" is one of Stoppard's finest. But it raises, in an acute form, the question asked by Peacock's Mr. Milestone: Does it matter if you walk only once around the grounds, or twice?

Arcadia is wonderfully inventive and funny, full of the epigrams, puns, and verbal pyrotechnics characteristic of Stoppard. From beginning to end, Stoppard's highly individual love affair with the English language never slackens.

—Anne Barton

Stoppard's plays, even **Rosencrantz and Guildenstern Are Dead,** now a prescribed text in many British schools, have provoked mixed reactions from academics and theater critics alike. No one has ever denied the cleverness and consummate craftsmanship of his twenty-odd works for radio, television, and the stage, or the urgency of Stoppard's ambition to achieve what he calls "the perfect marriage between the play of ideas and farce or perhaps even high comedy" ["Ambushes for an Audience: Towards a High Comedy of Ideas," in *Theatre Quarterly* (May-July 1974)]. His detractors, on the other hand, accuse him of game-playing for its own sake, of being persistently overweight with intellectual baggage, and of emptiness and chill. It has been said that he dodges political issues—an allegation harder to sustain after **Every Good Boy Deserves Favour** (1977), **Professional Foul** (1977), **Cahoot's Macbeth** (1979), and **Squaring the Circle** (1980-1981)—that most of his women are caricatures, and that when he does take them seriously (Annie in **The Real Thing,** 1982, or the protagonist of **Hapgood**), they fail to convince. Most consistent of all have been complaints that his plays, however masterfully constructed, are difficult for audiences to follow in the theater, or even (in some cases) on the printed page.

Stoppard has defended himself by pointing out that he writes in more than one mode, that it is inappropriate to judge an exquisite farce mechanism such as **The Real Inspector Hound** as though it aspired to the condition of high comedy, and that his real interest lies less in character than in dialogue and "the felicitous expression of ideas" ["Full Stoppard," an interview with Stephen Schiff (May 1989), reprinted in *Tom Stoppard in Conversation,* edited by Paul Delaney, 1994]. When various philosophical journals sniped at his account of Wittgenstein and British logical positivism as incorporated in **Jumpers,** he was able to take comfort from the fact that no less a figure than A.J. Ayer instantly rose to his defense. (A lingering distrust of academics remains evident in **Arcadia**'s portrait of Nightingale, the arrogant and insensitive Sussex don.) Stoppard has always maintained that his work, for all its dazzle, is grounded in humane and moral concerns, a claim that on the whole seems justified. Altogether more debatable is his insistence that, although he may in some

instances want to mystify audiences (he has admitted to creating a number of deliberately incomprehensible first scenes), his plays are meant to communicate in the theater, with no need for elucidation through recourse to the published text. Certainly **Arcadia,** despite its readily available surface fun, is not easy to appreciate fully the first time around in its acted or (indeed) even its printed form.

Audiences are not required to digest a great deal of plot in **Arcadia**—certainly nothing resembling the narrative perplexities of **Hapgood,** Stoppard's last full-length play. Basically, what happens is that in 1809, the young tutor in residence at Sidley Park, Byron's schoolfellow Septimus Hodge, is detected in an al fresco "carnal embrace" with the wife of Ezra Chater, a visiting poetaster. A duel is avoided only because Mrs. Chater collides that night with her equally lustful hostess, Lady Croom, on the threshold of Lord Byron's bedroom, and Byron and the two Chaters hastily leave the house. During all this, Mr. Noakes, the landscape architect, is preparing to replace Capability Brown's Arcadian paradise at Sidley Park with grounds in the picturesque style of Salvator Rosa: irregular, gloomy, and mock-wild, complete with a Gothic hermitage for which a resident hermit has yet to be found.

Meanwhile, Thomasina, the nubile and brilliant Croom daughter, quietly pursues the missing mathematical proof for Fermat's last theorem, questioning Newtonian physics, and feeling her way both toward what is now called the Second Law of Thermodynamics, and those iterated algorithms from which (with the help of computers) fractal mathematics and chaos theory have, in our own time, been born. The only character in the play to express enthusiasm for Mr. Noakes's plans, she does so not, like Peacock's Miss Tenorina, out of a Romantic passion for mossy, Gothic structures and woods "thick, intricate and gloomy," but because Noakes's jagged shapes and unkempt trees speak to her own developing sense that there is something wrong with the tidy symmetries of Euclidean geometry.

In Stoppard's interspersed scenes set in the present, two very different guests at Sidley Park try to piece together what happened there between 1809 and 1812. Hannah Jarvis, author of a popular book about Byron's mistress Lady Caroline Lamb, is hoping to write about the unidentified recluse (the "idiot in the landscape," or perhaps he represents "the Age of Enlightenment banished into the Romantic wilderness"?) who ended up living and dying in Mr. Noakes's hermitage. Bernard Nightingale, hot on the trail of academic fame, believes he can prove that Byron killed Ezra Chater in a duel at Sidley Park and for that reason was obliged to leave England in haste. (Stoppard may shy away from novels these days; it seems likely nonetheless that Nightingale and Hannah owe something to Roland Michell and the prickly Maud Bailey, A.S. Byatt's two literary sleuths in *Possession,* which won the Booker Prize in 1990.) Neither Hannah nor Nightingale gets everything right, but Hannah comes far closer to the truth than her rival. That is largely because, despite her temperamental preference for the clipped and formal Italian garden which dominated Sidley Park before the arrival of either Capability Brown or Mr. Noakes, she shares with the long-dead Thomasina not only a fiercely logical mind but certain intuitive powers.

These last allow her to grasp truths (including that of Thomasina's brilliance) independently of reason. Valentine, a research mathematician and future Earl of Croom, who is working with data supplied by his family's game books, cannot credit Thomasina's breakthrough, even after the equations she scribbled in an old mathematics primer, run a few million times though his computer, provide him with a publishable paper. (Thomasina, he insists, could have possessed neither the requisite mathematics nor the computer.) Hannah's sympathetic insights, however, attract to her Gus, Valentine's younger brother, the totally mute, autistic boy in whom something of Thomasina's genius survives. (He improvises brilliantly on the piano, and can identify the site of Capability Brown's boathouse when all the experts fail.) It is Gus who bestows on Hannah at the end Thomasina's drawing of "Septimus holding Plautus," the puzzle's most important missing piece.

That audiences have tended, both in New York and London, to leave *Arcadia* with a newly purchased copy of the text in hand is not really surprising. Many of the New York reviewers, even some who did take the precaution of reading the play in advance, apparently failed to register that three separate moments of time are juxtaposed in the comedy: one day in 1812, as well as three in 1809, and one in the present. This matters. Lord Byron, a charismatic but obscure guest at Sidley Park in 1809, has returned from his travels in 1812 to become London's darling, the lionized author of *Childe Harold;* Ezra Chater has died of a monkey bite in Martinique; his widow has remarried, and Lady Croom has reluctantly transferred her attentions from Byron to an exiled Polish count. Most important of all, Thomasina, no longer a child, is about to turn seventeen and (failing just as her mother did to capture Lord Byron) has fallen in love with her tutor. It also matters that the young and voluble Augustus Coverly of 1812 should not be confused, as he was by one New York reviewer, with his silent twentieth-century namesake. (John Griffin plays both parts.)

In a play that seems obsessed with the number three (a palimpsest of three gardens, three instances of "carnal embrace" in the gazebo/hermitage, three important mathematical issues), it is by no means easy to keep straight the two groups of three letters upon which so much hangs: the two challenges and the clandestine note from Mrs. Chater from which Bernard Nightingale draws so many erroneous conclusions, all originally secreted by Septimus Hodge between the pages of Chater's dreadful poem *The Couch of Eros,* or the two by Septimus and one from Lord Byron that are written and almost immediately destroyed.

The plain fact is that once around the garden is not enough. It is true, as Peacock's Mr. Milestone pointed out, that the element of surprise must be greatly reduced on any repeated circuit. In the case of *Arcadia,* that can result from a return to the theater, or a second experience with the printed page. Once you know that Thomasina is going to die in a matter of hours after the curtain finally goes down on her first (and last) waltz, or (assuming you have not studied the cast list closely) that Lord Byron and Mrs.

Chater will never materialize, it is impossible to forget these things—even as it is impossible not to remember during a return visit to Beaumont and Fletcher's *A King and No King* (1611), or *Philaster* (1609) that Arbaces and Panthea are not really brother and sister and will be able to marry, or that the pageboy Bellario is a girl. Brilliant theater craftsmen that they were, Fletcher and his collaborator were entirely aware that few plays, unless they are notably unsuccessful, can enjoy a perpetual first night. They guarded against potential letdown by ensuring that to visit theirs twice would be distinctively different—and richer—than once. Audiences no longer ambushed by the unexpected can savor nuances and details invisible on the first occasion, because of the things that, now, they know. Like *Philaster* and *A King and No King, Arcadia* is in a sense not one play but two.

On balance, Nunn's cast in New York is stronger than the one he had in London. As Lady Croom, Lisa Banes is far superior to the National's tiresomely arch and mannered Harriet Walter, a fine actress horribly miscast. Billy Crudup makes a handsome and sensitive Septimus. As Hannah, Blair Brown projects the right mixture of defensiveness and acerbity, while Victor Garber succeeds vividly in reminding at least some members of the audience that almost every academic conference has its Nightingale.

Any production of *Arcadia* must, however, stand or fall on the performance of Thomasina. A child prodigy who (for once) is also entrancing, Stoppard's heroine is high-spirited and funny as well as nice. Aware even at thirteen of her tutor's passion for Lady Croom, and Lady Croom's for Byron, she is far too shrewd not to see through Septimus's bogus explanation of "carnal embrace." Yet she generously feigns ignorance when the accuracy of his revised description threatens to get him into trouble with her mother. ("It is plain that there are some things a girl is allowed to understand, and these include the whole of algebra, but there are others, such as embracing a side of beef, that must be kept from her until she is old enough to have a carcass of her own.") Nightingale would like to push every scientist in the world over a cliff ("except the one in the wheel-chair, I think I'd lose the sympathy vote"), but Thomasina cares about literature as well as equations. She weeps over the destruction of the great library at Alexandria and the lost plays of Aeschylus and Sophocles.

It is a wonderful part—but diabolically difficult for any actress to encompass as a whole. In London, Emma Fielding could manage the older Thomasina, but was unconvincing as the child of thirteen. With the diminutive Jennifer Dundas, it is the other way round: wholly persuasive in 1809, she finds it hard to mature into the adolescent Thomasina of 1812. Most of the part, however, lies in 1809. And Dundas's very last appearance, barefoot with her candle and white nightdress on a darkening stage, pleading with Septimus to teach her how to waltz, is magical.

Stoppard is said to prepare for writing a play as though for an examination, patiently absorbing the contents of a great number of background books. For *Arcadia,* he clearly informed himself scrupulously not only about landscape gardening and post-Newtonian mathematics but about the life of Byron, that potently absent presence. Certainly Thomasina seems to derive in part from Byron's tragic daughter, Ada. Byron's estranged wife, Annabella, had dabbled in mathematics (Byron called her his "Princess of Parallelograms"), but Ada's talents were far more considerable. In collaboration with Charles Babbage, she experimented eagerly in the field of early computer science—until the demands of her role as Countess of Lovelace, and contemporary ideas of what was appropriate to her sex, pushed such inquiries aside. She ended up gambling on the races, and being blackmailed when she lost more than she could afford. Her death was early and grim. Thomasina, had she lived longer, might not have escaped such a fate. In 1812, Lady Croom is already worrying that her daughter may be "educated beyond eligibility," and is eager to marry her off.

Arcadia constantly engages the imaginary in a dialogue with the historically true. Byron really was residing at his Newstead Abbey estate in April 1809, and no letters or other testimony indicate his exact whereabouts between the 10th and the 12th, when Stoppard brings him to "nearby" Sidley Park. He did (as Nightingale is aware) publish a review of Wordsworth in the July 1807 issue of *Monthly Literary Recreations* (Stoppard's *Picadilly Recreation*), and although no letter from Peacock is quoted in any essay on "hermits" in *The Cornhill Magazine* for 1862, that is precisely the publication in which such an essay might be found. Byron was indeed adding verses to the second edition of his satire *English Bards and Scotch Reviewers* in the spring of 1809, even if a stanza ridiculing "Ezra Chater" was not among them. "Darkness," on the other hand ("I had a dream, which was not all a dream. / The bright sun was extinguish'd . . ."), suggested by the "lost summer" of 1816, when a colossal volcanic explosion in Indonesia blotted out the sun, and New England in August was covered with snow, is an entirely genuine Byronic prefiguration of that law of entropy Thomasina deduces from the work of the French mathematician Fourier: the bleak and irreversible cooling of the world. Hannah is right to quote the first lines of "Darkness" to Valentine in an attempt to persuade him that genius, whether in great poets or a gifted child, can sometimes fling open the door of a house that has not yet been built.

That Stoppard is playing witty games here with his audience is true. But these games are no more frivolous at bottom than Gus's apple, casually abandoned on the schoolroom table after he gives it, wordlessly, to Hannah at the end of scene two: an object that gradually comes to symbolize Newton's discovery of the law of gravity, the late-twentieth-century geometry of natural forms, the perils of sexuality, any paradise that is lost, and the introduction of death into the world after the Fall.

Stoppard packs an immense amount of information into *Arcadia,* but his reticences—the things he deliberately refuses to let his audience, not just Nightingale and Hannah Jarvis, ever know—loom equally large. Did Thomasina burn to death on the night before her seventeenth birthday because she was waiting for Septimus to come to her in bed, despite his principled refusal during the waltz scene, and consequently fell asleep without putting out her can-

dle? Was it really the Second Law of Thermodynamics, as set forth in Thomasina's diagram, that transformed the young tutor at Sidley Park into its despairing hermit, wearing out the rest of his days "without discourse or companion save for a pet tortoise, Plautus by name," while he tried frenziedly by way of "good English algebra" to stave off the end of the world? Or was it, fundamentally, self-reproach and grief for Thomasina herself? Stoppard refuses to say.

The problem of finding a suitable inhabitant for Mr. Noakes's new hermitage enlivens *Arcadia* throughout. Lady Croom's complaint that she can scarcely advertise ("surely a hermit who takes a newspaper is not a hermit in whom one can have complete confidence") stirs memories of the delicious episode in Richard Graves's novel *Columella, or the Distressed Anchoret* (1779), in which an out-of-work recluse arrives for an interview but is found to have been dismissed from his last employment for getting the dairymaid with child and visibly spending more time drunk than in prayer. The eighteenth- and early nineteenth-century vogue for hermits tended toward the risible, whether it involved the professionals recorded at Painshill and Stowe, or amateurs such as Gilbert White's brother Henry, the rector of Fyfield, for whom it was a party trick. (In his diary for July 28, 1763, Gilbert records the success of a tea party "at the Hermitage," to which his guests came attired as shepherds and shepherdesses, and "the Hermit appear'd to great advantage.") But Septimus Hodge is not a risible figure.

All his attempts to disprove the Second Law of Thermodynamics are doomed: with heat, you can't "run the film backwards," as Valentine tries patiently to make Hannah understand. Time runs wastefully on in only one direction, and one day there will be no time left. Septimus was wrong to console Thomasina for the burning of the library at Alexandria by assuring her that nothing is ever irretrievably lost, that even the missing plays of Sophocles will somehow turn up again. "You can put back the bits of glass," as Valentine says, "but you can't collect up the heat of the smash. It's gone." In *Arcadia* itself, on the other hand, time does run backward at the dramatist's will. In one stage direction, Stoppard meticulously explains that whereas Repton always superimposed his "before" sketch on his "after," with Noakes that order is reversed. A small point, scarcely available in the theater, it locks into place within a larger scheme of scenes that move backward in time as freely as forward. They lead to that final convergence, when the four people the play loves—Septimus and Thomasina, Hannah and Gus—dance across the centuries, as couples, to music that belongs at one moment to our own epoch, and to Byron's in the next.

Indian Ink, the new stage version of Stoppard's radio play *In the Native State* (1991), which is currently running in London, alternates 1930 with the "mid-Eighties." *Arcadia*'s "the present day," by contrast, is appropriately open-ended. The play can tacitly absorb new pieces of information. On April 24, 1995, an article in appeared the London *Times* describing a courteous, white-bearded hermit who receives occasional visitors, beside the Wolverhampton ring road, in a tent supplied by the local authorities, while trying to understand the horror of what he saw in the Second World War. It does not say if he has a pet tortoise. When the proof of Fermat's last theorem for which Thomasina is searching at the start, "the most tantalizing problem in the history of mathematics," as it has been called, was finally found last year, by someone who had been grappling with it since the age of nine (Andrew Wiles, assisted by his former student Richard Taylor), the discovery merely enriched—without overtaking—Stoppard's high comedy of ideas.

FURTHER READING

Christiansen, Richard. "Simply Brilliant." *Chicago Tribune* (14 July 1993): 18.

> Praises Stoppard's interweaving of scientific and humanistic themes in *Arcadia*.

Feeney, Joseph J. "Longing for Heaven: Four New Plays." *America* 170, No. 3 (29 January 1994): 23-6.

> Finds that *Arcadia* suggests the possibility of heaven but "presumes annihilation or, more likely, a final entropy."

Feingold, Michael. "Entropical Fevers." *The Village Voice* XL, No. 15 (11 April 1995).

> Calls *Arcadia* "astute and achingly beautiful in its philosophic paradoxes," but suggests the plot "leans hard on credibility" at some points.

Gerard, Jeremy. A review of *Arcadia,* by Tom Stoppard. *Variety* 358, No. 9 (3 April 1995): 150.

> Identifies the "hunger for meaning and discovery" as the theme that links the two halves of *Arcadia*.

Gray, Mary W. Review of *Arcadia,* by Tom Stoppard. *Mathematical Intelligencer* 17, No. 2 (Spring 1995): 67-8.

> Commends Stoppard's portrayal of mathematicians and their work.

Greer, Herb. "Writers on Writers on. . . ." *National Review* XLV, No. 23 (29 November 1993): 71-2.

> Calls *Arcadia* light entertainment but praises "Stoppard's extraordinary skill at word-play and semantic ambiguity."

Kroll, Jack. "Mind Over Matter." *Newsweek* CXXV, No. 13 (3 April 1995): 64-5, 68.

> Favorably reviews *Arcadia,* arguing that "Stoppard's unique genius is to humanize ideas . . . to show how they are part of our flesh and bone, our passion and pathos."

Leithauser, Brad. "A House of Games." *Time* 145, No. 15 (10 April 1995): 78.

> Favorably characterizes *Arcadia* as a "sort of bifurcated detective story."

Lyons, Donald. "Algorithms of the Heart." *Wall Street Journal* (31 March 1995): A10.

> Favorably reviews *Arcadia*.

Rich, Frank. "On Thermodynamics, Byron and Oh, Yes, Sex." *New York Times* (8 July 1993): 13, 16.

> Argues that *Arcadia*'s "vast tapestry" obscures its central themes and that the secondary characters "make no independent impressions as people."

Scheck, Frank. "*Arcadia* Has Intellectual Heft but Fails to Arouse Emotion." *Christian Science Monitor* (7 April 1995): 13.

> Largely negative review.

In Memoriam

Robertson Davies

August 28, 1913—December 2, 1995

(Full name William Robertson Davies; has also written under the pseudonym Samuel Marchbanks) Canadian novelist, dramatist, essayist, journalist, short story writer, editor, and critic.

For further information on his life and works, see *CLC*, Volumes 2, 7, 13, 25, 42, and 75.

INTRODUCTION

A leading figure in Canadian literature and one of the first Canadian novelists to gain international recognition, Davies is best known for the three novels that comprise *The Deptford Trilogy* (1983): *Fifth Business* (1970), *The Manticore* (1972), and *World of Wonders* (1975). Typical of his fiction, these intricate narratives incorporate religious symbolism and the supernatural, underscore the mystery and wonder of life, and are infused with a Jungian sensibility that informs the individual's quest for identity. Davies was born in Thamesville, Ontario, and attended Queen's University in Kingston, Ontario, before enrolling in Balliol College, Oxford, England. After graduating in 1938, he served with a theater troupe for two years before returning to Canada. In 1942, Davies assumed editorship of the *Peterborough Examiner,* a newspaper for which he also later served as vice-president and publisher. During his twenty-year tenure at the *Examiner,* Davies wrote under the pen name Samuel Marchbanks, adopting a curmudgeonly persona for his humorous and extravagant attacks on provincial life, Canadian politics, and contemporary culture. In 1960 Davies began teaching English literature at Trinity College in Toronto, and the following year was appointed first master of Massey College, a graduate school at the University of Toronto, where he taught until his retirement in 1981. In the 1950s Davies began writing novels, the first three of which—*Tempest-Tost* (1951), *Leaven of Malice* (1954), and *A Mixture of Frailties* (1958)—comprise *The Salterton Trilogy* (1986), which examines life in the small university town of Salterton, Ontario. While *The Deptford Trilogy* begins with a seemingly inconsequential snowball fight, the three novels variously examine the extent to which the individual must accept the irrationality of the self in order to achieve mental and emotional well-being. The dominant themes in these books stem from Davies's fascination with the search for identity and his belief in the moral value of living a well-examined life. *The Cornish Trilogy,* like his first three novels, explores the lives of individuals living in a Canadian college town. Comprising *The Rebel Angels* (1981), *What's Bred in the Bone* (1985), and *The Lyre of Orpheus* (1988), Davies's third trilogy has been hailed by several

critics as the culmination of his literary philosophy, which, they argue, largely eschews the aesthetics of contemporary fiction for nineteenth-century Romanticism. Remarking on Davies's works, Michiko Kakutani wrote that Davies "has created a rich oeuvre of densely plotted, highly symbolic novels that not only function as superbly funny entertainments but also give the reader . . . a deeper kind of pleasure—delight, awe, religious intimations, a fine sense of the past, and of the boundless depth and variety of life."

PRINCIPAL WORKS

Shakespeare's Boy Actors (nonfiction) 1939
Shakespeare for Young Players: A Junior Course (nonfiction) 1942
The Diary of Samuel Marchbanks (journalism) 1947

Overlaid (drama) 1947
At the Gates of the Righteous (drama) 1948
Eros at Breakfast (drama) 1948
Fortune, My Foe (drama) 1948
Hope Deferred (drama) 1948
Eros at Breakfast, and Other Plays [first publication]
      (drama) 1949
The Table Talk of Samuel Marchbanks (journalism)
      1949
At My Heart's Core (drama) 1950
King Phoenix (drama) 1950
*Tempest-Tost (novel) 1951
A Masque of Aesop (drama) 1952
*Renown at Stratford: A Record of the Shakespeare Festival
      in Canada, 1953* [with Tyrone Guthrie and Grant
      Macdonald] (nonfiction) 1953
A Jig for the Gypsy (drama) 1954
*Leaven of Malice (novel) 1954
*Twice Have the Trumpets Sounded: A Record of the Strat-
      ford Shakespearean Festival in Canada, 1954* [with
      Tyrone Guthrie and Grant Macdonald] (nonfic-
      tion) 1954
Hunting Stuart (drama) 1955
*Thrice the Brinded Cat Hath Mew'd: A Record of the Strat-
      ford Shakespearean Festival in Canada, 1955* [with
      Tyrone Guthrie, Boyd Neal, and Tanya Moisei-
      witsch] (nonfiction) 1955
*A Mixture of Frailties (novel) 1958
†Love and Libel (drama) 1960
A Voice from the Attic (addresses, essays, and lectures)
      1960; also published as *The Personal Art: Reading to
      Good Purposes,* 1961
A Masque of Mr. Punch (drama) 1962
Samuel Marchbanks' Almanack (journalism) 1967
‡Fifth Business (novel) 1970
Stephen Leacock (nonfiction) 1970
Hunting Stuart, and Other Plays [first publication]
      (drama) 1972
‡The Manticore (novel) 1972
Question Time (drama) 1975
‡World of Wonders (novel) 1975
*One Half of Robertson Davies: Provocative Pronounce-
      ments on a Wide Range of Topics* (addresses, lec-
      tures, and short stories) 1977; also published as *One
      Half of Robertson Davies,* 1978
The Enthusiasms of Robertson Davies (journalism and
      essays) 1979
§The Rebel Angels (novel) 1981
*The Well-Tempered Critic: One Man's View of Theatre
      and Letters in Canada* (addresses, essays, and lec-
      tures) 1981
High Spirits (short stories) 1982
The Mirror of Nature (lectures) 1983
The Papers of Samuel Marchbanks (journalism and es-
      says) 1985
§What's Bred in the Bone (novel) 1985
§The Lyre of Orpheus (novel) 1988
Murther & Walking Spirits (novel) 1991
Reading and Writing (essays) 1993
The Cunning Man (novel) 1994

*These works were published as *The Salterton Trilogy* in 1986.

†This work is an adaptation of Davies's novel *Leaven of Malice.*

‡These works were published as *The Deptford Trilogy* in 1983.

§These works are collectively referred to as *The Cornish Trilogy.*

INTERVIEWS

Clyde H. Farnsworth   (essay date 15 December 1994)

SOURCE: "A Land Apart: A Canadian Looks South Sourly," in *The New York Times,* December 15, 1994, p. A4.

[*In the following essay, which was based on an interview with Davies, Farnsworth presents the novelist's views on Canadian culture and politics.*]

When American invaders crossed the Niagara frontier during the War of 1812, they came upon the family farm of one of the forebears of the author Robertson Davies and were astonished to find angry youths shooting at them from the farmhouse windows.

"They thought we'd be delighted to lay down the hateful British yoke, but they didn't think they were bringing another kind of yoke with them," said the man some consider to be Canada's greatest living writer.

Four of his ancestors fell in that engagement, the Battle of Stoney Creek, and he is proud that it helped to turn the tide against the invaders.

That Canadians are distinct from Americans is a sub-theme of his novels, the most famous of which are the Deptford trilogy, **Fifth Business, The Manticore** and **World of Wonders.** In the 11th and latest novel, **The Cunning Man,** the aging hero—not unlike his 81-year-old creator—rues the withering of Canada's British connection and the growth of the American connection "under the caress of the iron hand and buckskin glove."

Greg Gatenby, the literary scholar who directs the Harborfront International Reading Series in Toronto, said that "in anyone's delineation of the pantheon of Canadian writers, Davies holds a place close to Zeus."

With his magnificent snowy beard, great white mane and protuberant brow, Mr. Davies has a magisterial look as well. As he talked about his views of Canadian nationality on a recent day, wisps of sunlight filtered into his second-floor office above the red-brick quadrangle at Massey College, the University of Toronto's graduate college, where he is the founding master.

Mr. Davies, who was born in Ontario, said the biggest difference between Canada and the United States is in their underlying myths. "The myth of America is a very powerful one and one that we in Canada look toward with envy," he said. "You have your heroes. You have your great men of the past, you have your myth of tradition, of the conquering of the west, and the pioneer life and the gold rush life and all that sort of thing, which is enormously romantic, and nations feed on the romantic tradition."

"We don't go for heroes," he said. "As soon as a man begins to achieve some sort of high stature, we want to cut him down and get rid of him, embarrass him."

He also sees Canada as "very much a northern country—much more like Scandinavia or Russia than the United States." Moreover, he went on, "Canada is a socialist monarchy. You hate monarchies and socialism—and we're both."

Mr. Davies is just as eager to see Canada hold together as he is to avoid an American yoke.

"The present hullabaloo about Quebec is precisely that," he said. "It will not die down, but it will not come to anything."

He contends that economic considerations will keep Quebec in the fold. "What happens to the thousands of French Canadian civil servants who are no longer on the public payroll?" he said. "They're suddenly going to be without a job, and certainly the new Quebec wouldn't be able to provide them with comparable income. And what would Quebec do with its share of the national debt? They wouldn't want to shoulder it."

He also expects pressure from the United States. "I don't imagine for one instant that the United States wants a balkanized Canada to the north," he said. The United States says officially that it supports a strong and united Canada.

Quebec separatism is Canada's civil war, Mr. Davies said, but unlike the American Civil War, he predicted, it will not become violent. "Our civil war is a psychological one," he said. "It's a tough kind of war to fight because it's very wearing. There is never any letup. There is never any cease-fire. There is never any stopping to celebrate Christmas."

His comments about French Canadians underscore the observation of Richard C. Davis, professor of Canadian literature at the University of Calgary, that Mr. Davies "comes from a traditional male, English-Canadian base."

The French are "always complaining." Mr. Davies contended. "They have never got over the defeat on the Plains of Abraham," the battle in 1759 that established British rule in Canada.

"They're terribly unrealistic about this sort of thing, but they are also very shrewd and very practical," he said. "They know the dollar better than they know their mothers, and if they think that is threatened by leaving the dominion, they will stay."

Mr. Davies's reflections on politics come from a certain academic distance.

His cozy office is dominated by a large writing desk, bookcases and portraits of Shakespeare, Rabelais, Robert Burton—whose *Anatomy of Melancholy* provides inspiration for the latest novel—and John Cowper Powys, the 19th-century novelist whom Mr. Davies called "a great, great, undervalued man."

With the help of a secretary, he handles correspondence in the office and researches current projects. For example, he is now working on an article for the *Dictionary of Na-tional Biography* on a 19th-century English actor, Henry Irving. But his main creative work is done on his 150-acre estate in the hills of Caledon East, about an hour from downtown Toronto, where he lives with his wife, Brenda.

He taught literature at the university for 21 years and still confers with students, including many, he volunteers, who ask whether getting a job on a newspaper would harm their writing style.

A former editor of *The Peterborough Examiner,* as well as an actor and playwright, he tells them that journalism "teaches you to write more concisely and to get busy and write when you must, instead of just sitting around waiting for the inspiration, which isn't going to come."

And if students are making noise below, he has no qualms about opening his window, looking down sternly, beard flowing, and thundering, "God is watching!"

What has pushed Robertson Davies outside favoured-author status in [Canada], but made him an international literary doyen, is that he evinces a contempt for fashion and convention.

—Michael Coren, in "The Indiscreet Charm of Robertson Davies," in Saturday Night, *October, 1994*.

Mel Gussow   (essay date 5 February 1995)

SOURCE: " 'A Moralist Possessed by Humor': A Conversation with Robertson Davies," in *The New York Times Book Review,* February 5, 1995, pp. 24-5.

[*Gussow is an American journalist, nonfiction writer, and critic. In the following essay, which was based on an interview with Davies, Gussow discusses Davies's career and most recent novel,* The Cunning Man.]

Robertson Davies, unceasing in his creativity at the age of 81, fervently makes a case for the place of melodrama in our lives. "Very few people live in a mode of tragedy," he says, "and when they do, we pity them deeply. Very few people live in a mode of real comedy; they laugh a lot but their lives are not comic. Comedy is almost as cruel and exclusive as tragedy. Most of us live in a world of melodrama, a world of mingled laughter and tears, gain and deprivation and excitement—the hurly-burly of normal life."

Taking off from a poem by Henrik Ibsen, he believes that "a man's self-judgment" is "the conscience of a writer." Through a process of self-analysis that has been both painful and joyous, his life has provided him with the raw material for what he writes. Interwoven, with overlapping characters, his 11 novels can be regarded as a kind of masked autobiography. The books often begin in Canadian villages as small as his birthplace of Thamesville in southwest Ontario, but they soon open up to reveal allegorical allusions and magical transformations. Accidental incidents can have endless effects, and behind everything is the immutability of the human heart. A misaimed snowball in his 1970 novel *Fifth Business,* for example, sets off a chain of events. It becomes a defining moment, touching scores of lives and a trilogy of novels. In the case of his new novel, *The Cunning Man,* there are medical and spiritual mysteries. Skeptics need not enter Mr. Davies's bewitching world.

Sitting straight-backed in a chair in his office at Massey College of the University of Toronto, Mr. Davies, with his patriarchal white beard and flowing white hair, exuded eminence and a kind of actorly presence. Indeed, he began his professional life as an actor, and he has also been a playwright. As he does every week, he has come down to Toronto from his country home in Caledon, an hour out of town. After many years as the master of Massey College, he no longer teaches but still keeps quarters on campus. It was a wintry day, and he was prepared for a long, warming conversation. In common with his character Brocky Gilmartin in *The Cunning Man,* he regards language "as a great unfailing plaything," and his talk, strewn with literary and theatrical references, journeyed widely through his life and work.

When he acted at the Old Vic in the late 1930's, he was told by Tyrone Guthrie that if he continued performing he might have a future playing grotesques. He had specialized in eccentrics and characters far older than himself. "I was the kind of actor who liked to put on a lot of makeup and humps and things," he says. "I never liked just being me, because I didn't really feel there was any me to be." Giving up the stage, he began to play himself, a role he has lived to the fullest. Among other talents, he is an excellent reader of his own work, and is in great demand on the lecture circuit.

Although energized by an audience, he prefers to stay home, working. For him, writing is an obsession, one that began in childhood. As a member of a writing family, he was expected to be an author or at least a journalist, and he has been both during his long and varied career. Writing has remained his fate, his *anangke,* a Greek word that appears frequently in his new novel.

At one point, his great desire was to be a playwright. Despite some success with his plays in Canada, his one Broadway venture, *Love and Libel,* a dramatization of his novel *Leaven of Malice,* was a quick failure in 1960. When he went to New York for the opening, he realized "what an insignificant creature a playwright was in circumstances like that." He remembers being told by his star, Dennis King, that "he had to have 10 more sure laughs by tomorrow morning or he was going to walk out." At the same time, the audience for his fiction was growing. That gave him a sense of independence—and no back talk. Now he can say: "I like being a novelist for the same reason that Charles Dickens liked being a novelist. You can play all the parts, arrange the scenery, be the whole show and nobody gets in the way."

Reflecting on the sources of his art, he says: "Imagination is the thing by which I have lived and which informs every part of my life. It's as Henry James said, you have a little donnée and from that, things develop." Students often ask him where his ideas come from, "as if there were some hidden cache of notions that I pillage." Mr. Davies gets his ideas from what he observes, what he hears, from his memory and his dreams—from the ether of his imagination.

As with his other novels, *The Cunning Man* started with a mass of notes "about characters, phrases, turns of plot" and with an irresistible idea, in this case a priest who dies while celebrating Communion. The author wondered if he died from "ecstasy, old age, stress or poison." This was the catalyst for a book about two of his favorite subjects, religion and medicine, and the curative aspects of both. As usual, at the outset he had no idea of the outcome.

A "cunning man," as defined in a prefatory quote from Robert Burton's *Anatomy of Melancholy,* is a wise man and kind of village know-it-all. The protagonist, Dr. Jonathan Hullah, who uses Jungian as well as holistic principles in his practice, can sense, even smell, the nature of disease. He is an expert diagnostician, a quality he shares with his author. It is clear that Mr. Davies can look at a character and know what ails him and why, what is "bred in the bone" and what is contracted. For him, medicine has been a lifelong preoccupation: "I've always been interested in why some people seem to get along with a minimum of disease and others are, in the true meaning of the word, patients all their lives, sufferers."

When Mr. Davies was a student at Oxford University, he began reading the work of Georg Groddeck, an unconventional German physician and author who used psychoanalysis in his treatment of disease. Dr. Hullah is inspired by Groddeck and other doctors the author has known. Despite his great medical curiosity, Mr. Davies says he himself would have been "temperamentally unsuited" to the profession.

Although the author prefers to regard *The Cunning Man* as an independent work, his readers will quickly notice the connections to its immediate predecessor, *Murther & Walking Spirits*. Here again are the various Gilmartins and Hugh McWearie, the journalist who writes about religion. Characters also flow from other books. For example, Dunstan Ramsay, the schoolmaster protagonist of *Fifth Business,* makes a brief appearance. Mr. Davies is himself represented in Dr. Hullah's analysis of Victorian fiction. When he refers to Heroine's Disease, or death by Ingrowing Virtue, it is a borrowing from one of Mr. Davies's own speeches.

Mr. Davies has said he is "a moralist possessed by humor," a description that would serve equally for Dr. Hullah, who, he says, "is a moralist not because he dictates morals but because he observes what's wrong with his patients." For both the author and the character, physical and emotional causes of disease are inseparable. Throughout the book is the theme of unfulfillment, people who feel they have had a "Raw Deal" in life. "A tremendous number of people have a deep sense that they haven't had their due," says Mr. Davies. He is empathetic but also realistic: "As Hamlet says, if we all had our due, who should escape whipping?" In Mr. Davies's word coinage, the way to confront the Raw Deal is with "Drye Mocke," or ironic humor.

Coincident with the publication of **The Cunning Man,** a massive biography of the writer was published in Canada, *Robertson Davies: Man of Myth,* by Judith Skelton Grant. As thick as a Davies trilogy, it documents the writer's life in minute detail. Although Mr. Davies cooperated with Mrs. Grant during her 12-year project, the book does not leave him in a state of rapture, despite the biographer's admiration. He feels that she shortchanges his humor. Perhaps he would have preferred the subtitle "Man of Mirth."

"I don't wish to be disagreeable about Judith," he says, "but my whole life since childhood has been bathed in a kind of satirical, mordant attitude toward life, which is inherited from my parents. Judith was looking for fascinating things, for the times I had to escape from the caliph's harem—and my life has been like the lives of so many writers, one of quiet industry and indeed drudgery. All the adventures have been mental and emotional." The search of his biographer was for "police-court truth," he says, for the facts behind the fiction. "I used to say to her over and over again: fiction is not photography, it's oil painting."

Despite Mr. Davies's criticism, Mrs. Grant's book illuminates the currents of his career. In particular, she describes how people from his past are amalgamated into characters, how his art is bound up with his life.

After leaving the Old Vic in 1940, he returned to Canada with his wife, Brenda, who had been an actress and stage manager with the company. Entering journalism, he started writing his first million words, as a critic of all the arts and as a curmudgeonly columnist named Samuel Marchbanks. For many years he was editor and publisher of *The Peterborough* (Ontario) *Examiner,* one of the newspapers owned by his father. He also became a teacher, with 19th-century theater and literature as his specialty.

Gradually, he edged into fiction. His first novel, the antic **Tempest-Tost** (1952), about a Little Theater production of *The Tempest,* inspired the **Salterton Trilogy** and its comic treatment of the various effects of the arts on provincial Canadians. **Fifth Business,** which was the turning point of his career, was the first volume of the more challenging **Deptford Trilogy** (dealing with art forgery and magic), and **The Rebel Angels** (1982) was the first in the **Cornish Trilogy** (about, in his words, "money, the love thereof and the rich comedy that ensues"). A pivotal theme in his work is the continuity of lives. "One is a bead on a string," he says. "You partake of innumerable people in the past, and you contribute to goodness knows how many people in the future."

Like the ghost stories Mr. Davies invented for the annual Christmas celebration at Massey, his novels cast a spell, although admittedly some readers are not in his thrall. There are those who regard him as too much of a traditionalist, and he is still underappreciated in England. He has never won a Booker Prize and is not even listed in the *Oxford Companion to English Literature,* though four lesser-known, unrelated men named Davies are there, including Thomas Davies, the bookseller who introduced Boswell to Johnson in his shop. Being in such a book would "impress the neighbors," Mr. Davies says, "but you can make a fool of yourself worrying about things like that."

He reserves his ire for those who regard him as old-fashioned. "I suppose my writing doesn't follow any of the new twists," he says, "but I've seen so many of the new things become old things in quite a short time. They never seem to recognize that there's anything experimental in my books. For instance, **The Manticore** is the only book I know which attempts to tell the story of a man's life in terms of a Jungian analysis."

In fact, his books are filled with innovative shifts in narrative and point of view. In the middle of **The Cunning Man,** the book suddenly becomes epistolary, with one of the characters exchanging letters with the British sculptor Barbara Hepworth. Two angels tell the story in **What's Bred in the Bone,** and in **Murther & Walking Spirits** the protagonist is a lively though incorporeal ghost.

His biographer reports that Mr. Davies has often dreamed about his mother's ghost. Asked whether he believes in supernatural emanations, he says: "I believe in them the way Shakespeare believed in them. They're a way of exemplifying something which you know to be true but which is very hard to give substance to. Why does Hamlet see his father's ghost? It's in order that he may recognize what he knows in the depths of his own mind. It doesn't really mean that people are floating around in nighties looking for somebody to scare."

It is time for lunch, and he leads the way through the snow to the York Club, where he often eats, and where a crucial scene in **The Cunning Man** takes place. Described in the novel as "a famous refuge of the beleaguered well-to-do," it is richly paneled and has a genteel atmosphere. As he enters the dining room, people look up in recognition. (Later Mr. Davies says, with a hint of irony—or is it envy? —that when Ibsen went to his favorite restaurant, people stood up.) Before ordering, he takes out a tiny notebook and offers an example of the kind of thought he frequently jots down. He had talked to a bank teller whose "fingers were worn smooth by counting currency. Someone who had no fingerprints! That would be an interesting character in a mystery story."

He is fascinated by crime, and keeps a file of clippings. "There are only a certain limited number of crimes, and they're repeated endlessly in different variations without the splendor of art being brought to them," he says. Despite his interest in crime, he has never served on a jury. "Up here," he says, "newspapermen and butchers are exempt from jury duty." Briefly he speaks about the fluctuating reputations of writers: a comeback for Galsworthy, a disappearance for Hugh Walpole. He is a great reader, especially of work from the 19th and early 20th centuries. Currently he is reading Thackeray.

In Mr. Davies's new novel he quotes Wordsworth: "the still, sad music of humanity." Beneath all the myth, mysticism and humor, is that the true subject of his fiction? After a pause, he answers: "Yes, and it is a thing which partners Thoreau's remark that most men lead lives of quiet desperation. It's horrifying when you get to know somebody and find what sadness and despair and wan hope lie beneath an apparently cheerful surface."

He says he has never had writer's block. "You can't afford to run dry," he explains. One could hear the Drye Mocke of his mother's wisdom, "It is better to wear out than to rust out." For him, writing remains a pleasure; he finds it "restful." He keeps voluminous diaries and dictates many letters. As always, he produces about 12,000 words a week on his typewriter—and never plans to stop. He attributes his general good health partly to the Alexander technique (a method of body alignment and breathing often used by actors), which he and his wife have been studying and practicing for more than 30 years.

He is now working on a new article about Henry Irving for the *Dictionary of National Biography* and on a libretto for an opera based on *The Golden Ass* by Apuleius. As he contemplates his future adventures, he seems tantalized by the thought of the untold stories within **The Cunning Man**. Those stories could, of course, lead to a third book in a Toronto Trilogy.

Although Mr. Davies retains his infinite curiosity, he knows there are unaccountable elements in the world: "I'm fascinated by those who assume that man with his five senses and his remarkable ability to think and investigate will somehow put salt on the tail of all the secrets of the universe." It is his feeling that "mankind's perpetual desire for explanations and maps" impedes "making a step into the unknown."

OBITUARIES AND TRIBUTES

Jane Gross and Craig Turner   (obituary date 4 December 1995)

SOURCE: An obituary in *Los Angeles Times,* December 4, 1995, p. A16.

[*In the following obituary, Gross and Turner provide an overview of Davies's life and career.*]

Robertson Davies, one of Canada's most celebrated novelists and the master of multiple, eclectic careers in theater, journalism and academia, has died.

Davies died Saturday night of a stroke at the age of 82. He had been hospitalized with pneumonia.

Davies' breakthrough as a novelist came with the 1970 publication of **Fifth Business,** the first work in the renowned **Deptford Trilogy,** which traced the interconnected lives of three men in the fictional town of Deptford, Ontario, the province where the author was born, spent most of his life and died this weekend.

In the 1970s and again in the 1980s, he produced two more well received trilogies. His last work of fiction, **The Cunning Man,** was published in 1994.

Explaining how so many of his novels came to be trilogies, Davies said, "I found almost as soon as I had finished that it wasn't all I wanted to say."

Although he wrote plays, criticism and essays, his reputation rests on dense novels full of mysticism, absurdity and Canadiana.

He has been praised as a gifted storyteller who favored complex plots and shifting points of view, a man of strong moral sense, a repository of obscure facts and esoteric vocabulary and a writer who could move easily from bawdy humor to lofty abstraction. His wide-ranging interests included Jungian psychology, medicine, religion and crime, and his command of these subjects course through the novels.

Davies was among the first Canadian novelists to gain an international reputation and he used his stature to promote Canadian culture and defend Canadian nationalism.

His books were translated into 17 languages, and he was mentioned as a possible winner of the 1993 Nobel Prize in literature.

Responding last year to complaints about Canada's reputation for being boring, he noted trenchantly, "There's worse things than being dull. There's being crazy and we're not that."

"He thought life was fascinating," Davies' widow, Brenda, told the Canadian Press Assn. on Sunday. "Nowadays, not enough people think life is fascinating. They think it's dreadful. He was very keen that they should take a look at it as magical, fascinating and extraordinary."

Toronto critic Robert Fulford called Davies' death "like the abrupt disappearance of a mountain range from the Canadian landscape" in an appreciation he wrote for publication in today's *Toronto Globe and Mail.* In an interview, Fulford noted the "theatrical quality" Davies brought to his writing and to his life.

Long before Davies gained acclaim for his fiction, first in the United States and later in his homeland, he had made a mark on the stage in London; then as a columnist, editor and publisher of a small Canadian newspaper; and again as a professor and founding master of Massey College at the University of Toronto.

He was born in 1913 in Thamesville, Ontario. His father was a Welsh immigrant who worked his way up from printer's apprentice to one of the country's leading newspaper publishers, political activists and philanthropists.

Like the sons of many prominent Canadian families of the day, Davies traveled to England for his university degree, graduating from Oxford in 1938. He then moved to London, where he played small parts and wrote plays for the Old Vic Repertory Company. At that theater, he met Brenda Mathews, an Australian stage manager, and they were married in 1940.

Returning to Canada after the outbreak of World War II, he was excluded from military service by his poor eyesight. He gained attention as columnist, editor and eventually publisher of the *Peterborough Examiner,* one of his father's newspapers.

Newspaper work turned him into an easy, prolific writer; his curmudgeonly columns, written under the pen name of Samuel Marchbanks, were eventually compiled for his first three books.

From there, Davies turned his kaleidoscopic intellect to teaching, specializing in English drama from 1660 to 1914. He began as a visiting professor at the University of Toronto and then, for nearly two decades until he retired in 1981, as head of Massey College, a graduate school of the university, where he kept an office and continued to advise students until his death.

With a flowing snow-white beard, a protuberant brow and an actorly demeanor, Davies made an unforgettable impression. His prose was equally arresting.

"He had no imitators and he imitated no one," said Douglas Fetherling, a Toronto critic and essayist who has written a book on the Davies family.

He published the first of his 11 novels, *Tempest-Tost,* in 1951. That and *Leaven of Malice* and *A Mixture of Frailties* comprise the first of his three trilogies.

The second, the *Deptford Trilogy,* written in the 1970s, includes *The Manticore* and *World of Wonders* as well as *Fifth Business* In the 1980s came the *Cornish Trilogy: The Rebel Angels, What's Bred in the Bone* and *The Lyre of Orpheus*.

He was planning to write another book after Christmas dealing with his old age, his wife said. He is survived by his wife and three daughters.

Peter B. Flint   (obituary date 4 December 1995)

SOURCE: An obituary in *The New York Times,* December 4, 1995, p. B10.

[*In the following obituary, Flint focuses on Davies's works, noting his concern with themes of morality, evil, myth, love, and death.*]

Robertson Davies, the novelist, journalist and educator who became one of the first Canadian literary figures to gain an international following, died on Saturday at a hospital in Orangeville, Ontario, 50 miles northwest of Toronto. He was 82.

The cause was a stroke, his secretary, Moira Whalon, told The Associated Press. Mr. Davies, who lived in Toronto but had a home in Caledon East, near Orangeville, had entered the hospital last Tuesday, said a supervisor at the hospital where he died, the Dufferin-Caledon Health Care Corporation.

Mr. Davies published more than 30 volumes of fiction, including three trilogies, as well as plays, essays and criticism. He was once mentioned as a potential recipient of the 1993 Nobel Prize in literature, which went instead to the American novelist Toni Morrison.

Though he retired as an educator more than a decade ago, he had continued to write in recent years, and his last novel, *The Cunning Man* (Viking, 1995), made the bestseller lists this year. It is a chronicle of personal and social change in Toronto as reflected in the life of a doctor whose brilliant diagnostic skills rest on shamanism and Platonism as well as scientific medicine.

Mr. Davies was primarily a storyteller concerned with moral conflicts. Beneath its imaginative, enigmatic themes, his work, which was translated into 17 languages, was informed by the philosophy of Carl Jung, with its emphasis on self-knowledge, creative maturity and wisdom.

Describing his admiration for the Swiss psychiatrist, Mr. Davies said in 1985: "Jung's thought is very expansive, a sort of opening out of life, whereas so much psychoanalytical thinking is reductive: getting you back to the womb and a lot of trouble."

Mr. Davies once said the theme at the core of his work was "the isolation of the human spirit" and mankind's growth "from innocence to experience." Characters' actions are carried out "on their own volition and usually contrary to what is expected of them," he remarked. "The characters try to escape from early influences and find their own place in the world but are reluctant to do so in a way that will bring pain and disappointment to others."

Other concerns in Mr. Davies's work were evil as an expression of suppressed fears and wishes, the irreversible consequences of actions, and myth, sainthood, ambition, love, vengeance and death. With disarming ease, he could fuse a comedy of manners with Gothic melodrama, blend realism with illusions, and juxtapose low humor and lofty abstractions. Satirizing bourgeois Canadian provincialism was one of his favorite sports.

> **With disarming ease, Davies could fuse a comedy of manners with Gothic melodrama, blend realism with illusions, and juxtapose low humor and lofty abstractions. Satirizing bourgeois Canadian provincialism was one of his favorite sports.**
>
> **—Peter B. Flint**

Critics, mostly realists, assailed his mystical style as schematic and accused him of overstressing and overanalyzing the cerebral at the expense of emotions. He was also at times accused of being pedantic, repetitious, vague and antifeminist.

The tall, flamboyant, bearded Mr. Davies was also the editor and publisher of *The Peterborough Examiner* in Ontario from 1942 to 1962; a professor of English at Massey College, a prestigious postgraduate unit of the University of Toronto, from 1960 to 1981, and master of the college from 1962 to 1981, when he retired.

He completed three trilogies of novels, set in fictional Ontario villages, that have been reprinted by Penguin paperbacks. The first, called the **Salterton Trilogy** and written in the 1950's, included **Tempest-Tost,** about a bungled amateur staging of Shakespeare's late romance; **Leaven of Malice,** arising from a bogus engagement notice involving two warring families, and **A Mixture of Frailties,** focusing on a factory girl transformed into an opera star.

The Deptford Trilogy, written in the 1970's, included **Fifth Business, The Manticore** and **World of Wonders.** All three followed the course of lives that were partly defined by a childhood prank in which a boy threw a snowball containing a rock at a classmate but hit a pregnant woman instead. These three novels were considered by some critics and readers to be Mr. Davies's best works.

The third set of novels, the **Cornish Trilogy,** was written in the 1980's and includes **The Rebel Angels, What's Bred in the Bone** and **The Lyre of Orpheus.** The novels center on a painter and art forger who was also a spy. The books satirize gift-giving, foundations and grand opera.

In 1985, Michiko Kakutani wrote in *The New York Times* that Mr. Davies "has created a rich oeuvre of densely plotted, highly symbolic novels that not only function as superbly funny entertainments but also give the reader, in his character's words, a deeper kind of pleasure—delight, awe, religious intimations, a fine sense of the past, and of the boundless depth and variety of life."

Mr. Davies's other books included **A Voice From the Attic,** the attic being Canada (1960), **One Half of Robertson Davies** (1978), **The Enthusiasms of Robertson Davies** (1979) and **The Papers of Samuel Marchbanks** (1985). Mr. Davies often revived the character of Marchbanks, an irascible old bachelor who issued blistering opinions about people, particularly Canadians, from his isolated home in Skunk's Misery, Ontario. Mr. Davies created the character in his columns in *The Peterborough Examiner.*

In a 1991 novel, **Murther and Walking Spirits,** Mr. Davies's narrator is murdered in the first line, and his spirit thereafter moves about, learning of his ancestral Holland, Wales and North America, watching scenes from the dead's point of view and slowly gaining revenge.

A frequent composer of epigrams in his work, Mr. Davies once wrote about marriage: "People marry most happily with their own kind. The trouble lies in the fact that people usually marry at an age where they do not really know what their own kind is." Of the future, he wrote: "The world is full of people whose notion of a satisfactory future is, in fact, a return to an idealized past."

The writer, whose full name was William Robertson Davies, was born on Aug. 28, 1913, in the southern Ontario town of Thamesville. His parents were William Rupert Davies, a Welshman who became a publisher and Liberal senator, and the former Florence McKay, whose British loyalist family had fled to Canada from New York at the time of the American Revolution. Mr. Davies attended Upper Canada College and Queen's University in Kingston, Ontario, and he earned a bachelor of letters degree at Balliol College, Oxford.

He spent two years with the Old Vic theater in London, directing, acting and teaching, before returning in 1940 to Ontario, where he spent two more years as the literary editor of *Saturday Night,* a Toronto magazine. He then began editing *The Peterborough Examiner,* an evening daily owned by his family, and wrote a column. He also wrote several plays, with little success, and was an active sponsor of the Shakespeare Festival at Stratford, Ontario. He received many awards and honorary degrees and was the first Canadian to be named a member of the American Academy and Institute of Arts and Letters.

In discussing his careers in journalism and education, Mr. Davies was candid. Of newspapers, he once wrote that they "like to represent themselves as wonderfully romantic and hitched into world events," but "they are really an entertainment and manufacturing business. The news is what you can squeeze in before you have to go to press; it's not what's happening in the world."

As an educator, he said: "I'm a great believer in encouragement. A great number of young people who are very brilliant come from very humble families, and they have to fight family criticism."

Mr. Davies lived in the Toronto area for most of his life with his wife, the former Brenda Mathews, an Australian whom he married in London in 1940. In addition to his wife, he is survived by three daughters, Miranda, who lives in England; Jennifer Surridge of Mississauga, Ontario, and Rosamound Cunnington of Oakville, Ontario, and four grandchildren.

REVIEWS OF DAVIES'S RECENT WORKS

Anthony Bailey   (review date 17 November 1991)

SOURCE: "How the Dead See It," in *The New York Times Book Review,* November 17, 1991, p. 9.

[*Bailey is an English-born journalist, nonfiction writer, novelist, and critic. In the review below, he discusses* Murther & Walking Spirits, *remarking on the unexpected turns in Davies's plot and the protagonist's development.*]

The epigraph to Robertson Davies's new novel, **Murther & Walking Spirits,** is as apt as can be. It comes from the Samuel Butler who was a 17th-century poet and satirist: "Printers finde by experience that one Murther is worth two Monsters, and at least three Walking Spirits. For the consequence of Murther is hanging, with which the Rabble is wonderfully delighted. But where Murthers and Walking Spirits meet, there is no other Narrative can come near it."

Mr. Davies wastes no time in putting into effect this antique prescription for a best seller. His protagonist narrator, Connor Gilmartin, the entertainment editor of *The Colonial Advocate* ("the very good newspaper" in Toronto), is murdered in the first sentence. A few lines later, his spirit is on the loose, if not actually walking then flitting and eventually sitting for some days alongside his murderer, one Randal Allard Going, the paper's theater critic, who is also known as the Sniffer, from his habit of sniffing out literary influences in new plays and films. One of the Sniffer's conceits is to carry a walking stick whose handle conceals a cudgel. It is this weapon he has used without thinking on Gilmartin's temple when the editor surprises the critic in bed with Gilmartin's wife, Esme, an *Advocate* columnist on women's affairs.

This reviewer sniffs no influence here other than that of a great tradition of theatrical high jinks. Gilmartin immediately sees Going and Esme with new, albeit deceased eyes. While Going begins to weep hysterically over the corpse, Esme—claim and collected, if still naked—gets rid of the fingerprints. When her lover has managed to pull himself together, she sends him off: "He went . . . though his face was tense with pain. But then, who notices when they meet a theatre critic whose face is tense with pain? It is one of the marks of the profession."

Esme dons a nightgown, calls the police and gives a polished performance as the dismayed wife, telling of an intruder who struck her husband. She is believed. Gilmartin watches his own body carried away; despite his demise, he has been feeling hungry and recalls being told that the digestive process continues for 45 minutes or so after death. In the next few days, he observes his own funeral, the reactions of his fellow newspapermen and the skill with which Esme puts her bereavement to use, soon starting work on a how-to book for widows. Meanwhile, Going is in growing distress. Gilmartin decides that, insofar as his unaccustomed condition permits, he will hound his murderer.

The reader may well smack his or her chops gleefully in anticipation of a revenger's comedy. But this would fail to take full measure of Robertson Davies, by no means a predictable writer. It is roughly 300 pages before Gilmartin's spirit begins to exact retribution from Going. Instead, his ghost pursues the murderer as far as a local film festival and then perches beside him as the Sniffer watches a series of classic movies. Gilmartin remembers feeling, while alive, that in cinemas "the half-darkness . . . spoke of that world of phantasmagoria and dream grotto of which I was aware as a part of my own life, which I could touch only in dreams or waking reverie. But film could open the door to it." Nevertheless, he thinks, having to sit beside the Sniffer for eternity watching even dearly loved films might be hell indeed.

The reader whose spirits may also be plummeting at such a prospect is wrong again. For Mr. Davies has something in mind other than disembodied reflections on *The Battleship Potemkin* or Ibsen's grandson Tancred's movie version of *The Master Builder*. Such films may be what the Sniffer sees. Gilmartin, however, watches a program meant just for him: a sequence of stories that inform him about his ancestral Dutch, Welsh and North American past.

Despite being decorated with terms like "rapid cutting" and "montage," the ensuing treatments do not come across as essentially cinematic, but rather as a series of no-

vellas making use of a range of skillful fictional devices. In one, a loyalist family flees New York after the Revolutionary War and makes its arduous way to Canada by canoe. In another, an itinerant Methodist weaver-preacher in the mountains of North Wales adopts a poor lad named Gwylim ap Sion ap Emrys ap Dafydd ap Owain ap Hywel ap Rhodri ap Rhydderch ap Gryffyd and—mercifully—christens him Wesley Gilmartin. The Gilmartin line includes an honest tailor who goes broke and a dishonest servant who does well. Their lives are linked with trade and small shops; harried women make ends barely meet until a point when they no longer do. Then the Gilmartins emigrate to Canada and better fortune.

Once in a while, as Connor Gilmartin watches his "films," one may wonder a bit impatiently when the Sniffer will get his just deserts. Mr. Davies is a tremendously enticing storyteller, whether his characters are cajoling in Welsh brogue or portaging a canoe through the northern wilderness, but it's possible to ask now and then just how such and such an incident fits in the master plan of the book. On most occasions, however, the author, as if sensing our restiveness, provides an answer. Although suspicions are aroused that this is a brilliantly disguised family memoir, they can be set aside as unworthy, for one is in any event having a marvelous time hearing about these people, with a constant smile of either pleasure or amusement on the lips. And, toward the end, the weft in Mr. Davies's weaving helps make his pattern clear. Connor Gilmartin's spirit realizes that the family members he has always taken for granted, or seen merely as supporting players in his own personal drama, have starred in deeply felt shows of their own.

Having a spirit for a hero gives Mr. Davies creative opportunities. He looks at séances from the point of view of the departed (shades of Elvira in Noël Coward's *Blithe Spirit*); he examines so-called after-death experiences, varieties of ghosts and the speculations of Emanuel Swedenborg, the 18th-century Swedish scientist and religious philosopher, who believed in "a spiritual world populated exclusively by dead human beings, grouped in coherent societies." As far as this reader is concerned, Mr. Davies bestows upon his characters many likings that are wholly admirable: for the works of P. G. Wodehouse, for John Bunyan's Pilgrim hymn "He who would valiant be" and for a Wales that is wonderful despite being "too far, and too wet, and too unfashionable."

By the way, as is customary in a Robertson Davies work, there are splendid tidbits. We learn of the connection between laudanum and constipation and of Napoleon's love of the fake Scottish epic of Ossian. As for Canada, it produces no self-conscious exertions from Mr. Davies. Its people may be "inescapably" provincial, as Brochwel Gilmartin, father of Connor, thinks; but they are people who have importance as "patient lookers-on" and (unlike their southern neighbors?) "are not beguiled by the notion that the fate of mankind and of human culture lies wholly in our hands."

Although we have been waiting for the Sniffer's comeuppance, by the time it comes, in unexpected form, it no longer seems to matter so much. By then, Connor Gilmartin is aware of his own abbreviated life as a continuance of the lives of his forebears, and the unthinking act of murder that made him such a reflective spirit (and formed the *primum mobile* of this not at all spectral saga) scarcely requires vengeance.

William J. Scheick   (review date Autumn 1992)

SOURCE: "Life After Death," in *Canadian Literature,* No. 134, Autumn, 1992, pp. 153-54.

[*Scheick is an American educator and critic. In the review below, he comments favorably on* Murther & Walking Spirits.]

The narrator of Robertson Davies's new novel [*Murther & Walking Spirits*] discovers his wife and a subordinate *en flagrant délit,* and is fatally bludgeoned for his trouble. Instead of undergoing the proverbial review of his life, the narrator unexpectedly witnesses, as if watching a series of motion pictures, a review of the lives of his ancestors from the eighteenth century onward. In dying, ironically, he learns something profound about living, and he actually undergoes a change of self.

He learns the truth of Heraclitus's observation "that anything, if pursued beyond a reasonable point, turns into its opposite." Again and again, he beholds the continuous rise and fall and resurrection of human desire and achievement as generation after generation experiences success and loss, affection and contempt, female principles and male principles, life and death. In his own instance, aptly, life has not only led to the seemingly antithetical enigma of death, but death has led to closure with the very mystery of life. "We live and learn, yes. But we die and learn, too, it appears." Life after death is the discovery of "a sense of life more poignant and more powerful than anything" he ever knew while he was physically alive.

This revelation of the Herclitian monad of mutually constitutive oppositions exposes as well that every human life is in effect one drama within the *theatrum mundi.* Metaphors drawn from the stage and from the cinema abound in the narrator's account, suggesting that life is a dream reality, a medium less firm than we tend to think while we live the particular version we know as our existence. Life is as much an artwork, a fiction, as is any play or film or novel. The *matter* of this dream version of a life, especially the fate of mutually constitutive oppositions, may be reality, but the *manner* of personal development in terms of this matter includes a greater variety of production, performance, and persona than we tend to realize. Although archetypes, palimpsests, or influences underlie all of our behavior, nonetheless the "surface" version we re-enact at any given moment may range from a very rough to a quite refined "management of the scene" in which we play a part and for which we also have some directional responsibility.

The dying narrator, for example, eventually appreciates that the most trivial features of life are simultaneously the most noble, and that the most comic are also the most tragic: "There is no such thing as a person who is 'nobody very much.' Everybody is an agonist in one of Fate's time-worn games on the earth." No longer thinking himself "superior to others," he realizes that "these people are my people and I suffer with them, and I do not take sides." At the end of his narrative he feels, in the very marrow of his being, a love that is expressed as "charity and forgiveness."

This is the message of Davies's book. If life is essentially the same as art, then art should be essential in life. Art should encourage its audience to live "more consciously," especially through charity, forgiveness, and acceptance. "Literature is an essence, not a piquant sauce," we are told. Art, particularly the "shady sort of narrative" of "an unauthorized translation" (like Davies's book) can "open the door" to aspects of life that tend to be glimpsed "only in dreams or waking reverie."

Davies anticipates that his audience will be resistant, will prefer not to be "roughly translated" (transported), as if they were colonial emigrants or disembodied ghosts forced to abandon their perceived homeland for the shores of a seemingly crude New World of possibility. But the homeland of their present life, Davies indicates, is not the Original: it is merely a "rough translation" of a reality still open to advancement in human awareness. He encourages us to face this revision of our present version of the "possibly gaudy and certainly deeply felt show" of life with the same determination, based on mutually fearful and joyful expectations, as evinced by the early immigrants to Canada.

Murther & Walking Spirits is, accordingly, a thinking person's book. It seeks to integrate the passivity of the reader—ideally a "patient looker-on" (as in *Fifth Business*) listening to the "deeper monologue" within the narrator's discourse—with the reader's subsequent action in life as the real *dénouement* of the book. The reader, as is well-known about Davies's work, will learn something of Jungean theory, the heritage of art, and the author's passionate commitment to personal reformation. Beyond question, there is much that is very clever in this novel. Whether its audience will appreciate every move Davies makes here will be a matter of taste, I suspect, even if his narrative is designed to demonstrate that literature is an essence, not a piquant sauce. I have no doubt, however, that Part I will strike most readers as Davies at his aesthetic best.

Edmund Fuller   (review date Fall 1993)

SOURCE: "Reading Eloquently," in *The Sewanee Review,* Vol. CI, No. 4, Fall, 1993, pp. 124-6.

[*In the following favorable review of* Reading and Writing, *Fuller praises Davies's various insights into literary creation and appreciation.*]

"Nobody ever reads the same book twice" to my ear is Robertson Davies's best line in a small book [*Reading and Writing*] containing many excellent ones. Midway in a lucid lecture on reading, he is making the point that all great, and many simply good, books not only must be read but reread, many times in the case of the finest, at different times or stages of life.

Unlike a river the book is not changing constantly but the reader is. If he has read *The Brothers Karamazov* in early youth, as I did, he must read it again from decade to decade, for what he can perceive and understand in it will have deepened and broadened. *The Brothers* subjectively is my totem novel, revisited more than any other book, unless we might look upon the whole canon of Shakespeare as a single work for infinite seasons. By widely accepted custom the Bible is set apart from general literary rankings, though doing so poses some risk to the mind as well as to the soul.

Davies, the Canadian journalist, novelist, essayist, and retired master of Massey College of the University of Toronto, delivered the Tanner lectures at the University of Utah in 1992. As the respective subjects of the two lectures he chose Reading and Writing, which he declares are inseparably linked as in his title.

Prolific and versatile in prose, he acknowledges himself to be "a failed playwright"—but so was Henry James. James's novels are more readily dramatizable for stage or screen than are those of Davies, reasons for which he discusses candidly under "Writing." It is partly because, filled though his novels are with extraordinary characters, he does not traffic in heroes or heroines easily conformable to the expectations of Broadway, or, more especially, of Hollywood.

Davies is harsh about reviewers, acknowledging himself as a sometime practitioner of the sinful craft. His criticism of critics generally is just, not unduly reflecting his having been the occasional target of some harshness. Not from me. I have reviewed nearly all of his works with admiration. One was his fattest book, ***Papers of Samuel Marchbanks*** (540 pages), the pen name under which he wrote a wittily acerbic newspaper column for many years. My paradox is that I had no trouble getting into my available space what I wished to say about that or any other of his books. Yet my notes and markings reveal the impossibility of encompassing here all that I would like to say concerning these 64 pages about subjects that are deceptively simple. He has done such a fine job of compression that reducing it further is like trying to compress water. Therefore I say read it for yourself, but I don't quite throw up my hands.

He advises us to read what we like. If we don't like it, don't read it. If we do like it, read it well. Don't "gobble it." Pace yourself so that, in effect, you can hear as well as see. "Read eloquently." He adds, "I know this is heresy. People who teach reading are dead against what they call 'verbalizing.'" Yet writing has major attractions for the ear, even if not read aloud.

Don't try to read always and only the "best." The diet is too rich. "Our grandparents used to say that we must eat a peck of dirt before we die, and they were right. And you must read a lot of rubbish before you die, as well, because an exclusive diet of masterpieces will give you spiritual dyspepsia. How can you know that a mountain peak is glorious if you have never scrambled through a dirty valley?"

An observation on the rewards of poetry leads him to add the advice to read several books at once. "Keep on your table a book of poetry, as well as a novel, some essays, and perhaps a play or two. The notion that you have to read solemnly through one book before you can allow yourself to take up another is simple Puritanism."

It surprises me slightly that he does not discuss reading aloud with or to someone. Many have done so only in reading to young children. Now technology offers a plethora of talking books, which I concede are a boon to the sight-impaired. What I am thinking about and would like him to have mentioned, is the practice that my wife and I carried out for more than fifty-five years, of reading aloud together, turn about. We set apart varying times of an hour or more, except in impossible circumstances, to read aloud together daily, even though we each read widely on our own. We covered an extraordinary volume and diversity, from Evelyn Waugh's *Decline and Fall* to Gibbon's lengthier work. ("Always scribble, scribble, scribble! Eh! Mr. Gibbon?") We read Proust, Tolstoy, Walker Percy, and Mr. Davies. From time to time I alluded to this habit in a long-running review column and got occasional queries. "Why on earth do you do that?" The answer is that there is no better way to read, mark, and inwardly digest, or (to use a much abused word) share, than thus reading together. You can involve a whole family in it.

In "Writing" he also says many wise things. Answering a frequent question: "When do you write?" he says, simply, "I write when I can." For forty years he held full-time jobs and wrote at night and during snatched moments. He advises writers to be independent, get jobs, and support themselves, not to depend on patronage, including its modern equivalent, grants.

Borrowing a striking Russian word from Nabokov, Davies says that a successful novelist, taleteller, playwright, or poet, at any level of literary rank, must have *shamantsvo.* Clearly related to the word *shaman,* it means that a writer must be something of a wizard, a spell-caster, a worker of magic.

If I have interpolated too much that is personal, it is not to aggrandize myself, a sin of which he says, justly, that many reviewers are guilty; but I responded thus because he starts so many hares that one wishes to chase. Unable to compress him any further than this little book, you can only enlarge upon him. That's the best tribute I can pay to a small work that expresses some old insights in a fresh way, along with some altogether new ones, about those universal subjects Reading and Writing.

Isabel Colegate   (review date 5 February 1995)

SOURCE: "Mind, Body and Dr. Hullah," in *The New York Times Book Review,* February 5, 1995, pp. 1, 23.

[*Colegate is an English novelist and critic. In the review below, she praises Davies's handling of character and first-person narration in* The Cunning Man.]

Robertson Davies's new novel is as substantial and as entertaining as any he has written. ***The Cunning Man*** enlarges joyously on many of his familiar themes; the one that underlies all the others is his belief that religion and

Davies has always liked a spacious canvas;
his novels embrace whole lives, from
childhood to death, and they focus
resolutely on the growth of a character's
soul, the discovery of vocation, the search
for meaning in a world governed by
chance and necessity.

—*Michael Dirda, in "Caring For Bodies
and Souls," in* Book World—The
Washington Post, *January 22, 1995.*

science, poetry and medicine, theater and psychoanalysis
have a kind of meeting place where no one is quite sufficient without the others. The liveliest dogs in all those
fields, whether they recognize it or not, may be barking up
the same tree. Thus, a Toronto physician, Dr. Jonathan
Hullah, known to some of his friends as the Cunning Man,
comes to realize that this is the belief that underlies his unusual success in medical diagnosis: "Platonism, or . . . the
Perennial Philosophy, lay at the root of my medical practice. No—*was* the root of it."

In developing this theme, and to escape the undue weighti-
ness of what Dr. Hullah in one of his notebooks claims
particularly to wish to avoid—"one of those German
Bildungsromane, about the growth of a human spirit"—
Mr. Davies employs a number of devices to lighten and
brighten his narrative. He plays with chronology, pinning
his story on Hullah's conversations with a young journalist who has been commissioned to produce a series of articles about old Toronto. He conjures up a casebook in
which Dr. Hullah makes random notes as an *aide-
mémoire* and a working notebook toward something we
imagine will never be completed: an "anatomy of fiction"
in which the doctor enlarges on a number of more general
themes, some relevant to the action and some not particularly so.

In Jonathan Hullah, Robertson Davies has found what
must be one of the most congenial of his many alter egos.
He has always seemed comfortable with a first-person narrator, but however distinctly we may think we hear the authorial voice, Mr. Davies is too expert a novelist to take
his narrator for granted; the character has to be properly
fleshed out and accounted for. Jonathan Hullah was raised
in Sioux Lookout, a small township "nearly 2,000 miles
northwest of Toronto." His father was a mine manager,
his mother a good Christian. His youthful life was saved
by the intervention of Mrs. Smoke, an Indian wise woman
from a nearby reservation. She, hearing that the boy is suffering a dangerous attack of scarlet fever, and mindful of
his mother's good works among her Indian neighbors, en-
camps on the lawn of the Hullah home in a tent that
shakes and emits animal cries all through a winter night
of crisis, after which the boy recovers. Understandably
enough, he is left with a lifelong interest in what would
now be called alternative medicine, whether that of Mrs.
Smoke or of his favorite author, Robert Burton, the writer

of *The Anatomy of Melancholy,* who in 1621 was well
aware of the existence and powers of cunning men and
white witches.

In due course Hullah leaves the simplicities of his home
life for Colborne College in Toronto, a school as highpowered socially as it is academically. At first he is
laughed at as a wild man of the woods, but he soon finds
congenial spirits in two clever fellow pupils: Brochwel Gilmartin, a literature enthusiast, and Charlie Iredale, who
is already determined to become an Anglican priest. These
friends, firmly set in their differing backgrounds, widen
Hullah's horizons and encourage his powers of observation.

Gilmartin's prosperous family home is a muddle of books
and a profusion of vulgar ornamentation. Brocky's father,
a newspaper publisher whose heart is still in the Wales he
left as a child, has fierce differences with his wife, who
comes from a family of old loyalist stock that left the United States at the time of the American Revolution and who
still looks on the Old World with suspicion and some resentment. Charlie Iredale's mother is a martyr to good
taste, having been born and bred in the socially exalted
English-speaking circle of Montreal; his professor father
has "an Englishman's sense of Who's Who." There is not
a character among the many in this crowded novel who
is not similarly put in his or her place, socially speaking;
this concern with detail is one of the book's solid pleasures.

Dr. Hullah's memory is prodded from time to time by
Esme, the young journalist who, before long, marries the
son of Brocky Gilmartin. Hullah tells of his wartime service in Europe as a member of the Royal Canadian Army
Medical Corps, an experience that leads him to believe
that "the physician is the priest of our modern, secular
world. The Medical Corps insignia on my sleeve promised
a magic that the chaplain's cross had lost."

But the cross has not entirely lost its magic for Hullah
himself. Back in Toronto after the war, as he builds up a
reputation as an unorthodox but successful diagnostician,
he becomes a fairly regular participant in the services at
St. Aidan's Church. This congregation, part of the Anglican Church of Canada, and thus of the Church of England, is what in that church is known as "high"—as high
as you can get without toppling over into Roman Catholicism: "Lots of incense, of course; clouds of it whenever an
excuse arose. Holy water, sloshed about lavishly, especially at funerals. Processions with banners, and these were
no innocent advertisements for the Women's League or
the Infant Band, but handsomely embroidered depictions
of the Instruments of the Passion, of the Virgin as Rose
of the World, of the IXΘYC symbol and anything else
that a devout adherent of the church could be persuaded
to pay the Sisters of St. John to work, with infinite patience, on a silken background. Ornaments abounded:
chasubles, of course, with splendid orphreys to enrich
them; copes, it seemed, without number; dalmatics, hu-
meral veils and tunicles whenever possible."

The life of St. Aidan's, with its music, its ritual and the
unconventionality of many of its adherents, becomes a sig-

nificant feature of postwar Toronto. Letters, quoted at length, written by Miss Pansy Freake Todhunter to her friend Barbara Hepworth in England describe its activities in lively style. The Barbara Hepworth here is the real Barbara Hepworth, the artist. And Ernest Jones, referred to in disparaging terms by Dr. Hullah, is the real biographer of Freud, but there is no danger of faction here; perhaps it is rather a question of old scores to be paid. Miss Todhunter's letters are cheerily amusing, and her relationship with Emily Raven-Hart, the sculptor whom she loves and protects and finally mourns, is touchingly conveyed. Meanwhile, dear dull Toronto is being slowly transformed into a modern international city.

In the course of the transformation, the goings-on at St. Aidan's attract the attention of the new financial establishment, which sniffs out a connection between art and left-wing politics. But the drama that ensues is not a political one. The officiating priest dies at the altar, and Charlie Iredale pronounces him to have been a saint. This is where the inquiries made by Esme the journalist of Dr. Hullah and others have been tending, and in the final telling of the truth of the old story, the themes of this big novel come together—with music, ritual, theater and pure comedy—showing us religion doing good and religion gone wrong and, in the sad end of Charlie Iredale, exposing the danger of antinomianism, the tragedy of the good man who mistakes the voices in his head for the voices of angels.

Brocky's son, Gil (who might be but is not Hullah's son, his mother, Nuala, having been the love of Hullah's life), is dispatched somewhat gratuitously toward the end of the book, so we can see that Hullah, although wise, is not uncomfortably so; he can be overcome by wild thoughts of love for Esme, the widow. Saved from making a fool of himself by Esme's meeting with a handsome young millionaire, he settles down philosophically to continue his contemplation of life's spectacle.

This is a wise, humane and consistently entertaining novel. Robertson Davies's skill and curiosity are as agile as ever, and his store of incidental knowledge is a constant pleasure. Long may he continue to divert us.

Roz Kaveney   (review date 7 April 1995)

SOURCE: "Toronto Blessings," in *New Statesman & Society*, Vol. 8, No. 347, April 7, 1995, p. 56.

[*In the following mixed review of* The Cunning Man, *Kaveney argues that while Davies may be reactionary in his ideological orientation, he has an "exemplary sense" of how "ordinary people" experience and deal with pity and terror.*]

It would be easy to dislike Robertson Davies. He is the sort of Tory anarchist whose tolerance of what he calls the poor, the minorities, has more to do with smug urbanity than ethics. Through his narrators, he shows off recondite knowledge in the humanities, medicine and theology for longer than he deigns to tell what might be called a story. His characterisation is displayed by affluent white men (occasionally women) who sit around discussing how fortunate and gifted they are. And yet . . .

Davies' 11 novels display a sense of the workings of the world that justifies that sense of his own urbanity. When he sets out to tell you how a particular small world operates—the small travelling circus in *World of Wonders,* but also, in the present novel [*The Cunning Man*], the protagonist Jonathan Hullah's eccentric practice as a diagnostician—he does so with an absolute conviction that is its own authority.

When, further, he lifts the lid off the way things normally are and shows us the horrors that lurk beneath, he does so in ways that are genuinely upsetting. All the more so, because his sense of humour stays on duty at such moments. We are made complicitly amused by the grotesquerie that accompanies the horrible. When the London Blitz traps Hullah under tons of rubble in a hotel bath, he stays sane by endlessly reciting the obscene mnemonics of his medical training. Davies' moral authority comes partly from the fact that he both knows, and will tell, what such things are.

Davies is obsessed with being a provincial; that helps him avoid being as insufferable as he might be. His Toronto intellectuals perpetually compare themselves with London and New York and find themselves wanting. If *The Cunning Man* has anything as utilitarian as a theme, it is this sense of a city struggling to become a metropolis in its own right. (Its predecessor, *Murther and Walking Spirits,* exhibited the creation of a Canadian identity to the ghost of Hullah's murdered godson.) Chips and Emily, Hullah's sympathetic upper-crust English lesbian landladies, are second-rate artists. Still, they create a salon that crystallises Toronto musical life. And the sin that destroys Hullah's childhood friend Charlie is motivated by the desire to turn a good, dotty old parson into an authentic Anglican saint.

Like all Davies' narrators, Hullah is saved from complacency by clear sight. As a child cured of scarlet fever by a Native American woman's sweat lodge, as a schoolboy coaching Charlie through exams and reading saints' lives aloud to help him endure a painful operation, as an amateur student actor, an army psychiatrist, a lover, a friend and a mourner—in all these roles, Hullah is a paragon of embattled good sense and stoicism. If Davies is a reactionary writer whom modernism and PC have passed by, he is also a humanist novelist with an exemplary sense of the pity and terror of life, and of how quite ordinary people sense and cope with them.

Phil Baker   (review date 7 April 1995)

SOURCE: "A Doctor of Souls," in *The Times Literary Supplement,* No. 4801, April 7, 1995, p. 25.

[*In the following review, Baker comments favorably on* The Cunning Man.]

It is the morning of Good Friday, and the Mass of the Pre-Sanctified is in progress in Toronto, at St Aidan's, a church so High as to be controversial, with "a whiff of gunpowder amid the incense". Father Ninian Hobbes has just taken the Communion wafer into his mouth, when he suddenly drops to the ground. For a second, it looks like genuflection, but it is a heart-attack. Father Hobbes, believed by many to be nothing less than a modern-day saint, is dead.

Whodunit enthusiasts should already be suspecting a case of Death by Wafer, but Robertson Davies calmly shifts the emphasis away from the end of Father Hobbes to the life of the Cunning Man, Dr Jonathan Hullah, who is telling the Hobbes story to a young female journalist. Hullah's "Casebook" (for that is what we are reading [in **The Cunning Man**]: he bought a casebook, realized it was impracticable, and now uses it for his memoirs) is much concerned with the area that lies between religion and science. His old friend Charlie Iredale, a priest, is surprised to hear Hullah talking about the soul ("You, a doctor"), and this balance is pivotal throughout the novel.

As a boy, Hullah was near death with scarlet fever, but his life was saved by the local Indian "wise woman", Elsie Smoke. Mrs Smoke is in polar contrast with Doc Ogg, the family's alcoholic doctor. Ogg is one of several superbly comic figures in the book, despite being "a lonely man, for good reasons. He had a depressing personality and he was a bore." It is the well-meaning Ogg who encourages young Jonathan with the gift of an out-of-date medical textbook, and warns him that "Science rules the world. Cling to Science, boy, and keep clear of superstition." Mrs Smoke, on the other hand, refuses to take Jonathan as an apprentice, but she does frighten him with two snakes which she claims are his totem; a claim which later proves to be true, in the form of the Aesculapian staff.

It is not these schematic significances which give the book its near-greatness, although it is finely constructed. Davies's chosen affinities here are with Chaucer and Goethe, and his book combines the earthy worldliness of the one— the Miller's Tale features a couple of times—with the "humanism" of the other: the Aesculapian staff makes another entrance as a wand, in a stage production of Goethe's *Faust*. Humanism may be a compromised and beleaguered word these days, but it is an entirely positive term in here.

Hullah's humanism is vaguely Jungian and definitely anti-Freudian. His feelings about both schools are integrated lightly into the narrative (including a vignette of the onetime Toronto inhabitant Ernest Jones) and his antiFreudian digs never have that sour hobby-horse quality of Nabokov's. Davies is, quite quietly, less in sympathy with the idea that "Sex is Lord of All" than he is with the idea that illumination is to be found in silent forests, and that archetypes are to be found in everyday situations. He perceives that soldiers behave according to the soldierarchetype, for example, and that the Lilith archetype figures in the wet dreams that his school friends have (and which, incidentally, are to be the unexpected mainspring of the central murder story). Davies's anti-Freudian bias also extends, perhaps less knowledgeably, to the Decon-

structionists, and although the digs are good-natured, they still sound rather like John Bayley might if he talked in his sleep.

Hullah's own declared philosophy is "Platonism . . . the Perennial Philosophy". This is central to his medical practice, which cunningly treats the whole person. He gained experience as a wartime doctor with troops maimed by friendly fire, and he had unexpected success with recitations such as "Christmas Day in the Workhouse" (which caused him to be warned about sedition by his superiors: "About the government not doing enough in the way of social service. That kind of stuff"). It was also among these unlucky soldiers that he discovered that intractable free-floating grievance is a central human problem. Hullah's discussion of his "Paracelsian" practice, with due attention given to the four humours, occasionally sails close to New Age nonsense and to the insidious end of the "holistics" argument (the argument, in effect, that people get the illnesses they deserve; which may occasionally be salutary, but it is no less salutary to remember that people also get the illnesses they don't deserve). The idea that incurable resentment finds its vessel in socialism is not likely to win friends for Davies in all quarters, either.

For all that, Davies's entertaining novel is magnanimously written, and its incidents have the convincingly anecdotal tone of autobiography. It is relaxed and believable in its period detail ("What made her popular", Hullah remembers of a girl who made his friend's life a lovesick misery, "was that she had a very good 'line', for it was a time when girls had 'lines'") and it is rich in secondary characters and incidents: characters like the High Church homosexual Darcy Dwyer, an expert in acting, practical joking and the theory of sin, for example; and incidents like the Coburg Social Parlour's Seventh Annual Bad Breath Contest. Medical student Hullah is roped in to judge this as a practical joke, but he triumphs by delivering a magnificent impromptu oration. It is one of the several faces of theatre in the book, along with the drama of church ritual, the showmanship of successful doctoring, and above all the "Theatre of Life".

The story ends with Hullah an old man, newly disappointed in love but well able to appreciate this *theatrum mundi*. Doctor Hullah's Casebook is essentially a long *Bildungsroman* in which the physician attempts, if not to heal himself, at least to know himself. Although his title is explained in the text, Hullah and his creator are really far less in the business of cunning than of being selfconsciously wise: but of course wisdom, especially in its grey-bearded variety, sounds somewhat less glamorous than cunning.

Additional coverage of Davies's life and career is contained in the following sources published by Gale Research: *Bestsellers 1989,* No. 2; *Contemporary Authors,* Vols. 33-36, rev. ed.; *Contemporary Authors New Revision Series,* Vols. 17, 42; *Contemporary Literary Criticism,* Vols. 2, 7, 13, 25, 42, 75; *Dictionary of Literary Biography,* Vol. 68; *DISCovering Authors; Major 20th-Century Writers;* and *World Literature Criticism.*

Stanley Elkin

May 11, 1930—May 31, 1995

(Full name Stanley Lawrence Elkin) American novelist, short story writer, and essayist.

For further information on Elkin's life and works, see *CLC*, Volumes 4, 6, 9, 14, 27, and 51.

INTRODUCTION

Considered one of the best and most entertaining stylists in contemporary fiction, Elkin is renowned for works that transform grotesque situations and the vulgarity and alienation of mass culture into comic affirmations of humanity. His prose style is characterized by punning wordplay, Jewish idioms, and a blend of formal and colloquial language that many critics have found reminiscent of a sales pitch conceived as high art. The son of a jewelry salesman, Elkin was born in New York City and raised in Chicago. He began writing stories in elementary school, evincing early the interest in literature he pursued through college and graduate school at the University of Illinois at Urbana-Champaign. After serving in the United States Army between 1955 and 1957, he returned to teach literature at Washington University in St. Louis, Missouri, and complete his dissertation on William Faulkner for the University of Illinois. Before earning his doctoral degree in 1961, however, he went to Rome and London on what he called "a mother's grant" to do most of the writing for his first novel, *Boswell* (1964). Elkin taught literature and creative writing at Washington University for the rest of his life, becoming a full professor in 1969 and the Merle King Professor of Modern Letters in 1983. Elkin's fiction features many first-person narrators whose obsessive personalities are expressed through intense, humorous, eloquent speech peppered with the inflections and jargon of their professions. Exemplary in this regard is the novella *The Bailbondsman* from *Searches and Seizures* (1973), in which Alexander Main, known as "the Phoenician" in the Cincinnati criminal justice community, begins to realize what it means to age: "Where are my muscles, my smooth skin? Why doesn't desire die? . . . Why do I have this curiosity like a game leg? How can I cross-examine the universe when it jumps my bond?" Critics note that evolving, aging, and physical decay are among the main themes of Elkin's fiction. Diagnosed with multiple sclerosis in 1972, a disease which eventually confined him to a wheelchair and the custodial care of his wife, Elkin continued to write and teach and faced his condition with humor and determination. He wrote that "As long as you've got your health you've got your naivete. I lost the one, I lost the other, and maybe that's what led me toward revenge—a writer's revenge anyway, the revenge, I mean, of *style*."

PRINCIPAL WORKS

Boswell: A Modern Comedy (novel) 1964
Criers and Kibitzers, Kibitzers and Criers (short stories) 1966
A Bad Man (novel) 1967
The Dick Gibson Show (novel) 1971
The Making of Ashenden (novella) 1972
Searches and Seizures (novellas) 1973; also published as *Eligible Men: Three Short Novels*, 1974, and *Alex and the Gypsy*, 1977
The Franchiser (novel) 1976
The Living End (novel) 1979
Stanley Elkin's Greatest Hits (short story, novella, novel fragments) 1980
The First George Mills (novel) 1981
George Mills (novel) 1982
Early Elkin (short stories) 1985
Stanley Elkin's Magic Kingdom (novel) 1985
The Rabbi of Lud (novel) 1987

The Coffee Room (novella) 1988
The MacGuffin (novel) 1991
Pieces of Soap: Essays by Stanley Elkin (essays) 1992
Van Gogh's Room at Arles: Three Novellas (novellas) 1993
Mrs. Ted Bliss (novel) 1995

*This work contains the novella *The Making of Ashenden,* previously published separately and in *Searches and Seizures;* the short story "The Guest," previously published in *Criers and Kibitzers, Kibitzers and Criers;* and five excerpts from Elkin's novels: "Feldman & Son" is taken from *A Bad Man;* "Bernie Perk" from *The Dick Gibson Show;* "The Transient" from *Boswell;* "Mr. Softee" from *The Franchiser;* and "The Conventional Wisdom" from *The Living End.*

OBITUARIES AND TRIBUTES

William Grimes (obituary date 2 June 1995)

SOURCE: An obituary in *The New York Times,* June 2, 1995, p. A25.

[*In the following, Grimes reviews Elkin's life and career, noting that "his work veered toward parody and black humor—and his highly wrought sentences formed a dense, self-contained linguistic world."*]

Stanley Elkin, a stylistic virtuoso whose novels, short stories and novellas were at once lyrical, bleak and fantastic, died on Wednesday at Jewish Hospital in St. Louis. He was 65 and lived in University City, Mo.

The cause was heart failure, said his daughter, Molly.

Mr. Elkin, the author of *Criers and Kibitzers, Kibitzers and Criers, Searches and Seizures, The Magic Kingdom* and *The Franchiser,* was often described as a clear-eyed realist—even though his work veered toward parody and black humor—and his highly wrought sentences formed a dense, self-contained linguistic world. Although he paid scant attention to plot and incident, his deliberately preposterous fictional situations led him to explore the pain at the heart of the human condition. His long struggle with multiple sclerosis only deepened his preoccupation with suffering and mortality. Reviewing Mr. Elkin's second novel, *A Bad Man* (1967), in *The New York Times Book Review,* the critic Josh Greenfeld called the author "at once a bright satirist, a bleak absurdist and a deadly moralist."

Mr. Elkin was born in Brooklyn, where his father was a costume-jewelry salesman, and grew up on the South Shore of Chicago, where he began writing stories in grade school. After graduating from South Shore High School, he attended the University of Illinois at Urbana-Champaign, where he earned a bachelor's degree in English in 1952, a master's degree in 1953 and a doctorate in 1961. His dissertation dealt with religious themes and symbols in William Faulkner's novels. From 1955 to 1957 he was in the Army.

As an undergraduate, Mr. Elkin contributed stories to *Illini Writers,* the university's literary magazine, and acted in radio dramas on the college station.

In 1960, he became an instructor in the English department of Washington University in St. Louis, where he taught writing for the rest of his life. He became a full professor in 1969 and was named Merle King Professor of Modern Letters in 1983.

His first novel, *Boswell: A Modern Comedy* (1964), showed Mr. Elkin's penchant for concocting absurd situations with tragic potential. It thrust an updated version of Samuel Johnson's biographer into the modern world. Fearful of death, haunted by a sense of his own mediocrity, he surrounds himself with celebrities, including a professional wrestler nicknamed the Grim Reaper, and tries to organize a club of famous people.

Mr. Elkin won widespread critical praise for his second book, *Criers and Kibitzers, Kibitzers and Criers* (1966), a collection of nine stories, most of them sharply realized character sketches. Critics also admired *Searches and Seizures* (1973), a collection of three novellas, one of which, "The Bailbondsman," was made into the 1976 film *Alex and the Gypsy.*

His work often dealt in darkly comic fashion with the alienating effects of American mass culture and the mysterious power of cliche. The hero of *The Dick Gibson Show* (1971), a radio disk jockey who roams from station to station, is everywhere and nowhere. *The Franchiser* (1976) tells the exploits of Ben Flesh, who is so successful in creating a nationwide empire of franchises that by the end of the novel he cannot tell one state from another.

Flesh's enthusiasm for his products inspired one of Mr. Elkin's most memorable set-pieces:

> The *colors* of those ice creams! Chocolate like new shoes. Cherry like bright fingernail polish. We do a Maple Ripple it looks like finegrained wood, Peach like a light coming through a lampshade. You should see that stuff—the ice-cream paints bright as posters, fifty Day-Glo colors. You scoop the stuff up you feel like Jackson Pollock.

In 1972, Mr. Elkin, who had already survived a heart attack, was found to have multiple sclerosis, an illness that, over time, restricted him to a wheelchair and forced him to abandon the pen for the computer. It also provided him a metaphor that runs through much of his subsequent work. *The Magic Kingdom* (1985), for example, tells the story of a group of terminally ill children who are taken on an outing to Disneyland.

His other novels include *The Living End* (1979), *The Rabbi of Lud* (1987) and *The MacGuffin* (1993). His novel *George Mills* (1982), about 40 generations of blue-collar workers named George Mills, won the National Book Critics Circle Award. Several of his essays were collected in *Pieces of Soap* (1992), and in 1992 he published a collection of three novellas, *Van Gogh's Room at Arles.*

At the time of his death he had just completed a novel,

Mrs. Ted Bliss, which Hyperion is to publish in September.

In addition to his daughter, of Washington, he is survived by his wife, Joan; two sons, Philip, of Creve Coeur, Mo., and Bernard, of St. Louis; a sister, Diane Brandwein of Chicago, and two grandchildren.

Marie Arana-Ward   (essay date 5 June 1995)

SOURCE: "Stanley Elkin, Voice of the Little Guy," in *The Washington Post,* June 5, 1995, p. 2, sec. 2.

[*Arana-Ward is a staff-writer at* The Washington Post *and former editor of some of Elkin's books. In the following tribute, she discusses Elkin's personality and his desire for a broad readership, one that included more than just other writers.*]

The last time I saw Stanley Elkin, we were speeding through a late Manhattan night in a van. I was in the front next to the driver, looking out at the street ruts winter had left behind. Stanley was in an open space in the back, strapped into his wheelchair, which was, in turn, yoked to the floor. It was 1992, and we were returning from the National Book Award ceremony in a funk. It was the third time he had been nominated for the award, and the third time he had lost.

Bumping along in the dark, trussed up in his tux with a runner-up medal festooning his neck, Stanley was inconsolable. As the road got worse, I could hear his hands thwack against the armrests and his head flop from side to side. Soon he was bobbing like a balloon in the wind. "Goddamn New York potholes!" he finally roared, half in a rage, and half with diabolical glee. It was vintage Elkin—a moment that could have been pulled from the life of Bobbo Druff, city commissioner of streets and luckless hero of *The MacGuffin,* his novel that hadn't taken the prize that year.

Stanley Elkin died last week in St. Louis of complications arising from his 23-year struggle with multiple sclerosis. He was 65. Merle King Professor of Modern Letters at Washington University and easily one of the greatest virtuosos of the American language, he produced 10 novels, two volumes of novellas, one volume of short stories, one collection of essays, and three published scripts.

I was Elkin's editor for a time—an oxymoron if ever there was one, for Elkin's books needed no editing. They sprang full-blown from the man's head, magical riffs of irreverent wisdom. Their heroes, like him, are the powerless but shrewd, setting out into an unjust world like Brooklyn bred Don Quixotes: off to tilt at windmills with little more than a mouthful of fast talk.

For all his yearning to be known by the greater American public, however, Elkin remained a writer's writer: an artist who was envied and exalted by the literary world, but whose works went undiscovered by the common man they strived to depict. Cynthia Ozick said of him, "Stanley Elkin is no ordinary genius of language, laughter, and the irresistible American idiom; he is an ingenious genius—an inimitable sword-swallower, fire-eater, and three-ring circus of fecund wit."

Elkin was born in the Bronx and grew up in Chicago. He was the eldest son of a costume jewelry salesman, a hereditary fact that predisposed him (he always said) to looking at words as if they were glittering gewgaws ready for the stringing.

After graduating from South Shore High School in Chicago, he attended the University of Illinois at Urbana-Champaign, where he completed a BA (1952), a master's (1953) and a doctorate (1961) in English. He served in the U.S. Army from 1955 to 1957. He was a visiting professor at many colleges, including Yale, Smith and the University of Iowa, but for most of his career he was an English professor at Washington University in St. Louis, where he taught writing until his death last Wednesday.

Although he could be seriously funny, much of Elkin's work is about the angst at the heart of American mass culture. *Boswell,* his first novel (1964), tells the tale of a modern-day biographer whose gnawing sense of his own mortality and mediocrity leads him to surround himself with bizarre people he perceives to be famous. His second book, *Criers and Kibitzers, Kibitzers and Criers* (1966), is a much-loved collection of nine short stories—sketches of an array of oddballs—that Harvard's Helen Vendler has likened to a dazzling show of "naked bravado and ostentation."

George Mills (1982), the novel that won Elkin the National Book Critics Circle Award, is about 40 generations of workers who are all named George Mills and who are all trapped in their blue-collar jobs. In *The Magic Kingdom* (1985), a group of terminally ill children is taken to explore the surreal landscape of Disney World. In *The MacGuffin* (1991), the aforementioned Bobbo Druff combs city streets in an existential daze and wonders when the traffic and his life got so far out of control. Among Elkin's most recent works are *Pieces of Soap* (essays, 1992), *Van Gogh's Room at Arles* (novellas, 1993) and the forthcoming novel *Mrs. Ted Bliss,* to be published in September.

When Elkin was nominated for the PEN/Faulkner award in 1994 and didn't win, his daughter Molly (one of three children Elkin had with his wife Joan), went to the ceremony in his place. "My father couldn't be here," she told the audience, "because of his debilitating disease. . . . Oh, I don't mean that one," she added when a knowing hush descended on the room. "I mean his writer's ego." He couldn't bear the torment of watching someone else get the glory again.

And yet, it was that not-getting-the-glory-thing that sharpened his wit and fed his imagination. Here Stanley Elkin ultimately found a victory: He became America's past master at taking defeat and weaving it, word by word, onto filaments of gold. "As long as you've got your health," he wrote, "you've got your naivete. I lost the one, I lost the other, and maybe that's what led me toward revenge—a writer's revenge anyway, the revenge, I mean, of *style.*"

An excerpt from *The Bailbondsman*

The door opens and a little bell sounds. Like in a bakery or an old candy store. I don't suppose much of this registers on my clients, but perhaps I get to them subliminally. . . .

I look up casually and greet the newcomer, a man in a checkered sports coat, loud matching shirt and tie, new style cuffs on his flaring trousers. He has a sort of crew cut and looks for all the world like an off-duty cop. . . .

"Top of the morning," I tell him pleasantly.

"Top of the morning yourself." This man is not a policeman.

"Raise the blinds please, Mr. Crainpool [Mr. Crainpool is the narrator's assistant—he does not speak in this scene]. A little sunshine on the tough here. You had me fooled, son."

"You the Phoenician?"

"I am Mr. Alexander Main, the bailbusinessman."

"I'm from out of state."

"You're lost?"

"I'm Mafia, Pops."

"Mafia, wow."

"Wow? This is how you talk to a mobster?"

"One call on the hot line and you'll never talk out of the side of your mouth again. Me and the Don of all the Dons are like that. I call him Donny. Behave yourself. Nice folks don't come in off the street on a bright and sunny morning and say 'I'm Mafia, Pops.' Who are you, son? Where are you from?"

"Chicago. They call me 'the Golfer.' "

"The Golfer, eh? What do you shoot?"

"*People,*" we both say together. I turn to Mr. Crainpool. "Mr. Crainpool, do you hear this dialogue? What a business this is! The nearer the bone you go, lifewise and deathwise, the saltier the talk. Peppery. You could flavor meat with our exchanges."

Stanley Elkin, in his "The Bailbondsman," in Searches and Seizures, *Nonpareil, 1973.*

Geoffrey Wolff   (essay date 17 September 1995)

SOURCE: "Remembering Stanley Elkin, Master of Excess," in *The New York Times Book Review,* September 17, 1995, p. 43.

[*Wolff, an American novelist, biographer, essayist, and educator, was a close friend of Elkin's. In the following reminiscence, he describes the author's "extravagant" literary style and the irreverence, tenacity, and "breath-stopping candor" with which he lived his life.*]

It wasn't enough to have written many singular novels and collections of stories and novellas and essays, every piece of work surprising. It didn't suffice to be Merle King Professor of Modern Letters at Washington University in St. Louis. It was too paltry a blessing to be eligible for Social Security payments, too miserly a bounty to be celebrated by fellow writers for the richest, most supple and idiomatic and muscular and elegantly cadenced American sentences since William Faulkner's. Stanley Elkin, all appetite, wanted more. He confessed his longing to be a "crossover" artist, Art Tatum goes platinum, to be read by everybody, even by—perhaps especially by—people who don't read.

The first words of Stanley Elkin's first novel, **Boswell:** "Everybody dies, everybody. Sure." He didn't ask for much, just to be rich and famous and to live forever free of pain. As to rich and famous, who cares? He woke up from the free-of-pain dream a long time ago, so it seemed little enough to ask to live forever.

He died on May 31, but not before finishing and editing a new novel, **Mrs. Ted Bliss.** When he'd say he wanted to live forever, he meant the part that wrote, talked, listened, ate, loved and laughed. He was brutally clear about this: He was contemptuously indifferent to the part in libraries—reputation, classical standing. He wanted the fun now.

The first time I met Elkin he called me a liar. I could make believe that coming from a fiction writer this was a compliment, but it wasn't. This was 20-some years ago, at a little party given by Robert and Pilar Coover at Princeton, where Elkin was about to read aloud from his work. I had just introduced myself and told him I cherished his fiction. He stared at me, shook his head and said, "You sure got a funny way of showing it." I was ashamed to be taken for a suck-up, but mostly I was bewildered. What could he be talking about? Maybe he was suffering the before-reading jitters, maybe he didn't mean to insult me; but he seemed cool as cool could be, and soon I learned that he always meant what he said.

Bob Coover, overhearing our exchange, asked, "Stanley, do you know Geoffrey Wolff?"

"Oh, do I know this guy? I know him, but Geoffrey Wolff he ain't."

"Well, I am," I said.

"I know who you are," he said.

Who he knew I was was a bearded novelist, a young has-been who lived in Greenwich Village and had somewhere hedged his review of an Elkin novel with reservations. I could have stood being confused with Vladimir Nabokov or Edmund Wilson. But my doppelgänger was washed up the afternoon of the morning the poor mutt was said to have promise. From the certitude that I was this bozo, Stanley would not budge. All that night, even during his reading, he gave me the fisheye.

And what a reading! The bravura punch of it, the quicksilver riffs and unreserved investment in his characters gave me a welcome kick in the pants, a reminder of why I'd ever thought it was a good idea to read and write. Elkin did all the voices: his greatest tribute to a writer he liked—and he liked many—was to say that a writer gave to all his characters the best lines. Later, when his body wore out, he lost his pipes for reading aloud, but he never lost his pitch-perfect timing, his all-stops-out indulgence of his characters' music; he lavished attention on them as they lavished attention on themselves. Elkin's characters were *hot* for themselves, in perpetual estrus, as passionately single-minded (but sane) as the she-bear who sexually victimizes the lordly master of his game preserve in **The Making of Ashenden.** I write "she-bear." Elkin wrote:

"A black patent-leather snout like an electric socket."

"A long and even elegant run of purplish tongue, mottled, seasoned as rare delicatessen meat, that lolled idiotic inches out of the side of its mouth."

"A commitment of claw . . . the color of the heads of hammers."

"A low black piping of lip."

"A shallow mouth, logjam of teeth."

You know, like a bear? Reviewers (and some book editors) beat up on Stanley for his extravagance: too much of a muchness, don't you know, over-egging the custard. This is like criticizing the Matterhorn for being too pointy, the Pacific for being too damned wet. In *The Paris Review,* Stanley told his interviewer, Thomas LeClair, that one of his editors kept insisting, "Stanley, less is more." "I had to fight him tooth and nail in the better restaurants to maintain excess because I don't believe that less is more. I believe that *more* is more. I believe that less is less, fat fat, thin thin and enough is enough."

When he'd say he wanted to live forever, he meant the part that wrote, talked, listened, ate, loved and laughed. He was contemptuously indifferent to the part in libraries—reputation, classical standing. He wanted the fun now.

—Geoffrey Wolff

Another criticism, offered as an explanation when Stanley complained (and Stanley was a virtuoso of complaint, a great griever) of his narrow audience: He demanded too much of his readers, his conceits flew too fast, too far past the pull of gravity, beyond where common folk could follow. Hearing **The Bailbondsman** that night at Princeton I heard a wizard aria, a display of verbal pyrotechnics in which Phoenician grave robbers break into a Pharaoh's tomb and find a mummy: "Its open eyes seem not blind so much as distracted, as though its pupils, large and black as handballs, witness something going on extraordinarily

high in the sky. Its sweet lips look as if they taste their own goldenness." Stanley insisted, was right to insist: That's how this mummy would look to you, too, if only you'd focus.

After his reading, down the table at a Chinese restaurant, he shook his head at me. "Pretty cute," he said. "Geoffrey Wolff—now *there's* a likely handle!" Stanley's stubbornness, his tenacious commitment to his vision of human situations, was awesome.

By the time he'd done with me, spun his version of who I was, elaborated the tangled skein of my motives, I longed to be the devious character he supposed me to be. Once I'd surrendered unconditionally to his version of me, he forgave me for changing my name and sort of forgave me for the ugly review I never wrote. We became friends, I loved him.

In his masterpiece, **The Living End,** he out-Jobs Job, takes on heaven and hell, Lucifer and the Almighty. He doesn't deny God, but he finds Him disappointing, petty, distanced from His creations. Stanley was personal, always, finding in each person everything that was available, teasing it out, improvising on it. He made of the human beings he encountered what God would have made had God had the time and imagination. When I spent time with Stanley I felt enhanced, transfigured into my possibilities.

I once taught a student who had grown up near Stanley's house in St. Louis, where she'd been a friend of Stanley's daughter. She felt intimidated by her friend's dad, the way kids will. One afternoon, visiting Molly, she found herself alone in the house with Mr. Elkin, downstairs in the living room, where he couldn't see her. He was in an adjoining room alone with someone's baby. The door was open; he was talking: "How's the weather down there?" "Da-Da? Oooh, how advanced guard of you!" "While you're down, shine my shoes." "Here's lookin' at you, kiddo." "Just kidding." "Gee baby, ain't I good to you?" I'm pretty certain that hanging out with a drooler incapable of a complete sentence was not Stanley's idea of heaven (his idea of heaven was a place where "there are actually halos—like golden quoits, or, in the distance, the lovely green pastures, delicious as fairway"), but by this time he was a prisoner of his body, which was a prisoner of multiple sclerosis, and since he wasn't going anywhere on his legs, he might as well sightsee Baby World for all it was worth.

About his disease he was everything anyone could admire: forthright, offended, curious, mordant. After he needed a cane and leg brace, but before he got sentenced to a wheelchair, he would go from standing to sitting in a kind of backward swoon, terrifying to watch, an audacious act of faith. During a cocktail party at Bread Loaf, he had just managed this feat when a jogger came into the room, sweating theatrically, stretching, cooling down, rubbing his neck.

"Oh boy, oh boy," he said, wincing, looking down at Stanley. "My neck is killing me! Running on these mountain roads. . . ."

"I wept," Stanley said, "because I had no feet, until I met a chap had no shoes."

Stanley was capable of breath-stopping candor. He didn't know how to make nice, was without tact. A guest for dinner came late to the Elkins' house one night years ago. This good friend arrived breathless, emotionally shaken. He brought bad news about a writer celebrated for his gassy homilies on the obligation of the artist to promote morality. This bloviating sermonizer had that evening passed along word that he was afflicted with a killing disease. Guests at the table gasped, put on sad faces. Stanley didn't.

A man who could translate God into a petty bureaucrat, a fine-print artist of an Almighty, was not one to shrink from a violation of appropriate reverence. "God reads," Stanley said.

I hope so.

At a Stanley Elkin public reading:

The monks were serving mulled wine, baked potatoes and pizza, and Stanley Elkin was getting nervous. He hadn't expected that the reading in England, arranged by his friend and fellow novelist Robert Coover, would be held in a monastery, and he certainly hadn't expected his audience of students from the university of Kent to be augmented by monks, much less by teenage girls on a weekend retreat.

This was, Elkin recalls, in 1971 or 1972. Nothing he had read thus far from his novella "The Making of Ashenden" . . . could have offended virgin ears. It begins innocently enough as a spoof of the idle and fatuously rich, a drawingroom, almost Noël Coward comedy. But the refreshments had interrupted Elkin just before he got to the rough stuff: a graphic description, at once obscene, lyrical and hilarious, of sexual intercourse between his twit protagonist and an extremely demanding Kamchatkan brown bear.

What was he to do? What else *could* he do but resume reading as his audience tried to digest the incongruous comestibles? When he reached the end, more than stomachs were rumbling. "I know why you wrote that story," one girl protested. (Here Elkin, as he retells the tale, assumes a cockney accent.) "Because you're the antichrist!" University students jumped to Elkin's defense, a brawl nearly ensued, and the affronted monks not only refused payment for their fare but also canceled all future literary evenings.

Ken Emerson, in his "The Indecorous, Rabelaisian, Convoluted Righteousness of Stanley Elkin," in The New York Times Magazine, *March 3, 1991, pp. 40-1.*

REVIEWS OF ELKIN'S RECENT WORK

Meg Wolitzer   (review date 21 March 1993)

SOURCE: "The Roaring Anger of Not Being in Charge," in *The New York Times Book Review,* March 21, 1993, pp. 3, 19.

[*Wolitzer is an American novelist, critic, and author of children's literature. In the following review of* Van Gogh's Room at Arles, *she praises Elkin's prose style, humor, and compassionate understanding of his characters.*]

The cover of Stanley Elkin's 1985 novel read **Stanley Elkin's The Magic Kingdom,** which brings to mind titles like *Stephen King's "It"* and *Jacqueline Susann's Once Is Not Enough.* What was Mr. Elkin's book doing in that particular pantheon? His work had never achieved blockbuster status, or been turned into a mini-series or movie. Mr. Elkin is a star of a very different literary universe, where well-constructed and difficult books are revered, and where a dream double bill at the local multiplex would be "Donald Barthelme's Snow White" and "Samuel Beckett's Malone Dies." There was nothing big and glitzy about Mr. Elkin's darkly comic novel, which concerned a group of terminally ill children sent on a whirlwind Make-a-Wish Foundation-style trip to Disney World.

Now, eight years later, Mr. Elkin has written **Van Gogh's Room at Arles,** a subtle, complicated, often astonishing collection of three novellas. This time around, it almost makes sense to think of the book as "Stanley Elkin's Van Gogh's Room at Arles," not because it feels showy and sensational, but simply because the collection is so singular to its author, and the room in its title seems to belong as much to Stanley Elkin as to Vincent van Gogh.

The first novella, an exercise in helplessness and rage called **"Her Sense of Timing,"** takes place far from Arles. Jack Schiff, a professor of political geography at a university in St. Louis, is a victim of a debilitating disease that has left him a virtual invalid, largely dependent on the care of Claire, his wife of 36 years: "Even in restaurants Claire paid the check, figured the tip, signed the credit-card slip. His disease had turned him into some sort of helpless, old-timey widow, some nice, pre-lib, immigrant lady."

At the beginning of the novella, Claire has just announced that she's leaving Jack, and she proceeds to pack her suitcases and scram. What follows is a maddening and riotous account of Schiff's struggle to reconcile himself to being on his own for the first time in years. Not only has Claire left him in the lurch, but, even more horrible, she's departed on the eve of Schiff's annual party for his graduate students, a big, messy affair that Claire has always overseen. What will he do? How will he cope?

Schiff (and, cleverly, Mr. Elkin) turns to one of those companies that install emergency aid devices in the homes of the elderly or disabled. The S.O.S. Corporation swiftly dispatches a team to Schiff's house, and his relationship with its members, Bill and Jenny, becomes the source of much broad, dark humor. He's forced to rely on them for every little thing, and when it's time for him to pay for their services, he enlists them to go rummaging around the house for his checkbook:

"I think it may be in one of the drawers in the tchtchk."

"Say what?"

"The cabinet in the hall. We call it the tchtchk."

"That's a new one on me. You ever hear that, Jen? The choo-choo? Heck, I can't even pronounce it. How do you say that again?"

"Tchtchk. It doesn't mean anything."

"Just a pet name, eh? From your salad days. . . . It's just something you ought to bear in mind. . . . Well, that you *had* salad days. . . . That's why the good Lord usually lets us hold on to our memories. . . . So we can remember the times before our wives had to carry us around piggyback."

The word "tchtchk" summons up the private shorthand used by longtime couples, the secret language of marriage that usually can't be shared with anyone else, or even fully translated. Later in the novella, when Jenny casually refers to the "tchtchk" as though it were a common word, the moment is surprisingly affecting. Schiff starts to grow attracted to her, to come alive for the first time in years. Although he's in a wheelchair, in a position of potentially humiliating vulnerability, this "pre-lib, immigrant lady" slowly gains back a good measure of his American maleness and bravado.

That night at the graduate students' bash, which takes place despite his protests, Schiff finds himself attracted once again, this time to a student named Molly Kohm: "He was gathering courage, putting together a sort of schoolkid's nerve he hadn't used in years. . . . Yes, Schiff thought, I'm going to touch her. I'm going to reach over and hold her."

Mr. Elkin, who teaches at Washington University in St. Louis and who has written eloquently elsewhere about his own multiple sclerosis, here explores the ramifications of degenerative illness, from the purely physical difficulties of the smallest everyday actions to the roaring anger and frustration of not being in charge. The novella gamely confronts weakness and strength, and ends with—no surprise—a really good punch line.

Mr. Elkin's second novella, **"Town Crier Exclusive, Confessions of a Princess Manqué: 'How Royals Found Me "Unsuitable" to Marry Their Larry,' "** brings us a bit closer to France, at least in terms of geography. This is a tour de force about a woman who falls in love with Lawrence, Crown Patriciate of England. Coming as it does on the heels of a major British monarchy shakedown, the novella is timely and funny, although inhabiting the mind of Louise, the commoner who briefly nabs Prince Larry, is at least as arduous as occupying the body of Prof. Jack Schiff. Louise rambles on, relating choice tidbits to a supermarket tabloid, *Town Crier,* that has bought the rights to her story. As Mr. Elkin portrays her, Louise is a kind of breezy, souped-up Fergie-Diana hybrid, an ordinary woman plucked from the normal world and brought into the palace nuthouse. **"Town Crier Exclusive"** is a witty piece of work, studded with bits that lampoon the royal family. Some are based on actual events, such as a reference to an intruder sneaking into the Queen's bedroom to watch her sleep, while others are pure Elkin, as in a scene

in which the Prince's relatives discuss the upcoming wedding with the prospective bride and groom:

"Would it be all right, do you think, if we wore, well, jeans, to the wedding?"

"Jeans? To a Royal Wedding? In Westminster Abbey?"

"I told you he wouldn't go for it."

"Well, not jeans, or not jeans exactly. Regular morning coats and top hats for the boys, actually."

"And gorgeous gowns for the ladies. With these ravishing big hats and really swell veils."

"Just *cut* like jeans."

"From stone-washed denim."

"Oh, it would be such fun! The Sloane Rangers would just die!"

"Town Crier Exclusive" is often truly funny, but at times it's a little too thickly packed with ludicrous humor and circumlocutious side trips, and it does go on somewhat longer than it should. After a while, the clutter of Mr. Elkin's version of royal life becomes a little too much to take and, like Fergie and Diana bolting the palace gates for good, the reader finally wants out.

Mr. Elkin's strongest stuff is saved for last. The title novella concerns a professor named Miller who's won a foundation grant and been sent to an academic retreat in Arles, where, by a stroke of luck, he's assigned to van Gogh's bedroom. All the accouterments of the great man, depicted in his famous painting of the room—the basin, the pitcher, the bed—have been left for the less-than-great man to use. Miller is out of his element in every way; the retreat in Arles is a think-tank hideaway for intellectuals from all the great institutions: Harvard, Yale, Princeton, Booth Tarkington Community College. *Booth Tarkington Community College?* That's where Mr. Elkin's protagonist teaches.

All around him, other institute fellows proudly describe their work: "Myra Gynt, a composer from the University of Michigan, explained how it was her intention to set the lyrics of various Broadway showstoppers to the more formal music of the 12-tone scale." "Farrell Jones held forth regarding his conclusions about the parallels between the mood swings of manic-depressives and babies." A man in a wheelchair is in Arles to research a project on his theory that "world-class cities were almost never found on mountaintops." (Although he's not named, we can guess that he is meant to be Jack Schiff of **"Her Sense of Timing,"** whose reappearance is a self-referential wink to the reader.)

Finally, when it's Miller's turn in this game of rarefied show and tell, he fails miserably. He's been invited by the foundation to work on a study of the image of the community college among academics from prestigious universities, and at the end of his description of this vague, bogus-sounding project, Miller faints dead away.

A doctor is summoned who turns out to be Félix Rey, the

great-great-grandson of van Gogh's own doctor, Félix Rey. The young Rey is the spitting image of his ancestor, right down to the tips of his reddened ears. Over the course of Miller's stay in Arles, he becomes aware of other members of the Club of the Portraits of Descendants of People Painted by Vincent van Gogh. These characters haunt the edges of the novella like apparitions, creating an atmosphere reminiscent of parts of Joyce's story "The Dead," invoking the greatness of what's past and the mundane but moving humanness of what's still living.

In this novella, Mr. Elkin muscularly demonstrates his talents through his easy transitions from shtick to art and back again. He has great fun listing the catalogue of intellectuals, getting their names just right: "Samuels Kleist, a vernacular architect in his late 60's, Yalom and Inga Basset, pop psychiatrists. . . . Jesus Hans, statistics adviser to the third world." Mr. Elkin can also be highly poetic, a kind of borscht belt visionary who reaches for a real epiphany near the close of the novella:

> Miller decided to turn off the light. Low as the light had been, his eyes still had to adjust to this new black dark. What he saw now, the almost colorless configuration of shapes and masses, made a different and still stranger picture and, as dawn came and the light turned milky, and then, as the sun rose higher and the room experienced its gradual yellowing, it seemed almost to go through a process of queer simultaneity, of aging and renewal at once.

This time, Mr. Elkin doesn't go out with a punch line, but the humor lingers even as the novella closes with a long passage of charged and beautiful writing.

The three novellas in **Van Gogh's Room at Arles** are linked through shared themes and obsessions, with Mr. Elkin the ironic geographer lurking in a corner, overseeing the landscapes of his characters' lives. Mostly, though, the novellas are connected by Stanley Elkin's distinctive and unflagging voice. In his new book, that voice is big enough to fill the whole room.

Francine Prose   (review date July 1993)

SOURCE: A review of *Van Gogh's Room at Arles,* in *The Yale Review,* Vol. 81, No. 3, July, 1993, pp. 128-30.

[*Prose is an American novelist, short story writer, critic, and educator. In the following excerpt, she argues that* Van Gogh's Room at Arles *is Elkin's best book.*]

Stanley Elkin writes fiction that veers into manic lyricism while maintaining—Elkin insists on it—absolute precision of language. By now readers have learned to so value the rhythms of Elkin's sentences that they may find themselves moving their lips when they read, just as they were always taught not to. *Van Gogh's Room at Arles,* a trio of novellas, has passages of description so classically and recognizably *Elkin* that one can imagine some poor (or lucky) student in the future asked, on a multiple-choice exam, to identify where this pizza comes from:

> The tops of the pizza boxes had been torn from their bottoms, and everywhere, teetering on the arm of the sofa, on the coffee table, left on a seat cushion, on a stereo speaker, in the makeshift dishes, the smeared, greasy, bronzed mix-and-match of the cardboard china, lay pieces of cold, uneaten pizza like long slices of abstract painting, their fats congealing, fissures opening in their cooling yellow cheeses; burst bubbles of painterly cholesterol, chips of pepperoni raised on them like rusty scabs.

It's this exactness (and humor) that allows Elkin's work to go so far out on the edge, to evoke the most extreme emotions—rage, shame, lust, grief, fear—and never for a moment veer out of control. Elkin and his characters share a dogged determination to see things as they truly are, without piety or illusion, and a distrust of cant and sloppiness, especially where language is concerned. When a graduate student warns Schiff, a crippled professor, about the "devastating effects" that "negative energy" can have on someone "in his condition," Schiff replies, " 'Let me tell you something, Ms. Kohm. . . . Unless they're referring to alternative fuels or to how they're feeling, I'm always a little suspicious of, and embarrassed for, people who use terms like energy.' "

The three novellas remind one again of Walter Benjamin's interest in who's staying home, who's traveling, what kinds of tales they tell [earlier in the review, Prose refers to German critic and essayist Walter Benjamin who, in "his essay on Leskov, . . . makes—and quickly blurs—a distinction between two kinds of storytellers: the one who stays home and knows the local history, the other who leaves and comes back with a tale to tell. One is 'embodied in the resident tiller of the soil, and the other in the trading seaman' ")]. The title novella is very much about going someplace else: to the South of France, where a community-college professor on a foundation grant is given Vincent Van Gogh's last bedroom—and considerably more. In **"Town Crier Exclusive, Confessions of a Princess Manqué: 'How Royals Found Me "Unsuitable" to Marry Their Larry' "** the narrator, a young woman briefly engaged to the heir to the British throne, embarks on a dizzy, madcap whirl before slamming straight into a wall. And the hero of **"Her Sense of Timing"** feels lucky just to make it up the stairs; the paralyzed, wheelchair-bound Schiff, a professor of political geography, discovers that his wife has left him on the eve of their annual graduate-student party.

The protagonists of these short novels are more sinned against than sinning, and in a way they have it worse than Job: their comforters are also their tormentors. The same students who offer to take on every arduous detail of hosting Schiff's party wreck his house in a Bacchanalian orgy of nerdiness and "awful graduate-student food."

Stanley Elkin has always been fascinated by the details of what people do, by work, jobs, hustles, hucksters, and fast talkers. Two of these three stories concern academics, but while Elkin gleefully flails away at the follies of academia, these characters have more important things to do. The hard work of simply surviving and staying sane are their day jobs, as it were, and occupy the major part of their time and attention. (Though the characters are mostly middle-class—and in the second novella, royalty—there's nothing safe or bourgeois about Elkin's writing; you feel he'll say anything.)

One hopes many readers (that is, besides other writers) will appreciate the sheer bravery, the riskiness and difficulty of what Stanley Elkin attempts and succeeds at. Writers will no doubt find themselves considering how tricky it must have been to describe the effort required for Schiff to perform ordinary physical acts: what a challenge for an author to capture that effort without the faintest tinny echo of falseness or sentimentality. (Stanley Elkin has often been drawn to material—for example, the terminally ill children in *The Magic Kingdom*—that would be awful, hopeless, written by anyone else.) What it costs Schiff to get from his bed to the bathroom is immensely moving and frightening and at the same time horrifically funny. One thinks of Samuel Beckett's Molloy, dragging himself from place to place; like Beckett, Elkin is perpetually weighing damage against resilience. So Professor Schiff gives a play-by-play description of his travails to an imaginary audience of fans:

> Technically I'm still in the bathroom, though the wheels of the walker, and even its two hind legs, are over the threshold and out in the hall, heading south, my right foot on Steppp, my left, huff puff huff puff, on Draaaag. And I'm in the hall too, now, in the hall and making my adjustments, shifting my trajectory, handling the walker, raising it up off the carpet and swinging it east, bringing my body into alignment with the walker. All right. All right. Just about ready to move on. From here it's a fairly clean shot east to the bedroom, where I'll have to hang a north, then jockey from there northeast to the bed. You know something, folks? I'm not saying it's a blessing or promising rose gardens, merely mentioning in huff-puff passing that this disease could have done worse than chosen to be trapped in the body of a political geographer.

Van Gogh's Room at Arles is, think, Stanley Elkin's best book. It's certainly the easiest to read—it moves right along, it asks nothing. The title novella is so well constructed that when you realize (or *think* you realize) where it is going, you feel a shiver at the back of your neck that intensifies when you see what turn the book is *actually* taking: toward a sudden, illuminating glimpse of the accidental, visionary, and (for lack of a better word) religious nature of art. What Stanley Elkin has always done well he does even better here. No one is more deft at pacing a scene for comic timing, and these fictions include scenes (a foundation social event at which grantees describe their silly projects, Schiff's monster of a party) which build to stunning heights of comic humiliation. Throughout these novellas, everything builds; their cumulative power is astounding.

Maureen Howard   (review date 3 September 1995)

SOURCE: "Sunset Over Miami," in *Los Angeles Times Book Review,* September 3, 1995, pp. 1, 8.

[*Howard is American novelist, essayist, critic, and autobiographer whose works include the novels* Expensive Habits *(1986) and* Natural History *(1992). In the following highly*

---

positive review of Mrs. Ted Bliss, *she compares Elkin to Mark Twain and Herman Melville, describing him as "an American writer of the first rank."*]

Stanley Elkin died this past spring. He will remain an American writer of the first rank. I'm taking the long view that includes Melville and Twain—by all means Twain—not the myopic squint at who is to be taken seriously this season. Elkin, the funny man, deserves a large and lasting audience—readers who will be rewarded when they buy a ticket to the Elkin Vaudeville Show and find that they also hold a season subscription to the symphony.

Mrs. Ted Bliss, Elkin's last novel, stands as a brilliant end to the long career of a writer who saw the pitch of every assaulting sentence, the shape of each paragraph, as vital to the moment of his story.

The energy and imagination that Elkin invests in Mrs. Bliss, the most ordinary of women in ordinary circumstances—a Jewish widow living in a Miami condominium, a fixture in the life of family and friends—is extraordinary. A woman as central character is new territory for Elkin, who celebrated the ordinary guy in his stories and novels of hopeful hucksters and flamboyant losers who work the salesrooms of tawdry-yet-wondrous American life.

Elkin's franchiser, bail bondsman and talk-show host are defined by their professions, as Dickens often defined and limited his memorable comic figures—a Mr. Gradgrind, a Uriah Heep. So what is Elkin doing with this aging beauty who hasn't worked since she was a girl helping customers zip and button in a dress shop? With this woman addicted to cleaning house and meticulously caring for herself (two showers a day, lotion, talc)? With this harmless plush dinosaur in a pre-feminist landscape? He is working over the passive character, the blank slate, the outer limits of ordinary. With his old magic, he conjures the pathetically amusing Mrs. Bliss, transfiguring her in the course of her final years from bland to bold, from a hoot in pink polyester to a heroine of depth and grace. The naiveté of this unenlightened woman is made clear:

> Dorothy had not, beyond the universe of her own family, known all that many men, but even in her family had noticed the tendency of the women to leave the choicest cuts, ripest fruits, even the favorite most popular flavors of candy sour balls—the reds and purples, the greens and oranges—for the men. The most comfortable chairs around the dining room table. The coldest water, the hottest soup, the last piece of cake.

Mrs. Bliss, seldom called Dorothy, is an uncomplaining product of her narrow society back home in Chicago and in Miami's Condominium No. 1. Branded as wife and mother, she sees marriage as a trade-off: "Women honored the men who put food on the table, who provided the table on which the food was put, and the men saved them." Mrs. Bliss feels that she was saved from her dreary job in the dress shop by Ted. As it turned out, she was saved to become a background figure, a leftover who can't balance a checkbook, never mind the stock emotions of her life.

Mrs. Bliss would seem to be a Jewish version of Evan Connell's foolishly innocent and touching Mrs. Bridge, save for the fact that Elkin's Dorothy has large adventures. This isn't Kansas, folks—it's Miami, and the condo crowd of retirees is straight out of central casting. What can transpire beyond the next illness, predictable death, visit from the kids, card game, potluck in the rec room? A novel with an amazingly inventive structure in which, for starters, a stranger comes to the door with a proposition for Mrs. Ted Bliss. Unlike Elkin's criers and kibitzers—men always alive to the scam, whether conning or being conned—Dorothy is a dupe, a sitting duck.

The deal has to do with Ted's '78 Buick LeSabre, which Alcibiades Chitral wants to buy (actually, he supposedly wants the parking space in the condo that goes with the car). Chitral is one of the condo's "Latins." The Jewish Establishment, "stereotypical down to the ground," refers to all new neighbors—Venezuelans, Chileans, Colombians, Cubans—as Latins. Life as they have lived it by the pool in Miami is changing, has changed. Chitral turns out to be a drug lord, and his use of the LeSabre to stash his hold is a desecration of that beloved artifact, the family car. Mrs. Bliss sends him up for a mythic 100 years with her testimony.

Elkin has been criticized wrongly for his lack of plot; the fact is that he is not satisfied by a simple anecdotal story with ethnic overtones like the one he sets up here in the first pages. His interest lies in the *consequences* of plot, in what happens when the untoward incident disrupts the overly ordered life.

Will Dorothy Bliss now wake from her dull dream? Has she left the door ajar? Is she to be forever condemned to be as dumb as yet another Latino con artist sees her:

> She wasn't human, she was a cliché quivering in the corner. Of course she was a pillar of love. She was a pillar of love capable of any greed, nastiness, bad manners, gossip or folly. A patriot only to consanguinity, this cowering special pleader of blood who traded on her revenant, immemorial widowship and mommyhood.

In Elkin's best work, the slight of caricature gains the fullness of character. And so the story of Mrs. Ted Bliss goes on, as life goes on to transcend mere plot. In this last-lap-of-the-road *Bildungsroman,* Elkin explores the afterlife, life after the shocking event—the death of a loved one, the sentencing of the guilty.

The protected life of the survivor, Dorothy Bliss, is seemingly without dimension—without reference to mass death and mass guilt. Writ large in Dorothy's story, however, are the undercurrent of her insufficiency and the struggle to overcome her innocence. The discoveries she makes about neighbors and family, and, painfully, about herself, form a grand and continuing narrative that is set in motion after the Keystone Kops and robbers sale of the Buick to Chitral.

As Mrs. Bliss is set free of her constraints, so is the novelist set free of the programmed story, free to let Mrs. Bliss confront less-comfortable memories in which even the beloved Ted was not free of major misdemeanors. She is free to mourn the death of a son and free to discover that in the present she lives at an emotional as well as a geographic distance from family.

Elkin wrote against the constraint of plot, as did Melville, daring to stop the whale chase for a brilliant dissertation. So we have Mrs. Bliss set in play, visiting her dull, prosperous children, visiting a spick-and-span prison in which Chitral, who calls himself a "cliché," is given a Stanley Elkin riff:

> "Had you been here when we came to the New World we'd have made you slaves, stolen your gold and smashed your temples. We'd have wiped out your mathematics and astronomy and forbidden you access to your terrible gods. No

offense, ma'am, but there's something loathsome and repellent to persons like me in persons like you.

"Perhaps your passivity—I bear you no grudge, Widow Bliss, I've no bones to pick with your kind—is at odds with our conquistador spirit, something antithetical between our engagement and the Jew's torpid stupor, his incuriosity and dead-pan, poker-faced genius for suffering. . . ."

And on and on he rants, in possession of the author's stunning rhetoric, in sentences with cadences that scan; a lecture, or is it a sermon from the devil we create by roping ourselves off from those not of our kind? This novel is profoundly about the tags we hang on ourselves and others, sexually and racially; about the dishonest mumble of polite memories, polite words; about our separate dictions of discord: Chitral with his wild articulation, his lethal cultural overview; Mrs. Bliss with her Yiddish phrases, homey, shopworn, antique.

As I read **Mrs. Ted Bliss,** I felt that the writer, who suffered for many years with multiple sclerosis, knew that this was his last time on stage and that his voice must carry—unmiked, no replays—to the last row. Elkin believed in voice, in his voice as a writer. When you read Elkin—outrageous, forgiving, compassionate, always testing the possibilities of his characters and exploring the bounds of their stories and of fiction itself—you read Elkin prose, not laid-back minimal reportage.

"But life's tallest order," Elkin wrote, "is to keep the feelings up, to make the two dollars worth of euphoria go the distance. And life can't do that. So fiction does. And there, right there, is the real—I want to say 'only'—morality of fiction." Yet this last work, this posthumous novel (what a high old time he'd have with that category), ends on a moral note.

Dorothy, grown older and infinitely wiser than Mrs. Bliss, the well-preserved widow, sits with Louise Munez, once known to her as a strange girl in the small society of the condo. Louise is now a woman of 50. The semblance of family is long gone from Condominium No. 1 and at this particular moment everyone has fled. They sit alone waiting for Hurricane Andrew, the unpredictable act of nature or God. Mrs. Bliss opens her arms:

> In the darkness, she lifted her left hand to Louise's head and began to stroke the dry hair.

> Because everything else falls away. Family, friends, love falls away. Even madness stilled at last. Until all that's left is obligation.

Obligation, as in the promise to forbear, as in the observance of our humanity.

Mrs. Ted Bliss came to me with a notice announcing the author's publicity tour. Elkin was a master mimic. We will miss him in eight cities doing his clever takes on the cast of minor characters who surround Dorothy Bliss—the skimmers, the shysters, a fraudulent therapist. But let it be known that the sustained and sustaining performance

for Elkin's readers will be there, in perpetuity on the page. He went the distance.

Walter Goodman   (review date 17 September 1995)

SOURCE: "Twilight of a Baleboosteh," in *The New York Times Book Review,* September 17, 1995, p. 7.

[*Goodman is an American journalist and critic who frequently writes on television for* The New York Times. *In the following review of* Mrs. Ted Bliss, *he argues that, though it is not Elkin's best work, it is characteristically intelligent and funny and parts of it will "stay with you after you've given up on the plot."*]

Has any reviewer faced with a Stanley Elkin novel not tried to describe its intoxication with words, a River Joyce springing from the incidental, swelling through the uncharted, anticlimaxing in the unexpected? The high-flying riffs, the virtuoso vaudeville shticks, the shameless clichés, the daft dialogue, the obsessively accurate lists of everything and anything, the unsettling mix of the funny and the fraught? Readers exasperated with the patchy plots and mistrustful of characters who are the author's mouthpieces may still relish the show. And so it is with his final work [**Mrs. Ted Bliss**]. Consider:

> She spent endless hours (three or four a day) in her kitchen, preparing food, doing the dishes till they sparkled, mopping the floor, scouring the sink, wiping down the stove; yet she had never been a very good cook, only a driven taskmistress, seldom varying her menus and never, not even when she entertained guests, a recipe, obsessive finally, so finicky about the world whenever she was alone in it that she was never (this preceded her deafness) entirely comfortable outside the door to her apartment (where she conceived of the slipcovers on her living room furniture, and perhaps even of the fitted terry-cloth cover on the lid of the toilet seat in the bathrooms, as a necessary part of the furniture itself; for her the development of clear, heavy-duty plastic a technological breakthrough, a hinge event in science, up there with Kem cards, washable mah-jongg tiles, lifelong shmuts-dread, a first impression she must have taken as a child in Russia, a sense of actual biological trayf, fear of the Gentile, some notion of caste deeper than a Hindu's, a notion, finally, of *order*), something stubborn and stolid and profoundly resistant in her Slavic features, her adamant, dumb and disapproving stance like that of a farm animal or a very picky eater.

That's Mrs. Ted Bliss, eponymous heroine of the 17th book by Stanley Elkin, who died in May. An unusual central character for him: a woman, and such an old one—80, give or take, and a widow to boot—and such a Jewish one, who flavors her often sour reflections with bits of Yiddish, crunches of lump sugar sweetening the lemony glass of tea. Still healthy, *kayn aynhoreh,* but aware that she never much enjoyed her long life. Not particularly lovable, but *echt* Miami Beach.

Elkinites will have no trouble recognizing her unstoppable locutions as the streetwise, sheltered, tough, vulnerable, ironic, yearning lingo of other Jewish-American writers—Bellow, Roth, Malamud—with whom Elkin has reasonably been conjoined. The washers on these gents' samovars are shot; there's no turning them off.

Why "Mrs. Ted"? Well, that's the way Dorothy has thought of herself for all the decades of her marriage, to which she came as an unformed, unknowing, fearful, suspicious girl, and deep down nothing much has changed. No liberation for this missus. She turned into a *baleboosteh,* queen of the kitchen, raising her three children in the physical and emotional shelter provided by her butcher husband. A woman whose days are now filled with activity without action. A vain woman—but no fooling around, thanks.

Sex and age aside, Mrs. Ted is as occupied with death and disability as any other Elkin creation (pancreatic cancer in *George Mills;* Elkin's own disease, multiple sclerosis, in *The Franchiser* and in the short story **"Her Sense of Timing"**; all manner of harrowing afflictions in *The Magic Kingdom*). Like Rose Helen in *The MacGuffin,* Mrs. Ted is hard of hearing and isn't crazy about earpieces; her world has a way of fading in and out, depending on her own inclinations and the author's needs. As for death, what is Florida, where Mrs. Ted now lives alone in a seventh-floor condominium, but a last stop in the American dream? "Hey, who's fooling who? Nobody got out of this place alive." It's the living end.

Lincoln Road is *in extremis:*

> Half the shops were boarded up or turned into medical buildings where chiropractors and recreational therapeusisists kept their offices; and in Wolfie's almost the only people you ever saw were dried-up old Jewish ladies on sticks with loose dentures hanging down beneath their upper lips or riding up their jaws, and holding on for dear life to their fat doggie bags of rolls and collapsing pats of foiled, melting butter that came with their cups of coffee and single boiled egg, taking them back to the lone rooms in which they lived in old, whitewashed, three-story hotels far down Collins.

Ted, *olov hasholem,* has already been gone "too many years," and her dearly mourned son Marvin, *olov hasholem, olov hasholem,* was lost even earlier, to leukemia, finished off not only before the arrival of death with dignity but before pain management. "The *chozzers* gobbled up the red cells like there was no tomorrow. They had a picnic with him."

So what already is the plot? Don't ask. It has to do with Mrs. Ted, as dependent as ever on the tricky attentions of men, tiptoeing out of her condominium cocoon, taking a few nervous chances and in some shaky way being reconciled, more or maybe less, to her two surviving children and their families, not bad people, but insignificant beside the anguished memories of her Marvin.

The men are the main thing. Courtly, threatening, antic, they divert the reader briefly from Mrs. Ted's kvetching, fetching though it often is. Especially the elegant Latins, those Cesar Romeros who share the condo with the over-the-hill Jews: Alcibiades Chitral, maybe a drug lord, who wants Ted's Buick LeSabre for some dubious business; Hector Camerando, a big shot in jai alai and the dogs, who offers Mrs. Ted a tip or two; Tommy Auveristas, an importer, ho ho. Their "sexy, perky, tango air sent unmixed signals of something like risk and danger that sailed right over the Jews' heads." But not over Mrs. Ted's; her they hit right in her girlish heart.

Everything about these guys is shady, not to say obscure—except as incarnations of Mrs. Ted's suppressed longings. Their entrances excite her expectations and the reader's, only to disappoint both. The huggermugger about drugs and the Buick is as hard to follow or swallow as the unkosher dreck served at Tommy Auveristas's suspicious open house. The Latins' main accomplishment is to have taken lessons in rhetoric from Professor Elkin, only they were not A students: "No offense, ma'am," Señor Chitral says with undisguisedly offensive intent, "but there's something loathsome and repellent to persons like me in persons like you. Perhaps your passivity—I bear you no grudge, Widow Bliss, I've no bones to pick with your kind—is at odds with our conquistador spirit, something antithetical between our engagement and the Jew's torpid stupor, his incuriosity and deadpan, poker-faced genius for suffering, like a cartoon kike's stoicism struck in a shekel." Stage Latin?

Also on call and equally recognizable in the Jewish-American canon, there is Junior Yellin, the onetime untrustworthy partner of Ted, the unreformable black marketeer who gave Mrs. Ted an unforgettable feeling-up in her husband's butcher shop so long ago, and who now returns as a recreational therapeusisist, still hustling, nowadays treasure hunting on beaches taken up by

> women older than Dorothy on beach chairs of bright woven plastic, indifferent as stylites, their skin dark as scabs; men, the ancient retired, chilly in suits and ties; girls in thong bathing suits, their teenage admirers trailing behind them like packs of wild dogs; kids, overexcited, wild in the surf, their parents frantically waving their arms like coaches in Little League; waiters, kitchen help and house-keepers on smoke breaks; small clans of picnickers handing off contraband sandwiches, contraband beer; lovers kneading lotions and sun block into one another's flesh like a sort of sexual first aid.

Pardon the extended quotes, but how else to get across the essence and appeal of *Mrs. Ted,* as of other Elkiniana? Toward the end, in search of a climax, the author resorts to Hurricane Andrew as accompaniment to Mrs. Ted's final coming to terms. Tune out the *Sturm*-ing *und Drang*-ing. Nobody knew better than Elkin that life and careers rarely end on a big note.

Mrs. Ted Bliss may not be Stanley Elkin's best, but it is a smart, generous, melancholy, funny, even elegiac work by a prodigious practitioner. Passages—all right, shticks—stay with you after you've given up on the plot. There's Mrs. Ted out shopping with her visiting health-nut daughter-in-law, Ellen, who announces that her doctor recommends coffee high colonics. A few pages later, Mrs. Ted awakens to the smell of fresh coffee: "Great, thought Mrs. Ted Bliss, she's making herself an enema."

David Milofsky (review date Winter 1995)

SOURCE: A review of *Mrs. Ted Bliss,* in *Prairie Schooner,* Vol. 69, No. 4, Winter, 1995, pp. 150-53.

[*In the following highly positive review, Milofsky prefaces his comments on* Mrs. Ted Bliss *with a brief tribute to Elkin's life and works.*]

The king is dead—and I don't mean Elvis. Stanley Elkin, arguably the most wildly imaginative fiction writer of the post-war generation, passed from this planet May 31 and literature is poorer for it. To the end, however, Stanley had his laugh as the *New York Times* obit was shot through with inaccuracies, starting with the cause of death. "We told them Daddy died of heart failure," Elkin's daughter Molly said, "because only drunks die of pancreatitis. My father did a lot of things, but he was no drunk." Our newspaper of record also got Stanley's place of birth wrong ("Brooklyn," his wife Joan remarked. "Give me a break."), and the number of novels he wrote. Other than that, it was a great obituary, but then Stanley never had any luck with journalists. He was after a higher truth than they knew.

Yet—and this is a big yet—Elkin was misunderstood by his peers as well as by the popular press. Like God in his brilliant triptych, **The Living End,** Stanley never really found his audience, never won the Pulitzer and was a three-time runner up for the National Book Award. And while things like this aren't supposed to bother writers, ironically, Elkin, like Brecht, always wanted the large popular audience more than he did the approval of the faux intellectuals of academic literary salons ("I don't even know what metafiction is," he once complained in conversation). And when he did win a big award, the National Book Critics Circle prize in 1983, he couldn't resist saying, "I could be a wise guy and thank the three critics who actually reviewed **George Mills,** but I won't."

The fact that his failure to achieve a popular audience didn't make Elkin bitter is a tribute to him, both as writer and as man. He didn't indulge in the common cop-out of claiming that future generations would discover his genius, and he never lost his sense of humor about his own work. When an editor of a literary magazine wrote saying that he planned to devote an issue of his magazine to Elkin if Stanley would give him a piece of fiction for the issue, Stanley replied that he thought it "would be unseemly if I contributed to a Festschrift for me. And actually, I'm a very seemly guy." The Festschrift issue never appeared and Elkin never mentioned it again. It wasn't what mattered. Seemliness mattered.

Yet even among the literati Elkin was more admired than he was read and, in a sense, it's understandable, though every sentence he wrote was a small work of art. Elkin is hard in an age that wants things to be easy. And while it is true that his genius inheres in the fact that he thinks of things no one else could ever conceive—that his work simply isn't *like* anyone or anything else—some of those things are bizarre, to say the least. To put it baldly, in anyone else's hands, these plots wouldn't be very promising. Take **The Magic Kingdom** (1985), a novel about a group of terminally ill children given a trip to Disney World as

their dying wish. Or how about **The Rabbi of Lud,** in which the lowest ranking member of his class at the Jewish Theological Seminary is given a "flock" consisting of all the people in the largest Jewish cemetery in New Jersey? Or even the award-winning **George Mills,** which considers the life and times of "George, the lunch-pail kid," scion of forty generations of blue collar workers dating all the way back to the Crusades. The point doesn't have to do with silk purses but rather with the fact that this material is so unique that no one but Elkin would even attempt to fashion it into a novel. And yet he did. Over and over. Time and again. And each time we read in wonder, not understanding exactly what it was that was working there, though the more alert could admire Elkin's dazzling literary catalogues, extended metaphors and remarkable diction. Reading him you didn't even think you wanted to be like him; that was out of the question. You were just glad to be around him, even if it was only through his fiction.

Which brings us to the current volume **Mrs. Ted Bliss,** which was completed before Stanley's death and was published this fall by Hyperion. If the plots of the books mentioned above seemed less than promising, they were real page-turners compared to this one, which concerns a once-beautiful but now deaf widow (with a hearing aid "the size of a Walkman hanging out of her ear") living by herself in a Florida condominium after her husband's death. You wonder what they're going to do for jacket copy, for ads, for this novel. But if plot has been said to be Elkin's weakness in days gone by, it's a pleasure to report that **Mrs. Ted Bliss** has nothing but.

Dorothy Bliss's condo is split fairly evenly between elderly Jews and younger Hispanics, whom the Jews suspect of being drug dealers. One of these men, Archimedes Chitral, approaches Dorothy shortly after her husband's death and offers to buy Ted's Buick LeSabre, which has sat in its prime parking space untouched since his demise. Since Dorothy doesn't want to pay taxes on a car she doesn't drive, she agrees to a price she knows is wildly inflated and then discovers that Chitral is part of a drug ring and that the DEA has seized the car as evidence. In short order, she is called upon to appear in court and ends up involved with several of Chitral's colleagues, who offer her opportunities to bet on sure things at jai alai. Given that Dorothy was known to be beautiful in her youth, it still strains credulity that a seventy-five-year-old widow would draw the ardent attentions of such men. Yet Elkin makes it all believable, as usual, even ordinary.

More important than the plot, however, is the theme of Elkin's new book. For he is writing here about loss, and writing about it in a way that makes this a novel of witness. Mrs. Bliss makes it a point never to trivialize death, or use euphemisms. Whenever she speaks of the dead, which is often in her retirement community, she says that the person "lost his life," which is chillingly accurate. What **Mrs. Ted Bliss** is about is loss; loss of place, loss of friends, loss of social position, finally of life itself which gives rise to everything else. It is in its own way eerie to have Elkin speaking to us of loss from the grave, but that is unquestioningly what he is doing. And in this picture of a woman growing old alone, there is something heroic about simply going on as Dorothy does, as all of us in one way or another must.

Yet even in the midst of her loss, Dorothy must deal inevitably with her children, neighbors, all the detritus of life. Among the many brilliant things in this brilliant book, Elkin demonstrates the enormous amount of meshugaas parents, especially elderly parents, must absorb from their children. Even when children are senior citizens, parents, like Mrs. Bliss, must tolerate their children's petty bickering, their enthusiasms. One of Dorothy's sons becomes an orthodox Jew, though he wouldn't say kaddish for his father. Her daughter-in-law, who arrives for a visit, is a health food nut eager to give Dorothy enemas.

> Now she knew what they could do together while her daughter-in-law was there waiting for her stay-over Saturday discount. They could give each other enemas. First Ellen could give her a coffee-bean enema, then they'd trade off and Dorothy could give her daughter-in-law a lovely rice enema. Coffee beans, rice. It was six of one, half a dozen of the other. Tomorrow, tomorrow they would lay in provisions.

Even in the midst of such trials, however, Dorothy manages to keep a good humor and to honor her past, specifically her dead husband, who never appears in the novel, except in memory. That this is somewhat archaic in a time of liberated women doesn't bother Elkin and it doesn't bother Dorothy, though she has "sympathy with her gender." In Dorothy's culture, women dressed for men, cooked for men, indeed lived for men. ". . . even in her family [she] had noticed the tendency of the women to leave the choicest cuts, ripest fruits, even the most popular flavors of candy sourballs—the reds and purples the greens and oranges—for the men. The most comfortable chair, the coldest water, the hottest soup, the last piece of cake. . . . They worked combs through the boys' hair gently; they scratched their backs."

In return, the men worked and provided (Dorothy does not even know how to write a check at her husband's death), and died young. From this perspective, it doesn't seem like much of a bargain for anyone, but Elkin's not making deals; he's creating a world and it is one that is uniquely, brilliantly, his own.

The novel ends with Dorothy holed up in her condo with the building's security guard, the two holdouts when a hurricane hits southern Florida. The image of the small, deaf woman left alone with a stranger in the face of a natural disaster could stand for Elkin's grim view of human existence. ". . . everything else falls away. Family, friends, love fall away. Even madness stilled at last. Until all that's left is obligation."

Dorothy Bliss's obligation is to wait out life, as one would wait out a storm, with forbearance and wit. The same, of course, could be said of Elkin, who endured more pain and tragedy than anyone deserves. He once wrote, "As long as you've got your health, you've got your naivete. I lost the one, I lost the other and maybe that's what led me toward revenge—a writer's revenge, anyway, the revenge of style."

One hopes that was enough for him. Certainly the body of work he has left behind should satisfy anyone who's wondering as to the seriousness and importance of contemporary American fiction. Those of us who knew him mourn Stanley's death, but it's reassuring to know that he went out on top—and in style. *Mrs. Ted Bliss* is a touching, enduring book, a worthy epitaph to a tragic life.

> Additional coverage of Elkin's life and career is contained in the following sources published by Gale Research: *Contemporary Authors,* Vols. 9-12, rev. ed.; *Contemporary Authors New Revision Series,* Vols. 8, 46; *Contemporary Literary Criticism,* Vols. 4, 6, 9, 14, 27, 51; *Dictionary of Literary Biography,* Vols. 2, 28; *Dictionary of Literary Biography Yearbook, 1980; Major 20th-Century Writers;* and *Short Story Criticism,* Vol. 12.

James Merrill

March 3, 1926—February 6, 1995

(Full name James Ingram Merrill) American poet, novelist, dramatist, and memoirist.

For further information on Merrill's life and works, see *CLC,* Volumes 2, 3, 6, 8, 13, 18, and 34.

INTRODUCTION

Merrill is regarded as one of the most important poets of the twentieth century. Esteemed from the beginning of his fifty-year career for the formal and metrical precision of his work, he steadily developed his poetry's thematic depth so that, in such notable works as *The Fire Screen* (1969), *Braving the Elements* (1972), and *The Changing Light at Sandover* (1982), he was able to openly address autobiographical concerns, socio-political elements, and, in J. D. McClatchy's words, "the creation of an entire cosmogony." The son of Charles Merrill, co-founder of the New York stock brokerage firm now known as Merrill Lynch, Merrill was born into great wealth and consequently did not have to rely on his writing to earn a living. He decided early in life that poetry would be his vocation and pursued his study of literature at the prestigious Lawrenceville School in New Jersey and at Amherst College. *Jim's Book* (1942), his first collection of poems, was published privately when he was sixteen. After serving in the military during World War II, he returned to graduate from Amherst and begin writing full time. Critics note that Merrill began his literary career during a revival of interest in metaphysical poetry, exemplified by the works of English poets John Donne and Andrew Marvell. Merrill's first works reflected this influence, and, as Paul Christensen noted, they represented the poet's "elegant persona, his widely cultivated tastes, his voice of leisured travel and gracious living—the poetry, in gist, of an American aristocrat." The majority of critics argue that while his work never lost its "mandarin" qualities, Merrill's poetic sensibility expanded—particularly in *The Fire Screen* and thereafter—to give voice to his deepest passions and most imaginative speculations. *Braving the Elements,* for example, is noted for the ways in which content and voice dictate the use of relatively free poetic forms, which critics suspect is the result of increased emotional honesty and willingness to reveal intimate feelings. The poems eventually collected in *The Changing Light at Sandover* evolved over a period of twenty-five years. In the 1950s Merrill and David Jackson, his friend, companion, and collaborator, began experimenting with a Ouija board, transcribing "messages" from dead relatives and friends, famous literary figures, and mythological beings. Merrill edited these messages, fashioning them into poetry and publishing

them in the Pulitzer Prize-winning *Divine Comedies* (1976), the National Book Award-winning *Mirabell: Books of Number* (1978), and *Scripts for the Pageant* (1980). *The Changing Light at Sandover,* which adds some original material to these Ouija board poems, won the National Book Critics Circle Award. In addition to two novels and several dramatic works, Merrill also wrote *A Different Person* (1993), a memoir in which he discusses his decisive trip to Europe in the early 1950s, his relationships with his parents, and his homosexuality. In 1972, Helen Vendler wrote in praise of Merrill's career that "readers actively wait for his books: to know that someone out there is writing down your century, your generation, your language, your life—under whatever terms of difference—makes you wish for news of yourself, for those authentic tidings of invisible things, as Wordsworth called them, that only come in the interpretation of life voiced by poetry." Eulogizing his friend, McClatchy concluded: "What sustained Merrill was dedication to his calling, a high ambition, and a deeply moral purpose. If we give equal weight to each word, then this definition of a poet he once offered sums him up: 'a man choosing the words he lives by.' "

PRINCIPAL WORKS

Jim's Book: A Collection of Poems and Short Stories   (poetry and short stories)   1942
The Black Swan, and Other Poems   (poetry)   1946
First Poems   (poetry)   1951
The Bait   (drama)   1953
Short Stories   (poetry)   1954
A Birthday Cake for David   (poetry)   1955
The Immortal Husband   (drama)   1955
The Seraglio   (novel)   1957
The Country of a Thousand Years of Peace, and Other Poems   (poetry)   1959; revised edition, 1970
Selected Poems   (poetry)   1961
Water Street   (poetry)   1962
The Thousand and Second Night   (poetry)   1963
The (Diblos) Notebook   (novel)   1965
Violent Pastoral   (poetry)   1965
Nights and Days   (poetry)   1966
The Fire Screen   (poetry)   1969
Braving the Elements   (poetry)   1972
Two Poems: "From the Cupola" and "The Summer People"   (poetry)   1972
Yannina   (poetry)   1973
The Yellow Pages: 59 Poems   (poetry)   1974
Divine Comedies   (poetry)   1976
Metamorphosis of 741   (poetry)   1977
Mirabell: Books of Number   (poetry)   1978
Ideas, etc.   (poetry)   1980
Scripts for the Pageant   (poetry)   1980
*The Changing Light at Sandover   (poetry)   1982
From the Cutting Room Floor   (poetry)   1982
From the First Nine: Poems 1947-1976   (poetry)   1982
Marbled Paper   (poetry)   1982
Peter   (poetry)   1982
Santorini: Stopping the Leak   (poetry)   1982
Bronze   (poetry)   1984
Occasions and Inscriptions   (poetry)   1984
Play of Light   (poetry)   1984
Rendezvous   (poetry)   1984
Souvenirs   (poetry)   1984
Late Settings   (poetry)   1985
The Image Maker   (drama)   1986
†Recitative   (prose)   1986
The Inner Room   (poetry)   1988
A Different Person: A Memoir   (memoir)   1993
Selected Poems   (poetry)   1993
A Scattering of Salts   (poetry)   1995

*This work contains "The Book of Ephraim" from *Divine Comedies,* all of the poems in both *Mirabell: Books of Number* and *Scripts for the Pageant,* and an original epilogue, "Coda: The Higher Keys."

†This work was edited by J. D. McClatchy.

OBITUARIES AND TRIBUTES

Mel Gussow   **(obituary date 7 February 1995)**

SOURCE: An obituary in *The New York Times,* February 7, 1995, p. B12.

[*In the following obituary, Gussow describes Merrill as "heir to the lyrical legacy of W. H. Auden and Wallace Stevens."*]

James Merrill, the Pulitzer Prize-winning poet whose 14 books of verse established him as heir to the lyrical legacy of W. H. Auden and Wallace Stevens, died yesterday in Tucson, Ariz. He was 68 and had homes in Stonington, Conn., and New York City.

He had been in Tucson on vacation and died of a heart attack at the Arizona Health Sciences Center, said J. D. McClatchy, a friend and fellow poet.

One of the most admired of American poets, Mr. Merrill was known for the elegance of his writing, his moral sensibility and his ability to transform moments of autobiography into deeply meaningful poetry. He once described his poetry as "chronicles of love and loss."

He won every major award, including the Pulitzer, the Bollingen Prize, two National Book Awards and a National Book Critics Circle Award. He was a member of the National Institute of Arts and Letters. In 1966, he was named Connecticut's first poet laureate (his verse is filled with references to his home there and to other places he lived, including Key West, Fla., and Greece). His 15th volume of poetry, **A Scattering of Salts,** is scheduled to be published in March by Alfred A. Knopf.

He was also a novelist, playwright and essayist and in 1993 published a memoir of his early years, **A Different Person.**

When Mr. Merrill won the Bollingen Prize in 1973, he was praised for his "wit and delight in language, his exceptional craft, his ability to enter into personalities other than his own, and his sustained vitality." These are qualities that resonated throughout his long, productive career. In his work, he often mixed lyrical language with contemporary conversation. "His common style is a net of loose talk tightening to verse," wrote the critic Denis Donoghue, "a mode in which anything can be said with grace."

James Ingram Merrill was born in New York City in 1926. His father was Charles Merrill, a founder of the stock brokerage now known as Merrill, Lynch & Company. James Merrill, grew up in luxurious surroundings, and because of family wealth never had to depend on his writing to make a living. He had been, he said in his memoir, rich since he was 5 "whether I liked it or not," and added that he was "as American as lemon chiffon pie." Nothing deterred him from his desire to be a poet.

At the age of 11, he discovered opera, a first love before literature and a guiding force in his poetry. He went to Lawrenceville School, where one of his close friends and classmates was the novelist Frederick Buechner. Mr. Buechner later said that their friendly competition was an impetus for each becoming a writer. At Lawrenceville, the young poet privately published a book of poetry and stories.

Mr. Merrill's studies at Amherst College were interrupted by a year of service in the infantry in World War II. He returned to Amherst in 1945, published poems in *Poetry* and *The Kenyon Review,* and wrote a thesis on Marcel Proust, who remained an inspiration in his writing.

After graduating from Amherst summa cum laude, he formally began his career, and his writing remained unabated for the next 48 years. His first book, *First Poems* (1951), received mixed reviews. Perhaps in response to that reaction, he switched briefly to fiction and play-writing: his first play, *The Immortal Husband,* was done off Broadway in 1955 and his first novel, *The Seraglio,* was published in 1957.

His return to poetry came in 1959 with *The Country of a Thousand Years of Peace,* and he then made his breakthrough in 1963 with *Water Street.* Reviewing that collection in *The New York Times Book Review,* X. J. Kennedy said that Mr. Merrill had become "one of the American poets most worth reading."

In 1967, Mr. Merrill won his first National Book Award, for *Nights and Days.* That book was followed by *The Fire Screen* (1969) and *Braving the Elements* (1972).

In her review of *Braving the Elements* in *The New York Times Book Review,* Helen Vendler said that "in the last 10 years, with his last four books of poems," Mr. Merrill "has become one of our indispensable poets." He won the Bollingen Prize in 1973.

He won the Pulitzer Prize for *Divine Comedies* (1976), and his second National Book Award for *Mirabell: Books of Number* (1978). In a review in *The New Republic,* Charles Molesworth compared *Scripts for the Pageant* (1980) to "Yeats and Blake, if not Milton and Dante." Within these three books was a long connected poem, inspired by Mr. Merrill's sessions at a Ouija board with his companion, David Jackson. The trilogy was republished in 1982, with a new epilogue, as *The Changing Light at Sandover.*

When he was 24, Mr. Merrill undertook what became a two-and-a-half-year journey of discovery in Europe. In *A Different Person,* he reflected on that trip, on his family life, his relationship with his parents and his homosexuality.

Reviewing the book in *The New York Times Book Review,* Brigitte Weeks said it was "a beguiling and deceptively simple memoir." Referring to the author at 67 and his younger incarnation, she said that "both make exhilarating and charming traveling companions."

When his father died, Mr. Merrill used money from his inheritance to establish the Ingram Merrill Foundation to give grants to writers and painters.

He is survived by his mother, Hellen Plummer of Atlanta, and by a half-sister, a half-brother and a stepsister.

J. D. McClatchy   (essay date 27 March 1995)

SOURCE: "Braving the Elements," in *The New Yorker,* Vol. LXXI, No. 5, March 27, 1995, pp. 49-52, 59-61.

[*An American poet, critic, and educator, McClatchy was a close friend of Merrill's. In the following reminiscence, he discusses Merrill's development as a poet, surveying his life and works through personal insights and anecdotes.*]

The news that James Merrill had died last month in Arizona at the age of sixty-eight, of a sudden heart attack, caused a palpable shock in the literary world. Spontaneous tributes and readings sprang up all around the country. Disbelieving letters and phone calls crisscrossed the circle of professional writers. Not since a starry chapter closed in the nineteen-seventies with the deaths of W. H. Auden, Robert Lowell, and Elizabeth Bishop has the loss of an American poet been as momentous, or as widely acknowledged to be so.

That is in part because, however compelling Merrill's ambitions or demanding his methods, his readers always felt a sort of intimacy with him. For fifty years, the poet had used the details of his own life to shape a portrait that in turn mirrored back to us an image of our world and our moment. When his sixth book of poems, *Braving the Elements,* appeared, in 1972, Helen Vendler's review in the *Times* [see *The New York Times Book Review,* September 24, 1972] struck early what has since come to be the dominant note in appraisals of Merrill: "The time eventually comes, in a good poet's career, when readers actively long [Vendler used the word "wait"] for his books: to know that someone out there is writing down your century, your generation, your language, your life—under whatever terms of difference—makes you wish for news of yourself, for those authentic tidings of invisible things, as Wordsworth called them, that only come in the interpretation of life voiced by poetry."

For Merrill's funeral service, in Stonington, Connecticut, on a raw February afternoon, the little village church—its whitewashed interior suddenly looking rather Greek—was filled. A piping soprano sang "Bist du bei mir" to the plaintive accompaniment of a virginal, and Merrill's good friend the novelist Allan Gurganus delivered a brief eulogy. "Some people contain their grace," he said. "James dispersed his. It was a molecular nimbus he lived within, and he seemed, after nearly seven decades in there, largely unaware of its effervescent impact on the rest of us." Later, at the cemetery, where a mossy oblong of sod lay beside a tiny grave, friend after friend sprinkled a handful of dirt over the poet's ashes. One young poet, when it was his turn, also dropped into the grave a dime-store marble painted to resemble the globe.

For Merrill's friends, the shock has slowly subsided into the dull realization that there will be no more of his witty company. Yes, he was a great poet and knew he was meant to end up as books on a shelf. Those books—the last one, *A Scattering of Salts,* is, as it happens, to be published this week—have long since confirmed his mastery: he knew more about the language of poetry than anyone else since Auden and used it to make poems that will remain part of anyone's definition of the art. But so, too, his conversation. He liked, as he once said, "English in its billiard-table sense—words that have been set spinning against their own gravity." At a large dinner party or on a casual stroll with an old acquaintance or a perfect stranger, he had an uncanny, almost anarchic habit of turning everything upside down. By his slight adjustment of perspective or realignment of a syllable, the dire became droll. He rarely relaxed his instinctive habit of reversing a truth or upending the mawkish, and his face loved to anticipate—with its pursed smile and arched brow—the pleasure his remark was about to give.

Last season, for instance, at a Met performance of "Otello," the Desdemona was in trouble long before her tragic end. Carol Vaness became ill during the opera and decided to withdraw. Her Russian cover, hastily done up in such a way as to make her quite a different woman from Vaness, took over the last act. After the performance, Merrill, ambling up the aisle, turned to a friend and shook his head with a rueful giddiness: "Poor Desdemona! She changed the color of her hair, but it didn't save her marriage."

The crack is characteristic in more ways than one. To begin with, he was at the opera, and nothing over the years had given him more pleasure or, at the start, had taught him more. He began going to the Met when he was eleven, and one of his best-known poems, **"Matinees,"** describes its effect: "The point thereafter was to arrange for one's / Own chills and fever, passions and betrayals, / Chiefly in order to make song of them." Opera—its ecstasies and deceptions, its transcendent fires and icy grandeurs—is, above all, a stylized dramatization of our inner lives, our forbidden desires and repressed fears. It may seem surprising in a poet like Merrill, whose surfaces can be so elegant and elusive, but center stage in his work is passion. However his words may work to heighten and refine it, the urgency of the heart's desires is his constant subject.

All the obsessions and inventions of his work, from the delicacies of metaphor on to the creation of an entire cosmogony, fuelled a career as remarkable as any in American literary history.

—J. D. McClatchy

That Merrill would joke not about Desdemona's murder but about her failed marriage also points to a distant event that had come to shape his imagination. At about the time he starting going to the opera, his parents separated. A bitter divorce trial followed, and, because Merrill's father was one of the most powerful financiers in America—a cofounder of the great brokerage house of Merrill, Lynch— the story was national news. One tabloid even ran a photograph of young James with the caption "PAWN IN PARENTS' FIGHT." Again and again in the course of his career, Merrill revisited the scene, and nowhere more memorably than in his sequence of sonnets called **"The Broken**

Home." Thirty years after the fact, the poem manages a knowing shrug: "Always that same old story— / Father Time and Mother Earth, / A marriage on the rocks." But the poem's impulse here to mythologize the trauma is part of a larger scheme. It is as if the divorce represented Merrill's own split personality. As much his father's son as his mother's boy, he had a temperament that by turns revealed what we may as well call paternal and maternal sides. He was drawn equally to the rational and the fanciful, the passionate and the ironic, America and Europe. And, from the very beginning, his ambition as a poet was—like the child attempting to reconcile his warring parents—to harmonize those two sides of his life. More often than not, he preferred to remain of two minds about all matters. And the energy spent exploring these divisions and doublings, all the obsessions and inventions of his work, from the delicacies of metaphor on to the creation of an entire cosmogony, fuelled a career as remarkable as any in American literary history.

As children, most of us fantasize a glamorous alternative: our parents are royal and rich, we live in a palace, we are adored and powerful. But if those happen to be the *facts* of your life instead of your fantasies? Merrill's parents had a brownstone on West Eleventh Street and a stately Stanford White pile in Southampton—The Orchard—with a dozen bedrooms, with conservatories and rose arbors, cooks and chauffeurs. In his 1957 roman à clef, *The Seraglio,* Merrill portrays his father in his later years as a sort of pasha, surrounded by wife, ex-wives, mistresses, nurses, and flatterers—a man who loved his wives deeply but cheerlessly while counting on other women for companionship and fun. He was a man whose face "would have made the fortune of any actor. Frank, earnest, noble in repose, it was kept from plain tiresome fineness by being always on the verge of some unlikely humor, mischief or doltishness or greed." Merrill's mother, Hellen Ingram, was Charles Merrill's second wife, a Jacksonville beauty who had once been a newspaper reporter, and she kept close tabs on her son. It's almost natural that Merrill's childhood fantasies weren't the usual ones. If his ballad **"Days of 1935"** is a fair account of them, he imagined himself kidnapped, like the Lindbergh baby, and carried off to some shabby hideout by a gangster and his moll, with whose cheap looks—her rosebud chewing gum, his sallow, lantern-jawed menace—he falls in love, and from whose violent ways he longs not to be ransomed.

In a 1982 *Paris Review* interview, he said, "It strikes me now maybe that during much of my childhood I found it difficult to *believe* in the way my parents lived. They seemed so utterly taken up with engagements, obligations, ceremonies—every child must feel that, to some extent, about the grown-ups in his life." In fact, like most childhoods, his was lonely. He craved affection, and spent most of his time with a beloved governess, reading up on the Norse myths or devising plots to present in his marionette theatre. The loneliness—perhaps a necessary condition for any poet's working life—and a need to charm run right through his work. By the time he was eight, he was writing poems. By the time he was at Lawrenceville, he meant to make a career of it and told his father so. Charles Merrill had a volume of the boy's early poems and stories—called

Jim's Book—privately printed, to the young author's immediate delight and future chagrin. Later, distressed by his son's determination, Charles nonetheless took a businessman's approach. He secretly sent his son's fledgling work to several "experts," including the president of Amherst, and asked for their frank opinion. When they all agreed on a precocious talent, the patriarch was overheard to say proudly that he would rather have a poet for a son than a third-rate polo player.

Recently, Merrill had begun to notice in his shaving mirror each morning how much he had come to resemble his father: "a face no longer / sought in dreams but worn as my own" is how one poem puts it. He had never thought to look for that face earlier, since the young need always to consider themselves unique. In his memoir *A Different Person,* published two years ago, he remembers looking at himself in 1950:

> From the mirror stares inquiringly a slim person neither tall nor short, in a made-to-order suit of sandy covert cloth and a bowtie. My bespectacled face is so young and unstretched that only by concentration do the lips close over two glinting chipmunk teeth. My hair, dark with fair highlights, is close-cropped. I have brown eyes, an unexceptionable nose, a good jaw. My brow wrinkles when I am sad or worried, as now.
>
> Not that what I see dismays me. Until recently I've been an overweight, untidy adolescent; now my image in the glass is the best I can hope for. Something, however, tells me that time will do little to improve it. The outward bloom of youth upon my features will fade long before the bud-like spirit behind them opens—if ever it does. It is inside that I need to change. To this end I hope very diffidently to get away from the kind of poetry I've been writing.

The kind of poetry he was writing then—his *First Poems* appeared in 1951—was very much of its time. The aloof, lapidary glamour of the poems, their dissolves and emblems were meant both to disguise feelings only dimly known and to declare his allegiance to a line of poets that could be traced from Wallace Stevens back to the French Symbolists. But before long he had written a novel and had a couple of plays produced Off Broadway, and from both experiences he had learned to write a more fluent and inflected line, often coaxed by narrative.

In 1954, Merrill decided to abandon New York City. He moved, with his companion, David Jackson, to Stonington, a small coastal village—half fishing fleet, half Yankee clapboard—that a friend had suggested might remind him of a Mediterranean port. He and Jackson bought a house; they had a brass bed, a record player, a rowboat, a table and two chairs to work on, and no telephone. He loved the light glinting on Long Island Sound, and the cozy, settled routines of village life; the town, he said, was "full of clever wrinkled semi-famous people whom by the end of our second season we couldn't live without." In 1959, he and Jackson made another move—to Athens. They soon bought a house there, too, and for the next two decades spent half of each year in Greece.

> **From Merrill's college days on, his favorite writer had been Proust, for whom the only true paradise was a lost paradise. For both writers, love is not fully itself until it is lost, until it becomes memory, becomes art.**
>
> **—J. D. McClatchy**

Both moves were, in a sense, strategic withdrawals. Like his friend Elizabeth Bishop, Merrill did what he could to avoid having to lead a Literary Life. Stonington's bright calm began to give his work a more domestic focus. In the collection named for his address, *Water Street* (1962), there is a poem that speaks of his "dull need to make some kind of house / Out of the life lived, out of the love spent." Always aware that the word "stanza" is Italian for "room," Merrill put together poems that would shelter his memories. Increasingly, his poems were autobiographical, reaching back to his childhood or puzzling over some passing event or involvement. He eventually described his poems as "chronicles of love and loss," and that term aptly stresses his sense of a life lived and understood over time, and links his two recurrent themes. From Merrill's college days on, his favorite writer had been Proust, for whom the only true paradise was a lost paradise. For both writers, love is not fully itself until it is lost, until it becomes memory, becomes art.

If the familiarities of Stonington afforded both distance and security, Greece gave him something else. Here was a landscape of ravishing ruggedness, a culture of exotic simplicities. Better still, a language—he quickly mastered it—in which his accent wouldn't at once betray his class. He loved the anonymity it gave him; he loved the very sound of it: "kaló-kakó, cockatoo-raucous / Coastline of white printless coves / Already strewn with offbeat echolalia."

The poems set in Greece, vivid with local color, are the highlight of his two subsequent books—*Nights and Days* (1966) and *The Fire Screen* (1969). Landscapes as different as New Mexico, Rome, and Key West would later figure in his work as well. Merrill was a poet who looked out at a scene or around a room for prompting. "I always find when I don't like a poem I'm writing, I don't look any more into the human components," he told an interviewer. "I look more to the *setting*—a room, the objects in it." What was in front of his eyes would reveal what was in his mind. It was a quality he especially admired in the poems of Eugenio Montale—the way their "ladles and love letters, their furniture and pets" led finally deep into a labyrinth of feeling. The rooms of Merrill's Stonington house, which gave the impression of a *boutique fantasque,* were themselves an image of his inner life: a clutter of beloved totems. An immense Victorian mirror would reflect masterpiece and tchotchke, piles of books on the horsehair divan, a glass bowl filled with glass globes, bat-motif wallpaper, a Maxfield Parrish, a Tanagra figurine, a snapshot of his goddaughter, a Mogul miniature, a wooden nickel, cacti and shells, a Meissen plate, a lacquered Japanese travelling box, a windup toy bird, the upheld hand of a Buddha.

A couple of years ago, Allan Gurganus wrote to Merrill urging him to reread Tolstoy's novella "Family Happiness." The poet dutifully looked for it but could find it only in French, in one of the worn Pléïade editions he kept by his bed. When he opened to "Le Bonheur Conjugal," out fluttered a piece of paper on which, twenty years earlier, he had typed a stanza from Byron's poem "Beppo"—lines that he imagined at the time described a person he might grow to resemble:

> Then he was faithful, too, as well as amorous,
>   So that no sort of female could complain,
> Although they're now and then a little clamor-
>   ous;
>   He never put the pretty souls in pain;
> His heart was one of those which most enamour
>   us,
>   Wax to receive and marble to retain:
> He was a lover of the good old school,
> Who still become more constant as they cool.

Rather like his father, Merrill was a lover of the good old school. He'd found his own *bonheur conjugal* in 1953 with David Jackson. Jackson could play the piano, write a story, dash off a watercolor; he was ebullient, daring, funny, irresistible. Over their years together, strains in their relationship were sometimes apparent. But they stayed together—if, lately, at a certain distance from each other. It was as if Merrill were determined to keep for himself the kind of relationship his parents had thrown away. He was constant to his other lovers, as well. He'd had affairs before he met Jackson, and several afterward. (For the last dozen years, he was devoted to a young actor, Peter Hooten.) He had a way of turning each affair not only into an abiding friendship but into poetry. He wrote some of the most beautiful love poems of this century. He relished Borges's description of love as "a religion with a fallible god," and few poets have looked on love with such a vulnerable and wary eye:

> Where I hid my face, your touch, quick, merci-
>   ful
> Blindfolded me. A god breathed from my lips.
> If that was illusion, I wanted it to last long;
> To dwell, for its daily pittance, with us there,
> Cleaning and watering, sighing with love or
>   pain.
> I hoped it would climb when it needed to the
>   heights
> Even of degradation, as I for one
> Seemed, those days, to be always climbing
> Into a world of wild
> Flowers, feasting, tears—or was I falling, legs
> Buckling, heights, depths,
> Into a pool of each night's rain?
> But you were everywhere beside me, masked,
> As who was not, in laughter, pain, and love.

Merrill's sexuality was like a drop of dye let fall into a glass of water: it is subdued but suffuses everything. He wrote openly and seriously about homosexual love long before that was fashionable. In his memoir he writes, "As

in the classic account of Sarah Bernhardt descending a spiral staircase—she stood still and *it* revolved around her—my good fortune was to stay in one place while the closet simply disintegrated."

When I met Merrill, he was forty-six and had earned his first full measure of fame. *Nights and Days* had won the 1967 National Book Award, whose judges (W. H. Auden, James Dickey, and Howard Nemerov) singled out "his insistence on taking the kind of tough, poetic chances which make the difference between esthetic success or failure." And he had just published *Braving the Elements,* whose exquisite austerities mark a kind of extreme in his work. Dense and rapturous, the poems are set amid the hazards of history and romance. His narrative skills turn out Chekhovian vignettes like **"After the Fire"** or **"Days of 1971,"** where the end of an affair helps him to a wistful self-knowledge:

> "Proust's Law" (are you listening?) is two-fold:
>
> a) What least thing our self-love longs for most
> Others instinctively withhold;
>
> b) Only when time has slain desire
> Is his wish granted to a smiling ghost
> Neither harmed nor warmed, now, by the fire.

When *Braving the Elements* was awarded the 1973 Bollingen Prize, Merrill was the subject of a *Times* editorial attacking those who continue to "reward poetry that is literary, private, traditional." That has been a sentiment, a peculiarly American fear of the Fancy, that other readers have shared. Some early critics condescended to his work by calling it "bejewelled." Ironically, their contemptuous dismissal hinted at a larger truth. From the start, but nowhere more than in this book, Merrill took his bearings from the four elements—earth, air, fire, water—and in many of his poems the jewel is their embodiment. Crystal prism or emerald brooch, waterfall or geode, dragonfly or planet, or whatever other brilliant lens he chose, it was to inspect more carefully the natural world's wonders. He once told a young writer, "It's not the precious but the semiprecious one has to resist." And, like most strong poets, he seemed largely indifferent to his critics. He knew his worth, and disdained the lust for celebrity. "Think what one has to *do* to get a mass audience," he once noted wryly to his friend the critic David Kalstone. "I'd rather have one perfect reader. Why dynamite the pond in order to catch that single silver carp? Better to find a bait that only the carp will take."

He was a poet who trusted language to tell him what anything means. Rhyme, wordplay, paradox only help reveal the hidden wish of words. Indeed, the O.E.D. is the collective unconscious of English speakers, he would say, for all our ideas and feelings are to be found there, in the endless recombinations of our words. He was himself rather shy of ideas in poems. "Shaped by ideas like everyone else, I nevertheless avert my eyes from them," he joked, "as from the sight of a nude grandparent, not presentable, indeed taboo, until robed in images." Those images are an astonishment. He notes a hotel's "strange bed, whose recurrent dream we are," or describes a plot of zinnias as "pine cones in drag," or Kufic script as "all trigger tail and gold vowel-sac." His lines are animated with colloquial idiom and quicksilver wit. Their perfection of tone is made to seem offhanded, their weight of allusion and symbol is deftly balanced. If the surfaces of his poems sometimes seemed difficult, it may have been because for most of his career other poets were loudly trumpeting the virtues of the plain style. For his part, Merrill would say that the natural word order isn't "See Jane run." The more *natural* way to put it is actually more complex: "Where on earth can that child be racing off to? Why, it's little—you know, the neighbor's brat—Jane!" So, too, the syntax of his poems darts and capers. The effect on a reader can be vertiginous. The long feather boa of some intellectually complex sentence may suddenly give way to a tank-top phrase. Merrill would have agreed with George Balanchine, who once said that the true figure for the artist should be the gardener or the chef: you love everything because you need everything.

By the mid-seventies, his poems were growing longer. He attributed that change to "middle-age spread." But even he was surprised by the project that occupied him for seven years, from 1974 until 1980. In fact, it was a project that preëmpted him. Ever since moving to Stonington, he and David Jackson had, on spare evenings, sat down at a homemade Ouija board and chatted with the great dead. No sooner did Merrill write up these encounters, in the volume **Divine Comedies,** which won him the 1976 Pulitzer Prize, than the spirits demanded that he attend to more rigorous lessons they would give him. "Don't you think there comes a time when everyone, not just a poet, wants to get beyond the self?" Merrill said in an interview. "To reach, if you like, the 'god' within you? The board, in however clumsy or absurd a way, allows for precisely that. Or if it's still *yourself* that you're drawing upon, then that self is much stranger and freer and more farseeing than the one you thought you knew." Resisting the impulse to be either wholly skeptical or merely credulous, Merrill sat for the lessons. The curriculum ranged from subatomic particles to cosmic forces, and the cast included Akhenaton, Pythagoras, Montezuma, T. S. Eliot, Maria Callas, bats and unicorns, scientists and neighbors, God Biology and Mother Nature. In his epic account of it all, the poet managed to make the otherworldly revelations into a very human drama of acceptance, resistance, and ambivalence. And by the time he had gathered all seventeen thousand lines of his adventure into a single volume, **The Changing Light at Sandover** (1982), he had written what is—with the possible exception of Whitman's "Song of Myself"—the strangest and grandest American poem ever: at once eerie, hilarious, and heartbreaking.

A Scattering of Salts (to call it his last book instead of his latest sticks in my throat) is a wonderful anthology of Merrill's characteristic strengths as a poet. There are portraits and elegies, sonnets and free-verse riffs, high style and slang. There are pungent, elliptical little lyrics and the longer, loping narratives that were his specialty. In one he describes "family week" at a dude-ranch rehab center he is visiting to be with a friend, who has sought treatment there. The poet tries to adjust to the New Age therapies:

> This wide-angle moonscape, lawns and pool,
> Patients sharing pain like fudge from home—

> As if these were the essentials,

> As if a month at what it invites us to think
> Is little more than a fat farm for Anorexics,
> Substance Abusers, Love & Relationship Addicts
> Could help *you,* light of my life, when even your
>   shrink . . .

> The message, then? That costly folderol,
> Underwear made to order in Vienna,
> Who needs it! Let the soul hang out
> At Benetton—stone-washed, one size fits all.

It ends with a haunting, lovelorn speculation that blends the newest jargon with one of poetry's oldest images:

> And if the old patterns recur?
> Ask how the co-dependent moon, another night,
> Feels when the light drains wholly from her face.
> Ask what that cold comfort means to her.

Cozy chats over the Ouija board acknowledge death as an event but not as a fact. They might even be said to represent at some level a denial of death. But the three collections that Merrill published during the past decade take a more realistic look at mortality. This final book has a nearly Yeatsian vigor in the face of the end. What Merrill sees on the microscope slide is everything we dread. "Dread? It crows for joy in the manger. / Joy? The tree sparkles on which it will die."

The earnest young poet I was in 1972 found the James Merrill who had kindly invited me to dinner one spring night dauntingly sophisticated. His features were faintly elfin, and his voice—a soft, cultivated baritone—drew one instinctively toward its flickering brightness. He had read everything (I found out later that in his twenties he had taken one winter to read all of Dickens, another for Balzac) but skated past any ponderous discussion of literature—though he could quote at will whole swatches of Baudelaire or Da Ponte or Cole Porter. He never played The Poet in company but felt himself "more like a doctor at a dinner party, just another guest until his hostess slumps to the floor or his little beeper goes off." He rarely read a newspaper and didn't vote, yet was scornfully eloquent about the technocracy's myopic bureaucrats and "their sad knowledge, their fingertip control." He worked at his desk every day, and, even to the extent that he lived for pleasure, he lived rather simply. If he meant to be a dandy in his dress, the results were more often merely eccentric. Old Auden wore carpet slippers to the opera. You could spot Merrill there in mauve Birkenstocks over limegreen socks, neatly pressed corduroys with a Navajo belt buckle, a shirt from the Gap, a Venetian bow tie, a loden cape, and a baseball cap.

His chief pleasure was friendship. Over the years, his friends ranged from Alice Toklas and Maya Deren to Richard Wilbur and Alison Lurie. To each he was tender and loyal. His friends, in turn, responded in such coin as they happened to have in their pockets. In 1968, when Stephen Yenser sent him a fervently used book—a palm-size, velvet-covered, dogeared copy of "The Rubáiyat of Omar Khayyám," a poem Merrill adored—the poet responded in kind:

Fortunate those who back from a brief trip,
To equinoctial storms and scholarship,
Unwrap, first thing, a present from a friend,
And into Omar's honeyed pages dip.

Richard Howard once noted that the art of living was one of Merrill's unrivalled talents. "What one wants in this world," Merrill wrote, "isn't so much to 'live' as to . . . *be* lived, to be used by life for its own purposes. What has one to give but oneself ?" It was always to Merrill that his friends turned when they needed advice. Here, for instance, is part of a 1973 letter he sent me from Greece. I seem then to have been in the throes of some now forgotten crisis of the heart. How sweetly he edged up to my worries. He began by describing the crowded summer in Athens, and his being content to stay blithely above it. Then he expanded from details to his theme:

> The iron gates of life have seldom seen such traffic, to judge from the confused rumor that reaches us here in the shade of the pearly ones. The real absurdity, you will say (and I'll agree, it's all so novel), is to feel in one's bones how utterly a boundary has been crossed. Here one is in Later Life, and it's perfectly pleasant really, not for a moment that garden of cactus and sour grapes I'd always assumed it *must* be. Oh dear, this sort of thing is probably just what you mean by my being "recessed" into myself. But it's odd. I mean, the times of greatest recession into the self have always been, for me, times of helpless suffering, such as you're going through; when there's no escape from the self. Perhaps any circumstance, any frame of mind, content, pain, trust, distrust, is a niche that limits visibility—for both the occupant and the onlooker? I read your last letter, in any case, with pangs of recognition. There's no special comfort, is there? in being understood at times like these. One is so mortified by one's predicament, and at the same moment so curiously proud of its ramifications. You won't be ready yet to *like* the fact of belonging to a very large group who've all had—allowing for particular differences—the same general experience. Later on, when your sense of humor and proportion returns, that fact ought rather to please you: to have so shared in the—or at least *a*—human condition. Write me as much or as little about it as you see fit. As you say, the particulars should probably be saved for the couch. Don't waste time feeling superior to your doctor. You are no doubt cleverer and more presentable than he is, but (with any luck) he knows his business, and the shoes he is making for you will last and last.

The definition of a poet that Merrill once offered sums him up: "a man choosing the words he lives by."

—J. D. McClatchy

Of course, he gave a great deal more than advice to his friends. He was a soft touch, and had learned the difficult art of giving money away gracefully. By a friend's staggering medical bill or the down payment on a house, appeals from ballet companies or animal shelters, stories of neglected old poets on the skids or a young painter who needed equipment his sympathy was easily sparked. In 1956, he used a portion of his inheritance to establish the Ingram Merrill Foundation, whose board of directors was empowered to award grants to writers and artists. Over the years, hundreds of people were helped. The edge was given to the promising beginner.

What Merrill couldn't give away was the stigma that came with his wealth and privilege. Epicurus famously said that riches don't alleviate, only change, one's troubles. The fortune that gave Merrill the chance both to distance himself from the family who made it and to pursue an odd, intricate career was, I'd guess, a nagging source of embarrassment for him and may have occasioned, in turn, his aversion to grand hotels and restaurants, his recycled razor blades and Spartan diet. He used, long ago, to confuse his companions by declaring, "Thank goodness I come from poor parents." He meant that his parents' values had been formed—by the example of *their* parents, who were hard-working and middle-class—before they had money. In a sense, his own values were old-fashioned. What sustained Merrill was dedication to his calling, a high ambition, and a deeply moral purpose. If we give equal weight to each word, then this definition of a poet he once offered sums him up: "a man choosing the words he lives by."

When Merrill's ashes were sent back to be buried in Stonington, a box of papers came, too. Peter Hooten had gathered up poems and drafts from the poet's desk. Among them was a poem called **"Koi."** Behind the house he and Hooten had been renting in Tucson for the winter was a small ornamental pool of koi, the Japanese carp. The poem—the last he finished, a couple of weeks before he died—is about those fish and his little Jack Russell terrier, Cosmo. Of course, it wasn't written *as* a last poem, but circumstances give it a special poignancy.

Also sent home was his notebook. It is open now on my desk. He'd kept a series of notebooks over the years, their entries irregular, often fragmentary. Things overheard or undergone. Dreams, lists, lines. An image or anagram. The writing—even the handwriting—is swift and elegant. But the last page of this notebook is nearly indecipherable. Suddenly, at the end, you can *see* the difficulty he was having: the script is blurred, and that may be because he had lost his glasses. His breathing, too, was labored. On Friday, he'd been admitted to the hospital with a bout of acute pancreatitis. I spoke with him by telephone on Sunday, the night before he died, and asked about his breathing. He said that, though he'd been given oxygen, the doctors were not unduly concerned. The rest of the conversation was banter and gossip and plans for the future: a cataract operation, the new "Pelléas" at the Met. But his notebook tells another, more anxious story. The last page is dated "5.ii.95," the day before his death. There are two dozen lines, sketches for a poem to be titled "The Next to Last Scene." Typically, it starts by looking around the hospital room, and opens with what in retrospect seems an eerie line: "A room with every last convenience." It glances at TV set, cassette player, smiling lover. He would often, when drafting a poem, fill out the end of a line, knowing where he wanted to go but not exactly how he would get there. He'd done so here. I can make out "to see the other through." And then, the very last thing he wrote, "To set the other free."

To see the other through. To set the other free. Who or what is this "other"? The longer I gaze at the page, the more resonant these phrases become. Is it everything beyond and beloved by the self: the man in his life, the world's abundance, the ideal reader? Or all that burdens the soul, distracts the heart? Perhaps the psyche? Even the imagination? The impulse of Merrill's poems all along was both to brave the elements and to release them. Some poets try a change of style to force a change in their work. Merrill was a poet who instead sought fresh experience—a new landscape, a new lover—in order to abide by unexpected demands. At the same time, he sought to release, as if from a spell, the textures and colors of objects, the inner life of our arrangements, the hidden relationships among motives and emotions, the secrets of childhood and the energies of the unconscious.

It is still intolerable to think that there will be no more of his resplendent, plangent, mercurial, wise poems; that their author is like the mirror ceremonially broken at the end of *Sandover,* "giving up its whole / Lifetime of images." James Merrill gave his lifetime to language, and to the way its hard truths and mysterious graces come to constitute our lives. Only a few poets in each generation—and Merrill was preëminent in his—can use language to make a style, and style to make a whole world of flesh and spirit, a world as momentous as the heart's upheavals and heaven's order, or as casual as a dime-store marble.

Stephen Yenser   (tribute date 13 May 1995)

SOURCE: "Metamorphoses," in *Poetry,* Vol. CLXVI, No. 6, September, 1995, pp. 331-34.

[*An American critic, poet, and educator, Yenser was a friend of Merrill's and wrote the study* The Consuming Myth: The Work of James Merrill *(1987). In the following tribute, which was delivered at the New York Public Library on May 13, 1995, he offers his thoughts on why "James Merrill will be among the handful of poets by whom we remember this century."*]

Over the twenty-eight years that it was given me to know him, I had the occasion to introduce James Merrill a dozen times, at readings in locations ranging from New York through St. Louis to Los Angeles, and I got to know something about how to do that. I have no experience whatever in bidding him farewell. So I am not going to do that.

Once upon a time, three Amherst undergraduates gained clandestine entry to the former home of Martha Dickinson Bianchi, Emily Dickinson's niece. One of this small cohort had the temerity to take as a souvenir a manuscript sheet (found in an old secretary), which, we must trust,

was not in Dickinson's hand. The second borrowed a charming, small mirror. For his part, James Merrill, he later confided, rescued "a tiny wine glass." Was that the literal truth? Or was he somehow conflating the dregs of that romantic peccadillo with Emily Dickinson's famous description of the color of her eyes?

I believed him, when this story came to light, one evening thirty years later, on the island of Poros, when he and I were visiting an old Greek friend of his. James, Mina reminded him, had introduced her some years after the Amherst escapade, in New York, to the man who had salvaged the mirror, which Mina very much envied him. They got to know each other, but then she didn't see the man for some time, and when they did cross paths she learned that he had *given away* the precious object. She was dismayed, especially because, as he knew, she so admired Dickinson that she had translated her poems into German, and he could just as easily have passed it along to her. So this old injury was touched upon as we sat there in a library designed by her first husband as though for a set for the last act of *Mignon,* with thick walls, high ceilings, tremendous beams, plank floors, and a commanding fireplace with an exposed brass chimney. James, as gracious a guest as she was a hostess, assured her that the looking glass in question could *never* have "held the face" of the poet, as he put it. Mina, mollified, presently retired. Whereupon James admitted to me that, given the style of the mirror, "an oval framed by two sconces," he recalled, he thought it likely that it had indeed gazed deeply into Emily Dickinson's sherry-colored eyes.

Fluent in Greek and English and German, Mina had grown up in Russia and still had some of that language, and she had taught herself some Chinese and, in her mid-eighties, was translating Lao Tzu into Greek. Her second husband was a well-known American poet and translator; her brother had once seen the Abominable Snowman in the Himalayas and told me that he believed that the famous figure was an ascetic monk out gathering certain herbs in the snow; and while we were there, her son arrived, accompanied by a stunning young woman who was not his wife and who was never introduced. As some of you will have guessed, by then Mina had been—though she seemed not to know it—the model for the enchanting heroine in James's second novel, which he had begun fifteen years before, in the very house we were visiting.

This is a kind of parable. To go anywhere with James was to enter a realm where boundaries dissolved, intrigues multiplied, and the plot dipped and looped like the dragon kite we flew that afternoon from Mina's roof. If, that night, by the flickering, fickle light of the fire and a glass of Metaxis, I found myself following a flashlight through a hallway in a dark house in Amherst, I also walked from a room where we were talking about Czarist Russia into a guest house that I recognized from *The (Diblos) Notebook*—itself a book in which the reader shuttles between alleged fiction and purported diary, even as prose narrows into metrical channels that eventually flood back out into prose. No wonder that James loved myths of metamorphosis and doted on Scheherazade, felt a kinship with Nabokov and Calvino, and relished Venice. It is fitting that

Hermes should figure prominently in his later work. The divine messenger, the god of travel and the psychopomp, he crosses at will from one country to another and from this world to the next. And, lest we forget that night in Amherst, Hermes is the patron of thieves.

Which patronage, since it presupposes his ability to slip through customs and to invade private property with impunity, is one with the sanctioning of the radical imagination itself. Hermes' magical passport is also a seditious license. It permits the bearer to subvert genres (to turn poetry into prose, to translate a novel into verse). It also permits the bearer to cross borders as secure as those between power and art. (As the patron of commerce, Hermes could mediate between James and his stockbroker father, each of whom could make good sense of Wallace Stevens's dictum, "Money is a kind of poetry.") And it permits the bearer to negotiate differences as entrenched as those between the genders. (You'll remember for instance that at a crucial point in **"The Book of Ephraim"** a recruit named Theodore changes into an officer named Teddy, who in turn passes himself off as Mrs. Smith, who flashes a compact from Hermès and who later becomes Mrs. Myth. . . .)

I'm trying to suggest one reason that James Merrill will be among the handful of poets by whom we remember this century now ever more rapidly circling the drain. The principle that I'm getting at will *not* be caught to the extent that change is of its essence. One might call this principle—which allowed him to move so invisibly from his art to his life and back—Mercurial, or Hermetic, or Protean, or Ovidian. To put that another way, James echoed Keats when he called himself a "chameleon," and his own "negative capability" is everywhere in evidence; at the same time, he showed off his debt to Byron. Alone among poets in our time he was able to turn Byron into Keats. He crafted the consummate lyric, in which he loaded every rift with ore (to borrow Keats's theft of Spenser), and he wrote the wittily ramshackle narrative, and he sometimes, somehow, impossibly did both at once. At Auden's death, he came into the older poet's copy of the *Oxford English Dictionary,* which he treasured above all others, but his young love in his last years was the *American Heritage Dictionary,* with its "Appendix," which follows words back through their vivid etymological metamorphoses to their "origins." Having learned from him in this respect as in so many others, I can remind you that the words *diligence* and *elegance* derive from one root, just as the words *orgy* and *work* stem from a single source. I hardly need add that no modern poet whom I know could be so fittingly located at the center of those four ever-shifting winds: *diligence, orgy, elegance, work.*

As you will remember, **"The Book of Ephraim,"** a poem rife with recollection, concludes with a passage recounting how a thief breaks into James's house—in Stonington—but takes nothing. As the poem has it, "nothing's gone, or nothing we recall." That is, on one reading, nothing that we recall is gone. And then this poem, which is to my mind as likely to be recalled as anything in America in this century, ends with a vision of the Earth from an otherworldly vantage, almost as though viewed posthumously.

This is Earth as *magna mater,* described in terms that always remind me a little of Mina—and in a way of his own mother, whose presence (I paraphrase James, on this Mother's Day eve) permeates **"The Book of Ephraim."** My last words are his, from the end of **"Ephraim":**

> And look, the stars have wound in filigree
> The ancient, ageless woman of the world.
> She's seen us. She is not particular—
> Everyone gets her injured, musical
> "Why do you no longer come to me?"
> To which there's no reply. For here we are.

REVIEWS OF MERRILL'S RECENT WORKS

David Lehman   **(review date 12 September 1993)**

SOURCE: "Another Past Recaptured," in *Book World— The Washington Post,* September 12, 1993, p. 4.

[*Lehman is an American critic, poet, and educator whose works include* James Merrill: Essays in Criticism *(1983), for which he served as editor and a contributor, and* Signs of the Times: Deconstruction and the Fall of Paul de Man *(1991). In the following review of* A Different Person: A Memoir, *he lauds Merrill's prose style and his insights into love and passion.*]

Elegant, graceful, puckish, lithe, James Merrill has steadily put his sonnets and intricate stanzas at the service of poignant autobiographical themes and expansive narrative ends. With rare candor and rarer tact James Merrill has explored the broken home of his upper-class childhood, the romance of art and myth and dreams and travel, his aestheticism, his homosexuality and the whole rich gamut of experiences available to a man who was always spared the financial angst that plagues most poets.

The great surprise in Merrill's career came about as a result of his infatuation with the Ouija board. A thousand and one nights spent conjuring up spirits familiar and strange led him to construct an epic poem. Comprising three books and an epilogue, and running over 17,000 lines, *The Changing Light at Sandover* (1983) presents a vision of the afterlife—an apocalyptic dream of startling intensity—with a structure derived from Dante's *Divine Comedy* and with similarly cosmic ambitions, but with all the insouciance of a reveler at a mad hatter's tea party.

A year ago Merrill's publisher reissued *Sandover* along with an enlarged edition of his *Selected Poems* (this fall both have been brought out in paperback). Rereading the former, one is struck anew by how marvelously Merrill manages to mix lofty and low elements, proving that a poem of the highest seriousness may cheerfully make do with the stage machinery of sci-fi novels, operatic high-tech phantasmagoria, and genteel spiritualism of the sort that Noel Coward sent up in *Blithe Spirit.*

Merrill's latest offering is a book of prose—his best book of prose to date. (He is also the author of several novels and a miscellany of critical pieces and short stories.) *A Different Person* is a highly unusual and compelling example of a genre that has been flourishing of late, the personal memoir. Beautifully written, with insights into love and passion that place the poet in the company of Benjamin Constant and Stendhal, the book tells the story of the two-and-a-half years Merrill spent in Europe as a young man in his twenties. But it is not a mere impressionistic record; Merrill uses the European sojourn as an organizing convenience, a narrative center. His true aim here, as in his poems, is to know himself—to come to terms with his experiences, self-critically but with a vast capacity for puzzlement and wonder—and, in the process, to chart out the growth of a poet's mind.

The young poet had studied at Amherst, had taught at Bard and was floundering about, full of anxieties and sensibility, when he sailed to Europe in 1950 in search of his Jamesian destiny. He knew he would eventually come back, and that when he did he would be a different person—changed by his love affairs in Paris, his psychoanalysis in Rome, his deepening passion for the opera, his difficult relations with his formidable father, the founder of the giant brokerage firm that bears his name, and dowager mother. The son is terribly unsure of himself on page one, afraid of being alone, a good candidate for the writer's block that will indeed afflict him in Europe; by the book's conclusion, we have come in contact with the person who will write the poems.

In *Sandover,* Merrill alternated between upper and lower case type, using the former to record the sayings of his heavenly informants; typography reinforced the book's vision of an angelic hierarchy. Here, too, the typesetting makes a real difference. In *A Different Person* Merrill alternates between roman and italic type to distinguish time past from time present, the time of the action from the time of composition. The story of the European sojourn is told in roman—suitably, since the eternal city is a prime locale—with italic type reserved for the chapter-ending passages in which the poet comments from the vantage point of 40 years on.

Merrill's writing in *A Different Person* is full of inspired plays on words ("The Spanish steps uplifted their descender") and ingenious similes ("His manners were natural, even humble, like the hut of forest boughs that shelters a great wizard").

—David Lehman

Merrill's title yields multiple meanings. Every young man, studied by himself with 60 winters on his head, is a different person in the sense of L.P. Hartley's immortal line: "The past is a foreign country; they do things differently there." But Merrill was always conscious of his difference from others—and from parental expectation. "From the age of nineteen I've been made to feel . . . my difference from the rest of the world, a difference laudable and literary at noon, shocking and sexual at midnight," he writes. His mother strongly disapproved of his homosexuality, and some of the most moving pages in this book are devoted to the poet's continuing dialogues with her, some actual, some imaginary.

Merrill, whose affinity for Proust has often been noted, is a philosopher of love in the French tradition. He gives us, for example, "that curious but widespread law whereby people instinctively withhold what you want from them." In an extraordinary passage he wonders about his father's habit of maintaining warm relations with ex-spouses—his unwillingness to break with past amours. Recognizing the same tendency in himself, the poet suddenly feels "the pain my father must have caused his latest love by never quite relinquishing the bygone ones."

Merrill's prose style is nacreous, with some of the finest pearls concealed in subordinate phrases and incidental figures of speech. His writing is full of inspired plays on words ("the Spanish steps uplifted their descender") and ingenious similes ("His manners were natural, even humble, like the hut of forest boughs that shelters a great wizard"). Inveterate lover of opera that he is, Merrill regularly breaks the recitative of his life to launch an aria of reflection or heightened emotion.

An acquaintance of the poet, an Italian count, has arranged a visit to Sansepolcro, where Merrill sets eyes on Piero della Francesca's magnificent "Resurrection." The painting triggers off a passage in which the vocation of the artist and the mission of Jesus Christ are brilliantly compared and contrasted: "Deep down I feared that Jesus and I, both, had reached our zenith as children and that I would be hard put to avoid a terminal phase shot through, like his, by showmanship and self-promotion.

"Weren't those, however, among the traits I saw Jesus as sharing with the artists I most admired? Like Baudelaire he had a weakness for loose women. Like Mallarme he enthralled and mystified his disciples; like Oscar Wilde, courted ruin at the height of his fame. Like Proust he had dipped, with miraculous consequences, a cookie into a restorative cup."

For admirers of Merrill's poetry *A Different Person* will be indispensable. In a fascinating aside, he attributes the difficulty of his early work to "the need to conceal my feelings, and their objects"; the pronoun *you* recommended itself to him because it was "genderless as a figleaf," thus concealing the writer's homosexuality.

Merrill has always relied on rituals and parlor games to generate the stuff of poetry. In *A Different Person* he gives us the directions for a "game of Murder": "Each player draws a slip of paper from a bowl and examines it secretly. All the slips are blank but for two—one marked with a black dot for the Murderer, the other with an X for the Cross-Examiner. In darkness the players wander from room to room." The murderer hopes to escape undetected when he deals "a gently stylized blow to the heart" of his chosen victim. Then the questioning begins.

It was Merrill's luck to receive the slip of paper with the big black dot on it when he played the game of Murder in Rome. Merrill's description of that party reminds us of the surprising affinities that the artistic eye may discern between the rules of the game and those of a literary composition—and between a love affair and a crime of the heart.

W. S. Merwin   (review date 26 March 1995)

SOURCE: "The End of More than a Book," in *The New York Times Book Review,* March 26, 1995, p. 3.

[*Merwin is an esteemed American poet, playwright, essayist, memoirist, and translator. In the following review of* A Scattering of Salts, *he assesses Merrill's body of work and writes that this final collection of poems "seemed to be telling me that the extraordinary cumulative wealth of this corpus was arriving at a final form."*]

There may exist somewhere a cache of juvenilia by James Merrill, early verses, precocious but clumsy, scarcely formed, patently imitative, perhaps even pretentious. But it is hard to believe. First because Merrill, disciple of perfection that he was, might well have destroyed any such crudities unless he had been tempted to save them as relatively simple memorabilia, for we see his (and our) ambivalent attitudes toward childhood and childish things surfacing again and again through his poems: the venerable resolution to "let go / Of the dead dog, the lost toy" conflicts with the continuing seductiveness and lightplay of what is forever lost and still pulsing in the present. But in fact it is difficult to imagine Merrill ever writing anything raw, inept, infelicitous. His poetry seems to have begun always with something already pertinent and realized, because that was the way he was.

The page proofs of this latest collection of his poems, *A Scattering of Salts,* suggested such a conclusion repeatedly. It was not only the varied brilliance of the individual pieces. Taken together, the retrospective quality of them—a recurring allusion to a body of work that was part of the past, a note of summation and, in every sense, of setting—gave the volume an implication of finality that I kept refusing to take literally. It led me back to earlier poems of his, decade by decade, to all of his published poetry from the late 1940's on. The new book seemed to be telling me that the extraordinary cumulative wealth of this corpus was arriving at a final form; the image that recurs throughout his work, but flashes with piercing insistence in these late poems, is that of crystallization. While I was reading them and trying to persuade myself that what all this amounted to was merely a timely apprehension of mortality, word came of his sudden death. Heart.

Viewed from afterward, the immediate cause of death seems to have been prefigured in the poems, however skeptical one may be, or may try to be, about such notions. Tropes and asides all through this new book seem to be pointing to something of the sort, nowhere more directly than in the final poem, which opens:

> O heart green acre   sown with salt
> by the departing   occupier

> lay down your gallant   spears of wheat
> Salt of the earth.

Though he wrote poems after this manuscript was finished, and indeed was writing in bed in the hospital during the last few days of his life, these lines clearly address the end of something more than a book.

And his death, announcing completion in any case, at once puts the sequence of his writings into a new, sharp focus. A light goes out, another goes on, and suddenly we are looking at stills, in series. It is, as we knew, a large and dazzling achievement, and for all its variety and extent a remarkably coherent body of work. From the first poems that Merrill published in *Poetry* and *The Kenyon Review* at the end of the 40's, until those he was writing during the last year of his life, the tone, the charge and tension of the language, the formal turns and their manners of disclosure, are distinctively his. But during that period of almost half a century he used those qualities to project and articulate a constantly growing, unpredictable range of character, mood, subject, genre and experience.

To say he wrote with unfailing style would be like pointing out that his poems are in English, but to ponder even for a moment the role of deliberation in that style is to encounter the abiding mysteries of his personality and his art. The extremes, the poles, the contradictions that they fuse are far apart in ordinary life. His writing is verbally dense and formal and at the same time a current of white-water rapids, the utterance of a taut freedom. He spoke of loving to be carried away by language—his own language; of course, as it came to him. His poetry is compounded of immense personal reserve, dramatic transformation and startling autobiographical candor, in proportions and mixes that doubtless will excite scholarly speculation and disagreement for a long time to come. The mind that it represents to us is swift, decisive, in no way naïve, in command of a vast treasury of literary, linguistic, musical, visual, social, geographical and erotic education and experience, a profound respecter of conventions yet endlessly impatient with limitations.

> **To say Merrill wrote with unfailing style would be like pointing out that his poems are in English, but to ponder even for a moment the role of deliberation in that style is to encounter the abiding mysteries of his personality and his art.**
>
> **—W. S. Merwin**

It is almost 25 years since he first invited us to take seriously—whatever that may mean—a private pantheon whose dramatic revelations were set before us, in his account, through the medium of a teacup on a Ouija board under the fingers of Merrill himself and a very few intimates: a work within his work, first coalescing in the luminous, eerie, powerful alphabet of **"The Book of Ephraim,"** the series of poems that then evolved into *The Changing Light at Sandover,* whose subject is nothing less than cosmic existence and the play of love within it in this world and, the voices suggest, before and after it. **"Nine Lives,"** one of the poems in *A Scattering of Salts,* is a small encore to that enormous light show, and its introductory verses say some definite things about Merrill's own conception, or at least his late view, of the enterprise.

To begin with, he places it in the lineage of "the ancient comic theater." These poems are parts, roles, the words of performances and performers, among whom he himself figures, thrilled, as he says, "to find oneself again on stage, / In character, at this untender age." And here, as in the main cycle this poem alludes to, the characters, his own included, appear or simply speak out of what Prospero calls a deep "backward and abysm" of unmeasured and unspeaking darkness.

The stage itself, and the voices of theatrical personae, had fascinated him for years, perhaps since he fell in love with opera while he was still a child—something that he describes in this book—and he wrote plays, in a translucent masque-like mode, from the 50's on.

The prologue to **"Nine Lives"** invites the reader to attend it too as a piece of intimate theater—which may help to satisfy those who continue to worry about how they are supposed to take the Ouija-board pronouncements. Though how one is supposed to take them, in fact, is the kind of question that comedy, and theatrical presentation as a whole, raise and leave in the air. **"Nine Lives"** is another farewell: to a stage, a house in Athens, a history, an appetite, a mode, even to a subconscious. It is the breaking of a wand, ending the revels:

> To all, sweet dreams. The teacup-stirring eddy
> Is spent. We've dropped our masks, renewed our
>   vows
> To Letters, to the lives that letters house,
> Houses they shutter, streets they shade. Already
> Empty and dark, this street is. Dusty boughs
> Sleep in a pool of vigilance so bright
> An old tom skirts it. The world's his tonight.

Writing for a cast of voices also, and by no means incidentally, displayed another of Merrill's gifts, his mastery of rhyme. In theatrical speech and in the whole spectrum of his poetry it seems natural, a realization of the empirical sureness of his ear, of the liveliness and apparent ease of his voice and peace, of all their high comedy.

He is the obvious immediate heir of W. H. Auden, who is an orbiting character in the Sandover cycle, an avuncular if somewhat irascible benefactor. Merrill's other immediate forebears are less evident. There was Elizabeth Bishop, whom he revered as friend and poet; in this book, **"Overdue Pilgrimage to Nova Scotia"** is an elegy not only for her but for what she comes to signify, a world that is departing:

> Out from such melting backdrops
> It is the rare conifer stands whole, one sharp
> Uniquely tufted spoke of a dark snow crystal
> Not breathed upon, as yet, by our exhaust.
> Part of a scene that with its views and warblers,
> And at its own grave pace, but in your footsteps
> —Never more imminent the brink, more
>   sheer—
> Is making up its mind to disappear.

And before Bishop, perhaps her own mentor, Marianne Moore, whose "No Swan So Fine" may be refracted behind one of Merrill's first published poems, **"The Black Swan,"** in which:

> The blond child on
> The bank, hands full of difficult marvels, stays
> Now in bliss, now in doubt.
> His lips move: I love the black swan.

Before them I think of the poems of Byron, and of Pope, whom Merrill loved, as ancestors of his poems. But he was never derivative, never to be mistaken for another. He wrote of change from within it, watching the crystal turn, remembering it as it passed. His opus is work of utter integrity, and he was able to suspend within it wit, frivolity, apparent frivolity, irony, grief, a vast gatherum of the minutiae of existence including drag, the G.N.P. and the paper substitute Tyvek, without loss of style. Like every authentic voice of such substance and distinction, he calls into question all the words he suggests that might designate him, and he resettles them as he goes on taking his own place.

Additional coverage of Merrill's life and career is contained in the following sources published by Gale Research: *Contemporary Authors,* Vols. 13-16, rev. ed., 147 [obituary]; *Contemporary Authors New Revision Series,* Vols. 10, 49; *Contemporary Literary Criticism,* Vols. 2, 3, 6, 8, 13, 18, 34; *Dictionary of Literary Biography,* Vol. 5; *Dictionary of Literary Biography Yearbook, 1985;* **and** *Major 20th-Century Writers.*

May Sarton

May 3, 1912—July 16, 1995

(Born Eléanore Marie Sarton) Belgian-born American poet, memoirist, novelist, autobiographer, author of children's books, and dramatist.

For further information on Sarton's life and works, see *CLC*, Volumes 4, 14, and 49.

INTRODUCTION

A prolific author respected for her poetry, fiction, and autobiographical writings, Sarton examined such issues as the joy and pain associated with love, the necessity of solitude for creativity and identity, the conflict between body and soul, lesbianism, aging, and the role of women in American society. Sarton considered herself first and foremost a poet. Her earliest verse collections, *Encounter in April* (1937) and *Inner Landscape* (1939), evince her skill with various poetic forms. The collections *Land of Silence, and Other Poems* (1953), *A Private Mythology* (1966), *Halfway to Silence* (1980), and *Letters from Maine* (1984) reflect her travels around the world and are known for their attention to physical landscapes, spirituality, and domestic life. Sarton is also a respected novelist. In *Mrs. Stevens Hears the Mermaids Singing* (1965), which many critics consider Sarton's most accomplished novel, acclaimed poet Hilary Stevens prepares for and gives an interview about her career. Throughout the novel, Sarton considers the difficulties women face trying to balance a writing career with raising a family. Most recently, Sarton has garnered critical acclaim for her various journals and memoirs. *I Knew a Phoenix* (1959) relates events from Sarton's childhood and early adulthood, while *Plant Dreaming Deep* (1968) recounts her purchase of a farmhouse in rural New Hampshire. Her more recent autobiographical works focus on her daily life and failing health. *Recovering* (1980) and *After the Stroke* (1988) recount Sarton's emotional and physical recovery from cancer and a stroke. *Endgame* (1992) and *Encore* (1993) are similarly focused but deal as well with her fear of dying alone. Sarton was extremely popular with women and feminists—an acknowledged lesbian, she championed the rights of women in her writings—but suffered a certain measure of critical neglect. Nevertheless, as Mel Gussow observed: "[Sarton] was a stoical figure in American culture, writing about love, solitude and the search for self-knowledge."

PRINCIPAL WORKS

Encounter in April (poetry) 1937
The Single Hound (novel) 1938
Inner Landscape (poetry) 1939
The Bridge of Years (novel) 1946
Underground River (drama) 1947
The Lion and the Rose (poetry) 1948
Shadow of a Man (novel) 1950
A Shower of Summer Days (novel) 1952
Land of Silence, and Other Poems (poetry) 1953
Faithful Are the Wounds (novel) 1955
The Birth of a Grandfather (novel) 1957
I Knew a Phoenix: Sketches for an Autobiography (autobiography) 1959
Cloud, Stone, Sun, Vine: Poems, Selected and New (poetry) 1961
The Small Room (novel) 1961
Mrs. Stevens Hears the Mermaids Singing (novel) 1965; revised edition, 1974

A Private Mythology (poetry) 1966
Plant Dreaming Deep (autobiography) 1968
A Grain of Mustard Seed (poetry) 1971
A Durable Fire (poetry) 1972
As We Are Now (novel) 1973
Journal of a Solitude (journal) 1973
Collected Poems 1930-1973 (poetry) 1974
Punch's Secret (juvenilia) 1974
Crucial Conversations (novel) 1975
A Walk through the Woods (juvenilia) 1976
A World of Light: Portraits and Celebrations (autobiography) 1976
The House by the Sea (journal) 1977
A Reckoning (novel) 1978
Selected Poems of May Sarton (poetry) 1978
Halfway to Silence: New Poems (poetry) 1980
Recovering: A Journal, 1978-1979 (journal) 1980
Writings on Writing (essays) 1981
Anger (novel) 1982
At Seventy (journal) 1984
Letters from Maine (poetry) 1984
The Magnificent Spinster (novel) 1985
As Does New Hampshire, and Other Poems (poetry) 1987
After the Stroke (journal) 1988
The Education of Harriet Hatfield (novel) 1989
*Sarton Selected: An Anthology of the Journals, Novels, and Poems of May Sarton (anthology) 1991
Endgame: A Journal of the Seventy-ninth Year (journal) 1992
Collected Poems (1930-1993) (poetry) 1993
Encore: A Journal of the Eightieth Year (journal) 1993
Coming into Eighty (poetry) 1994
At 82 (journal) 1995

*This work was edited by Bradford Dudley Daziel.

INTERVIEW

May Sarton with Deborah Straw (interview date September 1990)

SOURCE: An interview in *Belles Lettres: A Review of Books by Women,* Vol. 6, No. 2, Winter, 1991, pp. 34-8.

[*In the interview below, originally conducted in September 1990, Sarton discusses various aspects of her career, life, and writing process.*]

May Sarton has written several novels, poems, and journal entries about aging. She has taken her readers into a world of physical breakdown, the letting go of activities, the acceptance, in peace, of the inevitable. She has written much about re-prioritizing. With her transparent style, she has shared both her joy and her anguish.

Now in her seventy-ninth year, Sarton feels she has been "catapulted into" old age. After a stroke five years ago, from which she entirely recovered, she has suffered a fibrillating heart and various internal problems. She has lost much of her immense physical energy.

Not so her psychic energy. For this interview, held over a weekend last September, she was full-spirited and gracious. After walking through her light-filled house (*The House by the Sea*), with its profusion of flowering plants and stuffed animals (many sent by friends and fans) and its piles of books stacked on all available chairs and tables, I came to sit facing her. A passionate woman, she answered my questions thoughtfully, and her occasional full-bodied laughter resonated through the old house.

Sarton is still writing, actually taping a new journal, which will appear on her eightieth birthday next spring. Poems come less often these days, but she had just completed one on friendship. This spring Norton is issuing **Sarton Selected,** an anthology that includes the entire **As We Are Now** and selections from the journals, poems and essays on her work. **The Single Hound,** her first novel (originally published in 1938) will also soon be reissued.

During the hours we talked, Sarton often stopped to answer the phone or to let her elusive cat, Pierrot, in or out, as we reflected on a life of literature.

. . . . .

[*Straw*]: *You first started publishing poetry when you were about seventeen, but you have said you were always writing. Why did you begin?*

[Sarton]: For the same reason I've always written. Those early poems were mostly for my first muses, who were my teachers at Shady Hill—Anne Thorp, who is later **The Magnificent Spinster,** and especially Katharine Taylor, the head of the school, who taught English in the ninth grade and was a good critic. I recited poetry when I was very young because Agnes Hocking believed in everybody learning poetry. We knew so many poems by heart, and I loved reciting them.

In fact, I think I must have been impossible. We were taken up by Boston because of my father and invited to Sunday dinners, where I would always say a poem. I would force myself on those poor ladies. One I particularly loved was Byron's "Greece"—it was quite dramatic.

Did your parents read a lot in the house, and did they read to you?

Yes, my mother read to me every night. George Sarton, the historian, was very much interested in the arts, and so was my mother. It was a rich environment from that point of view. I miss them terribly because I miss the conversation. I didn't always agree, but I certainly always wanted to listen.

Did your early experience in the theater influence your later writing?

It more influenced my ability to communicate with audiences, to project. The other thing it taught me was, (it's kind of arrogant to say but true) that I have charisma, so large audiences respond to me. Not that I had so many large audiences in the theater; I was an apprentice.

Have either of your two plays been produced?

No, but one won a prize.

Would you like to see them produced?

Well, I think they're old fashioned. One is a social commentary called *The Music Box Bird*. It's about the dividing up of the family's belongings. They all want an eighteenth century music box with a bird that emerges and sings. It's got quite a plot, and it's got good dialogue. But now it would have to be much more avant-garde in its actual production. It's an old-fashioned play with a regular old-fashioned set, a big library in a big house on an estate. The children all come together to fight over the things.

The second play is called *The Underground River,* and that's about the French Resistance. Its point was that socialists and communists could work together, but that was not the fashion. Nobody wanted it. That's the one that won the prize, and I'm really fond of it.

After graduating from high school, did you take any writing courses? What do you think of the increase in creative writing programs?

Never. I never went to college. I don't like all the writing programs. I don't think you're taught how to write. I think you learn by reading other people. There's so much loose ambition, so little self-criticism. So much that comes out of these courses is second rate. People have illusions. They have no idea of the competition. They have no idea about how stern you have to be with yourself, how critical.

When I taught at Wellesley, a two-hour seminar course in short stories, the first hour was always given to a great writer. The students had been assigned a story by Chekhov or Hemingway. And in the second half of class, we would critique a story of theirs. They always had a great writer with whom they could, to some extent, compare themselves.

Were there ever times in your life when you could have given up writing and done something entirely different?

No, I think I was born a poet. There are three things you are born with—music (composing), mathematics, and poetry. You don't choose; you're chosen. We know it so well about mathematics. Children will appear, even from very poor backgrounds, who have this genius.

Poetry is harder because if language has not been important in your childhood, early on, I think it may never happen. I think of poetry as my main thing, which I hope will be seen as time goes on.

You seem to be one of the most disciplined people I know. You've written almost fifty books in as many years.

Yes, I have written a lot, and I had to earn my living as well. I wasn't earning my living as a writer until I was sixty-five.

And I know you haven't gotten as much critical acclaim as you would have wished. How have you sustained that inner discipline?

Well, it kept me alive. And also I love doing it. It was obviously my gift, and I feel happy when I'm doing it.

But so many people would have felt discouraged.

You've got to be awfully tough. Anybody who's been through the attacks that I've been through has to be.

Kinds of Love was reviewed in *The Times* by a former editor of *Harper's Magazine,* who wrote, "This novel should have been privately printed. It has no interest for the general reader." And more damming than that. I was so angry I resigned from *The Times,* for whom I had been reviewing. I wrote to the head and said, "I'm sorry, but I can't review for you anymore because I felt this was really dishonest." That book could have been a best seller, and it was killed. That's very hard to take. The poems were well-reviewed up to the collection *Cloud, Stone, Sun, and Vine*. Karl Shapiro wrote, "May Sarton is a bad poet." What can you do?

How did you overcome all this?

I cried. It was Christmas Eve. Poor Judy, my friend with whom I lived. I felt so badly. It wrecked Christmas, but I couldn't help it. And I've just gone on.

Do you think it would have been as possible to be as productive if you had married or been in a full-time relationship for forty years?

Well, I lived with Judy for fifteen years. I did a great deal of work during that time. She was gone all day, so I was alone. Yes, I think it would have been possible. But what I think would not be possible, probably, is to have had a large family. I saw a very good show on PBS about teenage mothers. And one of the things that several of them said was, "I never thought it would be so hard."

I think I wouldn't have had it in me. I can imaging wanting to strangle a baby when it cried, but I hope I wouldn't have. And you're never out from under. You can't say, "We're leaving the baby for twenty-four hours. He'll be all right." You have to do all that arranging. It's bad enough with a cat.

To get to the question of how much can you have. I think one of the dangers in America is that we're brought up to think that we can have everything. You can be a politician, a mother, a wife, all these things, to be a good cook, a good hostess and put on dinners for twenty people, to look wonderful. But if you decide to do all that, you probably couldn't be a writer.

How much of your writing goes on in your head?

Not a lot. I've cast aside, I think, two novels, which I wrote about fifty pages each on. They just weren't going; they hadn't gotten their claws into me. You have to be so seized by it. It's such hard work. It's that invention over a long period of time. It's very much harder than writing a poem; there's no comparison. Because a poem you can finish. It may take a week or even more. But novels, you have to give that supreme effort day after day for a year or more.

How many drafts do you usually do of the poems and of the novels?

With the poems, sometimes fifty, but not so many now. I'm using free verse more. With the novel, I don't revise very much. I plan very carefully. Every day I do five pages. I've thought it out quite hard before I begin. That's the hard work. You spend an hour chewing pencils, and you're thinking, "What really is going to happen now? Why?" You have to think all the time.

But I also miss it when I'm not writing a novel because it's such an obsession. It's like a love affair. You think about it all the time. All these characters are with you, when you go to bed, when you wake up. You have an idea, "This should be done." I enjoy it, but it is very hard work.

You don't know how a novel will end, do you?

No, my novels are predicated on a question that I need to answer by writing the book. For example, with *Faithful Are the Wounds,* the question was, "How can a man be right and wrong at the same time?"

You write four of five hours a day on a novel. How is that time spent?

Three hours, mostly writing. But it is the thinking beforehand that is the hard work. You've got to get down to it each day. It sometimes keeps me awake at night. Inspiration comes with getting started. In other words, you think, "I can't write a line today. I'm too tired, too dull." And then you make yourself write a few lines.

And that's what I miss in saying this new journal. I miss the pen on the paper, scratching things out. I have an old Olivetti, which I love. It has such a light touch. Carolyn Heilbrun almost persuaded me into a computer, but I do think at nearly eighty, it's a bit late. And especially since I'm not a mechanical person at all. But using a tape recorder was a triumph. I didn't think I could do it.

You said once that the thing that destroys art is self-indulgence. Do you still feel that way?

Yes, I do. It's one of the things that frightens me about my present state because I almost have to be self-indulgent. I pay such a high price if I'm not. It's that trying to keep on an even keel. You've got to be able to discipline yourself, to require production. This is one of the things that people don't realize about a novel. You don't write a novel when you're inspired. You're inspired maybe once when you first conceive the idea. And after that, you push it out. When I'm writing a novel, it's under there all the time. It's like an obsession. I'm never not thinking about it.

Have you always had good relationships with your agents and publishers?

Yes, I have. It was a miracle with Diarmuid Russell. How did I find him? Well, he found me. He took an interest in my short stories, and he sold all my novels. He sold me to *The New Yorker.* He was a wonderful man, the son of AE, the poet. And he believed that in the end, good writers would pay. When other agents were looking for writers who would pay right away, he was looking for good writers. Just once he told me he didn't like something. I think he was wrong, but that was one out of many, many times.

> **What I tell people about poetry is, "If you want to read poets, read what you find nourishing. Don't read what you think is fashionable, or the thing to know. Be like an animal looking for food, for the kind of food it can digest."**
>
> **—May Sarton**

So you have an opinion about what women should be writing about today?

No. I think you just write about where you are. If there's something in you that needs to be connected with a place like Christ House in Washington D.C., then you do that. There's an inner voice that tells you, "This has to be done."

Do you keep up with what other women are writing, or can you just go ahead and write, feeling confident that yours is a new idea?

I don't keep up. I read what's sent me. And if there's a book like Nancy Mairs' new book, *Carnal Acts* I order it right away (I saw the review in the *Times*). Actually, I'm always looking for books that will nourish me, and they aren't necessarily by a woman. I keep away from journals. There are a lot of them, but I think *Anne Truitt's Daybook: The Journal of an Artist* is the best.

People think it's very easy. They ask me, "How can I get this journal published?" And my answer is, "You can't unless you're famous for some other reason."

I don't read much poetry now. There's a lot of it I don't like, and usually I go back to people like George Herbert, whom I love. The Civil War PBS series has made me want to go back to Whitman, who was a great influence when I was about fourteen. He certainly comes high on the list of my early influences.

What I tell people about poetry is, "If you want to read poets, read what you find nourishing. Don't read what you think is fashionable, or the thing to know. Be like an animal looking for food, for the kind of food it can digest."

In the journals, you have made parts of your life transparent and have talked about having a transparent style. How do you define transparent?

I don't want people to say, "What a wonderful style you have." I want them to say, "I could just see that tree you described." It's an entirely different thing. People have very brilliant styles, like Elizabeth Bowen, whom I greatly admired, but I'm afraid she's fading out. People don't know her name, and it's partly because it's a very self-conscious style. You're aware of the craft and of the brilliance of the woman who wrote the books. But it's different with Virginia Woolf because, in her case, the style is so much the person.

I know one of the dilemmas through the years has been all

the fan mail. It's hard for you to say "No." You get involved with so many people and, after a while, maybe you wish you hadn't with some of them. Has responding to all these people's needs helped you in any way as a writer?

I think it has. I never went to college; I'm very isolated. I don't belong to any social group. I realize that more and more. But the letters connect me in ways I would otherwise not be connected. I open my address book when I'm looking for an address, and I realize how many of what I consider my real friends I've made through the work. There are an awful lot of them, all over the place.

How have you been able to give so much time and energy to strangers without draining our own energy?

Well, I used to have a lot of energy. Second, it sort of got me started. I never answered more than two or three before working. It got the wheels oiled a bit.

Let's talk about your poetry. Have you written many poems that you've never published?

The woman who is working on my papers now is reading the early poems. I wrote them when I was fifteen of sixteen. I was amazed; they're really quite good. I just kept on writing the poems and sending them out, but I have never made a huge name, as you know. So I don't exist as a poet (except that I am read).

Do you think there is a resurgence of interest in poetry? Is there a particular need in the human spirit now for poetry?

Yes, I do. But I think there always is. It's hard to tell why there's an increasing interest. I get the same amount of mail about my own poetry, and publishers send me all the little magazines.

But the whole question of the public and private life is very complex. I was very lucky that I could read my poems and therefore touch an audience that perhaps wouldn't have otherwise known I existed. Perhaps they had read the journals, and then they were pulled out by the poems when they were read aloud. And this was lucky for me. It was better publicity than reviews, no doubt.

I remember one woman about fifty-five coming up to me in the Midwest, saying intensely, "You must do only this. Don't bother writing another novel. Just read your poems."

You've stopped doing the readings?

I've had to because of my voice. I'm very conscious of being crippled in that way. And that was something I was so sure of.

Another thing I want to say about the poetry. When I started writing poetry, it was always in the masculine, for example **"The Phoenix"** (*Collected Poems*) was masculine. It wasn't that I had decided to do that. It's just that it seemed as if the poet in me was the masculine in me. This was unconscious. And it took me until about ten years ago when somebody said, "But isn't it she, this or that, and not he?" that I realized this.

I was brought up, startled by this, and I said, "Well, it's quite true, of course. I've got to try to learn how to be a

woman and be proud of it." The part of that was writing the poems was really the man and proud of it. I was in the position of wooing the woman.

In the last ten years, have the subjects you have written about changed?

No, I don't think so. But the actual gender, the actual language, has changed. I'm trying to say now that it's great to be a woman, and I don't have to be a man to be a poet. So that's a big change.

Do you think the position of women writers in America is improving? Do you think there's a better opportunity for woman to be treated more fairly, to be reviewed more often?

I think the poets are getting a break and partly because they're very good.

I think it's very hard to be a woman poet. For example, my worst reviews have been from women, and my best have been from men. This applies to the novels as well. It's so hard for women that I think they're inevitably jealous. If you're good, they're jealous, and if you're bad, they're only too glad to jump on you. It gets you out of the competition. But it's not conscious. I don't think there's any, "Let's get May Sarton. She's doing too well."

The more I think about it, the more I realize how terribly lucky I was in London in the 1930s, just before the War. There I knew Elizabeth Bowen, Koteliansky (who got the Cresset Press to publish my poetry as well as my novels), Basil de Selincourt (a distinguished critic), and Virginia Woolf (who, of course, was not a backer). I didn't know her that well, nor do I know if she liked my work. But she was certainly a wonderful person to have known. I was like a spoiled child. I was really picked up. I was getting the praise that I never got here, and it was wonderful.

What do you think of the new genre, lesbian books?

I hate it. I suppose that's my wound, if you will. Don't forget when I was growing up, you simply couldn't come out as a lesbian. And you had to conquer in yourself a great deal of self-doubt, of wondering if it was a morally viable life. And also, I really don't like sex in any book, homosexual or heterosexual. It offends me; it does not excite me.

You wouldn't like to see your books under the category of lesbian books?

No, I wouldn't at all. I think the books are universal. And the proof of that is that so many people don't recognize me as a lesbian in the poetry.

I consider you successful. But how do you define success for yourself?

Being in the anthologies. That's it. Remember *Modern American Poetry* by Louis Untermeyer? For thirty years, that was taught in every high school. That's how people knew some of the names like Louise Bogan.

I've never been in a first-rate anthology, not even in the Norton poetry anthology. I am now in lesbian anthologies. I'm glad, but I'd much rather be in a general anthology.

But I am quoted constantly. Did you see the quote in John

LeCarre's *The Russia House?* When that kind of thing happens, which is very precious, I love it.

Do you have an idea why you're not in more of the anthologies? Why you haven't gotten more breaks?

I wish I knew. One of the things involved is that I'm not an American. I really am a European, and I think that shows in the work. The Europeans have wanted something from me which is not there. They would have liked me to write about the Wild West or about the South in the Civil War. Yet, here is this generally humanistic, middle-aged woman who is not even depicting a definite society. That's the reason there are no translations of me. Well, I do now have a Dutch publisher who is crazy about me. They are publishing the work, but, after all, that's a small country.

My novels have no plot in the ordinary sense, yet people can't put them down. There's little violence or sex—all the things that are in the air and that people want, I don't give.

Why have you not written about these things—sex, violence, drugs?

I don't know enough about them. You have to write from where you are. And my life was a university background, a European background. What really made me an American was going to live in Nelson, New Hampshire.

But, back to the European and American attitudes and to the rejections. It seems that your writing is universal.

Yes, but you see, if you were thinking of America, and you wanted to give a Swiss friend an idea of what we're all about, I think you wouldn't give me. Because I am too universal, in a way. I might as well be a Swiss writer.

The woman living alone has given me a kind of raison d'etre from the critical point of view, which I didn't have before. Carolyn Heilbrun has emphasized that.

There's a quote from Elizabeth Bowen, "My writing, I am prepared to think, may be a substitute for something that does not, as far as I know, exist . . . a so-called normal relation to society. My books are my relation to society" (from a letter to V. S. Pritchett, from The Mulberry Tree). *Do you feel that way?*

No. I suppose for me it's more like "My Letter to the World." Or, "I have a thing to tell," as Tom Wolfe put it. It's a great desire to communicate, certainly, and to bridge the silence and the isolation. I have a real need for that. I feel lonely a lot of the time.

This is something I didn't foresee, that old age would not be a time of ripeness and fulfillment, for health reasons. That has changed all my plans. The end of my life was to be a very serene time, and I would keep a meditative journal. Well, you can't tell. If I could get well now, I'd have a lot to say. I might even be able to write a novel, but I don't have the energy now. I still have hundreds of ideas. But the actual energy, what goes from the pen to the page, that energy isn't there anymore. I've got the pen, and I've got the page, but the thing that is in between, which is all important, is very rarely there.

Are there any good aspects of being "catapulted into" old age? Have you learned anything that is useful?

I don't think I really have. Overall, it's rather a negative experience. I think you should grow old in a good temper, gradually, one thing after another laid aside without any great struggle.

But here's a good thing. I've certainly become much more passive. I can accept not being able to do anything, which I couldn't have accepted years ago.

Are some things more valuable to you now?

Friendship. It was a trial, but I wrote the Christmas poem this year. It has to be done in August to get to the printer. I did it for twenty years on my own, and when the list became one thousand, I stopped. I said, "It's a factory now. It's not me." And then there was a long gap, maybe ten or fifteen years. Then my printer asked me, "Would you mind if we use this as a Christmas poem, and I'll give you some?" Now I send out two hundred.

It's a kind of writing on deadline, which is different than writing when inspiration comes?

Well, it's not bad to have to write sometimes. One of my favorites was **"The Light,"** which I wrote two years ago about the Christmas tree light. If the poem comes at Christmas, I keep it. . . . Some of my very best poems were those poems, for example, **"A Hard Death"** (from *A Grain of Mustard Seed*).

But I'll never be inspired for poetry again. There'll never be another muse.

But you have said that the sea will be your last muse.

No. It's cold; it's impersonal. I love it, you know, but it's not a muse. The poem **"Invocation"** that begins, "Never has the sea been maternal to me or kind" says it (from *The Silence Now*).

How do you know there won't be another woman as muse?

Well, I don't know it. But I think certain things die in you, certain means of response. And when you're in a state of extreme fatigue as I am, there isn't that spring that leaps up when I see something. It's peaceful, and sometimes I think of how much pain there was. All these love affairs were disasters, but I wrote all the poems. I was happy. I was doing what I most loved doing.

Are you talking about the illness and pain in the new journal?

I'm trying not to, but I can't help talking about it sometimes because often I can't do the journal at all, and I have to explain that "I spent yesterday in bed." I think it will help other people, like *After the Stroke.* People don't want to talk about what they're going through. That's also what I admire about Nancy Mairs. She's willing to let you in, and that's wonderfully generous. It's also perhaps feminine.

Do you have any more writing plans?

My letters to Juliette Huxley. That will be a major work,

and that's all ready to go. It is the legacy of an *amitie amoureuse.*

Is there anything else you might have liked to have done with your life?

No.

OBITUARY

Mel Gussow   (obituary date 18 July 1995)

SOURCE: An obituary in *The New York Times,* July 18, 1995, p. B12.

[*In the obituary below, Gussow surveys Sarton's life and career.*]

May Sarton, poet, novelist and the strongest of individualists, died on [July 16, 1995], at the York Hospital in York, Me., the town in which she had lived for many years. She was a stoical figure in American culture, writing about love, solitude and the search for self-knowledge. She was 83.

The cause of death was breast cancer, said Susan Sherman, a close friend and editor of her letters.

During a remarkably prolific career that stretched from early sonnets published in 1929 in *Poetry* magazine to **Coming Into Eighty** her latest collection of poems, in 1994, Ms. Sarton persistently followed her own path and was nurtured by an inner lyricism. She wrote more than 20 books of fiction and many works of nonfiction, including autobiographies and journals, a play and several screenplays. She was best known and most highly regarded as a poet.

Extremely popular on college campuses, she became a heroine to feminists. In 1965, when she revealed that she was a lesbian, she said she lost two jobs as a result. But as with so much in her life, she had no regrets.

In an interview with Enid Nemy in *The New York Times* in 1983, Ms. Sarton was described as "a commanding, no-nonsense figure with clear blue eyes and a shock of white hair," a woman who lived in "self-imposed loneliness" in a weathered clapboard house on the Maine coast. She had, it was said, a difficult life; her work has been virtually ignored by major critics and she gained her reputation primarily by word of mouth. The poet said, "Women have been my muse."

Recovering from a stroke, and while often in pain from other ailments, she continued to keep a journal, and in 1993 published **Encore: A Journal of the 80th Year.** In it, she said, "I write poems, have always written them, to transcend the painfully personal and reach the universal." She added, "It's hard to say goodbye to journals, and if I live to be 85 I might resume one for the joy of it."

In *The New York Times Book Review,* the novelist Sheila

Ballantyne, reviewing **Anger,** Ms. Sarton's 1982 novel, wrote:

> It is clear that May Sarton's best work, whatever its form, will endure well beyond the influence of particular reviews or current tastes. For in it she is an example: a seeker after truth with a kind of awesome energy for renewal, an ardent explorer of life's important questions. Her great strength is that when she achieves insight, one believes—because one has witnessed the struggle that preceded the knowledge.

Ms. Sarton was born in Wondelgem in Belgium in 1914, as Eléanore Marie Sarton. Her father was a Belgian historian of science, her mother an English artist and designer. With the outbreak of World War I, the Sartons emigrated to England and, in 1916, to the United States, where her name was Anglicized to Eleanor May Sarton. As she later recalled in **I Knew a Phoenix: Sketches for an Autobiography,** her mother carried with her from Belgium a copy of *Leaves of Grass,* and passed on a love of poetry to her daughter.

In 1918, the Sartons settled in Cambridge, Mass. At Shady Hill School in Cambridge, the young woman explored her passion for poetry, and then fell into difficulty at high school because she objected to a teacher's statement that Ibsen was immoral. The fact that she did not go to college was, she said, "a great piece of luck; this way, I'm ignorant but I'm fresh." Stage-struck, she joined Eva Le Gallienne's Civic Repertory Theater as an actress. After the company disbanded in the early 1930's, she founded the Apprentice Theater of the New School for Social Research. When her theater failed, she made frequent trips back to Europe, and continued to re-envision her experiences in poetry.

During the 1930's, two volumes of poetry, **Encounter in April** and **Inner Landscape** and a novel, **The Single Hound,** established themes that were to occupy her for a lifetime: the many forms of love and the uniqueness of the individual. To support her art, she wrote book reviews and taught creative writing. Her second novel, **The Bridge of Years,** published in 1946, was seemingly drawn from life, dealing with the effect of two world wars on a Belgian family. Many of her subsequent novels, including **The Small Room, Crucial Conversations** and **A Reckoning,** centered on women as protagonists. In these novels as well as in her poems, she confronted issues that foreshadowed feminist writing of subsequent decades.

Sarton was a stoical figure in American culture, writing about love, solitude and the search for self-knowledge.

—Mel Gussow

For Ms. Sarton, poetry was her life's work. As she said: "When you're a poet, you're a poet first. When it comes, it's like an angel." Although she never had the full recognition attained by many of her peers, and never won a Pulitzer Prize or a National Book Award, her work generally received favorable reviews and she had a loyal-readership. She was a member of the American Academy of Arts and Sciences and received 18 honorary degrees.

In *Encore* she admitted to being hypersensitive about criticism. As she once said, referring to a review of her novel, *A Reckoning,* a bad review "is a drop of poison and slowly gets into the system, day by day." But nothing could discourage her from writing, not even a series of illnesses. Through her later years, she chronicled her life in journals. In *After the Stroke* a journal published in 1988, she wrote that she had discovered "for the first time perhaps what it takes to grow old," and, approaching 75, was determined to "recover and go on creating."

Speaking about the "rewards of a solitary life," she said, "Loneliness is most acutely felt with other people, for with others, even with a lover sometimes, we suffer from our differences—differences of taste, temperament, mood." Quietly she waited for the moment to come "when the world falls away, and the self emerges again from the deep unconscious, bringing back all I have recently experienced to be explored and slowly understood, when I can converse again with my own hidden powers, and so grow, and so be renewed, till death do us part."

OVERVIEW

Valerie Miner   (essay date 1991)

SOURCE: "Spinning Friends: May Sarton's Literary Spinsters," in *Old Maids to Radical Spinsters: Unmarried Women in the Twentieth-Century Novel,* edited by Laura L. Doan, University of Illinois Press, 1991, pp. 155-68.

[*Miner is an American novelist, short story writer, editor, critic, and educator. In the essay below, she examines the ways in which Sarton represents lesbians and single women in her writings, noting in particular the relationship between her fiction and nonfiction.*]

> In the mirror she recognized her *self,* her life companion, for better or worse. She looked at this self with compassion this morning, unmercifully prodded and driven as she had been for just under seventy years.
>
> —May Sarton, *Mrs. Stevens Hears the Mermaids Singing*
>
> She who has chosen her Self, who defines her Self, by choice, neither in relation to children nor to men, who is Self-identified, is a Spinster. . . .
>
> —Mary Daly, *Gyn/Ecology*

Spinning a web of literary friendship, May Sarton gives renewed grace and power to single women. "With a hundred threads binding their lives to hers," as she says of one

character in *The Magnificent Spinster,* Sarton expands and interweaves the definitions of the words "spinster" and "friend." May Sarton's spinsters are vital, often romantic women engaged in the world as teachers, writers, mentors, colleagues, and social activists.

Cam Arnold devotes herself to writing a biographical novel about Jane Reid as an act of friendship and commemoration in *The Magnificent Spinster.* Hilary Stevens befriends a troubled young man in *Mrs. Stevens Hears the Mermaids Singing.* Caro Spencer risks her own safety to protect another resident of her dreary nursing home in *As We Are Now.* These characters, like Sarton herself, are old women who have used their lives productively, indeed exuberantly. Although some might assume a tension between their friendship and autonomy, it is precisely the self-sufficiency of Sarton and her protagonists that locates their deep and lasting friendships as the source and expression of their best selves. Being spinsters has allowed them to give to their neighbors with time and spirit unavailable to many of their contemporaries who have chosen to reproduce and live in cloistered families.

The identity of the sisterly spinster is enacted in Sarton's own friendship with her characters. Their stories raise provocative notions: spinsterhood as a vocation of social responsibility; companionship as an alternative to motherhood; lesbian bonding as an alternative to marriage; friendship as an alternative to any sexual partnership; and writing as an act of friendship.

In this essay, I explore the uneasy borders between fiction and memoir by observing reflections between the characters in Sarton's novels, *The Magnificent Spinster, As We Are Now,* and *Mrs. Stevens Hears the Mermaids Singing,* and the spinster self-portraits in her journals, *At Seventy, Journal of a Solitude,* and *I Knew a Phoenix.* In particular, I am interested in Sarton's representation of the lesbian spinster and the literary spinster.

May Sarton manages to create a special familiarity among writer, protagonist, and reader because of the way she balances her work on the boundaries of autobiography and fiction. "I think of myself as a maker of bridges—between the heterosexual and the homosexual world, between the old and the young," Sarton tells Karen Saum in an interview for the *Paris Review* [1983]. The flexible forms of Sarton's fiction allow unique access to all involved. Each of the three novels under discussion engages the audience in questions about purpose, process, and style of writing.

The Magnificent Spinster is a novel about Cam, a retired history professor, writing a novel about the life of her teacher Jane Reid. Here we learn not only about Cam and Jane but about the intricacies of conveying the qualities of a long friendship in fiction. Sarton is at her best shaping the distinctive temperaments of these friends—balancing Cam's rash enthusiasm and Jane's measured graciousness—revealing how the women complement and confound each other. *Mrs. Stevens Hears the Mermaids Singing* is an account of an extended interview with Hilary Stevens, an acclaimed old poet, in which the skeleton of her biography is constructed by the questions and answers, while the rest of her story is fleshed out by her own dramatic internal flashbacks. During the interview, Hilary Stevens reflects on past friendships while developing an incipient friendship with the interviewer Jenny Hare. *As We Are Now* is a novel written as a journal to be published after Caro Spencer dies. Of these three protagonists, Caro most closely resembles the stereotype of the spinster as an isolated, single, old woman, but the greatest drama of the book takes place within the friendships of her last months and in the fire she sets, destroying her grim nursing home and herself. Caro's final legacy—the journal—is a celebration of those precious relationships as well as a customary gift to those who might follow her into rest homes.

It is easy to find the seeds of these novels in Sarton's life. Jane Reid in *The Magnificent Spinster* is consciously modeled on Sarton's old friend and teacher Anne Longfellow Thorp. Thorp is lovingly described in *I Knew a Phoenix* and *Journal of a Solitude.* Sarton proceeds to discuss the difficult process of writing the novel about Thorp in *At Seventy.* Like the protagonist in *Mrs. Stevens,* Sarton lived for a time in England, where she found great artistic nourishment. She, too, had romances with both men and women and found women to be the sustaining muse for her poetry. The inspiration for Caro Spencer's decline in *As We Are Now* can be traced to a visit Sarton makes to a nursing home in *Journal of a Solitude.* Indeed, she has Caro's friend repeat the same words as Sarton's friend Perley Cole from *Journal:* " 'I never thought it would end like this.' " All these women share Sarton's white, middle-class, New England background.

Although Sarton's fiction is autobiographical in the sense of memory recalled, it is also autobiographical in the sense of premonition. She relates to the characters in her novels as friends and models for her own life. Mrs. Stevens, a poet verging on seventy, is finally receiving the acknowledgment Sarton desires for her own poetry. The novel, published when Sarton was fifty-three, allows the author to try on the kudos, to see how she would feel looking back at her life from the distance of seven decades. (The name of Hilary Stevens's protégé, Mar, is not so different from the name of his creator, May. Mar's name and personality signify the anger with which Sarton so closely identifies.) This book also permits Sarton to watch Hilary come out as a lesbian in her narrative, before she herself comes out in her journals. Once Sarton reaches her own seventies, she chooses the character Cam, a seventy-year-old woman, to write a novel about Jane, to teach her how to write the novel she herself wants to write about Anne Longfellow Thorp. One step further into old age, Sarton creates *As We Are Now,* an unflinching study of rest-home existence. In *At Seventy,* she writes about putting a deposit on a modern, flexible retirement community, no doubt partially in response to her experience struggling with Caro's limited choices. It is useful to remember that the Sarton portrayed in the journals is also a persona shaped by the author. Just as her fiction is autobiographical, her autobiography is a creation of imagination. No doubt the May Sartons who emerge in the work of those who dare to write biographies of this formidable woman will be different characters altogether.

Sarton, then, develops a unique intimacy with her charac-

ters, between her characters, between the characters and readers, and between herself and readers. All her prose—fiction and journal—is rendered in a straightforward, yet elegant style. Although some may regard her commitment to realism as old-fashioned, I see it as yet another gesture of friendship because she makes her ideas accessible to a broad range of readers.

> **Although Sarton's fiction is autobiographical in the sense of memory recalled, it is also autobiographical in the sense of premonition. She relates to the characters in her novels as friends and models for her own life.**
>
> **—Valerie Miner**

May Sarton's spinsters forgo marriage for a wider province. Like Louisa May Alcott, they believe that the pursuit of good work and public service is [as Blanche Wiesen Cook says in her "Incomplete Lives" in *The Women's Review of Books* (1985)] "a better husband than love." These middle-class women are friends rather than wives—friends over the backfence and in the public arena. Sarton, whose work seems more Edwardian than contemporary, grew up in an era of strong single women, both literary figures and political activists. In Britain as well as the United States, single women were among the most visible early twentieth-century feminists—working in settlement houses, living in single-sex communities, and campaigning for female suffrage. Sarton, whose mother was English and whose father was Belgian, comes from a bourgeois European background noted for championing eccentricity. Given her girlhood acquaintance with genteel, socially concerned women in Cambridge, Massachusetts, it is not surprising to find her stories focus on the contributions of publicly generous, personally modest women. In addition, her place as an only child probably helped cultivate an affinity for spinsterly solitude. In Sarton's recollections about her youth, one detects a pleasure in her own company and an aptitude for independence which prepared her for spinsterly success.

Her characters are solitary figures only when narrowly viewed. They are deeply engaged in serving others through education, social activism, and the arts. In *The Magnificent Spinster,* Cam challenges sexism among her contemporaries and fights against fascism in the Spanish Civil War. Both she and the subject of her novel, Jane, are dedicated teachers. Jane works with French orphans after World War I and helps Germans reconstruct their lives after World War II. Later Jane confronts Boston racism—and her own bigotry—through her growing friendship with Ellen, the African-American director of the Cambridge Community Center.

Sarton's spinsters are often understated about their social contributions. Not all her spinsters are as comfortable with singleness as Jane is. For instance, Hilary Stevens describes her spinsterhood as deviance in her interview with the young writers Jenny and Peter: " 'For the aberrant woman art is health, the only health! It is,' she waved aside Peter's attempt to interrupt, 'as I see it, the constant attempt to rejoin something broken off or lost, to make whole again.' " Earlier in the novel, Hilary reassures herself that life is not as bad as it might be, that she did not turn out like Aunt Ida, an artist who was institutionalized because she was suicidal: "Nevertheless, young Hilary reminded old Hilary, you have not done too badly, old thing. You did not break down like Aunt Ida; you kept going; you have worked hard, and you have made a garden, which would have pleased your mother; and once in a while you have been able to be of some use to another human being—Mar for instance." Despite her self-effacing presentation, Hilary has had a very successful writing career and is a stimulating, encouraging friend to numerous people, especially Mar, the defensive young artist. She also inspires her interviewer Jenny: " 'For some odd reason you've given me courage,' she [Jenny] said, 'courage to be myself, to do what I want to do!' "

In *As We Are Now,* Caro Spencer questions the value of her own life after she is put out to pasture:

> Did they always hate me, my family I mean, because I was different, because I never married. . . . A high-school teacher in a small town is (or was in the years when I taught math) not exactly suspect, but set apart. Only in the very last years when I was established as a dear old eccentric did I ever dare have a drink in public! And even among my colleagues, mostly good simple-minded fellows, I did not quite fit in. They had their own club and went off fishing together and on an occasional spree to New York, but of course they didn't want an old maid tagging along. . . .

Caro's tightly corseted self-image conceals the cosmopolitan attitudes she has developed in her wise travels and forty years of teaching. Precisely because of her reserved nature, her expressions of loyalty—such as defending a colleague facing dismissal for his homosexuality—are acts of courage. Once in the nursing home, she becomes friends with Standish Flint, another resident. His mistreatment makes her strength flare. "Yet, Caro, remember that anger is the wicked side of fire—you had fire and that fire made you a good teacher and a brave fighter sometimes. Fire can be purifying." It is this sacred fire which fuels the keeping of her diary and allows her to leave the world of her own accord.

In the journals, Sarton portrays *herself* as someone for whom solitude is a respite for nurturing social contribution—whether this is her art; her philanthropy to adopted families and needy friends; her support for HOME, a progressive housing project in Orland, Maine; or her advice to young writers. In *I Knew a Phoenix,* she honors spinsters who have influenced her life, including her teachers at Shady Hill School and the actor Eva Le Gallienne, who inspired her to give up college and join the theater. Like Sarton, these spinsters may be suspect in the outside world but only because their participation in that world is veiled by stereotype.

Because these women are unmarried, their class and generation dictate that they also be childless. For some, this state is a failure; for some a relief; for some an opportunity to "mother" in unique ways. The identity "childless" has taken on various meanings during their long lives. Sarton and her fictional spinsters grew up within an ethic which defined nonmothers as unnatural or barren. They have survived both world wars, experiencing the absence of men on the home front as well as the baby booms following the soldiers' return. They lived through eras when feminists questioned the maternal imperative and celebrated selfhood. More recently, some have found themselves in a period where women—including single heterosexuals and lesbians—are having a renewed romance with biological motherhood. Since Sarton and her characters are all WASPish women, under no pressure to compensate for the genocide of their culture, many would observe that their first contribution is the decision not to add to an already overpopulated world. Perhaps these women don't suffer the impulse to reproduce biologically because they have found other venues for self-creation.

In *Journal of a Solitude,* Sarton describes Anne Longfellow Thorp:

> For her, life itself has been the creation, but not in the usual mode as wife, mother and grandmother. Had Anne married she would have led a different life and no doubt a rich one, but she would not have been able to give what she does here and in the way she does. . . . Here is a personal largess, a largess of giving to life in every possible way, that makes her presence itself a present. . . . Perhaps the key is in her capacity to make herself available on any day, at any time, to whatever human joy or grief longs to be fulfilled or assuaged by sharing . . . [or] longs to pour itself out and to be understood. So a teddy bear will materialize as if by magic for a one-year-old who has stubbed a toe; so a young woman who cannot decide whom to marry can have a long talk in perfect peace; so a very old lady can discuss with gusto the coming presidential election and feel a fire to match her own rise up in Anne's blue eyes. The participation is never passive, shot through with a sudden gust of laughter as it often is, always vivid and original.

In contrast, Hilary Stevens is painfully conscious of her abnormality:

> "No, the crucial question seems to me to be this: what is the *source* of creativity in the woman who wants to be an artist? After all, admit it, a woman is meant to create children not works of art—that's what she has been engined to do, so to speak. A man with a talent does what is expected of him, makes his way, constructs, is an engineer, a composer, a builder of bridges. It's the natural order of things that he construct objects outside himself and his family. The woman who does so is aberrant."

Near the end of the book, Hilary says to Mar, " 'No, I

think I would have liked to be a woman, simple and fruitful, a woman with many children, a great husband, . . . and no talent!' " (Sarton's ellipsis).

But Sarton's portrayal of the spinster or lesbian as perverted softens with the years. *Mrs. Stevens* is the earliest of the three novels discussed here. By the time readers meet Caro and especially Cam and Jane, the portrait of the spinster as an estimable figure of solitary strength is less qualified. If one accepts the threads connecting these books, one detects three distinct moods—anxiety in *Mrs. Stevens,* fury in *As We Are Now,* and tranquillity in *The Magnificent Spinster*—revealing a marked emotional moment. Perhaps the self-criticism so raw in *Mrs. Stevens* is due to the fact that this was Sarton's "coming-out" novel, and the writing process was filled with special conflict. Perhaps, too, she came to a greater peace about her own identity as spinster and lesbian in the years between this novel and the other two.

In *As We Are Now,* spinsterhood is portrayed both as freedom and loneliness. Caro doesn't think much about children, but, from her attitudes regarding marriage, readers gather that her independence from men and children comes from the same instinct for self-containment. When Anna asks Caro why she never married, Caro pauses, "It was a hard question to answer. How could I tell her, perhaps that I am a failure, couldn't take what it would have cost to give up an authentic being, myself, to take in the stranger? That I failed because I was afraid of losing myself when in fact I might have grown through sharing an equality with another human being. And yet . . . do I really regret not marrying? No, to be quite honest, *no.*"

Similarly, in *The Magnificent Spinster,* Cam describes Jane's spinsterhood in terms of potential: "she did not resemble anyone's idea of a spinster, dried up, afraid of life, locked away. On the contrary it may have been her riches as a personality, her openness, the depth of her feelings that made her what she was, not quite the marrying kind . . . a free spirit" (Sarton's ellipsis). And, like Caro and Hilary, Jane serves many different people with her "extra" time. Long after she quits teaching, Jane makes a point of inviting children to her family's country retreat.

Sarton's journals also reflect an active relationship with younger people. One of the most touching parts of *At Seventy* is Sarton's description of a visit by "little Sarton," a girl named after her by parents who fell in love while reading her poetry. She also discusses the satisfactions of her friendship with a young scholar named Georgia:

> What is wonderful for me is to be with someone whose vision of life is so like mine, who reads avidly and with discrimination, who goes deeply into whatever is happening to her and her family and can talk about it freely, so it feels a little like a piece of music in which we are playing different instruments that weave a theme in and out, in almost perfect accord. I had this experience always with my mother when I came home and we could talk. And I feel so happy that perhaps I can be that kind of mother for Georgia.

The spinsters in these books are parents in the sense of being mentors and confidantes. While they lack some ma-

ternal satisfactions, such as the pleasure derived from physical resemblance between oneself and one's own offspring, they are freed from certain kinds of maternal guilt and legal responsibilities. In *The Magnificent Spinster,* Jane gently directs Cam. Both Hilary Stevens and Caro Spencer can look back to spinster aunts as inspirational yet admonitory examples. In her journals Sarton emerges as a wise, generous persona, a model for her readers.

In addition to the gratification of reproducing, mothers often look forward to being cosseted by their children in old age. What does a spinster do? Sarton offers various possibilities, from Jane, who is surrounded by loving friends until the end, to Caro, who creates her own end and arranges her own cremation. Caro's death is admirable, tragic, and—in keeping with Mary Daly's glorious self-definition of spinsterhood—transcendent. "Spinsters, too, learn to be at home on the road. Our ability to make our spirits our moving shelters will enable us to dispense with patriarchal shelters, the various homes that house the domesticated, the sick, the 'mentally ill,' the destitute."

For each of these characters—Hilary, Caro, Cam, and the Sarton of the journals—the absence of one's own children is a blessing and a loss. Each in her own way expresses ambivalence and conflict about this aspect of being a *single* woman. The childlessness is one more instance of her autonomy from the family, if not from the society.

Lesbian friendship is a sanctuary and a stigma for Sarton's spinsters. One conventional definition of spinster is a "woman who has rejected or who has been rejected by marriage." Today, however, marriage is so broadly rejected in favor of live-in, unmarried partnerships between women and men that the definition is outdated. If one reads "male-linked" for marriage, one has a clearer sense of the current popular definition. All lesbians, whether coupled or not, might claim to be spinsters. By choosing women, they have remained "unmarried" to, and unprotected by, male identity. (While many heterosexual feminists have fought for autonomy within their individual partnerships, they do have privileges unavailable to women who forgo such bonding with males.) Spinsters have historically been identified by what they are *not* (married) just as contemporary lesbians are ostracized for what they are not (male-linked). This "identity by lack" leaves room for the cultural imagination to conjure new labels. People often seem more threatened by dismissal of patriarchy than by antagonism to it and thus turn the sin of omission into a sin of commission, transforming the medieval spinster into a witch (consorting with the devil is more easily imaginable than not consorting with males at all) and the contemporary lesbian into a pervert. Witch-hunting spirals into gay-bashing. While few of today's lesbian spinsters are burned at the stake, they suffer enormous discrimination in employment, housing, and healthcare. To be a lesbian in the United States is to be "illegitimate," to be substantially without civil rights. Lesbians are declared unsuitable as teachers in certain areas and unfit to immigrate to this country. When lesbians aren't attacked, they, like other spinsters, are often ignored. Individually, some heterosexuals find lesbian bonding so threatening that they refuse to see it, and in an ironic twist on my theme, they interpret the intimacy between long-time partners as a tamer "friendship." Such women, particularly the older ones, are identified in their jobs and neighborhoods as "spinsters."

These novels reveal a multiplicity of lesbians, from Cam, who has a long-term relationship with Ruth in *The Magnificent Spinster,* to Caro, whose last great love is Anna ("I myself am on the brink of understanding things about love I have never understood before"), to Hilary, who struggles with her aberration. Writing *Mrs. Stevens* was a profound psychological and professional risk for Sarton, as she explains in *Journal of a Solitude*:

> On the surface my work has not looked radical, but perhaps it will be seen eventually that in a "nice, quiet, noisy way" I have been trying to say radical things gently so that they may penetrate without shock. The fear of homosexuality is so great that it took courage to write *Mrs. Stevens,* to write a novel about a woman who is not a sex maniac, a drunkard, a drug-taker, or in any way repulsive; to portray a homosexual who is neither pitiable nor disgusting, without sentimentality. . . . But I am well aware that I probably could not have "leveled" as I did in that book had I had any family (my parents were dead when I wrote it), and perhaps not if I had had a regular job. I have a great responsibility because I can afford to be honest. The danger is that if you are placed in a sexual context people will read your work from a distorting angle of vision. I did not write *Mrs. Stevens* until I had written several novels concerned with marriage and family life.

In fact, Sarton did lose teaching engagements as a result of the book's publication. Her poetry has been censored from school texts, not because of explicit sexual references but simply because she is now widely known as lesbian.

On the other hand, this visibility has brought many lesbian readers. The revelation also has freed her to write more openly about her own relationships in the journals. In *Journal of a Solitude* and *At Seventy,* she looks back on her primary partnership with Judith Matlock, an English professor. Matlock, lover, friend, and Friend (a committed Quaker) lived with Sarton for fifteen years.

Sarton, however, is not doctrinaire. The lesbian connections are honored without any of the throat-clearing fanfare of more didactic lesbian novels. Moreover, just as she poses lesbianism as an alternative to marriage, she poses nonsexual friendship as an alternative to sexual partnership. Comrades and companions are often valued over lovers. Sexual relationships are often set in the past or in the background of a story. The strongest relationship in *The Magnificent Spinster* is between Cam and Jane—a friendship of cherished mutual development. In *As We Are Now,* Caro's current friendship with Standish, Reverend Thornhill, and Lisa are more important than any sexual partnership. *Mrs. Stevens* ends as it began, showing Hilary cajoling young Mar. The last scene is filled with affection, hope, and a provocative sexual energy: "For a second they confronted each other, the bold blue eyes of Mar and the hooded gray eyes of Hilary. Then at the same instant,

each reached for a pebble and threw it down. The two pebbles struck the water about two feet apart, and they watched avidly as the two great widening ripples intersected."

In Sarton's journals, the sexual partnerships are also masked (as in the reference to "X" in *Journal of a Solitude*) or set in the past. Sarton is at her most vital when greeting friends in her house in Nelson, Massachusetts, or York, Maine. She frequently complains about her voluminous correspondence with people she has met through her books, but, of course, the descriptions of such correspondence are what prompt so many fans to write.

For Sarton, literary friendship is an *exchange* involving various levels of interaction with members of her audience as well as with her characters. She is neither puppeteer nor omniscient benefactor. She needs her readers. Sarton's most popular work is her journals, which resemble long letters addressed to a broad-based audience of friends.

—*Valerie Miner*

Like spinning wool or silk or webs, Sarton's writing is a process of *conserving* the essential while transforming it into something useful for herself and others. Sarton spins her stories with intelligence and craft. Much as early spinsters turned their wheels, she uses her hands and wit to recycle raw experience.

Cam describes her impulse to write about Jane:

> What then has driven me so late in life to write a novel? Quite simply the unequivocal need to celebrate an extraordinary woman whom I had the good fortune to know for more than fifty years until her death a year ago. . . .
>
> I realized that in a few years everyone who knew Jane would be dead. Who would remember her? In fifty years who would know she had existed? She never married. There would be no children and grandchildren to keep her memory alive. She was already vanishing like sand in the ocean. . . . Then, almost without thinking, I went into my study, forgetting all about lunch, and began to write. (third ellipsis Sarton's)

In *As We Are Now,* the most meaningful and candid connection Caro has is with readers—of her letters, her imaginary letters, and the journal which she intends to be read after her death. The journal is an epistle from hell. Her last act of friendship before setting fire to the rest home is to hide the journal in a refrigerator where it will not burn, where it will be preserved for others.

For Sarton, literary friendship is an *exchange* involving

various levels of interaction with members of her audience as well as with her characters. She is neither puppeteer nor omniscient benefactor. She needs her readers. Sarton's most popular work is her journals, which resemble long letters addressed to a broad-based audience of friends. Indeed, many pages contain fragments of letters she has received from her readers or descriptions of feelings these letters have evoked. The personal connections become even more direct. Sarton reclaims storytelling as an oral form in offering readings all over the country to standing-room-only crowds. She does booksignings where people wait two hours to exchange a word and get an autograph. She describes one of these events in *At Seventy*:

> At three the next afternoon she drove me to a very different part of the city, a slum that is being rehabilitated, and there I found myself among "my people" at the Crazy Ladies—a subway crush of young and old but mostly young in blue jeans and sweaters, crowding around to get *Journal of a Solitude* signed (that is one for the young) and of course *Anger.* Some had brought a great pile of my books from home. Many had things to say to me, but it was rather a rush as the line was long and the time short. At the end of two hours when I had not stopped making my mark, it looked as though the bookstore may have been saved (they are having a hard time), and everyone was happy. And on the way back to the Regency and Heidi, two women from the cooperative told me they thought they had sold $1,500 worth. Once more I felt lifted up on all the delightful caring of these people who read me.

> It cannot be denied that it is these days a very good life for an old raccoon of seventy.

Such encounters buffer Sarton against the pain and fury about what she considers the unfair treatment—not just negative evaluation—of her work by the reviewing establishment. She describes two more personal exchanges earlier in *At Seventy*:

> When Webster was here last winter he asked me shyly whether I would be willing to give him a signed copy of *A Reckoning* in exchange for the work done. I told him he was getting the lean end of the bargain, but he insisted the book would do it.

> In the same order of good happenings, Bob Johnson at the florist's left a round planter filled with spring plants, a hyacinth, two yellow primroses, and some lilies on the terrace, this time with a note to say how he felt about *Recovering*. What do critics matter when workmen and florists are moved to respond with their gifts to mine?

> I sometimes imagine I am the luckiest person in the world. For what does a poet truly want but to be able to give her gifts and find that they are accepted? Deprived people have never found their gifts or feel their true gifts are not acceptable. This has happened to me more than once in a love relationship and that is my definition of hell.

Mary Sarton's spinsters are friendly women. Being spinsters allows them time to attend to numerous and often unlikely people. Like that legendary spinster Charlotte, who rescues her friend by spinning magical words, May Sarton's spinsters tend to their friends *in* their writing and *through* their lives. We may hope the future of this tradition will be as luminous as its past, which extends at least as far back as Sappho, who wrote:

> Tell everyone
> Now, today, I shall
> sing beautifully for
> my friends' pleasure

REVIEWS OF SARTON'S RECENT WORK

Sue Halpern   (review date 21 June 1992)

SOURCE: "From a Cocoon of Pain," in *The New York Times Book Review,* June 21, 1992, p. 18.

[Halpern is an American novelist. In the review below, she discusses thematic and stylistic aspects of Sarton's journal Endgame.]

May Sarton, the 80-year-old author of more than 30 volumes of poetry and fiction, is perhaps best known for the journals that have chronicled her life of solitude on the coast and in the interior of New England, her passionate love for other women and her wrestle with the demons of creativity. Ms. Sarton's journals are consciously public documents. There is nothing secret about them. Her readers are real, not imagined. "I don't think this journal is very good. That is a real blow, because I had counted on it. I may be wrong, and I am correcting all the time," she writes deep into the latest volume, *Endgame: A Journal of the Seventy-ninth Year.* It would seem a strange remark from a diarist, except one who deliberately writes to be read.

It would be hard to say, too, what would make a journal "good" if Ms. Sarton herself hadn't already shown us in *Plant Dreaming Deep, Journal of a Solitude* and *Recovering: A Journal,* among others. They are reflective, honest, engaged and circumspect. Her journals portray a woman struggling to make a life, a fertile life, without the conventional soil of marriage and children. In them she exposes her frailties, not to elicit pity but because they are there. She is often angry and petulant, frustrated by her lack of critical success, undone by loneliness and the absence of family. She doesn't ask readers to like her, she asks them to know her, and she allows this knowledge by projecting the intimacy of her domestic life onto the page. Readers respond, sending her sacks of personal letters and bouquets of cut flowers and arriving uninvited at her house as if they were old friends.

In *Endgame,* as in her earlier journals, Ms. Sarton reveals how attentive to her public she is, and how grateful, and how thoroughly she requires their adoration—it is a kind of critical acclaim. Yet it comes at a price and with a paradox, for the author deeply, and loudly, resents the presumption of familiarity that results from offering her life both as an open book and in one. Writing in midwinter, after an unannounced visit by an adoring, gift-laden fan, Ms. Sarton feels "a wish to commit suicide—to run down the field and drown myself because I felt that there was no privacy anymore."

Part of Ms. Sarton's trouble on this particular day, and on just about every day she chronicles here, is that she is sick. *Endgame* is the journal of a plague year, in which the author is overwhelmed by constant diverticulitis, fluid in her lungs and other debilities of old age. Page after page, day upon day, she writes about her failing health—talks about it, really, because the tape recorder soon proves more congenial than the pen.

It doesn't take long for the reader, waiting for the "real action" to begin, to feel impatient and helpless in the face of Ms. Sarton's illnesses. It takes a while to understand that her illnesses *are* the action, and that this book is about what is happening *to* her, rather than what she is doing. What is happening to her is not pleasant, and it is sometimes maddening and repetitious, but in this it is true to life. It is not the diarist's duty to make her life more exciting than it really is. Her duty is to tell the truth.

"Sometimes there seems to be no reason for getting up," she writes on May 14, 11 days after her 78th birthday. On Oct. 11: "So this is the beginning of a new journal—the journal of a woman who now knows she will never get well." Feb. 1: "It seems as if the year were already on its way out. I haven't been talking to this little machine, because I have been so ill. . . . I live in a cocoon of pain most of the day and look forward immensely to the night."

Despite its inescapable focus on physical pain and chronic despair, there are salutary passages in *Endgame* about friends and neighbors and the ordinary stuff of daily life, which so richly populate Ms. Sarton's past journals. And there are moments when, as before, her passing thoughts bring insight and the shock of recognition that comes when one is in the presence of truth. Old age is about learning to accept dependence, Ms. Sarton observes. "Solitude without society would be meager."

Gardeners live in the future as well as the present. May Sarton has long been a gardener, and she persists in spite of her infirmities. "There's no doubt that old age is a journey into a foreign country, so that one is constantly being astonished by what is not possible," she writes. While it is still possible, though, Ms. Sarton continues to sink bulbs into the ground. She does this with the knowledge that they will survive her, *because* they will survive her, because they go against the grain of old age, because they promise beauty. And while she still can, she continues to plant words on the page, maybe not as easily or felicitously as she did in the past, but with the signal grace of defiance.

An excerpt from *Encore: A Journal of the Eightieth Year*

I had an interesting dream between nine-thirty and eleven when I went down to get Pierrot and he did not come. The dream was about Katharine Davis, oddly enough, who appears in the preface of the new *Sarton Selected*. In the dream-meeting with her and her friend, who was not her real friend but an imaginary dream-friend, I pretended not to be May Sarton. We had an interesting talk. At the end I said, "Do you know who I am?" She said, "Yes," and walked away, obviously crying. It was so vivid that, for once, I remembered it very clearly when I woke up.

Yesterday, lacking tulips all eaten by the deer, I, for the first time in weeks, ordered flowers—pink and lavender tulips—and they are good to have in the house because the daffodils are completely gone. The whole world of daffodils is not there and it is a terrible loss. This spring has been such a rewarding one, one day after another, as the great sequences follow each other, the lilacs now. They have suffered on this place although everywhere else they are flourishing. I think it was the icy winds in December that wounded my lilacs, which are old here anyway.

May Sarton, in her Encore: A Journal of the Eightieth Year, *W. W. Norton & Company, 1993.*

Nancy Schwartzkopff (review date September-October 1993)

SOURCE: A review of *Encore: A Journal of the Eightieth Year,* in *The Bloomsbury Review,* Vol. 13, No. 5, September-October, 1993, p. 22.

[*Schwartzkopff is an American editor. In the review below, she provides a favorable assessment of* Encore.]

May Sarton will never be a candidate for sainthood. She's crabby when she feels ill, snaps at people when she's under stress, and is vulnerable to the relentless undertow of depression. But her way of sharing herself, warts and all, has won her journal fans around the world. She takes the writing of journals seriously, feeling an obligation to be truthful with her readers.

> Knowing my journals would be read has provided a certain discipline for me. It has forced me to try to be honest with myself and thus with my readers, not to pretend that things are better than they are, but learn to evaluate without self-pity or self-glorification what has been happening to me.

Unlike *Journal of a Solitude* (1973), arguably her best and certainly her best-known journal, *Encore* is almost entirely concerned with the physical rather than the intellectual life. Sarton's daily struggle with horrendously painful digestive trouble is undeniably the focus of the book. She still drops in her concise social and political commentaries, but they don't have the passion of her younger and stronger days.

A dizzying parade of friends, fans, and paid and unpaid helpers marches relentlessly through *Encore*. Sarton by turns loves, needs, and resents her entourage. I was tempted to keep score of the positive and negative remarks made about each person, but that would be missing the point. Sarton's anger at others is almost always anger at her own frailty.

Considering herself a poet who also writes novels and journals, the resounding neglect Sarton's poetry has received for much of her life has caused her some bitterness. The serious critical attention that has begun in her later years is a sweet victory indeed. "They had ignored and treated me badly—but someday they would come to me. Someday is now, and they are coming to me." In June of 1992 her work was the focus of a three-day conference at Westbrook College, where Carolyn Heilbrun and Sandra Gilbert, among others, spoke. In the festivities following the conference, Sarton "drank Sandra's generous praise with the wine."

Aging is a topic that receives its share of attention in all of Sarton's journals. In *Encore* she contemplates

> old age and how much I enjoy the freedom of it. By that I mean the freedom to be absurd, the freedom to forget things because everyone expects you to forget, the freedom to be eccentric, if that is what you feel like, or, on the other hand, the freedom to be quite rigid and to say, "But this is the way I do things."

Other aspects of aging are not so positive, of course; she bitterly resents her lack of stamina and the demands put on her two hours a day of productive work time. Her faithful readers have watched her joy in solitude dip into panic at the thought of dying alone and not being found for days. We wince at her having to lie down to tend her much-loved garden, the pain of stooping being too great. But much as the body, racked by a stroke and battles with cancer and debilitating digestive trouble, may betray her advanced years, there is still plenty of life left in May Sarton. During her 80th year she buys a computer and learns word processing, travels to London, gives poetry readings, receives her 17th honorary doctorate, and most triumphantly begins once again to write poetry.

> It is like returning home after a long time in a foreign country where there was no music. . . . I do not cry as I used to because I could not write poetry any more. I did not think it would ever come back, but now of course it has. It is like a miracle.

Encore is, in spite of Sarton's ill health and increasing frailty, a celebration of life. In her 80th year she has reached "an extraordinary time of happiness and fulfillment, more than [she] ever dreamed possible."

Carolyn G. Heilbrun on Sarton's fidelity to the conventions of genre:

Little has so marked contemporary literature as the melding of genres. Once the "certainties" of a steadier time were revealed to rest upon arguable assumptions, the slippage of genre was inevitable. Today biography and fiction are met together; novel and poetry, like righteousness and peace, have kissed each other. Ambiguity dilutes taxonomy. We now read "it" because it is by Lessing or Pynchon, Mailer or Millett, not because we know precisely what "it" is.

Here as in so much else, May Sarton has been unusual. Moving between many genres, occasionally distilling the same offering from life into several distinct artistic forms, she has defended the boundaries of genre: her journals and memoirs, tales and novels, poetry and translations of poetry have retained their claim to form.

Carolyn G. Heilbrun, in her "May Sarton's Memoirs," in May Sarton: Woman and Poet, *edited by Constance Hunting, National Poetry Foundation, Inc., 1982.*

Andrea Lockett　(review date July 1994)

SOURCE: "Strange Monsters," in *Belles Lettres: A Review of Books by Women,* Vol. 9, No. 3, July, 1994, p. 37.

[*In the following review, Lockett offers praise for Sarton's* Collected Poems (1930-1993).]

Even the most devout reader of May Sarton's work may be relatively unfamiliar with her poetry. But Sarton, who has published 16 volumes of verse to date, considers herself a poet first and foremost. Thus, *Collected Poems (1930-1993)* is essential reading.

The earliest poems, five of which appeared in the prestigious *Poetry* magazine when Sarton was only 17, already display the excellent command of form and technique that define her work. But it is with the publication of later collections that we see the poet at her peak, penning such classics as **"Prisoner at a Desk," "Now I Become Myself," "In Time Like Air"** (the collection of the same name received a National Book Award nomination), and **"My Sisters, O My Sisters,"** one of the many poems that address the struggle and fullness of life as a woman and a writer:

> . . . And now we who are writing women and
> 　strange monsters
> Still search our hearts to find the difficult an-
> 　swers,
> To be through what we make more simply
> 　human,
> To come to the deep place where poet becomes
> 　woman,
> Where nothing has to be renounced or given
> 　over—
> . . . And that great sanity, that sun, the femi-
> 　nine power.

Because Sarton is primarily a lyric poet—using sonnets, songs, villanelles, and other traditional forms at a time when free verse is all the rage—she has often been overlooked or attacked by critics. But Sarton's forte is in tooling the complex and compelling music and imagery that is characteristic of most poems that have stood the test of time. Similarly, the content of the poems always goes straight to the marrow of human experience whether she is writing about **"Old Lovers at a Ballet,"** domestic joy (**"A Light Left On"**), struggling with her mother's death (**"Dream"**), remembering Virginia Woolf (**"Letter from Chicago"**), or celebrating an unusual and fortunate relationship (**"To an Honest Friend"**). The strict form of many of the poems provides a sturdy framework for the often shocking revelations about savagery behind the most apparently benign human gesture, the violent and destructive impulse that is often the springboard for creativity (see **"Binding the Dragon"**), and the "dark goddess" in all of us that demands to be served (**"Invocation to Kali"**). The earliest collections precede the tradition of confes-

sional poetry, whose most successful practitioners include Sexton and Plath, but which is often a weakness in the hands of less-skilled contemporary poets. Much of Sarton's work focuses on the external world—the rhythm of the seasons, the wonder of animals, history, and mythology. Even when she explores her interior terrain (one collection is, in fact, called *Inner Landscape*), it is in a way that remains accessible and useful to readers, affecting the deep subconscious of the audience as much as that of the writer. This is hard to do, and readers will find a good example of Sarton's skill in **"Divorce of Lovers,"** which propels us on an exhausting but finally enlightening exploration of the grief, denial, rage, pain, and acceptance that follow the end of a love affair. Sarton's is never a poetry of self-pity, never purely a poetry of self. Her poems display a European discipline married to an American energy and fervor. There is a transparence and transcendence to her work that invite us into the poet's mind, where we are surprised to find not just a window into her soul but a mirror reflecting ours.

Additional coverage of Sarton's life and career is contained in the following sources published by Gale Research: *Contemporary Authors,* Vols. 1-4, rev. ed.; *Contemporary Authors New Revision Series,* Vols. 1, 34; *Contemporary Literary Criticism,* Vols. 4, 14, 49; *Dictionary of Literary Biography,* Vol. 48; *Dictionary of Literary Biography Yearbook, 1981; Major 20th-Century Writers;* and *Something about the Author,* Vol. 36.

Stephen Spender

February 28, 1909—July 16, 1995

(Full name Stephen Harold Spender) English poet, critic, autobiographer, playwright, short story writer, novelist, translator, editor, travel writer, and nonfiction writer.

For further information on his life and works, see *CLC,* Volumes 1, 2, 5, 10, and 41.

INTRODUCTION

Admired for the lyricism and powerful images of his verse, Spender is often associated with "The Auden Generation"—an informal grouping of writers, including W. H. Auden, Christopher Isherwood, C. Day Lewis, and Louis MacNeice, who met at Oxford University during the late 1920s. Among the most influential writers of the 1930s, they were joined by their social and political beliefs rather than a common aesthetic criteria, and their writings display a Marxist stance toward such turbulent events as the Depression and the Spanish Civil War as well as the economics, unemployment, and politics of England on the brink of World War II. After leaving Oxford without a degree in 1930, Spender traveled to Berlin, having been attracted by the sexual freedom and the literary communities that thrived there during the Weimar Republic. While in Germany, he witnessed the rise of fascism, which culminated in Hitler's election to the chancellorship in 1933. Spender's poetry during this period includes *Twenty Poems* (1930), published while he was at Oxford, *Poems* (1933), and *Vienna* (1934), a four-part poem that blends details of the fascist suppression of socialist insurgency in Austria with Spender's personal conflicts. While these early works exemplify Auden Generation social and political concerns, they also evince Spender's more lyrical, personal approach and the tension between his attraction to Romantic lyricism and his desire to comment directly on the times. *The Still Centre* (1939), based on his experiences in the Spanish Civil War, records Spender's growing disillusionment with communism and resembles the World War I poetry of Wilfred Owen in its rejection of the heroic idea of war and emphasis on the inhumanity combat inflicts on the individual. Other pieces in *The Still Centre* display the more private reflections—his concern with the nature of existence and his search for a rational system of belief—that exemplify much of Spender's later verse. His later poetry is written primarily in free verse—Spender became progressively liberated from meter and rhyme—and although he uses common language, his poems often create abstract, surreal images that verge on obscurity. Poems from Spender's early and subsequent volumes were published in *Collected Poems, 1928-1985* (1985), a collection which led critics to assert that Spender's poetry of the

1930s, his most prodigious period, will be his most enduring. After World War II, Spender produced less poetry and directed his energies toward critical and autobiographical writing, editing such journals as *Horizon* and *Encounter,* and extensive lecturing at various universities in the United States and England. His most renowned works of nonfiction include his autobiography, *World within World* (1951), which has been extensively praised as a valuable document of literary and cultural history, as well as *The Thirties and After* (1978), *Letters to Christopher* (1981), and *Journals, 1939-1983* (1985), all of which offer insights into some of the most influential writers, public figures, and events of the twentieth century. His most recent works include *The Temple* (1988), a novel he wrote during the early 1930s, and *Dolphins* (1994), a collection of poems. Described as a political allegory, *The Temple* is set primarily in Germany during the Weimar period and centers on the sexual experiences of a young Englishman as it investigates the relationship between homosexuality and politics. Summing up Spender's career,

Julian Symons stated that "Spender's principal achievement seems to have been less his poems or any particular piece of prose than the candour of the ceaseless critical self-examination he has conducted for more than half a century in autobiography, journals, criticism, poems."

PRINCIPAL WORKS

Nine Experiments: Being Poems Written at the Age of Eighteen (poems) 1928

Twenty Poems (poems) 1930

Poems (poems) 1933; revised and enlarged edition, 1934

Vienna (poem) 1934

The Destructive Element: A Study of Modern Writers and Beliefs (criticism) 1935

The Burning Cactus (short stories) 1936

Forward from Liberalism (nonfiction) 1937

Trial of a Judge: A Tragedy in Five Acts (play) 1938

The Still Centre (poems) 1939

The Backward Son (novel) 1940

Selected Poems (poems) 1940

Life and the Poet (criticism) 1942

Ruins and Visions: Poems, 1934-1942 (poems) 1942

European Witness (nonfiction) 1946

Poems of Dedication (poems) 1947

The Edge of Being (poems) 1949

World Within World: The Autobiography of Stephen Spender (autobiography) 1951

Learning Laughter (nonfiction) 1952

The Creative Element: A Study of Vision, Despair, and Orthodoxy among Some Modern Writers (criticism) 1953

Collected Poems, 1928-1953 (poems) 1955, also published as *Collected Poems, 1928-1985* [revised and enlarged edition], 1985

The Making of a Poem (criticism) 1955

Engaged in Writing, and The Fool and the Princess (sketches) 1958

The Imagination in the Modern World: Three Lectures (lectures) 1962

The Struggle of the Modern (lectures) 1963

Chaos and Control in Poetry (criticism) 1966

The Generous Days: Ten Poems (poems) 1969; enlarged edition, 1971

The Year of the Young Rebels (nonfiction) 1969

Love-Hate Relations: A Study of Anglo-American Sensibilities (nonfiction) 1974

Eliot (criticism) 1975, also published as *T. S. Eliot,* 1976

The Thirties and After: Poetry, Politics, People, 1933-1970 (nonfiction) 1978

Henry Moore: Sculptures in Landscape (nonfiction) 1979

Letters to Christopher: Stephen Spender's Letters to Christopher Isherwood, 1929-1939, with "The Line of the Branch"—Two Thirties Journals (letters and journals) 1980

Journals, 1939-1983 (journals) 1985

In Irina's Garden with Henry Moore's Sculpture (nonfiction) 1986

**The Temple* (novel) 1988

Dolphins (poems) 1994

*The original draft of this novel was written during a period from 1929 to 1931. Spender revised it before publication.

INTERVIEW

Stephen Spender with Peter Marchant and Stan Sanvel Rubin (interview date 14 February 1978)

SOURCE: An interview in *Partisan Review,* Vol. LV, No. 1, 1988, pp. 45-54.

[*In the following interview, which was conducted on February 14, 1978 and later edited for inclusion in* Partisan Review, *Spender discusses his relationship with W. H. Auden, Christopher Isherwood, and other literary figures, and remarks on his career as a poet, critic, and teacher.*]

[*Rubin*]: *You published an autobiography,* **World Within World,** *in 1951. Are you working on another to bring that one up to date?*

[Spender]: I don't quite want to bring it up to date, because I think that people's lives get very boring in autobiographies at the point of their becoming famous figures; the latter half of that sort of "life" tends to be a list of your accomplishments and the places you've been to—a kind of travelogue, almost. I might avoid that by cutting up the original autobiography and putting in new material. But I'll have to read **World Within World** again to decide whether I can do that. I haven't read it since I wrote it in 1950.

[*Marchant*]: *You've had many lives—prep school, adolescence, Oxford, Germany, England in the thirties and its literary life, Spain, the Auxiliary Fire Service. Which has been the worst?*

I always think that prep school was, far and away, the worst. I was very unhappy at the boarding school I was sent to when I was nine. I was totally unsuited to go to a boarding school, and I felt as if I'd been sent to prison. I always used to think, well, I'll never be as unhappy again as I am here. As a matter of fact, a master once said that to me. He noticed that I was very unhappy and said, "Anyhow you can have this consolation, that you'll never be so unhappy again." And it turned out to be quite true. When I was twenty-one, I wrote to him and thanked him very much for having made that remark and said that it had got me through being at school. I felt like a prisoner really, imprisoned with all these other awful little boys.

Which has been the best period of your life?

I was probably happiest after I had left Oxford and was away from any kind of institution. Oxford in a way I liked because I made friends there, but I didn't make anything of Oxford. My ambition always was to be independent—

and to have a typewriter and a room of my own—and to start doing my own work.

I joined forces with Christopher Isherwood, who was living in Berlin and was rather lonely there—he wanted someone to talk to about literature and things. We lived very close to each other, and we met for every meal. That really was my life then—seeing Christopher Isherwood and getting on with my writing.

Had your relationship with Isherwood remained the same as it had been when you were an undergraduate?

Yes, I think my relationships with nearly all my friends have stayed the same. We're very fond of one another, and we meet whenever we can.

[*Rubin*]: *There is a popular image of the poet as always a youthful figure and yet, in fact, you are writing poetry well into old age, just as Frost and Eliot and Stevens did.*

In a way it's a phenomenon of living in the twentieth century. Poets tend to get terribly preoccupied in middle life. In early life one is neglected and, therefore, free from being called on the whole time, so one can get on with one's work. Then in old age one is also suddenly free again, and things are falling away from one. One interesting thing about being old is that one is invisible: if I get into an elevator, say, and it's full of young people, they don't look at me; they're looking at one another. That sense of being invisible is rather nice.

[*Marchant*]: *Has your view of yourself changed? In* **World Within World,** *the sense I had of you as an undergraduate was somebody very sensitive and shy, easily humiliated. Someone made the remark to you that artists thrive on humiliation.*

Yes, Auden said, "You will always be a poet because you will always be humiliated." I'm rather beyond being humiliated. But otherwise I think I am very much as I was.

[*Rubin*]: *You talk about not changing, but I wonder if your time in America has had any direct impact on your writing.*

I never felt very "English" as a writer. In fact, in my generation, to be young and a member of the English upper-middle class, the kind of person who goes to an English public school and to Oxford or Cambridge, meant that if you were not English—and by origin I am a quarter-German and a quarter-Jewish—one was made very conscious of being a bit of an outsider. Also I belonged to a time when people of my generation resented England very much—the public school system, the Conservative Party, all the governments of England between the two wars, the British Empire, the whole English upper-class code. Not feeling myself very English anyway, I always felt happier abroad than in England. During the war, as a matter of fact, if one was in England, one recovered a great feeling of England. I can think of Englishness as something almost sacred, but I always feel a bit of an outsider and not really English myself; therefore, wherever I am, I feel pretty well at home. If I go to Asia, for instance, I don't feel that I have a white face in contrast to these peoples of different colors; I really feel as if I'm almost one of them. I've never found it very difficult to bridge those gulfs, which

are supposed to exist. I've always felt myself rather international, I think.

[*Marchant*]: *You've been extraordinarily prolific—you've written seventy-five books—yet you describe yourself as being very social, finding it difficult to say "no" to invitations. What exactly is your work routine? How do you manage to write so much?*

If one has lived a fairly long time, there have been a great many days in one's life. I've probably written on the average an hour or two a day, every day of my life, and if you worked it out, one could have written seventy-five books, I think. On the whole, when I am working on something that I care about, I really am working at it, or thinking about it, the whole time. A friend of mine always says, "I think of you as having a certain expression on your face when you're pretending to listen to me." When I'm pretending to listen to people, I'm usually getting on with whatever I happen to be writing.

[*Rubin*]: *You've written and spoken about what you term the need for "pressure" in writing, which I understand to mean the tension between the content and the form. Do you perceive a difference in your own approach to fiction (which you've not written for some time) versus poetry or journalism? How do you handle these diverse forms of "pressure"?*

Journalism I do simply to make money, although one needn't necessarily. It could be like writing a letter, for instance, which I do. In fact, I really prefer writing things I'm not paid for, and what I like very much is writing letters to people. Writing for one person seems to me the ideal situation.

Actually I think one has to keep on more or less writing in a genre like fiction, and if one doesn't, one forgets how to write in that genre. I would like to write stories, but I have the feeling that fiction has developed a great deal since the time when I did write stories, and I don't really know how to start again. I have kept on writing poetry just about enough to feel that I don't have to ask myself, "How does one write a poem?"

[*Marchant*]: *You've also written a play* [**Trial of a Judge**], *about Germany in the thirties. Did you find it a struggle to write a play, that you didn't know how?*

I see a great many plays and feel very critical of them, in the sense that I know they are not written as they should be written.

You've said that you didn't much like Cabaret, *which is the Hollywood version of you and Isherwood in Berlin. Was your play any sort of reaction to that film?*

I always say to Christopher that I often have a good mind to call my play *My Berlin,* in contrast to his. I noticed in his last book that he really wanted me to leave Berlin, because he was afraid that I would use his material. In the middle of the play, which is entirely political, there is a sort of cabaret scene which impinges on Christopher Isherwood's kind of Berlin.

Was Isherwood pleased with Cabaret?

No, we both felt the same: nothing happens in *Cabaret*

that Christopher and I could have possibly afforded to do. Hollywood seems quite incapable of really doing anything about the lives of people like students who are comparatively poor. *Cabaret* is quite ridiculous. Jean Ross, the model for Sally Bowles, was a very unsuccessful performer in a cabaret, and really, I suppose one would have to say, a sort of whore, although I hate to say that because she was a person I adored. But that really is the way she made her money. In this movie she's the toast of Berlin and at the same time she's always asking for cigarettes because she's so poor. That kind of unreality I find depressing and painful. It seems a pity that Hollywood couldn't make something much more interesting out of what was real—the kind of life we did live.

[*Rubin*]: *What do you think now of the work that Isherwood, Auden, MacNeice, and you did in the thirties?*

On the whole, politics didn't help us at all in our writing. Isherwood and MacNeice kept very clear of politics, in fact. Auden wrote a great deal about politics, all of which he suppressed. I went over all the journalism and everything Auden had written in the thirties the other day, and I was amazed how much he'd done and how serious he was about politics. He was always trying to reconcile socialism with Christianity and that kind of thing. It was a major effort, but it didn't seem to help him in his work. When he stopped being interested in politics and went to America, there's immediately a sense of release and he can get on with being Auden, I think.

In a certain sense, I'm interested in politics, as a theme and as it provides material—some really horrifying material. The question is whether one can make something of it. I always thought I could make *one* thing of it, which was my great interest in the struggle going on in Nazi Germany, when I was there and after I left.

On the whole, does the world seem a better one, say, for a young writer than it was when you went to Oxford?

Yes, in the sense that even if young poets in England today don't have a spectacular success, they can still support themselves fairly well because the Arts Council pays for readings they give. We didn't have any opportunity of that kind. A few writers when I was young—and I happen to be one of them—really had very little difficulty because we were recognized almost immediately. But the ones who weren't recognized did have a very difficult time.

Back in the sixties, writing about the state of British poetry at that time, you singled out Ted Hughes, Philip Larkin, and Thom Gunn. Whom would you add to that list now?

There are quite a lot of poets who write quite interesting poems, but I don't think that there has been a major figure since Larkin and Gunn and Hughes.

[*Marchant*]: *Auden, in his first* Collected Poems, *talks about the "slim volume for which one is honestly grateful." Looking back on your years of writing and friendships, what seems to count the most?*

A selection of poems, perhaps, the autobiography, and that's about it, I think.

You were critical of Virginia Woolf, looking at Edith Ca-

vell's statue, and saying, "Patriotism isn't enough." You wanted to say to her, "Sensibility isn't enough." Doesn't she turn out to be right in the end? Aren't personal relationships what matter most?

No, I don't think she is right. I adored Virginia Woolf, and I very much like her work. But I don't think a work of just sensibility is enough.

[*Rubin*]: *You've written of the development in this century of the poet-critic and the critic-poet. You yourself have done a number of critical, or scholarly, books in the past few years regarding the state of the artist in society. Do you think, on the whole, that criticism has improved in our time?*

A lot of criticism that's written now I simply don't understand at all. I don't understand what's meant by "structuralism," for instance, and I don't think I want to. Unless I felt that understanding, say, structuralism would help me to write, I'd rather not know about it. So I'll give it the miss; I find that I give a lot of things the miss, and ten years later everyone's stopped being interested in them anyway.

But criticism did make great contributions to our understanding. Certainly the whole school of the New Criticism did, and one learned really quite a lot from it. I'm not interested now in either writing or reading criticism at all. I don't know whether that's just personal or whether it reflects something of the present state of affairs.

[*Marchant*]: *Did Auden encourage you to write more criticism?*

No, Auden was not at all interested in criticism. He wrote some himself, of course, but it was always written from an extremely personal point of view; it was a kind of commonsense criticism, multiplied by a certain zany quality of Auden himself. But I don't think he read any literary criticism.

I know very few writers who really are interested in criticism, in spite of everything that's said. Robert Graves didn't read criticism; I'm sure Yeats didn't either. I don't think Eliot read anyone else's criticism very much.

There was a time when writers had to pretend that they were interested in criticism, because the critics, especially the New Critics, were so formidable.

One does learn to read more critically, but over a long period of time. I think that I understand what Eliot was trying to do in his poetry, really through reading his criticism. So to that extent, his criticism has been helpful. Also the whole idea that poetry is the manipulation of language and that what you are doing only exists within the language itself—I think I've learned that through the analyses of people's poems made by critics.

[*Rubin*]: *In other words, Eliot is rather an exception in writing criticism and poetry.*

Well, Eliot was always writing his best criticism from the point of view of a poet who was, as it were, clearing space for himself to write his poetry. In that way, his early criticism is very like the criticism you get in Keats's letters, for instance. It's the criticism of a working poet who's setting goals for himself.

What is it that turned you toward those critical studies that you've done?

Being in part a journalist, I have the awful habit of thinking of books that I would like to read and then I make the mistake of thinking that I can write them. For instance, **Love-Hate Relations** about American and English relations is really a very good idea for a book which someone else ought to have written, but which I wrote myself. I don't have any scholarship at all; I'm really very unscholarly. And I think that book suffers from my lack of scholarship; I'm not really qualified to write that sort of book. I regret that I spent so much time writing about what were quite good ideas but for which I lacked the scholarship or the intellectual stamina. I wish that if I had written criticism I'd have written first-class criticism.

[*Marchant*]: *I admire enormously your detachment. It's genuinely professional. I like your story of Eliot's reaction to a negative review that you wrote of his work. I wish you could tell it.*

During the 1930s we worshipped Eliot—Auden, myself, and all our friends—but one disagreed with him often about his opinions. He wrote a very opinionated book, called *After Strange Gods,* which he himself regretted later on. It was an attack on D. H. Lawrence and various writers whom we admired, written from a very moralizing and politically reactionary point of view. It was a series of lectures delivered at the University of Virginia, where he probably thought these views would be well accepted at that time. I attacked this book—I've forgotten what I said—but then I felt very bad about my criticism and wrote to Eliot, saying that I was sorry that I felt the way I did and regretted having published the review. He wrote me back a very nice letter in which he said: "You must always write exactly what you think about me, and it makes absolutely no difference to our personal friendship." I thought that showed Eliot's very high standards. Auden once said to me that of all the older literary people whom we'd known since we were very young, Eliot was the only one who had always behaved decently and had been consistently friendly to us all through his life, and I think that was true.

Did Auden also feel that whether you liked or disliked his work that it oughtn't affect your personal relationship?

Oh, yes, I'm sure he'd feel that. Auden probably wouldn't approve of my writing an attack on Eliot; Auden himself really never wrote attacks on people. Maybe it was just diplomacy, but I think he felt that on the whole it wasn't worth doing. He felt, and I think there's some truth in it, that destructive criticism almost always misfires. With very few exceptions, if a thing is bad, it's better to leave it alone and not attack it.

I remember at one point when I was editing I considered asking F. R. Leavis—although he probably would have refused—to write a column every month to say what he thought about literature. Auden said, "You know, that would be an absolutely irresponsible thing to do, because

Leavis is a critic who is very good on what he likes, but who is completely unfair about what he doesn't like. You would just be exposing yourself to publishing most unfair attacks on people." I think that on the whole Auden felt that's true of most critics.

You wrote criticism of Isherwood's book, which you didn't like, and he was hurt and angered by that.

I'm not quite sure that I agree with him about his belief, and I'm not even sure how far he agrees with himself. However, he believes that if you are personal friends with people, you should write only favorably about their work. If a friend writes a book that you don't like, you just shouldn't write about it. I don't absolutely agree, because it may be important to do so. One can think of controversies in the history of the arts in which an attack made by someone who was a personal friend of someone else has played a very important role. For instance, Nietzsche's attack on Wagner is marvelous and interesting, because Nietzsche was such a friend of Wagner at one time and so admired his work.

I'm not sure whether I agree with Isherwood, but I think that if there was serious reason to attack someone with whom one had a personal friendship one might want to do so. For instance, one might have attacked the whole cult of sensibility which we were talking about in Virginia Woolf. One might want to analyze it in the work of E. M. Forster, Virginia Woolf, and others in Bloomsbury and stage an attack on it, in spite of the fact that one had been so friendly with the people concerned.

She really attacked you and MacNeice and Auden in "Letter to a Young Poet."

That's right. She did, but we didn't have any resentment toward her for her having done it.

You took it as a wish to be helpful, to offer "constructive criticism"?

No, I don't think it was. She was fond of me, but I don't think she knew the others. No, I think that when she was alone in her study writing she said things she would not have even felt if one had been in the same room. We were absolutely unharmed by this attack, because from our point of view all that essay showed was that Virginia Woolf, great genius as she was and perceptive critic as she was, really knew nothing about modern poetry. It was the kind of attack that didn't hurt at all.

But it sounds as if you are very much helped by what your friends say of your work in progress. Just as at Oxford, your group read each other's work and were critical, even so now. You write for a few people and care intensely about what they say.

I think that the only criticism which is really helpful in one's life and which usually occurs when one's very young is the criticism of a group of writers who are friends and very interested in each other's work, who even to some extent identify with one another so that one shares the sense of success of any other member of the group. In this kind of criticism, the "critic" is almost criticizing his own work in criticizing yours.

You can have groups of friends who are all absolutely lacking in any critical sense, and then the effect is disastrous, because they become a mutual admiration society, encouraging the worst tendencies in each other. I'm not sure but that the Beats weren't like that. I can't think that anyone in that group had a real understanding of what the others were doing—perhaps Ginsberg did, but I doubt it. We were very lucky because Auden was an enormously intelligent and very intellectual person. He had an intelligence comparable to that of Bertrand Russell.

[*Rubin*]: *You've been a teacher at several points in your career. How do you approach that role?*

I try to understand what should be the development of the particular student. I don't treat all the students as though they are the same but try to help each student to realize the potentiality of writing the kind of thing which I feel he can write—to discover his own voice, as it were. I don't feel that everyone should be taught to do just formal verse or free verse.

I'm beginning to think that it's very important today to teach students that it's difficult to write, because they tend to think poetry is a kind of lottery and that if you write enough of it maybe some of it will be good. That's really rather how I felt when I was about sixteen. I try now to share selections of poetry with my students to show them a particular difficulty which the poet had to overcome, regardless of how easy the writing looks.

You said earlier that you regret the time you invested in your critical studies. How do you feel about your tenure at Encounter?

It was quite enjoyable, but it was rather a waste of time, really. It was playing the role of being self-important and selecting other people's work and so on. I had to work with its political editor, who was appointed by an organization called the Congress for Cultural Freedom; this meant one was always involved in a kind of fight with the political side. I always think that's a rather miserable business in a magazine when one side, representing the arts, is fighting against the other, representing politics. The politicians always think that theirs is the "serious" side of the magazine, on which the literature is merely so much froth. Also, as literature is supposed to be permanent and politics is day-to-day, one is always being asked to postpone publication of a poem or story, because it will be just as good in ten years' time as it is today, whereas the article on Vietnam has to be published immediately. I'm very glad to be away from that. I'd much rather be teaching.

OBITUARIES AND TRIBUTES

Eric Pace (obituary date 18 July 1995)

SOURCE: An obituary in *The New York Times*, July 18, 1995, p. B11.

[*Pace is an American journalist. In the obituary below, he surveys Spender's life and career.*]

Sir Stephen Spender, the British poet, critic and novelist, died Sunday at St. Mary's Hospital in London. He was 86.

He had been taken to the hospital after collapsing at his home in north London, a spokesman for the hospital said.

In the 1930's, Stephen Spender was one of a small number of young poets who gave a new direction to English letters by insisting that poetry be linked to political and social concerns and other aspects of the larger world.

In yesterday's issue of *The Guardian,* the scholar and critic Sir Frank Kermode wrote that Mr. Spender's writings on politics, "and on the relation of artists to politics, remain the most considered and the most serious of any by the young writers of the period."

In 1930 Mr. Spender, as he was then—he went on to be knighted in 1983—drew wide attention when his *Twenty Poems* was published; two years later, some of his poems and those by W. H. Auden, C. Day Lewis and others were included in an anthology, *New Signatures,* published by Leonard and Virginia Woolf's Hogarth Press.

Mr. Spender, Auden, Louis MacNeice and a few others came to be known as the Oxford poets, since they had all studied there at around the same time.

Sometimes Mr. Spender was described as "Shelleyan" because of the fervor of his call for sweeping change and of his lyrical way with words. Because of that lyricism, coupled with his good looks, he was also once labeled "the Rupert Brooke of the Depression," in a barbed reference to the handsome British war poet who died during World War I.

Mr. Spender often wrote about the world around him—which he saw with sorrow and anger. In 1934, he wrote a long narrative poem, *Vienna,* about a recent Socialist uprising in that city. And in **"The Landscape Near an Aerodrome"** he almost lovingly described the descent a plane with "furred antennae feeling its huge path / Through dusk."

Later, during World War II, he wrote of his feelings about politics in a series of articles on "Books and the War." He began one article with these words:

> We are living in a political age. That is to say political beliefs and events play a part in the lives of contemporaries which religious and spectacular warnings of the working out of doom amongst the great used to play in the past.
>
> Poets are faced, then, with the problem of transforming into the comprehensive terms of the imagination the chaos of this politically observed world.

In the late 1920's, Mr. MacNeice described Mr. Spender as "redeeming the world by introspection," and he remained involved with the world and its continuing need for redemption in his poetry and prose, as critic and commentator. And although he gained less worldly renown than did his friend Auden, his poems appeared widely in anthologies.

Appraisals of Mr. Spender and his writings have varied spectacularly. The worldly British man of letters Cyril Connolly said, "One must compare him to Goethe and Gide, artists who combine sensuality with puritanism, loving with willing, innocence with guile."

But the grumpy conservative novelist Evelyn Waugh wrote, "To watch him fumbling with our rich and delicate English language is like seeing a Sèvres vase in the hands of a chimpanzee."

Mr. Spender, who was shy and generous as well as modest, called Waugh's jibe "horrible" but added, "I do write with great difficulty and have absolutely no conviction that I write well."

Stephen Harold Spender was born on Feb. 28, 1909 in London, into a noted Liberal family that was in comfortable but not, according to his autobiography, particularly happy circumstances. His mother died when he was 12 and his father not many years later; Stephen and his three siblings were left under the care of their maternal grandmother, Hilda Schuster. He grew up tall and handsome, attended schools in Norfolk and London and went on to University College at Oxford.

There he met Mr. MacNeice, Auden, Isaiah Berlin and Christopher Isherwood, who became his friends and literary colleagues. With the help of a small independent income, he left Oxford in 1931 to devote himself entirely to poetry writing. He went frequently to Germany, where he spent time with Isherwood, whose experiences of that era led eventually to his Berlin stories and the play I Am a Camera, which was made into the musical Cabaret.

Mr. Spender's first prose book was a 1934 volume of essays, The Destructive Element, which commented on the poetry of T. S. Eliot, James Joyce, W. B. Yeats and others. His first collection of short stories, The Burning Cactus, came out in 1936. The following year saw the publication of his Forward From Liberalism, an exposition of his political thinking, which led to an invitation to join the British Communist Party.

It was an association that lasted only a few weeks. "I wrote something for The Daily Worker attacking the party," he recalled later, "and that was the last I heard of my membership." In 1950, he, Arthur Koestler, André Gide and others contributed to a book of essays, The God That Failed, relating their disillusionment with Communism.

As it was for many of his contemporaries, the Spanish Civil War for Mr. Spender was a searing experience. Evading a British Foreign Office ban on visas, he went to Spain in 1937 as a delegate to an International Writers' Congress in Barcelona.

Later that year, he edited Poems for Spain with John Lehmann, and in 1938 wrote Trial of a Judge, a five-act play in verse about Nazi Germany.

In 1939, he was a founder of the literary magazine Hori-

zon, of which he was co-editor, with Cyril Connolly, until 1941.

Mr. Spender was a pacifist, and he served as a fireman in London during most of World War II. He continued to write and to have works published as the war went on, including two collections of poems and his translations of work by other poets, including Rainer Maria Rilke and Federico García Lorca.

Just after the war, in 1946, there appeared Mr. Spender's book European Witness, which included an analysis of the situation of German intellectuals under Hitler. One of his most acclaimed poems, "Elegy for Margaret," dedicated to his terminally ill sister-in-law, was published that year in Poems of Dedication.

His 1949 volume of verse, Edge of Being: Poems, was less well received by the critics. His autobiography, World Within World, published in 1951, also received mixed reviews, but critics agreed that it was worth reading, if only for its incisive sketches of the stars of the British literary world.

Mr. Spender continued to write prose—like Learning Laughter, about a trip to Israel—as well as poetry, and a volume with his collected poems was published in 1953.

In 1953 also, he and Irving Kristol founded Encounter, an anti-Communist intellectual journal that soon wielded influence far out of proportion to its small circulation (about 40,000). It published everyone from Nancy Mitford to Mr. Koestler on topics ranging from semantic snobbery to Britain's future.

In 1967, Mr. Spender cut his ties to the magazine when it was disclosed that it had been partly supported by funds supplied indirectly by the Central Intelligence Agency.

His poetry, meanwhile, was generating other diverse appraisals. The Times Literary Supplement, in 1971, asked whether it did not make "better sense" to look at his work as basically personal introspection, "as attempts at redemptive and quasi-religious self-searching, than it ever did to see them as coming primarily from social or political concerns."

The critic David Daiches, writing in 1958, cited what he called Mr. Spender's "limited range" but praised his "quiet control in descriptive or confessional verse that has its own appeal."

In his later years, Mr. Spender produced far more prose than poetry, including The Creative Element: A Study of Vision, Despair and Orthodoxy Among Some Modern Writers (1953); a sympathetic look at student rebellion, The Year of the Young Rebels (1969); Love-Hate Relations: English and American Sensibilities, and The Thirties and After (1978).

In 1993, Viking published a novel by David Leavitt, an American, entitled While England Sleeps, and Sir Stephen—as he was by then—asserted that the novelist had committed plagiarism by using material from his autobiography.

Sir Stephen also filed suit in Britain against Viking Penguin, which was obliged to withdraw the book. In an out-of-court settlement reached early in 1994, Viking also agreed not to keep on selling the novel in its original form anywhere in the world.

In an essay published in *The New York Times Book Review* in September 1994, Sir Stephen contended that Mr. Leavitt's novel was "closely derived in plot and text from about 30 pages of my autobiography, concerning my relationship with a man I call Jimmy Younger."

"My book," Sir Stephen added, "describes how after my marriage to Inez Pearn, my friend, who was also my former lover, joined the International Brigade and fought in the Spanish Civil War."

Events involving Jimmy, Sir Stephen wrote, were "almost exactly transcribed in Mr. Leavitt's novel, though the character in the novel was named Edward."

For his part, Mr. Leavitt had contended that "When writing historical fiction about a period in which one did not live, one obviously has to look into the past—to eavesdrop on history itself."

In his essay in *The Times Book Review,* Sir Stephen wrote, "No one would disagree with him there, but doing so surely does not mean finding some past person's autobiography and presenting a great part of it as one's own current fiction."

"Mr. Leavitt's fantasy accretions to my autobiography, which I find pornographic, certainly do not correspond to my experience or to my idea of literature," Sir Stephen observed, adding: "Authors of the 1990's, like Mr. Leavitt, who are entirely free to exploit a wave of popular interest, would do well to understand that writers as recently as the 1950's ran considerable risks of being prosecuted" under intolerant British laws.

"It was for this reason that in 1950, while prepared to take the risk for myself, I gave my former lover the pseudonym Jimmy Younger in *World Within World.* My autobiography was received in 1951 as ahead of its time in its frankness, admired as such by some reviewers, attacked by others for what was seen as excessive candor."

By March 1995, Mr. Leavitt made 17 editorial changes in the novel's text, and a revised edition is to be published by Houghton Mifflin in the fall.

Meanwhile, in September 1994, St. Martin's Press reissued *World Within World* in the United States, with a new introduction by Sir Stephen. At that time St. Martin's also published *Dolphins,* a book of his recent poems. It was his first new volume of poetry in nine years, and it also came out in Britain in 1994.

With the passage of time, *World Within World* has proved to be in many ways Sir Stephen's most enduring prose work because it gives the reader revealing glimpses of its author, Auden and Mr. Isherwood and of what it was like to be a British poet in the 1930's.

In his new introduction to the 1994 edition, Sir Stephen wrote, "Our ideal was always to make out of experience artifacts—verbal objects as poems or fictions—which within themselves would have transcended their origins whether these were politics or sex or history."

But he added this caution: "It is quite wrong to be nostalgic about the Thirties on the grounds that during that decade many young people felt there were political causes worth fighting and dying for. Auden's description of the Thirties, sitting in a bar in New York in September 1939, as a 'low dishonest decade' at least deglamorizes it. The young should take the Thirties as a warning rather than as a cause for envy."

In addition to writing, Mr. Spender lectured widely, in Europe and Asia and at universities in the United States, where he also was a visiting professor on several campuses. He was a professor of English literature at University College of London University from 1970 to 1977.

He was named a Commander of the British Empire in 1962 and in 1971 was awarded the Queen's Gold Medal for Poetry. In 1965, he was the first non-American to serve as Consultant in Poetry in English to the Library of Congress.

Mr. Spender's first marriage, to Agnes Marie Pearn, known as Inez, ended in divorce in 1939. In 1941 he married Natasha Litvin, a pianist. She, their son, Matthew Francis, and their daughter, Elizabeth, survive.

The Times, London   (obituary date 18 July 1995)

SOURCE: An obituary in *The Times,* London, July 18, 1995, p. 19.

[*In the obituary below, the critic surveys Spender's life and career.*]

Latterly the reputation of Stephen Spender had been very much that of critic, lecturer, scholar and ambassador for culture, a role reflected in the seemingly belated knighthood bestowed on him in 1983. But these were functions which usefully filled the void left by his waning powers as a poet. As a creative artist Spender will always be indissolubly linked with the 1930s and his impressive stature and handsome features made him the physically dominating presence in the aesthetes' group which gathered around Auden and Isherwood at Oxford in those days. It was the decade when politics invaded the innermost recesses of literature, but as a poet Spender's inspiration was intensely personal, and he could never bring himself to wave flags or chant slogans for very long. His characteristic note was one of compassion for the deprived and the defeated, coupled with a painfully honest examination of his own motives.

Spender's sincerity sometimes exposed him to ridicule, leading him to write verse which was gauche or exaggeratedly lachrymose, but it was a price which he was willing to pay; and at his best he records the helpless anguish of the Thirties more directly than any other English poet of the period, with the true voice of feeling. Later he turned to writing in a more purely lyrical and reflective vein, often with great tenderness. In the opinion of many good judges, his finest work is to be found in the wartime collection, **Ruins and Visions** (1941) and in **Poems of Dedication** (1946).

Stephen Harold Spender was the second son of Edward Harold Spender. His uncle was J. A. Spender, the editor of the *Westminster Gazette,* and he grew up in the afterglow of Edwardian Liberalism. It was a comfortable and cultivated atmosphere which he described, not without irony, in his autobiography, **World Within World** (1951).

His interest in poetry was first aroused at a very early age, and confirmed during adolescence when he came heavily under the influence of his maternal grandmother, Hilda Schuster, a woman of cosmopolitan breadth of culture. He was educated at University College School, Hampstead, and University College, Oxford, and while an undergraduate he came into the orbit of the figure who was to become his close friend, W. H. Auden; he also got to know other aspiring poets who were later to figure in the public mind as members of the Auden group.

Together with Louis MacNeice he edited *Oxford Poetry* in 1929; in 1930 he edited it with Bernard Spencer. Another important friendship was with Christopher Isherwood, who has left an amusing glimpse of the youthful Spender in his memoir *Lions and Shadows* of 1938. Like Isherwood, he was drawn to Germany and lived there for two years after leaving Oxford. The intellectual and artistic ferment of the Weimar Republic fired his imagination, and he also found himself witnessing the rise of Hitler at first hand. Subsequent periods spent in Vienna confirmed his sense of the impending catastrophe of Nazism.

Along with other poets of his generation, Spender first became known to a wider public through Michael Robert's anthology *New Signatures* in 1932. A first volume, **Poems,** published in the following year, was enthusiastically received, and critics began to refer to the new triumvirate of Auden, Spender and Day Lewis. A little later MacNeice's name was added to the list, and the mythical composite MacSpaunday was complete.

Like other literary schools, the movement was less concerted and less tightly-knit than journalistic legend would suggest, but there was undoubtedly great excitement in the air. The technical lessons of Eliot, Hopkins and Wilfred Owen had been absorbed; the crosscurrents of Marxism and psychoanalysis were flowing with unprecedented vigour. Above all, the sense of deepening international crisis arising from the Nazi threat to civilised behaviour brought home to writers a sharp new sense of social responsibility.

Spender was in the vanguard, as a regular contributor to *New Writing* and *New Verse;* he also turned to prose, and wrote one of the few volumes of "committed" Thirties literary criticism which is still worth reading, **The Destructive Element** (1935). His growing radicalism was passionately if not always lucidly summed up in **Forward from Liberalism** (1936), an early Left Book Club selection. When the Civil War broke out he went to Spain and carried out propaganda work for the Republicans. He was also induced by Harry Pollitt in person to join the Communist Party, an unhappy experience from which he emerged disenchanted, and which he was to describe many years later in his contribution to R.H.S.Crossman's symposium *The God that Failed* (1949).

On the whole Spender's shorter poems of protest—a good example is **"An Elementary School Classroom"**—have worn better than more ambitious efforts such as his verseplay **Trial of a Judge** (1937). He published several collections during the 1930s, and became a well-known figure in literary London. T.S.Eliot and Leonard and Virginia Woolf were among those who encouraged him, and he was also taken up, perhaps inevitably, by Lady Ottoline Morrell.

He was one of the founders of *Horizon,* and from 1939 to 1941 helped Cyril Connolly to edit it. From 1941 to 1944 he was a fireman with the National Fire Service and then worked in a wartime branch of the Foreign Office. In 1947 he became a counsellor with the Section of Letters of Unesco. Between 1953 and 1967 he was coeditor of *Encounter,* first with Irving Kristol and then with Melvin Lasky, but resigned when it became apparent, despite the latter's denials, that the magazine had received money from the CIA.

He tended to bring a poet's vagueness to the administrative details of editing, but his disinterested love of literature, his generous appreciation of younger talent, and his wide range of artistic connections contributed greatly to the magazine's success. He had a knack of spotting talent in writers both at home and abroad, and was always anxious to get the voices of new writers heard in the pages of *Encounter.* In later years he continued the struggle for intellectual freedom in the columns of *Index on Censorship.*

Latterly he spent much of his time travelling and teaching. He was a tireless delegate to conferences, and few men have done more to consolidate international literary relations. He was particularly popular in America, where he had a wide circle of friends and admirers, and was much in demand as a lecturer, undertaking tours of the country until only a few years ago. At various times he was Elliston Professor of Poetry at the University of Cincinnati, Beckman Professor at the University of California, and Visiting Lecturer at Northwestern University, Illinois. In 1965 he was appointed Consultant in Poetry to the Library of Congress in Washington, the first foreigner to be thus honoured. He was an honorary member of Phi Beta Kappa (Harvard). In France his achievements were recognised by an honorary DLitt from the University of Montpellier.

But the apogee of his career as an academic—which is what he had by then almost entirely become—was his appointment as Professor of English at University College London in 1970. While in this post, which he held until 1977, he published a number of more formal editions and studies such as **A Choice of Shelley's Verse** (1971); **D. H. Lawrence, novelist, poet, prophet** (ed 1973) and **T. S. Eliot** (1975). After this period there were lighter-hearted essays such as his voyage to China with David Hockeny which produced their joint **China Diary** in 1982.

Spender had been appointed CBE in 1962 but his services to literature were more fully recognised in his knighthood of 1983.

His **Collected Poems** had been published in 1955; a subsequent volume of verse, **The Generous Days,** in 1971 and **Collected Poems, 1930-1985** in 1985. The publication of a collection, **The Dolphins,** celebrated his 85th birthday last year. Besides poetry, he also published volumes of fiction, reportage, and translations from the German, notably of Schiller and Rilke. But he had also produced a version of Sophocles's *Oedipus Trilogy* which was performed at the Oxford Playhouse in 1983. His outstanding prose work is **World Within World,** which is likely to remain one of the classic memoirs of its period, although his **Journals, 1939-1983** (1985) also make absorbing reading.

More recently he had published a novel **The Temple** which appeared in 1988 but had been written 59 years previously. The story of a young bisexual boy depicted in his wanderings down the Rhine and along the Baltic littoral in the Indian Summer of Weimar libertarianism, it had originally attracted the attention of Auden and Isherwood but their criticisms of it were enough to make its modest author shelve it. It had to wait for another, and completely different, age to see the light of day, revised by Spender along the lines Auden and Isherwood had suggested so many years before.

Spender was in the headlines even more recently when, in 1993, the American novelist David Leavitt published a novel *While England Sleeps* which, Spender claimed, infringed the copyright of his own **World Within World.** Leavitt had written of a friendship between two men in the 1930s closely resembling that described in Spender's autobiographical work, but emphasising the relationship as a specifically homosexual one. Invoking a part of the 1988 Copyright Act banning "distortion or mutilation" of an artistic work, Spender secured the suppression of Leavitt's book in 1994 after a four-month legal action, and its publishers Viking Penguin agreed to stop selling it anywhere in the world.

Spender had a notable gift for friendship, and numbered among his intimates not only writers, but some of the most distinguished artists, musicians, philosophers and scholars of his time. With the young he was invariably kind and helpful, while he was always an unstinting and dependable supporter of good causes, both private and public. One quality is not altogether apparent from his writing: strangers who expected him to be sombre or withdrawn must often have been surprised to find that in conversation he was extremely witty, and an agreeably worldly raconteur. Physically he was very striking: he had a handsome profile and piercing blue eyes, and there can have been few literary gatherings where he was not the tallest man in the room.

He married first, Agnes Marie (Inez) Penn. The marriage was dissolved and he married secondly, in 1941, the pianist Natasha Litvin. She and their son and daughter, married to Barry Humphries, survive him.

Peter Parker   **(essay date 23 July 1995)**

SOURCE: "The Vital Art of Witness," in *The Observer,* July 23, 1995, p. 16.

[*Parker is an English nonfiction writer and biographer. In the following tribute, he remarks on Spender's character.*]

In 1974 I arrived at University College London to read English, I had devoured Christopher Isherwood's Berlin books at school and had just seen *Cabaret* for the third time, and now I could attend commentary and analysis seminars conducted by Stephen Spender. On one occasion we were looking at a poem by WH Auden, and I remember thinking: but this man actually *knew* Auden; he may even have read the poem in manuscript at the time it was written.

Whether he had or not, Spender (who died last Sunday [July 16]) seemed far more interested in what a group of gauche students had to say about it than in providing his own, privileged insights, and had to be coaxed into a personal response. It was this modesty, this genuine interest in what other people might think, that made him such a good teacher.

It also made him extremely good company, as I discovered when I started working on a biography of Isherwood, and found myself asking the sort of questions I'm glad I hadn't at UCL. What was Sally Bowles 'really like'? And what about Otto Nowak? And Mr Norris? And all the other people whom I needed to disentangle from Isherwood's beguiling portraits of them?

Spender's vagueness was legendary, but like much else about him, starting with his height, it seemed exaggerated. Having outlived the majority of his literary contemporaries, he spent a great deal of time answering questions about them, almost always with immense patience, courtesy and good humour. His own bruising experiences as the subject of a *soidisant* biography made him understandably cautious when dealing with people seeking information, and he was quite capable of deploying strategic amnesia in order to avoid answering questions.

His astuteness was immediately apparent when I first arranged to question him about Isherwood. He invited me to lunch at the Savile Club, plied me with drink, and rattled off a number of indiscreet recollections and observations, perfectly well aware that club rules prevented me from taking notes.

This was a sort of game, or perhaps a test, and later conversations, both on and off the record, provided the sort of insights about people that could have been reached only after knowing them really intimately and thinking about their characters for many years. 'Oh dear,' he would say in mock-alarm, gesturing at my silently eavesdropping tape-recorder, 'Is that thing still on?'

It was not merely that he had lived such a long time that made him a vital witness of the past, however. His observations were always acute and usually very funny. 'The trouble with the Lehmanns,' he once said, 'is that they think they're the Brontës, when they're really the Marx Brothers.' His analysis of both friends and foes arose from a genuine interest in human nature, and he would frequently qualify or refine his thoughts, the phone sometimes ringing weeks later: 'I've been thinking again about Christopher . . .'

Obituaries have described Stephen Spender as 'the last link of a golden generation', which is not strictly true (happily, Edward Upward is still alive and still writing at the age of 91). He did, however, represent continuity, partly because, unlike Auden and Isherwood whose emigration to America in 1939 sealed off the decade, he remained swimming in the strong current of English literary life right up until his death. Indeed, although it seems absurd to suggest that someone who lived into his eighty-sixth year died before his time, what many people are now mourning is not so much the loss of a causeway to the past, as the shocking disappearance of someone who was very much of the present.

Of the triumvirate that dominated the Thirties, Spender was at once the most sympathetic and the most representative. Auden's brilliant dogmatism and Isherwood's stylish aloofness are as fresh today as they ever were, but what Spender diagnosed as his own 'combination of convictions and hesitation', particularly as recounted in his recklessly frank autobiography, *World Within World* (1951), most accurately reflects the idealism and confusion of the decade.

This willing self-exposure often made Spender seem foolish, but while many unkind things were said about him during his long and very public life, few were as damning (or as funny) as the things he said about himself. Far from self-aggrandising, his stories about the famous people he had known usually displayed him at a disadvantage. 'In my deepest friendships,' he wrote in a characteristic essay, 'I have been conscious of being "taken with a pinch of salt". Sometimes it is disconcerting to be laughed at when one is serious, but as long as it is done affectionately, one is grateful to people who enable one to see oneself a little from the outside.'

REVIEWS OF SPENDER'S RECENT WORKS

Edward Timms   (review date 17 March 1988)

SOURCE: "Wonderland," in *London Review of Books,* March 17, 1988, pp. 8-9.

[*Timms is an English educator and critic. In the following review, he discusses Spender's novel* The Temple, *and suggests that there exists a "dialectic between cultural decorum and artistic innovation."*]

'Mayn't your politics simply be the result of sexual maladjustment?' This question, unobtrusively formulated in Stephen Spender's *Forward from Liberalism* (1937), lurks as a sub-text in some of the most significant writings of his generation. For authors like Auden, Isherwood and Spender, the struggle for sexual freedom was a stimulus to political dissent. Around 1930, the centre of gravity both of their lives and of their writings was displaced to Weimar Germany, where a Reichstag committee on the penal code had resolved to lift the criminal sanctions against homosexuals. Germany was the country where sexual freedom and social progress seemed to go hand in hand. And the fact that the Soviet Union had been the first European country to revoke the laws against homosexuality gave Communism a particular appeal. In conservative Britain, by contrast, male homosexuals risked imprisonment and disgrace. And a crippling system of censorship made it impossible to write frankly about feelings.

This embargo on telling the truth lasted until more liberal legislation allowed the veterans of the Thirties to lift the veil on their double lives. Isherwood's *Christopher and his Kind* (1977) gives the most vivid account of the Weimar sub-culture, where 'Berlin meant Boys.' His earlier autobiographical writings, as he ruefully acknowledges, had been exercises in 'avoiding the truth'. Similar equivocations had characterised Spender's autobiography, *World within World,* published in 1951. Even at that date it was not possible to be explicit about the 'personal problems' for which he and Isherwood had found a cure in Germany.

These omissions are remedied in *The Temple,* an autobiographical novel based on those liberating German experiences, drafted in 1929-31 and now published for the first time—almost sixty years after the event. One of the consequences of censorship, Spender recalls in his Introduction, 'was to make us wish to write precisely about those subjects which were most likely to result in our books being banned'. When an early version of the novel was submitted to Geoffrey Faber, the publisher's response was that the book was both pornographic and libellous. Thus the manuscript gathered dust for three decades, until in the early Sixties—'during some financial crisis of the kind to which poets are liable'—it was sold to the University of Texas. And there it might have lain indefinitely, if a friend had not happened in 1985 to remind Spender of its existence. The novel now published is based on the original draft, extensively rewritten with the final section transposed from the golden summer of 1929 to the more sombre Germany of 1932.

Set mainly in Hamburg, with an idyllic interlude in the Rhineland, *The Temple* openly explores that homosexual sub-culture which Isherwood had dealt with so allusively in his Berlin novels of the Thirties. Spender's narrative lacks the vitality of *Goodbye to Berlin* or *Mr Norris changes trains.* Its merit is that it engages far more directly with the political implications of sexual dissent. In an 'English Prelude' set in Oxford, Paul (Spender's autobiographical persona) is lectured by his friend Wilmot (representing Auden) on the dangers of repression. 'England's No Good,' Wilmot proclaims. 'Germany's the Only Place for Sex.' After Paul's arrival in Germany, this is confirmed by his second mentor William Bradshaw (Isherwood): 'Everybody in Berlin is equal . . . It all comes down to sex.'

Sexuality, in this view, is an egalitarian force. 'Nakedness is the democracy of the new Germany,' Paul reflects after he has been taken to the open-air swimming pool by his Hamburg host, the young businessman Ernst Stockmann. Only elderly frumps like Ernst's mother are heard to disapprove of this permissiveness. The younger generation, particularly Ernst's bevy of homosexual friends, exult in the new attitude towards the body. 'We Germans are tired,' observed Joachim, the photograper whose Bauhaus-style studio is the scene of orgiastic parties. 'After the War and years of starvation, perhaps we need to swim and to lie in the sum and make love.' It is Joachim's sensuously-sculpted photographs which bring it home to the previously repressed Paul that the male body is a 'temple'. Joachim, too, is modelled on a historical personage—the photographer Herbert List whose evocative image of a young man bathing is on the dust-jacket of the novel.

There is a strong suggestion in **The Temple** that this cult of the body has political implications of a left-wing kind. Repeated references are made to Magnus Hirschfeld, the campaigner for homosexual freedom who was one of the gurus of the Left in the Weimar cultural revolution. Paul, like Wilmot and Bradshaw, seems to share these radical sympathies; and the same is true of many of their German friends. Ernst Stockmann, who like Paul is partly of Jewish descent, is attracted by socialism and communism. For Joachim, too, during the election campaign of November 1932, the only manifesto which makes any sense is that of the Communist Party. The position of the Nazis is represented by an apostle of Nordic purity named Hanussen, who regards sexual deviance with revulsion. Hannussen is dedicated to the destruction of all those who have 'fouled German blood: Jews and Bolsheviks, decadents, expressionists, homosexuals'.

The correlations between sexual and political dissidence become most explicit during the episode in the Rhineland when Paul and Joachim encounter an irresistible lad in lederhosen named Heinrich. The ensuing affair between Heinrich and Joachim, registered by Paul in terms that hint at a paradise regained, unexpectedly acquires a political dimension when Heinrich declares: 'I am a Communist.' This inspires Paul to compose a poem which transposes the tryptich of male friendship into a political allegory:

> Under the domed sky and athletic sun
> Three stand naked: the new, bronzed German,
> The Communist clerk, and myself, being English.

The poem anticipates that within ten years Communism, represented by Heinrich, will emerge as a redemptive force to destroy the bourgeois world of Paul and Joachim:

> The third—this clerk with world-offended
>   eyes—
> Builds with red hands his heaven: makes our bones
> The necessary scaffolding for peace.

It seems likely that these lines expressed the political drift of **The Temple** in the early version of 1929-31. For this poem, entitled **'In 1929'**, was included in Spender's **Poems,** published by Faber in 1933. And it anticipates that guarded commitment to Communism which was to become explicit in **Forward from Liberalism** four years later. If Spender had been able to publish **The Temple** in its original form, it might have come to seem a period piece: an evocation of that golden summer when, as the Introduction puts it, 'Germany seemed a paradise where there was no censorship and young Germans enjoyed extraordinary freedom.' The author who has now completed the novel is not the impressionable young Englishman of 1929, however, but a Tiresias who has foresuffered all. With the bleakness of hindsight he endows the pursuit of sexual liberation with undertones of aridity and disillusionment.

Thus the ideas of Auden and Isherwood, culture-heroes of the Thirties, acquire a bitter retrospective irony. 'Wilmot knew all about the complexes of Freudian guilt . . . One must not be repressed. Repression led to cancer.' Paul himself expounds the theory to Ernst, shortly before the scene in which they make love: 'If you do not feel guilt . . . you will not catch a disease from an infected partner.' The love-making that follows turns out to be 'arid' and 'repulsive' (Paul almost prefers intercourse with Irmi, the token woman in the homosexual sub-culture). And as the summer wears on, the cult of 'sun and air and water and making love' propounded by the more congenial Joachim also loses its charm. During the Rhineland idyll, Paul gets sunstroke, which leads him to record in his notebook: 'Now I no longer imagined the sun as a healer, but as evil, poisonous, serpent-like.'

This disillusionment with the hedonistic cult of the body is underscored by growing doubts about its ideological implications. After being in Germany for two months, Paul begins to find these 'brand-new Germans' who 'worship their body as if it were a temple' rather 'ludicrous'. And why is it that the members of the German Youth movement contorting their bodies on the beach are 'mostly middle-aged'? His dreams of the political transformation which might be brought about beneath 'the athletic sun' begin to fade when he discovers, on his return to Hamburg in 1932, that Heinrich with his long fair hair was probably never a Communist at all and collapse entirely when Joachim explains that Heinrich has now in fact become a Nazi. Although still sharing Joachim's studio-flat, Heinrich keeps a storm-trooper's uniform in the cupboard and spends almost every weekend with Hanussen, the fanatic of sexual and racial purification.

In the final section of the novel, the political implications of sexual dissidence become the central theme. Heinrich is not the only member of the homosexual sub-culture who is drifting into the orbit of Nazism. Perhaps, Paul muses, Joachim may be partly to blame for the patronising way he has treated the boys he picks up. In paying for the favours of Heinrich, Joachim has 'subsidised the mirror image of his darkest self'—his 'wicked, sensual, animal existence'. Perhaps he drove Heinrich into a position where he had no choice but to 'sink down into the anonymous mass of his fellow evil-doers—the storm-troopers'.

The problem is compounded by Joachim's own ambiguous response. His reaction on discovering Heinrich's Nazi uniform in his flat is to spit all over it. But when Heinrich returns with a Nazi thug named Horst to smash up the flat in retaliation, Joachim is betrayed by the ambivalence of his own emotions. For he finds Horst—'dressed in black leather'—sexually attractive, even in the ensuing orgy of destruction.

This culminating scene, with its undertones of masochistic fantasy, can be read as an allegory of the submission of the Weimar Republic to the brutal onslaught of Fascism. Joachim can only stand and watch as Horst smashes up his precious Bauhaus furniture. 'Perhaps I was too busy looking at Horst,' he subsequently explains, still nursing the knife-wound which the Nazi has inflicted on him:

> His uniform was too black to look like any Nazi uniform I had seen. It went with his hair and his eyes and the little straight moustache . . . I kept on wondering whether I was attracted to Horst . . . He must be WONDERFULLY strong.

It is on this note that the novel ends. Paul returns to England while Joachim—though still claiming to be anti-Nazi—is 'going to hunt for Horst'.

Set mainly in Hamburg, with an idyllic interlude in the Rhineland, *The Temple* openly explores that homosexual subculture which Christopher Isherwood had dealt with so allusively in his Berlin novels of the Thirties.

—*Edward Timms*

The quest for emotional liberation culminates in a sombre political allegory. The equation of homosexual attachment with progressive politics is discredited by Joachim's crypto-fascist fantasies. Through Horst, Spender invokes the dangerous glamour of a masculinity which gains its erotic appeal from muscle-power, uniforms and black leather. We are obliquely reminded that homosexuality made its own contribution to Nazism, at least among the storm-troopers, led by the notorious Ernst Röhm, while the figure of Hanussen represents the more puritanical faction in the Nazi movement, dedicated to the elimination of 'degenerate' homosexuals.

The golden dreams of youth are recorded in *The Temple* with the disillusioned eye of age. Its hybrid form is a source of critical rigour, but entails a loss of vitality. In addition, episodes already familiar from *World within World* recur in *The Temple* in a format which is too reminiscent of the biographical record. Telling the truth, it seems, may be inimical to telling a good story. This connects with the disturbing paradox of creativity and censorship. The Spender of the Eighties is able to write about sexuality in terms denied to an earlier generation: but the freedom to describe characters 'struggling to attain orgasm' or 'gummy from intercourse' is no guarantee of artistic success.

Can it be that the censorship which weighed so heavily on homosexual authors during the Thirties was a stimulus to the imagination? The question is likely to occur to any reader who contrasts the naive enthusiasms recorded by Isherwood in *Christopher and his Kind* ('Berlin meant Boys') with the subtleties of his early novels. If *Mr Norris changes trains* is a landmark in modern fiction, this is partly attributable to the legislation which obliged Isherwood to suppress the homosexuality of his authorial voice. This resulted in a novel of enthralling ambiguity, arising from the tension between the studied detachment of the narrator and the passions which convulse all around him. It is this tension that is lacking in *The Temple,* which places Paul's quest for emotional liberation at the centre of narrative sympathy—only to leave that quest largely unfulfilled.

Can it be that the quality of the writing is inversely proportional to the freedom of sexual utterance enjoyed by the author? This hypothesis seems to be confirmed by the work of other European modernists, not only Auden and Isherwood, Virginia Woolf and E.M. Forster, but Proust and Gide, Thomas Mann, Musil and Hesse. Trapped in the tortuous syntax of a patriarchal society, their texts enact a struggle for emotional expression which is all the more impressive for its ambiguity. Resistance is the matrix of desire, linguistic decorum the stimulus to imaginative subversion. It was surely for this, rather than for any overt celebration of sexuality, that *Ulysses* was banned. Joyce's images of sexual ambivalence subvert the established order far more effectively than any homosexual tract.

It is this dimension of ambivalence, with its concomitant textual density, that is lacking in *The Temple.* When we are told that Paul (in bed for the first time with Ernst) 'came very quickly', the sexual experience enacts the precipitation of the text. There is no withholding of meaning. The figure of Paul, even as he hovers between homo-erotic and heterosexual impulses, lacks the complexity of thought and feeling which we might have expected from the author of *World within World.* The earlier autobiography, though still constrained by what Spender calls 'decent and conspiratorial convention', offers a more complex picture of the author's 'secret selves'.

There is, in short, a dialectic between cultural decorum and artistic innovation which tends to be overlooked by the advocates of uninhibited self-expression. To say this is not to minimise the anguish suffered over so many decades by those classified as sexual deviants. The criminalisation of homosexuality is certainly one of the most mournful chapters in the history of European civilisation. Ninety years ago Oscar Wilde was condemned to walk the treadmill at Pentonville Prison six hours a day for alleged indecency. Less than fifty years ago, after the Nazi seizure of power, homosexuals in Germany were being sent in their thousands to concentration camps, in accordance with 'the Nordic principle that degenerates should be exterminated.' And now a public panic-stricken about Aids, unwilling to acknowledge that promiscuity (not homosexuality) is the cause, has singled out the gay community as a scapegoat.

How then should artists and writers react to the current measures designed to exclude works which 'promote homosexuality' from our schools, libraries and theatres? For an answer, we might turn back to Spender's *World within World,* which challenges those who operate with simplistic 'psychiatric labels' and affirms sexual ambivalence as a fundamental birthright:

> I have come to wonder whether many contemporaries in labelling themselves do not also condemn themselves to a kind of doom of being that which they consider themselves in the psychological textbook. For example, I suspect that many people feel today that a conception of friendship which can be labelled homosexual, on account of certain of its aspects, excludes normal sexual relationships; and conversely that the heterosexual relationship should preclude those which might be interpreted as homosexual . . . Yet when we look into the lives of men and women in the past, we see that relationships which today would be labelled abnormal existed side by side with the normal. Men labelled themselves less and adjusted themselves more.

A writer 'vividly aware of an ambivalence' in his attitudes towards men and women may be in the best position to subvert the simplistic categories imposed by society on our polymorphous emotional endowment: 'The relationship of a man with the "otherness" of a woman is a relationship of opposite poles. Yet I never lost my desire to share my creative and intellectual adventures with a man, whose search was the same as mine.' Echoing Goethe, Spender insists on the value of both polarity and identity. It is narrowness of emotional sympathy that is questioned, in *World within World* and—by implication—in *The Temple.* The narcissistic cult of the body seems arid, but truths in manhood darkly join, deep-seated in our mystic frame.

David Perkins (review date March-April 1989)

SOURCE: A review of *The Temple,* in *The Bloomsbury Review,* Vol. 9, No. 2, March-April, 1989, p. 21.

[*In the following review, Perkins comments favorably on* The Temple *and argues that its message regarding the repression of cultural and sexual freedom is relevant to contemporary America.*]

Some books are an honor to review, and Stephen Spender's *The Temple* is one of them. Poet, critic, journalist, playwright—there are few writing hats that Spender has not worn, and he has worn them all with dauntless grace and style.

The Temple was written, in part, by the youthful Spender at a time when he was discovering life—and sex—along with two other famous buddies of his, W.H. Auden and Christopher Isherwood, in the final halcyon days of the Weimer Republic. I say "in part" by the youthful Spender, because the novel took an interesting course over the years before finally finding the light of publication. "Dear Mrs. Grundy"-laden England had driven the three to Germany to unfetter their youth. "In the early twenties," Spender wryly comments in his introduction, "Prohibition resulted in young Americans like Hemingway and Scott Fitzgerald leaving America and going to France or Spain. For them, drink; for us [the English], sex." Spender's publisher liked the novel, but was afraid it might be too libelous and pornographic (Ah, there will always be an England!), and the

manuscript was never published. In a fit of poverty, something which happens all too often to even the best of poets, Spender sold his papers in 1962 to, of all places, the University of Texas, where the novel was rediscovered by John Fuller, who brought it back to the attention of Spender. Spender then requested a copy of his own manuscript, liked it, and, with some minor tinkering afforded by the wisdom of hindsight, it has finally arrived in Spender's spectacular canon.

The novel is thinly disguised autobiography, and, is even *more* fascinating for that; it is, in Spender's words, "a complex of memory, fiction, and hindsight." Spender's famous colleagues turn up, not much disguised, as Simon Wilmot (Auden) and William Bradshaw (Isherwood). Auden/Wilmot is beautifully and lovingly caricatured. "Terribly untidy in appearance," Wilmot made "pronouncements with almost absurd emphasis on certain words as though they were Holy Writ." Criticizing the poetry of Siegfried Sassoon, Wilmot says, "Siggy's No Use. His war poems Simply Won't Do." And, reiterating one of the themes of the novel, "Germany's the Only Place for Sex. England's No Good."

Beyond these wonderful insights into one of the most well-known triumvirates in English letters, there is a portrait of the world in the eye of the storm between two world wars. It is a novel of awakening—awakening to sex, yes (terribly sophisticated and very catholic regarding just who one might have sex with)—but also an awakening to the presence of evil in the world and to the possibilities and difficulties of love and friendship.

At times, the undercurrent of the growth of Nazism is eerily and frighteningly similar to the growth of conservatism that has taken place in this country over the past few years. As one of the major characters, Joachim, remarks to Paul/Spender, "It is what you are in your own being that counts. The terrible thing is that there are so many people today who are Nazis in their hearts even without belonging to the Party." The sun-drenched sexual freedom of 1929 Germany was followed by the worst oppression in modern history. The sexual expression, both homo- and heterosexual, which is at the heart of this novel, parallels America's recent past, and stares into face of an increasingly homophobic and repressive future not unlike the Germany which goose-stepped into the 1930s. The anti-Semitic comments which appear increasingly in our culture (witness the response to Scorsese's *The Last Temptation of Christ*), left unchecked and unchallenged will only proliferate, and the lessons are doomed to be repeated over and over until they are learned. The lesson of history, *The Temple* dares to tell us, is one that has not yet been absorbed. The consequences are dire.

Julian Symons (review date 18 February 1994)

SOURCE: "A Self-lacerating Frankness," in *The Times Literary Supplement,* No. 4742, February 18, 1994, p. 10.

[*Symons is an English novelist, short story writer, poet, critic, and biographer. In the review below, he comments on the poetry collection* Dolphins *and commends Spender's life-long dedication to critical self-evaluation.*]

"Lines for Roy Fuller", one of the poems in Stephen Spender's new collection [*Dolphins*], reminded me of the powerful effect Spender's *Poems* of 1932 had on the youthful Fuller. He knew a good many passages by heart: so did I, and we used to cap each other's quotations. There is a suggestion of the influence those early poems had on our generation in Fuller's autobiography, when he says a poem of Spender's about the unemployed helped to advance "the concept of a poetry of direct social function" reaching beyond "the provision of stimulating or consolatory sounds and images". Nowadays it might be felt that to write about unemployment without being unemployed would be an act of condescension; then we were more innocent or more generous. The indignation and idealism of these poems, and the assurance that seemed to lie behind them, probably made a more immediate impression than Auden's first collection, even among those who recognized Auden as the more talented poet.

The poem for Fuller first appeared as part of a tribute on his seventieth birthday. The version printed here is considerably different, but both confirm a feeling that Spender characteristically composes with his eye off the original subject. "Lines of yours I first read were of war / In Africa": that opening is markedly inaccurate, for Roy Fuller saw no shots fired in anger in Africa. The subsequent lines about soldiers silhouetted against the sky, their killing machines, and a final vision of the resemblance of the scene to a painting by Carpaccio—all these are "sounds and images" imported by the poet, quite irrelevant to what theoretically prompted them.

The point is worth making because the approach is typical. If Stephen Spender ever intended to create a poetry of "direct social function", the idea was long ago abandoned in favour of a concern to express in verse his own true beliefs and attitudes, about which he remains permanently uncertain. Much the longest, and much the finest, poem in his new collection is a life of Rimbaud done in short dramatic scenes, beginning with Verlaine's botched attempt to shoot him ("Mad aunt! Crazed shepherdess! Fuck off!" Rimbaud cries), and moving back and forwards in time to include mother-love, the Commune, rejection of Parisian literary life, contrasts between Communist beliefs and capitalist actions, gun-running in Africa, death. "I am / The poem made solid that is real", Rimbaud tells his mother. The reality is gold, hard cash, abandonment of any idea that the poet may be "Visionary, Prophet, Magus of / One unreal final ultimate / Of Hell or Heaven".

The sequence is successful in part because Spender can have found no difficulty in imagining himself both Rimbaud and Verlaine, in part because of his strong dramatic sense. Elsewhere there are one or two successful poems that don't attempt very much, and some sadly slack writing. "Nature abhors a vacuum" is a truism/cliché one might hope any poet would avoid, but here it pops up twice. Frequently there is what appears a straining to produce a "poetic" image, so that branches in a wood "seemed high as a cathedral", and in another poem the writer stands "silent, thinking of / Images to recall this moment", images which duly appear. So this must be a

disappointing collection for those who admire the early poems and are moved by the passionate raw emotion in some later ones such as **"No Orpheus, No Eurydice"** and **"The Double Shame"**. Yet as one looks back, Spender's principal achievement seems to have been less his poems or any particular piece of prose than the candour of the ceaseless critical self-examination he has conducted for more than half a century in autobiography, journals, criticism, poems.

Spender's principal achievement seems to have been less his poems or any particular piece of prose than the candour of the ceaseless critical self-examination he has conducted for more than half a century in autobiography, journals, criticism, poems.

—*Julian Symons*

Valentine Cunningham's *British Writers in the Thirties* (1988) excepts Spender from a general condemnation of his circle, on the ground of his honesty. Spender went to Spain and, Cunningham says, wrote unheroic poems about his experiences there, pieces distinct from what he calls the "potential bogusness" of stay-at-homes, who produced mock-heroic pieces like Day Lewis's "The Volunteer" and Jack Lindsay's "On Guard For Spain". Cunningham calls Auden a Spanish tripper, and remarks on the "disconcerted aloofness" of his poem about the Civil War. Spender got his friend out of a Spanish prison, never adopted anything like a heroic attitude, and was the first among his colleagues to deny publicly any merit in "the attempt to make poetry serve a cause". Those who died in the war, he said, were not heroes but simply "freezing or rotted lumps of isolated insanity".

At times, the frankness seems almost deliberately self-lacerating. Who else would have cared to reprint between book covers forty years after the event the article he wrote in the *Daily Worker* on joining the Communist Party in 1937, with its general acceptance that the Party line was sacred, and its belief in the official version at the first of the Moscow trials of dissidents? What other British writer would in 1951 have dared to write with candour about his earlier homosexuality, as Spender did in his memorable autobiography, *World Within World*? None of his close contemporaries, certainly, who admitted their past activities only when the climate had made it safe to do so. And his journals, published over the past half-century and more, are valuable not only as an evocation of one kind of literary life during the period, but as a ruthless examination of the character of Stephen Spender. The figure created is generous but self-distrustful and self-deprecating. His opinions are sometimes contradictory, but we are never in doubt that they express what he thought at the time. The second paragraph of a journal started when war began in 1939 states that he finds it hard to put words on paper; sometimes can't spell them. "I feel as if I could not write again". Perhaps he *did* feel like that at the time, but this is the first of nearly 500 pages. Does one wish that consciousness of this possible absurdity had prompted deletion of the sentence? Certainly not. That Spender had these feelings, in those first wartime days, is an element in the self-portrait.

His attractive waywardness and sharp perceptions are shown throughout the journals: for instance, in a gently ironic aside about Conrad Aiken, after Aiken had said subtly deprecatory things about his old friend Tom Eliot. Aiken, Spender observes, is a sort of Greek Chorus to Eliot's fame. "The Greek Chorus is capable, of course, of acid comment." Friends, even close friends, are not immune from criticism, although this is often self-involved and sometimes contradicted. Sonia Orwell and Auden are cases in point. A pungent character sketch of Sonia Orwell says she attacks people at parties "with a virulence which goes beyond the decencies of the particular gathering", attacks that cover "some kind of underlying changeless virginity" but make her behave at times like a school prefect or bossy hospital nurse. Not a particular friend, one might think. But a quarter of a century later, Spender dedicated a book to her in affectionate terms, and on her death, after a page of fairly cool speculation about her love affairs or lack of them, and mention of her pretentiousness, ends up surprisingly with "she remained underneath the warmhearted generous spontaneous person she was all her life".

Slightly comic—one can never be sure with Spender whether or not the comedy is deliberate—is the effect of a question after a lecture asking whether he had really liked Auden. He woke in the night, thinking: "*Did* I really like Wystan?" Auden had been such an important factor in Spender's life as a writer that one would have thought the question could hardly arise, but Spender's shrewd conclusion after half a page of speculation is that his relationship to Auden is "that of a somewhat battered observer".

He has a witty phrase earlier in relation to Auden's obsessively rigid adherence to exact times for eating, drinking, going to bed, rising: "Auden had an open mind about sex but a closed one about clocks".

Perhaps the shadow of Auden has always fallen over Spender as poet, and affected his work. It has not done so in an obvious way, for unlike some other contemporaries—Day Lewis the prime example—who produced poems that were faint carbon copies of the master's, Spender avoided from the beginning Auden's tricks of language, metrical experiments, intricate poetic forms. A Spender poem frequently starts with something physically seen, which is then transformed through an image or a series of images into an expression of personal feeling. Of course, the procedure varies, but he is almost never concerned with the problems of (say) the sonnet or the sestina, or with strict metres. Even the occasional use of rhyme seems casual, rarely integral to the poem. The journals contain a good many ideas and speculations among their accounts of places visited, people met, lectures given, but they are never concerned with the technique of poetry, and it would seem that this was not a subject that (with the exception of the form of verse drama) greatly interested Spender.

The freedom gained in this way was at first beneficial, but in the end limiting or even damaging. What seems at times an almost passionate determination to avoid "a poetry of direct social function", combined with a fading of intensity in the images that have been so important to Spender's finest poetry, has led to the production of some distinctly low-temperature verse. Stephen Spender's poetic output, more than that of most writers, needs sieving. The right kind of selection would show him to be, as he has been for a couple of decades, an underrated poet.

Additional coverage of Spender's life and career is contained in the following sources published by Gale Research: *Concise Dictionary of British Literary Biography, 1945-1960; Contemporary Authors,* Vols. 9-12, rev. ed.; *Contemporary Authors New Revision Series,* Vol. 31; *Contemporary Literary Criticism,* Vols. 1, 2, 5, 10, 41; *Dictionary of Literary Biography,* Vol. 20; and *Major 20th-Century Writers.*

Obituaries

In addition to the authors represented in the In Memoriam section of the *Yearbook,* the following notable writers died during 1995:

Kingsley William Amis
April 16, 1922—October 22, 1995
English novelist, poet, critic, essayist, nonfiction writer, short story writer, and journalist

Because of his acerbic wit and iconoclastic attitude toward many aspects of modern society, Amis influenced and became identified with the post-World War II group of working-class British writers known as the "Angry Young Men." Jim Dixon, the disgruntled hero of Amis's first novel *Lucky Jim* (1954), became for many readers a symbol of rebellion against the conservative establishment. As his career progressed, however, Amis began to shock liberal admirers with his increasingly reactionary social and political observations. Although the object of his satirical comedy remained social manners and mores, in particular cultural snobbishness, in his later period Amis focused his pessimistic yet comic scrutiny on many modern trends. His intense anti-feminist rhetoric in *Stanley and the Women* (1984) offended many English critics and made American publishers reluctant to distribute the novel. "You can't make nasty remarks, or humorous or critical remarks, about a group without seeming to be attacking it," Amis complained in a 1986 interview. "Look at the things I'm supposed to have attacked: universities, Americans, women, young people, old people. . . . I mean, you wouldn't bother to be critical about something which you didn't like to start with." His other writings include *Take a Girl Like You* (1960), *New Maps of Hell* (1961), *The Green Man* (1969), *Jake's Thing* (1978), *Memoirs* (1991), and *You Can't Do Both* (1994). [For further information on Amis's life and career, see *CLC,* Volumes 1, 2, 3, 5, 8, 13, 40, and 44.]

Toni Cade Bambara
March 25, 1939—December 9, 1995
American short story writer, novelist, scriptwriter, editor, and author of children's books

Lauded for her insightful depictions of African-American life, Bambara focused on contemporary political, racial, and feminist issues in her writing. Initially recognized for her short fiction, she later garnered critical acclaim for her work in other literary genres and other media. Beverly Guy-Sheftall stated that Bambara's "particular vision—as a teacher, writer, mother, world traveler, social critic, community worker, and humanist—can provide alternative ways perhaps of viewing certain aspects of [African-American] culture." *Gorilla, My Love* (1972), Bambara's most widely-read volume, collects short stories she wrote between 1959 and 1970. Focusing largely on the developmental experiences of young people, *Gorilla, My Love* includes the popular and often-anthologized tales "Raymond's Run" and the title story. In a 1979 interview with Sheftall, Bambara explained her preference for short stories: "I prefer the short story genre because it's quick, it makes a modest appeal for attention, it can creep up on you on your blind side." Eleanor Traylor, chairperson of the English department at Howard University, described Bambara as "quite skilled and adept in the use of language as an unmasking element as well as a revealing element. Her allusions are ancient, drawn from the entire ancient world—Greece, Africa, Asia and from the Native American and African American heritage." [For further information on Bambara's life and career, see *CLC,* Volumes 19 and 88.]

Brigid Antonia Brophy
June 12, 1929—August 7, 1995
Anglo-Irish novelist, critic, essayist, journalist, short story writer, and dramatist

With her first novel, *Hackenfeller's Ape* (1953), Brophy won praise for her wit and creative use of language. The novel depicts a scientist whose attempts to civilize an ape result in problems both for himself and the ape. Her novel *Flesh* (1962) examines eccentricities of human behavior by depicting the transformation of an introverted young man into a hedonist. These novels, along with *The Snow Ball* (1964), a comedy of manners that parallels themes in Mozart's opera *Don Giovanni,* established Brophy as a critic of middle-class morality and hypocrisy. Like George Bernard Shaw, whom she once acknowledged as a major influence, Brophy wrote social criticism with the moral intent of promoting a better world. Brophy's style has been compared with the satirical elegance of Ronald Firbank, who was the subject of Brophy's critical biography, *The Prancing Novelist* (1973). The work that generated the most critical commentary, however, was *Fifty Works of English and American Literature We Could Do Without* (1967), in which she collaborated with her husband, art historian Michael Levey, and Charles Osborne of *London Magazine.* While critics agreed that a few of the classics "debunked" in the study were unworthy of the high literary status they enjoyed, they also derided the trio's reliance on facetious analysis based on subjective opinion. Brophy's other works include *The Finishing Touch* (1963), *Palace without Chairs: A Baroque Novel* (1978), *A Guide to Public Lending Right* (1983), and *Baroque 'n' Roll, and Other Essays* (1987). [For further information on Brophy's life and career, see *CLC,* Volumes 6, 11, and 29.]

Emil M. Cioran
April 8, 1911—June 20, 1995
Rumanian-born philosopher and essayist

Considered a master of the personal, unsystematic philosophical discourse exemplified in the writings of Friedrich Nietzsche, Søren Kierkegaard, and Ludwig Wittgenstein, Cioran posited a comprehensively pessimistic view of existence and was particularly censorious of Western civilization. Primarily an essayist and aphorist, he sought to subvert conventional thought on such topics as alienation, consciousness, history, language, literature, religion, and death. In *Précis de décomposition* (1949; *A Short History of Decay*) he suggested that Western society is in irrevocable decline, its decay abetted by religion—or any cause—that inflames passions which inspire people to persecute dissenters or start wars. *La tentation d'exister* (1956; *The Temptation to Exist*) continues his exploration of the downfall of societies and includes commentaries on such topics as mystics, exile, and the history of the Jewish people. Cioran surveyed political regimes throughout history in *Histoire et utopie* (1960; *History and Utopia*) and concluded that all forms of government are fatally flawed. Civilization, he maintained, has hastened ruin by dissipating humanity's violent instincts, and therefore its vitality. Critic Daniel Stern remarked: "[Cioran] is the creator of a curving pessimism so profound and ironic as to almost meet a serious optimism at the other end of its arc. His aphorisms are lucid medicines that have no intent to cure. Thus, pure . . . , they are valuable remedies for the mind." [For further information on Cioran's life and career, see *CLC,* Volume 64.]

Donald Alfred Davie
July 17, 1922—September 18, 1995
English poet, critic, editor, and translator

Davie was well respected for both his creative and his critical contributions to contemporary literature. His belief that the poet "is responsible to the community in which he writes for purifying and correcting the spoken language" is evidenced by the classical formalism of his first volume of poetry, *The Brides of Reason* (1955), and is the focus of his first critical work, *The Purity of Diction in English Verse* (1952). In *The Purity of Diction,* Davie argues for a return to the prose-like syntax, formal structures, and conservative metaphors of the eighteenth-century Augustan poets. In the 1950s Davie was associated with the Movement, a group of poets including Philip Larkin, Kingsley Amis, and Thom Gunn who believed in the importance of these qualities. In contrast to English poets of the 1940s who were influenced by imagism and symbolism, the Movement poets emphasized restrained language, traditional syntax, and the moral and social implications of poetic content. Describing the appeal of Davie's poetry, critic John Lucas explained that "Davie is very readable, perhaps because his literary, donnish qualities compel him to take the reader seriously, so that although you often feel talked at you never feel talked down to." Davie's editor Michael Schmidt said, "He will be remembered as a man who stood up for poetry at a time when it needed defending." Davie's notable collections include *Essex Poems* (1969), *In the Stopping Train* (1977), and *To Scorch or Freeze* (1988). [For further information on Davie's life and career, see *CLC*, Volume 5, 8, 10, and 31.]

Michael Ende
November 12, 1929—August 28, 1995
German novelist, screenwriter, film critic, and actor

Best known for his children's fiction, Ende was the author of the international best seller *The Neverending Story*, first published in 1979 and filmed in 1984. He took up writing in the late 1950s after failing to make a career of acting, and produced his first children's book, the award-winning *Jim Knopf and Lukas the Locomotive Engineer*, in 1960. Ende produced *The Neverending Story* while living in self-imposed exile near Rome. While serving as an advisor during the filming of the book, he became displeased with the adaptation and divorced himself from the project. [For further information on Ende's life and career, see *CLC*, Volume 31.]

Gavin Ewart
February 4, 1916—October 23, 1995
English poet and editor

Ewart was known as a skilled writer of light verse. He began writing poetry while a student at Wellington College and published his first book, *Poems and Songs*, in 1939. After serving in England's Royal Artillery in World War II, he did not produce another work until *Londoners* in 1964. From then on he maintained a steady output, producing work often described as technically masterful. His major poems are collected in *The Gavin Ewart Show: Selected Poems, 1939-1985* and *Collected Poems: 1980-1990*. [For further information on Ewart's life and career, see *CLC*, Volumes 13 and 46.]

Walter Braden Finney
October 2, 1911(?)—November 16, 1995
American novelist

Finney, who published under the name Jack Finney, is best known for his second novel, *The Body Snatchers*, which was published in 1955 and served as basis for the classic science fiction film *The Invasion of the Body Snatchers* (1956). *Time and Again* (1970), a time-travel thriller, also proved widely successful; its sequel, *From Time to Time* (1995), appeared shortly before Finney's death. *Time and Again* was also adapted for film, as were a number of Finney's other works, including *Five against the House* (1954), *Assault on a Queen* (1959), and *Good Neighbor Sam* (1963).

Charles Gordone
October 12, 1925—November 17, 1995
American dramatist, actor, and director

Gordone's second produced play, *No Place to Be Somebody* (1970), won the Pulitzer Prize, making him the first African-American author to be so honored. The play generated much critical and popular attention for its polemical treatment of racial issues. A lifelong social and political activist, Gordone continued to write and direct plays and later taught English and theater at Texas A&M University. *No Place to Be Somebody* remains his best-known and most influential work. [For further information on Gordone's life and career, see *CLC*, Volumes 1 and 4.]

Jane Kenyon
May 23, 1947—April 23, 1995
American poet

Kenyon was the poet laureate of New Hampshire, where she had lived on a farm for the past two decades. Her poems often address such themes as domesticity, the rhythms of rural life, suffering, mental illness, and spirituality. Critics have described her work, which ranges from short narratives to meditations, as melancholic and introspective. Her works include: *From Room to Room* (1978), *The Little Boat* (1986), *Let Evening Come* (1990), and *Constance* (1993).

Howard Koch
December 12, 1901—August 17, 1995
American screenwriter, radio writer, playwright and memoirist

Best known for his work as co-writer of the screenplay to the film *Casablanca* (1942), Howard Koch also wrote the radio adaptation of H. G. Wells's classic *The War of the Worlds* (1898) which caused a nationwide panic when broadcast by Orson Welles in 1938. After graduating from Columbia University, Koch began working as a lawyer, writing stage plays in his spare time. By the early 1930s he moved to radio, writing for Orson Welles and his Mercury Theater of the Air. In the 1940s Koch began writing for films, joining Warner Bros. to work on such films as *The Letter* (1940), *Sergeant York* (1941), *Rhapsody in Blue* (1945), and *The Best Years of Our Lives* (1946). In 1942 he shared an Academy Award with Julius and Philip Epstein for writing *Casablanca,* the classic wartime film starring Humphrey Bogart as an expatriate barowner and Ingrid Bergman as his lost love. In 1951 Koch was blacklisted and not allowed to work in Hollywood following an investigation by the House Un-American Activities Committee into communist influence in the film industry. He moved to Europe where he wrote under the pseudonym Peter Howard until the early 1960s. Koch's memoirs, titled *As Time Goes By*—after the song sung by Sam the piano player (Dooley Wilson) in *Casablanca*—appeared in 1979. Toward the end of his life Koch found that mementoes from his early years as a writer were in demand. In 1988 he auctioned off the original manuscript to his *The War of the Worlds* radio adaptation for $143,000; in 1994, his Oscar for *Casablanca* earned $184,000 at auction.

Andrew Lytle
December 26, 1902—December 12, 1995
American novelist, essayist, and magazine editor

One of the founding members of the literary group known as the Agrarians, Andrew Lytle was a novelist whose best known works include *The Long Night* (1936), *At the Moon's Inn* (1941), *A Name for Evil* (1947), and *The Velvet Horn* (1957). Lytle was born in Murfreesboro, Tennessee, a city founded by his ancestors, and attended Vanderbilt University, Oxford University, and Yale's School of Drama. As a struggling young writer, Lytle supported himself by acting in New York. In 1930 he contributed an essay on the small farm to the anthology *I'll Take My Stand.* The book sparked a nationwide discussion about the agrarian versus urban lifestyles and led to the founding of the Agrarians, a group of writers who warned that urbanization was leading America to centralized politics and a standardized culture. The Agrarians included such prominent writers as Robert Penn Warren, John Crowe Ransom, and Allen Tate. Lytle taught at the University of the South in Sewanee from 1942 to 1944, leaving to found the writing program at the University of Florida. In 1960 Lytle returned to the University of the South and assumed editorship of the *Sewanee Review,* an academic journal he brought to national renown. Lytle's memoirs, *A Wake for the Living,* appeared in 1975.

Louis Malle
October 30, 1932—November 23, 1995
French film director and screenwriter

Louis Malle was among the most prominent and successful directors to emerge from the so-called "New Wave" of French cinema in the late 1950s and early 1960s. His work is characterized by the combination of apparently dissimilar impulses: one toward provocation and the disturbance of the audience—which he tried to achieve by tackling such controversial themes as child prostitution, incest, suicide, and collaboration with the Nazis—and one toward romance and nostalgia for the lost innocence of childhood. Among his best known films are *The Lovers* (1958), *Le feu follet* (1963), *Le souffle au coeur* (1971), *Lacombe Lucien* (1974), *Pretty Baby* (1978), *Atlantic City* (1980), *My Dinner with Andre* (1981), *Au Revoir, Les Enfants* (1987), and *Damage* (1992). Born to a financially-prominent family, Malle took a diploma in film and rejected pressure to enter his family's sugar-refining business. In 1953 he began working with Jacques-Yves Cousteau, filming the explorer's underwater projects; their film *Le monde de silence* (1956) won a Cannes Grand Prix award. In 1957, Malle directed his first feature film, *Ascenseur pour l'echafaud,* a thriller that earned him the Prix Delluc. Later successes included *Atlantic City,* winner of the top prize at the Venice Film Festival, *My Dinner with Andre,* the record of a single dinner conversation between two men, and *Au Revoir, Les Enfants,* the story of a Jewish boy betrayed to the Nazis by his French classmates.

Vladimir Yemelyanovich Maximov
December 9, 1930—March 26, 1995
Russian short story writer, novelist, playwright, and journalist

A leading Russian journalist and dissident during the late Soviet era, Maximov began his writing career in 1961 with a literary anthology that included the short story "Man Is Alive," a work that was successfully adapted for the stage. In 1968, while working as a journalist on the Soviet literary review *Oktyabr,* he resigned in protest over the Soviet invasion of Czechoslovakia and was expelled from the Soviet Writers' Union and stripped of his citizenship in 1975. After moving to Paris, Maximov founded *Continent,* a Russian literary review that published the works of fellow Soviet dissidents, notably that of Andrei Sakharov. His best known novels are *Karantin* (*Quarantine,* 1981), *Sem dnei tvozenia* (*Seven Days of Creation,* 1974), which is an unflattering look at Soviet society; and *Adieu from Nowhere,* an account of his turbulent teenage years. His last work *Nomad to the End* was published in Russia just before his death.

Edith Pargeter
September 20, 1913—October 15, 1995
English novelist, short story writer, travel writer, and translator

A prolific writer in a variety of genres, Pargeter achieved her greatest popularity with the medieval mystery novels she wrote under the pseudonym Ellis Peters. These mysteries feature the character Brother Cadfael, a twelfth-century Benedictine monk and former worldly layman who uses his secular experience, great intellect, and uncanny powers of observation to rescue young lovers who have become enmeshed in crimes at Shrewsbury Abbey. Set in her home town in western England, the Cadfael stories—which began in 1977 with *A Morbid Taste for Bones* and ended, some twenty-one volumes later, with *Brother Cadfael's Penance* (1994)—are consistently praised for their historical accuracy. Also under the name of Ellis Peters, Pargeter wrote another popular series of novels featuring the contemporary detective George Felse, his wife Bunty, and their son Dominic. In addition to her fiction, Pargeter translated a number of modern Czechoslovakian writers, including Jan Neruda, Bohumil Hrabel, and Ivan Klíma.

John Patrick
May 17, 1905—November 7, 1995
American playwright and screenwriter

Pulitzer Prize and Tony award-winning American playwright of *Teahouse of the August Moon* (1953), Patrick authored more than 1000 dramas for NBC Radio during the 1930s and more than 30 stage plays, including the popular *Curious Savage* (1950), *Hasty Heart* (1945), and the 1969 comedy *Love Is a Time of Day.* As a Hollywood screenwriter his credits include the screen adaptation of *Teahouse of the August Moon* (1956), *Three Coins in the Fountain* (1954), *Love Is a Many Splendored Thing* (1955), *High Society* (1956), which is the musical adaptation of Philip Barry's *The Philadelphia Story*; Gene Kelly's musical film *Les Girls* (1957), *The World of Suzie Wong* (1960), *Parrish* (1961), *Gigot,* with Jackie Gleason (1962); *The Main Attraction* (1963), and *The Shoes of the Fisherman* (1968). When queried about which of his many awards and honors was his favorite, Patrick answered: "The First Prize International Stock Show Senior Yearling Bull. This is the toughest award, when you win this, you know you've done something."

Donald Eugene Pendleton
December 12, 1927—October 23, 1995
American novelist

Pendleton's *The Executioner: War Against the Mafia* (1969) became the first of 38 novels in the "Executioner" series, virtually inventing the genre of the modern action-adventure novel. The main character, Mack Boland, went on to become the protagonist of over 150 more novels written by a variety of authors. Pendleton also created two detective series; one followed the exploits of the psychic detective Ashton Ford, while the other followed Joe Copp, a private detective. Writing under the pseudonyms Stephan Gregory and Dan Britain, Pendleton also published *The Sex Goddess* (1967), *Religion and the Sexual Life* (1968), *The Sexuality Gap* (1968), *Hypnosis and the Free Female* (1969), and *Civil War II: The Day It Finally Happened* (1971). His last book, *To Dance With Angels* (1990), was a collaborative effort with his wife and discusses the couple's experiences with channeling and talking with spirits.

Kenule Beeson Saro-Wiwa
October 10, 1941—November 10, 1995
Nigerian playwright, poet, novelist, short story writer, essayist, and author of children's books

Saro-Wiwa is best known for his acute, often humorous, satires of Nigerian life in which he attacks such social ills as corruption, inefficiency, materialism, and the lack of rights for minorities. One of his most popular works was the television soap opera *Basi & Co.,* which Saro-Wiwa both wrote and produced. The series concerns a group of lazy young men in Lagos who spend their time devising schemes for becoming rich. Saro-Wiwa also wrote a series of books, known as "The Adventures of Mr. B.," based on the characters from the television series. His other works include *Sozaboy: A Novel in Rotten English* (1985), which concerns a young man recruited to fight in the Biafran Army during the Nigerian civil war; *A Forest of Flowers* (1986), a short story collection that portrays the lives of ordinary people; and *Prisoners of Jebs* (1988), a satirical farce about an island prison full of writers, journalists, military officials, and governmental personnel from throughout the African continent. Saro-Wiwa, who had been demanding compensation from the Nigerian government and international oil companies for environmental damage to the homeland of the Ogoni people, had been in a Nigerian prison for over a year when he was executed by the state.

Topics in Literature: 1995

The *Bell Curve* Controversy

INTRODUCTION

With the publication of *The Bell Curve* (1994) by Richard J. Herrnstein and Charles Murray, *The Decline of Intelligence in America* (1994) by Seymour W. Itzkoff, and *Race, Evolution, and Behavior* (1994) by J. Philippe Rushton, debate over the relationship between genetics and intelligence has been re-ignited. Although the precise subject matter of the books differs, the authors share several controversial convictions: intelligence—the ability to reason, think abstractly, and organize information—can be quantitatively measured and expressed as I.Q.; intelligence is largely immutable and at least partially heritable, therefore linked to race; I.Q. scores correlate, although weakly, with job performance and rates of birth, crime, participation in the political process, and welfare dependency; and society must allow for topics regarding intelligence and race to be freely debated. The authors of *The Bell Curve*, which has so far received the most attention, postulate that present trends in reproduction in the United States favor the eventuality of a nation split between a ruling caste of high-I.Q. "meritocrats" and a large, powerless underclass that lacks the intelligence to prosper in a society dominated by sophisticated machines. Democracy will disintegrate in such a society, Herrnstein and Murray warn, while racial hatred and alienation will grow as America becomes a "custodial" state. The authors draw much of their evidence from the National Longitudinal Survey of Youth, a study of more than twelve thousand high school students who were tested in 1979 and have had their progress tracked ever since; and the Armed Forces Qualification Test, a general intelligence test which the military uses to predict success in military training schools. The authors argue that core intelligence has been the single most important determinate of success in the National Longitudinal Survey and that the Armed Forces Qualification Test has proven to be an extremely reliable predictor. The term "bell curve," from which the book's title derives, refers to the shape of a normal distribution graph, which bulges in the middle and narrows at the edges. The majority of people, being of average intellect, form the bulge in the middle, while the low and high achievers make up the bell's edges. As Malcolm W. Browne has noted, Herrnstein and Murray "frequently refer to bell curves to make a point: that predictions about any individual based exclusively on his or her I.Q. are virtually useless. It is only when weak correlations between intelligence and job success are applied to large groups of people that they have predictive value. Within statistically large groups of people, the authors say, the pervasive influence of I.Q. on human society becomes evident."

Critical reaction to *The Bell Curve* has generally been negative, with many commentators denouncing the book as a racist product of conservative ideology. However, as Christopher Winship has argued, "much of *The Bell Curve* is not about race at all, and parts of it have been misrepresented." Winship and other critics note that a sizeable portion of the book deals solely with the relationship between behavior and I.Q. among whites and that Herrnstein and Murray believe that only sixty percent, not one hundred percent, of intelligence is genetically determined. One of the most contentious claims in *The Bell Curve* is that intelligence is, for the most part, not improvable. Numerous critics have attacked Herrnstein and Murray's bleak prognosis, arguing that educational programs for disadvantaged children like Head Start do make a difference and that society can work to alter the social environment and therefore positively influence the population's general intelligence. One of the major problems with such statistical studies as Herrnstein and Murray's, scholars argue, is the difficulty of isolating determinate factors in a system as complex as human society and the resulting danger of overlooking other variables. Herrnstein and Murray have been criticized as well for failing to discuss and substantiate the theoretical basis behind their claims regarding intelligence and for ignoring significant studies in the fields of genetics, psychometrics, sociology, and psychology which would compromise their conclusions. Remarking on the durability of their arguments, Stephen Jay Gould has commented: "Intelligence, in their formulation, must be depictable as a single number, capable of ranking people in linear order, genetically based, and effectively immutable. If any of these premises are false, their entire argument collapses. . . . The central argument of *The Bell Curve* fails because most of the premises are false." Still, several opponents of *The Bell Curve*'s conclusions, such as Gregg Easterbrook, are grateful for Herrnstein and Murray's work, since it brings "the arguments about race, inheritance, and IQ out into the open . . . because the more you know about this line of thought, the less persuasive it becomes."

REPRESENTATIVE WORKS DISCUSSED BELOW

Brigham, Carl
A Study of American Intelligence (nonfiction) 1923
Gould, Stephen Jay
The Mismeasure of Man (nonfiction) 1981

Herrnstein, Richard J.
  Crime and Human Nature (nonfiction) 1985
  The Bell Curve: Intelligence and Class Structure in America [with Charles Murray] (nonfiction) 1994
Itzkoff, Seymour W.
  The Decline of Intelligence in America: A Strategy for National Renewal (nonfiction) 1994
Jensen, Arthur R.
  Educability and Group Differences (nonfiction) 1973
  Bias in Mental Testing (nonfiction) 1980
Murray, Charles
  Losing Ground: American Social Policy 1950-1980 (nonfiction) 1984
  The Bell Curve: Intelligence and Class Structure in America [with Richard J. Herrnstein] (nonfiction) 1994
Rushton, J. Philippe
  Race, Evolution, and Behavior: A Life History Perspective (nonfiction) 1994
Wright, Michael
  The Moral Animal (nonfiction) 1994
Young, Michael
  The Rise of the Meritocracy, 1870-2033: An Essay on Education and Equality (nonfiction) 1958

CRITICISM

Richard J. Herrnstein and Charles Murray **(essay date 10 October 1994)**

SOURCE: "Race, Pathology and IQ," in *The Wall Street Journal,* October 10, 1994, p. A14.

[*In the following essay, Herrnstein and Murray contend that IQ test results are the most reliable predictor of socioeconomic success and failure in society.*]

"But what about race?" we are asked whenever we try to talk about *The Bell Curve.* Part of the correct answer is that there are many interesting questions involving race and intelligence. Racial differences in means and distributions on IQ tests are a reality. As far as anyone can tell, they are not artifacts of test bias. Some of them call for a rethinking of policy, especially affirmative action. All of these topics are discussed at length in the book.

But another part of the correct answer to "What about race?" is that racial issues are secondary. People find it hard to accept this at face value. The topic of race and IQ, relegated to whispers for so many years, is in danger of becoming a test of one's intellectual machismo. If we try to talk about something else, many assume, it must be because we are afraid. So let us say it as loudly and clearly as the printed page permits: If tomorrow the U.S. consisted entirely of blue-eyed blonds, the crucial themes of *The Bell Curve* would remain unchanged. The increasing value of brains in the marketplace would remain. The driving role of cognitive stratification would remain. The prospects for a state in which high and moderate IQ taxpayers would become custodians of an underclass domi-

nated by low IQ individuals would remain as grim—postponed for a few years, perhaps, if the nation consisted entirely of blue-eyed blonds, but no more than that.

Here is the reality: Approximately 75% of the American population still consists of whites of European origin. Within that non-Latino white population, here is what IQ means for the problems that are identified with the underclass:

The first lesson, drawn from a massive database known as the National Longitudinal Survey of Youth, is that low intelligence is a stronger precursor of poverty than low socioeconomic background. Or, to put it another way: If you have to choose, is it better to be born smart or rich? The answer is unequivocally "smart." A white youth who was reared in a home in which his parent or parents were chronically unemployed, worked at only menial jobs and had not gotten past the ninth grade, but who is himself of average intelligence—an IQ of 100—has nearly a 90% chance of being out of poverty by his early 30s. The high rates of poverty that afflict certain segments of the white population are determined more by intelligence than by socioeconomic background.

The correlation between IQ and employment patterns is also strong, with white males in the bottom 5% of IQ having three times the chance of being out of the labor force as men in the top 5%—*after* taking socioeconomic and educational background into account. Why are young men out of the labor force? One obvious possibility is physical disability. Yet here too cognitive ability is a strong predictor: Of the men who described themselves as being too disabled to work, more than nine out of 10 were in the bottom quarter of the IQ distribution.

Illegitimacy, one of the central social problems of the times, is also strongly related to intelligence. White women in the bottom 5% of the cognitive ability distribution are six times as likely to have an illegitimate first child as those in the top 5%. Is this really a hidden effect of poverty? On the contrary, the independent role of intelligence in predicting illegitimacy is higher among poor white women than among white women in general.

The odds that a white woman in the top 5% of IQ will go on welfare within a year of the birth of her first child is one in a hundred; for a white woman in the bottom 5%, it is better than one in two. White women who remain childless or have babies within marriage have a mean IQ of 105. Those who have an illegitimate baby but never go on welfare have a mean IQ of 98. Those who go on welfare but do not become chronic recipients have a mean IQ of 94. Those who become chronic welfare recipients have a mean IQ of 92.

Not surprisingly, there are other tragic correlations. For example, low IQ among white mothers is related to low birthweight for their children, even after controlling for socioeconomic background, poverty and age of the mother. Evaluations of child well-being reveal that, while high IQ is by no means a prerequisite for being a good mother, the disquieting finding is that the worst environments for raising children, of the kind that not even the most resilient children can easily overcome, are concentrated in homes in which the mothers are at the low end of the intelligence distribution.

The list of social pathologies linked with intelligence goes on. Consistent with a large scientific literature, white males in the National Longitudinal Survey of Youth who had been sentenced to a correctional institution as juveniles had a mean IQ of 93, compared with 106 for those who had never been stopped by the police. Once IQ is held constant, the relationship of socioeconomic background to juvenile delinquency among whites was nearly zero.

The steep increases in such things as illegitimacy, welfare dependency and crime during the past 30 years are obviously not to be explained by intelligence, which did not plummet during the same period. But things did happen which put people at the low end of the intelligence scale—white and black alike—at much greater risk of those bad things happening to them.

In this story, then, race plays a minor role. The forbidden tends to be fascinating by virtue of being forbidden, and so it has been with race and IQ. As with most forbidden things, the reality is not merely as exciting as imagination has made it. If one wants to understand the trajectory of American life, one must first inquire about the condition of and changes within white America. It is among whites at both extremes of the bell curve that the role of intelligence will play out decisively.

Malcolm W. Browne (review date 16 October 1994)

SOURCE: "What is Intelligence, and Who Has It?," in *The New York Times Book Review,* October 16, 1994, pp. 3, 41, 45.

[*In the following review, Browne examines* The Bell Curve, *J. Philippe Rushton's* Race, Evolution, and Behavior, *and Seymour W. Itzkoff's* The Decline of Intelligence in America, *focusing on IQ testing and the role of genetics in determining the intellectual potential of a person or group.*]

One may loathe or share the opinions expressed in the three books under review, but one thing seems clear: The government or society that persists in sweeping their subject matter under the rug will do so at its peril.

The issues raised by the scholars who wrote these books bear intimately on America's near future: its quality of life, its citizens' sense of belonging, its economic survival and the very foundations of a democratic society. They believe that America is rapidly evolving a huge underclass, an intellectually deprived population of men and women whose cognitive abilities will never match the future needs of most employers and for whom American society seems to have less use each year. The prisoners of this new underclass, the authors fear, may be permanently doomed by their intellectual shortcomings to welfare dependency, poverty, crime and lives shorn of any hope of realizing the American dream.

The numbers are far from encouraging. Indicators of national intelligence in the United States have declined compared with similar measurements of intelligence in other countries. The demographer Daniel R. Vining Jr. has calculated that America's I.Q. scores have fallen about five points since intelligence tests first came into use at the beginning of this century, and the College Entrance Examination Board says that scores for the Scholastic Aptitude Test fell from 1962 to 1990 by 11 percent in the verbal section and 5 percent in the mathematics part. The Educational Testing Service does not call the S.A.T. an intelligence test, but the test is nevertheless supposed to measure something like native brainpower.

Worst of all, say the authors, the lowest intellectual levels of the population are strongly outbreeding the brightest, and if (as most psychologists believe) intelligence is partly inherited, America is losing the cognitive base essential to coping with national problems.

. . . . .

In *The Bell Curve: Intelligence and Class Structure in American Life,* Richard J. Herrnstein and Charles Murray write, "Mounting evidence indicates that demographic trends are exerting downward pressures on the distribution of cognitive ability in the United States and that the pressures are strong enough to have social consequences." It makes little difference whether people at the low end of the intelligence scale pass on their deficit genetically or environmentally, they say: "If women with low scores are reproducing more rapidly than women with high scores, the distribution of scores will, other things equal, decline, no matter whether the women with the low scores came by them through nature or nurture."

This thesis becomes especially unpalatable when one considers the authors' observation that a large proportion of this emergent underclass is black. Unless future accommodations between ethnic groups lead to a more harmonious social structure, Mr. Herrnstein and Mr. Murray say, the potential for racial hatred seems enormous.

However much one may disagree with this assessment, the possibility that the authors may be even partly right makes these three books worth plowing through and mulling over. The articulation of issues touching on group intelligence and ethnicity has been neither fashionable nor safe for the last three decades, but these scholars argue that the time has come to grasp the nettle of political heresy, to discard social myths and to come to grips with statistical evidence.

The authors suggest that unless we do something to correct present trends, America may soon be permanently split between an isolated caste of ruling meritocrats on one hand and a vast, powerless *Lumpenproletariat* on the other. Society, the authors predict, will have little use for this underclass in a world dominated by sophisticated machines and the bright human beings who tend them.

This grim future may already be unavoidable.

Seymour W. Itzkoff, whose book *The Decline of Intelligence in America: A Strategy for National Renewal* is the gloomiest of the group, writes: "Our problem is simple, but oh-so-difficult to discuss, let alone accept. We are a different people than we were 50 years ago. In truth, we are not the nation that we were. Relative to the rest of the developed and developing world, we probably no longer have the intellectual capital that can profit from the available educational resources."

These books are heavily laced with statistics, bibliographic citations and ideas requiring time to consider, and they are not light reading. The authors of *The Bell Curve* tell readers that they may limit their perusal to the summaries that precede each chapter, and that they may skip the main text. Still, *The Bell Curve* is 845 pages long, and a reader who skips even the appendixes will miss many of the points the authors are at pains to make.

The writers of these works are recognized by colleagues as serious scholars. Mr. Herrnstein, who died from lung cancer at the age of 64 this September, just before publication of *The Bell Curve,* was a professor of psychology at Harvard University; Mr. Murray, a fellow at the American Enterprise Institute whose views influenced the Reagan White House, is the author of *Losing Ground: American Social Policy 1950-1980;* J. Philippe Rushton, the firebrand of the quartet, is a professor of psychology at the University of Western Ontario, and Mr. Itzkoff is a professor of education at Smith College.

Although their books vary in viewpoint, the authors share a suite of controversial convictions. They believe that intelligence in some deep but ill-defined sense is a real attribute of human beings, not some artificial construct of the psychometricians who invented intelligence tests. (Mr. Itzkoff's loose definition of intelligence, very similar to that of the other authors, is expressed as the capacity "to think abstractly, to reason. . . . to organize large quantities of information into meaningful and useful systems.")

They believe that I.Q. can be quantitatively measured, and that intelligence is at least partly heritable. They say that numerical measurements of intelligence are statistically (albeit weakly) correlated with job performance, as well as with rates of birth, marriage, divorce, illegitimacy, crime, welfare dependency and participation in the political process.

The authors suggest that unless we do something to correct present trends, America may soon be permanently split between an isolated caste of ruling meritocrats on one hand and a vast, powerless *Lumpenproletariat* on the other.

—*Malcolm W. Browne*

Moreover, they say, intelligence test scores tend to vary with ethnic groups. In the United States, Asians generally score a few points higher than whites and blacks some 15 I.Q. points lower than whites. (Mr. Herrnstein and Mr. Murray mention in passing that "Ashkenazi Jews of European origins . . . test higher than any other ethnic group.") These relative standings have not changed appreciably over time, despite many profound changes during the last half-century in social and economic conditions. The authors acknowledge that an enriched social, educational, economic and intellectual environment can and does raise intelligence scores, but they insist that even when due allowance is made in terms of statistical comparisons of all other factors and measuring their relative weights, intelligence still seems to be strongly influenced by the genes of one's forebears.

This leads to the depressing inference by the authors that no matter how many remedial education programs are brought to bear on intellectually disadvantaged children, many of them will still be hamstrung by an ineradicable cognitive disability created by genetic bad luck.

Society, the authors argue, should accept this as a real possibility and learn to cope with it, rather than merely denouncing all intelligence studies and ignoring the data they yield. For one thing, they say, much of the Government money spent on education programs like Head Start (which was launched in 1964) is wasted, helping only the nation's bloated educational bureaucracies.

"The earliest returns on Head Start were exhilarating," Mr. Herrnstein and Mr. Murray write. "A few months spent by preschoolers in the first summer program seemed to be producing incredible I.Q. gains—as much as 10 points." The gain was so impressive that in 1966 Congress expanded the program, but by then, the authors of *The Bell Curve* say, "experts were noticing the dreaded 'fade-out,' the gradual convergence in test scores of the children who participated in the program with comparable children who had not. To shorten a long story, every serious attempt to assess the impact of Head Start on intelligence has found fade-out." Cognitive benefits "picked up in the first grade of school are usually gone by the third grade. By sixth grade, they have vanished entirely."

This leaves unanswered questions about whether the declining educational environment after Head Start may in itself account for the fading out of its beneficial effects, and it raises related questions about I.Q. itself: if it can be raised by education, how strongly is it linked to inheritance?

Taken individually, none of the propositions advanced in these books is necessarily a call to arms, but in combination they are explosive. The writers themselves, whose views have been widely known (among academics, at least) for many years, are no strangers to public rows, student boycotts, hostile demonstrations and even legal assaults. Aware of the storm of criticism their latest books may face, all four invoke mountains of statistics to fend off anticipated criticism from such critics as Stephen Jay Gould, the Harvard paleontologist who in *The Mismeasure of Man* (1981) charged that "determinist arguments for ranking people according to a single scale of intelligence, no matter how numerically sophisticated have recorded little more than social prejudice."

The authors cite many surveys suggesting significant correlations between low scores on intelligence tests and undesirable tendencies: a difficulty with learning, a likelihood of remaining impoverished and jobless, an involvement in all types of crime, a tendency not to vote or participate in community affairs, a high incidence of abusing or abandoning children and a record of producing far more children (most of them illegitimate) than can be supported.

Mr. Itzkoff believes that the least intelligent, least educable, poorest, most politically apathetic and abusive contingent of the population is reproducing faster than the smart, rich, politically active and nurturing contingent. He believes this has fueled a dysgenic trend: America's collective smartness is being diluted, gravely endangering the nation's ability to compete economically in international markets; for example, he says, America's declining ability to compete in the global sale of automobiles and other manufactured products, as well as its status as the world's leading debtor nation, are partly the result of the declining cognitive abilities of workers and administrators.

In his book, Mr. Itzkoff places most of the blame for America's alleged intellectual decline on what he sees as an economically and intellectually elite caste of misguided liberals. They have isolated themselves from American society, he says, by their paternalistic treatment of the underclass, by discounting the importance of traditional family values and by failing to raise enough bright, educated children to sustain national competence. Mr. Itzkoff's unabashedly conservative tract condemns liberals in government, in the news media and in society at large, and calls for an end to welfare programs, a radical reform of the academic and employment quota systems that are supported by affirmative action and a tightening of immigration standards, perhaps barring families deemed likely to become permanently dependent on the welfare system.

No such calls to action are urged by Mr. Rushton, the author of *Race, Evolution, and Behavior: A Life History Perspective,* or by Mr. Herrnstein and Mr. Murray. Nowhere do they advocate the measures championed by the eugenicists of the 1920's and 1930's, whose ideas were appropriated and perverted by the Nazis as the rationale for the Holocaust. Indeed, the authors of **The Bell Curve** say that the granting to any government or social institution of the power to decide who may breed and who may not is fraught with such obvious dangers as to be unacceptable.

Still, one suspects that the authors of these three books may have softened their agendas somewhat to parry the expected fury of liberal critics, fellow academics and hostile mobs. Given their conclusions about intellect and demographics, it is hard to believe that these writers would oppose a eugenically motivated program designed to influence patterns of reproduction.

They leave many subjects untouched, including the genetic opportunities created by molecular biology—a Pandora's box loaded with paradoxes and snares. For the first time in human history, it may soon be possible to confer resistance to disease upon living organisms and to free people of inherited scourges like sickle-cell anemia and Tay-Sachs disease. Most people would argue that society is justified in fighting physical disease, but what if we were to carry the war against disease a step farther? Is it wrong

to regard a hereditary predisposition to lower intelligence as a kind of genetic disease and to find ways to cure it?

Merely asking that question is enough to cause fear and outrage, and these authors, perhaps wisely, elect to leave it alone. Sooner or later, however, society may have to decide whether human beings have the right—perhaps even the duty—to strengthen our species' cognitive defenses against an increasingly dangerous global environment. Human beings evolved over the eons to defend themselves against changes in their environment, and things are still changing.

. . . . .

Meanwhile, there are matters of practical policy to consider, such as the merits of affirmative action. Psychometricians generally agree that blacks, on average, have scored lower than whites on intelligence tests and that whites have scored lower than Asians ever since such tests were devised early in this century. But it is often argued that standardized tests cannot measure intelligence, and that the tests administered in the United States are especially pointless because they are culturally biased against blacks and Hispanics. In 1971 the Supreme Court endorsed such criticisms and ruled that tests of general intelligence (as opposed to tests that solely measure fitness for particular jobs) are discriminatory and cannot be administered as a condition of employment.

Mr. Murray and Mr. Herrnstein argue, however, that charges of systematic bias in intelligence testing are refuted by objective analyses of the available data. They cite the Scholastic Aptitude Test as one of their examples. "If the S.A.T. is biased against blacks," they say, "it will *underpredict* their college performance." But "external evidence of bias has been sought in hundreds of studies," Mr. Herrnstein and Mr. Murray say. "It has been evaluated relative to performance in elementary school, in secondary school, in the university, in the armed forces, in unskilled and skilled jobs, in the professions. Overwhelmingly, the evidence is that the major standardized tests used to help make school and job decisions do not underpredict black performance, nor does the expert community find any other general or systematic difference in the predictive accuracy of tests for blacks and whites."

One of the strengths of **The Bell Curve** is that it devotes an entire section to the relationships between I.Q. and behavior among whites alone, thereby eliminating the complications arising from interracial comparisons. Analyses of data gathered from exclusively white demographic groups strongly suggest that even if one ignores race, socioeconomic status and family background, I.Q. does indeed correlate with birth rates, crime rates and many other things. Taken as a whole, the statistics are impressive; it seems hard to challenge the notion that I.Q. plays a statistically important role in the shaping of society.

Mr. Murray and Mr. Herrnstein draw extensively from the National Longitudinal Survey of Youth, which has focused on 12,686 high school students, picked as a representative sample of the high school population, who graduated between 1980 and 1982. These students, who were tested and measured at the outset of the study in 1979, have been tracked ever since. Based on the psychometric indicators and the personal histories of these young people, the authors found various suggestive correlations and concluded that the biggest influence on the lives of the people in their samples was the "g" factor—psychometricians' jargon for core intelligence.

Definitions of intelligence have always been controversial, as have been tests devised to measure it quantitatively. In 1904, the British psychometrician Charles Spearman conceived of a quality he called "g," or "general factor" of intelligence, which has remained part of the psychometrician's lexicon ever since. Spearman's idea was based on his finding that people tend to achieve similar scores on tests that may be very different in content but that contain questions requiring cognitive skill. Such questions were said to measure "g," and tests that emphasized this factor rather than calling for demonstrations of learned skills are said to be "g-loaded" tests.

"G-loaded" tests, the authors of these three books contend, are better predictors of job performance than tests for specific learned skills.

The Pentagon found the National Longitudinal Survey so useful that its experts used it in devising a general intelligence test known as the Armed Forces Qualification Test, which focuses on problem-solving aptitude and has been administered to all would-be recruits for many years. Mr. Herrnstein and Mr. Murray cite military statistics showing that the "strongly g-loaded" Armed Forces Qualification Test is an excellent predictor of success in military training schools, even including combat schools that stress physical performance. The statistics were assembled from the records of 472,539 service personnel and 828 military schools.

Statistics are so important to the subjects under discussion that Mr. Murray and Mr. Herrnstein offer readers a short course on the interpretation of standard deviations, regression analysis and kindred matters. Their title, *The Bell Curve,* refers to the shape of normal distribution graphs—bulging in the middle and thinning out at the edges—that are used to represent large numbers of individuals sorted according to any shared characteristic—weight, exposure to asbestos, taste in clothes or I.Q.

The authors frequently refer to bell curves to make a point: that predictions about any individual based exclusively on his or her I.Q. are virtually useless. It is only when weak correlations between intelligence and job success are applied to large groups of people that they have predictive value. Within statistically large groups of people, the authors say, the pervasive influence of I.Q. on human society becomes evident.

Statistics can be powerfully persuasive but they are as slippery as eels, often susceptible to opposing interpretations. In brief, it is sometimes difficult to tell good statistics from bad ones. Epidemiology, a branch of medicine that relies heavily on statistics and has had some brilliant successes but also some spectacular failures, is a case in point. Epidemiologists have successfully used statistical correlations to convince most people that smoking increases the incidence of certain diseases, for example, but when some epidemiologists pointed out a relationship between low doses of microwave radiation and disease, their claims were bitterly contested. Debates over the epidemiology of intelligence have fallen into the same witch's brew.

Herrnstein and Murray's book abounds with tables and graphs, but to gauge the validity of many of the inferences, the reader is often obliged to dig into the book's huge bibliography.

—Malcolm W. Browne

One of the main problems in assessing statistics is the risk of overlooking confounding variables. A graph demonstrating a positive correlation between intelligence test scores and academic achievement may be very persuasive until, perhaps, one looks at an equally impressive graph that shows a negative correlation between academic achievement and the level of environmental lead to which a student is exposed. Does the lead impair the learning process directly, or does it do so indirectly by reducing cognitive ability? Is it merely a coincidence that environmental lead levels are high in inner-city neighborhoods whose children do badly in school? In any study of I.Q., can an epidemiologist "control" for all the independent factors that may create spurious correlations, such as inequalities in schooling, nutrition, family environment and general health? Maybe so, but it is notoriously difficult for scientists who study intelligence to reach consensus about anything.

Despite its impressive (albeit numbing) mass of statistical arguments, *The Bell Curve* suffers from a consistent weakness: Its authors seem unsure whether they are addressing ordinary (but scientifically literate) readers or professional scholars. In their indecision, they offer either too little or too much information. Their book abounds with tables and graphs, but to gauge the validity of many of the inferences the authors present, a reader is often obliged to dig into the book's huge bibliography and seek out the original papers to which it refers, many of them available only at scientific libraries.

The book leaves unanswered questions a reader might have about such vital matters as sampling procedures. In a discussion of one of the statistical methods for gauging heritability, the authors write: "Nonspecialists need not concern themselves with nuts and bolts, but they may need to be reassured on a few basic points." What follows is partly a discussion of statistical analysis and partly a plea to the reader to accept certain inferences on faith.

Nevertheless, *The Bell Curve* makes a strong case that America's population is becoming dangerously polarized between a smart, rich, educated elite and a population of unintelligent, poor and uneducated people. The authors deplore this polarization, which, they feel, has begun to manifest itself in the polarization of the nation's services:

while the elite use private delivery services, go to private schools, live in gated communities and rely on arbitration by private lawyers to handle business disputes, the rest of the population uses the Federal postal service, goes to public schools, lives outside the gates of private communities and relies on public judicial process. Moreover, the authors note, America no longer has a conscript army—an institution which, with all its faults, was one of the great mixers of young men from all levels of society.

As the job market for the masses—the people at the low end of the intelligence spectrum—dries up, Mr. Herrnstein and Mr. Murray write, America's leaders are increasingly likely to create a "custodial" state that minimally nourishes, houses and cares for its despised underclass in the equivalent of an Indian reservation. The result, the authors contend, will be alienation and vicious racial hatred. Once a major segment of society becomes a permanent ward of the state, democracy must swiftly die.

Mr. Rushton's book, *Race, Evolution, and Behavior,* is incendiary. His thesis is that separate races of human beings evolved different reproductive strategies to cope with different environments, and that these strategies led to physical differences between races, including differences in brain size and hence in intelligence. Human beings who evolved in the warm but highly unpredictable environment of Africa adopted a strategy of high reproduction, while human beings who migrated to the hostile cold of Europe and northern Asia took to producing fewer children but nurturing them more carefully.

This, Mr. Rushton contends, gave rise to three major races (he scorns the phrase "ethnic groups")—mongoloids, caucasoids and negroids—and to physiological differences between the races (things like pelvis size, genital size and fertility rates) that are consonant with their rates of reproduction. He cites worldwide studies concluding that black women ovulate more often than white women, have more twins than white women, mature sexually faster than whites, and differ in other ways that affect their reproduction rates and strategies for child rearing. Among Mr. Rushton's conclusions are that whites, on average, emphasize nurture rather than numbers of offspring, while blacks, on average, are shaped by evolutionary selection pressures to produce more children but to nurture each one less. At the other extreme, some studies suggest that mongoloids evolved to produce even fewer offspring. One indicator, Mr. Rushton says, is a tendency to produce fraternal twins—twins conceived from two eggs in the same menstrual cycle. The rate of fraternal twins per 1,000 births for mongoloids is less than 4, for whites, approximately 8, and for negroids, more than 16, he says.

This is the kind of proposition that makes Mr. Rushton a constant target of furious protests. His classes in psychology at the University of Western Ontario have been barred by hostile demonstrators year after year, forcing him to lecture by videotape.

Mr. Rushton is nevertheless regarded by many of his colleagues as a scholar and not a bigot. The University of Western Ontario has consistently upheld his right to continue teaching. One of his papers on racial differences was presented at a 1989 meeting of the American Association for the Advancement of Science and caused an uproar, but demands to suppress the paper were rejected by Walter Massey, who at the time was president of the association. Mr. Massey, who is black, argued that no scientific organization has the right to act as a censor of scientific debate.

In their book, Mr. Murray and Mr. Herrnstein do not support Mr. Rushton's theories of human evolution, but they comment that "Rushton's work is not that of a crackpot or a bigot, as many of his critics are given to charging. . . . As science, there is nothing wrong with Rushton's work in principle; we expect that time will tell whether it is right or wrong in fact."

The most insistent plea of the four authors is for freedom of debate and an end to the shroud of censorship imposed upon scientists and scholars by pressure groups and an acquiescing society. Mr. Murray and Mr. Herrnstein write that "for the last 30 years, the concept of intelligence has been a pariah in the world of ideas," and that the time has come to rehabilitate rational discourse on the subject. It is hard to imagine a democratic society doing otherwise.

Mickey Kaus   (essay date 31 October 1994)

SOURCE: "Behind the Curve," in *The New Republic,* Vol. 211, No. 18, October 31, 1994, p. 4.

[*An essayist and nonfiction writer, Kaus is the author of* The End of Equality *(1992). In the following essay, he contends that* The Bell Curve *neglects the environmental factors that influence intelligence test results.*]

In *Losing Ground,* the 1984 book that made his name, Charles Murray pooh-poohed the role of race in America's social pathology. Instead, Murray blamed liberal welfare programs that trapped black and white alike in poverty. "Focusing on blacks cripples progress," he declared in a 1986 op-ed piece (titled "Not a Matter of Race"),

> because explanations of the special problems facing blacks nearly all begin with the assumption that blacks are different from everyone else, whether because of racism (as the apologists argue) or because of inherent traits (as the racists argue).

But that was then. Now, it turns out that Murray indeed thinks blacks face problems because they "are different from everyone else," and they are different "because of inherent traits (as the racists argue)"—or, at any rate, because of immutable traits. Elsewhere in this issue, and in a new book, ***The Bell Curve,*** Murray (and his co-author, the late Richard J. Herrnstein) argue that blacks have, on average, significantly lower "cognitive ability" than whites. Murray connects this disability with all sorts of pathologies (poverty, crime, illegitimacy) and predicts "the coming of the custodial state," in which a low-I.Q. underclass is maintained in a "more lavish version of the Indian reservation."

Just because many people (myself included) resist Murray's vision as alien and repellent doesn't mean he's wrong. But neither does it mean he's right. [*The New Re-*

public]'s editor apparently believes that disgust with the Murray-Herrnstein article reflects an unhealthy desire to suppress unpleasant truths. But the question isn't whether it is possible that some ethnic groups have, on average, higher mental abilities than others (it would be odd if every group came out the same). It's whether Murray is a reliable guide when it comes to exploring this possibility. The dishonest book he has coauthored, and the even more disingenuous article ["Race, Genes and I.Q.—An Apologia," *The New Republic,* October 31, 1994] this magazine has now published, reveal that he is not.

To make the pessimistic "ethnic difference" argument work, Murray and Herrnstein must demonstrate three things: (1) that there is a single, general measure of mental ability; (2) that the I.Q. tests that purport to measure this ability (and on which blacks score roughly fifteen points lower than whites) aren't culturally biased; and (3) that this mental ability is fixed across generations—classically, that it's "in the genes."

As a lay reader of *The Bell Curve,* I'm unable to judge fairly the first two claims. But it's pretty obvious that Murray and Herrnstein run into big trouble on step three, because they spend a lot of time trying to undermine a near-avalanche of evidence that the black-white difference in I.Q. is a function of environment rather than heredity. There is, for example, the convergence of black and white test scores over the past twenty years, which Murray admits has been so fast it is "likely" due to "environmental changes." There is the "Flynn effect"—rapidly rising test scores worldwide. French researchers have succeeded in boosting I.Q. twelve points by placing poor children in affluent homes. I.Q.s were also raised almost eight points by the Abecedarian Project, which offers intensive day care for five years.

And what is the evidence for a black-white *genetic* difference? Murray feebly offers "Spearman's hypothesis," which holds that blacks do worse on questions that tap into general mental ability. But, as Murray admits in the middle of a crucial—and virtually unintelligible—paragraph, . . . that only suggests the tests aren't biased. It doesn't show that the difference in ability isn't caused by the environment. The best Murray can do is declare it "improbable" that genes have no role, although he is "agnostic" as to how big a role.

The limited role of genes and the proven role of environment in the "black-white difference" would appear to be disastrously good news. What's an apocalyptic thinker to do? Here Murray has a bold, even brilliant, idea. Having failed in his effort to show that race differences in I.Q. are genetic, he simply declares "it matters little"! After all, what counts in the end isn't the source of I.Q. differences, but "how hard they are to change." And it is difficult to "manipulate the environment so that cognitive functioning is improved."

With this one dramatic move, Murray achieves two seemingly contradictory ends. He preserves his scary extrapolations—the prediction that the black-white gap will persist more or less indefinitely. And he defuses the charge that he believes in genetic inferiority. Just as by denying

of the role of race in *Losing Ground* Murray made himself seem a reasonable, race-neutral scholar, so by denying the importance of heredity in *The Bell Curve* he seems a nice, non-racialist fellow.

The only problem with the assertion that "it matters little whether the genes are involved" is that it's crazy. It matters a lot if the black-white difference is genetic, because genetic differences in mental ability are almost certainly much harder to alter. Yes, there are simple cures for some hereditary conditions, like baldness. But as yet there is no Rogaine for the brain. At a recent symposium on his book, Murray delivered a sweeping pronouncement . . . : "whether the black-white difference in test scores is produced by the genes or the environment has no bearing on any of the reasons why the black-white difference is worth worrying about." What about affirmative action? someone asked. Wasn't the argument that if blacks were artificially vaulted into the middle class, the environment in which the next generation was raised would change? Doesn't it matter for *that* argument if environment is the key? Gee, Murray responded. He hadn't thought of that example!

There are other, equally obvious policies that might change the black "environment" and therefore black I.Q. scores. Murray himself has proposed one of the more dramatic alterations: abolition of cash welfare, which he says would produce more responsible parents (which in turn might affect even prenatal nutrition).

If ethnic I.Q. differences are not genetic, in short, there is a good chance that by improving the awful environment in which many black children now grow up, America can move the two bell curves in Murray's graphs closer together—close enough for Americans to "live comfortably" by emphasizing common values (work, family, civility) rather than the creepy, half-baked tribalism Murray endorses in his [*The New Republic*] essay. Individualism and integration—why does that combination make Murray flinch?

Christopher Winship   (review date 15 November 1994)

SOURCE: "Lessons Beyond *The Bell Curve,*" in *The New York Times,* November 15, 1994, p. A29.

[*In the following review of* The Bell Curve, *Winship applauds the thoroughness of the authors' research, which argues a link between intelligence levels and social problems.*]

At a meeting of social scientists at the Harvard Business School last month, Richard Herrnstein's and Charles Murray's controversial book *The Bell Curve* came up. One group reported that in an earlier conversation they had thoroughly "trashed" it. Heads around the room nodded in approval. I asked the room at large—about 20 people—how many had actually read the book. Two raised their hands.

The condemnation of *The Bell Curve* in the media has been equally definitive, if presumably better informed.

Most of the analysis has focused on the question raised in the book of whether I.Q. is hereditary and whether racial differences in I.Q. are predominantly due to environmental or genetic factors. The consensus appears to be that the book's argument is inherently racist and that Mr. Herrnstein (who died in September) and Mr. Murray are academic charlatans.

Yet, while their treatment of these issues has been justly criticized, much of *The Bell Curve* is not about race at all, and parts of it have been misrepresented.

For example, a frequent assertion about *The Bell Curve* is that it argues that intelligence is essentially inherited. In fact, the authors make the weaker claim that, according to existing research, between 40 and 80 percent of intelligence is in the genes. They adopt the middle of this range, 60 percent, as reasonable. (If you think this amounts to arguing that intelligence is "essentially" inherited, ask yourself whether you would be "essentially" receiving the same pay if you received a 40 percent cut in salary.)

Mr. Herrnstein and Mr. Murray have been rightfully attacked for their shoddy and sometimes contradictory analysis of the relationship between race and intelligence. They acknowledge, for example, that there is no scientific way to determine even within broad ranges what proportion of the difference is due to environment and what proportion due to genes. After offering this critical warning, however, the authors conclude that the racial gap is more likely genetic than environmental—a divisive and irresponsible line of argument.

Yet, in spite of its serious flaws, *The Bell Curve* offers three potentially valuable insights that should not easily be dismissed. The first is that as a society we are becoming increasingly socially and economically stratified by level of cognitive ability. This is an observation that has been made by others from widely different political perspectives, including Secretary of Labor Robert Reich. The dramatic increase over the last two decades in the difference in incomes between high school and college graduates is strong evidence of this trend.

The second important assertion is that limited cognitive skills are strongly associated with myriad social problems. The authors find that among the poor, the unemployed, high schools dropouts, those in prison, women on welfare and unwed mothers, 40 to 65 percent fall in the bottom 20 percent of measured I.Q.

Most of these groups, by the way, contain more whites than blacks. Indeed, seeking to sidestep the race question altogether, the authors restricted a large part of their analysis to whites. They find, as other social scientists have using the same data, that cognitive ability is a strong predictor of various social problems even when other factors such as family background are taken into account. Given the strong suggestion of a link between intelligence and behavior, isn't further study of a possible causal relationship needed?

The third important claim in *The Bell Curve* is that cognitive ability is largely immutable. Although the authors may well be overly pessimistic about the possibility of improving intellectual ability, surely we would be naïve to think that simply increasing Federal funding for early childhood education, say, or for job-training programs

would be sufficient to compensate for the increasing gap between the highly educated and the barely literate in American society.

What are the consequences of ignoring such controversial but potentially important observations about our society? Twenty-nine years ago, Daniel Patrick Moynihan, then an aide in the Labor Department, wrote a report that argued for an aggressive social policy to address the rising number of out-of-wedlock births in the African-American community, then about 30 percent of the total. Today, nearly 70 percent of African-American children are born out of wedlock (as are 30 percent of white children, compared to about 12 percent in 1965).

However valid the warning, after the report was published Mr. Moynihan and his defenders were denounced as racists and the African-American family became a taboo subject for scholars for the next 20 years. As we now try to grapple with the desperate situation of many black families in this country, we are missing two decades of research that could have informed current policy.

The furor about *The Bell Curve* risks the same perils. Many scholars are likely to back away from research on cognitive skills and social outcomes; others will be inclined to present only findings consistent with the thesis that I.Q. and race differences of any kind are largely environmentally determined. This is hardly an atmosphere conducive to objective, rigorous scientific study.

Few of the most controversial assertions in *The Bell Curve* can be shown with any certainty to be either true or false. Only better, more unbiased and more sophisticated research can help us do this. We need to insure that neither the irresponsible statements in *The Bell Curve*—nor the media's vitriolic response to the book as a whole—prevents this research from being done.

In an era of increasing stratification by level of ability and income, it is critical that we understand what the relationship is, if any, between intelligence and entrenched social problems if we are to develop sensible public policy.

Alan Ryan   (review date 17 November 1994)

SOURCE: "Apocalypse Now?," in *The New York Review of Books,* Vol. XLI, No. 19, November 17, 1994, pp. 7-11.

[*Ryan is an educator, political scientist, and critic. In the following review of* The Bell Curve, *he contends that Herrnstein and Murray are using IQ research to support a political agenda that includes a racist meritocracy and the dismantling of the social welfare system.*]

The Bell Curve is the product of an obsession, or, more exactly, of two different obsessions. Richard Herrnstein—who died on September 24 of this year—was obsessed with the heritability of intelligence, the view that much the largest factor in our intellectual abilities comes in our genes. He was also convinced that there had been a liberal conspiracy to obscure the significance of genetically based differences in the intelligence of different races, social classes, and ethnic groups, and that all manner of educational and economic follies were being perpetrated in consequence. Charles Murray—who is energetically and noisily with us still—is obsessed with what he believes to be the destructive effects of the American welfare state.

The result of their cooperation is a decidedly mixed affair. The politics of *The Bell Curve* are at best slightly mad, and at worst plain ugly. Its literary tone wobbles uneasily between truculence and paranoia. Its intellectual pretensions are often ill founded. For all that, anyone who has an interest in the philosophy of science and a taste for public policy will enjoy much of *The Bell Curve;* it is full of interesting, if dubiously reliable, information, and it offers the always engaging spectacle of two practical-minded men firmly in the grip of irrational passion.

Richard Herrnstein's passion was the conviction that each person has a fixed or nearly fixed quantum of "cognitive ability," the intelligence whose quotient constitutes your IQ. Herrnstein began his career as a disciple of the behaviorist psychologist B.F. Skinner, and therefore as a devout environmentalist. Then he fell in love with "Spearman's *g.*" Charles Spearman was a turn-of-the-century British Army officer and statistician who thought that people possess varying amounts of general intelligence—or "*g*"—and invented statistical techniques to discover which intelligence tests most directly tap into this basic ability.

Skeptics have always said that *g* explains nothing: the fact that the performance of individuals on different tests is closely correlated, and predicts their success in school work and some occupational settings, is important and interesting. Talk of *g* adds nothing to the fact of the correlation. Herrnstein, however, was no skeptic in this matter. At the first mention of *g* he confesses that "its reality . . . was and remains arguable." But eleven pages later, he claims that *g* sits at the center of the mind's capacities "as an expression of a core mental ability much like the ability Spearman identified at the turn of the century," while eight pages on, after a further bout with the skeptics, he announces that it is universally accepted that "there is such a thing as a general factor of cognitive ability on which human beings differ."

Does it matter? Only to the extent that it reinforced Herrnstein's fascination with ethnicity. The more you think that talk of IQ is talk of a mysterious something that possesses the same reality as visible qualities like skin color or the curliness of the hair, the more obvious it will seem that ethnic groups that differ in such visible qualities must differ in intelligence too. By the same token, it bolsters the extraordinary fatalism that infuses *The Bell Curve*: once you discover that the average IQ of people in jail is 93, it's easy to believe that people with too little *g* are more or less doomed to social dysfunction. How other countries of the same ethnic composition as white America manage to commit fewer murders and yet jail far fewer of their citizenry remains for ever inexplicable. Conversely, a certain skepticism about what there is to IQ besides being good at certain sorts of tests may make us less superstitious about its importance.

Charles Murray is intoxicated by an apocalyptic vision of the American future, nicely summarized as "The Coming of the Custodial State." The anxieties about the widening

inequality produced by the American economy are ones that Mickey Kaus and Robert Reich long ago familiarized us with, but they are here run through Murray's wilder and darker imaginings to yield a vision of an incipient semifascist future that neither of them would recognize. American society is increasingly partitioned into a high-IQ, ever more affluent, upper caste, a hardpressed middle class, and a cognitively underprivileged underclass, whose criminality threatens the rest of us and whose unchecked breeding threatens to dilute the pool of talent, and so alarmingly on. The well-off migrate to enclaves of comfortable housing, which are walled-off, well-policed, and equipped with decent schools; the underclass are shut away in urban slums. The struggling middle class feels trapped.

The elite may hold liberal views and they may be willing to pay for help to the poor, but they will not live among them. The middle class have neither money to spend on the underclass nor tolerance of its ways. They will insist on coercive policing and a more punitive welfare system, and will want the underclass kept in whatever "hightech and more lavish version of the Indian reservation" it takes to keep them from preying on the respectable. The end result, Murray argues, is catastrophe: a version of the welfare state in which the incompetent have their lives managed without their consent.

> It is difficult to imagine the United States preserving its heritage of individualism, equal rights before the law, free people running their own lives, once it is accepted that a significant part of the population must be made permanent wards of the state.

This is a eugenicist, and not (in the usual sense) a racist, nightmare, for Murray believes that the bottom 10 percent of the white population is headed for the degradation that already afflicts the black urban underclass. The people he affectionately describes as "white trash" will need as much looking after as their black counterparts.

So far as I can see, none of Murray's anxieties about the direction of American domestic policy depends on the truth of Richard Herrnstein's ideas about the ontological status of *g,* and none of Herrnstein's claims about intelligence support Charles Murray's ideas about social policy. Murray himself seems to recognize this: "Like other apocalyptic visions, this one is pessimistic," he says, "perhaps too much so. On the other hand, there is much to be pessimistic about." That statement is a bit casual when it is used as the basis of social prophecy; there always has been much to be pessimistic about, but not much of it licenses the expectation of the imminent extinction of American civil liberties. For all the scientific apparatus with which they are surrounded, Murray's fears are closer to the ravings of Rush Limbaugh's audience than to Tocqueville's anxieties about "soft despotism."

Herrnstein and Murray don't explicitly contradict, each other, to be sure, but Murray was hostile to the welfare state long before he encountered Herrnstein; and Herrnstein's views on intelligence are in principle consistent with the politics of almost any persuasion from socialist to libertarian. Socialists might think that ineradicable differences in IQ should be met by making sure that the less clever were compensated with more education than the gifted, and with income supplements to make up for their difficulties in the competitive marketplace; libertarians might think we should treat such differences as the luck of the draw, no more worthy of treatment than the accident that makes some of us better baseball players than others. Between trying to obliterate their effects and letting them make whatever difference they make in the labor market, there are innumerable further alternatives.

Herrnstein and Murray have many common enemies—Head Start, open door immigration, unwed mothers, lax ideas about sexual morality, and the "dumbing down" of American secondary education—but *The Bell Curve* is very much not the work of one mind. Indeed, each of the authors is in more than one mind on more than one issue.

For all its oddities, *The Bell Curve* is a fluent piece of work. It is a still more fluent piece of publicity-seeking. The authors have tried to have their cake and eat it, and they have succeeded in a big way. They—this is largely Murray's achievement—claim to be frightened that they will stir up terrible controversy, but they have advertised their fears in such a way as to do just that. They insist that they have no urge to stir up racial dissension or give comfort to racists, but then say that their findings only reflect what people already think in their heart of hearts—which is, that blacks and white trash are born irremediably dumb, that black Americans have been overpromoted in the academy, that smarter white workers have been displaced by incompetent black ones at the behest of the federal government. A disagreeably wheedling tone is an unsurprising feature of such arguments.

Too often *The Bell Curve* relies on Herrnstein's real distinction as a psychologist to prop up what is essentially armchair sociology.

—*Alan Ryan*

There is a good deal of genuine science in *The Bell Curve;* there is also an awful lot of science fiction and not much care to make sure the reader knows which is which. What catches the eye of reviewers and reporters are Herrnstein's gloomy predictions about the declining intelligence of the American population, and Murray's prediction of imminent fascism. Fewer readers will notice the authors' throwaway admissions that these predictions are highly speculative, and only loosely rooted in the data they assemble. Take the connection between the fact that illegitimacy rises as IQ declines, and Murray's fears about the imminent collapse of the liberal state. It is, for a start, quite impossible—as is readily acknowledged by the authors—that the rising rate of illegitimate births in both the black and white American populations should in the first instance have had much to do with intelligence.

The rate remained almost stable between 1920 and 1960, at about 5 percent of all births, then took off sharply in the early 1960s to reach 30 percent in 1990. Herrnstein and Murray say, "If IQ is a factor in illegitimacy, as we will conclude it is, it must be in combination with other things (as common sense would suggest), because IQ itself has not changed nearly enough in recent years to account for the explosive growth in illegitimacy." They then evade the obvious implication that their obsession with IQ is largely irrelevant. They say "some of these 'other things' that have changed in the last three decades—broken homes and the welfare system being prime suspects—interact with intelligence, making it still more likely than before that a woman of low cognitive ability will have a baby out of wedlock." True, but largely beside the point; the social pressures they mention make it more likely that women of *any* degree of cognitive ability will have a baby out of wedlock. If the pressures operate more powerfully on women of lower intelligence, we want to know why this is so.

The interesting question is not one of genetics but one of changes in the culture; it is not what has happened to the intelligence of the mothers that needs explaining, but what happened in the early 1960s that so altered the incentives to have babies later rather than earlier and in wedlock rather than out. (It must mean something that divorce rates rose at the same speed during the same years.) That is the sociologist's territory, not the psychometrician's, and too often *The Bell Curve* relies on Herrnstein's real distinction as a psychologist to prop up what is essentially armchair sociology. A sociologist would at least wonder why the welfare system should be one of the "prime suspects" in the rising rate of illegitimacy when it has been *decreasingly* generous over the past thirty years; and a sociologist would at least notice that other Western societies such as Britain and the Netherlands have experienced rising illegitimacy rates, too. None of this suggests we ought not to worry about the propensity of the less clever to get pregnant out of wedlock, but it does suggest that we ought to attend to the real complexities of the social environment in which all this takes place.

Again, all readers will grasp the authors' insistence that Head Start programs haven't worked; fewer will notice that those failures are more partial than the authors say, and that the failures provide a better argument for seeking programs that work than they do for *The Bell Curve*'s conclusion that we should abandon the attempt to raise the IQs of the disadvantaged and devote virtually all our attention to the highly intelligent. The fashion in which such programs have failed is not analyzed with the scrupulousness one might wish. In essence, *The Bell Curve*'s data suggest that Head Start and other preschool programs can raise children's IQs quite sharply for a short period; once the children are in a regular school, their IQ scores drift back to something like the level they began at. For a believer in *g*, this is evidence that in the long run the quantum of cognitive ability, whatever it might be, simply reveals itself.

Someone who wanted to draw the opposite conclusion might think that the data only show that there is no cheap, one-shot environmental fix for deprivation. Environmental fixes are possible, but they take much longer to work, or where they work quickly, they need to be repeated so that they keep working. It may well be that a much more extensive transformation of the child's environment than Head Start and preschool programs can offer is needed to effect lasting changes in intelligence. There are suggestive data about the impact of adoption on the children of low-IQ mothers that might make one believe that is the case. If it is true, however, it provides an argument for affirmative action that renders *The Bell Curve* irrelevant from start to finish; for it suggests that one purpose in creating a larger black (or whatever) middle class is to create a better environment for the next generation and its descendants. The true beneficiaries of affirmative action on this view would be the children and the grandchildren of the people promoted today.

That could be quite wrong; it might be that the only effective environmental fix would be a national health service that gave babies a better prenatal and perinatal environment. It might even be that Charles Murray's "custodial state" would have to get into the act to insist that the mothers of children who are at risk should use such care. What one can certainly say is that the failure of Head Start to live up to its backers' most extravagant hopes is neither a knock-down argument for genetic determinism nor any sort of argument for abandoning the disadvantaged. Herrnstein and Murray argue elsewhere in *The Bell Curve* that American secondary education has "dumbed down" bright children, and so imply—what they elsewhere admit—that bad environments at least have an effect. After several hundred pages of this, one begins to wonder just what Herrnstein and Murray do believe other than that any old argument against helping the disadvantaged will do.

The sheer repetitiveness of its tables, graphs, and bar charts eventually dulls *The Bell Curve*'s impact for the conscientious reader; but Herrnstein and Murray do not expect—and perhaps do not really want—most of their readers to work their way through all 845 pages of their text. They say they want to make the reader's life easy. For readers whose minds go blank at the mention of multiple regression they provide a wonderfully lucid appendix on "Statistics For People Who Are Sure They Can't Learn Statistics." For readers in a particular hurry, they summarize their claims in some forty pages of italicized text spread across their twenty-two chapters.

Their main claims can be boiled down further still. They are essentially these: America is today a "meritocracy" in the sense that the best predictor of success in life is IQ; the various institutions that pass children up the ladder to success increasingly select the brightest children to train for entry to the best colleges, the best professional schools, and the most rewarding occupations. Where once the alumni of Harvard and Princeton were socially rather than mentally smarter than their peers, the students of the best colleges are today almost off the scale—inside the top 1 percent of their age group. Nor does IQ represent the result of training, or parental advantage; the social standing of our parents is a less reliable predictor of our future

economic success and failure than our IQ—it's good to have well-off parents *and* brains, but if you can only have one, take the brains.

More intriguingly, most indicators of our ability to function successfully in society correlate to a significant degree with IQ. Very few students with an average or above average IQ fail to complete high school; conversely, the students who fail to complete high school usually do so because they find it intellectually beyond them; unsurprisingly, they have higher levels of long-term unemployment, both when they are able-bodied and because they are more likely to be sick. Men with lower IQs show up disproportionately in prison, and that is not because the dim crooks get caught, since self-reported but otherwise undetected crime is also largely committed by the less bright. Crime, of course, is mainly a male activity, and *The Bell Curve* duly acknowledges that what IQ explains is which men are more likely to commit offenses, not why men do and women (generally) don't. Herrnstein and Murray's interest in women is mostly an interest in their propensity to produce children out of wedlock, to go on welfare, and to have difficult children. As ever, the less bright have higher rates of illegitimacy and less amenable children, and to nobody's surprise stay longer on welfare.

As for our relations with one another, the clever marry later, breed later, and stick together; the less bright marry in haste and repent in haste, or at any rate are twice as likely to get divorced within five years. One thing to remember in the face of all this—and usefully insisted on by the authors—is that IQ differences do not account for *much* of the difference in the fate or behavior of people; in statistical terms, IQ rarely accounts for as much as a fifth of the difference between one person and another, and usually for much less. The only thing with which IQ correlates very closely is our performance on tests that measure the same skills that IQ tests measure—which in a world full of lawyers and economists and scientifically trained professionals is surely likely to create a high-IQ caste of what Robert Reich labeled "symbolic analysts." Intelligence tests test for just that kind of intelligence. To the extent that other personal characteristics are involved in what happens to us, the impact of IQ is less. The importance of *any* contribution of IQ to the causation of social problems, however, is that when we are dealing with very large numbers it makes a difference whether we think the population we are dealing with is averagely bright, especially bright, or rather dim.

For readers who are convinced that any discussion of the heritability of intelligence is fundamentally, if covertly, a discussion of the inferior mental capacities of black Americans, Herrnstein and Murray seem at first to provide some measure of reassurance. All these gloomy results about the damage done by having lower intelligence than the average come from an analysis of the experiences of white Americans in the 1980s. Most of the data which Herrnstein and Murray use come from the National Longitudinal Survey of Labor Market Experience of Youth (NLSY), a study of some 12,500 Americans who were between fourteen and twenty-two in 1979 when the survey began, and whose progress has been followed ever since.

Its usefulness to Herrnstein and Murray is that "only the NLSY combined detailed information on the childhood environment *and* parental socioeconomic status *and* subsequent educational and occupational achievement and work history *and* family formation *and*—crucially for our interests—detailed psychometric measures of cognitive skills." The sample was used by the federal government to reassess its intelligence tests, so it fortuitously provides data on measured intelligence as well as on everything else that correlates with success and failure in the labor market. The NLSY covers all ethnic groups, but the first twelve chapters of *The Bell Curve* stick to the distribution of intelligence across the white American population in that sample. Only then do Herrnstein and Murray turn to the discussion of ethnic differences in IQ.

Of course, as the hubbub in the press suggests, the reassurance is less than skin deep; as soon as ethnic differences have been identified—the one that swamps all others is that the mean IQ of African Americans is 85 as against 100 for white Americans—the readers is in for two hundred pages of familiar complaints against affirmative action policies. Before we move on to these, some other findings are worth a brief look. The most familiar will be the fairly well-confirmed discovery that just as African Americans are one "standard deviation," i. e., 15 percent, less good than white Americans at tests of analytical and spatial intelligence, so East Asians—especially the Hong Kong Chinese—are anything up to one standard deviation better. If the white American average is set at 100, the black American average is 85, and the East Asian average 111-115. Ashkenazi Jews have similar scores to East Asians, but the scores of Oriental Jews in Israel show an embarrassing contrast.

Affirmative action greatly preoccupies Herrnstein and Murray. Oddly enough, they back away from an insistence on the genetic determination of IQ. All that matters is that IQ predicts performance and cannot be increased by short-term educational and environmental enrichment.

—Alan Ryan

Herrnstein and Murray don't dwell at length on the implications of their views for the social difficulties of black Americans, but they hardly need to. Once they have piled up the statistics on the disadvantages attendant on having an IQ much below 100, the case is made. Where they concentrate their attention is on the two related questions, whether we can do anything to raise IQ, and whether affirmative action policies in education and employment are worth the candle. In brief, their answer to both questions is no.

The greater part of the argument against remedial education is their argument against Head Start and analogous programs. But that argument, as we have seen, can be used to suggest that the programs should be more intensive, not abandoned. They acknowledge the possibility in principle of eugenicist programs, but flinch at the thought of putting into the hands of government the power to dictate such matters as who may and may not produce children—William Shockley gets a passing mention as someone who enjoyed shocking people by suggesting that we might pay the poor to be sterilized and might set up sperm banks to pass on the genes of geniuses (he contributed to a privately organized sperm bank: there is no record of the results). But Shockley is dismissed as excessively eccentric. Whether his proposal to pay the poor to be sterilized is more eccentric than Murray's proposal to abolish welfare payments and face the short-term consequences for the hapless children on the receiving end of the change, readers will judge for themselves.

Affirmative action greatly preoccupies Herrnstein and Murray. Oddly enough in discussing it, they back away from an insistence on the genetic determination of IQ. All that matters is that IQ predicts performance at work and in the academy, and cannot be increased by short-term educational and environmental enrichment. In academic matters, they are much bothered by the probability that the SAT scores of black students at the best universities are anything up to 200 points lower than those of their white peers, with obvious consequences for the clustering of black students among the least successful and therefore least happy members of the college community. Herrnstein and Murray argue that we do such students no favor by putting them in a situation where they are anxious in school and possess an undervalued credential when they leave.

Nor are Herrnstein and Murray any happier about affirmative action in employment. They launch a two-pronged attack. The first is to demonstrate that although the raw income data suggest that black Americans earn less than white Americans, the picture changes when we add in the distribution of intelligence. At this point, we find that black Americans earn relatively more than white Americans—that is, relative to their IQs. What you might call "dollars per IQ point" comes out in favor of African Americans. If your notion of justice is that people should be paid according to their IQs, then this is unjust. On the other hand, you might think that what matters is overall efficiency; and Herrnstein's other argument is that affirmative action damages efficiency. Given even halfway plausible assumptions, of course, it must do so; if IQ predicts competence, anything that makes us appoint people on some basis other than IQ produces some degree of incompetence. Old-fashioned class biases were denounced by British socialists precisely because they helped the incompetent to keep out the competent. Herrnstein advertises himself as an enthusiast for that view.

There is a lot to be said on both sides. In a highly competitive society like ours, it may be true that affirmative action causes anxiety in, say, the student who gets into a place like Princeton or Harvard with SATs well below those of his or her white peers. But this anxiety doesn't seem to affect athletes or "legacies," i. e., the children of alumni—

groups whose presence at such places Herrnstein is surprisingly happy about—which suggests that even if this generation of black students does less well in strictly academic terms than their white peers, there are better ways of reducing their anxieties than refusing to admit them in the first place. The same thought applies in employment. It may be that there are many black Americans struggling with jobs they cannot deal with and many white colleagues muttering about them under their breath. It may also be that these are the labor pains of a different sort of society from the one we have had for the past three centuries.

This, however, throws one back on the fundamental question raised by *The Bell Curve*—how seriously we should take its science. Is there an intelligence gap between black and white Americans that no passage of time and no social policy can close? If there were, would anything follow about the social policies a humane society should adopt? The answer seems to be that there is good reason to believe that there is a gap, but no conclusive reason to believe that it is unshrinkable; if there were, it would have a good many implications about the need to balance the search for efficiency against the desire for a more humane social order—but it would not dictate how we struck the balance and it would introduce no moral novelties into the calculation. In particular a belief in the importance of inherited differences in IQ need not encourage apocalyptic conservatism.

It is an under-remarked feature of arguments over the inheritability of intelligence that an obsession with the presumed incapacities of the poor, the children of the slums, the bastard offspring of dim servant girls, and all the rest was once characteristic of reformers and sexual radicals as much as of anxious conservatives. The unwillingness of the contemporary liberals and the left to think eugenically has everything to do with racism being disgusting and not much to do with logic. In 1916 Bertrand Russell condemned the inner city as a site of "race suicide," but meant only that the slums produced large numbers of undernourished, unfit, and ineducable children. It was a common hope of birth control pioneers that wanted children would be fitter and brighter children.

The label "eugenics" itself was coined by Darwin's cousin, Sir Francis Galton, to describe a program for improving the British stock. Nor was the idea foreign to the Fabians. It is not an ignoble hope that as the welfare state improves the physical health of the citizenry it will also make them brighter, more alert, more interested in their surroundings and themselves. One could fear that the most likely end result would be *Brave New World*, with its Alphas, Betas, and Gammas, but that would not be because eugenic science was disgusting, but because the science would be used by the wrong people for the wrong reasons. It is surely true that an interest in the connections between heredity and intelligence need not be malign. After all, our interest in hereditary disease usually stems from the wish to help the sufferers. One can readily imagine a benign educational program that addresses the different strengths and weaknesses of students more intelligently than contemporary schooling does. But if a concern for inherited intelligence

or the reverse need not be driven by panic and superstition, it usually has been.

In the United States, fear of new immigrants rather than optimism about the chances of raising the level of the whole population always seems to have driven the discussion; and fears of the "dilution" of the "pure-bred" white stock by Jewish or Negro blood were the common coin of academic discussion throughout the first forty years of this century. Herrnstein misrepresents this past and the complaint against it. He says that Stephen Jay Gould's famous attack on psychometrics in *The Mismeasure of Man* was unfair to the military psychologists of World War I and to the psychologists on Ellis Island, whom Gould accused of announcing that on first testing 80 percent of the Jews, Hungarians, Italians, and Russians were feebleminded, and that even on re-analysis, 50 percent were so. "The intelligence of the average 'third class' immigrant is low," said H. H. Goddard, "perhaps of moron grade." Gould, in essence, claimed that research into the supposed racial differences in intelligence was driven by panic and prejudice, and resulted in absurd findings. Herrnstein responds that the psychologists were looking only for mental defectives, and naturally reported cases of mental deficiency.

This, as Herrnstein knows, won't wash in the case of Carl Brigham, the Canadian military psychologist who came to the United States in World War I and stayed to become professor of psychology at Princeton and a leading figure in the work of the Educational Testing Service and the development of the SAT. Herrnstein diverts the argument from the point at issue by claiming that Brigham's book, *A Study of American Intelligence*, had less influence on the Immigration Restriction Act of 1924 than Gould supposed. But that is not the point. Brigham was a leading figure in World War I intelligence testing for the American Army, and Brigham held, and popularized, exactly the views that Gould complained of. Brigham knew that many people thought Jews were clever; having examined large numbers of Russian-born Americans in the war, he thought he knew better. His army sample was "at least one-half Jewish," he thought, and they "had an average intelligence below those from all other countries except Poland and Italy." Taking Negro draftees as his reference, he discovered that 39 percent of the Russian-born were below the Negro average, 42.3 percent of the Italian-born, and 46 percent of the Polish-born. This was not an eccentric's vision of the world but the respectable psychometrics of the day.

Brigham's estimates of the cognitive inferiority of black Americans were, as this would suggest, much greater than Herrnstein's—in which case, the unclosable gap has been closing. Even Brigham acknowledged that putting black Americans in a different environment made a difference to their tested intelligence; and other interwar studies confirmed Brigham's finding that northern blacks did better on his tests than southern blacks. Some even found that northern blacks scored higher on many tests than southern whites. None of this proves that there is no inbuilt difference in cognitive abilities between different human groups, though it is hard to believe that anything of the sort would follow the haphazard lines of self-reported ethnicity. What it does suggest is that either relative cognitive abilities change more rapidly than Herrnstein believed or that our estimates of them are less reliable than he thought.

One other thing it suggests is that we should worry less than Herrnstein did about the danger that American intelligence is declining. Herrnstein was an old-fashioned "deteriorationist," squarely in the Brigham tradition.

> When people die, they are not replaced one for one by babies who will develop identical IQs. If the new babies grow up to have systematically higher or lower IQs than the people who die, the national distribution of intelligence changes. Mounting evidence indicates that demographic trends are exerting downward pressure on the distribution of cognitive ability in the United States and that the pressure are strong enough to have social consequences.

Other evidence, also quoted by Herrnstein, suggests that intelligence levels are generally rising. As usual where the evidence points in both directions, Herrnstein and Murray urge us to accept the more frightening scenario.

Herrnstein's fears were partly those that recently alarmed Sir Keith Joseph, Mrs. Thatcher's former education minister. In Britain as elsewhere, the cleverer members of the population have fewer children than the less clever. If g is handed down in the genes, there will be less to go round in each generation. Even if each clever woman had as many children as each less clever woman, there would still be deterioration; the less clever have their children earlier, producing three generations of less bright children, while their intellectual superiors produce two. But Herrnstein also shared Brigham's more American anxieties: the wrong sort of immigrants have been flooding into the country. Small numbers of bright East Asians were no match for large numbers of less bright Latino and Caribbean migrants. Herrnstein knew that his critics would retort that all this was said about the Poles, the Russians, and the Italians a century ago; all he could say in reply was that this time the anxiety was justified.

The latent contradiction of *The Bell Curve*'s politics emerges when one contrasts Herrnstein's enthusiastic defense of meritocracy with Murray's final fantasy of a world in which we live in "clans" that are high on self-regard and cheerfully ignore the existence of cleverer and less clever people in the world. Herrnstein essentially wants the world in which clever Jewish kids or their equivalent make their way out of humble backgrounds and end up running Goldman Sachs or the Harvard physics department, while Murray wants the Midwest in which he grew up—a world in which the local mechanic didn't care two cents whether he was or wasn't brighter than the local math teacher. The trouble is that the first world subverts the second, while the second feels claustrophobic to the beneficiaries of the first. The authors are united only in their dislike of the mostly unnamed liberals who have been hostile to Herrnstein's obsessions with race and to Murray's obsessions with the welfare system. In short, *The Bell Curve* is not only sleazy; it is, intellectually, a mess.

Stephen Jay Gould   (review date 28 November 1994)

SOURCE: "Curveball," in *The New Yorker*, Vol. LXX, No. 39, November 28, 1994, pp. 139-49.

[*A paleontologist, educator, and critic, Gould is the author of* The Mismeasure of Man *(1981). In the following review, he charges that the authors of* The Bell Curve *used inadequate and biased data and that their conclusion "that minority groups exhibit lower IQs which are both hereditary and immutable and a threat to America's intellectual pool" is highly questionable.*]

The Bell Curve, by Richard J. Herrnstein and Charles Murray, subtitled "Intelligence and Class Structure in American Life," provides a superb and unusual opportunity to gain insight into the meaning of experiment as a method in science. The primary desideratum in all experiments is reduction of confusing variables: we bring all the buzzing and blooming confusion of the external world into our laboratories and, holding all else constant in our artificial simplicity, try to vary just one potential factor at a time. But many subjects defy the use of such an experimental method—particularly most social phenomena—because importation into the laboratory destroys the subject of the investigation, and then we must yearn for simplifying guides in nature. If the external world occasionally obliges by holding some crucial factors constant for us, we can only offer thanks for this natural boost to understanding.

So, when a book garners as much attention as *The Bell Curve,* we wish to know the causes. One might suspect the content itself—a startlingly new idea, or an old suspicion newly verified by persuasive data—but the reason might also be social acceptability, or even just plain hype. *The Bell Curve,* with its claims and supposed documentation that race and class differences are largely caused by genetic factors and are therefore essentially immutable, contains no new arguments and presents no compelling data to support its anachronistic social Darwinism, so I can only conclude that its success in winning attention must reflect the depressing temper of our time—a historical moment of unprecedented ungenerosity, when a mood for slashing social programs can be powerfully abetted by an argument that beneficiaries cannot be helped, owing to inborn cognitive limits expressed as low I.Q. scores.

The Bell Curve rests on two distinctly different but sequential arguments, which together encompass the classic corpus of biological determinism as a social philosophy. The first argument rehashes the tenets of social Darwinism as it was originally constituted. "Social Darwinism" has often been used as a general term for any evolutionary argument about the biological basis of human differences, but the initial nineteenth-century meaning referred to a specific theory of class stratification within industrial societies, and particularly to the idea that there was a permanently poor underclass consisting of genetically inferior people who had precipitated down into their inevitable fate. The theory arose from a paradox of egalitarianism: as long as people remain on top of the social heap by accident of a noble name or parental wealth, and as long as members of despised castes cannot rise no matter what their talents, social stratification will not reflect intellectual merit, and brilliance will be distributed across all classes; but when true equality of opportunity is attained smart people rise and the lower classes become rigid, retaining only the intellectually incompetent.

This argument has attracted a variety of twentieth-century champions, including the Stanford psychologist Lewis M. Terman, who imported Alfred Binet's original test from France, developed the Stanford-Binet I.Q. test, and gave a hereditarian interpretation to the results (one that Binet had vigorously rejected in developing this style of test); Prime Minister Lee Kuan Yew of Singapore, who tried to institute a eugenics program of rewarding well-educated women for higher birth rates; and Richard Herrnstein, a co-author of *The Bell Curve* and also the author of a 1971 *Atlantic Monthly* article that presented the same argument without the documentation. The general claim is neither uninteresting nor illogical, but it does require the validity of four shaky premises, all asserted (but hardly discussed or defended) by Herrnstein and Murray. Intelligence, in their formulation, must be depictable as a single number, capable of ranking people in linear order, genetically based, and effectively immutable. If any of these premises are false, their entire argument collapses. For example, if all are true except immutability, then programs for early intervention in education might work to boost I.Q. permanently, just as a pair of eyeglasses may correct a genetic defect in vision. The central argument of *The Bell Curve* fails because most of the premises are false.

Herrnstein and Murray's second claim, the lightning rod for most commentary, extends the argument for innate cognitive stratification to a claim that racial differences in I.Q. are mostly determined by genetic causes—small differences for Asian superiority over Caucasian, but large for Caucasians over people of African descent. This argument is as old as the study of race, and is almost surely fallacious. The last generation's discussion centered on Arthur Jensen's 1980 book *Bias in Mental Testing* (far more elaborate and varied than anything presented in *The Bell Curve,* and therefore still a better source for grasping the argument and its problems), and on the cranky advocacy of William Shockley, a Nobel Prize-winning physicist. The central fallacy in using the substantial heritability of within-group I.Q. (among whites, for example) as an explanation of average differences between groups (whites versus blacks, for example) is now well known and acknowledged by all, including Herrnstein and Murray, but deserves a re-statement by example. Take a trait that is far more heritable than anyone has ever claimed I.Q. to be but is politically uncontroversial—body height. Suppose that I measure the heights of adult males in a poor Indian village beset with nutritional deprivation, and suppose the average height of adult males is five feet six inches. Heritability within the village is high, which is to say that tall fathers (they may average five feet eight inches) tend to have tall sons, while short fathers (five feet four inches on average) tend to have short sons. But this high heritability within the village does not mean that better nutrition might not raise average height to five feet ten inches in a few generations. Similarly, the well-documented fifteen-point average difference in I.Q. between blacks and whites

in America, with substantial heritability of I.Q. in family lines within each group, permits no automatic conclusion that truly equal opportunity might not raise the black average enough to equal or surpass the white mean.

Disturbing as I find the anachronism of *The Bell Curve,* I am even more distressed by its pervasive disingenuousness. The authors omit facts, misuse statistical methods, and seem unwilling to admit the consequences of their own words.

> *The Bell Curve* is extraordinarily one-dimensional. It makes no attempt to survey the range of available data, and pays astonishingly little attention to the rich and informative history of its contentious subject.
>
> —*Stephen Jay Gould*

The ocean of publicity that has engulfed *The Bell Curve* has a basis in what Murray and Herrnstein, in an article in *The New Republic* last month, call "the flashpoint of intelligence as a public topic: the question of genetic differences between the races." And yet, since the day of the book's publication, Murray (Herrnstein died a month before the book appeared) has been temporizing, and denying that race is an important subject in the book at all; he blames the press for unfairly fanning these particular flames. In *The New Republic* he and Herrnstein wrote, "Here is what we hope will be our contribution to the discussion. We put it in italics; if we could, we would put it in neon lights: *The answer doesn't much matter.*"

Fair enough, in the narrow sense that any individual may be a rarely brilliant member of an averagely dumb group (and therefore not subject to judgment by the group mean), but Murray cannot deny that *The Bell Curve* treats race as one of two major topics, with each given about equal space; nor can he pretend that strongly stated claims about group differences have no political impact in a society obsessed with the meanings and consequences of ethnicity. The very first sentence of *The Bell Curve*'s preface acknowledges that the book treats the two subjects equally: "This book is about differences in intellectual capacity among people and groups and what those differences mean for America's future." And Murray and Herrnstein's *New Republic* article begins by identifying racial differences as the key subject of interest: "The private dialogue about race in America is far different from the public one."

Furthermore, Herrnstein and Murray know and acknowledge the critique of extending the substantial heritability of within-group I.Q. to explain differences between groups, so they must construct an admittedly circumstantial case for attributing most of the black-white mean difference to irrevocable genetics—while properly stressing that the average difference doesn't help in judging any particular person, because so many individual blacks score above the white mean in I.Q. Quite apart from the rhetorical dubiety of this old ploy in a shopworn genre—"Some of my best friends are Group X"—Herrnstein and Murray violate fairness by converting a complex case that can yield only agnosticism into a biased brief for permanent and heritable difference. They impose this spin by turning every straw on their side into an oak, while mentioning but downplaying the strong circumstantial case for substantial malleability and little average genetic difference. This case includes such evidence as impressive I.Q. scores for poor black children adopted into affluent and intellectual homes; average I.Q. increases in some nations since the Second World War equal to the entire fifteen-point difference now separating blacks and whites in America; and failure to find any cognitive differences between two cohorts of children born out of wedlock to German women, reared in Germany as Germans, but fathered by black and white American soldiers.

The Bell Curve is even more disingenuous in its argument than in its obfuscation about race. The book is a rhetorical masterpiece of scientism, and it benefits from the particular kind of fear that numbers impose on nonprofessional commentators. It runs to eight hundred and forty-five pages, including more than a hundred pages of appendixes filled with figures. So the text looks complicated, and reviewers shy away with a knee-jerk claim that, while they suspect fallacies of argument, they really cannot judge. In the same issue of *The New Republic* as Murray and Herrnstein's article, Mickey Kaus writes, "As a lay reader of *The Bell Curve*, I'm unable to judge fairly," and Leon Wieseltier adds, "Murray, too, is hiding the hardness of his politics behind the hardness of his science. And his science, for all I know, is soft. . . . Or so I imagine. I am not a scientist. I know nothing about psychometrics." And Peter Passell, in the *Times:* "But this reviewer is not a biologist, and will leave the argument to experts."

The book is in fact extraordinarily one-dimensional. It makes no attempt to survey the range of available data, and pays astonishingly little attention to the rich and informative history of its contentious subject. (One can only recall Santayana's dictum, now a cliché of intellectual life: "Those who cannot remember the past are condemned to repeat it.") Virtually all the analysis rests on a single technique applied to a single set of data—probably done in one computer run. (I do agree that the authors have used the most appropriate technique and the best source of information. Still, claims as broad as those advanced in *The Bell Curve* simply cannot be properly defended—that is, either supported or denied—by such a restricted approach.) The blatant errors and inadequacies of *The Bell Curve* could be picked up by lay reviewers if only they would not let themselves be frightened by numbers—for Herrnstein and Murray do write clearly, and their mistakes are both patent and accessible.

While disclaiming his own ability to judge, Mickey Kaus, in *The New Republic,* does correctly identify the authors' first two claims that are absolutely essential "to make the pessimistic 'ethnic difference' argument work": "(1) that there is a single, general measure of mental ability; (2) that

the I.Q. tests that purport to measure this ability . . . aren't culturally biased."

Nothing in *The Bell Curve* angered me more than the authors' failure to supply any justification for their central claim, the sine qua non of their entire argument: that the number known as *g,* the celebrated "general factor" of intelligence, first identified by the British psychologist Charles Spearman, in 1904, captures a real property in the head. Murray and Herrnstein simply declare that the issue has been decided, as in this passage from their *New Republic* article: "Among the experts, it is by now beyond much technical dispute that there is such a thing as a general factor of cognitive ability on which human beings differ and that this general factor is measured reasonably well by a variety of standardized tests, best of all by I.Q. tests designed for that purpose." Such a statement represents extraordinary obfuscation, achievable only if one takes "expert" to mean "that group of psychometricians working in the tradition of *g* and its avatar I.Q." The authors even admit that there are three major schools of psychometric interpretation and that only one supports their view of *g* and I.Q.

But this issue cannot be decided, or even understood, without discussing the key and only rationale that has maintained *g* since Spearman invented it: factor analysis. The fact that Herrnstein and Murray barely mention the factor-analytic argument forms a central indictment of *The Bell Curve* and is an illustration of its vacuousness. How can the authors base an eight-hundred-page book on a claim for the reality of I.Q. as measuring a genuine, and largely genetic, general cognitive ability—and then hardly discuss, either pro or con, the theoretical basis for their certainty?

Admittedly, factor analysis is a difficult mathematical subject, but it can be explained to lay readers with a geometrical formulation developed by L. L. Thurstone, an American psychologist, in the nineteen-thirties and used by me in a full chapter on factor analysis in my 1981 book *The Mismeasure of Man.* A few paragraphs cannot suffice for adequate explanation, so, although I offer some sketchy hints below, readers should not question their own I.Q. s if the topic still seems arcane.

In brief, a person's performance on various mental tests tends to be positively correlated—that is, if you do well on one kind of test, you tend to do well on the other kinds. This is scarcely surprising, and is subject to interpretation that is either purely genetic (that an innate thing in the head boosts all performances) or purely environmental (that good books and good childhood nutrition boost all performances); the positive correlations in themselves say nothing about causes. The results of these tests can be plotted on a multidimensional graph with an axis for each test. Spearman used factor analysis to find a single dimension—which he called g—that best identifies the common factor behind positive correlations among the tests. But Thurstone later showed that g could be made to disappear by simply rotating the dimensions to different positions. In one rotation Thurstone placed the dimensions near the most widely separated attributes among the tests, thus giving rise to the theory of multiple intelligences (verbal, mathematical, spatial, etc., with no overarching g). This theory (which I support) has been advocated by many prominent psychometricians, including J. P. Guilford, in the nineteen-fifties, and Howard Gardner today. In this perspective, g cannot have inherent reality, for it emerges in one form of mathematical representation for correlations among tests and disappears (or greatly attenuates) in other forms, which are entirely equivalent in amount of information explained. In any case, you can't grasp the issue at all without a clear exposition of factor analysis—and *The Bell Curve* cops out on this central concept.

As for Kaus's second issue, cultural bias, the presentation of it in *The Bell Curve* matches Arthur Jensen's and that of other hereditarians, in confusing a technical (and proper) meaning of "bias" (I call it "S-bias," for "statistical") with the entirely different vernacular concept (I call it "V-bias") that provokes popular debate. All these authors swear up and down (and I agree with them completely) that the tests are not biased—in the statistician's definition. Lack of S-bias means that the same score, when it is achieved by members of different groups, predicts the same thing; that is, a black person and a white person with identical scores will have the same probabilities for doing anything that I.Q. is supposed to predict.

But V-bias, the source of public concern, embodies an entirely different issue, which, unfortunately, uses the same word. The public wants to know whether blacks average 85 and whites 100 because society treats blacks unfairly—that is, whether lower black scores record biases in this social sense. And this crucial question (to which we do not know the answer) cannot be addressed by a demonstration that S-bias doesn't exist, which is the only issue analyzed, however correctly, in *The Bell Curve.*

The book is also suspect in its use of statistics. As I mentioned, virtually all its data derive from one analysis—a plotting, by a technique called multiple regression, of the social behaviors that agitate us, such as crime, unemployment, and births out of wedlock (known as dependent variables), against both I.Q. and parental socioeconomic status (known as independent variables). The authors first hold I.Q. constant and consider the relationship of social behaviors to parental socioeconomic status. They then hold socioeconomic status constant and consider the relationship of the same social behaviors to I.Q. In general, they find a higher correlation with I.Q. than with socioeconomic status; for example, people with low I.Q. are more likely to drop out of high school than people whose parents have low socioeconomic status.

But such analyses must engage two issues—the form and the strength of the relationship—and Herrnstein and Murray discuss only the issue that seems to support their viewpoint, while virtually ignoring (and in one key passage almost willfully hiding) the other. Their numerous graphs present only the form of the relationships; that is, they draw the regression curves of their variables against I.Q. and parental socioeconomic status. But, in violation of all statistical norms that I've ever learned, they plot *only* the regression curve and do not show the scatter of variation around the curve, so their graphs do not show anything about the strength of the relationships—that is, the

amount of variation in social factors explained by I.Q. and socioeconomic status. Indeed, almost all their relationships are weak: very little of the variation in social factors is explained by either independent variable (though the form of this small amount of explanation does lie in their favored direction). In short, their own data indicate that I.Q. is not a major factor in determining variation in nearly all the social behaviors they study—and so their conclusions collapse, or at least become so greatly attenuated that their pessimism and conservative social agenda gain no significant support.

Herrnstein and Murray actually admit as much in one crucial passage, but then they hide the pattern. They write, "It [cognitive ability] almost always explains less than 20 percent of the variance, to use the statistician's term, usually less than 10 percent and often less than 5 percent. What this means in English is that you cannot predict what a given person will do from his I.Q. score. . . . On the other hand, despite the low association at the individual level, large differences in social behavior separate groups of people when the groups differ intellectually on the average." Despite this disclaimer, their remarkable next sentence makes a strong casual claim. "We will argue that intelligence itself, not just its correlation with socioeconomic status, is responsible for these group differences." But a few per cent of statistical determination is not causal explanation. And the case is even worse for their key genetic argument, since they claim a heritability of about sixty per cent for I.Q., so to isolate the strength of genetic determination by Herrnstein and Murray's own criteria you must nearly halve even the few per cent they claim to explain.

My charge of disingenuousness receives its strongest affirmation in a sentence tucked away on the first page of Appendix 4, page 593: the authors state, "In the text, we do not refer to the usual measure of goodness of fit for multiple regressions, R^2, but they are presented here for the cross-sectional analyses." Now, why would they exclude from the text, and relegate to an appendix that very few people will read, or even consult, a number that, by their own admission, is "the usual measure of goodness of fit"? I can only conclude that they did not choose to admit in the main text the extreme weakness of their vaunted relationships.

Herrnstein and Murray's correlation coefficients are generally low enough by themselves to inspire lack of confidence. (Correlation coefficients measure the strength of linear relationships between variables; the positive values run from 0.0 for no relationship to 1.0 for perfect linear relationship.) Although low figures are not atypical for large social-science surveys involving many variables, most of Herrnstein and Murray's correlations are very weak—often in the 0.2 to 0.4 range. Now, 0.4 may sound respectably strong, but—and this is the key point—R^2 is the square of the correlation coefficient, and the square of a number between zero and one is less than the number itself, so a 0.4 correlation yields an r-squared of only .16. In Appendix 4, then, one discovers that the vast majority of the conventional measures of R^2, excluded from the main body of the text, are less than 0.1. These very low values of R^2 expose the true weakness, in any meaningful vernacular sense, of nearly all the relationships that form the meat of *The Bell Curve.*

Like so many conservative ideologues who rail against the largely bogus ogre of suffocating political correctness, Herrnstein and Murray claim that they only want a hearing for unpopular views so that truth will out. And here, for once, I agree entirely. As a card-carrying First Amendment (near) absolutist, I applaud the publication of unpopular views that some people consider dangerous. I am delighted that *The Bell Curve* was written—so that its errors could be exposed, for Herrnstein and Murray are right to point out the difference between public and private agendas on race, and we must struggle to make an impact on the private agendas as well. But *The Bell Curve* is scarcely an academic treatise in social theory and population genetics. It is a manifesto of conservative ideology; the book's inadequate and biased treatment of data displays its primary purpose—advocacy. The text evokes the dreary and scary drumbeat of claims associated with conservative think tanks: reduction or elimination of welfare, ending or sharply curtailing affirmative action in schools and workplaces, cutting back Head Start and other forms of preschool education, trimming programs for the slowest learners and applying those funds to the gifted. (I would love to see more attention paid to talented students, but not at this cruel price.)

The penultimate chapter presents an apocalyptic vision of a society with a growing underclass permanently mired in the inevitable sloth of their low I.Q.s. They will take over our city centers, keep having illegitimate babies (for many are too stupid to practice birth control), and ultimately require a kind of custodial state, more to keep them in check—and out of high-I.Q. neighborhoods—than to realize any hope of an amelioration, which low I.Q. makes impossible in any case. Herrnstein and Murray actually write, "In short, by *custodial state,* we have in mind a high-tech and more lavish version of the Indian reservation for some substantial minority of the nation's population, while the rest of America tries to go about its business."

> *The Bell Curve* is scarcely an academic treatise in social theory and population genetics. It is a manifesto of conservative ideology; the book's inadequate and biased treatment of data displays its primary purpose—advocacy.
>
> —*Stephen Jay Gould*

The final chapter tries to suggest an alternative, but I have never read anything more almost grotesquely inadequate. Herrnstein and Murray yearn romantically for the good old days of towns and neighborhoods where all people could be given tasks of value, and self-esteem could be found for people on all steps of the I.Q. hierarchy (so Forrest Gump might collect clothing for the church raffle, while Mr. Murray and the other bright ones do the planning and keep the accounts—they have forgotten about the town Jew and the dwellers on the other side of the tracks in many of these idyllic villages). I do believe in this concept of neighborhood, and I will fight for its return. I grew up in such a place in Queens. But can anyone seriously find solutions for (rather than important palliatives of) our social ills therein?

However, if Herrnstein and Murray are wrong, and I.Q. represents not an immutable thing in the head, grading human beings on a single scale of general capacity with large numbers of custodial incompetents at the bottom, then the model that generates their gloomy vision collapses, and the wonderful variousness of human abilities, properly nurtured, reëmerges. We must fight the doctrine of *The Bell Curve* both because it is wrong and because it will, if activated, cut off all possibility of proper nurturance for everyone's intelligence. Of course, we cannot all be rocket scientists or brain surgeons, but those who can't might be rock musicians or professional athletes (and gain far more social prestige and salary thereby), while others will indeed serve by standing and waiting.

I closed my chapter in *The Mismeasure of Man* on the unreality of g and the fallacy of regarding intelligence as a single-scaled, innate thing in the head with a marvellous quotation from John Stuart Mill, well worth repeating:

> The tendency has always been strong to believe that whatever received a name must be an entity or being, having an independent existence of its own. And if no real entity answering to the name could be found, men did not for that reason suppose that none existed, but imagined that it was something particularly abstruse and mysterious.

How strange that we would let a single and false number divide us, when evolution has united all people in the recency of our common ancestry—thus undergirding with a shared humanity that infinite variety which custom can never stale. E pluribus unum.

Andrew Ross   (review date 29 November 1994)

SOURCE: "Demography Is Destiny," in *The Village Voice*, Vol. XXXIX, No. 48, November 29, 1994, pp. 95-6.

[*In the following excerpt from a review of* The Bell Curve *and Robert T. Michael's* Sex in America, *Ross contends that the authors of the former have deliberately ignited racial controversies and questions their assessment of the relationship between genetics and intelligence.*]

The recent elections provided a brief respite from the platitude that politics are stage-managed entirely by cyborg pollsters and media spin surgeons. Left and right seem to be persuaded that an electoral swing of such proportions cannot be attributed wholly to the PR industry's numbers game, and that it must be related somehow to "values." This may be a faulty assumption. Not because the industry *does* dominate politics—a self-serving claim by industry professionals—but because values are themselves intimately related to the numbers game. When Mr. Gingrich vents off about the values of "normal" Americans, he doesn't even *need* to wheel in the heavy artillery of statistics. The values he cites are already imbued with peoples' desire to be part of (or their fear of being excluded from) a statistical majority. Indeed, the value system of North American culture has been systematically conditioned by the quantitative principle of proportional representation. How *else* would a concept like "minority culture" mean anything? The cult of the democratic majority is our civil software, and it prints out bell curves.

For confirmation, look no further than the two great conversation sponges of the election season, *The Bell Curve* itself and *Sex in America.* The aggregate newsprint already devoted to these books would fill a shallow grave, which is where many people think *The Bell Curve,* at least, belongs. Its authors, and their providers in the hoopla press, have campaigned hard as exhumers of truths persistently buried by the gatekeepers of polite, liberal society. Lifting a taboo here, exposing a shibboleth there, waving *their* data in the air like *we* just don't care, Murray and Herrnstein have been a publicist's wet dream. The anti-incumbency mood of a mid-term election favored their posturing as disenfranchised pariahs outside the intellectual Beltway, and their book has circulated like a Willie Horton ad, raising the policy-making temperature on immigration, welfare, the balance sheet of "positive" government, remedial education, crime, multiculturalism.

No one need read it to know what it says. Only reviewers, in a caffeine-rich stupor, will have been obliged to endure its 850 pages of lightweight prose and hand-me-down statistics. (Charles Lane ably examined its sources in the December 1 *New York Review of Books.*) *The Bell Curve* belongs to a genre of publication increasingly crucial to the PR industry, which scripts political life by reducing gigabyte scholarship to the minimal fraction of political RAM needed to access the public memory. We've been aware for some time of the process which can recycle, say, a single article into several forms—book, film, soundtrack, TV series—as it passes up the food chain of culture industries owned by the same transnational company. Given the oxygen of publicity, an analogous process can transform a policy-oriented article or book into a major political speech, or even The White House's paradigm of the month. Murray first took this express elevator 10 years ago when his *Losing Ground* provided academic ammo for the second, and worse, Reaganist round of welfare rollbacks. *The Bell Curve* came made to order; its success in dominating the mediasphere shows how finely tuned the publicity machine has become.

Books such as *The Bell Curve* aim specifically to reignite race fires, and in general to consume the energies of liberals and progressives in old battles. Murray and Herrnstein's barnacled appeals to genetic determinism are no more novel than their obsession with public policy involving race. What's new is the context of these appeals—notably an emergent industrial environment driven, in part, by biotechnology and genetic medicine. Despite *The Bell Curve*'s connection of genes and intelligence, the book makes no mention of hard science, least of all the kind of molecular biology that has reinvented our thinking about genetics in recent decades. In the splice-and-dice biotech labs, genetic material no longer has the fixed, immutable status it used to occupy in the theory books of destiny. If anything, industry boosters have reveled in the claim to be able to intervene in and modify the alleged connection between genes-and-anything, thereby opening up a whole new chapter in the history of eugenics.

> **Despite *The Bell Curve*'s connection of genes and intelligence, the book makes no mention of hard science, least of all the kind of molecular biology that has reinvented our thinking about genetics.**
>
> **—*Andrew Ross***

Murray and Herrnstein have good reasons for avoiding hard science, but their adversaries do not. Virtually none of the public commentary I have read on *The Bell Curve,* or any of the numerous gene-based books to hit the shelves this fall, has cited the relevance of this industrial environment to the wholesale revival of biologic and genetic determinism currently dominating public discussion. Of course, there is no direct causal relation among how biotech stocks are doing (rather badly, as it happens, but such vacillations are native to venture capitalism), the latest press releases from the labs, and the publication of books like *The Bell Curve,* Robert Wright's *The Moral Animal,* or J. Philippe Rushton's *Race, Evolution, and Behavior.* But there's obviously some affinity between ideology and economy here. In an age when R&D in basic science is the primary motor of capital investment—and when biotechnology, in particular, has been synonymous with the promise of an economic revolution—any public interest in genes is highly serviceable to the investors' cause. Familiarity does not only breed contempt, it also produces consent.

Given Herrnstein and Murray's focus on smartness and emergent "cognitive stratification" in a postindustrial society, it's also telling that they have nothing much to say about the industrial environment of information technology. Computers are designed and employed to outsmart knowledge workers, appropriating the functions of intelligent labor in much the same way as industrial machinery appropriated the skills and artisan know-how of manual workers and tradespeople. At the very moment that *The Bell Curve*'s cognitive elite is supposed to be assuming power, smartness is passing out of the human domain; it is increasingly an attribute of technology itself. The deindustrialization of wage labor that underpinned this transition took a heavy toll: the decimation of stable, working-class and middle-class employment, the deepening of class polarization, and the appearance of an informal economy shaped by racially inflected policies. Murray and Herrnstein have no time for such socioeconomic explanations. For them, the fact that poverty levels have barely budged since 1969 has nothing to do with top-down economic restructuring, it is simply the result of inheritable "cognitive disadvantages" combined with the increasing market value of intelligence.

Unlike Daniel Bell, who once forecast the benign rule of intelligence over capital, Murray and Herrnstein are not so enamored of the new smart elite. Ventriloquizing a page or two from the Great Book of Populism, *The Bell Curve* agonizes over the growing power of a smart affluent caste—one isolated from a dumbed-down populace they will learn to fear and resent, and immune to the traditional opposition of the intelligentsia, with whom they are destined to make a big-brained alliance. Well, the fact that CEOs are more educated these days may be something to worry about; capitalism will doubtless become even more efficient, i. e., ruthless. As for the intelligentsia, I honestly don't think we're going to see too many marriages of convenience between habitués of the Bohemian Grove and Ph.D.s from History of Consciousness programs—although the success of *The Bell Curve* will surely spawn many more unlikely alliances of the sort that brought together an IQ quack like Herrnstein and a welfare-basher like Murray.

Most disturbing to Murray and Herrnstein is their vision of a near-future "custodial state" featuring "a high-tech and more lavish version of the Indian reservation for some substantial minority of the nation's population," who will have become "permanent wards of the state" through welfare dependency. In the custodial state, it will finally be proved that inequalities related to genetic endowment can never be overcome. Murray and Herrnstein's recommendations: abandon all welfare and education programs aimed at the disadvantaged, institute a draconian immigration policy, and encourage rich women to have more babies. This is, of course, nothing but smelly old eugenics, scented with the statistical bouquet of dark-side social science.

Slightly more original is *The Bell Curve*'s version of conservative multiculturalism. Just as its authors put a right-wing spin on populist and left critiques of credentialism, so too they offer a racist gloss on radical claims to cultural justice based on some principle of "difference." They call it "wise ethnocentrism." It appeals to cultural difference as much as to biology, and we are likely to see more and more of it. Ethnic minority groups, Murray and Herrnstein argue, should be released from the injunction to assimilate, and should be encouraged to protect and sustain their "clannish" self-esteem. Cultures are different, they should remain so, and there is no need to compare one with another. Best not to mix at all, really. This new segregationism masquerades as tolerance for human variation.

Behind it lurks Murray's hankering after a Jeffersonian natural aristocracy and a caste order where everyone has a place and perceives that place to be a comfort zone. He insists that the only way to effect such a society is to change our value system by eradicating every last vestige of Jacobin faith in egalitarianism. Liberal guilt will be released like the gas of a balloon. Everyone will then cheerfully accept their point of distribution on the bell curves

of life. The gene pool, presumably, will replace the safety net.

As far as their book's impact on public consciousness goes, it doesn't matter much that Murray and Herrnstein's working definitions of "race" are at once hokey and Neanderthal. (They can be as bag-headed about white ethnicity as any other. In *The New Republic* they wrote, "The Scotch-Irish who moved to America tended to be cantankerous, restless, and violent.") When push comes to shove, they know that enough white people need the respectable cover of social science to vindicate their own racism. Murray and Herrnstein need not create a case, they need only reinforce racist perceptions already in the daily mind and hammered into policy-gab by the neoliberal likes of Senator Moynihan, who has recently been spouting nonsense about "speciation" among welfare clients.

Nor does it matter whether they come anywhere near to resolving that old chestnut—the exact ratio of genes: environment that is responsible for our social behavior (between 40 per cent and 80 per cent is genetic in their final estimate). If any of it is genetic, they say, then the whole situation is quite intractable, a thesis that makes the bulk of their book quite redundant. Welcome to the New Darwinism. If nothing else, *The Bell Curve* finally explains the meaning of Beavis and Butt-head: only white guys could be that stupid and still be alive. Forrest Gump? My point precisely.

A third of the way through the book, we are introduced to the people Murray likes to patronize: the good, middle-class citizen "that forms the spine of the typical American community, filling the seats at PTA meetings and the pews at church." . . .

Insofar as "the permissive society" still has meaning today, the winds of approval are blowing in the opposite direction. *The Bell Curve* and *Sex in America* are . . . gelid reminders that the permissions currently being issued are designed to reinstall racism and sexual conformity as the truly great American passions.

Gregg Easterbrook   (essay date December 1994)

SOURCE: "The Case Against *The Bell Curve*," in *The Washington Monthly*, Vol. 26, No. 12, December, 1994, pp. 17-25.

[*In the following essay, Easterbrook examines the intelligence data used in* The Bell Curve *and contends that it should "be seen as a tract advocating a political point of view, not a detached assessment of research."*]

Years ago, hoping to persuade this publication to hire me, I quit a decent job in Chicago and moved to Washington. Unemployed and low on money, I lived in a seedy neighborhood behind the Navy Yard in Southeast D.C. Because the editor of this magazine unaccountably took his time in acknowledging my merit as an applicant, to blow off steam I played basketball on the local court several hours each day. I was the only white player in the game, accepted at first as a charity case. After a few weeks on the blacktop, however, I was startled to discover other players wanting me on their team. After two months of daily basketball, I found myself able to hold my own in one-on-one matches against the hot players from nearby Eastern High School. I was squaring my shoulders for accurate jump shots, ducking under other players for layups—the sorts of coordinated, classy-looking moves I had never been able to do before and have not been able to do since.

It would hardly be a wild guess that practice had improved my game, and that lack of practice has since eroded it. Charles Murray and the late Richard Herrnstein would say, however, I had suddenly acquired basketball genes. Then just as suddenly, I lost them!

The Bell Curve should be seen not as racist or violating a taboo, but simply as an attempt to torment data to make it support a right-wing agenda.

—Gregg Easterbrook

Page after page of obstruent data and marching columns of Pearson correlations in the new book **The Bell Curve** by Murray and Herrnstein, which holds that success in life is mainly determined by inherited IQ and that statistically significant differences in inherited intellect exist among the races, imply that the issues at play in the IQ dispute are so sophisticated only readers of high intelligence can grasp them. This isn't so. Most common-sense aspects of the IQ debate are more significant than the statistical motes and jots—and being much better understood, are a sounder basis for social policy. The complex statistical claims of **The Bell Curve** have received extensive notice in initial reactions to the work. In the end the book's common-sense faults are more telling. Blacktop basketball offers an entry point for understanding why.

The reverse of the notion that blacks are born with less intelligence than whites is that blacks are born with more athletic potential. Well-meaning people who believe that whites are smarter than blacks often quickly add, "But look at how gifted blacks are physically," citing the undeniable black dominance of basketball. Yet if blacks have superior innate athletic ability, why are hockey, tennis, and many other lucrative sports largely dominated by whites? As the writer Farai Chideya will show in a forthcoming book, of the approximately 71,000 Americans who earn livings from sports (broadly defined to include golfers, skaters, and so on), only 10 percent are black.

A likely explanation for black success in basketball is not some mystically powerful jumping gene—natural selection may have favored strength and size in people, but what are the odds it ever favored jumping? —but that many blacks practice the sport intensely. For good or ill, thousands of black kids spend several hours per day through their youth playing basketball. By the time age 18 is reached, it shows: In general, blacks are really good at basketball. Meanwhile, hockey and tennis are usually

practiced in youth by whites, who in turn dominate these sports.

In all the complex arguments about inheritability and environment in IQ, the mundane, common-sense question of practice time is often overlooked. Other things being equal, what you practice is what you're good at. As Charles Darwin once wrote to his cousin Francis Galton, founder of the eugenics movement: "I have always maintained that, excepting fools, men [do] not differ much in intellect, only in zeal and hard work."

As a longtime basketball-league participant and a mediocre small-college football player, I have spent a notable portion of my life being knocked down, run past, and otherwise outperformed by black athletes. None ever struck me as possessing any mystical genetic athletic ability, though it may be that as a group they hold some small edge over whites. What often does strike me as a black basketball player in a pick-up game hits his shot and I miss mine is the thought: "He's taken that shot maybe five million times in his life, and I've taken it maybe five thousand." It's safe to say that if there had been no color barrier to college basketball in the 1940s and 1950s, blacks would not have dominated in those years, because at that time few blacks practiced basketball as much as the best white players of the period. By coincidence, the week before **The Bell Curve** was published, the "Science Times" section of *The New York Times* ran a prominent article on new research showing that the most accomplished violinists and other artistic performers spend significantly more time practicing than the less accomplished—though presumably they enjoy the advantage of genetic gifts. There seemed to me a pellucid connection between this research and the Herrnstein-Murray thesis.

Another missed connection concerns a 1990 flap at the University of California at Berkeley. There, a tenured anthropologist, Vincent Sarich, began to say that black success in basketball proved the inherited basis of talent, which in turn supported the view that whites could inherit superior mental faculties. Sarich's argument is revealingly faulty: He would tell classes that "There is no white Michael Jordan . . . nor has there ever been one." Actually there *was* a white Michael Jordan—the late Pete Maravich. Maravich scored much more than Jordan in college and had the same league-leading scoring average in the NBA, 31 points per game. Maravich had the same ability as Jordan to throw the no-look pass, to dunk in ways that appeared to defy certain laws of physics, and so on. Jordan became a sports legend because his college and pro teams were champions; this happened because Jordan was a highly disciplined defensive performer and an astute judge of the court situation. Maravich, in contrast, became something of a standing joke, even to sportswriters eager for white stars, because his teams always lost. Maravich was a hopelessly selfish performer, inert on defense and he never passed up a shot. The comparison between Jordan and Maravich both defies the stereotype of the white player as disciplined and the black player as the gunner, and undermines the notion of black genetic dominance generally.

So if white kids as a group spend more time practicing

schoolwork, should we then be surprised that they score better on school-related tests? Herrnstein and Murray acknowledge that 150 hours of extra study will raise the typical student's SAT score by 40 points—a commonsense confirmation that scholastic practice makes for scholastic success. True, the score-boosting effects of extra study on SAT tests reach a plateau beyond which further practice adds little. Yet seeing that behavior (study time) alters brain-test outcome, and then concluding as *The Bell Curve* does that brain performance is mainly genetic, is an inverted form of the logic that Stalin's favorite scientist, Trofim Lysenko, employed to contend that genetic characteristics are acquired during a person's life. That many white kids may spend more hours studying than many black kids may well be an argument that some minority parents are negligent in compelling their children to hit the books. But this is an argument about environment, not inheritance.

It is not racist for Herrnstein and Murray to study whether there are differences in inherited IQ. Some commentators have attempted to reject *The Bell Curve* out of hand on grounds of racism, and thereby avoid dealing with its discomfiting contentions. Yet obviously people talk about the mental abilities of various groups, usually in whispers; better to talk about this in the open. For this reason, in my affiliation with *The Atlantic Monthly*, I favored that magazine's publication of some of Herrnstein's earlier work. I agreed with the decision of *The New Republic* to put an excerpt from *The Bell Curve* on its cover. And I am glad Herrnstein and Murray (the principal author) wrote *The Bell Curve*, which is not a racist work, though it is fantastically wrong-headed. Bringing the arguments about race, inheritance, and IQ out into the open in Murray's straightforward writing style is a useful service—especially because the more you know about this line of thought, the less persuasive it becomes.

Now, other objections to *The Bell Curve*, concentrating on those not already raised by other commentators:

The Hollywood corollary. Perhaps black overrepresentation in basketball is essentially a fluke telling nothing about the general relationship between practice and achievement. Yet consider that blacks are also overrepresented in several performing arts, notably singing and comedy. Is this because they have superior singing and joking genes? It's hard to imagine why natural selection would have favored DNA for human song. On the other hand, African Americans as a group have spent generations learning various forms of performance. Most African culture is oral; and until recent decades, owing both to discrimination and poverty, when American blacks wanted entertainment they had to entertain each other. That is, they practiced song and comedy, and they got good at it.

Is everybody too dumb to know who's smart? In *The Bell Curve* there are numerous assertions that society has handicapped itself by failing to favor the smart. For instance, the book asserts that the American economy loses as much as $80 billion per year because a 1971 Supreme Court decision bars most forms of workplace IQ testing. High-IQ workers are more productive, Herrnstein and

Murray say; promoting them would increase productivity. But if high-IQ employees are more productive, that should be self-evident to employers regardless of tests. Are employers so dumb they don't promote the productive workers? On a commonsense basis, society has long been attuned to what can be accomplished by the smart, and almost always rewards this already.

The Hiram College contradiction. Early in *The Bell Curve* comes a section describing how in the fifties the freshman class at Harvard was not composed exclusively of the brightest of the bright; many were slow-witted kids entering on Dad-um's alumni connections. This was actually to the good, Murray writes, because it meant that many bright kids who otherwise would have been consolidated at Harvard instead had no choice but to attend Hiram or Kenyon or some other school, distributing IQ throughout society. These days, *The Bell Curve* says, owing to accurate SAT testing (which is now quite accurate, but only so far as it goes), Harvard gets the brightest of the bright, withdrawing the "cognitive elite" into a small, isolated world. This, the book says, is bad.

Yet later, in a section assailing affirmative action (*The Bell Curve* really despises affirmative action), Murray says that offering special admissions consideration to minority students is awful because it denies some worthy white students entry slots in the top schools. But isn't the effect that a percentage of smart kids end up at Hiram and Kenyon, distributing IQ throughout society? When some smart white kids were denied admission to Harvard because the sons of the landed had a special deal—in other words, when there was a patrician system that favored the affluent—that was great, according to *The Bell Curve.* Now that some smart white kids are denied admission to Harvard because the sons and daughters of *poverty* have a special deal—the new system no longer rigged in favor of the affluent—that's offensive, according to the same book.

Those inherited differences that have been confirmed are small. It's obvious that there exist inheritable physical differences among racial groups. But all such differences are too minor to mean anything, except as sources of the many forms of prejudice. Perhaps there are inherited mental differences among racial groups, but the observed pattern in physical differences suggests any mental differences would also be too minor to matter in practical terms. For instance, African Americans are on average about an inch and a half taller than Caucasian Americans. This distinction is real but just too small to make a difference except in highly competitive situations like, say, entry into the small number of slots in the National Basketball Association: There, a competition between two players of otherwise equal skills might end in the taller being selected. Similarly, suppose there really are on average a few points of difference between whites and blacks in IQ. This is too little to matter in practical terms, except in highly competitive situations like, say, entry into the small number of clerkships to the Supreme Court, where an extra margin of IQ might carry the day.

If this stuff is really true, it's whites that ought to feel inferior. The same IQ tests that Murray says show blacks one "standard deviation" (in this case, very roughly 15 percent) less smart than whites show white children duller than Asian-American children by almost the same margin. Simple-minded me might say that is mainly because of the phenomenal (probably excessive) study time many Asian-American parents impose on their kids. But if genes are the IQ destiny that *The Bell Curve* asserts, shouldn't whites be maneuvering to protect themselves against Asians, given that Asians already out-number Caucasians worldwide? Instead, nearly all of the book's prescriptive material focuses on reasons to retaliate politically against blacks: end affirmative action, shift money from compensatory education programs like Head Start to programs for the "gifted" (that is, white students), scale back welfare.

What's the mechanism? All human beings are physically similar because they share a line of descent and have all been subject to about the same "selection pressure" from evolution. For there to be significant inherent mental differences among racial groups, there would have to have been significantly different selection pressure. Scientists call this the "What's the mechanism?" question. Any researcher claiming to have found a substantial genetic difference among similar creatures is expected to propose a selection mechanism by which the differential arose.

Early in *The Bell Curve* controversy, *The New York Times* ran an op-ed article asserting that from an evolutionary standpoint, differential intellect among human groups could not have evolved in fewer than "hundreds of thousands of years." This is weak science: Most recent discoveries tend to support the notion that natural selection can operate relatively quickly in geologic terms. So differential intellect is not precluded. Yet neither Herrnstein and Murray nor any credentialed believer in the brain-gene theory has suggested how, on an evolutionary basis, black and white intelligence DNA could have diverged significantly.

The sole researcher asserting a hypothesis in this category is J. Philippe Rushton, a psychologist at the University of Western Ontario. *The Bell Curve* makes a point of praising Rushton as "not . . . a crackpot." But a crackpot is precisely what Rushton is. He believes that among males of African, European, and Asian descent, intellect and genital size are inversely proportional, and that evolution dictated this outcome in an as-yet-undetermined manner. Sound like something the 16-year-olds at your high school believed? That should not stop Rushton or any researcher from wondering if there might have been different selection pressures on different racial groups. But Rushton's "research" methods, defended by *The Bell Curve* as academically sound, are preposterous. For instance, Rushton has conducted surveys at shopping malls, asking men of different races how far their ejaculate travels. His theory is the farther the gush, the lower the IQ. Set aside the evolutionary absurdity of this. (Are we to presume that in prehistory low-IQ males were too dumb to find pleasure in full penetration, so their sperm had to evolve rocket-propelled arcs? Give me a break.) Consider only the "research" standard here. Is it possible that one man in a hundred actually knows, with statistical accuracy, the average

distance traveled by his ejaculate? Yet *The Bell Curve* takes Rushton in full seriousness.

Are the natives doltish as well as restless? Herrnstein and Murray note that not only do African-Americans score somewhat below white Americans on IQ tests but tribal black Africans score significantly low even in pure-logic tests designed to correct for language differences. (Mazes and so on.) Though many claims of cultural bias are exaggerated by the we're-all-victims lobby, here IQ tests would be expected to be of little reliability, considering the gulf between cultures as different as those of the United States and tribal Africa. Yet *The Bell Curve* takes the low scores of tribal Africans in earnest, implying this proves the existence of an entire continent of morons.

Just what mechanism of selection pressure would have caused this wide disparity? The authors do not say, gliding past this and all other complications of genetic science. More, they make a tee-hee implication, citing IQ scores among South African "coloureds," that American blacks are smarter than African blacks because of interbreeding with whites. Objection One: If black-white interbreeding in North America were substantial enough to transfer the presumed white intellect to the black gene pool, would not the same process have transferred the presumed black athletic gifts to the white gene pool, leading to an NBA dominated by guys named Blaine and Todd? Objection Two: Though geologic time would probably not be required for differential intellect to arise if a selection mechanism could be shown, a couple of centuries seems insufficient. That is, unions between whites and blacks since colonial times would be unlikely to account for African-Americans doing substantially better on IQ tests than tribal black Africans. The exposure of African-Americans to an educational system teaching (as it should) book-based culture would, on the other hand, explain it pretty neatly.

Geneticists don't claim genes explain IQ. "The people who say intelligence is genetic are the ones with no training in genetics," says Evan Balaban, a former professor of evolutionary biology at Harvard and now a fellow at The Neurosciences Institute, a research organization. Murray is a social scientist; Herrnstein was a psychologist. Balaban continues: "Any serious biologist would be horrified by the idea of using the little we know about genes as the basis for social policy. Current genetic research cannot even explain how basic body parts form." Nearly all contemporary discoveries about human genetics concern only markers or genes associated with protein coding, vastly less complicated than a developmental trait like intellect.

Troy Duster, a sociologist at the University of California at Berkeley who has studied the history of claims of inherited intellectual inferiority, notes that, "Since the turn of the century the people making political assertions about population genetics always reason backwards from the phenotype [observed trait] to the presence of a gene. This is the reverse of the way molecular biology reasons. Since molecular biologists have discovered genes for diseases like cystic fibrosis and Tay Sachs, the public has begun to believe biologists already understand the human genome. People like Herrnstein and Murray use the halo effect of that belief to give their views a sheen of modern genetics, when in truth their assertions run counter to what can be supported by modern genetics." I called prominent molecular biologists at Harvard, MIT, Penn State, Stanford, and the University of Washington, and all asserted that the notion of a traceable gene line for intelligence has no grounding in present research.

Telling in this regard is *The Bell Curve*'s misunderstanding of Mendelian genetics. The authors treat inheritance from parents as if it could be charted in straight lines: Smart parents A beget smart kids B, etc. This is a common blunder. Trait-inheritance charts more often look like zigzags, as phenotypes bounce around among offspring and may skip entire generations. Two red-haired parents may have two brunette children, each of whom in turn have one red- and one black-haired child, and so on. Herrnstein and Murray allude in a few sentences to the common outcome that the children of very bright parents may be only somewhat above average in intellect, but otherwise depict IQ as reliably passed through the generations in straight-line fashion. If IQ does pass down generations in straight lines, then the cause must be mainly the environment families create, since genetic traits don't express so predictably.

If IQ does pass down generations in straight lines, then the cause must be mainly the environment families create, since genetic traits don't express so predictably.

—*Gregg Easterbrook*

Nonsense dysgenics. A substantial doom section of *The Bell Curve* is devoted to "dysgenics," the reverse of eugenics—the fear that high fertility rates among those of low mental prowess will swamp society with dumbness. At least since Malthus, this has been a belief of the privileged classes whose concerns Murray and Herrnstein hold foremost. It was the central fear of Darwin's cousin Galton, and was a reputable paranoia among the educated in the United States as recently as the years when the Nazi use of eugenics became known. Even Norman Thomas, the most important American socialist of this century, in the thirties denounced the high rate of fertility among "those of a definitely inferior stock."

Yet during the very century in which, *The Bell Curve* says, dysgenics has run wild globally, overall scores on IQ tests have consistently risen by decade, among blacks as well as whites. Now, how can it be that overall IQ scores are going up, yet society simultaneously is being swamped by fertile dullards? One possible explanation is that in decrying high fertility rates among low-achieving inner-city women (a problem, to be sure, though first for the women themselves), *The Bell Curve* conveniently overlooks a parallel social phenomenon: the rise of the American black middle class. Today, for every one African-American

whose life pattern fits the dysgenic nightmare, there are roughly two following the eugenics prescription—moving out of the city, having smaller families, advancing financially and scholastically. Black middle class school achievement trails comparable white numbers, but a small trailer effect seems easily explained as a remnant of segregation.

Herrnstein and Murray say little about the black middle class, a significant group which for good or ill is busily embracing suburban American norms. The authors can't deal with this factor because not only would it foul up claims of dysgenics; dealing with it forces you to confront the fact that many studies show children's IQs tend to be higher in smaller families. This is what might be expected, as other things being equal smaller families offer children more attention and have better social and economic circumstances. That's er, ahem, nurture rather than nature, which falls outside the desired conclusion of *The Bell Curve.*

Spin disguised as scholarship. The most disquieting aspect of *The Bell Curve* is its insistence on phrasing as detached data analysis what is in truth an ideological argument about social policy. Ideology regarding social policy is fine, but should be presented as such. The authors of *The Bell Curve* adapt a weary tone of "we hate these conclusions, yet as scientists we are driven to them by impartial reading of neutral data." The data they offer as impartial has, however, been elaborately scrunched to fit the desired ideological boxes.

The book's main artifice in this regard is to present the work of those researchers who do conclude that IQ is mainly inherited and is the main determinant of life outcomes (there are a few such researchers, with full credentials), then describe their studies as generally accepted or no longer seriously contested by other researchers. This is duplicitous. Most academic researchers now accept the notion that IQ tests have become reasonably fair and reasonably predict performance in school. Beyond that there exists a fantastic range of opinions about what the tests really tell you. Many credentialed academic "psychometricians" (students of IQ) come to conclusions dramatically at odds with what Herrnstein and Murray think about IQ, genes, and mental determinism, Robert Sternberg of Yale probably standing as the leading example. *The Bell Curve* makes passing reference to the existence of prominent academics who would reject its thesis, but in the main represents to readers that few researchers now contest the notion that IQ rules. This borders on intellectual dishonesty.

Spin disguised, period. Murray's work on *The Bell Curve* was underwritten by a grant from the Bradley Foundation, which *National Journal* in 1993 described as "the nation's biggest underwriter of conservative intellectual activity." Bradley is a respectable foundation about whose financial support no author need apologize. But Bradley backs only one kind of work: that with right-wing political value. For instance, Bradley is currently underwriting William Kristol. *The Bell Curve* identifies Murray as a "Bradley Fellow" but gives readers no hint of the foundation's ideological requirements. Telling readers this would, needless to say, spoil the book's pretense of objective assessment of research.

Slipping down the slope from the respectable Bradley Foundation, Herrnstein and Murray praise some research supported by the Pioneer Fund, an Aryan crank organization. Until recently, Pioneer's charter said it would award scholarships mainly to students "deemed to be descended from white persons who settled in the original 13 states." Pioneer supports Rushton and backed the "Minnesota Twins" study, which purports to find that identical twins raised apart end up similar right down to personality quirks. The Aryan crank crowd has long been entranced by the Minnesota Twins project, as it appears to show that genes for mentation are entirely deterministic. Many academics consider the protocols used by the Minnesota Twins study invalid.

Lesser examples of disguised ideological agenda are common in *The Bell Curve.* For example, at one point Murray presents an extended section on problems within the D.C. Police Department, saying their basis lies in "degradation of intellectual requirements" on officer hiring exams. Information in this section is attributed to "journalist Tucker Carlson." No one who lives in Washington doubts its police department has problems, some of which surely stem from poor screening of applicants. But who is the source for the particularly harsh version of this problem presented in *The Bell Curve*? "Journalist Tucker Carlson" turns out to be an employee of the Heritage Foundation; he is an editor of its house journal *Policy Review.* Heritage, for those who don't know it, has a rigid hard-right ideological slant. Its *Policy Review* is a lively and at times insightful publication, but anyone regarding its content as other than pamphleteering would be a fool. The article *The Bell Curve* drawn from lampoons the intelligence of D.C. police officers because some cases have been dismissed owing to illegible arrest records. And just how many high-IQ white doctors have unreadable handwriting? If an article in *Policy Review* were an impartial source of social science observations, Murray would simply come out and say where his citation originates. Instead he disguises the source, knowing full well its doctrinaire nature.

Even the worst-case claimed by the brain-gene believers just doesn't sound so bad. Herrnstein and Murray estimate that intelligence is 60 percent nature, 40 percent nurture. Since genes get the majority number here, to them this clinches the argument for inborn intellectual determinism.

But think about this worst-case—intelligence as 40 percent nurture. "Forty percent variability based on environment would make intelligence an exceptionally pliant trait," Balaban says. It's known, for example, that better nutrition can improve height—but only by a few inches, about a five percent swing based on the potential range of human statures. If IQ swings by 40 percent owing to circumstances and life experiences, then human society has more control over intelligence than virtually anything else in its genetic inheritance. Thus, even *The Bell Curve*'s own contentions would seem solid ground upon which to support further attempts to improve the school and home environments of underprivileged children.

In the end, *The Bell Curve* should be seen not as racist or violating a taboo, but simply as an attempt to torment data to make it support a right-wing agenda. That's fine so far as it goes: Right-wing ideas have as much claim on society's attention as any other kind, and some of the conclusions Herrnstein and Murray offer are surely correct ones. (They're surely correct, for example, in contending that in most cases small, stable, "legitimate" parents-wedded families are in the best interests of the child.) It is essential, however, that *The Bell Curve* be seen as a tract advocating a political point of view, not a detached assessment of research. In that regard two final common-sense objections to the book are particularly strong:

You don't have to be real smart to grasp test-score convergence. For decades black scores on IQ and aptitude tests have been converging upward toward white scores, even as white scores rise. Exceptionally high intelligence is not required to theorize that this is happening because of improved educational opportunity.

The Bell Curve makes a passing mention of black IQ score increases, calls them encouraging, then quickly switches back to doom pronouncements about genetic determinism and the feeble-mindedness of minorities and the poor. Anything more than a passing mention of black IQ test convergence would have kicked the chair out from under the premise of Herrnstein and Murray's tract. If someday black scores stop rising toward white scores, that might be alarming. But this hasn't happened yet, and until it does all the marching data in *The Bell Curve* and similar works will contain a huge common-sense defect.

Even if **The Bell Curve** *were right about genes, then it's still wrong about policy.*

It turns out that since IQ testing became common, approximately in the 1920s, the scores of American blacks have shifted upward by about two "standard deviations"—that is, about twice as much positive shift as the negative gulf Herrnstein and Murray find between whites and blacks today. But then almost every American group's IQ score has upshifted by about two standard deviations in recent decades. Blacks, whites, yellows, reds, browns: According to IQ testing, we're all getting smarter dramatically fast. The explanation would seem obvious— quality and quantity (especially number of years of schooling) of education has gone up for everybody, so everybody now does better on tests of educational aptitude. Herrnstein and Murray reject this view, saying it must be mainly genes.

Suppose they're right. If rising IQ levels are mainly genetic, then some evolutionary force must be propelling genus *Homo* in the direction of more DNA for brainpower. Modern society rewards education and mental prowess, so evolution may now be rewarding the same. (Genes do not change during life, but changing circumstances influence which genes are deemed fit and passed to offspring—this is the definition of selection pressure.) Thus if *The Bell Curve* is correct about intellect being mainly genetic, then some aspect of modern social circumstances and government policy must be encouraging or at least neutral to a fantastic wave of improvements in the human genetic endowment for IQ.

Yet *The Bell Curve* concludes by calling for drastic changes in social circumstances and government policy—the very forces which, in Herrnstein and Murray's analysis, seem to be causing natural selection to favor IQ as never before. The book ends up mired in such illogic either because its authors do not understand the science of genetics on which they pretend to premise their case, or have produced what should properly be seen as an unusually lengthy promotional brochure for a rather unattractive political package.

Charles Murray   (essay date 2 December 1994)

SOURCE: "The Real 'Bell Curve'," in *The Wall Street Journal,* Vol. CCXXIV, No. 108, December 2, 1994, p. A14.

[*In the following essay, Murray responds to the negative criticism of* The Bell Curve.]

In the past few weeks, I have found myself occasionally leafing through *The Bell Curve* to reassure myself. Richard Herrnstein and I didn't really write the book people are saying we wrote, did we? We didn't.

The Bell Curve that you have read about in most publications is unrecognizably different from *The Bell Curve* that exists. I will not try to explain why it has been so blatantly misrepresented. I suspect that answer would require profound understanding of the American preoccupation with race. But at least I can outline some of the main ways in which the public commentary has kept people from understanding what the book is and says.

1. "**The Bell Curve** *is about race.*" *The Bell Curve* is about powerful, historically driven forces working at both tails of the bell curve that are fundamentally changing American life: Unless the nation comes to grips with the effects of these forces, American democracy is in danger. These forces have nothing to do with race.

This dominant theme is reflected in the book's organization. In all, *The Bell Curve* consists of 22 chapters. The first four chapters are about the cognitive stratification of American society. The next eight are about the relationship of IQ to social pathologies among whites—a device intended specifically so that the role of IQ in such topics as unemployment, school dropouts, family formulation, parenting, and crime could be contemplated without racial complications. Only then, 269 pages into the book, comes the first discussion of ethnic differences.

In all, ethnic differences are a major topic in four of the 22 chapters. In the two concluding chapters, the ones in which Richard Herrnstein and I describe in the broadest terms where we fear the nation is headed and what might be done about it, ethnic differences in IQ are mentioned once, indirectly, in a paragraph.

2. "**The Bell Curve** *says IQ is destiny.*" What we actually said, beginning in the Introduction, is how loosely an IQ score constrains an individual's achievements in life. We

wrote: "One of the problems of writing about intelligence is how to remind readers often enough how little an IQ score tells you about whether the human being next to you is someone whom you will admire or cherish"—which certainly has proved to be prophetic—and we italicized the core statement: "*Measures of intelligence have reliable statistical relationships with important social phenomena, but they are a limited tool for deciding what to make of any given individual.*" We repeated the message throughout the book.

3. "*Herrnstein and Murray ignore evidence that doesn't fit their thesis.*" While I cannot prove in a few words that *The Bell Curve*'s scholarship is fair and accurate, a few observations are pertinent.

First, you can check many such allegations for yourself. Take any article naming studies said to refute something in the book and see if we also discuss those studies. The answer will almost always be yes. Then compare what is claimed for the studies in the putative refutation and what *The Bell Curve* says about them. You will find that we generally give them as much real credit (in terms of actual statistical results, not the puffery) as is claimed for them in the critiques of the book.

Second, it should be remembered that Richard J. Herrnstein was one of the most respected psychologists of his generation. Aside from his pathbreaking work on rational choice theory, and aside from holding Harvard's oldest chair in psychology (he followed B.F. Skinner in it), he was for several years editor of *Psychological Bulletin,* a job for which the first requirements are scientific eminence and integrity.

4. "**The Bell Curve** *says that genes determine intelligence.*" The book's position on this point is explicit. We say that IQ is somewhere between 40% and 80% heritable—an example of wholly uncontroversial mainstream science. This means that a substantial portion of IQ is determined by environment, an implication we emphasized repeatedly and freely. The problem is not that genes determine everything, but that (1) as the environment becomes more uniform, the relative importance of genes is bound to rise, and (2) the differences in the environment that nurture intelligence have so far proved to be very difficult to manipulate through outside interventions. We look forward to a day when effective interventions will be found, and urge that the government sponsor the research that will lead to them.

> **The integrity of the book, we decided, depended on the reader having confidence that for once there would be no euphemisms, no self-censorship, no ducking of tough questions.**
>
> —*Charles Murray*

5. "**The Bell Curve** *says that race differences are mostly genetic.*" If you have not read the book and if you get your news from the *New York Times,* the *Washington Post, The Economist, Time, The New Yorker,* or any of the network evening news shows, that's what you'd think. No single allegation about **The Bell Curve** is more widespread. It is also untrue.

In some cases, the error can be put down to confusion. Because we say that IQ is 40% to 80% heritable and that ethnic differences in IQ cannot be attributed to test bias, many people reflexively assume that group differences must also be heritable. This assumption is wrong, and we open the discussion of genes and race with precisely that point ("A good place to start is by correcting a common confusion . . ."). Once again, we used italics for a key sentence: "*That a trait is genetically transmitted in individuals does not mean that group differences in that trait are also genetic in origin.*" The only way a commentator could have failed to miss it is by failing to read that key section of the book.

As I write, the most recent example of misrepresentation of our position is Stephen J. Gould's review in *The New Yorker.* Mr. Gould's characterization of our position is unambiguous: The claim that "racial differences in IQ are mostly genetic in origin" is said to be one of the two central arguments of the whole book. He goes on to say that "Herrnstein and Murray violate fairness by converting a complex case that can yield only agnosticism into a biased brief for permanent and heritable difference." Now, compare Mr. Gould's words with what Richard Herrnstein and I wrote in the crucial paragraph summarizing our views on genes and race:

"If the reader is now convinced that either the genetic or environmental explanations [of ethnic differences in IQ] have won out to the exclusion of the other, we have not done a sufficiently good job of presenting one side or the other. It seems highly likely to us that both genes and the environment have something to do with racial differences. What might the mix be? We are resolutely agnostic on that issue; as far as we can determine, the evidence does not yet justify an estimate."

I do not know how we could have stated our position more clearly. It is hard to think of an innocent explanation for Mr. Gould's characterization of it.

6. "**The Bell Curve** *was crafted to advance a political agenda.*" In reality, **The Bell Curve** provides a lot of ammunition for the political left. The data presented in the book showing that low-IQ people are statistically more vulnerable to everything from poverty to physical disability can easily be used to argue for a redistributive Rawlsian state involving more government intervention in people's lives, not more personal freedom. Mr. Herrnstein and I took another view, but we understood that our view had to be justified; it couldn't be treated as an inevitable conclusion. I suggest that you try to find any other book on social policy—virtually all of which are written by people with strong political views—that explicitly describes how and why the authors' political predispositions shape their

overall view of policy, as we do in the book's concluding chapter.

7. "**The Bell Curve** *is based on tainted sources.*" Charles Lane wrote an article in *The New York Review of Books* charging that **The Bell Curve** cites people who at some time or another had received funding from a foundation called the Pioneer Fund. The Pioneer Fund has in recent years supported some of the most important scholars of intelligence. But in the past—the worst charges involve events 50 and 60 years ago—the fund was allegedly associated with people of racist views.

Ergo . . . What? Apparently, Mr. Lane and *The New York Review of Books* want to set a new standard for scholarship: One must be able to vouch not only for the quality of a study one cites, or even for the integrity of its authors, but for the entire history of any institution that funded them at any point in their careers. Otherwise, one's work is to be discredited. It is not just through guilt by association, but guilt by association at third hand. I do not use scare words like "McCarthyism" lightly, but this is an appropriate occasion. *The New York Review of Books* has begun an intellectual witch hunt that should chill anyone who cares about scholarship.

8. "*At a time when racial tensions are running so high, writing* **The Bell Curve** *was irresponsible.*" This concern has been voiced by friends as well as critics, not just since publication but since we began work on the book. This attitude reflects precisely what came to bother us about too many in the cognitive elite: American intellectuals in universities and in the media alike are taking on the attitude of a priesthood, making judgments about what the common folk should be allowed to know. We emphatically rejected that view.

I should acknowledge that our own thinking on this issue evolved. At the outset, Mr. Herrnstein and I tried to pick and choose among topics, and even briefly thought about omitting ethnic differences altogether. We soon saw that was unrealistic. As time went on, we reached a conscious, explicit decision: If it was a topic that we knew readers would have questions about, and if we knew of solid data that bore on the topic, we would lay out our assessment of what was known with no holds barred.

The integrity of the book, we decided, depended on the reader having confidence that for once there would be no euphemisms, no self-censorship, no ducking of tough questions. As part of that decision, we said to ourselves that the question of irresponsibility must finally be determined by truth. As Mr. Herrnstein said shortly before his death: If what we say in **The Bell Curve** is not true, then there would be no responsible time to publish it. If what we say is true, there is no irresponsible time to publish it.

Michael Barone   (essay date 5 December 1994)

SOURCE: "Common Knowledge," in *National Review,* New York, Vol. XLVI, No. 23, December 5, 1994, pp. 32-3.

[*Barone is a lawyer, essayist, and critic. In the following essay, he favorably assesses* The Bell Curve *and claims that it encourages Americans to help the intellectually deficient.*]

Perhaps because I'm congenitally optimistic, I think *The Bell Curve*'s message is already widely understood, by the American people if not by the elite. Ordinary citizens know that some people are in significant ways more intelligent than others, that only a relative few are extremely bright or extremely dull, and that intelligence bunches up at the center. They know that intelligence is not randomly distributed among members of different identifiable racial and ethnic groups. These are lessons that are taught in everyday life, and you have to undergo a pretty sophisticated indoctrination and enlist in a tightly disciplined ideological army to believe otherwise.

Of course, most of our university and media elite have signed up for those forces. They have done so, I think, because they believe that ordinary people would take the admission that there are differences in average intelligence among the races as a license for racial discrimination. They evidently believe that many or most Americans long to return to the system of legally enforced racial segregation that prevailed in the American South until the mid 1960s. But that is nonsense. Ordinary people understand quite well what Herrnstein and Murray, mindful of their elite audience, feel obliged to state explicitly: that differences in average intelligence among the races do not justify discrimination against or for individuals of those races. Ordinary people know—everyday experience makes it quite plain to them—that some blacks are extremely bright and some non-blacks are extremely dull. They know that it is not rational to discriminate by race.

The Bell Curve is not an argument for racial discrimination. It is an argument *against* racial discrimination, against the one form of racial discrimination that is sanctioned by university and media and government and corporate elites: racial preferences and quotas. It shows that the discipline of psychology supports the inference suggested by (to take a vivid example) the preponderance of people of Chinese descent in mathematics departments: that abilities are not randomly distributed among different ethnic and racial groups. (If we assumed they were, we would have to suppose that an old boys' club of Chinese was plotting to keep the rest of us out of those math departments.) The case for racial quotas is that in a fair society desirable positions would be randomly distributed among all identifiable groups. Herrnstein and Murray confirm the ordinary citizen's intuition that this is absurd.

More specifically, by showing strong relationships between intelligence as measured by IQ tests and behaviors ranging from job performance to a propensity to commit crimes or bear children outside marriage, *The Bell Curve* makes a powerful case that the disproportionately low number of blacks in top positions and the disproportionately high number of blacks in prison (just under half our prisoners are black) do not result from racial discrimination. I hasten to add that, as a society and as individuals, we all have an obligation to remain alert to acts of individual unfairness, and we all have an obligation to do something about the continued existence of a criminal underclass, even though most of us are highly unlikely to be its individual victims. *The Bell Curve* does not deny, it affirms that nurture contributes importantly to intelligence; and just as we would have an obligation not to leave the Wild Boy of Aveyron in the woods, so we are obliged to do something (there is plenty of room to argue just what) to help those children fated to grow up in neighborhoods where the criminal underclass rules.

But it is quite another thing to say that statistical inequalities require racial preferences, radical social engineering, or economic redistribution, as the Left has long insisted. Will the elites get the message that *The Bell Curve* and the people are sending? Perhaps. The public response to the 1993 Clinton economic package made it clear the Democrats cannot raise taxes again. The response to the Clinton health-care plan made it plain that there is strong and enduring opposition to social engineering. And the 1994 election results prove that voters don't want more government.

Quotas remain a way of doing business for government and corporate elites and a way of asserting moral superiority for the university elite. But they are under attack in the courts, and anecdotal evidence suggests that elite institutions are quietly filling their minority places with high-scoring Asians rather than lower-scoring blacks. *The Bell Curve* argues to elites in their own language that the underpinnings of their regimes of racial preference are rotten. They are resisting the message and are not likely ever to admit it out loud. But it is possible that they will start behaving more the way sensible, ordinary people have been all along.

Ernest Van Den Haag (essay date 5 December 1994)

SOURCE: "Not Hopeless," in *National Review,* New York, Vol. XLVI, No. 23, December 5, 1994, pp. 38, 40.

[*In the following essay, Van Den Haag favorably assesses* The Bell Curve, *applauding it as thorough and accurate.*]

In 1971 Richard Herrnstein, co-author with Charles Murray of this weighty volume, published an article in *The Atlantic Monthly* arguing that success—status, income, power—now depends on intelligence. We are becoming a "meritocracy" with great hereditary inequalities. *The Bell Curve* lucidly organizes an immense amount of data demonstrating empirically that, despite costly efforts to stave it off, meritocracy is becoming a reality. Before continuing, let me dispose of two distractions which have produced hysterical and silly columns—e. g., in *The New Republic* (unexpected) and the *New York Times* (expected); although, to be fair, elsewhere the *Times* was rational.

1. *The Bell Curve* shows that cognitive ability measured by IQ tests reliably predicts success—professional, academic, pecuniary—and that, on average, African-Americans have an IQ about 15 points below that of Caucasians, whose IQ, in turn, is lower (by about 5 points) than that of East Asians. Success differs accordingly. However, the point would be the same if all low-and high-IQ persons were Caucasians. Ethnic differences in IQ cause political complications but do not otherwise affect the hereditary social stratification described and predicted by *The Bell*

Curve. (Incidentally, why should anyone expect all ethnic groups to have the same average IQ? Why not the same skin color?)

2. The authors establish the predictive validity of IQ tests for all groups and estimate that 60 per cent of the variation in measured intelligence is due to genetic differences, which means that nearly half of the variation depends on environmental factors. The proof of this point seems fairly conclusive, based on identical twins separated at birth and on adopted children. Yet if intelligence depended exclusively on environmental influences, if it were entirely an acquired trait, that would hardly make a difference. We have no way of influencing the average cognitive ability of any group, regardless of whether it depends on environmental or genetic factors. Whatever other benefits they may yield, Head Start and similar schemes do not permanently raise the IQ of disadvantaged groups. Perhaps in the future we will find a way to increase cognitive ability genetically or environmentally. So far we have not. Thus it matters little whether the cognitive ability of groups is inherited or acquired. (Needless to say, there may be a genius within a low-IQ group and dolts within a high-IQ group; what applies to averages does not apply to individuals.)

Without distractions, what does *The Bell Curve* tell us? Past societies have offered very unequal opportunities and, linked to them, very unequal outcomes. Education was distributed unequally, depending on parental status. So was everything else. Individual status was ascribed rather than achieved. Little depended on intelligence, much on inherited status and wealth. This has changed. Opportunity has become more and more equal, inherited social privileges less and less important. College education is widely distributed, and the best colleges are available to the talented poor. By now, intelligence on the average predicts outcomes better than parental privilege.

Liberals believed that, once opportunity was equal, outcomes would become equal too: they thought unequal outcomes were due largely to unequal opportunities. However, Herrnstein and Murray show conclusively that inequalities won't disappear. This may account for the liberal media's rancorous reception of *The Bell Curve.* Individuals are born not as *tabulae rasae,* as many liberals believe, but with different intelligences, which produce very unequal outcomes.

The prediction of *The Bell Curve* that people with low IQs have to become wards of the government is rank speculation.

—*Ernest Van Den Haag*

Equal opportunity redistributes social inequalities but does not diminish them. It may increase them. God is not an egalitarian, much as Jefferson thought it "self-evident" that He is. People are born unequally gifted. If they have equal opportunity to use their unequal gifts, major social inequalities are unavoidable.

These inequalities may be augmented because people usually marry others with similar IQs. The poor transmit their low IQs and therewith their poverty. Their fertility exceeds that of the more intelligent and produces a permanent and growing underclass. Unwed mothers have low IQs on the average and provide environments not likely to help their children. They help to perpetuate the underclass. Criminals also come from low-IQ groups. With our egalitarian ideology we will have major social problems with the increasing inherited inequalities predicted. Their congruence with ethnic groupings will accentuate political problems.

The data Herrnstein and Murray provide are convincing, but I do have reservations about their more speculative inferences. People with low IQs will not be left hopeless, as they imply. Many kinds of socio-economic success are independent of intelligence. A low-IQ youth may become a baseball player or a pop singer and do better than any professor. A low-IQ girl may become a supermodel. Such careers require neither stupidity nor intelligence. Sure, the (non-IQ) talents needed for these careers are rare and, therefore, such outcomes are statistically insignificant. But psychologically they generate hope, just as lotteries do. Success is possible, if not probable, for the low-IQ individual. Further, even those confined to the lowest jobs need not dwell in misery. In any future society practically all can be reasonably comfortable regardless of talent (unless they are highly self-destructive). The prediction of *The Bell Curve* that people with low IQs have to become wards of the government is rank speculation. We cannot predict future social policies and conflicts. Remember Karl Marx?

In any case, the structure of a future society does not really tell us how people will feel about it. The authors mention that intelligence is only one factor in prestige or self-esteem; but they hardly note that, in most high schools currently, intelligence is a negative factor, athletic ability (or attractiveness) a positive one in prestige and self-esteem. I do not know whether people in a future society will go far beyond these high-school evaluations. Will mathematicians be esteemed more and will they earn more than former high-school athletes?

The authors rightly commend individualism as an answer to group dissatisfactions based on low IQs and low success. Yet "affirmative action" and similar anti-individualist capers show that neither liberal politicians, nor bureaucrats, nor the favored groups want individualism. It would take another volume to explore why they have prevailed. Will they in the future? Charles Murray is just the man to explore this question.

James Q. Wilson   (essay date 5 December 1994)

SOURCE: "Acting Smart," in *National Review,* New York, Vol. XLVI, No. 23, December 5, 1994, pp. 46-8.

[*Wilson is an educator and author of* Families, Schools, and Delinquency Prevention *(1987). In the following essay, he favorably assesses* The Bell Curve, *contending that the book accurately reveals the differences in intelligence levels between racial groups and that low and high IQs actually determine success or failure in society.*]

Serious readers will ask four main questions about *The Bell Curve.* Is it true that intelligence explains so much behavior? How can IQ produce this effect? If it does, is there anything we should do differently in public policy? And will this nexus affect race relations?

My answer to the first question is unequivocally yes. I first became aware of the significance of low IQ as a predictor of ordinary criminality when I collaborated with the late Richard Herrnstein in writing *Crime and Human Nature*. Since we published that book in 1985, evidence showing that delinquents and other offenders have a lower measured intelligence, especially on the verbal component of the tests, has continued to accumulate. Now Herrnstein and Murray have shown that there are strong correlations between IQ and occupation level, school attainment, worker productivity, and possibly even political participation. These correlations exist within a given racial group (say, whites) and after matching people on the basis of their social class. (Controlling for social class means that the IQ—outcome link is even stronger than many of *The Bell Curve*'s graphs reveal, since IQ also partially determines a person's social class.) Herrnstein and Murray present their evidence abundantly, cautiously, and in painstaking detail. Though quibbles are possible, I find it very unlikely that their answers to this question will be confuted.

Herrnstein and Murray have shown that there are strong correlations between IQ and occupation level, school attainments and worker productivity. These correlations exist within a given racial group.

—*James Q. Wilson*

The second question seems to present a tougher challenge. How can IQ affect things that don't seem to involve much thinking, like stealing a radio, conceiving a child out of wedlock, or doing a poor job as a bricklayer? The answer, I think, is that even the simplest tasks require the mind to recall and process an enormous amount of information; even the most powerful temptations evoke from us very different degrees of vividness in imagining future consequences. We forget this when we adopt the language of "instinct," "social forces," "economic incentives." Though all of these factors are important, all are mediated by the human mind in complex ways. On average, bright people are more likely than not-so-bright ones to recall past experiences and use them to shape present actions, to foresee vividly the future consequences of actions, and to internalize rules of thumb for everything from how to lay

a straight line of bricks to how to prevent an unwanted pregnancy. There are many exceptions—bright people who give way to every temptation, not-so-bright people who follow the Ten Commandments scrupulously. But on average, IQ makes a difference across a wide range of human behaviors. How wide a range we have yet to learn.

My answer to the third question is, "It depends." To be exact, the public-policy implications depend on two things. One is how much of the variance in unhappy conditions—criminality, poverty, low worker productivity, and the like—can be explained by differences in intelligence. We know with certainty that IQ cannot explain all of the variance, because rates of crime, poverty, and illegitimacy change dramatically without corresponding changes in intelligence. But even allowing for these changes, the statistical techniques that Herrnstein and Murray use do not, for technical reasons, permit a good estimate of how much of the difference between two groups (say, white women on welfare and white women not on welfare) can be attributed to IQ differences.

The other point is that we do not know how policy measures designed to change the things that can be changed interact with IQ. For example, suppose having a low verbal IQ makes a young girl more likely to become a teenage mother, get on welfare, and remain poor. Knowing that we can't change IQ very much (as we have learned from virtually every study of pre-school education that has ever been done), we decide to change other things: we provide girls with sex education and contraception, enroll them in classes that teach them how to resist peer pressure, and develop apprenticeship programs that enable them to get jobs that do not require a lot of brain power. Such programs may work well with girls of ordinary talents, but how well will they work with girls of below-par talents? Or to put the same thing in other words, how heavily must we invest money and effort in a program to make up for whatever cognitive deficits the participants bring to it? Except for some isolated cases, we don't know the answer to that question. In those instances where one kind of investment (in pre-school education) has been shown to have enduring beneficial effects on behavior, the investment usually has been quite heavy—much heavier than in the standard Head Start project and, in many cases, lasting much longer.

Herrnstein and Murray agree with almost every other scholar that human behavior is the result of a complex interaction between nature and nurture. But they also remind us of a point that many laymen and some scholars forget: it is often just as hard to change nurture as it is to change nature, or even harder. Don't suppose for a moment that believing in the great importance of environmental factors facilitates planned social change. One example: almost everybody agrees that childhood experiences affect the risk of becoming a juvenile delinquent, a teenage mother, a school dropout. Now ask yourself: How do you change cold, discordant, abusive, neglectful parents into decent, loving, caring ones?

The answer to the fourth question is: Knowledge of the connection between intelligence and behavior shouldn't have any effect on race relations, but it probably will. In principle—and especially in the light of the principles on which the United States was founded—a person's group membership ought to have no effect on the assessment we make of that person. Yesterday the reader was dealing with a variety of individuals who were white, Oriental, or black. Today he reads *The Bell Curve.* Tomorrow, should his behavior toward these people change in any way? No. They are the same individuals, with the same strengths and weaknesses, that they were yesterday.

That, alas, is not always the way the world works. Some people, eager to have a generalizable reason for their dislike of a particular person, will impute to that person the average IQ of his ethic group as learned from Herrnstein and Murray. We call that racism. It is wrong. But it will happen. Some other people, eager to deny the reality of group (or even individual) differences, will want to deny the accuracy of *The Bell Curve* by assailing the motives of the authors. We call that an *ad hominem* argument. It is wrong. But it will happen.

In an ideal world, the book Herrnstein and Murray have written would pass into public consciousness with scarcely a ripple. "Of course," readers would say, "we know that people differ in intelligence and we know, from having watched them in school, on the job, and in the neighborhood that this difference will make a difference in how they behave." And then they would add: "But we are Americans, and in America it is your individual talents and inclinations, and only those, that count. So we don't have to change anything we are doing as individuals."

But this is not an ideal world, and so some conservative racists and some liberal multiculturalists (who are racists of a different kind) will make the wrong kind of fuss about this penetrating and magisterial book. Shame on them.

Arthur R. Jensen (essay date 5 December 1994)

SOURCE: "Paroxysms of Denial," in *National Review,* New York, Vol. XLVI, No. 23, December 5, 1994, pp. 48-50.

[*Jensen is a psychologist, educator, essayist, and author of* Bias in Mental Testing *(1979). In the following essay, he argues that* The Bell Curve *represents thorough research and draws accurate conclusions about inherited intelligence.*]

Commenting not as an advocate but as an expert witness, I can say that *The Bell Curve* is correct in all its essential facts. The graphically presented analyses of fresh data (from the National Longitudinal Survey of Youth) are consistent with the preponderance of past studies. Nowadays the factual basis of *The Bell Curve* is scarcely debated by the experts, who regard it as mainstream knowledge.

The most well-established facts: Individual differences in general cognitive ability are reliably measured by IQ tests. IQ is strongly related, probably more than any other single measurable trait, to many important educational, occupational, economic, and social variables. (Not mentioned in the book is that IQ is also correlated with a number of variables of the brain, including its size, electrical potentials, and rate of glucose metabolism during cognitive ac-

tivity.) Individual differences in adult IQ are largely genetic, with a heritability of about 70 per cent. So far, attempts to raise IQ by educational or psychological means have failed to show appreciable lasting effects on cognitive ability and scholastic achievement. The IQ distribution in two population groups socially recognized as "black" and "white" is represented by two largely overlapping bell curves with their means separated by about 15 points, a difference not due to test bias. IQ has the same meaning and practical predictive validity for both groups. Tests do not create differences; they merely reflect them.

The authors' crime, apparently, is that they argue with impressive evidence that the implications of IQ variance in American society can't be excluded from a realistic diagnosis of its social problems.

—*Arthur R. Jensen*

The conjunction of these facts is a troubling picture to most people. And rightly so. The book's penultimate chapter ("The Way We Are Headed"), in the light of the chapters that precede it, probably leaves most readers depressed and disturbed, and it should. I, for one, am not all that comforted by the final chapter's remedial recommendations for public policy, entirely sensible though they may be. In the present climate, they have a slim chance of being realized. Yet one hates to believe there may be no morally acceptable, feasible, and effective way to mitigate the most undesirable social consequences of the increasing IQ stratification of the nation's population. The phenomenon itself is almost inevitable in a technological civilization. It is simply more salient when there are large subpopulations that differ in mean IQ. The "custodial society," which the authors portray as the worst scenario for public policy (and which their recommendations are intended to prevent), is hardly an agreeable resolution to most Americans. Yet at present it seems that is "the way we are headed."

The topic of race differences in IQ occupies only a fraction of *The Bell Curve* and is not at all essential to its main argument. All the socially important correlates of IQ are demonstrated in the white population sample. But the mass media have pounced exclusively on the race issue and, with a few notable exceptions, by and large have gone into paroxysms of denial, trashing the factual basis of *The Bell Curve* in every conceivable way, as if obeying a categorical imperative to inoculate the public against it.

Although social problems involving race are conspicuously in the news these days, too few journalists are willing or able to discuss rationally certain possible causes. The authors' crime, apparently, is that they do exactly this, arguing with impressive evidence that the implications of IQ variance in American society can't be excluded from a realistic diagnosis of its social problems.

The media's spectacular denial probably arises from the juxtaposition of the book's demonstrations; first, that what is termed "social pathology"—delinquency, crime, drug abuse, illegitimacy, child neglect, permanent welfare dependency—is disproportionately concentrated (for whites and blacks alike) in the segment of the population with IQs below 75; and second, that at least one-fourth of the black population (compared to one-twentieth of the white population) falls below that critical IQ point in the bell curve. Because the smaller percentage of white persons with IQs below 75 are fairly well scattered throughout the population, many are guided, helped, and protected by their abler families, friends, and neighbors, whose IQs average closer to 100. Relatively few are liable to be concentrated in the poor neighborhoods and housing projects that harbor the "critical mass" of very low IQs which generates more than its fair share of social pathology. The "critical mass" effect exists mostly in the inner city, which has been largely abandoned by whites. Of course thinking citizens are troubled. Thinking about possible constructive remedies strains one's wisdom.

But can any good for anyone result from sweeping the problem under the rug? Shouldn't it be exposed to earnest, fair-minded public discussion? Our only real fear, I think, should be that such discussion might not happen. Consideration of the book's actual content is being displaced by the rhetoric of denial: name calling ("neo-nazi," "pseudo-scientific," "racism," "quackery"), sidetracks ("but does IQ really measure intelligence?"), non-sequiturs ("specific genes for IQ have not been identified, so we can claim nothing about its heritability"), red herrings ("Hitler misused genetics"), *ad hominem* attacks ("written in a conservative think tank"), falsehoods ("all the tests are biased"), hyperbole ("throwing gasoline on a fire"), and insults ("dishonest," "creepy," "indecent," "ugly").

The remedy for this obfuscation is simply to read the book itself. We should hope that President Clinton will do so before he speaks out on the subject again, or at least ask his science advisor's opinion of whether it is a serious work on important issues by qualified scholars. It would clear the air if the President asked the National Academy of Sciences to appoint a panel of experts to evaluate the factual claims of *The Bell Curve* and report its conclusions to the public. There is a precedent for such an action. Following the publication of my book *Bias in Mental Testing,* the NAS convened a panel of experts to examine the body of research it covered and issued a two-volume report confirming my main conclusions. A similar detailed examination of *The Bell Curve* seems warranted by the public's evident concern with the empirical substance of the argument and its meaning for the nation's future.

Loren E. Lomasky   (essay date 5 December 1994)

SOURCE: "Meritocracy That Works," in *National Review,* New York, Vol. XLVI, No. 23, December 5, 1994, pp. 52-3.

[*In the following essay, Lomasky applauds* The Bell Curve*'s suggestion of a social meritocracy in which intellec-tual and/or physical abilities are the deciding factors of success in life.*]

Some people succeed because of fortunate birth, some because of nuggets of good luck they find along the way. But high-level achievement mainly depends on ability. What makes one person more able to excel than another is, of course, partly a matter of upbringing and education, but there is overwhelming evidence that to a considerable extent it is a function of the mix of DNA in one's genes. People differ from one another along salient measures of achievement not only as individuals but also—though it may be politically injudicious to say so above a whisper—as members of racial groups. Although the spread between whites and blacks is much smaller than the variation within either group, at every level of achievement there is a clear disparity in representation between blacks and whites. The higher the level, the greater the disparity.

Is this the scenario of differential intelligence endowments leading to unequal positions in the American socio-economic hierarchy that Herrnstein and Murray describe at length in *The Bell Curve*? I think so, although the authors are not as clear as they might be on this point. But no matter; it wasn't meritocracy in the academy, business, or the professions I had in mind. Rather, I was talking basketball.

Boys of all sizes and complexions enjoy tossing balls toward baskets. Those who grow up to do so with the greatest success tend to be taller than average. They also tend to be darker. In high school, more so in college, and most of all at the professional level, basketball is an African-American's game—not exclusively, but to an extent that no advanced degree in statistics is needed to discern. It's not obvious why this is so. Some speculate that basketball achievement is a product of a subculture that celebrates athletic success; others point to the urban concentration of blacks, making them likelier to gravitate toward the "city game." But one may also suspect that there is a considerable genetic component to basketball achievement and that it is not distributed evenly across races.

It would be facile to conclude simply that different groups do well in different fields, and that's that. While athletic ability is a local talent, general intelligence is, as the authors of *The Bell Curve* demonstrate, globally advantageous. Those blessed with an above-average IQ will occupy most of the highest positions of power and prestige this society affords, whereas only a very few men will prosper as a result of the ability to run and jump and shoot. Still, reflecting on the minor meritocracy that is the National Basketball Association may promote clearer thinking concerning larger issues.

First, no deep understanding of the relative contributions of heredity and environment is required to figure out who deserves to play and who should ride the bench. What matters for a meritocratic activity is the capacity to contribute, whatever its ultimate ground may be. Herrnstein and Murray apparently concur.

But second, even if there were convincing evidence of a heritable component in basketball talent unevenly distributed among racial groups, it would not follow that investment of resources in the less well-endowed is futile. The authors seem to believe otherwise, but that conclusion follows only if the purpose of such investment is to equalize levels of achievement across groups. Herrnstein and Murray are not leftist egalitarians, so their confusion on this point is surprising.

Let me try to clarify it. Because of an extreme disparity in natural endowments, no amount of coaching will allow the Harvard University basketball team to play on equal terms with the Boston Celtics. It does not follow that all available coaching resources ought to be put into the latter and none into the former. It does not even follow that the proportional return on investment in nurturing the skills of the Celtics will be greater than the return on the same investment in the Harvard team. The origins of endowments imply nothing about whether and how they ought to be cultivated.

If the aim of social policy is to raise the abilities of the less well-off, without trying to achieve parity across races and classes, then speculation concerning the genetic basis of cognitive abilities is largely beside the point. What matters is evidence concerning the cost-effectiveness of attempts to raise the positions of the less talented. And virtually across the board, the Great Society's grand initiatives have shown themselves to be impotent, if not counterproductive. No one has more eloquently or urgently catalogued that failure than Charles Murray, and the cogency of his indictment of the welfare state in *Losing Ground* owed nothing to any deep inspection of chromosomes. It depicted people as responsive to the incentives they confront and to the moral atmosphere in which they take their bearings, not as passive servants of their genome. *The Bell Curve* tends to blur rather than enhance that message.

In the NBA, unlike at HHS, there are no affirmative-action programs, quotas, or overseers of political correctness. Roster positions, playing time, and salaries are distributed on the basis of ability to perform on the court. That meritocratic principle seems to work well, far better than government education, housing, and single-parent subsidy programs. In few areas of American life are racial animosities less evident. That is no accident, and it could have turned out otherwise.

Several decades ago, when the infusion of black talent into the league began, some team owners worried that the predominantly white fans would not support a team on which black athletes were the majority. Some recommended what in other contexts is now called a "racially sensitive" policy. Those suggestions weren't heeded, possibly because the technical term for a team that allocates positions based on race is "loser." It is now abundantly clear that the warnings were wrong.

Both on the floor and in the seats, sports arenas feature more amicable interracial mixing than almost any other venue in the country. Star performers such as Magic Johnson, Michael Jordan, and Charles Barkley have achieved enormous popularity among black and white fans alike. Precisely because allocation of basketball positions is guided by rebounding, not race, the success of players isn't contaminated by a suspicion that it is undeserved. This is a meritocracy that works. Is it too much to hope that the lessons of its success might someday be generalized?

Lisa Graham McMinn and Mark R. McMinn (essay date 12 December 1994)

SOURCE: "For Whom the Bell Curves," in *Christianity Today,* Vol. XXXVIII, No. 14, December 12, 1994, p. 19.

[*Lisa Graham McMinn is an American sociologist and Mark K. McMinn is an American psychologist. In the following essay, they fault* The Bell Curve *for asserting that "intelligence is of utmost importance for success."*]

In *The Bell Curve,* Richard Herrnstein and Charles Murray suggest blacks are less intelligent than whites and assert that intelligence cannot be improved significantly enough to merit policies designed to help blacks.

The authors' conservatism may give *The Bell Curve* a stronger than usual hearing among some evangelicals, but the methodology and the implications of their findings ought to raise serious concerns.

Many of Herrnstein and Murray's arguments are not new—they are the 1994 version of what other researchers have proposed over the post century. Nor are their methods and conclusions universally accepted by scholars. Thomas Sowell challenged Arthur Jensen's claim in 1969 of black/white IQ differences by tracing 50 years of European immigrants. Sowell found that as ethnic groups rose categorically in socioeconomic status, so did their IQ scores. Jerome Sattler, one of the leading authorities on intelligence testing, argues that we cannot determine genetic IQ differences among races as long as systematic differences in opportunity and environment persist.

Whether or not the authors intended it, *The Bell Curve* perpetuates racism. Herrnstein and Murray would have us abandon programs like Head Start for disadvantaged children, differential financial aid for black college students, and affirmative action. They argue that affirmative action is "manifestly unfair" and is "leaking a poison into the American soul." Yet their acceptance of the validity of intelligence testing leaks a different type of poison—one that demoralizes people of color and undermines efforts to overcome the effects of 250 years of oppression.

How should we as Christians respond? First, we need to think critically about claims regarding intelligence and success. One of the most insidious themes of *The Bell Curve* is the authors' assertion that intelligence is of utmost importance for success. Such intellectual chauvinism devalues the Christian teaching that one's character is vastly more important than what one knows. History has shown us smart people of all races who were also cruel and despotic, while some of our heroes have been men and women whose honor outshone their intelligence. Jesus taught that the one who is to be greatest must be a servant. Christians should guard against a fascination with IQ that results in neglecting character, humility, and service.

Second, Christians have more important tasks than merely measuring or debating intelligence. Herrnstein and Murray's kind of research can yield precise answers to the wrong questions. Christians need to go beyond debunking Herrnstein and Murray's questionable scholarship (a necessary but insufficient task) to seek after the *right* questions that direct us toward reconciliation and justice. What does it mean to believe that all people, regardless of intelligence, are created in the image of God? How can we do justice, love kindness, and walk humbly with God (Mic. 6:8)?

Especially in the aftermath of the media blitz surrounding publication of *The Bell Curve,* Christians need to break out of racial boundaries and involve themselves in intentional, ongoing, committed interracial relationships. In a fallen world, the human tendency to demean others will find no shortage of support. Where others will use *The Bell Curve* to reinforce stereotypes of blacks, the church must stand firm on the truth that all people are precious in God's sight.

F. Allan Hanson (essay date January-February 1995)

SOURCE: "Testing, *The Bell Curve,* and the Social Construction of Intelligence," in *Tikkun,* Vol. 10, No. 1, January-February, 1995, pp. 22-7.

[*Hanson, an American educator and critic, is the author of* Testing Testing: Social Consequences of the Examined Life *(1993). In the following essay, he faults* The Bell Curve *for arguing that intelligence testing is an accurate and valid measurement of human intelligence.*]

At some gut level, many middle- and upper-class white Americans apparently harbor the conviction that they are more intelligent than people of the lower class and ethnic minorities (especially of African descent). While its obviously racist and anti-democratic connotations are sufficient to keep this attitude under wraps most of the time, periodically works grounded in psychometrics (the branch of psychology devoted to measuring differences among people) encourage this sentiment to re-emerge with an apparent mantle of scientific respectability. The most notorious of several recent eruptions has been sparked by the publication of Richard J. Herrnstein and Charles Murray's book, *The Bell Curve.*

Herrnstein and Murray are only the latest in a 125-year-long succession of social scientists dedicated to the enterprise of postulating intellectual differences between classes and races. Important predecessors include Francis Galton, H. L. Goddard, Lewis Terman, and Arthur Jensen. Herrnstein himself articulated the main theme of *The Bell Curve* twenty-one years ago, when he predicted that the importance of inherited mental abilities for achieving high income and prestige in our society would inexorably open a social rift between an intellectually gifted ruling class and a dull underclass.

Despite a bulky 800-plus pages bulging with statistics and charts, *The Bell Curve* conveys a very simple message: The ills of society—poverty, unemployment, unmarried parenthood, crime—are causally connected to the low intelligence of the people who manifest them. From this put-down of the lower class, Herrnstein and Murray go on to make the highly controversial claim that races differ in intelligence, and particularly that Blacks are significantly less intellectually endowed than whites.

Indisputably, intelligence test scores vary directly with socioeconomic status. If people are sorted into groups defined by $10,000 increments in annual family income, average intelligence test scores increase with each step up the income ladder. It is also true that, on average, Ashkenazi Jews score between a half and a full standard deviation (about 7 to 15 I.Q. points) higher on intelligence tests than other whites, and whites average a full standard deviation higher than Blacks.

The interpretation of these facts forms the heart of the debate over *The Bell Curve.* Herrnstein and Murray insist that they mean that upper-class people, on average, are more intelligent than lower-class people, and that this difference goes a long way in explaining the affluence of the one group and the chronic crime, dependence on welfare, unmarried parenthood, and other social problems of the other.

In fact, Herrnstein and Murray's thesis about different levels of mental ability between rich and poor, white and Black, is wholly predicated on the notion that intelligence is an independently existing human characteristic that is accurately measured by intelligence tests. But that fundamentally misconstrues the nature of intelligence tests and what they measure, throwing the entire argument of *The Bell Curve* off track. Some reflections on the nature of tests in general, and intelligence tests in particular, will make this clear.

Tests are always indirect measures. What we wish to know from a test—the target information—and what we learn directly from it—the test result—are never identical. Test results represent target information. This is particularly obvious in a lie detector test, in which the test result consists of information about certain physiological changes— in blood pressure, pulse and respiration rates, and so on—as measured by a polygraph machine. The target information is whether or not the subject is telling the truth. The assumption underlying the test is that the test result tells us something about the target information: that certain physiological perturbations, when associated with responses to certain questions, signify deception.

The moment it is recognized that a gap exists between test result and target information, it becomes clear that the relation between the two is not one-to-one. Other variables may intervene. Thus, one of the biggest debates about polygraph tests is whether it is possible to weed out "false positives"—honest individuals whose physiological responses manifest the same pattern as that associated with deception, but for other reasons.

There is a similar gap in intelligence testing. The point of an intelligence test is not to learn if the subject knows the meaning of the exact words found on that test, or can solve the particular mathematical problems or identify the patterns among the specific numbers and shapes that appear there. Performance on the test is assumed to represent the subject's ability to define words or solve problems of these types, and that, in turn, is taken to represent the subject's level of some largely inherited capacity called "general intelligence." Thus, the gap between test results (right and wrong answers on a particular test) and target information (general intelligence, or I.Q.) is wide indeed, and dependent upon many variables. The most important of them is learning.

Literally every answer on an intelligence test depends on what a person has learned. Vocabulary and reading comprehension questions probe how well the individual has learned to read; quantitative questions explore how much mathematics the individual has learned; questions in logic have to do with how well the person has learned to think systematically; spatial relations problems concern how well the subject has learned to visualize shapes, compare, and mentally transpose them. Of course, intelligence or aptitude tests aim to tap learning that is more broadly applicable and loosely specified than "achievement" tests such as, say, tests limited to addition and subtraction of fractions or American colonial history. It remains true, however, that any mental test, including the most general intelligence test, is inevitably limited to measuring what the test-taker has learned.

Recognizing this, it becomes apparent that the score on an intelligence test indicates much more than an individual's innate intelligence. What the individual has learned may reflect inherited abilities to some degree but other factors are critical, such as opportunities and motivation to learn. These depend on a variety of considerations such as the rewards and encouragements the individual has received for learning, personal relationships with parents and teachers, if and when the individual was exposed to subject matter that stimulated interest, and how much time and how many facilities, books, instruments, and other resources have been made available for learning.

Herrnstein and Murray acknowledge that intelligence is not entirely inherited; they attribute about 40 per cent of it to environmental factors. So they would be likely to chalk up what has just been said to the environmental component in intelligence. Their recognition of an environmental factor is mitigated, however, by their claim that intelligence remains stable throughout life after about age ten. Thus, they imply that the environmental impact on intelligence occurs only in relatively early childhood.

Herrnstein and Murray's thesis about different levels of mental ability between rich and poor, white and Black, is wholly predicated on the notion that intelligence is an independently existing human characteristic that is accurately measured by intelligence tests.

—F. Allan Hanson

Given that tests can only measure what has been learned, it seems appropriate to reverse the direction of causality that Herrnstein and Murray propose. Far from differences

in intelligence (as indicated by intelligence test scores) causing class differences, it is more likely that class membership (with all the discrepancies in opportunities to learn that that entails) causes differences in intelligence test scores.

This way of phrasing causal connection intentionally begs the question of the relation between intelligence test scores and intelligence, since that topic requires careful, separate consideration. The most basic flaw in *The Bell Curve* is its concept of intelligence as a single, independently existing human trait that is accurately measured by intelligence tests. Intelligence is better understood as an artifact of intelligence testing. This is not to say that there is no such thing as intelligence. It exists, but it has been brought into being by intelligence tests.

Consider a thought experiment that constructs a new test and imagines its consequences. We will call our test the New Intelligence Test, or NIT. It is intended to surpass current tests by sampling more widely from the full range of cognitive ability, and particularly its practical applications in everyday life. The NIT consists of eight sections:

> A name recall scale tests ability to remember the names of persons to whom the subject has just been introduced;
>
> A mathematics section tests the subject's ability to solve problems of arithmetic and algebra;
>
> In the exposition of ideas section, the subject is given five minutes to read a complex idea—such as a page from Rousseau describing his distinction between self-love (*amour de soi*) and selfishness (*amour-propre*)—and thirty minutes to present a clear and accurate written account of it, with original examples;
>
> The small-talk scale evaluates subjects' ability to carry on an interesting conversation with someone they have just met;
>
> In the follow-the-directions scale, the subject is told once, at the speed of ordinary conversation, to do a task consisting of six distinct steps, and is evaluated on how well the task is accomplished;
>
> A bullshitting scale assesses skill at participating in a discussion with two other people on a topic about which the subject knows nothing;
>
> The adult sports scale evaluates the subject's ability to play golf or tennis, with suitable adjustments for male and female subjects;
>
> The presiding scale assesses ability to run a business meeting, including matters such as maintaining focus of discussion, building consensus, and finishing on time.

The test result is reported as a composite score generated from the outcomes of the NIT's eight sections.

The ability or human capacity tested by the NIT is certainly nothing inconsequential. If the appropriate studies were done, it would doubtless turn that high NIT scores correlate positively (probably more positively than I.Q. scores) with desirable social outcomes such as success in the university, in business or professional life, high income, and election to public office. But it is also obvious that what the NIT tests is not a single quality or capacity of persons. It is rather a set of distinct qualities, which have been measured by the several sections of the NIT and combined into a single score for convenience in reporting NIT results.

But assume now that the NIT were to catch on in a big way—that it came, for example, to be widely used for college and graduate admissions and for hiring and promotion purposes by law firms, government, and corporations. In such an event, the different abilities measured by the NIT would not remain static. People would spare no effort in preparing for the test, in the hope of achieving the rewards awaiting those who excel on it. They would bone up on arithmetic and algebra, master techniques for remembering the names of strangers, hone skills of bullshitting, take golf and tennis lessons, learn how to run successful business meetings. School curricula would shift in the direction of more training in the areas covered by the NIT. (If they did not, irate parents would demand to know why their children were not being taught something useful.) Kaplan and Princeton Review would explode into the marketplace with courses that promise dramatic improvement in one's NIT scores.

All of this dedicated effort would have a palpable effect. Although the NIT obviously measures several quite different abilities, people would knit them together as they strive to improve them all in order to raise their NIT scores. Because NIT scores are reported as simple numbers, they would begin to imagine these several abilities to be one. They would name it . . . perhaps "NITwit." Given its relevance for success in life, it would be valued as a thing of great importance. People would worry about how much of it they possess; they would look for promising signs of it in their children and envy evidence of its abundance in other people's offspring.

Not only would a new mental category swim into the social consciousness. The empirical amount of it possessed by individuals would literally increase as, in preparing for the NIT, they got better at following directions, playing golf, expounding on ideas, engaging in small talk, and the rest of it. And, of course, as individuals increase these skills, NIT scores would go up. There would be rejoicing in the land as today's average NIT scores exceed those achieved in the past or by test-takers in other countries . . . until, perhaps, an apogee is passed and national consternation about declining NIT scores sets in. Given all these transformations and developments, it is fair to say that NITwit would become a new, singular, personal trait—an objective reality literally constructed by NIT testing. Perhaps the ultimate development (and the ultimate absurdity, but it unquestionably would happen) would be the marketing of rival tests that claim to measure NITwit faster, cheaper, or more accurately than the NIT.

The foregoing discussion of the NIT has, of course, its facetious moments. But its purpose is entirely serious. It demonstrates two fundamental characteristics of all mental testing. One is that test results inevitably reflect what test-takers have learned. The other is that, when a given test becomes sufficiently important, whatever that test tests gets reified as a single quality or thing. This has been the experience of "intelligence" in the real world. Because of intelligence tests, several different abilities (to solve mathematical problems, to comprehend texts, to compare shapes, to sort ideas or objects into classes, to define words, to remember historical events, and to do all of these things rapidly) have been welded together to form a new, unitary mental characteristic called "intelligence." People place great emphasis on it because intelligence tests serve as the basis for offering or denying educational and career opportunities and other social rewards. Precisely as with NITwit in our thought experiment, intelligence has been fashioned into an objectively real personal trait by the practice of intelligence testing.

We have distinguished two very different ways of understanding the relation between intelligence, intelligence tests, race, and social class. They agree that intelligence test scores increase as one goes up the social ladder, but disagree as to why. The sociological explanation I support is that, on average, opportunities to learn increase with higher socioeconomic status. (The Black/white difference in average intelligence test scores is then attributable to the fact that the socioeconomic status distribution of Blacks is lower than that of whites.) To say that intelligence increases with socioeconomic class is true in a sense, but it is potentially misleading because of the common tendency to think of intelligence as an independently existing human trait. On the contrary, general intelligence is nothing but a social construct produced by intelligence testing. "Intelligence" rises with socioeconomic status only because intelligence test scores do. And that is explicable not by any difference in largely innate cognitive potential between people of different classes (and races), but by different opportunities to learn.

In contrast, *The Bell Curve* and other works in its genre take intelligence test scores to be accurate measures of an independently existing human trait called general intelligence. The fact that scores are lower for certain ethnic minorities and for the lower class indicates that people in those conditions are, on average, less intelligent than others. Moreover, low intelligence is an explanatory factor for poverty, crime, welfare dependence, and other social problems that tend to cluster in the lower class, as well as for the disproportionate representation of certain ethnic minorities (especially Blacks) in the lower class.

This point of view is perverse as well as erroneous. Its endorsement of the idea that ethnic groups and social classes differ in intellectual capacity fuels a combination of smug condescension and hostility toward minorities and those who live in poverty. This has closed opportunities for millions and has driven racism, class discrimination, and eugenic programs such as immigration quotas and enforced sterilization.

One the last century, each eruption of the discriminatory idea that some races and classes are less intelligent than others has been met with vigorous opposition, as have the contentions of *The Bell Curve.* It appears that this time, as in the past, after a relatively brief popular infatuation with the idea, scholarly counter-arguments will ultimately succeed in beating it back. But, if history is any indicator, in twenty years or so the issue will pop up again.

Perhaps it has not been defeated decisively because the critiques dealing with challenges to statistics and alternative explanations have not struck at its roots. Those consist not of ideas or propositions but of a social *practice*: intelligence testing. The practice of intelligence testing itself has produced both the concept of intelligence as a single thing and test results indicating that that thing systematically varies among ethnic groups and social classes. Thus, the most effective way to lay this spurious and socially disruptive issue to rest once and for all is to change the practice of intelligence testing.

While it may be inconvenient to do without the efficiency and economy achieved by large-scale intelligence testing, some institutions show signs that they are beginning to wean themselves from it. Antioch, Bard, Hampshire, and Union colleges, together with some two dozen others, no longer require applicants to submit SAT or ACT scores, and Harvard Business School has dropped the GMAT (Graduate Management Aptitude Test) as an application requirement. These schools make their selections on the basis of academic records, written statements by applicants, and letters of recommendation, and they manage to operate their admissions programs effectively without intelligence tests.

A movement is afoot in the primary and secondary schools to assess children not in terms of standardized intelligence tests, but according to portfolios they develop with examples of their best work in a variety of subjects. If this becomes widespread, the conventional notion of intelligence as a single, quantifiable entity will begin to fade, as people focus on children's different talents—in such areas as music, visual art, the use of language, mathematical skills, athletics, and interpersonal relations.

Developments of this sort would not signal the end of all testing. In addition to other evidence of accomplishments (such as portfolios), tests will doubtless continue to play a role in decisions about school promotions and graduation as well as competition among aspirants for scholarships, admission to selective colleges and training programs, or employment in desirable jobs. The tests, however, would not be designed to measure anything like "general intelligence." They would aim to assess how well individuals have succeeded in mastering knowledge or skills that have been presented to them in academic courses, technical, or artistic training programs. Different individuals would, of course, perform at different levels on these tests, and this would be taken into account along with other qualifications in deciding who will receive scarce rewards and opportunities.

To implement practices such as these would not require sea changes in attitudes about assessment. The alternative perspective is already well established. Consider how evaluation works in a typical American college course. Depending on the discipline, students are usually graded on the basis of some combination of the following: problems or questions to be completed and handed in at regular intervals, laboratory reports, term papers, performance in

discussion groups, and tests. The notion of general intelligence plays no role in the process. When students do not perform adequately and one wishes to understand why, the first questions have to do with how much interest they have in the subject matter and how much effort they put into it. If it is clear that they are interested and are trying hard, investigation turns next to their preparation. Have they developed good study habits? Do they have the requisite background for this course? Have they learned the particular modes of thinking and analysis that are used in this discipline?

Academic advisers account for the great majority of cases of unsuccessful course performance in terms of one or another of these lines of investigation. Only for the few cases that remain does the question of sheer ability or "intelligence" come up. And even then, the matter is posed in terms of the particular talents appropriate for a specific subject matter (ability to do mathematics, to draw, to interpret literature, and so on) rather than general intelligence.

If the attitudes represented in this process were to become commonplace, it is likely that we would lose the habit of thinking of general intelligence as an all-important, single trait that is distributed unequally among the population. Instead, we would evaluate quality of performance in terms of a variety of factors, only one of which is native ability in that particular area. Such a change in thinking would drastically curtail the destructive view that some people are irredeemably inferior to others by birth, and perhaps even by race. It would place primary responsibility for achievement squarely on the individual's effort and hold out the promise that, if given a fair opportunity, the degree of one's own determination is the major factor in achieving one's goals.

The model of the college classroom does not apply to larger evaluation programs in one crucial regard. It is a given that all of the students enrolled in a single course have the opportunity to receive the same instruction. This, of course, does not hold when large numbers from different localities and backgrounds are being assessed. They will have been exposed to a variety of different experiences and curricula in schools that are anything but uniform in the quality of education they provide. The question is how to achieve a fair evaluation of how well people have acquired academic, technical, artistic, or other skills when some of them have had much richer opportunities to acquire them than others. No simple answer exists. The only satisfactory long-range solution is to provide all primary- and secondary-school children with equal educational opportunities. And that will require much more than just fixing the schools. It also involves fostering supportive home and community environments.

Whether or not those ends will ever be achieved, doing away with testing for general intelligence would preclude the periodic eruption of facile explanations such as that crime, poverty, and other social problems are attributable to low intelligence. It would spare us from fighting the battle of *The Bell Curve* all over again in twenty years' time, and would help fix attention on our real challenges to eradicate race and class discrimination and to enrich environments, providing all Americans with an equal opportunity to develop their talents.

Jack Fischel   (essay date 10 February 1995)

SOURCE: "Strange 'Bell' Fellows," in *Commonweal,* Vol. CXXIII, No. 3, February 10, 1995, pp. 16-17.

[*Fischel is an American educator. In the following essay, he faults* The Bell Curve *for its "poorly disguised political agenda" which fosters racism.*]

Eugenics is as American as apple pie—well, stale apple pie. Margaret Sanger, the founder of Planned Parenthood, was notoriously enamored of it. Even Norman Thomas, a putative champion of the common man, bemoaned the tendency of "those of a definitely inferior stock" to go on reproducing themselves. Now come the new kids on the genetic block, *The Bell Curve* authors Charles Murray and Richard Herrnstein. Their explanations for the economic and social disparities in American society are hardly new. Thirty years ago Richard Hofstadter examined the long history of such schemes in his classic *Social Darwinism in American Society* [*Social Darwinism in American Thought, 1860-1915* (1944), revised as *Social Darwinism in American Thought* (1955)], exposing the undemocratic agendas of those who advanced such views. Given this history and their own carefully qualified presentation of the statistical evidence, it is somewhat astonishing that Murray and Herrnstein still advance their findings as a basis for public-policy making. Indeed, what seems unqualified is *The Bell Curve*'s poorly disguised political agenda.

The controversy over *The Bell Curve* is most immediately reminiscent of the furor created by the work of the psychologist Arthur Jensen and the social theorizing of the Nobel Prize-winning physicist William Shockley in the 1960s. Jensen traveled the country arguing that whites scored fifteen points higher than blacks on IQ tests. Shockley proposed that government offer cash incentives to the so-called "welfare queens" to undergo sterilization. Whatever its professed aims, *The Bell Curve* will inevitably enlist, as did Jensen and Shockley, the enthusiastic support of those who are committed to proving the racial superiority of whites over blacks.

That should remind us that not so long ago eugenics was considered a legitimate branch of science, and that prior to World War II eugenic research was popular on both sides of the Atlantic. In the United States, for example, the Rockefeller Foundation played an important role in establishing eugenics institutions in Weimar Germany and continued to support this type of research even after the Nazi seizure of power. Hitler, in particular, corresponded with American eugenicists and relied on their "expertise" in promoting his racial policies. Eugenics was widely discredited only after its pseudoscientific claims were seen to culminate in the horror of Nazi genocide.

Despite the experience with the Nazi use of eugenics, marginal groups in the United States have continued to preach the gospel of race-science. The eugenics movement here has been kept alive through the efforts of an institution called The Pioneer Fund, established in 1937 by Wickliffe

Draper, a New England merchant and two eugenicists, Harry Laughlin and Henry Fairfield Osborn. Draper's fortune was used to bankroll "research" on precisely the kinds of questions *The Bell Curve* examines. The early leadership of the fund praised much of what was done in Nazi Germany in the name of racial "science." For example, both Laughlin and Osborn defended the passage of the Nuremberg Laws of 1935 by pointing out that in America, thirty-two states prohibited marriage and sexual intercourse between blacks and whites. It is surprising, given its track record, that the fund continues to operate, and still adheres to its founding goal of "improv[ing] the character of the American people by encouraging the procreation of descendants of the white persons who settled the original thirteen colonies. . . ."

Following World War II, the Pioneer Fund aligned itself with those opposed to the Supreme Court's 1954 desegregation ruling in *Brown v. The Board of Education of Topeka.* After the passage of the Civil Rights Act of 1964, it began to actively oppose government programs for the poor such as Head Start. The academic performance of black students, the fund contended, was the result of irreversible genetic deficiencies and government funding for remedial programs was consequently a waste of taxpayers' money. It was during this time that the fund provided Jensen with research grants, which over the years amounted to more than $1 million. Others who were and remain recipients of Pioneer grants include Linda Gottfredson of the University of Delaware, Seymour Itzkoff of Smith College, Garrett Hardin of the University of California at Santa Barbara, Michael Levin of CUNY, and Richard Lynn of the University of Ulster in Northern Ireland.

The Bell Curve is an exhaustively documented book that relies on hundreds of perfectly reputable sources. It is also true, however, that Herrnstein and Murray use the work of many social scientists connected with the Pioneer Fund. According to Charles Lane ("The Tainted Sources of *The Bell Curve*," the *New York Review of Books,* December 1, 1994), no fewer than seventeen researchers cited in *The Bell Curve*'s bibliography have contributed to *Mankind Quarterly,* a journal founded and funded by people, Lane writes, "who believe in the genetic superiority of the white race." Since 1978 the journal has been edited by Roger Pearson, a British anthropologist who has expressed both anti-Semitic and white supremacist views. Furthermore, Pearson's Institute for the Study of Man, which publishes *Mankind Quarterly,* is another Pioneer Fund project and fund award recipients Itzkoff and Lynn both sit on the journal's editorial board. Research articles by Richard Lynn in *Mankind Quarterly* are liberally cited in *The Bell Curve.*

Neither Herrnstein nor Murray received money from the Pioneer Fund, but their use of sources from academic racialists throws a disturbing light on *The Bell Curve.* Inadvertently, perhaps, the authors have contributed to the rehabilitation of eugenic ideas once widely discredited. If the eugenicists of the 1920s and '30s favored government policies to prevent undesirable groups from overwhelming the "native stock," the contemporary heirs to such views seem eager to attack affirmative action, welfare, and programs such as Aid to Families with Dependent Children, arguing once again that money spent on the "inferior" is money wasted.

Will the arguments put forth in *The Bell Curve* enter the public policy debate in Washington today? House Speaker Newt Gingrich's recent praise for the civil rights revolution of the 1960s would seem to suggest that even a conservative "revolutionary" like Gingrich is not about to revisit a politics that explicitly embraces the idea of racial inferiority. Still, like the "scientific" studies on racial differences that have preceded it, *The Bell Curve* will undoubtedly give encouragement to both the crudest and the most subtle forms of racism.

Adrian Wooldridge   (essay date 27 February 1995)

SOURCE: "Bell Curve Liberals," in *The New Republic,* Vol. 212, No. 9, February 27, 1995, pp. 22-4.

[*An American journalist, Wooldridge is the author of* Measuring the Mind: Education and Psychology in England 1850-1990. *In the following essay, he favorably assesses* The Bell Curve's *conclusions about the importance of IQ testing as society's primary means of identifying talented individuals. Wooldridge also discusses the evolution of IQ testing in Western society, America's political reliance on egalitarian educational programs, and the role of an intellectual meritocracy in the development of society.*]

Opposition to the use of I.Q. testing goes back as far as testing itself. Its practitioners have been accused of, among other things, misusing science to justify capitalist exploitation; allowing their obsession with classification to blind them to the huge variety of human abilities; encouraging soulless teaching; and, worst of all, inflaming racial prejudices and justifying racial inequalities. To this school of thinking, *The Bell Curve* was a godsend. Charles Murray and Richard J. Herrnstein succeeded more effectively than even Stephen Jay Gould and Richard Lewontin in linking I.Q. testing firmly in people's minds with spectacularly unpopular arguments: that different racial groups have different I.Q. averages; that America is calcifying into rigid and impermeable castes; that the promise of American life is an illusion. The more society realizes the dream of equal opportunities, the more it breaks down into incommensurate groups, segregated not just by the accident of the environment, but by the unforgiving logic of genes.

But there is another, more enlightened tradition in the history of I.Q. testing, a tradition that was once the darling of liberals. It linked I.Q. testing with upward mobility, child-centered education, more generous treatment of the handicapped, humane welfare reform and, above all, the creation of a meritocracy. Indeed, it could be argued that it is this enlightened tradition that reflects the real essence of I.Q. testing, uncontaminated by local prejudices and unscientific conjectures. In ignoring this, in demonizing the purveyors of I.Q., liberals have betrayed their own political and moral tradition.

This liberal incarnation of I.Q. testing can be seen at its most articulate and influential in England, where its expo-

nents held sway over educational policymaking from the 1930s until the early 1960s. These I.Q. testers found their political inspiration in the meritocratic ideal, a revolt against patronage and particularism and a plea for individual justice. During the course of their attempts to wrest control of the civil service from the landed aristocracy in the mid-nineteenth century, Whig reformers such as Lord Macaulay, a historian, and Charles Trevelyan, a mandarin, argued that positions should be allocated on the basis of examination results and that the exams should be designed to test "the candidate's powers of mind" rather than to "ascertain the extent of his metaphysical reading."

By the twentieth century, the left took up this mission. During its early years, the Labour Party saw its main role as constructing a ladder of merit, stretching from the slums to Oxbridge and regulated by objective examinations, so that the able could find their natural level. Sidney and Beatrice Webb wanted to turn Britain's educational system into a gigantic "capacity-catching machine," capable of "rescuing talented poverty from the shop or the plough" and channeling it into the national elite. H. G. Wells argued that "the prime essential in a progressive civilization was the establishment of a more effective selective process for the privilege of higher education." R. H. Tawney, the doyen of socialist educationalists, welcomed I.Q. tests for pointing to the huge number of talented working-class children who were overlooked in the existing system.

The psychometrists argued that I.Q. tests were powerful instruments of meritocratic reform. I.Q. tests were particularly useful in spotting promising working-class children held back in school by poverty in the home, and in providing them with a secure ladder up the social system. Far from being defenders of the status quo, the psychometrists believed in the inevitability of social mobility. The random element in Mendelian inheritance combined with regression to the mean ensured that children would differ in significant ways from their parents. The psychologist Cyril Burt calculated that, in order to ensure that people were doing the sort of jobs for which their abilities marked them out, almost one-quarter of their children would have to end up in different social classes from their parents. The really conservative theory of abilities is not hereditarianism, after all, but environmentalism: if parents can transmit all their advantages to their children, educational as well as material, then social mobility will always be something of a freak.

Perhaps the biggest practical experiment involving I.Q. tests occurred in Britain in the wake of the Second World War, and the result was a huge increase in social mobility. The Second World War generated a widespread feeling that, if Britain was to justify the sacrifices of its people and also survive as an economic power, it must turn itself into a real meritocracy. The 1944 Education Act tried to satisfy this feeling, decreeing that children should be educated according to their "age, ability and aptitude." People across the political spectrum agreed that this did not mean sending all children to the same school, but rather, assigning them to schools suited to their particular talents.

Confronted with popular and ministerial pressure to recruit children on the basis of raw ability, Britain's elite grammar schools increasingly turned to psychologists to refine their traditional examinations. By 1952 almost all local education authorities had incorporated an intelligence test into their selection exams. Even leftist critics of the tests were forced on close examination to admit that they were doing a good job. The psychologists Alfred Yates and Douglas Pidgeon, for example, argued that "the 'examination' in its best forms comes out as a highly reliable and remarkably valid instrument of prediction, considering what it is expected to do." By relying on I.Q. tests, the grammar schools gradually transformed themselves into thoroughly meritocratic institutions, recruiting their pupils from an ever-wider section of society (outraged contemporaries complained that the schools were being flooded with "spivs" and "smart alecks") and providing the chosen ones with a highly efficient escalator into the universities and the national elite.

Moreover, the I.Q. testers were determined to change the nature of Britain's elite, not just to rationalize recruitment into it. They had no truck with the well-connected, muddle-headed, scientifically illiterate old fogies who dominated the establishment, and wanted to replace them with carefully selected and properly trained meritocrats. Passionate supporters of the moderns against the ancients, they argued that, if it was to have any chance of surviving as a serious country, Britain needed to put much more emphasis on teaching science. One of their greatest disappointments was that Conservative R. A. Butler succeeded in protecting the traditional grammar school curriculum, with its obsession with literary and classical education, from reform in the Education Act of 1944.

Unlike Murray and Herrnstein, the I.Q. liberals were enthusiastic about spending money on the welfare state in general, and public education in particular. They argued for raising the school-leaving age, improving teacher training, increasing the number of nursery schools, gearing instruction to the individual needs of "backward" as well as precocious learners and providing regular medical inspection for school children.

I.Q. testers also tended to be passionate devotees of child-centered education. Though they are often associated with classification and selection, the tests in fact embodied a much broader theory of aptitude development. Their earliest supporters were relentless critics of traditional pedagogy, complaining that it was designed for the convenience of adults rather than the needs of children, and arguing that teaching should be based on the unfolding abilities of children, as revealed by I.Q. tests. Alfred Binet invented I.Q. tests to identify slow-learning children who were having a miserable time trying to keep up with more able contemporaries. One of the first to popularize I.Q. tests in the United States was Granville Stanley Hall, the pioneer of the child-study movement and an enthusiastic advocate of child-centered education. Jean Piaget used I.Q. tests to explore children's idiosyncratic views of the world. Progressive teachers turned to them in their battle against giant classes and stuffy teaching methods.

Until the 1950s these psychologists found their most passionate supporters on the left and their bitterest opponents on the right. Labour intellectuals such as R. H. Tawney pointed to intelligence tests to prove that Britain was being disgracefully profligate with the talents of its population. T. S. Eliot argued that an educational system that sorts people according to their native capacities would disorganize society and debase education, breaking the bonds of class and tradition and creating a society of mobile, atomized individuals. Edward Welbourne, a particularly crusty Cambridge don, was even more direct: confronted with the news that a student was interested in I.Q. tests, he snorted, "Huh. Devices invented by Jews for the advancement of Jews."

Why were Britain's intelligence testers so much more palatable than their American colleagues? Partly because they were outsiders, marginal to Britain's snobbish social and scientific establishment. British psychologists turned to I.Q. tests precisely because they thought that the establishment's traditional methods of spotting talent—examination essays, Latin translations, viva voce examinations—were hopelessly biased in favor of the well-taught rather than the promising poor. In America, psychologists were loaded with scientific honors and academic resources. In Britain, they were starved of resources and shunted aside.

Britain also boasted a group of first-rate biologists, such as Lancelot Hogben, J.D. Bernal and J.B.S. Haldane, whose sympathies lay distinctly on the left. They wielded huge influence with both the scientific establishment and the popular media—Haldane, for example, was both a fellow of the Royal Society and a hyperactive newspaper columnist—and they ensured that anybody who wanted to pronounce on controversial questions such as the relationship between race and intelligence had to pass the highest possible test of intellectual rigor and scientific probity. Significantly, the most bigoted British intelligence testers fled to the United States: William McDougall, a psychologist with something of a fetish for blond, blue-eyed types, left Oxford for Harvard, and Raymond Cattell, who argued, in print, that the race was being swamped by "sub-men," later followed him to the States. (Cattell lives in the United States still; a list of supporters of *The Bell Curve* in *The Wall Street Journal* included his name.)

Yet, for all their progressive sentiments, the intelligence testers fell afoul of two of the most powerful constituencies of the postwar left: the communitarians and the egalitarians. Communitarians such as Michael Young, the author of the 1945 Labour manifesto and now ennobled as Lord Young of Dartington, argued that the 11-plus, an I.Q. test taken by all of Britain's 11-year-olds, was breaking down working-class communities and churning out alienated, confused, anxiety-ridden scholarship winners. Indeed, his 1959 indictment of intelligence testing, *The Rise of Meritocracy,* foreshadows many of the central concerns of *The Bell Curve,* arguing that, as society becomes more efficient at allocating positions according to ability, the elite lose any sense of social responsibility (after all, they have nobody to thank for their success but themselves), and the poor lose any sense of self-respect.

Egalitarians argued that individual differences are the result of social circumstances rather than genetic inheritance, and that comprehensive schools would produce a much more equal society. After a long struggle between meritocrats and egalitarians for the soul of the party, Labour finally came down on the side of egalitarianism in the mid-1960s, with Labour Minister Tony Crosland declaring that he would not rest until he had destroyed "every fucking grammar school in England. And Wales. And Northern Ireland."

Yet the Labour Party's rejection of meritocracy has hardly been a success. Communitarianism embodies a nostalgic quest for a lost world, before social mobility turned neighbors into strangers and village greens into asphalt jungles. It also smacks rather too much of the traditional Tory complaint about people not knowing their place. Egalitarian reforms have also proved strikingly counterproductive. The comprehensive schools, introduced by the Labour government in the 1960s, have replaced selection by ability with selection by neighborhood, hardly a triumph for social justice. When Conservatives tried to reintroduce selection by ability in Solihull in the mid-1980s they were met with howls of protest from middle-class parents, who argued that they had paid inflated prices for their houses so that they could get their children into good schools, and didn't want their children's school places commandeered by riffraff.

Policymakers on both sides of the Atlantic would do well to look again at the more enlightened tradition of intelligence testing. The more insightful on the left, led by U.S. Labor Secretary Robert Reich, but including the British Labour Party's new leader, Tony Blair, have realized they need to rethink ideas about the state. In a world of gigantic capital flows and globe-spanning production networks, the left has no choice but to abandon its traditional belief in picking industrial sectors or industries to support. Instead of investing in winning companies, the state should make sure it invests in winning people: ensuring that the educational system spots outstandingly promising children and allows them to make the most of their talents.

Given this agenda, the left can hardly afford to ignore I.Q. tests, which, for all their inadequacies, are still the best means yet devised for spotting talent wherever it occurs, in the inner cities as well as the plush housing estates, and ensuring that that talent is matched to the appropriate educational streams and job opportunities. The left, indeed, should be up in arms about *The Bell Curve.* But they should be up in arms because Murray and Herrnstein have kidnapped what ought to be one of the left's most powerful tools for opening opportunities, and have tried to turn it into an excuse for closing doors.

Ned Block   (essay date December-January 1995-1996)

SOURCE: "Race, Genes, and IQ," in *Boston Review,* Vol. XX, No. 6, December-January, 1995-1996, pp. 30-5.

[*In the following essay, Block faults* The Bell Curve*'s explanation of the influence of genetics and heritability in determining intelligence.*]

According to *The Bell Curve,* Black Americans are genetically inferior to Whites. That's not the only point in Richard Herrnstein and Charles Murray's book. They also argue that there is something called "general intelligence" which is measured by IQ tests, socially important, and 60 percent "heritable" within Whites. (I'll explain heritability below.) But my target here is their claim about Black genetic inferiority. It has been subject to wide-ranging criticism since the book was first published last year. Those criticisms, however, have missed its deepest flaws. Indeed, the Herrnstein/Murray argument depends on conceptual confusions about the genetic determination of human behavior that have not been fully addressed—in fact, have been tacitly accepted to some degree—by many of the book's sharpest critics.

Before getting to the confusions, let's first be clear about the conclusion itself. In a recent article on "The Real Bell Curve," Charles Murray grumbles about critics, such as Stephen Jay Gould, who read the book as saying that racial differences in IQ are mostly genetic. Murray answers by quoting from the book:

> If the reader is now convinced that either the genetic or environmental explanations have won out to the exclusion of the other, we have not done a sufficiently good job of presenting one side or the other. It seems highly likely to us that both genes and environment have something to do with racial differences. What might the mix be? We are resolutely agnostic on that issue; as far as we can determine, the evidence does not yet justify an estimate.

In this passage, Herrnstein and Murray are "resolutely agnostic" about whether bad environment or genetic endowment is *more* responsible for the lower IQs of Blacks. But they indicate no agnosticism at all about whether *part of the IQ difference* between Blacks and Whites is genetic; and given their way of thinking about the matter, this means that they are not at all agnostic about *some* Black genetic inferiority.

The Herrnstein-Murray argument for genetic IQ differences is based on two facts: IQ is 60 percent heritable within the White population; and there is a stable, 15-point difference between average IQs of Whites and Blacks. With IQ largely genetic in Whites, it is natural to conclude—according to Herrnstein and Murray—that the Black-White difference, too, is at least partly genetic. Their argument has more to it; they raise issues about the pattern and the magnitude of the differences that I will get to later. But the most important flaws in the more complex version are fully visible in this simple argument.

Herrnstein's and Murray's argument depends on thinking of the 15-point IQ difference as divisible into a genetic chunk and an environmental chunk. This picture suggests the following three alternatives:

> Extreme Environmentalism: Blacks are genetically on a par with Whites, so the IQ gap is all environmental.

> Extreme Geneticism: Blacks are environmentally on a par with Whites, so the IQ gap is all genetic.

> The Reasonable View: Blacks are worse off both

genetically and environmentally, so some of the gap is genetic, some environmental.

The 60 percent heritability of IQ is thought to exclude *Extreme Environmentalism*. Well-known environmental effects on IQ, together with differences between Black and White environments acknowledged by Herrnstein and Murray, exclude *Extreme Geneticism*. So we are left with *The Reasonable View*—which postulates some Black genetic inferiority.

Notice, however, that the statement of alternatives blots out a crucial possibility: that Blacks are much worse off than Whites environmentally and better off genetically. Allowing this option, we get a different set of alternatives: genetically, Blacks are either worse off, or better off, or equal to Whites. I don't say that it is likely that Blacks are genetically better off than Whites, but it is possible, and—a very important point—what you consider possible affects what you think is an extremist position. Moreover, the critics of Herrnstein and Murray have tended to trip over this possibility. For example, in a *New York Times* op-ed critique that describes *The Bell Curve* as "bogus" and "nothing but a racial epithet," Bob Herbert insists that "the overwhelming consensus of experts in the field is that environmental conditions account for most of the disparity when the test results of large groups are compared." In effect, he uses known environmental effects on IQ to argue for a low degree of Black genetic inferiority: in effect, he accepts a version of *The Reasonable View*. Even Stephen Jay Gould, in his otherwise excellent article in *The New Yorker,* missteps here. Apparently accepting *The Bell Curve*'s way of conceiving the issue, he complains that Herrnstein and Murray wrongly minimize the large environmental malleability of IQ. He says that they turn "every straw on their side into an oak, while mentioning but downplaying the strong circumstantial case for substantial malleability and little average genetic difference." Gould does not do enough to guard against the natural interpretation of "little average genetic difference" in the context of discussion of *The Bell Curve* as little average genetic inferiority of Blacks. Several critics in *The New Republic* (October 31, 1994), in turn, wonder about the size of the "genetic component of the Black-White difference," thereby buying into the same way of thinking.

If you accept *The Bell Curve*'s way of putting the options, then the idea that environmental differences between Blacks and Whites are big enough to account for 15 IQ points looks like extremism. But given the actual alternatives—that Blacks are genetically on a par with Whites, or worse off, or better off—zero genetic difference doesn't seem extremist at all.

But isn't the idea of Black genetic superiority in IQ a desperate and pathetic attempt to exploit a mere logical possibility? Consider a parallel case. Toe number is genetic in sloths and humans, and humans are observed to have five toes whereas diurnal sloths are observed to have three. Is there any real possibility that the genetic toe difference between humans and sloths goes in the opposite direction from the observed toe-number gap? It could be that the three-toed sloth evolved six toes, but we observe only three because of a thalidomide-like chemical which has polluted

their food during the years in which we have observed them. But this possibility is only worth mentioning as an example of something extremely unlikely. This example suggests a principle that, though never articulated, underlies all of Herrnstein's and Murray's thinking on genes and IQ:

> Fundamental Principle: If a characteristic is largely genetic and there is an observed difference in that characteristic between two groups, then the genetic difference between the two groups is very likely to go in the same direction as the observed difference.

Applying this principle to the case of IQ: given the substantial heritability of IQ (recall, 60 percent within the White population), if East Asians are superior in measured IQ, then, according to the *Fundamental Principle,* they are highly likely to be genetically superior; and if Blacks are inferior in measured IQ, then they are highly likely to be genetically inferior in IQ.

Heritability within one group implies nothing about the explanation of differences between groups.

—*Ned Block*

But while the *Fundamental Principle* seems intuitively plausible, it is either irrelevant to the Herrnstein-Murray argument, or simply false. To see the problem, we need first to understand a crucial ambiguity in the term "genetic." That term has two senses, and in the next section, I describe those senses in some detail. To put the point schematically for now: the claim that a trait is "genetic" can mean either that *the trait itself* is fixed by a person's genes—the trait is *genetically determined*—or that *differences in the trait in some populations* can be traced to genes—the trait shows a high degree of *heritability*. Once that distinction is in place, the problems for the *Principle* follow. Again, to put the point schematically for now: if "genetic" is used to mean *genetically determined,* then IQ is not genetic because it is not fixed by a person's genes, and the *Principle* is therefore irrelevant. If "genetic" is used to mean *heritable,* then IQ is genetic but the *Principle* is false because heritability within one group implies nothing about the explanation of differences between groups. In neither case, however, does the *Principle* support *The Bell Curve*'s claim about genetic differences in IQ.

To understand *The Bell Curve*'s fallacy, we need to distinguish the ordinary idea of genetic determination and the scientific concept of heritability, on which all Herrnstein's and Murray's data rely. Genetic determination is a matter of what causes a characteristic: number of toes is genetically determined because our genes cause us to have five toes. Heritability, by contrast, is a matter of what causes differences in a characteristic: heritability of number of toes is a matter of the extent to which genetic differences cause variation in number of toes (that some cats have five toes, and some have six). Heritability is, therefore, defined as a fraction: it is the ratio of genetically caused variation to total variation (including both environmental and genetic variation). Genetic determination, by contrast, is an informal and intuitive notion which lacks quantitative definition, and depends on the idea of a normal environment. A characteristic could be said to be genetically determined if it is coded in and caused by the genes and bound to develop in a normal environment. Consequently, whereas genetic determination in a single person makes sense—my brown hair color is genetically determined—heritability makes sense only relative to a population in which individuals differ from one another—you can't ask "What's the heritability of my IQ?"

For example, the number of fingers on a human hand or toes on a human foot is genetically determined: the genes code for five fingers and toes in almost everyone, and five fingers and toes develop in any normal environment. But the heritability of number of fingers and toes in humans is almost certainly very low. That's because most of the variation in numbers of toes is environmentally caused, often by problems in fetal development. For example, when pregnant women took thalidomide some years ago, many babies had fewer than five fingers and toes. And if we look at numbers of fingers and toes in adults, we find many missing digits as a result of accidents. But genetic coding for six toes is rare in humans (though apparently not in cats). So genetically caused variation appears to be small compared to environmentally caused variation. If someone asks, then, whether number of toes is genetic or not, the right answer is: "it depends what you mean by *genetic.*" The number of toes is genetically determined, but heritability is low because genes are not responsible for much of the variation.

Conversely, a characteristic can be highly heritable even if it is not genetically determined. Some years ago, when only women wore earrings, the heritability of having an earring was high because differences in whether a person had an earring were "due" to a genetic (chromosomal) difference. Now that earrings are less gender-specific, the heritability of having an earring has no doubt decreased. But neither then nor now was having earrings genetically determined in anything like the manner of having five fingers. The heritability literature is full of cases like this: high measured heritabilities for characteristics whose genetic determination is doubtful. For example, the same methodology that yields 60 percent heritability for IQ also yields 50 percent heritability of academic performance and 40 percent heritability of occupational status. Obviously, occupational status is not genetically determined: genes do not code for working in a printed circuit factory.

More significantly, a child's environment is often a heritable characteristic, strange as this may seem. If degree of musical talent is highly heritable and if variation in the number of music lessons a child gets depends on variation in musical talent, then the number of music lessons that a child gets may be heritable too, despite not being genetically determined. In fact, recent studies of heritabilities of various features of childrens' environments show substan-

tial heritabilities for many environmental features—for example, the "warmth" of the parents' behavior toward the child. Even number of hours of TV watched and number and variety of a child's toys shows some heritability. If this seems unintelligible, think of it this way: variation in these environmental properties is in part due to variation in heritable characteristics of the child, and so the environmental characteristics themselves are heritable. Readers of *The Bell Curve* often suppose that a heritable characteristic is one that is passed down in the genes, but this identification is importantly flawed. The number and variety of a child's toys is not passed down in the genes. Heritability is a matter of the causation of differences, not what is "passed down".

I have given examples of traits that are genetically determined but not heritable and, conversely, traits that are heritable but not genetically determined. Do these weird examples have any relevance to the case of IQ? Maybe there is a range of normal cases, of which IQ is an example, for which the oddities that I've pointed to are simply irrelevant.

Not so! In fact IQ is a great example of a trait that is *highly heritable but not genetically determined.* Recall that what makes toe number genetically determined is that having five toes is coded in and caused by the genes so as to develop in any normal environment. By contrast, IQ is enormously affected by normal environmental variation, and in ways that are not well understood. As Herrnstein and Murray concede, children from very low socio-economic status backgrounds who are adopted into high socio-economic status backgrounds have IQs dramatically higher than their parents. The point is underscored by what Herrnstein and Murray call the "Flynn Effect:" IQ has been rising about 3 points every 10 years worldwide. Since World War II, IQ in many countries has gone up 15 points, about the same as the gap separating Blacks and Whites in this country. And in some countries, the rise has been even more dramatic. For example, average IQ in Holland rose 21 points between 1952 and 1982. In a species in which toe number reacted in this way with environment (imagine a centipede-like creature which added toes as it ate more) I doubt that we would think of number of toes as genetically determined.

It is worth emphasizing the solidity of the data about the large IQ increases in Holland. The 21 point increase reported by Flynn is based on comprehensive testing of all Dutch 18-year-olds who pass a medical exam (and there has been no change in the pass rate). The test used is Raven's Progressive Matrices, a widely respected "nonverbal test that is an especially good measure of g [general intelligence]." Even Richard Lynn, the arch-Jensenist who is the source of much of *The Bell Curve*'s data on race concedes this point. He says, "The magnitude of the increase has generally been found to be about IQ points per decade, making fifteen points over a fifty year period. There have, however, been some larger gains among 18-year-old conscripts in The Netherlands and Belgium amounting to seven IQ points per decade." Lynn also mentions that similar results have been found in France. Herrnstein and Murray concede that "In some countries, the upward drift since World War II has been as much as a point a year for some spans of years." In an area where the facts are often contested, it is notable that this set of facts seems to be accepted by both sides.

One very important conclusion from the Flynn data is that no one understands very much about how environmental variation differentially affects IQ. The cause of the large increases in Holland is simply unknown. Even Herrnstein and Murray concede that "relatively little [of the environmental variation in IQ] can be traced to the shared environments created by families. It is, rather, a set of environmental influences *mostly unknown at present,* that are experienced by individuals as individuals" (emphasis added). Indeed, the crucial factor that has enabled the research that Herrnstein and Murray report to exist at all is the fact that one can measure the heritability of a characteristic without having much of an idea of what the characteristic is. To calculate the heritability of IQ, we do not need to know what IQ tests measure; we need only be able to measure IQ—whatever it is—in various circumstances.

A few additional observations about heritability and IQ will underscore the need for great caution in drawing any inferences about the sources of differences in IQ. A common method for measuring heritability relies on comparisons of the correlations of IQ among one-egg twins raised by their biological parents compared with two-egg twins raised by their biological parents. Suppose you give IQ tests to two children and they get the same score. One has a one-egg (identical) twin, the other has a two-egg (fraternal) twin. Suppose that you can predict the score of the one-egg twin reliably, but that your prediction of the score of the two-egg twin is much less reliable. This difference would be an indication of high heritability of IQ because one-egg twins share all their genes whereas two-egg twins normally share half their genes.

Environmental differences, including the sort that affect Black Americans, are known to have large effects on IQ.

—Ned Block

Heritability studies of IQ within White populations in the US and northern Europe have tended to yield moderately high heritabilities: Herrnstein's and Murray's 60 percent is a reasonable figure. But it is important to note that no one would do one of these heritability studies in a mixed Black/White population. The reason is straightforward: if you place a pair of Black one-egg twins in different environments "at random," you automatically fail to randomize environments. The Black twins will bring part of their environment with them; they are both Black and will be treated as Black.

Moreover, heritability—unlike genetic determination—can be very different in different populations. For exam-

ple, the heritability of IQ could be decreased if half the population were chosen at random to receive IQ lowering brain damage: by damaging the brains of some people, you make the environmentally caused variation larger. Or suppose we could make a million clones of Newt Gingrich, raising them in very different environments so there would be some variation in IQ, all of it environmentally caused. So heritability in that population would be zero because the ratio of genetic variation to total variation is zero if the genetic variation is zero. To take a real example, the heritability of IQ increases throughout childhood into adulthood. One study gives heritability figures of under 20 percent in infancy, about 30 percent in childhood, 50 percent in adolescence, and a bit higher in adult life. Studies of older twins in Sweden report an 80 percent heritability figure for adults by age 50 as compared to a 50 percent heritability for children. One possible reason for the rise in heritability is that although the genetic variation remains the same, environmental variation decreases with age. Children have very different environments; some parents don't speak to their children, others are ever verbally probing and jousting. Adults in industrialized countries, by contrast, are to a greater degree immersed in the same culture (e. g., the same TV programs). With more uniform environments, the heritability goes up. I hope these points remove the temptation (exhibited in *The Bell Curve*) to think of the heritability of IQ as a constant (like the speed of light). Heritability is a population statistic just like birth rate or number of TVs and can be expected to change with changing circumstances. There is no reason to expect the heritability of IQ in India to be close to the heritability of IQ in Korea.

These issues are pathetically misunderstood by Charles Murray. In a CNN interview reported in *The New Republic* (January 2, 1995), Murray declared "When I—when we—say 60 percent heritability, it's not 60 percent of the variation. It is 60 percent of the IQ in any given person." Later, he repeated that for the average person, "60 percent of the intelligence comes from heredity" and added that this was true of the "human species," missing the point that heritability makes no sense for an individual and that heritability statistics are population-relative. In a letter to the editor in which Murray complains about being quoted out of context (January 30, 1995), Murray quotes more of what he had said: ". . . your IQ may have been determined overwhelmingly by genes or it may have been—yours personally—or overwhelmingly by environment. That can vary a lot from individual to individual. In the human species as a whole, you have a large genetic component." *The Bell Curve* itself does not make these embarrassing mistakes. Herrnstein, the late coauthor, was a professional on these topics. But the upshot of part of this essay is that the book's main argument depends for some of its persuasive force on a more subtle conflation of heritability and genetic determination. And Murray's confusion serves to underscore just how difficult these concepts can be, even for someone so numerate as Murray.

What's the upshot of the distinction between genetic determination and heritability for the argument of *The Bell Curve*? Recall the sloth example: Toe number is genetic in sloths and in humans; there is a difference in toe number; so the toe-number difference is genetic. This is a good argument: it strains the imagination to suppose that the genetic toe difference between sloths and humans goes in the opposite direction from the observed toe difference. It is ludicrous to suppose that our genes code for two, despite the five we see at the beach. So in this sense the Herrnstein and Murray argument works for the concept of genetic determination. But the data on genes and IQ are about heritability, not genetic determination.

Is IQ genetically determined as well as heritable? No! As I already pointed out, IQ is very reactive to changes in environments in the normal range. Recall the example of the large rise in Holland. Further, the claim that IQ is genetically determined is not the kind of quantitative claim on which Herrnstein and Murray would want to base their claims about genes and race.

If "genetic" means genetically determined, then, IQ is not genetic in Whites or anyone else (and in any case the issue is not quantitative), so the *Fundamental Principle* is irrelevant. If "genetic" means heritable, however, then IQ is largely genetic (among Whites in the US at least). But in the next section I will show that in this sense of "genetic," the argument does not work because the *Fundamental Principle* is false.

In a 1969 article in the *Harvard Educational Review*, Arthur Jensen started off the current controversy by arguing from heritability within Whites to genetic differences between Whites and Blacks. Richard Lewontin responded a year later with a graphic illustration of why this is a mistake. Suppose you buy a bag of ordinary seed corn from a hardware store. Grow one handful of it in a carefully controlled environment in which the seeds get uniform illumination and uniform nutrient solution. The corn plants will vary in height, and because the environment is uniform, the heritability of height will be 100 percent. Now take another handful of corn from the same bag, and grow it in a similarly uniform environment but with a uniformly *poor* nutrient solution. Again, the plants will vary in height, but all will be stunted. Once more the heritability of height is 100 percent. Despite the 100 percent heritabilities of height within each group, the difference in height between the groups is entirely environmentally caused. So we can have total heritability within groups, substantial variation between groups, but no genetic difference between the groups.

The application to race is obvious: heritability is high within Whites. But as Lewontin's example shows, high heritability within groups licenses no conclusion about how to explain differences between groups. —none, in particular, about genetic explanations of the differences. Nor does it dictate the direction of any genetic difference between groups. The stunted corn could have been genetically taller, with the genetic advantage outweighed by the environmental deprivation.

In Lewontin's example, it is assumed that there is no genetic difference between the two groups of corn. But suppose we knew nothing about two groups except that they differed by 15 points in IQ and that IQ had some heritability in both, and we had to guess the causes. For all I've said so far, it would make sense to guess that the lower scoring group was disadvantaged both genetically and environmentally. In the next section, I'll show that even this weak principle is wrong. However, the principle has no application to the racial question because we know lots more than nothing: we know that the environment can have huge effects on IQ (e. g., the Flynn Effect of 3 points per decade and the 21 point increase in Holland), and that Blacks are environmentally disadvantaged in a way that has been shown to count. But without being able to measure the effect of being treated as sub-normal, and of an historical legacy of slavery and discrimination, how do we know whether its average effect is sufficient to lower Black IQ 15 points, or less than that—or more than that? Given the social importance of this issue, guessing is not appropriate.

Herrnstein and Murray have heard appeals to the legacy of slavery and discrimination. And they have a response which appeals both to the *pattern* of racial differences and their *magnitude*.

First, the pattern. They remind us that the Black/White IQ difference is smallest at the lowest socioeconomic levels. And this leads them to ask: "Why, if the Black/White difference is entirely environmental, should the advantage of the 'White' environment compared to the 'Black' be greater among the better off and better educated Blacks and Whites? We have not been able to think of a plausible reason. An appeal to the effects of racism to explain ethnic differences also requires explaining why environments poisoned by discrimination and racism for some other groups—against the Chinese or the Jews in some regions of America, for example—have left them with higher scores than the national average."

But these facts are not hard to understand. Blacks and Whites are to some extent separate cultural groups, and there is no reason to think that a measure like socioeconomics status means the same thing for every culture. Herrnstein and Murray mention the work of John Ogbu, an anthropologist who has distinguished a number of types of oppressed minorities. A key category is that of "caste-like" minorities who are regarded by themselves and others as inferior, and who, if they are immigrants, are not voluntary immigrants. This category includes the Harijans in India, burakumin and Koreans in Japan, and the Maori in New Zealand. He distinguishes them from groups like Chinese and Jews who are voluntary immigrants and have a culture of self-respect. If higher socioeconomic status Blacks still are to some extent part of a caste-like minority, then they will be at an environmental disadvantage relative to higher socio-economic status Whites. But low status Blacks and Whites are more likely to share a caste background. As Henry Louis Gates, Jr., points out (*New Republic*, October 31, 1994), affirmative action has had the effect of quadrupling the size of the Black middle class since 1967. Most middle class Blacks have arrived in the middle classes relatively recently, many of them under less than ideal conditions for the development of self-respect. It would be surprising if children of these newly middle-class Blacks were to have fully escaped their caste background in so short a time.

Ogbu notes that where IQ tests have been given, "the children of these caste-like minorities score about 10-15 points . . . lower than dominant group children." He notes further that differences remain "when minority and dominant group members are of similar socio-economic background." But when "members of a caste-like minority group emigrate to another society, the twin problem of low IQ test scores and low academic achievement appears to disappear." Data suggest that burakumin who have emigrated to this country do "at least as well at school and the work place" as other Japanese.

As to the magnitude: Herrnstein and Murray calculate that "the average environment of blacks would have to be at the sixth percentile of the distribution of environments among whites . . . for the racial differences to be entirely environmental." And they believe that "differences of this magnitude and pattern are implausible." That is, 94 percent of Whites would have to have an environment that is better for the development of IQ than the environment of the average Black—if the 15 point difference is to be explained environmentally. Herrnstein and Murray think this is implausible because when you look at environmental measures—for example, parental income, school quality—you do not find that 94 percent of Whites have a better environment than the average Black. But this calculation ignores the effect of being in Ogbu's category of a caste-like minority. Compare the Dutch 18-year-olds of 1982 with their fathers' cohort, the 18-year-olds of 1952. The difference is entirely environmental despite the probable substantial heritability within each group. Using the same procedures as Herrnstein and Murray, Flynn calculates that 99 percent of the 1982 group had to have a better environment for the development of IQ that the average member of the 1952 group. Given differences of this magnitude among people of a uniform culture who are separated by only a single generation, is it really so implausible that 94 percent of Whites have an environment better than a Black at the 50th percentile?

Environmental differences, then, including the sort that affect Black Americans, are known to have large effects on IQ. Moreover, we currently have no way to quantify these effects. So we should draw no conclusion about the probability of any Black genetic IQ advantage or disadvantage. As applied to the case of IQ, then, the *Fundamental Principle* is false: the combination of high heritability within the White population, and persistent Black-White differences, does not support a case for genetic differences.

Earlier, I commented that if we knew nothing at all about two groups except that they differed by 15 points in IQ and that IQ is heritable in both, and we had to guess the causes, it might seem sensible to guess that the lower scoring group was disadvantaged both genetically and environmentally. I have been emphasizing that in the case of Black-White IQ differences, we know much more than "nothing at all." I want now to show that even if we knew nothing, any such guess would be misguided, for reasons that go to the heart of the notion of heritability.

Let's start with an example. Consider a culture in which red-haired children are beaten over the head regularly, but all other children are treated well. This effect will increase the measured heritability of IQ because red-haired identical twins will tend to resemble one another in IQ (because they will both have low IQs) no matter what the social class of the family in which they are raised. The effect of a red-hair gene on red hair is a "direct" genetic effect because the gene affects the color via an internal biochemical process. By contrast, a gene affects a characteristic indirectly by producing a direct effect which interacts with the environment so as to affect the characteristic. In the hypothetical example, the red-hair genes affect IQ indirectly. In the case of IQ, no one has any idea how to separate out direct from indirect genetic effects because no one has much of an idea how genes and environment affect IQ. For that reason, we don't know whether or to what extent the roughly 60 percent heritability of IQ found in White populations is indirect heritability as opposed to direct heritability.

The methodology used to measure heritability obscures this ignorance by counting differences in characteristics as caused by genetic differences whenever there is a genetic difference, even if there is also an environmental difference. This distorts the ways we normally think about causation. For instance, the heritability methodology focuses on the difference between the red-hair genes and genes for other hair colors, not on the fact that red-haired children—unlike blond children—are beaten.

Earlier I said that wearing earrings used to be highly heritable because differences were "due" to the XY/XX difference. I put quotes around "due" because it is a by-product of the methodology for measuring heritability to adopt a tacit convention that genes are taken to dominate environment. When virtually only women were wearing earrings, variation in earrings was as much social as genetic, but counted as highly heritable. If there is a genetic difference in the causal chains that lead to different characteristics, the difference counts as genetically caused even if the environmental differences are just as important. If we adopted the opposite convention—concluding from any environmental difference in two causal chains that the differences are environmentally caused—then we could not use current methodology for measuring heritability, because we have no general method of detecting indirect genetic effects using current techniques. Heritabilities using the two different conventions would be radically different if there are substantial indirect genetic effects.

Recall the examples mentioned earlier about the measured heritabilities of such quantities as number of hours of watching TV. No one should suppose that there is variation in genes for watching TV; this is a case of indirect effects. Consider further the fact that no one would do a heritability study on a mixed Black/White population. I mentioned earlier that if you place a pair of Black one-egg twins in different homes, you automatically fail to randomize environments, because the Black twins will bring part of their environment with them; they are both Black and will be treated as Black. This is an indirect genetic effect par excellence. Implicitly, everyone in this field recognizes that, yet more subtle possibilities of indirect effects are typically ignored.

Recall that heritability is defined as a fraction: variation due to genetic differences divided by total variation. The measure of variation that is always used (though alternatives are available) is a statistical quantity known as *variance*. One factor that raises variance is a positive correlation between genetic and environmental variables. Suppose that children whose genes give them an advantage in musical talent tend to have parents who provide them with an environment conducive to developing that talent—music lessons, concerts, a great CD collection, musical discussion over dinner, etc. Suppose further that other children who have a genetic disadvantage also have an environment that stultifies their musical talents. The correlation between genes and environment will move children towards the extremes of the distribution, increasing the variance in musical skills.

Variance due to gene/environment correlation (gene/environment "covariance") should not be counted in the genetic component of the variance, and there are a variety of methods of separating out such variance. It is common in behavior genetics to distinguish among a number of different types of covariance. The kind just mentioned, in which parents provide genes for musical talent and an environment that develops it, is called "passive" covariance because it doesn't depend on what the child does. Reactive covariance is a matter of the environment reacting to the child's qualities, as when a school gives extra music classes to children who exhibit musical talent. With active covariance, the child creates a gene-environment correlation, as when a musically talented child practices musical themes in the imagination or pays attention to the musical environment. Passive covariance can be controlled in heritability calculations by attention to adoption studies in which the double-advantage/double-disadvantage does not exist. But reactive and active covariance cannot be measured without specific hypotheses about how the environment affects IQ. And as I observed, little is known—as all parties to the disagreements about genetics and IQ agree—about how the environment affects IQ. So distinguishing reactive and active covariance is, on the whole, beyond the reach of the empirical methods of our era's "behavior genetics," for those methods do not include an understanding of what IQ is—whether it is information-processing capacity, or whether it has more to do with how information-processing capacity is deployed, e. g. whether it is mainly attention—or how the environment affects it.

These points about covariance assume that there are genes for IQ and that these genes may affect the environment so as to produce effects on IQ that are correlated with the ones that the genes themselves produce. But this way of presenting the issue seriously underestimates its significance. For as the red hair example illustrates, indirect genetic effects needn't work through anything that should be thought of as "IQ genes."

Because we don't know much about how variation in environment differentially affects IQ, we can only guess about how variation in genes differentially affects IQ indirectly, via the environment. Suppose that a child's perceived attractiveness and self-confidence strongly affects how adults interact with children in a way that largely accounts for the variation in IQ. Of course, adults could give some children more attention than others without producing IQ differences, but differences might result from variations in adult attention. Suppose further that personal attractiveness and self-confidence are highly heritable. Then we would have an indirect effect *par excellence,* and such an effect could, for all we know, largely account for the heritability of IQ. Without an understanding of how the environment affects IQ, we simply have no way of determining how much of the variance in IQ is indirect genetic variance of this sort. Of course, if we knew that some specific adult behavior that is triggered by some specific heritable property of children was responsible for a large component of IQ variation, then we could measure that behavior. But there is no theory of intelligence or IQ that would allow us to have any synoptic grip on such factors.

The upshot is that there may be a large component of heritability due to indirect genetic effects, including (but not limited to) gene-environment correlation, that is outside the boundaries of what can be measured given the mainly atheoretical approach available today. Where does the "gene-environment covariance" show up in heritability calculations? Answer: active and reactive effects that we don't know how to measure *inevitably are included in the genetic component.* This is often regarded by behavior geneticists as perfectly OK. In practice, if researchers were to actually identify an "un-meritocratic" effect such as the red-hair indirect effect mentioned earlier, they would undoubtedly count the variance produced by the effect as covariance rather than genetic variance. But we have no idea how much of the 60 percent of the variance in IQ that is said to be genetic is of this sort. So in practice, covariance due to indirect effects that people know how to measure— at least if it is flagrantly non-meritocratic—is not counted in the heritability; but other indirect effects are counted as genetic. So what counts as genetic variance (inflating heritability) is a matter of *value judgments* and of what effects we know about. Surely this makes heritability a lousy scientific concept.

In effect, the field has adopted as an axiom that *heritability of IQ can be measured by current methods.* Without this assumption, the right conclusion would be that since we cannot separate indirect genetic effects (including certain kinds of gene/environment covariance) from pure genetic variance, no heritability estimate can be made. Why does the field adopt this axiom? I can not help thinking that part of the explanation is that behavior genetics is a young field, struggling for acceptance and funding, and heritability is a flag that attracts attention to it. Let us return to the speculation that the 60 percent heritability of IQ (within Whites) is entirely indirect and due to differential treatment of children on the basis of heritable characteristics. Then the direct heritability of IQ would be zero and we would have no reason to think that anything that could be called genes *for* IQ (e. g., genes for information-processing capacity) vary in the White population, and no reason to look for genetic differences to explain the 15-point difference between Blacks and Whites. Instead, we would have reason to look for differences in the ways adults interact with children to explain the Black-White IQ difference. So indirect heritability suggests an environmental hypothesis about the measured Black-White IQ difference, one that could perhaps be the object of social policy. Are there reasons to expect indirect genetic effects in the Black-White difference? I mentioned the obvious example of genes for skin color above. But there may be less obvious indirect effects as well. There are many more low-birth-weight Black babies than White babies. Nothing known appears to rule out a genetic explanation. If Blacks are more likely to have genes for low-birth-weight babies, perhaps the effect could be neutralized by diet or by drug intervention in pregnancy. Certainly, no one should think of genes for low birth weight as "IQ genes".

Herrnstein and Murray worry about pollution of the gene pool by immigrants and by large numbers of children of low IQ parents. But if the heritability of IQ is mainly indirect, their emphasis on genes is misguided.

—Ned Block

The points I've just made about indirect heritability show why, as I said at the beginning of this section, any inferences from heritability statistics to genetic disadvantage would be misguided. Such inferences seem plausible if we assume that the heritability of IQ within Whites reflects differences in IQ caused by differences in IQ genes. But the points about indirect heritability show that we don't know whether any of the variation within Whites is due to variation in IQ genes. If we have no real grip on the kinds of causal mechanisms that produce the 60 percent heritability within Whites, we can have no confidence in any extrapolation to Blacks.

Let's call a person's genome (his total set of genes) genetically inferior with respect to IQ if that genome yields low IQ in any normal environment. But what is to count as a normal environment? In the example discussed earlier, genes for red hair yield low IQ within environments that are normal in the environment of the hypothetical society, but in environments that we would consider normal, the red-hair genes are irrelevant to IQ. What if the heritabilities observed for IQ are a result of indirect effects that can be changed by changing social practice? Then phrases like "genetically inferior in IQ" and "genetic disadvantage in IQ" will only apply to genomes such as that of Down's Syndrome that yield low IQ no matter what the social practices.

The same points apply to recent reports of a gene for homosexuality—for example, a *New York Times* article headlined "New Evidence of a 'Gay Gene.'" Brothers who are both gay turn out to be more likely to share some genetic material on their X chromosomes. But the shared genetic material could code for physical or psychological characteristics that interact with our highly contingent social structures in a way that increases the probability that

its possessor will be gay. Perhaps the shared material makes both brothers more attractive to gays, or perhaps it increases their interest in bodily fitness, which puts them in contact with a gay culture that also values fitness. Or perhaps it is a gene for early puberty, causing boys to mature at an age at which it happens to be socially acceptable for boys to be friends with other boys but not with girls. If the effect is indirect, it might disappear in another cultural setting.

The point about indirect heritability also casts doubt on Herrnstein's and Murray's ideas about genetic social stratification among Whites. If the 60 percent heritability does not reflect IQ genes, then there is no reason to suppose that social classes differ at all in IQ genes. Herrnstein and Murray worry about pollution of the gene pool by immigrants and by large numbers of children of low IQ parents. But if the heritability of IQ is mainly indirect, their emphasis on genes is misdirected. If we lived in a culture that damaged the brains of red-haired children, it would be perverse to complain about genetic pollution when large numbers of red-haired immigrants arrived. Instead, we should try to change the social practices that deprive those with certain genes of an equal chance.

FURTHER READING

Criticism

Beardsley, Tim. "For Whom the Bell Curve Really Tolls." *Scientific American* 272, No. 1 (January 1995): 14, 16-7.
> Critiques Herrnstein and Murray's *The Bell Curve.* Beardsley questions the concept of biological determinism and the authors' reading of statistics relating to education, intelligence, and economic performance.

Berger, Brigitte. "Methodological Fetishism." *National Review* XLVI, No. 23 (5 December 1994): 54-6.
> Calls *The Bell Curve* a "narrow and deeply flawed book" and offers alternative explanations for Herrnstein and Murray's data.

Brimelow, Peter. "For Whom the Bell Tolls." *Forbes* 154, No. 10 (24 October 1994): 153-58, 163.
> Favorably reviews *The Bell Curve* and argues that the American emphasis on equality of opportunity has clouded the issue of ability.

Csikszentmihalyi, Mihaly. "Scales of Inequality." *Washington Post Book World* (6 November 1994): 2.
> Examines Herrnstein and Murray's claims, presented in *The Bell Curve,* regarding the rigidity of IQ and trends in American society.

Finn, Chester E., Jr. "For Whom It Tolls." *Commentary* 99, No. 1 (January 1995): 76-80.
> Comments favorably on *The Bell Curve,* asserting that it is "a trove of useful information, insight, and analysis" on the role intelligence tests play in identifying the intellectually elite and the underclass.

Glazer, Nathan. "Is Intelligence Fixed?" *National Review* XLVI, No. 23 (5 December 1994): 50-2.

Contends that intelligence is an inherited factor, but questions the assumption, as presented in *The Bell Curve*, that it cannot be altered.

Gould, Stephen Jay. "Ghosts of Bell Curves Past." *Natural History* 104, No. 2 (February 1995): 12, 14, 16-9.

Discusses the history of intelligence testing and the theory of genetic determinism with reference to the work of Joseph-Authur Gobineau, Alfred Binet, and Lewis M. Terman.

Hacker, Andrew. "White on White." *The New Republic* 211, No. 18 (31 October 1994): 13-4.

Faults Herrnstein and Murray, authors of *The Bell Curve*, for sidestepping issues of genetic difference among Americans of European descent.

Hirsch, E. D. "Good Genes, Bad Schools." *The New York Times* (29 October 1994): 19.

Laments *The Bell Curve*'s tone of "social inevitability" and discusses the limitations of the studies analyzed by Herrnstein and Murray.

Hofer, Myron A. "Behind the Curve." *The New York Times* (26 December 1994): A39.

Faults Herrnstein and Murray for ignoring significant research in genetics, brain sciences, and psychology in their analysis in *The Bell Curve* of intelligence and its mutability.

Hudson, Liam. "The Wretched Connection." *The Times Literary Supplement*, No. 4783 (2 December 1994): 5-6.

Questions the link between poverty and IQ levels that Herrnstein and Murray suggest in *The Bell Curve*.

Judis, John B. "Taboo You." *The New Republic* 211, No. 18 (31 October 1994): 18.

Charges that Herrnstein and Murray's *The Bell Curve* promotes ideas based on "pseudo-scientific racism."

Lacayo, Richard. "For Whom the Bell Curves." *Time* 144, No. 17 (24 October 1994): 66-7.

Unfavorably reviews *The Bell Curve*, concluding that it will be remembered "for some dubious premises and toxic conclusions" about the relationship between intelligence and race.

Lane, Charles. "The Tainted Sources of *The Bell Curve*." *The New York Review of Books* XLI, No. 20 (1 December 1994): 14-9.

Discusses the credibility of *The Mankind Quarterly*, one of Herrnstein and Murray's sources for *The Bell Curve*.

Locke, Edwin A. Review of *The Bell Curve*, by Richard J. Herrnstein and Charles Murray. *Personnel Psychology* 48, No. 1 (Spring 1995): 177-82.

Favorably reviews *The Bell Curve* and refutes claims that Herrnstein and Murray are promoting racist ideas.

Loury, Glenn. "A Political Act." *The New Republic* 211, No. 18 (31 October 1994): 12-3.

Argues that Herrnstein and Murray "unnecessarily invite the questioning of their motives by introducing extraneous and unproductive speculation into what should be a discussion of the facts."

Morganthau, Tom. "IQ: Is It Destiny?" *Newsweek* CXXIV, No. 17 (24 October 1994): 53-5.

Discusses the relationship between intelligence, race, and class as presented in Herrnstein and Murray's *The Bell Curve*.

"The 'Bell Curve' Agenda." *The New York Times* (24 October 1994): A16.

Contends that Herrnstein and Murray's *The Bell Curve* fails to build a convincing, scientific case for the relationship between genetics and intelligence.

Nisbett, Richard. "Blue Genes." *The New Republic* 211, No. 18 (31 October 1994): 15.

Argues that there exists considerable scientific evidence to refute the claims Herrnstein and Murray make about cognitive abilities and race in *The Bell Curve*.

Reed, Adolph, Jr. "Looking Backward." *The Nation* 259, No. 18 (28 November 1994): 654-57, 659-62.

Disputes Herrnstein and Murray's argument in *The Bell Curve* that intelligence is genetically inherited and unchangeable.

Reiland, Ralph R. "Charles Murray and Albert Einstein." *The Humanist* 55, No. 2 (March-April 1995): 3-4.

Contends that IQ deviations between races change over time and that environment plays a greater role than heredity in determining IQ.

Siegel, Lee. "For Whom the Bell Curves: The New Assault on Egalitarianism." *Tikkun* 10, No. 1 (January-February 1995): 27-9, 84, 94, 96.

Charges that Herrnstein and Murray use distorted statistics and contradictory data in *The Bell Curve* to support what "appears to be a growing reactionary counter-culture: an anti-egalitarian movement that, under the guise of a call for civic harmony and order, weaves a fantasy of immutable hierarchy and preordained limitations on individuals."

Wieseltier, Leon. "The Lowerers." *The New Republic* 211, No. 18 (31 October 1994): 20, 22-4.

Contends that Herrnstein and Murray's arguments in *The Bell Curve* are unoriginal, that they ignore diversity within communities, and that they fall prey to the temptation to regard problems in America's inner cities as "historically or scientifically inevitable."

Wolfe, Alan. "From P. C. to P. R." *The New Republic* 211, No. 18 (31 October 1994): 17.

Discusses Herrnstein and Murray's examination of the relationship between genetics and intelligence. Wolfe concludes that the authors of *The Bell Curve* are obsessed with race.

Weisberg, Jacob. "Who, Me? Prejudiced?" *New York* Magazine 27, No. 41 (17 October 1994): 26-7.

Charges that Herrnstein and Murray's contention in *The Bell Curve* that "blacks are innately less intelligent than whites" is "grist for racism of every variety."

The Holocaust and the Atomic Bomb: Fifty Years Later

INTRODUCTION

The fiftieth anniversary of the end of World War II has sparked renewed interest in the Holocaust and in a reexamination of the United States's use of atomic weapons against Japan. Foremost among the new works about the Holocaust is the plethora of personal accounts published in recent years, including the definitive edition of Anne Frank's *The Diary of a Young Girl* (1995). Many of these personal accounts search for an explanation or self-knowledge and some raise the theme of identity for Jews who survived by passing as gentiles. Though most of these works center on the Jewish experience, a growing number address the experiences of non-Jews, including aggressors, bystanders, and victims. *Death Dealer* (1992), for instance, is the memoir of the commandant of Auschwitz; *"The Good Old Days"* (1991) collects letters and diaries of German soldiers who witnessed or took part in atrocities; while Gordon Horwitz's *In the Shadow of Death* (1990) examines the lives of the Austrians living near Mauthausen, a concentration camp whose inmates were not primarily Jewish. Remarking on this interest in non-Jewish actors and victims, István Deák has stated that it "is not the uniqueness of the Jewish Holocaust that is being challenged but the tendency of earlier writers to remain strictly within the confines of the Jewish tragedy." Lawrence Langer's collection of essays *Admitting the Holocaust* (1994) and his anthology *Art from the Ashes* (1994) have been the focus of debate concerning Langer's definition of proper responses to the Holocaust. While some critics have praised Langer for focusing on the physical reality of Jewish suffering and for dismissing attempts to find hope or metaphors of transcendence in the Holocaust, others contend that Langer's criteria for appropriate modes or techniques of representation are too strict. Michael André Bernstein, for example, argues that "the basic premises and arguments of *Admitting the Holocaust . . .* are both seriously flawed on their own terms and potentially harmful in the ways they seek to circumscribe the range of appropriate discourses about the Shoah."

Recent literature on the atomic bombing of Japan tends to fall into two categories, those that address the human side of the tragedy and those that analyze the decision to use the bomb. Robert Jay Lifton and Greg Mitchell's *Hiroshima in America* (1995), for instance, offers an account of why the bomb was used and suggests that the effect on the American public can be described as denial and psychic numbing—closing one's self off from painful emotions and memories. Other works, such as John Whittier

Treat's discussion of Japanese literature on the bomb in *Writing Ground Zero* (1995) and Michihiko Hachiya's *Hiroshima Diary* (1955), discuss the Japanese reaction to the bomb. As for the American literary response to the atomic bomb, Lifton and Mitchell have argued that "Hiroshima is everywhere in postwar and contemporary fiction—in its themes of futurelessness and absurdity, and its predilection for violent or vengeful behavior by heroes and anti-heroes alike. . . . [T]he 'usual place' for Hiroshima in Western literature is 'the unconscious.'" Although few works of fiction specifically address the American attack, a number of poets have found a direct means of expression; common themes in their poems, which have been collected in *Atomic Ghost* (1995), include despair and the need for collective guilt. The debate over the rationale and the morality of America's use of the atomic bomb focuses on two arguments: on the one hand the need to force Japan to surrender and thus avoid an invasion of the mainland, which, it is argued, would have resulted in unacceptably high numbers of American casualties; on the other hand, the contention that Japanese surrender was imminent regardless of the bomb and that the attack was carried out primarily to display American strength to the Soviets. Historians have offered explanations based on the analysis of decisions represented in documents as well as the personalities of the major actors. However, considering the controversy over a Smithsonian exhibit on the *Enola Gay,* the B-29 used to drop the bomb on Hiroshima, the American public is far from reaching a consensus on the decision's motivation and morality. Remarking on the numerous attempts to explain the attack, Michael Sherry has stated: "Why, then, did the United States use atomic bombs in 1945? The truth is that no single reason prevailed, in part because no single individual prevailed."

REPRESENTATIVE WORKS DISCUSSED BELOW

Allen, Thomas B. and Norman Polmar
   Code-Name Downfall: The Secret Plan to Invade Japan—and Why Truman Dropped the Bomb (nonfiction)   1995
Alperovitz, Gar
   The Decision to Use the Atomic Bomb and the Architecture of an American Myth (nonfiction)   1995
Aubrac, Lucie
   Outwitting the Gestapo (autobiography)   1993
Begley, Louis

Wartime Lies   (novel)   1991

Bernstein, Jeremy
   Hitler's Uranium Club: The Secret Recordings at Farm Hall [editor]   (nonfiction)   1995

Bradley, John
   Atomic Ghost: Poets Respond to the Nuclear Age [editor]   (poetry)   1995

Deutschkron, Inge
   Outcast: A Jewish Girl in Wartime Berlin   (memoir)   1990

Eliach, Yaffa
   Hasidic Tales of the Holocaust   (short stories and interviews)   1982

Fein, Helen
   Accounting for Genocide: National Responses and Jewish Victimization During the Holocaust   (nonfiction)   1979

Fermi, Rachel and Esther Samra
   Picturing the Bomb: Photographs from the Secret World of the Manhattan Project   (photographs)   1995

Frank, Anne
   Het achterhuis [*The Diary of Anne Frank*]   (diaries)   1947; also published as *The Diary of a Young Girl: The Definitive Edition* [enlarged edition], 1995
   Anne Frank's Tales From the Secret Annex   (short stories)   1983
   The Diary of Anne Frank: The Critical Edition   (diaries)   1989

Friedman, Saul S.
   Amcha: An Oral Testament of the Holocaust   (interviews)   1979

Gilbert, Martin
   The Holocaust   (history, diaries, and memoirs)   1984

Hachiya, Michihiko
   Hiroshima Diary: The Journal of a Japanese Physician, Aug. 9-Sept. 30, 1945   (journal)   1955

Hackett, David A.
   The Buchenwald Report [editor and translator]   (nonfiction)   1995

Hillesum, Etty
   Het verstoorde leven: Dagboek van Etty Hillesum, 1941-1943 [*An Interrupted Life: The Diaries of Etty Hillesum, 1941-1943*]   (diaries)   1981

Horwitz, Gordon J.
   In the Shadow of Death: Living Outside the Gates of Mauthausen   (nonfiction)   1990

Höss, Rudolf
   Death Dealer: The Memoirs of the SS Kommandant at Auschwitz   (memoir)   1992

Klee, Ernst, Willi Dressen, and Volker Riess
   "The Good Old Days": The Holocaust as Seen by Its Perpetrators and Bystanders [editors]   (letters and diaries)   1991

Korczak, Janusz
   Ghetto Diary   (journal)   1978

Kowalski, Isaac
   Anthology on Armed Jewish Resistance, 1939-1945   (autobiographies, biographies, letters, and memoirs)   1984

Langer, Lawrence L.
   Admitting the Holocaust: Collected Essays   (essays)   1994

Art from the Ashes: A Holocaust Anthology [editor]   (diaries, memoirs, poetry, and prose)   1994

Lifton, Robert Jay and Greg Mitchell
   Hiroshima in America: Fifty Years of Denial   (nonfiction)   1995

Linden, R. Ruth
   Making Stories, Making Selves: Feminist Reflections on the Holocaust   (nonfiction)   1993

Nobile, Philip
   Judgment at the Smithsonian: The Uncensored Script of the Smithsonian's 50th Anniversary Exhibit of the Enola Gay [editor]   (nonfiction)   1995

Ōe, Kenzaburo
   Hiroshimo nōto [*Hiroshima Notes*]   (essays)   1963

Ringelblum, Emmanuel
   Notes from the Warsaw Ghetto   (journal)   1958

Ritner, Carol and John K. Roth
   Different Voices: Women and the Holocaust   (essays, memoirs, poetry, and prose)   1993

Rosenberg, Blanca
   To Tell at Last: Survival under False Identity, 1941-45   (autobiography)   1993

Rotem, Simha "Kazik"
   Memoirs of a Warsaw Ghetto Fighter: The Past Within Me   (memoirs)   1995

Rothchild, Sylvia
   Voices from the Holocaust [editor]   (interviews)   1981

Senesh, Hannah
   Hannah Senesh: Her Life and Diary   (journal)   1972

Szeman, Sherri
   The Kommandant's Mistress   (novel)   1993

Takaki, Ronald
   Hiroshima: Why America Dropped the Atomic Bomb   (nonfiction)   1995

Tec, Nechama
   In the Lion's Den: The Life of Oswald Rufeisen   (biography)   1990

Tedeschi, Giulana
   There Is a Place on Earth: A Woman in Birkenau   (autobiography)   1992

Treat, John Whittier
   Writing Ground Zero: Japanese Literature and the Atomic Bomb   (criticism)   1995

Wood, E. Thomas, and Jankowski, Stanislaw M.
   Karski: How One Man Tried to Stop the Holocaust   (biography)   1994

Wyden, Peter
   Stella: One Woman's True Tale of Evil, Betrayal, and Survival in Hitler's Germany   (biography)   1992

Yamazaki, James and Louis B. Fleming
   Children of the Atomic Bomb: An American Physician's Memoir of Nagasaki, Hiroshima, and the Marshall Islands   (memoir)   1995

Zassenhaus, Hiltgunt
   Walls: Resisting the Third Reich—One Woman's Story   (autobiography)   1993

*This work has also been published as *Diary of a Young Girl* and *Anne Frank: The Diary of a Young Girl*.

THE HOLOCAUST REMEMBERED

István Deák   (review date 8 October 1992)

SOURCE: "Strategies of Hell," in *The New York Review of Books,* Vol. XXXIX, No. 16, October 8, 1992, pp. 8, 10-3.

[*A Hungarian-born educator and historian, Deák specializes in Eastern European history. In the review below, he discusses books focusing on gentile bystanders and persecutors as well as Jewish collaborators and survivors.*]

Three years have passed since my review in these pages of fifteen books selected from the enormous Holocaust literature published during the 1980s; hundreds more on the subject have since appeared. [For Deák's earlier reviews and commentary, see "The Incomprehensible Holocaust," *The New York Review,* September 28, 1989, and the subsequent "Exchanges" on December 21, 1989; February 1, March 29, and September 27, 1990; and April 25, 1991.] Writing about the Holocaust has become an industry in itself, one with a terrible and never ending fascination. Perhaps, however, a change is taking place in the general character of such works. While survivors' memoirs, historical accounts, and philosophical, theological, and psychological studies continue to appear, interest has been growing in previously neglected subjects, such as the experience of ordinary non-Jews who were involved in the Holocaust, whether as murderers, collaborators, bystanders, or saviors. Then, too, more writers have felt the need to discuss the fate of millions of non-Jewish victims of Nazism and to make at least passing references to other cases of genocide. It is not the uniqueness of the Jewish Holocaust that is being challenged but the tendency of earlier writers to remain strictly within the confines of the Jewish tragedy.

More and more studies discuss the adventures of Jews who survived by "passing," and who, as a consequence, lived simultaneously in two worlds. The best known examples of this recent trend are Louis Begley's *Wartime Lies,* a chilling, witty novel about a Jewish boy and his aunt who survive the Nazi years in Poland by acquiring false Aryan papers, and Agnieszka Holland's more recent film, *Europa, Europa,* about a Jewish boy who survived by becoming a member of the Hitler youth organization. But while Begley's novel, however much it may be based on experience, does not claim to be other than fiction, the appeal of *Europa, Europa* as an exciting adventure story is marred, at least in my opinion, by its claim to be entirely true. I simply do not believe that a circumcised Jewish boy could have avoided, year after year, the rigorous medical inspections and the male-bonding nudity that were regular features of the Hitler Jugend training camps. It is also a bit too much to have a long lost brother turn up in a concentration camp uniform not a second too late before the young Jewish hero, captured by the Red Army as a Nazi soldier, is to be shot dead.

Some of the books under review tell no less unlikely sounding stories, yet they are thoroughly documented and so must be believed. Jews in hiding often had no choice but to share the fate of the ethnic group within which they had found shelter. Jewish women who were passing as non-Jewish Germans were raped by the liberating Soviet soldiers who claimed to be avenging Nazi atrocities. Jews pretending to be Polish Christians were persecuted and in some cases murdered by Germans, Ukrainians, and Lithuanians, and by Soviet soldiers eager to kill Poles. Jewish refugees serving in Soviet partisan units were in danger of being shot by Polish, Ukrainian, or Lithuanian partisans fighting both Nazis and Communists. If they joined other resistance groups, they risked being executed by Soviet partisans as suspected German or Polish agents. As he assumed one role after another, the hero of *In the Lion's Den,* the young Galician Jew Oswald Rufeisen, was in danger as a Jew, a Pole, a German policeman, a nun, a Soviet partisan, and a Bolshevik commissar.

Jews in disguise invariably confronted the moral dilemma of having to identify, at least outwardly, with Gentile spectators of the Holocaust and sometimes even with the Jew-killers. The more effective their disguise, the more some were in doubt about their own identity. Success in passing often hinged, after all, on the degree of one's past familiarity with non-Jewish cultures. The Berlin Jewish girl hiding with Christian friends and shielded by her "Aryan" looks and manners felt she was primarily German. For some young Jews who survived the war in a Polish monastery or convent, a hastily acquired Christian piety became a genuine commitment. Other Jews survived by assisting the oppressors: Stella, the young woman described in Peter Wyden's book [*Stella: One Woman's True Tale of Evil, Betrayal, and Survival in Hitler's Germany*], hunted down Jews in Berlin on behalf of the Gestapo.

Recent Holocaust literature pays more attention than previously to the question of how widespread was the desire among Europeans to see an end to a large Jewish presence in their midst. All the evidence indicates that millions upon millions of Europeans, not only the Germans, were keen for this to happen. No doubt, most of these people hoped for a nonviolent solution of the Jewish question; they were even prepared to absorb a small number of Jews into Gentile society. Yet without a widespread consensus that it was desirable to be rid of most Jews, the Nazi extermination program would have been far less successful. Nor would the Final Solution have succeeded to the degree it did without the callousness and even, in some cases, the anti-Semitism of the British and American political leaders, foreign services, professional associations, trade unions, press, and public. [In a footnote, Deák continues: "The American historian Bruce F. Pauley reminds us in his new and important book, *From Prejudice to Persecution: A History of Austrian Anti-Semitism* (1992), that the US laws passed in the 1920s to restrict immigration were aimed to a large extent at the Jews from Eastern Europe. These laws and the many American state laws forbidding racial intermarriage were closely watched and applauded by Austrian anti-Semites. Public opinion polls conducted in the US between 1938 and 1942 revealed that only one third of the population would have opposed anti-Semitic legislation if the government had proposed it. Finally, between July 1938 and May 1939, the worst period of open anti-Jewish excesses in Nazi Germany, from 66 to 77 percent of the American public was opposed to raising the immigration quota to help Jewish refugees, even children. Pauley quotes . . . from a work, published in 1935, by a great scholar of anti-Semitism, Count Richard Coudenhove-Calergi: '[T]he overwhelming majority of non-Jewish Europeans today are more or less anti-Semitically disposed.' "]

One question still to be adequately addressed is whether the rejection of the Jews was a special phenomenon that can be explained by many centuries of anti-Semitism, or whether it was a particularly odious phase in a continuous process of ethnic purification that had been taking place for years in many parts of Europe. A case can be made for both propositions. That millions of European children were brought up thinking that the Jews were responsible for killing Christ, for example, surely would have affected popular attitudes at the time of the Holocaust. The general trend toward ethnic purification has not only been neglected, however, but seems to bear a particularly heavy share of responsibility.

The desire of the European nations to rid their lands of all types of minorities was given a major impetus by the French Revolution; but the movement became infinitely more vociferous and violent in our century. The French Jacobins and their nineteenth-century nationalist imitators in Europe aimed at assimilating such ethnic minorities as the Bretons and Jews in France, or the Romanians, Slavs, Germans, and Jews in Hungary; they would punish only those among the minorities who openly resisted assimilation. After World War I, the aim of the groups in power changed increasingly to forcible absorption, expulsion, or annihilation. The campaigns for ethnic purification undertaken during and immediately after World War II affected the lives of more than a hundred million people, including Poles and other Slavs killed, persecuted, or displaced by the Germans; Germans killed by East Europeans; Ukrainians and others killed by the Soviets and Soviets killed by Ukrainians; Serbs killed by Croats and Croats killed by Serbs—to name only some of the most terrible cases. Among them, the Jews, being both wholly defenseless and the object of an official Nazi policy obsessively bent on eliminating them, were the most unfortunate group of victims; but the fate of the others deserves more attention than it has had so far.

Recent Holocaust literature pays more attention than previously to the question of how widespread was the desire among Europeans to see an end to a large Jewish presence in their midst. All the evidence indicates that millions upon millions of Europeans, not only the Germans, were keen for this to happen.

—Istvàn Deàk

Among the more recent studies discussing the personal lives and character of the murderers, *"The Good Old Days"* [edited by Ernst Klee, Willi Dressen, and Volker Riess] is particularly informative, in part because it is based on letters, diaries, and other documents that have been intelligently selected by three German compilers: a young writer, a jurist deeply involved in the investigation of National Socialist crimes, and a historian.

The photographs in the book tell even more about the behavior of the German soldiers than the documents. Wartime hangings with the executioners grinning under the gallows have long been a favorite photographic subject, but never was there more demand for such snapshots than during World War II. Scores of amateurish photographs depict SS and Wehrmacht soldiers posing beneath people hanging from a rope, or they record, in monotonously repetitive sequences, the mowing down of rows upon rows of shivering, half-clad women and children. The pictures were taken in spite of official orders not to do so, or to talk about what had taken place. It is true, as the records in *"The Good Old Days"* show, that the German murder squads sometimes delegated the job of execution to local East Europeans, but more often they did the work themselves.

In the accounts of mass murder, satisfaction over a job well done often mingles with self-pity over having had to perform such a demanding and unappreciated task. In fact, the murder assignments were unrewarding: policemen complained of not having received the cigarettes, schnapps, and sausages given the SS men following a successful joint massacre. Many members of the *Einsatzgruppen,* or murder squads, were not from the SS but were professional police and other middle-aged men drafted into the police forces. They were generally neither well paid nor well fed; not all had the opportunity to rob their victims. Few among them belonged to the Nazi Party and not all were convinced National Socialists.

As the documents show, these men killed to please their superiors; or because they knew that there were plenty of volunteers in regular army units ready to take their places, or because they feared to appear as weaklings. The SS man or policeman who did not like the idea of machine-gunning defenseless adults and smashing the heads of infants found that it was easy to say no. The worst that could happen to such recalcitrants was transfer to another unit. Others were sent home for being soft (*"wegen zu grosser Weichheit"*). In none of the vast literature on the Holocaust is there, so far as I know, the record of a single case of a German policeman or member of the SS having been severely reprimanded, imprisoned, or sent to the front—much less shot—for his refusal to participate in mass murder.

"Today gypsies, tomorrow partisans, Jews and suchlike riff-raff," notes one diarist. What both murderers and German military onlookers often objected to was not the killing itself but the methods used. Hence the gradual progression from pogrom-like clubbings and axings, which were usually left to Latvian, Lithuanian, or Ukrainian civilians, to machine-gunning by Germans and their uniformed auxiliaries, and, finally, to the setting up of death camps where efficient industrial killing could be carried out.

During the first months of the war in the East, when killings still took place in public, German sailors from the Baltic ports and soldiers from far away garrisons indulged in what *"The Good Old Days"* describes as execution tourism. These visitors raised objections to the officers in charge only when they observed that arms and legs, some of them still moving, were sticking out of the makeshift graves. The ground above the graves, some of the spectators noticed, continued to heave for several hours after the executions.

In perhaps the most distressing account in *"The Good Old Days,"* two German divisional chaplains, one Catholic, the other Protestant, report on their investigation undertaken at the request of two lower-ranking military chaplains, again one a Catholic and the other Protestant, who were themselves acting upon the request of some soldiers, into the case of ninety Jewish orphans, in a Ukrainian village in August 1941. The children's parents had been killed by the SS at the request of the local army command only a day or two earlier. The two divisional chaplains, like the two other clerics before them, visited the house in which the starving and thirsty children were locked up, but left without offering them even a cup of water. They were scandalized by the atrocious conditions in which the children were held, but even more by the fact that the incessant wailing of the children could be heard by both soldiers and civilians. In their separate reports to the chief of staff of the 295th Infantry Division, the divisional chaplains insisted that locals not be allowed to enter the house "in order to avoid the conditions there being talked about further," and "I consider it highly undesirable that such things should take place in full view of the public eye."

Because two army divisional chaplains, i.e., high-ranking officers, were involved in the affair, there was a thorough investigation by the divisional general staff. Finally, the commander of the Sixth Army himself, Field Marshal von Reichenau, ruled that the execution of the children should be carried out as planned, although of course in an orderly manner. In a remarkable act of interservice cooperation, the Wehrmacht dug the grave, the SS arranged the executions, and the local militia were ordered to do the shooting. "The Ukrainians were standing round trembling," noted the SS lieutenant supervising the affair ("I had nothing to do with this technical procedure"), and when they finally fired, they did so poorly. "Many children were hit four or five times before they died," reported the lieutenant.

What strikes one is the full cooperation offered by regular army units, the high proportion of Austrians in the murder squads, and how lightly, if at all, the murderers and their accomplices were punished after the war. [In a footnote, Deák adds: "On the National Socialist fanaticism, murderous activities, and postwar self-acquittal of the German regular army from generals down to ordinary soldiers, read Omer Bartov's devastating but scholarly indictment: *Hitler's Army: Soldiers, Nazis, and War in the Third Reich* (1991)."] The two Catholic chaplains who re-

ported on the Jewish orphans were both ordained as bishops in the German Federal Republic.

Members of the SS and police murder squads were recruited from every sort of occupation. Several unit commanders were doctors of law; others had risen through the ranks. Many officers and men suffered acutely under the stress of their assignment: "The wailing was indescribable. I shall never forget the scene throughout my life. . . . I particularly remember a small fair-haired girl who took me by the hand. She too was shot later," complained the SS lieutenant supervising the execution of the children in the Ukrainian village. Others, however, remained steadfast: "Strange, *I am completely unmoved. No pity, nothing.* That's the way it is and then it's all over," wrote the Austrian Felix Landau in his diary on July 12, 1941. He was more worried, however, about his "Trudchen" cheating on him during his absence.

The Germans in *"The Good Old Days"* were generally low in the Nazi hierarchy. This is not so for Rudolph Höss, the commander of Auschwitz, whose memoirs have now been issued, the publisher tells us, in their first complete translation into English. It would have been useful, however, had the editor of *Death Dealer* pointed out precisely in what way his version differs from that of the 1959 English-language edition. Still, this edition is usefully supplemented by diagrams, a detailed chronology of the events at Auschwitz-Birkenau, and the minutes of the January 1942 Wannsee Conference, at which representatives of the major German ministries and other services were told about the progress of the Final Solution.

Höss was sentenced to death by a Polish court and hanged, in 1947, in Auschwitz. He was similar to the murderers included in *"The Good Old Days"* in his limited intelligence, his desperate efforts to please his superiors, his determination not to appear weak, and his many prejudices. He was different because, unlike the average SS man and policeman, he was an "Old Combatant" and a dedicated National Socialist. Next to Adolf Eichmann, whose police and court hearings have filled thousands of pages, Höss is the best-documented Nazi killer. He wrote his lengthy autobiography, which is supplemented by detailed portraits of fellow SS leaders and, among other things, a report on the confusing rank order of the various SS service branches, while in a Polish prison. A Polish psychologist and the prosecuting attorney both suggested that he give an account of himself, but unlike Eichmann, who basically answered questions, Höss was free to put down whatever he wished. The result combines a considerable amount of accurate information and some genuine insights into his past with remarkable historical distortions. Like many other Nazi leaders, Höss had little sense of statistical reality, especially in connection with the Jews, whose numbers he vastly overestimated. He and Eichmann expected the arrival in Auschwitz of 4 million Jews from Romania, 2.5 million from Bulgaria, and 3 million from Hungary. In fact, there were no more than 1.5 million Jews in the three countries.

Höss was born into a devout Catholic middle-class family in Baden-Baden. He soon became "disgusted" with the Church, he writes, but remained forever a believer of sorts.

Having distinguished himself as a front-line soldier in World War I, he joined the Free Corps of right-wing veterans after the war and began the typical career of a Nazi leader. He took part in the fighting in the Baltic countries between 1918 and 1921, which he describes correctly as one of the most brutal and vicious wars in modern history, a *bellum omnium contra omnes* involving Russian Whites and Reds, German Free Corps, Poles, Latvians, and other local forces. Later, because he took part in the murder of a man who had allegedly betrayed the Nazi terrorist Leo Schlageter to the French authorities in the Ruhr, he spent six years in Weimar Germany's prisons, an experience that taught him, he says, to respect the rights of prisoners.

A party member since 1922, Höss joined the SS in 1934 and was soon sent by Himmler to help set up one of the first concentration camps in Germany. In 1940 he was made commander of the new camp at Auschwitz. Höss writes that, at Auschwitz, his "children could live free and easy," and that his wife "had her flower paradise," but as for himself, he was never really happy. He resented the conflicting instructions he received: one day he was ordered to exterminate all the Jews; then he was told to select for slave labor all persons strong enough to work. He complains constantly about the greed, sloth, corruption, and intrigues of his underlings, and his memoirs largely consist of criticism of the inefficiency and brutality of the SS and the Kapos, the prisoners who were put in charge of the others. There is no evidence to show that he ever tried to alleviate the atrocious camp conditions, and he himself invented new methods of torture. Still, an imprisoned Polish artist assigned to work in the Höss household told the editor of this book that the family had treated him as a guest, and he had been invited to dine with the commander.

As Höss tells it, he felt sorry for all his victims: the Russian POWs and Polish political prisoners whom he had gassed as a rehearsal for the gassing of the Jews; the Gypsies, for whom he had much sympathy, but whom he sent to the gas chambers nevertheless; the prisoners in the Women's Camp who were worse off even than the men ("I have always had a great respect for women in general"); and even the Jews whom he alternately admired and despised. True contempt and dislike he reserved for his fellow SS officers.

In his farewell letters to his family and in his "Final Thoughts," Höss declared himself a National Socialist and had this to say about the Holocaust: "Today I realize that the extermination of the Jews was wrong, absolutely wrong. It was exactly because of this mass extermination that Germany caused itself the hatred of the entire world. The cause of anti-Semitism was not served by this act at all, in fact, just the opposite. The Jews have come much closer to their final goal." Standing on the gallows, he apologized to the Polish people. As Steven Paskuly, the editor of the memoirs notes in his epilogue, Höss, who greatly admired the Jehovah's Witnesses for their courage in the camp, thought of himself as a soldier of faith, a true believer whose religion was National Socialism.

An impressive work exclusively devoted to bystanders is Gordon J. Horwitz's *In the Shadow of Death*. His subjects are the Austrians in and around Mauthausen, a town located close to a notorious Nazi concentration camp, although not one primarily for Jews. Only 40,000 of the 119,000 people who died there between 1938 and 1945 were Jews, and therefore the people who lived near the camp (or camps, since Mauthausen had many subsidiary establishments) did not necessarily think of the camp inmates as Jews.

Set up in 1938, soon after the *Anschluss* of Austria, the Mauthausen camp housed German and Austrian criminals, "asocials," political prisoners, homosexuals, Jehovah's Witnesses, and later, Poles, Spanish republican refugees handed over to the Germans by Vichy France, Soviet and other POWs, as well as, of course, Jews. With a large stone quarry at its center, Mauthausen camp was a thriving business enterprise for the SS but it was also a particularly brutal place. One form of punishment consisted of having to run up the 186 steps of the quarry shouldering a heavy slab of stone. The SS called those who fell, were pushed, or leaped into the pit "Parachute Troops" (*Fallschirmjäger*). In 1940 a gas chamber was set up in nearby Castle Hartheim, at first to kill only mentally ill and retarded Germans and Austrians, but later camp inmates as well. Subsequently, a gas chamber was set up in Mauthausen camp itself, with Soviet POWs as its first victims.

The center of Mauthausen, a small town of about 1,800, almost exclusively Catholic, inhabitants (there had been no Jews there before the war), was three miles away from the camp. The local people, as Horwitz's interviews and documents show, regularly witnessed atrocities being committed whenever new arrivals were driven across the town, or whenever local farmers and workers had to go near the quarry. A public road led directly across the camp, and although those using it were forbidden to linger, they heard and saw enough for the atrocities to become widely known and often discussed. Even in the early years of the camp, inmates were shot in full view of the peasants and left to die on the roadside. Eleanore Gusenbauer, a farmer, filed a complaint in 1941 about the tortures and the random shootings: "I am anyway sickly and such a sight makes such a demand on my nerves that in the long run I cannot bear this. I request that it be arranged that such inhuman deeds be discontinued, or else be done where one does not see it."

Complaining was not without its risks: some who protested what they saw happening were sentenced to a stay in a concentration camp, and when a man called Winklehner threw bread and cigarettes to the inmates, he was taken to Dachau camp, where he died. All in all, however, the locals learned to live with the camp. They resented the rowdiness of the SS but profited from the business the SS brought to the town. The civilians employed at Castle Hartheim soothed their consciences with the knowledge that they were not directly involved in the gassings. Near Hartheim, parts of human bodies littered the countryside and tufts of hair flew out of the chimney onto the street; but neither this nor the smell of burning flesh prevented the staging of popular candlelight festivals at the castle. Even the monks at the famous Benedictine monastery nearby at Melk accepted the sight and stench of the local subsidiary camp and crematorium.

On February 2, 1945, when hundreds of Soviet officers escaped from the camp, townspeople joined in the hunt. Only a dozen made it to freedom, thanks in part to a couple of brave local inhabitants, who thus helped persons who were clearly seen as the enemy. During World War I, Mauthausen had served as a giant POW camp; it must have been difficult for the townspeople to distinguish between prisoners of war, common criminals, political prisoners, and innocent victims. Still, the passivity and silence of most of the population is disheartening and so is that wave of acute anti-Semitism that swept the region immediately after the war, as it did throughout Europe from the Netherlands to Poland. Today, despite some efforts by the Austrian government to preserve the memory of the camp, no one really wants to talk about what happened in Mauthausen. Horwitz, who managed, after much effort, to find revealing sources, concludes: "The efforts [to address the past] are minimal compared to the enormity of the deliberate silences, evasions, and distortions of a generation that slowly mutely fades into the grave."

In the extensive literature on collaboration, a special place has always been reserved for Jewish collaborators. Perhaps the most dreadful accounts to appear on this subject are not about the Jewish Councils or the concentration camp Kapos but about the Jewish retrievers (*Abholer*), raiders (*Ordner*), stool pigeons (*Spitzel*), and catchers (*Greifer*) in Berlin, who brought other Jews to the collection centers and prevented escapes. The most trusted among them did the work of the Gestapo by detecting and arresting Jews who tried to pass as non-Jews. The "catchers" included the blonde, blue-eyed Stella Goldschlag, the subject of Peter Wyden's book [*Stella: One Woman's True Tale of Evil, Betrayal, and Survival in Hitler's Germany*]. Wyden is himself from Berlin; his family came to New York just before the outbreak of the war, and Stella, for whom he had a secret passion, was one of his friends and classmates in the luxurious private high school that Jewish upper-class youngsters attended after the Nazis had dismissed them from the state schools.

The picture drawn by Wyden of Berlin's Jewish upper class is not flattering, but he candidly admits that he doesn't know how he himself would have behaved had he been left in Berlin to face the Nazis. The Jewish elite had been too successful for their own good, Wyden argues in *Stella,* and too certain of their niche in German society. They were contemptuous of the Jewish refugees from the East and many among them were anti-Semitic.

Assimilated Jews, in Berlin or elsewhere, had enormous difficulties coping with their sudden decline to the level of the most downtrodden of East European Jews. How was a person called Siegfried to react to the Nazi order adding the middle name Israel to his first name? How was the decorated veteran of the First World War to behave when kicked in the behind, in public, by young SA louts who had never even been soldiers? Those who could emigrated; others became Zionists; still others kept affirming their devotion to the fatherland that had deserted them; some tried to join their persecutors.

At first, young Stella Goldschlag lived a semi-illegal life: during the day, she wore the yellow star while working in a factory, but at night she was a free and immensely attractive German woman who went to parties using an assumed name. Later, when she tried to live entirely as an Aryan German, she was arrested, tortured to reveal the names of those who had provided her with false papers, and at last talked into helping the Gestapo. Soon she was out in the streets, dressed elegantly, haunting the cafés and other places where Jews attempting to pass for Gentiles tended to gather. Together with other upper-class Jews in her team, she caught and delivered to the Gestapo people who had often been her friends and former classmates. What makes the story particularly harrowing is that Stella and her friends carried revolvers, probably the only Jews in the world so equipped by the Nazis. They needed the guns not only to make arrests but also to defend themselves.

Today it may seem almost inconceivable that these catchers never even thought of turning the guns on their masters, yet, for them, the notion of shooting German policemen would have been no less inconceivable. Like so many other victims, they also admired and desperately tried to imitate their oppressors. For other, worse-off victims of totalitarianism, they felt only contempt. After the war, Stella claimed that she had only tried to protect her parents. Yet, as Wyden shows, she continued in her job and became more active than ever after her parents had been sent to Theresienstadt. Stella and her friends enjoyed what they were doing because it gave them power and allowed them to identify with the dashing Nazis.

A surprising number of Jews survived the war in Berlin, the city that Hitler most wanted to be *judenfrei.* At least 1,400 managed to stay in hiding; several thousand others remained unharmed because they were married to Christians; thousands survived in camps in and near the capital; and hundreds got through the war in a Jewish hospital that was oddly allowed to exist. Immediately after the end of fighting, Stella was arrested and tried by the Soviet occupation authorities: she spent ten years in various East German camps and prisons. Following her release, she was tried twice by a West Berlin court and because she was sentenced each time to the same ten years she had already spent in Soviet custody, she was not again put in prison. Wyden visited her repeatedly in her comfortable West German apartment in 1990 and 1991: still attractive, mendacious, a professed "victim of the Jews," but very much isolated. Her daughter is a public health nurse in Israel; she says she hates her mother and has fantasies about killing her.

Those who migrated from Germany and Austria before the war tended to have money, the right connections, and relatives abroad who were both devoted to them and well-to-do. People like Stella's family, who had less money and no foreign friends, usually stayed put and were mostly killed. The unfairness of it all was one reason for Stella's bitterness and hatred. In Wyden's account, Berlin Gentiles applauded when Stella and the Gestapo were catching Jews. This is quite different from the picture that emerges from Inge Deutschkron's *Outcast,* a simple and

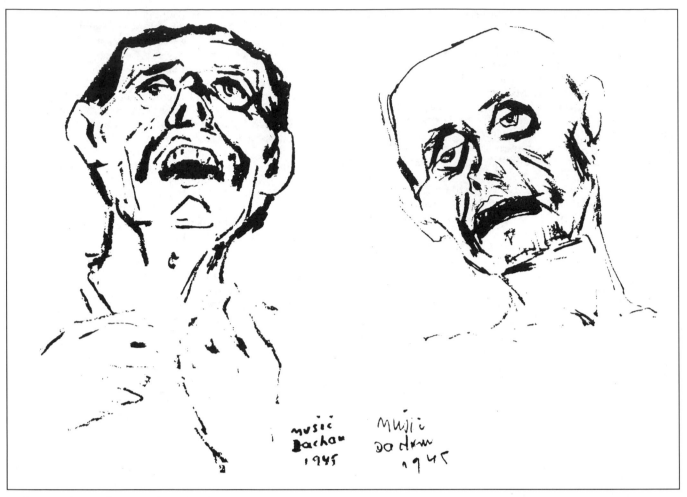

Drawings by an unknown prisoner of Dachau concentration camp; given by survivors to Dr. Marcus J. Smith, the First American Army physician to enter the camp after its liberation.

charming memoir by a Jewish woman of how she survived as a girl in her late teens in wartime Berlin.

The daughter of a teacher, Inge Deutschkron found a job in a workshop for the blind in 1941. Then and later, she writes, she met with almost invariable kindness on the part of non-Jewish Berliners. Seeing her wearing a yellow star, a man insisted that she take his place in the subway, which she was, of course, not allowed to do. People slipped apples and meat stamps into her pocket. After the deportations to the East had begun, in October 1941, Inge and her mother went into hiding. Scores of Gentile acquaintances and people she did not know at all took enormous risks in giving work to the two women and in feeding and sheltering them. They were forced to change residences repeatedly, for no one could take the risk of keeping them for more than a few months; but the two women always found volunteers to take them in. If there is any bitterness in Inge Deutschkron's account, it is mostly directed against the Jewish communal authorities, whom she accuses of having helped the authorities organize the deportations.

Toward the end of the war, the bombings and the influx of German refugees from the East made the situation of mother and daughter not very different from that of the other Germans, and when the Red Army arrived, they, too, were roughed up by Soviet soldiers. Unsentimental, resilient, aware that luck can make all the difference, Inge Deutschkron, who now lives in Israel, has remained a true Berliner. [In a footnote, Deák adds: "Bruce Pauley writes in *From Prejudice to Persecution* that 5,000 Jewish 'U-boats' or 'submarines' survived in Berlin, but only 700 in Vienna, a city that, before the war, had housed considerably more Jews. Even if we take into consideration the unreliability of all statistical data on annihilation and survival, and the differing conditions in the two cities, we have no reason to doubt that a Jew in hiding was more likely to find assistance among the notoriously cynical Berliners than among the Viennese."]

Myrna Goldenberg   (review date Winter 1993-94)

SOURCE: "Choices, Risks, and Conscience," in *Belles Lettres: A Review of Books by Women,* Vol. 9, No. 2, Winter, 1993-94, pp. 42-5, 48.

[*In the following review, Goldenberg discusses several works written by women, both personal narratives and fiction, that examine Nazi Germany and the Holocaust.*]

We are witnessing a flood of books about the Holocaust. Even the trickle of books by and about women during the Third Reich is slowly widening to a stream. Sometimes the stream yields crystalline gems and sometimes murky flotsam. The seven books reviewed here range from jewels to dregs, from rescue to survival, from ethnography to journalism, and from authenticity to sexational fiction.

Lucie Aubrac's and Hiltgunt Zassenhaus's important autobiographical chronicles of their defiance of the Nazis [*Outwitting the Gestapo* and *Walls: Resisting the Third Reich—One Woman's Story*] leave the reader breathless. Aubrac outwitted Klaus Barbie, the infamous head of the Vichy Gestapo (aka the Butcher of Lyon) by rescuing her husband, Raymond, who was second to Jean Moulin in command of the French Resistance. The Free French, headquartered in Lyon, has been the subject of extensive scrutiny since the capture of Barbie in 1982. Francine du Plessix Gray's insightful and moving analysis of "the hypocritical amnesia indulged in by the French nation to obliterate the truths of its collaboration with Nazism and of its deep complicity in the Holocaust" in "The Rise and Fall of Klaus Barbie" (*Adam & Eve and the City,* New York: Simon and Schuster, 1987) stands among the most substantial. With *Outwitting the Gestapo,* Aubrac joins Gray.

A creative and well-regarded history teacher, Aubrac narrates her tale with skill and precision. We follow her visiting Raymond in prison, teaching her eager young students, "interviewing" Barbie, keeping house, bribing Nazi guards, feeding her infant son, and listening to her rescued husband describe the torture sessions that lasted for weeks on end, while Barbie and his girlfriend became more and more sexually stimulated with each brutalizing blow delivered to Raymond. Aubrac was in the eighth month of her pregnancy when she and a few of her male colleagues in the Resistance pulled off the daring rescue. She had used her pregnancy as a ploy to gain entry to the offices of high-ranking Gestapo to get information on her husband's whereabouts. She was in her ninth month when she, Raymond, and their son flew to England—and freedom.

Aubrac not only sheds light on the French Resistance and some of its heroes and traitors, but she also writes from the perspective of a woman who was misunderstood in her time. When her comrades tell her "You fight like a man," she responds, "Why is it that the greatest compliment a man can pay a woman is to tell her: you write, you work, you act like a man." "Perfectly at ease as a woman," she answered her comrade in no uncertain terms, "What I did was a woman's job, and what's more, a pregnant woman's, something that would never happen to you." Through her narrative and her ironic comments, she reminds us that women, even those active in the underground, added their resistance job to their full-time jobs and their routine household duties, which were increasingly more difficult to do in times of shortage and deprivation. Perhaps *Outwitting the Gestapo* will stimulate the publication of more resistance narratives by women.

Republished after a 20-year hiatus, Zassenhaus's *Walls* complements Aubrac's book. The timing is perfect. Here we have an account of a young German woman who would not compromise her principles. During the war, her three brothers were summoned to defend the Reich while she sneaked medicines and food to Scandinavian prisoners of war.

Without a shred of self-importance and as if resistance were a normal, everyday response, Zassenhaus tells what "happens to be [her] story," beginning with the first day of Hitler's rise to power, January 30, 1933. The windows of their house had been plastered with "thick, yellow paper, printed over and over with swastikas. Overnight [their] house had been dimmed by unknown Nazi hands." Late for school because she tried futilely to scrape the windows, she began a career of defying the Nazis. She refused to salute Heil Hitler the next morning and made a "desperate movement" with her left arm that broke the glass of an open window and caused a minor riot in the classroom. The 1930s had taught her family to be cautious of the Nazis. They were denied university scholarships because they were not party members, so they ate less—and less well.

Eventually, Zassenhaus's degree in Scandinavian languages led to her appointment as "official interpreter to the Court of Hamburg," which, in turn, led to regular but dangerous visits to prisons to distribute mail that she was supposed to have censored. She actually added encouraging comments to mail that came from Scandinavia to the POWs and pleading messages to the mail leaving Germany for Scandinavia. She managed to smuggle letters from starved Jews in ghettos to their families and friends in Scandinavia to request food and clothing parcels before mass deportations began. Zassenhaus risked severe reprisals, and worse. Amazingly, she enrolled in medical school and continued her studies along with episode after episode of resistance work. *Walls* unfolds the hideousness of the Third Reich and the ridiculousness of its civilian zealots. Zassenhaus's courage as she dodges Gestapo and informers unifies the book, creating a backdrop against which the homefront tries to endure. Her ironic and restrained wit reveals her energy, intelligence, clear head, and unshakable faith in justice.

Nora Waln's *The Approaching Storm* is an abrupt change in perspective, sensibility, and insight. First published in 1939, *Storm* tells of Waln's years as a long-term visitor in Germany while her husband, an Englishman retired from government service in China, fulfilled a passion—the study of music in Germany. During these years, Waln, a successful journalist and a Pennsylvania Quaker, observed Germany and its neighboring countries closely. She tracked the spread of Nazism, noting its impact on all facets of life, from art to education, and pointedly described the vast differences between the Germany she found and the Germany she expected to find. Her keen eye and her compulsive need to research and report the historical perspective on German culture and history lead to painful conclusions. In fact, the book is sad. Reader and author witness the imposition of "instant and blind obedience to the Fuehrer's every command" by a German population too willing to accept the new order.

Waln, however, is almost unbelievably romantic, peppering the book with an optimism based on naive generalizations and wishful thinking. She generalizes that Germans are exceptionally and historically kind to animals; "Fundamentally, Germans are good"; and "The good in [Nazism] will endure. All other elements the German people will discard. They are not an ignorant mass. They are an educated populace." She closes her book on Christmas 1938, with a plea to her readers to pray for the Germans. Although she bemoans the militarization of Germany, she denies its reality and fails to confront the implications of incarcerating dissidents in concentration camps. Distressed that "pacificism is treason in Germany now," she holds on to the possibility that the dissidents will swell in numbers and prevail. *Storm* is valuable because of its eyewitness authenticity, but it is limited by its romanticism and naiveté.

Two survivor accounts contrast sharply with resistance stories and journalistic analyses. Blanca Rosenberg's *To Tell at Last: Survival Under False Identity, 1941-45* is the harrowing story of a young Jewish mother who evades the Nazis from one Polish city to the next until she winds up in Heidelberg, Germany, where she works as a maid until liberation. She had tried—and failed—to keep her infant son alive both in the ghetto and in hiding. She had witnessed the SS, aided by their Ukrainian guards, throw babies at concrete walls. She had witnessed the SS use children for target practice and then machine-gun the men who tried to stop the slaughter. She was helped by gentiles who gave her false identity papers, but she found that she had "forgotten how to be free, to act normally, to tread the sidewalks instead of the gutter, to look people in the eye without baring [her] fears."

She adjusted to a temporary respite from hell—"From Hades to the metropolis [Lvov] was too long a step"—but her compassion led her to recognize and help other Jews in hiding, thus making her vulnerable to capture. Her misery was bearable because she shared her danger and despair with Maria, her closest friend. They lived in Warsaw during the uprising. Using false papers, they worked as saleswomen in department stores, scrubwomen in hospitals, and maids in German households. They nurtured, lied, and took incredible risks for each other. They saved each other's lives and emigrated to the United States, where they both became social workers. Blanca's narrative gives life to Maria, and to their families and friends who did not survive.

There is a Place on Earth: A Woman in Birkenau by Giuliana Tedeschi is breathtaking. If its subject were not Auschwitz/Birkenau, it would be a beautiful book. It is, as most survivor narratives by women are, a vivid, realistic depiction of courage and sisterhood in the face of degradation and brutality. But Tedeschi's writing is extraordinarily sensitive—and feminist. Her metaphors assure us that the author is a woman: "Prison life is like a piece of knitting whose stitches are strong as long as they remain woven together; but if the woolen strand breaks, the invisible stitch that comes undone slips off among the others

and is lost." She is acutely connected to her feelings as well as to the beauty of family, community, and nature.

She writes of surrogate families; the prison rebellion on October 7, 1944, that began with women passing powder to the men who used it to blow up one of the gas chambers; Mala, the prisoner who had escaped with her lover but was caught and then tried to cut her veins before being hanged; the "pathological obsession with recipes and imaginary meals"; and of childbirth in the barracks, a horrible irony to be born just to die. Her barrackmate Edith delivered an eight-pound boy who "opened his eyes, wailed, and immediately closed them again forever." The fear of being used by Nazi doctors for their heinous experiments terrorized Tedeschi: "I was overcome by a wild desperation. My deepest, most intimate femininity was anguished and rebelled. I thought of my body brutally mutilated, its vitality hacked away, of being forced to surrender that most female function that nature had imposed to the monstrous violence these Germans in their hatred and scorn had coldly devised for us. . . . Memories of early motherhood, its infinite, overwhelming sweetness, flooded back like a torture, a physical need."

While incarcerated in the several concentration camps, Tedeschi despaired of the miraculous. But she was wrong—her survival and ability to rebuild her life is itself a miracle. She returned to Turin, Italy, where she taught Latin and Greek in the same high school for 40 years.

The last two books are unique, one interestingly so; the other, disastrously. R. Ruth Linden's *Making Stories, Making Selves* is actually two books in one, connected loosely by the author's growing consciousness of herself as a Jew, an awareness that was prompted by her awareness of the Holocaust. The first is an autobiographical account that focuses on her family's Jewish identification and her own emergence as a feminist. By 1982, she stopped using Robin, her first name, and began calling herself Ruth, signifying to herself "and others [her] desire to explore what it means to be a Jew and to live Jewishly." This process was enhanced by her gradual involvement with an oral history project to interview survivors. The second part of the book deals with the interviewing experience, its effect on her emotionally and intellectually.

Making Stories, Making Selves is a very personal book. We observe Linden learning about the Holocaust and then learning about her process of trying to understand survival and the victory of living freely. An unusual approach, this work is a primer on ethnographic research methodology. Although it is less about the Holocaust than it is about feminist ethnography, it is valuable analysis of "survival [of] the Holocaust [as] a social process; it could not be done alone." We witness Linden's intellectual development as she experiences intellectual and spiritual growth as a social process. This tight process—this interdependence of substance and process—is "polyvocal—collectively woven braids in which individual lives and memories are intertwined." They are, indeed.

Finally, *The Kommandant's Mistress,* by Sherri Szeman, is a moral embarrassment. Reminiscent of *Sophie's Choice* and *The White Hotel,* the book sensationalizes the Holocaust, weaving a lurid tale of a death-camp (presumably Auschwitz) kommandant who snatches a Jewish deportee from the selection ramp, rapes her in a guard tower, and then keeps her in his office, which is located in his house, for the remainder of the war. Of course, the complications include his wife and children, the mistress's hidden poems, the pressure from her campmates to participate in sabotage, the postwar accounts of the kommandant and his former mistress, and references to the crematoria, the Sonderkommando revolt, the Wannsee Conference, Ilse Koch's lampshades made from the skin of Jewish victims, and other items related to the Holocaust. Szeman is undoubtedly a gifted craftswoman who controls point of view skillfully, even brilliantly, but her work is offensive. Her improbable, sex-drenched plot betrays the memory of the dead and assaults their survivors.

Clearly, it is challenging to write about the Holocaust. The subject is depressing and threatening, and it is not easy to find words to describe and evaluate the unspeakable.

When the writer begins with honesty, the result is a historical document that requires respectful critical analysis. When the artist couples respect with her gift of insight and skill, the result is enduring truth.

By the very nature of the topic, Holocaust writing is often judged as either overwhelmingly moving or disappointingly ineffective; there is hardly any middle ground of response. . . . [The] most outstanding difference . . . is that good literature reflects a certain sentiment while the lesser material is sentimental. The distinction is crucial.

—Harry James Cargas, in "The Holocaust in Fiction," in Holocaust Literature: A Handbook of Critical, Historical, and Literary Writings, **edited by Saul S. Friedman, Greenwood Press, 1993.**

Helen Brent   (review date Winter 1993-94)

SOURCE: A review of *Different Voices: Women and the Holocaust,* in *Belles Lettres: A Review of Books by Women,* Vol. 9, No. 2, Winter, 1993-94, p. 46.

[*Below, Brent remarks favorably on the book under review.*]

When Carol Rittner read John Roth and Michael Berenbaum's *Holocaust: Religious and Philosophical Implications,* she asked the age-old inevitable question, "Where are the women?" They weren't in that book, nor are their experiences reflected in most of the books about the Holocaust. Indeed, although women survivors have never been silent and their narratives are no longer rare, their stories and experiences did not receive much attention, nor were

they anthologized. But Jewish women were doubly vulnerable: they were victims of both Nazi atrocities and misogyny. They experienced "different horrors" but the "same Hell," a description that underpins and unifies *Different Voices: Women and the Holocaust* (edited by Carol Rittner and John K. Roth).

Rittner and Roth compiled the answer to her question in *Different Voices,* a book that will become a touchstone in feminist and Holocaust studies. It is good literature, good history, and good philosophy. Its three sections are flanked by an insightful prologue and epilogue, a chronology, and demographic tables.

With the exception of Etty Hillesum, who was transported from Westerbork to Auschwitz (where she was gassed on November 30, 1943), all the voices, Jews and non-Jews, in part one, "Voices of Experience," are witness survivors. First-person accounts of survival and active resistance are stated simply, even quietly, but with stunning effect. We hear recent voices, like Ida Fink's and Sara Nomberg-Przytyk's, but *Different Voices* also rediscovers voices long out of print, like Pelagia Lewinska describing clothes so lice-infested that these bugs formed patterns of stripes and plaids on the fabric, mud-filled ditches into which the SS kicked women and nearly drowned them, piles of excrement that "inspired" Terence Des Pres's term Excremental Assault, and an "average" pain-filled work day at Auschwitz.

"Voices of Interpretation" is primarily composed of brilliant, scholarly essays by contemporary women historians whose point of vision reflects gender. Their studies of the intersection of gender and racism have much to teach us about vulnerability, pseudo-science, false patriotism, and spirituality. Magda Trocme epitomizes courage and goodness. Vera Laska calls herself "a gatherer of memories," but she is also a hero and a scholar. Sybil Milton, Marion Kaplan, Claudia Koonz, and Gisela Bock explore the historical records to answer Rittner's question as well as other pivotal questions on the significance of gender during the Holocaust.

Finally, "Voices of Reflection" offers artistic and thoughtful responses to the Nazi horror. Irena Klepfisz's poetry comments profoundly on the unspeakable; Charlotte Delbo tells us of the indelibility of Auschwitz on her senses and soul; and Joan Ringelheim seeks some reason behind the statistics and poses difficult questions for the scholar.

Yes, women's voices are missing, but this book, the first anthology of its kind (at least, in English), portends the beginning of more rediscoveries, more narratives of women's courage and caring, and more research into the catastrophe that haunts our memory and shapes our paths to the future.

Laurence Kutler   (essay date 1993)

SOURCE: "Holocaust Diaries and Memoirs," in *Holocaust Literature: A Handbook of Critical, Historical, and Literary Writings,* edited by Saul S. Friedman, Greenwood Press, 1993, pp. 521-32.

The assessing of autobiographical writing in the form of memoirs, records of oral interviews, and diaries for the period of the Holocaust is a little like sailing a boat in the fog. Without an eye on the lighthouse, one can easily be distracted and make errors in judgment causing disaster. A sailor's best rule of thumb is to have adequate maps to guide his or her approach toward a safe harbor.

The same situation confronts the historian of the Holocaust. Not enough time has elapsed for a corpus to have formed that can serve the function of history. J. Huizinga, a Dutch historian, has tried to propose a definition of history that can serve our purpose: "History is the intellectual form in which a civilization renders account to itself of the past" ["A Definition of the Concept of History," in *Philosophy and History: Essays Presented to Ernst Cassavier,* 1936]. The nature of the "intellectual form" and the accountability factor are the notions that are of the greatest concern. What did Huizinga mean by "intellectual form," and what standard could be meant? To whom are the writers of memoirs, diaries, and interviews accountable? These are some of the questions that need to be addressed before criteria can be established to identify which writings among those who survived and those who did not can be judged to have made a significant contribution to the historiography of the Holocaust.

Thus, like the sailor with maps to guide him or her to safe harbor, the historian needs a set of criteria that will serve as a guide for a proper methodology. Without it, the practitioner of history will steer off course. The following statements are useful in identifying memoirs or diaries that render an account of themselves to the past and serve us as sufficiently historical:

1. Diary and memoir writing is a specific form of tradition.

2. Diaries and memoirs are not concerned primarily with the accurate reporting of events; they also involve apology and self-justification.

3. Diary writing and memoirs concern themselves with causes of events and circumstances. This could be a reflection upon events or a moralizing tendency.

4. Diary and memoir writing will incorporate or reflect upon national consciousness or fate.

Returning briefly to Huizinga's definition, I am confronted with the notion of what constitutes an "intellectual form." Diaries, memoirs, or records of oral interviews qualify as intellectual forms since they are clear forms of individual expression set to paper with the purpose of communicating ideas. The standard of such writings must be tested by the value of the information gained and the place it has in the genre.

To what degree do the writings render account to the past? In order for this question to be answered, the collections have to be assessed in terms of presentation and of judgments of events and individual behavior. But more, the manuscripts should be accountable to the facts. Diary and memoir writing as a specific form of tradition is well accounted for, especially in Jewish tradition. In the worst of times this vulnerable people has responded to oppression by recording events as they unfold in an appeal not to its contemporaries but to the judgment of history. The book of Ecclesiastes is an example from late biblical times. *The Wars of the Jews* is a written account by Josephus of the wars against Rome presented apologetically to the Roman world. The medieval period saw a continuation of this tradition. Thus we have Moses Maimonides in his *Epistle to the Yemenites* encouraging these people to remain stolid in the face of persecution, Solomon Bar Samson telling of the Kiddush ha-Shem who were massacred in Mainz in May 1096, and Nathan Hanover recounting the horrors of the Chmielnicki pogroms in his *Vale of Tears.* On the eve of World War II Polish Jewry's greatest scholar, Simon Dubnow, advised his contemporaries to record everything for posterity. Whether or not they had ever read Dubnow, countless Jews heeded his advice.

Personal observations may be flawed by bias, hearsay, rumor, or outright error. While severe trauma may sharpen the senses momentarily, extended periods of starvation, disease, threats, and shifts from location to location can also result in confusion. As a result, some of those who experienced Elie Wiesel's "other planet" misplaced rivers and camps. Some survivors remember what they think they should remember. In retrospect, some of the jottings seem mundane—concern over food, housing, family—but none of them were unimportant. The diaries humanize the numbers. Six million people become individuals with passions and agonies that we can understand. In Holland a town clerk left a last inscription in the community notebook on December 31, 1942: "For we are left but few of many. We are counted as sheep for the slaughter, to be killed and to perish in misery and shame. May deliverance come to Jews speedily in our days."

About the time Abraham Toncman was pondering the fate of his people in Holland, a little girl who wanted to be a movie star was setting down her most personal thoughts in a journal. From 1942 to August 1944, Anne Frank complained about the crowding and discipline in the annex above her father's store in Amsterdam. But she also expressed hope when the Allies landed at Normandy. A teenager, she was falling in love, and she longed for a world without hate, where she might live as a Jew and Zionist. For many educators, *The Diary of Anne Frank* is the starting point for making the Holocaust relevant for young people.

Virtually the same aspirations are found in *Hannah Senesh: Her Life and Diary* (1972). The eleven-year journal (1933-44) of a young Jewish woman from Budapest contains some of the most moving writing on the Holocaust ever recorded. Older and more mature than Anne Frank, she expressed concern about anti-Semitism in the prewar period. Hannah Senesh steeled herself to racism by becoming an ardent Zionist and emigrating to Palestine. When her homeland was occupied by the Nazis, she volunteered to return to Hungary as a commando. There in November 1944 she was executed by a firing squad. Her poem "Blessed Is the Match" has inspired a book by the same name written by Marie Syrkin and has been incorporated into Reform Judaism's Hanukkah service. But a much more compelling statement is found in her 1941 poem "To Die" written at Nahalal, where Senesh speaks of the contrast between warm, sunny skies and the terrible consequences of war. She concludes, however, that she is willing to sacrifice herself for her home, her land, and her people.

Two other journals merit special mention. Few documents are as poignant as Janusz Korczak's *Ghetto Diary* (1978). The notes of the gentle pediatrician from Warsaw were published posthumously, Korczak having accompanied 190 orphan children to death at Treblinka in the summer of 1942. Korczak (whose real name was Henryk Goldszmit) wrote of sick and abandoned children who needed to be tended, of reading stories over and over to them, of people lying on the streets dying of starvation, of his own personal torment whether to use euthanasia on his orphans, and of his hope for a world where no child would be barred from playing with any other. As if anticipating those who would deny the facts of Nazi genocide, Korczak concluded thoughtfully, "What matters is that all this did happen."

Korczak, Senesh, and Anne Frank were not professional historians. But Emmanuel Ringelblum was, and his writings, recovered between 1946 and 1950 from milk jars buried during the war, constitute a conscious effort on the part of a trained historian to document what occurred in the Warsaw ghetto. A Labor Zionist who worked for the Jewish Historical Institute before the war, Ringelblum served as the model for the fictional character Noach Levinson in John Hersey's inspirational novel *The Wall*. Like Levinson, Ringelblum organized intellectual meetings in the ghetto where Peretz and Sholom Aleichem were discussed. Ringelblum's journal, however, transcends Hersey's novel because it is fact. From its masked opening in January 1940, addressed to Ringelblum's father, to the final entries posted in December 1942, *Notes from the Warsaw Ghetto* (1958) tracks the progressive dehumanization of the largest concentration of Jews in Europe. The reader learns of expedience that compromised leaders of the Judenrat who though that they were sacrificing a few of their people to save the whole, and of the same expedience that forced overburdened families to turn a deaf ear to the whimpering of children freezing on stoops below. The reader learns how Jewish businessmen like Kohn and Heller and policemen like Jacob Leikin collaborated with the Nazis hoping to emerge richer and unscathed at war's end while volunteers at the Joint Distribution Committee, CENTOS children's aid, and TOZ medical aid worked valiantly in the most primitive conditions to help their fellow Jews. We learn what they were reading in that doomed quarter (the memoirs of Lloyd George, Napoleon, Tolstoy), how they regretted being herded into the ghetto, and how they wondered if the free world truly appreciated their plight.

Neither Ringelblum's notes nor *The Warsaw Diary of Chaim A. Kaplan* (1965) nor *The Warsaw Diary of Adam Czerniakow* (1979) cover the desperate uprising of May 1943. For that the reader should consult Philip Friedman's *Martyrs and Fighters* (1954), which includes lengthy extracts from Marek Edelman's *The Ghetto Fights* (1946), Melekh Neustadt's *Hurbn un oyfshtand fun di Yidn in Varshe* (1948), Tuvya Borzykowski's *Tsvishn falndike vent* (1949), and SS General Jürgen Stroop's report titled *Es gibt keinen judischen Wohnbezirk in Warschau mehr* (1943). Ringelblum's notes do not possess the sweep of history; no grand conclusions are offered. They are the words of a man afraid, a family man, who hoped that they would have value for posterity. Just as Anne Frank's diary has achieved epic status in literature, so too Ringelblum's notes merit a special place in historiography.

The postwar reminiscences of Holocaust survivors form an incredibly large corpus. Ever expanding, these works may be broken into individual accounts and collections edited by professional scholars. Among the more notable memoirs that tell the tale of Jews in Poland are Alexander Donat's *The Holocaust Kingdom* (1963), Leon Wells's *The Janowska Road* (1963), Bernard Goldstein's *The Stars Bear Witness* (1949), Oscar Pinkus's *House of Ashes* (1964), Vladka Meed's *On Both Sides of the Wall* (1979), Joseph Ziemian's *The Cigarette Sellers of Three Crosses Square* (1975), Sara Zyskind's *Stolen Years* (1981), Matylda Engleman's *End of the Journey* (1980), Halina Birenbaum's *Hope Is the Last to Die* (1971), Jack Eisner's *The Survivor* (1980), Izaak Goldberg's *The Miracle Versus Tyranny* (1978), George Topas's *The Iron Furnace* (1990), and Tadeusz Pankiewicz's *The Cracow Ghetto Pharmacy* (1987). The story of Jews in Hungary is told in Rudolf Vrba and Alan Bestic's *I Cannot Forgive* (1968), Georgia Gabor's *My Destiny* (1982), Livia Jackson's *Elli* (1980), and Gizelle Hersh and Peggy Mann's *Gizelle, Save the Children* (1980). For the Ukraine, see Paul Trepman's *Among Men and Beasts* (1978) and Mel Mermelstein's *By Bread Alone* (1979). For Latvia, see Gertrude Schneider's *Journey into Terror* (1980) and Frida Michelson's *I Survived Rumboli* (1982). The story of Czechoslovakia is told by Hana Demetz in *The House on Prague Street* (1980) and Saul Friedlander in *When Memory Comes* (1979). On the Jews of Holland, see Marga Minco's *Bitter Herbs* (1960), Etty Hillesum's *An Interrupted Life* (1984), and Jona Oberski's *Childhood* (1983). On France, see Joseph Joffo's *A Bag of Marbles* (1974) and Sim Kessel's *Hanged at Auschwitz* (1972). Among the more gripping concentration-camp memoirs are Filip Muller's *Eyewitness Auschwitz* (1979), Kitty Hart's *Return to Auschwitz* (1981), Eugene Heimler's *Concentration Camp* (1961), Germaine Tillion's *Ravensbrück* (1975), Fania Fenelon's *Playing for Time* (1977), Luba Gurdus's *The Death Train* (1978), Primo Levi's *Survival in Auschwitz* (1973), and Isabella Leitner's *Fragments of Isabella: A Memoir of Auschwitz* (1978). Other recommended works that have a single person's perspective include Elie Cohen's *The Abyss* (1973), William Perl's *The Four-Front War* (1979), Peter Schweifert's *The Bird Has No Wings* (1976), Ilse Koehn's *Mischling, Second Degree* (1978), Judith Strick Dribben's *A Girl Called Judith Strick* (1970), and Charlotte Delbo's *None of Us Will Return* (1968).

A second approach to memoirs is for historians, psychologists, or community leaders to interview a number of survivors for the purpose of making some sense of the Holocaust. A number of these texts stress the heroic response of Jews to the Nazis. They range from the very good (including Yuri Suhl's *They Fought Back: The Story of the Jewish Resistance in Nazi Europe* [1967], Anny Latour's *The Jewish Resistance in France (1940-1944)* [1981], Marie Syrkin's *Blessed Is the Match* [1947], and Eric Boehm's *We Survived* [1949]) to the more pedestrian (Ina Friedman's *Escape or Die* [1982], Reba Karp's *Holocaust Stories: Inspiration for Survival* [1986], and Milton Meltzer's *Never to Forget* [1976]). Some of the works have a clinical orientation, including the excellent *Survivors, Victims, and Perpetrators: Essays on the Nazi Holocaust* (1980) edited by Joel Dimsdale, Sarah Moskovitz's *Love Despite Hate: Child Survivors of the Holocaust and Their Adult Lives* (1983), Claudine Vegh's *I Didn't Say Goodbye: Interviews with Children of the Holocaust* (1984), and Shelly Lore's *Jewish Holocaust Survivors' Attitudes Toward Contemporary Beliefs About Themselves* (1984).

The late 1970s witnessed the appearance of a spate of Holocaust memoirs. For more than a quarter-century, many Holocaust survivors were disinclined to speak about their wartime experiences. They concentrated on rebuilding their lives, and raising children. Once these children were grown and out of the home, the survivors were faced with their own mortality. Now they were eager to talk, and the result was the publication of books like Dorothy Robinowitz's *New Lives: Survivors of the Holocaust Living in America* (1976), Lucy Steinitz and David Szonyi's *Living After the Holocaust: Reflections by the Post-War Generation in America* (1976), Isaiah Trunk's *Jewish Responses to Nazi Persecution* (1978), and Helen Epstein's *Children of the Holocaust* (1979).

Following along these lines in his book *The Holocaust,* Martin Gilbert attempts to gather testimony from survivors in order to constitute a record of the Holocaust. The book gives a brief historical overview of Hitler's rise to power and continues to the 1945 death marches. The book employs diary accounts to substantiate conditions throughout. Interspersed with events are also memoirs, for example, Zindel Grynzspan recalling October 27, 1938, when he and his family were expelled from Germany, or Eric Luca's account of storm troops defiling a synagogue.

Gilbert also utilizes some of the chronicles from the ghettos. For example, the Lodz chronicle is cited in his chapter "Write and Record," which were Simon Dubnow's last words before being shot in the back in December 1941. Gilbert ends his book with the following rationale: "The survivors tell their story to their children, set it down in memoirs and testimonies, relive it in nightmares. . . . Each survivor faces the past, and confronts the future with a burden which those who do not go through the torment, cannot measure. 'I may bear indelible scars in body and soul' Cordelia Edvardson has written [in Gilbert's *The Holocaust*]; 'but I do not intend to reveal them to the world—least of all the Germans. That is the pride of the survivor. Hitler is dead but I am alive.' "

In *Voices from the Holocaust* Sylvia Rothchild employs a tripartite system of "Life Before the Holocaust," "Life During the Holocaust," and "Life in America." As editor, Rothchild allows survivors to relate their testimonies. She edits 650 hours of conversation in a gripping fashion that conveys to the reader a feeling that he or she, too, is "a kind of survivor." Stories are told by survivors from France, Greece, Hungary, Denmark, Czechoslovakia, Poland, Holland, Yugoslavia, Germany, Austria, Italy, Russia, and the United States. Some have lived in Israel or South America. The preface gives the self-justification of the survivors "to our sons . . . may they never know the heartaches and agonies their parents suffered during those years except by reading this transcript or listening to the tapes," or "I tell you the only thing that kept me going is the burning desire to tell, to bear witness."

In excerpts from "Life Before the Holocaust," Rothchild offers a precise description of the survivors' place in society. A sense of loss and nostalgia is expressed. These tapes, transcribed in written form, offer impressions of European life in much the same way as other European Jews have related them. They are accounts full of social insights. Life is simplified with statements such as "We loved each other and helped each other. And then the Germans came" or "At my job everything was normal."

The moralizing tendencies of the survivors in this volume take on important messages. "Do not hate! Do not harm! Share with others less fortunate." "Remember the past and learn from it." Rothchild states that they share their painful memories of the dark places in recent history in the hope that things may never be so dark again. Sometimes the survivors reflect upon their experiences and feel strongly toward Israel. Their work in support of Israel may in fact bring about a personal redemption. For Stephen Ross from Dodz, Poland, freedom in America necessitates a state in Israel.

In *Amcha: An Oral Testament of the Holocaust,* Saul Friedman attempts to fill a lacuna in Holocaust studies. Friedman communicates the story of the mass of Jews who survived the Holocaust, the common folk "who lived on the periphery of colossal events." The book is limited, for the most part, to survivors who were acquaintances of Friedman in Youngstown.

Three themes are evinced in *Amcha* by the survivors: (1) widespread anti-Semitism, (2) an ingenuous attitude on the part of Jews themselves, and (3) resistance manifested in a variety of ways. The survivors' accounts include accuracies and inaccuracies as to events and places, but these are not the important criteria for this chapter. A search for apology and self-justification, integral themes for our genre, do turn up. Siep Jongeling from Holland expressed the view that "the Germans are not all bad people. I have no objections to Germans as long as they don't want to impose their will on me." Leon Lieberman theorized on survival: "In Buchenwald, you gotta survive. When I came in they [the Germans] noticed my number. They gave me credit for this and gave me a better job."

The book is also filled with reflections on life after the Holocaust. Morris Weinerman, the friendly carpenter from Youngstown, expresses his feelings: "I still have dreams. It has been a long time, and all the time I have been free. But in the dreams right away I am surrounded. All the time I am caught again. . . . We do not forget." Optimism is expressed by Esther Bittman Shudmak: "I don't think that anything like that would happen again. People now have access to ammunition and guns. People protect themselves more than in those days. I think now people care more about others in general."

Isaac Kowalski's *Anthology on Armed Jewish Resistance, 1939-1945* is a repository of accounts on Jewish resistance by partisans and underground activists. The book contains memoirs, letters, testimonies, biographies, and autobiographies of the resistance movement. This work depicts the Jew as a fighter with a three-fold battle: fighting the Nazi invaders, facing the indigenous population who hated him, and struggling to exist within the partisan movement.

The anthology serves the aim of an apology, that is, to explain the situation of the partisans and their raison d'être to the Western community. To this end, Kowalski attempts to portray the Jewish partisan as a fighting soldier. He seeks to bury the lie that the Jew was not a fighting man. The romantic notion of Ph.D.'s as glamorous fighting warriors, "the new chivalry," is ferreted out in the book time and again.

The volume allows the partisans to speak for themselves, to enable the reader to sense the tension and to recapture the moment. Jewish heroism is paraded in Sobibor, the trenches, the ghettos, and at the front. The tendency to moralize, albeit in a grim fashion, is evinced in the book of Anthon Schmidt: "Every man must die once. One can die as a hangman or as a man helping others. I'd die for helping other men."

Revenge is also a value justification. Norman Salsitz took a machine gun and fired salvo after salvo into the Germans: "Their party was over. At this moment with the gun still hot in my hands I no longer felt like a victim. I had settled my score with the *Scharffuhrer* and my pact with G-d who had let me down so many times."

In Helen Fein's book *Accounting for Genocide,* the reader is asked to confront the Holocaust as an event challenging earlier notions of history. "To understand the implications of the Holocaust, the reader must grapple with its success." The book's main interest to us is the part that explores the responses of Jews, drawn from first-person records in Warsaw, the Netherlands, and Hungary. She records Ringelblum's diary on the Warsaw ghetto as well as the diary of Chaim Kaplan.

The section on the Warsaw ghetto employs memoirs and diaries interspersed as a literary device within a running narrative by the author. Fein even goes so far as to use excerpts from novels. Fein's book does not lend itself to the type of literary criterion that we have posed. It is essentially a work for sociologists that uses personal accounts of the victims to reconstruct the social psychology of the camp inmates.

A literary work of merit can be found in Yaffa Eliach's *Hasidic Tales of the Holocaust*. She utilizes a long tradition of oral story telling circulating among the Hasidic communities and puts these tales and interviews down in print. The original interviews were conducted in nine languages and numerous dialects. The tales fall into four major parts reflecting four stages: ancestors and faith, friendship, the spirit alone, and the Gates of Freedom.

In the first part, "Ancestors and Faith" shows the reaction of the Jew, the innocent victim, when he encounters his executioners. Our first criterion of diary writing being a form of tradition is nowhere so exemplified as in this volume. The Hasidic tale with its themes of love, optimism, and faith in God ultimately triumphs in the world of the Holocaust.

The writing of autobiography, memoirs, and diaries is an enterprise that is essentially reflective. Not only do these authors engage in the task of writing about experience but also offer us their own thoughts of that experience. Thus different attitudes are adopted by these authors, conditioned by the momentous and monstrous experience that they all shared. They are rendering accounts about occurrences (history) while having participated in these events and in turn being shaped by these events. Thus the type of writing described here is not history but the reflective subjective passion of the participant.

The authors share a burning and important question that is rarely evinced: What is this account for? For whom is it intended? The attempts to address these issues are the raison d'être of these authors and are in fact the thread that ties this type of historiography together.

The autobiographers seek an explanation; they seek self-knowledge. In their quest for this gnosis they render an account of human action so that human understanding can profit. The accounts of history in any of the forms studied here are for posterity. They are for the present readers. They make an attempt to reach out across time to an audience so that the audience can be made aware of particular and subjective events. But they are also an exercise in self-awareness. The tension between these two objectives gives genesis to the passion in the literature. The reader then has the task of explaining the connection between the narrative of the individuals and their reason for its rendition.

Historical research can also benefit from the memoirs and diaries cited here. These are in fact statements of eyewitnesses and, as such, contemporary with the events that they attest. Praise is due for these sources because they are not derivative. If they lack the sound judgment and interpretation of historians, they do so because there is a distinction between the two methods. Our authors do not use the tools of the modern historiographer by collecting evidence and evaluating it. Instead, they turn to personal accounts and reflect back on them. The researcher will need to avail himself or herself of the patrimony of memoirs, diaries, and other accounts in order to evaluate the history of this period. This evaluation will allow a "lost" civilization to speak to new generations, render account of itself, and thereby fulfill J. Huizinga's definition of history. The researcher will then have contributed to the understanding of the period known as the Holocaust.

Walter Reich   (review date 29 January 1995)

SOURCE: "In the Maw of the Death Machine," in *The New York Times Book Review*, January 29, 1995, pp. 1, 25-6.

[*Reich is a Polish-born American psychiatrist and nonfiction writer. In the following review of Lawrence L. Langer's* Admitting the Holocaust *and* Art from the Ashes, *he praises Langer for focusing on the physical reality of the Holocaust.*]

During the last five decades, many writers have tried to make sense of the Holocaust through philosophical, religious, psychological, symbolic and literary formulations. Often, they have tried to find *some* good in that epoch of profound evil, *some* way of distilling hope, or at least consolation, from that vast sea of despair. They have struggled with the meaning of memory, the limits of spiritual strength, the rupture of history, the ontology of survival.

But in the process, they have too frequently lost sight of what actually happened, of how the suffering was actually felt, of how death actually came, of who actually caused it and of how it was actually carried out. There was, in fact, nothing metaphorical about the Germans' systematic murder of six million Jews, nothing metaphysical or literary. The Jews were terrorized, humiliated, herded, enslaved, tortured, shot, gassed and burned; then their bones were ground up, mingled with their ashes and dumped into ponds or pits. There was nothing uplifting about any of this, no saving spiritual grace, no redeeming human nobility. Yes, some Jews, in the face of certain death, and with almost no support from anyone, resisted the ferocious German onslaught; but they rarely had a chance to accomplish much more than a gesture, and their efforts were overwhelmed by the murderous force of the Germans.

The problem with literary and philosophical abstractions of the Holocaust is that they tend to obscure the event's reality, immensity and singularity. Other events since then, also terrible but not comparable in scope, focus or planning, have been called holocausts as well; the misbegotten efforts at universalization and interpretation have too often yielded not understanding but rather a diminished appreciation of the intensity of history's most fiercely inhuman episode and of the extent of modern civilization's extraordinary potential for evil.

So it is important that Lawrence L. Langer has given us two books—a collection of essays [*Admitting the Holocaust: Collected Essays*] and an anthology of readings [*Art from the Ashes: A Holocaust Anthology*]—to bring us back from the vacancy of words to the density of physical reality. These books provide a sense of how Europe's Jews experienced, on a daily basis, the pressure of the Holocaust's ever-tightening vise, and of how they were extruded, finally, into the German death machine that processed them, with an ineluctable and brilliant efficiency, into ashes and ground-up bones.

In the introduction to his collection of essays, *Admitting the Holocaust,* Mr. Langer, a professor emeritus of English at Simmons College in Boston and the author of *Holocaust*

Testimonies: The Ruins of Memory, reminds us of our tendency, understandable but misleading, to adopt in dealing with the Holocaust "a persisting myth about the triumph of the spirit that colors the disaster with a rosy tinge and helps us to manage the unimaginable without having to look at its naked and ugly face."

Mr. Langer writes about our need to speak about survivors rather than victims, or of martyrdom rather than murder; to "evoke the redemptive rather than the grievous power of memory"; and to "build verbal fences between the atrocities of the camps and ghettos and what we are mentally willing—or able—to face." He stresses that one of the most difficult realities for us to grasp is that during the Holocaust Jews never had real choices—that they were all marked for murder, and that if they chose the line moving to the right, say, rather than the left, or chose to submit to the Germans in some way, they might put off their deaths for a while but not for very long.

In these essays, Mr. Langer illuminates the literature of the Holocaust—the chroniclers of the ghettos and the camps, the writers of Holocaust fiction and poetry, and the representations of the Holocaust in film. He deplores the television drama *Holocaust,* shown 17 years ago, which portrayed "well-groomed and sanitized men and women filing into the gas chamber," but applauds Steven Spielberg's recent film *Schindler's List* for its focus "on the steady fear that drains all feeling when one's daily diet is the ruthless and impulsive cruelty of the murderers."

No less valuable is Mr. Langer's other gift to us—*Art From the Ashes: A Holocaust Anthology.* In one remarkable volume, perfectly suited for anyone studying the Holocaust, he collects personal accounts, many of them by Holocaust survivors, like Elie Wiesel and Primo Levi, but some by people who were devoured in the cataclysm and whose writings were found where they had hidden them. Mr. Langer also collects Holocaust-related fiction, poetry and art, some by figures who have become well known, like Paul Celan, as well as work by others whose efforts are more obscure but no less compelling. Some of the accounts in Mr. Langer's anthology have been translated into English only in the last few years. Three of them are, in the unadorned record they leave, utterly gripping.

One of these is the diary of Abraham Lewin, found after the war. It describes the daily terror of the great deportation, which began on July 22, 1942, and lasted 54 days, of 300,000 of Warsaw's Jews to the gas chambers in Treblinka. On Aug. 12, Lewin pauses briefly to focus on his wife: "Eclipse of the sun, universal blackness. My Luba was taken away during a blockade. . . . It looks like she was taken directly into the train. . . . I have no words to describe my desolation. I ought to go after her, to die. But I have no strength to take such a step." Yet, in the same entry, Lewin quickly returns to the tragedy of his people: "The 'action' goes on in the town at full throttle. All the streets are being emptied of their occupants. Total chaos. Each German factory will be closed off in its block and the people will be locked in their building. Terror and blackness. And over all this disaster hangs my own private anguish." Lewin's last entry is dated Jan. 16, 1943, after which he and his teen-age daughter were probably caught in a roundup and sent to Treblinka.

Admitting the Holocaust and *Art from the Ashes* provide a sense of how Europe's Jews experienced, on a daily basis, the pressure of the Holocaust's ever-tightening vise, and of how they were extruded, finally, into the German death machine that processed them, with an ineluctable and brilliant efficiency, into ashes and ground-up bones.

—*Walter Reich*

Another diarist, Jozef Zelkowicz, provides a description of the deportation in 1942, from the ghetto in Lodz, Poland, of 20,000 Jews. Before that deportation, the ghetto's leader, Mordechai Chaim Rumkowski, believing he could save the majority of the ghetto's inhabitants by convincing the Germans that their labor would be useful to them, pleaded with the Jews of Lodz to give up their children under age 10 and their old people so that the rest, who could work, would be saved. Zelkowicz quotes Rumkowski's speech to the assembled residents, who realized that deportation meant death: " 'The ghetto has been afflicted with a great sorrow. We are being asked to give up the best that we possess—children and old people. . . . I must stretch forth my arms and beg: Brothers and sisters, yield them to me! Fathers and mothers, yield me your children.' (Enormous and fearful weeping among the crowd.) . . . 'I have to cut off limbs in order to save the body! I have to take children, because otherwise—God forbid—others will be taken.' (Terrible wails.)"

The next day, Zelkowicz records, the "action" in the Lodz ghetto began: "Over on Rybna Street the police have to take them out of apartments. There they are encountering resistance. There they have to cut living, palpitating limbs from bodies. There they wrench infants from their mothers' breasts. . . . People scream. And the screams are terrible and fearful and senseless. . . . The whole ghetto is one enormous spasm. The whole ghetto jumps out of its own skin and plunges back within its own barbed wires. Ah, if only a fire would come and consume everything! If only a bolt from heaven would strike and destroy us altogether! . . . Everyone is ready to die."

In the end, giving up the children and the old people didn't stop the deportations to the gassing centers; the German intention, from the beginning, was to kill everyone, productive worker or not. The terrible choice Rumkowski thought he was making for the ghetto turned out to be no choice at all.

A third diarist, Avraham Tory, describes the roundup, in October 1941, of 10,000 Jews in the Lithuanian city of Kaunas (Kovno, in Yiddish), who were taken to a killing site known as the Ninth Fort, where Lithuanians, working

for the Germans, executed them: "In the fort, the wretched people were immediately set upon by the Lithuanian killers. . . . They forced them to strip naked, pushed them into pits which had been prepared in advance and fired into each pit with machine guns.. . . The murderers did not have time to shoot everybody in one batch before the next batch of Jews arrived. . . . They were pushed into the pit on top of the dead, the dying and those still alive from the previous group. So it continued, batch after batch, until the 10,000 men, women and children had been butchered."

Compared with these firsthand accounts, fiction could be, one would think, only a pallid version of reality. Yet the fiction Mr. Langer collects in his anthology, much of it by survivors themselves, like Aharon Appelfeld, highlights the reality of the Holocaust with stunning intensity. In a story by an Auschwitz survivor, Arnost Lustig, a character listens to the sounds of people being shot outside his barracks and knows that the snow coming down is mingling with the ashes from a crematorium's nearby chimney: "I felt the snow, the ashes and the silence around me. I felt the urge to go outside, for which the guard would immediately shoot me before I got to the barbed wire. I wanted to touch with my lips a sliver of ash or snowflake."

And the poetry Mr. Langer collects evokes it all. Dan Pagis, a Romanian Jew who survived three years in German concentration camps, wrote in Hebrew. Here, in its entirety, is the breath-stopping poem called "Written in Pencil in the Sealed Railway-Car":

> here in this carload
> i am eve
> with abel my son
> if you see my other son
> cain son of man
> tell him that i

The most profound tragedy of the Holocaust is that it happened. But it is not yet finished. Its victims' mouths remain open. And so long as they speak, and even when they don't, we are driven, and privileged, to listen.

Michael Burleigh   (review date 5 May 1995)

SOURCE: "The Unbelieved," in *The Times Literary Supplement*, No. 4805, May 5, 1995, p. 8.

[*An English educator and historian, Burleigh has written extensively on Nazi Germany. In the following review, he discusses E. Thomas Wood and Stanislaw M. Jankowski's* Karski, *the biography of a Polish underground agent, and* The Buchenwald Report, *a study of the SS concentration camp system combined with testimony of Buchenwald inmates, edited and translated by David A. Hackett.*]

Karski is the remarkable story of a modest man who has become a "professional hero", which the journalist authors tell with sympathy and verve, even if their hyperbolic subtitle ["How One Man Tried to Stop the Holocaust"] is rather discordant. Jan Kozielewski (also known as Witold Karski) was born in 1914 in the industrial city of Lodz in Poland. Educated by the Jesuits and at the University of Lwow, where he witnessed (and later regretted doing nothing about) attacks on Jews by right-wing students, Kozielewski joined the fast stream in the Polish foreign service in 1938 and, top of his class, seemed set to become an ambassador at an early age.

The war intervened. With his horse-artillery battery decimated by the Luftwaffe, Kozielewski fled eastwards, and found himself in an NKVD prison camp in central Ukraine. Concealing his rank from Stalin's class-warriors, Kozielewski bluffed his way back to Poland. (Many of his fellow officer inmates were subsequently murdered at Kalinin, Kharkov and Katyn.) Immediately reimprisoned by Stalin's Nazi allies, Kozielewski escaped from a moving train, returning to Warsaw where his elder brother—the city police chief—gradually inducted him into the underground. Adventures already tantamount to the Polish equivalent of a good war were shortly eclipsed by other acts of extraordinary heroism.

Jan Kozielewski became Witold Kucharski (the name of a student contemporary who was conveniently marooned abroad), a name which, by the loss of a syllable, produced his *nom de guerre*. Karski's intelligence, languages, mnemonic skills and ability "to wither into the background" equipped him to act as a courier for the faction-ridden Polish underground. During briefing sessions, he would listen straight-faced as the socialists relayed their fears of a post-war fascist coup, while their nationalist allies spoke darkly of a Blum-style popular front behind which lurked Jews and freemasons, intelligence he would store in his head as he trekked over the Tatras mountains and then half-way across Europe.

Inevitably, operations involving guides and safe houses ran the risk of betrayal. In June 1940, a Slovakian peasant turned Karski over to the Gestapo. The latter battered him with rubber truncheons, kicked out several of his teeth and broke a few ribs. During a period of respite from one such session, Karski extracted a razor-blade he had concealed in his boot, and sawed through his wrists in a desperate attempt at suicide. This resulted in a crucial period in hospital, from which his underground contacts were able to liberate him. Thirty-two people were subsequently tortured and shot for alleged or actual involvement in his escape. Underground security procedures meant that he was effectively quarantined for seven months on a country estate, where he had to take such precautions as keeping his sleeves rolled down even on the hottest of days lest anyone spot the giveaway scars on his arms.

Resuming his work as a courier, in August 1942, Karski met leaders of Warsaw's Jewish underground whose physical appearance enabled them to operate outside the ghetto. So agitated that their pacing shadows danced on the dimly lit walls, the Zionist and Bundist leaders were adamant that "not a single leader of the United Nations should be able to say that they did not know that we were being murdered in Poland and could not be helped except from the outside", and that therefore Karski would have to be smuggled into the Warsaw Ghetto. After crawling through a tunnel forty yards long, Karski and a companion shuffled through the densely packed streets, past people in whom life consisted of a faint rustle beneath layers of rags, only their clothing separating them from the corpses that littered the streets. Members of the Hitler Youth amused themselves by taking potshots at faces incautious enough to venture near a window. In addition to returning twice to this nightmare, Karski followed the odour of evil to its operative centre: journeying to Lublin, he disguised himself as a Ukrainian militiaman and, accompanied by a guard who had been bribed, entered a holding camp at Izbica used to regulate the flow of Jews to the Belzec extermination camp. Hundreds of people were being loaded into boxcars whose floors had been covered with quicklime. They would either go directly to Belzec or slowly expire in some railway siding *en route* to it. What he saw led to an immediate mental breakdown, so apparent it put both his and his escort's lives in jeopardy. Afterwards he washed the experience from his body with water, and from his mind with vodka.

Disguised as a French volunteer worker, Karski made his way via Berlin to Paris. A dentist had injected his mouth with a substance that induced tumescence, which, together with the missing teeth, would plausibly offset the need to speak halting French during a long train journey. After he had crossed into Spain, British and American secret service agents escorted him to Gibraltar and thence to an RAF base outside London. Members of the Polish government in exile arranged meetings between Karski and ever more illustrious interlocutors. It became obvious that the latter were planning to disburden the Poles of eastern territories in order to oblige their Soviet ally. Although Karski's celebrity as a hero was used to attract the interest of senior British government figures, this strategy proved counter-productive, in the sense that it allowed senior British politicians deftly to switch the conversation from issues of substance regarding Poland's future borders or the fate of the Jews to the courier's personal exploits, with Eden on one occasion telling him to step nearer the window because "I want to see what an authentic hero of this war looks like".

The same pattern was repeated in Washington. Top policy-makers were invited to dine with Karski at the Polish ambassador's residence in order to whet the appetite of a President who was fascinated with the minutiae of cloak-and-dagger existence. On one such occasion, there was a curious exchange between ambassador Ciechanowski and Supreme Court Justice Felix Frankfurter over Karski's graphic description of the fate of the Jews: "Mr Ambassador. I did not say this young man is lying. I said I am unable to believe him. There is a difference." Karski finally met Roosevelt. Demonstrating his unique capacity to transcend local Polish perceptions and prejudices, Karski explained the difference between Nazi policy towards Poles and Jews: "the Germans want to ruin the Polish state as a state; they want to rule over a Polish people deprived of its elites. . . . With regard to the Jews, they want to devastate the biological substance of the Jewish nation." Although Karski succeeded in holding the President's attention for an hour and a quarter, Roosevelt was predictably fascinated by the possibilities of equipping aircraft with skis to land in Poland; non-committal about both Poland's future borders or the plight of the Jews; and evasive on the subject of "wily" Uncle Joe's agents' efforts to subvert the Polish underground from within. Karski left overawed but also disappointed.

Since his numerous speaking engagements in America had blown his cover in Occupied Europe, Karski reconciled himself to a career as a propagandist and publicist. There are a few tantalizing references to wartime Manhattan, including drinking sessions with the young Leonard Bernstein. He wrote an account of his exploits, entitled *Story of a Secret State* (1944), although his literary agent persuaded him to drop a chapter on nefarious Communist activities, while his publisher none too subtly indicated that he should include something on his romantic life, muttering "Pity" on being told that these matters had a low priority in the cells of the Gestapo. Only thirty-four and somewhat adrift at the end of the war, Karski eventually resumed his studies and in 1953 joined the faculty at Georgetown University. Nicknamed "McCarthyski" by some of his students, he divided his time between teaching, buying and renovating old houses, and lecture tours in the Third World on behalf of the US Information Service. He had various on-going links with the Pentagon and CIA. In 1978, Karski contributed his spell-binding forty-minute interview to Claude Lanzmann's *Shoah,* where the trauma of what he had seen in the Warsaw Ghetto is palpable. Since the early 1980s, Karski has been fêted by various Jewish communities, and in Israel where a tree bears his name in the Avenue of the Righteous.

Economically written and well researched, the book does not explore in any detail why Karski risked his life on so many occasions, or what obliged him to insert the fate of Poland's Jews into the agenda of his various reports from the underground, even when this took up time his Polish political masters, who were never very far from his shoulders, would have wanted devoted to other issues.

Karski's powerful story ends in the routinized world of academic Holocaust conferences and the bestowing of belated thanks by grateful nations. *The Buchenwald Report* takes us back fifty years to when the actuality of these horrors was just being revealed. Shortly after the liberation of the camp on April 11, 1945, a report was compiled at the instigation of an intelligence unit from the Psychological Warfare Department of the US Army. It was designed to provide "in-depth analysis of the inner workings of Buchenwald and, by extension, of the entire Nazi concentration camp system". A team under the Austrian, conservative, Catholic inmate Eugen Kogon drew up the analytical and descriptive Main Report, which, following the suggestion of Richard Crossman, Kogon reworked and published as *Der SS-Staat* (1946, translated into English as *The Theory and Practice of Hell*). This drew upon the oral testimony of 104 prisoners interviewed while they were still in the camp. The documents containing the testimony went missing, and came to light again in 1983; they are published and translated for the first time, together with the Main Report, in David Hackett's well-organized edition that will be an invaluable source for future historians of the SS concentration-camp empire. Buchenwald was built by prisoner labour on a heavily wooded mountain above Weimar, housing at one point during the war nearly 90,000 people. It gradually spawned a number of eccentric

facilities, such as an angora-rabbit station; a zoo; a personal falconry for Hermann Goering; and a vast riding hall where Ilse Koch, the commandant's wife, could prance around in front of mirrors to the tune of an SS band for half an hour twice a week. The SS guards disposed of a sculpture studio, which did a nice line in marble items for Himmler's desk—Viking long ships and painted porcelain—and well-stocked cellars and larders. The 150 guard dogs had considerably better food than the inmates, who, on liberation day, treated themselves to a load of dog biscuits.

Corruption in the camp was endemic; sadistic abuse by SS men, including more than their share of rheumy-eyed drunks and syphilitic sexual perverts, was a fact of everyday life. Virtually every piece of testimony by a prisoner bears witness to the "hands-on" nature of their approach, much of it of an extraordinary, psychopathic savagery, or else done merely to offset boredom, as when guards tossed prisoners' caps near the fencing and then ordered them to retrieve them in order to watch people being shot. The detail in the prisoner accounts is of a matter-of-fact, and frequently sickening, immediacy that leaves the mind reeling at human ingenuity in cruelty. Comparing these two very different accounts from the Second World War, we should all be thankful the values embodied in Jan Karski prevailed, and that, at least in western and much of eastern Europe, the bullies and murderers have been relegated to the margins.

Michael André Bernstein   (review date 5 May 1995)

SOURCE: "Against Comfort," in *The Times Literary Supplement,* No. 4805, May 5, 1995, pp. 9-10.

[*Bernstein is an Austrian-born Canadian educator and critic. In the following review of Simha "Kazik" Rotem's* Memoirs of a Warsaw Ghetto Fighter *and Lawrence Langer's* Admitting the Holocaust *and* Art from the Ashes, *Bernstein focuses on Langer's criteria for valid responses to the Holocaust.*]

In the epilogue to *Memoirs of a Warsaw Ghetto Fighter: The past within me,* [Rotem's] gripping account of his time as the nineteen-year-old head courier of the Jewish Fighting Organization (ZOB) which planned and led the Warsaw Ghetto Uprising, Simha Rotem gives a bitter description of his arrival in Israel in the months just before statehood: "I was interrogated about everyone who had been killed, but I was never asked, even remotely, about those who had survived. . . . This was why, even after learning Hebrew, I didn't talk very much. I preferred not to tell about myself and where I had spent the war years." Rotem's shock at such a reception is hardly surprising, but the nearly universal lack of curiosity about a survivor of the single most famous armed Jewish insurrection against the Nazis surely is. In recent years, after all, we have often been told that out of a deep embarrassment at how a doomed European Jewry went meekly "like lambs to the slaughter", Jews in the post-war world, and especially in Israel, have over-emphasized the limited and largely symbolic acts of defiance by those few who chose to fight back against their murderers.

This, at any rate, is clearly Lawrence Langer's view, and the essays collected in *Admitting the Holocaust* emphatically, and it must be said, somewhat repetitively, insist on what he calls "the current disproportionate emphasis on resistance during the Holocaust", as well as on the utter untenability of the categories of individual choice or meaningful action by Jews caught up in the German machinery for their wholesale extermination. Langer, who writes that our task is "not to acknowledge heroic lives, but to mount melancholy deaths", thereby implicitly aligns himself with those who, already in 1947, were not concerned to ask Rotem about the few ghetto fighters who had survived, but solely about the myriad victims of the genocide.

Each of the chapters in *Admitting the Holocaust* was originally published as a separate article between 1983 and 1994, and the book usefully reprints such still pertinent essays as "Kafka as Holocaust Prophet: A Dissenting View". But the oldest of Langer's texts, like "The Americanization of the Holocaust on Stage and Screen", with its sustained critique of such commercially aimed ventures as *Judgment at Nuremberg,* the theatre and film versions of *The Diary of Anne Frank,* and the appalling television series *Holocaust,* could have been omitted without significant loss, since condemnation of their facile sentimentalizations is by now a commonplace in any serious writing on the Shoah. But even the more recent essays suffer from Langer's tendency to insist that he stands virtually alone in recognizing the evasiveness and irrelevance of conventional tropes of consolation, martyrdom and dignity-in-suffering when confronting the Holocaust.

Paradoxically, while stressing the emptiness of any notion of "heroism" in a context of industrialized mass extermination, Langer's own rhetoric stakes out a dubious claim to a singular intellectual-moral fortitude in being able to confront the bleak truth from which he thinks the rest of us turn our eyes. Langer so persistently indicts "us" for our "elaborate fantasies about the dignity of dying under or living through such miserable circumstances", for "the nostalgia that invades so many of our memories of the Holocaust", and for "the rhetorical shield of heroism that protects us", that by the end his book reads like an extended polemic against an "us" whose naive and wilful blindness seem little more than the projective fantasies of a polemic in search of easy targets.

It is hard to know what prompts Langer's certainty that "we go on using a discourse of consolation" based on "ideas like natural innocence, innate dignity, the innovative spirit, and the triumph of art over reality", in order to construct a "normalized or sanitized" interpretation of the Nazi genocide, since he provides little evidence for what he takes as the near-universality of such a strategy. Doubtless such voices exist, although it is hard to imagine how one might go about "sanitizing" the Holocaust, but they are neither as numerous nor as influential as Langer seems to believe, and when he frames his realization about the infernal universe of the Holocaust with phrases like "though I realize this statement may sound radical, unorthodox, or threatening to many readers", his insistence seems particularly misplaced. In this case, the "radical

statement" that Langer thinks may "threaten" us is his rejection of interpretations that "read the Holocaust through the values implied in the stories of Jesus and Job"—as though these really were the archetypes habitually invoked in texts about the Shoah. Nowadays, I am afraid, everyone, at least in the American academy, longs to sound "radical, unorthodox, and threatening", and if it is sad to see a figure of Langer's distinction adopt the same vocabulary, it is still more distressing to see an interpretation of the Holocaust advertise itself in such tones. Langer is absolutely right to refuse to find any "lesson about the value of suffering for the growth of the human spirit" in the Holocaust, but he is attacking a stance whose moral obtuseness has been broadly recognized. Indeed, one would be hard pressed to find any traces of so callous an attitude in the many scrupulously researched and carefully thought-through works that are currently shaping our understanding of the Shoah.

Langer's dismissive invocation of the Job and Jesus stories as exemplary narratives of redemptive suffering, although a curiously contrived target for so extended a critique, is characteristic of the basic premises and arguments of *Admitting the Holocaust,* and these premises and arguments are both seriously flawed on their own terms and potentially harmful in the ways they seek to circumscribe the range of appropriate discourses about the Shoah. Together, the theoretical positions staked out in this book, and the specific instantiations of those positions gathered in *Art from the Ashes,* Langer's deeply moving anthology of memoirs, diaries, fiction, drama, poetry and painting, both from and about the Shoah, seek to establish something close to a "canon" of appropriate responses. And, like all powerful attempts at canonization, Langer's, too, is as proscriptive as it is responsive, as confident of its criteria for excluding as of its grounds for granting admission.

To his great credit, Langer openly argues his case both *for* the perspectives he thinks face up to "the rupture in human values" enacted by the Holocaust, and *against* those he rejects for their unwillingness or inability to give up the search for some "mental comfort" in their accounts of the ghettos and death camps. And because he reiterates his fundamental principles so forcefully, Langer makes it possible to question them in an equally direct way. Put in the starkest terms, such a questioning would make three distinct but related counter-claims, claims that move outward in widening circles from the field of Holocaust studies to more general positions about the function of culture today. (1) Even if what Langer calls "a culture of consolation" ever was a regnant orthodoxy in texts about the Holocaust, which is questionable, such a discourse manifestly no longer occupies that role. (2) Jews *did* react in very different ways to the Nazi assault, and it is as crucial to learn about, record and understand those individual differences as it is to stress the common death which the Nazis tried to inflict on the entire Jewish people. (3) "The idea of rupture [and] the discourse of ruin", far from meeting with widespread resistance, actually occupy a central place in our culture's self-representation. The urge towards unbridled violence, the lust for domination, and the impotence of culture to act as a brake on our most savage instincts, have long constituted an enormous, if not actually the major, portion of our intellectual conversation about history as well as about the human psyche. To indict culture because of its helplessness either to prepare one for, or somehow actually to restrain, an event as lethal and cataclysmic as the Holocaust profoundly misunderstands the relationship between culture and lived experience; very little about either cultural or individual human values can be learned from how they bear up in a situation *in extremis,* and the Shoah is not an appropriate, let alone a privileged, gauge for the authenticity or legitimacy of those values.

Although Langer likes to initiate his arguments through rhetorical questions such as "does Holocaust 'remembrance' have redemptive power?", the problem is less the coercive nature of his question than the tendentiousness of its crucial terms. The existence of a "redemptive" view of art and culture is not in dispute, and it has been the subject of several probing critiques like Leo Bersani's study *The Culture of Redemption* (1990). But even at its most self-assured, the view that art can endow inherently painful or simply insignificant and transitory experiences with a compensatory dignity has always been thought of as applying only to an individual's private existence, never to the agony of a whole people. Holocaust "remembrance", like Holocaust scholarship and art, is not redemptive in the sense of repairing an injury, but rather in the sense of rescuing an irreparable catastrophe from the universal oblivion its perpetrators intended for it. But more generally, we need to be clear that narrated desolation, just like narrated hope, is an arranged mode of representation, and

that, consciously or unconsciously, each relies on formal devices of structuring, lexical and tonal decisions, and specific emphases. At issue, in other words, is not what Langer seems to regard as an artificial and self-deluding rhetoric versus an unmediatedly "natural" one, but rather the truly difficult question of decorum in its full ethical sense: the ongoing attempt to work out which modes and techniques of representation are appropriately responsive to the exigencies of so monstrous a series of events.

> **The basic premises and arguments of *Admitting the Holocaust* are both seriously flawed on their own terms and potentially harmful in the ways they seek to circumscribe the range of appropriate discourses about the Shoah.**
>
> —*Michael André Bernstein*

This is why it is particularly disturbing to watch Langer essentially "write out" of Holocaust testimony those witnesses whose responses do not match his particular criteria. A characteristic example is his treatment of Etty Hillesum (1914-43), a young Dutch Jewess who kept a set of diaries (translated as *An Interrupted Life: The Diaries of Etty Hillesum*) during her internment in the Dutch transit camp at Westerbork, from which she was finally deported to be murdered in Auschwitz. Hillesum maintained simultaneous love affairs with two significantly older men in Westerbork, read works by Dostoevsky and St Augustine, and was determined to maintain as much of her erotic, intellectual and emotional vitality as possible. But precisely her efforts to sustain the values by which she had lived before Westerbork prompt Langer to discredit her testimony. For him, "our hindsight . . . makes her buoyancy seem pathetic and exasperating rather than praiseworthy". Langer believes that any attempt to maintain one's psychological continuity in the face of irrevocable annihilation can only be a form of evasion, and any report that does not register the total demolition of one's being is profoundly dishonest and must be rejected accordingly.

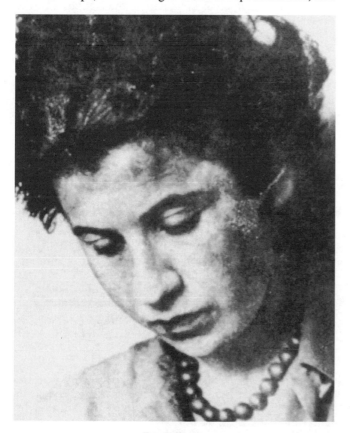

Etty Hillesum.

Although it is entirely legitimate to criticize post-war historians, scholars and writers on the Holocaust for error of fact or inappropriateness of tone, Langer's dismissal of the "breathtaking naïveté" of this testimony from a woman who died in the Shoah, and his judgment that "her verbalized courage approaches rhetoric" is deeply troublesome. So intent is Langer on his own rhetoric of condemnation that he completely loses touch with any sense of decorum, and after criticizing Hillesum's "arrogance of tone and style", he goes so far as to suggest that her "bland conclusions . . . may remind some" of the callousness of a post-war German prosecutor unable to understand the enormity of what the Nazis had done.

For Langer, a recorded experience of the Holocaust seems

to be significant only in so far as it bears witness to 6 million similar fates, and although he criticizes Terrence Des Pres for "creating a collective identity called 'the survivor'", Langer in effect de-individualizes both victim and survivor precisely by denying anyone the right to experience the Holocaust except through the categories and terms he himself has judged appropriate. And perhaps the most important of these categories, central to both *Admitting the Holocaust* and *Art from the Ashes*, is encapsulated in Jean Améry's famous phrase, "No bridge led from death in Auschwitz to *Death in Venice*". But Améry's dictum, for all its dark brilliance, needs to be carefully questioned, not merely recited; and finally, perhaps, it may open, rather than shut off, a whole series of questions on the relationship between pre-Nazi culture and the Holocaust.

Améry seems to indict Mann's novella, and metonymically culture as a whole, for the absence of such a bridge. But would not a culture that provided this "bridge" be much more alarming? What if, in other words, there were not a chasm, but rather, as has been argued by many, a *continuity* between the Nazi atrocities and the highest forms of German creativity? But in this context, I am less concerned to explore that question than to ask in more general terms why we ought to require of any work of art that it serve as a preparation for, or a link to, the experience of torture and genocide. And yet—though neither Langer's prefatory account of Primo Levi's life and work, nor the excerpt by Levi included in *Art from the Ashes* would let one suspect it—culture, in the specific form of Dante's lines about Ulysses in *Inferno* XXVI, *did* help Levi, if only briefly, even in Auschwitz. Levi's recollection of Dante's great canto did not provide a bridge *to* Auschwitz; instead it gave him a momentary bridge *back* to a different way of thinking about himself, a way that enabled him still to answer in the affirmative the question, "Is this a man?" I am far from sentimentalizing Levi's experience by invoking this episode, but I also think it cannot be elided without distorting our understanding of his testimony.

Clearly, neither Hillesum's diaries nor Simha Rotem's memoirs would find a place in Langer's anthology, but neither could the "Canto d'Ulisse" chapter from *Survival in Auschwitz*, and this is exactly what marks the limits of the anthology's authoritativeness. But the writing and art that stay within Langer's grounds for inclusion are generously and thoughtfully represented. In its scope and breadth, *Art from the Ashes* is the single most significant anthology of Holocaust writing yet published in English, and reading it is an almost unendurably painful, yet necessary, glimpse into what Langer rightly says is not an "anti-world, but the world as Nazi Germany decided it should be". That any voices at all have come back to us from that world is itself amazing, and although Langer's impulse to legislate what constitutes a legitimate response, even by the victims, must be rejected, his gathering of these voices represents an act of both vital remembrance and historical continuity.

ANNE FRANK REVISITED

Yasmine Ergas (essay date 1987)

SOURCE: "Growing up Banished: A Reading of Anne Frank and Etty Hillesum," in *Behind the Lines: Gender and the Two World Wars*, edited by Margaret Randolph Higonnet and others, Yale University Press, 1987, pp. 84-95.

[*In the essay below, Ergas compares the diaries of Etty Hillesum and Anne Frank, focusing on such themes as femininity, identity, and persecution.*]

Memories help us live. Oddly, they need not be our own, seared as they are into the lives of those who were not there. Wars, for example: long after the bombing has stopped and the shell-shocked cities have been reconstructed, children learn to remember scenes of devastation they never witnessed. Persecution, too: age-old fears come to haunt generations born and bred in safety. Partly experienced and partly borrowed, memories are selective—mental notebooks we keep to honor the past, but equally to keep track of ourselves. "*Remember what it was to be me:* that is always the point," Joan Didion said of her jottings [in *Slouching towards Bethlehem*, 1981], and the same could well be said of what we choose to recall.

Diaries serve a double function, reminding both author and reader of a past self. Anne Frank and Etty Hillesum tracked their personal routes along transitory moments, and we in turn trace in their diaries the signposts to the present. Although the differences between then and now, between them and us, are enormous, these diaries still feed the memories of many today.

An Interrupted Life and *The Diary of a Young Girl* bear witness to life as it was lived in parallel to the Nazi concentration camps. They are not "camp" stories, permeated by the horrors of Auschwitz or Dachau. Instead, they tell of the attempt to maintain or construct normalcy in a rapidly bestializing civil society. From them we learn of persecution and war as they once intertwined with the processes of growing up female and Jewish.

What do they tell us? Synopses of such works are always difficult. For portrayals of the authors, let me refer you to the texts themselves. My intent is to unravel something of what they say about developing identities in the context of genocide. The diaries talk of maintaining individuality, forging personalities, coming to terms with femininity when persecution straitjackets its victims into a racial identity intended to be all-encompassing and all-defining. Although Anne Frank and Etty Hillesum repeatedly attempt to fashion and review their ways of being women, gender ultimately recedes to second place. As Nazism casts them, they must cast themselves: first and foremost as Jews.

These diaries speak, then, of the intersection of war and persecution. War is not for everyone the same. For persecuted groups, its contours are dictated by banishment. Their men and boys do not defend their countries at the front; they are not the nation's warriors. Their women and girls do not courageously nurse the wounded in battle, send their beloveds patriotic messages sealed with state approval, or otherwise join the country's effort. They may escape, resist, or submit. But they must always confront the condition of having been singled out—in this case, for annihilation.

Both young women, relatively affluent, of cultured milieux, and trapped in German-occupied Holland, Etty and Anne recorded the passages that led from individual lives to a collective fate. Etty Hillesum began writing first, at the age of twenty-seven. Her diaries, abridged by her Dutch publisher, were written between March, 1941, and October, 1942. The book also includes a few letters written later, up until her deportation on September 7, 1943. When Anne Frank started her diary on June 14, 1942, Etty was close to ending her own. And by the time the Frank household was deported—on August 4, 1944— Etty has been dead in Auschwitz, eight months.

Their styles are very different. Anne receives a diary for her thirteenth birthday. Within a week the diary has acquired a name, Kitty, and been properly introduced, via Anne's descriptions, to the entire family. Kitty is Anne's confidante in a friendship initiated in freedom and continued in the cloistered captivity of the *Achterhuis* or Secret Annexe where the family, together with a colleague of Otto Frank's, Mr. Van Daan, his wife, and their adolescent son, Peter, find refuge. [In a footnote, Ergas adds: "Frank portrays Kitty's character in a short story written in hiding: see *Anne Frank's Tales from the Secret Annexe,* 1983."] (Some time after going into hiding, they invited Albert Dussel, a dentist of late middle age, to join them.) Notwithstanding occasional doubts, Anne possesses the "instinct for reality" that is the hallmark of a diary keeper. Everyday life is not too prosaic to be carefully recorded. She chronicles its details, patterning the day's events into a coherent narrative. The narrative is its own point, although it also often serves as the springboard for moral reflections, laying the foundations of *Selbstbildung,* of construction of the self or of self-improvement.

Etty hardly ever reports a day's events and never provides an introduction to her cast of characters. Like a diver going off the deep end, she plunges in with "Here goes, then." A series of reflections follows, written at all times of day and night. Etty is not addressing a paper standin for a best friend as she records impressions and feelings in a nervous reworking of her spiritual and moral self. Her diaries are written in the mode of annotations designed to evoke a full range of associations rather than to record each day's passing. "That may seem rather clumsily put, but I know what I mean," she comments after a particularly elliptical entry, making the point of her writing clear.

A variety of factors must have contributed to the two women's divergent approaches. The one conjures up her alter ego as an imaginary penpal, while the other seeks to fathom and reorder her innermost self. For Etty, turning inward is painful: "So many inhibitions," she remarks at the outset, "so much fear of letting go, of allowing things to pour out of me, and yet that is what I must do if I am ever to give my life a reasonable and satisfactory purpose. It is like the final, liberating scream that always sticks

bashfully in your throat when you make love." For Anne, the diary is an immediate source of joy: "Now I must stop. Bye-bye, we're going to be great pals!" she ends her first entry.

Despite their differences, Anne and Etty share a propensity to harp on the limitations inherent in women's attitudes toward men and to set themselves on routes of less fettered freedom. For Anne, the captive community in which she lives provides the models from whom she fully intends to differ: her mother, Mrs. Van Daan, even her much-admired sister. The pettiness of their concerns strikes her, as does the triviality of their accomplishments. "If God lets me live," she exclaims in April, 1944, "I shall attain more than Mummy has ever done, I shall not remain insignificant." A few days earlier she remarked in a similar vein: "I want to get on; I can't imagine that I would have to lead the same sort of life as Mummy and Mrs. Van Daan and all the women who do their work and are forgotten." The road to significance leads, Anne thinks, through working "in the world and for mankind"; the road to life after death, she hopes, can be paved by writing. Femininity rarely threatens these aspirations: there are no obvious traces of female fear of success. [In a footnote, Ergas adds: "Nonetheless, describing Kitty, who 'wants to work in a factory, like those jolly chattering girls she sees passing by the window,' Anne does say, 'Kitty's mother always says that a girl doesn't get a husband if she's too clever, and that, Kitty thinks, would be just awful' (*Anne Frank's Tales from the Secret Annexe*)."] Just before scorning her mother's "insignificance," Anne affirms confidence in herself. "I know what I want, I have a goal, an opinion, I have a religion and love. Let me be myself and then I am satisfied. I know that I'm a woman, a woman with inward strength and plenty of courage."

Like Anne, Etty is impatient with the conventional bonds of womanhood. While also referring critically to her mother, she frequently proffers general comments on the "not at all simple . . . role of women," whose marks she recognizes in herself—unlike Anne. Passing "a beautiful, well-groomed, wholly feminine, albeit dull woman, I completely lose my poise. Then I feel that my intellect, my struggle, my suffering, are oppressive, ugly, unwomanly; then I, too, want to be beautiful and dull, a desirable plaything for a man." This desiring to be desired Etty dismisses as "only a primitive instinct." Reflecting on traditional feminine conditioning, she looks forward to an "essential emancipation of women." "We still have to be born as human beings, that is the great task that lies before us."

This want of emancipation notwithstanding, Etty's lifestyle seems largely unhampered by patriarchal constraints. Her reviewers often cite as indicators of her sexual liberty her dual involvement with her mentor, Speier, and Papa Han, her kindly and elderly landlord; and her entries allude to several earlier experiences. She pursued her psychological and spiritual liberation in tandem with her studies. Having already earned a degree in law at the University of Amsterdam, she enrolled in the Faculty of Slavonic Languages before turning to psychology. She lived in Papa Han's house with four friends, in an arrangement similar to that often found around university campuses today. The way to free femininity may have been arduous and uncharted, but it was open. So it appeared, at least, as described by Anne and Etty, upper-middle-class girls of "enlightened" and cultured backgrounds. But, while the future of women revealed avenues of possibility, that of the Jews appeared increasingly walled in by political foreclosures.

The diaries of Anne Frank and Etty Hillesum talk of maintaining individuality, forging personalities, coming to terms with femininity when persecution straitjackets its victims into a racial identity intended to be all-encompassing and all-defining.

—*Yasmine Ergas*

Branded as a special enemy in occupied lands, the Jews were sharply set off from their societies. As the racial laws were strengthened, demarcations became more rigid. Race prevailed as the ordering societal criterion. Yet Etty had been keeping a diary for six months before she talked of herself as a Jew, and even then the mention is more metaphorical than factual. On walking through south Amsterdam, she wrote, "I felt like an old Jew, wrapped up in a cloud. No doubt that's recorded somewhere in our mythology: a Jew moving along, wrapped up in a cloud." Over the course of many months, however, her Jewishness impinges on her sense of self at an accelerating pace, finally becoming the implicit referent when she says *we*. For Etty, "Jew"—once a seemingly marginal connotation—had been transformed into the ineluctable answer to the question "who am I?" In July, 1942, she wrote: "What is at stake is our impending destruction and annihilation, we can have no more illusions about that. They are out to destroy us completely, we must accept that and go on from there."

A fortnight earlier, Anne had introduced herself to the as yet unnamed Kitty. "Sketching in the brief story of my life," a sentence and a half sufficed for the family's vital statistics: her parents' ages at marriage, the births of her elder sister, Margot, and of herself. Immediately she launched into a description of their lives, "as we are Jewish." Friday evening dinners or Passover festivities do not ensue. Of the forty-five lines that Anne dedicates to this presentation, thirty are devoted to the Nazi racial laws and their repercussions. "As we are Jewish," Anne explains, the Franks had left Germany in 1933. But the rest of the family stayed behind, "so life was filled with anxiety." With the arrival of the Germans in Holland, "the sufferings of us Jews really began. Anti-Jewish decrees followed each other in quick succession," and she lists them. To be a Jew, a persecuted Jew, is an essential component of Anne's sense of self: it prescribes the coordinates by which she locates herself in the world.

Anne chafes against the racial yoke represented by the yellow star. "Surely the time will come when we are people again, and not just Jews," she writes well into 1944, longing not for the obliteration of Jewish identity but for the restoration of individuality. Etty invokes that time too, in a letter from Westerbrok. [In a footnote, Ergas notes that "Westerbrok was a 'transit camp' in the east Netherlands to which Jews were deported before being sent to other camps. For histories of the Netherlands during the Second World War focusing on policies toward the Jews, see J. Presser, *The Destruction of the Dutch Jews,* 1969; and Helen Fein, *Accounting for Genocide: National Responses and Jewish Victimization during the Holocaust,* 1979."] "The outside world probably thinks of us as a grey, uniform, suffering mass of Jews, and knows nothing of the gulfs and abysses and subtle differences that exist between us. They could never hope to understand." To understand, that is, how differences persist notwithstanding the iron rule of racial caste. [In a footnote, Ergas states: "The Nazis did differentiate. Etty's parents, for instance, fruitlessly hoped to be admitted to Barneveld, a temporary refuge for the privileged. Even at the camps particular powers and protection were given to some: kapos, entertainers, physicians, technicians. Ultimately, however, these distinctions only articulated and bolstered the general category of 'Jew.' "]

Collective identities imply common destinies. As the Nazi persecution intensified, the futures Anne and Etty envisaged changed. In April, 1942, Etty could anticipate the day when, chancing upon an anemone preserved in the pages of her diary, she would remember Speier's fifty-fifth birthday. [In a footnote, Ergas explains: "Speier, a Jewish psychochirologist, had moved to Amsterdam from Germany. Etty began as his patient, worked temporarily as his secretary, and remained devoted to him until his death. He, however, was engaged to a young woman in London, and, although emotionally involved with Etty, remained 'faithful to her [his fiancée] above everything else.' "] Looking back upon this happy moment of her youth, she would then be, Etty foresaw, a matron who had attained a clearly imagined moment of the future. That future represented a personal development woven from the idiosyncratic yearnings of an aspiring writer endowed with intense spiritualist tendencies and strong passions. "I am sure," she wrote in the early summer, "that one day I shall go to the East." But within a matter of weeks the prospect of walking through Japanese landscapes had faded. The future was reduced to the question of survival or death as persecution crystallized the awareness that reordered experience, the anticipation of imminent mass murder. On "July 3, 1942, Friday evening, 8:30" she describes the rupture that has sundered her life's apparent continuities. "Yes, I am still at the same desk, but it seems to me that I am going to have to draw a line under everything and continue in a different tone." "Every day I shall put my papers in order and every day I shall say farewell."

Anne undergoes a similar transition. In the summer of 1944 the young girl who "did so want to grow into a real young woman" senses her impending doom and recalls her obligations. "I must uphold my ideals, for perhaps the time will come when I shall be able to carry them out," she reminds herself, having stared disaster in the face. "I see the world gradually being turned into a wilderness. I hear the ever approaching thunder, which will destroy us too, I can feel the suffering of millions and yet, if I look up into the heavens, I think that it will all come right." Months earlier, she had equated the time when it would "all come right" with survival and testimony. In April she had written: "If we bear all this suffering and if there are still Jews left, when it is over, then Jews instead of being doomed will be held up as an example." Distinguishing herself from Margot, who wished to be a midwife in Palestine, Anne dreamed that May of a year in Paris and one in London, learning languages and studying the history of art, seeing "beautiful dresses" and "doing all kinds of exciting things." Hopes of an individual, lighthearted future remained, hostage of an uncertain collective fate.

The leaden quality of that fate contrasted sharply with the possibilities feminine identity seemed to hold in store. Reading Anne and Etty it seems, however, that persecution provided a greater impetus to searches that stretched Jewish spirituality than to social experiments that yielded transformative models of femininity. Bound to a hunted community at once racial and religious, Anne and Etty seek the transcendental meaning that can endow their lives with reason, value, and significance. In a novel written in hiding, Anne grapples with the divisiveness of race. The tale of Cady—who appears in many ways indistinguishable from her narrator—breaks off in grief when the heroine's friend Mary is deported. " 'Mary, forgive me, come back.' Cady no longer knew what to say or think. For this misery she saw so clearly before her eyes there were no words . . . she saw a troop of armed brutes . . . and in among them, helpless and alone, Mary, Mary who was the same as she was" [*Anne Frank's Tales from the Secret Annexe*].

Anne's fiction echoes her diary. On November 26, 1943, she dreamed of her deported school friend, Lies. Lies's imploring gaze mesmerized Anne, now anguished and incapable of offering help, wracked by grief and an emotion we term today "survivor's guilt." [In a footnote, Ergas adds: "For a succinct discussion of survivor's guilt, see Robert J. Lifton, 'The Concept of the Survivor,' in *Survivors, Victims, and Perpetrators: Essays on the Nazi Holocaust,* ed. Joel E. Dimsdale, 1980."] Like Anne in her dream, Cady ranks among the privileged. But between them there is an important distinction: Cady is a Christian. As Anne's double on the other side of the racial divide, she incarnates a pedagogy of the persecuted. A Christian emphasizing anti-Semitism's savagery, she epitomizes the moral stance Anne must have recognized in the Christian friends on whose unfaltering loyalty the Secret Annexe depended. Anne became conscious of the growing precariousness of such a stance when the news of spreading, virulent Dutch anti-Semitism reached the family's refuge. Insisting that "one must always look at things from both sides," she tried to explain to Kitty the alleged behavior of those Jews who, by betraying resistance secrets or otherwise acting wrongly, had incurred the wrath of the Germans on the Netherlands. Anne did look at things from both sides, through Cady: as a Jew taking on the persona of a Christian and as a Christian seeing herself in the person of a Jew. [In a footnote, Ergas continues: "Pleading for under-standing toward individual Germans, Etty insisted that they were also suffering. Of 'that kosher German soldier with his bag of carrots and cauliflowers at the kiosk' who had told her friend Lies that 'she reminded him of the late rabbi's daughter whom he had nursed on her deathbed for days and nights on end,' Etty says: 'I knew at once: I shall have to pray for this German soldier . . . German soldiers suffer as well. There are no frontiers between suffering people, and we must pray for them all.' "]

Strikingly, in this only fictional piece to mention Jews, Anne does not clearly identify as one herself. Here the *Tales* and the *Diary* differ: with the exception of Cady's story, Anne refrains from literary forays into the matter of her own race. But, although no one ever utters a *kiddush,* religiosity surfaces throughout fables and short stories animated by Anne's psychological twins: fairies, elves, bears, and little girls. Belief in God repeatedly issues from their voyages in search of self. "In the field, amid the flowers, beneath the darkening sky, Krista is content. Gone is fatigue . . . the little girl dreams and thinks only of the bliss of having, each day, this short while alone with God and nature." The first-person protagonist of "Fear" comes to a similar conclusion. Having fled her city home in the midst of violent bombings, she finally rests in the countryside. Later, when war is over, fear appears as "a sickness for which there is only one remedy . . . look at nature and see that God is much closer than most people think." Locked into the Secret Annexe, Anne could not indulge longings for nature and personal space. The claustrophobic world of confinement forced the quest for meaning— and identity—inward.

Exploring spirituality introspectively and untrammeled by religious observance, Anne developed beliefs at most loosely related to Judaism. Embracing practices and systems of signification proper to Christianity, Etty even more evidently strained the limits of her received religion. The morning of Good Friday, 1942, she recounts having knelt in prayer and recalls the bathroom's "rough coconut matting." Hesitantly, she confesses to success, for the struggle to bow down in prayer has long engaged her and is central to the allegory she has been weaving, the tale of "the girl who could not kneel." In October of that year she equates kneeling with prayer. Her story, she says, is strange: "the girl who could not kneel. Or its variation: the girl who could not pray." Like her practices, her beliefs assume Christian tonalities. "I have broken my body like bread and shared it out among men. And why not, they were hungry and had gone without for so long," the last diary entry notes before her sacrificial closing words: "We should be willing to act as balm for all wounds." The Christian hues of her faith notwithstanding, Etty never disavows Judaism, nor does she dwell on its potential conflicts with her spiritual trajectory. On the contrary, referring to her love for Speier she exclaimed at the end of April, 1942, "I am so glad that he is a Jew and I a Jewess."

While the grip of racial Jewishness tightened, its hold as an organized religion weakened. Practice was largely impossible. The Franks, who took a menorah into hiding, complemented Chanukah candle-lightings with Christmas celebrations. Perhaps privileged Dutch and German

Jews like Etty or Anne were already too distant from the Jewish religious tradition to perpetuate it in such trying conditions and on their own. And yet, Anne's father oversaw her nightly prayers. Many factors must have fashioned their spiritualities. Certainly, persecuted Jews found innumerable solutions to the question all were asking: "God Almighty, what are You doing to us?" The words escaped Etty in Westerbrok.

Somehow, every Jew had to find an answer. And every answer found remained that of a Jew. No matter how apostate individual Jews' beliefs, the Nazi persecution had established the supremacy of descent over faith in the definition of the Jewish community. [In a footnote, Ergas states: "Anti-Semitic persecutions have not always been based on race: the Spanish Inquisition, for instance, focused on beliefs. At that time, as the history of the Marranos shows, conversion provided an escape."] For all her spiritual trespassing into Christian domains, Etty, like Anne, stayed within that community. In the practical activity of evolving beliefs, with untold others they explored possible religiosities of the unobservant Jew.

By contrast, persecution provided Anne and Etty with few opportunities for the practical remodeling of their identities as women. Where soldiers are drawn from populations neatly cleaved along lines of gender, age, and health, when war leads ablebodied men to battle and leaves all others at home, persecuted groups are promiscuously amassed into communities of fear. Nazi anti-Semitism did not emancipate Jewish women. Slave labor cannot be equated with enlistment for factory jobs or other patriotic—and remunerative—tasks. For Jewish women, barriers affecting labor-force participation were not lifted. They were not called upon to occupy posts men left vacant. They were not integrated into labor organizations. They did not axiomatically gain special powers over their households, head communities and families, bring in vital wages, reorganize living arrangements, support dependents. They were not awarded childcare services, nutrition programs, widows' pensions. They were not extolled by ideologies that elevated their status while catalyzing their support. In their struggles to survive extermination, Jewish women often found themselves alone, responsible for the shelter of others, or otherwise pivotal to collective moral and material economies. Nazism undid the patriarchal family as it ripped apart the fabric of Jewish life. But gender roles were not systematically rewoven by women darning the holes that men's absences opened. War befits women, some have argued, pitching bellicose Minervas and triumphant Nikes against romantic portrayals of pacifist Geas. At a minimum, they claim, war has benefited women in the twentieth century and in the West. Yet neither economically nor socially nor politically did the Nazi war reallocate power to Jewish women.

Persecution brought Etty a new job as a clerical employee of the Jewish Council, with its attendant emotional responsibilities toward the deportees with whom she worked and lived at Westerbrok. Lowly as her position may have been in the Council's hierarchy, it conferred petty powers and offered her temporary security. But it also tainted her with the guilt of collaboration and of that, too, she was

sporadically aware. Before entering into this Nazi-created employment, Etty had worked, earned money, and overseen her own living arrangements. As a woman, under Nazism, she never gained; as a Jew, she only lost.

Anne lost too. Like others in hiding or attempting escape, the Franks lived within a drastically narrowed circle of social relations. Here familial or quasi-familial bonds strengthened into clandestine enclaves of solidarity. With everyone's safety at the mercy of the others' fealty and sense of responsibility, a general flattening of social status ensued. The Secret Annexe housed an extended ménage that partially reshuffled gender roles. Otto Frank and Mr. Van Daan peeled potatoes alongside their wives: testimony more to the loss of their external, head-of-the-household functions than to their wives' elevation. However, many other tasks retained their conventional gender markings. Protection, for example, remained a manly duty. [In a footnote, Ergas adds: "The permanence of conventional gender roles is clear in Anne's description of the Annexe's response to an attempted burglary."] Peeling potatoes and protecting the household need not clash, and in the Annexe clandestine life restricted role-playing and the potential for role conflict.

In this context of limited activity, there were few occasions for Anne to realize her emancipatory desires. Her diary and short stories provided writing practice, an informal apprenticeship for the career she wished to undertake. Lessons, from math to shorthand, broadened the scope of her abilities. Her mother proved a source of frustration and rivalry, her father of affection, Mrs. Van Daan of contempt, and Albert Dussel of irritation. With Peter, the Van Daans' adolescent son, she navigated through a sentimental journey clouded by parental disapproval. Yet all these elements spurring Anne's development pale by comparison to her world before confinement or even to the war-ridden world of her non-Jewish peers. Stripped of every right, amid the debris of their decimated milieux, Anne and Etty were killed. Women, but most of all Jews, on every possible count for them Nazism and war entailed losing.

As the persecuted resist the progressive diminishment of self, they struggle against the temporal scansions that are imposed upon them. They do not walk in step with the drumbeat of battles and bombs. For persecution proceeds at its own pace, and the persecuted are mobilized not to the call of the nation but to the cumulation of special prohibitions and obligations. [In a footnote, Ergas adds: "Persecution marches in uneasy synchrony with war. The Wehrmacht complained bitterly that extermination policies drained the German military effort. See Saul Friedlander, *Reflections of Nazism: An Essay on Kitsch and Death,* 1984. For a synthetic discussion of the economic, administrative, and psychological obstacles the Nazis had to overcome in implementing their extermination policies, see Raul Hilberg, 'The Nature of the Process,' in Dimsdale, ed., *Survivors.*"] Some, like Anne and her family, meticulously plan for invasion. For over a year, the Franks stocked food, clothes, and furniture in the Secret Annexe. Or, like Etty, they tenaciously cling to everyday life. "I cannot take in how beautiful the jasmine is," she wrote on

July 1, 1942, "but there is no need to. It is enough simply to believe in miracles in the 20th century. And I do, even though the lice will be eating me up in Poland before long." Others join the Resistance, engaging their oppressors in armed struggle. No matter which stance they take, persecution, more than war, orders their public experience.

Persecution imposes its measure on personal time, too. Anne divided life into before, during, and after hiding. Memory reigned over "before." Routines provided a modicum of activity to make time pass in the present. Her passion for Peter, like the radio broadcasts announcing the war's events, anticipated a time to come "after." Ultimately, writing for both Etty and Anne bridged the time of persecution and that which followed, transforming their diaries from tools of authorial apprenticeship into testimonials to the present and instruments of its transcendence. Etty kept her diary to remain her "own witness, marking well everything that happens in this world." She was determined to "know this century of ours inside and out" and describe it. Finally, her diary condensed her aspirations, the legacy she bequeathed in fulfillment of a promise made in the summer of 1942, when she vowed: "When I have survived it all, I shall write stories about these times that will be like faint brush strokes against the great wordless background of God, Life, Death, Suffering, and Eternity." Anne, too, planned a testimonial, hoping "to publish a book entitled *Het Achterhuis* after the war"—the book her diary became.

Tales of persecution are crucial to the European memory of World War II. It is a memory periodically fanned by the celebrations of antifascist resistances (where they existed), national holidays, the capture or escape of a Nazi war criminal. And by a few, enduring testimonies. Such testimonies are provided by the *Diary of Anne Frank* and Etty Hillesum's *An Interrupted Life*. Like many memoirs of war, they bespeak a remote "other" path to, or through, adulthood: one produced by fragments of past normalities as they shatter into conflict and loss. But, unlike war literature at large, these memoirs evoke the specific horrors of anti-Semitic persecution four decades ago. Their protagonists have become emblematic of the journey through banishment and exile that so frequently ended in death. Their words resonate today, and not simply because they left lessons about our possible tomorrows. Rather, they resonate because we remember, and what we remember colors who we are.

Sylvia Patterson Iskander   (essay date Summer 1991)

SOURCE: "Anne Frank's Autobiographical Style," in *Children's Literature Association Quarterly,* Vol. 16, No. 2, Summer, 1991, pp. 78-81.

[*In the following essay, Iskander examines Frank's style, noting its relation to the classic tenets of biography developed by Samuel Johnson and James Boswell.*]

Anne Frank's *Diary of a Young Girl,* originally entitled *Het Achterhuis* (*The Secret Annex*), presents a self portrait that captivates most readers initially because of their foreknowledge of the tragic conclusion of this young girl's life

Anne Frank.

and the other horrors of the Holocaust. Subsequently, Anne's revelation of her unique personality and her unusual circumstances rivet readers to the *Diary,* proclaiming it a classic. [In an endnote, Iskander states: "Anne's diary is unique, even though other diaries exist from World War II. The others are either written by diarists older than teenagers, such as twenty-seven-year old Etty Hillesum's *An Interrupted Life* (about her life in Amsterdam from 1941 to 1943), or they are not yet available in English. Still others recollect life as a teenager, such as Jack Eisner's *The Survivor* (about his teen years in Warsaw), but these were either written, or revised, years after the war."] An examination of Anne's writing techniques reveals, in addition, a thoroughly professional style, which also contributes significantly to the book's merit. Anne's style, in fact, is so unusual for a thirteen to fifteen-year-old that her authorship has been questioned. Extensive handwriting analysis, however, has verified the *Diary*'s authenticity. Although sometimes censored for its politics or ideology, its attitude toward adults, and its revelation of sexual maturation, the *Diary,* if excised only slightly as Otto Frank, Anne's father, has indicated and if accurately translated, is an achievement of rare and precious worth.

The complete, unexpurgated *Diary,* now available in Dutch, appeared in English for the first time published by Doubleday in June, 1989. I believe that it reveals more of her autobiographical talent, for Anneliese Marie Frank employed many and varied techniques, some acquired, no doubt, from her own reading. Under her father's tutelage,

Anne studied several excellent histories and biographies, which probably influenced her style; she specifically mentions in the *Diary*: Karl Brandi's *The Emperor Charles V,* Zsolt Harsányi's biographies of Galileo and Franz Liszt, Karl Tschuppik's *Maria Theresa,* and others. Her reading—of books originally published in English, German, French, Hungarian, Swedish, as well as Dutch, of myths and legends, popular young-adult novels, articles on psychology, movie and theater magazines, a young people's annual, plays, and even the Bible—impressed Anne, whose assimilation of them with her own intuition enabled her to create her remarkable journalistic style.

Anne cannot be compared as a theorist to the eighteenth-century English masters of biography and autobiography, Samuel Johnson and James Boswell, whose innovations in the field established the still-current criteria, but she actually utilized most of their theories about style, perhaps absorbing them from the biographies that she read. Whether she developed her style on her own or from her reading of European writers following in the Johnson/Boswell tradition, we may never know. One possible explanation, however, is that she absorbed much of this tradition through her reading of Professor Brandi's biography of Emperor Charles V, over which he labored forty years while at Göttingen University in Germany. Göttingen, founded by George II of England and Hanover in 1734, certainly contained by the early twentieth century, most of Johnson's and Boswell's works, for its collection has long been noted for its rich English holdings. Brandi emulates Johnson's ideas in including not just the significant events, but also the minutiae of his subject's daily life; his stated goal is to paint not a hero's portrait, but a man's with frailties and virtues.

Anne also emulates the eighteenth-century biographers in various ways; her introspective method, for one, reveals her ability to view herself as an outsider, her awareness of a prospective audience, her desire to be a writer, and her abundant possession of the autobiographer's primary prerequisite: knowledge of self. Though sometimes confused by her own conflicting emotions, typical of the teen years, she possesses a relentless interest, curiosity, and objectivity which provoke her to examine her own activities and thoughts intimately, an examination which places her diary among the best of this century's with the distinction of being the most translated Dutch book.

Although Anne "assimilate[s] external events," such as news of the war, in the *Diary,* her most unusual characteristic is her ability to view life as an outsider; for example, she speaks of her younger self on 7 March 1944, as "a different Anne who has grown wise within these walls"; she says, "that Anne [was] an amusing, but very superficial girl, who has nothing to do with the Anne of today"; and she continues, "I look upon my life up till the New Year, as it were, through a powerful magnifying glass." Her introspection is evident also on 7 May 1944, when she has been chastised by her father; she comments, "It's right that for once I've been taken down from my inaccessible pedestal, that my pride has been shaken a bit, for I was becoming much too taken up with myself again. What Miss Anne does is by no means always right!" This young woman admits to knowing her own faults (14 June 1944) "better than anyone, [she says] but the difference is that I also know that I want to improve, shall improve, and have already improved a great deal." This statement is perhaps self-justification, perhaps a sincere attempt to present herself in a better light for the implied reader.

Doubtless Anne had a view of posterity reading her diary. On 29 July 1943, she writes in a postscript to her journal entry, "Will the reader take into consideration that when this story was written [about Mrs. Van Daan's bad qualities] the writer had not cooled down from her fury!" Her awareness of potential readers is again divulged when she cross references a dream about Peter Wessel. In the 28 April 1944 entry, she urges herself or the implied reader to see "the beginning of January" for her first account of the dream. Further, her creation of Kitty, a stylistic stroke of genius, was influenced, I believe, by the epistolary style in the first book of Cissy van Marxveldt's *Joop ter Heul* series; Anne says on 20 June 1942, "I want this diary to be my friend, and I shall call my friend Kitty." Joop, in the opening book of van Marxveldt's still popular series of adolescent novels, also writes to a fictitious friend "Net," and another in her school club is named "Kitty." Anne's imaginary correspondent is more than just a name for her diary; this "friend" presumably is a pseudo-interviewer; for example, the 6 April 1944 entry commences with this address to Kitty: "You asked me what my hobbies and interests were, so I want to reply." Later she suggests to "Kits" that her diary with all its nonsense should be entitled "The unbosomings of an ugly duckling." Regardless of title, Anne's awareness of audience extended even to a desire to publish her diary after the war. The version, unexpurgated by her father, from which a few excerpts were published in English prior to 1989 reveal Anne's adherence to Johnson's and Boswell's repugnance for panegyric in biography. Otto Frank, perhaps not less aware than Anne of the audience's need for absolute truth in autobiography, was, however, more aware of the invasion of privacy of persons still living.

Anne incorporates many other autobiographical techniques expounded by Samuel Johnson and aptly illustrated by James Boswell. She not only adheres to Johnson's dictum that the autobiographer is the best biographer because he possesses knowledge of self, but also her diary provides evidence of Johnson's beliefs as stated in *The Rambler,* No. 60, that any man is a fit subject for biography, that no detail is too minute to be included, and that biography should be didactic. To these dicta in his immortal *Life of Johnson,* Boswell added the results of his own phenomenal memory, his ability at recreating conversation and depicting dramatic scenes, his strong sense of personal pride, and his great confidence in his writing ability.

All of these qualities and characteristics describe Anne as well. Her knowledge of self is evident to herself and to others as she questions her identity, like all teens, when she ponders her attractiveness to boys, her writing ability, and even her chances for surviving the war. No detail is too small for inclusion; for example, Anne's reading of Nico van Suchtelen's tale of a young girl from a small town, entitled *Eva's Youth,* in which Eva's monthly period is openly discussed may have been the impetus for her frank revelations about her budding sexuality. Anne enumerates other details, such as her birthday gifts, the food eaten on numerous occasions, even the order of the bathroom queue. In regard to the didactic purpose of autobiography, Anne's strong desire for peace and freedom evince in the reader a profound sense of injustice for Anne and the members of the Annex and a sense of horror for the atrocities of the Holocaust; the moral lessons are evident to the reader, even though Anne may not always have been conscious of them as she wrote.

Like Boswell, Anne recreates actual or at least typical conversations, sets dramatic scenes, and describes the various personalities in the Annex trying to live together harmoniously, such as the following brief but discerning description, which she labels, "the views of the five grownups":

> Mrs. Van Daan: "This job as queen of the kitchen lost its attraction a long time ago. It's dull to sit and do nothing, so I go back to my cooking again. . . . Nothing but ingratitude and rude remarks do I get in return for my services. I am always the black sheep, always the guilty one. Moreover, according to me, very little progress is being made in the war; in the end the Germans will still win. I'm afraid we're going to starve, and if I'm in a bad mood I scold everyone."
>
> Mr. Van Daan: "I must smoke and smoke and smoke, and then the food, the political situation, and Keril's moods don't seem so bad. Keril is a darling wife." . . .
>
> Mrs. Frank: "Food is not very important, but I would love a slice of rye bread now, I feel so terribly hungry. If I were Mrs. Van Daan I would have put a stop to Mr. Van Daan's everlasting smoking a long time ago. But now I must definitely have a cigarette, because my nerves are getting the better of me. The English make a lot of mistakes, but still the war is progressing. I must have a chat and be thankful I'm not in Poland."
>
> Mr. Frank: "Everything's all right. I don't require anything. Take it easy, we've ample time. Give me my potatoes and then I will keep my mouth shut. Put some of my rations on one side for Elli. The political situation is very promising. I'm extremely optimistic!"
>
> Mr. Dussel: "I must get my task for today, every thing must be finished on time. Political situation 'outschtänding' and it is 'eempossible' that we'll be caught."

These thumbnail sketches describing the five adults in the Annex are a tribute to Anne's ability to capture in a few lines the essence of the characters with their differing and conflicting personalities.

In contrast, another scene depicts the kind-hearted Peter and the realistic Anne in a conversation typical of teenagers everywhere, interesting because it lacks the sophistication of the earlier description. Anne's writing style here matches the girl herself as she faces her boyfriend: immature, somewhat argumentative, a bit unsure:

> Peter so often used to say, "Do laugh, Anne!" This struck me as odd, and I asked, "Why must I always laugh?"
>
> "Because I like it; you get such dimples in your cheeks when you laugh; how do they come, actually?"
>
> "I was born with them. I've got one in my chin too. That's my only beauty!"
>
> "Of course not, that's not true."
>
> "Yes, it is, I know quite well that I'm not a beauty; I never have been and never shall be."
>
> "I don't agree at all, I think you're pretty."
>
> "That's not true."
>
> "If I say so, then you can take it from me it is."

Anne exhibits a lack of confidence in her beauty when flirting with Peter and in her fear that she will never achieve her life-long dream to go to Hollywood; yet she exhibits a strong sense of confidence in her writing ability and her critical faculties. She says on 4 April 1944: "I know that I can write, a couple of my stories are good, my descriptions of the 'Secret Annexe' are humorous, there's a lot in my diary that speaks, but—whether I have real talent remains to be seen. . . . I am the best and sharpest critic of my own work. I know myself what is and what is not well written. . . . I want to go on living even after my death! And therefore I am grateful to God for giving me this gift, this possibility of developing myself and of writing, of expressing all that is in me. . . . [W]ill I ever be able to write anything great, will I ever become a journalist or a writer? I hope so, oh, I hope so very much." Her self-criticism and her desire for publication, perhaps encouraged by Dutch Minister Bolkesteim's appeal on 28 March 1944 over Radio Orange (the Dutch government's radio exiled to London) for diaries and letters written during the war, may have been the impetus for her to begin revising the *Diary* for later publication; these revisions on single sheets of paper, rather than the orange plaid diary proper, formed the basis for the first publication.

Other techniques Anne employed are, to coin Samuel Richardson's phrase, "writing to the moment," creating a sense of immediacy; for example, she apologizes to Kitty saying "that my style is not up to standard today. I have just written down what came into my head." She skips days even up to a month if nothing eventful happens, showing her selectivity of detail; she tells Kitty, "I have deserted you for a whole month, but honestly, there is so little news here that I can't find amusing things to tell every day," a statement that also reveals her awareness of potential audience.

Anne's presentation of a typical day in her life suggests her objectivity and her awareness of an overall view of life in the Annex; her descriptions of people, such as Peter, events, ideas, fears, hopes, reveal the best in Anne's style. She says of Peter, "When he lies with his head on his arm with his eyes closed, then he is still a child; when he plays with Boche [the cat], he is loving; when he carries potatoes or anything heavy, then he is strong; when he goes and watches the shooting, or looks for burglars in the darkness, then he is brave; and when he is so awkward and clumsy, then he is just a pet." Anne's ability to summarize salient points, such as the rules for Jews in Amsterdam, the rules under which the group in the Secret Annex lived, or even the summary of Anne's life itself about six months before she was arrested by the Green Police and taken to Westerbork, Auschwitz, and finally Bergen-Belson, is proof of her objectivity, both toward herself and others.

These stylistic techniques, coupled with the poignancy of the death of such a talented young fifteen-year-old girl and the horrors of the Holocaust, have justified the sale of over fifteen million copies, the book's translation into more than fifty languages, the play, film, and ballet based on the *Diary,* the Chagall lithograph and Pieter d'Hont statue, the 1978 exhibition in Japan and the exhibition "Anne Frank in the World, 1929-1945," which toured the United States in the late 1980s, the conversion of the home in Amsterdam to the Anne Frank Museum with its half a million visitors annually, the establishment of the Anne Frank Foundation in the Netherlands with its New York branch, the publication of Anne's other writings in a collection entitled *Tales from the Secret Annex,* and, last but not least, the enduring interest in Anne Frank and her writing.

Patricia Hampl   (review date 5 March 1995)

SOURCE: "The Whole Anne Frank," in *The New York Times Book Review,* March 5, 1995, pp. 1, 21.

[*Hampl is an American educator, poet, and memoirist. In the following review, she comments on the new edition of Anne Frank's* Diary *and discusses the book's publication history.*]

On Tuesday, March 28, 1944, Gerrit Bolkestein, Education Minister of the Dutch Government in exile, delivered a radio message from London urging his war-weary countrymen to collect "vast quantities of simple, everyday material" as part of the historical record of the Nazi occupation.

"History cannot be written on the basis of official decisions and documents alone," he said. "If our descendants are to understand fully what we as a nation have had to endure and overcome during these years, then what we really need are ordinary documents—a diary, letters."

In her diary the next day, Anne Frank mentions this broadcast, which she and her family heard on a clandestine radio in their Amsterdam hiding place. "Ten years after the war," she writes on March 29, "people would find it very amusing to read how we lived, what we ate and what we talked about as Jews in hiding."

The word "amusing" reads strangely now, chillingly. But her extraordinary commitment to the immediacy of individual experience in the face of crushing circumstance is precisely what has made Anne Frank's *Diary* [now titled *The Diary of a Young Girl: The Definitive Edition*]—since the first edition of the book appeared in the Netherlands in 1947—the single most compelling personal account of the Holocaust (an account now augmented by this "Definitive Edition," published on the 50th anniversary of her

death in Bergen-Belsen and containing entries not present in the earlier standard version).

Bolkestein's broadcast galvanized Anne Frank, or perhaps ignited an idea she already had: her diary, at first a private confidante, now struck her as a source for a book. "I'd like to publish a book called 'The Secret Annex,' " she writes on May 11, 1944. "It remains to be seen whether I'll succeed, but my diary can serve as the basis." She immediately set about organizing the diary entries, giving the residents of the "Secret Annex" pseudonyms like characters in a novel, rearranging passages for better narrative effect.

She was still engaged in this work when the hiding place was raided by the Gestapo on Aug. 4, 1944. Miep Gies, one of the office employees in the Frank spice and pectin firm who had been protecting the Jews hidden above the office, gathered all the diary notebooks and papers left in disarray by the Gestapo. She hid them in her desk for the rest of the war. After Anne's father, Otto Frank, returned to Amsterdam late in 1945, Miep Gies returned all the papers to him. He was the sole survivor of the eight people who had sheltered together for over two years in the annex.

Anne Frank had been keeping her diary since June 12, 1942, the day her parents gave her a red-and-white plaid notebook for her 13th birthday. Less than a month later the diary went with her into hiding.

From the first, she addressed the notebook as a trusted girlfriend: "I'll begin from the moment I got you, the moment I saw you lying on the table among my other birthday presents." A few days later this anonymous "you" becomes the imaginary "Kitty," and the entries turn into letters, giving the diary the intimacy and vivacity of a developing friendship. The growing relationship, of course, is with her own emerging self. As John Berryman said, the *Diary* has at its core a subject "even more mysterious and fundamental than St. Augustine's" in his classic *Confessions:* namely, "the conversion of a child into a person."

Otto Frank, in preparing the first edition of the diary, was compelled, partly by his own sense of discretion and partly by the space limitations imposed on him by the original Dutch publisher, to limit the book. The restored entries, constituting, according to the publisher, 30 percent more material, do not alter our basic sense of Anne Frank, but they do give greater texture and nuance—and punch—to some of the hallmark concerns of the diary.

There are more searching passages about her erotic feelings and her urgent curiosity about sexuality, more emphatic distancing from her dignified but apparently critical mother. None of these new entries, however, surpass the urgency shown in the standard version about the need to accomplish real work as a woman: "I can't imagine having to live like Mother, Mrs. van Daan and all the women who go about their work and are then forgotten," she writes on April 5, 1944. "I need to have something besides a husband and children to devote myself to! . . . I want to be useful or bring enjoyment to all people, even those I've never met. I want to go on living even after my death!"

The new material also includes sketches of short stories

she was writing in the Secret Annex. The additions are not always whole entries or complete new letters to Kitty. Sometimes passages of only a few lines are set in a text already familiar. But the effect underscores the acuity of Anne Frank's eye, the keen relish of her descriptive powers. In one of her habitual reviews of the "inmates" of the annex, she regards the fussy dentist Dussel with the coolness of a practiced novelist: "One of my Sunday morning ordeals is having to lie in bed and look at Dussel's back when he's praying. . . . A praying Dussel is a terrible sight to behold."

Even her transports over her first kiss, with Peter van Daan, the son of the family sharing the Franks' hiding space, are subject to her mordant observation: "Oh, it was so wonderful. I could hardly talk, my pleasure was too intense; he caressed my cheek and arm, a bit clumsily." Only a born writer would snap that clear-eyed "a bit clumsily" into place, along with the body's first rhapsodic shiver of delight.

In 1986, a "Critical Edition" of the *Diary* was published that meticulously presented Anne's original diary (designated by its editors diary *a*), the version she was working on for her proposed book "The Secret Annex" (diary *b*), and the edition her father eventually published and which all the world has come to know (diary *c*). This monumental task included as well exhaustive scientific examination of the original documents to prove what should never have been questioned in the first place: that this is indeed the work of a girl named Anne Frank who lived and eventually died as she prophetically sensed she would: "I hear the approaching thunder that, one day, will destroy us too, I feel the suffering of millions."

The earlier "Critical Edition" is the book for research, but this "Definitive Edition," smoothly translated anew by Susan Massotty, is the reader's edition, unencumbered by notes, with only the barest afterword to conclude the story that Anne Frank was unable to finish herself.

The *Diary,* now 50 years old, remains astonishing and excruciating. It is a work almost sick with terror and tension, even as it performs its miracle of lucidity.

On Feb. 12, 1944, Anne Frank writes Kitty, "I feel as if I were about to explode. . . . I walk from one room to another, breathe through the crack in the window frame. . . . I think spring is inside me." The crack in the window frame was her purchase on the world: she put her nose to it and drew in life.

It is uncanny how, reading the *Diary,* one falls into escape fantasies for Anne Frank and the inhabitants of the Secret Annex. No wonder that in his 1979 novel *The Ghost Writer,* Philip Roth sustains an entire section devoted to a detailed fabrication about how, after all, Anne Frank survived, how she came to America, how she lives among us still in disguise. It is unthinkable and disorienting to know that this life was crushed.

All that remains is this diary, evidence of her ferocious appetite for life. It gnaws at us still.

Merle Rubin   (review date 15 March 1995)

SOURCE: "Anne Frank, More Comprehensively," in *The Christian Science Monitor,* March 15, 1995, p. 14.

[*In the review below, Rubin describes Anne Frank's* Diary *as a "prototype for the sufferings of millions of European Jews."*]

Anne Frank was not a survivor, to borrow a term overused in present-day parlance. She was born in Germany in 1929, fled with her family to the Netherlands at the age of four, and was flushed out of the secret annex where they had hidden for two years to die in a concentration camp in 1945, a few months short of her 16th birthday. Yet, as even the most cursory reading of her diary amply demonstrates, she had all of the qualities that are supposed to characterize survivorship: intelligence, courage, honesty, compassion, resilience, resourcefulness, and a good sense of humor.

Anne Frank hoped to become a writer. In the spring of 1944, after hearing a radio broadcast of the Dutch government-in-exile about the importance of letters and diaries as documents, she began revising and expanding her own diary to provide a broader picture of the times. Anne's father, Otto Frank, the only member of the immediate family to survive the camps, recovered the diary after the war and from her two versions prepared a third.

Some passages from the manuscripts were omitted: comments Otto Frank deemed disrespectful to his late wife, critical remarks about others whose feelings might be hurt, and some of Anne's direct references to sexual matters, such as menstruation and birth control.

First published in 1947, *Anne Frank: The Diary of a Young Girl* became an international bestseller, a prizewinning play, and a film. In 1986, the Netherlands State Institute for War Documentation prepared a new "critical" edition of the diary. Over 700 pages long, it presents the three parallel texts (Anne's first version, her revised version, and her father's combined version) printed on the same page for comparison and is complete with background material about the Frank family and the editing and publishing history of the diary.

The present Definitive Edition, featuring a new English translation somewhat more direct and earthy than the previous one, includes much of the material that was left out of the 1947 edition. Unlike the Critical Edition, designed for scholarly use, the Definitive Edition is for the general reader who simply wants to read Anne's diary from its beginning (on her 13th birthday in June 1942) to its abrupt cessation just a few days before the Gestapo invaded the hiding place in August 1944.

The story of this particular Jewish girl remains a kind of prototype for the sufferings of millions of European Jews in the years that Hitler pursued his plan to exterminate every last one of them.

Even apart from the larger role it has played, Anne Frank's diary would still command attention as a remarkable, candid, lively, and insightful portrait of a gifted, quirky, spirited teenager watching herself grow up. The girl who kept this journal was in many respects a very typical adolescent: fun-loving, impatient with her parents, more than a little boy-crazy. But at the same time she had extraordinary powers of self-analysis, self-criticism, and self-expression. Countless readers are familiar with Anne's poignant declaration: " . . . in spite of everything I still believe that people are really good at heart."

Anne's hopefulness seems all the more impressive in the context of so much else that she witnessed and recognized: "I don't believe the war is simply the work of politicians and capitalists," wrote the 14-year-old. "Oh no, the common man is every bit as guilty. . . . There's a destructive urge in people, the urge to rage, murder and kill. And until all of humanity, without exception, undergoes a metamorphosis, . . . everything that has been carefully built up, cultivated and grown will be cut down and destroyed, only to start all over again."

THE ATOMIC BOMB AND AMERICAN MEMORY

Michael R. Beschloss   (review date 30 July 1995)

SOURCE: "Did We Need to Drop It?," in *The New York Times Book Review,* July 30, 1995, pp. 10-11.

[*An American historian, Beschloss has written extensively on American diplomatic history. In the review below, he remarks on Gar Alperovitz's* The Decision to Use the Atomic Bomb and the Architecture of an American Myth *and Thomas B. Allen and Norman Polmar's* Code-Name Downfall.]

For 20 years after Harry Truman ordered the atomic bomb dropped on Japan in August 1945, most American scholars and citizens subscribed to the original, official version of the story: the President had acted to avert a horrendous invasion of Japan that could have cost 200,000 to 500,000 American lives. Then a young political economist named Gar Alperovitz published a book of ferocious revisionism, *Atomic Diplomacy: Hiroshima and Potsdam* (1965). While acknowledging the paucity of evidence available at the time, he argued that dropping the atomic bomb "was not needed to end the war or to save lives" but was Truman's means of sending a chastening message to the Soviet Union.

Now, in *The Decision to Use the Atomic Bomb,* Mr. Alperovitz, who is the president of the National Center for Economic Alternatives, writes that "oversimplified versions of my argument (together with some obvious graduate-student errors) were pounced upon by critics who could not abide criticism of the Hiroshima decision." Benefiting from documentary discoveries of the past 30 years and the less fractious post-cold war atmosphere, he has produced a more ambitious and far-reaching work. As the author notes, his earlier book focused on "how the bomb influenced diplomacy." With the advantage of greater hindsight and documentation, this volume seeks to deal more comprehensively with the decision to drop the bomb and to suggest why the public clings so tenaciously to the original explanation of why Truman gave the order. With piquant irony, he has chosen the same title that Truman's first Secretary of War, Henry L. Stimson, used in a famous 1947 essay in *Harper's* that did much to establish the original version of the story in the public mind. Mr. Alperovitz has lost none of his instinct for provocative judgments about one of the century's paramount historical controversies. He has written what will almost certainly serve as a bible for the next generation of revisionist scholars, a book that is elegantly documented (with the aid of seven research collaborators) and intensely argued.

Fifty years after Hiroshima and Nagasaki, Mr. Alperovitz declares that a final answer to why the atomic bomb was used is "neither essential nor possible." He continues with a more debatable premise: "What is important is whether, when the bomb was used, the President and his top advisers understood that it was not required to avoid a long and costly invasion, as they later claimed and as most Americans still believe." More orthodox historical critiques of the atomic bomb decision sometimes question the estimates of casualties to be expected from a full-scale invasion of Japan. The argument goes that if these appraisals were inflated, the President had less business justifying the horror of the bomb as a way of saving lives. This debate is less interesting to Mr. Alperovitz. He insists that without use of the bomb, Japan might still have been made to surrender before the first American landing on the island of Kyushu, planned for November 1945. He notes that many American military leaders then and later felt that using atomic weapons against Japan was unnecessary.

But, Mr. Alperovitz argues, Truman and his Secretary of State, James F. Byrnes, were struck by the notion that ending World War II without dropping the atomic bomb would not have brought added strength to American diplomacy against the Soviet Union in Europe. More than in the earlier book, Byrnes is the villain of this piece. Mr. Alperovitz insists that a decision not to drop the bomb could actually have bolstered American diplomatic objectives in Asia—for example, by helping to create the atmosphere for a more harmonious post-war American-Soviet relationship. He criticizes Truman for failing to issue a more explicit warning to Japan about the bomb and for attacking Hiroshima rather than a nonurban target, as his Army Chief of Staff, Gen. George C. Marshall, had suggested.

As evidence of the link between the bomb decision and diplomacy toward Moscow, Mr. Alperovitz points to Truman's postponement of his Potsdam meeting with Stalin and Churchill until July 1945, when the new weapon would have been tested. At Potsdam, after hearing about the first successful detonation in New Mexico, Truman turned suddenly more truculent. According to Stimson, Churchill marveled that the President "was a changed man. He told the Russians just where they got on and off and generally bossed the whole meeting." Truman confided to his crony and reparations negotiator Edwin Pauley that the bomb "would keep the Russians straight." Mr. Alperovitz argues that "the U.S. feeling of cheerfulness rather than frustration" over differences with the Soviets at Potsdam "makes little sense unless one realizes that top policy makers were thinking ahead to the time when the force of the new weapon would be displayed."

But how might Truman, if he were disinclined to use the bomb, have ended the war without the large number of casualties required, by any estimate, for the invasion of Japan? Mr. Alperovitz says that the President could have shown himself a lot more eager to welcome the Soviets into the Asian conflict. Franklin D. Roosevelt, for example, had wanted Stalin to help pin the Japanese down on the Chinese mainland, making it harder for them to reinforce their home armies when the Americans invaded.

Mr. Alperovitz suggests that on the issue of Soviet participation in the Japanese war, Truman zigged and zagged after taking office in April 1945. In mid-June, American officials like General Marshall were arguing that a Soviet war declaration might "prove to be the decisive blow to force a Japanese surrender." But at Potsdam, Mr. Alperovitz writes, Truman sought to delay a Soviet war declaration: although it might have precluded the use of the bomb on Japan, it would have given Stalin a large foothold in east Asia. Mr. Alperovitz says that the timing of the Hiroshima bombing—Aug. 6, 1945—was no accident. Two days later the Soviet Union declared war on the Japanese and then crossed the border into Manchuria.

Mr. Alperovitz offers another alternative for ending the war without using the bomb: relaxing the unconditional surrender demand issued by Roosevelt in 1943 at Casablanca. He suggests that the President might have provided assurances that if Tokyo surrendered, the Japanese Emperor, Hirohito, would be permitted to retain his throne. This idea indeed found strong support among Truman's advisers. Stimson proposed that Truman allow the Japanese "a constitutional monarchy under the present dynasty if it be shown to the complete satisfaction of the world that such a government will never again conspire to aggression." Mr. Alperovitz notes that in mid-August, after the bombs had been dropped and the Russians had entered the conflict, Truman and Byrnes were willing to provide assurances about the Emperor. Doesn't the fact that these weren't provided earlier, when they might have helped end the war, indicate an eagerness to drop the bomb?

Mr. Alperovitz gives less weight than other scholars to the arguments against such an offer. As the Stanford historian Barton Bernstein has recently noted in the journal *Diplomatic History,* the Tokyo regime of mid-summer 1945 was badly split over what kind of American peace offer, if any, to accept. At that point, granting a concession on the Emperor's role could have drawn the United States into extended bargaining with the Japanese leaders. Haggling with a regime that Roosevelt and Truman had denounced as criminal, that had attacked Pearl Harbor and that had committed well-publicized atrocities was the kind of thing the unconditional surrender doctrine had been drafted to avoid. Not irrationally, Truman told Churchill that he did not think the Japanese had "any military honor after Pearl Harbor." (And there is also the possibility that ambiguity over Hirohito's role might have impeded America's ability

to occupy the country and reform the political system from the ground up.)

Mr. Alperovitz devotes considerable space to showing how Stimson's article in *Harper's,* misleading official memoirs and the American Government's refusal over the years to release certain classified documents helped enshrine the original explanation of the atomic bomb decision. Yet, as energetically as he argues his case, he is unlikely to convert those who do not believe that finding an alternative to the atomic bomb should have been an overarching priority for Truman in the summer of 1945.

Moreover, Mr. Alperovitz's new volume lacks what the Harvard historian Charles S. Maier has called the "shock value" of his earlier one. One reason is that we are more skeptical about the motives of our leaders and the origins of the cold war than we were in 1965. But another is the degree to which Mr. Alperovitz's views have pushed other scholars to re-examine their assumptions about Hiroshima and Nagasaki.

In *Code-Name Downfall,* Thomas B. Allen and Norman Polmar, the authors of *CNN: War in the Gulf* and *Rickover: Controversy and Genius,* reveal new sidelights on the planning to invade Japan. Amid some purple prose (the book begins, "The United States was plunged into despair on Sunday, Dec. 7, 1941," and later says, "MacArthur's life and career were a parade of superlatives"), they show how the fall of Okinawa in July 1945 became the prelude to the planned landing by seven Army and three Marine divisions on Kyushu and the 17-division landing on the main Japanese island of Honshu, the latter action scheduled for March 1946. They describe the fictitious attacks and feints devised to deceive the foe, and the possible American use of poison gas, anthrax germs and atomic weapons during the invasion. Told of Hiroshima, one American planner said he wanted "six of these things" for the Kyushu landing. Ignorant of the danger of radiation to his own troops, General Marshall pondered using atomic bombs on Kyushu before the Americans came ashore.

Mr. Allen and Mr. Polmar explain that before the atomic bombs were dropped the Pentagon expected to be faced with Japanese resistance until November 1946. Grimly recalling a March 1945 bombing attack on the Japanese capital, General Marshall said, "We had 100,000 people killed in Tokyo in one night, and it had seemingly no effect whatsoever."

The authors also describe Truman's effort to assess the possible casualties that would result from a full-scale invasion. Whereas Mr. Alperovitz laments Truman's manipulation of casualty estimates after his retirement (in 1959 he argued that the bomb saved "millions of lives"), Mr. Allen and Mr. Polmar are more intrigued by the manipulation of casualty estimates before Truman made his decision. They note a "worst-case scenario" in June 1945 that estimated the number of battle casualties at 220,000, but caution that the military was not averse to reshaping casualty estimates in order to influence Truman's thinking on whether or not to invade Japan: "High estimates would make the invasion a far less attractive alternative to the bomb."

The authors display little ambivalence about the question raised by the second half of their subtitle, "And Why Truman Dropped the Bomb." They dispose of the immensely complex problem of whether or not the bomb should have been dropped in a few paragraphs, writing, "As for the use of the atomic bomb as an implied threat to the Soviet Union, geopolitics may have been on the minds of some of Truman's advisers, but the war and American lives were on his mind. Preparations for the massive amphibious assault on Japan were under way, and Truman went to Potsdam in July seeking assurance that Stalin would enter the war against Japan. Then Truman learned on July 16 that the atomic bomb would work, and he ordered it used. It was a weapon, and it *might* end the war without an invasion." Mr. Allen and Mr. Polmar conclude that Kyushu "would have been the bloodiest invasion in history" and "could have been surpassed by the assault of Honshu." The debate goes on.

Michael Sherry   (review date 30 July 1995)

SOURCE: "Guilty Knowledge," in *The New York Times Book Review,* July 30, 1995, pp. 11-12.

[*An American educator and historian, Sherry has written extensively on American involvement in World War II. In the following review of Robert Jay Lifton and Greg Mitchell's* Hiroshima in America *and Ronald Takaki's* Hiroshima, *Sherry contends that both books fail to address the full complexity of the atomic bomb issue.*]

Must we return to the question Ronald Takaki [in his *Hiroshima: Why America Dropped the Atomic Bomb*] raises in his subtitle? We seem to be stuck with coming back to it in a ritualistic, even fetishistic fashion, even though the ground has been so worked that there appears little new to say, except to shore up earlier interpretations—or reshape them in the light of current politics. Asking why we dropped the atomic bomb long ago became less a way to say anything new than a way to expiate our guilt or reassert our virtue. Revisiting the question also revisits the period when the world's fate seemed to hinge on what the United States did (even those who, like Mr. Takaki, Robert Jay Lifton and Greg Mitchell, challenge Americocentrism slip into it at times).

But many younger people haven't covered this ground before. Like other questions about America's past—why the North won the Civil War, how Japan pulled off Pearl Harbor—this one continues to draw succeeding generations (though, like historians, they ponder the question in ways that often reflect as much the time they live in as the past they presumably examine).

Surprisingly, the veteran scholars of the question have written the fresher book—awkwardly organized, repetitive, but page by page highly readable. In *Hiroshima in America*, Dr. Lifton and Mr. Mitchell offer a sweeping account not only of why the atomic bomb was used but of "what Hiroshima means—and has done—to America." In their view, the bomb plunged the nation into a half-

century of troubled denial of its capacity to inflict—and to ignore—mass death.

These basic claims and concepts are hardly new. Dr. Lifton, the author of *Death in Life: Survivors of Hiroshima,* and *The Protean Self,* has long presented "denial" (refusing to accept a fact or event) and "psychic numbing" (distancing oneself by sealing off emotions and memories) as keys to American responses to the bomb. In this book, he and Mr. Mitchell, the author of *The Campaign of the Century,* on Upton Sinclair's California gubernatorial race in 1934, are sometimes too glib. They applaud those who bristled at the use of the bomb for recognizing that "human survival was now at issue." But in fact many of those who supposedly perpetuated the nation's denial simply drew a different conclusion from that same recognition. Truman used the threat to human survival to justify a mighty drive to outgun the Kremlin in nuclear weapons. And while Dr. Lifton and Mr. Mitchell argue that Secretary of War Henry L. Stimson needed terms for the bomb like "the thing," "the dreadful" and "the diabolical" to sustain "his own psychic numbing," Stimson's terms don't seem to me bland or deceptive.

Concepts like denial and psychic numbing inadvertently work against themselves by making the general American response to the bomb seem natural. "Psychic numbing" is given a totalizing quality, used to explain almost everything, down to the United States' alleged indifference to "the 1990's genocides in Bosnia and Rwanda." And "denial" operates to divide Americans into the healthy few ("enlightened scientists") who appreciated the bomb's evil and the pathological many who did not. Artifacts of the atomic age as much as insights into it, these terms succeed more as polemical devices than as historical explanations.

Dr. Lifton and Mr. Mitchell, do, however, breathe new life and specificity into the terms. If their framework is top-heavy, they offer such keen insights into so many particulars, especially in men like Truman and Maj. Gen. Leslie R. Groves, the director of the Manhattan Project, that their book makes compelling reading.

One of the more interesting sections of Ronald Takaki's *Hiroshima* also turns on insight into personality. Mr. Takaki's reading of American leaders, especially Truman, as caught in the cult of "masculinity" is effective, though it overlooks how such a reading might apply to Japanese and Soviet leaders. Short, graceful and generally evenhanded, *Hiroshima* will nicely inform the novice on the basic issues. But the book presents problems, even as an introductory primer. Mr. Takaki barely mentions the Soviet Union's role in ending the Pacific war, widely noted at the time but later erased by Americans proud (or fearful) of the role their weapon played. He claims to draw on "recently declassified military documents," but most have long been available. Even on the role of racial ideology in the decision, Mr. Takaki, an Asian-American scholar of race turning to a subject long dominated by an unchanging cast of white male experts, mostly recycles familiar findings. In the end, he favors critics of the use of the bomb and fails to capture how so many Americans gratefully received the news and celebrated it.

Why did the United States use atomic bombs in 1945? The truth is that no single reason prevailed, in part because no single individual prevailed.

—*Michael Sherry*

In *Hiroshima in America,* perhaps more than Dr. Lifton and Mr. Mitchell realize, denial emerges less as an emotional reaction to terrifying news than as a political construct, guiding Americans toward celebration of the bomb and then to a reliance on it in cold-war policy making. Their book helps us understand why veterans' groups demanded that stories of Japanese atrocities be included in the Smithsonian's *Enola Gay* exhibit to quell doubts about the use of the atomic bomb. Atrocity stories have been at the core of Americans' atomic bomb discourse since its start. American authorities released them to justify the ferocious firebombing of Japan that preceded Hiroshima, and did so again after Aug. 6 and at key points later when public anxiety arose about the bomb's use. Such stories had a genuine place in moral debate, yet the timing of their release, as opposed to their content, suggests a ritual reassertion of American virtue rather than an interest in the atrocities per se. (Perhaps this is why atrocity survivors often felt used and then ignored rather than really heard.) In 1945, as in 1995, disturbing evidence of the effects of radiation, of American P.O.W.'s killed in the atomic blasts, of the improbability that any invasion of Japan would be needed, as well as film footage of the damage to Hiroshima and Nagasaki, was played down or censored outright.

Why did a great nation confident of its virtue resort to such deception? The cynic can respond, rightly, that great powers routinely do such things, and Washington's embrace of nuclear weapons as the counter to Soviet power vastly enhanced the temptation to deceive. Yet the conclusion is also inescapable that many Americans were hardly confident of the nation's virtue. However unsurprising politically, the recurring need to stack the deck betrays profound doubts, among defenders of the bomb's use as well as critics, from Truman in 1945 to the Smithsonian's opponents in 1995.

Both *Hiroshima* and *Hiroshima in America* also remind us how silly the claim was, in the debate over the Enola Gay exhibit, that critics of the bomb's use are now and have always been liberals, antimilitarists and the politically correct. Before Hiroshima, Gen. George C. Marshall, Gen. Dwight D. Eisenhower and Adm. William D. Leahy, among other military officials, questioned or opposed use without warning. After Hiroshima, doubts or denunciations emerged from the conservative columnist David Lawrence, the theologian Reinhold Neibuhr, Monsignor Fulton J. Sheen (a cold-war hawk who judged the claim that the bomb's use saved lives "precisely the argument Hitler used in bombing Holland") and the diplomat John Foster Dulles. Even among crewmen of the atomic bomb

flights there was a wide range of reactions. They all would have found curious the idea that endorsing the bomb's use was a litmus test of patriotism or loyalty. The harsh assertion of that test today testifies to the rancor of the 1990's, not to the realities of the 1940's. Moreover, as Dr. Lifton and Mr. Mitchell shrewdly point out, the litmus test notion is oddly "self-diminishing for the veterans," for it "shifts the credit for defeating the Japanese" to the bomb makers and away from "the U.S. soldiers, pilots and seamen who had defeated the enemy, at great cost, in one battle after another."

Why, then, did the United States use atomic bombs in 1945? The truth is that no single reason prevailed, in part because no single individual prevailed. For some, like Secretary of State James F. Byrnes, the primary justification was to intimidate the Soviet Union and crowd it out of the Pacific war, as Gar Alperovitz's new book, *The Decision to Use the Atomic Bomb,* emphasizes. For others, like the physicist J. Robert Oppenheimer, it was to shock the world into forging international control of atomic weapons. For men like George Marshall, it was to gain quick victory, not only to save American lives but to address war-weariness at home. For still others—Secretary Stimson at times—it was the fatalistic sense that the firebombing of Japan's cities had already crossed the moral and political line that blocked use of such a terrible weapon. Rarely mentioned by officials—though certainly well known to them—was a visceral sense that the Japanese were a subhuman foe who deserved atomic retribution for the crime of Pearl Harbor and much else.

For many leaders, these reasons to use the bomb coexisted in a jumbled fashion over the summer of 1945—each rising or falling with the moment, none clearly singled out, especially by Truman, who erratically grabbed and discarded the various rationales offered. Only after the war did the saving of American lives—not even mentioned, Dr. Lifton and Mr. Mitchell point out, in Truman's long initial statement on the bomb's use—get wrenched from this murky web and enshrined as the principal justification, as leaders worked to uphold the purity of American motives. As Dr. Lifton and Mr. Mitchell note, once the bomb was successfully tested on July 16, invasion of Japan was not an option even if the war had dragged on: "For what sane power, with the atomic weapon securely in its arsenal," the sociologist Kai Erikson has asked, "would hurl a million or more of its sturdiest young men on a heavily fortified mainland?"

The nub of the "why" question—bothersome to men like Stimson but erased in more recent political debate—involves the timing of American assurances to Japan that it could retain its emperor system. By July 1945, American leaders sensed that Japan was a defeated nation: ferociously bombed, economically strangled and desperate to find a way to surrender without losing its monarchy. Before Hiroshima, the Truman Administration would not offer assurances about the Emperor, at least not in a form clear enough to convey anything meaningful. After Nagasaki, the Soviet entry into the war and Japan's inquiry about peace terms, assurances were forthcoming. (Later, Truman erroneously claimed that Japan's leaders "were offered the terms, which they finally accepted, well in advance of the dropping of the bomb.") That shift in the American approach, not just the bomb's use and Russia's entry, led to surrender.

The disquieting likelihood (though neither Dr. Lifton and Mr. Mitchell nor Ronald Takaki suggest it) is that the use of the bomb allowed the United States to offer surrender terms it previously withheld, giving the bomb as decisive an impact in Washington as in Tokyo. Before Hiroshima, the Administration was hamstrung by (among other things) a fear that softening the surrender terms would enrage Americans long fed promises of "unconditional surrender" and images of Japanese "fanaticism." Having carried out the final assault, having proved their atomic mastery (to the Soviet Union, among others), having "repaid" (as Truman put it) Japan for its treachery, American leaders freed themselves to be flexible—now they would not lose face by relaxing the surrender terms. Saving American lives, though a general goal of American policy, did not dictate the immediate decision to use the atomic bomb. Instead, American leaders bombed themselves into accepting Japan's surrender terms.

Suzanne Mantell   (essay date 31 July 1995)

SOURCE: "Fifty Years of the Nuclear Age," in *Publishers Weekly,* Vol. 242, No. 31, July 31, 1995, pp. 23-4.

[*In the excerpt below, Mantell surveys works published in 1995 that center on the development of the atomic bomb, the victims in Japan, and the American decision to carry out the attack.*]

The 50th anniversary of the dropping of the atomic bomb on Hiroshima and Nagasaki is almost upon us. Many related books have been published in the half-decade since the bombings, including acclaimed and widely read volumes such as John Hersey's *Hiroshima* (Knopf), Robert J. Lifton's *Death in Life: Survivors of Hiroshima* (UNC paperback) and Richard Rhodes's *The Making of the Atomic Bomb* (S&S). But an event this momentous demands attention over and over again, often, as is the case this commemorative year, from new and different angles.

The crop of books that will be published on Aug. 6 or soon thereafter can be divided roughly into two kinds: those that put a human face onto nuclear tragedy, and those that analyze what happened, in an attempt to understand why America did it. Boundaries, however, are not always clear-cut.

Volume Two of the Library of America's two-volume *Reporting World War II: American Journalism,* coming in October, is published in celebration of the war's end and makes newly available John Hersey's famous report on the human consequences of the destruction, published originally in 1946 as an entire issue of the *New Yorker.* Volume I, covering the years 1938-1944, contains material published during the war; together, the books contain 191 pieces by nearly 90 writers.

Hiroshima Notes by 1994 Nobel Prize winner Kenzaburo Oe, coming from Marion Boyars with an Aug. 6 publication date, humanizes the war through a combination of reportage and reflection. Oe—who was 10 and far from the blast when the bomb dropped—visited Hiroshima several times in the 1960s to interview survivors and the doctors who cared for them and their children. This is the first American edition of the book; in Japan, where it was published in the mid-1960s, it is in its 30th printing, with 700,000 copies sold to date. Oe has written a new introduction for the American edition. . . .

The Manhattan Project physicists who developed the bomb left a legacy beyond the scientific one—namely, their children and grandchildren. Now two of these offspring have created books that reflect their families' involvement.

Rachel Fermi, granddaughter of the physicist Enrico Fermi, has produced, with Esther Samra, *Picturing the Bomb: Photographs from the Secret World of the Manhattan Project* (Abrams). Richard Rhodes wrote the introduction to this photographic scrapbook filled with previously unseen pictures that were found in family albums and discovered in laboratory archives. Included are snapshots of the physicists and their families, and historical documentation of the first A-bomb explosions. Both Fermi and Samra are photographers.

A more verbal view of that era comes to us from Claudio G. Segré, who grew up in the shadow of his father, Emilio, who shared a 1959 Nobel Prize in physics with Owen Chamberlain for their work on antimatter. Segré also discovered Element 43 and several others. In the memoir, *Atoms, Bombs & Eskimo Kisses,* a September release from Viking, the younger Segré tries to answer the questions, "What was it like to live at Los Alamos while the atomic bomb was being built? What was it like to have Fermi, Niels Bohr and Robert Oppenheimer over for dinner?" Segré is a historian at the University of Texas at Austin, so his memoir looks at his own past and his complicated relationship with his father with the light of history shining down on it. . . .

A firsthand account in the Hersey-Oe genre (and the first eyewitness account published in the West, according to the publisher) is the University of North Carolina Press's *Hiroshima Diary: The Journal of a Japanese Physician, Aug. 9-Sept. 30, 1945* by Michihiko Hachiya, M.D., translated by Dr. Warner Wells, due Aug. 6 in a new paperback edition with a new foreword by MIT scholar John W. Dower. Immediately after the bombing, the author kept a diary in which he chronicled his attempts to aid the victims. The book has been in print continuously since it was first published in 1955.

Duke University Press publishes the memories of another medical witness in James Yamazaki's *Children of the Atomic Bomb: An American Physician's Memoir of Nagasaki, Hiroshima, and the Marshall Islands,* out in August. Written with Louis B. Fleming, the book is an attempt by Yamazaki, an L.A. pediatrician, to understand and document the impact of nuclear explosions on children, particularly those in utero at the time of the explosions.

Dominating the second category of book, those that want to figure out what was behind Truman's decision to drop the bomb, is Gar Alperovitz's *The Decision to Use the*

Atomic Bomb and the Architecture of an American Myth, a book that Knopf embargoed prior to its Aug. 6 publication because of arrangements with ABC for a Peter Jennings special, and with the *New York Times Magazine* for an excerpt.

Alperovitz, a historian and president of the National Center for Economic Alternatives, probes the reasons we dropped the bomb and looks anew at the historic controversy about whether the war with Japan could have been ended by other means. In the second half of the 847-page volume, he tries to find out why Americans continue to believe that it was necessary to bomb Japan to put an end to the war, and why we resist thinking otherwise.

Alperovitz says that as the 50th anniversary of the bombing approached, he felt it was "simply wrong" to continue to pass over the troubling question of why we did it. He takes as a given that the use of the bomb was not needed to prevent an invasion and reckons that understanding what happened has less to do with the past and everything to do with the future.

Robert Jay Lifton returns to the subject of the bomb in Putnam's just-published *Hiroshima in America: Fifty Years of Denial,* written with Greg Mitchell, a journalist who specializes in nuclear issues. Lifton and Mitchell want to understand how Americans have responded to the use of the bomb over the past 50 years. Their book reviews the official narrative of the bombing; offers a detailed analysis of the process by which Truman made his decision and then defended it; and examines the bombing's moral, psychological and political legacy. . . .

Similar in intent to both the Alperovitz and the Lifton-Mitchell books is a Little, Brown August release, Ronald Takaki's *Hiroshima: Why America Dropped the Atomic Bomb.* Takaki, a professor of ethnic studies at UC-Berkeley, uses original documents to consider the ways in which stereotypes of the Japanese influenced the decision of policy makers to drop the bomb and the public's subsequent acceptance of the decision. Like the other analysts, Takaki takes the position that Truman ordered the bomb to be dropped as a show of strength against the Soviet Union, rather than as a way to end the war quickly and avoid massive casualties. . . .

A title that touches on the bomb through German eyes is *Hitler's Uranium Club: The Secret Recordings at Farm Hall,* annotated by writer and physicist Jeremy Bernstein, due from the American Institute of Physics in October. The book, which is being marketed to the lay reader, uses recently declassified intelligence reports to refute the theory that Germany had developed its own bomb during the war.

The book contains verbatim conversations that took place among 10 top German scientists who were held in captivity at Farm Hall in England before, during and after the bombing of Japan. The tapes indicate the Germany didn't have the correct math to build the bomb, despite the claims of Werner Heisenberg, who had been in charge of the Reich's nuclear program, that he and his researchers purposefully stalled the project in order to keep the weapon out of Hitler's hands.

Finally, we come to *Judgment at the Smithsonian: The Uncensored Script of the Smithsonian's 50th Anniversary Exhibit of the Enola Gay,* edited by journalist Philip Nobile with an afterword by Barton J. Bernstein, a paperback original that was first scheduled for October release by the publisher, Marlowe & Company (distributed by PGW), but then made available June 27. The date was changed to coincide with the opening of the revamped Smithsonian exhibit, whose original wall labels were altered after veterans' groups and others objected to them on the grounds that they were too critical of the U.S. and insufficiently patriotic. In reproducing the original labels, the book is a testament—like all of these books, in their different ways—to the public's right to know.

Ian Buruma   (review date 21 September 1995)

SOURCE: "The War Over the Bomb," in *The New York Review of Books,* Vol. XLII, No. 14, September 21, 1995, pp. 26-34.

[*Buruma is a Dutch-born journalist and nonfiction writer who specializes in the study of Japanese culture. Below, he discusses the bombing of Nagasaki and remarks on several books about the atomic bombing of Japan, focusing on questions concerning the motivation, purpose, and necessity of the attacks.*]

The flight of the bomber called *Bock's Car* on August 9, 1945, from Tinian to Nagasaki was blessed but not smooth. In a Quonset hut at the air base before takeoff Chaplain Downey had prayed for the success of the plane's mission. "Almighty God, Father of all mercies," he said, "we pray Thee to be gracious with those who fly this night." He also said: "Give to us all courage and strength for the hours that are ahead; give to them rewards according to their efforts. Above all else, our Father, bring peace to Thy world."

But things went wrong from the start. A fuel pump wasn't working. So the captain, Major Charles "Chuck" Sweeney ("cheerful Irish grin"), decided to rendezvous with escort planes over Japan and refuel in Okinawa on the way back. The skies were thundery and turbulent. The rendezvous was missed: the planes lost contact and much time. The primary target, Kokura, an industrial city in northern Kyushu, was covered by smoke from a bombing raid on a neighboring city. Fuel was running low, but Sweeney flew his B-29 bomber on to the second target on the list: Nagasaki.

A thick deck of clouds had rendered Nagasaki invisible, too. "Skipper" Sweeney had to think fast. Fuel was running out. Ditching his load in the ocean was one possibility. But he decided against it. "After all," he said, "anything is better than dumping it in the water." He would ignore his orders, which stipulated that the target had to be visible, and drop the "Fat Man" by radar. Then, suddenly, Kermit "Bea" Beahan ("slow Texas drawl"; "crack bombardier"; "ladies' man"), shouted: "I've got it. I see the city. I'll take it now. . . ."

And so the "Fat Man" went down, slowly at first. It took a while for things to happen. Internal radar fuses had been

Yasuko Yamagata's version of the immediate consequences of the atomic bomb in Hiroshima.

activated in the bomb to sense its height. Chuck Sweeney was impatient. "Oh, my God," he said to his copilot, Charles "Donald Duck" Albery ("a deeply religious man"), "did we goof it up?" Moments later, the sky lit up, the plane was rocking like a rowing boat in a storm, and Sweeney could relax at last. "Well, Bea," said "Donald Duck" to the bombardier, "there's a thousand Japs you've just killed." [This and preceding quotes are from *Nagasaki: The Forgotten Bomb,* by Frank Chinnock, 1970.]

The "Fat Man," a plutonium bomb, exploded about three miles from the center of Nagasaki, above an area called Urakami, sometimes referred to in Nagasaki as Urakami-mura, or Urakami village. The pressure generated by the bomb at the hypocenter—the point directly under the blast—was about ten tons per square meter. The heat at ground level reached 4,000 degrees Celsius. People near the hypocenter were vaporized. Others, who were not so lucky, died more slowly, often after shedding their skins like snakes. Some died weeks or months, or even years, later of various kinds of cancer. Altogether up to 70,000 people are thought to have died as a result of the bombing of Nagasaki. About half of them died on the day itself.

The landscape of Urakami, separated by mountains from Nagasaki proper, was marked by Mitsubishi weapons factories and the largest cathedral in east Asia. Urakami was a district with a low reputation. Its population included a large number of poor Roman Catholics and even poorer outcasts. It was as though a bomb had fallen on Harlem, leaving the rest of Manhattan relatively unscathed. Some residents of Nagasaki quietly voiced the opinion that the bomb had "cleaned up" Urakami. In August 1945, there were 14,000 Catholics in Nagasaki. More than half were killed by the bomb. There are 70,000 Catholics living in Nagasaki today. Southern Kyushu is still the only part of Japan with a large Christian minority.

The first missionary to reach Kyushu was Francis Xavier, who landed there in 1549. His high hopes for Japan were not disappointed. By the turn of the century about 300,000 Japanese had been converted to the Roman faith. Even Hideyoshi, the "Barbarian-slaying" Shogun himself, was seen in his palace fingering a rosary. This did not stop him from crucifying twenty-six Japanese and European priests in Nagasaki in 1597. Like his more ferocious successors, he was afraid that Japanese Christians might help Spanish invaders take over Japan—a fear that Dutch traders did their best to encourage.

After 1612 persecution began in earnest. Christianity was banned. Men, women, and children were burned to death while singing praises to the Lord. Priests were suspended upside down in pits of excrement or boiling sulfur, cut open, and bled to death, unless they agreed to renounce their faith and trample on images of Christ. A Christian peasant rebellion in 1632 was put down (with Dutch help) so brutally that hardly any of the 40,000 rebels survived. Naturally, missionary work became impossible and priests could no longer attend to their flock.

Even so, small communities of "hidden Christians" hung on, often reverting in time to folk religion: local deities were worshiped in the name of Jesus; a kind of Christian cargo cult developed, with fisherfolk praying for the return of priests in black ships. Only after Americans (in black ships) and Europeans had pried Japan open in the latter half of the nineteenth century did Japanese Christians dare to declare themselves. But they remained an often harassed and poor minority, forced to do religiously polluted work in the meat and leather trades, which were normally reserved for outcasts. The ban on Christianity was formally lifted in 1873. Twenty years later, the Nagasaki Christians managed to collect enough money to start construction of a wood and redbrick cathedral on a hill in Urakami. It was completed in 1925. It was above this cathedral that the "Fat Man" exploded.

Twice a day, the one surviving Angelus bell rings out from the new Cathedral. Visiting Nagasaki this summer I walked from the Cathedral to Peace Park. It is built on the site of an old prison, whose foundation stones recently emerged during the construction of an underground garage. The appearance of these prison foundations caused a political row in Nagasaki: Should they be preserved as a reminder of the war (among the prisoners were Koreans and Chinese)? A compromise was reached: the car park was completed, and a slab of the old prison wall is displayed in Peace Park, among the monuments and memorials.

Compared to the one in Hiroshima, Nagasaki Peace Park is a small and subdued affair. There is the "Peace Statue," a large white figure pointing his right hand at the sky and extending his left hand sideways. According to a booklet on sale in the Peace Park bookstore, the right hand points to the nuclear threat and the left hand symbolizes eternal peace. The folded right leg and the extended left leg "symbolize meditation and the initiative to stand up and rescue the people of the world." In the rest of the park are various sculptures, some of them donated by countries that no longer exist: the German Democratic Republic, Czechoslovakia, the USSR. Two kindly ladies and an elderly man had set up a long table in front of the Soviet "Statue of Peace." They invited "all the people who love peace," including small children on school excursions, to sign an antinuclear petition to be sent to Washington.

But there is much less of this kind of thing than in Hiroshima, which is dominated by memorials to the bomb victims and messages of salvation. The main reason people visit Hiroshima is the bomb. This is not true of Nagasaki. Hiroshima, not Nagasaki, has become the mecca of international antinuclear activism. The Hiroshima bomb came

first. It fell in the center of the city. More people died there—and few of them were despised Christians or outcasts. People say: "No more Hiroshimas." They rarely say: "No more Nagasakis."

Instead of dwelling on the bomb, Nagasaki has turned its history of foreign missionaries, Dutch traders, Chinese merchants, and Madame Butterfly into a tourist attraction. Nagasaki takes pride in once having been the nearest thing in Japan to a cosmopolitan city. When the rest of the country was sealed off from the outside world between the early seventeenth and mid-nineteenth centuries, Nagasaki kept a Dutch trading post on Dejima Island. Western science first entered Japan through Nagasaki in the form of medical texts, which Japanese scholars learned to read by memorizing Dutch dictionaries. After Japan opened up, village girls acquired Russian by serving Russian sailors as prostitutes, and outcasts acquired foreign languages by supplying the Europeans with meat. Nagasaki had a large Chinatown, now a cute, touristy pastiche of its former self. A celebrated entertainer from Nagasaki, who sings French *chansons* and wears women's clothes, claims to be the reincarnation of a seventeenth-century Christian martyr, thought to have been the incarnation of *Deusu,* the Lord. The most popular souvenirs in Nagasaki include all manner of Christian trinkets, as well as a sponge-cake called *castella,* introduced by the Portuguese four hundred years ago.

Nagasaki's most famous survivor was a Christian named Nagai Takashi. He became a symbol of his city's suffering, just as a schoolgirl, named Sasaki Sadako, became a symbol of Hiroshima. Sadako was two years old when the bomb exploded a mile from her home. She died of leukemia ten years later, but not before trying to fold one thousand paper cranes, as symbols of longevity. Her monument in Hiroshima Peace Park is covered in thousands of paper cranes, folded by schoolchildren from all over Japan.

Dr. Nagai was a professor of radiology at the University of Nagasaki when the city was bombed. He had contracted leukemia before the war, perhaps as a result of his laboratory work, but radiation from the bomb cured the symptoms. Dr. Nagai was a devout Catholic and a Japanese patriot who exhorted his students to fight their hardest for the nation. He was devastated by Japan's defeat. But then, as he wrote in his best-selling book *The Bells of Nagasaki,* he had a flash of religious inspiration. The bomb, he decided, was "a great act of Divine Providence," for which Nagasaki "must give thanks to God." He declared that Nagasaki, "the only holy place in Japan," had been chosen as a sacrificial lamb "to be burned on the altar of sacrifice to expiate the sins committed by humanity in the Second World War." In this vision, Dr. Nagai added the Catholic victims of the bomb to the long list of Nagasaki martyrs. They were the spiritual heirs of believers who had been crucified for their faith.

> How noble, how splendid was that holocaust of August 9, when flames soared up from the cathedral, dispelling the darkness of war and bringing the light of peace! In the very depth of our grief we reverently saw here something beautiful,

something pure, something sublime. Eight thousand people, together with their priests, burning with pure smoke, entered into eternal life. All without exception were good people whom we deeply mourn.

The symptoms of leukemia returned, and Dr. Nagai retired to a tiny hut near the cathedral, where he wrote his many books and was visited by dignitaries ranging from Emperor Hirohito to Helen Keller. *The Bells of Nagasaki* was completed in 1946, but out of fear that accounts of the nuclear bombings would encourage anti-American attitudes, the US occupation authorities only allowed it to be published in 1949. Two years later Dr. Nagai died. His hut is now a shrine, visited by Japanese schoolchildren and tourists from all over the world, who peer through the window at the bone-white image of the Virgin Mary next to his bed.

I asked Father Calaso, a Spanish priest who has lived in Nagasaki for many years, what he thought of Dr. Nagai's vision. He answered that it was "theologically correct. We cannot know why the bomb was good, but God cannot will anything evil." Of course, as John Whittier Treat points out in his excellent book *Writing Ground Zero*, a critical discussion of Japanese writing about the bomb, the Christian idea of martyrdom was not the only response of Nagasaki bomb survivors. Treat contrasts Nagai's Christian idealism with the existential despair of such non-Christian writers as Hayashi Kyoko, who express not just their own "leukemia of the soul" but also their fear that the atomic disease will be carried by future generations. Hayashi's view is radically secular. In a short story entitled "In the Fields," she writes: "These are deliberate wounds precisely calculated and inflicted by human beings. On account of these calculations, the very life that we would pass on to our children and grandchildren has sustained injury."

Nevertheless the mood of Christian resignation has affected Nagasaki. There are social reasons for this, too. Like many Jewish survivors of the Holocaust who returned to their native countries in Europe, Nagasaki Christians did not wish to dwell on their suffering lest it expose them to the public gaze. They did not want to stand out in a society obsessed with bloodlines and social conformity. It was difficult enough finding marriage partners for your children, if you were a bomb survivor, being a Catholic could only make things worse. So there is something to the cliché that "Hiroshima is angry, while Nagasaki prays." Compared to Hayashi's *Angst*, Dr. Nagai's beatitude makes the past easier to bear. We are told of *Bock's Car*'s crew: "Today, they are all deeply religious men" [Chinnock].

Religion was linked to the nuclear bombs from the beginning. Witnessing the first successful nuclear explosion in New Mexico, Dr. J. Robert Oppenheimer famously quoted from the Bhagavad-Gita: "Now I am become Death the destroyer of worlds." President Truman, announcing the bombing of Hiroshima, thanked God that the weapon had "come to us instead of to our enemies; and we pray that He may guide us to use it in His ways and for His purposes." Arthur H. Compton, a member of the Interim Committee for Atomic Bomb Policy, believed that "God

had fought on our side during the war, supplying free men with weapons that tyranny could not produce."

What Truman and Compton had in common with Dr. Nagai—but absolutely not with Hayashi Kyoko—was the convenient view that God, not man, was ultimately responsible for the bomb. Opponents of the bomb often express themselves in equally religious terms. Treat quotes a poem from Nagasaki which goes: "In the Cathedral in the ruins of boundless expanse, I stayed one night cursing God." The bomb has been described on many occasions as a transgression of religious taboos, indeed a sin against God. In 1946, the Federal Council of Churches special committee explicitly said so: "As the power that first used the atomic bomb under these circumstances, we have sinned grievously against the laws of God and against the peoples of Japan." The Roman Catholic hierarchy concluded at the Second Vatican Council in 1965 that "every act of war directed to the indiscriminate destruction of whole cities or vast areas with their inhabitants is a crime against God and man."

Even if one leaves God out of it, it is hard to disagree that deliberate mass murder of civilians by so-called conventional or nuclear bombing is a war crime. But "strategic bombing," including the use of the two atomic bombs, was not an act of God. It was the result of political decisions, taken by human beings acting under particular circumstances. The trouble with focusing on God, sin, transgression, and other moral or religious aspects of this strategy is that it makes it very hard to discuss the politics and the historical circumstances dispassionately. This is especially true when politicians, newspaper columnists, peace activists, and veterans enter the debate. Too often emotional moralism sets the tone.

Many defenders of the atomic bombs, beginning with President Truman himself, have tried to justify their use on moral grounds: i.e., that the bombings saved half a million, or even a million, American lives by preventing an invasion. These probably inflated figures are supposed to make the bombings of Hiroshima and Nagasaki seem like acts of mercy. And opponents tend to boost their moral condemnation by adding evidence of bad faith: i.e., that the bombings were acts of racism, or scientific experiments, or merely opening shots of the coming cold war, or that they served no purpose at all. In other words, it is not enough for some critics to call the attacks on Hiroshima and Nagasaki a sin against God and man; to strengthen the moral case, they must be shown to have been unnecessary and politically reprehensible, too. Many critics find it impossible to accept, for example, that the A-bombing was a war crime that actually might have helped to bring the war to a quicker end. By the same token, political reasons, however justified, are not enough for some defenders of the bomb to feel vindicated. To them, the bombs must show that God was on our side, that only the purest of motives prevailed.

I think this helps to explain the debacle over the projected *Enola Gay* exhibition at the Smithsonian Institution. The fault does not lie with the authors of the original text prepared by the Smithsonian to accompany the exhibition, now published as part of *Judgment at the Smithsonian*.

Newt Gingrich was wrong: the script was not in the least anti-American, nor did it "espouse a set of values that are essentially destructive" [these views were expressed to Fred Barnes in *The New Republic,* March 13, 1995]. Historians—unlike many veterans, journalists, and politicians—have been debating the history of the bomb for years without invoking God or the Devil. And their different views are admirably and concisely reflected in the Smithsonian script. All the controversies about the atomic bombing are touched upon: whether it was an act of racism; whether the bombs were dropped to warn the Soviets, and keep them from invading Japan; whether Truman should have paid more attention to Japanese peace initiatives; and whether there were better ways than nuclear bombing of ending the war swiftly.

The Smithsonian consensus—evenhanded to the point of banality—is that racist attitudes existed, but that Roosevelt would have used the bomb on Germany if necessary. On the Soviet factor, the Smithsonian concludes that " 'atomic diplomacy' against the Soviets provided one more reason for Truman not to halt the dropping of the bomb." The Smithsonian writers believe it is possible the war *might* have ended without the bombings if the Allies had guaranteed the Japanese emperor's position. And it is not sure whether a warning demonstration—dropping the bomb in Tokyo Bay, for instance—would have sufficed. But despite all these "hotly contested" issues, its conclusion is that "the bombing of Hiroshima and Nagasaki . . . played a crucial role in ending the Pacific War quickly."

Here and there the Smithsonian text is too glib. I don't think Japanese forces kept on fighting because they feared that unconditional surrender would mean "the annihilation of their culture." Japanese forces had no choice. They went on fighting because their supreme commanders feared the annihilation of their power. Still, the projected Smithsonian exhibition would have provided an invaluable opportunity for the Hiroshima debate to break out of academic circles and reach a wider audience. This opportunity was lost when the Smithsonian caved in to protests from such organizations as the American Legion and the Air Force Association. The text was withdrawn and only the Hiroshima bomber is displayed now, without context or explanation, as just another great American plane, like the Spirit of St. Louis and the *Kitty Hawk Flyer.* This is a shame, for not only has it discouraged open discussion in the US, but it has fueled the self-righteousness of Japanese apologists for the Pacific War. If Americans refuse to question *their* war record, they ask, then why should Japanese risk the reputation of Japanese soldiers by questioning theirs?

Of course, none of this has anything to do with intellectual curiosity (the primary function of a museum, I should think), but everything to do with national pride. The American Legion and its intellectual defenders in the press were less interested in an argument than in a celebration. They wanted it to be taken for granted that the bomb was right and just. Barton Bernstein points out in a thoughtful concluding essay to *Judgment at the Smithso-*

nian that the dispute was not simply about history but about "a symbolic issue in a 'culture war.' " He writes that

> many Americans lumped together the seeming decline of American power, the difficulties of the domestic economy, the threats in world trade and especially Japan's successes, the loss of domestic jobs, and even changes in American gender roles, and shifts in the American family. To a number of Americans, the very people responsible for the [Smithsonian] script were the people who were changing America. The bomb, representing the end of World War II and suggesting the height of American power, was to be celebrated. . . . Those who in any way questioned the bomb's use were, in this emotional framework, the enemies of America. The Air Force Association, the Legion, many individual vets, segments of Congress, and parts of the media accepted, and promoted, that interpretation.

Unfortunately, the editor of *Judgment at the Smithsonian,* Philip Nobile, is no less emotional than the conservatives he deplores. Reading his introduction, I almost felt sympathetic to the American Legion. Nobile not only believes the bombings were a moral outrage, which would be a respectable position. He goes further: he believes that anyone who defends Truman's decision is morally outrageous. To him, the defenders of the Hiroshima and Nagasaki bombings are not just wrong, they are "white male American intellectuals," who seek to "deny" Hiroshima. Paul Fussell, who argued that the bomb saved American lives, including his own, which might well be true, is smeared as the "Robert Faurisson of Hiroshima denial." This is not just nasty, it is dishonest. Faurisson is a right-wing extremist who maintains that the gas chambers never existed. Whatever the merits of Fussell's argument, he never denied that the bomb was dropped or that countless civilians died. To equate Fussell with Faurisson, or Paul Tibbetts, pilot of the *Enola Gay,* with Rudolf Hoess, commandant at Auschwitz, as Nobile does, is to kill the debate. For how can you argue with bad faith? But then Nobile is as little interested in a debate as the American Legion. Like them, he is concerned with moral gestures, not of celebration in his case, but of atonement, repentance, and so forth. He bandies about words like "original sin."

Robert Jay Lifton and Greg Mitchell, in their analysis of Hiroshima's legacy in America, are not nasty, just woolly and moralistic. They believe that the bombings were morally offensive, and so the reasons for dropping them must necessarily have been politically misguided, dishonest, and irrational. Lifton takes it for granted that the bombs did not hasten the end of the war, since the Japanese would have surrendered anyway, if only Truman had listened to Joseph Grew, the former ambassador to Japan, and promised the Japanese they could keep their imperial system. He thinks that the Potsdam Declaration was mere propaganda, since it did not mention the atom bomb, the entry of Russia into the war, or the Emperor, "each of which would have pressed the Japanese towards surrender."

Was this really as obvious as Lifton and Mitchell, as well as many serious critics of Truman A-bomb policy, claim?

Some historians, such as Gar Alperovitz, believe that the Potsdam Declaration was designed to be unacceptable to the Japanese, so that the US would have time to drop the bomb and demonstrate its supremacy to the increasingly aggressive Soviet Union. [In a footnote, Buruma states: "Gar Alperovitz first set out his ideas in *Atomic Diplomacy: Hiroshima and Potsdam.* His new book, *The Decision to Use the Atomic Bomb,* goes over the same ground in more detail, as well as dealing with postwar myths about the bomb."] Truman, on the advice of his secretary of state, James Byrnes, withheld a guarantee of the Emperor's status. In *The Decision to Use the Atomic Bomb,* Alperovitz repeats over and over that Truman did this, fully aware "that a surrender was not likely to occur." The implication is that Truman did not want the Japanese to surrender before the bomb was used. On his way to Potsdam, in July 1945, Truman heard the news that the first atomic bomb had been successfully tested at Alamogordo, New Mexico. With the bomb in his pocket, so to speak, he believed that the "Japs will fold up before Russia comes in." Which was precisely what he wanted.

Alperovitz makes his case for the above scenario with mountains of documentary quotes. He shows how Truman's desire to involve the Soviet Red Army in forcing a Japanese surrender cooled as soon as he heard the good news from Alamogordo. That the Soviet Union played a part in Truman's calculations is neither a new nor an especially controversial observation. Most historians agree with Alperovitz that "even those who still wished for Russian help (to say nothing of those who opposed it) began to see the atomic bomb as a way not only to end the war, but perhaps to end it as soon as possible—preferably before the Russians attacked, and certainly, if feasible, before the Red Army got very far in its assault."

But to say that Truman deliberately withheld a guarantee of the Emperor's status at Potsdam so that he could drop his bomb is to assume it was clear the Japanese would have surrendered *with* such a guarantee. Alperovitz has no difficulty finding quotes from US officials who thought so, but there is no reason to believe that they were right, and consequently that Truman was wrong, or merely Machiavellian, to press for an unconditional surrender. There is no evidence that Japan would have surrendered, even with a guarantee of the Emperor's status, and there are good reasons to believe that it would not. As long as the Japanese were not ready to surrender on terms acceptable to the Allies, Truman had no option but to insist on a sharp ultimatum, bomb or no bomb.

What we know is that even some members of the so-called peace faction in the Japanese war cabinet were remarkably casual about the Potsdam terms—and not only because of the lack of guarantees for the Emperor. One of the "moderates," Navy Minister Yonai, said there was no need to rush because "Churchill has fallen, America is beginning to be isolated. The government therefore will ignore [the Potsdam Proclamation]" ["Japan's Delayed Surrender: A Reinterpretation," by Herbert P. Bix, *Diplomatic History* (Spring 1995)]. Even after the bombing of Nagasaki on August 9, half the Supreme War Leadership Council was still determined to fight on. Japan may have been "licked"

militarily, as Eisenhower and other Americans said at the time, and later, but this did not mean it would give up. Instead of preparing for surrender, the Japanese government exhorted the population to defend the "divine land," in mass suicide actions if necessary. The press kept up a daily Die-for-the-Emperor campaign. Thomas B. Allen and Norman Polmar describe in their book *Code-Name Downfall* how Japanese schoolchildren were trained to fight the enemy with bamboo spears, kitchen knives, firemen's hooks, or, as a last resort, feet and bare knuckles. Children were told: "If you don't kill at least one enemy soldier, you don't deserve to die." Eight hundred thousand troops, including home defense forces, were gathered in Kyushu to resist an American invasion. If it had come to a final battle in Japan, after more months of firebombing and starvation, the human cost to the Japanese—leaving aside the Allies for a moment—would have been horrendous.

If saving Japanese lives was not Truman's concern, it didn't particularly bother the Japanese leaders either. The debate inside the Leadership Council at a crisis meeting on August 9 was not about whether to surrender but about whether to insist on one condition (retention of the imperial system, or *kokutai*) or four, including the demand that there be no Allied occupation. There had to be a unanimous decision. Without absolute consensus, the government would fall, more time would be wasted, and more lives lost. This is the Emperor's own account of the meeting, which took place in the sticky heat of an underground bomb shelter. The Emperor sat stiffly in front of a gilded screen, while his ministers sweated in their dress uniforms:

> The meeting went on until two o'clock in the morning of August 10, without reaching an agreement. Then Suzuki asked me to break the deadlock and come to a decision. Apart from Prime Minister Suzuki, the participants were Hiranuma, Yonai, Anami, Togo, Umezu and Toyoda. Everyone agreed on the condition to preserve the *kokutai*. Anami, Toyoda and Umezu insisted on adding three more conditions: that Japan would not be occupied, and that the task of disarming our armed forces and dealing with war crimes would be in our own hands. They argued that at the present stage of the war, there was enough room for negotiation. Suzuki, Yonai, Hiranuma and Togo disagreed. I believed it was impossible to continue the war . . . [In a footnote, Buruma explains: "The Emperor gave this self-serving account before the Tokyo War Crimes Tribunal was convened. The text was circulated among General MacArthur's staff but then disappeared, until it turned up in America after Hirohito's death. The full text was published in Tokyo in *Showa Tenno Dokuhakuroku,* 1991."]

And so, finally, after two atomic bombings, the Emperor spoke out in favor of the peace faction. It had become impossible to carry on the war. Not only had Hiroshima been obliterated, but on the day Nagasaki was bombed, the Soviet Union had declared war on Japan. Some have argued that this, rather than the nuclear bombs, forced Japan's surrender. Perhaps, but the August 9 meeting had been convened before the Soviet declaration of war, and Alperovitz tells us that the Emperor, "on hearing of the Hiroshima bombing," had already "agreed the time had come to surrender." In the Emperor's own account, he mentions both the Soviets and the bombs: "The people were suffering terribly, first from bombings getting worse by the day, then by the appearance of the atomic bomb. Because of these factors, and the fact that the Soviet Union had unleashed a war in Manchuria, we could not but accept the terms of Potsdam" [*Showa Tenno Dokuhakuroku*]. In his broadcast to the nation, on August 15, the Emperor left the Soviet Union unmentioned, but referred to the bombs:

> The enemy has begun to use a new and most cruel bomb to kill and maim extremely large numbers of the innocent . . . if the war were to be continued, it would cause not only the downfall of our nation but also the destruction of all human civilization . . . it is according to the dictate of time and fate that We have resolved to pave the way for a grand peace for all the generations to come by enduring the unendurable and suffering what is insufferable.

The Emperor's decision to accept surrender is called the *seidan,* or sacred resolution. The Japanese war cabinet needed the voice of God to make up its mind. And as the above words show, the supreme descendant of the Japanese gods, in his divine benevolence, would save not only the Japanese nation but all human civilization. As a result of the bombs, the Japanese had been transformed from aggressors to saviors, a magnificent feat of public relations. In fact, official Japanese reasoning was more complicated than the Emperor's speech suggests. The ruling elite of Japan, with the Emperor as its active high priest, was afraid that the Japanese people, exhausted, hungry, and sick of war, might become unruly. The atomic bombs offered a perfect excuse to end the war on terms that would not destroy the elite. Admiral Yonai Mitsumasa, a member of the peace faction, said on August 12, 1945:

> I think the term is perhaps inappropriate, but the atomic bombs and the Soviet entry into the war are, in a sense, gifts from the gods. This way we don't have to say that we quit the war because of domestic circumstances. Why I have long been advocating control of the crisis of the country is neither for fear of an enemy attack nor because of the atomic bombs and the Soviet entry into the war. The main reason is my anxiety over the domestic situation. So, it is rather fortunate that now we can control matters without revealing the domestic situation. [Bix, *Diplomatic History*]

It is not certain that a warning, or demonstration of the bomb, would have been enough of an excuse for the peace faction and the Emperor to stand up to the die-hards. Oppenheimer could think of no demonstration "sufficiently spectacular" to bring about surrender. Assistant Secretary of War John McCloy disagreed; he recommended a demonstration. The least one can say is that it would surely have been worth a try. For 200,000 deaths was a high price to pay for a gift from the gods.

Alperovitz, among others, suggests that an earlier war declaration by the Soviet Union, coupled with an Ameri-

can promise to protect the Emperor, would have been enough to make Japan give in. After all, the Emperor was protected after the Japanese surrender, so why not before? As soon as Japan showed its readiness to accept the Potsdam terms on August 10, so long as the Emperor would be protected, Truman was so eager to end the war that the Emperor's authority was recognized, "subject to the Supreme Commander of the Allied Powers" (SCAP).

Alperovitz finds this change of policy "puzzling." If then, why not before? But there is quite a difference between recognizing the Emperor's authority as a condition of surrender, and doing so under the auspices of SCAP, after Japan was defeated. For now the US was in control of the institution. The result was not entirely positive. SCAP, that is to say General MacArthur, used his powers to protect Emperor Hirohito not only from prosecution for war crimes but even from appearing as a witness. This had serious consequences, for so long as the Emperor, in whose name the war had been waged, could not be held accountable, the question of war guilt would remain fuzzy in Japan, and a source of friction between Japan and its former enemies.

Alperovitz thinks that Truman's uncompromising position at Potsdam had given "hard-line army leaders a trump card against early surrender proposals. The army could continue to argue that the Emperor-God might be removed, perhaps tried as a war criminal, possibly even hanged." Here I think he is missing the point. The hardliners, as well as the peace faction, were fighting to preserve a *kokutai,* which was hardly benign. Indeed, it was the very system that brought war to Asia. Herbert Bix, one of the most knowledgeable historians of the Japanese imperial system, has argued—I think, rightly—that even the peace faction wanted to retain an authoritarian system, which would have left substantial power in the Emperor's hands. He writes:

> If Grew and the Japan crowd [in Washington] had gotten their way, and the principle of unconditional surrender had been contravened, it is highly unlikely that Japan's post-surrender leaders, now the "moderates" around the throne, would ever have discarded the Meiji Constitution and democratized their political institutions.

Although Truman might have looked better in retrospect if he had guaranteed the Emperor's status earlier, before dropping the atomic bombs, such a guarantee alone was unlikely to have pushed Japan toward surrender before August 9. The hardliners rejected the idea of an Allied occupation, let alone the submission of the imperial institution to a foreign ruler. Indeed, some of the die-hards, including War Minister Anami, continued to argue against the surrender until August 14, when the Emperor, once again, spoke in favor of peace. After that, Anami resisted no more, and committed suicide in the traditional manner of a samurai.

Those who claim that Truman should have been more flexible tend to misunderstand the role of the imperial institution. Alperovitz writes that the Japanese regarded their emperor as a god, "more like Jesus or the incarnate

Buddha," and that the US demand for unconditional surrender "directly threatened not only the person of the Emperor but such central tenets of Japanese culture as well." In fact, the Emperor was never regarded as anything like the Buddha; he was more like a priest-king, a combination of the Pope and a constitutional monarch. Alperovitz quotes, with approval, John McCloy's proposal in 1945 that "the Mikado" be retained "on the basis of a constitutional monarchy." But Emperor Hirohito already was a constitutional monarch. The problem was his other function, as the pope of Japanese nationalism. His position during the 1930s and early 1940s had less to do with central tenets of Japanese culture than with a political ideology, based in large part on nineteenth-century European nationalism. It was not culture or religion that the Japanese leaders tried to protect, but their own position in the *kokutai*. Without the Emperor, their power would have lacked any legitimacy. Since it was Truman's aim to break their power, he had to break the *kokutai* first.

The question at the heart of Alperovitz's book is "whether, when the bomb was used, the president and his top advisers understood that it was not required to avoid a long and costly invasion, as they later claimed and as most Americans still believe." He has proved that avoiding an invasion was not Washington's only aim. Secretary of State Henry Stimpson's statement (to McCloy) in May 1945 makes that pretty clear. The US, he said, had "coming into action a weapon which will be unique." The "method now to deal with Russia was to . . . let our actions speak for words." And the US might have to "do it in a pretty rough and realistic way." There is no doubt that at Potsdam Truman saw the bomb as a joker in his pack.

But Alperovitz does not prove conclusively that the Soviet Union was the only reason for dropping the bomb. There were other considerations, which did involve the possibility of an invasion. Truman wanted to end the war swiftly to stop the Soviet advance in East Asia, but also because Americans were getting tired of fighting. Truman worried that the prospect of a prolonged war in the Far East, including an eventual invasion, would put pressure on him to accept a Japanese surrender on less than favorable terms. In other words, before Hiroshima, Truman did think the defeat of Japan, on American terms, might require a long battle. The problem with Alperovitz's analysis is that he pays too little attention to the political situation in wartime Japan. In his famous book *Atomic Diplomacy*, published in 1965, there is only one reference to Prime Minister Suzuki, and none to his die-hard opponents Anami, Umezu, and Toyoda. His new tome still only mentions them in passing.

Alperovitz's case that the bomb was not dropped to prevent a final bloody battle rests entirely on the assumption that Truman and his advisers knew perfectly well that the Japanese were on the verge of capitulation before the destruction of Hiroshima. Closer examination of what went on in Tokyo shows that the Japanese were not. So long as there was no unanimity in the war cabinet and the Emperor remained silent, the war would go on. And so long as the hard-liners prevailed, any attempt by members of the

peace faction, such as Foreign Minister Togo, to negotiate for peace had to be vague, furtive, and inconclusive. Alperovitz makes a great deal of Togo's dispatches in July 1945 to Sato Naotake, ambassador to Moscow, conveying the Emperor's wish to discuss peace terms through the good offices of Moscow. He makes less of the fact that Ambassador Sato told his foreign minister that the mission was hopeless since Japan had nothing specific to discuss. And he makes nothing at all of the other reason for approaching Moscow: important members of the peace faction, including Admiral Yonai, still hoped to forge a Japanese-Soviet alliance against the US and Britain. [In a footnote, Buruma adds: "Japanese historians have paid attention to this, most recently in a discussion in the September issue of the monthly magazine *Gendai*."]

So I do not believe it was an irrational policy on Truman's part to insist on unconditional surrender. But analyzing rational policies is not the business of a professor of psychiatry and psychology, so Robert Jay Lifton ignores these political considerations, and dwells on such issues as Truman's "denial of death," or James Byrnes's "totalistic relationship with the weapon," or "the formation of separate, relatively autonomous selves" in the personality of Henry Stimson. From this psychiatric perspective, anyone mad enough to drop an atomic bomb, even in 1945, when any means to end the war had to be considered, must be a mental patient. And the policy of a mental patient has to be touched with madness.

Lifton and Mitchell claim, like Alperovitz, that since the successful test of the atomic bomb, "Truman and Byrnes began to focus on how to end the war sufficiently quickly that the Soviets would not gain a foothold in Japan." But again the authors do not consider the reasons why. To them it is but one more example of Truman's irrational state of mind, because he was suppressing his feelings and "any tendency to reflect," since he had been bad at sports as a child and was afraid of being "a sissy." Even if all these things were true, there were still compelling reasons for wishing to stop Soviet troops from entering Japan. There was concern in Washington about the swift expansion of the Soviet Empire in Eastern and Central Europe. The US ambassador to the Soviet Union, W. Averill Harriman, called it a "barbarian invasion." He believed, quite correctly, that Soviet control of other countries meant the extinction of political liberties in those countries and a dominant Soviet influence over their foreign relations. As subsequent events in China and the Korean peninsula have shown, Truman was right to worry about Soviet power in northeast Asia. It certainly would not have suited US interests, or those of Japan for that matter, if the Japanese archipelago had been divided into different occupation zones, with Stalin's troops ensconced in Hokkaido.

As he did in his book on the "genocidal mentality" of nuclear scientists and strategists [*The Genocidal Mentality*, by Robert Jay Lifton and Eric Markusen, 1990], Lifton uses the phrase "nuclearism," which he describes as "a spiritual faith that the ultimate power of the emerging weapon could serve not only death and destruction but also continuing life." Believers in this faith, such as Truman, feel like "merging with a source of power rivaling that of any deity." They are, in short, possessed. Here Lifton and Mitchell are close to the religious position of Dr. Nagai: the atomic bombs over Hiroshima and Nagasaki were propelled by a force beyond human reason. Having established that, the authors can dispense with political arguments and concentrate on the corruption of American life by irrational forces. They can write that the "nurturing of this deified object [i.e., the bomb], as our source of security and ultimate power over death, became the central task of our society," without contemplating what the world would have been like if the sole possessors of this object had been the likes of Joseph Stalin.

Perhaps it helps to be a Nagasaki Catholic to take a more complex view of sin. Loyalty to their own deity must have given some Japanese Christians a skeptical view of Japanese politics when the *kokutai* was at the height of its divine imperial pretensions. One of the most controversial and interesting Nagasaki Catholics is the ex-mayor Motoshima Hitoshi. I first interviewed him seven years ago, in Nagasaki, when Emperor Hirohito was dying. Motoshima had just said in public that the Emperor bore some responsibility for the war and, by not ending it soon enough, for the fates of Hiroshima and Nagasaki. A conservative politician, he was disowned by the Liberal Democratic Party and blackballed by various patriotic organizations of which he was a member. He also received threats from right-wing extremists. One year later, he was shot in the back by one of them, and barely survived. This is the "Japanese culture" that remains from the war. It is no longer the main political-tendency, but it is still intimidating enough to silence critics of the imperial system and other remnants of the old *kokutai,* which General MacArthur helped to protect.

This summer, Motoshima looked less robust than I remembered him, perhaps because of the assassination attempt, perhaps because of his recent loss of the mayoral election. He began by reading the late Emperor's statement of August 15, 1945, about the "new and most cruel bomb." He tapped the text with his finger and said the bomb did bring the war to an end. But then he made another point. The atomic bombs, he said, had done away with the idea of a good war. He himself had believed in a Japanese victory. Although he had been tormented as a Christian child by teachers who forced him to declare who was holier, Jesus or the Emperor, Motoshima was a patriot. He served in an army propaganda unit. But the atomic bombs had turned war into an absolute evil, like the Holocaust in Europe. He illustrated this view at a recent press conference in Tokyo, by comparing the innocent victims of Hiroshima and Nagasaki to the Jews killed at Auschwitz. The Japanese press made nothing of this. But the Western correspondents were full of indignation: yet another Japanese whitewash, they thought, another sob story of the Japanese as victims.

I asked him about this. Was there really no difference between the citizens of a nation that started a war and people who were killed for purely ideological reasons? Had he himself not said that the Japanese people bore responsibility for the war, as well as their emperor? He answered my question by asking me whether I thought Jewish soldiers in Hitler's army had been responsible for the war in Europe. Clearly, the precise nature of the European Holocaust had rather escaped him. But when pressed by others he has acknowledged that there was a difference between the atomic bombings and the Holocaust. The US was not planning to exterminate the entire Japanese people. The question remains, however, whether there is a fundamental moral difference between dropping atomic bombs on Hiroshima and Nagasaki and many thousands of incendiary bombs on, say, Tokyo.

Truman's decision to drop the atomic bombs was the climax of a horrible strategy, started by Germany and Japan, that had left much of Europe, parts of China, and most of Japan in ruins.

—*Ian Buruma*

Miyazaki Kentaro, the son of bomb survivors, and a historian specializing in the "hidden Christian" communities in Japan, saw no moral difference. All forms of carpet bombing were a sin. But like the former mayor, he blamed the Japanese government for starting the war, and saw no reason to criticize the US. I also asked the opinion of Father Sebastian Kawazoe, the priest at Urakami Cathedral. Like Motoshima, with whom he went to school, Kawazoe was born on one of the Goto Islands, in a family of hidden Christians. He had the same straight, almost rough, manner of speaking as the ex-mayor. He told me most Catholics had not been keen supporters of the war. But they had to be careful, for they were always being treated as spies. He, too, saw no moral distinction between A-bombs and other forms of terror bombing.

I dwell on this point because I think it clarifies our thinking about the past. If we see the atomic bombs as morally unique, as something fundamentally different, in ethical terms, from large numbers of incendiary bombs or napalm bombs dropped on civilians, it is difficult to analyze the actions of men, such as Truman, who saw the A-bomb attacks as a logical extension of strategic bombing. [In a footnote, Buruma adds: "In his article, 'Understanding the Atomic Bomb and the Japanese Surrender: Missed Opportunities, Little-Known Near Disasters, and Modern Memory,' in *Diplomatic History* (Spring 1995), Barton Bernstein emphasizes that in 1945, American leaders were not seeking to avoid the use of the A-bomb. Its use did not create ethical or political problems for them.' "] McGeorge Bundy wrote about this in his book *Danger and Survival,* in a chapter entitled "The Decision to Drop the Bombs on Japan."

> Both military and political leaders came to think of urban destruction not as wicked, not even as a necessary evil, but as a result with its own military value. Distinctions that had seemed clear when the Germans bombed Rotterdam were

gradually rubbed out in the growing ferocity of the war.

This, rather than theological jargon about original sin or "nuclearism," is the nub of the matter. Truman, in response to an American advocate of "the Christian tradition of civilized war," said there was no such thing, that war "has always been a matter of slaughter of innocents and never civilized." This sounds good, a moral *cri de coeur* from a tough-minded, peace-loving leader, but it is disingenuous. For there is a difference between killing innocents in the heat of battle and killing them deliberately, in huge numbers, as a form of terror. Tens of thousands died horribly in Dresden without any apparent military or political justification. The possibility that the carnage in Hiroshima and Nagasaki might have brought the war to a speedier end made these mass killings expedient, perhaps, but no less morally disturbing. This does not mean, however, that it would have been any more ethical to go on fire-bombing Japanese cities, as Curtis LeMay, an opponent of the A-bomb strategy, wanted. More than 100,000 civilians had already died in one night in May, when LeMay's B-29s torched Tokyo with incendiary bombs. Truman's decision to drop the bombs was the climax of a horrible strategy, started by Germany and Japan, that had left much of Europe, parts of China, and most of Japan in ruins.

It would make sense for the Nagasaki Catholics, who suffered disproportionately from the A-bomb, to be active in the antinuclear peace movement. Actually they are not. Motoshima, who is a campaigner for world peace, is an exception. Father Kawazoe, himself a survivor, said: "I don't take part in the peace movement. It is used by people to expand their own sect. They talk about peace, but you don't know what's behind it." While acknowledging the checkered record of the Christian Church—"60 percent bad, 40 percent good"—he also said: "We Christians have a history of oppression, but we don't make a living out of our suffering. Emphasizing one's own suffering is just a way to win sympathy."

This is a bit harsh on the survivors in Peace Park, who devote their time to telling schoolchildren about the bomb. But as I watched those same schoolchildren, lined up in straight rows in front of the "Peace Statue" and solemnly shouting lines they had memorized about loving peace, I was reminded of demonstrations in the former East Berlin, where the masses marched past their leaders, raising their fists and bellowing slogans about "people's friendship." These peace ceremonies have become ritual gestures to ward off nuclear evil: "People who love peace, please sign your name here."

There is nothing in Nagasaki to tell those schoolchildren why the bomb was dropped, or what led up to it. It is indeed hard to explain why the bomb had to be dropped on Nagasaki. There is no evidence that it hastened the end of the war. Carl Spaatz, the commanding general of the US Army Strategic Air Forces, is quoted by Alperovitz as saying (to Averill Harriman) that he had no idea why a bomb had been dropped on Nagasaki. We will never know to what extent the fate of Nagasaki influenced the Emperor's decision to tell his soldiers to lay down their arms. But some historical context, some indication of what those Japanese soldiers had done to others, would not have been amiss. Instead, all one really hears in Nagasaki is the sound of prayer. And one only needs to walk past the Peace Park monuments, from China, the USSR, Bulgaria, Cuba, Poland, Czechoslovakia, and the German Democratic Republic, to see how peace has been exploited.

On my last day in Nagasaki, I visited Urakami Cathedral, where Father Kawazoe was celebrating Mass. The cathedral was full, with more women than men. The women wore old-fashioned veils, a custom that has virtually died out in Europe. Almost all these people were descended from families who had clung to their faith through centuries of persecution. It was a moving spectacle, even if one had no special feeling for the Catholic Church. Father Kawazoe was preaching that God's will could not be known, and it was useless to expect favors from Him. God was not like some local deity, whom one could ask for a good catch or an abundant crop. I was puzzled by this. Here was a Japanese priest, in the Cathedral of a modern, sophisticated city, talking to people as though they were villagers on Goto Island who had to be weaned from their native gods.

I left the Cathedral feeling touched, but also with a sense

The mushroom cloud over Nagasaki, August, 1945.

of sadness and futility. Outside were some of the remains of the old Cathedral: a blackened statue of Christ, with a chipped nose and dark stumps where there had once been fingers; and there a damaged Saint Agnes; and there, in the grass, the charred heads of decapitated angels. People used to believe that Armageddon was a prerogative of God, or of the gods. Now we know it is in the hands of man. Hardly a consolation.

Erika Lenz   (review date September-October 1995)

SOURCE: A review of *Atomic Ghost: Poets Respond to the Nuclear Age,* in *The Bloomsbury Review,* Vol. 15, No. 5, September-October, 1995, p. 28.

[*In the following positive review of* Atomic Ghosts, *an anthology of poems that examine the use of nuclear weapons and nuclear power, Lenz applauds the collection's structure and guiding principles.*]

This year—the 50th anniversary of the bombing of Hiroshima—arrives for a public so familiar with "the bomb," nuclear power, and their dangers as to create the illusion that microscopic atom-play is commonplace, a simple fact of life. The smallness—and paradoxically monstrous scale—of atomic and nuclear power is precisely what makes its impact so hard to grasp. To an average person living in the nineties, the effect of this technology on our day-to-day lives seems minor.

Atomic Ghost serves to remind us of the danger of this sort of denial, especially in a culture that often fails to pass down important stories to younger generations. Editor John Bradley writes in his Preface that the main impetus for this book was a student of his who didn't know about Hiroshima:

> Her question made me realize that there are Americans who have no idea . . . how we are still dealing with the consequences, and the "ghosts." . . . Her question made me realize that I have an obligation . . . to see that future generations will know, and that they in turn will teach their children. How else, I wonder, can we have peace, can we have a future, if we do not remember?

To this end, Bradley collects an impressive array of emerging and established poets from several cultures, including Philip Levine, David Mura, Nanao Sakaki, Lucien Stryk, Antler, Jorie Graham, Adrienne Rich, Gregory Corso, Gary Snyder, Galway Kinnell, Carolyn Forché, and others. As Bradley presents a variety of visions about the bomb, he also displays the range of styles and techniques in contemporary poetry. Poems range from lyric to conversational narrative, from 10 lines to 10 pages, from overtly political to highly personal. The collection also includes many translations, predominantly from Japanese poets. Bradley combines this array of personal visions into a chorus of witnesses that powerfully demonstrates the complexity of the nuclear issue.

Some readers of poetry might be put off by 300 pages of poetry on the same subject. Although this anthology is certainly not light reading, Bradley has created—with his keen editorial eye and sensitivity to the reader's experience—a surprisingly readable collection. The success of this anthology lies in both its contents and its structure. The various poets' approaches differ enough to keep the reader interested and challenged. In addition, by arranging this collection into six loosely chronological sections, Bradley creates a subtle "nuclear primer"—one more interesting than could be found in any history text because the lessons carry the weight of personal experience. For the reader unfamiliar with the development of this technology and the history of its use, this order facilitates entering directly into the experience of several generations. For those already all too aware of the dangers, this book provides an opportunity to explore multiple perspectives. Perhaps more significant than the historical element, however, is the emotional structure of the book. The sections, beginning with "Creation" and ending with "Prayer for Continuation," are consciously arranged to enable what Terry Tempest Williams describes in her Introduction as "a collective ritual, a ceremony to heal ourselves through poetry."

Like most anthologies, some poems in *Atomic Ghost* are better than others. A few succumb to the prosaic weight of historical detail. A large percentage, however, are strong poems by strong writers. Most retain subtlety and control where there could be a blinding rage that might overpower the aesthetic. Far from inundating the reader with tiresome activist diatribes, Bradley has chosen poems in which there is often only a lateral connection to the subject at hand. This is particularly effective and demonstrates the insidious, often nearly invisible, impact of nuclear technology. Despite this subtlety, it's apparent that for these poets there's a very real imperative to write. As Marc Kaminsky asks in his poem "Questions,"

> if I fail
> to work all the horror
> into a play
> of voices in which the living and the dead
> live again
> who will forgive me?

At the base of all these poems lies the struggle to remind us that nuclear technology is not only a creation of humankind in the physical realm, but it also has an undeniable life in the mind. At the end of his poem "The Lightning," James Grabill repeats, "life as we see it, atomic war," reminding us of the equation between the two. Human dynamics created the bomb, and almost simultaneously, the bomb created a new human dynamic. Life and nuclear technology are now inseparable; these poets remind us that to deny this is to deny the true nature of the life we now live. Together in *Atomic Ghost,* their voices join in protest, awe, and grief, and by doing so, work to keep the machine of history from repeating itself through the power of collective memory.

Robert Jay Lifton and Greg Mitchell   (essay date 1995)

SOURCE: "Appendix: Cultural Responses to Hiroshima," in *Hiroshima in America: Fifty Years of Denial,* G. P. Putnam's Sons, 1995, pp. 359-81.

[*An American psychiatrist, nonfiction writer, and critic, Lifton received a National Book Award for* Death in Life: Survivors of Hiroshima *(1968). Mitchell is an American journalist and critic as well as the editor of* Nuclear Times *magazine. In the following excerpt, the critics discuss the American literary response to the atomic bombing of Japan.*]

Television and cinema have slighted Hiroshima, but fiction has virtually ignored it. There is no major American novel about Hiroshima. Indeed, few American novels of any stature explore the consequences of using the atomic bomb. Only a handful of fiction writers have utilized Hiroshima or Los Alamos as a setting, or explored the emotions and attitudes of the scientists, the policy makers, or the airmen who dropped the bomb. The few novels that have approached the subject have all been forgotten.

"Hiroshima has had nothing like the literary impact of other great military events," Paul Brians recently observed in his book *Nuclear Holocausts: Atomic War in Fiction.* Brians chronicles over eight hundred "nuclear novels," most of them science fiction. Less than a dozen explore the building or use of the bomb; few of them sold particularly well or remained long in print. In contrast, Brians notes, some people read a dozen Civil War novels *every year,* and he asks: Where are the Hiroshima "buffs"?

There are reasons for this, of course, including moral ambivalence "Evil has no place, it seems, in our national mythology," asserts Tim O'Brien, author of the novel *The Nuclear Age.* Another factor is the technological nature of the atomic attacks. The bombing of Japan may have been efficient but it was hardly "stirring"; it involved only a small group of airmen, not vast armies; and it was uncomfortably one-sided. Still, it can be said that, as with cinema, Hiroshima is everywhere in postwar and contemporary fiction—in its themes of futurelessness and absurdity, and its predilection for violent or vengeful behavior by heroes and antiheroes alike. One critic has observed that the "usual place" for Hiroshima in Western literature is "the unconscious."

Like Hiroshima films, Hiroshima fiction often seems inappropriate to the subject, treating a revolutionary event far too realistically. What happened to Hiroshima is impossible to make explicit. (One recalls Walt Whitman's comment on the Civil War: "The real war will never get into the books.") Of the few published novels, most focus on the scientists—not the decision makers, the pilots, or the Japanese victims.

If there are any major novels exploring the decision to drop the bomb or the *Enola Gay*'s mission to Hiroshima, no bibliographer has yet uncovered them. Many novelists of the postwar era seemed to follow the advice of William Faulkner's 1950 Nobel Prize acceptance speech. Faulkner lamented that "the young man or woman writing today has forgotten the problems of the human heart in conflict with itself which alone can make good writing because only that is worth writing about, worth the agony and the sweat." There were no longer "problems of the spirit. There is only the question: When will I be blown up?" Faulkner offered this advice to the modern writer:

He must teach himself that the basest of all things is to be afraid; and, teaching himself that, forget it forever, leaving no room in his workshop for anything but the old verities and truths of the heart . . . Until he does so, he labors under a curse.

Others, however, believed that the "curse" itself must *not* be forgotten but rather addressed, directly or subversively. Alfred Kazin wrote: "I don't care for novelists who ignore what H. G. Wells himself called the 'queerness' that has come into contemporary life since the bomb." Kazin scored the "dimness," "flatness," and "paltriness" of many reputable novelists, calling them "ways of escape" from the nuclear reality.

The work of fiction most directly related to, and inspired by, Hiroshima—and certainly reflective of Kazin's notion of "queerness"—is a short story written by James Agee called "Dedication Day." Significantly, it was conceived in the immediate aftermath of Hiroshima, before the event was covered over and it was easier for a writer to act as witness. Agee wrote in a feverish rage. The day after the attack on Hiroshima, he informed a *Time* colleague that it was "the worst thing that ever happened—so far: anyhow, that it pretty thoroughly guarantees universal annihilation, within not many years." As an American, he felt he was personally implicated in the killing of thousands of civilians. It was Agee who wrote the first *Time* magazine essay on Hiroshima [published in the August 20, 1945 issue], which brilliantly . . . rendered the splitting of American conscience no less than the atom. A few days later, he started work on what he called "a story . . . about the atomic bomb." This subject was "the only thing much worth writing or thinking about."

A satirical fantasy, "Dedication Day" (which was published in Dwight Macdonald's *Politics* in 1946) depicts the postwar celebration of the bomb in which any attempt to atone for Hiroshima must be viewed as evidence of madness.

The time is 1946. A great arch designed by Frank Lloyd Wright, made of fused uranium and meant to mark "the greatest of human achievements," is about to be dedicated in Washington, D.C., near the Capitol. Reporters, generals, statesmen (including Truman and Conant), and enthusiastic citizens gather. Agee spares no aspect of the American way of life: advertising, religion, science, the military, psychiatry, art. Vendors sell Good Humor bars. Church leaders offer prayers. The first major television hookup in history carries the event to New York City. But all is not well. A pregnant woman faints and miscarries. A bugler, assigned to play "Reveille," feels impelled to play "Taps."

An Eternal Fuse—which symbolizes America's growing nuclear-weapons arsenal—will feed a memorial flame. Made of cotton, it burns so swiftly that it must be manufactured on the spot, in an "irradiated workshop" directly beneath the arch. These keepers of the flame toil in twelve-hour shifts, behind glass, always under the gaze of tourists. One shift is made up of disabled American veterans. The other is composed of Japanese survivors "of the experiments at Hiroshima and Nagasaki," who had "been forgiven." The survivors have become a popular tourist attraction because of "those strange burns which have excited, in Americans, so much friendly curiosity."

The dedication ceremonies, however, are marred by "a pathetic incident." One of the scientists who invented the bomb, and had been seeking atonement ever since Hiroshima—which struck his colleagues as "a little queer in the head"—now insists on joining the Japanese custodians of the flame. To humor him, officials oblige. Tourists, watching him among the survivors, tearing at his hair and beating his face with his fists, try to cheer him up by flashing the V for Victory sign. Officials, feeling that "the intended dignity, charm, and decorum of the exhibit" is threatened, decide to send the scientist to a sanitarium. This he accepts, in return for being allowed to throw the switch that starts the burning of the Eternal Fuse. General Groves, who was to have performed this task, agrees to step aside.

Alas, a few minutes after he throws the switch, the scientist is found next to the great spool of cotton, dead, by his own hand. Pinned to his laboratory coat is a note revealing that "he regarded his suicide as obligatory—as, indeed, a kind of religious or ethical 'sacrifice,' through which he hoped to endow the triumphal monument with a new and special significance and . . . once more (as he thought) to assist the human race." As the scientist is buried with full honors at the Trinity site, philosophers and clergymen embark on a campaign of "controlled ridicule," pointing to the scientist as an object lesson for anyone "liable to the grievous error of exaggerated scrupulousness." Yet the narrator of Agee's story concludes that this view of the scientist was too harsh:

> For misguided and altogether regrettable though his last days were—a sad warning indeed to those who turn aside from the dictates of reason, and accept human progress reluctantly—he was nevertheless, perhaps, our last link with a not-too-distant past in which such conceptions as those of "atonement," and "guilt," and "individual responsibility" still had significance.

Richly symbolic, if erratic, "Dedication Day" makes plain the "intensity and bitterness of Agee's feelings about the atomic bomb," Paul Boyer has observed. "The story's topographical structure—official celebrations aboveground contrasting with strange and disturbed goings-on underground—metaphorically suggests his sense of the complexity and partially hidden nature of the American response to the bomb." Yet the story would find only a limited audience, and Agee lamented his inability to turn it into a more complete work, in the end dubbing it a "Rough Sketch for a Moving Picture." More than anything, it offers eloquent evidence, according to Boyer, "of Agee's difficulty in translating anguish and dread into literature." Few have made this kind of attempt, regarding Hiroshima, since.

Agee fared no better with two other projects he began and then abandoned: a nonfiction book on the bomb and a treatment for a nuclear holocaust film, starring his friend Charles Chaplin (entitled *Scientists and Tramp*). Few serious writers shared Agee's passion and sense of personal

connection to the atomic bombings. One who did was Kurt Vonnegut, Jr.

His book *Cat's Cradle,* published in 1963 shortly after the Cuban missile crisis, is probably the only widely read novel overtly related to Hiroshima. Many who read *Cat's Cradle* years ago probably still recall how it ends: with crystals of a substance called ice-nine destroying the world. Many forget how the book begins: with the narrator interviewing Americans about what they were doing on August 6, 1945 (he's writing a book on this subject). This leads him to the children of Dr. Felix Hoenikker, one of the inventors of the A-bomb, who, as it turns out, also created ice-nine. Dr. Hoenikker doesn't have much use for people. When confronted with Oppenheimer's notion that the atomic scientists had "known sin," he replies: "What is sin?"

Vonnegut, educated as a chemist, based Hoenikker on the famous scientist Irving Langmuir, whom he met when he worked at General Electric after the war. "I want scientists to be more moral," Vonnegut once told an interviewer. The end of the world, or of distant planets, due to human greed or miscalculation would figure prominently in many of his novels.

This is not surprising, because Vonnegut is probably the only major fiction writer who personally experienced a near-apocalypse: the firebombing of Dresden, which he witnessed as a prisoner of war. This inspired his most acclaimed novel, *Slaughterhouse Five,* and surely influenced his lifetime obsession with nuclear weapons, global self-destruction, and human conscience. The parallels between Dresden and Hiroshima are obvious. Vonnegut has said that in response to Dresden he became a pacifist. Later, he instructed his sons that they were not to take part in massacres or work for companies that make "massacre machinery"; further, "the news of massacres of enemies" was "not to fill them with satisfaction or glee."

Another response to the bombing of Dresden: Vonnegut no longer believed what his government said. After all, the U.S. had claimed that it was not bombing civilians in the war; and later, when Vonnegut tried to obtain information on what had actually happened in Dresden, he ran into a government stonewall. Told that this information was still top secret, Vonnegut exclaimed: "Secret? My God—from whom?"

Vonnegut was "sickened" by Hiroshima. Having observed city bombings in Europe, he knew immediately "what bullshit it was" when he heard Truman's reference to Hiroshima as a military base. He compares his reaction to that of "being a devout Christian and then seeing some horrible massacres conducted by Christians after a victory." In *Slaughterhouse Five,* Vonnegut quoted the first six paragraphs of Truman's August 6 announcement in their entirety—probably the widest airing this text had received since August 1945—and followed it with quotes by two Allied generals justifying the firebombing of Dresden as a "military necessity." Later, a fictional character comments on the Dresden raid: "Pity the men who had to *do* it."

Slaughterhouse Five is a survivor's effort to make sense of a world dominated by the threat of holocaust and the reality of numbing. It is about feeling and not feeling, about remembering and not remembering.

Like *Slaughterhouse Five,* Joseph Heller's *Catch-22* has never been considered a "nuclear" book, but its themes of absurd death and amoral bureaucracy could not be more relevant to Hiroshima. Catch-22 itself represents the dilemma facing all Americans in a nuclear era of secrecy and powerlessness: "Catch-22 says they have a right to do anything we can't stop them from doing." This includes ordering the use of nuclear weapons. As Heller shows, the American airmen in World War II had as much to fear from their own generals as they did from the enemy: an apt metaphor for the nuclear age.

The essence of both *Catch-22* and *Slaughterhouse Five,* Alfred Kazin observed, is that though both are ostensibly about World War II, "they are really about The Next War, and thus about a war that will be without limits and without meaning, a war that will end only when no one is alive to fight it." In *Closing Time,* his recent sequel to *Catch-22,* Heller made this manifest. He portrayed General Leslie Groves engaged in a project to build an attack plane that flies so fast "you can bomb someone yesterday." An admiral asks arms merchant Milo Minderbinder if it can destroy the world. "I'm afraid not, sir," he replies. "We can make it uninhabitable, but we can't destroy it." "I can live with that!" the admiral replies.

This, in a sense, has been the grim message of countless postapocalypse novels: Ray Bradbury's *The Martian Chronicles* (1950), Nevil Shute's *On the Beach* (1957), Russell Hoban's *Riddley Walker* (1980), Bernard Malamud's *God's Grace* (1982), and Denis Johnson's *Fiskadoro* (1985), among others, as well as accidental nuclear war novels such as *Fail-Safe* (1962). By now, the publishing pattern is predictable: nuclear novels appear when the bomb appears most threatening (for example, the fallout scare and "missile gap" of the late 1950s and early 1960s) and virtually disappear when the terror subsides. "The all-time high point of nuclear war fiction," according to Paul Brians, was 1984—not coincidentally a time of antinuclear fervor. But that trend quickly collapsed. Not much prose on this subject has appeared since the mid-1980s. And even at its high-water mark, nuclear fiction evaded Hiroshima.

In contrast, a number of major poets have written brilliantly on nuclear concerns, and they have invoked Hiroshima far more often than the novelists. This is especially significant when one considers that the tradition of political poetry in this country was "very, very thin" until Vietnam, as Galway Kinnell has observed [in *Literature Under the Nuclear Cloud,* 1984]. The subject of nuclear war is "inherently very difficult," Kinnell explains. "If a poem is to be useful, it has to give hope, but if it is to be realistic, it has to cause despair. Despair is built into the subject."

American poets have applied themselves to Hiroshima more imaginatively and persistently than filmmakers and fiction writers, perhaps because they are not constrained by the historical or documentary narrative common to those other forms of expression. They can attempt to get at the meaning of Hiroshima in a more personal, creative, imagistic, even fractured way—an approach the event practically demands. *Atomic Ghost,* a 1995 anthology, includes more than one hundred "nuclear" poems, with many (written by well-known poets such as Philip Levine, Mary Jo Salter, and Denise Levertov) relating specifically to Hiroshima.

Shortly after Hiroshima, Randall Jarrell informed a friend that he felt "so rotten about the country's response" to the atomic bombings that he wished he could become "a naturalized cat or dog." That year (in "Losses") he wrote of men in "bombers named for girls" carrying out missions to burn cities to the ground. The following year (in "1945: The Death of the Gods") he pondered the end of the world "when rockets rise like stars." Robert Frost, in "U.S. 1946 King's X," observed the hypocrisy of those who "invented a new Holocaust" yet believed that no other country had the right to use the bomb. John Berryman (in "The Dispossessed") considered individual versus collective guilt for Hiroshima and Nagasaki.

Years passed, but prominent poets would not let go of Hiroshima Robert Penn Warren's poem "New Dawn" rendered the flight of the *Enola Gay* in a dispassionate, documentary-like manner. Beat poets, on the other hand, railed angrily, vulgarly, against the bomb in the 1950s, but rarely invoked Hiroshima.

In the late 1980s, Marc Kaminsky created a cycle of poems about *hibakusha* called "The Road from Hiroshima." Campbell McGrath examined how the atomic bombings had psychologically affected his entire generation in "Nagasaki, Uncle Walt, the Eschatology of America's Century," noting that young people had "invested so much in World War III it seems a shame to miss it."

Also in the 1980s, two prominent poets, Galway Kinnell and Carolyn Forché, made highly significant visits to Hiroshima and Nagasaki. Already antinuclear in spirit, they achieved a more direct artistic witness in the two cities. Indeed, the subtle brilliance of the poems that resulted shows the value, even the necessity, of such witness in exploring what happened in Hiroshima. "One of the things I've learned," Kinnell said afterward, "is that if one doesn't feel despair, one has not really understood what's happened in the world. From now on, it is certain that a kind of despair has to be a component of hope." That sense is expressed in the powerful poem "The Fundamental Project of Technology," which grew out of his visit, marked by the memorable repetition of the phrase "a white flash sparkled."

"We are the poets of the Nuclear Age," Carolyn Forché exclaimed in 1984, shortly after returning from Hiroshima, "perhaps the last poets, and some of us fear what the Muse is telling us. Some of us are finding it harder to write. . . . There is no metaphor for the end of the world and it is horrible to search for one." Nevertheless, she would compose one of the most haunting poems about Hiroshima, "The Garden Shukkei-en." An American visits a place in Hiroshima with a survivor who "has always been afraid to come here." Forché writes:

> It is the river she most

remembers, the living
and the dead both crying for help.

The poem ends, however, with the hopeful line, "it is the bell to awaken God that we've heard ringing." Forché is telling us that Hiroshima can provide illumination, can "awaken God," and that the Hiroshima bell tolls for everyone. That is precisely the message Americans have resisted for so long and must now address after fifty years have passed.

FURTHER READING

Bibliography

Bennett, James R., and Clark, Karen. "Hiroshima, Nagasaki, and the Bomb: A Bibliography of Literature and the Arts." *Arizona Quarterly* 46, No. 3 (Autumn 1990): 33-64.

> Lists bibliographies, historical works, criticism, personal narratives, literature, and films concerning the atomic bombing of Japan.

Criticism

Creager, Ellen. "Revealing Details." *Chicago Tribune* (21 March 1995): Sec. 5, p. 5.

> Reviews *The Diary of a Young Girl: The Definitive Edition* and states that the restored fragments reveal "a new depth to Anne's dreams, irritations, hardship and passions."

Deák, István. "Witnesses to Evil." *New York Review of Books* XXXIX, No. 17 (22 October 1992): 40-3.

> Reviews four books: *In the Lion's Den: The Life of Oswald Rufeisen,* a biography of a Jewish survivor who later became a Catholic priest; *Perpetrators, Victims, Bystanders: The Jewish Catastrophe, 1933-1945,* a history of the Holocaust; and two books concerning the Holocaust experiences of gentiles, *A Mosaic of Victims: Non-Jews Persecuted and Murdered by the Nazis* and *Out of the Inferno: Poles Remember the Holocaust.*

———. "Holocaust Heroes." *New York Review of Books* XXXIX, No. 18 (5 November 1992): 22-6.

> Reviews eight books focusing on various aspects of Jewish and gentile experiences of the Holocaust in Italy, Norway, Poland, and Yugoslavia.

Doctorow, E. L. "Mythologizing the Bomb." *The Nation* 261, No. 5 (14 August 1995): 1, 170-73.

> Speculates on the events and individuals who will be recorded in America's "mythology" of the atomic bomb and the hydrogen bomb.

Friedman, Saul S., ed. *Holocaust Literature: A Handbook of Critical, Historical, and Literary Writings.* Westport, Conn.: Greenwood Press, 1993, 677 p.

> Includes bibliographic essays on various aspects of Holocaust studies including sections on conceptual approaches, area studies, and education and the arts.

Gilman, Sander L. "The Dead Child Speaks: Reading *The Diary of Anne Frank.*" *Studies in American Jewish Literature* 7, No. 1 (1988): 9-25.

> Discusses the reaction of such authors as Meyer Levin and Philip Roth to Anne Frank's *Diary* and comments on the literary works of these authors that make reference to Anne Frank.

Graver, Lawrence. *An Obsession with Anne Frank: Meyer Levin and the "Diary."* Berkeley: University of California Press, 1995, 254 p.

> Examines the dispute between Meyer Levin and Otto Frank regarding the adaptation of Anne Frank's *Diary* for the theater.

Klein, Thomas, and Darsa, Jan. "Holocaust Literature: The Perils of Breaking the Silence." *The CEA Critic* 56, No. 2 (Winter 1994): 31-41.

> Discusses the distinguishing characteristics of and methods for teaching Holocaust literature.

Kremer, S. Lillian. *Witness through the Imagination: Jewish-American Holocaust Literature.* Detroit: Wayne State University Press, 1989, 392 p.

> Discusses works dealing with the Holocaust by such writers as Cynthia Ozick, Chaim Potok, Saul Bellow, and Bernard Malamud.

Kwitny, Jonathan. "Shattering the Myth of the Bomb." *Los Angeles Times Book Review* (6 August 1995): 10, 15.

> Favorably reviews Robert Jay Lifton and Greg Mitchell's *Hiroshima in America* and Gar Alperovitz's *The Decision to Use the Atomic Bomb and the Architecture of an American Myth.*

Merkin, Daphne. "Witness to the Holocaust." *The New York Times Book Review* (17 December 1995): 7.

> Reviews Elie Wiesel's memoir *All Rivers Run to the Sea.*

Modern Language Studies XXIV, No. 4 (Fall 1994).

> Special issue devoted to Holocaust literature.

Musleah, Rahel. " 'The Hidden Children' of the Holocaust, from Their Point of View." *New York Times* (8 January 1995): 15.

> Favorably reviews Maxine Rosenberg's *Hiding to Survive,* a book for children that relates the stories of thirteen Jewish children who survived the Holocaust in hiding.

Niebuhr, Gustav. "Whose Memory Lives When the Last Survivor Dies?" *The New York Times* (29 January 1995): Sec. 4, p. 5.

> Argues that "both the Auschwitz death camp and the Enola Gay are physical relics that demand explanation, for it is in the telling of their stories that people and nations come to understand themselves."

Reid, T. R. "The Atomic Bomb." *Book World—The Washington Post* (6 August 1995): 6.

> Reviews six books dealing with the atomic bombing of Japan.

Sloan, James Park. "Kosinski's War." *The New Yorker* LXX, No. 32 (10 October 1994): 46-8, 50-3.

> Remarks on the controversy over the factual accuracy of the events related in Jerzy Kosinski's Holocaust novel *The Painted Bird.*

Weigley, Russell F. "Unleashing Destruction." *Book World—The Washington Post* (6 August 1995): 1, 11.

> Contends that, in *The Decision to Use the Atomic Bomb,*

Gar Alperovitz "relies more on repeated assertion than on convincing proof when he argues that America did not need to use the bomb in order to end the war without worse loss of life than the bombing itself caused."

The Vietnam War in Literature and Film

INTRODUCTION

The United States's involvement in the Vietnam War, which ended in April, 1975 when the last American soldiers were withdrawn, has been the subject of an extensive and diverse body of creative works in a variety of genres, including drama, fiction, film, and poetry. Many of these efforts share such themes as a search for meaning and authenticity as well as a lack of faith in traditional values and forms. Vietnam War poetry, for instance, is primarily confessional, sardonic, and empirical rather than idealistic or transcendent, and the poems generally seek to instruct rather than delight or provide the affirmation and closure typical of traditional lyrics. Common subjects include atrocities and mass violence as well as records of sensory details and character sketches that evoke the soldier's experience in Vietnam. Efforts to confront anguish, guilt, post-traumatic stress disorder, the conflict between poetic and political uses of language, and the reconciliation of memory with the present are among the poetry's common themes. W. D. Ehrhart's "The Generals' War," for instance, points with contempt at the ironic distinction between "paper orders" and their actual execution in the field, while Bruce Weigl's "Song of Napalm" shows wartime memories infiltrating a domestic scene. Commenting on the lessons Vietnam veteran poets have to offer, Lorrie Smith has stated: "By rooting Vietnam in our collective consciousness and connecting it to contemporary American life, these poets insist that their memories form part of our past, their anguish part of our present. . . . If we ask and listen and respond, we may finally relinquish our illusions of national innocence and personal neutrality and begin to chart a truer history of our involvement with Vietnam."

Vietnam War fiction shares many concerns with the poetry, particularly the search for meaning and the emphasis on finding explanations for the conflict's conduct and outcome. "Vietnam affected our literary imagination in ways that no other war has," Jerome Klinkowitz has stated, "and the result has been a body of fiction that relies on various innovative formal devices, similar to the experimental features that characterize other postmodern fiction, to capture a sense of that war's assault on language and on our sense of reality." Some of the more prominent writings about the war include Graham Greene's *The Quiet American* (1955), which focuses on American involvement before the introduction of troops; Robin Moore's *The Green Berets* (1965), one of the few positive portrayals of American involvement; Tim O'Brien's *Going after Cacciato* (1978), a formally innovative work that combines the pro-

tagonist's memories of combat with an imaginary journey to Paris as it dramatizes the main character's coming to terms with the horrors of war; and John Del Vecchio's *The 13th Valley* (1982), a naturalistic account centering on the fate of a single patrol. Other works, such as Bobbie Ann Mason's *In Country* (1984) and Larry Heinemann's *Paco's Story* (1986), address the problems of veterans attempting to reenter civilian life. In their discussions of Vietnam War fiction, critics have remarked on the appropriation and reinterpretation of American myths, particularly those associated with the American frontier—in *Going after Cacciato,* for instance, the protagonist "goes West" in search of the deserter Cacciato—and have argued that the most provocative fiction about the war ultimately goes beyond the story of combat in a foreign environment to offer insight into the evolution of American society during the 1960s and 1970s.

Discussion regarding drama and film about the conflict center on themes of alienation from society due to military training and combat experience and the reinterpretation of American myths. Considered the most prominent playwright on the Vietnam experience, David Rabe addresses all of these themes in *The Basic Training of Pavlo Hummel* (1968), which dramatizes Hummel's failed search for identity and belonging in the social structure of the military and the unreliability of traditional assumptions and myths on which an understanding of reality is based. As J. W. Fenn has stated: "The overwhelmingly dominant themes of the war plays became those of both individual and social disintegration, internecine conflict, psychological fragmentation, alienation, and isolation; and a loss of cultural identity." In their commentaries on Vietnam War films, critics have highlighted such common elements as the binary opposition between the American military's technological superiority and the guerrilla warfare practiced by the Vietnamese, the futility and ineffectiveness of American involvement, and the depiction of the war and its veterans as catalysts for violence in the United States. Commentators have noted as well the explicit use and debunking of the American frontier mythos in such films as Michael Cimino's *The Deer Hunter* (1978), Francis Coppola's *Apocalypse Now* (1979), and Oliver Stone's *Platoon* (1986). The parallels between James Fenimore Cooper's *The Deerslayer* (1841) and *The Deer Hunter* are evident in the title as well as the protagonist's attachment to the wilderness. In *Apocalypse Now,* Coppola presents the American initiative in Vietnam in terms of Western/European man's attempt to civilize and exploit the "savage" wilderness; the film is based on Joseph Conrad's novella *Heart of Darkness* (1902) and thus casts in an

American context Conrad's themes of the hubris and folly of empire and colonization. Stone, on the other hand, contrasts competing views of American involvement and associates the right-wing military viewpoint with Sergeant Barnes, who speaks with a Western accent, plays poker, and drinks whiskey. As W. J. Hug has written, "In one way or another, the War in Vietnam becomes in each of [these films] America's failed effort to resurrect the frontier."

REPRESENTATIVE WORKS DISCUSSED BELOW

Balk, H. Wesley and Ronald J. Glasser
    The Dramatization of 365 Days   (drama)   1972
Barry, Jan and W. D. Ehrhart
    Demilitarized Zones: Veterans After Vietnam [editors]
        (poetry)   1976
Berry, David
    G. R. Point   (drama)   1975
Bunting, Josiah
    The Lionheads   (novel)   1972
Caputo, Philip
    Indian Country   (novel)   1987
Cimino, Michael
    The Deer Hunter   (film)   1978
Cole, Tom
    Medal of Honor Rag   (drama)   1975
Coppola, Francis
    Apocalypse Now   (film)   1979
Del Vecchio, John
    The 13th Valley   (novel)   1982
DiFusco, John
    Tracers   (drama)   1980
Ehrhart, W. D.
    To Those Who Have Gone Home Tired   (poetry)
        1984
    Carrying the Darkness [editor]   (poetry)   1985
    Unaccustomed Mercy: Soldier Poets of the Vietnam War
        [editor]   (poetry)   1989
    Just For Laughs   (poetry)   1990
Greene, Graham
    The Quiet American   (novel)   1955
Halberstam, David
    One Very Hot Day   (novel)   1967
Heinemann, Larry
    Paco's Story   (novel)   1986
Herr, Michael
    Dispatches   (nonfiction)   1978
Huong, Duong Thu
    *Novel Without a Name   (novel)   1995
    *Paradise of the Blind   (novel)   1995
Kellogg, Ray and John Wayne
    The Green Berets   (film)   1968
Kennedy, Adrienne
    An Evening with Dead Essex   (drama)   1973
Komunyakaa, Yusef
    Dien Cai Dau   (poetry)   1988
Kubrick, Stanley

†*Full Metal Jacket*   (film)   1987
Mailer, Norman
    Why Are We in Vietnam   (novel)   1967
Mann, Emily
    Still Life   (drama)   1980
Mason, Bobbie Ann
    In Country   (novel)   1984
McClure, James
    Private Wars   (drama)   1979
Moore, Robin
    The Green Berets   (novel)   1965
Mura, David
    After We Lost Our Way   (poetry)   1989
Nemerov, Howard
    War Stories: Poems About Long Ago and Now   (poetry)
        1987
Ninh, Bao
    *The Sorrow of War: A Novel of North Vietnam
        (novel)   1995
O'Brien, Tim
    Going after Cacciato   (novel)   1978
Rabe, David
    The Basic Training of Pavlo Hummel   (drama)   1968
    Sticks and Bones   (drama)   1969
    Streamers   (drama)   1976
Rottmann, Larry, Jan Barry, and Basil T. Pacquet
    Winning Hearts and Minds: War Poems by Vietnam Veterams [editors]   (poetry)   1972
Schaeffer, Susan Fromberg
    Buffalo Afternoon   (novel)   1989
Sloan, James Park
    War Games   (novel)   1971
Stanford, Frank
    The Battlefield Where the Moon Says I Love You
        (poem)   1977
Stone, Oliver
    Platoon   (film)   1986
Weigl, Bruce
    Executioner   (poetry)   1976
    A Romance   (poetry)   1979
    The Monkey Wars   (poetry)   1985
Woods, William Crawford
    The Killing Zone   (novel)   1970
Wright, Stephen
    Meditations in Green   (novel)   1983

*These works were originally written and published in Vietnamese.

†The screenplay for this film was co-written by Michael Herr, Gustav Hasford, and Kubrick. The film is based on Hasford's novel *The Short-timers* (1979).

OVERVIEW

Philip K. Jason   (essay date 1991)

SOURCE: An introduction to *Fourteen Landing Zones: Approaches to Vietnam War Literature,* edited by Philip K. Jason, University of Iowa Press, 1991, pp. ix-xix.

[*In the essay below, Jason outlines the major issues and trends in Vietnam War literature and its criticism.*]

There has always been a literature of war. The classical epics are among its early prototypes. In American literature, Whitman's *Drum-Taps,* Melville's *Battle-Pieces,* and Crane's *The Red Badge of Courage* form the nucleus of a significant literature of the Civil War—yet Whitman was the only major writer who put himself in some proximity to the horrors of battle. Melville was only a casual visitor, and Crane was born years after the war's close. From this beginning (though we could go back further), the war literature of American writers has been a mixture of testimony, commentary, and imaginative reconstruction. Though many more creative works about the Civil War were written, only these nineteenth-century visions of that war are read today—and Melville's just barely. The distant reconstructions of that past include Michael Shaara's Pulitzer Prize novel of 1974, *The Killer Angels,* which treats the battle of Gettysburg, and Stephen Vincent Benét's verse narrative, *John Brown's Body,* winner of a Pulitzer in 1928.

America's best-known literary treatment of World War I is *A Farewell to Arms,* though Hemingway's service was primarily as a volunteer Red Cross ambulance driver. Somewhat less celebrated are John Dos Passos's *Three Soldiers* and E. E. Cummings's *The Enormous Room.* James Jones's *From Here to Eternity* and *The Thin Red Line* are among our classics of World War II, as are John Hersey's *A Bell for Adano, Hiroshima,* and *The Wall.* Alongside of Kurt Vonnegut's *Slaughterhouse-Five,* Irwin Shaw's *The Young Lions,* Norman Mailer's *The Naked and the Dead,* and Joseph Heller's *Catch-22* are the retrospective epic treatments by Herman Wouk (*The Winds of War* and *War and Remembrance*) as well as *The Caine Mutiny Court Martial* drama based on his earlier novel. Of more recent vintage is Marge Piercy's highly acclaimed *Gone to Soldiers* (1987). *M*A*S*H* is our major imaginative rendering of the Korean "conflict," though it is often imagined by the viewers of the television series as a work about Vietnam.

This short checklist of well-known literary responses to our earlier wars reminds us by its very brevity that the winnowing processes of popular and critical acclaim canonize only a small percentage of the imaginative works written on any subject. The rest are left to special-interest readers and scholars. How will the writings on the Vietnam War be filtered? Which will survive—and why? The critical enterprise now underway, to which the present volume is an addition, has begun to engage these questions.

Why is there such a rich literature about the Vietnam War, a war that for so many years no one wanted to hear about at all? How did that experience stir the nation and discover so many interpreters? There are no conclusive answers to such questions, though some suggestions may be offered.

In the two decades between the end of World War II and our military buildup in Vietnam, the American educational system reached out to embrace greater numbers. The proportion of young men and women who achieved a higher literacy (at the expense of a smaller elite no longer attaining the highest literacy) may account for the great number of significant literary responses to the Vietnam War.

Though we read much about the demography of the armed services during the war that describes the disproportionate sacrifice of the disadvantaged and the dropouts, the number of enlistees (and even draftees) who had some college education was not insignificant, and the educational attainment of the young officer corps was high. Which is to say that many of those who went to Vietnam had the equipment to turn their experiences into literary documents. And many others would, upon return, gain the skills needed to shape and reshape their memories.

We should note as well that among its literary fashions the sixties ushered in a personal journalism that employed novelistic techniques. Norman Mailer's *The Armies of the Night* (1968) is a classic of this kind. Such a genre was ready-made for the memoirs of the war and for the many autobiographical novels—often memoirs in thin disguise. (Ironically, Mailer's *The Naked and the Dead,* published twenty years earlier, is a model for most of the "old-fashioned" realistic-naturalistic combat narratives of Vietnam. Mailer's own treatment of this war is trendily oblique; his 1967 *Why Are We in Vietnam* is a grotesque stateside adventure in macho bloodletting, thus, a study in American character.) The related genre of the nonfiction novel—Truman Capote's *In Cold Blood* (1966) and William Styron's *The Confessions of Nat Turner* (1967)—also influenced the literary climate in which the first writings about the Vietnam War were nourished. And one can hardly imagine the stylistic hijinks of Michael Herr's *Dispatches* without the earlier work of Tom Wolfe.

Aside from anything one might say about the magnitude of cultural upheaval caused by the war, the circumstances of literacy and literature in the United States during the war years help explain the great numbers of writings and the generic outlines of this body of work—a corpus that began to gain momentum in the late seventies and a decade later became a significant facet of American publishing. The growing commercial viability of Vietnam fiction allowed early works like Ward Just's *Stringer* (1974) to be brought out ten years later in paperback and introduced a new generation of readers to Graham Greene's classic, *The Quiet American* (1955).

In fact, many bookstores have "Vietnam" shelves. The "Vietnam: Ground Zero" series by Eric Helm, now approaching twenty titles (including *The Raid, Incident at Plei Soi, Cambodian Sanctuary,* and *Payback*), is representative of the mass-market success of Vietnam material. The developing "Wings over Nam" series by Cat Branigan lengthens the bandwagon. Indeed, every paperback house has its Vietnam titles, both fiction and nonfiction, both serious and escapist. There are even a couple of bookstores dedicated exclusively to Vietnam War publications, and a few college libraries have undertaken special collections of Vietnam material. New Vietnam-related works keep tumbling onto the bookstore shelves. In 1989, Lucian K. Truscott IV's *Army Blue,* John Amos's *The Medallion,* and Franklin Allen Leib's *The Fire Dream* were among the most conspicuous, while 1990 has brought Tim

O'Brien's *The Things They Carried* and Gustav Hasford's *The Phantom Blooper.*

Of course, given the economics of publishing, it is easier to find a copy of James Webb's *Fields of Fire* than John Balaban's Lamont Prize poetry collection, *After Our War.* The same concern for the ledger that led Avon Books to drop W. D. Ehrhart's excellent poetry anthology, *Carrying the Darkness* (since reissued by Texas Tech Press), led Zebra Books to bring out a mass-market edition of his memoir, *Vietnam-Perkasie,* first published by a small press in North Carolina. Many titles receive a second life as they become the basis for films. Ron Kovic's *Born on the Fourth of July* is a recent (and worthy) beneficiary of this marketing system. And who can tell what motivated the Bantam hardback publication of Steve Mason's *Johnny's Song,* a collection of mediocre poems wrapped in the flag and destined for coffee tables?

A number of works about the war have earned and gained recognition, most notably Robert Stone's *Dog Soldiers,* Tim O'Brien's *Going after Cacciato,* Gloria Emerson's *Winners and Losers,* Larry Heinemann's *Paco's Story,* and Neil Sheehan's *A Bright Shining Lie*—all winners of National Book Awards. Pulitzer Prizes have been awarded to Sheehan's book and also to Frances FitzGerald's *Fire in the Lake.*

The battle among scholars and politicians who have tried to explain this war is a battle for our collective memory—for the "truth" that future generations will share about the reasons for, conduct of, and outcome of this conflict. Our novelists, playwrights, and poets are significant players in this engagement—few, if any, are above a political or moral vision, and many works are overtly propagandistic.

Certainly, the fact that the war was "witnessed" by the American public on television and, however tentatively, in movies does not escape the notice of the literary and dramatic artists who approach it. The constant allusions to John Wayne movies in Gustav Hasford's *The Short-Timers* and elsewhere, the Ozzie and Harriet game played by David Rabe in *Sticks and Bones* in which the television doesn't work and David's movie can't be seen, the concern with photographic and cinematic images in Stephen Wright's *Meditations in Green,* Emmett's obsession with "M*A*S*H" reruns in Bobbie Ann Mason's *In Country,* and Sgt. Krummel's comment in James Crumley's *One to Count Cadence* that the maimed Vietcong "flipped out of the tree like a Hollywood stunt man" all remind us of the different planes of perception, intersecting and overlaying, through which the truths of the war are offered us. Indeed, some of the most significant literary art is reportage (Jonathan Schell's *The Real War* and Gloria Emerson's *Winners and Losers* come immediately to mind), and some of that is fundamentally concerned with the act of reporting, of representing, the war to the public. Thus, works like Michael Herr's *Dispatches* are, at one level, about the limits of perception and representation.

The works that will last, one must suppose, will be those that transcend the representation of a particular arena of military engagement. The more provocative stories that unfold in the literature of the Vietnam War are not simply or finally stories of armed conflict in a distant land. They are stories about American society as it evolved through the sixties and seventies. They are understandings, and sometimes underminings, of American myths. Many of the critical responses . . . are alert to the ways in which the literature confronts the myths of American innocence, American invulnerability, and American righteousness. In particular, Maria S. Bonn's "A Different World: The Vietnam Veteran Novel Comes Home" [in *Fourteen Landing Zones,* 1991] addresses the lost myth of an American homeland that could be depended on to nurture its returning soldiers.

Writing about the early collection of Vietnam War fiction, *Free Fire Zone* (1973) [in "Truth Is the First Casualty," *The Nation* (November 19, 1973)], Jerry Griswold observed, "These writers have ceased to believe in the myth of an imperfectible America, and their stories are meant to make uncomfortable the complacent who do believe in it." He went on to note that these writers "can't be comfortable in their disbelief either." The myth of a fair-minded, egalitarian America is threatened by literary reflections of an American society that tolerated and even fostered racism and sexism. Jacqueline E. Lawson's " 'She's a Pretty Woman . . . for a Gook': The Misogyny of the Vietnam War" uncovers the tragedy of a sexist America in the memoirs of Vietnam War veterans. Though Lawson does not here treat the imaginative literature of the war, her approach is one that can be applied to a significant portion of the poetry, drama, and fiction. Katherine Kinney's " 'Humping the Boonies': Sex, Combat, and the Female in Bobbie Ann Mason's *In Country*" provides a specific application of feminist reading that complements Lawson's overview. These essays [collected in *Fourteen Landing Zones*] are evidence of how much the feminist consciousness has to tell us about who we are.

The more provocative stories that unfold in the literature of the Vietnam War are not simply or finally stories of armed conflict in a distant land. They are stories about American society as it evolved through the sixties and seventies. They are understandings, and sometimes underminings, of American myths.

—*Philip K. Jason*

The dominant literature of the war—whether autobiography or fiction, whether by veteran or not—is cast in the dominant genre of prose narrative. Lorrie Smith and Don Ringnalda question the effectiveness of narrative to contain or release the Vietnam experience. Smith's "Resistance and Revision in Poetry by Vietnam War Veterans" argues that lyric utterance best serves the social and personal purposes of the veteran writer. Ringnalda, in "Doing It Wrong Is Getting It Right: America's Vietnam War Drama," looks closely at the limits of the master narrative and maintains that the oblique approaches of the dramatists have been more significantly expressive of this war's central traits. Both essays [which also appear in *Fourteen Landing Zones*] survey the vision and technical invention of major voices in the maverick genres.

Does war narrative have its own traditions that are passed on from one generation of writers to the next? John Clark Pratt makes one set of connections in "Yossarian's Legacy: *Catch-22* and the Vietnam War," along the way defining a significant subgenre. Pratt's own novel, with its peculiar mixture of private, generic, and more broadly literary allusions, is the subject of James R. Aubrey's "Conradian Darkness in John Clark Pratt's *The Laotian Fragments*." Owen W. Gilman, Jr., in "Vietnam and John Winthrop's Vision of Community," asks which species of narrative is likely to have the most profound impact. He makes a case for the "typological" narrative, finding in the Puritan vision of Winthrop an unexpected but instructive model.

The Vietnam conflict happened over there, but it happened here as well. Many fought against the war, and many who fought in it also fought with themselves. These are the concerns of Jacqueline R. Smetak's "The (Hidden) Antiwar Activist in Vietnam War Fiction." Many veterans carried the war home, and all citizens lived in the shadows of its stateside reverberations. Matthew C. Stewart underscores the former situation in "Realism, Verisimilitude, and the Depiction of Vietnam Veterans in *In Country*." Stuart Ching, in " 'A Hard Story to Tell': The Vietnam War in Joan Didion's *Democracy*," examines one literary work that illustrates the latter perspective. While this war was an American moment in Asia, it was first of all an Asian ordeal. In his "Darkness in the East: The Vietnam Novels of Takeshi Kaiko," an analysis of works by an important Japanese writer, Mark A. Heberle drives this realization home.

The human capacity for violence is nothing new, though the actors and victims change. What seems different in the literature of the Vietnam War is how directly and minutely atrocities are described and how conscious the writer (witness or perpetrator) is of the horror and of the moral implications of the event and of its record in language. In his "Line of Departure: The Atrocity in Vietnam War Literature," Cornelius A. Cronin demonstrates this awareness by contrasting Vietnam War narratives with a representative narrative of World War II. Kali Tal, on the other hand, doubts that traditional literary criticism can meaningfully explore what our traumatized participant-writers have created. In "Speaking the Language of Pain: Vietnam War Literature in the Context of a Literature of Trauma," Tal argues the limits of critical approaches that tend to the unraveling of metaphor. Insisting that the writings of veterans and those of nonveterans comprise radically separate categories, she begins the task of finding a new approach by linking the literature of Vietnam veterans to that of other survivor literatures, particularly the literature of the Holocaust and the literature of sexual abuse.

Along with the representative works treated in these essays are scores of others deserving of attention. The list, which I won't attempt to give, contains enormous variety.

It includes David A. Willson's *REMF Diary*, a comic portrait of rear echelon service; Wayne Karlin's *Lost Armies*, a haunting psychological thriller of the war's long aftermath of suffering; and the lyrical sequence *Fatal Light* by Richard Currey (all 1988).

Though battlefield stories still dominate the body of Vietnam War literature and thus the attention of critics, it is clear that the focus of Vietnam War criticism is shifting as that of the literature itself has shifted. The shift, among writers who were veterans of the war, follows their own experience from the war they fought to the war they took home. Among both veteran and nonveteran writers, one movement is to a vision of larger perspective: works that integrate the Vietnam War into a reading of the larger American story. Susan Fromberg Schaeffer's novel, *Buffalo Afternoon* (1989), is one such effort. Walter MacDonald's collection of poems, *After the Fall of Saigon* (1988), is another.

The history of criticism on Vietnam War literature is, of course, not a very long one. The key titles are James C. Wilson's *Vietnam in Prose and Film* (1982), Philip Beidler's *American Literature and the Experience of Vietnam* (1982), John Newman's annotated bibliography of *Vietnam War Literature* (1982; 2d ed. 1988), John Hellmann's *American Myth and the Legacy of Vietnam* (1986), Timothy J. Lomperis's *"Reading the Wind": The Literature of the Vietnam War* (1987), Thomas Myers's *Walking Point: American Narratives of Vietnam* (1988), Susan Jeffords's *The Remasculinization of America: Gender and the Vietnam War* (1989), and Sandra M. Wittman's *Writing about Vietnam: A Bibliography of the Literature of the Vietnam Conflict* (1989). These titles, referred to by many of the essayists in [*Fourteen Landing Zones*], are only the beginning of what promises to be a provocative engagement with the literature, with history itself, and with methodological problems. Collections of critical essays edited by William J. Searle (*Search and Clear*, 1988), Jeffrey Walsh and James Aulich (*Vietnam Images: War and Representation*, 1989), Stephen H. Knox (*Vietnam Studies*, 1990), and Owen W. Gilman, Jr., and Lorrie Smith (*America Rediscovered*, 1990) preceded [*Fourteen Landing Zones*].

This scholarship is serving the great interest in Vietnam studies of all kinds that are proliferating at American colleges and universities. That interest comes, in part, from the curiosity of those born about 1970 who are now in college, which is to say old enough to be fighting in a war. The eighteen-year-olds who lived through the Tet Offensive are now entering middle age. The cadre of young officers (some of whom became authors) was four or five years older. They, and the larger group who came to majority during the 1965 to 1975 period, are the Vietnam Generation. *Vietnam Generation*, a quarterly journal, has become the major clearinghouse for interdisciplinary studies on the war's centrality to contemporary American culture. The first general anthology for classroom use, Nancy Anisfield's *Vietnam Anthology: American War Literature*, appeared in 1987. Robert M. Slabey's *America in Vietnam/Vietnam in America: Reading and Teaching the Vietnam War* was planned for release in 1990.

The academics' debate over how the war should be taught, which works should be canonical in Vietnam studies, and which works will find a place in the canon of American literature is obviously connected to the struggle for the national memory. While the discussion is often heated, few new fields of study have engaged so many scholars in cooperative endeavors. Unfortunately, there has been little encouragement from the most powerful professional organizations; scholars proposing panels for Modern Language Association meetings have experienced only limited success. The annual combined meeting of the American Culture Association and Popular Culture Association has become the major forum for scholarly discussion in this area, and many of the articles in [*Fourteen Landing Zones*] (as in those mentioned above) originated as papers delivered at ACA/PCA meetings.

For all of the activity in Vietnam War studies, more work needs to be done to discover and assess literature that provides both perspectives on the Vietnamese and Vietnamese perspectives. Literary representations of the Vietnamese range from racist slurs to outright admiration of these people as a skilled and valiant enemy to total disrespect for a seemingly inept ally. These valuations tend to be collective: generic. Few Vietnamese are seen up close. Typical figures are Kit Carson scouts (Vietcong turncoats working with American military units) and prostitutes. Among the few works that provide rich treatments of Vietnamese characters is David Halberstam's *One Very Hot Day* (1968). And, of course, we have yet to pay much attention to Vietnamese accounts of the war.

In the September/October 1989 issue of *Poets & Writers Magazine,* Wendy Larsen, coauthor of *Shallow Graves: Two Women and Vietnam* (1986), took out an ad in which she announced that the title was out of print. She offered signed hardcover copies for ten dollars. A critical success (and even issued in paperback), this book told Americans more than we wanted to know about noncombatant life and about Vietnamese culture. It revealed, beyond Larsen's own experience in Vietnam, the outlook and life story of a Vietnamese woman, Tran Thi Nga, whom Larsen employed and then befriended. While critics rightly complain that the Vietnamese are largely missing from this body of literature, not many readers are prepared to accept their most significant appearances.

As a field of special study, the appraisal of war literature has had sporadic growth. Indeed, fields of literary study centered on the *subject matter* of the literature tend to be considered as marginal, transient, suspect endeavors. While literary criticism becomes more and more concerned with theory and methodology, the questions about what literary works *express* receive less and less attention and little respect. Scholars who are concerned with myth, paradigm, and genre are making valuable contributions to our understanding of Vietnam War literature. Indeed, the essays [in *Fourteen Landing Zones*] make that apparent. Yet often these and other approaches seem designed to dignify a pursuit by mainstreaming it into an appropriately rarified critical channel. Some critics seem a bit nervous about the "humanities" approach to literature, which asks us to find in our study of artworks keys to understanding

the human condition. Certainly it is what the literature of war tells us (*shows* us) that claims our attention and concern. Each of the essays in [*Fourteen Landing Zones*] shares that assumption.

Douglas Wapniak, the overeducated sergeant in Susan Fromberg Schaffer's *Buffalo Afternoon,* is constantly asking questions, theorizing, and jotting things down in his notebook. An oddball to those around him, Wapniak has a sense of history. To all the other men, their LT is just "Lieutenant," but Wapniak wants to know his full name. When asked why, Wapniak replies:

> "Some day this war's going to be important. People are going to study this war. Right now there might be complaints about it, but people are looking at it. This war won't go away. When people come back to look at it, when they see how important it was, what significance it had, they're going to want to know *names.* They're going to want to know who made it possible, because, believe me, Lieutenant, there's meaning in this war. Mankind's never going to be the same after this war. I don't know what it means yet. Nobody does, but it means something. We ought to sit down and talk about this. I've given it a lot of thought."

With hindsight, Schaeffer has made her character prophetic. She has also anticipated the argument against her ambition. A man like Douglas Wapniak is prepared to test the authenticity of Vietnam War narratives. Is a nonparticipant and nonobserver, like Schaeffer, prepared to write one? Of what value, and to whom, is the test of authenticity? Is Lt. Howard Hollingshead's name the issue, or is it the "something" that the war means? If the latter, then we have to look for this meaning together in the recollections of the grunt and in the visions and insights of all those writers and thinkers who have dedicated their talents to the search.

During the Vietnam War, an LZ or landing zone was an area designated for helicopter set-downs to insert troops near suspected enemy forces. Often a small clearing in the jungle, the LZ—meant to be secure enough for the immediate purpose—was often vulnerable as the noise of the propellers signaled arrival. From the LZ, squads would fan out to accomplish their mission of interdiction or intelligence gathering. Each zone marked a stage of approach toward a defined objective. From these clearings, trails were discovered—or created—and followed cautiously to uncertain destinations.

PROSE

Jerome Klinkowitz   (essay date 1986)

SOURCE: "Writing Under Fire: Postmodern Fiction and the Vietnam War," in *Postmodern Fiction: A Bio-Bibliographical Guide,* edited by Larry McCaffery, Greenwood Press, 1986, pp. 79-92.

[*An American educator and critic, Klinkowitz has written extensively on contemporary American fiction and edited* Writing Under Fire: Stories of the Vietnam War *(1978). In the essay below, he surveys novels published during American involvement in the Vietnam War and focuses his analysis on innovative approaches to plot and structure.*]

American novels and stories about Vietnam reveal a common, desperate search for meaning—a search for any shred of authenticity in this experience—that may be traced back decades before "our" Vietnam War and that extends forward to the decade that has now passed since the American withdrawal from Vietnam. Although many important novels about Vietnam have recently appeared—Tim O'Brien's *Going After Cacciato* (1978), Robert Butler's *The Alleys of Eden* (1981), John Cassidy's *A Station in the Delta* (1979), Charles Durden's *No Bugles, No Drums* (1976), Winston Groom's *Better Times Than These* (1978), among others—this article focuses on the fiction published during our actual involvement there. But the central thesis of this article remains true for more recent works: Vietnam affected our literary imagination in ways that no other war has, and the result has been a body of fiction that relies on various innovative formal devices, similar to the experimental features that characterize other postmodern fiction, to capture a sense of that war's assault on language and on our sense of reality.

The first Western novelist to write about Vietnam was André Malraux, who as early as 1930 saw that the Indochina experience could be a metaphor for man's anguished alienation from an absurd society within a meaningless universe. Malraux's *The Royal Way* (1930) was the beginning of a line of books that followed the Western involvement in Vietnam from colonial exploitation to ideologically based warfare. By 1966 Norman Mailer could state [in *Cannibals and Christians,* 1966], "If World War II was like *Catch-22,* this war will be like *Naked Lunch.*" Malraux's anguished alienation had become a full-blown nightmare, suggesting that this shard of the Asian continent was indeed bound up with the subconscious of Europe and America, and that to deal with it in art would take on the dimensions of a dark encounter with the more unpleasant aspects of our lives.

The processes of art inevitably tell us more about ourselves than the matter at hand. But the Indochina experience is especially self-revealing, and with Malraux's *The Royal Way* the measure of self begins. In the jungles of what we now call Thailand, Cambodia, and Vietnam, Malraux explores the roots of what two subsequent generations of novelists must face: "that fabulous aura of scandal, fantasy, and fiction which always hovers about the white man who has played a part in the affairs of independent Asiatic states." The jungle itself is a strange and exotic contrast to the civilizations of the West, a place where Malraux's protagonist finds that he was "growing aware of the essential oneness of the forest and had given up trying to distinguish living beings from their setting, life that moves from life that oozes." Even in 1930 Vietnam is a place where "some unknown power assimilated the trees with fungoid growths upon them, and quickened the restless movements of all the rudimentary creatures darting to and fro

upon a soil like marsh-scum amid the steaming vegetation of a planet in the making." In such a place one asks, "Here what act of man had any meaning, what human will but spent its staying power?"

The overt action in *The Royal Way* is colonial adventure. The soldier of fortune, Perken, would plunder the land of its treasures and organize a military force to become its political ruler as well. But as in every subsequent Vietnam fiction there is a deeper current turning back upon the characters. As Perken explains his motives to his skeptical assistant Claude:

> "And then—only try to grasp all that this country really is. Why, I'm only just beginning to understand their erotic rites, the process of assimilation by which a man comes to identify himself, even in his sensations, with the woman he possesses—till he imagines *he is she,* yet without ceasing to be himself! There's nothing in the world to match it—sensual pleasure strained to the point where it becomes intolerable, the breaking-point of pain! No, for me these women aren't merely bodies; they're . . . instruments. And I want . . ." Claude guessed his unseen gesture, the gesture of a hand crushing out life. ". . . as I once wanted to conquer men."

> What he's really after, Claude mused, is self-annihilation. I wonder is he more aware of it than he admits. Anyhow he'll achieve it easily enough.

Perken's immediate quest fails. He cannot take his plunder out of Vietnam, and his private army is decisively beaten. But his greatest defeat is just as Claude supposed:

> Frenzied with self-centered passion, her body was withdrawing itself from him irrevocably. Never, never would he apprehend, never share, this woman's sensations; never could the frenzy which thrilled her body be for him anything but a proof of the unbridgeable gulf between them. Without love there can be no passion. Carried away by forces he could not control, unable even to make her realize his presence by tearing himself away from her, he too closed his eyes, thrown back upon himself as on a noxious drug, drunk with a wild desire violently to crush out of existence this stranger's face that urged him on to death.

It would be 35 years before American fiction came to grips so closely with these dark matters of the self. Westerners in this novel took their first steps into an experience destined to constrain and diminish their imperial selves, but the challenge was irresistible.

Two dozen novels about the war were published during America's active involvement in it. In 1965, Robin Moore first introduced the war to a literary audience with *The Green Berets,* which concluded: "What the outcome in Vietnam will be is anybody's guess, but whatever happens, Special Forces men will continue to fight Communism and make friends for America in the underdeveloped nations that are the targets of Communist expansion." The war did not turn out that way, and neither did our country's appreciation of it. Coming to a final understanding, and expressing it in art, has become an ongoing effort as arduous as any trial described in the existential novels of Kafka, Sartre, or Malraux. From a European perspective it would have been nothing new. But in Vietnam, America lost its innocence and by that process grew immeasurably in its art.

Some historians date the beginning of American involvement in Vietnam from 1954, with Vice-President Richard M. Nixon's advocacy of intervention at Dien Bien Phu against Eisenhower's wish to remain neutral. Graham Greene's Vietnam novel of 1955, *The Quiet American,* witnesses the awesomely quiet birth of American interest in this country recently deserted by the French. The narrator is a British journalist, seasoned by events in his personal life as well as by his nation's experience, before whom the quiet American Agency for International Development (AID) official, Pyle, is the epitome of collective innocence: "He was absorbed already in the dilemmas of democracy and the responsibilities of the West; he was determined—I learned that very soon—to do good, not to any individual person, but to a country, a continent, a world. Well, he was in his element now, with the whole universe to improve." This innocence, of course, is Pyle's downfall. As the journalist tells him, "I wish sometimes you had a few bad motives; you might understand a little more about human beings. And that applies to your country too, Pyle." Innocence, we learn, "is like a dumb leper who has lost his bell, wandering the world, meaning no harm." The young, well-intentioned man with a crew cut and a black dog at his heels is as out of date as an Errol Flynn movie where the hero "rescued a girl and killed his enemy and led a charmed life. It was what they call a film for boys, but the sight of Oedipus emerging with his bleeding eyeballs from the palace at Thebes would surely give a better training for life today." Vietnam was already gaining a reputation as "an experience," and Americans were from the first cast as hapless (if dangerous) innocents.

Greene's novel portrays the personal and national havoc created by Pyle's "involvement," the consequences of which are a vivid preview of what was to happen from 1962 to Christmas week of 1972. During these same years *The Quiet American* went through 17 printings in the United States; but few Americans came forward to write a Vietnam novel with such a measured and controlled view. The first attempt was Robin Moore's *The Green Berets.* Its tone was set by the dust-jacket advertisement, boasting that Moore "was paid the 'supreme compliment' of being sent along as the second Special Forces 'sergeant' on all-Vietnamese or Montagnard patrols. On one such patrol Moore so distinguished himself that the Montagnard commander offered him the rare privilege of cutting off the ear of a dead VC!"

In the years since 1965 Robin Moore has remained an apologist for the war in Vietnam. David Halberstam is not. A journalist in Vietnam the same time as Moore, Halberstam incurred Administration disapproval for his Saigon dispatches, which Graham Greene characterized as not taking at all "the conventional line about the American presence in Vietnam." In 1967 Halberstam wrote *One Very Hot Day,* a novel that follows an American advisor

through a day's patrol—the same role Moore took for his own book, but with very different results. Halberstam's Captain Beaupré is the first American literary character to face Malraux's jungle, the first to sense that "the heat was the enemy of all white men, but it was more an enemy of his, he had less resistance and resilience." It is 1963; he is only a military advisor; and there is a strict limit to his tour of duty, so the magnitude of Malraux's primeval landscape need be nothing more than "his imagination turning Vietnam into 365 days of this." But the artificial limits on time and on his military role are distressing. "He wished the troops would go faster, would move it out, and he wished he were a real officer, someone who could give commands and then see them obeyed, who could send a patrol here and another there, could make the troops go fast, go slow, be brave, be strong; wished to be hated, to be feared, even to be loved, but to be an officer and in charge." His experience is perplexing, because Vietnam is a different kind of war for him. A veteran of World War II and Korea, the sergeant can instruct his young lieutenant (a scene that is to reappear in several Vietnam fictions) in just how strange things are compared to the war against Hitler:

> We didn't know how simple it was, and how good we had it. Sure we walked but in a straight line. Boom, Normandy beaches, and then you set off for Paris and Berlin. Just like that. No retracing, no goddam circles, just straight ahead. All you needed was a compass and good sense. But here you walk in a goddam circle, and then you go home, and then you go out the next day and wade through a circle, and then you go home and the next day you go out and reverse the circle you did the day before, erasing it. Every day the circles get bigger and emptier. Walk them one day, erase them the next. In France you always knew where you were, how far you had walked, and how far you had to go. But this goddam place, Christ, if I knew how far I had walked, it would break my heart. From Normandy to Berlin and back, probably.

Halberstam's novel also begins the search for structure common to most subsequent Vietnam novels: how to organize this war that defies all previous military and political patterns. The novelist starts with basics, a single day's patrol, but on it his veteran sergeant loses all sense of purpose and achievement. Even in the simplest of conventional terms, the experience of Vietnam makes little sense.

Whether experienced by journalists on Guggenheims or by literate infantrymen on patrol, Vietnam proved to be a war unlike any other. Tom Mayer, a representative of the first group, writes about such difficulties in his collection of stories, *The Weary Falcon* (1971), which includes the situation of "the US Marines landing at Chu Lai where the troops came storming out of the amtracks and up the beach like John Wayne in 'The Sands of Iwo Jima' only to find twenty photographers on the top of the first dune taking pictures of it all." In similar terms William Pelfrey's *The Big V* (1972) fails as a realist combat novel, because the war, measured first against its familiar image on television, never has the chance to escape the tired pop-art cliches assigned to every act. "I fired one round on semiautomatic. His body jerked erect, almost like a gangster blown back by a sawed-off shotgun, only screaming, hoarse, with his mouth gaping; more like an Indian, his arms flying up and dropping the rifle." Pelfrey's narrator can find no vocabulary for the war beyond that of its television images because his vision extends no further than the video-adventures of his youth. That Vietnam was fought on such a level is less frightening than the thought that it was so comprehended, by soldiers and citizens alike.

Vietnam affected our literary imagination in ways that no other war has, and the result has been a body of fiction that relies on various innovative formal devices to capture a sense of that war's assault on language and on our sense of reality.

—*Jerome Klinkowitz*

Outstripping the politics and military theories of earlier wars and older generations, the truth of Vietnam became a test of the artist's imagination. Hence, three of the best books about the war were written by authors who were never there as participants, and who remove the action of their books to points of broader perspective. In *The Prisoners of Quai Dong* (1967) Victor Kolpacoff suggests the sense of Vietnam by writing about a military jail, where the order of life has all the tedium, uncertainty, and senselessness of the war going on outside—particularly when the narrator is asked to participate in the interrogation/torture of a Viet Cong suspect. William Eastlake's *The Bamboo Bed* (1969) finds an even more appropriate perspective on this surreal war—above the jungle combat, above even the monsoon engulfing that action, in a rescue helicopter used for inflight trysts by a modern Captain Tarzan and Nurse Jane. The ship is more noted for the people it has not rescued, including an infantry company directed by its captain into a ritualistic re-creation of Custer's Last Stand, with the Viet Cong as obliging Indians. Asa Baber sets his *The Land of a Million Elephants* (1970) in a place of make-believe not unlike Vietnam in its geography, and quite like Vietnam in its role in our international fantasies. Baber's strategists submit that America has been deadened by civil unrest and political assassination: "I submit that if you had a National Blood Pressure Monitor at the moment people heard the news you would have found virtually no response. No orgasm."

Baber's depiction of the lack of imaginative possibilities in Vietnam may be closest to the truth of what the war really meant. But within the limits of actual events, it remained the role of fictionists to find a structure. Ronald J. Glasser's *365 Days* (1971) admitted the problem: "There is no novel in Nam, there is not enough for a plot, nor is there really any character development. If you survive 365 days without getting killed or wounded you simply go home and take up again where you left off." Yet within

this artificially imposed structure of a duty tour Glasser sketches many aspects of the war: the suicidal role of helicopter pilots, the medics' psychotic altruism, and the case of a veteran commander who against the military silliness of Vietnam applies World War II tactics with great success until he is fragged by his most decidedly Vietnam-era troops. Airmen's routines—bombing Vietnam on office-hour schedules, from comfortable bases in Thailand while intimately involved in affairs back home in Washington, D.C., or Schenectady, New York—are used by George Davis as the structure for *Coming Home* (1971). In counterpoint, Davis places the problems of a black officer, unique even in the Vietnam-era Air Force, for whom "this war is like Harvard. Nothing in it seems real. Everything is abstract. Everything is an argument or a question."

In terms of structure, the most successful novel to portray the military situation in Vietnam is Josiah Bunting's *The Lionheads* (1972). A major and former commander in Vietnam teaching history at West Point, Bunting finds the essence of the Vietnam insanity simply by viewing it through the traditional form of Army chain-of-command. His novel begins at the top, where a major general knows that

> commanding a Division in the combat theatre can be the capstone of an excellent career of service, leading to one further assignment . . . or, if he truly distinguishes himself, the assignment will lead to another promotion—the big step to three stars (only 15 percent of two-star generals are promoted to the three star rank). . . . He wants to be Chief of Staff—of the Army.

With the visit of a branch secretary imminent, the general mounts a campaign, the implications of which are carried down-staff with the orders. At brigade, he charges one of his colonels in the manner of a sales director: "Your body-count is a standing joke. Tell you what, Robertson, you have one week to produce." Among the three brigades, there is a scramble for the division's helicopter assets; inevitably, one brigade is shorted and sustains a frightening number of deaths, but overall the casualties are "moderate" enough for the general to claim a significant victory. As the battle has progressed from planning to execution, Bunting has followed the action down to company, platoon, and squad, until he reaches what the Army calls the "real sharp individual"—the soldier in the field, in this case PFC Compella, the single person in the book devoid of all but purely human ambitions. In the first chapter, at division, he has been temporarily assigned as an aide, displaying maps for the coming battle. "PFC Compella notes that the officers take no notice of him, but follow only the movements of the tip of his pointer as it plots the new locations on the briefing map." His presence is as unreal as the deaths orchestrated by these same commanders. At the novel's conclusion, when he himself is the fine point of the war's action, the officers again take no note, for he is killed on a day for rejoicing, when casualties are light. His experience in Vietnam is absolute but unmeasurable.

But the Vietnam experience was bewildering even to the military. To Army veterans, the war made little sense. Confused sergeants, whose 20 years of service span the end of World War II, Korea, and the beginnings of Vietnam, are familiar characters in fiction emerging from the war—and in few cases do they find a solution, or even an understanding of what is going on. The larger dimensions of America's involvement remain the province of the professional novelist. Two young novelists wrote their first books about the war, James Park Sloan with *War Games* (1971) and William Crawford Woods with *The Killing Zone* (1970). Both have since broadened their writing careers, but these first novels are two of the best to come out of the Vietnam War.

For *War Games* Sloan faces the familiar problem of finding a structuring device. This is why his protagonist has joined the Army—he has two theories to test, one of which he hopes to use for a novel:

Theory One

The timid hero goes to Vietnam like a sissy dipping his toe in the pool. Suddenly he realizes that he can be a cold-water swimmer. This happens because Vietnam provides him with a character-molding experience. It is both purposeful and earthshaking. There is a flash of insight. He realizes that he is now fully mature. He has become a soldier and a man.

This is only a hypothesis. Then there is Theory Two.

Theory Two

A tough-minded young man, who unsuspectingly has above-average sensitivity goes to Vietnam. For the first time in his life he encounters genuine brutality and tragedy—perhaps his first tragic love affair. The experience shocks him into his own humanity. There is a flash of insight. He comes home in total revulsion at war and probably writes a book.

This story of his book becomes the story of his attempts to write the definitive novel of Vietnam, and its structure becomes natural and unique to the young college dropout ripping off the Army in Vietnam. Discovering that if the service does dental work on any tooth it is responsible for the care of that tooth, and the two adjacent, for the rest of the soldier's life, Sloan's protagonist begins a program of systematically complaining about every third tooth. The organization of his dental chart becomes the structure of his novel.

The chart is the most real thing in the book. Like other writers before him, Sloan finds that there are many unreal things in this new war: airliners that race the sun across the Pacific, serving breakfast every hour; APO mail that sends the same letter back and forth across the world 27 times; a peacetime army staffed by uniformed civil servants who must suddenly fight for their careers; and dozens of other incongruities that suggest that Vietnam and its war are a world apart from anything America has previously known. Officially, the Army contrives its own unreality to match. It is a nonlinear war, with no objectives to seize or end-date in sight:

Each departure is festive in its own way. . . . Since the rotations after one-year tours are staggered, victory is a continuous process. It is thus

more sustained than the sword tendering, paper signing, and ticker-tape marching of previous wars. On the other hand, it is followed by an equally continuous reappraisal.

The service treats it as a game, a matter of duration and a simple modal exercise:

We lead by a steady three-to-one. Which is good, but not good enough. Any worse and there would be alarm. Any better and the statistics would be checked. . . . I never bother with the facts. When a town comes up on my roster, I put the monthly battle there. That's the way it is with this war.

Sloan's protagonist learns that if he is to have a real war, he must make it up himself. "I shall remember to cite Hamlet: devise the play, then act in it!" As he makes progress through his war, which has become his novel, he wonders, "Have I begun inventing things? A man who goes to war should return with tales to tell. . . . Is my life merging with my imagination?" He fears that he is "tramping, step by step, in the direction of the implausible." On patrol with a group of ARVN rangers, his dream catches up with him: sickened by his allies' torture of villagers and disgusting acts with animals, he sets his rifle on automatic fire and destroys them all. For this he expects court-martial and execution, but at least he has performed a significant act in this otherwise insignificant war.

The writer and his "separate war" are saved by his new boss, Colonel Rachow, who has authored the Army manual *Creative Leadership and Collective Tunnel Vision,* and who in other times "would have been magnificent . . . as a paper lawyer in the twelfth century. Or perhaps as the head of a noble family encroaching on its vassals." Rachow sympathizes with the protagonist's behavior because he can articulate many of the young soldier's feelings about the unreal war against Vietnam:

War, said Rachow, has ceased to be tied down by facts. It has become metaphysical; one might say a platonic form. He asked me to picture an amphibious landing across Lake Michigan. Then imagine, he said, such things as landings by Martians; invaders from liquid planets formed of molten lava, surprised and threatened by our exploration. This is the future of military planning. War is no longer waged merely to achieve ends; it is waged as proof of its own possibility.

Moreover, technologically "war had come to a state of entropy! It was more and more complex, but in the process its energy was spent. If he had known sooner, he might have quit the army and written a book—on the war which had made his profession obsolete." And so Sloan's protagonist ends his tour with the creation of his small novel about a small war, *War Games.*

In *The Killing Zone* William Crawford Woods employs even more artifice to come to terms with this most artificial of wars. A confused sergeant stands at the center of the action, which Woods places not in Vietnam but rather in a New Jersey training camp where the strategies of Vietnam are first rehearsed. Sergeant Melton has rejected a career that would have led him to Josiah Bunting's managerial officer caste of Vietnam. Instead, he finds himself first sergeant of a company with no executive officer, its C.O. having been stricken with a heart attack on the golf course; and so he is in a position of command when a new lieutenant arrives to test a demonstration plan of computerized warfare—a plan being implemented in the Vietnam War for which the inductees are training. The war and its methods, of course, are like no other. The lieutenant helping to plan it is equally new:

> Twenty-four years old. BS and MS in electrical engineering from the University of California. Master's thesis on some military application of information retrieval. ROTC commission deferred until after graduate school. Part-time programmer for Armed Resources Corporation—one of those ambiguous concerns that hide in the rolling countryside of Maryland and Virginia within fifteen minutes by chopper of the Pentagon.

Lieutenant Track's experiment is to find out how closely and how well a computer can perform with a small line unit in a rapidly changing combat situation. The unit chosen is led by Sergeant Cox, who is of Track's age but in spirit is more akin to Melton's Army. Despite the strange nature of the war and the even more incongruous circumstances in which one trains for it ("the training area . . . was a parking lot; they were learning to kill like cavemen in a place where the pizza truck would stop that night,"), he resists computerized warfare in favor of the personal virtues of soldiery.

Track's computer plans an action, issues plastic-headed wargame ammunition, and follows the training exercise with all the deliberation of a division commander, receiving information from the field and determining the best strategies to continue. But an error is made: the operator has not routinely cleared the computer's storage, and as a result two boxes of live ammunition have been used. There is no way the computer can discover or correct its action. That remains the prerogative of the common foot soldier, in this case Sergeant Cox, who has but one way to save his men from total slaughter:

> He had been hit four times by the gunner who was still firing when he reached him. Mr. Track's computer had provided an unbeatable realism which had gone into his belly, and one bit of realism had ruined his left arm, taken it out altogether. So it was with the rifle in one hand that he came over the barrel, calmly, indifferently, almost sweetly, and with practiced smoothness and precision slid the bayonet into the boy's chest. . . . The sergeant and the private fell together behind the finally silent gun.

Because he has attacked the technology itself, Sergeant Cox can affirm both himself and the real matter of death, each of which the military technicians of the Vietnam War try to efface. *The Killing Zone* probably stands as the best novel to define, amid the surreal confusion of a war planned by computers and practiced in parking lots, what field remains for honor. The villains are those who disavow such honor, whether they be technocrat lieutenants

who fight weekday wars with weekends in New York, or a military establishment that has lost sight of the purpose of soldiering. Again, the sergeants, both young and old, suffer. But in Woods' novel their acts have meaning and their minds comprehend the meaning of what's going on. The lieutenant can drive away in his red Corvette, radio blaring; the first sergeant remains, to write letters of bereavement but also to understand:

> Melton paused, because the melody from Track's radio was surfacing in his mind, and he wanted to name it. It mingled with the others, then came clearer. Rock and roll, or what they now called just rock, the new music—he hated most of it—but he had heard before, and liked, this quiet tune—there it was: "Ruby Tuesday," by the Rolling Stones. A really beautiful song.

The fact that amateur and professional writers of all ages and abilities wrote on every aspect of the war in a wide range of styles and modes demonstrates that writing, that telling stories, is an essential reflex to the human dilemma. More specifically, these works of fiction argue that literature is a person's private weapon against lies and hypocrisy, that a precise and concrete use of language is a moral act. The Vietnam conflict made less of an immediate impression on domestic America than any other war in history; there was no mobilization of the homefront, and America was, simultaneously, going through one of the most culturally fertile periods in recent times. In his book *Standard Operating Procedure: Notes of a Draft-Age American* (1971), James S. Kunen ponders what he will be able to tell his future grandchildren:

> They won't understand why the war did not become the center of our lives, why stopping it did not pre-empt all other concerns, why opposition did not progress far beyond *dissent*. They won't understand how it was possible that, while the war was going on, a new football league grew and merged with the old, hemlines rose and fell amid great controversy, and the nation rediscovered romance.

The task of making such explanations ultimately falls on literary artists. The peculiar nature of Vietnam, both at home and abroad, has made that task all the more difficult. But long after the politics, economics, military theories, and sociologies of the war have been outdated, the fictions of those artists will remain as evidence of how the war affected our imagination. And for all its struggles, their writing is perhaps our most reliable record of just what Vietnam was.

Walter Hölbling   (essay date 1989)

SOURCE: "Literary Sense-Making: American Vietnam Fiction," in *Vietnam Images: War and Representation,* edited by Jeffrey Walsh and James Aulich, The Macmillan Press, Ltd., 1989, pp. 123-40.

[*Hölbling is the author of* The Discourse of War in Recent American Novels *(1987). In the following essay, he discusses the different types of literary responses the Vietnam war has engendered and relates them to American cultural myths and previous war literature.*]

Since 1941 the United States has been more-or-less continuously involved in a series of military conflicts around the world. The resulting public awareness of war has contributed to the production of an ever-growing number of fictional accounts that deal with war or war-like situations. One of the assumptions of this essay is that stories of war display essential cultural concepts, expectations and self-images more prominently than other kinds of fiction, as the extreme situation of war provides occasions for scrutinising and putting into words the individual and collective values in whose name the state demands that its citizens risk their lives for the common good. Thus, novels of war can be considered as fictional models of a nation's (or people's) 'storifying of experience', as acts of literary sense-making (or questioning) in response to historical problems of national importance. The literary conventions employed by these texts in their attempt to understand a specific historical situation reveal specific cultural idiosyncrasies in plot patterns, motifs, symbol systems, and so on. If they have sufficient explanatory power, these models of literary sense-making persist as persuasive conventions, even in the face of political and historical change.

Michael Herr says in *Dispatches* that 'war stories, after all, are stories about people'—stories, that is, like other stories, but about people in an extreme situation that is still (thank God) considered the exception rather than the rule. In this exceptional situation of war the state demands that its citizens (usually the younger ones) risk their lives for the common good—something that goes beyond the usual requirements for proving yourself a valuable member of the community. Such situations are traditionally an occasion for questioning the validity of those individual and collective values and self-concepts in whose name one might die prematurely, and the whole matter is complicated by the perceptions of the enemy, which ignorance makes all the more alien and terrifying.

The Vietnam conflict is exceptional in at least three respects: (1) no war since the Civil War caused such a rift in American public opinion and led to such a massive and heated public debate for and against; (2) it was the first war the United States conclusively lost; and (3) never before did Americans think they knew so much about their military opponents, only to discover that they knew very little. Even if Frances Fitzgerald's critical stance in *Fire in the Lake* does appear somewhat harsh at times, many of her comments are born out by the language, concepts and general attitudes evident in the majority of fictions about the war. Denise Levertov's poem 'What Were They Like?' succinctly catches the inadequacy of the rather vague ideas Americans held about the country in which—and supposedly for which—they were fighting.

The outcome of this conflict has had far-reaching effects on US domestic, foreign and military policy, and the nation's self-image still seems to be in the process of recomposing itself from a broad spectrum of critical as well as revisionist public opinions. Just remember the kaleidoscope of articles, commentaries and speeches in 1985, on the occasion of the tenth anniversary of the fall of Saigon.

In short, the overall impact of the Vietnam conflict on the United States not only justifies but demands that students of American Studies familiarise themselves with the fictional models responding to this unique historical experience.

Ideological positions are obviously important in this kind of fiction, as there were two camps—and little in between—from the beginning. Though there is not much in the way of explicit ideological argument in most of the novels, with the notable exception of John Briley's *The Traitors* (1967), it certainly makes some difference whether you focus your analyses around novels in the vein of *The Green Berets* or of *Bamboo Bed* or of *Close Quarters* or of *The 13th Valley*. To put into perspective the achievements of American fiction on Vietnam, it is necessary to have some knowledge not only of the political and sociocultural background but also—maybe even more so—of the literary conventions of American war fiction as they developed up to the Second World War. What Paul Fussell, in an essay on First World War British literature, called 'cultural paradigms', determine the fictional design, as does the familiar habit of conceiving of a new war in terms of the previous one. [In an endnote, Hölbling adds: 'Fussell defines "cultural paradigms" as "systems of convention and expectation that largely determine which objective phenomena become part of the individual's experience—what people 'make of things', how they fit their experience into the conceptual frames their culture has taught them to consider suitable for making sense of the world".'] In relation to Vietnam, Second World War models soon turned out to be inadequate, though this did not prevent a sizable group of authors from using them. Even so-called experimental fictions such as *Catch-22* and *Slaughterhouse-Five* were not easily assimilable to the new experience, as is shown by the ambitious failure of Eastlake's *Bamboo Bed*. The peculiar combination of massive high-tech destruction and guerrilla warfare in an exotic environment, along with the one-year rotation system and the increasingly doubtful political and moral premises of the involvement, made general public consent, as in the Second World War, impossible.

Here, perhaps, is the place to digress a little from the immediate topic and to focus on some of the 'cultural paradigms' developed in earlier American war narratives—particularly as the specific conditions of Vietnam stimulated American authors to look to the past for adequate fictional models. They turned to central American myths and self-concepts, originally embodied in the religiously motivated Indian-war narratives of the seventeenth and eighteenth centuries, then secularised in the pioneer stories of Western fiction, and nowadays happily and profitably thriving in the comic-strip and formula-story section of popular literature. To understand the appeal of such models we have to go back to the original narratives and the way they responded to the 'American experience'. In the words of Richard Slotkin, [in *Regeneration through Violence: The Mythology of the American Frontier, 1600-1830*, 1973], 'The Indian wars proved to be the most acceptable metaphor for the American experience. To all of the complexities of that experience, it offered simplicity of dramatic contrast and direct confrontation of opposites.'

Slotkin considers the Indian narratives 'the first coherent myth-literature developed in America for American audiences' and argues that in the hands of eloquent preachers such as Increase Mather it became 'a primary vehicle for the American Puritan's mythology'. Of the several components of this myth, the most important from our point of view are the *sense of mission,* the *conviction of being engaged in a just war* in a *unique historical situation,* and *racial warfare.*

The early settlers' sense of mission made partners of Bible and sword, as is shown by the following passage from John Underhill's *Newes from America* (1638):

> Many were burnt in the fort, both men, women, and children. Others forced out. ... which our soldiers received and entertained with the sword. Down fell men, women, and children. . . . Great and doleful was the bloudy sight to the view of young soldiers that never had been in war, to see so many souls lie gasping on the ground, so thick, in some places, that you could hardly pass along. . . . Sometimes the Scripture declareth women and children must perish with their parents. Sometime the case alters; but we will not dispute it now. We had sufficient light from the word of God for our proceedings.

By the end of the eighteenth century, the struggle for souls had largely given way to the struggle for soil in the name of democracy and civilisation. This 'errand into the wilderness' retained from the earlier struggle the elements of racial warfare and the sense of the unique historical occasion, soon to become known as 'manifest destiny'. Underpinned by the symbol system of 'cultivating the wilderness' or 'the progress of civilisation', it justified the use of collective violence, as well as heroic individual actions by outstanding figures such as Daniel Boone, Davy Crockett and Kit Carson, in the gradual destruction of the aboriginal culture.

It is interesting to note that, just as official US histories never refer to the 300 or so years of war with the Indians *as* war (unless other nations were involved), so the engagement in Vietnam remained to the end a 'conflict', as a state of war was never officially declared. One could thus state, somewhat facetiously, that the two longest military engagements in US history—the Indian wars and the war in Vietnam—were, until recently, never acknowledged as what they in fact were, and one might be tempted to take a rather critical view of the myth of the Pax Americana, rather as Edmund Wilson does in his book *Patriotic Gore* (1962). Recent American historical writings such as Russell Weigley's *The American Way of War* (1977) and David Kennedy's *Over Here* (1980), a study of the socio-cultural context of the First World War, present a more realistic appraisal of the American past.

The literary legacy of the First World War was rich and proved adaptable to the experience of the next generation of authors, who, sooner than expected after the 'war to end all wars', were having one of their own. As Malcolm Cowley remarks [in *The Literary Situation,* 1958], somewhat tongue-in-cheek,

> One might say that a great many novels of the

Second World War are based on Dos Passos for structure, since they have collective heroes in the Dos Passos fashion, and since he invented a series of structural devices for dealing with such heroes in unified works of fiction. At the same time, they are based on Scott Fitzgerald for mood, on Steinbeck for humor, and on Hemingway for action and dialogue.

Given the broad national consensus, in the Second World War, that war against the Nazis and Fascists in Europe and the Japanese imperialists in the Pacific was justified on political and moral grounds, it must be considered a sign of the intellectual honesty of those concerned that the fiction about this war voiced any criticisms at all. The general climate of the Cold War years was not very conducive to critical voices or texts, yet authors such as Norman Mailer and J. H. Burns, and, in a different vein, Irwin Shaw, Stefan Heym, Alfred Hays and John Hersey, are among those who, while supporting the war goals, point out the potentially dangerous effects on the victors. Not unexpectedly, they remain—like their predecessors after the First World War—an influential minority. Most American novels about the Second World War are conventional war stories imbued with the myths summarised by Ward Just in his book *Military Men:*

> Since American wars are never undertaken for imperialist gain (myth one), American soldiers always fight in a virtuous cause (myth two) for a just and goalless peace (myth three). . . . American wars are always defensive wars, undertaken slowly and reluctantly, the country a righteous giant finally goaded beyond endurance by foreign adventurers.

To conclude this brief synopsis of 'cultural paradigms' and literary conventions, the dominant perceptions of war in fiction and Hollywood films in the years before and during the Vietnam involvement were those of these myths.

Apart from their use of traditional concepts and conventional narrative techniques, war stories of the kind just outlined also share two other premises. One is a basically unchallenged belief in the leading role of the United States in a teleologically progressive history of mankind; the other is what might be called a 'realist' position concerning the relation of literature to historical events—i.e. the assumption that historical events are 'objective', that their chronological sequence is meaningful in and of itself, and that the task of fiction in relation to historical events is the *post factum* revelation of this meaning by various traditional literary techniques. Against this understanding of literature as a more or less well-wrought, ancillary explanation of official historical events, a small but distinct group of writers see the task of fiction not as the representation of familiar facts but as the creation of (literary) answers in response to, not in imitation of, events of national historical importance. To some extent all these writers share the assumption that meaning is created not by the mere chronological sequence of events but by the way those events are 'spoken of'—i.e. the order and sense we give to them according to our (culturally diverse) modes of conceptualising and contextualising. Inevitably this means that the meta-fictional dimension tends to dominate these authors' texts, which make the reader aware of how fictional discourse constitutes itself.

Robin Moore's *The Green Berets* (1965) is typical of the conventional war story. Its animated cartoon heroes have the same basic characteristics as the heroes of James Jones's gritty combat novels and share James Bond's explosive professional self-sufficiency. A well-blended concoction of macho American stereotypes serves up patriotism, adventure, secret-mission suspense and heroic individualism, with more than enough brutalising rhetoric to drive home *how* tough and professional these guys really are who successfully complete one dangerous mission after another on the new frontiers of democracy. Moving expertly in the dangerous limbo on the outer edge of civilised society, these supermen embody the heroic frontier man, the 'good gunman' as state marshal, the stubborn 'good detective', and their ilk. They fight for law and order in spite of their corrupt or weak superiors and the bungling military bureaucracy; and, if they seem much like the enemy in their use of deceit and brutality, they are usually more efficient, and the end justifies the means. Yet they are basically good comrades, with a soft spot for gentle women and helpless children. Moore dutifully differentiates between 'good good guys' and 'bad good guys', whose names usually suggest non-WASP ethnic groups and their supposed characteristics: Korn and Schmelzer have German names and Nazi tendencies; Ossidian, with an American name, is cruel and sly; men with Mexican or Italian names are passionate and crafty.

The Green Berets' enemies are 'Communists (C), black hordes, monkeys', or the Vietnamese in general—gooks', 'dinks', female 'slanteyes': inferior, sub-human creatures who are conceded to have human qualities only when dying in 'brilliant white pools of napalm'. Then 'human torches cry their last'. There is no doubt that they will share the fate of their literary predecessors, the devilish 'injuns'. Strangely enough, the danger never ceases, though scores of black-pyjama'd fanatics are blown to kingdom come on the Berets' perfectly executed missions.

By his use of symbol systems based on a trivialised version of historical racial warfare, Moore demonstrates his fundamental failure (or unwillingness) to understand the real issues of the Vietnam conflict and reduces the representatives of a foreign culture to abstract embodiments of evil, the exotic and the inferior. In consequence, the American heroes become equally abstract, stereotyped agents of the 'good cause'. The success of Moore's book, which by 1975 had sold 3.2 million copies and is still selling (a new edition was published by Ballantine in 1983), was reflected in a movie version starring John Wayne, and shows that its perception of the American involvement in Vietnam as another just mission in the fight for democracy and freedom was shared by a statistically significant number of Americans. The more recent success of *Rambo: First Blood II*, of which Moore's novel is in some ways a forerunner, is evidence that this viewpoint is still widely held.

> **The loss of values and traditional symbol systems for sense-making is a trademark of much Vietnam fiction. The same is true of a good deal of 'faction' based on the war, especially that written after its end.**
>
> —*Walter Hölbling*

In what may be considered an inner-American counterpoint to Moore's well-written vision of American success, Norman Mailer in *Why are we in Vietnam?* (1967) employs a stylised sixties hipster idiom that suggests an extreme situation of a different kind. In order to render the anonymous information overload of a repressive post-industrial society geared to maximum performance, Mailer chooses a kind of electronic-stream-of-consciousness technique for his fictional psychoanalysis of the collective American unconscious. His comprehensive understanding of war—he once called 'form in general' the 'record of war'—indicates that for him 'war' is the life principle, understood as the dialectic interaction of opposing forces manifest in individual struggles, in cosmic events, in politics, and even in the artist's struggle for adequate literary form. In his attempt to express the irrationalities he sees as underlying the American involvement in Vietnam, Mailer employs a highly idiosyncratic form of genital-scatological symbolism which brings together contemporary concepts from Reich, Marcuse, N. O. Brown and McLuhan. The result is a generously four-letter-worded discourse, delivered by a protean 'narrative voice', that explodes a fair number of traditional American myths and self-images. And, while one may argue about the validity of some of Mailer's criticism, there is little doubt that his novel provides a fascinating, if not very optimistic, fictional analysis of the complex struggle of American youth for an identity of their own in a decade that deprived them of the values held by their parents.

The loss of values and traditional symbol systems for sense-making is a trademark of much Vietnam fiction. The same is true of a good deal of 'faction' based on the war, especially that written after its end, such as Michael Herr's *Dispatches*. Herr, sharing his readers knowledge of the outcome of the Vietnam conflict, sets out not to glorify but to understand and tell the truth, according to his personal experience. His book is quite a contrast to Moore's, and, even allowing for the rather different perspectives and attitudes of the authors, it is obvious that the war Herr writes about is not the same one as Moore had in mind. In addition, the two texts provide ample ground for comparison of fictional strategies. Moore's book follows the success-story formula: all missions are carefully planned and smoothly executed in a sort of ideal war. The linear narrative discourse suggests definite beginnings, goals and ends—'Mission completed, Sir!' —and it does not matter that no end is in sight. With Herr, we get no supermen but brave and occasionally quietly heroic soldiers who try to survive in a war that does not make sense. Employing collage and montage techniques that do not belong to the standard repertoire of media correspondents (except the 'new journalists'), *Dispatches* shows the formidable difficulties involved in writing traditional 'stories' about this war which was, as one reviewer put it, 'all circumference, had no center, and was therefore difficult to filter through unified plot and point of view' (E. Pochloda, in *The Nation,* no. 25 (1978) p. 344). The ordered reality that Moore's discourse presupposes does not exist in Herr's Vietnam:

> The spokesmen spoke in words that had no currency left as words, sentences with no hope of meaning in the sane world, and if much of it was sharply queried by the press, all of it got quoted. The press got all the facts (more or less), it got too many of them. But it never found a way to report meaningfully about death, which of course is really what it was all about. The most repulsive, transparent gropes for sanctity in the midst of the killing received serious treatment in the papers and on the air. The jargon of progress got blown into our heads like bullets, and by the time you waded through all the Washington stories and all the Saigon stories, all the Other War stories and the corruption stories and the stories about brisk new gains in ARVN effectiveness, the suffering was somehow unimpressive. And after enough years of that, so many that it seemed to have been going on forever, you got to a point where you could sit there in the evening and listen to the man say that American casualties for the week had reached a six-week low, only eighty G.I. s had died in combat, and you'd feel like you'd just gotten a bargain.

The problems implied here—a certain numbing indifference, the inability to decide which story to believe and how to tell it, the fact that war has become a habit—show the combined effects of information overload, moral uncertainty, and lack of motivation and of definite strategic goals. All of this leads to an entropy of meaning not unlike that exhibited in the works of contemporary fiction writers such as Pynchon, Barth, Barthelme and Vonnegut. The borderline between 'story' and 'history' blurs in direct relation to the extent to which official interpretations of reality and individual experience are moving apart, and the individual can no longer use common cultural symbol systems to explain events to himself and others.

After Herr's excellent, if puzzled and puzzling, 'factual' account, let us turn to the novel which I think provides the most powerful literary expression so far of the specific characteristics of the US experience in Vietnam: Tim O'Brien's *Going after Cacciato.* Its sensitive narrator-protagonist, Paul Berlin, is dropped into a world he thinks he knows from various secondary sources: his father's tales of the Second World War, movies and television series (*Iwo Jima, Hogan's Heroes, M*A*S*H*), daily media coverage, and supposedly true-to-life simulatory training in boot camp. His attempts to understand the reality of Vietnam by applying the rules of this media-created 'reality' fail abysmally and lead him to a terrifying awareness of his fundamental ignorance. A fellow soldier's 'death of fright' which Paul witnesses on his first patrol becomes, for him, the 'ultimate war story'. Like the key motifs in

---

Daniel L. Zins on Tim O'Brien's early career:

Drafted in 1968, Tim O'Brien served in Vietnam in 1969, and in the fall of 1970 he enrolled in Harvard University's doctoral program in government. During his first year of graduate school O'Brien began writing *If I Die in a Combat Zone,* a memoir of his Vietnam experiences. Taking a year off from Harvard in 1973-74 to work as a general assignment reporter for the *Washington Post,* O'Brien also found time to write *Northern Lights,* his first novel. Realizing that the form of *If I Die* did not allow him to get at important psychological truths or to fully explore the meaning of his Vietnam experiences, and convinced that the life of the imagination is half of war—indeed, half of *any* kind of experience—O'Brien gave his fertile imagination free rein in *Going After Cacciato.*

Daniel L. Zins, in "Imagining the Real: The Fiction of Tim O'Brien," in The Hollins Critic, *Vol. XXIII, No. 3, June, 1986. pp. 1-2.*

---

earlier war novels—Dresden in *Slaughterhouse-Five,* Snowden's death in *Catch-22,* Hennessy's death at the beginning of *The Naked and the Dead,* or the retreat from Caporetto in *A Farewell to Arms*—this experience makes the protagonist shockingly aware of his own precarious situation.

The figure of the sensitive and critical intellectual has been with American war fiction ever since Andrews in the Dos Passos novel *Three Soldiers,* but O'Brien introduces a number of new elements. In order to involve the reader in his protagonist's attempts at sense-making, i.e. his 'storifying of experience', he uses two clearly distinguishable modes of literary discourse. One renders Berlin's *memories* of the past events ('what happened'), the other his *imaginative* pursuit of Cacciato across Eurasia to Paris ('what might have happened'). The two levels interact and interfere with each other: while imaginatively leaving the dangerous world of war in his pseudo-legitimate pursuit of the deserter Cacciato, Berlin (mostly involuntarily) remembers—and finally comes to terms with—the horrors of war in an alien environment. O'Brien's innovation here lies in the way he uses his sophisticated 'dialog of discourses' to juxtapose the 'factual' and the 'fictional' modes of literary sense-making. The discourse of Berlin's memory recalls the phenomenological style of the Hemingway tradition and consciously places itself in the context of previous war fictions. Let me give an example of what I mean by this.

In one passage Paul remembers a firebreak during a patrol in hilly terrain that has been devastated by aerial bombardment—the caustic Doc Peret christens it the 'World's Greatest Lake Country'. Cacciato, the prototypical young innocent-ignorant American soldier, casts an improvised fishing-line into one of the bomb-craters filled with rain-water:

> He tied a paperclip to a length of string, baited
> it up with bits of ham, then attached a bobber
> fashioned out of an empty aerosol can labeled
> *Secret*. Cacciato moved down to the lip of the
> crater. He paused as if searching for proper wa-
> ters, then flipped out the line. The bobber made
> a splashing sound.

The obvious allusion here is to Hemingway's famous short story 'Big Two-Hearted River', where Nick Adams, back from the war, attempts to regain his bearings in the world by the familiar ritual of trout fishing. Also evident are the contrasts in style and semantic differences between Cacciato's acts and Nick's preparations for trout fishing.

For both, the ritual of fishing is meant to reconstitute their sense of personal identity, yet its respective forms and directions take quite different turns. Hemingway's Nick, symbolically placed with the burned land around Seyney behind him and the swamp before him, is able to determine his position in the world—the river and the camp-site—by doing the right things, or rather by 'doing things right', and thus establishes a working relationship with his natural environment. Compared to this, the very material Cacciato uses for fishing—some string, a paperclip, a piece of canned ham, an empty aerosol can—signifies more than just a low grotesque version of Yankee ingenuity. In the world of the seventeen-year-old Cacciato, no piece of un-touched nature is left between the burned land and the swamp; both have been fused in the lifeless wasteland of the 'World's Greatest Lake Country'. Interaction with such an environment to constitute one's identity must take a different form from Nick's parallel attempt; Cacciato's fishing becomes an ambiguous symbolic gesture. On the one hand an act of individual self-assertion, this clinging to a familiar ritual is on the other an expression of boyish helplessness and withdrawal into oneself. The situational inadequacy of the youth's behaviour makes it a striking image of his despair.

Opposed, and sometimes complementary, to the disturbing memories of despair and death, Paul Berlin's imaginative discourse creates an alternative reality on the occasion of a night watch. Berlin makes it clear that his imaginings are more than mere escapist daydreaming or pretending:

> Not a dream, but an idea. An idea to develop,
> to tinker with and build and sustain, to draw out
> as an artist draws out his visions. . . . It was a
> working out of the possibilities. It wasn't dream-
> ing and it wasn't pretending. . . . It was a way
> of asking questions.

While Berlin's memories contain all the horrors of war, his imaginings are full of the popular myths and stereotypes a twenty-year-old may come up with in his attempts to build 'a smooth arc from war to peace'. We see the 'story within stories' unfold before us, flounder along and, finally, shatter on the senselessness of war. With a sharp eye for the incongruences between popular myths and histori-cal realities, O'Brien inverts the motif of the American Westward movement. 'Going West' does not lead Caccia-to and his pursuers to untouched new continents but to

Paris: the city where American independence was official-ly ratified in 1783; the city that served as the symbol of Eu-ropean culture in the First World War and was celebrated by Americans in the Second; but in 1968 the city where negotiations for peace in Vietnam were bogged down around the notorious oval conference table. Paris as the literal 'vanishing point' of Cacciato's and Paul Berlin's imaginative journey—'Imagination, like reality, has its limits'—is a sign that the American Westward movement has come full circle, and a reminder of the ironical fact that the United States, itself a former colony, took over from France as the colonising power in Indo China. At the end of the novel, Cacciato, the enigmatic symbol of inno-cence and ignorance, is missing in action. Thus O'Brien, while leaving open the possibility that Cacciato may still be alive, makes it clear that in relation to the American involvement in Vietnam traditional concepts of the 'just war', the 'unique historical mission' and the 'crusade for democracy' have lost their power of providing explanato-ry symbol systems. Now they are stories, overtaken by his-torical realities. Paul Berlin, while still unable to make sense of the war, has finally taken a significant step toward self-definition: his imaginative questioning of the realities of war has yielded no easy solutions, but a heightened awareness that helps him distinguish clearly between what happened and what might have happened. By such means O'Brien's novel manages to interrelate, as far as it is possi-ble, main elements of the two major modes of writing about war, the 'factual' and the 'imaginative', that have been employed by American authors since the Second World War.

This is not achieved in John Del Vecchio's *The 13th Valley* (1982). Here is an example of the attempt to write a 'natu-ralist epic' about Vietnam, in the tradition of Dos Passos, Irwin Shaw, Mailer's *The Naked and the Dead* and James Jones's *The Thin Red Line*. The novel's merits are obvi-ous, but even more so its final failure to grasp the special quality of the American experience in Vietnam. Intention-ally or not, Del Vecchio uses two levels of discourse that are hermetically sealed off against each other. One is that of the traditional story of a patrol in enemy country, with all its ups and downs, details of army life, equipment, weapons and so on, and a (somewhat melodramatic) finale in which most of the main characters and half the compa-ny die heroically in fulfilment of their duty; of the major figures, only the Ishmael-like Chellini survives to tell the tale. None of the usual problems that Americans were fac-ing in Vietnam exists on this level of the novel: US soldiers fight North Vietnamese regulars in an otherwise uninhab-ited mountain valley, so it's soldiers against soldiers in a campaign that might have taken place in the Second World War or perhaps Korea.

All the real problems of Vietnam are mentioned in the sec-ond level of discourse—that of meditation and discussion, camp-fire talks and so forth. Here we learn about social, cultural, ethical, political and military problems—racial antagonism, anti-war protest, personal problems, and the like; but all this leaves the level of action curiously unaf-fected. In keeping these two discourses apart, Del Vecchio employs a kind of narrative immunisation strategy which allows him to avoid tackling the real issues of the American experience in Vietnam without leaving them out of the picture altogether.

In a way, this seems to exemplify a major trend in the United States ever since the Vietnam veterans, enraged by the national public welcome given to the returning Iranian hostages in 1980, came out of the closet. To me there are signs of an easy kind of revisionism which (not altogether unintentionally, I assume) links two completely different things. What I mean is that there is a tendency, in rehabilitating the Vietnam veterans, to present the war itself in a more positive light. Just to make my point clear: I am definitely *for* the long-overdue rehabilitation of the veterans, but would argue that they are being exploited and abused all over again if this is used to justify an unjustifiable war. (*Rambo: First Blood II* is a typical product of this trend. [In an endnote, Hölbling adds: 'The most recent American movie about Vietnam, *Platoon,* provides a much-needed counterpoint to *Rambo: First Blood II;* so far the most balanced of commercial movie releases on this topic, it seems to indicate that the American Vietnam trauma may begin to receive a different treatment from that of "regeneration through (cinematic) violence".']) It seems that the painful truth that more than 50,000 young Americans died in a war which still defies explanation by standard American self-concepts is not easily acknowledged. There is a great temptation to confuse means and ends, and to sanction the Vietnam War by doing justice to those who had to fight it.

Let me conclude by summing up what I consider to be the main characteristics of the 'well-made novels' and more critical and questioning works on war in American fiction since the beginning of the US involvement in Vietnam. The Vietnam experience has not only influenced writings on that war, but has also, I believe, been highly significant for perceptive American writers (such as Heller, Vonnegut and Pynchon) dealing with the Second World War in novels published while the Vietnam War was in progress.

The mainstream consists of works written in the traditional mimetic modes, based on the assumption that war, as a specific historical event, takes its place in a (usually vaguely implied) teleological process of history, and that the task of fiction is to tell 'what it was really like' with the help of traditional literary techniques. Seen in this perspective, war is an exceptional historical situation interrupting an otherwise more or less civilised evolutionary progress toward a higher state of civilisation; indeed, it is explained by the need to defend this peaceful development against dangerous disturbances. In the novels that take this point of view we usually receive information about the characters' civilian lives before (and sometimes after) the war, follow them through basic training and into combat, learn about their problems and thoughts—all of this in the context of a linearly progressive narrative that feeds the reader's desire for mimetic illusion with (seemingly) realistic details of places, dates, the military hierarchy, technological equipment, battlefields, and so forth. It all adds up to the idea that the war—like the world as a whole—is explainable; actions and events follow the familiar pattern of cause and effect, and, if anything goes wrong, we know why. The fictional world is basically that of the nine-teenth-century realist novel, where events proceed in linear sequence, if sometimes parallel in time, and are presented by means of a corresponding plot structure. We either follow the protagonists chronologically through the war years (James Webb, *Fields of Fire*) or, again chronologically, follow them through a specific campaign or mission (Josiah Bunting, *The Lionheads;* John Briley, *The Traitors,* Del Vecchio, *The 13th Valley*), which has a definite beginning and end corresponding to the sequence of events in time and space. Whether or not the novel is critical of the army or war goals is irrelevant to this dimension of the text, but it is manifest in the use the novel makes of patriotic imagery, characterisation, ideological rhetoric and (happy) endings.

The sense of an ending in war—and of closure in the narrative—implies that at least those who survive return to business as usual; it also suggests that the world of war is categorically different from the world of peace. Other rules of conduct apply, and one has to adjust, even if it may be difficult. A fair number of novels add distinctly Freudian overtones to the world of war, describing it as a space where men temporarily change (back) into fighting animals, rely on their instincts, and live out their aggressions and drives in words and in actions. The higher purpose of their relapse into a culturally anachronistic state is, of course, to ensure the continuing existence of that advanced cultural state from which they have temporarily descended. War is a regrettable yet necessary means of ensuring the progress of humankind. It is this basically optimistic understanding of war as a concrete historical event limited in time and space and sanctioned by transcending goals that makes its horror, its irrationalities and the suffering it causes acceptable to the reader.

Unlike the mainstream novels, the innovative texts use war as a complex metaphor for our contemporary industrialised information society, in which traditional distinctions between 'peace' and 'war' are rapidly losing their validity. What were formerly thought of as acts of 'warlike' behaviour now appear to be variants of basic problem-solving strategies on a scale that ranges from individual verbal aggression to the collective use of violence organised and sanctioned by the state. As R. E. Canjar puts it in a recent article ['The Modern Way of War, Society, and Peace,' *American Quarterly,* 36, no. 3 (1984)],

> War in short, is neither an emotional, moral, or political aberration; it is the socialized production of violence and its monopoly use by the state. . . . Both corporate social life and corporate social death are materially produced by social means. It is for this reason that such phenomena as the military-industrial complex occur. It has less to do with conspiracies than it is a routine outcome of a production process in which the means, methods, labor, technology and organizations simultaneously serve, and often fail to distinguish between, the production of life and the production of death.

War in this sense is no longer a limited historical event but threatens to become a way of life; accordingly, in the more innovative war novels (and in related works such as Pynchon's *Gravity's Rainbow*), war is global and ever-

DOWN IN THE VALLEY—An RTO, a squad leader and platoon leader of Co. D, 2nd Bn. (Ambl.), 327th Inf., stop to check their position during a patrol near FB Rendezvous. (U.S. Army Photo by SP4 John Del Vecchio)

Photograph taken by John M. Del Vecchio that shows soldiers looking down on the Khe Ta Laou River Valley, the setting for Del Vecchio's novel The 13th Valley.

present. Peace exists only temporarily in the shape of ideal spaces contrasting with the fictional world of war— Alaska, Sweden, Tralfamadore, Paris—and inevitably turns out to be but a projection of the narrator/ protagonist's wishful thinking. The absence of peaceful spaces (and times) corresponds to the absence of a teleological concept of history in which war can be given a place and meaning, and within which the individual can understand himself and his actions as contributing to a collective goal definable in terms of commonly accepted symbol systems.

Such prerequisites for joint action are no longer functional in these texts. Meaning, if it exists at all, is constituted only in a highly individualised, sometimes hermetically solipsist, 'totality of vision', on both the textual and the meta-textual level. The advanced deconstruction of collectively or even intersubjectively valid codes produces a multitude of equally valid, idiosyncratic symbol systems and discourses. They resemble the pluralist structures in complex (post-)industrial societies, where a heightened sense of individuality corresponds to a reciprocal loss of collective agreement upon common goals. One result is a kaleido-

scopic supply of information that leaves the individual with practically infinite options for sense-making or, viewed differently, with an entropy of meaning. The innovative authors translate this insight into the structure and discourse of their novels and point to the roots of violent aggression in our everyday patterns of communication and socialisation. The reader, involved in the texts by force of their continuous deferral of definite meaning, comes to realise that language is indeed, as John Hawkes once put it, 'the most powerful kind of actuality' ['John Hawkes: An Interview,' in *The Contemporary Writer: Interview with Sixteen Novelists and Poets,* edited by L.S. Dembo and Cyrena N. Pondrom, 1972]. On a more radical level, whatever kind of reality these texts present, the simple truth is impressed upon the reader that the very concept of 'reality' only exists because there is a perceiving and reflecting human consciousness. The literary discourse on war, creating fictional models of speechless confrontation, powerfully reminds us of the primal necessity to interact by signs rather than by wordless acts of destruction: far from being the 'motor of history', war threatens the very foundations of meaningful communication.

Philip D. Beidler   (essay date 1990)

SOURCE: "Re-Writing America: Literature as Cultural Revision in the New Vietnam Fiction," in *America Rediscovered: Critical Essays on Literature and Film of the Vietnam War,* edited by Owen W. Gilman, Jr. and Lorrie Smith, Garland Publishing, Inc., 1990, pp. 3-9.

[*Beidler is the author of* American Literature and the Experience of Vietnam *(1982). In the essay below, he argues that Tim O'Brien's* Going After Cacciato *and Stephen Wright's* Meditations in Green *are works of cultural revision that offer the "prospect of a new imaginative fiction of the American experience of Vietnam."*]

"We can truly be transformed, and even possibly redeemed, by electing to write at times of what happened—but also of what might have happened, what could have happened, what should have happened, and also what can be kept from happening or what can be made to happen. . . . Words are all we have." These words happen to be mine, although they have their origin in the words of the fine novelist, Tim O'Brien, who in turn had earlier made them the words, in his *Going After Cacciato,* of the fictional protagonist, Paul Berlin. In them we find a call and a challenge to a new art that would be a kind of ultimate cultural revision, an art that, even as it acknowledges the painful memory of the experience of Vietnam, would make possible the imaginative projection of that memory into new dimensions of consciousness, individual and collective, often providing equally new insights into knowledge, meaning, and value. It is a call, in the fullest terms of artistic possibility, to do nothing less than re-write ourselves, and apace, to re-write America.

The project of cultural revision so defined supplies the artistic agenda for Vietnam fiction even in a number of extremely early and highly experimental works such as Norman Mailer's *Why Are We in Vietnam?,* James Crumley's *One to Count Cadence,* and William Eastlake's *The Bamboo Bed.* It certainly continues to dictate the evolution of variously experimental styles in subsequent novels such as Charles Durden's *No Bugles, No Drums,* John Clark Pratt's *The Laotian Fragments,* and David Winn's *Gangland,* not to mention, on the other side of what might be called the meta-fictive coin, Michael Herr's *Dispatches.* It is in Tim O'Brien's award-winning *Going After Cacciato,* however, and in Stephen Wright's more recent and comparably acclaimed *Meditations in Green,* that we find the issue most fully elaborated. In them, we are confronted with the prospect of a new imaginative fiction of the American experience of Vietnam that indeed might ultimately reify itself into redemptory cultural fact.

The better known of the two works, *Going After Cacciato,* makes its creative task clear from the outset:

> Paul Berlin, whose only goal was to live long enough to establish goals worth living for still longer, stood high in the tower by the sea, the night soft all around him, and wondered, not for the first time, about the immense powers of his own imagination. A truly awesome notion. Not a dream, an idea. An idea to develop, to tinker with and build and sustain, to draw out as an artist draws out his visions.

Thus begins a novel that, as one quickly sees, is actually two, or possibly three, novels, each of which, moreover, can be read only in terms of its other or others. In a guard tower by the South China Sea, Specialist Fourth Class Paul Berlin stands lonely vigil and thinks out at once a fact-book and a fantasy-book, a book of memory and a book of imagination. Connected by frequent interchapters in what perhaps might be considered a third book—entitled, appropriately, "The Observation Post," —the other two flow in and out of each other at will until all boundaries of consciousness seem dissolved. What results is a whole far greater than the sum of its parts, one in which Berlin rewrites himself and his America into new realms of individual and collective insight.

The domain of fact or memory is a nightmare-continuum of particular horrors. Frenchie Tucker gets shot through the nose. Bernie Lynn dies of a tunnel wound, shot from his chest straight down into his vitals. Billy Boy Watkins dies of fright on the field of battle, screaming his dreadful scream, trying to lace back on the boot that holds what used to be his foot. Buff winds up ass-high in the air, "like a praying Arab in Mecca," his upturned helmet holding all that remains of his disposable humanity in the muck of his shot-away face.

Then, as if all along, enter *and* exit Cacciato. "Dumb as a bullet," says one G.I. "Dumb as a month-old oyster fart," says another. Dumb, perhaps, but apparently not crazy. Or maybe just dumb and crazy enough to think he can pull it off. "Split, departed," says Doc Peret, and somehow, incredibly, miraculously, "Gone to Paris." So, in *Going After Cacciato,* the real quickly begins to meld into the imaginative, the factually just plausible into the fictively just possible. Cacciato goes. Berlin and the others follow. Apace, Berlin ponders: "what part was fact and what part was the extension of fact? And how were facts separated from possibilities? What had really happened and what merely might have happened? How did it end?"

The fictive road to Paris does somehow magically end there, and in the negotiations that ultimately terminate American participation in the war. At the same time, the novel remains firmly anchored in the experience of the battlefield and centered on the movement of Berlin's particular experiential consciousness toward the recognition of new possibilities of acceptance and understanding. Within this twofold movement, the complex play of style re-engenders that whole vast collocation of memory, myth, metaphor, slogan, political shibboleth, and popular cliché that was in fact America in Vietnam.

It will be remembered, for example, that "The Road to Paris" was the literal expression used by bureaucratic and journalistic phrase-makers to describe the tortuous, and often nearly absurd labors—including some prolonged squabbling over the shape and dimensions of a conference table—of getting the peace talks set in motion. It will also be remembered that "The Road to" any number of places once supplied the title to any number of innocently ridiculous American movies that made comedy, in some of the bleakest times of war, out of danger and dire predicament. Here Berlin finds his Dorothy Lamour—it is hard in fact to think of the new model as being clothed in anything but a sarong—in Sarkin Aung Wan, his Vietnamese companion and spiritual guide. He persistently finds himself playing pensive Crosby to wisecracking Hope in the nimble Doc Peret. Peril mixes with pratfall all the way. They and the rest of Cacciato's pursuers barely escape death at the hands of the Shah's dreaded Savak. They miraculously avoid detection as they slip ashore in Greece. They traverse the breadth of Europe looking over their shoulders for pursuers.

In Asia itself, they have already fallen, Alice-in-Wonderland-like, through "A Hole in the Road to Paris" and have wound up seeing "the Light" at the end of General Westmoreland's "Tunnel." The "Light" turns out to be a periscope manned by an aged Vietnamese who is himself a deserter condemned there now for ten years. Berlin, looking through the eyepiece and seeing in imagination, he realizes, Bernie Lynn and Frenchie Tucker in precisely the same moment of his experiential memory of their descent and death, understands for a split second that here the Americans have the chance to see the war from the other side. It is too late. Berlin's platoon commander, a sick, aging relic of American wars, destroys the periscope with six rounds from his M-16. Shortly, they all fall back out of the Hole on the Road to Paris, and, the lesson of perspective lost, continue on their weary, imperiled way.

Such fantasy wordplay is also grounded in mythic memories of other times and other wars and empires as well. One of the roads on the Road to Paris turns out to be the Road to Mandalay. What they ultimately seek, the most recent in a long line of historical belligerents, is the "Peace of Paris." Shortly after they arrive, Berlin finds a *New York Herald-Tribune* carrying news of the death of Eisenhower. On the front page are two pictures, one of Eisenhower as a cadet at West Point, the other of "him riding into Paris, the famous grin, the jeep swamped by happy Frenchmen."

Berlin reads on. So at the end, even as at the beginning, he sees, it remains all of a piece, the world, himself, his America: "The world went on. Old facts warmed over. Nixon was President. In Chicago, a federal grand jury had handed down indictments against eight demonstrators at the Democratic convention the previous summer. He'd missed that—the whole thing had happened while he was in basic training. Tear gas and cops, something like that. No matter: Dagwood still battled Mr. Dithers. What changed? The war went on. 'In an effort to bring the Peace Talks to a higher level of dialogue, the Secretary of Defense has ordered the number of B-52 missions over the North to be dropped from 1,800 to 1,600 a month;' meanwhile, in the South, it was a quiet week, with sporadic and light action confined to the Central Highlands and Delta.

Dust jacket for Tim O'Brien's Going After Cacciato.

Only 204 more dead men. And Ike. Ike was dead and an era had ended."

So it goes in "The Observation Post." Still, if nothing has really changed, a very great deal may have been learned and gained. The mythic cycle may persist, but one may also still elect not to succumb to its grim dominion. Like Yossarian, Berlin elects to persevere. "Insight, vision. What you remember is what you see, and what you see depends on what you remember. A cycle, Doc Peret had said. A cycle that has to be broken. And this requires a fierce concentration on the process itself: focus on the order of things, sort out the flow of events so as to understand how one thing led to another, search for that point at which what happened had been extended into a vision of what might have happened." Persevere. Seek the possibility in the face of all of it still to be able to say the two words with which the novel ends: "Maybe so."

Apropos of the mode of fiction that over the last two decades or so we have come to call "magical realism," an alternate title for *Going After Cacciato* might be "Henry Fleming meets Jorge Luis Borges and/or Gabriel Garcia Marquez and/or Italo Calvino." A comparable gloss on Stephen Wright's *Meditations in Green* might be something like "Johnny Appleseed meets the Fabulous Furry Freak Brothers." It is a drug-addled American pastorale, a whole lurid apocalypse of collective myth. At the same time, this general nightmare, through the shaping and transforming process of imaginative art, ultimately does come, magically, miraculously, by the novel's end, to bear also the generative promise of new creation.

As with *Going After Cacciato, Meditations in Green* quickly turns out to be a novel that is several novels, again each of which can only be read in terms of the others. It begins with one of a series of inter-chapters entitled "Meditations in Green." It then moves to two other narratives, one emanating from a first-person narrator and another from a third-person narrator. The former announces himself early on: "I, your genial narrator, wreathed in a beard of smoke, look into the light and recite strange tales from the war back in the long ago time." It is, as we soon find out, perhaps one of the most familiar of Vietnam litanies: "Dear Mom, Stoned Again." His book is a book of imagination. At the same time, he is also the other narrator as well. There, his book is a book of memory. The two merge and interflow in and out of each other to form, as the inter-chapters remind us, a series of meditations in green, and one ultimately in which the institutional war-green, the olive drab of death and old destruction becomes the fruitional green of promise, the peace-green of life and new creation.

In the book of memory—Vietnam—we are given the whole stoned, lurid spectacle. The setting is in a military intelligence unit that specializes in photo-interpretation and physical torture. The narrator-protagonist, Griffin, and his fellow draftees who work there spend their lives in a near-permanent state of drugged hallucination. The unit commander dies on take-off in a plane most likely sabotaged by a homicidal G.I. Grunts from the Spook House drive around in their jeep with decomposing Viet Cong corpses sitting in the back seat. The corpses are wearing party hats. Weird Wendell, enlisting fellow G.I.'s and base-camp Vietnamese, makes a make-believe war-movie with a cast of thousands. During the last scene the idiotic make-believe comes hideously real. His creative endeavors interrupted by an actual Viet Cong attack on the base camp, Wendell keeps filming. A plane takes a direct hit from a mortar round. He films the pilot being incinerated in his cockpit. He films a U.S. Captain and "a genuine VC in black shorts locked in a lover's clench on the gravel outside the O club and stabbing one another at intervals with long knives." In an ensuing explosion, Wendell himself falls, mangled, mortally wounded. He dies giving camera directions and quoting from a cherished copy of *Atlas Shrugged*. Over in the chapel, a real film has been playing all the while, spectatorless. Griffin wonders how it came out. He does not know that it has self-destructed, as has Wendell's, on the last frame. In fact, as in fantasy, —or, if you will, in fantasy as in fact, —it is Vietnam, the movie: "The screen was blank, a rectangle of burning light."

Back in the world, both initially and for a good part of the novel to come, we are forced to comprehend what seems an equally nightmarish mixup of fact *and* phantasmagoria. Literally and litcrarily, they blend across a whole stoned, echolalic spectrum. Trips, Griffin's war buddy, endlessly stalks after and plots lovingly various forms of demise for a figure he takes to be his old NCO nemesis, Sergeant Antrim. Griffin finds a friend and possible soulmate named Huette Mirandella. Her nickname: Huey. More neo-Shakespearean horseplay shows up in a botanic psychologist named Arden. As in Vietnam, so back in the world, it can only get crazier and crazier. Trips continues his mad quest. Huey pronounces "all this plant jive" thus far but "words, words, words." It is time, she challenges Griffin, to "test how green your thumb really is."

As the novel would have it, the exhortation is, both figuratively and quite literally, the crucial seed planted in the fertile ground of ever-creating consciousness. Out of a nightmare memory of old death comes a generative thrusting forth of imagination into imagings and envisionings of new life.

As in *Going After Cacciato,* the book of fact and the book of imagination in *Meditations in Green* merge at the novel's end, and with comparable result. Outside, nothing much probably does change a very great deal. Given the way the world goes, the operative question may well always be the one recorded at the bottom line of the last of the novel's meditations in green: "Who has a question for Mr. Memory?" In life, this may indeed always be the basic issue. At the same time, however, through the generative power of art, there has now emerged also the possibility that such a going back might become the stuff of a going ahead as well. And that going ahead for Stephen Wright, as with Dylan Thomas, will lie in "the green fuse that drives the flower," the vision of an art that would come to touch on nothing less than the eternal springs of creation. Here may yet reside, one may be bold enough to believe, the answer to what Griffin announces near the end as "Problem of the Age." Question: "how to occupy the diminishing interval between fire and wind and flags." Answer: Imagine. Create. Make it happen. "I think my thumb has always been green," he exclaims. The dream of a new imaginative possibility has come to germination:

> In the spring I'll wander national highways, leather breeches around my legs, pot on my head, sowing seeds from the burlap bag across my shoulder, resting in the afternoon in the shade of a laurel tree. At night I carve peace pipes from old cypress branches. Everywhere the green fuses are burning and look now, snipping rapidly ahead of your leaping eye, the forged blades cutting through the page, the transformation of this printed sheet twisted about a metal stem for your lapel your hat your antenna, a paper emblem of the widow's hope, the doctor's apothecary, the veteran's friend: a modest flower.

In the play of the text, the extending of experiential and cultural memory into new dimensions of imaginative possibility, the veteran's flower newly engenders itself out of the memorial of death into the promise of new life. Flower Power indeed. The veteran's friend, his dream, his creation, his gift to you: peace.

Robert A. Wright on anti-intellectualism in Vietnam fiction:

The recurrent anti-intellectualism of Vietnam fiction, a theme which has somehow gone unnoticed by most scholars of this literature, attests to the seriousness of the breach between literary artists and historians. The trend began as far back as 1955 with Graham Greene's prophetic *The Quiet American,* the first and perhaps finest novel on the American involvement in Indochina. Greene prefaced this work by saying that it was "a story and not a piece of history." The tenor of the work suggests, however, that he knew what he was writing was both historical and prescient. From the unheeded legacy of the French war and Alden Pyle's unwavering faith in the domino theory, to the horror of napalm bombing, Greene was meticulous in recounting the Americans' growing role in the war in this crucial period. Although there is much truth to the recent suggestion that Greene's "commitment to history provides *The Quiet American* with its very powerful critical perspective," it is equally apparent that he viewed intellectuals' treatment of the war with marked, if ambivalent, disdain. . . . Greene writes: "[Pyle] had an enormous respect for what he called serious writers. That term excluded novelists, poets, and dramatists unless they had what he called a contemporary theme, and even then it was better to read the straight stuff. . . . [Pyle] never saw anything he hadn't learned in a lecture hall, and his writers and lecturers made a fool of him."

Robert A. Wright, in " 'History's Heavy Attrition': Literature, Historical Consciousness and the Impact of Vietnam," in Canadian Review of American Studies, *Vol. 17, No. 3, Fall, 1986.*

Marilyn Durham   (essay date 1990)

SOURCE: "Narrative Strategies in Recent Vietnam War Fiction," in *America Rediscovered: Critical Essays on Literature and Film of the Vietnam War,* edited by Owen W. Gilman, Jr. and Lorrie Smith, Garland Publishing, Inc., 1990, pp. 100-08.

[*In the following essay, Durham discusses point-of-view in three novels about Vietnam veterans—Larry Heinemann's* Paco's Story, *Philip Caputo's* Indian Country, *and Bobbie Ann Mason's* In Country.]

Literature of the Vietnam War, since it concerns experiences most readers have not personally lived through, must face an initial obstacle in engaging not only our interest, but more crucially our participation, in constructing its singular reality. As in all literary encounters, communication between writer and audience is a result of their active partnership, but Vietnam may be an especially difficult environment to share in that it is not only excessively foreign to most of us, but it may also be intensely painful. The war is a world which the majority of readers will not have physically entered, and if we are to make sense of it we must do more than read about it; we must become complicit in mentally rebuilding it and imaginatively living in it. One wedge into an unknown universe is narrative point of view.

This strategy is handled variously, and with different results, in three novels which explore the impact of the war on veterans and their families. *Paco's Story* by Larry Heinemann, *Indian Country* by Philip Caputo, and *In Country* by Bobbie Ann Mason all focus on the efforts of a returning soldier to reinsert himself into normal life. We learn much about the war experiences of each veteran, but we learn more about the emotional and physical fallout of Vietnam for themselves and the people they come home to. In each book, narrative strategy calibrates the intensity of our engagement in each story and its truth. Heinemann and Mason isolate one voice to draw us into their narrative structures, and this focus invites our sympathy, identification, and ultimate insight into the speaker's experience. We feel privileged to know the storyteller's world from the inside, to see it from behind his own eyes. Caputo's detached and omniscient narrator, on the other hand, and the author's movement from one character's consciousness to another, separate a reader from that one insistent vision necessary to our complete understanding. This resulting distance between story and reader precludes our full participation in *Indian Country.*

The voice which narrates *Paco's Story* does so with a special authority: he was there with Paco, at Fire Base Harriette, when the company was attacked, leaving Paco the only survivor. The soldier who speaks to us was killed we learn, and Paco's story is told to us by a ghost, surrounded by the other ghosts of Paco's company. We don't know the ghost's name and we don't know who James is (the speaker constantly addresses this friend), but we do know these are men who fought with Paco, who humped the jungle with him, who set the ambushes, and who raped the VC prisoner. The unstinting realism and concreteness of the narrative conjures an image of a ghostly storyteller, surrounded by a circle of intimates, concerned with revealing the truth. This authority and experiential immediacy draws us in; the expression is so vital and heartfelt because so intensely *lived* that we experience its pain and its beauty through a special lens. It is the lens of a friend, of a loving commentator, a wistful voice which sounds its loss while following the survivor. It is in no way what omniscient narration often becomes: a detached Olympian voice, surveying and reporting. This speaker was on that hill when it was attacked, he lost his life while Paco held on to his, and every fact he reports about Paco resonates with the narrator's awareness of his own dissolution.

While this intimacy is encouraged between reader and narrator, however, his haunting revelations assume a cosmic significance, increasing his stature and diminishing our own. While on the one hand we might imagine we were listening in on a terrifying yet eloquent conversation among intimates, at the same time we are reminded that this is a conversation in heaven or hell—somewhere in the after life—in another world where soldiers gather to stand vigil over survivors of firefights. This tells us that the events at Fire Base Harriette were no mere local affair, but form part of a global even universal perspective. This is a broadening of our consciousness. But we simultaneously hear, smell, taste, and feel the moment concretely—which is a way of focusing our consciousness. The narrative strategy in *Paco's Story* makes us feel as if we'd been there—in detail—while at the same time forcing us to locate "there" in a larger meaning. Narrative voice and language work to narrow and expand the center of consciousness, and this rhythm akin to the inhale-exhale of the human body, breathes life into *Paco's Story*.

The narrator begins his account with "the first clean fact" and follows it with a riotous series of facts about life in Vietnam. But the central fact of the massacre, that night when Alpha Company was evaporated, leaving behind only Paco alive, that fact is withheld until the end of the first chapter. After following the man's patter, happily drawn into his rollicking account and even laughing with him, we begin to squirm for we now learn *he* was one of the "disappeared": "When the mother fuckers hit we didn't go *poof* of a piece; rather, we disappeared like sand dunes in a stiff and steady offshore ocean breeze—one goddamned grain at a time." The individual crystals of the imagery point to each soldier's separate consciousness and the speaker makes us feel each shell's impact and each life extinguished. But lest we conclude this was an isolated event with only local import, he ends the chapter implying that, on the contrary, it resounds throughout the universe. The cosmic range of Alpha Company's dissolution is suggested when the ghost says: "Oh, we dissolved all right, everybody but Paco, but our screams burst through the ozone . . . the aurora borealis . . . frequency-perfect out into God's Everlasting Cosmos." And, he adds, "we're pushing up daisies for half a handful of millenia" while that "blood-curdling scream is rattling all over God's ever-loving Creation like a BB in a boxcar, only louder." We know now that this voice ranges over "God's ever-loving Creation" and is uttering a terrible truth. We have reveled in his chattiness throughout the first chapter, then we are brought up short when we realize he speaks from

the dead. You'd better believe that we begin to listen more closely to the rest.

It is striking, given this awful solemnity and power our narrator suddenly seems to assume, that over the course of the story he creates an intimacy among reader, Paco, and storyteller which directly engages our senses and emotions. After Paco's return to the United States, he rides a bus as far as his money will take him and alights at a small town named Boone. And, here, incredibly, beauty enters this story as the narrator lovingly describes the arrival of spring and the birth of new life Paco perceives around him. The small ugly town where Paco bitterly encounters prejudice and rejection is yet suffused with a luminosity and energy which nature cannot withhold even where a blighted humanity has set up shop. Spots of beauty enter the narrative as Paco enters Boone and stands at the edge of a "broad panorama of farmland and woods, greening up, with the warmth of the lowering sun full in his face, the shadows elongated. The bright spring sky is beginning to cloud over, and a clean moist rain smell fills the air."

The ghostly voice pauses often to look about, and these introspective interruptions invite us to share his wonder at nature's loveliness, as, for example, when Paco stops to watch the rainbows in the mist playing below the bridge. As the story progresses, James is not mentioned as often, the attention lavished on the tactile effect of words increases, and this caress of the landscape enables us to live in Paco's pores. We are again in the midst of an ordinary life. Before we meet Paco on the bus and enter the green world with him, the disembodied voice of the narrator dissolving into the cosmos has clothed the story in apocalyptic colors. However, when we travel behind Paco's eyes, we luxuriate in the ripeness of the warm plums a fellow-traveller hugs to herself in sleep.

The sensual awareness intensifies when Paco enters The Texas Lunch and brings the spring sunshine in the door with him:

> And just now that strong, clean, spring-showery
> yellow light streaks straight in the back door,
> a sudden sharp presence that makes everyone
> blind, startled, lighting up everything.

The narrator invites us to take "this whole image" into our hearts and feel its life-force: "Right this moment, James we could stand in the middle of the street at the edge of the shadow of that bright, late-afternoon light . . . ." Although this voice has constantly intruded on the story and reminded us of his ghostly role, we are brought up short at this heightening of the experiential immediacy of the narrative. "We could stand"—he says, it's like we're right there, James, so *feel* it. He urgently brings home Paco's sensations to us, but his intrusion evokes the gathering of the dead Alpha Company. Part of what he wants us to notice is the beauty of young, rain-drenched Betsy Sherburne, her shining locks catching the light as Paco gazes at her. And yes, we savor her loveliness at the same time that we feel the loss of this earthly beauty by the narrator and his cronies. Thus, the concrete sensual enjoyment we gain from the minute observation of this day and our awareness of the narrator's distance from this earthly pleasure reinforces the tragedy of Paco's story. It is a mo-

Larry Heinemann in late August or early September 1967, in Suoi Dau, near the Nui Ba Den.

ment in time which transports us beyond time and keeps our eyes firmly fixed on the ghosts of those who no longer live in our time.

This lifelike narrative strategy controls the force of the impact, and while Heinemann achieves a visceral thrust with his ghostly narrator, Philip Caputo creates a highly gripping but somehow artificial structure which manages to maintain its distance from a reader. The omniscient voice of *Indian Country* relates Chris Starkman's tale with the sweep of a camera's eye rather than the passion of a participant. The point of view changes and throughout the book this move through a series of voices is logical but repels our efforts to identify with any one voice. We listen to an external and all-knowing consciousness, to Chris' thoughts, to the mind of his wife June, and to the ruminations of the old Ojibwa Indian Louis, grandfather to Bonny George St. Germaine who was Chris's best friend. This consistent shift in narrative focus allows the story to be told from many different angles but at the same time has an alienating effect. The change in focus reminds us that a narrative construct is being built and diminishes our ability to absorb the persona of the teller and thus make the story our own. There is no central witness to whom we can attach our emotions. While reading *Indian Country* we are always aware that revelations are orchestrated; we are being shown rather than immersed in experience.

Chris, naturally, is the character whose thoughts we ex-

plore most frequently. We often find ourselves understanding the man as he explains himself, but the insightful—yet sanitized—voice of the omniscient narrator repeatedly intrudes on Chris's speculations to clarify a point or strengthen a moral lesson. For example, Chris wrestles with the injustice of a society in which his Indian friend Bonny George must go to Vietnam while he, a middle-class white kid of the same age, can stay home and go to college. We witness this struggle in Chris's mind and become a part of it when our sympathies are pulled toward Bonny; then the narrator breaks in to comment sonorously on the social and political realities of modern America. We are again reminded that these people are characters in a novel and we are being manipulated to feel something for them. We lose sight of Chris because his protective storyteller who knows all has dwarfed the young man's role.

In a special moment of beauty and communion between Chris and Bonny, with the aurora borealis splashed across the night sky, the narrator breaks the spell by observing:

> they stood as silent and transfixed as the first human beings ever to behold the wonder of creation . . . for what was he and what was Bonny George?

Chris doesn't think to himself "what am *I*," instead we watch Chris staring at the stars and notice a conspicuously philosophic and didactic statement being put into his head. The intrusion closes the moment off—we have not felt it from inside Chris.

Another distancing technique is the series of long retrospective sections which explain how these characters became the people they are. So, for example, we follow Chris into the woods and spend the day with him "cruising timber" for a lumber company, and when he breaks for lunch he suddenly "remembers" in great detail the events between the last time we saw him in the woods with Bonny George and the present walk through the forest.

Our immediate reactions are similarly blunted by the way sentences from the Bible will suddenly enter the narrative when Chris thinks of his father. Lucius Starkman, a pacifist minister who bitterly disapproved of Chris's enlistment, casts his son out of his heart when Chris returns from Vietnam, and much of *Indian Country* concerns Chris's efforts to reconcile himself to the differences between his father and himself. Biblical quotations, always in italicized print, intrude on Chris' stream of consciousness, and although they often fit the context of Chris's thoughts, they don't seem fully integrated, breaking our absorption in the way Chris' mind is presently working. Chris may be hearing his father's voice, but the words have no flesh for us because we don't know the man who spoke them well enough. The device is finally artificial and ineffective, rendering the distance between reader and story palpable.

The most destructively intrusive narrative element is Caputo's handling of the ghosts. As Chris's mental state deteriorates, he retreats into the safe camaraderie he felt in Vietnam among his fellow soldiers, D.J., Hutch and Ramos. He begins by simply talking to them, but as his withdrawal from reality intensifies, he hallucinates the three figures. Their appearance is not revealed "from the inside" however, as they grow before Chris's disturbed mind, but we experience them from a clinical perspective (as if a psychiatrist were observing a patient). The emphasis on insanity reminds us, again, that we are watching Chris twist in the wind rather than understanding the source of the movement. Chris lashes himself with this fear of insanity when he first sees the ghosts, then blacks out. When he awakens, the narrator reports, he had relaxed

> and his mind, working with supernatural speed, grasped the truth in the apparent contradiction that the three men were real and illusory at the same time. He had entered a realm in which distinctions between the imaginary and its opposite did not exist. The instantaneousness with which he came to this understanding astonished him.

The narrator explains that Chris had grasped this truth rather than showing Chris's mind moving toward it. The "instantaneousness" is indeed astonishing because the reader has not been made to see how it happened, and this explanatory mode generated by the intrusive narrator lessens the impact of the ghosts' appearance and conventionalizes their role in the narrative.

Bobbie Ann Mason makes us feel the impact of the war by firmly centering her narrative perspective in the awakening consciousness of Samantha Hughes, aged 17. *In Country* differs from *Paco's Story* and *Indian Country* in that the focal character is not a returning soldier, but the daughter of a soldier killed in Vietnam before she was born. The story reveals Sam's discovery, through his letters and journals and her own "growing up," of the father she never knew and the war which killed him. Living in Sam's mind allows us to participate in her learning process and forces us to recognize our own difficulties in sorting out Vietnam. She is no soldier and neither are most of us; thus, her move toward insight replicates our own epistemological journey, and her personal connection with the war deepens our emotional response. Mason guides Sam, and us, through the paces logically by filtering all input through Sam's eyes and finally through her heart. When the book ends with Sam's visit to the Vietnam War memorial in Washington, we feel that each step on the road to this climactic encounter has been earned by both Sam and reader.

In the beginning of the story we find Sam living with her uncle Emmett, another Vietnam veteran, whose behavior frightens her because she can't understand the source of his conflicts—the war. One effect she becomes fairly sure of, however, is his poor health: the skin rash, headaches and digestive problems she attributes to his exposure to Agent Orange. We follow her efforts to draw Emmett out on his war experiences and her increasing involvement with his vet friends, all of whom exhibit permanent scars from the war. As she grows closer to Emmett and his friends, her reflections on the world are colored by her knowledge of what happened to these men in Vietnam and what continues to happen to them and their families "back in the world."

Mason collects Sam's conclusions in one short scene when she shows us how Sam's stream of consciousness is continually invaded by the war. The veterans organize a dance to benefit the son of Buddy Mangrum, a child recently hospitalized due to complications arising from his father's contamination by Agent Orange. Sam's thoughts are these as she sits in the darkened gymnasium:

> The entwined red and white and blue streamers flowed in the breeze from the air conditioner. Buddy Mangrum's kid's intestines were twisted like that.

Sam's world has been darkened by realizing the impact of the war on soldiers and their families, and because we are close companions of her mind, we share her insights. We have no need for instruction because we have collected the same data due to Mason's narrative strategy.

Sitting and watching the vets at the dance, Sam thinks of a party she decided not to attend and to the present she never bought.

> You could work hard wrapping a package and buy some pretty paper and a nice ribbon and a name tag, but the person would just rip it all up to see what was inside. Packaging was supposed to deceive, Sam thought, but it never did.

One kind of packaging reminds her of another sort and she muses, "Her father came back from the war in a plastic bag. Attractive and efficient. A good disguise." The shadows in the gymnasium are unsettling because "in the corners it was dark, like a foxhole where an infantryman would lie crouched for the night, under his poncho, spread above." Sam vividly imagines the nocturnal scramblings of jungle creatures, frequently illuminated by "the tracers beaming across the sky, identifying the crisscross path of a distant firefight. The strobe light was like that. The pain in Emmett's head." She moves from the gym to Vietnam, then back again as she collides with the fallout from that jungle experience: her uncle's psychological scars.

Sam's thoughts are impinged upon by her new knowledge about her father, and the transitions between ideas seem logical, almost organic. The lessons we draw maintain the narrative integrity and avoid the artificial imposition we felt occasionally in *Indian Country.* Mason's method is a gentler entangling of reader in the narrative web than Heinemann's shocking entrapment of the reader with his ghostly scream. Both books, though, involve us in an intimate exploration of the truth.

We share Sam's awareness of at least one painful truth: the sheer waste of human lives, among those killed in Vietnam and among those who returned. She feels the hurt most deeply due to her desire for Tom, a veteran whose memories prevent him from making love to Sam. His impotence brings home the war to Sam:

> The sadness of his affliction hit her then like a truck. She thought of all the lives wasted by the war. She wanted to cry, but then she wanted to yell and scream and kick. She could imagine fighting, but only against the war. All the boys getting killed, on both sides. And boys getting mutilated. And then not being allowed to grow up. That was it—they didn't get to grow up and become regular people.

Sam has aged considerably throughout *In Country,* and it is our participation in her growing up which renders the cut-off of young lives even more poignant, and at the same time, more tangible. College students identify with Sam and the meaning of Vietnam is brought home to them, with a special urgency, it seems, because Mason's narrative strategy invites them into Sam's consciousness.

In *Walking Point: American Narratives of Vietnam,* Thomas Myers comments on the importance of this collusion between writer and reader:

> . . . there is in even the most powerful writing something that language cannot reach or explicate, an experience that words point toward but that only the reader's own creative energies can begin to trace.

The aesthetic rendering of experience which *Paco's Story* and *In Country* employ makes the most of these "creative energies." Our partnerships with these authors result in concrete connections with the narrative universe of Heinemann and Mason, while Caputo's *Indian Country* remains, at least for this reader, largely unknown territory.

Jonathan Mirsky   (review date 21 September 1995)

SOURCE: "No Trumpets, No Drums," in *The New York Review of Books,* Vol. XLII, No. 14, September 21, 1995, pp. 58-61.

[*In the review below, Mirsky remarks on three novels by Vietnamese writers about the Vietnam war.*]

Reading these novels makes one raise a long-neglected question: How did the North Vietnamese win the war? If Robert McNamara has read them he must be even more baffled; he says in his recent memoir that he realized almost from the beginning that few Americans, including himself, knew much about the Vietnamese. His critics have condemned him for this, noting how just when the war started the White House and State Department scorned journalists like Bernard Fall and Jean Lacouture, who had come to know the country during the French War, or academic specialists like George Kahin and David Marr, who had studied Vietnamese nationalism. Nor did the military listen to its own experts, like Colonel David Hackworth or John Vann, who had fought the North Vietnamese and warned that unless the Americans adopted the tactics and perhaps the strategy of their enemy they would lose the war.

Dean Rusk admitted he had underestimated what he called the enemy's "tenacity"—they endured the equivalent of ten million American dead, told his son—but he insisted that the cause had been just. North Vietnam's General Giap, in his own writings and in interviews with foreigners, including the American journalist Morley Safer, spoke of his soldiers' enormous sacrifices. Asked if these bothered him, Giap literally brushed the question aside as if he were brushing away a fly. Others on the American side, such as General Westmoreland, continue to insist that all the Americans needed was the will to win and no betrayals back home.

Maybe McNamara was right. The novels under review [Bao Ninh's *The Sorrow of War: A Novel of North Vietnam* and Duong Thu Huong's *Novel Without a Name* and *Paradise of the Blind*] deepen the mystery of how the Vietnamese stuck it out and won. Here is a song North Vietnamese soldiers were singing in 1974, when the war was nearly over, which goes:

> Oh, this is war without end,
> War without end.
> Tomorrow or today,
> Today or tomorrow.
> Tell me my fate,
> When will I die.

That same year, Bao Ninh, the soldier-author of *The Sorrow of War,* wrote, "Victory after victory, withdrawal after withdrawal. The path of war seemed endless, desperate and leading nowhere. . . . the soldiers waited in fear, hoping they would not be ordered in as support forces, to hurl themselves into the arena to almost certain death."

In the late eighteenth century, the official history of the Chinese Emperor Qianlong described the Vietnamese as an "unreliable people," always keen to fight invaders. In 1874, Paulin Vial, a French observer of the colonial war, described bands of Vietnamese appearing as if from no-where to attack local officials and suddenly disappearing.

Understanding the tenacious character of the Vietnamese remains just as elusive as ever. I became aware of this again this past May when I talked to Hong Kong officials in charge of what they call "the orderly repatriation" of the over 20,000 Vietnamese boat people, of the original 40,000, who are still in the colony's detention camps. The repatriations are anything but orderly. In April 1994 those to be flown back to Hanoi resisted so vigorously that more than 200 of them were gassed or beaten badly enough to require hospital care—the authorities admitted this only after a local newspaper published the extent of the inju-ries—and ever since it has been usual for the security men and women to carry some of the repatriated Vietnamese kicking and shouting onto the planes. Not long ago when the plane landed in Hanoi the passengers resisted so hard that the Vietnamese authorities nearly refused to accept them.

On May 20 and 21, 1995, well over 2,000 Hong Kong po-lice and Correctional Services officers entered the White-head Detention Centre to move 1,500 Vietnamese, mostly women and children, to another center before flying them to Hanoi. They suddenly found themselves attacked by 6,000 inmates, many from other, supposedly sealed-off sections of the camp, who had cut wires and burrowed under fences and were armed with homemade spears and clubs. They injured over 130 officers. The Vietnamese were subjected to more than 3,000 rounds of gas; the repa-triation efforts had to be called off for the night and began again the next morning.

The inmates' resistance was blamed on their knowing that the American Congress was considering legislation to per-mit more boat people to enter the US. The deputy secre-tary for security in Hong Kong said the Congress was "raising false hopes." He was asked repeatedly how the Vietnamese had made the weapons or cut the wires or or-ganized their forces in a well-supervised and patrolled camp. He said he didn't know.

I suggested to the deputy secretary that after many years of supervising the Vietnamese and repeated encounters with their resistance, the government seemed to know very little about them. His briefing reminded me, I said, of the Saigon briefings by the Americans during the war, called the "Five o'Clock Follies," in which the briefers confessed incredulity that yet another of their well-planned operations had failed. When I asked him if he or his colleagues had bothered to read anything about the Vietnamese and their surprising capacity to keep resisting and to be what Qianlong's historian had called "unreli-able," the deputy secretary told me he had no time for such questions.

We do not get much closer to the answer in these books. Instead what we find is the fear, desperation, disillusion, and comradeship that one often meets among combat sol-diers, together with the corruption and hypocrisy among the commanders and officials back home that are equally familiar.

The Sorrow of War is the best-known of the recent novels from Hanoi about the war, and the author, Bao Ninh, has every reason to have written bitterly about it. In 1967 he was one of the five hundred soldiers of the Glorious 27th Youth Brigade, of whom ten survived the war. This is his first novel and he has explained in interviews with foreign-ers that although the book has sold well in Vietnam, he has had an uneasy relationship with the authorities be-cause of it.

No wonder: much of the book is about the grim experi-ences of Kien, an infantry officer who in 1975 goes back to the battlefield to find and bury the dead. We also learn about his growing up in Hanoi and then, after the war, his attempts to write a novel about what he has seen. The parts about his difficulties as a writer become tedious, but the rest of the book has considerable imaginative power.

This is particularly striking when we read of Kien's expe-riences on B3 battlefield in the Central Highlands as his Missing in Action Remains-Gathering Team enters the Jungle of Screaming Souls. Kien had been there before. "It was here at the end of the dry season of 1969, that his 27th Battalion was surrounded and almost totally wiped out. Ten men survived from the Lost Battalion after fierce, horrible, barbarous fighting." The men were sprayed with napalm and clustered together terrified. Some went mad; others were blown to bits or were shot one by one from helicopters. The frantic battalion commander blew his brains out in front of Kien, after yelling, "Better to die than surrender, my brothers! Better to die!"

Western readers will then find themselves in a Vietnamese spirit world that is probably wholly unfamiliar to them. The destroyed battalion, Bao writes, was never mentioned again, "though numerous souls of ghosts and devils were born in that deadly defeat . . . refusing to depart for the Other World." Sobbing and whispering filled the nights in what came to be called the Jungle of Screaming Souls. The burial group—secretly—built an altar and burned incense. Bitterly, Kien remembers the propaganda of the time: "We won, the enemy lost. The enemy will surely lose. The North had a good harvest, a bumper harvest. The people will rise up and welcome you. Those who don't just lack awareness."

The soldiers were happy only when away from the front, playing cards, talking about sex, and painting mustaches on one another with lampblack. But at any minute a card player could be called away and "burned alive in a T54 tank, his body turned to ash. No grave or tomb for them to throw the cards onto." Desertions were common, "as though soldiers were being vomited out, emptying the in-sides of whole platoons." The soldiers "had created an al-most invincible fighting force because of their peasant na-ture, by volunteering to sacrifice their lives. They had sim-ple, gentle, ethical outlooks on life. . . . yet they never had a say in deciding the course of the war."

Even the capture of Saigon, a brief moment of exhilaration for Kien, was marked by his comrades with drunkenness, looting, destruction. The victorious troops enjoyed "their greatest prize: sleep."

Then comes an episode that for most American readers will seem both unexpected and familiar. When the soldiers returned to Hanoi after their victory, most of them had been years in the field; the trip home was the happiest moment of their years in the army. But they immediately found

> a common emotion of bitterness. There had been no trumpets for the victorious soldiers, no drums, no music. That might have been tolerated, but not the disrespect shown them. The general population just didn't care about them. Nor did their own authorities.

An army driver harangues Kien. The dead, he said, had died for a corrupt society. "This kind of peace? In this kind of peace it seems people have unmasked themselves and revealed their true, horrible selves. So much blood, so many lives sacrificed—for what?" In addition to the known dead, there are 300,000 North Vietnamese MIAs, in contrast with the famous 2,000 still-missing Americans.

The returned soldiers were exhorted to avoid reconciliation with the South. This we have read before, in the memoirs of former NLF leaders like Truong Nhu Tang, author of *Journal of a Vietcong,* who described how their part in the war was ignored. The northern soldiers were warned, writes Bao Ninh, "to guard against the idea of the South having fought valiantly or been meritorious in any way." So much for the assurances to antiwar Americans from the North Vietnamese during the war that the Southern struggle was simply being aided by the North, and that a regime based on a southern coalition headed by the Vietcong would take over.

In fact, the only idyllic moment in *The Sorrow of War* takes place in the South. In the midst of terrible fighting, Kien's unit stumbles into a remote coffee plantation in the Central Highlands, a pretty place with a house on stilts surrounded by flowers. The soldiers are dirty and sweaty, and are offered a meal and coffee by the owner and his wife, Northerners who had come south.

The owner tells them, "We just live a simple life, growing coffee, sugarcane, and flowers. . . . Thanks to Heaven, thanks to the land and the trees and nature, and thanks to our hands . . . we are self-sufficient. We don't need help from any government. . . . You are Communists. . . . You're human too. You want peace and a calm life, families of your own."

When the soldiers leave, enchanted, one of them who had studied economic planning before the war bursts out, "That's the way to live! What a peaceful, happy oasis. My lecturers with all their Marxist theories will pour in and ruin all this if we win. I'm horrified to think of what will happen to that couple. They'll soon learn what the new political order means."

Duong Thu Huong's *Novel Without a Name* also begins in a terrible place ridden with spirits: the Gorge of Lost Souls. In both books the soldiers kill and eat an orangutan as if carrying out a rite. In Bao's book, it looks "like a fat woman with ulcerous skin, the eyes, half-white, half-grey, still rolling." In *Novel Without a Name* the creature is minced into salad and boiled into soup; its hands look like a child's, and taste, or so Duong imagines, like human flesh.

Like Bao Ninh, Duong Thu Huong spent seven years at the front in a Communist Youth Brigade; she is one of three survivors of a unit of forty men and women. Her novels, once popular, are now difficult to obtain in Hanoi. In recent years she has spent months in prison for sending "state secrets" abroad, and has been expelled from the Party.

Her central character is platoon leader Quan, who has been in the field for ten years and spends a brief home leave deep in disillusion. When Quan and his friends went off to war, "drunk on our youth, . . . marching toward a glorious future," the mothers in his village wept. Vietnam had been chosen by History, the young recruits imagined, and would become humanity's paradise when the war ended. "The deeper we plunged into the war, the more the memory of that first day haunted us. The more we were tortured by the consciousness of appalling indifference . . . We had renounced everything for glory. It was this guilt that bound us to one another." Ten years later he admits to himself, "I had been defeated from the beginning . . . I had never really committed myself to war."

It is common in the West to ascribe the stubbornness of the Vietnamese, their ability to just keep coming, to their long history of opposing foreign invaders, beginning with the elephant-riding Truong sisters, who fought the Han armies almost two thousand years ago. This is indeed a long tradition, and some historians note that nationalism was present in Vietnam before it appeared anywhere else. But a cynical comrade of Quan's looks at past heroes differently:

> We country folk have gagged ourselves, our stomachs and our mouths, even our penises. But when it comes to the generals, they know how to take advantage of a situation. Wherever they go . . . they make sure they have plenty of women. In the old days they had concubines; now they call them "mission comrades." . . . For so long, it's just been misery, suffering, and more suffering. How many have died since the great De Tham, Phan, and Nguyen Thai Hoc— how many lives were sacrificed to gain independence? The colonialists had only just left Vietnamese soil and these little yellow despots already had a foothold.

In Hanoi on leave, Quan listens to two members of the official elite chatting on a train. One, a highly placed intellectual, describes real power: "All you need to do is mount a podium perched above a sea of rippling banners. Bayonets sparkling around you. Cannons booming. Now that's the ultimate gratification: the gratification of power. Money. Love."

His companion is shocked at this cynicism. The intellectual goes on: " 'We demolished the temples and emptied the pagodas so we could hang up portraits of Marx, enthrone a new divinity for the masses. . . . But just for a laugh, do you know what kind of a man Karl Marx was in real life? Well, he was a debauched little dwarf. . . .' The two men doubled over laughing."

Confronted by a military officer who accuses them of defaming Marx, they show him their identity cards and send him away. The intellectual winks at his companion: "Well? Did you see that? A nation of imbeciles. They need a religion to guide them and a whip to educate them."

In Duong Thu Huong's novel we find hints of how the experienced North Vietnamese soldiers, whose time in the field—until they were killed—greatly exceeded their enemy's, managed to win. Quan remembers that in the jungle, as the opposing forces crept near each other, "We found one another by smell . . . we opened fire like madmen . . . toward the place where the wind carried a foreign scent, the smell of the enemy." Equally revealing are the stories of fatal errors. The previous year a North Vietnamese unit had been detected "because instead of pissing into the bushes one guy had done it into a wild-flower that camouflaged an American sensor." In his book on soldiering, *About Face: The Odyssey of an American Warrior,* Colonel David H. Hackworth writes that he ordered his soldiers in Vietnam not to smoke or to use after-shave, thus preventing telltale smells from giving the enemy an advantage. But Quan also speaks more than once of "equilibrium in extermination . . . the supreme art of war. One of ours for seven of theirs." This is puzzling when we consider who actually lost more men. After a particularly bloody engagement, when his unit took heavy losses, Quan says, "We knew from experience that we had to redress the balance . . . Annihilation had to be evenly distributed. This insane thirst had taken hold of everyone without exception."

Duong Thu Huong's most famous novel, *Paradise of the Blind,* was published in Hanoi in 1988. Set in the Soviet Union and Vietnam in the Eighties, its central character, Hang, is a "guest worker" in a Russian factory, where she works to support her mother, a Hanoi street peddler, who has sacrificed her health and most of her money to advance her brother's career. He is now a corrupt bureaucrat. The author has said in interviews that the man is modeled on a well-known official, and she hopes he has read her book.

Although Ms. Duong describes herself as a writer of the second rank, hers is the best Vietnamese novel I've read, mainly because of its portrait of the heroine's Aunt Tam. Just as Hang's mother adores her brother simply because he is the family's last male, Aunt Tam worships her niece because she carries her dead father's blood. When they first meet, "Her wizened face, which ordinarily must have been quite severe, was ecstatic, reverent. 'She's a drop of his blood. My niece,' she murmured."

Both Hang's mother and her aunt show their reverence for their male relatives with food, which is meticulously described. Aunt Tam makes little Hang a meal. "It was a feast worthy of a Tet banquet: steamed chicken, fried chicken, pork pâté, cinnamon pâté, spring rolls seasoned with rice powder, spicy cold salads, asparagus, vermicelli, and sautéed side dishes."

Hang stares at her aunt's feet. "Horrible deep, ugly furrows separated the soles of her feet into flaky layers. . . . At the same time, they were dainty feet, thin and elegant. Rich now, she could afford to wear imported plastic san-

dals from Thailand, a luxury in this village. Still, they could never hide her past."

Aunt Tam is immensely strong. She "carried two mahogany stools. I saw the muscles and veins in her arms ripple. But she walked down the steps slowly, gingerly; the feet of the two stools didn't even brush the ground until she placed them in the center of the courtyard. Few men could have matched her strength."

The mother and the aunt had been victims of the Communist land reform in the late Fifties, which had "ripped through the village like a squall, devastating fields and rice paddies, sowing only chaos and misery in its wake." For the victims, "All it took was one malicious remark to push them over the edge, to catapult them from the ranks of the innocent spectators into the pit of the accused. They knew that they were being stalked, that at any moment they could meet with humiliation, sorrow, even death." The villagers whom the Party, in this case represented by Hang's corrupt uncle, select to carry out this appalling campaign—which was eventually repudiated—are drawn from among the most debased and selfish local people. All they care about is getting ahead. The uncle warns Hang's mother: "If you continue to mix with these landowners, they will denounce me to my superiors. My authority and my honor will be ruined."

Hang watches everything closely, not just her aunt's feet and muscles. She describes how the villagers plunge their hands into the paddy mud to test its temperature; one crack of thunder and they know they have to rush to shore up the dikes. "Devotion like this is impossible to explain. No matter, for it was this love that assured the survival of an entire way of life." But she knows how difficult and hopeless the peasant's world can seem. "Everywhere, an indescribable backwardness hung in the air, immaterial yet terrifyingly present: It would be like this for eternity. . . . cold, stubborn, a sluggish, liquid sweetness escaping all control, ready at any moment to drown those unable to rise to its surface."

And always, as in *The Sorrow of War* and *Novel Without a Name,* we are told of the corruption of the Party. Hang's shameless uncle comes to Moscow on an official junket, which he uses for stockpiling goods to sell when he returns to Hanoi. A Vietnamese student condemns the uncle: "Where does it come from, your need to humiliate us. In the name of what? . . . You say our dances are decadent. But haven't you done some dancing yourself? Invisible dances, infinitely more decadent. . . . It's the dance of the overlords. . . ." He explains such petty officials to Hang: "Little Sister, you must understand, even if it hurts. Your uncle is like a lot of people I've known. . . . They are their own tragedy. Ours, as well."

The officials in Hong Kong who claim the boat people in the local camps are simply "economic migrants" who must be forcibly returned to Vietnam should read Duong Thu Huong's *Paradise of the Blind,* which describes life only a few years ago. The author has been banned and imprisoned for writing of her own sadness. In *Paradise of the Blind,* Hang says, "I saw my village, this cesspool of ambition, all the laughter and tears that had drowned in these bamboo groves." She recalls a woman whose house was seized by a greedy local official and who then hacked him to death and hanged herself. "In the middle of a blazing inferno, I saw it again: the vision of a woman twisting from the end of a rope."

The war has long since ended. It is time, Hang decides, to take leave of it and much else in Vietnam, if only in fantasy. "I can't squander my life tending these faded flowers, these shadows, the legacy of past crimes. . . . I sat down . . . and dreamed of different worlds, of the cool shade of a university auditorium, of a distant port where a plane could land and take off. . . ."

The "tenacity" of the Vietnamese is to be found not only in stories of war but in Duong Thu Huong's persistence, under threat of prison, in writing as she does here. Perhaps it is through the work of writers and poets that we will best understand the qualities of the Vietnamese. The feelings Duong describes are close to those of the North Vietnamese soldier who wrote the following poem [published in *Poems from Captured Documents,* edited and translated by Thanh T. Nguyen and Bruce Weigl, 1994], which was found by the American army in 1967. It seems likely that the man had been either killed, wounded, or captured.

> Today, first day of the year
> I write to celebrate the Spring
> I'm already weary of.
> In the New Year I may have luck
> But much unhappiness as well.
> I have no choice but to live this new year.
> Older but still trapped in this life.
> I'm tired of you, new year, and you, spring.

FILM AND DRAMA

David E. Whillock   (essay date 1988)

SOURCE: "Defining the Fictive American Vietnam War Film: In Search of a Genre," in *Literature/Film Quarterly,* Vol. 16, No. 4, 1988, pp. 244-50.

[*In the following essay, Whillock analyzes themes and images in Vietnam combat films and points out the disparities between these films and World War II combat films.*]

> What should the Vietnam War look like on film? What were the motifs, visual, and thematic, that would emerge as dominant, that would reappear in film after film—with greater or lesser variations—to evolve into a codified 'Vietnam style'?
>
> Gilbert Adair *Vietnam on Film*

The "visual style" that Adair alludes to is the concept of genre and its application to films about Vietnam. One of the major academic pursuits in critical discourse is the application of categories to certain "like" narratives in literature and cinema studies. This "pursuit" has become a major source for critical discourse in film. However, while such discourse should be predicated upon precise stan-

dardization, terms such as genre are often used with idiosyncratic designation.

Three areas that deserve attention when attempting to apply a precise standardization to films about the Vietnam war are found in three general questions: what is the technical term "genre" and how is it applied to critical concerns in film study; is there a commonality of these films that would categorize them into groups for comparison and contrast; and what, if anything, is the standardization that is constant throughout the categories developed. A discussion of the term "genre" and its specific application to film studies will be beneficial in answering the question: Is there a Vietnam war film genre?

Historically, the term genre was borrowed from literary criticism; etymologically, it came from Latin/French roots related to the concept of "kind" or "type". The Greeks used the term to describe the three main topics of poetry—lyric, epic, and drama—each represented a distinct form of presentation. Through transformations of such literary critics as Northrop Frye, the term evolved to distinguish between the novel, short story, essay and possibly film. A more modern application is found in Thrall and Hibbard's classic *Handbook to Literature* which contends that "Genre classification implies that there are groups of formal or technical characteristics existing among works of the same kind regardless of time or place of composition, author, or subject matter. . . ." These definitions underscore the idea of "type." Critically there is a distinction between certain kinds of feature films as compared to other feature films (i.e. a western from a detective story) but these definitions do not focus on the precise standardization that would separate one narrative structure from another.

The distinction between the use of genre in literary criticism and film criticism is found in the writings of film critics John Cawelti, Stanley Solomon, and Stuart Kaminsky. Kaminsky in *American Film Genres* presents an argument for this distinction. He writes that the "usage [of the term] will result in a change of meaning for the word genre, particularly when it is applied to film analysis." Instead of the literary distinction between genres as the form of presentation (novel, short story, essay or radio and television play), a film genre will be distinct by a film's motifs and styles within the presentation (such as comedy, western, detective, science fiction and war films). Thus, for a film genre, subject matter is a valued critical dimension. However, the distinction cannot be based on a single motif or style, but a series of motifs and styles which are similar in all members of the classification. These styles will give a body of "like" films structure and design that will be immediately recognized as a western genre or, in this discussion, a war-film genre.

In order to adapt the use of generic criticism to film, the basis of determining what a film genre is should be clarified. Kaminsky suggests that genres in film criticism must be rigorously defined.

> Genre in film, if it is to have meaning, must have a limited scope, a limited definition. These films must have clearly defined constants so that the

traditions and forms within them can be clearly seen and not diluted into abstractions.

A soap commercial that has a man with a horse and a cowboy hat located in a desert is not necessarily a western. As Kaminsky points out, there has to be a strict distinction, a set of operating elements, to make the film or the commercial a western. The basic implication to this definition is that there needs to be a corpus or body of films that include enough of the "defined constants" to constitute a genre. Thus, a film genre will have recurring motifs that are alike. For the film critic, these motifs are a combination of two distinct elements: icon and convention.

An icon is defined by Solomon [in *Beyond Formula,* 1976] as a "visual symbol used from film-to-film." These are physical symbols that represent something else, a deeper reality. For example, a visual symbol (icon), such as the badge in the Western, stands for something deeper than its surface image: the badge stands for law and order in an otherwise wild and uncivilized western town. Thus, each distinct genre will have its own specific recurring icons which share meanings.

The second element found in a generic film is the convention. [In *The Six Gun Mystique,* 1971] Cawelti defines the conventions as ". . . elements which are known to both the creator and his audience before hand—they consist of things like favorite plots, stereotyped characters, accepted ideas, commonly known metaphors and other linguistic devices, etc." Among the most common conventions are familiar themes, characters, and narrative structure.

To consider a body of works as a constituted genre all three critics agree that there have to be enough elements of what Kaminsky calls "defined constants." These elements are the recurring icons and conventions (motifs and themes) from film-to-film. By investigating these recurring icons and conventions, the question of what a Vietnam war film should "look like" can be considered.

There are two opposing arguments about the study of Vietnam war films that the critic must confront before a critical analysis is attempted. The arguments are, first, that there are too few Vietnam movies to warrant study; and second, there are too many indistinct films about the Vietnam war to warrant study. This is because nearly every American feature film made during the conflict, specifically in the decade of 1965-1975, directly or indirectly reflects some aspects of the war's political make-up and therefore could be relevant to the Vietnam war. As our purpose is to discuss the Vietnam war film and its possible generic form, a discussion of these opposing arguments might prove fruitful in focusing the discussion.

The first argument that there are too few films to study as a corpus of work has some (albeit little) credence if the critic focuses the study on the films that specifically confront the war. These few films would place their characters and story development in the physical surrounding of Vietnam during the conflict. What is of particular interest about these specific films is that there was only a single film made during the actual conflict. This film, *The Green Berets* (1968), is one of nine that were eventually released for an American audience. The other seven include *The*

Boys of Company C (1977), *Go Tell the Spartans* (1978), *Apocalypse Now* (1979), *The Killing Fields* (1983), *Purple Hearts* (1984), *Platoon* (1986), *Full Metal Jacket* (1987), and *Hamburger Hill* (1987).

Why so few? In part, this may be due to the lack of coherent means of dealing with the war. One speculation worth considering is articulated by Julian Smith in his book *Looking Away: Hollywood and Vietnam.* He says that "for lack of a formula, a way to handle the war, Hollywood turned elsewhere." In essence Hollywood turned away from movies about the direct confrontation of the war towards the effects of the war at home. This "lack of formula" can possibly be traced back to the age old literary problem of "closure." While formulas of films about other wars have been successful, films about the Vietnam war leave the viewer with a sense of unfinished business, that is, the feeling that loose ends are not tied and the prospect of possible closure fades with the end credits.

Lawrence Suid in his dissertation "The Film Industry and the Vietnam War" [Case Reserve University, 1980] discusses another possible cause of the lack of Vietnam war films:

> Not only have few films been made that deal with Vietnam in any way, but even fewer have portrayed combat in any significant way. As much as anything, this reflects the nature of the war itself. In other American wars of the 20th century, there was a clearly defined homefront and clearly defined war zone. Perhaps in some way reflecting the lack of battle lines in Vietnam itself, the combat war seems tightly interwoven with the nation's response to it at home.

The second reason, a "lack of distinction" between the war fronts, leads us into the argument that there are too many films about the war and that these films are very indistinct: they overlap all problems, that are portrayed through violence at home, of the Vietnam war.

This argument, concerning the inclusion of films which reflect the war on American society as a whole, is indeed a strong consideration when discussing the possibility of a Vietnam war film genre. Siegfried Kracaur in *From Caligari to Hitler* underscores the ability of a film reflecting a society's mass desires when he writes: "The films of a nation reflect its mentality in a more direct way than any other media." The cinema becomes a crucial index to the desires and concerns of a society's mass population. The Vietnam war films are no exception. They reflect the seemingly indistinguishable concerns of Vietnam as a combat zone, the returning vet, the furor over the involvement in Southeast Asia, and the growing violence that threatens to shred the very fiber of American freedom and ideology. Yet, while every film produced during that time underscores a possible ideology or apology, there are four distinct categories that become evident when investigating films with a common theme of the Vietnam Era. They include: The Vietnam Veteran; the effects of the war at home; the revenge film (POW film), and the combat film. A closer discussion of each category focuses on the distinctions more clearly.

The films investigating the Vietnam veteran, and his struggle in the reintegration into society is the theme of many Vietnam films. The veteran has been chosen through society's disapproval of combat films to tell us what the war is really like. The individual in these films is changed by the war experience and challenged to come back to the folds of society and accept the rules and guidelines that give it existence. However, this unconditional acceptance of routine life does not come easy and only through time and understanding does society and the veteran reach a mutual understanding. Some of the films that represent this thematic category include *Coming Home, The Deer Hunter, Gardens of Stone,* and *Heroes.*

Films that reflect the effects of the war at home are those that use the Vietnam veteran for violence, or the Vietnam war as a catalyst for violence in the United States. The returning veteran in these films is the misunderstood hero or anti-hero. The veteran is asked to conform immediately without any concern for his past experiences in combat or his "chip on the shoulder" attitude about authority. Some of these characters are more patient than others and are slow to anger. However, the veteran will eventually reach his point of no return and begin his violent struggle. Films in this category include *Rolling Thunder, First Blood, Taxi Driver,* and *Billy Jack.* The other type of effects of the war at home is reflected in the anti-culture films of the period. These films include college uprisings and road trips (usually on a motorcycle). These films nearly always include naked bodies and plenty of leather and drugs. Examples of these films include *Easy Rider, Chrome and Hot Leather,* and *The Strawberry Statement.*

The revenge films are another important category of films. They add closure to the Vietnam experience. With their myth-building narratives, these films convey the illusion that the war is understood ten years later and that one man has the ability to succeed in the jungles of Southeast Asia when the combined efforts of the United States military failed to do so. The Vietnam war in these films becomes a simple problem to understand. The war is presented as a catharsis of our national frustration through the individual's ability to completely destroy the enemy in the hero's self-styled mission to save the POW's and restore American pride simultaneously. The viewing American public can now see the war and from the vantage point of a winner, they now can put the Vietnam war in perspective with newer and more successful military ventures both on and off the screen. Select films that underscore this category are *Uncommon Valor, Good Guys Wear Black,* and *Rambo: First Blood Part II.*

At the other end of this same ideological thought is a film that portrays the prisoner of war in a more "realistic" way. This film (to date there is only one) attempts to achieve its Manichean philosophy through the recounting of the POW experience and the atrocities that these men endured by the North Vietnamese, visiting Cuban advisors, and Hollywood celebrities. The film is *Hanoi Hilton.*

The combat film portrays Americans in the midst of the conflict during the years of our Vietnam involvement. These films place their characters for the majority of the film in war-torn Vietnam or Cambodia and the narrative of all of these films takes place during the years of Ameri-

can involvement in the conflict. The combat films include *The Green Berets, The Boys of Company C, Go Tell The Spartans, Apocalypse Now, The Killing Fields, Purple Hearts, Platoon, Full Metal Jacket,* and *Hamburger Hill.*

Though these distinctions may separate the vast number of films of the Vietnam era into categories, the question of genre is still not resolved. By examining the combat films of the Vietnam war in juxtaposition to the generic structure (icons and conventions) found in the combat films of the Second World War, insight into the question of genre may become clearer. Several considerations in this examination include the possibility that the Vietnam war combat film is indeed a distinct genre; the combat films are a subheading in the overall genre of war films; or that these films are neither a distinct generic form nor a subheading of the war film genre.

As discussed earlier, an icon is that physical visual element within like films that recurs and shares a common meaning. In the war film, icons are usually the machinery of war. In the Second World War combat films, the icons would include the .45 automatic, the M-1 carbine, and the American military dress. In comparison, the Vietnam war combat film icons would include the M-16, the Huey-B helicopter, and the more modern version of the American combat military dress. Each of these visual elements represents in some fashion the machinery of the American military versus the military machines of the opposing countries.

In the Vietnam war film specifically, these icons represent the American military omnipotence versus the village culture of the Vietnamese. As presented in the American Vietnam war film, the visual elements underscore the binary opposition between the American modern technological army and the guerrilla warfare of the Vietcong. The icons in these films is a constant visual reminder of the amount of technology used so inefficiently. This point becomes a common innertextual discussion in the combat American Vietnam war film. The ability for technical "overkill" in Vietnam was not enough for an assured victory. This innertext is found specifically in *The Boys of Company C, Apocalypse Now, Platoon,* and *Full Metal Jacket.* While the icons found in the Vietnam war film remain alike, the conventions begin to underline the discrepancies among the separate combat films of the Vietnam war.

Conventions have been defined as "familiar shared images and meanings" which "assert an ongoing continuity of values" [Cawelti]. These "shared images and meanings" consist of the themes and motifs common from film-to-film. Kaminsky, in his discussion of the war film genre, states that there are five conventions that are similar in all war films. These conventions include the mission, the justification for involvement of the war, the development of the symbiotic relationships within the unit to survive, the stark and open landscape, and the elevation of characters above the madness and violence of the war.

In the combat Vietnam war film, this list of conventions does not apply. Based on an analysis of three of these—the justification for involvement of the war, the stark and open landscape, and the elevation of characters above the madness and violence of the war—the argument can be made that there is not at present a Vietnam war genre, or that the Vietnam war film is not a sub-genre of the war film.

The concept of justification that permeates the war films about World War Two does not exist in most of the Vietnam war films. The only film that involves itself with justification is *The Green Berets.* In the last scene, Wayne's Colonel Kirby discusses life and death philosophy with a Vietnamese mascot named Hamchuck. As the "Ballad of the Green Berets" swells in the background, and the sun sets on the ocean with a visual of Wayne and mascot outlined in the foreground, the mascot asks Wayne (Kirby) what will happen to him (the mascot). Wayne gives the mascot the green beret of a fallen comrade (and the mascot's keeper) saying that he will take care of him; after all says Wayne "you are why we're here." How much more justification would anyone want?

By contrast, in *Apocalypse Now* there is an intense monologue by Kurtz to Willard about the ineffectiveness of the American involvement both militarily and politically. For example, he tells of a village that cut the arms off of the children who received shots from the American troops. In most of the films about the Vietnam war, the futility of American involvement is a working convention. The later films about the American involvement in Vietnam are ideologically at the opposite pole in justifying the war. In a sense these later films (from *The Boys of Company C* to *Full Metal Jacket*) are a justification against the war.

While *Apocalypse Now* investigates the futility of the war without considering a mediating factor between the two binary positions, *Platoon* gives an attempt to "heal the wounds" caused by the opposing views. After presenting the two points of view about the war through the characters of Barnes and Elias, the closing monologue by the film's mediator and narrator, Chris Taylor, is an attempt to seal the ideological cracks of the 1970s. After surviving a night time Vietcong attack and a direct hit of napalm on his position by the United States, Taylor (Charlie Sheen) privately debates both sides of the war. Within this discussion he presents himself as a child "born of two fathers" (the two ideological positions) and only by coming to terms with himself will the opposing positions be successfully resolved. Only through self acceptance will the chasm over the war be bridged. While the war is not justified (it is in fact condemned), the direct confrontation between the two points of view are permutated to a closer resolve.

The second convention, the stark and open landscape, also does not exist in the Vietnam film. The Vietnam film takes place in a dense jungle where the enemy is hidden or nonexistent. Indeed, one of the conventions of many Vietnam war films is the lack of visual contact with the enemy. Only his effects are left to be dealt with. Unlike the World War Two film, there are no formal rules in jungle fighting. The differences between the World War Two film and Vietnam in location is best exemplified when comparing *The Sands of Iwo Jima,* with *Apocalypse Now* and *Platoon.* In Iwo Jima the jungles of this Pacific Island are devastated or nonexistent. The symbol of the destruction of war

and the loss of life is expressionistically shown. The location of Iwo Jima is an extension of the clarity for the justification of why we are fighting (all things are clearly visible). Conversely, the Vietnam film is full of beauty and dense jungle. One scene in *Apocalypse Now* views a helicopter thousands of feet from the ground; the jungle is green and lush and perfect for the hidden enemy; the bombed out craters are filled with water and have become lakes in this mixture of Disneyland and hell. In *Platoon,* as the American soldiers move their way through the dense jungle, their view is extremely limited by that lush jungle. In one scene, Taylor nearly walks into a Vietcong bunker complex without seeing it in advance. The jungle becomes a perfect cover for the enemy, and a representation of the "lack of clarity" for the war in Vietnam.

The last convention is the elevation of characters above the madness and violence of war. The World War Two film uses its justification to elevate itself above the madness. After all we are fighting for the just cause of liberty. There is for the war film a passionate cause, justifiable, for the destruction found in the war film.

The Vietnam War film, excluding *The Green Berets,* does not have the same sense to elevate the characters above the madness and insanity of the war. *The Boys of Company C, Go Tell the Spartans, Apocalypse Now, The Killing Fields, Purple Hearts, Platoon,* and *Full Metal Jacket* all portray their characters as conspirators within the "dirty" war. In *Apocalypse Now,* Willard becomes more like the animal he seeks the closer he gets to his prey. The insanity is part of the reason for the war's existence. This insane madness gives the film its theme and its lure. In *Killing Fields* both Schanberg and Pran are witness to on-the-spot executions by the Khmer Rouge and the "mistaken" bombing of a Cambodian village. The sense of insanity of both of these films spirals deeper when the audience witnesses an attack on the village in *The Killing Fields* by Khmer Rouge and the soldiers are drinking bottles of Coca-Cola as they fight. In *Apocalypse Now,* the Chief is killed when his modern assault boat is attacked by hidden natives with archaic spears. In *Full Metal Jacket* the whole premise of the movie is the concept of comic insanity in a war gone mad with no end in sight.

Applying the definitions of icon and convention, there is presently no Vietnam War genre. Using Kaminsky's generic description of the war film, the Vietnam war film is not a sub-genre of the overall war film genre either. Perhaps one of the reasons for this is the problematic resolve to use old cinematic language for new concepts. The producers of *The Green Berets* were interested in gaining support for the war through a tried and true formula. They attempted to present to the American public the Vietnam war wrapped in the language of the Second World War. After the hostile acceptance of the film, Hollywood decided to be less controversial and left the presentation of the combat in the Vietnam war for a future generation. The studios went to the veteran and coming home films to discuss the war in Vietnam.

The next attempt to present the Vietnam war on film developed a new cinematic language. [In an endnote, Whillock states: "This is not to ignore the other important films about the Vietnam era. *The Deer Hunter* and *Coming Home* deserve high regard in the way they presented the effects of the war at home. However, the focus of this writing is on the combat films and the language used in their presentation."] While *The Boys of Company C* and *Go Tell the Spartans* were quick and dirty films that tried to get an advantage from the secrecy and controversy over the long production of *Apocalypse Now,* they remain important because of the form in which they presented their content. No longer were the formulas of the Second World War films attempted in the films about Vietnam. Instead a new approach was taken and built upon throughout the later films. These common themes include the oppositions between the American and Vietcong's methods of war (civilized warfare versus savagery); distinctions between environments in the films (controlled environment versus uncontrolled environment); and character relations (the representation of binary ideological points of view). Despite the presence of common themes and motifs in the later films about combat in the Vietnam war, they are not yet fully formalized as conventions. With the new interest in Vietnam war films, these themes may indeed become the formula for the combat Vietnam war film.

J. W. Fenn   (essay date 1992)

SOURCE: "The Vietnam War: Plays of Initiation," in *Levitating the Pentagon: Evolutions in the American Theatre of the Vietnam War Era,* University of Delaware Press, 1992, pp. 137-67.

[*In the following excerpt, Fenn focuses on David Rabe's* The Basic Training of Pavlo Hummel *(1968) and* Streamers *(1976) as he remarks on themes and structures common to Vietnam War dramas.*]

The significant dramas dealing with the actualities of the Vietnam War were written by playwrights who had firsthand knowledge of the conflict. These authors, of whom few had written previous works for the theatre, undertook to dramatize the ordeal and its consequences for both the combatants and the home community. These writers confronted the fact of war directly and chronicled in dramatic terms its psychological horror. Their plays, which attempted to portray the magnitude of the event and its immediate and long-lasting effects on both the individual and the collective American psyche, best illustrate how the theatre eventually managed to come to terms with Vietnam.

The dramas that deal directly with the War experience, are essentially of three types and are characterized, both thematically and dramatically, by variations on structural principles described by Arnold van Gennep in his *Rites of Passage.* In the plays dealing with the men who served in Vietnam, a tripartite pattern is observable—that of separation, experience, and reintegration. Typically, these plays document the consequences for an individual as he undergoes the transitional stage of induction into the army, the extracultural exposure overseas, and reintegration into the society from which he has been alienated as a consequence of his military training and experience. Major themes of these pieces include the individual's psychological recon-

ditioning as he is indoctrinated into the military order, the trauma of his overseas experience, and the problems associated with reassimilation into a society whose ethics and values, perceptions, and modes of behavior have become alien to him.

A recurring motif associated with the rites-of-passage motif that typifies all of these plays is that there is a failure of myth and ritual to support and sustain the process of transition, which invariably creates problems of adjustment in the men who undergo the ordeal. The novitiates find themselves in an existential void, isolated and alienated, separated by their experience from the old order, but never fully integrated into the new. Man's attempt at gaining or regaining a place in a cultural construct is prevalent in virtually all major plays dealing with Vietnam. Works focusing on the theme of separation rites are represented by David Rabe's *The Basic Training of Pavlo Hummel* (1968) and *Streamers* (1976); those describing rites of experience include H. Wesley Balk's and Ronald J. Glasser's *The Dramatization of 365 Days* (1972), David Berry's *G. R. Point* (1975), and John DiFusco's (et al) *Tracers* (1980). Rites of reintegration are prominent in David Rabe's *Sticks and Bones* (1969), Adrienne Kennedy's *An Evening with Dead Essex* (1973), Tom Cole's *Medal of Honor Rag* (1975), James McClure's *Private Wars* (1979), and Emily Mann's *Still Life* (1980).

The term "passage" in Gennep's *Rites of Passage* is better rendered in English translation as "transition." Van Gennep undertook an analysis of the ceremonies that accompanied an individual's "life crises" and noted that a pattern, or schema, was present. He distinguished three major phases of this schema: separation (*séparation*), transition (*marge*), and incorporation (*agrégation*). In the general pattern of transition from one state of existence to another there are three main phases: the act of separation from the previous environment, instruction and a gradual conditioning as the novitiate is taught the "ground rules" of the new social order, and a process of reintegration into the society in which he will function as a fully-accredited individual. The relation of the individual to his collective group or society is dependent on modes of social intercourse that are established through rites of transition.

In the Vietnam plays of separation the military is depicted as a self-contained social unit, as distinct from the society that it serves as one culture is from another. Draftees undergo rites of initiation that replace the social codes of the civilian order with a new set of behavioral patterns predicated on a different set of requirements for survival. The recruits are effectively integrated into a new social hierarchy through a systematic desymbolization and replacement of the signifiers of their former cultures, and they are assimilated into a new society that has its own distinct terms of reference. The recruit is stripped of his premilitary identity, programmed with new criteria of desirable behavior, and in essence is acculturated to a new social order predicated on a cultural mythology separate and distinct from that of the civilian world.

David Rabe was a war veteran, who, after his tour of duty was over, intended to return to Vietnam as a press correspondent. Yet he admits to extreme difficulty in his attempts at recording his impressions of the battlefield, citing the inability of language to describe them: "In no way could I effect the cannon, the shuddering tent flaps." He notes [in his introduction to *The Basic Training of Pavlo Hummel* and *Sticks and Bones,* 1973] that trying to describe the sensations at the time was similar to attempting to replay "desperate and painful events in your skull while they continued to occur in front of you." In his Vietnam plays Rabe places less emphasis on reconstruction of battlefield scenes, but describes instead the painful psychological transformations undergone by the combat troops who underwent and endured mind-wrenching experiences.

The protagonists of many dramas about Vietnam find themselves in an existential void, isolated and alienated, separated by their experience from the old order, but never fully integrated into the new. Man's attempt at gaining or regaining a place in a cultural construct is prevalent in virtually all major plays dealing with Vietnam.

—J. W. Fenn

Both of David Rabe's "initiation" plays, *The Basic Training of Pavlo Hummel* (1968) and *Streamers* (1976), deal with the process of induction into the military and the irrevocable changes that the men undergo in this process. The set of mythic constructs upon which reality is based is shown to be every bit as arbitrary and unreliable as those of the civilian world. Both plays illustrate the concerns that became so prevalent in the works dealing with the consequences of Vietnam for both the individual and his society: the stress resulting from the social conflict put excruciating and irresistible pressure on the fabric of reality itself. The overwhelmingly dominant themes of the war plays became those of both individual and social disintegration, internecine conflict, psychological fragmentation, alienation, and isolation; and a loss of cultural identity.

In the opening scene of *Hummel,* a grenade, later identified as a "M-twenty-six-A-two fragmentation" type, is thrown into a bordello in which the title character is consorting with a prostitute. The grenade has been thrown by a "Sergeant Wall," with whom "Pavlo," a PFC, has had an altercation concerning rights to the brothel girl, "Yen." The fragmentation of social order implicit in such an act corresponds well—in both a dramatic and thematic sense—to the destructive mechanism of a fragmentation grenade accommodating the physical disintegration of both man and his weapon, and the psychological fractionalization associated with the breakdown of social order. The nature of the weapon and the state of Pavlo's mind create a raw irony as corporeal and psychological disintegration occur simultaneously.

The subsequent action of the play is developed through a series of flashbacks drawn from Pavlo's fragmented consciousness, a disjointed collection of his perceptions that date from his childhood and mark his progress through his army training and war experiences. These disjointed expressionistic flashbacks chronicle the soldier's conditioning as a civilian, his experience as a recruit in basic training, and his life as a front line soldier. Emerging from the dying Pavlo's mind, these flashbacks are orchestrated by a choral figure and alter ego named "Ardell," a Black sergeant who appears immediately after the explosion, and returns periodically during Pavlo's military indoctrination to comment on his situation and to advise him on his course of action.

Ardell orders Pavlo to attention, and the soldier springs from his dying position to answer in ritualized military terminology questions concerning his identity and status. He names the officers of his company, battalion, platoon, and squad by rote, and adds his height, weight, and complexion type. Ardell immediately takes Pavlo to task about the occasion of his death and his failure to avoid being killed by the grenade:

> *Ardell:* You had that thing in your hand, didn't you? What was you thinkin' on you had that thing in your hand?
>
> *Pavlo:* About throwin' it. About a man I saw when I was eight years old who came through the neighbourhood with a softball team called the Demons, and he could do anything with a softball underhand that most big-leaguers could do with a hardball overhand. He was fantastic.

Pavlo's death is subsequently demonstrated to be a consequence of his confusion of cultural realities. In his mind, the grenade has become only a harmless baseball, and instead of disposing of it or taking evasive action as his military training would demand, his response is delayed because of his uncertainty about the cultural construct in which he is functioning. In effect, his out of context "basic training"—his cultural conditioning, has killed him. The "Pavlovian" conditioning process of basic training has overlapped with that of the previous culture and proved to be a source of confusion, inaction, and ultimate destruction.

There are also sexual concerns associated with Pavlo's confusion and uncertainty in his own identity; these problems are directly related to both his civilian and military basic training, and are revealed to be the source of his impotency and his problems in relating to women. Ardell's "You had that thing in your hand, didn't you?" reflects Pavlo's inadequacy in the bordello. In his fight with the sergeant, Pavlo kicked Wall in the groin, and the incapacitated NCO resorted to the use of the grenade. The internecine war has its roots in sexual frustration—a constant source of anxiety associated with the soldiers' reconditioning to new codes of sexual standards and behavior in the cultural construct of military society. A definitive characteristic of Rabe's plays, as well as of many others that treat the War, is the consistent theme of the sexual repression of the American male—the fixation on a somewhat vague and uncertain perception of manhood—and the consequences stemming from this confusion. . . .

The process of basic military training is revealed to be a paradigm of the conditioning mechanism of the larger culture, and the most obvious and significant ramification is the equation of sexual maturity and vitality and the exercise of martial power. Rifle training is continually couched in sexual references:

> This an M-sixteen rifle, this is the best you country got. . . . You got to have feelin' for it, like it a good woman to you. . . . You got to love this rifle, Gen'lmen, like it you pecker and you love to make love [sic].

Sexual passions and the passions of killing are a popular equation in Vietnam War dramas, and also in nonfictional accounts where soldiers have reported experiencing orgasms in the heat of battle.

The theme of sexual repression of the American male provides much of the subtext of *Hummel*. For most of the recruits, initiation into the military is closely related to rites of puberty, and the power inherent in the gun is readily associated with terms of sexual libido. A corporal who has been to Vietnam arouses Pavlo with the observation, "Can of bug spray buys you all the ass you can handle in some places . . . You give 'em a can of bug spray, you can lay their fourteen-year-old daughter." For many men, in fiction as in fact, the first sexual encounter occurs within the context of military experience. Staged concurrently with the sergeant's instruction on the use of the rifle is a brothel scene in which Pavlo embraces Yen. Rabe's stage direction suggests, "*Something of Pavlo's making love to Yen is in his* [the sergeant's] *marching.*"

Pavlo's death in the brothel results from the fragmentation of his lower body and genitals, and the mutilation of the sexual organs is a frequent theme both in the dramas and in nonfictive accounts of battle. This threat, while representing a serious danger under actual war conditions, is closely associated with the subliminal fears of the human male, and a basic concept of Freud's anxiety theory of "castration complex." The mutilation of the sexual organs is also prominent in certain of van Gennep's analyses of rites of passage, and changes in social status, particularly maturity, are often accompanied and demonstrated by such mutilation. In the war dramas, injuries of this kind are imbued with a symbolic significance, since they infer not only the emasculation of the individual, but also the enervation of his culture.

Pavlo is revealed to be a misfit in civilian life, and his problems follow him into the army. Unsuccessful with women in the civilian world, he also has problems with rifle drill:

> You mother rifle. You stupid fucking rifle. Mother! Stupid mother, whatsamatter with you? I'll kill you! Rifle, please. Work for me, do it for me. I know what to do, just do it.

His inability to relate to women is reflected in his lack of coordination in handling his rifle. Threatening, then cajoling, his pleas to his rifle assume the attributes of an adolescent's verbal foreplay. He brags to his fellow recruits about an affair that he had with a girl before joining the army, but it is unclear whether the story is contrived in order to enhance his manhood in his comrade's eyes, or whether it actually represents his civilian initiation into manhood.

In an effort to belong, to become one of the group, Pavlo invents stories calculated to elicit the awe and respect of his fellows. He tells of his uncle Roy, who, he says, has been executed at San Quentin:

> He killed four people in a barroom brawl usin' broken bottles and table legs and screamin', jus' screamin'. He was mean, man. He was rotten; and my folks been scared the same thing might happen to me; all their lives, they been scared. I got that same look in my eyes like him.

Pavlo also relates to his fellows tales of criminal exploits: he has, he says, stolen twenty-three cars. In response to his juvenile bragging, he elicits the comment from his fellows: "Shut up, Hummel! . . . you don't talk American, you talk Hummel! Some goddamn foreign language!"

Pavlo genuinely tries to become part of the new system: he studiously memorizes his General Orders; he volunteers for menial duties, and he undergoes supplementary physical training. His actions, however, have the opposite effect intended. Failing to realize that the assimilation of an individual by a group can only be realized through proper ritual and communal assent, he does not succeed in his attempts at integration with his fellow men and with the military system. Pavlo's problem is that he attempts to accomplish through a process of rationalization what must be undertaken subconsciously: an implicit surrendering to the rituals of incorporation inherent in the drill and its cadence.

In the course of *Pavlo Hummel* the conditioning process of the military is seen to be a product of the repetitive mind-numbing but habit-forming process of close-order drill. The intellectual facility of the mind must be subsumed to the process of conditioned automatic reflex, in essence, Pavlovian conditioning. In the rhythms and lyrics of the drill cadence are expressed the recruits' identity, function and sense of purpose. The Drill Sergeant commands: "I GONNA DO SOME SINGIN', GEN'LMEN, I WANT IT COMIN' BACK TO ME LIKE WE IN GRAND CANYON—AND YOU MY MOTHER-FUCKIN' ECHO." Marching refrains include: "LIFT YOUR HEAD AND HOLD IT HIGH / ECHO COMPANY PASSIN' BY"; "MOTHER, MOTHER WHAT'D I DO? / THIS ARMY TREATIN' ME WORSE THAN YOU"; "SAW SOME STOCKIN'S ON THE STREET / WISHED I WAS BETWEEN THOSE FEET"; "STANDIN' TALL AND LOOKIN' GOOD / WE BELONG IN HOLLYWOOD." Even the passage of time is measured collectively: "LORD HAVE MERCY I'M SO BLUE / IT SIX MORE WEEKS TILL I BE THROUGH." Through the rhythms and the repeated chants expressed communally by the men as they march, they are moulded into an homogeneous and distinct society.

The first act of the two-act play presents Pavlo's problems in becoming assimilated into his new social order. In an expressionistic scene, he fantasizes with his psychological mentor, Ardell, about aspects of biological warfare training. In testing Pavlo's reactions to hypothetical situations, Ardell vividly describes a "radiation attack." Pavlo recoils in horror, "No, no," but, as men rise about him, the denial becomes a response to an accusation of a stolen wallet. Pavlo's stories of theft have now been taken at face value, and he is severely beaten by the other recruits. His failed attempts to integrate into the new society stem from his insistence on his individuality, which is antithetical to the process of regimentation in the military order. He subsequently realizes that integration is not a function of individual striving, but of collective assent.

In his search for belonging Pavlo desperately wants to be privy to the esoteric knowledge that he believes is part of the military mystique. He senses that identification with the military will validate him as a man, and will endow him with the self-esteem and sexual prowess that has eluded him in civilian life. In conversation with the returned Vietnam corporal, he is told of an event that happened in-country: an old Vietnamese with a young girl approach a US patrol; the girl is crying. As they draw near, according to the corporal, a US sergeant drops to his knees and "lets go two bursts—first the old man, then the kid—cuttin' them both right across the face, man you could see the bullets walkin'. It was somethin.' " Pavlo does not understand why the sergeant shot the two Vietnamese, and the corporal explains: "Satchel charges, man. The both of them front and back. They had enough TNT on them to blow up this whole damn state."

The incident becomes the source of a consuming passion for Pavlo: he *must* understand how the sergeant was aware that the pair was carrying explosives. In wonderment, he accosts a fellow recruit,

> Can you imagine that, Hinkel? Just knowin'. Seein' nothin', but bein' sure enough to gun down two people. They had TNT on 'em, they was stupid slopeheads. That Sergeant Tinden saved everybody's life.

He is sure that integration into the army and experience in action will lead him to the arcane knowledge that Sergeant Tinden possesses, a knowledge which has eluded him in civilian life. . . .

Both Pavlo's civilian and military lives are portrayed as a series of disillusionments as "facts of the mind" continue to be contradicted by the immediate experience. The central dramatic metaphor of the play continues in force as Pavlo resumes his quest to gain esoteric knowledge and to establish definitive parameters of existence. When he is shipped overseas to Vietnam, he is designated a medical orderly, but is dissatisfied with that posting because he is denied the battle experience that he feels will lead him to the desired arcane knowledge. Fellow members of his medical unit treat him with disdain when, in an attempt to demonstrate his battle expertise, he suggests setting up "fields of fire" about the camp hospital. It is only after he goads his Captain about the latter's training as ROTC rather than OCS that he is transferred to an active combat unit.

The later movement of Act II consists of a surrealistic montage of scenes of battle, demonstrations of Sergeant Towers's drill instructions, events occurring in the bordello, and periodic appearances by Ardell. The juxtaposed and overlapping scenes illustrate the quickening pace of Pavlo's psychological disintegration as his mind begins to recall and to replay formative incidents in his life. The montage effect reduces human consciousness to a series of mental impressions that lack rational structure, coherent relationship, logical progression, or chronological order or continuity.

The avid pursuit of his quest for knowledge has the effect of Pavlo distinguishing himself on the battlefield through his heroic efforts as a medical orderly retrieving the wounded and the bodies of the dead. In the act of recovering the body of a comrade, he himself is wounded by a knife thrust from a fleeing Viet Cong. As he lies, bleeding, Ardell appears and chastises him over his quest for the esoteric knowledge that Pavlo thinks will give him critical insights into the nature of existence. As Pavlo moans in agony, Ardell comments:

> The knowledge comin', baby. I'm talkin' about what your kidney know, not your fuckin' fool's head. I'm talkin' about your skin and what it sayin', thin as paper. We melt, we tear and rip apart. Membrane baby. Cellophane. Ain't that some shit.

Ardell points out the elemental distinction between innate knowledge, the knowledge of the "kidney," and the arbitrary perceptions which are products of the mind, and limited to it. . . .

Under the stress of battle experience, Pavlo's sensations become more distorted and jumbled. He shoots a Vietnamese farmer believing the latter to be approaching with satchel charges under his clothes, but his judgement call is never vindicated. Ardell notes, "You don't know what he's got under his clothes." Pavlo's mental equilibrium totally disintegrates in a confusion of images when, believing he is shooting at the Vietnamese farmer, the target image changes to a fellow soldier, and ultimately he incurs the wounds himself. Taking aim at the farmer, he cries:

> I fuckin' shoot him. He's under me. I'm screamin' down at him. RYAN, RYAN. And he's lookin' up at me. His eyes squinted like he knows by my face what I'm sayin' matters to me so maybe it matters to him. And then, all of a sudden, see, he starts to holler and shout like he's crazy, and he's pointin' at his foot, so I shoot it. (*He fires again.*) I shoot his foot and then he's screamin' and tossin' all over the ground, so I shoot into his head. (*Fires.*) I shot his head. And I get hit again. I'm standin' there over him and I get fuckin' hit again. They keep fuckin' hittin' me.

Pavlo's mental disintegration is complete when he can no longer distinguish cause from effect, illusion from reality, or friend from foe.

The problem and consequences of not being able to identify and distinguish one's enemy are further revealed when Ardell, commenting on Pavlo's inability to differentiate between the farmer, the soldier, and himself observes, "When you shot into his head, you hit into your own head, fool." Ardell adds that Pavlo shot the farmer not because he had made a judgement call, but because the Viet Cong had shot his comrade, Ryan, two weeks earlier. Pavlo's action is not based on an intuitive and esoteric knowledge, but purely on blind, brutal vengeance. The Drill Sergeant tells of an incident that happened in the Korean War in which a group of American POWs cast one of their wounded into a snow bank to freeze because his screaming disturbed their sleep. He tells the men, "You got to watch out for the enemy."

The essence of Ardell's and Tower's speeches is that war so conditions men to brutality that discernment of truth is neither problematic nor necessary. The men are programmed to react automatically to a given situation, and judgmental humanistic values have no place in combat. Sergeant Tinden, in the tale recited by the corporal, would have shot the old man and young girl in any case, either on pure suspicion, or in an act of vengeance. The esoteric knowledge that has inspired Pavlo's quest is revealed to be that of unthinking, conditioned, and unquestioned brutality. Knowing and identifying one's enemy is the key to survival. For the soldier, the enemy is the indecision and uncertainty that springs from humanistic instincts that are incompatible with the realities of war. . . .

Pavlo's insecurity can be traced back to his childhood conditioning in the family environment. At the time of Pavlo's leave, after his basic training, Mickey taunts him with, "You know, if my father hadn't died, you wouldn't even exist," and, in reference to the mother, adds,

> All those one-night stands. You ever think of that? Ghostly pricks. I used to hear'em humpin' the old whore. I probably had my ear against the wall the night they got you goin'.

Pavlo's search for identity has a very real base in a legalistic as well as in a psychological sense, and it becomes further apparent that his motivation for joining the army was the result of a direct confrontation with his mother. In the bordello, after Pavlo has kicked Sergeant Wall in the groin, he turns to Ardell, and boasts,

> Did I do it to him Ardell? The triple Hummel? Got to be big and bad. A little shuffle. Did I ever tell you? Thirteen months a my life ago. . . . What she did, my ole lady, she called Joanna a slut and I threw kitty litter, screamin'—cat shit—Happy Birthday! She called that sweet church-goin' girl a whore. To be seen by her now, up tight with this odd-lookin whore, feelin' good and tall, ready to bed down. Feelin'—

Evidently the mother, in response to Pavlo's first association with a girl, Joanna, has projected onto Pavlo's relationship those very attributes that she has been accused of herself. In having sex with a Vietnamese girl, in the most degrading manner possible, Pavlo is taking revenge on all that is implied in his mother's idolization of the screen images that have portrayed America's heroic exploits in former wars. In addition, given Pavlo's imaginative nature and the unsubstantiated, tenuous truth of the relationship between Joanna and Pavlo, the mother may well have not been attacking the relationship itself, but her son's self-sustaining *myth* of the relationship, his own "life-lie." The

ultimate revelation is that Pavlo has fled into the army in search of all the things that have eluded him in civilian life, and that what was unattainable in his previous existence, remains even more elusive in his new milieu.

The fragmentation grenade explodes and Ardell relates subsequent events involving the preparation and transport of Pavlo's body home. At the end of his speech, he turns to Pavlo and asks whether he has anything to say:

> *Ardell:* What you think a gettin' your ass blown clean off a freedom's frontier? What you think a bein' R.A. Regular Army lifer . . . ?
>
> *Pavlo:* Shit!
>
> *Ardell:* And what you think a all the 'folks back home,' sayin' you a victim . . . you an animal . . . you a fool?
>
> *Pavlo:* They shit!

Pavlo then expands his observations into his own existentialist philosophy: "It all shit."

Pavlo has found neither purpose nor substance in his military career and faces the same existential void that he found in civilian life. Access to another culture, the substitution of one form of conditioning for another, has neither increased his knowledge nor made him more capable of coping with existence. Like many other plays of the period and genre, *The Basic Training of Pavlo Hummel* deals less with the actualities of the War than with the problems of the individual in a given social structure. Individual problems of integration, of belonging, of identity, purpose, and function are exacerbated but not caused by larger external conflicts. The conclusion, "It all shit," reflects the absurdist existential condition of the individual, who, overcome with the complexities of existence, pursues a futile and desperate search for recognition, belonging, and fulfilment.

Rabe's later play, *Streamers,* while similarly depicting problems of initiation into a new cultural construct and the existential limbo that surrounds all of human experience, portrays characters who seem to be unaware of the process in which they are entangled, and who fail to arrive even at Pavlo's limited conclusion concerning the nature of existence. In *Streamers,* there is no communally agreed upon existential norm to which the individual can aspire: the inductees are isolated in their own consciousness and alienated from each other in the matrix of the holding camp where they are temporarily stationed. Rabe's philosophy and motif in his works owe much to Beckett, and *Streamers,* in particular, is heavily indebted to *Waiting for Godot.*

Although *Streamers* is an extremely complex work in its examination of the relationships between individuals in a given society, it is technically the most realistic play of Rabe's Vietnam trilogy. Rather than springing from the mind of a dying soldier, the action is chronologically structured according to the dictates of the "well-made play." Dialogue is realistic, the setting natural, and the situation credible. It is that very facade of normality, however, that serves as a counterpoint to the subliminal aspects of the work. Although the events are grounded in an objective realism, the characters themselves exist within individual subjective frames of reference between which there is little communication, resonance, or empathy.

The title and central metaphor of *Streamers* is inherent in a parody of Stephen Foster's song "Beautiful Dreamer." An adaptation of Foster's lyrics expresses the existentialist philosophy of the work: "Beautiful Streamers" is sung by two alcoholic Regular Army sergeants who have become totally acculturated to the routine of army life, and who unconditionally accept the parameters of life experience as defined by military protocol. The lyrics reveal the veterans' fatalistic attitude and are ultimately only an expression of hollow bravado; they are a verbal denial of the presence of death that lurks in the minds of airborne troops, for whom the thin ribbon of fabric trailing from a pack indicates a parachute that has failed to deploy. The men attempt, through a communal liturgical expression, to overcome the ever-present terrors associated with their military calling.

> Beautiful streamer, / Open for me,
> The sky is above me, / But no canopy.
> Counted ten thousand, / Pulled on the cord.
> My chute didn't open, / I shouted "Dear Lord."
> Beautiful streamer, / This looks like the end,
> The earth is below me, / My body won't [b]end.
> Just like a mother / Watching o'er me,
> Beautiful streamer, / Ohhhhh, open for me.

An expression of resolution in the face of death, the lyrics reflect the existential philosophy of the soldier; a man who has supposedly been conditioned to his own mortality by his army training. In the context of the play, the human condition is defined through the experience of the intense but brief period that exists between the moment of emergence from the secure matrix of the airplane to the impact that marks the end of mortal existence. The image owes much to Beckett, as the umbilical cord or "streamer" symbolizes the link between the womb of the airplane and the tomb of the earth. As Vladimir observes in *Godot,* "Astride of a grave and a difficult birth. Down in the hole, lingeringly, the grave-digger puts on the forceps . . . the air is full of our cries." In counterpoint to an unremitting existential dilemma the one constant is the relentless force of gravity.

The single set of *Streamers* is a barracks-room in an army camp in Virginia. The action involves recent boot camp graduates presently being held in a "holding company"—the transitional stage between the completion of basic training and to a regular unit overseas. The unit ensconced in the room is a microcosm of American society: men of disparate backgrounds are forced into a crucible by the dictates of military necessity incurred by the omnipresent war. Vietnam provides justification for such military installations, since the fighting of wars requires their continued existence; in terms of philosophical symbolism; it is also the source of an ominous, all-encompassing fear that dominates the lives of the soldiers. In this miniature world reside men whose tensions and anxieties are normally dissipated in the larger civilian culture; however, within the confines of the claustrophobic barracks environment social distinctions and inequalities that are normally con-

trolled or diffused are exacerbated and erupt into random and chaotic violence. . . .

Streamers encompasses a microcosmic world that reflects the problems extant in American society when the stresses associated with Vietnam were beginning to erupt in violent confrontations in the street. In a sense, this work is also an analogy, as it describes, in terms of the barracks-room, the situation in contemporary America where racial strife, doubts about the society, and Vietnam occupied the individual and collective consciousness. For the men in the barracks-room, however, social tensions are real, immediate, and personally threatening. Not yet comprising an homogeneous group, they continually attempt to cope with the mental stress of cultural isolation. In the dramas of battlefield experience, that isolation becomes all the more terrifying as the immediate threat of carnage and destruction further exacerbates psychological disintegration.

W. J. Hug　(essay date 1993)

SOURCE: "Images of the Western in Selected Vietnam Films," in *Continuities in Popular Culture: The Present in the Past & the Past in the Present and Future,* edited by Ray B. Browne and Ronald J. Ambrosetti, Bowling Green State University Popular Press, 1993, pp. 176-90.

[*In the excerpt below, Hug discusses the links and correspondences between Vietnam War films and Hollywood westerns.*]

Film makers have often portrayed twentieth-century America at war in images reminiscent of the nation's frontier past. Gary Cooper's Sergeant York, the peaceable, soft-spoken primitive whose skills in the wilderness make him a hero in the trenches, is a son of the Leatherstocking transported to the Western Front. Slim Pickens as the fanatical cowboy bomber pilot of Stanley Kubrick's *Dr. Strangelove* begins the nuclear holocaust with an apocalyptic last ride astride a warhead. In more recent films about America at war—those depicting the war in Vietnam—the nation's conquest of the frontier and its involvement in Southeast Asia have been linked with particular consistency. From John Wayne's *Green Berets,* with it Special Forces camp called "Dodge City," to Kubrick's *Full Metal Jacket,* wherein marines in Vietnam joke about themselves as players in a western movie, references to the American West and the western recur time and time again.

One likely explanation for this recurrence lies in the fabric of broad correspondences between the circumstances of the Vietnam War and those of the conquest of the American frontier. As John Hellmann has shown in *American Myth and the Legacy of Vietnam,* these correspondences made Southeast Asia a latter-day correlative or extension of the American West, and the American soldier a correlative of the western hero. Both the frontier experience and the Vietnam experience involved American military efforts to extend and maintain socio-political "spheres of influence." In both cases, the targets were primitive, non-Anglo-Saxon cultures inhabiting primeval landscapes. Both cultures were stereotypically assumed to be ethnically inferior—"redskins" in one instance, "gooks" in the other—and therefore in special need of Americanization, particularly the South Vietnamese, who after the French withdrawal from Indochina lay in danger of communist subversion. In the American West and in Southeast Asia, the nation's military effort was relatively large-scale, bureaucratically managed, and fought with technologically advanced weapons, from repeating rifles and gatling guns to napalm; in contrast, native responses generally consisted of sporadic guerilla campaigns frequently conducted with more primitive weapons, like bows and arrows or booby traps. While western fiction and films often highlight later stages of the Americanizing process—the arrival of settlers, the establishment of law and order in small, frontier communities—the initial stages—subduing the wilderness and the natives, confining them to reservations—are always assumed facts and thus part of every western's context. In Vietnam films, these initial stages are consistently in the forefront, as the narratives highlight American soldiers' combat experiences against the Viet Cong or North Vietnamese regulars, or their relations with the Vietnamese natives in the rural villages.

Perceived in these terms, stories about Americans on the frontier and stories about Americans in Vietnam involve similar tensions. Most broadly, these can be subsumed within the tension between civilization and wilderness; in more specific terms, they may include the tension between white and non-white, between the technological and the primitive, between complex and distant bureaucracies and simpler, localized administrative structures. The play of these tensions emerges most vividly in the stories' protagonists. Like the archetypal American hero of the West, the American hero in Vietnam is almost inevitably a man in the middle: he must choose whether to employ his considerable skills in violence to promote the spread of the American Way with its promise of safety, stability, and equality on the one hand and its imperialist and capitalist ambiguities on the other, or to retreat in favor of the wilderness, where good and bad emerge in far more elemental forms. In the majority of westerns and in at least one Vietnam film—Wayne's *Green Berets*—the issue is simple, even simplistic, a choice so obvious as to leave no choice. The American Way, as embodied in the stoical sheriff or the tough Special Forces commander, is so virile and morally upright as to be irresistible, while the denizens of the wilderness—whether they be red or yellow—are so savage as to be utterly repulsive. However, in some Vietnam films as in some of the more ambitious westerns, the choice is not this clear-cut. In these works, the American endeavor to civilize the wilderness is distinctly flawed, perhaps by administrative corruption or clumsiness, or a powerful individual's obsession. In western narrative, the scheming banker, the swindling Indian agent, and the rapacious cattle baron have appeared so often as to be cliches. In stories about Vietnam, the noncom or the commander with a we-must-destroy-the-village-in order-to-save-it mentality has become more and more familiar. On the other hand, the wilderness in such works often has a pastoral allure embodied in the nomadic or agrarian simplicity and close-knit communities of the Indian or Vietnamese villagers.

Confronted with situations as complicated as these, the hero's choice becomes a far more difficult proposition. The

moral awareness which is essential to his heroism enables him to distinguish the flaws in the pioneer endeavor and the appeal of the wilderness. His growing alienation from endeavor makes his participation in it more and more of a dilemma—he cannot accept the very system he feels duty-bound to defend. In the best Vietnam narratives as in the best westerns, the dilemma is irresolvable. The hero may die fighting for a cause he sees as tainted, or, having defended it successfully, he may withdraw, into the wilderness and/or perhaps into himself. In these situations he becomes a figure of potentially tragic stature.

Of course this summary of correspondences between western and Vietnam narratives identifies only in the broadest terms the characteristic tensions of civilization and wilderness and the hero's involvement with them. These issues may be handled in very different ways from one story to another. Narrative structure, point of view, portrayal of character, socio-political perspective may all vary widely, as may the mode of presentation—i.e., tragic, epic, elegiac, comic, parodic, etc. To take three instances from western narrative as examples, Cooper's romantic saga of the Leatherstocking is certainly tragic and elegiac; Owen Wister's pseudo-realistic novel *The Virginian* is, in terms of its happy resolution in the hero's marriage, classically comic; Mel Brooks' postmodern send-up of the western, *Blazing Saddles*, vacillates between the parodic and the satiric. Yet all three adhere generally to the suggested paradigm. Less diversity has emerged in Vietnam films produced thus far. Since the war became such a painful element in the national consciousness, the notion of portraying American soldiers' experiences in Vietnam in an upbeat fashion has seemed grotesque. Nevertheless, some diversity has emerged. In two of the more ambitious films yet made about the Vietnam War, the correspondences between Americans on the western frontier and Americans in Southeast Asia are given distinctly different modes of presentation. In Michael Cimino's *The Deer Hunter*, the dilemma of the young Green Beret Michael Vronsky (Robert DeNiro) is portrayed in tragic and elegiac terms reminiscent of Cooper. In Francis Coppola's *Apocalypse Now*, Colonel Kilgore (Robert Duvall), the swaggering leader of an air Cavalry unit, is depicted in terms of the western mock-heroic.

Since *The Deer Hunter*'s release in 1978, many reviewers and critics have noted the deer hunter/Deerslayer parallel: like Natty Bumppo as well as his literary and cinematic progeny, Michael Vronsky is a solitary hero uncomfortable in his society and allied with the wilderness, from which he derives his skills in violence and his strict code of behavior. These are embodied in Michael's notion of "one shot," his catch phrase for the grace, skill, and integrity necessary to stalk and kill a deer with a single bullet. Circumstances dictate that he, like the Leatherstocking, must defend his society against the primitive inhabitants of the wilderness; Michael emerges from the conflict a melancholy and perhaps even tragic figure whose fate raises troubling questions about the society he has fought for. Some critics have taken *The Deer Hunter*'s relations to the western still further, linking the film not only with Cooper's novels but with the classic Hollywood westerns of John Ford and Howard Hawks, works with far less ambivalent social and political implications. In these discussions, *The Deer Hunter* emerges as something of a swan song for the Hollywood western, a eulogy for the simplicity and vigor of the frontier endeavor as depicted in such films. Though the parallels drawn between Cimino's film and those of Ford and Hawks are sometimes far-fetched (*The Deer Hunter* and *Rio Bravo*?), they have been valuable not only in defining *The Deer Hunter* within its cinematic tradition, but in suggesting the possibility of broad correspondences, of the sort outlined above between western and Vietnam narratives. . . .

If Cimino's *Deer Hunter* portrays the western hero tragically and elegiacally to mourn America's endeavor in Vietnam, Francis Ford Coppola's *Apocalypse Now* portrays him satirically to ridicule it. Though neither of Coppola's main characters—the military assassin Captain Willard (Martin Sheen) or his victim Colonel Kurtz (Marlon Brando)—is depicted overtly in western terms, both are caught up in versions of the western hero's classic predicament. In his own way, each is at odds with the pioneer cause he fights for, the American effort to civilize and democratize the wilderness. Willard has witnessed and understood the absurdity of the war effort, yet for him no other sort of life is any longer possible. As he admits in the film's voice-over, he'd gone stateside after his first tour in Vietnam only to find himself incapable of returning to the domestic roles of husband and father, so he and his wife divorced. Furthermore, the nation as he thought he'd known it no longer existed, so he'd asked for another tour in Vietnam. Like the western hero unsuited to civilized life and suspicious of civilization, Willard returns to the wilderness. Kurtz, the special Forces colonel whom Willard is assigned to kill, represents an analogous case. Frustrated at the bureaucratic clumsiness of the American war effort and at the bureaucrats' pretensions to a lofty morality in conducting it, he surrenders to the primitive ferocity of the wilderness. Kurtz becomes a renegade, crossing into Cambodia so that he may carry on the war with the utter savagery he believes essential to victory.

To draw forth these western implications latent in his major characters and to comment on the Vietnam conflict itself, Coppola creates a minor character who is explicitly, even bombastically western—Colonel Kilgore (Robert Duvall), head of the air cavalry unit that carries Willard and his boat on one leg of his quest to kill Kurtz. Unlike these men who have found themselves at odds with America's pioneer endeavor in Vietnam, Kilgore revels in it, to the point of arrogance. As Gilbert Adair has noted, Kilgore plays to the hilt the historical and cinematic role of swashbuckling cavalry officer leading the fight against the savages on the frontier. His uniform, his style of leadership, his relations with his men, and even his enthusiasm for surfing suggest an extravagant and ultimately satiric rendering of the George-Custer-cum-Roy-Rogers western hero of the Saturday matinees—a simplified, homogenized descendant of the classical western hero, utterly pleased with his part in the ambivalent conflict of civilization and wilderness. Kilgore's dandyism in dress and manner recalls the flashiness of the historical Custer and of the Hollywood cavalry officers who were his progeny. The broad-brimmed Stetson, the yellow dickey reminiscent of the

cavalryman's bandanna, the pistol and holster on the hip, the swaggering oblivion to personal danger—all ironically conjure the heroic image of the gallant soldier conquering the western plains. He strives to impart the western mystique to his command as well, maintaining a company bugler also replete with Stetson, and even orchestrating nights around the campfire. In a scene recalling countless western films, Kilgore strums a guitar as he and his men lounge around a fire amidst the Asian wilderness, drinking and swapping stories of their exploits. In battle he is every bit as fearless as his idealized and vacuous predecessors; after his unit attacks a Vietnamese coastal village and lands to mop up, he stands upright, oblivious to enemy artillery and small-arms fire, while his men duck for cover. All of this, in a film about another time and another war, could be straight heroism; in Coppola's depiction of Vietnam, however, it becomes mock-heroic. The conventional elements in Kilgore's character are so overstated—particularly from the more skeptical perspective that grew out of Vietnam and Watergate—as to be bombastic pretense. Kilgore becomes the satiric embodiment of the corrupted pioneer endeavor he defends. . . .

Though *Apocalypse Now* and *The Deer Hunter* approach the Vietnam conflict through different modes of western presentation—the satiric as opposed to the tragic and elegiac—their mutual reliance on images and themes from the western produces visions of the war that dovetail. Both films employ the western to comment on perceived absurdities of the American involvement: Coppola's lampoons them, while Cimino's laments them. In their depictions of the nation's effort in Vietnam as failed extension of America's effort on the frontier, the two films not only resonate with ironic echoes of Wayne's *Green Berets*; they define a *leitmotif* for later Vietnam films like Oliver Stone's *Platoon* and Stanley Kubrick's *Full Metal Jacket*. Through the character of Barnes (Tom Berenger), a sergeant fanatically committed to the war, Stone associates visual and aural imagery reminiscent of the frontier with a militant right-wing stance. The film's more urban and politically liberal white characters have no recognizable accents and spend their free time smoking marijuana as they listen to rock music; Barnes, however, speaks in a thick western accent, plays poker and drinks whiskey saloon-style, while he listens to country-and-western music, most notably Merle Haggard's "Okie from Muskogee." The corruption of this latter-day cowboy's jingoist notion of Vietnam as a new frontier emerges vividly after he allows an atrocity in a Vietnamese village: when Elias (Willem DaFoe), a kindly and liberal sergeant outraged at the crime, threatens him with court-martial, Barnes kills his accuser and blames the Viet Cong for the death. As another embodiment of America's pioneer endeavor gone wrong, Barnes is not far removed from Kilgore.

Kubrick's *Full Metal Jacket* handles western references in similar and sometimes more overt ways. In fact, two particular scenes late in the work explicitly define the historical, psychological, and cinematic relations between the Old West and Southeast Asia which all these films address. Preliminary allusions to the West and the western establish the motif: the opening credits roll to a country-and-western song "Goodbye Sweetheart, Hello Vietnam" proclaiming "America has heard the bugle call" just as it had on the frontier—both Kilgore and Barnes would love it. The film's central character, an anonymous marine draftee (Matthew Modine) does swaggering imitations of John Wayne's cowboy *persona,* for which he earns the name "Joker" from his drill instructor; another draftee whom we learn comes from Texas is christened "Cowboy." Later, after Joker has arrived in Vietnam, a fellow marine has his camera snatched as he and Joker haggle with a prostitute outside a Saigon cafe called the "Las Vegas": moral decadence in Vietnam is linked to the most famous resort town of America's New West and the decadence often associated with it.

These seemingly random allusions—and in fact the western references in every film we've considered—are thrust into context by two scenes near the end of the film. Joker, now a reporter for *Stars and Stripes,* is sent with a camera crew to cover a marine counterattack in the city of Hue during the Tet offensive. As he and a cameraman film a unit of troops huddled behind a pile of fallen brickwork, they come upon a marine whom Joker had known in boot-camp. With a wry gallows humor, the soldier peers into the camera and asks Joker in a tone of mock-reverence, "Is that you, John Wayne?" His buddies immediately pick up on the joke and extend it:

"I'll be General Custer."

"I'll be a horse"—this from a black marine.

"Who'll be the indians?"

"We'll let the gooks be the indians."

This little scene, lasting less than a minute, comically condenses the complex of interrelations between the frontier and Vietnam which Kubrick's film and these others to varying extents address; Kubrick's verdict on the American involvement emerges in an episode that soon follows. After shooting the combat footage, Joker and his crew tape interviews with several marines concerning their feelings about the War; among them is another of Joker's friends from bootcamp, Cowboy, the soldier from Texas. In light of the previous western allusions in the film, his comments, which posit an implicit contrast between his home state and Vietnam, take on particular significance. "I hate Vietnam," he says, peering into the camera in quiet, puzzled disappointment; "there's not one horse in this whole country." In Cowboy's frustration at a petty disparity between Southeast Asia and his home in what was once the Old West, Kubrick creates an ingenious miniature of the disillusionment that permeates all of these films. In one way or another, the War in Vietnam becomes in each of them America's failed effort to resurrect the frontier. The western will probably remain a viable motif in representations of the nation's future conflicts.

POETRY

Lorrie Smith   (essay date November-December 1986)

SOURCE: "A Sense-Making Perspective in Recent Poetry by Vietnam Veterans," in *The American Poetry Review,* Vol. 15, No. 6, November-December, 1986, pp. 13-8.

[*In the essay below, Smith comments on the distinctive traits of Vietnam veteran poetry and analyzes the work of W. D. Ehrhart and Bruce Weigl.*]

Amid the flurry of special magazine issues, photo retrospectives, and television documentaries commemorating the tenth anniversary of the fall of Saigon, one back-page item brought into focus our continuing failure to make sense of the Vietnam War. An ABC News-*Washington Post* poll found that "while most Americans believe U.S. involvement in the war was a mistake, one out of three does not know on whose side we fought." Among adults thirty years old and younger, "48 percent did not know that the U.S. fought on the side of South Vietnam." Although the recent visibility of Vietnam in the media temporarily bestowed the illusion that we could "relive the era" and assess "the legacy of Vietnam," these disturbing figures suggest that the war remains as remote now as when fabricated body counts and official double-talk masqueraded as fact.

It is now commonplace to observe the violence done to language, hence thinking and moral judgement, during the Vietnam era, to regret the euphemism, tautology, jargon, and illogic epitomized by phrases like "peace offensive," "destroying a town to save it," and "kill ratio" [In an endnote, Smith adds: "See, for instance, Thomas Merton, 'War and the Crisis of Language,' in Robert Ginsberg, ed., *The Critique of War,* 1969. The corruption of language, which, as Orwell pointed out, always peaks in periods of war, is a major preoccupation of poets in this era."] Likewise, we now know, the ubiquitous visual images of our first T.V. war did little to clarify these obfuscations. Instead, our responses to atrocity were numbed by redundancy or made safe by bland newscasters. With such forces confounding our ability to imagine the war fully while it was happening, it is natural that our retrospective view is one of suppression and denial, an almost willful collective amnesia only rarely jarred by intruding reports of MIA remains or Agent Orange. When we do choose to look back at Vietnam, the past is often cast in light of the prevailing conservatism of the eighties. Men have been known, for instance, to invent Vietnam military service records on their resumés, tailoring a once-unpopular war to a new vogue for patriotism. Such slippery psychic and cultural holds on history inevitably generate myths which distort the real significance of the war, narratives which too easily master and enclose its anguish. Most popular media treatments of Vietnam are incomplete versions of history at best; slick, sensational, or sentimental fictions at worst. A new generation—the forty-eight percent whose misconceptions are tallied in this survey—may already be succumbing to the mass-market fantasies of Hollywood, persuaded by *Rambo* that American machismo still wields force in Southeast Asia and may yet redeem our tarnished myth of military glory.

Though a growing body of personal memoir and oral history is beginning to map a more accurate historical terrain, our knowledge of Vietnam remains fragmented and its full cost unmeasured. Journalist Pete Hamill suggests [in "Vietnam, Vietnam," *Vanity Fair* (April 1985)] why the actuality of this war continues to be so elusive: "The truth of the war was internalized, mythic, surrealistic, allusive; its darkest furies, deepest grief, and most brutal injuries could not be photographed. This war belongs to the printed page." Questioning the putative objectivity of documentary and film—our most visible attempts to come to terms collectively with the Vietnam Era—Hamill suggests that the war might be recovered more fully in imaginative literature. In fact, one valuable and largely untapped source of truth about the war lies in poetry by Vietnam soldiers and veterans. The protest poetry of stateside poets like Denise Levertov, Robert Duncan, Robert Bly, Galway Kinnell, and Allen Ginsberg provides one chapter in the story of our national trauma, but the war for them was a necessarily distant moral and ideological cause. [In an endnote, Smith adds: "There is no sustained study of poetry by participants in the war, and few critics have distinguished it from the general body of Vietnam literature. Cary Nelson, in *Our Last First Poets: Vision and History in Contemporary American Poetry,* 1981, grounds his book's argument in an introductory discussion of 'Whitman in Vietnam' but admits the work of veterans is outside his scope. James F. Mersmann, in *Out of the Vietnam Vortex,* 1979, also bypasses veterans' poetry. Jeffrey Walsh's *American War Literature 1914-Vietnam,* 1982, looks briefly at several poets. Philip D. Beidler's *American Literature and the Experience of Vietnam,* 1982, is a more penetrating and far-reaching study of Vietnam literature as a project of cultural myth-making. Though he concentrates mainly on fiction, he examines the work of poets D. C. Berry, Michael Casey, John Balaban, and Bruce Weigl. John Felstiner considers veteran poets in 'American Poetry and the War in Vietnam,' *Stand* 19:2 (1978), and in 'Bearing the War in Mind,' *Parnassus* 6:2 (1979)."] Like the letters in *Dear America: Letters Home from Vietnam* [edited by Bernard Edelman, 1985], poems by Vietnam veterans provide a repository of first-hand knowledge about the war and retain the living contexts of history by naming people, battles, dates, and places. Beyond this project of anamnesia, however, veteran-poets have begun to locate the larger significations of the war in American history and consciousness. Theirs is a poetry of witness but also, at its best, of retrospective and heuristic vision.

The enormous outpouring of poetry by participants in the Vietnam War is a singular event in American literary history. Though previous wars have all had their lyric rememberers—Whitman, e. e. cummings, Karl Shapiro, Richard Eberhart, Randall Jarrell—there is no corresponding *body* of poetry by war veterans and few workable literary models for the Vietnam poet. Even the British poets of the First World War, whose poetry and whose war were in many ways akin to the Vietnam veterans', had considerably more literary and cultural resources to support their enterprise. As Paul Fussell has pointed out [in

The Great War and Modern Memory, 1975], the age of serious readers, a coherent and continuous national literature, and an assumed consensus of values was shattered after World War I; indeed, such supports may never have been available to the American poet, as Whitman discovered.

While war poetry naturally treats archetypal themes of life and death, it must also respond to the specific conditions of its time and the needs of its contemporary audience. The Second World War can be read as a coherent narrative of struggle and victory, because the soldier-poet's suffering made sense in terms of shared national values; the culture glorified the soldier's sacrifices, helped expiate his guilt, and welcomed him back as a hero. But the peculiar qualities of the Vietnam War further complicate poetic sense-making. In addition to being appropriated and distorted by the media and effaced in our collective memory, the war itself took place in a hermetic microcosm where all normal points of reference—ethical, logical, even linguistic—were suspended. (In soldiers' argot and throughout these poems, "the world" refers to any place outside Vietnam.) Fighting a war to which his country did not assent, returning to ambivalence, scorn, or silence, the veteran has been left alone to make what sense he can of his private *agon.* Thus the Vietnam veteran attempting to bring poetic language to bear on his experience of the war faces a dual problem of memory and form, historical representation and literary representation. As Philip Beidler observes [in *American Literature and the Experience of Vietnam,* 1982], "It would become the task of the Vietnam writer to create a landscape that never was, one might say—a landscape of consciousness where it might be possible to accommodate experience remembered within a new kind of imaginative cartography endowing it with large configurings of value and signification." For such a project and such a war, irony seems too redundant, pathos too weak, realism too unrealistic, epic scope too broad, mythic redemption too spurious. The veteran's recourse, most often, is an anti-poetry stripped of transfiguring metaphor but enriched by the accuracy of a witnessing moral vision. Its content is empirical rather than idealistic, its epiphanies sardonic rather than transcendent. Indeed, most Vietnam veteran poets shun the traditional affirmations and consolations of lyricism. Their motives are decidedly to instruct rather than to delight—a stance entirely appropriate for a subject which is, after all, political.

Not surprisingly, as Beidler demonstrates in his chronological study of Vietnam literature, the perspective of veteran writers gains a wider angle with time and distance. Three stages mark progressively more complex and mature responses to the war. The many poems written under the pressure of battle and directly after the war constitute a poetry of close-up witness providing visceral description for the reader and, one suspects, catharsis for many writers. Driven by a need to pin down the ambiguous facts and experiences of war, many soldiers recorded the texture of life in Vietnam: its decimated landscapes and torn bodies, its mud and monsoons, its prostitutes and peasants, its moments of fear, frustration, and comradeship. Whether written by poets with evident literary training or by less sophisticated writers, these early poems are uniformly prosaic but enlivened—often quite artfully—by anecdotal realism, satire, wry or deadpan humor, soldiers' slang, obscenity, and catalogues of concrete details. [In an endnote, Smith states: "This empirical, colloquial style marks most of the poems collected in the three anthologies of veterans' poetry: Larry Rottmann, Jan Barry, and Basil Paquet, eds., *Winning Hearts and Minds: War Poems by Vietnam Veterans,* 1972, Jan Barry and W.D. Ehrhart, eds., *Demilitarized Zones: Veterans After Vietnam,* 1976, and W.D. Ehrhart, ed., *Carrying the Darkness,* 1985."] Though few soldiers could shape their war-time experiences into larger patterns of meaning at the time (it is helpful to remember that the average age of the Vietnam GI was nineteen), their topography of physical detail and event is essential to a deeper imaginative penetration of Vietnam.

If the only poems to come out of the war were these, we might dismiss veteran poets as chroniclers locked in a moment of the past. But several poets emerged in the seventies with a broader mediating perspective, negotiating between the extremes of concreteness and artifice, quotidian and universal. Such a stance is most apparent in volumes conceived as sequences, whose formal coherence begins to give shape to the still-near past. Two have gained recognition by the academic establishment—Michael Casey's *Obscenities,* a Yale Younger Poet selection, and John Balaban's *After our War,* a Lamont Poetry selection. Many others remain largely ignored: *How Audie Murphy Died in Vietnam* (1973) by McAvoy Layne, *The Long War Dead: An Epiphany* (1976) by Bryan Alec Floyd, *War Story* (1977) by Gerald McCarthy, *Vinh Long* (1976) by Perry Oldham, and *saigon cemetery* (1972) by D.C. Berry are particularly significant. Each gains the advantage of an extended and ordered vision composed of vignettes, character sketches, and sensory details which evoke the soldier's life in Vietnam. Resisting traditional forms of lyric affirmation and closure in individual poems, they discover meaning in larger structures of sequential or interlocking poems: Layne's mock-heroic *Bildungsroman* of draftee-turned-Maoist Audie Murphy, Casey's cryptic account of a year's tour of duty, Floyd's elegant elegies to each member of his platoon. Each finds a way to organize the random and often senseless experience of Vietnam into a meaningful form. Still located in Vietnam, they predict the even broader sense-making perspective of more recent poetry, by veterans who have gone on to explore how the memory of Vietnam impinges on the present and to gauge the extent to which, in Cary Nelson's terms, "history has usurped" visionary poetic language and form. Veteran-poets' continuing engagement with the moral and political questions raised by Vietnam dismantles the popular myth that we have regained our national innocence and forces us to scrutinize our well-meaning but still unexamined consensus that U.S. involvement in Vietnam was a mistake. By continuing to bring the war home and inviting our own empathic response, they map our common ground of history.

Two veterans have emerged in the eighties as leading poets of the Vietnam War, their differences staking a range of possible retrospective treatments of the war. W.D. Ehrhart is a founder of Vietnam Veterans Against the War, an important editor and advocate of veterans' poetry, and

a highly polemical poet. His collection of previous and new poems, *To Those Who Have Gone Home Tired,* traces one representative veteran's growth from naiveté to disillusionment, anger, and political activism. In an attempt to find cultural contexts for his *angst,* Ehrhart connects two converging continuums: his personal coming of age and the destructive flow of history. Bruce Weigl re-presents Vietnam with more dense and resonant language. In his two recent volumes, *A Romance* and *The Monkey Wars,* Weigl takes memory itself as his main theme and insistently links Vietnam with contemporary life in America. Both ground their poems in the immediacy of the war but move beyond a mere litany of atrocities to imagine the war's continuing and palpable presence in American life. The anaesthetized flatness of earlier veterans' poetry has evolved into a broader range of responses which measure and connect the war's psychic, cultural, political, and literary costs. Refusing to recuperate a past before war or a poetry untinged by its anguish, Ehrhart and Weigl both extend the possibilities and expose the limitations of a lyric response to Vietnam.

Ehrhart's poems set in Vietnam are often typical of the poetry of direct and graphic witness. One "Sergeant Jones," for instance, is described as "The kind of guy the young enlisted men / admire: / he can hit a gook at 50 yards / with a fuckin' .45." The sinister shift in diction, of course, exposes and condemns this callow but common sentiment. While many early poems from the front are curiously devoid of protest, Ehrhart early on places his personal experiences in a larger political context. In "The Generals' War," Ehrhart speaks with contempt of the ironic disjunction between "Paper orders passed down and executed" and the actual execution of soldiers "straggling back in

W. D. Ehrhart during Operation Pike, south of Hoi An, in August, 1967.

plum-colored rags, / one-legged, in slings, on stretchers, / in green plastic bags." Such outright bitterness extends to Ehrhart's poems written after he returns from the war. He first attempts to make sense of his personal fall from innocence, to retrieve the lost ideals of his small-town youth and reconcile them with the bare facts of war. "To the Asian Victors" presents an emblematic crisis of identity and dilemma of cultural dispossession:

> I remember the dead, I
> remember the dying.
>
> But I cannot ever quite remember
> what I went looking for,
> or what it was I lost
> in that alien land that became
> more I
> than my own can ever be again.

Since nothing in American culture helps Ehrhart assimilate his experience, he turns to his enemy, in one poem cursing the "cock-eyed" North Vietnamese gunner who sent him "back alive among a people / I can never feel / at ease with anymore," and pleading "do not let it all come down / to nothing." But the war's meaning, Ehrhart realizes, must lie closer to home, so he shifts the battleground to America. Speaking on behalf of his fellow veterans and addressing the American public directly, he inveighs against the culture that piously celebrates its Bicentennial while ignoring the veteran next door. His voice is often collective, his position a combative us-against-them which points up our complicity and complacency: "they always assume the war is over, / not daring to imagine our wounds, / or theirs, if it is not." Though justifiably angry, Ehrhart is also willing to help us overcome our amnesia and heal our collective wounds. In "The Teacher," he recounts an oath made after the war "to teach you / all I know— / and I know things / worth knowing." Yet he fumbles and asks for his students' patience "until I find a voice that speaks / the language / that you speak." Implicit in this exchange is our need to meet the veteran halfway in dialogue, to decode a language which is not, after all, so inaccessible.

Between his nightmarish memories of Vietnam and his longing for empathy at home, Ehrhart does find consoling moments of love, self-knowledge, and comradeship. In "A Confirmation," a long, blank verse narrative reminiscent in setting and situation of Hemingway's "The Big Two-Hearted River," the speaker camps with a fellow veteran he hasn't seen since the war on a river "tumbling through the darkness toward the sea / that laps the shores of Asia." Their companionship differentiates these veterans from Hemingway's shell-shocked Nick Adams, replacing his code of tough reticence with one of compassion and vulnerability. Hammering stakes and catching fish become, as in Hemingway, masculine rituals—here binding the two men in the present by recalling their shared experiences in Vietnam. Like Hemingway's skittish veteran, Ehrhart has a moment of near-panic; after a half-hour struggle to catch a rainbow trout, "I throw the fish back / in the awkward silence, and you / slip your arm around my shoulders / gently for a moment, knowing why." Away from society, sharing both an "awkward silence" and a "perfect stillness," the two men find common mean-

ings for their private anguish. Ehrhart's poem echoes— and perhaps even pays oblique tribute to—veteran poets of an earlier war. Like Wilfred Owen, Siegfried Sassoon, and Isaac Rosenberg, Vietnam veterans must reanimate the dead ideals of their fathers with their own darker meanings, salvaging

> something worth clinging to
> out of the permanent past of stillborn dreams:
> the ancient, implacable wisdom
> of ignorance shattered forever, a new
> reverence we were never taught
> by anyone we believed, a frail hope
> we gave each other, communion
> made holy by our shame.

The healing power of love, nature, and friendship may be effective in Ehrhart's own life, but his most recent poems suggest that such personal consolations are insufficient to counter the force of history or to correct the mistakes of the past. He is openly didactic in his call for a reformation of our national vision and policies. In "A Confirmation," he says "good-bye" to "high school history"; his recent poems attempt to correct the history books with "what I know." Thus, Vietnam figures in many poems as an important node on a continuum of self-destructive events in American history: imperialistic aggression, the disinheritance of Native Americans, the build-up of nuclear armaments. Ehrhart does more than protest or propagandize, however. By claiming his own place in history and inscribing his personal fall within the story of our national will to destruction, he reminds us that the veteran is a truthful witness to history, his war an active force in the present. "The Invasion of Grenada" never mentions that recent military escapade but instead uses what he knows about Vietnam to make a broader statement at once personal and political:

> I didn't want a monument,
> not even one as sober as that
> vast black wall of broken lives . . .
>
> What I wanted was a simple recognition
> of the limits of our power as a nation
> to inflict our will on others.
> What I wanted was an understanding
> that the world is neither black-and-white
> nor ours.
> What I wanted was an end to monuments.
> But no one
> ever asked me what I wanted.

Ehrhart manages to be didactic but not dogmatic, lyrical but not transcendental; his plain-spoken, chastising style is appropriate for a moral and political re-conception of Vietnam.

> Both W. D. Ehrhart and Bruce Weigl
> ground their poems in the immediacy of
> the war but move beyond a mere litany of
> atrocities to imagine the war's continuing
> and palpable presence in American life.
> The anaesthetized flatness of earlier
> veterans' poetry has evolved into a
> broader range of responses which measure
> and connect the war's psychic, cultural
> political, and literary costs.
>
> —*Lorrie Smith*

Bruce Weigl's poems begin at the point of assimilating the war into large imaginative and historical constructs. Like Ehrhart, he continually goes back to the war in an attempt to go beyond it and, like Ehrhart, his efforts to reconcile past and present, memory and imagination, often end in dilemma. In his 1976 volume, *Executioner,* poems about America and Vietnam are gathered in two separate sections. In his latest volumes, however, Weigl juxtaposes Vietnam's cloying jungle with Midwest factory towns whose slag heaps, smokestacks, bars, and graveyard shifts recall the grey landscapes of James Wright and Philip Levine. Whether viewed from Vietnam or Ohio, the war penetrates all of Weigl's observations. Linked by peculiarly American brands of violence and pathos, the two places are not so far apart. The dark underside of Vietnam is finally, as in Ehrhart, a monstrous exaggeration and a logical extension of the more banal forms of violence and moral depletion of home.

In both recent volumes, Weigl images the war as a monkey on his back—a tenacious memory, potent and insidious as a drug; a carnivalesque *Doppelgänger,* both intimate and repugnant; a symbol of man's unregenerate brutality. The climactic poem of *A Romance,* "Monkey," is a fractured nightmare in which language nearly disintegrates under the pressures of psychic and physical pain. Present reflection and past experience intermingle as Weigl searches for a way to live with and speak of the war. Memory erupts in disconnected flashes or is suppressed altogether as the speaker tries to "Forget the stinking jungle." He compulsively conjugates the verb "to be" and grasps the activities of daily life in an attempt to fix reality and to fend off memory and desire: "I am you are he she it is / they are you are we are . . . Good times bad times sleep / get up work / sleep get up / good times bad times." The poem finally places the war in time, expressing present fatigue as the speaker remembers the past:

> I'm twenty-five years old,
> quiet, tired of the same mistakes,
> the same greed, the same past.
> The same past with its bleat
> and pound of the dead,
> with its hand grenade
> tossed into a hootch on a dull Sunday

Like Ehrhart, Weigl longs for a thoughtful and responsive

audience, but he goes further to address a sympathetic interlocutor and to pull us intimately into the poem: "I'm tired and I'm glad you asked." The speaker finds temporary release from the redundancies of battle and nightmare only through fantasy that finally itself dissolves into further repetitions:

> my monkey my beautiful
> monkey he saved me lifted
> me above the punji
> sticks above the mines
> above the ground burning
> above the dead above
> the living above the
> wounded dying the wounded
> dying.

Though he survives the war and transcends it in imagination, the fighting continues—with or without him—stripped to the archetypal motions of all wars, a cartoon endlessly re-run, a game of king-of-the-mountain never resolved. "Monkey" runs down and endlessly around with a weary cynicism that colors many of Weigl's later war poems:

> Men take hill away from smaller men.
> Men take hill and give to fatter man.
> Men take hill. Hill has number.
> Men run up hill. Run down.
>
> (*A Romance*)

The alternating impulses to immerse himself in actuality and to rise "above the / wounded dying" in Keatsian flights of imagination structure many of Weigl's war poems. Though he soars toward transcendence in many passages, he almost always falls. In "Him, on the Bicycle," the speaker is riding "In a liftship near Hue" when "the door gunner sees movement / . . . four men running, carrying rifles / one man on a bicycle." The poem then leaps to a fantasy in which the speaker becomes one with his enemy and the two fly past the battleground like Butch Cassidy and the Sundance Kid:

> He pulls me out of the ship,
> there's firing far away.
> I'm on the back of the bike
> holding his hips.
>
> . . . . .
>
> His hat flies off,
> I catch it behind my back,
> put it on, I want to live forever!

The real and the imaginary fuse, however, in a final ambiguous image in which the Vietnamese man may either be literally torched by the gunner or apotheosized in the speaker's fantasy. He disappears "Like a blaze / streaming down the trail."

The Monkey Wars pushes this oscillation of flight and fall toward a darker view of the limitations of transcendent and redemptive imagination. In the first poem, "Amnesia," Vietnam has obliterated the memory of a world before war, much as it effaced Ehrhart's past in "To the Asian Victors":

> If there was a world more disturbing than this

Where black clouds bowed down and swallowed
    you whole
And overgrown tropical plants
Rotted, effervescent in the muggy twilight and
    monkeys
Screamed something
That came to sound like words to each other
Across the triple-canopy jungle you shared,
You don't remember it.

The enervated speaker is caught between his lost past and an impotent yearning for the future; between them, mentioned only obliquely, lies Vietnam, the monkey, as he says in another poem, "no myth this time, / Grinning, howling, never letting go." The speaker yearns to "Fly up to . . . the crows calling autumn into place," but lacks "the strength and will." In "Burning Shit at An Khe," the speaker does manage to escape temporarily from the literal and symbolic "shit" which he is ordered to burn because "You had to do something / Because it just kept piling up / And it wasn't our country, it wasn't / Our air thick with the sick smoke." He sinks "deep to my knees" until

    . . . it all came down on me, the stink
            And the heat and the worthlessness
    Until I slipped and climbed
            Out of that hole and ran
    Past the olive drab
            Tents and trucks and clothes and ev-
    erything
    Green as far from the shit
            As the fading light allowed.

But the speaker suddenly shifts to the present, where the remembered actuality of the war blocks his escape:

    Only now I can't fly.
            I lay down in it
    And finger paint the words of who I am
            Across my chest
    Until I'm covered and there's only one smell,
            One word.

Several other poems remember Vietnam in sharp focus. Always, however, the details of war yield larger symbolic significations in retrospect. In "The Last Lie," Weigl observes a soldier hurling a can of C-rations into the face of a begging girl: he "laughed / And fingered the edge of another can / Like it was the seam of a baseball / Until his rage ripped / Again into the faces of children / Who called to us for food." With one deft simile, Weigl transmutes the sanctioned violence of the war into an all-American pastime. Even in poems not directly about Vietnam, the language of battle and the memory of terror shadow all present thoughts. In "Snowy Egret," a young boy's clandestine hunting of an egret re-enacts a soldier's naive killing. The final lines draw us in and expand beyond this incident to condemn all such "innocent" atrocities, to insist on our complicity, and to elegize our collective fall:

    What a time we share, that can make a good boy
            steal away,
    Wiping out from the blue face of the pond
    What he hadn't even known he loved, blasting
    Such beauty into nothing.

In the final poem of *The Monkey Wars*, "Song of Na-

palm," the war infiltrates a tender domestic and pastoral scene. Again, Vietnam is the glass through which the present is seen darkly, the obstacle which keeps the speaker from flying freely into the future. Standing in the doorway with his wife after a storm, Weigl sees with double vision: "branches / Crisscrossed the sky like barbed wire / But you said they were only branches." Though it seems for a moment "the old curses . . . swung finally away from me," Weigl cannot finally shake his monkey. Past and present collapse together in equations of literal rather than figurative correspondence:

    But still the branches are wire
    And thunder is the pounding mortar,
    Still I close my eyes and see the girl
    Running from her village, napalm
    Stuck to her dress like jelly,
    Her hands reaching for the no one
    Who waits in waves of heat before her.

As the poem's darkly ironic title suggests, the lyric imagination utterly fails to ameliorate or transform the memory of Vietnam; napalm is "like jelly" because it *is* jelly. At stake, and paralyzed as in "Amnesia," are the speaker's future and, implicitly, the possibilities of a salvific poetic vision which might unify past and present, anguish and affirmation:

    So I can keep on living,
    So I can stay here beside you,
    I try to imagine she runs down the road and
            wings
    Beat inside her until she rises
    Above the stinking jungle and her pain
    Eases, and your pain, and mine.

    But the lie swings back again.
    The lie works only as long as it takes to speak
    And the girl runs only as far
    As the napalm allows
    Until her burning tendons and crackling
    Muscles draw her up
    Into that final position
    Burning bodies so perfectly assume. Nothing
    Can change that; she is burned behind my eyes
    And not your good love and not the rain-swept
            air
    And not the jungle green
    Pasture unfolding before us can deny it.

For Ehrhart and Weigl, the war will not go away simply because we forget it or refuse to think of it, nor can lyricism sustain "the lie" or reclaim the innocent "green / Pasture unfolding" now violated forever by the "stinking jungle." The veteran poet's witnessing vision can, however, guard against the peculiarly American habit of denying history. His memories and nightmares and dilemmas are ours as well, drawing us intimately into the fallen history we share—"her pain . . . and your pain, and mine"—and reminding us, as Hemingway did for an earlier generation, that his war took place "in our time." By rooting Vietnam in our collective consciousness and connecting it to contemporary American life, these poets insist that their memories form part of our past, their anguish part of our present. Vietnam veterans do, indeed, "know things / worth knowing." If we ask and listen and respond, we may finally relinquish our illusions of national innocence and personal neutrality and begin to chart a truer history of our involvement with Vietnam.

Stephen P. Hidalgo   (essay date Fall 1993)

SOURCE: "Agendas for Vietnam War Poetry: Reading the War as Art, History, Therapy, and Politics," in *Journal of American Culture,* Vol. 16, No. 3, Fall, 1993, pp. 5-13.

[*In the following essay, Hidalgo focuses on language and sensemaking in his discussion of Vietnam War poetry.*]

This is about the margins of the poem, as much as it is about the poem itself, at once *act* and *artifact,* as is every written or recorded spoken word. At its margins the poem rests within the consciousness of the author and retrieves evidence of the poet's own implied situatedness in his or her social, political, and historical context, functioning as a source of meaning. Within the context, the poet of war experience, Veteran or protestor, endures a kind of social, political, and historical marginalization which the war poem seeks to invert, redefining the center of common experience out of its socially and psychologically repressed margins. If the poem is an *artifact,* it is not an "object," Wendell Berry insisted in 1974 ("The Specialization of Poetry" [in *Standing By Words,* 1983]), but a relevant understanding, a vision, and more, as Czeslaw Milosz concluded in *The Witness of Poetry* (1983), "a passionate pursuit of the real" carried by a "historical force . . . inventing means against destruction." Still earlier, in 1968, in "Leaping Up into Political Poetry," [*American Poetry: Wildness and Domesticity,* 1990] Robert Bly had explained the political poem as an appeal to a common contextual reality, a "leaping up" into "the life of the nation . . . , but as a psyche larger than the psyche of anyone living." Adrienne Rich in 1984, in "Blood, Bread, and Poetry," [*Blood, Bread, and Poetry: Selected Prose,* 1986] also has agreed with Berry that the implied contextual relevance of the poem is as important as its supposed autonomous status as an esthetic object.

In the recent war poem, self-reflexiveness offers to acknowledge the unsatisfactory nature, even the meaninglessness, of war experience; meaning is deferred from the experience the poem embodies to the enframing context—a field of cultural and political relationships in flux, that evolves the poet's own imaginative and therapeutic need. This context is summoned to validate every war poem, much as every photograph of atrocity is validated by its context, factual or invented. In Vietnam War poems, meaning is characteristically formed in the poem as question, paradox, or challenge to interpretation rather than as the illustration of a paraphrasable maxim, as it would be in the philosophical poems preferred by critical defenders of the primacy of esthetic sensibility, such as Jonathan Holden in *Style and Authenticity in Postmodern Poetry* (1986). War poems, after all, are not often about experiences esthetically pleasing in actuality, although some war poems are, as for instance this excerpt from John Balaban's "The Dragonfish":

> Brown men shock the brown pools with nets.
> Fishing for mudfish, carp and *ca loc,*

> they step and stalk the banks; hurl;
> stand, then squat heronlike in the
> shadow-stretching, red evening dusk.
>   (Ehrhart, ed., *Unaccustomed Mercy*)

If the imagery captures a pastoral moment of revery as the mind's retreat from violence, the poem goes on to unmask the precariousness of the moment, as "guerrillas of the Front hide" among the "rain-eaten tombs" that stand "Far out in deserted paddies / more cratered than the moon." Even here, the scarred consciousness of the narrator shapes the poem's content out of raw experience to disclose the insecurity of a moment of esthetic remembrance.

Esthetic demands characteristically impose a kind of revisionism on the memory of actual experiences, as much by an interpretive selection of details as by the re-formative function of language, as Paul Fussell has pointed out about the poems and novels of two World Wars (*The Great War and Modern Memory; Wartime*). A desire to cultivate resistance to the revisionary force of esthetics may perhaps account for Vietnam Veteran poet W.D. Ehrhart's concern to distance himself from the demands of poetry as an art form, a concern which he shares with Wilfred Owen, among poets of World War I, but a concern which, fortunately for literature, Ehrhart sometimes fails to fulfill. But so radical is Ehrhart's concern about the revisionary force of esthetics that in a roughly grotesque poem, "The Heart of the Matter" (*Just for Laughs*) he graphically burlesques the writing of a poem as an atrocity cruel in itself, the cutting out of a human heart. Comparably, many if not most Vietnam War poems are consciously antiesthetic in recording or responding to experienced atrocities or acts of mass violence. Such experience as most Vietnam War poems offer is directed into dialogue with its context, a dialogue by implication engaged in the margins of the poem of war remembrance, where, in the poet's consciousness, the war is still being fought.

Susanne Langer in *Feeling and Form* noted that poetry as "virtual experience"—the equivalence of felt experience that is the meaning of the poem—differs from discursive uses of language to remember actual experience in that poetry most definitively illustrates Saussure's idea of meaning as linguistic coherence, rather than Peirce's sense of meaning as reference to things. Poetry is particularly designed, in fact, often by esthetic device, for establishing distance between virtual experience (the poem) and actual experience. Thus, poetry is inherently revisionistic of the experience that it purports to be about, or, as Plato insisted in *The Republic,* poetry "lies." Even allowing for referential meaning as a function of language in the poem, meaning still functions as coherent interpretation of linguistic structures, and always therefore entails, in the act of verbalization, revision of the experience to which it refers. Common sense shows further that where language records remembered experiences, memory itself revises, glorifies or diminishes, idealizes or suppresses experienced content. In consequence, poetry may paradoxically be the form of linguistic expression most allied with memory in being the closest thing to its own method, showing forth both the advantages and problems of linguistic constructions of remembered experience. Frank Kermode suggests this, in *Poetry, Narrative, History,* when he claims that a poem may be history, and history may be viewed as a poem.

By its nature, poetry is self-referential in a high degree, and often self-reflexive about its revisionistic approach to experience in the ways that it presents itself as language counter to ordinary discourse, beyond the usual function of words as referential signs. Poetry about the Vietnam War—by veterans or protestors—highlights the poem's self-reflexive distance by a wide range of devices including direct assaults on the tenability of any language about war experience. For instance, D.F. Brown's "Patrols" encapsulates the whole cycle of war experience as its consequence, an accounting for the bodies of casualties, urging: "This is where stacking pays off. / Invent numbers each time you need one. / Sunlight more than names, any name" (*Unaccustomed Mercy*). In this poem, the wordless identity, the "name" of each combatant fashioned by war experience, remains inarticulate, beyond the reach of language.

By far the most common self-reflexive device is the violation of the imagistic poem with confessional intrusions, as in Bruce Weigl's "Song of Napalm" (*Unaccustomed Mercy*). Such intrusions, "trying to say this straight: for once / I was sane enough," confess poetic speech about atrocities to be a guilty act—as an act that obscures memory ("So I can keep on living"), or as an act of erasure ("I try to imagine"), or as an act guilty in its resort to the medium of public language ("The lie works only as long as it takes to speak"), a medium defiled in that the seemingly ineradicable duplicity of public language was itself material cause for the string of wars of hidden atrocity in Southeast Asia. Cary Nelson in *Our Last First Poets* (1981) assesses such confessional acknowledgements to be the root of authenticity in the Vietnam War protest poem, as a valid record of experience. This judgement implies not only that a frustrated search for meaning is basic to the experience of modern war, but that the poem as a formal evocation of virtual experience is irremovably enclosed within a larger context of discursive public language that contributes to its meaning. To this language of context, the reader who values Vietnam War poems as acts of sensemaking, as critics like Philip D. Beidler clearly do, must have interpretive recourse.

Since, in addition to esthetic concerns, a multitude of interpretive needs—political or therapeutic ones, for instance—qualify historically valid memory within the poem, Vietnam War poems regularly incur revisionism by selection and focus, rather than by extending their scope to explore the range of existential potency within memory as in the classical poem of history as epic. Instead, individual works focus either on one subjective perceptual response, as in Ehrhart's "Our gravel-crunching boots tear great holes in the darkness" ("Night Patrol," *Unaccustomed Mercy*); or on one set of perceptual contradictions offered as irony, as in this excerpt from Komunyakaa's "Thanks" [in *Unaccustomed Mercy*]:

> thanks for the dud
> handgrenade tossed at my feet
> outside Chu Lai. I'm still
> falling through its silence.

Sometimes Vietnam War poems offer a collage of conflicting perceptions offered as surrealism by the blurring of distinctions among perceiving subjects (as in Frank Stanford's long poem *The Battlefield Where the Moon Says I Love You*). Vietnam War poems (and novels, films, and plays) offer a wide scope of experience only in the collective assessment of them. Thus the validity of the poem as memory, including its use for purposes like "teaching the Vietnam War," is afforded by its enclosure within a larger dialogue that necessarily includes not only other Vietnam War poems, but also fiction, personal narrative, and "objective" history. Poetry functions in this dialogue to constructively question all verbal (and thereby revisionist) representations of experience, as it constantly discloses to us the interpretive function of sense-making as a project. Like other literary forms, but more intensely than they, poetry reminds us of the centrality and the severe limits of personal perceptiveness and of memory in making sense of experience.

The particularly literary faculties of formative perception that poetry brings to the project of historical memory—its sensitivity to the inclusive resonances of words, its discovery of a value within detail that equals the scope of actual experience, and its property to form of these a virtual experience by balancing, as Wallace Stevens explains (in "The Noble Rider and the Sound of Words," 1942), the imagination as a "violence" from within against the "pressure" of reality as a "violence" from without—these faculties invoke tensions between language and experience that are not unique to poetry, but are typical of all projects of linguistic sense-making. In the Vietnam War poem, these tensions are brought to a symptomatic crisis that includes the recognition of a traumatic exchange of functions between reality and imagination—sometimes as a mental escape that saves the speaker's sanity, as in Vietnam veteran poet Bruce Weigl's "Him, on the Bicycle" (*Unaccustomed Mercy*), an American soldier sees from a helicopter "four men running, carrying rifles, / one man on a bicycle." In revery, the bicycler "pulls me out of the ship; / . . . I'm on the back of the bike / holding his hips." When the bicycler's hat flies off, the rider catches and wears it, crying out, "I want to live forever!"

Alternatively, the violent displacement of imagination by the need for attentiveness to mortal realities, and the corresponding displacement of reality by imagination may imply war consciousness as a form of life-sustaining insanity, as in David Mura's artful "Lan Nguyen: The Uniform of Death (1971)":

> In the river, my face
> is twisted, mottled green,
> a mango rotted eight days in the jungle's oven.
>
> . . .
>
> I think we should fight underwater,
> crawling at the river bottom,
> moving heavily, flies caught in honey.
> (*After We Lost Our Way*)

A therapeutic recollection of war consciousness as saving madness, but reshaped, like Mura's fantastic musing, into an esthetic revery, redistancing itself from madness as a mutual displacement between imagination and reality, as it recovers the same exchange in the revisionary form of a lyric poem, is offered in this excerpt from Bruce Weigl's "Monkey":

> my Vietnamese monkey . . .
> he's my little brown monkey
> he came here from heaven
> to give me his spirit imagine
> my monkey my beautiful
> monkey he saved me lifted
> me above the punji
> sticks above the mines
> above the ground burning
> above the dead above
> the living above the
> wounded dying the wounded
> dying.
>
> (*Unaccustomed Mercy*)

The recovered interchange between imagination and reality here implies also a partial displacement of cultural identity through emulation of the Vietnamese out of the need to survive. In all these excerpts, the crisis of tension between imagination and reality in the poem reveals the underlying tensions among conflicting needs of sense-making: therapeutic, esthetic, political, and historical. Call these needs "agendas," and number them as potentially infinite as the reach of human imagination. As agendas multiply within Vietnam War poems, exploring tensions among these agendas should raise more perceptive questions about the nature of these tensions, as conflicts potentially revelatory about the perennial, psychologically self-propagating phenomenon of modern war.

Much Vietnam poetry, particularly poems in early anthologies like *Winning Hearts and Minds,* 1972, is therapeutic in the original motive (Ehrhart, "Soldier Poets"). These poems use inscription in the poem to assuage the unheeded anguish of veterans and to overcome symptoms like the long-term traumatic amnesia characteristic of many cases of Vietnam PTSD, and perhaps most importantly, to come to terms with guilt—either "survivor guilt" or the guilt incurred by deeds of violence, culpable or not as acts of war, as both Robert Jay Lifton (*Home From the War*) and Hendin and Haas (*Wounds of War*) observe. The shock of self-recognition in such therapeutic poems, when published, may incur a parallel self-recognition from its readership as unacknowledged psychological victims and as active or passive contributors to the War in Vietnam. This use of the poem gestures toward what Kali Tal has termed "cultural therapy."

Still, as Paul Jay has pointed out about autobiography in *Being in the Text,* all therapeutic stories are partly fictional retellings, and thus are essentially acts of mnemonic revision. As a result, therapeutic assessments of the War in Vietnam inevitably conflict with each other, as, for example, the post-traumatic therapeutic needs of veterans and disaffected citizens conflict, at least in immediate ends, with Richard M. Nixon's postulation (*No More Vietnams*) of "Vietnam syndrome" as an alleged national pathological weakness of will following the American withdrawal from Indochina. All such therapeutic agendas potentially threaten the need for a history that goes beyond political

motives for historical revisionism—specifically to cover mistakes and protect reputations. Consequently, John Carlos Rowe's and Rick Berg's charge, in *The Vietnam War and American Culture,* that "therapeutic" agendas towards remembering Vietnam are abetting historical revisionism, should not surprise us. It is a liability of any valid history that, while sharpening factual content, it can never remove the influence of reshaping reassessments on its final product. Even those historical accounts that Robert A. Divine, in "Historiography: Vietnam Reconsidered," [*The Vietnam Reader,* edited by Walter Capps, 1991] has called "postrevisionist histories" are only superior in that they are more acutely discerning of our needs for history in adjudicating among revisionary recastings of our collective story as history.

Much Vietnam poetry is therapeutic. These poems use inscription in the poem to assuage the unheeded anguish of veterans and to overcome symptoms like the long-term traumatic amnesia characteristic of many cases of Vietnam PTSD, and perhaps most importantly, to come to terms with guilt.

—Stephen P. Hidalgo

Vietnam War poems intended as therapeutic assessments reveal still unmet needs for a valid history of the conflict, and offer at times penetrating, concise insights into the problems of historical revisionism. Specifically, many poems as examples of acknowledged post-traumatic recovery reinterpret a persistence of remorse not as "Vietnam syndrome" but as potentially a new maturity of reflection toward the problem of modern war, in lines like Gerald McCarthy's "the war still follows me / Never in anything have I found / a way to throw off the dead" (*Unaccustomed Mercy*); or in C.K. Williams's:

> There is a world that uses its soldiers and widows for
> flour, its orphans for building stones, its legs for pens.
> . . . When we come home, we are half way.
> Our screams heal the torn silence. We are the scars
>
> (Williams);

or W.D. Ehrhart's:

> We are the ones you sent to fight a war
> you did not know a thing about . . .
> When you awake,
> we will still be here
>
> (*Unaccustomed Mercy*);

or again:

> . . . all of us
> looking for a reason.

We never found one. Presidents
come and go away like snowdrifts;

or again:

Oh, we're still haggling over pieces
of the lives sticking out
beyond the margins of our latest
history books—but no one haggles
with the authors;

or Howard Nemerov's ironic apology for the failure of
Americans to "learn from history" because we can periodically reinvent ourselves:

. . . we are not the same people as them
That fed our sons and honor to Vietnam

. . .

And history will not blame us if once again
The light at the end of the tunnel is the train.
              (Nemerov [*War Stories,* 1987])

A few Vietnam poems offer qualitative prescriptions for
the reform of historical processes, like Wendell Berry's
call in "The Morning's News" for a "deathlier knowledge" (*Collected Poems*).

Even more illuminating, perhaps, are the questions raised
by Vietnam War poetry about the allegedly irreconcilable
conflict between political and poetic uses of language.
Against recent critical attempts to see poetry as felicitously in retreat from the unbearable horrors of politics (Terrence Des Pres in *Praises and Dispraises*), M.L. Rosenthal
in 1971 (" 'The Unconsenting Spirit' " [*Our Life in Poetry,*
1991]) found poetry's involvement with political questions
to be one of its most valuable, permanent contributions in
the modern era. Robert Bly and Adrienne Rich both acknowledge William Butler Yeats as their poetic ancestor,
in his political engagement as well as in esthetic concerns.
Moreover, that political language and poetic language
function in much the same way has been argued most
forcefully by Wallace Stevens ("The Noble Rider and the
Sound of Words" [in *The Necessary Angel,* 1951]), who in
suggesting that both move their audience to a virtual experience that acquires collective validity, adds the qualifying
observation that "social obligation" represents "a phase of
the pressure of reality which a poet . . . is bound to resist
or evade today." The poet, Stevens concludes, "fulfills
himself only as he sees his imagination become the light
in the minds of others. His role, in short, is to help people
to live their lives." Stevens's desire is to see poetry and politics as separate, potentially complementary domains.

But the conditions of poetry and politics in the contemporary world repeatedly put them at odds as agendas for
finding meaning. Poetry demands an inclusive sensitivity
to resonances of meaning in the selection of words, and
typically draws poetic meaning out of cohering resonances
among the words selected, modulated by recognizable
form, whether conventional genres, patterns of repetition,
or the suggestion of an analogue. In contrast, George Orwell noted as early as 1946 ("Politics and the English Language") the fragmenting and meaning-evacuating influence that mass politics and its propaganda discourse exert-
ed on words as vessels of sense pertinent to experience.

Added to this, Daniel Boorstin noted in 1961, in *The
Image,* a discrepancy arises between television images as
political terms and the realities that mass audiences take
them to accurately present—with the consequent diminishment of the role of the political leader from statesman
to custodian of a public image. Walter J. Ong in 1967, in
The Presence of the Word, confirmed Boorstin's analysis,
suggesting a discrepancy between television images perceived as spontaneous and their rehearsed and preplanned
actual format. Modern and contemporary poems are presumed to discover their form spontaneously in the act of
constituting them, and often rely, as poetry traditionally
has relied, on the transformation of a creditably real descriptive image into figurative sense—based on a confidence in language that political uses of television have
tended to discredit. By 1969, Thomas Merton, in "War
and the Crisis of Language" [in *Thomas Merton on Peace,*
1971] noted a wide discrepancy between the intense language of need arising in the experience of personal lives,
manifest in poetry as the antiformal, antilinguistic confessional mode, and the false language of self-fulfillment as
verbal autonomy offered by televised political speeches
and advertising.

As an alternative to the formlessness of the confessional
mode, with its tendency to slide into sentimentality and
self-pity, Vietnam War poems have preferred the ironic
application of dysfunctional political language. Galway
Kinnell, in "The Dead Shall Be Raised Incorruptible," be-
queaths a new poetic legacy:

My tongue
goes to the Secretary of the Dead
to tell the corpses, "I'm sorry, fellows,
the killing was just one of those things
difficult to pre-visualize."

                              (*Selected Poems*)

And continuing the black comedy, Michael Casey, in
"Road Hazard" literalizes concrete circumstances behind
the mask of political euphemism, as "the Nuoc Mau / Citizens standing around this scene / Holding their noses"
(*Unaccustomed Mercy*). Kinnell's and Casey's words
sharply focus as dissonance the contrast between human
experience and dysfunctional political language, and at
the same time are analogously ironic acknowledgements
of the poet's own crisis of language in failing to find terms
that offer redeeming sense to the memory of horrors. The
real conflict here is not between the linguistic methods of
sense making used by the poet and by the politician, but
between their recognized sense-making needs. As an act
of language, poetic sense-making parallels political sense-
making in these instances, revealingly, as instances of linguistic failure. Paradoxically, the poems succeed through
their failure to make sense of the senseless.

It may be that in contrast to our experience of fragmented
political language in the twentieth century, we usually assume poetic language to be all constitutive, after Benedetto Croce, and word-creative, as urged by Stéphane Mallarmé. But the high modernists, who took Croce and Mallarmé most seriously, produced almost universally an esthetic of fragmentation, since acts of poetry are based on a particularly irremediable linguistic tension. The distance

which constitutes "virtual experience" out of actual experience generates a special status for the language of the poem, which, when it reaches a level of conventionality, we call "poetic diction." But since Wordsworth, poetry as a constitutive function of language has been held in tension with its avowed need to approximate the language of spoken use, a task historically incurred by the awkwardness of sense created by artificial poetic dictions, but also, as some recent poets have argued, by the recognition that words cannot be wholly removed from their normal multiple and fragmenting discursive functions by incorporating them into a "special" vocabulary as components of an esthetic object. If the poem is an act of sense-making, it must make sense by transformations that rely on vocabularies in use in its context.

David Jones, a veteran of World War I, felt poems set words apart for a mystical, sacramental function that he called "anathemata," from the Greek meaning "outcasts." Jones textured unusual terms from dialects ancient and modern, blending them with soldiers' argot, and thus collected words like wounded, cast-off soldiers, to give them, in war poems like *In Parenthesis,* new meaning and new wholeness within the poem. But Jones, like Eliot, Pound, and other high modernists, achieves wholeness by shifting the fractures within languages and within words to more esthetic alignments. David Jones self-consciously acknowledges the persistence of linguistic fragmentation better than most high modernist poets, and also succeeds better than most in conceding the irremediable distance generated between the poem's virtual experience and the actual experience it "images" or the "history" it claims to "contain," as Pound claimed for *The Cantos.*

Vietnam War poetry, like David Jones's war poems, applies the contextual realignment of fragmented language, but plays off complex self-reflexive ironies against this poetics of fragmentation in its postmodern search to revitalize the community-constitutive functions of song and story in the poem. How can Eliot's "falling towers" help but be recalled in a poem made out of refunctioned fragments of linguistic dysfunction and cultural disintegration, as in a passage from Yusef Komunyakaa's "After the Fall"?

> Dzung leaves the Continental Hotel
> in a newspaper dress.
> Hoping for a hard rain,
> she moves through broken colors
> flung to the ground,
> mixing up the words to Trinh's
> "Mad Girl's Love Song"
> & "Stars Fell on Alabama,"
> trying to bite off her tongue.
>   (*Unaccustomed Mercy*)

Call this a jazz oratorio. Poetry and politics are playing in concert here, ringing changes off of the same fragmentation, blending snatches of a Vietnamese love song with an African-American lament, laying down the same dissonances, and absconding into the same revealed wordlessness—the melting of the newspaper clothing and the biting off of the singer's tongue.

Political terms—and here cultural terms are political terms—are ruptured and recollected, are reconstituted with dynamic force into an anti-language, a set of self-consciously euphemistic analogies for torn psyches and wounded lives. Wholeness, implied by negation, is invoked as an absence. The absence is redemptive as laughter is, or the blues—the door out of the absurd, conjecturing the possibility of other actual worlds, and more satisfying virtual experiences (poems) as well.

The escape from the conventionally esthetic demands of poesis is simultaneously an escape from corrupt and corrupting politics. Characteristic of the compatibility of poetics and politics in this capacity are W.D. Ehrhart's complementary pronouncements: about poesis, that he is not interested in mere poetry; about politics, that he will never trust our government again. Consider this a special case of negative capability. This double-absconding from poetry and politics, in the processes of writing political poetry and establishing a poetic reputation, offers not so much a condemnation of poetry or politics, but a repudiation of corrupting or distorting circumstances within both.

The escape from conventional meaning suggested within the "virtual experience" offered by the Vietnam War poem is an escape into dialogue, into the larger discursive context in which the poem is situated, where it offers its challenge to other sense-making agendas. A recent poem by W.D. Ehrhart, "Not Your Problem," offers a new ironic use of dissonance in that, while about El Salvador, the setting is never identified, and (but for the detail of "ink" that brands "voters," an ironic analogue for the poem) could as well have been Vietnam:

> Not Your Problem
>
> Avoid this place.
>
> Here time travels in tiny circles
> like the hands of a clock.
>
> Here dust rises like smoke
> until it rains;
> then we lie down in mud
> and dream of dust.
>
> Here our children will never learn
> to read or write; their teeth
> will rot from their heads;
> they will join the army, or die
> like us beneath foreign bombs.
>
> Here men with guns at night
> make sleeping people in houses
> disappear.
>
> Here voters are branded with ink,
> and those unmarked are found
> days later in trash dumps.
> Here being poor is a crime
> unless we are also quiet;
> almost everyone is poor,
> and we can hear a bullet
> being chambered a mile away.
>
> We will change all this.
>
> You won't want to be here
> when we do.

(*Just for Laughs* reprinted by permission of
the author)

A convergence between observation and memory drives
this poem, as in the images of enforced conscription and
heedless bombing of civilians—"children" who "will join
the army or die / like us beneath foreign bombs"—which
suggests in its strong parallel to the Vietnam War, the pro-
generation of violence, the parenting of one war by another. In an ironic psychological displacement of motive, the
civilians' hearing is sharpened so that they "can hear a
bullet / being chambered a mile away"—sharpened not by
natural fear but by guilt over the "crime" of "poverty,"
as though they had uncannily acquired the Vietnam veteran observer's own survivor guilt. Paradoxically, the desire
to see things change for succeeding generations emerges
as a need to escape being an active agent of the change;
survival creates, in conflict with its actual demands, a felt
need to escape from even the politics of war's trauma.

Absence, escape, is the sense-making gesture of this
poem—escape at once from the untenability of making
pleasurable esthetic experiences out of intolerable human
experience, and escape from the corrupting influence of
political dishonesty. Critically, the margins of the poem,
and the conflicts of guilt there sustained, emerge as primary interpretant of its virtual experience. Further, the context of an evolving politics of Vietnam veterans concerned
with questioning the strategy, legality, wisdom, or morality of the conduct of the Vietnam War; with appropriate
acknowledgement of veterans' sacrifices; with the accom-
modation of veterans' health needs, not only from physical
wounds but from PTSD and Agent Orange Syndrome;
with some accountability for POW's thought to be missing; and with a re-examination of American government
policy toward future limited foreign military engagements
(or "dirty little wars") renders the concluding lines more
than a simple gut yearning to be elsewhere. "You won't
want to be here" is a complex accusation, not urging non-
involvement, but convicting the speaker and possibly the
reader of the wrong forms of destructive, paradoxical in-
volvement/noninvolvement.

Intermittent American television voyeurism, punctuating
a years-long scarcity of informed coverage by the American press of the now cooled conflict in El Salvador, is a
further implied irony drawn from the poem's discursive
context to enrich the image of absence. The "poor" don't
need television if they "can hear a bullet / being chambered a mile away." It is the wealthy North Americans
who need television as a spur to humane accountability.
The poem offers an escape from guilty paralysis *into* political dialogue. The poem's "virtual experience" might best
be characterized as despair. But the meaning of the poem
is escape from despair in the recognition of it, and in the
asking "must it be so?" Language in the poem, in Wendell
Berry's terms ("Unspecializing Poetry" [in *Standing By
Words,* 1983]), "is the vector that carries vision into and
(since no action fully enacts vision) out of action."

In "A Poem of Difficult Hope" (1990), a celebratory cri-
tique of Hayden Carruth's poem "On Being Asked to
Write a Poem Against the War in Vietnam," Wendell
Berry argues:

A person who marks his trail into despair remembers hope—and thus has hope, even if only
a little. . . . the poem preserves the poet's
wholeness of heart in the face of his despair. And
it shows us how to do so as well.

(*What Are People For?*)

And earlier he acknowledges:

Protest that endures, I think, is moved by a
hope . . . of preserving qualities in ones own
heart and spirit that would be destroyed by ac-
quiescence.

Wendell Berry thinks of the poem, as expression of conscience, as an action, not just the constituting of a verbal
artifact to preserve a "virtual experience." It must be more
than an esthetically valuable act of making, because our
consciences are more than esthetic, and had best be more
than just invented. Expressing one's conscience, moreover, is an action with political implications; in this case,
it encourages the reader to persevere.

How can one be plainly political in the poem without taking on the dishonesty of political-linguistic processes?
Moreover, what does the quest for linguistic acuity in converting actual into virtual experience as poetry sets forth,
in Eliot's words, "to purify the dialect of the tribe," serve
in terms of the practice of politics in an age of holocausts?
By redirecting the poem towards its discursive context,
Vietnam War poems find new ways of making political
and poetic agendas come together in the poem. But rather
than answering the most important political questions,
poems can only propose new ways of asking them.

FURTHER READING

Bibliography

Calloway, Catherine. "Vietnam War Literature and Film: A
Bibliography of Secondary Sources." *Bulletin of Bibliography*
43, No. 3 (September 1986): 149-58.
    Provides listings for criticism on Vietnam War literature
    organized according to drama, film, poetry, and prose.

Colonnese, Tom, and Hogan, Jerry. "Vietnam War Literature, 1958-1979: A First Checklist." *Bulletin of Bibliography*
38, No. 1 (January-March 1981): 26-31, 51.
    Bibliography of book-length works and short fiction
    dealing with the Vietnam War.

Criticism

Asahina, Robert. "The Basic Training of American Playwrights: Theater and the Vietnam War." *Theater* 9, No. 2
(Spring 1978): 30-7.
    Surveys plays about the Vietnam War from the 1960s
    through the 1970s and concludes that "as far as the
    question of the war was concerned, [David Rabe] was
    the only playwright really concerned with the art of the
    theater rather than with the form or the content of the
    media."

Beidler, Philip D. "Truth-Telling and Literary Values in the

Vietnam Novel." *South Atlantic Quarterly* 78, No. 2 (Spring 1979): 141-56.

> Considers the combination of experimental and traditional novelistic techniques employed in David Halberstam's *One Very Hot Day*, Josiah Bunting's *The Lionheads*, William Eastlake's *The Bamboo Bed*, and Charles Durden's *No Bugles, No Drums*.

————. *Re-Writing America: Vietnam Authors in Their Generation*. Athens: University of Georgia Press, 1991, 333 p.

> Examines the work of major Vietnam War novelists, dramatists, poets, and nonfiction writers and discusses "the ways in which [their] work continues to place many of them at the forefront of current American literary endeavor."

Carter, Susanne. "Variations on Vietnam: Women's Innovative Interpretations of the Vietnam War Experience." *Extrapolation* 32, No. 2 (1991): 170-83.

> Discusses the deviations from realism that several women novelists and short story writers have followed in their works about the Vietnam War.

Carton, Evan. "Vietnam and the Limits of Masculinity." *American Literary History* 3, No. 2 (Summer 1991): 294-318.

> Examines the idea that for some soldiers the Vietnam experience was "an enacted dream of *undifferentiation*—of a human solidarity beyond (or before) ideological, linguistic, and sexual division."

Critique, Special Issue: The Fiction of Vietnam XXIV, No. 2 (Winter 1983).

> Contains essays on several novels, including Robert Stone's *Dog Soldiers*, Tim O'Brien's *Going After Cacciato*, and Larry Heinemann's *Close Quarters*.

Franklin, H. Bruce. "The Vietnam War as American Science Fiction and Fantasy." *Science Fiction Studies* 17, No. 52 (November 1990): 341-59.

> Discusses depictions of the Vietnam War in science fiction and fantasy literature and argues that "American SF very explicitly defined the war, which unalterably redefined American SF."

Genre, Special Topics: The Vietnam War & Postmodern Memory XXI, No. 4 (Winter 1988).

> Includes essays on Vietnam War fiction, films, nonfiction, and television documentaries as well as excerpts from Robert Olen Butler's novel *The Deuce* and R. S. Carlson's *Was That Someplace You Were? Selected Poems 1968-1987*.

Gilman, Owen W., Jr., and Smith, Lorrie, eds. *America Rediscovered: Critical Essays on Literature and Film of the Vietnam War*. New York: Garland Publishing, 1990, 386 p.

> Contains essays covering a wide range of topics on Vietnam War fiction, film, and poetry.

Herzog, Tobey C. *Vietnam War Stories: Innocence Lost*. New York: Routledge, 1992, 238 p.

> Analyzes novels and personal narratives dealing with the Vietnam War in terms of major cultural and literary themes.

Hölbling, Walter W. "The Impact of the Vietnam War on U.S. Fiction: 1960s to 1980s." In *Literature and War*, edited by David Bevan, pp. 193-209. Atlanta, Ga.: Rodopi, 1990.

> Examines contemporary American writing on the Vietnam War which not only acknowledges "the uniqueness of the Vietnam experience" but also places "it in the context of other cultural and literary movements of the past decades."

Jeffords, Susan. " 'Things Worth Dying For': Gender and the Ideology of Collectivity in Vietnam Representation." *Cultural Critique*, No. 8 (Winter 1987-88): 79-103.

> Argues that although battle appears to erase differentiations based on race and class, the bonds of collectivity exhibited in Vietnam War literature are distinctly masculine and gender exclusive.

Johannessen, Larry R. "Young-Adult Literature and the Vietnam War." *English Journal* 82, No. 5 (September 1993): 43-9.

> Divides adolescent Vietnam War literature into four types—combat narratives, the war at home, refugee experiences, and the war's legacies—and discusses the most common devices authors use to convey meaning.

Journal of American Culture, Special Issue: Poetry and the Vietnam War 16, No. 3 (Fall 1993).

> Issue includes essays on Vietnam War poets and poetry and contains several poems.

Katzman, Jason. "From Outcast to Cliché: How Film Shaped, Warped and Developed the Image of the Vietnam Veteran, 1967-1990." *Journal of American Culture* 16, No. 1 (Spring 1993): 7-24.

> Surveys the portrayal of Vietnam veterans in television and film, noting that early works tended to depict veterans as villains or losers while more recent efforts have attempted realistic explanations of veterans' problems.

Krasteva, Yonka K. "Rediscovering America in Personal Narratives about Vietnam." *North Dakota Quarterly* 60, No. 1 (Winter 1992): 161-73.

> Examines Philip Caputo's *A Rumor of War*, Michael Herr's *Dispatches*, and Ron Kovic's *Born on the Fourth of July* in terms of American culture. Krasteva concludes that "ultimately these books are about how to come to terms with disorder and chaos both in our physical and psychological world."

Literature/Film Quarterly 20, No. 3 (1992).

> Special issue devoted to Vietnam War films, with essays on such works as Francis Coppola's *Apocalypse Now* and Brian DePalma's *Casualties of War*.

Martin, Andrew. *Receptions of War: Vietnam in American Culture*. Norman: University of Oklahoma Press, 1993, 192 p.

> Investigates connections between historical themes and contemporary issues in Vietnam War film, literature, and television in an effort to illuminate "the process through which an unpopular war has come to be received in popular culture."

McInerney, Peter. " 'Straight' and 'Secret' History in Vietnam War Literature." *Contemporary Literature* 22, No. 2 (Spring 1981): 187-204.

> Remarks on history, structure, questions of authenticity, and the meaning of facts in several works, including Michael Herr's *Dispatches*, Ron Kovic's *Born on the Fourth of July*, and Philip Caputo's *A Rumor of War*.

Muse, Eben J. "From Lt. Calley to John Rambo: Repatriating the Vietnam War." *Journal of American Studies* 27, No. 2 (August 1993): 88-92.

Focuses on the portrayal of soldiers and veterans in several Vietnam War films.

Pratt, John Clark. "The Lost Frontier: American Myth in the Literature of the Vietnam War." In *The Frontier Experience and the American Dream: Essays on American Literature,* edited by David Mogen, Mark Busby, and Paul Bryant, pp. 236-47. College Station, Texas: Texas A&M University Press, 1989.

Surveys Vietnam War novels and argues that "the literature of the Vietnam War is filled with American characters who enter Vietnam as traditional frontier huntsmen, then become men trying merely to survive in a wilderness they do not understand."

Price, Joanna. "Remembering Vietnam: Subjectivity and Mourning in American New Realist Writing." *Journal of American Studies* 27, No. 2 (August 1993): 173-86.

Discusses Jayne Anne Phillips's *Machine Dreams* and Bobbie Ann Mason's *In Country,* focusing on themes of identity and mourning.

Reitinger, Douglas W. "Paint It Black: Rock Music and Vietnam War Film." *Journal of American Culture* 15, No. 3 (Fall 1992): 53-9.

Remarks on the degree of success or failure of various filmmakers in thematically integrating rock music into their films about the Vietnam War.

Rowe, John Carlos. " 'Bringing It All Back Home': American Recyclings of the Vietnam War." In *The Violence of Representation: Literature and the History of Violence,* edited by Nancy Armstrong and Leonard Tennenhouse, pp. 197-218. New York: Routledge, 1989.

Focuses on Vietnam War films in his analysis of the interpretation and use of the Vietnam War in American culture.

————, and Berg, Rick, eds. *The Vietnam War and American Culture.* New York: Columbia University Press, 1991, 275 p.

Collection of essays that analyzes literary works and other media sources in a multidisciplinary approach that the editors refer to as "cultural criticism."

Spark, Alasdair. "Vietnam: The War in Science Fiction." In *Science Fiction, Social Conflict and War,* edited by Philip John Davies, pp. 113-31. Manchester, England: Manchester University Press, 1990, 184 p.

Remarks on the history of the Vietnam War as a subject of science fiction.

Tal, Kalí. "The Mind at War: Images of Women in Vietnam Novels by Combat Veterans." *Contemporary Literature* 31, No. 1 (Spring 1990): 76-96.

Examines images of women in several Vietnam War novels in an effort to elucidate "the connection those images have with the author's process of healing from the trauma of combat."

☐ Contemporary Literary Criticism

Indexes

Literary Criticism Series
Cumulative Author Index
Cumulative Topic Index
Cumulative Nationality Index
Title Index, Volume 91

How to Use This Index

The main references

Calvino, Italo
1923-1985.....CLC 5, 8, 11, 22, 33, 39,
73; SSC 3
---

list all author entries in the following Gale Literary Criticism series:

BLC = *Black Literature Criticism*
CLC = *Contemporary Literary Criticism*
CLR = *Children's Literature Review*
CMLC = *Classical and Medieval Literature Criticism*
DA = *DISCovering Authors*
DC = *Drama Criticism*
HLC = *Hispanic Literature Criticism*
LC = *Literature Criticism from 1400 to 1800*
NCLC = *Nineteenth-Century Literature Criticism*
PC = *Poetry Criticism*
SSC = *Short Story Criticism*
TCLC = *Twentieth-Century Literary Criticism*
WLC = *World Literature Criticism, 1500 to the Present*

The cross-references

See also CANR 23; CA 85-88;
obituary CA 116
---

list all author entries in the following Gale biographical and literary sources:

AAYA = *Authors & Artists for Young Adults*
AITN = *Authors in the News*
BEST = *Bestsellers*
BW = *Black Writers*
CA = *Contemporary Authors*
CAAS = *Contemporary Authors Autobiography Series*
CABS = *Contemporary Authors Bibliographical Series*
CANR = *Contemporary Authors New Revision Series*
CAP = *Contemporary Authors Permanent Series*
CDALB = *Concise Dictionary of American Literary Biography*
CDBLB = *Concise Dictionary of British Literary Biography*
DLB = *Dictionary of Literary Biography*
DLBD = *Dictionary of Literary Biography Documentary Series*
DLBY = *Dictionary of Literary Biography Yearbook*
HW = *Hispanic Writers*
JRDA = *Junior DISCovering Authors*
MAICYA = *Major Authors and Illustrators for Children and Young Adults*
MTCW = *Major 20th-Century Writers*
NNAL = *Native North American Literature*
SAAS = *Something about the Author Autobiography Series*
SATA = *Something about the Author*
YABC = *Yesterday's Authors of Books for Children*

Literary Criticism Series
Cumulative Author Index

A. E............................TCLC 3, 10
See also Russell, George William

Abasiyanik, Sait Faik   1906-1954
See Sait Faik
See also CA 123

Abbey, Edward   1927-1989......CLC 36, 59
See also CA 45-48; 128; CANR 2, 41

Abbott, Lee K(ittredge)   1947-......CLC 48
See also CA 124; CANR 51; DLB 130

Abe, Kobo   1924-1993.....CLC 8, 22, 53, 81
See also CA 65-68; 140; CANR 24;
DAM NOV; MTCW

Abelard, Peter   c. 1079-c. 1142 ... CMLC 11
See also DLB 115

Abell, Kjeld   1901-1961............CLC 15
See also CA 111

Abish, Walter   1931-..............CLC 22
See also CA 101; CANR 37; DLB 130

Abrahams, Peter (Henry)   1919- .....CLC 4
See also BW 1; CA 57-60; CANR 26;
DLB 117; MTCW

Abrams, M(eyer) H(oward)   1912-... CLC 24
See also CA 57-60; CANR 13, 33; DLB 67

Abse, Dannie   1923-.......CLC 7, 29; DAB
See also CA 53-56; CAAS 1; CANR 4, 46;
DAM POET; DLB 27

Achebe, (Albert) Chinua(lumogu)
1930- .....CLC 1, 3, 5, 7, 11, 26, 51, 75;
BLC; DA; DAB; DAC; WLC
See also AAYA 15; BW 2; CA 1-4R;
CANR 6, 26, 47; CLR 20; DAM MST,
MULT, NOV; DLB 117; MAICYA;
MTCW; SATA 40; SATA-Brief 38

Acker, Kathy   1948- ....CLC 45
See also CA 117; 122

Ackroyd, Peter   1949-..........CLC 34, 52
See also CA 123; 127; CANR 51; DLB 155;
INT 127

Acorn, Milton   1923-.........CLC 15; DAC
See also CA 103; DLB 53; INT 103

Adamov, Arthur   1908-1970......CLC 4, 25
See also CA 17-18; 25-28R; CAP 2;
DAM DRAM; MTCW

Adams, Alice (Boyd)   1926- ... CLC 6, 13, 46
See also CA 81-84; CANR 26; DLBY 86;
INT CANR-26; MTCW

Adams, Andy   1859-1935.........TCLC 56
See also YABC 1

Adams, Douglas (Noel)   1952- ... CLC 27, 60
See also AAYA 4; BEST 89:3; CA 106;
CANR 34; DAM POP; DLBY 83; JRDA

Adams, Francis   1862-1893.......NCLC 33

Adams, Henry (Brooks)
1838-1918 ......TCLC 4, 52; DA; DAB;
DAC
See also CA 104; 133; DAM MST; DLB 12,
47

Adams, Richard (George)
1920- ....CLC 4, 5, 18
See also AAYA 16; AITN 1, 2; CA 49-52;
CANR 3, 35; CLR 20; DAM NOV;
JRDA; MAICYA; MTCW; SATA 7, 69

Adamson, Joy(-Friederike Victoria)
1910-1980 ....CLC 17
See also CA 69-72; 93-96; CANR 22;
MTCW; SATA 11; SATA-Obit 22

Adcock, Fleur   1934-..............CLC 41
See also CA 25-28R; CAAS 23; CANR 11,
34; DLB 40

Addams, Charles (Samuel)
1912-1988 ....CLC 30
See also CA 61-64; 126; CANR 12

Addison, Joseph   1672-1719 .... LC 18
See also CDBLB 1660-1789; DLB 101

Adler, Alfred (F.)   1870-1937......TCLC 61
See also CA 119

Adler, C(arole) S(chwerdtfeger)
1932-......................CLC 35
See also AAYA 4; CA 89-92; CANR 19,
40; JRDA; MAICYA; SAAS 15;
SATA 26, 63

Adler, Renata   1938-............CLC 8, 31
See also CA 49-52; CANR 5, 22; MTCW

Ady, Endre   1877-1919 ....TCLC 11
See also CA 107

Aeschylus
525B.C.-456B.C........CMLC 11; DA;
DAB; DAC
See also DAM DRAM, MST

Afton, Effie
See Harper, Frances Ellen Watkins

Agapida, Fray Antonio
See Irving, Washington

Agee, James (Rufus)
1909-1955 ....TCLC 1, 19
See also AITN 1; CA 108; 148;
CDALB 1941-1968; DAM NOV; DLB 2,
26, 152

Aghill, Gordon
See Silverberg, Robert

Agnon, S(hmuel) Y(osef Halevi)
1888-1970 ....CLC 4, 8, 14
See also CA 17-18; 25-28R; CAP 2; MTCW

Agrippa von Nettesheim, Henry Cornelius
1486-1535 ....LC 27

Aherne, Owen
See Cassill, R(onald) V(erlin)

Ai   1947-.................CLC 4, 14, 69
See also CA 85-88; CAAS 13; DLB 120

Aickman, Robert (Fordyce)
1914-1981 ....CLC 57
See also CA 5-8R; CANR 3

Aiken, Conrad (Potter)
1889-1973 ... CLC 1, 3, 5, 10, 52; SSC 9
See also CA 5-8R; 45-48; CANR 4;
CDALB 1929-1941; DAM NOV, POET;
DLB 9, 45, 102; MTCW; SATA 3, 30

Aiken, Joan (Delano)   1924-........CLC 35
See also AAYA 1; CA 9-12R; CANR 4, 23,
34; CLR 1, 19; DLB 161; JRDA;
MAICYA; MTCW; SAAS 1; SATA 2,
30, 73

Ainsworth, William Harrison
1805-1882 ....NCLC 13
See also DLB 21; SATA 24

Aitmatov, Chingiz (Torekulovich)
1928-......................CLC 71
See also CA 103; CANR 38; MTCW;
SATA 56

Akers, Floyd
See Baum, L(yman) Frank

Akhmadulina, Bella Akhatovna
1937-......................CLC 53
See also CA 65-68; DAM POET

Akhmatova, Anna
1888-1966 ....CLC 11, 25, 64; PC 2
See also CA 19-20; 25-28R; CANR 35;
CAP 1; DAM POET; MTCW

Aksakov, Sergei Timofeyvich
1791-1859 ....NCLC 2

Aksenov, Vassily
See Aksyonov, Vassily (Pavlovich)

Aksyonov, Vassily (Pavlovich)
1932-....................CLC 22, 37
See also CA 53-56; CANR 12, 48

Akutagawa Ryunosuke
1892-1927 ....TCLC 16
See also CA 117

Alain   1868-1951 ....TCLC 41

Alain-Fournier....................TCLC 6
See also Fournier, Henri Alban
See also DLB 65

Alarcon, Pedro Antonio de
1833-1891 ....NCLC 1

Alas (y Urena), Leopoldo (Enrique Garcia)
1852-1901 ....TCLC 29
See also CA 113; 131; HW

Albee, Edward (Franklin III)
1928-......CLC 1, 2, 3, 5, 9, 11, 13, 25,
53, 86; DA; DAB; DAC; WLC
See also AITN 1; CA 5-8R; CABS 3;
CANR 8; CDALB 1941-1968;
DAM DRAM, MST; DLB 7;
INT CANR-8; MTCW

Alberti, Rafael   1902- ....CLC 7
See also CA 85-88; DLB 108

Albert the Great   1200(?)-1280.... CMLC 16
See also DLB 115

Alcala-Galiano, Juan Valera y
See Valera y Alcala-Galiano, Juan

Alcott, Amos Bronson 1799-1888 .. **NCLC 1**
See also DLB 1

Alcott, Louisa May
1832-1888 .... **NCLC 6; DA; DAB;
DAC; WLC**
See also CDALB 1865-1917; CLR 1, 38;
DAM MST, NOV; DLB 1, 42, 79; JRDA;
MAICYA; YABC 1

Aldanov, M. A.
See Aldanov, Mark (Alexandrovich)

Aldanov, Mark (Alexandrovich)
1886(?)-1957 .... **TCLC 23**
See also CA 118

Aldington, Richard 1892-1962...... **CLC 49**
See also CA 85-88; CANR 45; DLB 20, 36,
100, 149

Aldiss, Brian W(ilson)
1925- .... **CLC 5, 14, 40**
See also CA 5-8R; CAAS 2; CANR 5, 28;
DAM NOV; DLB 14; MTCW; SATA 34

Alegria, Claribel 1924-........... **CLC 75**
See also CA 131; CAAS 15; DAM MULT;
DLB 145; HW

Alegria, Fernando 1918-........... **CLC 57**
See also CA 9-12R; CANR 5, 32; HW

Aleichem, Sholom .... **TCLC 1, 35**
See also Rabinovitch, Sholem

Aleixandre, Vicente
1898-1984 .... **CLC 9, 36; PC 15**
See also CA 85-88; 114; CANR 26;
DAM POET; DLB 108; HW; MTCW

Alepoudelis, Odysseus
See Elytis, Odysseus

Aleshkovsky, Joseph 1929-
See Aleshkovsky, Yuz
See also CA 121; 128

Aleshkovsky, Yuz .... **CLC 44**
See also Aleshkovsky, Joseph

Alexander, Lloyd (Chudley) 1924- .. **CLC 35**
See also AAYA 1; CA 1-4R; CANR 1, 24,
38; CLR 1, 5; DLB 52; JRDA; MAICYA;
MTCW; SAAS 19; SATA 3, 49, 81

Alfau, Felipe 1902-............... **CLC 66**
See also CA 137

Alger, Horatio, Jr. 1832-1899..... **NCLC 8**
See also DLB 42; SATA 16

Algren, Nelson 1909-1981 .... **CLC 4, 10, 33**
See also CA 13-16R; 103; CANR 20;
CDALB 1941-1968; DLB 9; DLBY 81,
82; MTCW

Ali, Ahmed 1910-................ **CLC 69**
See also CA 25-28R; CANR 15, 34

Alighieri, Dante 1265-1321 .... **CMLC 3**

Allan, John B.
See Westlake, Donald E(dwin)

Allen, Edward 1948-.............. **CLC 59**

Allen, Paula Gunn 1939-.......... **CLC 84**
See also CA 112; 143; DAM MULT;
NNAL

Allen, Roland
See Ayckbourn, Alan

Allen, Sarah A.
See Hopkins, Pauline Elizabeth

Allen, Woody 1935-........... **CLC 16, 52**
See also AAYA 10; CA 33-36R; CANR 27,
38; DAM POP; DLB 44; MTCW

Allende, Isabel 1942- .... **CLC 39, 57; HLC**
See also CA 125; 130; CANR 51;
DAM MULT, NOV; DLB 145; HW;
INT 130; MTCW

Alleyn, Ellen
See Rossetti, Christina (Georgina)

Allingham, Margery (Louise)
1904-1966 .... **CLC 19**
See also CA 5-8R; 25-28R; CANR 4;
DLB 77; MTCW

Allingham, William 1824-1889 ... **NCLC 25**
See also DLB 35

Allison, Dorothy E. 1949-......... **CLC 78**
See also CA 140

Allston, Washington 1779-1843.... **NCLC 2**
See also DLB 1

Almedingen, E. M. .... **CLC 12**
See also Almedingen, Martha Edith von
See also SATA 3

Almedingen, Martha Edith von 1898-1971
See Almedingen, E. M.
See also CA 1-4R; CANR 1

Almqvist, Carl Jonas Love
1793-1866 .... **NCLC 42**

Alonso, Damaso 1898-1990 .... **CLC 14**
See also CA 110; 131; 130; DLB 108; HW

Alov
See Gogol, Nikolai (Vasilyevich)

Alta 1942-..................... **CLC 19**
See also CA 57-60

Alter, Robert B(ernard) 1935-...... **CLC 34**
See also CA 49-52; CANR 1, 47

Alther, Lisa 1944-.............. **CLC 7, 41**
See also CA 65-68; CANR 12, 30, 51;
MTCW

Altman, Robert 1925-............. **CLC 16**
See also CA 73-76; CANR 43

Alvarez, A(lfred) 1929-.......... **CLC 5, 13**
See also CA 1-4R; CANR 3, 33; DLB 14,
40

Alvarez, Alejandro Rodriguez 1903-1965
See Casona, Alejandro
See also CA 131; 93-96; HW

Alvaro, Corrado 1896-1956 .... **TCLC 60**

Amado, Jorge 1912-..... **CLC 13, 40; HLC**
See also CA 77-80; CANR 35;
DAM MULT, NOV; DLB 113; MTCW

Ambler, Eric 1909-........... **CLC 4, 6, 9**
See also CA 9-12R; CANR 7, 38; DLB 77;
MTCW

Amichai, Yehuda 1924- ...... **CLC 9, 22, 57**
See also CA 85-88; CANR 46; MTCW

Amiel, Henri Frederic 1821-1881 .. **NCLC 4**

Amis, Kingsley (William)
1922-1995 ..... **CLC 1, 2, 3, 5, 8, 13, 40,
44; DA; DAB; DAC**
See also AITN 2; CA 9-12R; 150; CANR 8,
28; CDBLB 1945-1960; DAM MST,
NOV; DLB 15, 27, 100, 139;
INT CANR-8; MTCW

Amis, Martin (Louis)
1949- .... **CLC 4, 9, 38, 62**
See also BEST 90:3; CA 65-68; CANR 8,
27; DLB 14; INT CANR-27

Ammons, A(rchie) R(andolph)
1926- .... **CLC 2, 3, 5, 8, 9, 25, 57**
See also AITN 1; CA 9-12R; CANR 6, 36,
51; DAM POET; DLB 5; MTCW

Amo, Tauraatua i
See Adams, Henry (Brooks)

Anand, Mulk Raj 1905-........... **CLC 23**
See also CA 65-68; CANR 32; DAM NOV;
MTCW

Anatol
See Schnitzler, Arthur

Anaya, Rudolfo A(lfonso)
1937- .... **CLC 23; HLC**
See also CA 45-48; CAAS 4; CANR 1, 32,
51; DAM MULT, NOV; DLB 82; HW 1;
MTCW

Andersen, Hans Christian
1805-1875 .... **NCLC 7; DA; DAB;
DAC; SSC 6; WLC**
See also CLR 6; DAM MST, POP;
MAICYA; YABC 1

Anderson, C. Farley
See Mencken, H(enry) L(ouis); Nathan,
George Jean

Anderson, Jessica (Margaret) Queale
.... **CLC 37**
See also CA 9-12R; CANR 4

Anderson, Jon (Victor) 1940- .... **CLC 9**
See also CA 25-28R; CANR 20;
DAM POET

Anderson, Lindsay (Gordon)
1923-1994 .... **CLC 20**
See also CA 125; 128; 146

Anderson, Maxwell 1888-1959 ..... **TCLC 2**
See also CA 105; DAM DRAM; DLB 7

Anderson, Poul (William) 1926- .... **CLC 15**
See also AAYA 5; CA 1-4R; CAAS 2;
CANR 2, 15, 34; DLB 8; INT CANR-15;
MTCW; SATA-Brief 39

Anderson, Robert (Woodruff)
1917- .... **CLC 23**
See also AITN 1; CA 21-24R; CANR 32;
DAM DRAM; DLB 7

Anderson, Sherwood
1876-1941 .... **TCLC 1, 10, 24; DA;
DAB; DAC; SSC 1; WLC**
See also CA 104; 121; CDALB 1917-1929;
DAM MST, NOV; DLB 4, 9, 86;
DLBD 1; MTCW

Andouard
See Giraudoux, (Hippolyte) Jean

Andrade, Carlos Drummond de ...... **CLC 18**
See also Drummond de Andrade, Carlos

Andrade, Mario de 1893-1945..... **TCLC 43**

Andreae, Johann V. 1586-1654 ...... **LC 32**

Andreas-Salome, Lou 1861-1937... **TCLC 56**
See also DLB 66

Andrewes, Lancelot 1555-1626 .... **LC 5**
See also DLB 151

Andrews, Cicily Fairfield
See West, Rebecca

Author Index

Andrews, Elton V.
See Pohl, Frederik

Andreyev, Leonid (Nikolaevich)
1871-1919 .... **TCLC 3**
See also CA 104

Andric, Ivo 1892-1975 .... **CLC 8**
See also CA 81-84; 57-60; CANR 43;
DLB 147; MTCW

Angelique, Pierre
See Bataille, Georges

Angell, Roger 1920- .... **CLC 26**
See also CA 57-60; CANR 13, 44

Angelou, Maya
1928- .... **CLC 12, 35, 64, 77; BLC; DA;
DAB; DAC**
See also AAYA 7; BW 2; CA 65-68;
CANR 19, 42; DAM MST, MULT,
POET, POP; DLB 38; MTCW; SATA 49

Annensky, Innokenty Fyodorovich
1856-1909 .... **TCLC 14**
See also CA 110

Anon, Charles Robert
See Pessoa, Fernando (Antonio Nogueira)

Anouilh, Jean (Marie Lucien Pierre)
1910-1987 ...... **CLC 1, 3, 8, 13, 40, 50**
See also CA 17-20R; 123; CANR 32;
DAM DRAM; MTCW

Anthony, Florence
See Ai

Anthony, John
See Ciardi, John (Anthony)

Anthony, Peter
See Shaffer, Anthony (Joshua); Shaffer,
Peter (Levin)

Anthony, Piers 1934- .... **CLC 35**
See also AAYA 11; CA 21-24R; CANR 28;
DAM POP; DLB 8; MTCW; SAAS 22;
SATA 84

Antoine, Marc
See Proust, (Valentin-Louis-George-Eugene-)
Marcel

Antoninus, Brother
See Everson, William (Oliver)

Antonioni, Michelangelo 1912- ..... **CLC 20**
See also CA 73-76; CANR 45

Antschel, Paul 1920-1970
See Celan, Paul
See also CA 85-88; CANR 33; MTCW

Anwar, Chairil 1922-1949 .... **TCLC 22**
See also CA 121

Apollinaire, Guillaume .. **TCLC 3, 8, 51; PC 7**
See also Kostrowitzki, Wilhelm Apollinaris
de
See also DAM POET

Appelfeld, Aharon 1932- .... **CLC 23, 47**
See also CA 112; 133

Apple, Max (Isaac) 1941- .... **CLC 9, 33**
See also CA 81-84; CANR 19; DLB 130

Appleman, Philip (Dean) 1926- ..... **CLC 51**
See also CA 13-16R; CAAS 18; CANR 6,
29

Appleton, Lawrence
See Lovecraft, H(oward) P(hillips)

Apteryx
See Eliot, T(homas) S(tearns)

Apuleius, (Lucius Madaurensis)
125(?)-175(?) .... **CMLC 1**

Aquin, Hubert 1929-1977......... **CLC 15**
See also CA 105; DLB 53

Aragon, Louis 1897-1982....... **CLC 3, 22**
See also CA 69-72; 108; CANR 28;
DAM NOV, POET; DLB 72; MTCW

Arany, Janos 1817-1882........ **NCLC 34**

Arbuthnot, John 1667-1735......... **LC 1**
See also DLB 101

Archer, Herbert Winslow
See Mencken, H(enry) L(ouis)

Archer, Jeffrey (Howard) 1940- .... **CLC 28**
See also AAYA 16; BEST 89:3; CA 77-80;
CANR 22; DAM POP; INT CANR-22

Archer, Jules 1915- .... **CLC 12**
See also CA 9-12R; CANR 6; SAAS 5;
SATA 4, 85

Archer, Lee
See Ellison, Harlan (Jay)

Arden, John 1930- .... **CLC 6, 13, 15**
See also CA 13-16R; CAAS 4; CANR 31;
DAM DRAM; DLB 13; MTCW

Arenas, Reinaldo
1943-1990 .... **CLC 41; HLC**
See also CA 124; 128; 133; DAM MULT;
DLB 145; HW

Arendt, Hannah 1906-1975 .... **CLC 66**
See also CA 17-20R; 61-64; CANR 26;
MTCW

Aretino, Pietro 1492-1556 .... **LC 12**

Arghezi, Tudor.................... **CLC 80**
See also Theodorescu, Ion N.

Arguedas, Jose Maria
1911-1969 .... **CLC 10, 18**
See also CA 89-92; DLB 113; HW

Argueta, Manlio 1936-............ **CLC 31**
See also CA 131; DLB 145; HW

Ariosto, Ludovico 1474-1533........ **LC 6**

Aristides
See Epstein, Joseph

Aristophanes
450B.C.-385B.C......... **CMLC 4; DA;
DAB; DAC; DC 2**
See also DAM DRAM, MST

Arlt, Roberto (Godofredo Christophersen)
1900-1942 .... **TCLC 29; HLC**
See also CA 123; 131; DAM MULT; HW

Armah, Ayi Kwei 1939- .... **CLC 5, 33; BLC**
See also BW 1; CA 61-64; CANR 21;
DAM MULT, POET; DLB 117; MTCW

Armatrading, Joan 1950-.......... **CLC 17**
See also CA 114

Arnette, Robert
See Silverberg, Robert

**Arnim, Achim von (Ludwig Joachim von
Arnim)** 1781-1831 .... **NCLC 5**
See also DLB 90

Arnim, Bettina von 1785-1859.... **NCLC 38**
See also DLB 90

Arnold, Matthew
1822-1888 ..... **NCLC 6, 29; DA; DAB;
DAC; PC 5; WLC**
See also CDBLB 1832-1890; DAM MST,
POET; DLB 32, 57

Arnold, Thomas 1795-1842 ...... **NCLC 18**
See also DLB 55

Arnow, Harriette (Louisa) Simpson
1908-1986 .... **CLC 2, 7, 18**
See also CA 9-12R; 118; CANR 14; DLB 6;
MTCW; SATA 42; SATA-Obit 47

Arp, Hans
See Arp, Jean

Arp, Jean 1887-1966............... **CLC 5**
See also CA 81-84; 25-28R; CANR 42

Arrabal
See Arrabal, Fernando

Arrabal, Fernando 1932- ... **CLC 2, 9, 18, 58**
See also CA 9-12R; CANR 15

Arrick, Fran..................... **CLC 30**
See also Gaberman, Judie Angell

Artaud, Antonin (Marie Joseph)
1896-1948 .... **TCLC 3, 36**
See also CA 104; 149; DAM DRAM

Arthur, Ruth M(abel) 1905-1979.... **CLC 12**
See also CA 9-12R; 85-88; CANR 4;
SATA 7, 26

Artsybashev, Mikhail (Petrovich)
1878-1927 .... **TCLC 31**

Arundel, Honor (Morfydd)
1919-1973 .... **CLC 17**
See also CA 21-22; 41-44R; CAP 2;
CLR 35; SATA 4; SATA-Obit 24

Asch, Sholem 1880-1957 .... **TCLC 3**
See also CA 105

Ash, Shalom
See Asch, Sholem

Ashbery, John (Lawrence)
1927- ...... **CLC 2, 3, 4, 6, 9, 13, 15, 25,
41, 77**
See also CA 5-8R; CANR 9, 37;
DAM POET; DLB 5; DLBY 81;
INT CANR-9; MTCW

Ashdown, Clifford
See Freeman, R(ichard) Austin

Ashe, Gordon
See Creasey, John

Ashton-Warner, Sylvia (Constance)
1908-1984 .... **CLC 19**
See also CA 69-72; 112; CANR 29; MTCW

Asimov, Isaac
1920-1992 ...... **CLC 1, 3, 9, 19, 26, 76**
See also AAYA 13; BEST 90:2; CA 1-4R;
137; CANR 2, 19, 36; CLR 12;
DAM POP; DLB 8; DLBY 92;
INT CANR-19; JRDA; MAICYA;
MTCW; SATA 1, 26, 74

Astley, Thea (Beatrice May)
1925- .... **CLC 41**
See also CA 65-68; CANR 11, 43

Aston, James
See White, T(erence) H(anbury)

Asturias, Miguel Angel
1899-1974 . . . . **CLC 3, 8, 13; HLC**
See also CA 25-28; 49-52; CANR 32;
CAP 2; DAM MULT, NOV; DLB 113;
HW; MTCW

Atares, Carlos Saura
See Saura (Atares), Carlos

Atheling, William
See Pound, Ezra (Weston Loomis)

Atheling, William, Jr.
See Blish, James (Benjamin)

Atherton, Gertrude (Franklin Horn)
1857-1948 . . . . **TCLC 2**
See also CA 104; DLB 9, 78

Atherton, Lucius
See Masters, Edgar Lee

Atkins, Jack
See Harris, Mark

Atticus
See Fleming, Ian (Lancaster)

Atwood, Margaret (Eleanor)
1939- . . . . . **CLC 2, 3, 4, 8, 13, 15, 25, 44,**
84; DA; DAB; DAC; PC 8; SSC 2; WLC
See also AAYA 12; BEST 89:2; CA 49-52;
CANR 3, 24, 33; DAM MST, NOV,
POET; DLB 53; INT CANR-24; MTCW;
SATA 50

Aubigny, Pierre d'
See Mencken, H(enry) L(ouis)

Aubin, Penelope 1685-1731(?) . . . . **LC 9**
See also DLB 39

Auchincloss, Louis (Stanton)
1917- . . . . **CLC 4, 6, 9, 18, 45**
See also CA 1-4R; CANR 6, 29;
DAM NOV; DLB 2; DLBY 80;
INT CANR-29; MTCW

Auden, W(ystan) H(ugh)
1907-1973 . . . . . . **CLC 1, 2, 3, 4, 6, 9, 11,**
14, 43; DA; DAB; DAC; PC 1; WLC
See also CA 9-12R; 45-48; CANR 5;
CDBLB 1914-1945; DAM DRAM, MST,
POET; DLB 10, 20; MTCW

Audiberti, Jacques 1900-1965 . . . . . . **CLC 38**
See also CA 25-28R; DAM DRAM

Audubon, John James
1785-1851 . . . . **NCLC 47**

Auel, Jean M(arie) 1936- . . . . **CLC 31**
See also AAYA 7; BEST 90:4; CA 103;
CANR 21; DAM POP; INT CANR-21

Auerbach, Erich 1892-1957 . . . . **TCLC 43**
See also CA 118

Augier, Emile 1820-1889 . . . . **NCLC 31**

August, John
See De Voto, Bernard (Augustine)

Augustine, St. 354-430 . . . . . **CMLC 6; DAB**

Aurelius
See Bourne, Randolph S(illiman)

Austen, Jane
1775-1817 . . . . . **NCLC 1, 13, 19, 33, 51;**
DA; DAB; DAC; WLC
See also CDBLB 1789-1832; DAM MST,
NOV; DLB 116

Auster, Paul 1947- . . . . **CLC 47**
See also CA 69-72; CANR 23, 51

Austin, Frank
See Faust, Frederick (Schiller)

Austin, Mary (Hunter)
1868-1934 . . . . **TCLC 25**
See also CA 109; DLB 9, 78

Autran Dourado, Waldomiro
See Dourado, (Waldomiro Freitas) Autran

Averroes 1126-1198 . . . . **CMLC 7**
See also DLB 115

Avicenna 980-1037 . . . . **CMLC 16**
See also DLB 115

Avison, Margaret 1918- . . . . **CLC 2, 4; DAC**
See also CA 17-20R; DAM POET; DLB 53;
MTCW

Axton, David
See Koontz, Dean R(ay)

Ayckbourn, Alan
1939- . . . . **CLC 5, 8, 18, 33, 74; DAB**
See also CA 21-24R; CANR 31;
DAM DRAM; DLB 13; MTCW

Aydy, Catherine
See Tennant, Emma (Christina)

Ayme, Marcel (Andre) 1902-1967 . . . **CLC 11**
See also CA 89-92; CLR 25; DLB 72

Ayrton, Michael 1921-1975 . . . . **CLC 7**
See also CA 5-8R; 61-64; CANR 9, 21

Azorin . . . . **CLC 11**
See also Martinez Ruiz, Jose

Azuela, Mariano
1873-1952 . . . . **TCLC 3; HLC**
See also CA 104; 131; DAM MULT; HW;
MTCW

Baastad, Babbis Friis
See Friis-Baastad, Babbis Ellinor

Bab
See Gilbert, W(illiam) S(chwenck)

Babbis, Eleanor
See Friis-Baastad, Babbis Ellinor

Babel, Isaak (Emmanuilovich)
1894-1941(?) . . . . . . **TCLC 2, 13; SSC 16**
See also CA 104

Babits, Mihaly 1883-1941 . . . . **TCLC 14**
See also CA 114

Babur 1483-1530 . . . . **LC 18**

Bacchelli, Riccardo 1891-1985 . . . . . **CLC 19**
See also CA 29-32R; 117

Bach, Richard (David) 1936- . . . . **CLC 14**
See also AITN 1; BEST 89:2; CA 9-12R;
CANR 18; DAM NOV, POP; MTCW;
SATA 13

Bachman, Richard
See King, Stephen (Edwin)

Bachmann, Ingeborg 1926-1973 . . . . . **CLC 69**
See also CA 93-96; 45-48; DLB 85

Bacon, Francis 1561-1626 . . . . **LC 18, 32**
See also CDBLB Before 1660; DLB 151

Bacon, Roger 1214(?)-1292 . . . . . . **CMLC 14**
See also DLB 115

Bacovia, George . . . . **TCLC 24**
See also Vasiliu, Gheorghe

Badanes, Jerome 1937- . . . . **CLC 59**

Bagehot, Walter 1826-1877 . . . . . . **NCLC 10**
See also DLB 55

Bagnold, Enid 1889-1981 . . . . **CLC 25**
See also CA 5-8R; 103; CANR 5, 40;
DAM DRAM; DLB 13, 160; MAICYA;
SATA 1, 25

Bagritsky, Eduard 1895-1934 . . . . . **TCLC 60**

Bagrjana, Elisaveta
See Belcheva, Elisaveta

Bagryana, Elisaveta . . . . **CLC 10**
See also Belcheva, Elisaveta
See also DLB 147

Bailey, Paul 1937- . . . . **CLC 45**
See also CA 21-24R; CANR 16; DLB 14

Baillie, Joanna 1762-1851 . . . . **NCLC 2**
See also DLB 93

Bainbridge, Beryl (Margaret)
1933- . . . . **CLC 4, 5, 8, 10, 14, 18, 22, 62**
See also CA 21-24R; CANR 24;
DAM NOV; DLB 14; MTCW

Baker, Elliott 1922- . . . . **CLC 8**
See also CA 45-48; CANR 2

Baker, Nicholson 1957- . . . . **CLC 61**
See also CA 135; DAM POP

Baker, Ray Stannard 1870-1946 . . . **TCLC 47**
See also CA 118

Baker, Russell (Wayne) 1925- . . . . . . **CLC 31**
See also BEST 89:4; CA 57-60; CANR 11,
41; MTCW

Bakhtin, M.
See Bakhtin, Mikhail Mikhailovich

Bakhtin, M. M.
See Bakhtin, Mikhail Mikhailovich

Bakhtin, Mikhail
See Bakhtin, Mikhail Mikhailovich

Bakhtin, Mikhail Mikhailovich
1895-1975 . . . . **CLC 83**
See also CA 128; 113

Bakshi, Ralph 1938(?)- . . . . **CLC 26**
See also CA 112; 138

Bakunin, Mikhail (Alexandrovich)
1814-1876 . . . . **NCLC 25**

Baldwin, James (Arthur)
1924-1987 . . . . . . **CLC 1, 2, 3, 4, 5, 8, 13,**
15, 17, 42, 50, 67, 90; BLC; DA; DAB;
DAC; DC 1; SSC 10; WLC
See also AAYA 4; BW 1; CA 1-4R; 124;
CABS 1; CANR 3, 24;
CDALB 1941-1968; DAM MST, MULT,
NOV, POP; DLB 2, 7, 33; DLBY 87;
MTCW; SATA 9; SATA-Obit 54

Ballard, J(ames) G(raham)
1930- . . . . **CLC 3, 6, 14, 36; SSC 1**
See also AAYA 3; CA 5-8R; CANR 15, 39;
DAM NOV, POP; DLB 14; MTCW

Balmont, Konstantin (Dmitriyevich)
1867-1943 . . . . **TCLC 11**
See also CA 109

Balzac, Honore de
1799-1850 . . . . **NCLC 5, 35, 53; DA;**
DAB; DAC; SSC 5; WLC
See also DAM MST, NOV; DLB 119

Baxter, John
See Hunt, E(verette) Howard, (Jr.)

Bayer, Sylvia
See Glassco, John

Baynton, Barbara 1857-1929 . . . . . **TCLC 57**

Beagle, Peter S(oyer) 1939- . . . . **CLC 7**
See also CA 9-12R; CANR 4, 51;
DLBY 80; INT CANR-4; SATA 60

Bean, Normal
See Burroughs, Edgar Rice

Beard, Charles A(ustin)
1874-1948 . . . . **TCLC 15**
See also CA 115; DLB 17; SATA 18

Beardsley, Aubrey 1872-1898 . . . . . **NCLC 6**

Beattie, Ann
1947- . . . . **CLC 8, 13, 18, 40, 63; SSC 11**
See also BEST 90:2; CA 81-84; DAM NOV,
POP; DLBY 82; MTCW

Beattie, James 1735-1803 . . . . **NCLC 25**
See also DLB 109

Beauchamp, Kathleen Mansfield 1888-1923
See Mansfield, Katherine
See also CA 104; 134; DA; DAC;
DAM MST

Beaumarchais, Pierre-Augustin Caron de
1732-1799 . . . . **DC 4**
See also DAM DRAM

Beaumont, Francis 1584(?)-1616 . . . . . . **DC 6**
See also CDBLB Before 1660; DLB 58, 121

Beauvoir, Simone (Lucie Ernestine Marie
Bertrand) de
1908-1986 . . . . **CLC 1, 2, 4, 8, 14, 31, 44,
50, 71; DA; DAB; DAC; WLC**
See also CA 9-12R; 118; CANR 28;
DAM MST, NOV; DLB 72; DLBY 86;
MTCW

Becker, Jurek 1937- . . . . **CLC 7, 19**
See also CA 85-88; DLB 75

Becker, Walter 1950- . . . . **CLC 26**

Beckett, Samuel (Barclay)
1906-1989 . . . . . . **CLC 1, 2, 3, 4, 6, 9, 10,
11, 14, 18, 29, 57, 59, 83; DA; DAB;
DAC; SSC 16; WLC**
See also CA 5-8R; 130; CANR 33;
CDBLB 1945-1960; DAM DRAM, MST,
NOV; DLB 13, 15; DLBY 90; MTCW

Beckford, William 1760-1844 . . . . **NCLC 16**
See also DLB 39

Beckman, Gunnel 1910- . . . . **CLC 26**
See also CA 33-36R; CANR 15; CLR 25;
MAICYA; SAAS 9; SATA 6

Becque, Henri 1837-1899 . . . . **NCLC 3**

Beddoes, Thomas Lovell
1803-1849 . . . . **NCLC 3**
See also DLB 96

Bedford, Donald F.
See Fearing, Kenneth (Flexner)

Beecher, Catharine Esther
1800-1878 . . . . **NCLC 30**
See also DLB 1

Beecher, John 1904-1980 . . . . **CLC 6**
See also AITN 1; CA 5-8R; 105; CANR 8

Beer, Johann 1655-1700 . . . . **LC 5**

Beer, Patricia 1924- . . . . **CLC 58**
See also CA 61-64; CANR 13, 46; DLB 40

Beerbohm, Henry Maximilian
1872-1956 . . . . **TCLC 1, 24**
See also CA 104; DLB 34, 100

Beerbohm, Max
See Beerbohm, Henry Maximilian

Beer-Hofmann, Richard
1866-1945 . . . . **TCLC 60**
See also DLB 81

Begiebing, Robert J(ohn) 1946- . . . . . **CLC 70**
See also CA 122; CANR 40

Behan, Brendan
1923-1964 . . . . **CLC 1, 8, 11, 15, 79**
See also CA 73-76; CANR 33;
CDBLB 1945-1960; DAM DRAM;
DLB 13; MTCW

Behn, Aphra
1640(?)-1689 . . . . . . **LC 1, 30; DA; DAB;
DAC; DC 4; PC 13; WLC**
See also DAM DRAM, MST, NOV, POET;
DLB 39, 80, 131

Behrman, S(amuel) N(athaniel)
1893-1973 . . . . **CLC 40**
See also CA 13-16; 45-48; CAP 1; DLB 7,
44

Belasco, David 1853-1931 . . . . **TCLC 3**
See also CA 104; DLB 7

Belcheva, Elisaveta 1893- . . . . **CLC 10**
See also Bagryana, Elisaveta

Beldone, Phil "Cheech"
See Ellison, Harlan (Jay)

Beleno
See Azuela, Mariano

Belinski, Vissarion Grigoryevich
1811-1848 . . . . **NCLC 5**

Belitt, Ben 1911- . . . . **CLC 22**
See also CA 13-16R; CAAS 4; CANR 7;
DLB 5

Bell, James Madison
1826-1902 . . . . **TCLC 43; BLC**
See also BW 1; CA 122; 124; DAM MULT;
DLB 50

Bell, Madison (Smartt) 1957- . . . . . . **CLC 41**
See also CA 111; CANR 28

Bell, Marvin (Hartley) 1937- . . . . . **CLC 8, 31**
See also CA 21-24R; CAAS 14;
DAM POET; DLB 5; MTCW

Bell, W. L. D.
See Mencken, H(enry) L(ouis)

Bellamy, Atwood C.
See Mencken, H(enry) L(ouis)

Bellamy, Edward 1850-1898 . . . . . . **NCLC 4**
See also DLB 12

Bellin, Edward J.
See Kuttner, Henry

Belloc, (Joseph) Hilaire (Pierre)
1870-1953 . . . . **TCLC 7, 18**
See also CA 106; DAM POET; DLB 19,
100, 141; YABC 1

Belloc, Joseph Peter Rene Hilaire
See Belloc, (Joseph) Hilaire (Pierre)

Belloc, Joseph Pierre Hilaire
See Belloc, (Joseph) Hilaire (Pierre)

Belloc, M. A.
See Lowndes, Marie Adelaide (Belloc)

Bellow, Saul
1915- . . . . . . **CLC 1, 2, 3, 6, 8, 10, 13, 15,
25, 33, 34, 63, 79; DA; DAB; DAC;
SSC 14; WLC**
See also AITN 2; BEST 89:3; CA 5-8R;
CABS 1; CANR 29; CDALB 1941-1968;
DAM MST, NOV, POP; DLB 2, 28;
DLBD 3; DLBY 82; MTCW

Belser, Reimond Karel Maria de
See Ruyslinck, Ward

Bely, Andrey . . . . **TCLC 7; PC 11**
See also Bugayev, Boris Nikolayevich

Benary, Margot
See Benary-Isbert, Margot

Benary-Isbert, Margot 1889-1979 . . . **CLC 12**
See also CA 5-8R; 89-92; CANR 4;
CLR 12; MAICYA; SATA 2;
SATA-Obit 21

Benavente (y Martinez), Jacinto
1866-1954 . . . . **TCLC 3**
See also CA 106; 131; DAM DRAM,
MULT; HW; MTCW

Benchley, Peter (Bradford)
1940- . . . . **CLC 4, 8**
See also AAYA 14; AITN 2; CA 17-20R;
CANR 12, 35; DAM NOV, POP;
MTCW; SATA 3

Benchley, Robert (Charles)
1889-1945 . . . . **TCLC 1, 55**
See also CA 105; DLB 11

Benda, Julien 1867-1956 . . . . **TCLC 60**
See also CA 120

Benedict, Ruth 1887-1948 . . . . **TCLC 60**

Benedikt, Michael 1935- . . . . **CLC 4, 14**
See also CA 13-16R; CANR 7; DLB 5

Benet, Juan 1927- . . . . **CLC 28**
See also CA 143

Benet, Stephen Vincent
1898-1943 . . . . **TCLC 7; SSC 10**
See also CA 104; DAM POET; DLB 4, 48,
102; YABC 1

Benet, William Rose 1886-1950 . . . **TCLC 28**
See also CA 118; DAM POET; DLB 45

Benford, Gregory (Albert) 1941- . . . . **CLC 52**
See also CA 69-72; CANR 12, 24, 49;
DLBY 82

Bengtsson, Frans (Gunnar)
1894-1954 . . . . **TCLC 48**

Benjamin, David
See Slavitt, David R(ytman)

Benjamin, Lois
See Gould, Lois

Benjamin, Walter 1892-1940 . . . . . . **TCLC 39**

Benn, Gottfried 1886-1956 . . . . **TCLC 3**
See also CA 106; DLB 56

Bennett, Alan 1934- . . . . . **CLC 45, 77; DAB**
See also CA 103; CANR 35; DAM MST;
MTCW

Bennett, (Enoch) Arnold
1867-1931 . . . . **TCLC 5, 20**
See also CA 106; CDBLB 1890-1914;
DLB 10, 34, 98, 135

Bennett, Elizabeth
See Mitchell, Margaret (Munnerlyn)

Bennett, George Harold　1930-
See Bennett, Hal
See also BW 1; CA 97-100

Bennett, Hal . . . . **CLC 5**
See also Bennett, George Harold
See also DLB 33

Bennett, Jay　1912- . . . . **CLC 35**
See also AAYA 10; CA 69-72; CANR 11,
42; JRDA; SAAS 4; SATA 41;
SATA-Brief 27

Bennett, Louise (Simone)
1919- . . . . **CLC 28; BLC**
See also BW 2; DAM MULT; DLB 117

Benson, E(dward) F(rederic)
1867-1940 . . . . **TCLC 27**
See also CA 114; DLB 135, 153

Benson, Jackson J.　1930- . . . . **CLC 34**
See also CA 25-28R; DLB 111

Benson, Sally　1900-1972 . . . . **CLC 17**
See also CA 19-20; 37-40R; CAP 1;
SATA 1, 35; SATA-Obit 27

Benson, Stella　1892-1933 . . . . **TCLC 17**
See also CA 117; DLB 36, 162

Bentham, Jeremy　1748-1832 . . . . . **NCLC 38**
See also DLB 107, 158

Bentley, E(dmund) C(lerihew)
1875-1956 . . . . **TCLC 12**
See also CA 108; DLB 70

Bentley, Eric (Russell)　1916- . . . . **CLC 24**
See also CA 5-8R; CANR 6; INT CANR-6

Beranger, Pierre Jean de
1780-1857 . . . . **NCLC 34**

Berendt, John (Lawrence)　1939- . . . . **CLC 86**
See also CA 146

Berger, Colonel
See Malraux, (Georges-)Andre

Berger, John (Peter)　1926- . . . . . . **CLC 2, 19**
See also CA 81-84; CANR 51; DLB 14

Berger, Melvin H.　1927- . . . . **CLC 12**
See also CA 5-8R; CANR 4; CLR 32;
SAAS 2; SATA 5

Berger, Thomas (Louis)
1924- . . . . **CLC 3, 5, 8, 11, 18, 38**
See also CA 1-4R; CANR 5, 28, 51;
DAM NOV; DLB 2; DLBY 80;
INT CANR-28; MTCW

Bergman, (Ernst) Ingmar
1918- . . . . **CLC 16, 72**
See also CA 81-84; CANR 33

Bergson, Henri　1859-1941 . . . . **TCLC 32**

Bergstein, Eleanor　1938- . . . . **CLC 4**
See also CA 53-56; CANR 5

Berkoff, Steven　1937- . . . . **CLC 56**
See also CA 104

Bermant, Chaim (Icyk)　1929- . . . . . . **CLC 40**
See also CA 57-60; CANR 6, 31

Bern, Victoria
See Fisher, M(ary) F(rances) K(ennedy)

Bernanos, (Paul Louis) Georges
1888-1948 . . . . **TCLC 3**
See also CA 104; 130; DLB 72

Bernard, April　1956- . . . . **CLC 59**
See also CA 131

Berne, Victoria
See Fisher, M(ary) F(rances) K(ennedy)

Bernhard, Thomas
1931-1989 . . . . **CLC 3, 32, 61**
See also CA 85-88; 127; CANR 32;
DLB 85, 124; MTCW

Berriault, Gina　1926- . . . . **CLC 54**
See also CA 116; 129; DLB 130

Berrigan, Daniel　1921- . . . . **CLC 4**
See also CA 33-36R; CAAS 1; CANR 11,
43; DLB 5

Berrigan, Edmund Joseph Michael, Jr.
1934-1983
See Berrigan, Ted
See also CA 61-64; 110; CANR 14

Berrigan, Ted . . . . **CLC 37**
See also Berrigan, Edmund Joseph Michael,
Jr.
See also DLB 5

Berry, Charles Edward Anderson　1931-
See Berry, Chuck
See also CA 115

Berry, Chuck . . . . **CLC 17**
See also Berry, Charles Edward Anderson

Berry, Jonas
See Ashbery, John (Lawrence)

Berry, Wendell (Erdman)
1934- . . . . **CLC 4, 6, 8, 27, 46**
See also AITN 1; CA 73-76; CANR 50;
DAM POET; DLB 5, 6

Berryman, John
1914-1972 . . . . . . **CLC 1, 2, 3, 4, 6, 8, 10,
13, 25, 62**
See also CA 13-16; 33-36R; CABS 2;
CANR 35; CAP 1; CDALB 1941-1968;
DAM POET; DLB 48; MTCW

Bertolucci, Bernardo　1940- . . . . **CLC 16**
See also CA 106

Bertrand, Aloysius　1807-1841 . . . . **NCLC 31**

Bertran de Born　c. 1140-1215 . . . . . **CMLC 5**

Besant, Annie (Wood)　1847-1933 . . . **TCLC 9**
See also CA 105

Bessie, Alvah　1904-1985 . . . . **CLC 23**
See also CA 5-8R; 116; CANR 2; DLB 26

Bethlen, T. D.
See Silverberg, Robert

Beti, Mongo . . . . **CLC 27; BLC**
See also Biyidi, Alexandre
See also DAM MULT

Betjeman, John
1906-1984 . . . **CLC 2, 6, 10, 34, 43; DAB**
See also CA 9-12R; 112; CANR 33;
CDBLB 1945-1960; DAM MST, POET;
DLB 20; DLBY 84; MTCW

Bettelheim, Bruno　1903-1990 . . . . . . **CLC 79**
See also CA 81-84; 131; CANR 23; MTCW

Betti, Ugo　1892-1953 . . . . **TCLC 5**
See also CA 104

Betts, Doris (Waugh)　1932- . . . . **CLC 3, 6, 28**
See also CA 13-16R; CANR 9; DLBY 82;
INT CANR-9

Bevan, Alistair
See Roberts, Keith (John Kingston)

Bialik, Chaim Nachman
1873-1934 . . . . **TCLC 25**

Bickerstaff, Isaac
See Swift, Jonathan

Bidart, Frank　1939- . . . . **CLC 33**
See also CA 140

Bienek, Horst　1930- . . . . **CLC 7, 11**
See also CA 73-76; DLB 75

Bierce, Ambrose (Gwinett)
1842-1914(?) . . . . **TCLC 1, 7, 44; DA;
DAC; SSC 9; WLC**
See also CA 104; 139; CDALB 1865-1917;
DAM MST; DLB 11, 12, 23, 71, 74

Billings, Josh
See Shaw, Henry Wheeler

Billington, (Lady) Rachel (Mary)
1942- . . . . **CLC 43**
See also AITN 2; CA 33-36R; CANR 44

Binyon, T(imothy) J(ohn)　1936- . . . . **CLC 34**
See also CA 111; CANR 28

Bioy Casares, Adolfo
1914- . . . **CLC 4, 8, 13, 88; HLC; SSC 17**
See also CA 29-32R; CANR 19, 43;
DAM MULT; DLB 113; HW; MTCW

Bird, Cordwainer
See Ellison, Harlan (Jay)

Bird, Robert Montgomery
1806-1854 . . . . **NCLC 1**

Birney, (Alfred) Earle
1904- . . . . **CLC 1, 4, 6, 11; DAC**
See also CA 1-4R; CANR 5, 20;
DAM MST, POET; DLB 88; MTCW

Bishop, Elizabeth
1911-1979 . . . . . . **CLC 1, 4, 9, 13, 15, 32;
DA; DAC; PC 3**
See also CA 5-8R; 89-92; CABS 2;
CANR 26; CDALB 1968-1988;
DAM MST, POET; DLB 5; MTCW;
SATA-Obit 24

Bishop, John　1935- . . . . **CLC 10**
See also CA 105

Bissett, Bill　1939- . . . . **CLC 18; PC 14**
See also CA 69-72; CAAS 19; CANR 15;
DLB 53; MTCW

Bitov, Andrei (Georgievich)　1937- . . . **CLC 57**
See also CA 142

Biyidi, Alexandre　1932-
See Beti, Mongo
See also BW 1; CA 114; 124; MTCW

Bjarme, Brynjolf
See Ibsen, Henrik (Johan)

Bjornson, Bjornstjerne (Martinius)
1832-1910 . . . . **TCLC 7, 37**
See also CA 104

Black, Robert
See Holdstock, Robert P.

Blackburn, Paul　1926-1971 . . . . . . **CLC 9, 43**
See also CA 81-84; 33-36R; CANR 34;
DLB 16; DLBY 81

Black Elk　1863-1950 . . . . **TCLC 33**
See also CA 144; DAM MULT; NNAL

Black Hobart
See Sanders, (James) Ed(ward)

Blacklin, Malcolm
See Chambers, Aidan

Bourget, Paul (Charles Joseph)
1852-1935 . . . . **TCLC 12**
See also CA 107; DLB 123

Bourjaily, Vance (Nye) 1922- . . . . **CLC 8, 62**
See also CA 1-4R; CAAS 1; CANR 2;
DLB 2, 143

Bourne, Randolph S(illiman)
1886-1918 . . . . **TCLC 16**
See also CA 117; DLB 63

Bova, Ben(jamin William) 1932- . . . . **CLC 45**
See also AAYA 16; CA 5-8R; CAAS 18;
CANR 11; CLR 3; DLBY 81;
INT CANR-11; MAICYA; MTCW;
SATA 6, 68

Bowen, Elizabeth (Dorothea Cole)
1899-1973 . . . . . . **CLC 1, 3, 6, 11, 15, 22;**
SSC 3
See also CA 17-18; 41-44R; CANR 35;
CAP 2; CDBLB 1945-1960; DAM NOV;
DLB 15, 162; MTCW

Bowering, George 1935- . . . . **CLC 15, 47**
See also CA 21-24R; CAAS 16; CANR 10;
DLB 53

Bowering, Marilyn R(uthe) 1949- . . . **CLC 32**
See also CA 101; CANR 49

Bowers, Edgar 1924- . . . . **CLC 9**
See also CA 5-8R; CANR 24; DLB 5

Bowie, David . . . . **CLC 17**
See also Jones, David Robert

Bowles, Jane (Sydney)
1917-1973 . . . . **CLC 3, 68**
See also CA 19-20; 41-44R; CAP 2

Bowles, Paul (Frederick)
1910- . . . . **CLC 1, 2, 19, 53; SSC 3**
See also CA 1-4R; CAAS 1; CANR 1, 19,
50; DLB 5, 6; MTCW

Box, Edgar
See Vidal, Gore

Boyd, Nancy
See Millay, Edna St. Vincent

Boyd, William 1952- . . . . **CLC 28, 53, 70**
See also CA 114; 120; CANR 51

Boyle, Kay
1902-1992 . . . . . **CLC 1, 5, 19, 58; SSC 5**
See also CA 13-16R; 140; CAAS 1;
CANR 29; DLB 4, 9, 48, 86; DLBY 93;
MTCW

Boyle, Mark
See Kienzle, William X(avier)

Boyle, Patrick 1905-1982 . . . . **CLC 19**
See also CA 127

Boyle, T. C. 1948-
See Boyle, T(homas) Coraghessan

Boyle, T(homas) Coraghessan
1948- . . . . **CLC 36, 55, 90; SSC 16**
See also BEST 90:4; CA 120; CANR 44;
DAM POP; DLBY 86

Boz
See Dickens, Charles (John Huffam)

Brackenridge, Hugh Henry
1748-1816 . . . . **NCLC 7**
See also DLB 11, 37

Bradbury, Edward P.
See Moorcock, Michael (John)

Bradbury, Malcolm (Stanley)
1932- . . . . **CLC 32, 61**
See also CA 1-4R; CANR 1, 33;
DAM NOV; DLB 14; MTCW

Bradbury, Ray (Douglas)
1920- . . . . **CLC 1, 3, 10, 15, 42; DA;**
DAB; DAC; WLC
See also AAYA 15; AITN 1, 2; CA 1-4R;
CANR 2, 30; CDALB 1968-1988;
DAM MST, NOV, POP; DLB 2, 8;
INT CANR-30; MTCW; SATA 11, 64

Bradford, Gamaliel 1863-1932 . . . . . **TCLC 36**
See also DLB 17

Bradley, David (Henry, Jr.)
1950- . . . . **CLC 23; BLC**
See also BW 1; CA 104; CANR 26;
DAM MULT; DLB 33

Bradley, John Ed(mund, Jr.)
1958- . . . . **CLC 55**
See also CA 139

Bradley, Marion Zimmer 1930- . . . . . **CLC 30**
See also AAYA 9; CA 57-60; CAAS 10;
CANR 7, 31, 51; DAM POP; DLB 8;
MTCW

Bradstreet, Anne
1612(?)-1672 . . . . . . **LC 4, 30; DA; DAC;**
PC 10
See also CDALB 1640-1865; DAM MST,
POET; DLB 24

Brady, Joan 1939- . . . . **CLC 86**
See also CA 141

Bragg, Melvyn 1939- . . . . **CLC 10**
See also BEST 89:3; CA 57-60; CANR 10,
48; DLB 14

Braine, John (Gerard)
1922-1986 . . . . **CLC 1, 3, 41**
See also CA 1-4R; 120; CANR 1, 33;
CDBLB 1945-1960; DLB 15; DLBY 86;
MTCW

Brammer, William 1930(?)-1978 . . . . **CLC 31**
See also CA 77-80

Brancati, Vitaliano 1907-1954 . . . . . **TCLC 12**
See also CA 109

Brancato, Robin F(idler) 1936- . . . . . **CLC 35**
See also AAYA 9; CA 69-72; CANR 11,
45; CLR 32; JRDA; SAAS 9; SATA 23

Brand, Max
See Faust, Frederick (Schiller)

Brand, Millen 1906-1980 . . . . **CLC 7**
See also CA 21-24R; 97-100

Branden, Barbara . . . . **CLC 44**
See also CA 148

Brandes, Georg (Morris Cohen)
1842-1927 . . . . **TCLC 10**
See also CA 105

Brandys, Kazimierz 1916- . . . . **CLC 62**

Branley, Franklyn M(ansfield)
1915- . . . . **CLC 21**
See also CA 33-36R; CANR 14, 39;
CLR 13; MAICYA; SAAS 16; SATA 4,
68

Brathwaite, Edward Kamau 1930- . . . **CLC 11**
See also BW 2; CA 25-28R; CANR 11, 26,
47; DAM POET; DLB 125

Brautigan, Richard (Gary)
1935-1984 . . . . **CLC 1, 3, 5, 9, 12, 34, 42**
See also CA 53-56; 113; CANR 34;
DAM NOV; DLB 2, 5; DLBY 80, 84;
MTCW; SATA 56

Braverman, Kate 1950- . . . . **CLC 67**
See also CA 89-92

Brecht, Bertolt
1898-1956 . . . . . . **TCLC 1, 6, 13, 35; DA;**
DAB; DAC; DC 3; WLC
See also CA 104; 133; DAM DRAM, MST;
DLB 56, 124; MTCW

Brecht, Eugen Berthold Friedrich
See Brecht, Bertolt

Bremer, Fredrika 1801-1865 . . . . . **NCLC 11**

Brennan, Christopher John
1870-1932 . . . . **TCLC 17**
See also CA 117

Brennan, Maeve 1917- . . . . **CLC 5**
See also CA 81-84

Brentano, Clemens (Maria)
1778-1842 . . . . **NCLC 1**
See also DLB 90

Brent of Bin Bin
See Franklin, (Stella Maraia Sarah) Miles

Brenton, Howard 1942- . . . . **CLC 31**
See also CA 69-72; CANR 33; DLB 13;
MTCW

Breslin, James 1930-
See Breslin, Jimmy
See also CA 73-76; CANR 31; DAM NOV;
MTCW

Breslin, Jimmy . . . . **CLC 4, 43**
See also Breslin, James
See also AITN 1

Bresson, Robert 1901- . . . . **CLC 16**
See also CA 110; CANR 49

Breton, Andre
1896-1966 . . . . . **CLC 2, 9, 15, 54; PC 15**
See also CA 19-20; 25-28R; CANR 40;
CAP 2; DLB 65; MTCW

Breytenbach, Breyten 1939(?)- . . **CLC 23, 37**
See also CA 113; 129; DAM POET

Bridgers, Sue Ellen 1942- . . . . **CLC 26**
See also AAYA 8; CA 65-68; CANR 11,
36; CLR 18; DLB 52; JRDA; MAICYA;
SAAS 1; SATA 22

Bridges, Robert (Seymour)
1844-1930 . . . . **TCLC 1**
See also CA 104; CDBLB 1890-1914;
DAM POET; DLB 19, 98

Bridie, James . . . . **TCLC 3**
See also Mavor, Osborne Henry
See also DLB 10

Brin, David 1950- . . . . **CLC 34**
See also CA 102; CANR 24;
INT CANR-24; SATA 65

Brink, Andre (Philippus)
1935- . . . . **CLC 18, 36**
See also CA 104; CANR 39; INT 103;
MTCW

Brinsmead, H(esba) F(ay) 1922- . . . . **CLC 21**
See also CA 21-24R; CANR 10; MAICYA;
SAAS 5; SATA 18, 78

Brittain, Vera (Mary)
1893(?)-1970 . . . . CLC 23
See also CA 13-16; 25-28R; CAP 1; MTCW

Broch, Hermann 1886-1951 . . . . . . TCLC 20
See also CA 117; DLB 85, 124

Brock, Rose
See Hansen, Joseph

Brodkey, Harold 1930- . . . . CLC 56
See also CA 111; DLB 130

Brodsky, Iosif Alexandrovich 1940-
See Brodsky, Joseph
See also AITN 1; CA 41-44R; CANR 37;
DAM POET; MTCW

Brodsky, Joseph . . CLC 4, 6, 13, 36, 50; PC 9
See also Brodsky, Iosif Alexandrovich

Brodsky, Michael Mark 1948- . . . . . CLC 19
See also CA 102; CANR 18, 41

Bromell, Henry 1947- . . . . CLC 5
See also CA 53-56; CANR 9

Bromfield, Louis (Brucker)
1896-1956 . . . . TCLC 11
See also CA 107; DLB 4, 9, 86

Broner, E(sther) M(asserman)
1930- . . . . CLC 19
See also CA 17-20R; CANR 8, 25; DLB 28

Bronk, William 1918- . . . . CLC 10
See also CA 89-92; CANR 23

Bronstein, Lev Davidovich
See Trotsky, Leon

Bronte, Anne 1820-1849 . . . . NCLC 4
See also DLB 21

Bronte, Charlotte
1816-1855 . . . . NCLC 3, 8, 33; DA;
DAB; DAC; WLC
See also AAYA 17; CDBLB 1832-1890;
DAM MST, NOV; DLB 21, 159

Bronte, Emily (Jane)
1818-1848 . . . . NCLC 16, 35; DA; DAB;
DAC; PC 8; WLC
See also AAYA 17; CDBLB 1832-1890;
DAM MST, NOV, POET; DLB 21, 32

Brooke, Frances 1724-1789 . . . . LC 6
See also DLB 39, 99

Brooke, Henry 1703(?)-1783 . . . . LC 1
See also DLB 39

Brooke, Rupert (Chawner)
1887-1915 . . . . . . TCLC 2, 7; DA; DAB;
DAC; WLC
See also CA 104; 132; CDBLB 1914-1945;
DAM MST, POET; DLB 19; MTCW

Brooke-Haven, P.
See Wodehouse, P(elham) G(renville)

Brooke-Rose, Christine 1926- . . . . . . CLC 40
See also CA 13-16R; DLB 14

Brookner, Anita
1928- . . . . CLC 32, 34, 51; DAB
See also CA 114; 120; CANR 37;
DAM POP; DLBY 87; MTCW

Brooks, Cleanth 1906-1994 . . . . . CLC 24, 86
See also CA 17-20R; 145; CANR 33, 35;
DLB 63; DLBY 94; INT CANR-35;
MTCW

Brooks, George
See Baum, L(yman) Frank

Brooks, Gwendolyn
1917- . . . . . . CLC 1, 2, 4, 5, 15, 49; BLC;
DA; DAC; PC 7; WLC
See also AITN 1; BW 2; CA 1-4R;
CANR 1, 27; CDALB 1941-1968;
CLR 27; DAM MST, MULT, POET;
DLB 5, 76; MTCW; SATA 6

Brooks, Mel . . . . CLC 12
See also Kaminsky, Melvin
See also AAYA 13; DLB 26

Brooks, Peter 1938- . . . . CLC 34
See also CA 45-48; CANR 1

Brooks, Van Wyck 1886-1963 . . . . . . CLC 29
See also CA 1-4R; CANR 6; DLB 45, 63,
103

Brophy, Brigid (Antonia)
1929-1995 . . . . CLC 6, 11, 29
See also CA 5-8R; 149; CAAS 4; CANR 25;
DLB 14; MTCW

Brosman, Catharine Savage 1934- . . . . CLC 9
See also CA 61-64; CANR 21, 46

Brother Antoninus
See Everson, William (Oliver)

Broughton, T(homas) Alan 1936- . . . CLC 19
See also CA 45-48; CANR 2, 23, 48

Broumas, Olga 1949- . . . . CLC 10, 73
See also CA 85-88; CANR 20

Brown, Charles Brockden
1771-1810 . . . . NCLC 22
See also CDALB 1640-1865; DLB 37, 59,
73

Brown, Christy 1932-1981 . . . . CLC 63
See also CA 105; 104; DLB 14

Brown, Claude 1937- . . . . CLC 30; BLC
See also AAYA 7; BW 1; CA 73-76;
DAM MULT

Brown, Dee (Alexander) 1908- . . CLC 18, 47
See also CA 13-16R; CAAS 6; CANR 11,
45; DAM POP; DLBY 80; MTCW;
SATA 5

Brown, George
See Wertmueller, Lina

Brown, George Douglas
1869-1902 . . . . TCLC 28

Brown, George Mackay 1921- . . . . CLC 5, 48
See also CA 21-24R; CAAS 6; CANR 12,
37; DLB 14, 27, 139; MTCW; SATA 35

Brown, (William) Larry 1951- . . . . . . CLC 73
See also CA 130; 134; INT 133

Brown, Moses
See Barrett, William (Christopher)

Brown, Rita Mae 1944- . . . . . CLC 18, 43, 79
See also CA 45-48; CANR 2, 11, 35;
DAM NOV, POP; INT CANR-11;
MTCW

Brown, Roderick (Langmere) Haig-
See Haig-Brown, Roderick (Langmere)

Brown, Rosellen 1939- . . . . CLC 32
See also CA 77-80; CAAS 10; CANR 14, 44

Brown, Sterling Allen
1901-1989 . . . . CLC 1, 23, 59; BLC
See also BW 1; CA 85-88; 127; CANR 26;
DAM MULT, POET; DLB 48, 51, 63;
MTCW

Brown, Will
See Ainsworth, William Harrison

Brown, William Wells
1813-1884 . . . . NCLC 2; BLC; DC 1
See also DAM MULT; DLB 3, 50

Browne, (Clyde) Jackson 1948(?)- . . . CLC 21
See also CA 120

Browning, Elizabeth Barrett
1806-1861 . . . . . NCLC 1, 16; DA; DAB;
DAC; PC 6; WLC
See also CDBLB 1832-1890; DAM MST,
POET; DLB 32

Browning, Robert
1812-1889 . . . . NCLC 19; DA; DAB;
DAC; PC 2
See also CDBLB 1832-1890; DAM MST,
POET; DLB 32; YABC 1

Browning, Tod 1882-1962 . . . . CLC 16
See also CA 141; 117

Brownson, Orestes (Augustus)
1803-1876 . . . . NCLC 50

Bruccoli, Matthew J(oseph) 1931- . . CLC 34
See also CA 9-12R; CANR 7; DLB 103

Bruce, Lenny . . . . CLC 21
See also Schneider, Leonard Alfred

Bruin, John
See Brutus, Dennis

Brulard, Henri
See Stendhal

Brulls, Christian
See Simenon, Georges (Jacques Christian)

Brunner, John (Kilian Houston)
1934-1995 . . . . CLC 8, 10
See also CA 1-4R; 149; CAAS 8; CANR 2,
37; DAM POP; MTCW

Bruno, Giordano 1548-1600 . . . . LC 27

Brutus, Dennis 1924- . . . . CLC 43; BLC
See also BW 2; CA 49-52; CAAS 14;
CANR 2, 27, 42; DAM MULT, POET;
DLB 117

Bryan, C(ourtlandt) D(ixon) B(arnes)
1936- . . . . CLC 29
See also CA 73-76; CANR 13;
INT CANR-13

Bryan, Michael
See Moore, Brian

Bryant, William Cullen
1794-1878 . . . . . NCLC 6, 46; DA; DAB;
DAC
See also CDALB 1640-1865; DAM MST,
POET; DLB 3, 43, 59

Bryusov, Valery Yakovlevich
1873-1924 . . . . TCLC 10
See also CA 107

Buchan, John 1875-1940 . . . TCLC 41; DAB
See also CA 108; 145; DAM POP; DLB 34,
70, 156; YABC 2

Buchanan, George 1506-1582 . . . . LC 4

Buchheim, Lothar-Guenther 1918- . . . CLC 6
See also CA 85-88

Buchner, (Karl) Georg
1813-1837 . . . . NCLC 26

Buchwald, Art(hur) 1925- . . . . CLC 33
See also AITN 1; CA 5-8R; CANR 21;
MTCW; SATA 10

Cary, (Arthur) Joyce (Lunel)
    1888-1957 .... **TCLC 1, 29**
    See also CA 104; CDBLB 1914-1945;
    DLB 15, 100

Casanova de Seingalt, Giovanni Jacopo
    1725-1798 .... **LC 13**

Casares, Adolfo Bioy
    See Bioy Casares, Adolfo

Casely-Hayford, J(oseph) E(phraim)
    1866-1930 .... **TCLC 24; BLC**
    See also BW 2; CA 123; DAM MULT

Casey, John (Dudley) 1939-........ **CLC 59**
    See also BEST 90:2; CA 69-72; CANR 23

Casey, Michael 1947-.............. **CLC 2**
    See also CA 65-68; DLB 5

Casey, Patrick
    See Thurman, Wallace (Henry)

Casey, Warren (Peter) 1935-1988 ... **CLC 12**
    See also CA 101; 127; INT 101

Casona, Alejandro................. **CLC 49**
    See also Alvarez, Alejandro Rodriguez

Cassavetes, John 1929-1989....... **CLC 20**
    See also CA 85-88; 127

Cassill, R(onald) V(erlin) 1919-... **CLC 4, 23**
    See also CA 9-12R; CAAS 1; CANR 7, 45;
    DLB 6

Cassirer, Ernst 1874-1945 .... **TCLC 61**

Cassity, (Allen) Turner 1929- .... **CLC 6, 42**
    See also CA 17-20R; CAAS 8; CANR 11;
    DLB 105

Castaneda, Carlos 1931(?)-........ **CLC 12**
    See also CA 25-28R; CANR 32; HW;
    MTCW

Castedo, Elena 1937- .... **CLC 65**
    See also CA 132

Castedo-Ellerman, Elena
    See Castedo, Elena

Castellanos, Rosario
    1925-1974 .... **CLC 66; HLC**
    See also CA 131; 53-56; DAM MULT;
    DLB 113; HW

Castelvetro, Lodovico 1505-1571..... **LC 12**

Castiglione, Baldassare 1478-1529 ... **LC 12**

Castle, Robert
    See Hamilton, Edmond

Castro, Guillen de 1569-1631........ **LC 19**

Castro, Rosalia de 1837-1885 ..... **NCLC 3**
    See also DAM MULT

Cather, Willa
    See Cather, Willa Sibert

Cather, Willa Sibert
    1873-1947 .... **TCLC 1, 11, 31; DA;**
                      DAB; DAC; SSC 2; WLC
    See also CA 104; 128; CDALB 1865-1917;
    DAM MST, NOV; DLB 9, 54, 78;
    DLBD 1; MTCW; SATA 30

Catton, (Charles) Bruce
    1899-1978 .... **CLC 35**
    See also AITN 1; CA 5-8R; 81-84;
    CANR 7; DLB 17; SATA 2;
    SATA-Obit 24

Cauldwell, Frank
    See King, Francis (Henry)

Caunitz, William J. 1933- .... **CLC 34**
    See also BEST 89:3; CA 125; 130; INT 130

Causley, Charles (Stanley) 1917-..... **CLC 7**
    See also CA 9-12R; CANR 5, 35; CLR 30;
    DLB 27; MTCW; SATA 3, 66

Caute, David 1936-.............. **CLC 29**
    See also CA 1-4R; CAAS 4; CANR 1, 33;
    DAM NOV; DLB 14

Cavafy, C(onstantine) P(eter)
    1863-1933 .... **TCLC 2, 7**
    See also Kavafis, Konstantinos Petrou
    See also CA 148; DAM POET

Cavallo, Evelyn
    See Spark, Muriel (Sarah)

Cavanna, Betty .... **CLC 12**
    See also Harrison, Elizabeth Cavanna
    See also JRDA; MAICYA; SAAS 4;
    SATA 1, 30

Cavendish, Margaret Lucas
    1623-1673 .... **LC 30**
    See also DLB 131

Caxton, William 1421(?)-1491(?)..... **LC 17**

Cayrol, Jean 1911-.............. **CLC 11**
    See also CA 89-92; DLB 83

Cela, Camilo Jose
    1916- .... **CLC 4, 13, 59; HLC**
    See also BEST 90:2; CA 21-24R; CAAS 10;
    CANR 21, 32; DAM MULT; DLBY 89;
    HW; MTCW

Celan, Paul ...... **CLC 10, 19, 53, 82; PC 10**
    See also Antschel, Paul
    See also DLB 69

Celine, Louis-Ferdinand
    .... **CLC 1, 3, 4, 7, 9, 15, 47**
    See also Destouches, Louis-Ferdinand
    See also DLB 72

Cellini, Benvenuto 1500-1571 .... **LC 7**

Cendrars, Blaise .... **CLC 18**
    See also Sauser-Hall, Frederic

Cernuda (y Bidon), Luis
    1902-1963 .... **CLC 54**
    See also CA 131; 89-92; DAM POET;
    DLB 134; HW

Cervantes (Saavedra), Miguel de
    1547-1616 .... **LC 6, 23; DA; DAB;**
                       DAC; SSC 12; WLC
    See also DAM MST, NOV

Cesaire, Aime (Fernand)
    1913- .... **CLC 19, 32; BLC**
    See also BW 2; CA 65-68; CANR 24, 43;
    DAM MULT, POET; MTCW

Chabon, Michael 1965(?)- .... **CLC 55**
    See also CA 139

Chabrol, Claude 1930-............ **CLC 16**
    See also CA 110

Challans, Mary 1905-1983
    See Renault, Mary
    See also CA 81-84; 111; SATA 23;
    SATA-Obit 36

Challis, George
    See Faust, Frederick (Schiller)

Chambers, Aidan 1934- .... **CLC 35**
    See also CA 25-28R; CANR 12, 31; JRDA;
    MAICYA; SAAS 12; SATA 1, 69

Chambers, James 1948-
    See Cliff, Jimmy
    See also CA 124

Chambers, Jessie
    See Lawrence, D(avid) H(erbert Richards)

Chambers, Robert W. 1865-1933... **TCLC 41**

Chandler, Raymond (Thornton)
    1888-1959 .... **TCLC 1, 7**
    See also CA 104; 129; CDALB 1929-1941;
    DLBD 6; MTCW

Chang, Jung 1952- .... **CLC 71**
    See also CA 142

Channing, William Ellery
    1780-1842 .... **NCLC 17**
    See also DLB 1, 59

Chaplin, Charles Spencer
    1889-1977 .... **CLC 16**
    See also Chaplin, Charlie
    See also CA 81-84; 73-76

Chaplin, Charlie
    See Chaplin, Charles Spencer
    See also DLB 44

Chapman, George 1559(?)-1634...... **LC 22**
    See also DAM DRAM; DLB 62, 121

Chapman, Graham 1941-1989 ...... **CLC 21**
    See also Monty Python
    See also CA 116; 129; CANR 35

Chapman, John Jay 1862-1933 ..... **TCLC 7**
    See also CA 104

Chapman, Walker
    See Silverberg, Robert

Chappell, Fred (Davis) 1936-.... **CLC 40, 78**
    See also CA 5-8R; CAAS 4; CANR 8, 33;
    DLB 6, 105

Char, Rene(-Emile)
    1907-1988 .... **CLC 9, 11, 14, 55**
    See also CA 13-16R; 124; CANR 32;
    DAM POET; MTCW

Charby, Jay
    See Ellison, Harlan (Jay)

Chardin, Pierre Teilhard de
    See Teilhard de Chardin, (Marie Joseph)
    Pierre

Charles I 1600-1649 .... **LC 13**

Charyn, Jerome 1937- .... **CLC 5, 8, 18**
    See also CA 5-8R; CAAS 1; CANR 7;
    DLBY 83; MTCW

Chase, Mary (Coyle) 1907-1981 ...... **DC 1**
    See also CA 77-80; 105; SATA 17;
    SATA-Obit 29

Chase, Mary Ellen 1887-1973....... **CLC 2**
    See also CA 13-16; 41-44R; CAP 1;
    SATA 10

Chase, Nicholas
    See Hyde, Anthony

Chateaubriand, Francois Rene de
    1768-1848 .... **NCLC 3**
    See also DLB 119

Chatterje, Sarat Chandra 1876-1936(?)
    See Chatterji, Saratchandra
    See also CA 109

Chatterji, Bankim Chandra
    1838-1894 .... **NCLC 19**

Clarke, Marcus (Andrew Hislop)
　1846-1881 .... **NCLC 19**

Clarke, Shirley　1925- .... **CLC 16**

Clash, The
　See Headon, (Nicky) Topper; Jones, Mick;
　Simonon, Paul; Strummer, Joe

Claudel, Paul (Louis Charles Marie)
　1868-1955 .... **TCLC 2, 10**
　See also CA 104

Clavell, James (duMaresq)
　1925-1994 .... **CLC 6, 25, 87**
　See also CA 25-28R; 146; CANR 26, 48;
　DAM NOV, POP; MTCW

Cleaver, (Leroy) Eldridge
　1935- .... **CLC 30; BLC**
　See also BW 1; CA 21-24R; CANR 16;
　DAM MULT

Cleese, John (Marwood)　1939- ..... **CLC 21**
　See also Monty Python
　See also CA 112; 116; CANR 35; MTCW

Cleishbotham, Jebediah
　See Scott, Walter

Cleland, John　1710-1789 .... **LC 2**
　See also DLB 39

Clemens, Samuel Langhorne　1835-1910
　See Twain, Mark
　See also CA 104; 135; CDALB 1865-1917;
　DA; DAB; DAC; DAM MST, NOV;
　DLB 11, 12, 23, 64, 74; JRDA;
　MAICYA; YABC 2

Cleophil
　See Congreve, William

Clerihew, E.
　See Bentley, E(dmund) C(lerihew)

Clerk, N. W.
　See Lewis, C(live) S(taples)

Cliff, Jimmy .... **CLC 21**
　See also Chambers, James

Clifton, (Thelma) Lucille
　1936- .... **CLC 19, 66; BLC**
　See also BW 2; CA 49-52; CANR 2, 24, 42;
　CLR 5; DAM MULT, POET; DLB 5, 41;
　MAICYA; MTCW; SATA 20, 69

Clinton, Dirk
　See Silverberg, Robert

Clough, Arthur Hugh　1819-1861 .. **NCLC 27**
　See also DLB 32

Clutha, Janet Paterson Frame　1924-
　See Frame, Janet
　See also CA 1-4R; CANR 2, 36; MTCW

Clyne, Terence
　See Blatty, William Peter

Cobalt, Martin
　See Mayne, William (James Carter)

Cobbett, William　1763-1835 ..... **NCLC 49**
　See also DLB 43, 107, 158

Coburn, D(onald) L(ee)　1938- ...... **CLC 10**
　See also CA 89-92

Cocteau, Jean (Maurice Eugene Clement)
　1889-1963 .... **CLC 1, 8, 15, 16, 43; DA;**
　DAB; DAC; WLC
　See also CA 25-28; CANR 40; CAP 2;
　DAM DRAM, MST, NOV; DLB 65;
　MTCW

Codrescu, Andrei　1946- .... **CLC 46**
　See also CA 33-36R; CAAS 19; CANR 13,
　34; DAM POET

Coe, Max
　See Bourne, Randolph S(illiman)

Coe, Tucker
　See Westlake, Donald E(dwin)

Coetzee, J(ohn) M(ichael)
　1940- .... **CLC 23, 33, 66**
　See also CA 77-80; CANR 41; DAM NOV;
　MTCW

Coffey, Brian
　See Koontz, Dean R(ay)

Cohan, George M.　1878-1942 ..... **TCLC 60**

Cohen, Arthur A(llen)
　1928-1986 .... **CLC 7, 31**
　See also CA 1-4R; 120; CANR 1, 17, 42;
　DLB 28

Cohen, Leonard (Norman)
　1934- .... **CLC 3, 38; DAC**
　See also CA 21-24R; CANR 14;
　DAM MST; DLB 53; MTCW

Cohen, Matt　1942- .... **CLC 19; DAC**
　See also CA 61-64; CAAS 18; CANR 40;
　DLB 53

Cohen-Solal, Annie　19(?)- .... **CLC 50**

Colegate, Isabel　1931- .... **CLC 36**
　See also CA 17-20R; CANR 8, 22; DLB 14;
　INT CANR-22; MTCW

Coleman, Emmett
　See Reed, Ishmael

Coleridge, Samuel Taylor
　1772-1834 ..... **NCLC 9, 54; DA; DAB;**
　DAC; PC 11; WLC
　See also CDBLB 1789-1832; DAM MST,
　POET; DLB 93, 107

Coleridge, Sara　1802-1852 .... **NCLC 31**

Coles, Don　1928- .... **CLC 46**
　See also CA 115; CANR 38

Colette, (Sidonie-Gabrielle)
　1873-1954 ...... **TCLC 1, 5, 16; SSC 10**
　See also CA 104; 131; DAM NOV; DLB 65;
　MTCW

Collett, (Jacobine) Camilla (Wergeland)
　1813-1895 .... **NCLC 22**

Collier, Christopher　1930- .... **CLC 30**
　See also AAYA 13; CA 33-36R; CANR 13,
　33; JRDA; MAICYA; SATA 16, 70

Collier, James L(incoln)　1928- ..... **CLC 30**
　See also AAYA 13; CA 9-12R; CANR 4,
　33; CLR 3; DAM POP; JRDA;
　MAICYA; SAAS 21; SATA 8, 70

Collier, Jeremy　1650-1726 .... **LC 6**

Collier, John　1901-1980 .... **SSC 19**
　See also CA 65-68; 97-100; CANR 10;
　DLB 77

Collins, Hunt
　See Hunter, Evan

Collins, Linda　1931- .... **CLC 44**
　See also CA 125

Collins, (William) Wilkie
　1824-1889 .... **NCLC 1, 18**
　See also CDBLB 1832-1890; DLB 18, 70,
　159

Collins, William　1721-1759 .... **LC 4**
　See also DAM POET; DLB 109

Collodi, Carlo　1826-1890 .... **NCLC 54**
　See also Lorenzini, Carlo
　See also CLR 5

Colman, George
　See Glassco, John

Colt, Winchester Remington
　See Hubbard, L(afayette) Ron(ald)

Colter, Cyrus　1910- .... **CLC 58**
　See also BW 1; CA 65-68; CANR 10;
　DLB 33

Colton, James
　See Hansen, Joseph

Colum, Padraic　1881-1972 .... **CLC 28**
　See also CA 73-76; 33-36R; CANR 35;
　CLR 36; MAICYA; MTCW; SATA 15

Colvin, James
　See Moorcock, Michael (John)

Colwin, Laurie (E.)
　1944-1992 .... **CLC 5, 13, 23, 84**
　See also CA 89-92; 139; CANR 20, 46;
　DLBY 80; MTCW

Comfort, Alex(ander)　1920- .... **CLC 7**
　See also CA 1-4R; CANR 1, 45; DAM POP

Comfort, Montgomery
　See Campbell, (John) Ramsey

Compton-Burnett, I(vy)
　1884(?)-1969 ...... **CLC 1, 3, 10, 15, 34**
　See also CA 1-4R; 25-28R; CANR 4;
　DAM NOV; DLB 36; MTCW

Comstock, Anthony　1844-1915 .... **TCLC 13**
　See also CA 110

Comte, Auguste　1798-1857 .... **NCLC 54**

Conan Doyle, Arthur
　See Doyle, Arthur Conan

Conde, Maryse　1937- .... **CLC 52**
　See also Boucolon, Maryse
　See also BW 2; DAM MULT

Condillac, Etienne Bonnot de
　1714-1780 .... **LC 26**

Condon, Richard (Thomas)
　1915- .... **CLC 4, 6, 8, 10, 45**
　See also BEST 90:3; CA 1-4R; CAAS 1;
　CANR 2, 23; DAM NOV;
　INT CANR-23; MTCW

Congreve, William
　1670-1729 .... **LC 5, 21; DA; DAB;**
　DAC; DC 2; WLC
　See also CDBLB 1660-1789; DAM DRAM,
　MST, POET; DLB 39, 84

Connell, Evan S(helby), Jr.
　1924- .... **CLC 4, 6, 45**
　See also AAYA 7; CA 1-4R; CAAS 2;
　CANR 2, 39; DAM NOV; DLB 2;
　DLBY 81; MTCW

Connelly, Marc(us Cook)
　1890-1980 .... **CLC 7**
　See also CA 85-88; 102; CANR 30; DLB 7;
　DLBY 80; SATA-Obit 25

Connor, Ralph .... **TCLC 31**
　See also Gordon, Charles William
　See also DLB 92

Conrad, Joseph
    1857-1924 .... **TCLC 1, 6, 13, 25, 43, 57;**
                        DA; DAB; DAC; SSC 9; WLC
    See also CA 104; 131; CDBLB 1890-1914;
        DAM MST, NOV; DLB 10, 34, 98, 156;
        MTCW; SATA 27

Conrad, Robert Arnold
    See Hart, Moss

Conroy, Pat 1945-............ **CLC 30, 74**
    See also AAYA 8; AITN 1; CA 85-88;
        CANR 24; DAM NOV, POP; DLB 6;
        MTCW

Constant (de Rebecque), (Henri) Benjamin
    1767-1830 .... **NCLC 6**
    See also DLB 119

Conybeare, Charles Augustus
    See Eliot, T(homas) S(tearns)

Cook, Michael 1933- .... **CLC 58**
    See also CA 93-96; DLB 53

Cook, Robin 1940- .... **CLC 14**
    See also BEST 90:2; CA 108; 111;
        CANR 41; DAM POP; INT 111

Cook, Roy
    See Silverberg, Robert

Cooke, Elizabeth 1948- .... **CLC 55**
    See also CA 129

Cooke, John Esten 1830-1886 ..... **NCLC 5**
    See also DLB 3

Cooke, John Estes
    See Baum, L(yman) Frank

Cooke, M. E.
    See Creasey, John

Cooke, Margaret
    See Creasey, John

Cooney, Ray .... **CLC 62**

Cooper, Douglas 1960-............ **CLC 86**

Cooper, Henry St. John
    See Creasey, John

Cooper, J. California............... **CLC 56**
    See also AAYA 12; BW 1; CA 125;
        DAM MULT

Cooper, James Fenimore
    1789-1851 .... **NCLC 1, 27, 54**
    See also CDALB 1640-1865; DLB 3;
        SATA 19

Coover, Robert (Lowell)
    1932- .. CLC 3, 7, 15, 32, 46, 87; SSC 15
    See also CA 45-48; CANR 3, 37;
        DAM NOV; DLB 2; DLBY 81; MTCW

Copeland, Stewart (Armstrong)
    1952- .... **CLC 26**

Coppard, A(lfred) E(dgar)
    1878-1957 .... **TCLC 5; SSC 21**
    See also CA 114; DLB 162; YABC 1

Coppee, Francois 1842-1908 ...... **TCLC 25**

Coppola, Francis Ford 1939-....... **CLC 16**
    See also CA 77-80; CANR 40; DLB 44

Corbiere, Tristan 1845-1875 ..... **NCLC 43**

Corcoran, Barbara 1911-.......... **CLC 17**
    See also AAYA 14; CA 21-24R; CAAS 2;
        CANR 11, 28, 48; DLB 52; JRDA;
        SAAS 20; SATA 3, 77

Cordelier, Maurice
    See Giraudoux, (Hippolyte) Jean

Corelli, Marie 1855-1924........ **TCLC 51**
    See also Mackay, Mary
    See also DLB 34, 156

Corman, Cid................... **CLC 9**
    See also Corman, Sidney
    See also CAAS 2; DLB 5

Corman, Sidney 1924-
    See Corman, Cid
    See also CA 85-88; CANR 44; DAM POET

Cormier, Robert (Edmund)
    1925- ..... **CLC 12, 30; DA; DAB; DAC**
    See also AAYA 3; CA 1-4R; CANR 5, 23;
        CDALB 1968-1988; CLR 12; DAM MST,
        NOV; DLB 52; INT CANR-23; JRDA;
        MAICYA; MTCW; SATA 10, 45, 83

Corn, Alfred (DeWitt III) 1943-.... **CLC 33**
    See also CA 104; CANR 44; DLB 120;
        DLBY 80

Corneille, Pierre 1606-1684.... **LC 28; DAB**
    See also DAM MST

Cornwell, David (John Moore)
    1931- .... **CLC 9, 15**
    See also le Carre, John
    See also CA 5-8R; CANR 13, 33;
        DAM POP; MTCW

Corso, (Nunzio) Gregory 1930-... **CLC 1, 11**
    See also CA 5-8R; CANR 41; DLB 5, 16;
        MTCW

Cortazar, Julio
    1914-1984 ...... **CLC 2, 3, 5, 10, 13, 15,**
                        33, 34; HLC; SSC 7
    See also CA 21-24R; CANR 12, 32;
        DAM MULT, NOV; DLB 113; HW;
        MTCW

CORTES, HERNAN 1484-1547..... **LC 31**

Corwin, Cecil
    See Kornbluth, C(yril) M.

Cosic, Dobrica 1921- .... **CLC 14**
    See also CA 122; 138

Costain, Thomas B(ertram)
    1885-1965 .... **CLC 30**
    See also CA 5-8R; 25-28R; DLB 9

Costantini, Humberto
    1924(?)-1987 .... **CLC 49**
    See also CA 131; 122; HW

Costello, Elvis 1955-.............. **CLC 21**

Cotter, Joseph Seamon Sr.
    1861-1949 .... **TCLC 28; BLC**
    See also BW 1; CA 124; DAM MULT;
        DLB 50

Couch, Arthur Thomas Quiller
    See Quiller-Couch, Arthur Thomas

Coulton, James
    See Hansen, Joseph

Couperus, Louis (Marie Anne)
    1863-1923 .... **TCLC 15**
    See also CA 115

Coupland, Douglas 1961-..... **CLC 85; DAC**
    See also CA 142; DAM POP

Court, Wesli
    See Turco, Lewis (Putnam)

Courtenay, Bryce 1933-........... **CLC 59**
    See also CA 138

Courtney, Robert
    See Ellison, Harlan (Jay)

Cousteau, Jacques-Yves 1910-...... **CLC 30**
    See also CA 65-68; CANR 15; MTCW;
        SATA 38

Coward, Noel (Peirce)
    1899-1973 ....**CLC 1, 9, 29, 51**
    See also AITN 1; CA 17-18; 41-44R;
        CANR 35; CAP 2; CDBLB 1914-1945;
        DAM DRAM; DLB 10; MTCW

Cowley, Malcolm 1898-1989 .... **CLC 39**
    See also CA 5-8R; 128; CANR 3; DLB 4,
        48; DLBY 81, 89; MTCW

Cowper, William 1731-1800....... **NCLC 8**
    See also DAM POET; DLB 104, 109

Cox, William Trevor 1928- ... **CLC 9, 14, 71**
    See also Trevor, William
    See also CA 9-12R; CANR 4, 37;
        DAM NOV; DLB 14; INT CANR-37;
        MTCW

Coyne, P. J.
    See Masters, Hilary

Cozzens, James Gould
    1903-1978 .... **CLC 1, 4, 11**
    See also CA 9-12R; 81-84; CANR 19;
        CDALB 1941-1968; DLB 9; DLBD 2;
        DLBY 84; MTCW

Crabbe, George 1754-1832....... **NCLC 26**
    See also DLB 93

Craig, A. A.
    See Anderson, Poul (William)

Craik, Dinah Maria (Mulock)
    1826-1887 .... **NCLC 38**
    See also DLB 35; MAICYA; SATA 34

Cram, Ralph Adams 1863-1942.... **TCLC 45**

Crane, (Harold) Hart
    1899-1932 .... **TCLC 2, 5; DA; DAB;**
                        DAC; PC 3; WLC
    See also CA 104; 127; CDALB 1917-1929;
        DAM MST, POET; DLB 4, 48; MTCW

Crane, R(onald) S(almon)
    1886-1967 .... **CLC 27**
    See also CA 85-88; DLB 63

Crane, Stephen (Townley)
    1871-1900 .... **TCLC 11, 17, 32; DA;**
                        DAB; DAC; SSC 7; WLC
    See also CA 109; 140; CDALB 1865-1917;
        DAM MST, NOV, POET; DLB 12, 54,
        78; YABC 2

Crase, Douglas 1944-............. **CLC 58**
    See also CA 106

Crashaw, Richard 1612(?)-1649...... **LC 24**
    See also DLB 126

Craven, Margaret
    1901-1980 .... **CLC 17; DAC**
    See also CA 103

Crawford, F(rancis) Marion
    1854-1909 .... **TCLC 10**
    See also CA 107; DLB 71

Crawford, Isabella Valancy
    1850-1887 .... **NCLC 12**
    See also DLB 92

Crayon, Geoffrey
    See Irving, Washington

Creasey, John 1908-1973.......... **CLC 11**
    See also CA 5-8R; 41-44R; CANR 8;
        DLB 77; MTCW

Crebillon, Claude Prosper Jolyot de (fils)
1707-1777 . . . . **LC 28**

Credo
See Creasey, John

Creeley, Robert (White)
1926- . . . . . **CLC 1, 2, 4, 8, 11, 15, 36, 78**
See also CA 1-4R; CAAS 10; CANR 23, 43;
DAM POET; DLB 5, 16; MTCW

Crews, Harry (Eugene)
1935- . . . . **CLC 6, 23, 49**
See also AITN 1; CA 25-28R; CANR 20;
DLB 6, 143; MTCW

Crichton, (John) Michael
1942- . . . . **CLC 2, 6, 54, 90**
See also AAYA 10; AITN 2; CA 25-28R;
CANR 13, 40; DAM NOV, POP;
DLBY 81; INT CANR-13; JRDA;
MTCW; SATA 9

Crispin, Edmund . . . . **CLC 22**
See also Montgomery, (Robert) Bruce
See also DLB 87

Cristofer, Michael 1945(?)- . . . . **CLC 28**
See also CA 110; DAM DRAM; DLB 7

Croce, Benedetto 1866-1952 . . . . . . **TCLC 37**
See also CA 120

Crockett, David 1786-1836 . . . . **NCLC 8**
See also DLB 3, 11

Crockett, Davy
See Crockett, David

Crofts, Freeman Wills
1879-1957 . . . . **TCLC 55**
See also CA 115; DLB 77

Croker, John Wilson 1780-1857 . . **NCLC 10**
See also DLB 110

Crommelynck, Fernand 1885-1970 . . **CLC 75**
See also CA 89-92

Cronin, A(rchibald) J(oseph)
1896-1981 . . . . **CLC 32**
See also CA 1-4R; 102; CANR 5; SATA 47;
SATA-Obit 25

Cross, Amanda
See Heilbrun, Carolyn G(old)

Crothers, Rachel 1878(?)-1958. . . . . **TCLC 19**
See also CA 113; DLB 7

Croves, Hal
See Traven, B.

Crowfield, Christopher
See Stowe, Harriet (Elizabeth) Beecher

Crowley, Aleister. . . . . **TCLC 7**
See also Crowley, Edward Alexander

Crowley, Edward Alexander 1875-1947
See Crowley, Aleister
See also CA 104

Crowley, John 1942-. . . . . **CLC 57**
See also CA 61-64; CANR 43; DLBY 82;
SATA 65

Crud
See Crumb, R(obert)

Crumarums
See Crumb, R(obert)

Crumb, R(obert) 1943-. . . . . **CLC 17**
See also CA 106

Crumbum
See Crumb, R(obert)

Crumski
See Crumb, R(obert)

Crum the Bum
See Crumb, R(obert)

Crunk
See Crumb, R(obert)

Crustt
See Crumb, R(obert)

Cryer, Gretchen (Kiger) 1935-. . . . . . **CLC 21**
See also CA 114; 123

Csath, Geza 1887-1919. . . . . **TCLC 13**
See also CA 111

Cudlip, David 1933-. . . . . **CLC 34**

Cullen, Countee
1903-1946 . . . . . . **TCLC 4, 37; BLC; DA;
DAC**
See also BW 1; CA 108; 124;
CDALB 1917-1929; DAM MST, MULT,
POET; DLB 4, 48, 51; MTCW; SATA 18

Cum, R.
See Crumb, R(obert)

Cummings, Bruce F(rederick) 1889-1919
See Barbellion, W. N. P.
See also CA 123

Cummings, E(dward) E(stlin)
1894-1962 . . . . . . **CLC 1, 3, 8, 12, 15, 68;
DA; DAB; DAC; PC 5; WLC 2**
See also CA 73-76; CANR 31;
CDALB 1929-1941; DAM MST, POET;
DLB 4, 48; MTCW

Cunha, Euclides (Rodrigues Pimenta) da
1866-1909 . . . . **TCLC 24**
See also CA 123

Cunningham, E. V.
See Fast, Howard (Melvin)

Cunningham, J(ames) V(incent)
1911-1985 . . . . **CLC 3, 31**
See also CA 1-4R; 115; CANR 1; DLB 5

Cunningham, Julia (Woolfolk)
1916- . . . . **CLC 12**
See also CA 9-12R; CANR 4, 19, 36;
JRDA; MAICYA; SAAS 2; SATA 1, 26

Cunningham, Michael 1952- . . . . **CLC 34**
See also CA 136

Cunninghame Graham, R(obert) B(ontine)
1852-1936 . . . . **TCLC 19**
See also Graham, R(obert) B(ontine)
Cunninghame
See also CA 119; DLB 98

Currie, Ellen 19(?)-. . . . . **CLC 44**

Curtin, Philip
See Lowndes, Marie Adelaide (Belloc)

Curtis, Price
See Ellison, Harlan (Jay)

Cutrate, Joe
See Spiegelman, Art

Czaczkes, Shmuel Yosef
See Agnon, S(hmuel) Y(osef Halevi)

Dabrowska, Maria (Szumska)
1889-1965 . . . . **CLC 15**
See also CA 106

Dabydeen, David 1955- . . . . **CLC 34**
See also BW 1; CA 125

Dacey, Philip 1939- . . . . **CLC 51**
See also CA 37-40R; CAAS 17; CANR 14,
32; DLB 105

Dagerman, Stig (Halvard)
1923-1954 . . . . **TCLC 17**
See also CA 117

Dahl, Roald
1916-1990 . . . . . . **CLC 1, 6, 18, 79; DAB;
DAC**
See also AAYA 15; CA 1-4R; 133;
CANR 6, 32, 37; CLR 1, 7; DAM MST,
NOV, POP; DLB 139; JRDA; MAICYA;
MTCW; SATA 1, 26, 73; SATA-Obit 65

Dahlberg, Edward 1900-1977. . . **CLC 1, 7, 14**
See also CA 9-12R; 69-72; CANR 31;
DLB 48; MTCW

Dale, Colin. **TCLC 18**
See also Lawrence, T(homas) E(dward)

Dale, George E.
See Asimov, Isaac

Daly, Elizabeth 1878-1967. . . . . **CLC 52**
See also CA 23-24; 25-28R; CAP 2

Daly, Maureen 1921-. . . . . **CLC 17**
See also AAYA 5; CANR 37; JRDA;
MAICYA; SAAS 1; SATA 2

Damas, Leon-Gontran 1912-1978 . . . **CLC 84**
See also BW 1; CA 125; 73-76

Dana, Richard Henry Sr.
1787-1879 . . . . **NCLC 53**

Daniel, Samuel 1562(?)-1619. . . . . **LC 24**
See also DLB 62

Daniels, Brett
See Adler, Renata

Dannay, Frederic 1905-1982 . . . . **CLC 11**
See also Queen, Ellery
See also CA 1-4R; 107; CANR 1, 39;
DAM POP; DLB 137; MTCW

D'Annunzio, Gabriele
1863-1938 . . . . **TCLC 6, 40**
See also CA 104

Danois, N. le
See Gourmont, Remy (-Marie-Charles) de

d'Antibes, Germain
See Simenon, Georges (Jacques Christian)

Danvers, Dennis 1947-. . . . . **CLC 70**

Danziger, Paula 1944- . . . . **CLC 21**
See also AAYA 4; CA 112; 115; CANR 37;
CLR 20; JRDA; MAICYA; SATA 36,
63; SATA-Brief 30

Da Ponte, Lorenzo 1749-1838. . . . **NCLC 50**

Dario, Ruben
1867-1916 . . . . **TCLC 4; HLC; PC 15**
See also CA 131; DAM MULT; HW;
MTCW

Darley, George 1795-1846. . . . . **NCLC 2**
See also DLB 96

Daryush, Elizabeth 1887-1977. . . . **CLC 6, 19**
See also CA 49-52; CANR 3; DLB 20

**Dashwood, Edmee Elizabeth Monica de la
Pasture** 1890-1943
See Delafield, E. M.
See also CA 119

de Montherlant, Henry (Milon)
See Montherlant, Henry (Milon) de

Demosthenes 384B.C.-322B.C. . . . **CMLC 13**

de Natale, Francine
See Malzberg, Barry N(athaniel)

Denby, Edwin (Orr) 1903-1983 . . . . . **CLC 48**
See also CA 138; 110

Denis, Julio
See Cortazar, Julio

Denmark, Harrison
See Zelazny, Roger (Joseph)

Dennis, John 1658-1734 . . . . **LC 11**
See also DLB 101

Dennis, Nigel (Forbes) 1912-1989 . . . . **CLC 8**
See also CA 25-28R; 129; DLB 13, 15;
MTCW

De Palma, Brian (Russell) 1940- . . . . **CLC 20**
See also CA 109

De Quincey, Thomas 1785-1859 . . . **NCLC 4**
See also CDBLB 1789-1832; DLB 110; 144

Deren, Eleanora 1908(?)-1961
See Deren, Maya
See also CA 111

Deren, Maya . . . . **CLC 16**
See also Deren, Eleanora

Derleth, August (William)
1909-1971 . . . . **CLC 31**
See also CA 1-4R; 29-32R; CANR 4;
DLB 9; SATA 5

Der Nister 1884-1950 . . . . **TCLC 56**

de Routisie, Albert
See Aragon, Louis

Derrida, Jacques 1930- . . . . **CLC 24, 87**
See also CA 124; 127

Derry Down Derry
See Lear, Edward

Dersonnes, Jacques
See Simenon, Georges (Jacques Christian)

Desai, Anita 1937- . . . . . . **CLC 19, 37; DAB**
See also CA 81-84; CANR 33; DAM NOV;
MTCW; SATA 63

de Saint-Luc, Jean
See Glassco, John

de Saint Roman, Arnaud
See Aragon, Louis

Descartes, Rene 1596-1650 . . . . **LC 20**

De Sica, Vittorio 1901(?)-1974 . . . . . **CLC 20**
See also CA 117

Desnos, Robert 1900-1945 . . . . **TCLC 22**
See also CA 121

Destouches, Louis-Ferdinand
1894-1961 . . . . **CLC 9, 15**
See also Celine, Louis-Ferdinand
See also CA 85-88; CANR 28; MTCW

Deutsch, Babette 1895-1982 . . . . **CLC 18**
See also CA 1-4R; 108; CANR 4; DLB 45;
SATA 1; SATA-Obit 33

Devenant, William 1606-1649 . . . . **LC 13**

Devkota, Laxmiprasad
1909-1959 . . . . **TCLC 23**
See also CA 123

De Voto, Bernard (Augustine)
1897-1955 . . . . **TCLC 29**
See also CA 113; DLB 9

De Vries, Peter
1910-1993 . . . . **CLC 1, 2, 3, 7, 10, 28, 46**
See also CA 17-20R; 142; CANR 41;
DAM NOV; DLB 6; DLBY 82; MTCW

Dexter, Martin
See Faust, Frederick (Schiller)

Dexter, Pete 1943- . . . . **CLC 34, 55**
See also BEST 89:2; CA 127; 131;
DAM POP; INT 131; MTCW

Diamano, Silmang
See Senghor, Leopold Sedar

Diamond, Neil 1941- . . . . **CLC 30**
See also CA 108

Diaz del Castillo, Bernal 1496-1584 . . **LC 31**

di Bassetto, Corno
See Shaw, George Bernard

Dick, Philip K(indred)
1928-1982 . . . . **CLC 10, 30, 72**
See also CA 49-52; 106; CANR 2, 16;
DAM NOV, POP; DLB 8; MTCW

Dickens, Charles (John Huffam)
1812-1870 . . . . . . **NCLC 3, 8, 18, 26, 37,**
50; DA; DAB; DAC; SSC 17; WLC
See also CDBLB 1832-1890; DAM MST,
NOV; DLB 21, 55, 70, 159; JRDA;
MAICYA; SATA 15

Dickey, James (Lafayette)
1923- . . . . **CLC 1, 2, 4, 7, 10, 15, 47**
See also AITN 1, 2; CA 9-12R; CABS 2;
CANR 10, 48; CDALB 1968-1988;
DAM NOV, POET, POP; DLB 5;
DLBD 7; DLBY 82, 93; INT CANR-10;
MTCW

Dickey, William 1928-1994 . . . . . . **CLC 3, 28**
See also CA 9-12R; 145; CANR 24; DLB 5

Dickinson, Charles 1951- . . . . **CLC 49**
See also CA 128

Dickinson, Emily (Elizabeth)
1830-1886 . . . . . . **NCLC 21; DA; DAB;**
DAC; PC 1; WLC
See also CDALB 1865-1917; DAM MST,
POET; DLB 1; SATA 29

Dickinson, Peter (Malcolm)
1927- . . . . **CLC 12, 35**
See also AAYA 9; CA 41-44R; CANR 31;
CLR 29; DLB 87, 161; JRDA; MAICYA;
SATA 5, 62

Dickson, Carr
See Carr, John Dickson

Dickson, Carter
See Carr, John Dickson

Diderot, Denis 1713-1784 . . . . **LC 26**

Didion, Joan 1934- . . . . . **CLC 1, 3, 8, 14, 32**
See also AITN 1; CA 5-8R; CANR 14;
CDALB 1968-1988; DAM NOV; DLB 2;
DLBY 81, 86; MTCW

Dietrich, Robert
See Hunt, E(verette) Howard, (Jr.)

Dillard, Annie 1945- . . . . **CLC 9, 60**
See also AAYA 6; CA 49-52; CANR 3, 43;
DAM NOV; DLBY 80; MTCW;
SATA 10

Dillard, R(ichard) H(enry) W(ilde)
1937- . . . . **CLC 5**
See also CA 21-24R; CAAS 7; CANR 10;
DLB 5

Dillon, Eilis 1920-1994 . . . . **CLC 17**
See also CA 9-12R; 147; CAAS 3; CANR 4,
38; CLR 26; MAICYA; SATA 2, 74;
SATA-Obit 83

Dimont, Penelope
See Mortimer, Penelope (Ruth)

Dinesen, Isak . . . . **CLC 10, 29; SSC 7**
See also Blixen, Karen (Christentze
Dinesen)

Ding Ling . . . . **CLC 68**
See also Chiang Pin-chin

Disch, Thomas M(ichael) 1940- . . . **CLC 7, 36**
See also AAYA 17; CA 21-24R; CAAS 4;
CANR 17, 36; CLR 18; DLB 8;
MAICYA; MTCW; SAAS 15; SATA 54

Disch, Tom
See Disch, Thomas M(ichael)

d'Isly, Georges
See Simenon, Georges (Jacques Christian)

Disraeli, Benjamin 1804-1881 . . **NCLC 2, 39**
See also DLB 21, 55

Ditcum, Steve
See Crumb, R(obert)

Dixon, Paige
See Corcoran, Barbara

Dixon, Stephen 1936- . . . . . **CLC 52; SSC 16**
See also CA 89-92; CANR 17, 40; DLB 130

Dobell, Sydney Thompson
1824-1874 . . . . **NCLC 43**
See also DLB 32

Doblin, Alfred . . . . **TCLC 13**
See also Doeblin, Alfred

Dobrolyubov, Nikolai Alexandrovich
1836-1861 . . . . **NCLC 5**

Dobyns, Stephen 1941- . . . . **CLC 37**
See also CA 45-48; CANR 2, 18

Doctorow, E(dgar) L(aurence)
1931- . . . . . **CLC 6, 11, 15, 18, 37, 44, 65**
See also AITN 2; BEST 89:3; CA 45-48;
CANR 2, 33, 51; CDALB 1968-1988;
DAM NOV, POP; DLB 2, 28; DLBY 80;
MTCW

Dodgson, Charles Lutwidge 1832-1898
See Carroll, Lewis
See also CLR 2; DA; DAB; DAC;
DAM MST, NOV, POET; MAICYA;
YABC 2

Dodson, Owen (Vincent)
1914-1983 . . . . **CLC 79; BLC**
See also BW 1; CA 65-68; 110; CANR 24;
DAM MULT; DLB 76

Doeblin, Alfred 1878-1957 . . . . **TCLC 13**
See also Doblin, Alfred
See also CA 110; 141; DLB 66

Doerr, Harriet 1910- . . . . **CLC 34**
See also CA 117; 122; CANR 47; INT 122

Domecq, H(onorio) Bustos
See Bioy Casares, Adolfo; Borges, Jorge
Luis

Domini, Rey
See Lorde, Audre (Geraldine)

Duffy, Maureen 1933- . . . . **CLC 37**
See also CA 25-28R; CANR 33; DLB 14;
MTCW

Dugan, Alan 1923- . . . . **CLC 2, 6**
See also CA 81-84; DLB 5

du Gard, Roger Martin
See Martin du Gard, Roger

Duhamel, Georges 1884-1966 . . . . **CLC 8**
See also CA 81-84; 25-28R; CANR 35;
DLB 65; MTCW

Dujardin, Edouard (Emile Louis)
1861-1949 . . . . **TCLC 13**
See also CA 109; DLB 123

Dumas, Alexandre (Davy de la Pailleterie)
1802-1870 . . . . **NCLC 11; DA; DAB;
DAC; WLC**
See also DAM MST, NOV; DLB 119;
SATA 18

Dumas, Alexandre
1824-1895 . . . . **NCLC 9; DC 1**

Dumas, Claudine
See Malzberg, Barry N(athaniel)

Dumas, Henry L. 1934-1968 . . . . . **CLC 6, 62**
See also BW 1; CA 85-88; DLB 41

du Maurier, Daphne
1907-1989 . . . . **CLC 6, 11, 59; DAB;
DAC; SSC 18**
See also CA 5-8R; 128; CANR 6;
DAM MST, POP; MTCW; SATA 27;
SATA-Obit 60

Dunbar, Paul Laurence
1872-1906 . . . . . . **TCLC 2, 12; BLC; DA;
DAC; PC 5; SSC 8; WLC**
See also BW 1; CA 104; 124;
CDALB 1865-1917; DAM MST, MULT,
POET; DLB 50, 54, 78; SATA 34

Dunbar, William 1460(?)-1530(?) . . . . **LC 20**
See also DLB 132, 146

Duncan, Lois 1934- . . . . **CLC 26**
See also AAYA 4; CA 1-4R; CANR 2, 23,
36; CLR 29; JRDA; MAICYA; SAAS 2;
SATA 1, 36, 75

Duncan, Robert (Edward)
1919-1988 . . . . **CLC 1, 2, 4, 7, 15, 41, 55;
PC 2**
See also CA 9-12R; 124; CANR 28;
DAM POET; DLB 5, 16; MTCW

Duncan, Sara Jeannette
1861-1922 . . . . **TCLC 60**
See also DLB 92

Dunlap, William 1766-1839 . . . . **NCLC 2**
See also DLB 30, 37, 59

Dunn, Douglas (Eaglesham)
1942- . . . . **CLC 6, 40**
See also CA 45-48; CANR 2, 33; DLB 40;
MTCW

Dunn, Katherine (Karen) 1945- . . . . . **CLC 71**
See also CA 33-36R

Dunn, Stephen 1939- . . . . **CLC 36**
See also CA 33-36R; CANR 12, 48;
DLB 105

Dunne, Finley Peter 1867-1936 . . . . **TCLC 28**
See also CA 108; DLB 11, 23

Dunne, John Gregory 1932- . . . . **CLC 28**
See also CA 25-28R; CANR 14, 50;
DLBY 80

**Dunsany, Edward John Moreton Drax
Plunkett** 1878-1957
See Dunsany, Lord
See also CA 104; 148; DLB 10

Dunsany, Lord . . . . **TCLC 2, 59**
See also Dunsany, Edward John Moreton
Drax Plunkett
See also DLB 77, 153, 156

du Perry, Jean
See Simenon, Georges (Jacques Christian)

Durang, Christopher (Ferdinand)
1949- . . . . **CLC 27, 38**
See also CA 105; CANR 50

Duras, Marguerite
1914- . . . . **CLC 3, 6, 11, 20, 34, 40, 68**
See also CA 25-28R; CANR 50; DLB 83;
MTCW

Durban, (Rosa) Pam 1947- . . . . **CLC 39**
See also CA 123

Durcan, Paul 1944- . . . . **CLC 43, 70**
See also CA 134; DAM POET

Durkheim, Emile 1858-1917 . . . . . . **TCLC 55**

Durrell, Lawrence (George)
1912-1990 . . . . **CLC 1, 4, 6, 8, 13, 27, 41**
See also CA 9-12R; 132; CANR 40;
CDBLB 1945-1960; DAM NOV; DLB 15,
27; DLBY 90; MTCW

Durrenmatt, Friedrich
See Duerrenmatt, Friedrich

Dutt, Toru 1856-1877 . . . . **NCLC 29**

Dwight, Timothy 1752-1817 . . . . . . **NCLC 13**
See also DLB 37

Dworkin, Andrea 1946- . . . . **CLC 43**
See also CA 77-80; CAAS 21; CANR 16,
39; INT CANR-16; MTCW

Dwyer, Deanna
See Koontz, Dean R(ay)

Dwyer, K. R.
See Koontz, Dean R(ay)

Dylan, Bob 1941- . . . . . . **CLC 3, 4, 6, 12, 77**
See also CA 41-44R; DLB 16

Eagleton, Terence (Francis) 1943-
See Eagleton, Terry
See also CA 57-60; CANR 7, 23; MTCW

Eagleton, Terry . . . . **CLC 63**
See also Eagleton, Terence (Francis)

Early, Jack
See Scoppettone, Sandra

East, Michael
See West, Morris L(anglo)

Eastaway, Edward
See Thomas, (Philip) Edward

Eastlake, William (Derry) 1917- . . . . . **CLC 8**
See also CA 5-8R; CAAS 1; CANR 5;
DLB 6; INT CANR-5

Eastman, Charles A(lexander)
1858-1939 . . . . **TCLC 55**
See also DAM MULT; NNAL; YABC 1

Eberhart, Richard (Ghormley)
1904- . . . . **CLC 3, 11, 19, 56**
See also CA 1-4R; CANR 2;
CDALB 1941-1968; DAM POET;
DLB 48; MTCW

Eberstadt, Fernanda 1960- . . . . **CLC 39**
See also CA 136

Echegaray (y Eizaguirre), Jose (Maria Waldo)
1832-1916 . . . . **TCLC 4**
See also CA 104; CANR 32; HW; MTCW

Echeverria, (Jose) Esteban (Antonino)
1805-1851 . . . . **NCLC 18**

Echo
See Proust, (Valentin-Louis-George-Eugene-)
Marcel

Eckert, Allan W. 1931- . . . . **CLC 17**
See also CA 13-16R; CANR 14, 45;
INT CANR-14; SAAS 21; SATA 29;
SATA-Brief 27

Eckhart, Meister 1260(?)-1328(?) . . **CMLC 9**
See also DLB 115

Eckmar, F. R.
See de Hartog, Jan

Eco, Umberto 1932- . . . . **CLC 28, 60**
See also BEST 90:1; CA 77-80; CANR 12,
33; DAM NOV, POP; MTCW

Eddison, E(ric) R(ucker)
1882-1945 . . . . **TCLC 15**
See also CA 109

Edel, (Joseph) Leon 1907- . . . . . . **CLC 29, 34**
See also CA 1-4R; CANR 1, 22; DLB 103;
INT CANR-22

Eden, Emily 1797-1869 . . . . **NCLC 10**

Edgar, David 1948- . . . . **CLC 42**
See also CA 57-60; CANR 12;
DAM DRAM; DLB 13; MTCW

Edgerton, Clyde (Carlyle) 1944- . . . . **CLC 39**
See also AAYA 17; CA 118; 134; INT 134

Edgeworth, Maria 1768-1849 . . . **NCLC 1, 51**
See also DLB 116, 159; SATA 21

Edmonds, Paul
See Kuttner, Henry

Edmonds, Walter D(umaux) 1903- . . **CLC 35**
See also CA 5-8R; CANR 2; DLB 9;
MAICYA; SAAS 4; SATA 1, 27

Edmondson, Wallace
See Ellison, Harlan (Jay)

Edson, Russell . . . . **CLC 13**
See also CA 33-36R

Edwards, Bronwen Elizabeth
See Rose, Wendy

Edwards, G(erald) B(asil)
1899-1976 . . . . **CLC 25**
See also CA 110

Edwards, Gus 1939- . . . . **CLC 43**
See also CA 108; INT 108

Edwards, Jonathan
1703-1758 . . . . **LC 7; DA; DAC**
See also DAM MST; DLB 24

Efron, Marina Ivanovna Tsvetaeva
See Tsvetaeva (Efron), Marina (Ivanovna)

Ehle, John (Marsden, Jr.) 1925- . . . . **CLC 27**
See also CA 9-12R

Ehrenbourg, Ilya (Grigoryevich)
See Ehrenburg, Ilya (Grigoryevich)

Ehrenburg, Ilya (Grigoryevich)
1891-1967 . . . . **CLC 18, 34, 62**
See also CA 102; 25-28R

Eriksson, Buntel
See Bergman, (Ernst) Ingmar

Ernaux, Annie 1940- .... **CLC 88**
See also CA 147

Eschenbach, Wolfram von
See Wolfram von Eschenbach

Eseki, Bruno
See Mphahlele, Ezekiel

Esenin, Sergei (Alexandrovich)
1895-1925 .... **TCLC 4**
See also CA 104

Eshleman, Clayton 1935- .... **CLC 7**
See also CA 33-36R; CAAS 6; DLB 5

Espriella, Don Manuel Alvarez
See Southey, Robert

Espriu, Salvador 1913-1985......... **CLC 9**
See also CA 115; DLB 134

Espronceda, Jose de 1808-1842... **NCLC 39**

Esse, James
See Stephens, James

Esterbrook, Tom
See Hubbard, L(afayette) Ron(ald)

Estleman, Loren D. 1952- .... **CLC 48**
See also CA 85-88; CANR 27; DAM NOV,
POP; INT CANR-27; MTCW

Eugenides, Jeffrey 1960(?)- .... **CLC 81**
See also CA 144

Euripides c. 485B.C.-406B.C. .... **DC 4**
See also DA; DAB; DAC; DAM DRAM,
MST

Evan, Evin
See Faust, Frederick (Schiller)

Evans, Evan
See Faust, Frederick (Schiller)

Evans, Marian
See Eliot, George

Evans, Mary Ann
See Eliot, George

Evarts, Esther
See Benson, Sally

Everett, Percival L. 1956- .... **CLC 57**
See also BW 2; CA 129

Everson, R(onald) G(ilmour)
1903- .... **CLC 27**
See also CA 17-20R; DLB 88

Everson, William (Oliver)
1912-1994 .... **CLC 1, 5, 14**
See also CA 9-12R; 145; CANR 20; DLB 5,
16; MTCW

Evtushenko, Evgenii Aleksandrovich
See Yevtushenko, Yevgeny (Alexandrovich)

Ewart, Gavin (Buchanan)
1916-1995 .... **CLC 13, 46**
See also CA 89-92; 150; CANR 17, 46;
DLB 40; MTCW

Ewers, Hanns Heinz 1871-1943 ... **TCLC 12**
See also CA 109; 149

Ewing, Frederick R.
See Sturgeon, Theodore (Hamilton)

Exley, Frederick (Earl)
1929-1992 .... **CLC 6, 11**
See also AITN 2; CA 81-84; 138; DLB 143;
DLBY 81

Eynhardt, Guillermo
See Quiroga, Horacio (Sylvestre)

Ezekiel, Nissim 1924-............. **CLC 61**
See also CA 61-64

Ezekiel, Tish O'Dowd 1943- .... **CLC 34**
See also CA 129

Fadeyev, A.
See Bulgya, Alexander Alexandrovich

Fadeyev, Alexander.............. TCLC 53
See also Bulgya, Alexander Alexandrovich

Fagen, Donald 1948-............. **CLC 26**

Fainzilberg, Ilya Arnoldovich 1897-1937
See Ilf, Ilya
See also CA 120

Fair, Ronald L. 1932-............. **CLC 18**
See also BW 1; CA 69-72; CANR 25;
DLB 33

Fairbairns, Zoe (Ann) 1948- .... **CLC 32**
See also CA 103; CANR 21

Falco, Gian
See Papini, Giovanni

Falconer, James
See Kirkup, James

Falconer, Kenneth
See Kornbluth, C(yril) M.

Falkland, Samuel
See Heijermans, Herman

Fallaci, Oriana 1930-............. **CLC 11**
See also CA 77-80; CANR 15; MTCW

Faludy, George 1913-............. **CLC 42**
See also CA 21-24R

Faludy, Gyoergy
See Faludy, George

Fanon, Frantz 1925-1961..... **CLC 74; BLC**
See also BW 1; CA 116; 89-92;
DAM MULT

Fanshawe, Ann 1625-1680 .... **LC 11**

Fante, John (Thomas) 1911-1983 ... **CLC 60**
See also CA 69-72; 109; CANR 23;
DLB 130; DLBY 83

Farah, Nuruddin 1945-....... **CLC 53; BLC**
See also BW 2; CA 106; DAM MULT;
DLB 125

Fargue, Leon-Paul 1876(?)-1947 ... **TCLC 11**
See also CA 109

Farigoule, Louis
See Romains, Jules

Farina, Richard 1936(?)-1966 .... **CLC 9**
See also CA 81-84; 25-28R

Farley, Walter (Lorimer)
1915-1989 .... **CLC 17**
See also CA 17-20R; CANR 8, 29; DLB 22;
JRDA; MAICYA; SATA 2, 43

Farmer, Philip Jose 1918-....... **CLC 1, 19**
See also CA 1-4R; CANR 4, 35; DLB 8;
MTCW

Farquhar, George 1677-1707........ **LC 21**
See also DAM DRAM; DLB 84

Farrell, J(ames) G(ordon)
1935-1979 .... **CLC 6**
See also CA 73-76; 89-92; CANR 36;
DLB 14; MTCW

Farrell, James T(homas)
1904-1979 .... **CLC 1, 4, 8, 11, 66**
See also CA 5-8R; 89-92; CANR 9; DLB 4,
9, 86; DLBD 2; MTCW

Farren, Richard J.
See Betjeman, John

Farren, Richard M.
See Betjeman, John

Fassbinder, Rainer Werner
1946-1982 .... **CLC 20**
See also CA 93-96; 106; CANR 31

Fast, Howard (Melvin) 1914- ...... **CLC 23**
See also AAYA 16; CA 1-4R; CAAS 18;
CANR 1, 33; DAM NOV; DLB 9;
INT CANR-33; SATA 7

Faulcon, Robert
See Holdstock, Robert P.

Faulkner, William (Cuthbert)
1897-1962 ..... **CLC 1, 3, 6, 8, 9, 11, 14,
18, 28, 52, 68; DA; DAB; DAC; SSC 1;
WLC**
See also AAYA 7; CA 81-84; CANR 33;
CDALB 1929-1941; DAM MST, NOV;
DLB 9, 11, 44, 102; DLBD 2; DLBY 86;
MTCW

Fauset, Jessie Redmon
1884(?)-1961 .... **CLC 19, 54; BLC**
See also BW 1; CA 109; DAM MULT;
DLB 51

Faust, Frederick (Schiller)
1892-1944(?) .... **TCLC 49**
See also CA 108; DAM POP

Faust, Irvin 1924-................. **CLC 8**
See also CA 33-36R; CANR 28; DLB 2, 28;
DLBY 80

Fawkes, Guy
See Benchley, Robert (Charles)

Fearing, Kenneth (Flexner)
1902-1961 .... **CLC 51**
See also CA 93-96; DLB 9

Fecamps, Elise
See Creasey, John

Federman, Raymond 1928- ...... **CLC 6, 47**
See also CA 17-20R; CAAS 8; CANR 10,
43; DLBY 80

Federspiel, J(uerg) F. 1931-........ **CLC 42**
See also CA 146

Feiffer, Jules (Ralph) 1929-.... **CLC 2, 8, 64**
See also AAYA 3; CA 17-20R; CANR 30;
DAM DRAM; DLB 7, 44;
INT CANR-30; MTCW; SATA 8, 61

Feige, Hermann Albert Otto Maximilian
See Traven, B.

Feinberg, David B. 1956-1994...... **CLC 59**
See also CA 135; 147

Feinstein, Elaine 1930-........... **CLC 36**
See also CA 69-72; CAAS 1; CANR 31;
DLB 14, 40; MTCW

Feldman, Irving (Mordecai) 1928-.... **CLC 7**
See also CA 1-4R; CANR 1

Fellini, Federico 1920-1993..... **CLC 16, 85**
See also CA 65-68; 143; CANR 33

Felsen, Henry Gregor 1916- .... **CLC 17**
See also CA 1-4R; CANR 1; SAAS 2;
SATA 1

Forez
See Mauriac, Francois (Charles)

Forman, James Douglas 1932- ...... **CLC 21**
See also AAYA 17; CA 9-12R; CANR 4,
19, 42; JRDA; MAICYA; SATA 8, 70

Fornes, Maria Irene 1930- ...... **CLC 39, 61**
See also CA 25-28R; CANR 28; DLB 7;
HW; INT CANR-28; MTCW

Forrest, Leon 1937- .... **CLC 4**
See also BW 2; CA 89-92; CAAS 7;
CANR 25; DLB 33

Forster, E(dward) M(organ)
1879-1970 ..... **CLC 1, 2, 3, 4, 9, 10, 13,
15, 22, 45, 77; DA; DAB; DAC; WLC**
See also AAYA 2; CA 13-14; 25-28R;
CANR 45; CAP 1; CDBLB 1914-1945;
DAM MST, NOV; DLB 34, 98, 162;
DLBD 10; MTCW; SATA 57

Forster, John 1812-1876 .... **NCLC 11**
See also DLB 144

Forsyth, Frederick 1938- ...... **CLC 2, 5, 36**
See also BEST 89:4; CA 85-88; CANR 38;
DAM NOV, POP; DLB 87; MTCW

Forten, Charlotte L. .... **TCLC 16; BLC**
See also Grimke, Charlotte L(ottie) Forten
See also DLB 50

Foscolo, Ugo 1778-1827.......... **NCLC 8**

Fosse, Bob .... **CLC 20**
See also Fosse, Robert Louis

Fosse, Robert Louis 1927-1987
See Fosse, Bob
See also CA 110; 123

Foster, Stephen Collins
1826-1864 .... **NCLC 26**

Foucault, Michel
1926-1984 .... **CLC 31, 34, 69**
See also CA 105; 113; CANR 34; MTCW

Fouque, Friedrich (Heinrich Karl) de la Motte
1777-1843 .... **NCLC 2**
See also DLB 90

Fourier, Charles 1772-1837 ...... **NCLC 51**

Fournier, Henri Alban 1886-1914
See Alain-Fournier
See also CA 104

Fournier, Pierre 1916- .... **CLC 11**
See also Gascar, Pierre
See also CA 89-92; CANR 16, 40

Fowles, John
1926- ...... **CLC 1, 2, 3, 4, 6, 9, 10, 15,
33, 87; DAB; DAC**
See also CA 5-8R; CANR 25; CDBLB 1960
to Present; DAM MST; DLB 14, 139;
MTCW; SATA 22

Fox, Paula 1923-................ **CLC 2, 8**
See also AAYA 3; CA 73-76; CANR 20,
36; CLR 1; DLB 52; JRDA; MAICYA;
MTCW; SATA 17, 60

Fox, William Price (Jr.) 1926- ..... **CLC 22**
See also CA 17-20R; CAAS 19; CANR 11;
DLB 2; DLBY 81

Foxe, John 1516(?)-1587 .... **LC 14**

Frame, Janet .... **CLC 2, 3, 6, 22, 66**
See also Clutha, Janet Paterson Frame

France, Anatole .... **TCLC 9**
See also Thibault, Jacques Anatole Francois
See also DLB 123

Francis, Claude 19(?)- .... **CLC 50**

Francis, Dick 1920- .... **CLC 2, 22, 42**
See also AAYA 5; BEST 89:3; CA 5-8R;
CANR 9, 42; CDBLB 1960 to Present;
DAM POP; DLB 87; INT CANR-9;
MTCW

Francis, Robert (Churchill)
1901-1987 .... **CLC 15**
See also CA 1-4R; 123; CANR 1

Frank, Anne(lies Marie)
1929-1945 .... **TCLC 17; DA; DAB;
DAC; WLC**
See also AAYA 12; CA 113; 133;
DAM MST; MTCW; SATA-Brief 42

Frank, Elizabeth 1945-............. **CLC 39**
See also CA 121; 126; INT 126

Franklin, Benjamin
See Hasek, Jaroslav (Matej Frantisek)

Franklin, Benjamin
1706-1790 ..... **LC 25; DA; DAB; DAC**
See also CDALB 1640-1865; DAM MST;
DLB 24, 43, 73

Franklin, (Stella Maraia Sarah) Miles
1879-1954 .... **TCLC 7**
See also CA 104

Fraser, (Lady) Antonia (Pakenham)
1932- .... **CLC 32**
See also CA 85-88; CANR 44; MTCW;
SATA-Brief 32

Fraser, George MacDonald 1925-.... **CLC 7**
See also CA 45-48; CANR 2, 48

Fraser, Sylvia 1935-.............. **CLC 64**
See also CA 45-48; CANR 1, 16

Frayn, Michael 1933-...... **CLC 3, 7, 31, 47**
See also CA 5-8R; CANR 30;
DAM DRAM, NOV; DLB 13, 14;
MTCW

Fraze, Candida (Merrill) 1945-..... **CLC 50**
See also CA 126

Frazer, J(ames) G(eorge)
1854-1941 .... **TCLC 32**
See also CA 118

Frazer, Robert Caine
See Creasey, John

Frazer, Sir James George
See Frazer, J(ames) G(eorge)

Frazier, Ian 1951-................ **CLC 46**
See also CA 130

Frederic, Harold 1856-1898...... **NCLC 10**
See also DLB 12, 23; DLBD 13

Frederick, John
See Faust, Frederick (Schiller)

Frederick the Great 1712-1786 ..... **LC 14**

Fredro, Aleksander 1793-1876..... **NCLC 8**

Freeling, Nicolas 1927- .... **CLC 38**
See also CA 49-52; CAAS 12; CANR 1, 17,
50; DLB 87

Freeman, Douglas Southall
1886-1953 .... **TCLC 11**
See also CA 109; DLB 17

Freeman, Judith 1946-........... **CLC 55**
See also CA 148

Freeman, Mary Eleanor Wilkins
1852-1930 .... **TCLC 9; SSC 1**
See also CA 106; DLB 12, 78

Freeman, R(ichard) Austin
1862-1943 .... **TCLC 21**
See also CA 113; DLB 70

French, Albert 1943- .... **CLC 86**

French, Marilyn 1929-...... **CLC 10, 18, 60**
See also CA 69-72; CANR 3, 31;
DAM DRAM, NOV, POP;
INT CANR-31; MTCW

French, Paul
See Asimov, Isaac

Freneau, Philip Morin 1752-1832.. **NCLC 1**
See also DLB 37, 43

Freud, Sigmund 1856-1939 .... **TCLC 52**
See also CA 115; 133; MTCW

Friedan, Betty (Naomi) 1921-...... **CLC 74**
See also CA 65-68; CANR 18, 45; MTCW

Friedlaender, Saul 1932- .... **CLC 90**
See also CA 117; 130

Friedman, B(ernard) H(arper)
1926-....................... **CLC 7**
See also CA 1-4R; CANR 3, 48

Friedman, Bruce Jay 1930-.... **CLC 3, 5, 56**
See also CA 9-12R; CANR 25; DLB 2, 28;
INT CANR-25

Friel, Brian 1929-........... **CLC 5, 42, 59**
See also CA 21-24R; CANR 33; DLB 13;
MTCW

Friis-Baastad, Babbis Ellinor
1921-1970 .... **CLC 12**
See also CA 17-20R; 134; SATA 7

Frisch, Max (Rudolf)
1911-1991 ..... **CLC 3, 9, 14, 18, 32, 44**
See also CA 85-88; 134; CANR 32;
DAM DRAM, NOV; DLB 69, 124;
MTCW

Fromentin, Eugene (Samuel Auguste)
1820-1876 .... **NCLC 10**
See also DLB 123

Frost, Frederick
See Faust, Frederick (Schiller)

Frost, Robert (Lee)
1874-1963 .... **CLC 1, 3, 4, 9, 10, 13, 15,
26, 34, 44; DA; DAB; DAC; PC 1; WLC**
See also CA 89-92; CANR 33;
CDALB 1917-1929; DAM MST, POET;
DLB 54; DLBD 7; MTCW; SATA 14

Froude, James Anthony
1818-1894 .... **NCLC 43**
See also DLB 18, 57, 144

Froy, Herald
See Waterhouse, Keith (Spencer)

Fry, Christopher 1907-........ **CLC 2, 10, 14**
See also CA 17-20R; CAAS 23; CANR 9,
30; DAM DRAM; DLB 13; MTCW;
SATA 66

Frye, (Herman) Northrop
1912-1991 .... **CLC 24, 70**
See also CA 5-8R; 133; CANR 8, 37;
DLB 67, 68; MTCW

Gasset, Jose Ortega y
See Ortega y Gasset, Jose

Gates, Henry Louis, Jr. 1950-...... **CLC 65**
See also BW 2; CA 109; CANR 25;
DAM MULT; DLB 67

Gautier, Theophile
1811-1872 .... **NCLC 1; SSC 20**
See also DAM POET; DLB 119

Gawsworth, John
See Bates, H(erbert) E(rnest)

Gay, Oliver
See Gogarty, Oliver St. John

Gaye, Marvin (Penze) 1939-1984 ... **CLC 26**
See also CA 112

Gebler, Carlo (Ernest) 1954-....... **CLC 39**
See also CA 119; 133

Gee, Maggie (Mary) 1948-........ **CLC 57**
See also CA 130

Gee, Maurice (Gough) 1931-....... **CLC 29**
See also CA 97-100; SATA 46

Gelbart, Larry (Simon) 1923-... **CLC 21, 61**
See also CA 73-76; CANR 45

Gelber, Jack 1932-........ **CLC 1, 6, 14, 79**
See also CA 1-4R; CANR 2; DLB 7

Gellhorn, Martha (Ellis) 1908-.. **CLC 14, 60**
See also CA 77-80; CANR 44; DLBY 82

Genet, Jean
1910-1986 ... **CLC 1, 2, 5, 10, 14, 44, 46**
See also CA 13-16R; CANR 18;
DAM DRAM; DLB 72; DLBY 86;
MTCW

Gent, Peter 1942-................ **CLC 29**
See also AITN 1; CA 89-92; DLBY 82

Gentlewoman in New England, A
See Bradstreet, Anne

Gentlewoman in Those Parts, A
See Bradstreet, Anne

George, Jean Craighead 1919-...... **CLC 35**
See also AAYA 8; CA 5-8R; CANR 25;
CLR 1; DLB 52; JRDA; MAICYA;
SATA 2, 68

George, Stefan (Anton)
1868-1933 .... **TCLC 2, 14**
See also CA 104

Georges, Georges Martin
See Simenon, Georges (Jacques Christian)

Gerhardi, William Alexander
See Gerhardie, William Alexander

Gerhardie, William Alexander
1895-1977 .... **CLC 5**
See also CA 25-28R; 73-76; CANR 18;
DLB 36

Gerstler, Amy 1956-.............. **CLC 70**
See also CA 146

Gertler, T. .... **CLC 34**
See also CA 116; 121; INT 121

Ghalib......................... **NCLC 39**
See also Ghalib, Hsadullah Khan

Ghalib, Hsadullah Khan 1797-1869
See Ghalib
See also DAM POET

Ghelderode, Michel de
1898-1962 .... **CLC 6, 11**
See also CA 85-88; CANR 40;
DAM DRAM

Ghiselin, Brewster 1903-.......... **CLC 23**
See also CA 13-16R; CAAS 10; CANR 13

Ghose, Zulfikar 1935-............. **CLC 42**
See also CA 65-68

Ghosh, Amitav 1956-............. **CLC 44**
See also CA 147

Giacosa, Giuseppe 1847-1906 ...... **TCLC 7**
See also CA 104

Gibb, Lee
See Waterhouse, Keith (Spencer)

Gibbon, Lewis Grassic .... **TCLC 4**
See also Mitchell, James Leslie

Gibbons, Kaye 1960- .... **CLC 50, 88**
See also DAM POP

Gibran, Kahlil
1883-1931 .... **TCLC 1, 9; PC 9**
See also CA 104; 150; DAM POET, POP

Gibran, Khalil
See Gibran, Kahlil

Gibson, William
1914-........ **CLC 23; DA; DAB; DAC**
See also CA 9-12R; CANR 9, 42;
DAM DRAM, MST; DLB 7; SATA 66

Gibson, William (Ford) 1948-... **CLC 39, 63**
See also AAYA 12; CA 126; 133;
DAM POP

Gide, Andre (Paul Guillaume)
1869-1951 .... **TCLC 5, 12, 36; DA;**
DAB; DAC; SSC 13; WLC
See also CA 104; 124; DAM MST, NOV;
DLB 65; MTCW

Gifford, Barry (Colby) 1946-....... **CLC 34**
See also CA 65-68; CANR 9, 30, 40

Gilbert, W(illiam) S(chwenck)
1836-1911 .... **TCLC 3**
See also CA 104; DAM DRAM, POET;
SATA 36

Gilbreth, Frank B., Jr. 1911-....... **CLC 17**
See also CA 9-12R; SATA 2

Gilchrist, Ellen 1935-.. **CLC 34, 48; SSC 14**
See also CA 113; 116; CANR 41;
DAM POP; DLB 130; MTCW

Giles, Molly 1942-.............. **CLC 39**
See also CA 126

Gill, Patrick
See Creasey, John

Gilliam, Terry (Vance) 1940-....... **CLC 21**
See also Monty Python
See also CA 108; 113; CANR 35; INT 113

Gillian, Jerry
See Gilliam, Terry (Vance)

Gilliatt, Penelope (Ann Douglass)
1932-1993 .... **CLC 2, 10, 13, 53**
See also AITN 2; CA 13-16R; 141;
CANR 49; DLB 14

Gilman, Charlotte (Anna) Perkins (Stetson)
1860-1935 .... **TCLC 9, 37; SSC 13**
See also CA 106; 150

Gilmour, David 1949-............ **CLC 35**
See also CA 138, 147

Gilpin, William 1724-1804...... **NCLC 30**

Gilray, J. D.
See Mencken, H(enry) L(ouis)

Gilroy, Frank D(aniel) 1925-........ **CLC 2**
See also CA 81-84; CANR 32; DLB 7

Ginsberg, Allen
1926- ...... **CLC 1, 2, 3, 4, 6, 13, 36, 69;**
DA; DAB; DAC; PC 4; WLC 3
See also AITN 1; CA 1-4R; CANR 2, 41;
CDALB 1941-1968; DAM MST, POET;
DLB 5, 16; MTCW

Ginzburg, Natalia
1916-1991 .... **CLC 5, 11, 54, 70**
See also CA 85-88; 135; CANR 33; MTCW

Giono, Jean 1895-1970........ **CLC 4, 11**
See also CA 45-48; 29-32R; CANR 2, 35;
DLB 72; MTCW

Giovanni, Nikki
1943- ...... **CLC 2, 4, 19, 64; BLC; DA;**
DAB; DAC
See also AITN 1; BW 2; CA 29-32R;
CAAS 6; CANR 18, 41; CLR 6;
DAM MST, MULT, POET; DLB 5, 41;
INT CANR-18; MAICYA; MTCW;
SATA 24

Giovene, Andrea 1904-............ **CLC 7**
See also CA 85-88

Gippius, Zinaida (Nikolayevna) 1869-1945
See Hippius, Zinaida
See also CA 106

Giraudoux, (Hippolyte) Jean
1882-1944 .... **TCLC 2, 7**
See also CA 104; DAM DRAM; DLB 65

Gironella, Jose Maria 1917-....... **CLC 11**
See also CA 101

Gissing, George (Robert)
1857-1903 .... **TCLC 3, 24, 47**
See also CA 105; DLB 18, 135

Giurlani, Aldo
See Palazzeschi, Aldo

Gladkov, Fyodor (Vasilyevich)
1883-1958 .... **TCLC 27**

Glanville, Brian (Lester) 1931- ...... **CLC 6**
See also CA 5-8R; CAAS 9; CANR 3;
DLB 15, 139; SATA 42

Glasgow, Ellen (Anderson Gholson)
1873(?)-1945 .... **TCLC 2, 7**
See also CA 104; DLB 9, 12

Glaspell, Susan (Keating)
1882(?)-1948 .... **TCLC 55**
See also CA 110; DLB 7, 9, 78; YABC 2

Glassco, John 1909-1981 .... **CLC 9**
See also CA 13-16R; 102; CANR 15;
DLB 68

Glasscock, Amnesia
See Steinbeck, John (Ernst)

Glasser, Ronald J. 1940(?)- .... **CLC 37**

Glassman, Joyce
See Johnson, Joyce

Glendinning, Victoria 1937-........ **CLC 50**
See also CA 120; 127; DLB 155

Glissant, Edouard 1928-....... **CLC 10, 68**
See also DAM MULT

Gloag, Julian 1930- .... **CLC 40**
See also AITN 1; CA 65-68; CANR 10

Glowacki, Aleksander
See Prus, Boleslaw

Glueck, Louise (Elisabeth)
1943- . . . . CLC 7, 22, 44, 81
See also CA 33-36R; CANR 40;
DAM POET; DLB 5

Gobineau, Joseph Arthur (Comte) de
1816-1882 . . . . NCLC 17
See also DLB 123

Godard, Jean-Luc 1930- . . . . CLC 20
See also CA 93-96

Godden, (Margaret) Rumer 1907- . . . CLC 53
See also AAYA 6; CA 5-8R; CANR 4, 27,
36; CLR 20; DLB 161; MAICYA;
SAAS 12; SATA 3, 36

Godoy Alcayaga, Lucila 1889-1957
See Mistral, Gabriela
See also BW 2; CA 104; 131; DAM MULT;
HW; MTCW

Godwin, Gail (Kathleen)
1937- . . . . CLC 5, 8, 22, 31, 69
See also CA 29-32R; CANR 15, 43;
DAM POP; DLB 6; INT CANR-15;
MTCW

Godwin, William 1756-1836 . . . . . NCLC 14
See also CDBLB 1789-1832; DLB 39, 104,
142, 158

Goethe, Johann Wolfgang von
1749-1832 . . . . NCLC 4, 22, 34; DA;
DAB; DAC; PC 5; WLC 3
See also DAM DRAM, MST, POET;
DLB 94

Gogarty, Oliver St. John
1878-1957 . . . . TCLC 15
See also CA 109; 150; DLB 15, 19

Gogol, Nikolai (Vasilyevich)
1809-1852 . . . . NCLC 5, 15, 31; DA;
DAB; DAC; DC 1; SSC 4; WLC
See also DAM DRAM, MST

Goines, Donald
1937(?)-1974 . . . . CLC 80; BLC
See also AITN 1; BW 1; CA 124; 114;
DAM MULT, POP; DLB 33

Gold, Herbert 1924- . . . . CLC 4, 7, 14, 42
See also CA 9-12R; CANR 17, 45; DLB 2;
DLBY 81

Goldbarth, Albert 1948- . . . . CLC 5, 38
See also CA 53-56; CANR 6, 40; DLB 120

Goldberg, Anatol 1910-1982 . . . . CLC 34
See also CA 131; 117

Goldemberg, Isaac 1945- . . . . CLC 52
See also CA 69-72; CAAS 12; CANR 11,
32; HW

Golding, William (Gerald)
1911-1993 . . . . CLC 1, 2, 3, 8, 10, 17, 27,
58, 81; DA; DAB; DAC; WLC
See also AAYA 5; CA 5-8R; 141;
CANR 13, 33; CDBLB 1945-1960;
DAM MST, NOV; DLB 15, 100; MTCW

Goldman, Emma 1869-1940 . . . . . . TCLC 13
See also CA 110; 150

Goldman, Francisco 1955- . . . . CLC 76

Goldman, William (W.) 1931- . . . . CLC 1, 48
See also CA 9-12R; CANR 29; DLB 44

Goldmann, Lucien 1913-1970 . . . . . . CLC 24
See also CA 25-28; CAP 2

Goldoni, Carlo 1707-1793 . . . . LC 4
See also DAM DRAM

Goldsberry, Steven 1949- . . . . CLC 34
See also CA 131

Goldsmith, Oliver
1728-1774 . . . . . LC 2; DA; DAB; DAC;
WLC
See also CDBLB 1660-1789; DAM DRAM,
MST, NOV, POET; DLB 39, 89, 104,
109, 142; SATA 26

Goldsmith, Peter
See Priestley, J(ohn) B(oynton)

Gombrowicz, Witold
1904-1969 . . . . CLC 4, 7, 11, 49
See also CA 19-20; 25-28R; CAP 2;
DAM DRAM

Gomez de la Serna, Ramon
1888-1963 . . . . CLC 9
See also CA 116; HW

Goncharov, Ivan Alexandrovich
1812-1891 . . . . NCLC 1

Goncourt, Edmond (Louis Antoine Huot) de
1822-1896 . . . . NCLC 7
See also DLB 123

Goncourt, Jules (Alfred Huot) de
1830-1870 . . . . NCLC 7
See also DLB 123

Gontier, Fernande 19(?)- . . . . CLC 50

Goodman, Paul 1911-1972 . . . . CLC 1, 2, 4, 7
See also CA 19-20; 37-40R; CANR 34;
CAP 2; DLB 130; MTCW

Gordimer, Nadine
1923- . . . . CLC 3, 5, 7, 10, 18, 33, 51, 70;
DA; DAB; DAC; SSC 17
See also CA 5-8R; CANR 3, 28;
DAM MST, NOV; INT CANR-28;
MTCW

Gordon, Adam Lindsay
1833-1870 . . . . NCLC 21

Gordon, Caroline
1895-1981 . . . CLC 6, 13, 29, 83; SSC 15
See also CA 11-12; 103; CANR 36; CAP 1;
DLB 4, 9, 102; DLBY 81; MTCW

Gordon, Charles William 1860-1937
See Connor, Ralph
See also CA 109

Gordon, Mary (Catherine)
1949- . . . . CLC 13, 22
See also CA 102; CANR 44; DLB 6;
DLBY 81; INT 102; MTCW

Gordon, Sol 1923- . . . . CLC 26
See also CA 53-56; CANR 4; SATA 11

Gordone, Charles 1925-1995 . . . . . . CLC 1, 4
See also BW 1; CA 93-96; 150;
DAM DRAM; DLB 7; INT 93-96;
MTCW

Gorenko, Anna Andreevna
See Akhmatova, Anna

Gorky, Maxim . . . . TCLC 8; DAB; WLC
See also Peshkov, Alexei Maximovich

Goryan, Sirak
See Saroyan, William

Gosse, Edmund (William)
1849-1928 . . . . TCLC 28
See also CA 117; DLB 57, 144

Gotlieb, Phyllis Fay (Bloom)
1926- . . . . CLC 18
See also CA 13-16R; CANR 7; DLB 88

Gottesman, S. D.
See Kornbluth, C(yril) M.; Pohl, Frederik

Gottfried von Strassburg
fl. c. 1210- . . . . CMLC 10
See also DLB 138

Gould, Lois . . . . CLC 4, 10
See also CA 77-80; CANR 29; MTCW

Gourmont, Remy (-Marie-Charles) de
1858-1915 . . . . TCLC 17
See also CA 109; 150

Govier, Katherine 1948- . . . . CLC 51
See also CA 101; CANR 18, 40

Goyen, (Charles) William
1915-1983 . . . . CLC 5, 8, 14, 40
See also AITN 2; CA 5-8R; 110; CANR 6;
DLB 2; DLBY 83; INT CANR-6

Goytisolo, Juan
1931- . . . . CLC 5, 10, 23; HLC
See also CA 85-88; CANR 32;
DAM MULT; HW; MTCW

Gozzano, Guido 1883-1916 . . . . PC 10
See also DLB 114

Gozzi, (Conte) Carlo 1720-1806 . . NCLC 23

Grabbe, Christian Dietrich
1801-1836 . . . . NCLC 2
See also DLB 133

Grace, Patricia 1937- . . . . CLC 56

Gracian y Morales, Baltasar
1601-1658 . . . . LC 15

Gracq, Julien . . . . CLC 11, 48
See also Poirier, Louis
See also DLB 83

Grade, Chaim 1910-1982 . . . . CLC 10
See also CA 93-96; 107

Graduate of Oxford, A
See Ruskin, John

Graham, John
See Phillips, David Graham

Graham, Jorie 1951- . . . . CLC 48
See also CA 111; DLB 120

Graham, R(obert) B(ontine) Cunninghame
See Cunninghame Graham, R(obert)
B(ontine)
See also DLB 98, 135

Graham, Robert
See Haldeman, Joe (William)

Graham, Tom
See Lewis, (Harry) Sinclair

Graham, W(illiam) S(ydney)
1918-1986 . . . . CLC 29
See also CA 73-76; 118; DLB 20

Graham, Winston (Mawdsley)
1910- . . . . CLC 23
See also CA 49-52; CANR 2, 22, 45;
DLB 77

Grant, Skeeter
See Spiegelman, Art

Granville-Barker, Harley
1877-1946 . . . . TCLC 2
See also Barker, Harley Granville
See also CA 104; DAM DRAM

Grass, Guenter (Wilhelm)
1927- ..... **CLC 1, 2, 4, 6, 11, 15, 22, 32, 49, 88; DA; DAB; DAC; WLC**
See also CA 13-16R; CANR 20;
DAM MST, NOV; DLB 75, 124; MTCW

Gratton, Thomas
See Hulme, T(homas) E(rnest)

Grau, Shirley Ann
1929- .... **CLC 4, 9; SSC 15**
See also CA 89-92; CANR 22; DLB 2;
INT CANR-22; MTCW

Gravel, Fern
See Hall, James Norman

Graver, Elizabeth 1964-........... **CLC 70**
See also CA 135

Graves, Richard Perceval 1945- .... **CLC 44**
See also CA 65-68; CANR 9, 26, 51

Graves, Robert (von Ranke)
1895-1985 ...... **CLC 1, 2, 6, 11, 39, 44, 45; DAB; DAC; PC 6**
See also CA 5-8R; 117; CANR 5, 36;
CDBLB 1914-1945; DAM MST, POET;
DLB 20, 100; DLBY 85; MTCW;
SATA 45

Gray, Alasdair (James) 1934- ...... **CLC 41**
See also CA 126; CANR 47; INT 126;
MTCW

Gray, Amlin 1946- .... **CLC 29**
See also CA 138

Gray, Francine du Plessix 1930-.... **CLC 22**
See also BEST 90:3; CA 61-64; CAAS 2;
CANR 11, 33; DAM NOV;
INT CANR-11; MTCW

Gray, John (Henry) 1866-1934 .... **TCLC 19**
See also CA 119

Gray, Simon (James Holliday)
1936- .... **CLC 9, 14, 36**
See also AITN 1; CA 21-24R; CAAS 3;
CANR 32; DLB 13; MTCW

Gray, Spalding 1941- .... **CLC 49**
See also CA 128; DAM POP

Gray, Thomas
1716-1771 ...... **LC 4; DA; DAB; DAC; PC 2; WLC**
See also CDBLB 1660-1789; DAM MST;
DLB 109

Grayson, David
See Baker, Ray Stannard

Grayson, Richard (A.) 1951-....... **CLC 38**
See also CA 85-88; CANR 14, 31

Greeley, Andrew M(oran) 1928-.... **CLC 28**
See also CA 5-8R; CAAS 7; CANR 7, 43;
DAM POP; MTCW

Green, Brian
See Card, Orson Scott

Green, Hannah
See Greenberg, Joanne (Goldenberg)

Green, Hannah .... **CLC 3**
See also CA 73-76

Green, Henry................. **CLC 2, 13**
See also Yorke, Henry Vincent
See also DLB 15

Green, Julian (Hartridge) 1900-
See Green, Julien
See also CA 21-24R; CANR 33; DLB 4, 72;
MTCW

Green, Julien............... **CLC 3, 11, 77**
See also Green, Julian (Hartridge)

Green, Paul (Eliot) 1894-1981...... **CLC 25**
See also AITN 1; CA 5-8R; 103; CANR 3;
DAM DRAM; DLB 7, 9; DLBY 81

Greenberg, Ivan 1908-1973
See Rahv, Philip
See also CA 85-88

Greenberg, Joanne (Goldenberg)
1932- .... **CLC 7, 30**
See also AAYA 12; CA 5-8R; CANR 14, 32; SATA 25

Greenberg, Richard 1959(?)-....... **CLC 57**
See also CA 138

Greene, Bette 1934- .... **CLC 30**
See also AAYA 7; CA 53-56; CANR 4;
CLR 2; JRDA; MAICYA; SAAS 16;
SATA 8

Greene, Gael .... **CLC 8**
See also CA 13-16R; CANR 10

Greene, Graham
1904-1991 .... **CLC 1, 3, 6, 9, 14, 18, 27, 37, 70, 72; DA; DAB; DAC; WLC**
See also AITN 2; CA 13-16R; 133;
CANR 35; CDBLB 1945-1960;
DAM MST, NOV; DLB 13, 15, 77, 100, 162; DLBY 91; MTCW; SATA 20

Greer, Richard
See Silverberg, Robert

Gregor, Arthur 1923-.............. **CLC 9**
See also CA 25-28R; CAAS 10; CANR 11;
SATA 36

Gregor, Lee
See Pohl, Frederik

Gregory, Isabella Augusta (Persse)
1852-1932 .... **TCLC 1**
See also CA 104; DLB 10

Gregory, J. Dennis
See Williams, John A(lfred)

Grendon, Stephen
See Derleth, August (William)

Grenville, Kate 1950-............. **CLC 61**
See also CA 118

Grenville, Pelham
See Wodehouse, P(elham) G(renville)

Greve, Felix Paul (Berthold Friedrich)
1879-1948
See Grove, Frederick Philip
See also CA 104; 141; DAC; DAM MST

Grey, Zane 1872-1939 .... **TCLC 6**
See also CA 104; 132; DAM POP; DLB 9;
MTCW

Grieg, (Johan) Nordahl (Brun)
1902-1943 .... **TCLC 10**
See also CA 107

Grieve, C(hristopher) M(urray)
1892-1978 .... **CLC 11, 19**
See also MacDiarmid, Hugh; Pteleon
See also CA 5-8R; 85-88; CANR 33;
DAM POET; MTCW

Griffin, Gerald 1803-1840 .... **NCLC 7**
See also DLB 159

Griffin, John Howard 1920-1980.... **CLC 68**
See also AITN 1; CA 1-4R; 101; CANR 2

Griffin, Peter 1942- .... **CLC 39**
See also CA 136

Griffiths, Trevor 1935-......... **CLC 13, 52**
See also CA 97-100; CANR 45; DLB 13

Grigson, Geoffrey (Edward Harvey)
1905-1985 .... **CLC 7, 39**
See also CA 25-28R; 118; CANR 20, 33;
DLB 27; MTCW

Grillparzer, Franz 1791-1872...... **NCLC 1**
See also DLB 133

Grimble, Reverend Charles James
See Eliot, T(homas) S(tearns)

Grimke, Charlotte L(ottie) Forten
1837(?)-1914
See Forten, Charlotte L.
See also BW 1; CA 117; 124; DAM MULT,
POET

Grimm, Jacob Ludwig Karl
1785-1863 .... **NCLC 3**
See also DLB 90; MAICYA; SATA 22

Grimm, Wilhelm Karl 1786-1859 .. **NCLC 3**
See also DLB 90; MAICYA; SATA 22

Grimmelshausen, Johann Jakob Christoffel
von 1621-1676 .... **LC 6**

Grindel, Eugene 1895-1952
See Eluard, Paul
See also CA 104

Grisham, John 1955- .... **CLC 84**
See also AAYA 14; CA 138; CANR 47;
DAM POP

Grossman, David 1954- .... **CLC 67**
See also CA 138

Grossman, Vasily (Semenovich)
1905-1964 .... **CLC 41**
See also CA 124; 130; MTCW

Grove, Frederick Philip .... **TCLC 4**
See also Greve, Felix Paul (Berthold
Friedrich)
See also DLB 92

Grubb
See Crumb, R(obert)

Grumbach, Doris (Isaac)
1918- .... **CLC 13, 22, 64**
See also CA 5-8R; CAAS 2; CANR 9, 42;
INT CANR-9

Grundtvig, Nicolai Frederik Severin
1783-1872 .... **NCLC 1**

Grunge
See Crumb, R(obert)

Grunwald, Lisa 1959-............. **CLC 44**
See also CA 120

Guare, John 1938- .... **CLC 8, 14, 29, 67**
See also CA 73-76; CANR 21;
DAM DRAM; DLB 7; MTCW

Gudjonsson, Halldor Kiljan 1902-
See Laxness, Halldor
See also CA 103

Guenter, Erich
See Eich, Guenter

Guest, Barbara 1920- . . . . **CLC 34**
See also CA 25-28R; CANR 11, 44; DLB 5

Guest, Judith (Ann) 1936- . . . . **CLC 8, 30**
See also AAYA 7; CA 77-80; CANR 15;
DAM NOV, POP; INT CANR-15;
MTCW

Guevara, Che . . . . **CLC 87; HLC**
See also Guevara (Serna), Ernesto

Guevara (Serna), Ernesto 1928-1967
See Guevara, Che
See also CA 127; 111; DAM MULT; HW

Guild, Nicholas M. 1944- . . . . **CLC 33**
See also CA 93-96

Guillemin, Jacques
See Sartre, Jean-Paul

Guillen, Jorge 1893-1984 . . . . **CLC 11**
See also CA 89-92; 112; DAM MULT,
POET; DLB 108; HW

Guillen (y Batista), Nicolas (Cristobal)
1902-1989 . . . . . **CLC 48, 79; BLC; HLC**
See also BW 2; CA 116; 125; 129;
DAM MST, MULT, POET; HW

Guillevic, (Eugene) 1907- . . . . **CLC 33**
See also CA 93-96

Guillois
See Desnos, Robert

Guiney, Louise Imogen
1861-1920 . . . . **TCLC 41**
See also DLB 54

Guiraldes, Ricardo (Guillermo)
1886-1927 . . . . **TCLC 39**
See also CA 131; HW; MTCW

Gumilev, Nikolai Stephanovich
1886-1921 . . . . **TCLC 60**

Gunesekera, Romesh . . . . **CLC 91**

Gunn, Bill . . . . **CLC 5**
See also Gunn, William Harrison
See also DLB 38

Gunn, Thom(son William)
1929- . . . . **CLC 3, 6, 18, 32, 81**
See also CA 17-20R; CANR 9, 33;
CDBLB 1960 to Present; DAM POET;
DLB 27; INT CANR-33; MTCW

Gunn, William Harrison 1934(?)-1989
See Gunn, Bill
See also AITN 1; BW 1; CA 13-16R; 128;
CANR 12, 25

Gunnars, Kristjana 1948- . . . . **CLC 69**
See also CA 113; DLB 60

Gurganus, Allan 1947- . . . . **CLC 70**
See also BEST 90:1; CA 135; DAM POP

Gurney, A(lbert) R(amsdell), Jr.
1930- . . . . **CLC 32, 50, 54**
See also CA 77-80; CANR 32;
DAM DRAM

Gurney, Ivor (Bertie) 1890-1937 . . . **TCLC 33**

Gurney, Peter
See Gurney, A(lbert) R(amsdell), Jr.

Guro, Elena 1877-1913 . . . . **TCLC 56**

Gustafson, Ralph (Barker) 1909- . . . . **CLC 36**
See also CA 21-24R; CANR 8, 45; DLB 88

Gut, Gom
See Simenon, Georges (Jacques Christian)

Guterson, David 1956- . . . . **CLC 91**
See also CA 132

Guthrie, A(lfred) B(ertram), Jr.
1901-1991 . . . . **CLC 23**
See also CA 57-60; 134; CANR 24; DLB 6;
SATA 62; SATA-Obit 67

Guthrie, Isobel
See Grieve, C(hristopher) M(urray)

Guthrie, Woodrow Wilson 1912-1967
See Guthrie, Woody
See also CA 113; 93-96

Guthrie, Woody . . . . **CLC 35**
See also Guthrie, Woodrow Wilson

Guy, Rosa (Cuthbert) 1928- . . . . **CLC 26**
See also AAYA 4; BW 2; CA 17-20R;
CANR 14, 34; CLR 13; DLB 33; JRDA;
MAICYA; SATA 14, 62

Gwendolyn
See Bennett, (Enoch) Arnold

H. D. . . . . **CLC 3, 8, 14, 31, 34, 73; PC 5**
See also Doolittle, Hilda

H. de V.
See Buchan, John

Haavikko, Paavo Juhani
1931- . . . . **CLC 18, 34**
See also CA 106

Habbema, Koos
See Heijermans, Herman

Hacker, Marilyn
1942- . . . . **CLC 5, 9, 23, 72, 91**
See also CA 77-80; DAM POET; DLB 120

Haggard, H(enry) Rider
1856-1925 . . . . **TCLC 11**
See also CA 108; 148; DLB 70, 156;
SATA 16

Hagiwara Sakutaro 1886-1942 . . . . **TCLC 60**

Haig, Fenil
See Ford, Ford Madox

Haig-Brown, Roderick (Langmere)
1908-1976 . . . . **CLC 21**
See also CA 5-8R; 69-72; CANR 4, 38;
CLR 31; DLB 88; MAICYA; SATA 12

Hailey, Arthur 1920- . . . . **CLC 5**
See also AITN 2; BEST 90:3; CA 1-4R;
CANR 2, 36; DAM NOV, POP; DLB 88;
DLBY 82; MTCW

Hailey, Elizabeth Forsythe 1938- . . . **CLC 40**
See also CA 93-96; CAAS 1; CANR 15, 48;
INT CANR-15

Haines, John (Meade) 1924- . . . . **CLC 58**
See also CA 17-20R; CANR 13, 34; DLB 5

Hakluyt, Richard 1552-1616 . . . . **LC 31**

Haldeman, Joe (William) 1943- . . . . . **CLC 61**
See also CA 53-56; CANR 6; DLB 8;
INT CANR-6

Haley, Alex(ander Murray Palmer)
1921-1992 . . . . **CLC 8, 12, 76; BLC; DA;**
DAB; DAC
See also BW 2; CA 77-80; 136; DAM MST,
MULT, POP; DLB 38; MTCW

Haliburton, Thomas Chandler
1796-1865 . . . . **NCLC 15**
See also DLB 11, 99

Hall, Donald (Andrew, Jr.)
1928- . . . . **CLC 1, 13, 37, 59**
See also CA 5-8R; CAAS 7; CANR 2, 44;
DAM POET; DLB 5; SATA 23

Hall, Frederic Sauser
See Sauser-Hall, Frederic

Hall, James
See Kuttner, Henry

Hall, James Norman 1887-1951 . . . **TCLC 23**
See also CA 123; SATA 21

Hall, (Marguerite) Radclyffe
1886-1943 . . . . **TCLC 12**
See also CA 110; 150

Hall, Rodney 1935- . . . . **CLC 51**
See also CA 109

Halleck, Fitz-Greene 1790-1867 . . **NCLC 47**
See also DLB 3

Halliday, Michael
See Creasey, John

Halpern, Daniel 1945- . . . . **CLC 14**
See also CA 33-36R

Hamburger, Michael (Peter Leopold)
1924- . . . . **CLC 5, 14**
See also CA 5-8R; CAAS 4; CANR 2, 47;
DLB 27

Hamill, Pete 1935- . . . . **CLC 10**
See also CA 25-28R; CANR 18

Hamilton, Alexander
1755(?)-1804 . . . . **NCLC 49**
See also DLB 37

Hamilton, Clive
See Lewis, C(live) S(taples)

Hamilton, Edmond 1904-1977 . . . . **CLC 1**
See also CA 1-4R; CANR 3; DLB 8

Hamilton, Eugene (Jacob) Lee
See Lee-Hamilton, Eugene (Jacob)

Hamilton, Franklin
See Silverberg, Robert

Hamilton, Gail
See Corcoran, Barbara

Hamilton, Mollie
See Kaye, M(ary) M(argaret)

Hamilton, (Anthony Walter) Patrick
1904-1962 . . . . **CLC 51**
See also CA 113; DLB 10

Hamilton, Virginia 1936- . . . . **CLC 26**
See also AAYA 2; BW 2; CA 25-28R;
CANR 20, 37; CLR 1, 11, 40;
DAM MULT; DLB 33, 52;
INT CANR-20; JRDA; MAICYA;
MTCW; SATA 4, 56, 79

Hammett, (Samuel) Dashiell
1894-1961 . . . . **CLC 3, 5, 10, 19, 47;**
SSC 17
See also AITN 1; CA 81-84; CANR 42;
CDALB 1929-1941; DLBD 6; MTCW

Hammon, Jupiter
1711(?)-1800(?) . . . . **NCLC 5; BLC**
See also DAM MULT, POET; DLB 31, 50

Hammond, Keith
See Kuttner, Henry

Hamner, Earl (Henry), Jr. 1923- . . . **CLC 12**
See also AITN 2; CA 73-76; DLB 6

Hampton, Christopher (James)
1946- .... **CLC 4**
See also CA 25-28R; DLB 13; MTCW

Hamsun, Knut .... **TCLC 2, 14, 49**
See also Pedersen, Knut

Handke, Peter 1942- .. **CLC 5, 8, 10, 15, 38**
See also CA 77-80; CANR 33;
DAM DRAM, NOV; DLB 85, 124;
MTCW

Hanley, James 1901-1985 ... **CLC 3, 5, 8, 13**
See also CA 73-76; 117; CANR 36; MTCW

Hannah, Barry 1942- .... **CLC 23, 38, 90**
See also CA 108; 110; CANR 43; DLB 6;
INT 110; MTCW

Hannon, Ezra
See Hunter, Evan

Hansberry, Lorraine (Vivian)
1930-1965 ...... **CLC 17, 62; BLC; DA;
DAB; DAC; DC 2**
See also BW 1; CA 109; 25-28R; CABS 3;
CDALB 1941-1968; DAM DRAM, MST,
MULT; DLB 7, 38; MTCW

Hansen, Joseph 1923- .... **CLC 38**
See also CA 29-32R; CAAS 17; CANR 16,
44; INT CANR-16

Hansen, Martin A. 1909-1955 ..... **TCLC 32**

Hanson, Kenneth O(stlin) 1922- .... **CLC 13**
See also CA 53-56; CANR 7

Hardwick, Elizabeth 1916- .... **CLC 13**
See also CA 5-8R; CANR 3, 32;
DAM NOV; DLB 6; MTCW

Hardy, Thomas
1840-1928 ...... **TCLC 4, 10, 18, 32, 48,
53; DA; DAB; DAC; PC 8; SSC 2; WLC**
See also CA 104; 123; CDBLB 1890-1914;
DAM MST, NOV, POET; DLB 18, 19,
135; MTCW

Hare, David 1947- .... **CLC 29, 58**
See also CA 97-100; CANR 39; DLB 13;
MTCW

Harford, Henry
See Hudson, W(illiam) H(enry)

Hargrave, Leonie
See Disch, Thomas M(ichael)

Harjo, Joy 1951- .... **CLC 83**
See also CA 114; CANR 35; DAM MULT;
DLB 120; NNAL

Harlan, Louis R(udolph) 1922- ..... **CLC 34**
See also CA 21-24R; CANR 25

Harling, Robert 1951(?)- .... **CLC 53**
See also CA 147

Harmon, William (Ruth) 1938- ..... **CLC 38**
See also CA 33-36R; CANR 14, 32, 35;
SATA 65

Harper, F. E. W.
See Harper, Frances Ellen Watkins

Harper, Frances E. W.
See Harper, Frances Ellen Watkins

Harper, Frances E. Watkins
See Harper, Frances Ellen Watkins

Harper, Frances Ellen
See Harper, Frances Ellen Watkins

Harper, Frances Ellen Watkins
1825-1911 .... **TCLC 14; BLC**
See also BW 1; CA 111; 125; DAM MULT,
POET; DLB 50

Harper, Michael S(teven) 1938- .. **CLC 7, 22**
See also BW 1; CA 33-36R; CANR 24;
DLB 41

Harper, Mrs. F. E. W.
See Harper, Frances Ellen Watkins

Harris, Christie (Lucy) Irwin
1907- .... **CLC 12**
See also CA 5-8R; CANR 6; DLB 88;
JRDA; MAICYA; SAAS 10; SATA 6, 74

Harris, Frank 1856-1931 .... **TCLC 24**
See also CA 109; 150; DLB 156

Harris, George Washington
1814-1869 .... **NCLC 23**
See also DLB 3, 11

Harris, Joel Chandler
1848-1908 .... **TCLC 2; SSC 19**
See also CA 104; 137; DLB 11, 23, 42, 78,
91; MAICYA; YABC 1

**Harris, John (Wyndham Parkes Lucas)
Beynon** 1903-1969
See Wyndham, John
See also CA 102; 89-92

Harris, MacDonald .... **CLC 9**
See also Heiney, Donald (William)

Harris, Mark 1922- .... **CLC 19**
See also CA 5-8R; CAAS 3; CANR 2;
DLB 2; DLBY 80

Harris, (Theodore) Wilson 1921-.... **CLC 25**
See also BW 2; CA 65-68; CAAS 16;
CANR 11, 27; DLB 117; MTCW

Harrison, Elizabeth Cavanna 1909-
See Cavanna, Betty
See also CA 9-12R; CANR 6, 27

Harrison, Harry (Max) 1925- ...... **CLC 42**
See also CA 1-4R; CANR 5, 21; DLB 8;
SATA 4

Harrison, James (Thomas)
1937- .... **CLC 6, 14, 33, 66; SSC 19**
See also CA 13-16R; CANR 8, 51;
DLBY 82; INT CANR-8

Harrison, Jim
See Harrison, James (Thomas)

Harrison, Kathryn 1961- .... **CLC 70**
See also CA 144

Harrison, Tony 1937- .... **CLC 43**
See also CA 65-68; CANR 44; DLB 40;
MTCW

Harriss, Will(ard Irvin) 1922- ...... **CLC 34**
See also CA 111

Harson, Sley
See Ellison, Harlan (Jay)

Hart, Ellis
See Ellison, Harlan (Jay)

Hart, Josephine 1942(?)- .... **CLC 70**
See also CA 138; DAM POP

Hart, Moss 1904-1961 .... **CLC 66**
See also CA 109; 89-92; DAM DRAM;
DLB 7

Harte, (Francis) Bret(t)
1836(?)-1902 .... **TCLC 1, 25; DA; DAC;
SSC 8; WLC**
See also CA 104; 140; CDALB 1865-1917;
DAM MST; DLB 12, 64, 74, 79;
SATA 26

Hartley, L(eslie) P(oles)
1895-1972 .... **CLC 2, 22**
See also CA 45-48; 37-40R; CANR 33;
DLB 15, 139; MTCW

Hartman, Geoffrey H. 1929- .... **CLC 27**
See also CA 117; 125; DLB 67

Hartmann von Aue
c. 1160-c. 1205 .... **CMLC 15**
See also DLB 138

Hartmann von Aue 1170-1210.... **CMLC 15**

Haruf, Kent 1943- .... **CLC 34**
See also CA 149

Harwood, Ronald 1934- .... **CLC 32**
See also CA 1-4R; CANR 4; DAM DRAM,
MST; DLB 13

Hasek, Jaroslav (Matej Frantisek)
1883-1923 .... **TCLC 4**
See also CA 104; 129; MTCW

Hass, Robert 1941- .... **CLC 18, 39**
See also CA 111; CANR 30, 50; DLB 105

Hastings, Hudson
See Kuttner, Henry

Hastings, Selina .... **CLC 44**

Hatteras, Amelia
See Mencken, H(enry) L(ouis)

Hatteras, Owen .... **TCLC 18**
See also Mencken, H(enry) L(ouis); Nathan,
George Jean

Hauptmann, Gerhart (Johann Robert)
1862-1946 .... **TCLC 4**
See also CA 104; DAM DRAM; DLB 66,
118

Havel, Vaclav
1936- .... **CLC 25, 58, 65; DC 6**
See also CA 104; CANR 36; DAM DRAM;
MTCW

Haviaras, Stratis .... **CLC 33**
See also Chaviaras, Strates

Hawes, Stephen 1475(?)-1523(?) ..... **LC 17**

Hawkes, John (Clendennin Burne, Jr.)
1925- ...... **CLC 1, 2, 3, 4, 7, 9, 14, 15,
27, 49**
See also CA 1-4R; CANR 2, 47; DLB 2, 7;
DLBY 80; MTCW

Hawking, S. W.
See Hawking, Stephen W(illiam)

Hawking, Stephen W(illiam)
1942- .... **CLC 63**
See also AAYA 13; BEST 89:1; CA 126;
129; CANR 48

Hawthorne, Julian 1846-1934 ..... **TCLC 25**

Hawthorne, Nathaniel
1804-1864 .... **NCLC 39; DA; DAB;
DAC; SSC 3; WLC**
See also CDALB 1640-1865; DAM MST,
NOV; DLB 1, 74; YABC 2

Haxton, Josephine Ayres 1921-
See Douglas, Ellen
See also CA 115; CANR 41

Hayaseca y Eizaguirre, Jorge
See Echegaray (y Eizaguirre), Jose (Maria Waldo)

Hayashi Fumiko 1904-1951 .... **TCLC 27**

Haycraft, Anna
See Ellis, Alice Thomas
See also CA 122

Hayden, Robert E(arl)
1913-1980 ...... **CLC 5, 9, 14, 37; BLC; DA; DAC; PC 6**
See also BW 1; CA 69-72; 97-100; CABS 2; CANR 24; CDALB 1941-1968; DAM MST, MULT, POET; DLB 5, 76; MTCW; SATA 19; SATA-Obit 26

Hayford, J(oseph) E(phraim) Casely
See Casely-Hayford, J(oseph) E(phraim)

Hayman, Ronald 1932- .... **CLC 44**
See also CA 25-28R; CANR 18, 50; DLB 155

Haywood, Eliza (Fowler)
1693(?)-1756 .... **LC 1**

Hazlitt, William 1778-1830 ...... **NCLC 29**
See also DLB 110, 158

Hazzard, Shirley 1931- .... **CLC 18**
See also CA 9-12R; CANR 4; DLBY 82; MTCW

Head, Bessie 1937-1986 ... **CLC 25, 67; BLC**
See also BW 2; CA 29-32R; 119; CANR 25; DAM MULT; DLB 117; MTCW

Headon, (Nicky) Topper 1956(?)- ... **CLC 30**

Heaney, Seamus (Justin)
1939- ...... **CLC 5, 7, 14, 25, 37, 74, 91; DAB**
See also CA 85-88; CANR 25, 48; CDBLB 1960 to Present; DAM POET; DLB 40; MTCW

Hearn, (Patricio) Lafcadio (Tessima Carlos)
1850-1904 .... **TCLC 9**
See also CA 105; DLB 12, 78

Hearne, Vicki 1946- .... **CLC 56**
See also CA 139

Hearon, Shelby 1931- .... **CLC 63**
See also AITN 2; CA 25-28R; CANR 18, 48

Heat-Moon, William Least .... **CLC 29**
See also Trogdon, William (Lewis)
See also AAYA 9

Hebbel, Friedrich 1813-1863 ..... **NCLC 43**
See also DAM DRAM; DLB 129

Hebert, Anne 1916- ... **CLC 4, 13, 29; DAC**
See also CA 85-88; DAM MST, POET; DLB 68; MTCW

Hecht, Anthony (Evan)
1923- .... **CLC 8, 13, 19**
See also CA 9-12R; CANR 6; DAM POET; DLB 5

Hecht, Ben 1894-1964 .... **CLC 8**
See also CA 85-88; DLB 7, 9, 25, 26, 28, 86

Hedayat, Sadeq 1903-1951 .... **TCLC 21**
See also CA 120

Hegel, Georg Wilhelm Friedrich
1770-1831 .... **NCLC 46**
See also DLB 90

Heidegger, Martin 1889-1976 ...... **CLC 24**
See also CA 81-84; 65-68; CANR 34; MTCW

Heidenstam, (Carl Gustaf) Verner von
1859-1940 .... **TCLC 5**
See also CA 104

Heifner, Jack 1946- .... **CLC 11**
See also CA 105; CANR 47

Heijermans, Herman 1864-1924 ... **TCLC 24**
See also CA 123

Heilbrun, Carolyn G(old) 1926-..... **CLC 25**
See also CA 45-48; CANR 1, 28

Heine, Heinrich 1797-1856 .... **NCLC 4, 54**
See also DLB 90

Heinemann, Larry (Curtiss) 1944- .. **CLC 50**
See also CA 110; CAAS 21; CANR 31; DLBD 9; INT CANR-31

Heiney, Donald (William) 1921-1993
See Harris, MacDonald
See also CA 1-4R; 142; CANR 3

Heinlein, Robert A(nson)
1907-1988 ...... **CLC 1, 3, 8, 14, 26, 55**
See also AAYA 17; CA 1-4R; 125; CANR 1, 20; DAM POP; DLB 8; JRDA; MAICYA; MTCW; SATA 9, 69; SATA-Obit 56

Helforth, John
See Doolittle, Hilda

Hellenhofferu, Vojtech Kapristian z
See Hasek, Jaroslav (Matej Frantisek)

Heller, Joseph
1923- .... **CLC 1, 3, 5, 8, 11, 36, 63; DA; DAB; DAC; WLC**
See also AITN 1; CA 5-8R; CABS 1; CANR 8, 42; DAM MST, NOV, POP; DLB 2, 28; DLBY 80; INT CANR-8; MTCW

Hellman, Lillian (Florence)
1906-1984 ...... **CLC 2, 4, 8, 14, 18, 34, 44, 52; DC 1**
See also AITN 1, 2; CA 13-16R; 112; CANR 33; DAM DRAM; DLB 7; DLBY 84; MTCW

Helprin, Mark 1947- ..... **CLC 7, 10, 22, 32**
See also CA 81-84; CANR 47; DAM NOV, POP; DLBY 85; MTCW

Helvetius, Claude-Adrien
1715-1771 .... **LC 26**

Helyar, Jane Penelope Josephine 1933-
See Poole, Josephine
See also CA 21-24R; CANR 10, 26; SATA 82

Hemans, Felicia 1793-1835 ...... **NCLC 29**
See also DLB 96

Hemingway, Ernest (Miller)
1899-1961 .... **CLC 1, 3, 6, 8, 10, 13, 19, 30, 34, 39, 41, 44, 50, 61, 80; DA; DAB; DAC; SSC 1; WLC**
See also CA 77-80; CANR 34; CDALB 1917-1929; DAM MST, NOV; DLB 4, 9, 102; DLBD 1; DLBY 81, 87; MTCW

Hempel, Amy 1951- .... **CLC 39**
See also CA 118; 137

Henderson, F. C.
See Mencken, H(enry) L(ouis)

Henderson, Sylvia
See Ashton-Warner, Sylvia (Constance)

Henley, Beth .... **CLC 23; DC 6**
See also Henley, Elizabeth Becker
See also CABS 3; DLBY 86

Henley, Elizabeth Becker 1952-
See Henley, Beth
See also CA 107; CANR 32; DAM DRAM, MST; MTCW

Henley, William Ernest
1849-1903 .... **TCLC 8**
See also CA 105; DLB 19

Hennissart, Martha
See Lathen, Emma
See also CA 85-88

Henry, O. .... **TCLC 1, 19; SSC 5; WLC**
See also Porter, William Sydney

Henry, Patrick 1736-1799 .... **LC 25**

Henryson, Robert 1430(?)-1506(?).... **LC 20**
See also DLB 146

Henry VIII 1491-1547 .... **LC 10**

Henschke, Alfred
See Klabund

Hentoff, Nat(han Irving) 1925-..... **CLC 26**
See also AAYA 4; CA 1-4R; CAAS 6; CANR 5, 25; CLR 1; INT CANR-25; JRDA; MAICYA; SATA 42, 69; SATA-Brief 27

Heppenstall, (John) Rayner
1911-1981 .... **CLC 10**
See also CA 1-4R; 103; CANR 29

Herbert, Frank (Patrick)
1920-1986 ...... **CLC 12, 23, 35, 44, 85**
See also CA 53-56; 118; CANR 5, 43; DAM POP; DLB 8; INT CANR-5; MTCW; SATA 9, 37; SATA-Obit 47

Herbert, George
1593-1633 .... **LC 24; DAB; PC 4**
See also CDBLB Before 1660; DAM POET; DLB 126

Herbert, Zbigniew 1924- .... **CLC 9, 43**
See also CA 89-92; CANR 36; DAM POET; MTCW

Herbst, Josephine (Frey)
1897-1969 .... **CLC 34**
See also CA 5-8R; 25-28R; DLB 9

Hergesheimer, Joseph
1880-1954 .... **TCLC 11**
See also CA 109; DLB 102, 9

Herlihy, James Leo 1927-1993 ...... **CLC 6**
See also CA 1-4R; 143; CANR 2

Hermogenes fl. c. 175- .... **CMLC 6**

Hernandez, Jose 1834-1886 ...... **NCLC 17**

Herodotus c. 484B.C.-429B.C..... **CMLC 17**

Herrick, Robert
1591-1674 ..... **LC 13; DA; DAB; DAC; PC 9**
See also DAM MST, POP; DLB 126

Herring, Guilles
See Somerville, Edith

Herriot, James 1916-1995 .... **CLC 12**
See also Wight, James Alfred
See also AAYA 1; CA 148; CANR 40; DAM POP; SATA 86**

Herrmann, Dorothy 1941-......... **CLC 44**
See also CA 107

Herrmann, Taffy
See Herrmann, Dorothy

Hersey, John (Richard)
1914-1993 .... **CLC 1, 2, 7, 9, 40, 81**
See also CA 17-20R; 140; CANR 33;
DAM POP; DLB 6; MTCW; SATA 25;
SATA-Obit 76

Herzen, Aleksandr Ivanovich
1812-1870 .... **NCLC 10**

Herzl, Theodor 1860-1904........ **TCLC 36**

Herzog, Werner 1942-............ **CLC 16**
See also CA 89-92

Hesiod c. 8th cent. B.C.-......... **CMLC 5**

Hesse, Hermann
1877-1962 .... **CLC 1, 2, 3, 6, 11, 17, 25,**
69; DA; DAB; DAC; SSC 9; WLC
See also CA 17-18; CAP 2; DAM MST,
NOV; DLB 66; MTCW; SATA 50

Hewes, Cady
See De Voto, Bernard (Augustine)

Heyen, William 1940- .... **CLC 13, 18**
See also CA 33-36R; CAAS 9; DLB 5

Heyerdahl, Thor 1914-............ **CLC 26**
See also CA 5-8R; CANR 5, 22; MTCW;
SATA 2, 52

Heym, Georg (Theodor Franz Arthur)
1887-1912 .... **TCLC 9**
See also CA 106

Heym, Stefan 1913-.............. **CLC 41**
See also CA 9-12R; CANR 4; DLB 69

Heyse, Paul (Johann Ludwig von)
1830-1914 .... **TCLC 8**
See also CA 104; DLB 129

Heyward, (Edwin) DuBose
1885-1940 .... **TCLC 59**
See also CA 108; DLB 7, 9, 45; SATA 21

Hibbert, Eleanor Alice Burford
1906-1993 .... **CLC 7**
See also BEST 90:4; CA 17-20R; 140;
CANR 9, 28; DAM POP; SATA 2;
SATA-Obit 74

Higgins, George V(incent)
1939- .... **CLC 4, 7, 10, 18**
See also CA 77-80; CAAS 5; CANR 17, 51;
DLB 2; DLBY 81; INT CANR-17;
MTCW

Higginson, Thomas Wentworth
1823-1911 .... **TCLC 36**
See also DLB 1, 64

Highet, Helen
See MacInnes, Helen (Clark)

Highsmith, (Mary) Patricia
1921-1995 .... **CLC 2, 4, 14, 42**
See also CA 1-4R; 147; CANR 1, 20, 48;
DAM NOV, POP; MTCW

Highwater, Jamake (Mamake)
1942(?)-..................... **CLC 12**
See also AAYA 7; CA 65-68; CAAS 7;
CANR 10, 34; CLR 17; DLB 52;
DLBY 85; JRDA; MAICYA; SATA 32,
69; SATA-Brief 30

Higuchi, Ichiyo 1872-1896....... **NCLC 49**

Hijuelos, Oscar 1951- ...... **CLC 65; HLC**
See also BEST 90:1; CA 123; CANR 50;
DAM MULT, POP; DLB 145; HW

Hikmet, Nazim 1902(?)-1963....... **CLC 40**
See also CA 141; 93-96

Hildesheimer, Wolfgang
1916-1991 .... **CLC 49**
See also CA 101; 135; DLB 69, 124

Hill, Geoffrey (William)
1932- .... **CLC 5, 8, 18, 45**
See also CA 81-84; CANR 21;
CDBLB 1960 to Present; DAM POET;
DLB 40; MTCW

Hill, George Roy 1921-........... **CLC 26**
See also CA 110; 122

Hill, John
See Koontz, Dean R(ay)

Hill, Susan (Elizabeth)
1942-................. **CLC 4; DAB**
See also CA 33-36R; CANR 29;
DAM MST, NOV; DLB 14, 139; MTCW

Hillerman, Tony 1925-............ **CLC 62**
See also AAYA 6; BEST 89:1; CA 29-32R;
CANR 21, 42; DAM POP; SATA 6

Hillesum, Etty 1914-1943 .... **TCLC 49**
See also CA 137

Hilliard, Noel (Harvey) 1929-...... **CLC 15**
See also CA 9-12R; CANR 7

Hillis, Rick 1956-............... **CLC 66**
See also CA 134

Hilton, James 1900-1954........ **TCLC 21**
See also CA 108; DLB 34, 77; SATA 34

Himes, Chester (Bomar)
1909-1984 .... **CLC 2, 4, 7, 18, 58; BLC**
See also BW 2; CA 25-28R; 114; CANR 22;
DAM MULT; DLB 2, 76, 143; MTCW

Hinde, Thomas .... **CLC 6, 11**
See also Chitty, Thomas Willes

Hindin, Nathan
See Bloch, Robert (Albert)

Hine, (William) Daryl 1936-....... **CLC 15**
See also CA 1-4R; CAAS 15; CANR 1, 20;
DLB 60

Hinkson, Katharine Tynan
See Tynan, Katharine

Hinton, S(usan) E(loise)
1950- .... **CLC 30; DA; DAB; DAC**
See also AAYA 2; CA 81-84; CANR 32;
CLR 3, 23; DAM MST, NOV; JRDA;
MAICYA; MTCW; SATA 19, 58

Hippius, Zinaida .... **TCLC 9**
See also Gippius, Zinaida (Nikolayevna)

Hiraoka, Kimitake 1925-1970
See Mishima, Yukio
See also CA 97-100; 29-32R; DAM DRAM;
MTCW

Hirsch, E(ric) D(onald), Jr. 1928-... **CLC 79**
See also CA 25-28R; CANR 27, 51;
DLB 67; INT CANR-27; MTCW

Hirsch, Edward 1950- .... **CLC 31, 50**
See also CA 104; CANR 20, 42; DLB 120

Hitchcock, Alfred (Joseph)
1899-1980 .... **CLC 16**
See also CA 97-100; SATA 27;
SATA-Obit 24

Hitler, Adolf 1889-1945......... **TCLC 53**
See also CA 117; 147

Hoagland, Edward 1932-.......... **CLC 28**
See also CA 1-4R; CANR 2, 31; DLB 6;
SATA 51

Hoban, Russell (Conwell) 1925- .. **CLC 7, 25**
See also CA 5-8R; CANR 23, 37; CLR 3;
DAM NOV; DLB 52; MAICYA;
MTCW; SATA 1, 40, 78

Hobbs, Perry
See Blackmur, R(ichard) P(almer)

Hobson, Laura Z(ametkin)
1900-1986 .... **CLC 7, 25**
See also CA 17-20R; 118; DLB 28;
SATA 52

Hochhuth, Rolf 1931-........ **CLC 4, 11, 18**
See also CA 5-8R; CANR 33;
DAM DRAM; DLB 124; MTCW

Hochman, Sandra 1936-......... **CLC 3, 8**
See also CA 5-8R; DLB 5

Hochwaelder, Fritz 1911-1986...... **CLC 36**
See also CA 29-32R; 120; CANR 42;
DAM DRAM; MTCW

Hochwalder, Fritz
See Hochwaelder, Fritz

Hocking, Mary (Eunice) 1921- ..... **CLC 13**
See also CA 101; CANR 18, 40

Hodgins, Jack 1938-.............. **CLC 23**
See also CA 93-96; DLB 60

Hodgson, William Hope
1877(?)-1918 .... **TCLC 13**
See also CA 111; DLB 70, 153, 156

Hoffman, Alice 1952-............. **CLC 51**
See also CA 77-80; CANR 34; DAM NOV;
MTCW

Hoffman, Daniel (Gerard)
1923-................. **CLC 6, 13, 23**
See also CA 1-4R; CANR 4; DLB 5

Hoffman, Stanley 1944-............ **CLC 5**
See also CA 77-80

Hoffman, William M(oses) 1939- ... **CLC 40**
See also CA 57-60; CANR 11

Hoffmann, E(rnst) T(heodor) A(madeus)
1776-1822 .... **NCLC 2; SSC 13**
See also DLB 90; SATA 27

Hofmann, Gert 1931-............. **CLC 54**
See also CA 128

Hofmannsthal, Hugo von
1874-1929 .... **TCLC 11; DC 4**
See also CA 106; DAM DRAM; DLB 81,
118

Hogan, Linda 1947-............. **CLC 73**
See also CA 120; CANR 45; DAM MULT;
NNAL

Hogarth, Charles
See Creasey, John

Hogg, James 1770-1835.......... **NCLC 4**
See also DLB 93, 116, 159

Holbach, Paul Henri Thiry Baron
1723-1789 .... **LC 14**

Holberg, Ludvig 1684-1754 .... **LC 6**

Holden, Ursula 1921-............. **CLC 18**
See also CA 101; CAAS 8; CANR 22

Kane, Wilson
See Bloch, Robert (Albert)

Kanin, Garson 1912- . . . . **CLC 22**
See also AITN 1; CA 5-8R; CANR 7;
DLB 7

Kaniuk, Yoram 1930- . . . . **CLC 19**
See also CA 134

Kant, Immanuel 1724-1804 . . . . . . **NCLC 27**
See also DLB 94

Kantor, MacKinlay 1904-1977 . . . . . . **CLC 7**
See also CA 61-64; 73-76; DLB 9, 102

Kaplan, David Michael 1946- . . . . . . **CLC 50**

Kaplan, James 1951- . . . . **CLC 59**
See also CA 135

Karageorge, Michael
See Anderson, Poul (William)

Karamzin, Nikolai Mikhailovich
1766-1826 . . . . **NCLC 3**
See also DLB 150

Karapanou, Margarita 1946- . . . . **CLC 13**
See also CA 101

Karinthy, Frigyes 1887-1938 . . . . . . **TCLC 47**

Karl, Frederick R(obert) 1927- . . . . . **CLC 34**
See also CA 5-8R; CANR 3, 44

Kastel, Warren
See Silverberg, Robert

Kataev, Evgeny Petrovich 1903-1942
See Petrov, Evgeny
See also CA 120

Kataphusin
See Ruskin, John

Katz, Steve 1935- . . . . **CLC 47**
See also CA 25-28R; CAAS 14; CANR 12;
DLBY 83

Kauffman, Janet 1945- . . . . **CLC 42**
See also CA 117; CANR 43; DLBY 86

Kaufman, Bob (Garnell)
1925-1986 . . . . **CLC 49**
See also BW 1; CA 41-44R; 118; CANR 22;
DLB 16, 41

Kaufman, George S. 1889-1961 . . . . . **CLC 38**
See also CA 108; 93-96; DAM DRAM;
DLB 7; INT 108

Kaufman, Sue . . . . **CLC 3, 8**
See also Barondess, Sue K(aufman)

Kavafis, Konstantinos Petrou 1863-1933
See Cavafy, C(onstantine) P(eter)
See also CA 104

Kavan, Anna 1901-1968 . . . . . . **CLC 5, 13, 82**
See also CA 5-8R; CANR 6; MTCW

Kavanagh, Dan
See Barnes, Julian

Kavanagh, Patrick (Joseph)
1904-1967 . . . . **CLC 22**
See also CA 123; 25-28R; DLB 15, 20;
MTCW

Kawabata, Yasunari
1899-1972 . . . . . **CLC 2, 5, 9, 18; SSC 17**
See also CA 93-96; 33-36R; DAM MULT

Kaye, M(ary) M(argaret) 1909- . . . . . **CLC 28**
See also CA 89-92; CANR 24; MTCW;
SATA 62

Kaye, Mollie
See Kaye, M(ary) M(argaret)

Kaye-Smith, Sheila 1887-1956 . . . . . **TCLC 20**
See also CA 118; DLB 36

Kaymor, Patrice Maguilene
See Senghor, Leopold Sedar

Kazan, Elia 1909- . . . . **CLC 6, 16, 63**
See also CA 21-24R; CANR 32

Kazantzakis, Nikos
1883(?)-1957 . . . . **TCLC 2, 5, 33**
See also CA 105; 132; MTCW

Kazin, Alfred 1915- . . . . **CLC 34, 38**
See also CA 1-4R; CAAS 7; CANR 1, 45;
DLB 67

Keane, Mary Nesta (Skrine) 1904-
See Keane, Molly
See also CA 108; 114

Keane, Molly . . . . **CLC 31**
See also Keane, Mary Nesta (Skrine)
See also INT 114

Keates, Jonathan 19(?)- . . . . **CLC 34**

Keaton, Buster 1895-1966 . . . . **CLC 20**

Keats, John
1795-1821 . . . . **NCLC 8; DA; DAB;**
DAC; PC 1; WLC
See also CDBLB 1789-1832; DAM MST,
POET; DLB 96, 110

Keene, Donald 1922- . . . . **CLC 34**
See also CA 1-4R; CANR 5

Keillor, Garrison . . . . **CLC 40**
See also Keillor, Gary (Edward)
See also AAYA 2; BEST 89:3; DLBY 87;
SATA 58

Keillor, Gary (Edward) 1942-
See Keillor, Garrison
See also CA 111; 117; CANR 36;
DAM POP; MTCW

Keith, Michael
See Hubbard, L(afayette) Ron(ald)

Keller, Gottfried 1819-1890 . . . . **NCLC 2**
See also DLB 129

Kellerman, Jonathan 1949- . . . . **CLC 44**
See also BEST 90:1; CA 106; CANR 29, 51;
DAM POP; INT CANR-29

Kelley, William Melvin 1937- . . . . . . **CLC 22**
See also BW 1; CA 77-80; CANR 27;
DLB 33

Kellogg, Marjorie 1922- . . . . **CLC 2**
See also CA 81-84

Kellow, Kathleen
See Hibbert, Eleanor Alice Burford

Kelly, M(ilton) T(erry) 1947- . . . . **CLC 55**
See also CA 97-100; CAAS 22; CANR 19,
43

Kelman, James 1946- . . . . **CLC 58, 86**
See also CA 148

Kemal, Yashar 1923- . . . . **CLC 14, 29**
See also CA 89-92; CANR 44

Kemble, Fanny 1809-1893 . . . . **NCLC 18**
See also DLB 32

Kemelman, Harry 1908- . . . . **CLC 2**
See also AITN 1; CA 9-12R; CANR 6;
DLB 28

Kempe, Margery 1373(?)-1440(?) . . . . . **LC 6**
See also DLB 146

Kempis, Thomas a 1380-1471 . . . . **LC 11**

Kendall, Henry 1839-1882 . . . . **NCLC 12**

Keneally, Thomas (Michael)
1935- . . . . . . **CLC 5, 8, 10, 14, 19, 27, 43**
See also CA 85-88; CANR 10, 50;
DAM NOV; MTCW

Kennedy, Adrienne (Lita)
1931- . . . . **CLC 66; BLC; DC 5**
See also BW 2; CA 103; CAAS 20; CABS 3;
CANR 26; DAM MULT; DLB 38

Kennedy, John Pendleton
1795-1870 . . . . **NCLC 2**
See also DLB 3

Kennedy, Joseph Charles 1929-
See Kennedy, X. J.
See also CA 1-4R; CANR 4, 30, 40;
SATA 14, 86

Kennedy, William 1928- . . . **CLC 6, 28, 34, 53**
See also AAYA 1; CA 85-88; CANR 14,
31; DAM NOV; DLB 143; DLBY 85;
INT CANR-31; MTCW; SATA 57

Kennedy, X. J. . . . . **CLC 8, 42**
See also Kennedy, Joseph Charles
See also CAAS 9; CLR 27; DLB 5;
SAAS 22

Kenny, Maurice (Francis) 1929- . . . . **CLC 87**
See also CA 144; CAAS 22; DAM MULT;
NNAL

Kent, Kelvin
See Kuttner, Henry

Kenton, Maxwell
See Southern, Terry

Kenyon, Robert O.
See Kuttner, Henry

Kerouac, Jack . . . . . **CLC 1, 2, 3, 5, 14, 29, 61**
See also Kerouac, Jean-Louis Lebris de
See also CDALB 1941-1968; DLB 2, 16;
DLBD 3

Kerouac, Jean-Louis Lebris de 1922-1969
See Kerouac, Jack
See also AITN 1; CA 5-8R; 25-28R;
CANR 26; DA; DAB; DAC; DAM MST,
NOV, POET, POP; MTCW; WLC

Kerr, Jean 1923- . . . . **CLC 22**
See also CA 5-8R; CANR 7; INT CANR-7

Kerr, M. E. . . . . **CLC 12, 35**
See also Meaker, Marijane (Agnes)
See also AAYA 2; CLR 29; SAAS 1

Kerr, Robert . . . . **CLC 55**

Kerrigan, (Thomas) Anthony
1918- . . . . **CLC 4, 6**
See also CA 49-52; CAAS 11; CANR 4

Kerry, Lois
See Duncan, Lois

Kesey, Ken (Elton)
1935- . . . . . . **CLC 1, 3, 6, 11, 46, 64; DA;**
DAB; DAC; WLC
See also CA 1-4R; CANR 22, 38;
CDALB 1968-1988; DAM MST, NOV,
POP; DLB 2, 16; MTCW; SATA 66

Kesselring, Joseph (Otto)
1902-1967 . . . . **CLC 45**
See also CA 150; DAM DRAM, MST

Kessler, Jascha (Frederick) 1929- . . . . **CLC 4**
See also CA 17-20R; CANR 8, 48

Lamb, Charles
      1775-1834 . . . . **NCLC 10; DA; DAB;
                              DAC; WLC**
   See also CDBLB 1789-1832; DAM MST;
   DLB 93, 107; SATA 17

Lamb, Lady Caroline   1785-1828 . . **NCLC 38**
   See also DLB 116

Lamming, George (William)
      1927- . . . . **CLC 2, 4, 66; BLC**
   See also BW 2; CA 85-88; CANR 26;
   DAM MULT; DLB 125; MTCW

L'Amour, Louis (Dearborn)
      1908-1988 . . . . **CLC 25, 55**
   See also AAYA 16; AITN 2; BEST 89:2;
   CA 1-4R; 125; CANR 3, 25, 40;
   DAM NOV, POP; DLBY 80; MTCW

Lampedusa, Giuseppe (Tomasi) di . . . **TCLC 13**
   See also Tomasi di Lampedusa, Giuseppe

Lampman, Archibald   1861-1899 . . **NCLC 25**
   See also DLB 92

Lancaster, Bruce   1896-1963 . . . . **CLC 36**
   See also CA 9-10; CAP 1; SATA 9

Landau, Mark Alexandrovich
   See Aldanov, Mark (Alexandrovich)

Landau-Aldanov, Mark Alexandrovich
   See Aldanov, Mark (Alexandrovich)

Landis, John   1950- . . . . **CLC 26**
   See also CA 112; 122

Landolfi, Tommaso   1908-1979 . . . **CLC 11, 49**
   See also CA 127; 117

Landon, Letitia Elizabeth
      1802-1838 . . . . **NCLC 15**
   See also DLB 96

Landor, Walter Savage
      1775-1864 . . . . **NCLC 14**
   See also DLB 93, 107

Landwirth, Heinz   1927-
   See Lind, Jakov
   See also CA 9-12R; CANR 7

Lane, Patrick   1939- . . . . **CLC 25**
   See also CA 97-100; DAM POET; DLB 53;
   INT 97-100

Lang, Andrew   1844-1912 . . . . **TCLC 16**
   See also CA 114; 137; DLB 98, 141;
   MAICYA; SATA 16

Lang, Fritz   1890-1976 . . . . **CLC 20**
   See also CA 77-80; 69-72; CANR 30

Lange, John
   See Crichton, (John) Michael

Langer, Elinor   1939- . . . . **CLC 34**
   See also CA 121

Langland, William
      1330(?)-1400(?) . . . . . . **LC 19; DA; DAB;
                                 DAC**
   See also DAM MST, POET; DLB 146

Langstaff, Launcelot
   See Irving, Washington

Lanier, Sidney   1842-1881 . . . . **NCLC 6**
   See also DAM POET; DLB 64; DLBD 13;
   MAICYA; SATA 18

Lanyer, Aemilia   1569-1645 . . . . . . **LC 10, 30**
   See also DLB 121

Lao Tzu . . . . **CMLC 7**

Lapine, James (Elliot)   1949- . . . . **CLC 39**
   See also CA 123; 130; INT 130

Larbaud, Valery (Nicolas)
      1881-1957 . . . . **TCLC 9**
   See also CA 106

Lardner, Ring
   See Lardner, Ring(gold) W(ilmer)

Lardner, Ring W., Jr.
   See Lardner, Ring(gold) W(ilmer)

Lardner, Ring(gold) W(ilmer)
      1885-1933 . . . . **TCLC 2, 14**
   See also CA 104; 131; CDALB 1917-1929;
   DLB 11, 25, 86; MTCW

Laredo, Betty
   See Codrescu, Andrei

Larkin, Maia
   See Wojciechowska, Maia (Teresa)

Larkin, Philip (Arthur)
      1922-1985 . . . . . **CLC 3, 5, 8, 9, 13, 18, 33,
                          39, 64; DAB**
   See also CA 5-8R; 117; CANR 24;
   CDBLB 1960 to Present; DAM MST,
   POET; DLB 27; MTCW

Larra (y Sanchez de Castro), Mariano Jose de
      1809-1837 . . . . **NCLC 17**

Larsen, Eric   1941- . . . . **CLC 55**
   See also CA 132

Larsen, Nella   1891-1964 . . . . . **CLC 37; BLC**
   See also BW 1; CA 125; DAM MULT;
   DLB 51

Larson, Charles R(aymond)   1938- . . . **CLC 31**
   See also CA 53-56; CANR 4

Las Casas, Bartolome de   1474-1566 . . **LC 31**

Lasker-Schueler, Else   1869-1945 . . **TCLC 57**
   See also DLB 66, 124

Latham, Jean Lee   1902- . . . . **CLC 12**
   See also AITN 1; CA 5-8R; CANR 7;
   MAICYA; SATA 2, 68

Latham, Mavis
   See Clark, Mavis Thorpe

Lathen, Emma . . . . **CLC 2**
   See also Hennissart, Martha; Latsis, Mary
   J(ane)

Lathrop, Francis
   See Leiber, Fritz (Reuter, Jr.)

Latsis, Mary J(ane)
   See Lathen, Emma
   See also CA 85-88

Lattimore, Richmond (Alexander)
      1906-1984 . . . . **CLC 3**
   See also CA 1-4R; 112; CANR 1

Laughlin, James   1914- . . . . **CLC 49**
   See also CA 21-24R; CAAS 22; CANR 9,
   47; DLB 48

Laurence, (Jean) Margaret (Wemyss)
      1926-1987 . . . . **CLC 3, 6, 13, 50, 62;
                              DAC; SSC 7**
   See also CA 5-8R; 121; CANR 33;
   DAM MST; DLB 53; MTCW;
   SATA-Obit 50

Laurent, Antoine   1952- . . . . **CLC 50**

Lauscher, Hermann
   See Hesse, Hermann

Lautreamont, Comte de
      1846-1870 . . . . **NCLC 12; SSC 14**

Laverty, Donald
   See Blish, James (Benjamin)

Lavin, Mary   1912- . . . . . . **CLC 4, 18; SSC 4**
   See also CA 9-12R; CANR 33; DLB 15;
   MTCW

Lavond, Paul Dennis
   See Kornbluth, C(yril) M.; Pohl, Frederik

Lawler, Raymond Evenor   1922- . . . . **CLC 58**
   See also CA 103

Lawrence, D(avid) H(erbert Richards)
      1885-1930 . . . . **TCLC 2, 9, 16, 33, 48, 61;
                       DA; DAB; DAC; SSC 4, 19; WLC**
   See also CA 104; 121; CDBLB 1914-1945;
   DAM MST, NOV, POET; DLB 10, 19,
   36, 98, 162; MTCW

Lawrence, T(homas) E(dward)
      1888-1935 . . . . **TCLC 18**
   See also Dale, Colin
   See also CA 115

Lawrence of Arabia
   See Lawrence, T(homas) E(dward)

Lawson, Henry (Archibald Hertzberg)
      1867-1922 . . . . **TCLC 27; SSC 18**
   See also CA 120

Lawton, Dennis
   See Faust, Frederick (Schiller)

Laxness, Halldor . . . . **CLC 25**
   See also Gudjonsson, Halldor Kiljan

Layamon   fl. c. 1200- . . . . **CMLC 10**
   See also DLB 146

Laye, Camara   1928-1980 . . . **CLC 4, 38; BLC**
   See also BW 1; CA 85-88; 97-100;
   CANR 25; DAM MULT; MTCW

Layton, Irving (Peter)
      1912- . . . . **CLC 2, 15; DAC**
   See also CA 1-4R; CANR 2, 33, 43;
   DAM MST, POET; DLB 88; MTCW

Lazarus, Emma   1849-1887 . . . . **NCLC 8**

Lazarus, Felix
   See Cable, George Washington

Lazarus, Henry
   See Slavitt, David R(ytman)

Lea, Joan
   See Neufeld, John (Arthur)

Leacock, Stephen (Butler)
      1869-1944 . . . . **TCLC 2; DAC**
   See also CA 104; 141; DAM MST; DLB 92

Lear, Edward   1812-1888 . . . . **NCLC 3**
   See also CLR 1; DLB 32; MAICYA;
   SATA 18

Lear, Norman (Milton)   1922- . . . . . . **CLC 12**
   See also CA 73-76

Leavis, F(rank) R(aymond)
      1895-1978 . . . . **CLC 24**
   See also CA 21-24R; 77-80; CANR 44;
   MTCW

Leavitt, David   1961- . . . . **CLC 34**
   See also CA 116; 122; CANR 50;
   DAM POP; DLB 130; INT 122

Leblanc, Maurice (Marie Emile)
      1864-1941 . . . . **TCLC 49**
   See also CA 110

Levi, Peter (Chad Tigar) 1931-..... **CLC 41**
See also CA 5-8R; CANR 34; DLB 40

Levi, Primo
1919-1987 .... **CLC 37, 50; SSC 12**
See also CA 13-16R; 122; CANR 12, 33;
MTCW

Levin, Ira 1929-............... **CLC 3, 6**
See also CA 21-24R; CANR 17, 44;
DAM POP; MTCW; SATA 66

Levin, Meyer 1905-1981 .... **CLC 7**
See also AITN 1; CA 9-12R; 104;
CANR 15; DAM POP; DLB 9, 28;
DLBY 81; SATA 21; SATA-Obit 27

Levine, Norman 1924-............... **CLC 54**
See also CA 73-76; CAAS 23; CANR 14;
DLB 88

Levine, Philip 1928-.. **CLC 2, 4, 5, 9, 14, 33**
See also CA 9-12R; CANR 9, 37;
DAM POET; DLB 5

Levinson, Deirdre 1931-........... **CLC 49**
See also CA 73-76

Levi-Strauss, Claude 1908- .... **CLC 38**
See also CA 1-4R; CANR 6, 32; MTCW

Levitin, Sonia (Wolff) 1934- .... **CLC 17**
See also AAYA 13; CA 29-32R; CANR 14,
32; JRDA; MAICYA; SAAS 2; SATA 4,
68

Levon, O. U.
See Kesey, Ken (Elton)

Lewes, George Henry
1817-1878 .... **NCLC 25**
See also DLB 55, 144

Lewis, Alun 1915-1944........... **TCLC 3**
See also CA 104; DLB 20, 162

Lewis, C. Day
See Day Lewis, C(ecil)

Lewis, C(live) S(taples)
1898-1963 ..... **CLC 1, 3, 6, 14, 27; DA;**
DAB; DAC; WLC
See also AAYA 3; CA 81-84; CANR 33;
CDBLB 1945-1960; CLR 3, 27;
DAM MST, NOV, POP; DLB 15, 100,
160; JRDA; MAICYA; MTCW;
SATA 13

Lewis, Janet 1899-............... **CLC 41**
See also Winters, Janet Lewis
See also CA 9-12R; CANR 29; CAP 1;
DLBY 87

Lewis, Matthew Gregory
1775-1818 .... **NCLC 11**
See also DLB 39, 158

Lewis, (Harry) Sinclair
1885-1951 ..... **TCLC 4, 13, 23, 39; DA;**
DAB; DAC; WLC
See also CA 104; 133; CDALB 1917-1929;
DAM MST, NOV; DLB 9, 102; DLBD 1;
MTCW

Lewis, (Percy) Wyndham
1884(?)-1957............... **TCLC 2, 9**
See also CA 104; DLB 15

Lewisohn, Ludwig 1883-1955...... **TCLC 19**
See also CA 107; DLB 4, 9, 28, 102

Lezama Lima, Jose 1910-1976 ... **CLC 4, 10**
See also CA 77-80; DAM MULT;
DLB 113; HW

L'Heureux, John (Clarke) 1934-.... **CLC 52**
See also CA 13-16R; CANR 23, 45

Liddell, C. H.
See Kuttner, Henry

Lie, Jonas (Lauritz Idemil)
1833-1908(?) .... **TCLC 5**
See also CA 115

Lieber, Joel 1937-1971............. **CLC 6**
See also CA 73-76; 29-32R

Lieber, Stanley Martin
See Lee, Stan

Lieberman, Laurence (James)
1935-.................... **CLC 4, 36**
See also CA 17-20R; CANR 8, 36

Lieksman, Anders
See Haavikko, Paavo Juhani

Li Fei-kan 1904-
See Pa Chin
See also CA 105

Lifton, Robert Jay 1926-.......... **CLC 67**
See also CA 17-20R; CANR 27;
INT CANR-27; SATA 66

Lightfoot, Gordon 1938-.......... **CLC 26**
See also CA 109

Lightman, Alan P. 1948-.......... **CLC 81**
See also CA 141

Ligotti, Thomas (Robert)
1953-.............. **CLC 44; SSC 16**
See also CA 123; CANR 49

Li Ho 791-817.................... **PC 13**

Liliencron, (Friedrich Adolf Axel) Detlev von
1844-1909 .... **TCLC 18**
See also CA 117

Lilly, William 1602-1681.......... **LC 27**

Lima, Jose Lezama
See Lezama Lima, Jose

Lima Barreto, Afonso Henrique de
1881-1922 .... **TCLC 23**
See also CA 117

Limonov, Edward 1944-.......... **CLC 67**
See also CA 137

Lin, Frank
See Atherton, Gertrude (Franklin Horn)

Lincoln, Abraham 1809-1865..... **NCLC 18**

Lind, Jakov .... **CLC 1, 2, 4, 27, 82**
See also Landwirth, Heinz
See also CAAS 4

Lindbergh, Anne (Spencer) Morrow
1906-..................... **CLC 82**
See also CA 17-20R; CANR 16;
DAM NOV; MTCW; SATA 33

Lindsay, David 1878-1945........ **TCLC 15**
See also CA 113

Lindsay, (Nicholas) Vachel
1879-1931 ... **TCLC 17; DA; DAC; WLC**
See also CA 114; 135; CDALB 1865-1917;
DAM MST, POET; DLB 54; SATA 40

Linke-Poot
See Doeblin, Alfred

Linney, Romulus 1930-........... **CLC 51**
See also CA 1-4R; CANR 40, 44

Linton, Eliza Lynn 1822-1898.... **NCLC 41**
See also DLB 18

Li Po 701-763.................. **CMLC 2**

Lipsius, Justus 1547-1606 .... **LC 16**

Lipsyte, Robert (Michael)
1938-............... **CLC 21; DA; DAC**
See also AAYA 7; CA 17-20R; CANR 8;
CLR 23; DAM MST, NOV; JRDA;
MAICYA; SATA 5, 68

Lish, Gordon (Jay) 1934-.. **CLC 45; SSC 18**
See also CA 113; 117; DLB 130; INT 117

Lispector, Clarice 1925-1977...... **CLC 43**
See also CA 139; 116; DLB 113

Littell, Robert 1935(?)- .... **CLC 42**
See also CA 109; 112

Little, Malcolm 1925-1965
See Malcolm X
See also BW 1; CA 125; 111; DA; DAB;
DAC; DAM MST, MULT; MTCW

Littlewit, Humphrey Gent.
See Lovecraft, H(oward) P(hillips)

Litwos
See Sienkiewicz, Henryk (Adam Alexander
Pius)

Liu E 1857-1909................ **TCLC 15**
See also CA 115

Lively, Penelope (Margaret)
1933-................... **CLC 32, 50**
See also CA 41-44R; CANR 29; CLR 7;
DAM NOV; DLB 14, 161; JRDA;
MAICYA; MTCW; SATA 7, 60

Livesay, Dorothy (Kathleen)
1909-........... **CLC 4, 15, 79; DAC**
See also AITN 2; CA 25-28R; CAAS 8;
CANR 36; DAM MST, POET; DLB 68;
MTCW

Livy c. 59B.C.-c. 17........... **CMLC 11**

Lizardi, Jose Joaquin Fernandez de
1776-1827 .... **NCLC 30**

Llewellyn, Richard
See Llewellyn Lloyd, Richard Dafydd
Vivian
See also DLB 15

Llewellyn Lloyd, Richard Dafydd Vivian
1906-1983 .... **CLC 7, 80**
See also Llewellyn, Richard
See also CA 53-56; 111; CANR 7;
SATA 11; SATA-Obit 37

Llosa, (Jorge) Mario (Pedro) Vargas
See Vargas Llosa, (Jorge) Mario (Pedro)

Lloyd Webber, Andrew 1948-
See Webber, Andrew Lloyd
See also AAYA 1; CA 116; 149;
DAM DRAM; SATA 56

Llull, Ramon c. 1235-c. 1316..... **CMLC 12**

Locke, Alain (Le Roy)
1886-1954 .... **TCLC 43**
See also BW 1; CA 106; 124; DLB 51

Locke, John 1632-1704 .... **LC 7**
See also DLB 101

Locke-Elliott, Sumner
See Elliott, Sumner Locke

Lockhart, John Gibson
1794-1854 .... **NCLC 6**
See also DLB 110, 116, 144

MacBeth, George (Mann)
1932-1992 . . . . **CLC 2, 5, 9**
See also CA 25-28R; 136; DLB 40; MTCW;
SATA 4; SATA-Obit 70

MacCaig, Norman (Alexander)
1910- . . . . **CLC 36; DAB**
See also CA 9-12R; CANR 3, 34;
DAM POET; DLB 27

MacCarthy, (Sir Charles Otto) Desmond
1877-1952 . . . . **TCLC 36**

MacDiarmid, Hugh
. . . . **CLC 2, 4, 11, 19, 63; PC 9**
See also Grieve, C(hristopher) M(urray)
See also CDBLB 1945-1960; DLB 20

MacDonald, Anson
See Heinlein, Robert A(nson)

Macdonald, Cynthia 1928- . . . . . . **CLC 13, 19**
See also CA 49-52; CANR 4, 44; DLB 105

MacDonald, George 1824-1905 . . . . . **TCLC 9**
See also CA 106; 137; DLB 18; MAICYA;
SATA 33

Macdonald, John
See Millar, Kenneth

MacDonald, John D(ann)
1916-1986 . . . . **CLC 3, 27, 44**
See also CA 1-4R; 121; CANR 1, 19;
DAM NOV, POP; DLB 8; DLBY 86;
MTCW

Macdonald, John Ross
See Millar, Kenneth

Macdonald, Ross . . . . . **CLC 1, 2, 3, 14, 34, 41**
See also Millar, Kenneth
See also DLBD 6

MacDougal, John
See Blish, James (Benjamin)

MacEwen, Gwendolyn (Margaret)
1941-1987 . . . . **CLC 13, 55**
See also CA 9-12R; 124; CANR 7, 22;
DLB 53; SATA 50; SATA-Obit 55

Macha, Karel Hynek 1810-1846 . . **NCLC 46**

Machado (y Ruiz), Antonio
1875-1939 . . . . **TCLC 3**
See also CA 104; DLB 108

Machado de Assis, Joaquim Maria
1839-1908 . . . . **TCLC 10; BLC**
See also CA 107

Machen, Arthur . . . . **TCLC 4; SSC 20**
See also Jones, Arthur Llewellyn
See also DLB 36, 156

Machiavelli, Niccolo
1469-1527 . . . . . . **LC 8; DA; DAB; DAC**
See also DAM MST

MacInnes, Colin 1914-1976 . . . . . . **CLC 4, 23**
See also CA 69-72; 65-68; CANR 21;
DLB 14; MTCW

MacInnes, Helen (Clark)
1907-1985 . . . . **CLC 27, 39**
See also CA 1-4R; 117; CANR 1, 28;
DAM POP; DLB 87; MTCW; SATA 22;
SATA-Obit 44

Mackay, Mary 1855-1924
See Corelli, Marie
See also CA 118

Mackenzie, Compton (Edward Montague)
1883-1972 . . . . **CLC 18**
See also CA 21-22; 37-40R; CAP 2;
DLB 34, 100

Mackenzie, Henry 1745-1831 . . . . **NCLC 41**
See also DLB 39

Mackintosh, Elizabeth 1896(?)-1952
See Tey, Josephine
See also CA 110

MacLaren, James
See Grieve, C(hristopher) M(urray)

Mac Laverty, Bernard 1942- . . . . **CLC 31**
See also CA 116; 118; CANR 43; INT 118

MacLean, Alistair (Stuart)
1922-1987 . . . . **CLC 3, 13, 50, 63**
See also CA 57-60; 121; CANR 28;
DAM POP; MTCW; SATA 23;
SATA-Obit 50

Maclean, Norman (Fitzroy)
1902-1990 . . . . **CLC 78; SSC 13**
See also CA 102; 132; CANR 49;
DAM POP

MacLeish, Archibald
1892-1982 . . . . **CLC 3, 8, 14, 68**
See also CA 9-12R; 106; CANR 33;
DAM POET; DLB 4, 7, 45; DLBY 82;
MTCW

MacLennan, (John) Hugh
1907-1990 . . . . **CLC 2, 14; DAC**
See also CA 5-8R; 142; CANR 33;
DAM MST; DLB 68; MTCW

MacLeod, Alistair 1936- . . . . . **CLC 56; DAC**
See also CA 123; DAM MST; DLB 60

MacNeice, (Frederick) Louis
1907-1963 . . . . . . **CLC 1, 4, 10, 53; DAB**
See also CA 85-88; DAM POET; DLB 10,
20; MTCW

MacNeill, Dand
See Fraser, George MacDonald

Macpherson, James 1736-1796 . . . . . . **LC 29**
See also DLB 109

Macpherson, (Jean) Jay 1931- . . . . . . **CLC 14**
See also CA 5-8R; DLB 53

MacShane, Frank 1927- . . . . **CLC 39**
See also CA 9-12R; CANR 3, 33; DLB 111

Macumber, Mari
See Sandoz, Mari(e Susette)

Madach, Imre 1823-1864 . . . . **NCLC 19**

Madden, (Jerry) David 1933- . . . . **CLC 5, 15**
See also CA 1-4R; CAAS 3; CANR 4, 45;
DLB 6; MTCW

Maddern, Al(an)
See Ellison, Harlan (Jay)

Madhubuti, Haki R.
1942- . . . . **CLC 6, 73; BLC; PC 5**
See also Lee, Don L.
See also BW 2; CA 73-76; CANR 24, 51;
DAM MULT, POET; DLB 5, 41;
DLBD 8

Maepenn, Hugh
See Kuttner, Henry

Maepenn, K. H.
See Kuttner, Henry

Maeterlinck, Maurice 1862-1949 . . . **TCLC 3**
See also CA 104; 136; DAM DRAM;
SATA 66

Maginn, William 1794-1842 . . . . . . **NCLC 8**
See also DLB 110, 159

Mahapatra, Jayanta 1928- . . . . **CLC 33**
See also CA 73-76; CAAS 9; CANR 15, 33;
DAM MULT

Mahfouz, Naguib (Abdel Aziz Al-Sabilgi)
1911(?)-
See Mahfuz, Najib
See also BEST 89:2; CA 128; DAM NOV;
MTCW

Mahfuz, Najib . . . . **CLC 52, 55**
See also Mahfouz, Naguib (Abdel Aziz
Al-Sabilgi)
See also DLBY 88

Mahon, Derek 1941- . . . . **CLC 27**
See also CA 113; 128; DLB 40

Mailer, Norman
1923- . . . . . . **CLC 1, 2, 3, 4, 5, 8, 11, 14,
28, 39, 74; DA; DAB; DAC**
See also AITN 2; CA 9-12R; CABS 1;
CANR 28; CDALB 1968-1988;
DAM MST, NOV, POP; DLB 2, 16, 28;
DLBD 3; DLBY 80, 83; MTCW

Maillet, Antonine 1929- . . . . . . **CLC 54; DAC**
See also CA 115; 120; CANR 46; DLB 60;
INT 120

Mais, Roger 1905-1955 . . . . **TCLC 8**
See also BW 1; CA 105; 124; DLB 125;
MTCW

Maistre, Joseph de 1753-1821 . . . . **NCLC 37**

Maitland, Sara (Louise) 1950- . . . . . . **CLC 49**
See also CA 69-72; CANR 13

Major, Clarence
1936- . . . . **CLC 3, 19, 48; BLC**
See also BW 2; CA 21-24R; CAAS 6;
CANR 13, 25; DAM MULT; DLB 33

Major, Kevin (Gerald)
1949- . . . . **CLC 26; DAC**
See also AAYA 16; CA 97-100; CANR 21,
38; CLR 11; DLB 60; INT CANR-21;
JRDA; MAICYA; SATA 32, 82

Maki, James
See Ozu, Yasujiro

Malabaila, Damiano
See Levi, Primo

Malamud, Bernard
1914-1986 . . . . . . **CLC 1, 2, 3, 5, 8, 9, 11,
18, 27, 44, 78, 85; DA; DAB; DAC;
SSC 15; WLC**
See also AAYA 16; CA 5-8R; 118; CABS 1;
CANR 28; CDALB 1941-1968;
DAM MST, NOV, POP; DLB 2, 28, 152;
DLBY 80, 86; MTCW

Malaparte, Curzio 1898-1957 . . . . . **TCLC 52**

Malcolm, Dan
See Silverberg, Robert

Malcolm X . . . . **CLC 82; BLC**
See also Little, Malcolm

Malherbe, Francois de 1555-1628 . . . . . **LC 5**

Mallarme, Stephane
1842-1898 . . . . **NCLC 4, 41; PC 4**
See also DAM POET

Martinez Sierra, Gregorio
　　1881-1947 .... **TCLC 6**
　　See also CA 115

Martinez Sierra, Maria (de la O'LeJarraga)
　　1874-1974 .... **TCLC 6**
　　See also CA 115

Martinsen, Martin
　　See Follett, Ken(neth Martin)

Martinson, Harry (Edmund)
　　1904-1978 .... **CLC 14**
　　See also CA 77-80; CANR 34

Marut, Ret
　　See Traven, B.

Marut, Robert
　　See Traven, B.

Marvell, Andrew
　　1621-1678 ...... **LC 4; DA; DAB; DAC;**
　　　　　　　　　　　　　　　PC 10; WLC
　　See also CDBLB 1660-1789; DAM MST,
　　POET; DLB 131

Marx, Karl (Heinrich)
　　1818-1883 .... **NCLC 17**
　　See also DLB 129

Masaoka Shiki .... **TCLC 18**
　　See also Masaoka Tsunenori

Masaoka Tsunenori 1867-1902
　　See Masaoka Shiki
　　See also CA 117

Masefield, John (Edward)
　　1878-1967 .... **CLC 11, 47**
　　See also CA 19-20; 25-28R; CANR 33;
　　CAP 2; CDBLB 1890-1914; DAM POET;
　　DLB 10, 19, 153, 160; MTCW; SATA 19

Maso, Carole 19(?)- .... **CLC 44**

Mason, Bobbie Ann
　　1940- .... **CLC 28, 43, 82; SSC 4**
　　See also AAYA 5; CA 53-56; CANR 11,
　　31; DLBY 87; INT CANR-31; MTCW

Mason, Ernst
　　See Pohl, Frederik

Mason, Lee W.
　　See Malzberg, Barry N(athaniel)

Mason, Nick 1945- .... **CLC 35**

Mason, Tally
　　See Derleth, August (William)

Mass, William
　　See Gibson, William

Masters, Edgar Lee
　　1868-1950 ...... **TCLC 2, 25; DA; DAC;**
　　　　　　　　　　　　　　　PC 1
　　See also CA 104; 133; CDALB 1865-1917;
　　DAM MST, POET; DLB 54; MTCW

Masters, Hilary 1928- .... **CLC 48**
　　See also CA 25-28R; CANR 13, 47

Mastrosimone, William 19(?)- ..... **CLC 36**

Mathe, Albert
　　See Camus, Albert

Matheson, Richard Burton 1926- ... **CLC 37**
　　See also CA 97-100; DLB 8, 44; INT 97-100

Mathews, Harry 1930- .... **CLC 6, 52**
　　See also CA 21-24R; CAAS 6; CANR 18,
　　40

Mathews, John Joseph 1894-1979... **CLC 84**
　　See also CA 19-20; 142; CANR 45; CAP 2;
　　DAM MULT; NNAL

Mathias, Roland (Glyn) 1915- ..... **CLC 45**
　　See also CA 97-100; CANR 19, 41; DLB 27

Matsuo Basho 1644-1694 .... **PC 3**
　　See also DAM POET

Mattheson, Rodney
　　See Creasey, John

Matthews, Greg 1949- .... **CLC 45**
　　See also CA 135

Matthews, William 1942- .... **CLC 40**
　　See also CA 29-32R; CAAS 18; CANR 12;
　　DLB 5

Matthias, John (Edward) 1941- ..... **CLC 9**
　　See also CA 33-36R

Matthiessen, Peter
　　1927- .... **CLC 5, 7, 11, 32, 64**
　　See also AAYA 6; BEST 90:4; CA 9-12R;
　　CANR 21, 50; DAM NOV; DLB 6;
　　MTCW; SATA 27

Maturin, Charles Robert
　　1780(?)-1824 .... **NCLC 6**

Matute (Ausejo), Ana Maria
　　1925- .... **CLC 11**
　　See also CA 89-92; MTCW

Maugham, W. S.
　　See Maugham, W(illiam) Somerset

Maugham, W(illiam) Somerset
　　1874-1965 ...... **CLC 1, 11, 15, 67; DA;**
　　　　　　　　　　　　　DAB; DAC; SSC 8; WLC
　　See also CA 5-8R; 25-28R; CANR 40;
　　CDBLB 1914-1945; DAM DRAM, MST,
　　NOV; DLB 10, 36, 77, 100, 162; MTCW;
　　SATA 54

Maugham, William Somerset
　　See Maugham, W(illiam) Somerset

Maupassant, (Henri Rene Albert) Guy de
　　1850-1893 ..... **NCLC 1, 42; DA; DAB;**
　　　　　　　　　　　　　DAC; SSC 1; WLC
　　See also DAM MST; DLB 123

Maurhut, Richard
　　See Traven, B.

Mauriac, Claude 1914- .... **CLC 9**
　　See also CA 89-92; DLB 83

Mauriac, Francois (Charles)
　　1885-1970 .... **CLC 4, 9, 56**
　　See also CA 25-28; CAP 2; DLB 65;
　　MTCW

Mavor, Osborne Henry 1888-1951
　　See Bridie, James
　　See also CA 104

Maxwell, William (Keepers, Jr.)
　　1908- .... **CLC 19**
　　See also CA 93-96; DLBY 80; INT 93-96

May, Elaine 1932- .... **CLC 16**
　　See also CA 124; 142; DLB 44

Mayakovski, Vladimir (Vladimirovich)
　　1893-1930 .... **TCLC 4, 18**
　　See also CA 104

Mayhew, Henry 1812-1887 ...... **NCLC 31**
　　See also DLB 18, 55

Mayle, Peter 1939(?)- .... **CLC 89**
　　See also CA 139

Maynard, Joyce 1953- .... **CLC 23**
　　See also CA 111; 129

Mayne, William (James Carter)
　　1928- .... **CLC 12**
　　See also CA 9-12R; CANR 37; CLR 25;
　　JRDA; MAICYA; SAAS 11; SATA 6, 68

Mayo, Jim
　　See L'Amour, Louis (Dearborn)

Maysles, Albert 1926- .... **CLC 16**
　　See also CA 29-32R

Maysles, David 1932- .... **CLC 16**

Mazer, Norma Fox 1931- .... **CLC 26**
　　See also AAYA 5; CA 69-72; CANR 12,
　　32; CLR 23; JRDA; MAICYA; SAAS 1;
　　SATA 24, 67

Mazzini, Guiseppe 1805-1872 .... **NCLC 34**

McAuley, James Phillip
　　1917-1976 .... **CLC 45**
　　See also CA 97-100

McBain, Ed
　　See Hunter, Evan

McBrien, William Augustine
　　1930- .... **CLC 44**
　　See also CA 107

McCaffrey, Anne (Inez) 1926- ...... **CLC 17**
　　See also AAYA 6; AITN 2; BEST 89:2;
　　CA 25-28R; CANR 15, 35; DAM NOV,
　　POP; DLB 8; JRDA; MAICYA; MTCW;
　　SAAS 11; SATA 8, 70

McCall, Nathan 1955(?)- .... **CLC 86**
　　See also CA 146

McCann, Arthur
　　See Campbell, John W(ood, Jr.)

McCann, Edson
　　See Pohl, Frederik

McCarthy, Charles, Jr. 1933-
　　See McCarthy, Cormac
　　See also CANR 42; DAM POP

McCarthy, Cormac 1933- ..... **CLC 4, 57, 59**
　　See also McCarthy, Charles, Jr.
　　See also DLB 6, 143

McCarthy, Mary (Therese)
　　1912-1989 ... **CLC 1, 3, 5, 14, 24, 39, 59**
　　See also CA 5-8R; 129; CANR 16, 50;
　　DLB 2; DLBY 81; INT CANR-16;
　　MTCW

McCartney, (James) Paul
　　1942- .... **CLC 12, 35**
　　See also CA 146

McCauley, Stephen (D.) 1955- ..... **CLC 50**
　　See also CA 141

McClure, Michael (Thomas)
　　1932- .... **CLC 6, 10**
　　See also CA 21-24R; CANR 17, 46;
　　DLB 16

McCorkle, Jill (Collins) 1958- ...... **CLC 51**
　　See also CA 121; DLBY 87

McCourt, James 1941- .... **CLC 5**
　　See also CA 57-60

McCoy, Horace (Stanley)
　　1897-1955 .... **TCLC 28**
　　See also CA 108; DLB 9

McCrae, John 1872-1918 .... **TCLC 12**
　　See also CA 109; DLB 92

McCreigh, James
See Pohl, Frederik

McCullers, (Lula) Carson (Smith)
1917-1967 .... **CLC 1, 4, 10, 12, 48; DA;
DAB; DAC; SSC 9; WLC**
See also CA 5-8R; 25-28R; CABS 1, 3;
CANR 18; CDALB 1941-1968;
DAM MST, NOV; DLB 2, 7; MTCW;
SATA 27

McCulloch, John Tyler
See Burroughs, Edgar Rice

McCullough, Colleen 1938(?)- ...... **CLC 27**
See also CA 81-84; CANR 17, 46;
DAM NOV, POP; MTCW

McDermott, Alice 1953- .... **CLC 90**
See also CA 109; CANR 40

McElroy, Joseph 1930- .... **CLC 5, 47**
See also CA 17-20R

McEwan, Ian (Russell) 1948- ... **CLC 13, 66**
See also BEST 90:4; CA 61-64; CANR 14,
41; DAM NOV; DLB 14; MTCW

McFadden, David 1940- .... **CLC 48**
See also CA 104; DLB 60; INT 104

McFarland, Dennis 1950- .... **CLC 65**

McGahern, John
1934- .... **CLC 5, 9, 48; SSC 17**
See also CA 17-20R; CANR 29; DLB 14;
MTCW

McGinley, Patrick (Anthony)
1937- .... **CLC 41**
See also CA 120; 127; INT 127

McGinley, Phyllis 1905-1978 ...... **CLC 14**
See also CA 9-12R; 77-80; CANR 19;
DLB 11, 48; SATA 2, 44; SATA-Obit 24

McGinniss, Joe 1942- .... **CLC 32**
See also AITN 2; BEST 89:2; CA 25-28R;
CANR 26; INT CANR-26

McGivern, Maureen Daly
See Daly, Maureen

McGrath, Patrick 1950- .... **CLC 55**
See also CA 136

McGrath, Thomas (Matthew)
1916-1990 .... **CLC 28, 59**
See also CA 9-12R; 132; CANR 6, 33;
DAM POET; MTCW; SATA 41;
SATA-Obit 66

McGuane, Thomas (Francis III)
1939- .... **CLC 3, 7, 18, 45**
See also AITN 2; CA 49-52; CANR 5, 24,
49; DLB 2; DLBY 80; INT CANR-24;
MTCW

McGuckian, Medbh 1950- .... **CLC 48**
See also CA 143; DAM POET; DLB 40

McHale, Tom 1942(?)-1982 ...... **CLC 3, 5**
See also AITN 1; CA 77-80; 106

McIlvanney, William 1936- .... **CLC 42**
See also CA 25-28R; DLB 14

McIlwraith, Maureen Mollie Hunter
See Hunter, Mollie
See also SATA 2

McInerney, Jay 1955- .... **CLC 34**
See also CA 116; 123; CANR 45;
DAM POP; INT 123

McIntyre, Vonda N(eel) 1948- ..... **CLC 18**
See also CA 81-84; CANR 17, 34; MTCW

McKay, Claude
.... **TCLC 7, 41; BLC; DAB; PC 2**
See also McKay, Festus Claudius
See also DLB 4, 45, 51, 117

McKay, Festus Claudius 1889-1948
See McKay, Claude
See also BW 1; CA 104; 124; DA; DAC;
DAM MST, MULT, NOV, POET;
MTCW; WLC

McKuen, Rod 1933- .... **CLC 1, 3**
See also AITN 1; CA 41-44R; CANR 40

McLoughlin, R. B.
See Mencken, H(enry) L(ouis)

McLuhan, (Herbert) Marshall
1911-1980 .... **CLC 37, 83**
See also CA 9-12R; 102; CANR 12, 34;
DLB 88; INT CANR-12; MTCW

McMillan, Terry (L.) 1951- ..... **CLC 50, 61**
See also BW 2; CA 140; DAM MULT,
NOV, POP

McMurtry, Larry (Jeff)
1936- .... **CLC 2, 3, 7, 11, 27, 44**
See also AAYA 15; AITN 2; BEST 89:2;
CA 5-8R; CANR 19, 43;
CDALB 1968-1988; DAM NOV, POP;
DLB 2, 143; DLBY 80, 87; MTCW

McNally, T. M. 1961- .... **CLC 82**

McNally, Terrence 1939- ... **CLC 4, 7, 41, 91**
See also CA 45-48; CANR 2;
DAM DRAM; DLB 7

McNamer, Deirdre 1950- .... **CLC 70**

McNeile, Herman Cyril 1888-1937
See Sapper
See also DLB 77

McNickle, (William) D'Arcy
1904-1977 .... **CLC 89**
See also CA 9-12R; 85-88; CANR 5, 45;
DAM MULT; NNAL; SATA-Obit 22

McPhee, John (Angus) 1931- ...... **CLC 36**
See also BEST 90:1; CA 65-68; CANR 20,
46; MTCW

McPherson, James Alan
1943- .... **CLC 19, 77**
See also BW 1; CA 25-28R; CAAS 17;
CANR 24; DLB 38; MTCW

McPherson, William (Alexander)
1933- .... **CLC 34**
See also CA 69-72; CANR 28;
INT CANR-28

Mead, Margaret 1901-1978 .... **CLC 37**
See also AITN 1; CA 1-4R; 81-84;
CANR 4; MTCW; SATA-Obit 20

Meaker, Marijane (Agnes) 1927-
See Kerr, M. E.
See also CA 107; CANR 37; INT 107;
JRDA; MAICYA; MTCW; SATA 20, 61

Medoff, Mark (Howard) 1940- ... **CLC 6, 23**
See also AITN 1; CA 53-56; CANR 5;
DAM DRAM; DLB 7; INT CANR-5

Medvedev, P. N.
See Bakhtin, Mikhail Mikhailovich

Meged, Aharon
See Megged, Aharon

Meged, Aron
See Megged, Aharon

Megged, Aharon 1920- .... **CLC 9**
See also CA 49-52; CAAS 13; CANR 1

Mehta, Ved (Parkash) 1934- .... **CLC 37**
See also CA 1-4R; CANR 2, 23; MTCW

Melanter
See Blackmore, R(ichard) D(oddridge)

Melikow, Loris
See Hofmannsthal, Hugo von

Melmoth, Sebastian
See Wilde, Oscar (Fingal O'Flahertie Wills)

Meltzer, Milton 1915- .... **CLC 26**
See also AAYA 8; CA 13-16R; CANR 38;
CLR 13; DLB 61; JRDA; MAICYA;
SAAS 1; SATA 1, 50, 80

Melville, Herman
1819-1891 ..... **NCLC 3, 12, 29, 45, 49;
DA; DAB; DAC; SSC 1, 17; WLC**
See also CDALB 1640-1865; DAM MST,
NOV; DLB 3, 74; SATA 59

Menander
c. 342B.C.-c. 292B.C. .... **CMLC 9; DC 3**
See also DAM DRAM

Mencken, H(enry) L(ouis)
1880-1956 .... **TCLC 13**
See also CA 105; 125; CDALB 1917-1929;
DLB 11, 29, 63, 137; MTCW

Mercer, David 1928-1980 .... **CLC 5**
See also CA 9-12R; 102; CANR 23;
DAM DRAM; DLB 13; MTCW

Merchant, Paul
See Ellison, Harlan (Jay)

Meredith, George 1828-1909 ... **TCLC 17, 43**
See also CA 117; CDBLB 1832-1890;
DAM POET; DLB 18, 35, 57, 159

Meredith, William (Morris)
1919- .... **CLC 4, 13, 22, 55**
See also CA 9-12R; CAAS 14; CANR 6, 40;
DAM POET; DLB 5

Merezhkovsky, Dmitry Sergeyevich
1865-1941 .... **TCLC 29**

Merimee, Prosper
1803-1870 .... **NCLC 6; SSC 7**
See also DLB 119

Merkin, Daphne 1954- .... **CLC 44**
See also CA 123

Merlin, Arthur
See Blish, James (Benjamin)

Merrill, James (Ingram)
1926-1995 .... **CLC 2, 3, 6, 8, 13, 18, 34,
91**
See also CA 13-16R; 147; CANR 10, 49;
DAM POET; DLB 5; DLBY 85;
INT CANR-10; MTCW

Merriman, Alex
See Silverberg, Robert

Merritt, E. B.
See Waddington, Miriam

Merton, Thomas
1915-1968 .. **CLC 1, 3, 11, 34, 83; PC 10**
See also CA 5-8R; 25-28R; CANR 22;
DLB 48; DLBY 81; MTCW

Merwin, W(illiam) S(tanley)
    1927- . . . **CLC 1, 2, 3, 5, 8, 13, 18, 45, 88**
    See also CA 13-16R; CANR 15, 51;
    DAM POET; DLB 5; INT CANR-15;
    MTCW

Metcalf, John   1938- . . . . **CLC 37**
    See also CA 113; DLB 60

Metcalf, Suzanne
    See Baum, L(yman) Frank

Mew, Charlotte (Mary)
    1870-1928 . . . . **TCLC 8**
    See also CA 105; DLB 19, 135

Mewshaw, Michael   1943- . . . . **CLC 9**
    See also CA 53-56; CANR 7, 47; DLBY 80

Meyer, June
    See Jordan, June

Meyer, Lynn
    See Slavitt, David R(ytman)

Meyer-Meyrink, Gustav   1868-1932
    See Meyrink, Gustav
    See also CA 117

Meyers, Jeffrey   1939- . . . . **CLC 39**
    See also CA 73-76; DLB 111

Meynell, Alice (Christina Gertrude Thompson)
    1847-1922 . . . . **TCLC 6**
    See also CA 104; DLB 19, 98

Meyrink, Gustav . . . . **TCLC 21**
    See also Meyer-Meyrink, Gustav
    See also DLB 81

Michaels, Leonard
    1933- . . . . **CLC 6, 25; SSC 16**
    See also CA 61-64; CANR 21; DLB 130;
    MTCW

Michaux, Henri   1899-1984 . . . . . . **CLC 8, 19**
    See also CA 85-88; 114

Michelangelo   1475-1564 . . . . **LC 12**

Michelet, Jules   1798-1874 . . . . . . **NCLC 31**

Michener, James A(lbert)
    1907(?)- . . . . **CLC 1, 5, 11, 29, 60**
    See also AITN 1; BEST 90:1; CA 5-8R;
    CANR 21, 45; DAM NOV, POP; DLB 6;
    MTCW

Mickiewicz, Adam   1798-1855 . . . . . **NCLC 3**

Middleton, Christopher   1926- . . . . . . **CLC 13**
    See also CA 13-16R; CANR 29; DLB 40

Middleton, Richard (Barham)
    1882-1911 . . . . **TCLC 56**
    See also DLB 156

Middleton, Stanley   1919- . . . . **CLC 7, 38**
    See also CA 25-28R; CAAS 23; CANR 21,
    46; DLB 14

Middleton, Thomas   1580-1627 . . . . **DC 5**
    See also DAM DRAM, MST; DLB 58

Migueis, Jose Rodrigues   1901- . . . . . **CLC 10**

Mikszath, Kalman   1847-1910 . . . . . **TCLC 31**

Miles, Josephine
    1911-1985 . . . . **CLC 1, 2, 14, 34, 39**
    See also CA 1-4R; 116; CANR 2;
    DAM POET; DLB 48

Militant
    See Sandburg, Carl (August)

Mill, John Stuart   1806-1873 . . . . . **NCLC 11**
    See also CDBLB 1832-1890; DLB 55

Millar, Kenneth   1915-1983 . . . . **CLC 14**
    See also Macdonald, Ross
    See also CA 9-12R; 110; CANR 16;
    DAM POP; DLB 2; DLBD 6; DLBY 83;
    MTCW

Millay, E. Vincent
    See Millay, Edna St. Vincent

Millay, Edna St. Vincent
    1892-1950 . . . . . . **TCLC 4, 49; DA; DAB;**
                         DAC; PC 6
    See also CA 104; 130; CDALB 1917-1929;
    DAM MST, POET; DLB 45; MTCW

Miller, Arthur
    1915- . . . . **CLC 1, 2, 6, 10, 15, 26, 47, 78;**
              DA; DAB; DAC; DC 1; WLC
    See also AAYA 15; AITN 1; CA 1-4R;
    CABS 3; CANR 2, 30;
    CDALB 1941-1968; DAM DRAM, MST;
    DLB 7; MTCW

Miller, Henry (Valentine)
    1891-1980 . . . . **CLC 1, 2, 4, 9, 14, 43, 84;**
                    DA; DAB; DAC; WLC
    See also CA 9-12R; 97-100; CANR 33;
    CDALB 1929-1941; DAM MST, NOV;
    DLB 4, 9; DLBY 80; MTCW

Miller, Jason   1939(?)- . . . . **CLC 2**
    See also AITN 1; CA 73-76; DLB 7

Miller, Sue   1943- . . . . **CLC 44**
    See also BEST 90:3; CA 139; DAM POP;
    DLB 143

Miller, Walter M(ichael, Jr.)
    1923- . . . . **CLC 4, 30**
    See also CA 85-88; DLB 8

Millett, Kate   1934- . . . . **CLC 67**
    See also AITN 1; CA 73-76; CANR 32;
    MTCW

Millhauser, Steven   1943- . . . . **CLC 21, 54**
    See also CA 110; 111; DLB 2; INT 111

Millin, Sarah Gertrude   1889-1968 . . **CLC 49**
    See also CA 102; 93-96

Milne, A(lan) A(lexander)
    1882-1956 . . . . **TCLC 6; DAB; DAC**
    See also CA 104; 133; CLR 1, 26;
    DAM MST; DLB 10, 77, 100, 160;
    MAICYA; MTCW; YABC 1

Milner, Ron(ald)   1938- . . . . **CLC 56; BLC**
    See also AITN 1; BW 1; CA 73-76;
    CANR 24; DAM MULT; DLB 38;
    MTCW

Milosz, Czeslaw
    1911- . . . **CLC 5, 11, 22, 31, 56, 82; PC 8**
    See also CA 81-84; CANR 23, 51;
    DAM MST, POET; MTCW

Milton, John
    1608-1674 . . . . . . **LC 9; DA; DAB; DAC;**
                            WLC
    See also CDBLB 1660-1789; DAM MST,
    POET; DLB 131, 151

Min, Anchee   1957- . . . . **CLC 86**
    See also CA 146

Minehaha, Cornelius
    See Wedekind, (Benjamin) Frank(lin)

Miner, Valerie   1947- . . . . **CLC 40**
    See also CA 97-100

Minimo, Duca
    See D'Annunzio, Gabriele

Minot, Susan   1956- . . . . **CLC 44**
    See also CA 134

Minus, Ed   1938- . . . . **CLC 39**

Miranda, Javier
    See Bioy Casares, Adolfo

Mirbeau, Octave   1848-1917 . . . . . . **TCLC 55**
    See also DLB 123

Miro (Ferrer), Gabriel (Francisco Victor)
    1879-1930 . . . . **TCLC 5**
    See also CA 104

Mishima, Yukio
    . . . . **CLC 2, 4, 6, 9, 27; DC 1; SSC 4**
    See also Hiraoka, Kimitake

Mistral, Frederic   1830-1914 . . . . . . **TCLC 51**
    See also CA 122

Mistral, Gabriela . . . . **TCLC 2; HLC**
    See also Godoy Alcayaga, Lucila

Mistry, Rohinton   1952- . . . . . . **CLC 71; DAC**
    See also CA 141

Mitchell, Clyde
    See Ellison, Harlan (Jay); Silverberg, Robert

Mitchell, James Leslie   1901-1935
    See Gibbon, Lewis Grassic
    See also CA 104; DLB 15

Mitchell, Joni   1943- . . . . **CLC 12**
    See also CA 112

Mitchell, Margaret (Munnerlyn)
    1900-1949 . . . . **TCLC 11**
    See also CA 109; 125; DAM NOV, POP;
    DLB 9; MTCW

Mitchell, Peggy
    See Mitchell, Margaret (Munnerlyn)

Mitchell, S(ilas) Weir   1829-1914 . . **TCLC 36**

Mitchell, W(illiam) O(rmond)
    1914- . . . . **CLC 25; DAC**
    See also CA 77-80; CANR 15, 43;
    DAM MST; DLB 88

Mitford, Mary Russell   1787-1855 . . **NCLC 4**
    See also DLB 110, 116

Mitford, Nancy   1904-1973 . . . . **CLC 44**
    See also CA 9-12R

Miyamoto, Yuriko   1899-1951 . . . . . **TCLC 37**

Mo, Timothy (Peter)   1950(?)- . . . . . . **CLC 46**
    See also CA 117; MTCW

Modarressi, Taghi (M.)   1931- . . . . . . **CLC 44**
    See also CA 121; 134; INT 134

Modiano, Patrick (Jean)   1945- . . . . . **CLC 18**
    See also CA 85-88; CANR 17, 40; DLB 83

Moerck, Paal
    See Roelvaag, O(le) E(dvart)

Mofolo, Thomas (Mokopu)
    1875(?)-1948 . . . . **TCLC 22; BLC**
    See also CA 121; DAM MULT

Mohr, Nicholasa   1935- . . . . **CLC 12; HLC**
    See also AAYA 8; CA 49-52; CANR 1, 32;
    CLR 22; DAM MULT; DLB 145; HW;
    JRDA; SAAS 8; SATA 8

Mojtabai, A(nn) G(race)
    1938- . . . . **CLC 5, 9, 15, 29**
    See also CA 85-88

Moliere
    1622-1673 . . . . . **LC 28; DA; DAB; DAC;**
                             WLC
    See also DAM DRAM, MST

Molin, Charles
See Mayne, William (James Carter)

Molnar, Ferenc 1878-1952 . . . . **TCLC 20**
See also CA 109; DAM DRAM

Momaday, N(avarre) Scott
1934- . . . **CLC 2, 19, 85; DA; DAB; DAC**
See also AAYA 11; CA 25-28R; CANR 14,
34; DAM MST, MULT, NOV, POP;
DLB 143; INT CANR-14; MTCW;
NNAL; SATA 48; SATA-Brief 30

Monette, Paul 1945-1995 . . . . **CLC 82**
See also CA 139; 147

Monroe, Harriet 1860-1936 . . . . . . **TCLC 12**
See also CA 109; DLB 54, 91

Monroe, Lyle
See Heinlein, Robert A(nson)

Montagu, Elizabeth 1917- . . . . **NCLC 7**
See also CA 9-12R

Montagu, Mary (Pierrepont) Wortley
1689-1762 . . . . **LC 9**
See also DLB 95, 101

Montagu, W. H.
See Coleridge, Samuel Taylor

Montague, John (Patrick)
1929- . . . . **CLC 13, 46**
See also CA 9-12R; CANR 9; DLB 40;
MTCW

Montaigne, Michel (Eyquem) de
1533-1592 . . . . . . **LC 8; DA; DAB; DAC;**
WLC

See also DAM MST

Montale, Eugenio
1896-1981 . . . . **CLC 7, 9, 18; PC 13**
See also CA 17-20R; 104; CANR 30;
DLB 114; MTCW

Montesquieu, Charles-Louis de Secondat
1689-1755 . . . . **LC 7**

Montgomery, (Robert) Bruce 1921-1978
See Crispin, Edmund
See also CA 104

Montgomery, L(ucy) M(aud)
1874-1942 . . . . **TCLC 51; DAC**
See also AAYA 12; CA 108; 137; CLR 8;
DAM MST; DLB 92; JRDA; MAICYA;
YABC 1

Montgomery, Marion H., Jr. 1925- . . **CLC 7**
See also AITN 1; CA 1-4R; CANR 3, 48;
DLB 6

Montgomery, Max
See Davenport, Guy (Mattison, Jr.)

Montherlant, Henry (Milon) de
1896-1972 . . . . **CLC 8, 19**
See also CA 85-88; 37-40R; DAM DRAM;
DLB 72; MTCW

Monty Python
See Chapman, Graham; Cleese, John
(Marwood); Gilliam, Terry (Vance); Idle,
Eric; Jones, Terence Graham Parry; Palin,
Michael (Edward)
See also AAYA 7

Moodie, Susanna (Strickland)
1803-1885 . . . . **NCLC 14**
See also DLB 99

Mooney, Edward 1951-
See Mooney, Ted
See also CA 130

Mooney, Ted . . . . **CLC 25**
See also Mooney, Edward

Moorcock, Michael (John)
1939- . . . . **CLC 5, 27, 58**
See also CA 45-48; CAAS 5; CANR 2, 17,
38; DLB 14; MTCW

Moore, Brian
1921- . . . . . . **CLC 1, 3, 5, 7, 8, 19, 32, 90;**
DAB; DAC
See also CA 1-4R; CANR 1, 25, 42;
DAM MST; MTCW

Moore, Edward
See Muir, Edwin

Moore, George Augustus
1852-1933 . . . . **TCLC 7; SSC 19**
See also CA 104; DLB 10, 18, 57, 135

Moore, Lorrie . . . . **CLC 39, 45, 68**
See also Moore, Marie Lorena

Moore, Marianne (Craig)
1887-1972 . . . . **CLC 1, 2, 4, 8, 10, 13, 19,**
47; DA; DAB; DAC; PC 4
See also CA 1-4R; 33-36R; CANR 3;
CDALB 1929-1941; DAM MST, POET;
DLB 45; DLBD 7; MTCW; SATA 20

Moore, Marie Lorena 1957-
See Moore, Lorrie
See also CA 116; CANR 39

Moore, Thomas 1779-1852 . . . . **NCLC 6**
See also DLB 96, 144

Morand, Paul 1888-1976 . . . . **CLC 41**
See also CA 69-72; DLB 65

Morante, Elsa 1918-1985 . . . . **CLC 8, 47**
See also CA 85-88; 117; CANR 35; MTCW

Moravia, Alberto . . . . . . **CLC 2, 7, 11, 27, 46**
See also Pincherle, Alberto

More, Hannah 1745-1833 . . . . **NCLC 27**
See also DLB 107, 109, 116, 158

More, Henry 1614-1687 . . . . **LC 9**
See also DLB 126

More, Sir Thomas 1478-1535 . . . . **LC 10, 32**

Moreas, Jean . . . . **TCLC 18**
See also Papadiamantopoulos, Johannes

Morgan, Berry 1919- . . . . **CLC 6**
See also CA 49-52; DLB 6

Morgan, Claire
See Highsmith, (Mary) Patricia

Morgan, Edwin (George) 1920- . . . . . **CLC 31**
See also CA 5-8R; CANR 3, 43; DLB 27

Morgan, (George) Frederick
1922- . . . . **CLC 23**
See also CA 17-20R; CANR 21

Morgan, Harriet
See Mencken, H(enry) L(ouis)

Morgan, Jane
See Cooper, James Fenimore

Morgan, Janet 1945- . . . . **CLC 39**
See also CA 65-68

Morgan, Lady 1776(?)-1859 . . . . . . **NCLC 29**
See also DLB 116, 158

Morgan, Robin 1941- . . . . **CLC 2**
See also CA 69-72; CANR 29; MTCW;
SATA 80

Morgan, Scott
See Kuttner, Henry

Morgan, Seth 1949(?)-1990 . . . . **CLC 65**
See also CA 132

Morgenstern, Christian
1871-1914 . . . . **TCLC 8**
See also CA 105

Morgenstern, S.
See Goldman, William (W.)

Moricz, Zsigmond 1879-1942 . . . . . **TCLC 33**

Morike, Eduard (Friedrich)
1804-1875 . . . . **NCLC 10**
See also DLB 133

Mori Ogai . . . . **TCLC 14**
See also Mori Rintaro

Mori Rintaro 1862-1922
See Mori Ogai
See also CA 110

Moritz, Karl Philipp 1756-1793 . . . . . . **LC 2**
See also DLB 94

Morland, Peter Henry
See Faust, Frederick (Schiller)

Morren, Theophil
See Hofmannsthal, Hugo von

Morris, Bill 1952- . . . . **CLC 76**

Morris, Julian
See West, Morris L(anglo)

Morris, Steveland Judkins 1950(?)-
See Wonder, Stevie
See also CA 111

Morris, William 1834-1896 . . . . **NCLC 4**
See also CDBLB 1832-1890; DLB 18, 35,
57, 156

Morris, Wright 1910- . . . **CLC 1, 3, 7, 18, 37**
See also CA 9-12R; CANR 21; DLB 2;
DLBY 81; MTCW

Morrison, Chloe Anthony Wofford
See Morrison, Toni

Morrison, James Douglas 1943-1971
See Morrison, Jim
See also CA 73-76; CANR 40

Morrison, Jim . . . . **CLC 17**
See also Morrison, James Douglas

Morrison, Toni
1931- . . . . **CLC 4, 10, 22, 55, 81, 87;**
BLC; DA; DAB; DAC
See also AAYA 1; BW 2; CA 29-32R;
CANR 27, 42; CDALB 1968-1988;
DAM MST, MULT, NOV, POP; DLB 6,
33, 143; DLBY 81; MTCW; SATA 57

Morrison, Van 1945- . . . . **CLC 21**
See also CA 116

Mortimer, John (Clifford)
1923- . . . . **CLC 28, 43**
See also CA 13-16R; CANR 21;
CDBLB 1960 to Present; DAM DRAM,
POP; DLB 13; INT CANR-21; MTCW

Mortimer, Penelope (Ruth) 1918- . . . . **CLC 5**
See also CA 57-60; CANR 45

Morton, Anthony
See Creasey, John

Mosher, Howard Frank 1943- . . . . . . **CLC 62**
See also CA 139

Mosley, Nicholas 1923- . . . . **CLC 43, 70**
See also CA 69-72; CANR 41; DLB 14

Moss, Howard
1922-1987 . . . . **CLC 7, 14, 45, 50**
See also CA 1-4R; 123; CANR 1, 44;
DAM POET; DLB 5

Mossgiel, Rab
See Burns, Robert

Motion, Andrew (Peter) 1952- . . . . . . **CLC 47**
See also CA 146; DLB 40

Motley, Willard (Francis)
1909-1965 . . . . **CLC 18**
See also BW 1; CA 117; 106; DLB 76, 143

Motoori, Norinaga 1730-1801 . . . . **NCLC 45**

Mott, Michael (Charles Alston)
1930- . . . . **CLC 15, 34**
See also CA 5-8R; CAAS 7; CANR 7, 29

Moure, Erin 1955- . . . . **CLC 88**
See also CA 113; DLB 60

Mowat, Farley (McGill)
1921- . . . . **CLC 26; DAC**
See also AAYA 1; CA 1-4R; CANR 4, 24,
42; CLR 20; DAM MST; DLB 68;
INT CANAR-24; JRDA; MAICYA;
MTCW; SATA 3, 55

Moyers, Bill 1934- . . . . **CLC 74**
See also AITN 2; CA 61-64; CANR 31

Mphahlele, Es'kia
See Mphahlele, Ezekiel
See also DLB 125

Mphahlele, Ezekiel 1919- . . . . . **CLC 25; BLC**
See also Mphahlele, Es'kia
See also BW 2; CA 81-84; CANR 26;
DAM MULT

Mqhayi, S(amuel) E(dward) K(rune Loliwe)
1875-1945 . . . . **TCLC 25; BLC**
See also DAM MULT

Mr. Martin
See Burroughs, William S(eward)

Mrozek, Slawomir 1930- . . . . **CLC 3, 13**
See also CA 13-16R; CAAS 10; CANR 29;
MTCW

Mrs. Belloc-Lowndes
See Lowndes, Marie Adelaide (Belloc)

Mtwa, Percy (?)- . . . . **CLC 47**

Mueller, Lisel 1924- . . . . **CLC 13, 51**
See also CA 93-96; DLB 105

Muir, Edwin 1887-1959 . . . . **TCLC 2**
See also CA 104; DLB 20, 100

Muir, John 1838-1914 . . . . **TCLC 28**

Mujica Lainez, Manuel
1910-1984 . . . . **CLC 31**
See also Lainez, Manuel Mujica
See also CA 81-84; 112; CANR 32; HW

Mukherjee, Bharati 1940- . . . . **CLC 53**
See also BEST 89:2; CA 107; CANR 45;
DAM NOV; DLB 60; MTCW

Muldoon, Paul 1951- . . . . **CLC 32, 72**
See also CA 113; 129; DAM POET;
DLB 40; INT 129

Mulisch, Harry 1927- . . . . **CLC 42**
See also CA 9-12R; CANR 6, 26

Mull, Martin 1943- . . . . **CLC 17**
See also CA 105

Mulock, Dinah Maria
See Craik, Dinah Maria (Mulock)

Munford, Robert 1737(?)-1783 . . . . **LC 5**
See also DLB 31

Mungo, Raymond 1946- . . . . **CLC 72**
See also CA 49-52; CANR 2

Munro, Alice
1931- . . . **CLC 6, 10, 19, 50; DAC; SSC 3**
See also AITN 2; CA 33-36R; CANR 33;
DAM MST, NOV; DLB 53; MTCW;
SATA 29

Munro, H(ector) H(ugh) 1870-1916
See Saki
See also CA 104; 130; CDBLB 1890-1914;
DA; DAB; DAC; DAM MST, NOV;
DLB 34, 162; MTCW; WLC

Murasaki, Lady . . . . **CMLC 1**

Murdoch, (Jean) Iris
1919- . . . . . . **CLC 1, 2, 3, 4, 6, 8, 11, 15,
22, 31, 51; DAB; DAC**
See also CA 13-16R; CANR 8, 43;
CDBLB 1960 to Present; DAM MST,
NOV; DLB 14; INT CANR-8; MTCW

Murnau, Friedrich Wilhelm
See Plumpe, Friedrich Wilhelm

Murphy, Richard 1927- . . . . **CLC 41**
See also CA 29-32R; DLB 40

Murphy, Sylvia 1937- . . . . **CLC 34**
See also CA 121

Murphy, Thomas (Bernard) 1935- . . . **CLC 51**
See also CA 101

Murray, Albert L. 1916- . . . . **CLC 73**
See also BW 2; CA 49-52; CANR 26;
DLB 38

Murray, Les(lie) A(llan) 1938- . . . . . **CLC 40**
See also CA 21-24R; CANR 11, 27;
DAM POET

Murry, J. Middleton
See Murry, John Middleton

Murry, John Middleton
1889-1957 . . . . **TCLC 16**
See also CA 118; DLB 149

Musgrave, Susan 1951- . . . . **CLC 13, 54**
See also CA 69-72; CANR 45

Musil, Robert (Edler von)
1880-1942 . . . . **TCLC 12; SSC 18**
See also CA 109; DLB 81, 124

Muske, Carol 1945- . . . . **CLC 90**
See also Muske-Dukes, Carol (Anne)

Muske-Dukes, Carol (Anne) 1945-
See Muske, Carol
See also CA 65-68; CANR 32

Musset, (Louis Charles) Alfred de
1810-1857 . . . . **NCLC 7**

My Brother's Brother
See Chekhov, Anton (Pavlovich)

Myers, L. H. 1881-1944 . . . . **TCLC 59**
See also DLB 15

Myers, Walter Dean 1937- . . . **CLC 35; BLC**
See also AAYA 4; BW 2; CA 33-36R;
CANR 20, 42; CLR 4, 16, 35;
DAM MULT, NOV; DLB 33;
INT CANR-20; JRDA; MAICYA;
SAAS 2; SATA 41, 71; SATA-Brief 27

Myers, Walter M.
See Myers, Walter Dean

Myles, Symon
See Follett, Ken(neth Martin)

Nabokov, Vladimir (Vladimirovich)
1899-1977 . . . . . **CLC 1, 2, 3, 6, 8, 11, 15,
23, 44, 46, 64; DA; DAB; DAC; SSC 11;
WLC**
See also CA 5-8R; 69-72; CANR 20;
CDALB 1941-1968; DAM MST, NOV;
DLB 2; DLBD 3; DLBY 80, 91; MTCW

Nagai Kafu . . . . **TCLC 51**
See also Nagai Sokichi

Nagai Sokichi 1879-1959
See Nagai Kafu
See also CA 117

Nagy, Laszlo 1925-1978 . . . . **CLC 7**
See also CA 129; 112

Naipaul, Shiva(dhar Srinivasa)
1945-1985 . . . . **CLC 32, 39**
See also CA 110; 112; 116; CANR 33;
DAM NOV; DLB 157; DLBY 85;
MTCW

Naipaul, V(idiadhar) S(urajprasad)
1932- . . . . **CLC 4, 7, 9, 13, 18, 37; DAB;
DAC**
See also CA 1-4R; CANR 1, 33, 51;
CDBLB 1960 to Present; DAM MST,
NOV; DLB 125; DLBY 85; MTCW

Nakos, Lilika 1899(?)- . . . . **CLC 29**

Narayan, R(asipuram) K(rishnaswami)
1906- . . . . **CLC 7, 28, 47**
See also CA 81-84; CANR 33; DAM NOV;
MTCW; SATA 62

Nash, (Frediric) Ogden 1902-1971 . . **CLC 23**
See also CA 13-14; 29-32R; CANR 34;
CAP 1; DAM POET; DLB 11;
MAICYA; MTCW; SATA 2, 46

Nathan, Daniel
See Dannay, Frederic

Nathan, George Jean 1882-1958 . . . **TCLC 18**
See also Hatteras, Owen
See also CA 114; DLB 137

Natsume, Kinnosuke 1867-1916
See Natsume, Soseki
See also CA 104

Natsume, Soseki . . . . **TCLC 2, 10**
See also Natsume, Kinnosuke

Natti, (Mary) Lee 1919-
See Kingman, Lee
See also CA 5-8R; CANR 2

Naylor, Gloria
1950- . . . . . . **CLC 28, 52; BLC; DA; DAC**
See also AAYA 6; BW 2; CA 107;
CANR 27, 51; DAM MST, MULT,
NOV, POP; MTCW

Neihardt, John Gneisenau
1881-1973 . . . . **CLC 32**
See also CA 13-14; CAP 1; DLB 9, 54

Nekrasov, Nikolai Alekseevich
1821-1878 . . . . **NCLC 11**

Nelligan, Emile 1879-1941 . . . . **TCLC 14**
See also CA 114; DLB 92

Nelson, Willie 1933- . . . . **CLC 17**
See also CA 107

Osborne, David
See Silverberg, Robert

Osborne, George
See Silverberg, Robert

Osborne, John (James)
1929-1994 ..... **CLC 1, 2, 5, 11, 45; DA;**
DAB; DAC; WLC
See also CA 13-16R; 147; CANR 21;
CDBLB 1945-1960; DAM DRAM, MST;
DLB 13; MTCW

Osborne, Lawrence 1958- .... **CLC 50**

Oshima, Nagisa 1932- .... **CLC 20**
See also CA 116; 121

Oskison, John Milton
1874-1947 .... **TCLC 35**
See also CA 144; DAM MULT; NNAL

Ossoli, Sarah Margaret (Fuller marchesa d')
1810-1850
See Fuller, Margaret
See also SATA 25

Ostrovsky, Alexander
1823-1886 .... **NCLC 30**

Otero, Blas de 1916-1979......... **CLC 11**
See also CA 89-92; DLB 134

Otto, Whitney 1955-.............. **CLC 70**
See also CA 140

Ouida .... **TCLC 43**
See also De La Ramee, (Marie) Louise
See also DLB 18, 156

Ousmane, Sembene 1923- .... **CLC 66; BLC**
See also BW 1; CA 117; 125; MTCW

Ovid 43B.C.-18(?).......... **CMLC 7; PC 2**
See also DAM POET

Owen, Hugh
See Faust, Frederick (Schiller)

Owen, Wilfred (Edward Salter)
1893-1918 ...... **TCLC 5, 27; DA; DAB;**
DAC; WLC
See also CA 104; 141; CDBLB 1914-1945;
DAM MST, POET; DLB 20

Owens, Rochelle 1936-............. **CLC 8**
See also CA 17-20R; CAAS 2; CANR 39

Oz, Amos 1939- ... **CLC 5, 8, 11, 27, 33, 54**
See also CA 53-56; CANR 27, 47;
DAM NOV; MTCW

Ozick, Cynthia
1928- .... **CLC 3, 7, 28, 62; SSC 15**
See also BEST 90:1; CA 17-20R; CANR 23;
DAM NOV, POP; DLB 28, 152;
DLBY 82; INT CANR-23; MTCW

Ozu, Yasujiro 1903-1963 .... **CLC 16**
See also CA 112

Pacheco, C.
See Pessoa, Fernando (Antonio Nogueira)

Pa Chin .... **CLC 18**
See also Li Fei-kan

Pack, Robert 1929-.............. **CLC 13**
See also CA 1-4R; CANR 3, 44; DLB 5

Padgett, Lewis
See Kuttner, Henry

Padilla (Lorenzo), Heberto 1932- ... **CLC 38**
See also AITN 1; CA 123; 131; HW

Page, Jimmy 1944-.............. **CLC 12**

Page, Louise 1955-.............. **CLC 40**
See also CA 140

Page, P(atricia) K(athleen)
1916- .... **CLC 7, 18; DAC; PC 12**
See also CA 53-56; CANR 4, 22;
DAM MST; DLB 68; MTCW

Paget, Violet 1856-1935
See Lee, Vernon
See also CA 104

Paget-Lowe, Henry
See Lovecraft, H(oward) P(hillips)

Paglia, Camille (Anna) 1947-....... **CLC 68**
See also CA 140

Paige, Richard
See Koontz, Dean R(ay)

Pakenham, Antonia
See Fraser, (Lady) Antonia (Pakenham)

Palamas, Kostes 1859-1943 .... **TCLC 5**
See also CA 105

Palazzeschi, Aldo 1885-1974....... **CLC 11**
See also CA 89-92; 53-56; DLB 114

Paley, Grace 1922-.... **CLC 4, 6, 37; SSC 8**
See also CA 25-28R; CANR 13, 46;
DAM POP; DLB 28; INT CANR-13;
MTCW

Palin, Michael (Edward) 1943-..... **CLC 21**
See also Monty Python
See also CA 107; CANR 35; SATA 67

Palliser, Charles 1947-............ **CLC 65**
See also CA 136

Palma, Ricardo 1833-1919........ **TCLC 29**

Pancake, Breece Dexter 1952-1979
See Pancake, Breece D'J
See also CA 123; 109

Pancake, Breece D'J............... CLC 29
See also Pancake, Breece Dexter
See also DLB 130

Panko, Rudy
See Gogol, Nikolai (Vasilyevich)

Papadiamantis, Alexandros
1851-1911 .... **TCLC 29**

Papadiamantopoulos, Johannes 1856-1910
See Moreas, Jean
See also CA 117

Papini, Giovanni 1881-1956....... **TCLC 22**
See also CA 121

Paracelsus 1493-1541.............. **LC 14**

Parasol, Peter
See Stevens, Wallace

Parfenie, Maria
See Codrescu, Andrei

Parini, Jay (Lee) 1948- .... **CLC 54**
See also CA 97-100; CAAS 16; CANR 32

Park, Jordan
See Kornbluth, C(yril) M.; Pohl, Frederik

Parker, Bert
See Ellison, Harlan (Jay)

Parker, Dorothy (Rothschild)
1893-1967 ..... **CLC 15, 68; SSC 2**
See also CA 19-20; 25-28R; CAP 2;
DAM POET; DLB 11, 45, 86; MTCW

Parker, Robert B(rown) 1932-...... **CLC 27**
See also BEST 89:4; CA 49-52; CANR 1,
26; DAM NOV, POP; INT CANR-26;
MTCW

Parkin, Frank 1940-.............. **CLC 43**
See also CA 147

Parkman, Francis, Jr.
1823-1893 .... **NCLC 12**
See also DLB 1, 30

Parks, Gordon (Alexander Buchanan)
1912- .... **CLC 1, 16; BLC**
See also AITN 2; BW 2; CA 41-44R;
CANR 26; DAM MULT; DLB 33;
SATA 8

Parnell, Thomas 1679-1718 .... **LC 3**
See also DLB 94

Parra, Nicanor 1914-........ **CLC 2; HLC**
See also CA 85-88; CANR 32;
DAM MULT; HW; MTCW

Parrish, Mary Frances
See Fisher, M(ary) F(rances) K(ennedy)

Parson
See Coleridge, Samuel Taylor

Parson Lot
See Kingsley, Charles

Partridge, Anthony
See Oppenheim, E(dward) Phillips

Pascoli, Giovanni 1855-1912 ...... **TCLC 45**

Pasolini, Pier Paolo
1922-1975 .... **CLC 20, 37**
See also CA 93-96; 61-64; DLB 128;
MTCW

Pasquini
See Silone, Ignazio

Pastan, Linda (Olenik) 1932- ...... **CLC 27**
See also CA 61-64; CANR 18, 40;
DAM POET; DLB 5

Pasternak, Boris (Leonidovich)
1890-1960 ...... **CLC 7, 10, 18, 63; DA;**
DAB; DAC; PC 6; WLC
See also CA 127; 116; DAM MST, NOV,
POET; MTCW

Patchen, Kenneth 1911-1972 ... **CLC 1, 2, 18**
See also CA 1-4R; 33-36R; CANR 3, 35;
DAM POET; DLB 16, 48; MTCW

Pater, Walter (Horatio)
1839-1894 .... **NCLC 7**
See also CDBLB 1832-1890; DLB 57, 156

Paterson, A(ndrew) B(arton)
1864-1941................ **TCLC 32**

Paterson, Katherine (Womeldorf)
1932-.................. **CLC 12, 30**
See also AAYA 1; CA 21-24R; CANR 28;
CLR 7; DLB 52; JRDA; MAICYA;
MTCW; SATA 13, 53

Patmore, Coventry Kersey Dighton
1823-1896 .... **NCLC 9**
See also DLB 35, 98

Paton, Alan (Stewart)
1903-1988 ...... **CLC 4, 10, 25, 55; DA;**
DAB; DAC; WLC
See also CA 13-16; 125; CANR 22; CAP 1;
DAM MST, NOV; MTCW; SATA 11;
SATA-Obit 56

Paton Walsh, Gillian 1937-
See Walsh, Jill Paton
See also CANR 38; JRDA; MAICYA;
SAAS 3; SATA 4, 72

Paulding, James Kirke 1778-1860.. **NCLC 2**
See also DLB 3, 59, 74

Paulin, Thomas Neilson 1949-
See Paulin, Tom
See also CA 123; 128

Paulin, Tom .... **CLC 37**
See also Paulin, Thomas Neilson
See also DLB 40

Paustovsky, Konstantin (Georgievich)
1892-1968 .... **CLC 40**
See also CA 93-96; 25-28R

Pavese, Cesare
1908-1950 ..... **TCLC 3; PC 13; SSC 19**
See also CA 104; DLB 128

Pavic, Milorad 1929- .... **CLC 60**
See also CA 136

Payne, Alan
See Jakes, John (William)

Paz, Gil
See Lugones, Leopoldo

Paz, Octavio
1914- .... **CLC 3, 4, 6, 10, 19, 51, 65;**
DA; DAB; DAC; HLC; PC 1; WLC
See also CA 73-76; CANR 32; DAM MST,
MULT, POET; DLBY 90; HW; MTCW

Peacock, Molly 1947-............. **CLC 60**
See also CA 103; CAAS 21; DLB 120

Peacock, Thomas Love
1785-1866 .... **NCLC 22**
See also DLB 96, 116

Peake, Mervyn 1911-1968...... **CLC 7, 54**
See also CA 5-8R; 25-28R; CANR 3;
DLB 15, 160; MTCW; SATA 23

Pearce, Philippa .... **CLC 21**
See also Christie, (Ann) Philippa
See also CLR 9; DLB 161; MAICYA;
SATA 1, 67

Pearl, Eric
See Elman, Richard

Pearson, T(homas) R(eid) 1956- .... **CLC 39**
See also CA 120; 130; INT 130

Peck, Dale 1967- .... **CLC 81**
See also CA 146

Peck, John 1941- .... **CLC 3**
See also CA 49-52; CANR 3

Peck, Richard (Wayne) 1934- ...... **CLC 21**
See also AAYA 1; CA 85-88; CANR 19,
38; CLR 15; INT CANR-19; JRDA;
MAICYA; SAAS 2; SATA 18, 55

Peck, Robert Newton
1928- .... **CLC 17; DA; DAC**
See also AAYA 3; CA 81-84; CANR 31;
DAM MST, JRDA; MAICYA; SAAS 1;
SATA 21, 62

Peckinpah, (David) Sam(uel)
1925-1984 .... **CLC 20**
See also CA 109; 114

Pedersen, Knut 1859-1952
See Hamsun, Knut
See also CA 104; 119; MTCW

Peeslake, Gaffer
See Durrell, Lawrence (George)

Peguy, Charles Pierre
1873-1914 .... **TCLC 10**
See also CA 107

Pena, Ramon del Valle y
See Valle-Inclan, Ramon (Maria) del

Pendennis, Arthur Esquir
See Thackeray, William Makepeace

Penn, William 1644-1718.......... **LC 25**
See also DLB 24

Pepys, Samuel
1633-1703 ..... **LC 11; DA; DAB; DAC;**
WLC
See also CDBLB 1660-1789; DAM MST;
DLB 101

Percy, Walker
1916-1990 .... **CLC 2, 3, 6, 8, 14, 18, 47,**
65
See also CA 1-4R; 131; CANR 1, 23;
DAM NOV, POP; DLB 2; DLBY 80, 90;
MTCW

Perec, Georges 1936-1982 .... **CLC 56**
See also CA 141; DLB 83

Pereda (y Sanchez de Porrua), Jose Maria de
1833-1906 .... **TCLC 16**
See also CA 117

Pereda y Porrua, Jose Maria de
See Pereda (y Sanchez de Porrua), Jose
Maria de

Peregoy, George Weems
See Mencken, H(enry) L(ouis)

Perelman, S(idney) J(oseph)
1904-1979 ... **CLC 3, 5, 9, 15, 23, 44, 49**
See also AITN 1, 2; CA 73-76; 89-92;
CANR 18; DAM DRAM; DLB 11, 44;
MTCW

Peret, Benjamin 1899-1959 .... **TCLC 20**
See also CA 117

Peretz, Isaac Loeb 1851(?)-1915... **TCLC 16**
See also CA 109

Peretz, Yitzkhok Leibush
See Peretz, Isaac Loeb

Perez Galdos, Benito 1843-1920... **TCLC 27**
See also CA 125; HW

Perrault, Charles 1628-1703 .... **LC 2**
See also MAICYA; SATA 25

Perry, Brighton
See Sherwood, Robert E(mmet)

Perse, St.-John .... **CLC 4, 11, 46**
See also Leger, (Marie-Rene Auguste) Alexis
Saint-Leger

Perutz, Leo 1882-1957........... **TCLC 60**
See also DLB 81

Peseenz, Tulio F.
See Lopez y Fuentes, Gregorio

Pesetsky, Bette 1932-............. **CLC 28**
See also CA 133; DLB 130

Peshkov, Alexei Maximovich 1868-1936
See Gorky, Maxim
See also CA 105; 141; DA; DAC;
DAM DRAM, MST, NOV

Pessoa, Fernando (Antonio Nogueira)
1888-1935 .... **TCLC 27; HLC**
See also CA 125

Peterkin, Julia Mood 1880-1961.... **CLC 31**
See also CA 102; DLB 9

Peters, Joan K. 1945-............. **CLC 39**

Peters, Robert L(ouis) 1924-........ **CLC 7**
See also CA 13-16R; CAAS 8; DLB 105

Petofi, Sandor 1823-1849....... **NCLC 21**

Petrakis, Harry Mark 1923-........ **CLC 3**
See also CA 9-12R; CANR 4, 30

Petrarch 1304-1374............ **PC 8**
See also DAM POET

Petrov, Evgeny .... **TCLC 21**
See also Kataev, Evgeny Petrovich

Petry, Ann (Lane) 1908- ...... **CLC 1, 7, 18**
See also BW 1; CA 5-8R; CAAS 6;
CANR 4, 46; CLR 12; DLB 76; JRDA;
MAICYA; MTCW; SATA 5

Petursson, Halligrimur 1614-1674 .... **LC 8**

Philips, Katherine 1632-1664....... **LC 30**
See also DLB 131

Philipson, Morris H. 1926-........ **CLC 53**
See also CA 1-4R; CANR 4

Phillips, David Graham
1867-1911 .... **TCLC 44**
See also CA 108; DLB 9, 12

Phillips, Jack
See Sandburg, Carl (August)

Phillips, Jayne Anne
1952- .... **CLC 15, 33; SSC 16**
See also CA 101; CANR 24, 50; DLBY 80;
INT CANR-24; MTCW

Phillips, Richard
See Dick, Philip K(indred)

Phillips, Robert (Schaeffer) 1938-... **CLC 28**
See also CA 17-20R; CAAS 13; CANR 8;
DLB 105

Phillips, Ward
See Lovecraft, H(oward) P(hillips)

Piccolo, Lucio 1901-1969.......... **CLC 13**
See also CA 97-100; DLB 114

Pickthall, Marjorie L(owry) C(hristie)
1883-1922 .... **TCLC 21**
See also CA 107; DLB 92

Pico della Mirandola, Giovanni
1463-1494 .... **LC 15**

Piercy, Marge
1936- .... **CLC 3, 6, 14, 18, 27, 62**
See also CA 21-24R; CAAS 1; CANR 13,
43; DLB 120; MTCW

Piers, Robert
See Anthony, Piers

Pieyre de Mandiargues, Andre 1909-1991
See Mandiargues, Andre Pieyre de
See also CA 103; 136; CANR 22

Pilnyak, Boris .... **TCLC 23**
See also Vogau, Boris Andreyevich

Pincherle, Alberto 1907-1990 ... **CLC 11, 18**
See also Moravia, Alberto
See also CA 25-28R; 132; CANR 33;
DAM NOV; MTCW

Pinckney, Darryl 1953- .... **CLC 76**
See also BW 2; CA 143

Pindar 518B.C.-446B.C......... **CMLC 12**

Powell, Anthony (Dymoke)
1905- . . . . CLC **1, 3, 7, 9, 10, 31**
See also CA 1-4R; CANR 1, 32;
CDBLB 1945-1960; DLB 15; MTCW

Powell, Dawn 1897-1965 . . . . CLC **66**
See also CA 5-8R

Powell, Padgett 1952- . . . . CLC **34**
See also CA 126

Power, Susan . . . . CLC **91**

Powers, J(ames) F(arl)
1917- . . . . CLC **1, 4, 8, 57; SSC 4**
See also CA 1-4R; CANR 2; DLB 130;
MTCW

Powers, John J(ames) 1945-
See Powers, John R.
See also CA 69-72

Powers, John R. . . . . CLC **66**
See also Powers, John J(ames)

Pownall, David 1938- . . . . CLC **10**
See also CA 89-92; CAAS 18; CANR 49;
DLB 14

Powys, John Cowper
1872-1963 . . . . CLC **7, 9, 15, 46**
See also CA 85-88; DLB 15; MTCW

Powys, T(heodore) F(rancis)
1875-1953 . . . . TCLC **9**
See also CA 106; DLB 36, 162

Prager, Emily 1952- . . . . CLC **56**

Pratt, E(dwin) J(ohn)
1883(?)-1964 . . . . CLC **19; DAC**
See also CA 141; 93-96; DAM POET;
DLB 92

Premchand . . . . TCLC **21**
See also Srivastava, Dhanpat Rai

Preussler, Otfried 1923- . . . . CLC **17**
See also CA 77-80; SATA 24

Prevert, Jacques (Henri Marie)
1900-1977 . . . . CLC **15**
See also CA 77-80; 69-72; CANR 29;
MTCW; SATA-Obit 30

Prevost, Abbe (Antoine Francois)
1697-1763 . . . . LC **1**

Price, (Edward) Reynolds
1933- . . . . CLC **3, 6, 13, 43, 50, 63**
See also CA 1-4R; CANR 1, 37;
DAM NOV; DLB 2; INT CANR-37

Price, Richard 1949- . . . . CLC **6, 12**
See also CA 49-52; CANR 3; DLBY 81

Prichard, Katharine Susannah
1883-1969 . . . . CLC **46**
See also CA 11-12; CANR 33; CAP 1;
MTCW; SATA 66

Priestley, J(ohn) B(oynton)
1894-1984 . . . . CLC **2, 5, 9, 34**
See also CA 9-12R; 113; CANR 33;
CDBLB 1914-1945; DAM DRAM, NOV;
DLB 10, 34, 77, 100, 139; DLBY 84;
MTCW

Prince 1958(?)- . . . . CLC **35**

Prince, F(rank) T(empleton) 1912- . . CLC **22**
See also CA 101; CANR 43; DLB 20

Prince Kropotkin
See Kropotkin, Peter (Alekseievich)

Prior, Matthew 1664-1721 . . . . LC **4**
See also DLB 95

Pritchard, William H(arrison)
1932- . . . . CLC **34**
See also CA 65-68; CANR 23; DLB 111

Pritchett, V(ictor) S(awdon)
1900- . . . . CLC **5, 13, 15, 41; SSC 14**
See also CA 61-64; CANR 31; DAM NOV;
DLB 15, 139; MTCW

Private 19022
See Manning, Frederic

Probst, Mark 1925- . . . . CLC **59**
See also CA 130

Prokosch, Frederic 1908-1989 . . . . CLC **4, 48**
See also CA 73-76; 128; DLB 48

Prophet, The
See Dreiser, Theodore (Herman Albert)

Prose, Francine 1947- . . . . CLC **45**
See also CA 109; 112; CANR 46

Proudhon
See Cunha, Euclides (Rodrigues Pimenta) da

Proulx, E. Annie 1935- . . . . CLC **81**

Proust, (Valentin-Louis-George-Eugene-)
Marcel
1871-1922 . . . . TCLC **7, 13, 33; DA;**
DAB; DAC; WLC
See also CA 104; 120; DAM MST, NOV;
DLB 65; MTCW

Prowler, Harley
See Masters, Edgar Lee

Prus, Boleslaw 1845-1912 . . . . TCLC **48**

Pryor, Richard (Franklin Lenox Thomas)
1940- . . . . CLC **26**
See also CA 122

Przybyszewski, Stanislaw
1868-1927 . . . . TCLC **36**
See also DLB 66

Pteleon
See Grieve, C(hristopher) M(urray)
See also DAM POET

Puckett, Lute
See Masters, Edgar Lee

Puig, Manuel
1932-1990 . . . CLC **3, 5, 10, 28, 65; HLC**
See also CA 45-48; CANR 2, 32;
DAM MULT; DLB 113; HW; MTCW

Purdy, Al(fred Wellington)
1918- . . . . CLC **3, 6, 14, 50; DAC**
See also CA 81-84; CAAS 17; CANR 42;
DAM MST, POET; DLB 88

Purdy, James (Amos)
1923- . . . . CLC **2, 4, 10, 28, 52**
See also CA 33-36R; CAAS 1; CANR 19,
51; DLB 2; INT CANR-19; MTCW

Pure, Simon
See Swinnerton, Frank Arthur

Pushkin, Alexander (Sergeyevich)
1799-1837 . . . . . NCLC **3, 27; DA; DAB;**
DAC; PC 10; WLC
See also DAM DRAM, MST, POET;
SATA 61

P'u Sung-ling 1640-1715 . . . . LC **3**

Putnam, Arthur Lee
See Alger, Horatio, Jr.

Puzo, Mario 1920- . . . . CLC **1, 2, 6, 36**
See also CA 65-68; CANR 4, 42;
DAM NOV, POP; DLB 6; MTCW

Pym, Barbara (Mary Crampton)
1913-1980 . . . . CLC **13, 19, 37**
See also CA 13-14; 97-100; CANR 13, 34;
CAP 1; DLB 14; DLBY 87; MTCW

Pynchon, Thomas (Ruggles, Jr.)
1937- . . . . . CLC **2, 3, 6, 9, 11, 18, 33, 62,**
72; DA; DAB; DAC; SSC 14; WLC
See also BEST 90:2; CA 17-20R; CANR 22,
46; DAM MST, NOV, POP; DLB 2;
MTCW

Qian Zhongshu
See Ch'ien Chung-shu

Qroll
See Dagerman, Stig (Halvard)

Quarrington, Paul (Lewis) 1953- . . . . CLC **65**
See also CA 129

Quasimodo, Salvatore 1901-1968 . . . CLC **10**
See also CA 13-16; 25-28R; CAP 1;
DLB 114; MTCW

Queen, Ellery . . . . CLC **3, 11**
See also Dannay, Frederic; Davidson,
Avram; Lee, Manfred B(ennington);
Sturgeon, Theodore (Hamilton); Vance,
John Holbrook

Queen, Ellery, Jr.
See Dannay, Frederic; Lee, Manfred
B(ennington)

Queneau, Raymond
1903-1976 . . . . CLC **2, 5, 10, 42**
See also CA 77-80; 69-72; CANR 32;
DLB 72; MTCW

Quevedo, Francisco de 1580-1645 . . . . LC **23**

Quiller-Couch, Arthur Thomas
1863-1944 . . . . TCLC **53**
See also CA 118; DLB 135, 153

Quin, Ann (Marie) 1936-1973 . . . . CLC **6**
See also CA 9-12R; 45-48; DLB 14

Quinn, Martin
See Smith, Martin Cruz

Quinn, Peter 1947- . . . . CLC **91**

Quinn, Simon
See Smith, Martin Cruz

Quiroga, Horacio (Sylvestre)
1878-1937 . . . . TCLC **20; HLC**
See also CA 117; 131; DAM MULT; HW;
MTCW

Quoirez, Francoise 1935- . . . . CLC **9**
See Sagan, Francoise
See also CA 49-52; CANR 6, 39; MTCW

Raabe, Wilhelm 1831-1910 . . . . TCLC **45**
See also DLB 129

Rabe, David (William) 1940- . . . CLC **4, 8, 33**
See also CA 85-88; CABS 3; DAM DRAM;
DLB 7

Rabelais, Francois
1483-1553 . . . . . . CLC **5; DA; DAB; DAC;**
WLC
See also DAM MST

Rabinovitch, Sholem 1859-1916
See Aleichem, Sholom
See also CA 104

Racine, Jean 1639-1699 . . . . LC **28; DAB**
See also DAM MST

Radcliffe, Ann (Ward) 1764-1823 . . NCLC **6**
See also DLB 39

Robinson, Jill 1936-............. **CLC 10**
See also CA 102; INT 102

Robinson, Kim Stanley 1952-...... **CLC 34**
See also CA 126

Robinson, Lloyd
See Silverberg, Robert

Robinson, Marilynne 1944-........ **CLC 25**
See also CA 116

Robinson, Smokey................. **CLC 21**
See also Robinson, William, Jr.

Robinson, William, Jr. 1940-
See Robinson, Smokey
See also CA 116

Robison, Mary 1949-.............. **CLC 42**
See also CA 113; 116; DLB 130; INT 116

Rod, Edouard 1857-1910......... **TCLC 52**

Roddenberry, Eugene Wesley 1921-1991
See Roddenberry, Gene
See also CA 110; 135; CANR 37; SATA 45;
SATA-Obit 69

Roddenberry, Gene................ **CLC 17**
See also Roddenberry, Eugene Wesley
See also AAYA 5; SATA-Obit 69

Rodgers, Mary 1931-.............. **CLC 12**
See also CA 49-52; CANR 8; CLR 20;
INT CANR-8; JRDA; MAICYA;
SATA 8

Rodgers, W(illiam) R(obert)
1909-1969.................... **CLC 7**
See also CA 85-88; DLB 20

Rodman, Eric
See Silverberg, Robert

Rodman, Howard 1920(?)-1985..... **CLC 65**
See also CA 118

Rodman, Maia
See Wojciechowska, Maia (Teresa)

Rodriguez, Claudio 1934-.......... **CLC 10**
See also DLB 134

Roelvaag, O(le) E(dvart)
1876-1931.................. **TCLC 17**
See also CA 117; DLB 9

Roethke, Theodore (Huebner)
1908-1963...... **CLC 1, 3, 8, 11, 19, 46;
PC 15**
See also CA 81-84; CABS 2;
CDALB 1941-1968; DAM POET; DLB 5;
MTCW

Rogers, Thomas Hunton 1927-..... **CLC 57**
See also CA 89-92; INT 89-92

Rogers, Will(iam Penn Adair)
1879-1935.................. **TCLC 8**
See also CA 105; 144; DAM MULT;
DLB 11; NNAL

Rogin, Gilbert 1929-.............. **CLC 18**
See also CA 65-68; CANR 15

Rohan, Koda.................... **TCLC 22**
See also Koda Shigeyuki

Rohmer, Eric.................... **CLC 16**
See also Scherer, Jean-Marie Maurice

Rohmer, Sax.................... **TCLC 28**
See also Ward, Arthur Henry Sarsfield
See also DLB 70

Roiphe, Anne (Richardson)
1935-...................... **CLC 3, 9**
See also CA 89-92; CANR 45; DLBY 80;
INT 89-92

Rojas, Fernando de 1465-1541..... **LC 23**

**Rolfe, Frederick (William Serafino Austin
Lewis Mary)** 1860-1913..... **TCLC 12**
See also CA 107; DLB 34, 156

Rolland, Romain 1866-1944...... **TCLC 23**
See also CA 118; DLB 65

Rolvaag, O(le) E(dvart)
See Roelvaag, O(le) E(dvart)

Romain Arnaud, Saint
See Aragon, Louis

Romains, Jules 1885-1972.......... **CLC 7**
See also CA 85-88; CANR 34; DLB 65;
MTCW

Romero, Jose Ruben 1890-1952... **TCLC 14**
See also CA 114; 131; HW

Ronsard, Pierre de
1524-1585.............. **LC 6; PC 11**

Rooke, Leon 1934-............ **CLC 25, 34**
See also CA 25-28R; CANR 23; DAM POP

Roper, William 1498-1578.......... **LC 10**

Roquelaure, A. N.
See Rice, Anne

Rosa, Joao Guimaraes 1908-1967... **CLC 23**
See also CA 89-92; DLB 113

Rose, Wendy 1948-......... **CLC 85; PC 13**
See also CA 53-56; CANR 5, 51;
DAM MULT; NNAL; SATA 12

Rosen, Richard (Dean) 1949-....... **CLC 39**
See also CA 77-80; INT CANR-30

Rosenberg, Isaac 1890-1918...... **TCLC 12**
See also CA 107; DLB 20

Rosenblatt, Joe................. **CLC 15**
See also Rosenblatt, Joseph

Rosenblatt, Joseph 1933-
See Rosenblatt, Joe
See also CA 89-92; INT 89-92

Rosenfeld, Samuel 1896-1963
See Tzara, Tristan
See also CA 89-92

Rosenthal, M(acha) L(ouis) 1917-... **CLC 28**
See also CA 1-4R; CAAS 6; CANR 4, 51;
DLB 5; SATA 59

Ross, Barnaby
See Dannay, Frederic

Ross, Bernard L.
See Follett, Ken(neth Martin)

Ross, J. H.
See Lawrence, T(homas) E(dward)

Ross, Martin
See Martin, Violet Florence
See also DLB 135

Ross, (James) Sinclair
1908-.................. **CLC 13; DAC**
See also CA 73-76; DAM MST; DLB 88

Rossetti, Christina (Georgina)
1830-1894..... **NCLC 2, 50; DA; DAB;
DAC; PC 7; WLC**
See also DAM MST, POET; DLB 35;
MAICYA; SATA 20

Rossetti, Dante Gabriel
1828-1882........ **NCLC 4; DA; DAB;
DAC; WLC**
See also CDBLB 1832-1890; DAM MST,
POET; DLB 35

Rossner, Judith (Perelman)
1935-.................... **CLC 6, 9, 29**
See also AITN 2; BEST 90:3; CA 17-20R;
CANR 18, 51; DLB 6; INT CANR-18;
MTCW

Rostand, Edmond (Eugene Alexis)
1868-1918...... **TCLC 6, 37; DA; DAB;
DAC**
See also CA 104; 126; DAM DRAM, MST;
MTCW

Roth, Henry 1906-1995....... **CLC 2, 6, 11**
See also CA 11-12; 149; CANR 38; CAP 1;
DLB 28; MTCW

Roth, Joseph 1894-1939.......... **TCLC 33**
See also DLB 85

Roth, Philip (Milton)
1933-...... **CLC 1, 2, 3, 4, 6, 9, 15, 22,
31, 47, 66, 86; DA; DAB; DAC; WLC**
See also BEST 90:3; CA 1-4R; CANR 1, 22,
36; CDALB 1968-1988; DAM MST,
NOV, POP; DLB 2, 28; DLBY 82;
MTCW

Rothenberg, Jerome 1931-....... **CLC 6, 57**
See also CA 45-48; CANR 1; DLB 5

Roumain, Jacques (Jean Baptiste)
1907-1944.............. **TCLC 19; BLC**
See also BW 1; CA 117; 125; DAM MULT

Rourke, Constance (Mayfield)
1885-1941................. **TCLC 12**
See also CA 107; YABC 1

Rousseau, Jean-Baptiste 1671-1741... **LC 9**

Rousseau, Jean-Jacques
1712-1778..... **LC 14; DA; DAB; DAC;
WLC**
See also DAM MST

Roussel, Raymond 1877-1933..... **TCLC 20**
See also CA 117

Rovit, Earl (Herbert) 1927-........ **CLC 7**
See also CA 5-8R; CANR 12

Rowe, Nicholas 1674-1718.......... **LC 8**
See also DLB 84

Rowley, Ames Dorrance
See Lovecraft, H(oward) P(hillips)

Rowson, Susanna Haswell
1762(?)-1824............... **NCLC 5**
See also DLB 37

Roy, Gabrielle
1909-1983..... **CLC 10, 14; DAB; DAC**
See also CA 53-56; 110; CANR 5;
DAM MST; DLB 68; MTCW

Rozewicz, Tadeusz 1921-........ **CLC 9, 23**
See also CA 108; CANR 36; DAM POET;
MTCW

Ruark, Gibbons 1941-............. **CLC 3**
See also CA 33-36R; CAAS 23; CANR 14,
31; DLB 120

Rubens, Bernice (Ruth) 1923-... **CLC 19, 31**
See also CA 25-28R; CANR 33; DLB 14;
MTCW

Rudkin, (James) David 1936-...... **CLC 14**
See also CA 89-92; DLB 13

Schwob, (Mayer Andre) Marcel
    1867-1905 .... TCLC 20
    See also CA 117; DLB 123

Sciascia, Leonardo
    1921-1989 .... CLC 8, 9, 41
    See also CA 85-88; 130; CANR 35; MTCW

Scoppettone, Sandra 1936-........ CLC 26
    See also AAYA 11; CA 5-8R; CANR 41;
    SATA 9

Scorsese, Martin 1942- .... CLC 20, 89
    See also CA 110; 114; CANR 46

Scotland, Jay
    See Jakes, John (William)

Scott, Duncan Campbell
    1862-1947 .... TCLC 6; DAC
    See also CA 104; DLB 92

Scott, Evelyn 1893-1963.......... CLC 43
    See also CA 104; 112; DLB 9, 48

Scott, F(rancis) R(eginald)
    1899-1985 .... CLC 22
    See also CA 101; 114; DLB 88; INT 101

Scott, Frank
    See Scott, F(rancis) R(eginald)

Scott, Joanna 1960- .... CLC 50
    See also CA 126

Scott, Paul (Mark) 1920-1978.... CLC 9, 60
    See also CA 81-84; 77-80; CANR 33;
    DLB 14; MTCW

Scott, Walter
    1771-1832 .... NCLC 15; DA; DAB;
                      DAC; PC 13; WLC
    See also CDBLB 1789-1832; DAM MST,
    NOV, POET; DLB 93, 107, 116, 144, 159;
    YABC 2

Scribe, (Augustin) Eugene
    1791-1861 .... NCLC 16; DC 5
    See also DAM DRAM

Scrum, R.
    See Crumb, R(obert)

Scudery, Madeleine de 1607-1701..... LC 2

Scum
    See Crumb, R(obert)

Scumbag, Little Bobby
    See Crumb, R(obert)

Seabrook, John
    See Hubbard, L(afayette) Ron(ald)

Sealy, I. Allan 1951- .... CLC 55

Search, Alexander
    See Pessoa, Fernando (Antonio Nogueira)

Sebastian, Lee
    See Silverberg, Robert

Sebastian Owl
    See Thompson, Hunter S(tockton)

Sebestyen, Ouida 1924-........... CLC 30
    See also AAYA 8; CA 107; CANR 40;
    CLR 17; JRDA; MAICYA; SAAS 10;
    SATA 39

Secundus, H. Scriblerus
    See Fielding, Henry

Sedges, John
    See Buck, Pearl S(ydenstricker)

Sedgwick, Catharine Maria
    1789-1867 .... NCLC 19
    See also DLB 1, 74

Seelye, John 1931-............... CLC 7

Seferiades, Giorgos Stylianou 1900-1971
    See Seferis, George
    See also CA 5-8R; 33-36R; CANR 5, 36;
    MTCW

Seferis, George .... CLC 5, 11
    See also Seferiades, Giorgos Stylianou

Segal, Erich (Wolf) 1937- .... CLC 3, 10
    See also BEST 89:1; CA 25-28R; CANR 20,
    36; DAM POP; DLBY 86;
    INT CANR-20; MTCW

Seger, Bob 1945-................. CLC 35

Seghers, Anna .... CLC 7
    See also Radvanyi, Netty
    See also DLB 69

Seidel, Frederick (Lewis) 1936-..... CLC 18
    See also CA 13-16R; CANR 8; DLBY 84

Seifert, Jaroslav 1901-1986..... CLC 34, 44
    See also CA 127; MTCW

Sei Shonagon c. 966-1017(?) ...... CMLC 6

Selby, Hubert, Jr.
    1928-......... CLC 1, 2, 4, 8; SSC 20
    See also CA 13-16R; CANR 33; DLB 2

Selzer, Richard 1928-............ CLC 74
    See also CA 65-68; CANR 14

Sembene, Ousmane
    See Ousmane, Sembene

Senancour, Etienne Pivert de
    1770-1846 .... NCLC 16
    See also DLB 119

Sender, Ramon (Jose)
    1902-1982 .... CLC 8; HLC
    See also CA 5-8R; 105; CANR 8;
    DAM MULT; HW; MTCW

Seneca, Lucius Annaeus
    4B.C.-65.............. CMLC 6; DC 5
    See also DAM DRAM

Senghor, Leopold Sedar
    1906-................. CLC 54; BLC
    See also BW 2; CA 116; 125; CANR 47;
    DAM MULT, POET; MTCW

Serling, (Edward) Rod(man)
    1924-1975 .... CLC 30
    See also AAYA 14; AITN 1; CA 65-68;
    57-60; DLB 26

Serna, Ramon Gomez de la
    See Gomez de la Serna, Ramon

Serpieres
    See Guillevic, (Eugene)

Service, Robert
    See Service, Robert W(illiam)
    See also DAB; DLB 92

Service, Robert W(illiam)
    1874(?)-1958 ...... TCLC 15; DA; DAC;
                       WLC
    See also Service, Robert
    See also CA 115; 140; DAM MST, POET;
    SATA 20

Seth, Vikram 1952-........... CLC 43, 90
    See also CA 121; 127; CANR 50;
    DAM MULT; DLB 120; INT 127

Seton, Cynthia Propper
    1926-1982 .... CLC 27
    See also CA 5-8R; 108; CANR 7

Seton, Ernest (Evan) Thompson
    1860-1946 .... TCLC 31
    See also CA 109; DLB 92; DLBD 13;
    JRDA; SATA 18

Seton-Thompson, Ernest
    See Seton, Ernest (Evan) Thompson

Settle, Mary Lee 1918- .... CLC 19, 61
    See also CA 89-92; CAAS 1; CANR 44;
    DLB 6; INT 89-92

Seuphor, Michel
    See Arp, Jean

Sevigne, Marie (de Rabutin-Chantal) Marquise
    de 1626-1696 .... LC 11

Sexton, Anne (Harvey)
    1928-1974 .... CLC 2, 4, 6, 8, 10, 15, 53;
                  DA; DAB; DAC; PC 2; WLC
    See also CA 1-4R; 53-56; CABS 2;
    CANR 3, 36; CDALB 1941-1968;
    DAM MST, POET; DLB 5; MTCW;
    SATA 10

Shaara, Michael (Joseph, Jr.)
    1929-1988 .... CLC 15
    See also AITN 1; CA 102; 125; DAM POP;
    DLBY 83

Shackleton, C. C.
    See Aldiss, Brian W(ilson)

Shacochis, Bob .... CLC 39
    See also Shacochis, Robert G.

Shacochis, Robert G. 1951-
    See Shacochis, Bob
    See also CA 119; 124; INT 124

Shaffer, Anthony (Joshua) 1926-.... CLC 19
    See also CA 110; 116; DAM DRAM;
    DLB 13

Shaffer, Peter (Levin)
    1926-...... CLC 5, 14, 18, 37, 60; DAB
    See also CA 25-28R; CANR 25, 47;
    CDBLB 1960 to Present; DAM DRAM,
    MST; DLB 13; MTCW

Shakey, Bernard
    See Young, Neil

Shalamov, Varlam (Tikhonovich)
    1907(?)-1982 .... CLC 18
    See also CA 129; 105

Shamlu, Ahmad 1925- .... CLC 10

Shammas, Anton 1951-............ CLC 55

Shange, Ntozake
    1948- .... CLC 8, 25, 38, 74; BLC; DC 3
    See also AAYA 9; BW 2; CA 85-88;
    CABS 3; CANR 27, 48; DAM DRAM,
    MULT; DLB 38; MTCW

Shanley, John Patrick 1950-....... CLC 75
    See also CA 128; 133

Shapcott, Thomas W(illiam) 1935- .. CLC 38
    See also CA 69-72; CANR 49

Shapiro, Jane...................... CLC 76

Shapiro, Karl (Jay) 1913- .. CLC 4, 8, 15, 53
    See also CA 1-4R; CAAS 6; CANR 1, 36;
    DLB 48; MTCW

Sharp, William 1855-1905 .... TCLC 39
    See also DLB 156

Sharpe, Thomas Ridley 1928-
    See Sharpe, Tom
    See also CA 114; 122; INT 122

Simic, Charles 1938-... **CLC 6, 9, 22, 49, 68**
See also CA 29-32R; CAAS 4; CANR 12,
33; DAM POET; DLB 105

Simmons, Charles (Paul) 1924-..... **CLC 57**
See also CA 89-92; INT 89-92

Simmons, Dan 1948-............. **CLC 44**
See also AAYA 16; CA 138; DAM POP

Simmons, James (Stewart Alexander)
1933-....................... **CLC 43**
See also CA 105; CAAS 21; DLB 40

Simms, William Gilmore
1806-1870 .... **NCLC 3**
See also DLB 3, 30, 59, 73

Simon, Carly 1945-............... **CLC 26**
See also CA 105

Simon, Claude 1913-...... **CLC 4, 9, 15, 39**
See also CA 89-92; CANR 33; DAM NOV;
DLB 83; MTCW

Simon, (Marvin) Neil
1927-.......... **CLC 6, 11, 31, 39, 70**
See also AITN 1; CA 21-24R; CANR 26;
DAM DRAM; DLB 7; MTCW

Simon, Paul 1942(?)-............. **CLC 17**
See also CA 116

Simonon, Paul 1956(?)-........... **CLC 30**

Simpson, Harriette
See Arnow, Harriette (Louisa) Simpson

Simpson, Louis (Aston Marantz)
1923-................. **CLC 4, 7, 9, 32**
See also CA 1-4R; CAAS 4; CANR 1;
DAM POET; DLB 5; MTCW

Simpson, Mona (Elizabeth) 1957-... **CLC 44**
See also CA 122; 135

Simpson, N(orman) F(rederick)
1919-..................... **CLC 29**
See also CA 13-16R; DLB 13

Sinclair, Andrew (Annandale)
1935-.................... **CLC 2, 14**
See also CA 9-12R; CAAS 5; CANR 14, 38;
DLB 14; MTCW

Sinclair, Emil
See Hesse, Hermann

Sinclair, Iain 1943-.............. **CLC 76**
See also CA 132

Sinclair, Iain MacGregor
See Sinclair, Iain

Sinclair, Mary Amelia St. Clair 1865(?)-1946
See Sinclair, May
See also CA 104

Sinclair, May.................. **TCLC 3, 11**
See also Sinclair, Mary Amelia St. Clair
See also DLB 36, 135

Sinclair, Upton (Beall)
1878-1968 ...... **CLC 1, 11, 15, 63; DA;
DAB; DAC; WLC**
See also CA 5-8R; 25-28R; CANR 7;
CDALB 1929-1941; DAM MST, NOV;
DLB 9; INT CANR-7; MTCW; SATA 9

Singer, Isaac
See Singer, Isaac Bashevis

Singer, Isaac Bashevis
1904-1991 .... **CLC 1, 3, 6, 9, 11, 15, 23,
38, 69; DA; DAB; DAC; SSC 3; WLC**
See also AITN 1, 2; CA 1-4R; 134;
CANR 1, 39; CDALB 1941-1968; CLR 1;
DAM MST, NOV; DLB 6, 28, 52;
DLBY 91; JRDA; MAICYA; MTCW;
SATA 3, 27; SATA-Obit 68

Singer, Israel Joshua 1893-1944 ... **TCLC 33**

Singh, Khushwant 1915-.......... **CLC 11**
See also CA 9-12R; CAAS 9; CANR 6

Sinjohn, John
See Galsworthy, John

Sinyavsky, Andrei (Donatevich)
1925-....................... **CLC 8**
See also CA 85-88

Sirin, V.
See Nabokov, Vladimir (Vladimirovich)

Sissman, L(ouis) E(dward)
1928-1976 .... **CLC 9, 18**
See also CA 21-24R; 65-68; CANR 13;
DLB 5

Sisson, C(harles) H(ubert) 1914-..... **CLC 8**
See also CA 1-4R; CAAS 3; CANR 3, 48;
DLB 27

Sitwell, Dame Edith
1887-1964 .... **CLC 2, 9, 67; PC 3**
See also CA 9-12R; CANR 35;
CDBLB 1945-1960; DAM POET;
DLB 20; MTCW

Sjoewall, Maj 1935-............... **CLC 7**
See also CA 65-68

Sjowall, Maj
See Sjoewall, Maj

Skelton, Robin 1925-............. **CLC 13**
See also AITN 2; CA 5-8R; CAAS 5;
CANR 28; DLB 27, 53

Skolimowski, Jerzy 1938-......... **CLC 20**
See also CA 128

Skram, Amalie (Bertha)
1847-1905 .... **TCLC 25**

Skvorecky, Josef (Vaclav)
1924-........... **CLC 15, 39, 69; DAC**
See also CA 61-64; CAAS 1; CANR 10, 34;
DAM NOV; MTCW

Slade, Bernard................. **CLC 11, 46**
See also Newbound, Bernard Slade
See also CAAS 9; DLB 53

Slaughter, Carolyn 1946-.......... **CLC 56**
See also CA 85-88

Slaughter, Frank G(ill) 1908- ...... **CLC 29**
See also AITN 2; CA 5-8R; CANR 5;
INT CANR-5

Slavitt, David R(ytman) 1935-.... **CLC 5, 14**
See also CA 21-24R; CAAS 3; CANR 41;
DLB 5, 6

Slesinger, Tess 1905-1945 .... **TCLC 10**
See also CA 107; DLB 102

Slessor, Kenneth 1901-1971........ **CLC 14**
See also CA 102; 89-92

Slowacki, Juliusz 1809-1849 ..... **NCLC 15**

Smart, Christopher
1722-1771 .... **LC 3; PC 13**
See also DAM POET; DLB 109

Smart, Elizabeth 1913-1986........ **CLC 54**
See also CA 81-84; 118; DLB 88

Smiley, Jane (Graves) 1949- .... **CLC 53, 76**
See also CA 104; CANR 30, 50;
DAM POP; INT CANR-30

Smith, A(rthur) J(ames) M(arshall)
1902-1980 .... **CLC 15; DAC**
See also CA 1-4R; 102; CANR 4; DLB 88

Smith, Anna Deavere 1950-........ **CLC 86**
See also CA 133

Smith, Betty (Wehner) 1896-1972... **CLC 19**
See also CA 5-8R; 33-36R; DLBY 82;
SATA 6

Smith, Charlotte (Turner)
1749-1806 .... **NCLC 23**
See also DLB 39, 109

Smith, Clark Ashton 1893-1961 .... **CLC 43**
See also CA 143

Smith, Dave................... **CLC 22, 42**
See also Smith, David (Jeddie)
See also CAAS 7; DLB 5

Smith, David (Jeddie) 1942-
See Smith, Dave
See also CA 49-52; CANR 1; DAM POET

Smith, Florence Margaret 1902-1971
See Smith, Stevie
See also CA 17-18; 29-32R; CANR 35;
CAP 2; DAM POET; MTCW

Smith, Iain Crichton 1928- .... **CLC 64**
See also CA 21-24R; DLB 40, 139

Smith, John 1580(?)-1631 .... **LC 9**

Smith, Johnston
See Crane, Stephen (Townley)

Smith, Joseph, Jr. 1805-1844 .... **NCLC 53**

Smith, Lee 1944-.............. **CLC 25, 73**
See also CA 114; 119; CANR 46; DLB 143;
DLBY 83; INT 119

Smith, Martin
See Smith, Martin Cruz

Smith, Martin Cruz 1942-.......... **CLC 25**
See also BEST 89:4; CA 85-88; CANR 6,
23, 43; DAM MULT, POP;
INT CANR-23; NNAL

Smith, Mary-Ann Tirone 1944-..... **CLC 39**
See also CA 118; 136

Smith, Patti 1946-............... **CLC 12**
See also CA 93-96

Smith, Pauline (Urmson)
1882-1959 .... **TCLC 25**

Smith, Rosamond
See Oates, Joyce Carol

Smith, Sheila Kaye
See Kaye-Smith, Sheila

Smith, Stevie .... **CLC 3, 8, 25, 44; PC 12**
See also Smith, Florence Margaret
See also DLB 20

Smith, Wilbur (Addison) 1933-..... **CLC 33**
See also CA 13-16R; CANR 7, 46; MTCW

Smith, William Jay 1918-.......... **CLC 6**
See also CA 5-8R; CANR 44; DLB 5;
MAICYA; SAAS 22; SATA 2, 68

Smith, Woodrow Wilson
See Kuttner, Henry

Smolenskin, Peretz 1842-1885.... **NCLC 30**

Smollett, Tobias (George) 1721-1771 .. **LC 2**
See also CDBLB 1660-1789; DLB 39, 104

Snodgrass, W(illiam) D(e Witt)
1926- .... **CLC 2, 6, 10, 18, 68**
See also CA 1-4R; CANR 6, 36;
DAM POET; DLB 5; MTCW

Snow, C(harles) P(ercy)
1905-1980 .... **CLC 1, 4, 6, 9, 13, 19**
See also CA 5-8R; 101; CANR 28;
CDBLB 1945-1960; DAM NOV; DLB 15,
77; MTCW

Snow, Frances Compton
See Adams, Henry (Brooks)

Snyder, Gary (Sherman)
1930- .... **CLC 1, 2, 5, 9, 32**
See also CA 17-20R; CANR 30;
DAM POET; DLB 5, 16

Snyder, Zilpha Keatley 1927- ...... **CLC 17**
See also AAYA 15; CA 9-12R; CANR 38;
CLR 31; JRDA; MAICYA; SAAS 2;
SATA 1, 28, 75

Soares, Bernardo
See Pessoa, Fernando (Antonio Nogueira)

Sobh, A.
See Shamlu, Ahmad

Sobol, Joshua .... **CLC 60**

Soderberg, Hjalmar 1869-1941 .... **TCLC 39**

Sodergran, Edith (Irene)
See Soedergran, Edith (Irene)

Soedergran, Edith (Irene)
1892-1923 .... **TCLC 31**

Softly, Edgar
See Lovecraft, H(oward) P(hillips)

Softly, Edward
See Lovecraft, H(oward) P(hillips)

Sokolov, Raymond 1941- .... **CLC 7**
See also CA 85-88

Solo, Jay
See Ellison, Harlan (Jay)

Sologub, Fyodor .... **TCLC 9**
See also Teternikov, Fyodor Kuzmich

Solomons, Ikey Esquir
See Thackeray, William Makepeace

Solomos, Dionysios 1798-1857 ... **NCLC 15**

Solwoska, Mara
See French, Marilyn

Solzhenitsyn, Aleksandr I(sayevich)
1918- ...... **CLC 1, 2, 4, 7, 9, 10, 18, 26,**
34, 78; DA; DAB; DAC; WLC
See also AITN 1; CA 69-72; CANR 40;
DAM MST, NOV; MTCW

Somers, Jane
See Lessing, Doris (May)

Somerville, Edith 1858-1949 ...... **TCLC 51**
See also DLB 135

Somerville & Ross
See Martin, Violet Florence; Somerville,
Edith

Sommer, Scott 1951- .... **CLC 25**
See also CA 106

Sondheim, Stephen (Joshua)
1930- .... **CLC 30, 39**
See also AAYA 11; CA 103; CANR 47;
DAM DRAM

Sontag, Susan 1933-... **CLC 1, 2, 10, 13, 31**
See also CA 17-20R; CANR 25, 51;
DAM POP; DLB 2, 67; MTCW

Sophocles
496(?)B.C.-406(?)B.C. .... **CMLC 2; DA;**
DAB; DAC; DC 1
See also DAM DRAM, MST

Sordello 1189-1269 .... **CMLC 15**

Sorel, Julia
See Drexler, Rosalyn

Sorrentino, Gilbert
1929- .... **CLC 3, 7, 14, 22, 40**
See also CA 77-80; CANR 14, 33; DLB 5;
DLBY 80; INT CANR-14

Soto, Gary 1952-........ **CLC 32, 80; HLC**
See also AAYA 10; CA 119; 125;
CANR 50; CLR 38; DAM MULT;
DLB 82; HW; INT 125; JRDA; SATA 80

Soupault, Philippe 1897-1990 ...... **CLC 68**
See also CA 116; 147; 131

Souster, (Holmes) Raymond
1921- .... **CLC 5, 14; DAC**
See also CA 13-16R; CAAS 14; CANR 13,
29; DAM POET; DLB 88; SATA 63

Southern, Terry 1924(?)-1995 .... **CLC 7**
See also CA 1-4R; 150; CANR 1; DLB 2

Southey, Robert 1774-1843 .... **NCLC 8**
See also DLB 93, 107, 142; SATA 54

Southworth, Emma Dorothy Eliza Nevitte
1819-1899 .... **NCLC 26**

Souza, Ernest
See Scott, Evelyn

Soyinka, Wole
1934- .... **CLC 3, 5, 14, 36, 44; BLC;**
DA; DAB; DAC; DC 2; WLC
See also BW 2; CA 13-16R; CANR 27, 39;
DAM DRAM, MST, MULT; DLB 125;
MTCW

Spackman, W(illiam) M(ode)
1905-1990 .... **CLC 46**
See also CA 81-84; 132

Spacks, Barry 1931-............... **CLC 14**
See also CA 29-32R; CANR 33; DLB 105

Spanidou, Irini 1946- .... **CLC 44**

Spark, Muriel (Sarah)
1918- .... **CLC 2, 3, 5, 8, 13, 18, 40;**
DAB; DAC; SSC 10
See also CA 5-8R; CANR 12, 36;
CDBLB 1945-1960; DAM MST, NOV;
DLB 15, 139; INT CANR-12; MTCW

Spaulding, Douglas
See Bradbury, Ray (Douglas)

Spaulding, Leonard
See Bradbury, Ray (Douglas)

Spence, J. A. D.
See Eliot, T(homas) S(tearns)

Spencer, Elizabeth 1921- .... **CLC 22**
See also CA 13-16R; CANR 32; DLB 6;
MTCW; SATA 14

Spencer, Leonard G.
See Silverberg, Robert

Spencer, Scott 1945-............. **CLC 30**
See also CA 113; CANR 51; DLBY 86

Spender, Stephen (Harold)
1909-1995 ...... **CLC 1, 2, 5, 10, 41, 91**
See also CA 9-12R; 149; CANR 31;
CDBLB 1945-1960; DAM POET;
DLB 20; MTCW

Spengler, Oswald (Arnold Gottfried)
1880-1936 .... **TCLC 25**
See also CA 118

Spenser, Edmund
1552(?)-1599 .... **LC 5; DA; DAB; DAC;**
PC 8; WLC
See also CDBLB Before 1660; DAM MST,
POET

Spicer, Jack 1925-1965 ...... **CLC 8, 18, 72**
See also CA 85-88; DAM POET; DLB 5, 16

Spiegelman, Art 1948- .... **CLC 76**
See also AAYA 10; CA 125; CANR 41

Spielberg, Peter 1929- .... **CLC 6**
See also CA 5-8R; CANR 4, 48; DLBY 81

Spielberg, Steven 1947- .... **CLC 20**
See also AAYA 8; CA 77-80; CANR 32;
SATA 32

Spillane, Frank Morrison 1918-
See Spillane, Mickey
See also CA 25-28R; CANR 28; MTCW;
SATA 66

Spillane, Mickey .... **CLC 3, 13**
See also Spillane, Frank Morrison

Spinoza, Benedictus de 1632-1677 .... **LC 9**

Spinrad, Norman (Richard) 1940-... **CLC 46**
See also CA 37-40R; CAAS 19; CANR 20;
DLB 8; INT CANR-20

Spitteler, Carl (Friedrich Georg)
1845-1924 .... **TCLC 12**
See also CA 109; DLB 129

Spivack, Kathleen (Romola Drucker)
1938- .... **CLC 6**
See also CA 49-52

Spoto, Donald 1941-.............. **CLC 39**
See also CA 65-68; CANR 11

Springsteen, Bruce (F.) 1949- ...... **CLC 17**
See also CA 111

Spurling, Hilary 1940-............. **CLC 34**
See also CA 104; CANR 25

Spyker, John Howland
See Elman, Richard

Squires, (James) Radcliffe
1917-1993 .... **CLC 51**
See also CA 1-4R; 140; CANR 6, 21

Srivastava, Dhanpat Rai 1880(?)-1936
See Premchand
See also CA 118

Stacy, Donald
See Pohl, Frederik

Stael, Germaine de
See Stael-Holstein, Anne Louise Germaine
Necker Baronn
See also DLB 119

Stael-Holstein, Anne Louise Germaine Necker
Baronn 1766-1817 .... **NCLC 3**
See also Stael, Germaine de

Stafford, Jean 1915-1979 ... **CLC 4, 7, 19, 68**
See also CA 1-4R; 85-88; CANR 3; DLB 2;
MTCW; SATA-Obit 22

Stafford, William (Edgar)
1914-1993 . . . . **CLC 4, 7, 29**
See also CA 5-8R; 142; CAAS 3; CANR 5,
22; DAM POET; DLB 5; INT CANR-22

Staines, Trevor
See Brunner, John (Kilian Houston)

Stairs, Gordon
See Austin, Mary (Hunter)

Stannard, Martin 1947- . . . . **CLC 44**
See also CA 142; DLB 155

Stanton, Maura 1946- . . . . **CLC 9**
See also CA 89-92; CANR 15; DLB 120

Stanton, Schuyler
See Baum, L(yman) Frank

Stapledon, (William) Olaf
1886-1950 . . . . **TCLC 22**
See also CA 111; DLB 15

Starbuck, George (Edwin) 1931- . . . . **CLC 53**
See also CA 21-24R; CANR 23;
DAM POET

Stark, Richard
See Westlake, Donald E(dwin)

Staunton, Schuyler
See Baum, L(yman) Frank

Stead, Christina (Ellen)
1902-1983 . . . . **CLC 2, 5, 8, 32, 80**
See also CA 13-16R; 109; CANR 33, 40;
MTCW

Stead, William Thomas
1849-1912 . . . . **TCLC 48**

Steele, Richard 1672-1729 . . . . **LC 18**
See also CDBLB 1660-1789; DLB 84, 101

Steele, Timothy (Reid) 1948- . . . . . . **CLC 45**
See also CA 93-96; CANR 16, 50; DLB 120

Steffens, (Joseph) Lincoln
1866-1936 . . . . **TCLC 20**
See also CA 117

Stegner, Wallace (Earle)
1909-1993 . . . . **CLC 9, 49, 81**
See also AITN 1; BEST 90:3; CA 1-4R;
141; CAAS 9; CANR 1, 21, 46;
DAM NOV; DLB 9; DLBY 93; MTCW

Stein, Gertrude
1874-1946 . . . . . . **TCLC 1, 6, 28, 48; DA;
DAB; DAC; WLC**
See also CA 104; 132; CDALB 1917-1929;
DAM MST, NOV, POET; DLB 4, 54, 86;
MTCW

Steinbeck, John (Ernst)
1902-1968 . . . . . . **CLC 1, 5, 9, 13, 21, 34,
45, 75; DA; DAB; DAC; SSC 11; WLC**
See also AAYA 12; CA 1-4R; 25-28R;
CANR 1, 35; CDALB 1929-1941;
DAM DRAM, MST, NOV; DLB 7, 9;
DLBD 2; MTCW; SATA 9

Steinem, Gloria 1934- . . . . **CLC 63**
See also CA 53-56; CANR 28, 51; MTCW

Steiner, George 1929- . . . . **CLC 24**
See also CA 73-76; CANR 31; DAM NOV;
DLB 67; MTCW; SATA 62

Steiner, K. Leslie
See Delany, Samuel R(ay, Jr.)

Steiner, Rudolf 1861-1925 . . . . **TCLC 13**
See also CA 107

Stendhal
1783-1842 . . . . **NCLC 23, 46; DA; DAB;
DAC; WLC**
See also DAM MST, NOV; DLB 119

Stephen, Leslie 1832-1904 . . . . **TCLC 23**
See also CA 123; DLB 57, 144

Stephen, Sir Leslie
See Stephen, Leslie

Stephen, Virginia
See Woolf, (Adeline) Virginia

Stephens, James 1882(?)-1950 . . . . . . **TCLC 4**
See also CA 104; DLB 19, 153, 162

Stephens, Reed
See Donaldson, Stephen R.

Steptoe, Lydia
See Barnes, Djuna

Sterchi, Beat 1949- . . . . **CLC 65**

Sterling, Brett
See Bradbury, Ray (Douglas); Hamilton,
Edmond

Sterling, Bruce 1954- . . . . **CLC 72**
See also CA 119; CANR 44

Sterling, George 1869-1926 . . . . **TCLC 20**
See also CA 117; DLB 54

Stern, Gerald 1925- . . . . **CLC 40**
See also CA 81-84; CANR 28; DLB 105

Stern, Richard (Gustave) 1928- . . . **CLC 4, 39**
See also CA 1-4R; CANR 1, 25; DLBY 87;
INT CANR-25

Sternberg, Josef von 1894-1969 . . . . . **CLC 20**
See also CA 81-84

Sterne, Laurence
1713-1768 . . . . . . **LC 2; DA; DAB; DAC;
WLC**
See also CDBLB 1660-1789; DAM MST,
NOV; DLB 39

Sternheim, (William Adolf) Carl
1878-1942 . . . . **TCLC 8**
See also CA 105; DLB 56, 118

Stevens, Mark 1951- . . . . **CLC 34**
See also CA 122

Stevens, Wallace
1879-1955 . . . . **TCLC 3, 12, 45; DA;
DAB; DAC; PC 6; WLC**
See also CA 104; 124; CDALB 1929-1941;
DAM MST, POET; DLB 54; MTCW

Stevenson, Anne (Katharine)
1933- . . . . **CLC 7, 33**
See also CA 17-20R; CAAS 9; CANR 9, 33;
DLB 40; MTCW

Stevenson, Robert Louis (Balfour)
1850-1894 . . . . . **NCLC 5, 14; DA; DAB;
DAC; SSC 11; WLC**
See also CDBLB 1890-1914; CLR 10, 11;
DAM MST, NOV; DLB 18, 57, 141, 156;
DLBD 13; JRDA; MAICYA; YABC 2

Stewart, J(ohn) I(nnes) M(ackintosh)
1906-1994 . . . . **CLC 7, 14, 32**
See also CA 85-88; 147; CAAS 3;
CANR 47; MTCW

Stewart, Mary (Florence Elinor)
1916- . . . . **CLC 7, 35; DAB**
See also CA 1-4R; CANR 1; SATA 12

Stewart, Mary Rainbow
See Stewart, Mary (Florence Elinor)

Stifle, June
See Campbell, Maria

Stifter, Adalbert 1805-1868 . . . . . . **NCLC 41**
See also DLB 133

Still, James 1906- . . . . **CLC 49**
See also CA 65-68; CAAS 17; CANR 10,
26; DLB 9; SATA 29

Sting
See Sumner, Gordon Matthew

Stirling, Arthur
See Sinclair, Upton (Beall)

Stitt, Milan 1941- . . . . **CLC 29**
See also CA 69-72

Stockton, Francis Richard 1834-1902
See Stockton, Frank R.
See also CA 108; 137; MAICYA; SATA 44

Stockton, Frank R. . . . . **TCLC 47**
See also Stockton, Francis Richard
See also DLB 42, 74; DLBD 13;
SATA-Brief 32

Stoddard, Charles
See Kuttner, Henry

Stoker, Abraham 1847-1912
See Stoker, Bram
See also CA 105; DA; DAC; DAM MST,
NOV; SATA 29

Stoker, Bram
1847-1912 . . . . **TCLC 8; DAB; WLC**
See also Stoker, Abraham
See also CA 150; CDBLB 1890-1914;
DLB 36, 70

Stolz, Mary (Slattery) 1920- . . . . **CLC 12**
See also AAYA 8; AITN 1; CA 5-8R;
CANR 13, 41; JRDA; MAICYA;
SAAS 3; SATA 10, 71

Stone, Irving 1903-1989 . . . . **CLC 7**
See also AITN 1; CA 1-4R; 129; CAAS 3;
CANR 1, 23; DAM POP;
INT CANR-23; MTCW; SATA 3;
SATA-Obit 64

Stone, Oliver 1946- . . . . **CLC 73**
See also AAYA 15; CA 110

Stone, Robert (Anthony)
1937- . . . . **CLC 5, 23, 42**
See also CA 85-88; CANR 23; DLB 152;
INT CANR-23; MTCW

Stone, Zachary
See Follett, Ken(neth Martin)

Stoppard, Tom
1937- . . . . . . **CLC 1, 3, 4, 5, 8, 15, 29, 34,
63, 91; DA; DAB; DAC; DC 6; WLC**
See also CA 81-84; CANR 39;
CDBLB 1960 to Present; DAM DRAM,
MST; DLB 13; DLBY 85; MTCW

Storey, David (Malcolm)
1933- . . . . **CLC 2, 4, 5, 8**
See also CA 81-84; CANR 36;
DAM DRAM; DLB 13, 14; MTCW

Storm, Hyemeyohsts 1935- . . . . **CLC 3**
See also CA 81-84; CANR 45;
DAM MULT; NNAL

Storm, (Hans) Theodor (Woldsen)
1817-1888 . . . . **NCLC 1**

Storni, Alfonsina
1892-1938 . . . . **TCLC 5; HLC**
See also CA 104; 131; DAM MULT; HW

Stout, Rex (Todhunter) 1886-1975 . . . **CLC 3**
See also AITN 2; CA 61-64

Stow, (Julian) Randolph 1935- .. **CLC 23, 48**
See also CA 13-16R; CANR 33; MTCW

Stowe, Harriet (Elizabeth) Beecher
1811-1896 . . . . . **NCLC 3, 50; DA; DAB;
DAC; WLC**
See also CDALB 1865-1917; DAM MST,
NOV; DLB 1, 12, 42, 74; JRDA;
MAICYA; YABC 1

Strachey, (Giles) Lytton
1880-1932 . . . . **TCLC 12**
See also CA 110; DLB 149; DLBD 10

Strand, Mark 1934- . . . . . . **CLC 6, 18, 41, 71**
See also CA 21-24R; CANR 40;
DAM POET; DLB 5; SATA 41

Straub, Peter (Francis) 1943- . . . . . . **CLC 28**
See also BEST 89:1; CA 85-88; CANR 28;
DAM POP; DLBY 84; MTCW

Strauss, Botho 1944- . . . . **CLC 22**
See also DLB 124

Streatfeild, (Mary) Noel
1895(?)-1986 . . . . **CLC 21**
See also CA 81-84; 120; CANR 31;
CLR 17; DLB 160; MAICYA; SATA 20;
SATA-Obit 48

Stribling, T(homas) S(igismund)
1881-1965 . . . . **CLC 23**
See also CA 107; DLB 9

Strindberg, (Johan) August
1849-1912 . . . . . . **TCLC 1, 8, 21, 47; DA;
DAB; DAC; WLC**
See also CA 104; 135; DAM DRAM, MST

Stringer, Arthur 1874-1950 . . . . **TCLC 37**
See also DLB 92

Stringer, David
See Roberts, Keith (John Kingston)

Strugatskii, Arkadii (Natanovich)
1925-1991 . . . . **CLC 27**
See also CA 106; 135

Strugatskii, Boris (Natanovich)
1933- . . . . **CLC 27**
See also CA 106

Strummer, Joe 1953(?)- . . . . **CLC 30**

Stuart, Don A.
See Campbell, John W(ood, Jr.)

Stuart, Ian
See MacLean, Alistair (Stuart)

Stuart, Jesse (Hilton)
1906-1984 . . . . **CLC 1, 8, 11, 14, 34**
See also CA 5-8R; 112; CANR 31; DLB 9,
48, 102; DLBY 84; SATA 2;
SATA-Obit 36

Sturgeon, Theodore (Hamilton)
1918-1985 . . . . **CLC 22, 39**
See also Queen, Ellery
See also CA 81-84; 116; CANR 32; DLB 8;
DLBY 85; MTCW

Sturges, Preston 1898-1959 . . . . **TCLC 48**
See also CA 114; 149; DLB 26

Styron, William
1925- . . . . **CLC 1, 3, 5, 11, 15, 60**
See also BEST 90:4; CA 5-8R; CANR 6, 33;
CDALB 1968-1988; DAM NOV, POP;
DLB 2, 143; DLBY 80; INT CANR-6;
MTCW

Suarez Lynch, B.
See Bioy Casares, Adolfo; Borges, Jorge
Luis

Su Chien 1884-1918
See Su Man-shu
See also CA 123

Suckow, Ruth 1892-1960 . . . . **SSC 18**
See also CA 113; DLB 9, 102

Sudermann, Hermann 1857-1928 . . **TCLC 15**
See also CA 107; DLB 118

Sue, Eugene 1804-1857 . . . . **NCLC 1**
See also DLB 119

Sueskind, Patrick 1949- . . . . **CLC 44**
See also Suskind, Patrick

Sukenick, Ronald 1932- . . . . . **CLC 3, 4, 6, 48**
See also CA 25-28R; CAAS 8; CANR 32;
DLBY 81

Suknaski, Andrew 1942- . . . . **CLC 19**
See also CA 101; DLB 53

Sullivan, Vernon
See Vian, Boris

Sully Prudhomme 1839-1907 . . . . . **TCLC 31**

Su Man-shu . . . . **TCLC 24**
See also Su Chien

Summerforest, Ivy B.
See Kirkup, James

Summers, Andrew James 1942- . . . . . **CLC 26**

Summers, Andy
See Summers, Andrew James

Summers, Hollis (Spurgeon, Jr.)
1916- . . . . **CLC 10**
See also CA 5-8R; CANR 3; DLB 6

Summers, (Alphonsus Joseph-Mary Augustus)
Montague 1880-1948 . . . . **TCLC 16**
See also CA 118

Sumner, Gordon Matthew 1951- . . . . **CLC 26**

Surtees, Robert Smith
1803-1864 . . . . **NCLC 14**
See also DLB 21

Susann, Jacqueline 1921-1974 . . . . . . **CLC 3**
See also AITN 1; CA 65-68; 53-56; MTCW

Su Shih 1036-1101 . . . . **CMLC 15**

Suskind, Patrick
See Sueskind, Patrick
See also CA 145

Sutcliff, Rosemary
1920-1992 . . . . **CLC 26; DAB; DAC**
See also AAYA 10; CA 5-8R; 139;
CANR 37; CLR 1, 37; DAM MST, POP;
JRDA; MAICYA; SATA 6, 44, 78;
SATA-Obit 73

Sutro, Alfred 1863-1933 . . . . **TCLC 6**
See also CA 105; DLB 10

Sutton, Henry
See Slavitt, David R(ytman)

Svevo, Italo . . . . **TCLC 2, 35**
See also Schmitz, Aron Hector

Swados, Elizabeth (A.) 1951- . . . . **CLC 12**
See also CA 97-100; CANR 49; INT 97-100

Swados, Harvey 1920-1972 . . . . **CLC 5**
See also CA 5-8R; 37-40R; CANR 6;
DLB 2

Swan, Gladys 1934- . . . . **CLC 69**
See also CA 101; CANR 17, 39

Swarthout, Glendon (Fred)
1918-1992 . . . . **CLC 35**
See also CA 1-4R; 139; CANR 1, 47;
SATA 26

Sweet, Sarah C.
See Jewett, (Theodora) Sarah Orne

Swenson, May
1919-1989 . . . . **CLC 4, 14, 61; DA; DAB;
DAC; PC 14**
See also CA 5-8R; 130; CANR 36;
DAM MST, POET; DLB 5; MTCW;
SATA 15

Swift, Augustus
See Lovecraft, H(oward) P(hillips)

Swift, Graham (Colin) 1949- . . . . **CLC 41, 88**
See also CA 117; 122; CANR 46

Swift, Jonathan
1667-1745 . . . . . . **LC 1; DA; DAB; DAC;
PC 9; WLC**
See also CDBLB 1660-1789; DAM MST,
NOV, POET; DLB 39, 95, 101; SATA 19

Swinburne, Algernon Charles
1837-1909 . . . . . . **TCLC 8, 36; DA; DAB;
DAC; WLC**
See also CA 105; 140; CDBLB 1832-1890;
DAM MST, POET; DLB 35, 57

Swinfen, Ann . . . . **CLC 34**

Swinnerton, Frank Arthur
1884-1982 . . . . **CLC 31**
See also CA 108; DLB 34

Swithen, John
See King, Stephen (Edwin)

Sylvia
See Ashton-Warner, Sylvia (Constance)

Symmes, Robert Edward
See Duncan, Robert (Edward)

Symonds, John Addington
1840-1893 . . . . **NCLC 34**
See also DLB 57, 144

Symons, Arthur 1865-1945 . . . . **TCLC 11**
See also CA 107; DLB 19, 57, 149

Symons, Julian (Gustave)
1912-1994 . . . . **CLC 2, 14, 32**
See also CA 49-52; 147; CAAS 3; CANR 3,
33; DLB 87, 155; DLBY 92; MTCW

Synge, (Edmund) J(ohn) M(illington)
1871-1909 . . . . **TCLC 6, 37; DC 2**
See also CA 104; 141; CDBLB 1890-1914;
DAM DRAM; DLB 10, 19

Syruc, J.
See Milosz, Czeslaw

Szirtes, George 1948- . . . . **CLC 46**
See also CA 109; CANR 27

Tabori, George 1914- . . . . **CLC 19**
See also CA 49-52; CANR 4

Tagore, Rabindranath
1861-1941 . . . . **TCLC 3, 53; PC 8**
See also CA 104; 120; DAM DRAM,
POET; MTCW

Taine, Hippolyte Adolphe
1828-1893 . . . . **NCLC 15**

Talese, Gay 1932-............... **CLC 37**
  See also AITN 1; CA 1-4R; CANR 9;
   INT CANR-9; MTCW

Tallent, Elizabeth (Ann) 1954- ..... **CLC 45**
  See also CA 117; DLB 130

Tally, Ted 1952-................. **CLC 42**
  See also CA 120; 124; INT 124

Tamayo y Baus, Manuel
  1829-1898 .... **NCLC 1**

Tammsaare, A(nton) H(ansen)
  1878-1940 .... **TCLC 27**

Tan, Amy 1952- .... **CLC 59**
  See also AAYA 9; BEST 89:3; CA 136;
   DAM MULT, NOV, POP; SATA 75

Tandem, Felix
  See Spitteler, Carl (Friedrich Georg)

Tanizaki, Jun'ichiro
  1886-1965 ...... **CLC 8, 14, 28; SSC 21**
  See also CA 93-96; 25-28R

Tanner, William
  See Amis, Kingsley (William)

Tao Lao
  See Storni, Alfonsina

Tarassoff, Lev
  See Troyat, Henri

Tarbell, Ida M(inerva)
  1857-1944 .... **TCLC 40**
  See also CA 122; DLB 47

Tarkington, (Newton) Booth
  1869-1946 .... **TCLC 9**
  See also CA 110; 143; DLB 9, 102;
   SATA 17

Tarkovsky, Andrei (Arsenyevich)
  1932-1986 .... **CLC 75**
  See also CA 127

Tartt, Donna 1964(?)-............. **CLC 76**
  See also CA 142

Tasso, Torquato 1544-1595 .... **LC 5**

Tate, (John Orley) Allen
  1899-1979 .... **CLC 2, 4, 6, 9, 11, 14, 24**
  See also CA 5-8R; 85-88; CANR 32;
   DLB 4, 45, 63; MTCW

Tate, Ellalice
  See Hibbert, Eleanor Alice Burford

Tate, James (Vincent) 1943-... **CLC 2, 6, 25**
  See also CA 21-24R; CANR 29; DLB 5

Tavel, Ronald 1940-............... **CLC 6**
  See also CA 21-24R; CANR 33

Taylor, C(ecil) P(hilip) 1929-1981... **CLC 27**
  See also CA 25-28R; 105; CANR 47

Taylor, Edward
  1642(?)-1729 ... **LC 11; DA; DAB; DAC**
  See also DAM MST, POET; DLB 24

Taylor, Eleanor Ross 1920-......... **CLC 5**
  See also CA 81-84

Taylor, Elizabeth 1912-1975 ... **CLC 2, 4, 29**
  See also CA 13-16R; CANR 9; DLB 139;
   MTCW; SATA 13

Taylor, Henry (Splawn) 1942-...... **CLC 44**
  See also CA 33-36R; CAAS 7; CANR 31;
   DLB 5

Taylor, Kamala (Purnaiya) 1924-
  See Markandaya, Kamala
  See also CA 77-80

Taylor, Mildred D. .... **CLC 21**
  See also AAYA 10; BW 1; CA 85-88;
   CANR 25; CLR 9; DLB 52; JRDA;
   MAICYA; SAAS 5; SATA 15, 70

Taylor, Peter (Hillsman)
  1917-1994 ..... **CLC 1, 4, 18, 37, 44, 50,**
                 71; SSC 10
  See also CA 13-16R; 147; CANR 9, 50;
   DLBY 81, 94; INT CANR-9; MTCW

Taylor, Robert Lewis 1912-....... **CLC 14**
  See also CA 1-4R; CANR 3; SATA 10

Tchekhov, Anton
  See Chekhov, Anton (Pavlovich)

Teasdale, Sara 1884-1933......... **TCLC 4**
  See also CA 104; DLB 45; SATA 32

Tegner, Esaias 1782-1846........ **NCLC 2**

Teilhard de Chardin, (Marie Joseph) Pierre
  1881-1955 .... **TCLC 9**
  See also CA 105

Temple, Ann
  See Mortimer, Penelope (Ruth)

Tennant, Emma (Christina)
  1937- .... **CLC 13, 52**
  See also CA 65-68; CAAS 9; CANR 10, 38;
   DLB 14

Tenneshaw, S. M.
  See Silverberg, Robert

Tennyson, Alfred
  1809-1892 .... **NCLC 30; DA; DAB;**
               DAC; PC 6; WLC
  See also CDBLB 1832-1890; DAM MST,
   POET; DLB 32

Teran, Lisa St. Aubin de .... **CLC 36**
  See also St. Aubin de Teran, Lisa

Terence 195(?)B.C.-159B.C...... **CMLC 14**

Teresa de Jesus, St. 1515-1582...... **LC 18**

Terkel, Louis 1912-
  See Terkel, Studs
  See also CA 57-60; CANR 18, 45; MTCW

Terkel, Studs .... **CLC 38**
  See also Terkel, Louis
  See also AITN 1

Terry, C. V.
  See Slaughter, Frank G(ill)

Terry, Megan 1932-.............. **CLC 19**
  See also CA 77-80; CABS 3; CANR 43;
   DLB 7

Tertz, Abram
  See Sinyavsky, Andrei (Donatevich)

Tesich, Steve 1943(?)-.......... **CLC 40, 69**
  See also CA 105; DLBY 83

Teternikov, Fyodor Kuzmich 1863-1927
  See Sologub, Fyodor
  See also CA 104

Tevis, Walter 1928-1984 .... **CLC 42**
  See also CA 113

Tey, Josephine................... **TCLC 14**
  See also Mackintosh, Elizabeth
  See also DLB 77

Thackeray, William Makepeace
  1811-1863 .... **NCLC 5, 14, 22, 43; DA;**
              DAB; DAC; WLC
  See also CDBLB 1832-1890; DAM MST,
   NOV; DLB 21, 55, 159; SATA 23

Thakura, Ravindranatha
  See Tagore, Rabindranath

Tharoor, Shashi 1956-............ **CLC 70**
  See also CA 141

Thelwell, Michael Miles 1939-..... **CLC 22**
  See also BW 2; CA 101

Theobald, Lewis, Jr.
  See Lovecraft, H(oward) P(hillips)

Theodorescu, Ion N. 1880-1967
  See Arghezi, Tudor
  See also CA 116

Theriault, Yves 1915-1983.... **CLC 79; DAC**
  See also CA 102; DAM MST; DLB 88

Theroux, Alexander (Louis)
  1939-..................... **CLC 2, 25**
  See also CA 85-88; CANR 20

Theroux, Paul (Edward)
  1941- .... **CLC 5, 8, 11, 15, 28, 46**
  See also BEST 89:4; CA 33-36R; CANR 20,
   45; DAM POP; DLB 2; MTCW;
   SATA 44

Thesen, Sharon 1946-............. **CLC 56**

Thevenin, Denis
  See Duhamel, Georges

Thibault, Jacques Anatole Francois
  1844-1924
  See France, Anatole
  See also CA 106; 127; DAM NOV; MTCW

Thiele, Colin (Milton) 1920-....... **CLC 17**
  See also CA 29-32R; CANR 12, 28;
   CLR 27; MAICYA; SAAS 2; SATA 14,
   72

Thomas, Audrey (Callahan)
  1935-.......... **CLC 7, 13, 37; SSC 20**
  See also AITN 2; CA 21-24R; CAAS 19;
   CANR 36; DLB 60; MTCW

Thomas, D(onald) M(ichael)
  1935-................. **CLC 13, 22, 31**
  See also CA 61-64; CAAS 11; CANR 17,
   45; CDBLB 1960 to Present; DLB 40;
   INT CANR-17; MTCW

Thomas, Dylan (Marlais)
  1914-1953 ... **TCLC 1, 8, 45; DA; DAB;**
           DAC; PC 2; SSC 3; WLC
  See also CA 104; 120; CDBLB 1945-1960;
   DAM DRAM, MST, POET; DLB 13, 20,
   139; MTCW; SATA 60

Thomas, (Philip) Edward
  1878-1917 .... **TCLC 10**
  See also CA 106; DAM POET; DLB 19

Thomas, Joyce Carol 1938-........ **CLC 35**
  See also AAYA 12; BW 2; CA 113; 116;
   CANR 48; CLR 19; DLB 33; INT 116;
   JRDA; MAICYA; MTCW; SAAS 7;
   SATA 40, 78

Thomas, Lewis 1913-1993 .... **CLC 35**
  See also CA 85-88; 143; CANR 38; MTCW

Thomas, Paul
  See Mann, (Paul) Thomas

Thomas, Piri 1928-............... **CLC 17**
  See also CA 73-76; HW

Thomas, R(onald) S(tuart)
  1913- .... **CLC 6, 13, 48; DAB**
  See also CA 89-92; CAAS 4; CANR 30;
   CDBLB 1960 to Present; DAM POET;
   DLB 27; MTCW

Trogdon, William (Lewis) 1939-
See Heat-Moon, William Least
See also CA 115; 119; CANR 47; INT 119

Trollope, Anthony
1815-1882 ..... **NCLC 6, 33; DA; DAB;**
DAC; WLC
See also CDBLB 1832-1890; DAM MST,
NOV; DLB 21, 57, 159; SATA 22

Trollope, Frances 1779-1863 ..... **NCLC 30**
See also DLB 21

Trotsky, Leon 1879-1940 .... **TCLC 22**
See also CA 118

Trotter (Cockburn), Catharine
1679-1749 .... **LC 8**
See also DLB 84

Trout, Kilgore
See Farmer, Philip Jose

Trow, George W. S. 1943- .... **CLC 52**
See also CA 126

Troyat, Henri 1911- .... **CLC 23**
See also CA 45-48; CANR 2, 33; MTCW

Trudeau, G(arretson) B(eekman) 1948-
See Trudeau, Garry B.
See also CA 81-84; CANR 31; SATA 35

Trudeau, Garry B. .... **CLC 12**
See also Trudeau, G(arretson) B(eekman)
See also AAYA 10; AITN 2

Truffaut, Francois 1932-1984 ...... **CLC 20**
See also CA 81-84; 113; CANR 34

Trumbo, Dalton 1905-1976 .... **CLC 19**
See also CA 21-24R; 69-72; CANR 10;
DLB 26

Trumbull, John 1750-1831 .... **NCLC 30**
See also DLB 31

Trundlett, Helen B.
See Eliot, T(homas) S(tearns)

Tryon, Thomas 1926-1991 .... **CLC 3, 11**
See also AITN 1; CA 29-32R; 135;
CANR 32; DAM POP; MTCW

Tryon, Tom
See Tryon, Thomas

Ts'ao Hsueh-ch'in 1715(?)-1763 .... **LC 1**

Tsushima, Shuji 1909-1948
See Dazai, Osamu
See also CA 107

Tsvetaeva (Efron), Marina (Ivanovna)
1892-1941 .... **TCLC 7, 35; PC 14**
See also CA 104; 128; MTCW

Tuck, Lily 1938- .... **CLC 70**
See also CA 139

Tu Fu 712-770 .... **PC 9**
See also DAM MULT

Tunis, John R(oberts) 1889-1975 ... **CLC 12**
See also CA 61-64; DLB 22; JRDA;
MAICYA; SATA 37; SATA-Brief 30

Tuohy, Frank .... **CLC 37**
See also Tuohy, John Francis
See also DLB 14, 139

Tuohy, John Francis 1925-
See Tuohy, Frank
See also CA 5-8R; CANR 3, 47

Turco, Lewis (Putnam) 1934- ... **CLC 11, 63**
See also CA 13-16R; CAAS 22; CANR 24,
51; DLBY 84

Turgenev, Ivan
1818-1883 .... **NCLC 21; DA; DAB;**
DAC; SSC 7; WLC
See also DAM MST, NOV

Turgot, Anne-Robert-Jacques
1727-1781 .... **LC 26**

Turner, Frederick 1943- .... **CLC 48**
See also CA 73-76; CAAS 10; CANR 12,
30; DLB 40

Tutu, Desmond M(pilo)
1931- .... **CLC 80; BLC**
See also BW 1; CA 125; DAM MULT

Tutuola, Amos 1920- ... **CLC 5, 14, 29; BLC**
See also BW 2; CA 9-12R; CANR 27;
DAM MULT; DLB 125; MTCW

Twain, Mark
..... **TCLC 6, 12, 19, 36, 48, 59; SSC 6;**
WLC
See also Clemens, Samuel Langhorne
See also DLB 11, 12, 23, 64, 74

Tyler, Anne
1941- .... **CLC 7, 11, 18, 28, 44, 59**
See also BEST 89:1; CA 9-12R; CANR 11,
33; DAM NOV, POP; DLB 6, 143;
DLBY 82; MTCW; SATA 7

Tyler, Royall 1757-1826 .... **NCLC 3**
See also DLB 37

Tynan, Katharine 1861-1931 .... **TCLC 3**
See also CA 104; DLB 153

Tyutchev, Fyodor 1803-1873 ..... **NCLC 34**

Tzara, Tristan .... **CLC 47**
See also Rosenfeld, Samuel
See also DAM POET

Uhry, Alfred 1936- .... **CLC 55**
See also CA 127; 133; DAM DRAM, POP;
INT 133

Ulf, Haerved
See Strindberg, (Johan) August

Ulf, Harved
See Strindberg, (Johan) August

Ulibarri, Sabine R(eyes) 1919- ..... **CLC 83**
See also CA 131; DAM MULT; DLB 82;
HW

Unamuno (y Jugo), Miguel de
1864-1936 .... **TCLC 2, 9; HLC; SSC 11**
See also CA 104; 131; DAM MULT, NOV;
DLB 108; HW; MTCW

Undercliffe, Errol
See Campbell, (John) Ramsey

Underwood, Miles
See Glassco, John

Undset, Sigrid
1882-1949 .... **TCLC 3; DA; DAB;**
DAC; WLC
See also CA 104; 129; DAM MST, NOV;
MTCW

Ungaretti, Giuseppe
1888-1970 .... **CLC 7, 11, 15**
See also CA 19-20; 25-28R; CAP 2;
DLB 114

Unger, Douglas 1952- .... **CLC 34**
See also CA 130

Unsworth, Barry (Forster) 1930- .... **CLC 76**
See also CA 25-28R; CANR 30

Updike, John (Hoyer)
1932- ...... **CLC 1, 2, 3, 5, 7, 9, 13, 15,**
23, 34, 43, 70; DA; DAB; DAC; SSC 13;
WLC
See also CA 1-4R; CABS 1; CANR 4, 33,
51; CDALB 1968-1988; DAM MST,
NOV, POET, POP; DLB 2, 5, 143;
DLBD 3; DLBY 80, 82; MTCW

Upshaw, Margaret Mitchell
See Mitchell, Margaret (Munnerlyn)

Upton, Mark
See Sanders, Lawrence

Urdang, Constance (Henriette)
1922- .... **CLC 47**
See also CA 21-24R; CANR 9, 24

Uriel, Henry
See Faust, Frederick (Schiller)

Uris, Leon (Marcus) 1924- ...... **CLC 7, 32**
See also AITN 1, 2; BEST 89:2; CA 1-4R;
CANR 1, 40; DAM NOV, POP; MTCW;
SATA 49

Urmuz
See Codrescu, Andrei

Urquhart, Jane 1949- .... **CLC 90; DAC**
See also CA 113; CANR 32

Ustinov, Peter (Alexander) 1921- .... **CLC 1**
See also AITN 1; CA 13-16R; CANR 25,
51; DLB 13

Vaculik, Ludvik 1926- .... **CLC 7**
See also CA 53-56

Valdez, Luis (Miguel)
1940- .... **CLC 84; HLC**
See also CA 101; CANR 32; DAM MULT;
DLB 122; HW

Valenzuela, Luisa 1938- ... **CLC 31; SSC 14**
See also CA 101; CANR 32; DAM MULT;
DLB 113; HW

Valera y Alcala-Galiano, Juan
1824-1905 .... **TCLC 10**
See also CA 106

Valery, (Ambroise) Paul (Toussaint Jules)
1871-1945 .... **TCLC 4, 15; PC 9**
See also CA 104; 122; DAM POET; MTCW

Valle-Inclan, Ramon (Maria) del
1866-1936 .... **TCLC 5; HLC**
See also CA 106; DAM MULT; DLB 134

Vallejo, Antonio Buero
See Buero Vallejo, Antonio

Vallejo, Cesar (Abraham)
1892-1938 .... **TCLC 3, 56; HLC**
See also CA 105; DAM MULT; HW

Valle Y Pena, Ramon del
See Valle-Inclan, Ramon (Maria) del

Van Ash, Cay 1918- .... **CLC 34**

Vanbrugh, Sir John 1664-1726 ...... **LC 21**
See also DAM DRAM; DLB 80

Van Campen, Karl
See Campbell, John W(ood, Jr.)

Vance, Gerald
See Silverberg, Robert

Vance, Jack .... **CLC 35**
See also Vance, John Holbrook
See also DLB 8

Von Rachen, Kurt
See Hubbard, L(afayette) Ron(ald)

von Rezzori (d'Arezzo), Gregor
See Rezzori (d'Arezzo), Gregor von

von Sternberg, Josef
See Sternberg, Josef von

Vorster, Gordon 1924-............ **CLC 34**
See also CA 133

Vosce, Trudie
See Ozick, Cynthia

Voznesensky, Andrei (Andreievich)
1933-................. **CLC 1, 15, 57**
See also CA 89-92; CANR 37;
DAM POET; MTCW

Waddington, Miriam 1917-........ **CLC 28**
See also CA 21-24R; CANR 12, 30;
DLB 68

Wagman, Fredrica 1937-........... **CLC 7**
See also CA 97-100; INT 97-100

Wagner, Richard 1813-1883....... **NCLC 9**
See also DLB 129

Wagner-Martin, Linda 1936-...... **CLC 50**

Wagoner, David (Russell)
1926-.................. **CLC 3, 5, 15**
See also CA 1-4R; CAAS 3; CANR 2;
DLB 5; SATA 14

Wah, Fred(erick James) 1939-...... **CLC 44**
See also CA 107; 141; DLB 60

Wahloo, Per 1926-1975 .... **CLC 7**
See also CA 61-64

Wahloo, Peter
See Wahloo, Per

Wain, John (Barrington)
1925-1994 .... **CLC 2, 11, 15, 46**
See also CA 5-8R; 145; CAAS 4; CANR 23;
CDBLB 1960 to Present; DLB 15, 27,
139, 155; MTCW

Wajda, Andrzej 1926-............. **CLC 16**
See also CA 102

Wakefield, Dan 1932-.............. **CLC 7**
See also CA 21-24R; CAAS 7

Wakoski, Diane
1937- ..... **CLC 2, 4, 7, 9, 11, 40; PC 15**
See also CA 13-16R; CAAS 1; CANR 9;
DAM POET; DLB 5; INT CANR-9

Wakoski-Sherbell, Diane
See Wakoski, Diane

Walcott, Derek (Alton)
1930- .... **CLC 2, 4, 9, 14, 25, 42, 67, 76;**
BLC; DAB; DAC
See also BW 2; CA 89-92; CANR 26, 47;
DAM MST, MULT, POET; DLB 117;
DLBY 81; MTCW

Waldman, Anne 1945- .... **CLC 7**
See also CA 37-40R; CAAS 17; CANR 34;
DLB 16

Waldo, E. Hunter
See Sturgeon, Theodore (Hamilton)

Waldo, Edward Hamilton
See Sturgeon, Theodore (Hamilton)

Walker, Alice (Malsenior)
1944-....... **CLC 5, 6, 9, 19, 27, 46, 58;**
BLC; DA; DAB; DAC; SSC 5
See also AAYA 3; BEST 89:4; BW 2;
CA 37-40R; CANR 9, 27, 49;
CDALB 1968-1988; DAM MST, MULT,
NOV, POET, POP; DLB 6, 33, 143;
INT CANR-27; MTCW; SATA 31

Walker, David Harry 1911-1992.... **CLC 14**
See also CA 1-4R; 137; CANR 1; SATA 8;
SATA-Obit 71

Walker, Edward Joseph 1934-
See Walker, Ted
See also CA 21-24R; CANR 12, 28

Walker, George F.
1947-......... **CLC 44, 61; DAB; DAC**
See also CA 103; CANR 21, 43;
DAM MST; DLB 60

Walker, Joseph A. 1935-.......... **CLC 19**
See also BW 1; CA 89-92; CANR 26;
DAM DRAM, MST; DLB 38

Walker, Margaret (Abigail)
1915-.................. **CLC 1, 6; BLC**
See also BW 2; CA 73-76; CANR 26;
DAM MULT; DLB 76, 152; MTCW

Walker, Ted.................... **CLC 13**
See also Walker, Edward Joseph
See also DLB 40

Wallace, David Foster 1962-....... **CLC 50**
See also CA 132

Wallace, Dexter
See Masters, Edgar Lee

Wallace, (Richard Horatio) Edgar
1875-1932 .... **TCLC 57**
See also CA 115; DLB 70

Wallace, Irving 1916-1990...... **CLC 7, 13**
See also AITN 1; CA 1-4R; 132; CAAS 1;
CANR 1, 27; DAM NOV, POP;
INT CANR-27; MTCW

Wallant, Edward Lewis
1926-1962 .... **CLC 5, 10**
See also CA 1-4R; CANR 22; DLB 2, 28,
143; MTCW

Walley, Byron
See Card, Orson Scott

Walpole, Horace 1717-1797.......... **LC 2**
See also DLB 39, 104

Walpole, Hugh (Seymour)
1884-1941 .... **TCLC 5**
See also CA 104; DLB 34

Walser, Martin 1927-............. **CLC 27**
See also CA 57-60; CANR 8, 46; DLB 75,
124

Walser, Robert
1878-1956 .... **TCLC 18; SSC 20**
See also CA 118; DLB 66

Walsh, Jill Paton................. **CLC 35**
See also Paton Walsh, Gillian
See also AAYA 11; CLR 2; DLB 161;
SAAS 3

Walter, Villiam Christian
See Andersen, Hans Christian

Wambaugh, Joseph (Aloysius, Jr.)
1937-.................... **CLC 3, 18**
See also AITN 1; BEST 89:3; CA 33-36R;
CANR 42; DAM NOV, POP; DLB 6;
DLBY 83; MTCW

Ward, Arthur Henry Sarsfield 1883-1959
See Rohmer, Sax
See also CA 108

Ward, Douglas Turner 1930-....... **CLC 19**
See also BW 1; CA 81-84; CANR 27;
DLB 7, 38

Ward, Mary Augusta
See Ward, Mrs. Humphry

Ward, Mrs. Humphry
1851-1920 .... **TCLC 55**
See also DLB 18

Ward, Peter
See Faust, Frederick (Schiller)

Warhol, Andy 1928(?)-1987........ **CLC 20**
See also AAYA 12; BEST 89:4; CA 89-92;
121; CANR 34

Warner, Francis (Robert le Plastrier)
1937-...................... **CLC 14**
See also CA 53-56; CANR 11

Warner, Marina 1946-............. **CLC 59**
See also CA 65-68; CANR 21

Warner, Rex (Ernest) 1905-1986.... **CLC 45**
See also CA 89-92; 119; DLB 15

Warner, Susan (Bogert)
1819-1885 .... **NCLC 31**
See also DLB 3, 42

Warner, Sylvia (Constance) Ashton
See Ashton-Warner, Sylvia (Constance)

Warner, Sylvia Townsend
1893-1978 .... **CLC 7, 19**
See also CA 61-64; 77-80; CANR 16;
DLB 34, 139; MTCW

Warren, Mercy Otis 1728-1814... **NCLC 13**
See also DLB 31

Warren, Robert Penn
1905-1989 .... **CLC 1, 4, 6, 8, 10, 13, 18,**
39, 53, 59; DA; DAB; DAC; SSC 4; WLC
See also AITN 1; CA 13-16R; 129;
CANR 10, 47; CDALB 1968-1988;
DAM MST, NOV, POET; DLB 2, 48,
152; DLBY 80, 89; INT CANR-10;
MTCW; SATA 46; SATA-Obit 63

Warshofsky, Isaac
See Singer, Isaac Bashevis

Warton, Thomas 1728-1790........ **LC 15**
See also DAM POET; DLB 104, 109

Waruk, Kona
See Harris, (Theodore) Wilson

Warung, Price 1855-1911........ **TCLC 45**

Warwick, Jarvis
See Garner, Hugh

Washington, Alex
See Harris, Mark

Washington, Booker T(aliaferro)
1856-1915 .... **TCLC 10; BLC**
See also BW 1; CA 114; 125; DAM MULT;
SATA 28

Washington, George 1732-1799...... **LC 25**
See also DLB 31

Wassermann, (Karl) Jakob
1873-1934 . . . . TCLC 6
See also CA 104; DLB 66

Wasserstein, Wendy
1950- . . . . CLC 32, 59, 90; DC 4
See also CA 121; 129; CABS 3;
DAM DRAM; INT 129

Waterhouse, Keith (Spencer)
1929- . . . . CLC 47
See also CA 5-8R; CANR 38; DLB 13, 15;
MTCW

Waters, Frank (Joseph)
1902-1995 . . . . CLC 88
See also CA 5-8R; 149; CAAS 13; CANR 3,
18; DLBY 86

Waters, Roger   1944- . . . . CLC 35

Watkins, Frances Ellen
See Harper, Frances Ellen Watkins

Watkins, Gerrold
See Malzberg, Barry N(athaniel)

Watkins, Paul   1964- . . . . CLC 55
See also CA 132

Watkins, Vernon Phillips
1906-1967 . . . . CLC 43
See also CA 9-10; 25-28R; CAP 1; DLB 20

Watson, Irving S.
See Mencken, H(enry) L(ouis)

Watson, John H.
See Farmer, Philip Jose

Watson, Richard F.
See Silverberg, Robert

Waugh, Auberon (Alexander)   1939- . . CLC 7
See also CA 45-48; CANR 6, 22; DLB 14

Waugh, Evelyn (Arthur St. John)
1903-1966 . . . . . . CLC 1, 3, 8, 13, 19, 27,
44; DA; DAB; DAC; WLC
See also CA 85-88; 25-28R; CANR 22;
CDBLB 1914-1945; DAM MST, NOV,
POP; DLB 15, 162; MTCW

Waugh, Harriet   1944- . . . . CLC 6
See also CA 85-88; CANR 22

Ways, C. R.
See Blount, Roy (Alton), Jr.

Waystaff, Simon
See Swift, Jonathan

Webb, (Martha) Beatrice (Potter)
1858-1943 . . . . TCLC 22
See also Potter, Beatrice
See also CA 117

Webb, Charles (Richard)   1939- . . . . . . CLC 7
See also CA 25-28R

Webb, James H(enry), Jr.   1946- . . . . CLC 22
See also CA 81-84

Webb, Mary (Gladys Meredith)
1881-1927 . . . . TCLC 24
See also CA 123; DLB 34

Webb, Mrs. Sidney
See Webb, (Martha) Beatrice (Potter)

Webb, Phyllis   1927- . . . . CLC 18
See also CA 104; CANR 23; DLB 53

Webb, Sidney (James)
1859-1947 . . . . TCLC 22
See also CA 117

Webber, Andrew Lloyd. . . . . CLC 21
See also Lloyd Webber, Andrew

Weber, Lenora Mattingly
1895-1971 . . . . CLC 12
See also CA 19-20; 29-32R; CAP 1;
SATA 2; SATA-Obit 26

Webster, John   1579(?)-1634(?) . . . . DC 2
See also CDBLB Before 1660; DA; DAB;
DAC; DAM DRAM, MST; DLB 58;
WLC

Webster, Noah   1758-1843 . . . . NCLC 30

Wedekind, (Benjamin) Frank(lin)
1864-1918 . . . . TCLC 7
See also CA 104; DAM DRAM; DLB 118

Weidman, Jerome   1913- . . . . CLC 7
See also AITN 2; CA 1-4R; CANR 1;
DLB 28

Weil, Simone (Adolphine)
1909-1943 . . . . TCLC 23
See also CA 117

Weinstein, Nathan
See West, Nathanael

Weinstein, Nathan von Wallenstein
See West, Nathanael

Weir, Peter (Lindsay)   1944- . . . . CLC 20
See also CA 113; 123

Weiss, Peter (Ulrich)
1916-1982 . . . . CLC 3, 15, 51
See also CA 45-48; 106; CANR 3;
DAM DRAM; DLB 69, 124

Weiss, Theodore (Russell)
1916- . . . . CLC 3, 8, 14
See also CA 9-12R; CAAS 2; CANR 46;
DLB 5

Welch, (Maurice) Denton
1915-1948 . . . . TCLC 22
See also CA 121; 148

Welch, James   1940- . . . . CLC 6, 14, 52
See also CA 85-88; CANR 42;
DAM MULT, POP; NNAL

Weldon, Fay
1933- . . . . CLC 6, 9, 11, 19, 36, 59
See also CA 21-24R; CANR 16, 46;
CDBLB 1960 to Present; DAM POP;
DLB 14; INT CANR-16; MTCW

Wellek, Rene   1903-1995. . . . . CLC 28
See also CA 5-8R; 150; CAAS 7; CANR 8;
DLB 63; INT CANR-8

Weller, Michael   1942- . . . . CLC 10, 53
See also CA 85-88

Weller, Paul   1958- . . . . CLC 26

Wellershoff, Dieter   1925- . . . . CLC 46
See also CA 89-92; CANR 16, 37

Welles, (George) Orson
1915-1985 . . . . CLC 20, 80
See also CA 93-96; 117

Wellman, Mac   1945- . . . . CLC 65

Wellman, Manly Wade   1903-1986 . . CLC 49
See also CA 1-4R; 118; CANR 6, 16, 44;
SATA 6; SATA-Obit 47

Wells, Carolyn   1869(?)-1942 . . . . . . TCLC 35
See also CA 113; DLB 11

Wells, H(erbert) G(eorge)
1866-1946 . . . . TCLC 6, 12, 19; DA;
DAB; DAC; SSC 6; WLC
See also CA 110; 121; CDBLB 1914-1945;
DAM MST, NOV; DLB 34, 70, 156;
MTCW; SATA 20

Wells, Rosemary   1943- . . . . CLC 12
See also AAYA 13; CA 85-88; CANR 48;
CLR 16; MAICYA; SAAS 1; SATA 18,
69

Welty, Eudora
1909- . . . . . . CLC 1, 2, 5, 14, 22, 33; DA;
DAB; DAC; SSC 1; WLC
See also CA 9-12R; CABS 1; CANR 32;
CDALB 1941-1968; DAM MST, NOV;
DLB 2, 102, 143; DLBD 12; DLBY 87;
MTCW

Wen I-to   1899-1946 . . . . TCLC 28

Wentworth, Robert
See Hamilton, Edmond

Werfel, Franz (V.)   1890-1945 . . . . . . TCLC 8
See also CA 104; DLB 81, 124

Wergeland, Henrik Arnold
1808-1845 . . . . NCLC 5

Wersba, Barbara   1932- . . . . CLC 30
See also AAYA 2; CA 29-32R; CANR 16,
38; CLR 3; DLB 52; JRDA; MAICYA;
SAAS 2; SATA 1, 58

Wertmueller, Lina   1928- . . . . CLC 16
See also CA 97-100; CANR 39

Wescott, Glenway   1901-1987. . . . . . . CLC 13
See also CA 13-16R; 121; CANR 23;
DLB 4, 9, 102

Wesker, Arnold   1932- . . CLC 3, 5, 42; DAB
See also CA 1-4R; CAAS 7; CANR 1, 33;
CDBLB 1960 to Present; DAM DRAM;
DLB 13; MTCW

Wesley, Richard (Errol)   1945- . . . . CLC 7
See also BW 1; CA 57-60; CANR 27;
DLB 38

Wessel, Johan Herman   1742-1785 . . . . LC 7

West, Anthony (Panther)
1914-1987 . . . . CLC 50
See also CA 45-48; 124; CANR 3, 19;
DLB 15

West, C. P.
See Wodehouse, P(elham) G(renville)

West, (Mary) Jessamyn
1902-1984 . . . . CLC 7, 17
See also CA 9-12R; 112; CANR 27; DLB 6;
DLBY 84; MTCW; SATA-Obit 37

West, Morris L(anglo)   1916- . . . . . CLC 6, 33
See also CA 5-8R; CANR 24, 49; MTCW

West, Nathanael
1903-1940 . . . . . TCLC 1, 14, 44; SSC 16
See also CA 104; 125; CDALB 1929-1941;
DLB 4, 9, 28; MTCW

West, Owen
See Koontz, Dean R(ay)

West, Paul   1930- . . . . CLC 7, 14
See also CA 13-16R; CAAS 7; CANR 22;
DLB 14; INT CANR-22

West, Rebecca   1892-1983 . . CLC 7, 9, 31, 50
See also CA 5-8R; 109; CANR 19; DLB 36;
DLBY 83; MTCW

Wong, Jade Snow 1922-.......... **CLC 17**
See also CA 109

Woodcott, Keith
See Brunner, John (Kilian Houston)

Woodruff, Robert W.
See Mencken, H(enry) L(ouis)

Woolf, (Adeline) Virginia
1882-1941 .... **TCLC 1, 5, 20, 43, 56;**
DA; DAB; DAC; SSC 7; WLC
See also CA 104; 130; CDBLB 1914-1945;
DAM MST, NOV; DLB 36, 100, 162;
DLBD 10; MTCW

Woollcott, Alexander (Humphreys)
1887-1943 .... **TCLC 5**
See also CA 105; DLB 29

Woolrich, Cornell 1903-1968....... **CLC 77**
See also Hopley-Woolrich, Cornell George

Wordsworth, Dorothy
1771-1855 .... **NCLC 25**
See also DLB 107

Wordsworth, William
1770-1850 .... **NCLC 12, 38; DA; DAB;**
DAC; PC 4; WLC
See also CDBLB 1789-1832; DAM MST,
POET; DLB 93, 107

Wouk, Herman 1915-......... **CLC 1, 9, 38**
See also CA 5-8R; CANR 6, 33;
DAM NOV, POP; DLBY 82;
INT CANR-6; MTCW

Wright, Charles (Penzel, Jr.)
1935- .... **CLC 6, 13, 28**
See also CA 29-32R; CAAS 7; CANR 23,
36; DLBY 82; MTCW

Wright, Charles Stevenson
1932- .... **CLC 49; BLC 3**
See also BW 1; CA 9-12R; CANR 26;
DAM MULT, POET; DLB 33

Wright, Jack R.
See Harris, Mark

Wright, James (Arlington)
1927-1980 .... **CLC 3, 5, 10, 28**
See also AITN 2; CA 49-52; 97-100;
CANR 4, 34; DAM POET; DLB 5;
MTCW

Wright, Judith (Arandell)
1915- .... **CLC 11, 53; PC 14**
See also CA 13-16R; CANR 31; MTCW;
SATA 14

Wright, L(aurali) R. 1939-......... **CLC 44**
See also CA 138

Wright, Richard (Nathaniel)
1908-1960 .... **CLC 1, 3, 4, 9, 14, 21, 48,**
74; BLC; DA; DAB; DAC; SSC 2; WLC
See also AAYA 5; BW 1; CA 108;
CDALB 1929-1941; DAM MST, MULT,
NOV; DLB 76, 102; DLBD 2; MTCW

Wright, Richard B(ruce) 1937-...... **CLC 6**
See also CA 85-88; DLB 53

Wright, Rick 1945-............... **CLC 35**

Wright, Rowland
See Wells, Carolyn

Wright, Stephen Caldwell 1946-.... **CLC 33**
See also BW 2

Wright, Willard Huntington 1888-1939
See Van Dine, S. S.
See also CA 115

Wright, William 1930-............ **CLC 44**
See also CA 53-56; CANR 7, 23

Wroth, LadyMary 1587-1653(?) ..... **LC 30**
See also DLB 121

Wu Ch'eng-en 1500(?)-1582(?)....... **LC 7**

Wu Ching-tzu 1701-1754 .... **LC 2**

Wurlitzer, Rudolph 1938(?)- ... **CLC 2, 4, 15**
See also CA 85-88

Wycherley, William 1641-1715.... **LC 8, 21**
See also CDBLB 1660-1789; DAM DRAM;
DLB 80

Wylie, Elinor (Morton Hoyt)
1885-1928 .... **TCLC 8**
See also CA 105; DLB 9, 45

Wylie, Philip (Gordon) 1902-1971... **CLC 43**
See also CA 21-22; 33-36R; CAP 2; DLB 9

Wyndham, John................ **CLC 19**
See also Harris, John (Wyndham Parkes
Lucas) Beynon

Wyss, Johann David Von
1743-1818 .... **NCLC 10**
See also JRDA; MAICYA; SATA 29;
SATA-Brief 27

Xenophon
c. 430B.C.-c. 354B.C......... **CMLC 17**

Yakumo Koizumi
See Hearn, (Patricio) Lafcadio (Tessima
Carlos)

Yanez, Jose Donoso
See Donoso (Yanez), Jose

Yanovsky, Basile S.
See Yanovsky, V(assily) S(emenovich)

Yanovsky, V(assily) S(emenovich)
1906-1989 .... **CLC 2, 18**
See also CA 97-100; 129

Yates, Richard 1926-1992 ..... **CLC 7, 8, 23**
See also CA 5-8R; 139; CANR 10, 43;
DLB 2; DLBY 81, 92; INT CANR-10

Yeats, W. B.
See Yeats, William Butler

Yeats, William Butler
1865-1939 ..... **TCLC 1, 11, 18, 31; DA;**
DAB; DAC; WLC
See also CA 104; 127; CANR 45;
CDBLB 1890-1914; DAM DRAM, MST,
POET; DLB 10, 19, 98, 156; MTCW

Yehoshua, A(braham) B.
1936- .... **CLC 13, 31**
See also CA 33-36R; CANR 43

Yep, Laurence Michael 1948-...... **CLC 35**
See also AAYA 5; CA 49-52; CANR 1, 46;
CLR 3, 17; DLB 52; JRDA; MAICYA;
SATA 7, 69

Yerby, Frank G(arvin)
1916-1991 .... **CLC 1, 7, 22; BLC**
See also BW 1; CA 9-12R; 136; CANR 16;
DAM MULT; DLB 76; INT CANR-16;
MTCW

Yesenin, Sergei Alexandrovich
See Esenin, Sergei (Alexandrovich)

Yevtushenko, Yevgeny (Alexandrovich)
1933- .... **CLC 1, 3, 13, 26, 51**
See also CA 81-84; CANR 33;
DAM POET; MTCW

Yezierska, Anzia 1885(?)-1970 ..... **CLC 46**
See also CA 126; 89-92; DLB 28; MTCW

Yglesias, Helen 1915-........... **CLC 7, 22**
See also CA 37-40R; CAAS 20; CANR 15;
INT CANR-15; MTCW

Yokomitsu Riichi 1898-1947 ...... **TCLC 47**

Yonge, Charlotte (Mary)
1823-1901 .... **TCLC 48**
See also CA 109; DLB 18; SATA 17

York, Jeremy
See Creasey, John

York, Simon
See Heinlein, Robert A(nson)

Yorke, Henry Vincent 1905-1974 ... **CLC 13**
See also Green, Henry
See also CA 85-88; 49-52

Yosano Akiko 1878-1942 .. **TCLC 59; PC 11**

Yoshimoto, Banana................ **CLC 84**
See also Yoshimoto, Mahoko

Yoshimoto, Mahoko 1964-
See Yoshimoto, Banana
See also CA 144

Young, Al(bert James)
1939- .... **CLC 19; BLC**
See also BW 2; CA 29-32R; CANR 26;
DAM MULT; DLB 33

Young, Andrew (John) 1885-1971.... **CLC 5**
See also CA 5-8R; CANR 7, 29

Young, Collier
See Bloch, Robert (Albert)

Young, Edward 1683-1765........... **LC 3**
See also DLB 95

Young, Marguerite (Vivian)
1909-1995 .... **CLC 82**
See also CA 13-16; 150; CAP 1

Young, Neil 1945-................ **CLC 17**
See also CA 110

Yourcenar, Marguerite
1903-1987 .... **CLC 19, 38, 50, 87**
See also CA 69-72; CANR 23; DAM NOV;
DLB 72; DLBY 88; MTCW

Yurick, Sol 1925-................. **CLC 6**
See also CA 13-16R; CANR 25

Zabolotskii, Nikolai Alekseevich
1903-1958 .... **TCLC 52**
See also CA 116

Zamiatin, Yevgenii
See Zamyatin, Evgeny Ivanovich

Zamora, Bernice (B. Ortiz)
1938- .... **CLC 89; HLC**
See also DAM MULT; DLB 82; HW

Zamyatin, Evgeny Ivanovich
1884-1937 .... **TCLC 8, 37**
See also CA 105

Zangwill, Israel 1864-1926........ **TCLC 16**
See also CA 109; DLB 10, 135

Zappa, Francis Vincent, Jr. 1940-1993
See Zappa, Frank
See also CA 108; 143

Zappa, Frank................. **CLC 17**
See also Zappa, Francis Vincent, Jr.

Zaturenska, Marya 1902-1982.... **CLC 6, 11**
See also CA 13-16R; 105; CANR 22

Zelazny, Roger (Joseph)
1937-1995 .... **CLC 21**
See also AAYA 7; CA 21-24R; 148;
CANR 26; DLB 8; MTCW; SATA 57;
SATA-Brief 39

Zhdanov, Andrei A(lexandrovich)
1896-1948 .... **TCLC 18**
See also CA 117

Zhukovsky, Vasily   1783-1852 .... **NCLC 35**

Ziegenhagen, Eric .... **CLC 55**

Zimmer, Jill Schary
See Robinson, Jill

Zimmerman, Robert
See Dylan, Bob

Zindel, Paul
1936- ..... **CLC 6, 26; DA; DAB; DAC;**
DC 5
See also AAYA 2; CA 73-76; CANR 31;
CLR 3; DAM DRAM, MST, NOV;
DLB 7, 52; JRDA; MAICYA; MTCW;
SATA 16, 58

Zinov'Ev, A. A.
See Zinoviev, Alexander (Aleksandrovich)

Zinoviev, Alexander (Aleksandrovich)
1922- .... **CLC 19**
See also CA 116; 133; CAAS 10

Zoilus
See Lovecraft, H(oward) P(hillips)

Zola, Emile (Edouard Charles Antoine)
1840-1902 ...... **TCLC 1, 6, 21, 41; DA;**
DAB; DAC; WLC
See also CA 104; 138; DAM MST, NOV;
DLB 123

Zoline, Pamela   1941- .... **CLC 62**

Zorrilla y Moral, Jose   1817-1893 .. **NCLC 6**

Zoshchenko, Mikhail (Mikhailovich)
1895-1958 .... **TCLC 15; SSC 15**
See also CA 115

Zuckmayer, Carl   1896-1977 .... **CLC 18**
See also CA 69-72; DLB 56, 124

Zuk, Georges
See Skelton, Robin

Zukofsky, Louis
1904-1978 .... **CLC 1, 2, 4, 7, 11, 18;**
PC 11
See also CA 9-12R; 77-80; CANR 39;
DAM POET; DLB 5; MTCW

Zweig, Paul   1935-1984 .... **CLC 34, 42**
See also CA 85-88; 113

Zweig, Stefan   1881-1942 .... **TCLC 17**
See also CA 112; DLB 81, 118

Literary Criticism Series
Cumulative Topic Index

This index lists all topic entries in Gale's *Classical and Medieval Literature Criticism, Contemporary Literary Criticism, Literature Criticism from 1400 to 1800, Nineteenth-Century Literature Criticism,* and *Twentieth-Century Literary Criticism.*

Topic Index

CLC Cumulative Nationality Index

Nationality Index

Nationality Index

Nationality Index

CLC-91 Title Index

Title Index

ISBN 0-8103-9269-0